VAX/VMS Internals and Data Structures

VERSION 4.4

VERSION 4.4

VAX/VMS Internals and Data Structures

Lawrence J. Kenah, Ruth E. Goldenberg, Simon F. Bate

Digital Press

9 8 7 6 5 4 3 2 1

Order number EY-8264E-DP.

Designed by David Ford. Production coordinated by Editorial Inc. Automatically typeset by York Graphic Services. Printed in the United States of America by the Alpine Press, Inc.

The painting on the front cover is Paul Klee, 1921, 69, "Fugue in Red," watercolor, Canson, 24.3 × 37.2 cm, signed lower left, private collection, Switzerland; copyright © 1987 by COSMOPRESS, Geneva.

The Digital logo, DEC, DECnet, VAX, and VMS are trademarks of Digital Equipment Corporation.

Library of Congress Cataloging-in-Publication Data

Kenah, Lawrence J.
    VAX/VMS internals and data structures.

    1. VAX/VMS (Computer operating system) 2. VAX-11
(Computer)—Programming. 3. Data structures (Computer
science) I. Goldenberg, Ruth.   II. Bate, Simon F.
III. Title.
QA76.76.063K47   1988   005.4′44   87-30378
ISBN 1-55558-008-4

Preface

The main topic of this book is the kernel of the VAX/VMS Version 4.4 operating system: process management; memory management; the I/O subsystem; the mechanisms that transfer control to, from, and among these; and the system services that support and complement them.

In explaining the operation of a subsystem, this book emphasizes the data structures manipulated by that subsystem. Most of the operations of VMS can be more easily understood once the contents of the various data structures are known. The book also provides a detailed description of the flow of some major routines and annotated excerpts from certain key routines.

The intended readers are system programmers and other users of VAX/VMS who wish to understand its components, mechanisms, and data structures. For system programmers, the book provides technical background helpful in activities such as writing privileged utilities and system services. Its detailed description of data structures should help system managers make better informed decisions when they configure systems for space- or time-critical applications. It should also help application designers appreciate the effects (in speed or in memory consumption) of different design and implementation decisions.

In addition, this book is intended as a case study of VMS for an advanced undergraduate or graduate course in operating systems.

It assumes that the reader is familiar with the VAX architecture, particularly its memory management, and the VMS operating system, particularly its system services.

The book is divided into nine parts, each of which describes a different aspect of the operating system.

- Part 1 presents an overview of the operating system and reviews those concepts that are basic to its workings.
- Part 2 describes the mechanisms used to pass control between user programs and the operating system, and within the system itself.
- Part 3 describes scheduling, timer support, process control, and lock management.
- Part 4 discusses memory management, with emphasis on system data structures and their manipulation by paging and swapping routines.
- Part 5 contains an overview of the I/O subsystem, paying particular attention to the I/O-related system services.
- Part 6 describes the life cycle of a process: its creation, the activation and termination of images within its context, and its deletion.

- Part 7 covers system initialization, powerfail recovery, and asymmetric multiprocessing support.
- Part 8 discusses the implementation of logical names and the internals of several miscellaneous system services.
- The appendixes include a summary of VMS data structures, a detailed layout of system and P1 virtual address space, and information on the use of listing and map files, and the conventions used in naming symbols.

This book does not include a discussion of VAXcluster Systems.

There is no guarantee that any data structure or subroutine described here will remain the same from release to release. With each new version of the operating system, a privileged application program that relies on details contained in this book should be rebuilt and tested prior to production use.

The VAX/VMS document set supplies important background information for the topics discussed in this book. The following provide an especially important foundation: *VAX/VMS System Services Reference Manual*, *Writing a Device Driver for VAX/VMS*, and the chapter in the *VAX/VMS Run-Time Library Routines Reference Manual* that describes condition handling.

The *VAX Architecture Reference Manual* (Digital Press, 1987) documents the VAX architecture in detail. An excellent description of the VAX architecture, as well as a discussion of some of the design decisions made for its first implementation, the VAX-11/780, is found in *Computer Programming and Architecture: The VAX-11* by Henry M. Levy and Richard H. Eckhouse, Jr., (Digital Press, 1980). This book also contains a bibliography of some of the literature dealing with operating system design.

There are several conventions used throughout this book. In all diagrams of memory, the lowest virtual address appears at the top of the page and addresses increase toward the bottom of the page. This convention means that the direction of stack growth is upward from the bottom of the page. In diagrams that display more detail, such as bytes within longwords, addresses also increase from right to left. That is, the lowest addressed byte (or bit) in a longword is on the right-hand side of a figure and the most significant byte (or bit) is on the left-hand side.

The word *executive* refers to those parts of the operating system that reside in system virtual address space. The executive includes the contents of the file SYS.EXE, device drivers, and other code and data structures loaded at initialization time, including RMS and the system message file.

The words *system* and *VMS system* are used to describe the entire VAX/VMS software package, including privileged processes, utilities, and other support software as well as the executive itself.

VAX/VMS consists of many different components, each a different file in a directory on the system disk. One component is the system image itself, SYS$SYSTEM:SYS.EXE. Other components include device drivers, the DCL command language interpreter, and utility programs.

The source modules from which these components are built, and their listings on microfiche, are divided into facilities. Each facility is a directory containing sources and command procedures to build one or more components. The facility [DRIVER], for example, contains sources for most of the device drivers. The facility [BOOTS] includes sources for the primary bootstrap program, VMB; the secondary bootstrap program, SYSBOOT; and the SYSGEN Utility. The facility [SYS] contains the sources that comprise SYS.EXE.

It is a convention of this book that a source module identified solely by file name is part of the [SYS] facility. Modules from all other facilities are identified by facility directory name and file name. For example, [DRIVER]LPDRIVER refers to the file which is the source for the line printer device driver. Appendix B discusses how to locate a module in the VAX/VMS source listing microfiche.

When either *process control block* or *PCB* is used without a modifier, it refers to the software structure used by the scheduler. The data structure that contains copies of the general registers (which the hardware locates through the PR$_PCBB register) is always called the hardware PCB.

In reference to access modes, the term *inner access modes* means those access modes with more privilege. The term *outer access modes* means those with less privilege. Thus, the innermost access mode is kernel and the outermost mode is user.

The term *SYSBOOT parameter* is used to describe any of the adjustable parameters that are used by the secondary bootstrap program SYSBOOT to configure the system. (These parameters are often referred to elsewhere as SYSGEN parameters.) These include both the dynamic parameters that can be changed on the running system and the static parameters that require a reboot in order for their values to change. These parameters are referred to by their parameter names rather than by the global locations where their values are stored. Appendix C relates parameter names to their corresponding global locations.

The terms *byte index*, *word index*, *longword index*, and *quadword index* refer to methods of VAX operand access that use context indexed addressing modes. That is, the index value is multiplied by 1, 2, 4, or 8 (depending on whether a byte, word, longword, or quadword is being referenced) as part of operand evaluation to calculate the effective address of the operand.

In general, the component called INIT refers to a module of that name in the executive and not to the volume initialization utility. When that utility program is referenced, it is clearly specified.

Three conventions are observed for lists:

• In lists such as this one, where there is no order or hierarchy, list elements are indicated by leading bullets (•). Sublists without hierarchy are indicated by dashes (—).

- Lists that indicate an ordered set of operations are numbered. Sublists that indicate an ordered set of operations are lettered.
- Numbered lists with the numbers enclosed in circles indicate a correspondence between the individual list elements and numbered items in a figure.

Front Cover Illustration

The cover of the Version 3.3 edition of this book displayed a painting by Hannes Beckmann. For the cover of the present Version 4.4 edition, the author has chosen "Fugue in Red," by Paul Klee, which like the Beckmann painting conveys a strong sense of structure.

"Fugue in Red" communicates a dynamism, a sense of flow, movement, and adaptability. The way in which the geometric elements of the painting repeat, with subtle variations in color and shape, suggests data structures, whose contents change with the current state of the system and the operation under way. Like the shapes in "Fugue in Red," the key structures of VMS are used again and again to express recurring contrapuntal themes as in a musical fugue.

Acknowledgments: Version 3.3 Edition

Our first thanks must go to Joe Carchidi for suggesting that this book be written, and to Dick Hustvedt, for his help and enlightening conversations.

We would like to thank John Lucas for putting together the initial versions of Chapters 7, 10, 11, and 29 and Vik Muiznieks for writing the initial versions of Chapters 5, 18, and 19.

Appreciation goes to all those who reviewed the drafts for the VAX/VMS Version 2.2 and the VAX/VMS Version 3.3 editions of this book. We would particularly like to thank Kathy Morse for reviewing the V2.2 volume in its entirety and Wayne Cardoza for reviewing this entire V3.3 edition. Our special thanks go to Ruth Goldenberg for reviewing both in their entirety, and for her many corrections, comments, and suggestions. [The V2.2 book was published in 1981. Digital Press published the first edition of the present volume, for V3.3, in 1984.]

We owe a lot of thanks to our editing staff, especially to Jonathan Ostrowsky for his labors in preparing the V2.2 book, and Betty Steinfeld for her help and suggestions. Many thanks go to Jonathan Parsons for reviewing and editing the present edition, and for all his help, patience, and suggestions.

We would like to thank the Graphic Services department at Spitbrook, particularly Pat Walker for her help in paging and production of the V2.2 book and Paul King for his help in transforming innumerable slides and rough sketches into figures. Thanks go to Kathy Greenleaf and Jackie Markow for converting the files to our generic markup language.

Thanks go to Larry Bohn, Sue Gault, Bill Heffner, Kathleen Jensen, and Judy Jurgens for their support and interest in this project.

Finally, we would like to thank all those who originally designed and implemented the VAX/VMS operating system, and all those who have contributed to later releases.

Lawrence J. Kenah
Simon F. Bate
August 1983

Acknowledgments: Version 4.4 Edition

First, I thank Larry Kenah for suggesting that I do this edition of the book, for providing such an excellent foundation to update, and for his astute review and responsive answers to my innumerable questions.

I was blessed with many dedicated reviewers, four of whom reviewed the entire book: Dick Buttlar, Wayne Cardoza, Kathy Morse, and Rod Shepardson. Rod Shepardson, moreover, revised Chapter 19, Appendixes D and E, and provided considerable update and enhancement to Chapter 18. Dick Buttlar also aided me in my struggles to format tables and tactfully suggested improvements to the book. Wayne Cardoza and Kathy Morse, who had critiqued earlier versions of the book, provided continuity, insight, and technical assistance and support.

A number of other people reviewed large portions of the book, significantly improving its quality: Stan Amway, Richard Bishop, George Claborn, Dan Doherty, Joy Dorman, Rod Gamache, and John Hallyburton. I also thank the many other reviewers and early readers who helped find errors and omissions.

Carl Rehbein helped update Chapters 5, 18, 19, and Appendixes C, D, and E.

Bob Kadlec, my manager, encouraged and supported me throughout this endeavor and intercepted many potential interrupts.

Joy Lanza edited the initial version of this edition and carefully, patiently shepherded the copy and artwork through its preliminary publication.

George Jakobsche acted as negotiator and facilitator and played an important part in catalyzing this edition of the book.

I thank all the people who produced this book. Alice Cheyer's meticulous editing corrected numerous errors that had escaped the rest of us. Carol Keller edited the artwork, polishing it and removing inconsistencies. Jonathan Weinert diligently orchestrated the entire production.

I would like to thank John Osborn and Mike Meehan of Digital Press for their strong support.

I am especially grateful to Chase Duffy of Digital Press for her comprehensive publishing experience and ready wit, which lightened the work.

My deepest thanks are to Jim Fraser, who wrote the final draft of several important sections, contributed much technical and editorial review, helped me through the gnarly bits, and, most important, supplied much gumption.

Finally, I, also, thank the original designers and implementers of VAX/VMS and the contributers to subsequent releases, those past and those to come.

Ruth E. Goldenberg
August 1987

Contents

Contents

Contents

Contents

PART I/Introduction

1 System Overview

For the fashion of Minas Tirith was such that it was built on
seven levels, each delved into a hill, and about each was set a
wall, and in each wall was a gate.

J.R.R. Tolkien, *The Return of the King*

This chapter introduces the basic components of the VAX/VMS operating
system. Special attention is paid to the features of the VAX architecture that
are either exploited by the operating system or exist solely to support an
operating system. In addition, some of the design goals that guided the implementation of the VMS operating system are discussed.

1.1 PROCESS, JOB, AND IMAGE

The fundamental unit in the implementation of scheduling on the VAX/VMS
operating system, the entity that is selected for execution by the scheduler, is
the process. If a process creates subprocesses, the collection of the creator
process, all the subprocesses created by it, and all subprocesses created by its
descendants, is called a job. The programs that are executed in the context of
a process are called images.

1.1.1 Process

A process is fully described by data structures which specify the hardware
and software context, and by a virtual address space description. This information is stored in several different places in the process and system address
space. The data structures that contain the various pieces of process context
are pictured in Figure 1-1.

1.1.1.1

Hardware Context. The hardware context consists of copies of the general
purpose registers, the four per-process stack pointers, the program counter
(PC), the processor status longword (PSL), and the process-specific processor
registers, including the memory management registers and the asynchronous
system trap (AST) level register. The hardware context is stored in a data
structure called the hardware process control block (hardware PCB), which is
used primarily when a process is removed from or placed into execution.

Another part of process context that is related to hardware is four per-
process stacks, one for each of the four access modes. Code executing in the
context of a process uses the stack associated with the process's current access mode.

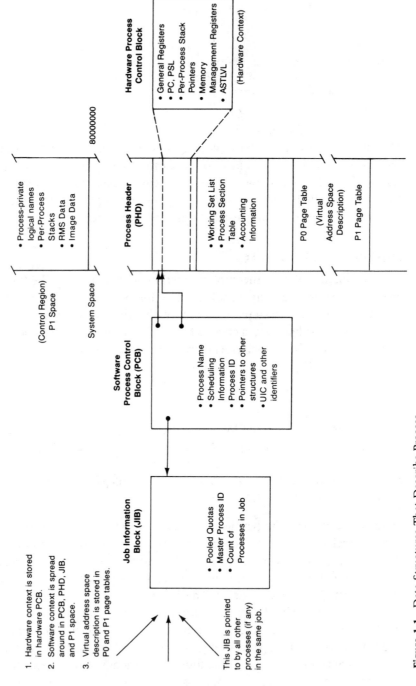

Figure 1-1 Data Structures That Describe Process Context

.1.1.2 **Software Context.** Software context consists of all the data required by various parts of the operating system to control that portion of common resources allocated to a given process. This context includes the process software priority, its current scheduling state, process privileges and "identifiers," quotas and limits, and miscellaneous information, such as process name and process identification.

The information about a process that must be in memory at all times is stored in a data structure called the software process control block (PCB). This information includes the software priority of the process, its unique process identification (PID), and the particular scheduling state that the process is in at a given point in time. The software PCB also records some process quotas and limits. Other quotas and limits are recorded in the job information block (JIB).

The PCB incorporates another data structure called an access rights block (ARB), which lists the identifiers that the process holds. Identifiers are names that specify to what groups a process belongs for purposes of determining access to files and other protected objects. Identifiers are described briefly in Section 1.4.1.4.

The information about a process that does not have to be permanently resident (swappable process context) is contained in a data structure called the process header (PHD). This information is needed when the process is resident and consists mainly of information used by memory management when page faults occur. The data in the process header is also used by the swapper when the process is removed from memory (outswapped) or brought back into memory (inswapped). The hardware PCB, which contains the hardware context of a process, including its page tables, is a part of the process header. Some information in the process header is nonpageable and available to suitably privileged code whenever the process is resident. The process page tables, however, are only accessible from that process's context.

Other process-specific information is stored in the P1 portion of the process virtual address space (the control region). This includes exception dispatching information, Record Management Services (RMS) data tables, and information about the image that is currently executing. Information that is stored in P1 space is only accessible when the process is executing (is the current process), because P1 space is process-specific.

.1.1.3 **Virtual Address Space Description.** The virtual address space of a process is described by the process P0 and P1 page tables, stored in the high address end of the process header. The process virtual address space is altered when an image is initially activated, during image execution through selected system services, and when an image terminates. The process page tables reside in system virtual address space and are, in turn, described by entries in the system page table. Unlike the other portions of the process header, the process page tables are themselves pageable, and they are faulted into the process working set only when they are needed.

1.1.2	**Image**

The programs that execute in the context of a process are called images. Images usually reside in files that are produced by the VAX/VMS Linker. When the user initiates image execution (as part of process creation or through a Digital command language (DCL) command in an interactive or batch job), a component of the executive called the image activator sets up the process page tables to point to the appropriate sections of the image file. The VMS operating system uses the same paging mechanism that implements its virtual memory support to read image pages into memory as they are needed.

1.1.3	**Job**

The collection of subprocesses that have a common root process is called a job. The concept of a job exists for the purpose of sharing resources. Some quotas and limits are shared among all processes in the same job. The current values of these quotas are contained in a data structure called a job information block (JIB) (see Figure 1-1) that is shared by all processes in the same job.

1.2	**FUNCTIONS PROVIDED BY VAX/VMS**

The VAX/VMS operating system provides services at many levels so that user applications may execute easily and effectively. The layered structure of the VAX/VMS operating system is pictured in Figure 1-2. In general, components in a given layer can make use of the facilities in all inner layers.

1.2.1	**Operating System Kernel**

The main topic of this book is the operating system kernel: the I/O subsystem, memory management, the scheduler, and the VAX/VMS system services that support and complement these components. The discussion of these three components and other miscellaneous parts of the operating system kernel focuses on the data structures that are manipulated by a given component. In describing what each major data structure represents and how that structure is altered by different sequences of events in the system, this document describes the detailed operations of each major piece of the kernel.

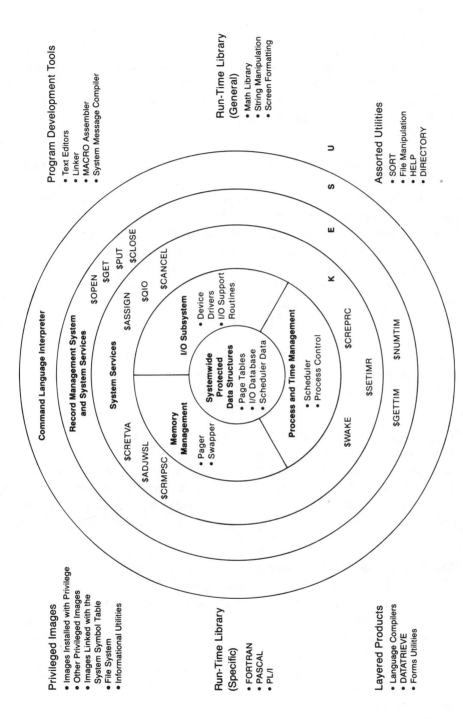

Figure 1-2 Layered Design of the VAX/VMS Operating System

7

1.2.1.1   **I/O Subsystem.** The I/O subsystem consists of device drivers and their associated data structures; device-independent routines within the executive;
and several system services, the most important of which is the $QIO re-
quest, the eventual I/O request that is issued by all outer layers of the system.
The I/O subsystem is described in detail from the point of view of adding a
device driver to a VMS operating system in the manual *Writing a Device
Driver for VAX/VMS*. Chapters 18 and 19 of this book describe some features
of the I/O subsystem that are not described in that manual.

1.2.1.2   **Memory Management.** The main components of the memory management
subsystem are the page fault handler, which implements the virtual memory
support of the VAX/VMS operating system, and the working set swapper,
which allows the system to utilize more fully the amount of physical memory that is available. The data structures used and manipulated by the pager
and swapper include the page frame number (PFN) database and the page
tables of each process. The PFN database describes each page of physical
memory that is available for paging and swapping. Virtual address space descriptions of each currently resident process are contained in their respective
page tables. The system page table describes the system space portion of virtual address space.

     System services are available to allow a user (or the system on behalf of the
user) to create or delete specific portions of virtual address space or map a file
into a specified virtual address range.

1.2.1.3   **Scheduling and Process Control.** The third major component of the kernel is
the process scheduler. It selects processes for execution and removes from
execution processes that can no longer execute. The scheduler also handles
clock servicing and includes timer-related system services. System services
are available to allow a process to create or delete other processes. Other
services provide one process the ability to control the execution of another.

1.2.1.4   **Miscellaneous Services.** One area of the operating system kernel that is not
pictured in Figure 1-2 involves the many miscellaneous services that are
available in the operating system kernel. Some of these services for such
tasks as logical name creation or string formatting are available to the user in
the form of system services. Others, such as pool manipulation routines and
certain synchronization techniques, are only used by the kernel and privileged utilities. Still others, such as the lock management system services, are
used throughout the system—by users' programs, system services, RMS, the
file system, and privileged utilities.

.2.2   **Data Management**

The VAX/VMS operating system provides data management facilities at two levels. The record structure that exists within a file is interpreted by the VAX Record Management Services (RMS), which exists in a layer just outside the kernel. RMS exists as a series of procedures located in system space, so it is in some ways just like the rest of the operating system kernel. Most of the procedures in RMS execute in executive access mode, providing a thin wall of protection between RMS and the kernel itself.

The placement of files on mass storage volumes is controlled by one of the disk or tape ancillary control processes (ACP) or by the Files-11 Extended QIO Processor (XQP). An ACP is implemented as a separate process because many of its operations must be serialized to avoid synchronous access conflicts. ACPs and the Files-11 XQP interact with the kernel both through the system service vector interface and by the use of utility routines not accessible to the general user.

The Files-11 XQP, new with VAX/VMS Version 4, controls the most commonly used "on-disk structure." (The placement of files on a block-structured medium, such as a disk volume or a TU58, is referred to as on-disk structure.) The XQP is implemented as an extension to the $QIO system service and runs in process context. A process's XQP file operations are serialized with those of other processes through lock management system services.

.2.3   **User Interface**

The interface that is presented to the user (as distinct from the application programmer who is using system services and Run-Time Library procedures) is a command language interpreter (CLI). The DCL CLI is available on all VAX/VMS systems. The monitor console routine (MCR) CLI, the command language used with RSX-11M, is available as an optional software product. Some of the services performed by a CLI call RMS or the system services directly; others result in the execution of an external image. These images are generally no different from user-written applications because their only interface to the executive is through the system services and RMS calls.

.2.3.1   **Images Installed with Privilege.** Some of the informational utilities and disk and tape volume manipulation utilities require that selected portions of protected data structures be read or written in a controlled fashion. Images that require privilege to perform their function can be installed (made known to the operating system) by the system manager so that they can perform their function in an ordinarily nonprivileged process environment. Images that fit this description include MAIL, MONITOR, VMOUNT (the volume mount utility), SET, and SHOW. Appendix A lists those images that are installed with privilege in a typical VMS system.

1.2.3.2   **Other Privileged Images.** Other images that perform privileged functions are not installed with privilege because their functions are less controlled and could destroy the system if executed by naive or malicious users. These images can only be executed by privileged users. Examples of these images include SYSGEN (for loading device drivers), INSTALL (which makes images privileged or shareable), or the images invoked by a CLI to manipulate print or batch queues. Images that require privilege to execute but are not installed with privilege in a typical VAX/VMS system are also listed in Appendix A.

1.2.3.3   **Images That Link with SYS$SYSTEM:SYS.STB.** Appendix A also lists those components that are linked with the system symbol table (SYS$SYSTEM: SYS.STB). These images access known locations in the system image (SYS.EXE) through global symbols and must be relinked each time the system itself is relinked. User applications or special components that include SYS.STB when they are linked, such as device drivers, must be relinked whenever a new version of the symbol table is released, usually at each major release of the VAX/VMS operating system.

1.2.4   **Interface among Kernel Subsystems**

The coupling among the three major subsystems pictured in Figure 1-2 is somewhat misleading because there is actually little interaction between the three components. In addition, each of the three components has its own data structures for which it is responsible. When one of the other pieces of the system wishes to access such data structures, it does so through some controlled interface. Figure 1-3 shows the small amount of interaction that occurs between the three major subsystems in the operating system kernel.

1.2.4.1   **I/O Subsystem Requests.** The I/O subsystem makes a request to memory management to lock down specified pages for a direct I/O request. The pager or swapper is notified directly when the I/O request that just completed was initiated by either one of them.

I/O requests can result in the requesting process being placed in a wait state until the request completes. This change of state requires that the scheduler be notified. In addition, I/O completion can also cause a process to change its scheduling state. Again, the scheduler would be called.

1.2.4.2   **Memory Management Requests.** Both the pager and swapper require input and output operations to fulfill their functions. The pager and swapper use

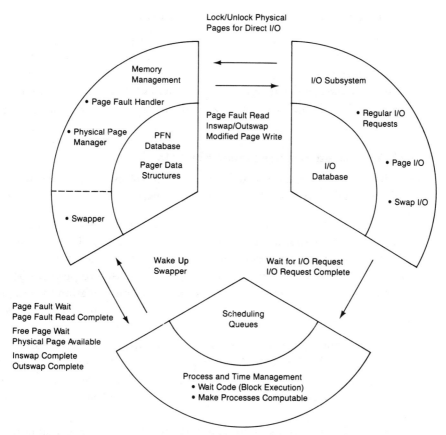

Figure 1-3 Interaction Between Components of VMS Kernel

special entry points into the I/O system rather than call $QIO. These entry points queue prebuilt I/O packets directly to the driver, bypassing unnecessary protection checks and preventing an irrelevant attempt to lock pages associated with these direct I/O requests.

If a process incurs a page fault that results in a read from disk or if a process requires physical memory and none is available, the process is put into one of the memory management wait states by the scheduler. When the page read completes or physical memory becomes available, the process is made computable again.

2.4.3   **Scheduler Requests.** The scheduler interacts very little with the rest of the system. It plays a more passive role when cooperation with memory management or the I/O subsystem is required. One exception to this passive role is that the scheduler awakens the swapper when a process that is not currently memory resident becomes computable.

1.3   **HARDWARE ASSISTANCE TO THE OPERATING SYSTEM KERNEL**

The method of implementing the many services provided by the VAX/VMS operating system illustrates the close connection between the hardware design and the operating system. Many of the general features of the VAX architecture are used to advantage by the VAX/VMS operating system. Other features of the architecture exist entirely to support an operating system.

1.3.1   **VAX Architecture Features Exploited by VMS**

Several features of the VAX architecture that are available to all users are used for specific purposes by the operating system:

- The general purpose calling mechanism is the primary path into the operating system from all outer layers of the system. Because all system services are procedures, they are available to all native mode languages.
- The memory management protection scheme is used to protect code and data used by more privileged access modes from modification by less privileged modes. Read-only portions of the executive are protected in the same manner.
- There is implicit protection built into special instructions that can only be executed from kernel mode. Because only the executive (and suitably privileged process-based code) executes in kernel mode, such instructions as MTPR, LDPCTX, and HALT are protected from execution by nonprivileged users.
- The operating system uses interrupt priority level (IPL) for several purposes. IPL is elevated so that certain interrupts are blocked. For example, clock interrupts must be blocked while the system time (stored in a quadword) is checked because this checking takes more than one instruction. Clock interrupts are blocked to prevent the system time from being updated while it is being checked.
- IPL is also used as a synchronization tool. For example, any routine that accesses certain systemwide data structures, such as the scheduler database, must raise IPL to 8 (called IPL$_SYNCH). The assignment of various hardware and software interrupts to specific IPL values establishes an order of importance to the hardware and software interrupt services that the VMS operating system performs.

Several other features of the VAX architecture are used by specific components of the operating system and are described in later chapters. They include the following:

- The change mode instructions (CHME and CHMK), which are used to decrease access mode (to greater privilege) (see Figure 1-4). Note that most exceptions and all interrupts also result in changing mode to kernel. Section 1.3.5 presents an introduction to exceptions and interrupts.

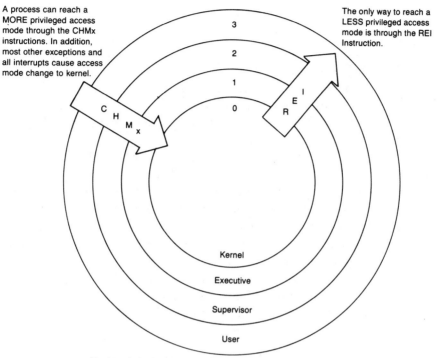

Access mode fields in the PSL are not directly accessible to the programmer or to the operating system.

A process can reach a MORE privileged access mode through the CHMx instructions. In addition, most other exceptions and all interrupts cause access mode change to kernel.

The only way to reach a LESS privileged access mode is through the REI Instruction.

The boundaries between the access modes are nearly identical to the layer boundaries pictured in Figure 1-2.
• Nearly all of the system services execute in kernel mode.
• RMS and some system services execute in executive mode.
• Command Language Interpreters normally execute in supervisor mode.
• Utilities, application programs, Run-Time Library procedures, and so on normally execute in user mode. Privileged utilities sometimes execute in kernel or executive mode.

Figure 1-4   Methods for Altering Access Mode

• The inclusion of many protection checks and pending interrupt checks in the single instruction that is the common exception and interrupt exit path, REI.
• Software interrupts.
• Hardware context and the single instructions (SVPCTX and LDPCTX) that save and restore it.
• The use of ASTs to obtain and pass information.

3.2   VAX Instruction Set

While the VAX instruction set, data types, and addressing modes were designed to be somewhat compatible with the PDP-11, several features that were missing in the PDP-11 were added to the VAX architecture. True context indexing allows array elements to be addressed by element number, with the hardware accounting for the size (byte, word, longword, or quadword) of each element. Short literal addressing was added in recognition of the fact that the majority of literals that appear in a program are small numbers. Variable length bit fields and character data types were added to serve the needs of several classes of users, including operating system designers.

The instruction set includes many instructions that are useful to any designer and occur often in the VMS executive. The queue instructions allow the construction of doubly linked lists as a common dynamic data structure. Character string instructions are useful when dealing with any data structure that can be treated as an array of bytes. Bit field instructions allow efficient operations on flags and masks.

One of the most important features of the VAX architecture is the VAX Calling Standard. Any procedure that adheres to this standard can be called from any native language, an advantage for any large application that requires the use of the features of a wide range of languages. The VMS operating system adheres to this standard in its interfaces to the outside world through the system service interface, RMS entry points, and the Run-Time Library procedures. System services and RMS services are written as procedures that can be accessed by issuing a CALLx to absolute location SYS$*service* in the process P1 virtual address space. Run-Time Library procedures are mapped into a process's P0 space, instead of being located in system space.

1.3.3 Implementation of VMS Kernel Routines

In Section 1.2.1, the VMS kernel was divided into three functional pieces plus the system service interface to the rest of the world. Alternatively, the operating system kernel can be partitioned according to the method used to gain access to each part. The three classes of routines within the kernel are procedure-based code, exception service routines, and interrupt service routines. Other systemwide functions, the swapping and modified page writing performed by the swapper, are implemented as a separate process that resides in system space. Figure 1-5 shows the various entry paths into the operating system kernel.

1.3.3.1 **Process Context and System State.** The first section of this chapter discussed the pieces of the system that are used to describe a process. Process context includes a complete address space description, quotas, privileges, scheduling data, etc. Any portion of the system that executes in the context of a process has all of these process attributes available.

There is a portion of the kernel, however, that operates outside the context of a specific process. Most routines that fall into this category are interrupt service routines, invoked in response to external events, regardless of the currently executing process. Portions of the initialization sequence also fall into this category. In any case, there are no process features, such as a kernel

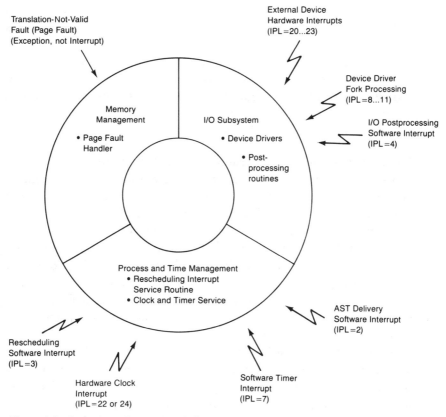

Figure 1-5   Paths into Components of VMS Kernel

stack or a page fault handler, available when these routines are executing.

Because of the lack of a process, this system state or interrupt state can be characterized by the following limited context:

- All stack operations take place on the systemwide interrupt stack.
- The primary indication that the CPU is in this state is contained in the PSL. The PSL indicates that the interrupt stack is being used, the current access mode is kernel mode, and the IPL is higher than 2.
- The system control block, the data structure that controls the dispatching of interrupts and exceptions, can be thought of as the secondary structure that describes system state.
- Code that executes in this so-called system context can only refer to system virtual addresses. In particular, there is no P1 space available, so the systemwide interrupt stack must be located in system space.
- No page faults are allowed. The page fault handler generates a fatal bugcheck if a page fault occurs and the IPL is above IPL 2.
- No exceptions are allowed (other than subset instruction emulation exceptions). Exceptions such as page faults are associated with a process. The

exception dispatcher generates a fatal bugcheck if an exception occurs above IPL 2 or while the processor is executing on the interrupt stack.

- ASTs, asynchronous events that allow a process to receive notification when external events have occurred, are not allowed. (The AST delivery interrupt is not requested when the processor is in system state and not granted until IPL drops below 2, an indication that the processor is leaving system state.)
- No system services are allowed in the system state.

1.3.3.2   **Process-Based Routines.** Procedure-based code (RMS services, Files-11 XQP, and system services) and exception service routines usually execute in the context of the current process (on the kernel stack when in kernel mode).

The system services are implemented as procedures and are available to all native mode languages. In addition, the fact that they are procedures means that there is a call frame on the stack. Thus, a utility subroutine in a system service can signal an error simply by putting the error status into R0 and issuing a RET instruction. All superfluous information is cleaned off the stack by the RET instruction. The system service dispatchers (actually the dispatchers for the CHMK and CHME exceptions) are exception service routines.

System services must be called from process context. They are not available from interrupt service routines or other code (such as portions of the initialization sequence) that execute outside the context of a process. One reason for requiring process context is that the various services assume that there is a process whose privileges can be checked and whose quotas can be charged as part of the normal operation of the service. Some system services reference locations in P1 space, a portion of address space only available while executing in process context.

The pager (the page fault exception handler) is an exception service routine that is invoked in response to a translation-not-valid fault. The pager thus satisfies page faults in the context of the process that incurred the fault. Because page faults are associated with a process, the system cannot tolerate page faults that occur in interrupt service routines or other routines that execute outside the context of a process. The actual restriction imposed by the pager is even more stringent. Page faults are not allowed above IPL 2. This restriction applies to process-based code executing at elevated IPL as well as to interrupt service code.

1.3.3.3   **Interrupt Service Routines.** By their asynchronous nature, interrupts execute without the support of process context (on the systemwide interrupt stack):

- I/O requests are initiated through the $QIO system service, which can be issued directly by the user or by some intermediary, such as RMS or the Files-11 XQP, on the user's behalf. Once an I/O request has been placed into a device queue, it remains there until the driver is triggered, usually by an interrupt generated in the external device.

Two classes of software interrupt service routines exist solely to support the I/O subsystem. The fork level interrupts allow device drivers to lower IPL in a controlled fashion. Final processing of I/O requests is also done in a software interrupt service routine.

- The timer functions in the operating system include support in both the hardware clock interrupt service routine and a software interrupt service routine that actually services individual timer requests.
- Another software interrupt performs the rescheduling function, where one process is removed from execution and another selected and placed into execution.

1.3.3.4   **Special Processes—Swapper and Null.** The swapper and the null processes are different from any other processes that exist in a VAX/VMS system. The differences lie not in their operations but in their limited context.

The limited context of either of these processes is partly because these two processes exist as part of the system image SYS.EXE. They do not have to be created with the Create Process system service. Specifically, their PCBs and process headers are assembled (in module PDAT) and linked into the system image. Other characteristics of these two processes are listed here:

- Their process headers are static. There is no working set list and no process section table. Neither process supports page faults. All code executed by either process must be locked into memory in some way. In fact, the code of both of these processes is part of the nonpaged executive.
- Both processes execute entirely in kernel mode, thereby eliminating the need for stacks for the other three access modes.
- Neither process has a P1 space. The kernel stack for either process is located in system space.
- The null process does not have a P0 space either. The swapper uses an array allocated from nonpaged pool as its P0 page table when it swaps, writes modified pages, and also during the part of process creation that takes place in the context of the swapper process.

Despite their limited contexts, both of these processes behave in a normal fashion in every other way. The swapper and the null processes are selected for execution by the scheduler just like any other process in the system. The swapper spends its idle time in the hibernate state until some component in the system recognizes a need for one of the swapper functions, at which time it is awakened. The null process is always computable but set to the lowest software priority in the system (priority 0). All CPU time not used by any other process in the system will be used by the null process.

1.3.3.5   **Special Subroutines.** There are several utility subroutines within the operating system related to scheduling and resource allocation that are called from both process-based code, such as system services, and from software interrupt service routines. These subroutines are constrained to execute with the limited context of interrupt or system state. An example of such a routine is SCH$QAST, which is called to queue an AST to a process. It may be invoked from IPL 4 and IPL 7 interrupt service routines, as well as from various system services.

1.3.4   **Memory Management and Access Modes**

The address translation mechanism is described in the *VAX Architecture Reference Manual*. Two side effects of this operation are of special interest to the VAX/VMS operating system. When a page is not valid, a translation-not-valid exception is generated that transfers control to an exception service routine that takes whatever steps are required to make the page valid. This exception transfers control from a hardware mechanism, address translation, to a software exception service routine, the page fault handler, and allows the operating system to gain control on address translation failures to implement its dynamic mapping of pages while a program is executing.

Before the address translation mechanism checks the valid bit in the page table entry, a protection check is made to determine whether the requested access will be granted. The check uses the current access mode in the PSL (PSL<25:24>), a protection code that is defined for each virtual page, and the type of access (read, modify, or write) to make its decision. This protection check allows the operating system to make read-only portions of the executive inaccessible to anyone (all access modes) for writing, preventing corruption of operating system code. In addition, privileged data structures can be protected from even read access by nonprivileged users, preserving system integrity.

1.3.5   **Exceptions, Interrupts, and REI**

The VAX exception and interrupt mechanisms are very important to the operation of VMS. Below is a comparison of the exception and interrupt mechanisms, followed by brief descriptions of features of the mechanisms which are used by VMS.

1.3.5.1   **Comparison of Exceptions and Interrupts.** The following list summarizes some of the characteristics of exceptions and interrupts:

• Interrupts occur asynchronously to the currently executing instruction stream. They are actually serviced between individual instructions or at well-defined points within the execution of a given instruction. Exceptions occur synchronously as a direct effect of the execution of the current instruction.

- Both mechanisms pass control to service routines whose addresses are stored in the system control block (SCB). These routines perform exception-specific or interrupt-specific processing.

- Exceptions are generally a part of the currently executing process. Their servicing is an extension of the instruction stream that is currently executing on behalf of that process. Interrupts are generally systemwide events that cannot rely on support of a process in their service routines.

- Because interrupts are generally systemwide, the systemwide interrupt stack is usually used to store the PC and PSL of the process that was interrupted. Exceptions are usually serviced on the per-process kernel stack. Which stack to use is usually determined by control bits in the SCB entry for each exception or interrupt.

- Interrupts cause a PC/PSL pair to be pushed onto the stack. Exceptions often cause exception-specific parameters to be stored in addition to a PC/PSL pair.

- Interrupts cause the IPL to change. Exceptions usually do not have an IPL change associated with them. (Machine checks and kernel-stack-not-valid exceptions elevate IPL to 31.)

- An interrupt can be blocked by elevating IPL to a value at or above the IPL associated with the interrupt. Exceptions, on the other hand, cannot be blocked. However, some exceptions can be disabled (by clearing associated bits in the PSL).

- When an interrupt or exception occurs, a new PSL is formed that summarizes the new IPL, the current access mode (usually kernel), the stack in use (interrupt or other), etc. One difference between exceptions and interrupts, a difference that reflects the fact that interrupts are not related to the interrupted instruction stream, is that the previous access mode field in the new PSL is set to kernel for interrupts while the previous mode field for exceptions reflects the access mode in which the exception occurred.

.3.5.2   **Other Uses of Exceptions and Interrupts.** In addition to the translation-not-valid fault used by memory management software, the operating system also uses the CHMK and CHME exceptions as entry paths to the executive. System services that must execute in a more privileged access mode use either the CHMK or CHME instruction to gain access mode rights (see Figure 1-4). The system handles most other exceptions by dispatching to user-defined condition handlers as described in Chapter 4.

Hardware interrupts temporarily suspend code that is executing so that an interrupt-specific routine can service the interrupt. Each interrupt has a priority level, or IPL, associated with it. The CPU raises IPL when it grants the interrupt. High-level interrupt service routines thus prevent the recognition of low-level interrupts. Low-level interrupt service routines can be interrupted by subsequent high-level interrupts. Kernel mode routines can also block interrupts at certain levels by specifically raising the IPL.

The VAX architecture also defines a series of software interrupt levels that can be used for a variety of purposes. The VMS operating system uses them for scheduling, I/O completion routines, and for synchronizing access to certain classes of data structures. Chapter 6 describes the software interrupt mechanism and its use.

1.3.5.3 **The REI Instruction.** The REI instruction is the common exit path for interrupts and exceptions. Many protection and privilege checks are incorporated into this instruction. Because most fields in the PSL are not accessible to the programmer, the REI instruction provides the only means for changing access mode to a less privileged mode (see Figure 1-4). It is also the only way to reach compatibility mode.

Although the IPL field of the PSL is accessible through the PR$_IPL processor register, execution of an REI is a common way that IPL is lowered during normal execution. Because a change in IPL can alter the deliverability of pending interrupts, many hardware and software interrupts are delivered after an REI instruction is executed.

1.3.6 **Process Structure**

The VAX architecture also defines a data structure called a hardware process control block that contains copies of all a process's general registers when the process is not active. When a process is selected for execution, the contents of this block are copied into the actual registers inside the processor with a single instruction, LDPCTX. The corresponding instruction that saves the contents of the general registers when the process is removed from execution is SVPCTX.

1.4 **OTHER SYSTEM CONCEPTS**

This chapter began by discussing the most important concepts in the VMS operating system, process and image. There are several other fundamental ideas that should be mentioned before beginning a detailed description of VMS internals.

1.4.1 **Resource Control**

The VAX/VMS operating system protects itself and other processes in the system from careless or malicious users, with hardware and software protection mechanisms, software privileges, and software quotas and limits.

1.4.1.1 **Hardware Protection.** The memory management protection mechanism that is related to access mode is used to prevent unauthorized users from modifying (or even reading) privileged data structures. Access mode protection is also used to protect system and user code and other read-only data structures from being modified by programming errors.

A more subtle but perhaps more important aspect of protection provided by the memory management architecture is that the process address space of one process (P0 space or P1 space) is not accessible to code running in the context of another process. When such accessibility is desired to share common routines or data, the operating system provides a controlled access through global sections. System virtual address space is addressable by all processes, although page-by-page protection may deny read or write access to specific system virtual pages for certain access modes.

1.4.1.2 **Process Privileges.** Many operations that are performed by system services could destroy operating system code or data or corrupt existing files if performed carelessly. Other services allow a process to adversely affect other processes in the system. The VMS operating system requires that processes wishing to execute these potentially damaging operations be suitably privileged. Process privileges are assigned when a process is created, either by the creator or through the user's in the authorization file.

These privileges are described in the *VAX/VMS System Manager's Reference Manual* and in the *VAX/VMS System Services Reference Manual.* The privileges themselves are specific bits in a quadword that is stored in the beginning of the process header. (The locations and manipulations of the several process privilege masks that the operating system maintains are discussed in Chapter 21.) When a VMS system service that requires privilege is called, the service checks to see whether the associated bit in the process privilege mask is set.

1.4.1.3 **Quotas and Limits.** The VMS operating system also controls allocation of its systemwide resources, such as nonpaged dynamic memory and page file space, through the use of quotas and limits. These process attributes are also assigned when the process is created. By restricting such items as the number of concurrent I/O requests or pending ASTs, VMS exercises control over the resource drain that a single process can exert on system resources, such as nonpaged dynamic memory. In general, a process cannot perform certain operations (such as queue an AST) unless it has sufficient quota (nonzero PCB$W_ASTCNT in this case). The locations and values of the various quotas and limits used by the operating system are described in Chapter 20.

1.4.1.4 **User Access Control.** The VMS operating system uses user identification code (UIC) for two different protection purposes. If a process wishes to perform some control operation (Suspend, Wake, Delete, etc.) on another process, it requires WORLD privilege to affect any process in the system. A process with GROUP privilege can affect only other processes with the same group number. A process with neither WORLD nor GROUP privilege can affect only other processes with the same UIC.

VMS also uses UIC as a basis for protection of various system objects, such as files, global sections, logical names, and mailboxes. The owner of a file, for example, specifies what access to the file she grants to herself, to other processes in the same group, and to other processes in the system.

A new Version 4 feature called an access control list (ACL) provides more selective levels of sharing. An ACL lists individual users or groupings of users who are to be allowed or denied access to a system object. ACLs specify sharing on the basis of UIC, as well as other groupings, known as identifiers, that can be associated with a process. As of Version 4.2, ACLs can be specified for files, directories, devices, global sections, and shareable logical name tables.

1.4.2   Other System Primitives

Several other simple tools used by the VMS operating system are mentioned freely throughout this book and are described in Chapters 2, 3, and 28.

1.4.2.1   Synchronization.
Any multiprogramming system must take measures to prevent simultaneous access to system data structures. The executive uses three synchronization techniques. By elevating IPL, a subset of interrupts can be blocked, allowing unrestricted access to systemwide data structures. The most common synchronization IPL used by the operating system is IPL 8, called IPL$_SYNCH.

For some data structures, elevated IPL is either an unnecessary tool or a potential system degradation. For example, processes executing at or above IPL 3 cannot be rescheduled (removed from execution). Once a process gains control of a data structure protected by elevated IPL, it will not allow another process to execute until it gives up its ownership. In addition, page faults are not allowed above IPL 2 and so any data structure that exists in pageable address space cannot be synchronized with elevated IPL.

The VMS executive requires a second synchronization tool to allow synchronized access to pageable data structures. This tool must also allow a process to be removed from execution while it maintains ownership of the structure in question. One synchronization tool that fulfills these requirements is called a mutual exclusion semaphore (or mutex). Synchronization, including the use of mutexes, is discussed in Chapter 2.

The VMS executive and other system components, such as the Files-11 XQP, RMS, and the job controller, use a third tool, the lock management system services, for more flexible sharing of resources among processes. The lock management system services provide a waiting mechanism for processes whose desired access to a resource is blocked. They also provide notification to a process whose use of a resource blocks another process. Most importantly, the lock management system services provide sharing of clusterwide resources. Chapter 13 describes the lock management system services.

1.4.2.2   **Dynamic Memory Allocation.** The system maintains several dynamic memory areas from which blocks of memory can be allocated and deallocated. Nonpaged pool contains those systemwide structures that might be manipulated by (hardware or software) interrupt service routines or process-based code executing above IPL 2. Paged pool contains systemwide structures that do not have to be kept memory resident. The process allocation region and the kernel request packet (KRP) lookaside list, both in process P1 space, are used for pageable data structures that will not be shared among several processes. Dynamic memory allocation and deallocation are discussed in detail in Chapter 3.

1.4.2.3   **Logical Names.** The system uses logical names for many purposes, including a transparent way of implementing a device-independent I/O system. The use of logical names as a programming tool is discussed in the *VAX/VMS System Services Reference Manual*. The internal operations of the logical name system services, as well as the internal organization of the logical name tables, are described in Chapter 28.

1.5   **LAYOUT OF VIRTUAL ADDRESS SPACE**

This section shows the approximate contents of the three different parts of virtual address space.

1.5.1   **System Virtual Address Space**

The layout of system virtual address space is pictured in Figure 1-6. Details such as the no-access pages at either end of the interrupt stack are omitted to avoid cluttering the diagram. Table F-2 in Appendix F gives a more complete description of system space, including these guard pages, system pages allocated by disk drivers, and other details.

This figure was produced from two lists provided by the System Dump Analyzer (SDA) Utility (the system page table and the contents of all global data areas in system space) and from the system map SYS$SYSTEM: SYS.MAP. The relationships between the variable size pieces of system space and their associated SYSBOOT parameters are given in Appendix F.

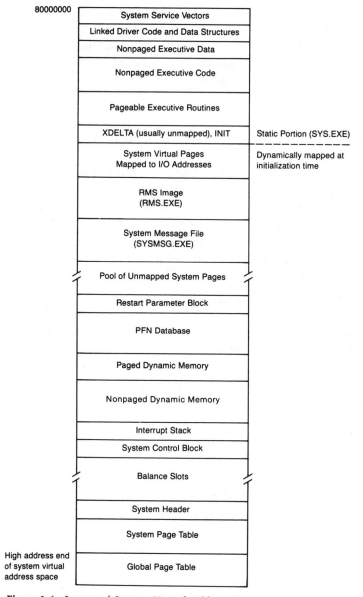

Figure 1-6 Layout of System Virtual Address Space

1.5.2   Control Region (P1 Space)

Figure 1-7 shows the layout of P1 space. This figure was produced mainly from information contained in module SHELL, which contains a prototype of a P1 page table that is used whenever a process is created. An SDA listing of process page tables was used to determine the order and size of the portions of P1 space not defined in SHELL.

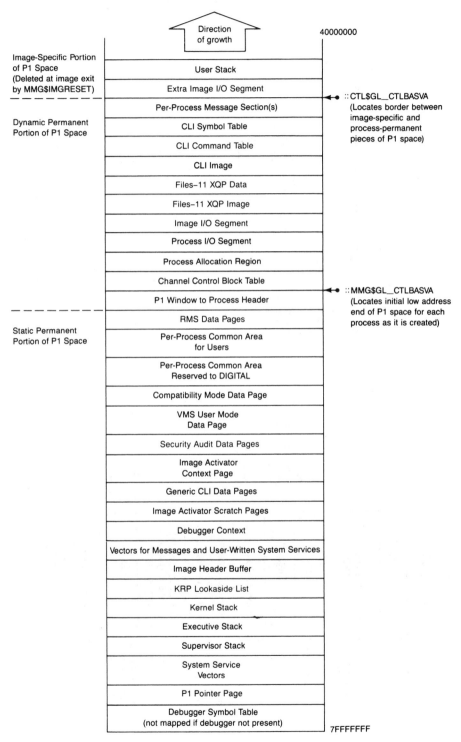

Figure 1-7   Layout of P1 Space

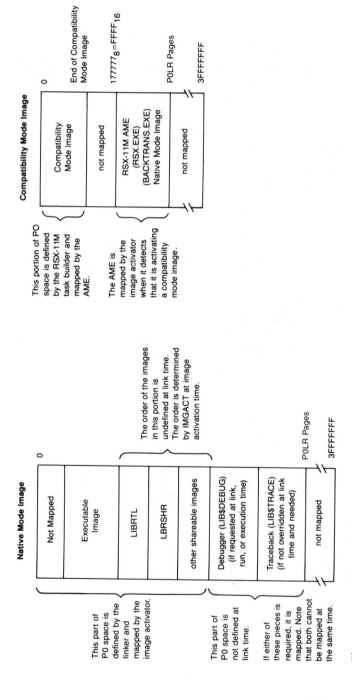

Figure 1-8 P0 Space Allocation

Some of the pieces of P1 space are created dynamically when the process is created. These include a P1 map of process header pages, a command language interpreter (CLI) if one is being used, a symbol table for that CLI, the process allocation region, and the process I/O segment. In addition, the Files-11 XQP and its data areas are mapped at process creation.

The two pieces of P1 space at the lowest virtual addresses (the user stack and any extra image I/O segment) are created dynamically each time an image executes and are deleted as part of image rundown. Appendix F contains a description of the sizes of the different pieces of P1 space. Table F-5 gives a complete description of P1 space, including details, such as memory management page protection and the name of the system component that maps a given portion.

1.5.3   Program Region (P0 Space)

Figure 1-8 shows a typical layout of P0 space for both a native mode image (produced by the VMS linker) and a compatibility mode image (produced by the RSX-11M task builder). This figure is much more conceptual than the previous two illustrations because the layout of P0 space depends upon the image being run.

By default, the first page of P0 space (0 to 1FF) is not mapped (protection set to No Access). This no-access page allows easy detection of two common programming errors, using zero or a small number as the address of a data location or using such a small number as the destination of a control transfer. (A link-time request or system service call can alter the protection of virtual page zero. Note also that page zero is accessible to compatibility mode images.)

The main native mode image is placed into P0 space, starting at address 200_{16}. Any shareable images that are position-independent and shared (for example, LIBRTL) are placed at the end of the main image. The order in which these shareable images are placed into the image is determined during image activation.

If the debugger or the traceback facility is required, these images are added at execution time (even if /DEBUG was selected at link time). This mapping is described in detail in Chapter 21.

2 Synchronization Techniques

> "Time," said George, "why I can give you a definition of time.
> It's what keeps everything from happening at once."
>
> Ray Cummings, *The Man Who Mastered Time**

One of the most important issues in the design of an operating system is synchronization. Especially in a system that is interrupt driven, certain sequences of instructions must be allowed to execute without interruption. The VMS operating system raises processor interrupt priority level (IPL) to block interrupts of equal and lower priority during the execution of critical code paths.

Any operating system must also take precautions to ensure that shared data structures are not being simultaneously modified by several routines or being read by one routine while another routine is modifying the structure. The VMS executive uses a combination of the following software techniques and features of the VAX hardware to synchronize access to shared data structures:

- Interlocked instructions
- Elevated IPL
- Serialized access
- Mutual exclusion semaphores, called mutexes
- VAX/VMS lock management system services

2.1 OVERVIEW

Synchronization is a term normally used to refer to the simultaneous occurrence of two or more events.

In a computer context, however, synchronization is the technique of blocking all but one of two or more events when their simultaneous occurrence might disrupt the proper operation of the system.

One fundamental computer synchronization problem is the requirement that a thread of execution change two storage locations as a single operation. If either is changed, but not both, the storage is temporarily inconsistent. If the thread of execution can be interrupted, after changing the first location

*Copyright © 1957 by Gabrielle Cummings; reprinted by courtesy of Forrest J Ackerman, 2495 Glendower Ave., Hollywood, CA 90027.

and before changing the second, by another thread of execution which uses or changes those locations, then access to those locations is not synchronized and system disruption can occur.

Another fundamental synchronization problem is the requirement that a thread of execution read a storage location and, depending on its value, write a new value into the location. If the thread can be interrupted after the read and before the write by another thread with the same intent toward that location, then access to that location is not synchronized and system disruption can occur. Specifically, the modification of one of the threads can overlay the modification of the other.

There are a number of situations for which synchronization is an issue. One example is a single CPU with multiple threads of execution simultaneously in progress. Another example is a system in which several independent CPUs share some storage. This category includes not only multiprocessor systems but also single CPU systems with intelligent I/O controllers.

Synchronization of memory and disk storage, though conceptually similar, are different problems requiring different techniques.

When data structures in memory which require synchronized access are accessed only by a single VAX CPU, VMS typically runs at raised IPL to block interrupts during the relevant instruction sequences, although it may use mutexes and locks where appropriate.

If a modification to a data structure accessed only by a single CPU can be made with one uninterruptible instruction, then IPL need not be raised. INSQUE and REMQUE are examples of such instructions; each is uninterruptible and each changes two or more memory locations.

Some types of single processor memory synchronization require specific techniques:

- A data structure accessed from interrupt service routines is protected by raising IPL to the highest interrupt level from which the structure is accessed (see Section 2.2.2).
- A data structure accessed by multiple processes from IPLs below 3 is protected by mutexes or lock management system services. Section 2.4 discusses mutexes and Section 2.5 briefly describes the lock management system services.
- A process-private data structure accessed from a non-AST thread of execution and an AST thread of execution must be protected against concurrent access. Access to the data structure can be synchronized by blocking AST delivery, either by raising IPL to 2 or through the Set AST Enable ($SETAST) system service. The concept of AST reentrancy and ways of achieving it are described in the *Guide to Creating Modular Procedures on VAX/VMS*.

When there are independent processors accessing data structures in memory, synchronization requires memory interlocks. A memory interlock is a mechanism to provide an atomic read-modify-write sequence to a location in shared memory. The VAX architecture provides a number of instructions which interlock memory. These consist of BBCCI, BBSSI, ADAWI, and INSQxI and REMQxI, the instructions that manipulate the self-relative queues. The operations of the interlocked instructions are described in detail in the *VAX Architecture Reference Manual.*

The following examples show synchronization of independent processors accessing the same memory:

- The DR32 is a general purpose, intelligent data port that connects a VAX internal memory bus to a bus accessible to foreign devices. An application program accesses the DR32 through command and response queues in VAX memory. Synchronizing access to the queues requires that both the DR32 and the application program use interlocked queue instructions. The user interface to the DR32 is documented in the *VAX/VMS I/O User's Reference Manual: Part II.*
- The CI adapter (for example, CI780) is a microcoded intelligent controller that connects a VAX to a CI bus and communicates with its counterparts on other nodes. The CI port driver communicates with the CI adapter through command and response queues. Both the CI adapter and the port driver must use interlocked queue instructions to access the queues.
- VMS systems sharing memory through MA780 controllers communicate through a data area located in shared memory. The data area describes mailboxes, global sections, and common event flag clusters created in the shared memory. VMS code on each processor executes interlocked instructions to prevent concurrent access to the data area. User processes accessing a global section in shared memory must also use interlocked instructions to synchronize their access to data in the global section. Chapter 14 describes shared memory support.
- VAX CPUs running asymmetric multiprocessing communicate through a shared data structure located in nonpaged pool. VMS code on each processor executes interlocked instructions to prevent concurrent access to the data structure. Chapter 27 describes asymmetric multiprocessing support.

Another important synchronization issue for VMS involves disk storage. Data structures on a shared disk (for example, files and records within files and the actual disk structure) are protected by lock management system services. This form of synchronization serves whether the disk is accessed by multiple processes on a single system or by multiple processes on multiple nodes of a VAXcluster. Lock management system services are the only clusterwide synchronization mechanism (see Section 2.5).

.2   **ELEVATED IPL**

The primary purpose for raising IPL is to block interrupts at the selected IPL value and all lower values of IPL. The operating system uses specific IPL values to synchronize access to certain structures. For example, by raising IPL to 23, all device interrupts are blocked, but interval timer interrupts at IPL 24 can still be granted.

The IPL, stored in the Processor Status Longword (PSL) register bits <20:16>, is altered by writing the desired IPL value to the privileged register PR$_IPL with the MTPR instruction. This change in IPL is usually accomplished in the operating system with one of two macros, SETIPL or DSBINT, whose macro definitions are as follows:

```
.MACRO SETIPL IPL = #31
       MTPR    IPL,S^#PR$_IPL
.ENDM  SETIPL


.MACRO DSBINT IPL = #31, DST = -(SP)
       MFPR    S^#PR$_IPL,DST
       MTPR    IPL,S^#PR$_IPL
.ENDM  DSBINT
```

The SETIPL macro changes IPL to the specified value. If no argument is present, IPL is elevated to 31. The DSBINT macro first saves the current IPL before elevating IPL to the specified value. If no alternate destination is specified, the old IPL is saved on the stack. The default IPL value is 31.

The DSBINT macro is usually used when a later sequence of code must restore the IPL to the saved value (with the ENBINT macro). This macro is especially useful when the caller's IPL is unknown. The SETIPL macro is used when the IPL will later be explicitly lowered with another SETIPL or simply as a result of executing an REI instruction. That is, the value of the saved IPL is not important to the routine that is using the SETIPL macro.

The ENBINT macro is the counterpart to the DSBINT macro. It restores the IPL to the value found in the designated source argument.

```
.MACRO ENBINT SRC = (SP)+
       MTPR SRC,S^#PR$_IPL
.ENDM  ENBINT
```

Occasionally it is necessary to save an IPL value (to be restored later by the ENBINT macro) without changing the current IPL. The SAVIPL macro performs this function:

```
.MACRO SAVIPL DST = -(SP)
       MFPR    S^#PR$_IPL,DST
.ENDM  SAVIPL
```

The successful use of IPL as a synchronization tool requires that IPL be raised (not lowered) to the appropriate synchronization level. Lowering IPL defeats any attempt at synchronization and also runs the risk of a reserved operand fault when an REI instruction is later executed. (An REI instruction that attempts to elevate IPL causes a reserved operand fault.)

Suppose a thread of execution modifying more than one location in a shared database raises IPL to x to block interrupts from other accessors of the database. The first thread of execution is interrupted after partially making its modifications by a second thread running in response to a higher priority interrupt. The shared database is now in an inconsistent state. If the second thread were to lower IPL to x in a mistaken attempt at synchronization and access the database, the second thread could receive incorrect data and/or corrupt the database.

Integrity of the database would, however, be maintained if the second thread of execution were to reschedule itself to run as the result of an interrupt at or below x and access the database from the rescheduled thread. "Forking" is the primary way in which an interrupt thread of execution reschedules itself to run at a lower IPL. Chapter 6 describes forking in more detail.

2.2.1 Use of IPL$_SYNCH

IPL 8 (IPL$_SYNCH) is the IPL at which the software timer routines execute. These routines service timer queue entries and handle quantum expiration. (The software timer interrupt is requested and granted at IPL 7, but the interrupt service routine raises IPL and runs primarily at IPL$_SYNCH. See Chapter 11 for further details.) IPL 8 is the level to which IPL must be raised for any routine to access several systemwide data structures, for example, the scheduler database. By raising IPL to 8, all other routines that might access the same systemwide data structure are blocked from execution until IPL is lowered. IPL 8 is also the IPL at which most driver fork processing occurs.

While the processor is executing at IPL 8, certain systemwide events such as scheduling and I/O postprocessing are blocked. However, other more important operations, such as hardware interrupt servicing, can continue.

In previous versions of VMS, the value of IPL$_SYNCH was 7. Almost all device driver fork processing occurred above IPL$_SYNCH, at IPL 8 and higher IPLs. Thus the time the system spent at IPL$_SYNCH did not affect I/O processing. With VMS V4, the value of IPL$_SYNCH has been changed to IPL 8. This change was made to enable three executive components to run at the same IPL: the distributed lock manager, system communications services (SCS), and the CI port driver.

On a VAXcluster, the lock manager must communicate clusterwide with its counterparts on other nodes to perform locking. The lock managers communicate using the message services of SCS. SCS is also used heavily by class and port drivers and runs at the same IPL they do, IPL$_SCS, or 8. The SCS port drivers must run at IPL 8 because some of them, for example, the UDA port driver, run at IPL 8 to synchronize access to shared UNIBUS resources and data structures.

In addition to having to communicate with SCS at IPL$_SCS, the lock manager has another constraint. Its actions (granting locks, queueing ASTs, placing processes into wait) result in modifications to the scheduler database, which is synchronized at IPL$_SYNCH. To simplify the interactions among the lock manager, SCS, and other threads of execution modifying the scheduler database, IPL$_SYNCH and IPL$_SCS were made the same value by changing the value of IPL$_SYNCH.

.2.2   Other IPLs Used for Synchronization

Table 2-1 lists several IPLs that are used for synchronization purposes by the system. Some of these levels are used to control access to shared data structures. Others are used to prevent certain events, such as a clock interrupt or process deletion, from occurring while a block of instructions is executed.

.2.2.1

IPL$_POWER. Routines in the operating system raise IPL to IPL$_POWER, or 31, to block all interrupts, including power failure, an IPL 30 interrupt. IPL is raised to this level only for a short period of time (usually less than ten instructions once the system is initialized).

- Device drivers use IPL 31 just before they call IOC$WFIxxCH to prevent a powerfail interrupt from occurring.

Table 2-1   Common IPL Values Used by VAX/VMS for Synchronization

Name	Value (decimal)	Meaning
IPL$_POWER	31	Disable all interrupts
IPL$_HWCLK[1]	24	Block clock and device interrupts
UCB$B_DIPL[2]	20–23	Block interrupts from specific devices
UCB$B_FIPL[2]	8–11	Device driver fork levels
IPL$_SYNCH	8	Synchronize access to certain system data structures
IPL$_QUEUEAST	6	Device driver fork IPL that allows drivers to elevate IPL to 8
IPL$_ASTDEL	2	Block delivery of ASTs (prevent process deletion)

[1]Interval timer interrupts occur at IPL 22 or 24, depending on processor type.
[2]These symbols are offsets into a device unit control block.

- The entire bootstrap sequence operates at IPL 31 to put the system into a known state before allowing interrupts to occur.
- Because the error logger routines can be called from anywhere in the executive, including fault service routines that execute at IPL 31 (such as machine check handlers), allocation of an error log buffer can only execute at IPL 31. A corollary of this requirement demands that the ERRFMT process execute at IPL 31 when it is altering data structures that describe the state of the error log buffer. (As Chapter 8 describes, the copy is done at two IPL levels. The error log buffer status flags and message counts are modified at IPL 31. Then IPL is lowered to 0; the contents of the error log buffer are copied to the ERRFMT process's P0 space, and the messages are formatted and written to the error log file.)

2.2.2.2   **IPL$_HWCLK.** When IPL is raised to 24, interval timer interrupts are blocked. On some VAX processors, the interval timer interrupts at IPL 22; on others it interrupts at IPL 24. See Table 11-2 for a list of processor types and associated interval timer IPLs. The software timer interrupt service routine uses IPL 24 when it is comparing two quadword system time values. This IPL prevents the system time from being updated while it is being compared to some other time value. (This precaution is required because the VAX architecture does not contain an uninterruptible compare quadword instruction.)

2.2.2.3   **Device IPL.** Device drivers will raise IPL to the level at which the associated device will interrupt to prevent the same device or other devices from generating interrupts while device registers are being read or written. This step usually precedes the further elevation of IPL to 31 just described.

2.2.2.4   **Fork IPL.** Fork IPL (a value specific to each device type) is used by the executive to synchronize access to each unit control block. These blocks are accessed by device drivers and by procedure-based code, such as the completion path of the $QIO system service and the Cancel I/O system service.

Device drivers also use their associated fork IPL as a synchronization level when accessing data structures that control shared resources, such as multi-unit controllers, datapath registers, or map registers. For this synchronization to work properly, all devices sharing a given resource must use the same fork IPL.

The use of fork IPL to synchronize access to unit control blocks works the same way that elevating IPL to IPL$_SYNCH does. That is, one piece of code elevates IPL to the specified fork IPL (found at offset UCB$B_FIPL) and blocks all other potential accesses to the UCB. Fork processing, the technique whereby device drivers lower IPL below device interrupt level in a manner consistent with the interrupt nesting scheme, also uses the serialization technique described in Section 2.3.

2.2.2.5   **IPL$_QUEUEAST.** In previous versions of VMS, IPL$_SYNCH, the IPL at which several systemwide databases were synchronized, was 7. Device drivers that needed to execute code at IPL$_SYNCH forked to IPL 6, so that they could raise IPL to IPL$_SYNCH. IPL 6 was named IPL$_QUEUEAST, since its primary use as a fork IPL 6 was AST enqueuing. The terminal driver, for example, might notify a requesting process about unsolicited input or a CTRL/Y through an AST (see Chapter 7). The mailbox driver might also queue an AST to notify a requesting process about unsatisfied reads and unsolicited writes to a mailbox. Queuing an AST to a process requires scheduler database modifications, which must be made at IPL$_SYNCH.

The IPL 7 interrupt could not be used to achieve the same result because it is reserved for software timer interrupts. So this synchronization technique used the first free IPL below 7, the IPL 6 software interrupt called IPL$_QUEUEAST.

In VMS V4, the value of IPL$_SYNCH was changed to 8 for the reason described in Section 2.2.1. As a result of this change, IPL$_QUEUEAST forking is generally unnecessary for serializing access to databases synchronized at IPL$_SYNCH. Fork processes running at IPL 8 could remain at 8; device interrupt service routines and fork processes running at IPLs above 8 could fork to 8. However, many instances of IPL$_QUEUEAST fork processing remain in VMS V4, unchanged from earlier versions. These result in placing a somewhat higher priority on I/O processing.

2.2.3   **IPL 2**

IPL 2 is the level at which the software interrupt associated with AST delivery occurs. When system service procedures raise IPL to 2, they are blocking the delivery of all ASTs, but particularly the kernel AST that causes process deletion. In other words, if a process is executing at IPL 2 (or above), that process cannot be deleted.

This technique is used in several places to prevent process deletion between the time that some system resource (such as system dynamic memory) is allocated and the time that ownership of that resource is recorded (such as the insertion of a data structure into a list). For example, the $QIO system service executes at IPL 2 from the time that an I/O request packet is allocated from nonpaged dynamic memory until that packet is queued to a unit control block or placed into the I/O postprocessing queue.

The memory management subsystem uses IPL 2 to inhibit the special kernel mode AST that is queued on I/O completion. This inhibition is necessary at times when the memory management subsystem has some knowledge of the process's working set and yet the execution of the I/O completion AST could cause a modification to the working set, thereby invalidating that knowledge.

IPL 2 also has significance for an entirely different reason: it is the highest IPL at which page faults are permitted. If a page fault occurs above IPL 2, a PGFIPLHI fatal bugcheck is issued. If there is any possibility that a page fault can occur, because either the code that is executing or the data that it references is pageable, then that code cannot execute above IPL 2. The converse of this constraint is that any code that executes above IPL 2, and all data referenced by such code, must be locked into memory in some way. Appendix B shows some of the techniques that the VMS executive uses to dynamically lock code or data into memory so that IPL can be elevated above IPL 2.

2.3 SERIALIZED ACCESS

The software interrupt mechanism described in Chapter 6 provides no method for counting the number of requested software interrupts. The VMS operating system uses a combination of software interrupts and doubly linked lists to cause several requests for the same data structure or procedure to be serialized. The most important example of this serialization in the operating system is the use of fork processes by device drivers. The I/O postprocessing software interrupt is a second example of serialized access.

2.3.1 Fork Processing

Fork processing is the technique that allows device drivers to lower IPL in a manner consistent with the interrupt nesting scheme defined by the VAX architecture. When a device driver receives control in response to a device interrupt, it performs whatever steps are necessary to service the interrupt at device IPL. For example, any device registers whose contents would be destroyed by another interrupt must be read before dismissing the device interrupt.

Usually, there is some processing that can be deferred. For DMA devices, an interrupt signifies either completion of the operation or an error. The code that distinguishes these two cases and performs error processing is usually lengthy and to execute at device IPL for extended periods of time would slow down the system. For non-DMA devices that do not interrupt at too rapid a rate, interrupt processing can be deferred in favor of other more important device servicing.

In either case, the driver signals that it wants to delay further processing until the IPL in the system drops below a predetermined value, the fork IPL associated with this driver. This signaling is accomplished by calling a routine in the executive that saves some minimal context including the address of the driver routine to be executed. The context is saved in a data structure called a fork block, shown in Figure 6-2. The fork block is then inserted at the end of the fork queue for that IPL value. A software interrupt at the appropriate IPL is requested. Chapter 6 describes fork processing in further detail.

I/O Postprocessing

Upon completion of an I/O request, there is a series of cleanup steps that must be performed. The event flag associated with the request must be set. A special kernel AST that will perform final cleanup in the context of the process that initially issued the $QIO call must be queued to the process. This cleanup must be completed for one I/O request before another is handled. In other words, I/O postprocessing must be serialized.

This serialization is accomplished by performing the postprocessing operation as a software interrupt service routine (at IPL 4). When a request is recognized as being complete, the I/O request packet is placed at the tail of the I/O postprocessing queue (at global listhead IOC$GL_PSBL), and a software interrupt at IPL 4 is requested.

When the device driver recognizes that an I/O request has completed (either successfully or unsuccessfully), it calls routine IOC$REQCOM, which makes the IPL 4 software interrupt request at fork IPL (IPL 8 to IPL 11), so the postprocessing interrupt is deferred until the IPL drops below 4.

Some I/O requests do not require driver action. When the Queue I/O Request ($QIO) system service or device-specific FDT routines detect that the request can be completed without driver intervention, or if they detect an error, they call one of the routines EXE$FINISHIO or EXE$FINISHIOC. These two routines execute at IPL 2, so the requested software interrupt is taken immediately. ACPs and Files-11 XQP also place I/O request packets into the postprocessing queue and request the IPL 4 software interrupt.

MUTUAL EXCLUSION SEMAPHORES (MUTEXES)

The synchronization techniques described so far all execute at elevated IPL, thus blocking certain operations, such as a rescheduling request, from taking place. However, in some situations requiring synchronization, elevated IPL is an unacceptable technique. One reason elevated IPL might be unacceptable is that the processor would have to remain at an elevated IPL for an indeterminately long time because of the structure of the data. For example, associating to a common event block cluster requires a search of the list of common event blocks (CEBs) for the specified CEB. This might be a lengthy operation on a system with many CEBs.

Furthermore, elevated IPL is unacceptable for synchronizing access to pageable data. The memory management subsystem does not allow page faults to occur when IPL is above 2. Thus, any pageable data structure cannot be protected by elevating IPL to IPL$_SYNCH. For these two reasons, another mechanism is required for controlling access to shared data structures.

The VMS operating system uses mutexes, mutual exclusion semaphores, for this purpose. Mutexes are essentially flags that indicate whether a given data structure is being examined or modified by one of a group of cooperating processes. The implementation allows either multiple readers or one writer

Table 2-2   List of Data Structures Protected by Mutexes

Data Structure	Global Name of Mutex[1]
Logical name table	LNM$AL_MUTEX
I/O database[2]	IOC$GL_MUTEX
Common event block list	EXE$GL_CEBMTX
Paged dynamic memory	EXE$GL_PGDYNMTX
Global section descriptor list	EXE$GL_GSDMTX
Shared memory global section descriptor table	EXE$GL_SHMGSMTX
Shared memory mailbox descriptor table	EXE$GL_SHMMBMTX
Not currently used	EXE$GL_ENQMTX
Line printer unit control block[3]	UCB$L_LP_MUTEX
Not currently used	EXE$GL_ACLMTX
System intruder lists	CIA$GL_MUTEX
Object rights block access control list[4]	ORB$L_ACL_MUTEX

[1]When a process is placed into an MWAIT state waiting for a mutex, the address of the mutex is placed into the PCB$L_EFWM field of the PCB. The symbolic contents of PCB$L_EFWM will probably remain the same for new releases, but the numeric contents change. The numeric values are available from the system map, SYS$SYSTEM: SYS.MAP.

[2]This mutex is used by the Assign Channel and Allocate Device system services when searching through the linked list of device data blocks and unit control blocks (UCBs) for a device. It is also used whenever UCBs are added or deleted, for example, during the creation of mailboxes and network devices.

[3]The mutex associated with each line printer unit does not have a fixed location like the other mutexes. As a field in the unit control block (UCB), its location and value depend on where the UCB for that unit is allocated.

[4]The mutex associated with each object rights block (ORB) does not have a fixed location like the other mutexes. As a field in the object rights block, its location and value depend on where the ORB is allocated.

of a data structure. Table 2-2 lists those data structures in the system that are protected by mutexes.

The mutex itself consists of a single longword that contains the number of owners of the mutex (MTX$W_OWNCNT) in the low-order word and status flags (MTX$W_STS) in the high-order word (see Figure 2-1). The owner count begins at −1 so that a mutex with a zero in the low-order word has one owner. The only flag currently implemented indicates whether a write operation is either in progress or pending for this mutex (MTX$V_WRT).

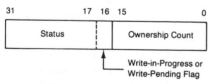

Figure 2-1   Format of Mutual Exclusion Semaphore (MUTEX)

4.1   Locking a Mutex for Read Access

When a process wishes to gain read access to a data structure that is protected by a mutex, it passes the address of that mutex to a routine called SCH$LOCKR (in module MUTEX). If there is no write operation either in progress or pending, the owner count of this mutex (MTX$W_OWNCNT) is incremented, the count of mutexes owned by this process (stored at offset PCB$W_MTXCNT in the software PCB) is also incremented, and control is passed back to the caller, unless this is the only mutex owned by this process (mutex count equals 1).

If this mutex is the first the process has locked and if the process is not a real-time process, its current and base priorities are saved in the PCB at offsets PCB$B_PRISAV and PCB$B_PRIBSAV and its priority is elevated to 16. The process receives a boost to hasten its execution and use of the mutex. The mutex is owned for as little time as possible to avoid blocking other processes which require it. The check on the number of owned mutexes prevents a process that gains ownership of two or more mutexes from receiving a permanent priority elevation to 16.

Routine SCH$LOCKR always returns successfully in the sense that, if the mutex is currently unavailable, the process is placed into a miscellaneous wait state (MWAIT) until the mutex is available for the process. When the process eventually gains ownership of the mutex, control is then passed back to the process. IPL is set to IPL$_ASTDEL (2) to prevent process deletion and suspension while the mutex is owned by this process. This preventative step must be taken because neither the Delete Process system service nor the Suspend Process system service checks whether the target process owns any mutexes. If the deletion or suspension were to succeed, the locked data structure would be lost to the system.

4.2   Locking a Mutex for Write Access

A process wishing to gain write access to a protected data structure passes the address of the appropriate mutex to a routine called SCH$LOCKW (in module MUTEX). This routine returns control to the caller with the mutex locked for write access if the mutex is currently unowned. In addition, both mutex counts (MTX$W_OWNCNT and PCB$W_MTXCNT) are incremented, the process software priority is possibly altered, and IPL is set to 2. An alternate entry point, SCH$LOCKNOWAIT, returns control to the caller with R0<0> cleared (indicating failure) if the requested mutex is already owned. For the regular entry point (SCH$LOCKW), if this mutex is owned, the process is placed into the mutex wait state (MWAIT). However, the write pending bit is set so that future requests for read access will also be denied. In a sense, this scheme is placing requests for write access ahead of requests for read access. However, all that this check really does is prevent a continuous stream of read accesses from keeping the mutex locked. When the mutex count does go to −1 (no owners), it is declared available, and the highest priority process waiting for the mutex is the one that will get first access to the mutex, independent of whether that process is requesting a read or a write access.

2.4.3 Mutex Wait State

When a process is placed into a mutex wait state, its stack is set up so that the saved PC is the entry point of either the read-lock routine or the write-lock routine. The PSL is adjusted so that the saved IPL is 2. The address of the mutex that is being requested is placed into the software PCB at offset PCB$L_EFWM. (Because the process is not waiting on an event flag, the field is available for this purpose.) Table 2-2 lists the system global names of mutexes whose addresses might be placed in PCB$L_EFWM.

2.4.4 Unlocking a Mutex

A process relinquishes ownership of a mutex by passing the address of the mutex to be released to a routine called SCH$UNLOCK (also in module MUTEX). This routine decrements the number of mutexes owned by this process recorded in its PCB. If this process does not own any more mutexes (PCB$W_MTXCNT contains zero), the saved base and current priorities (in fields PCB$B_PRIBSAV and PCB$B_PRISAV) are established as the p ɔcess's new base and current priorities. If there is a computable resident process with a higher priority than this process's restored priority, a rescheduling interrupt is requested. This situation is known as "delayed preemption" of the current process.

SCH$UNLOCK also decrements the number of owners of this mutex (MTX$W_OWNCNT). If the owner count of this mutex does not go to −1, there are other outstanding owners of this mutex, so control is simply passed back to the caller.

If the count does become −1, this value indicates that this mutex is currently unowned. If the write-in-progress bit is clear, this indicates that there are no processes waiting on this mutex and control is passed back to the caller. (A waiting writer would set this bit. A potential reader is only blocked if there is a current or pending writer.) If there are other processes waiting for this mutex, SCH$UNLOCK scans the MWAIT queue to locate each process whose PCB$L_EFWM field contains the address of the unlocked mutex. For each process SCH$UNLOCK finds, it reports the availability of the mutex by invoking a scheduler routine. The scheduler routine changes the process's state to computable.

If the priority of any of the processes removed from the mutex wait state is greater than or equal to the priority of the current process, a rescheduling pass will occur that will select the highest priority process for execution. As previously noted, there is no difference between processes waiting for read access or write access. The criterion that determines who will get first chance at ownership of the mutex is software priority.

.4.5   Resource Wait State

The routines that place a process into a resource wait state and make resources available share some code with the mutex locking and unlocking routines and will be briefly described here. Chapter 10 describes system resources which processes allocate.

When a process tries to acquire a resource that is unavailable, the resource-allocating routine (for example, EXE$ALLOCBUF in the case of nonpaged pool) dispatches to SCH$RWAIT, passing it the number of the unavailable resource (in the case of nonpaged pool, RSN$_NPDYNMEM). The resource-allocating routine must have already pushed a PSL onto the stack and raised IPL to IPL$_SYNCH.

SCH$RWAIT (in module MUTEX) stores the resource number (instead of a mutex address) in PCB$L_EFWM and changes the process's state to MWAIT. (See Table 10-2 for a list of the resource names and numbers.) In addition, SCH$RWAIT sets the bit corresponding to the resource number in the systemwide resource wait mask SCH$GL_RESMASK. SCH$RWAIT then branches to SCH$WAITL.

SCH$WAITL (in module SYSWAIT) saves the process's context, inserts its PCB into the MWAIT queue, and causes a new process to be selected for execution. The PC and PSL saved in the waiting process's hardware PCB are determined by the caller of routine SCH$RWAIT.

When such a resource becomes available, the resource-deallocating routine (for example, EXE$DEANONPAGED) must call SCH$RAVAIL to ensure that all processes waiting for the resource are made computable. SCH$RAVAIL (in module MUTEX) clears the bit corresponding to the resource number in the resource mask. If the bit was previously clear, there are no waiters and SCH$RAVAIL returns to its invoker. If the bit was previously set, there are processes waiting on this resource. The same routine that frees processes waiting on a mutex is entered at this point. Offset PCB$L_EFWM now contains a resource number instead of a mutex address, but this difference is a conceptual difference that is invisible to the code that is actually executing.

The MWAIT state queue is scanned for all processes whose PCB$L_EFWM field matches the number of the recently freed resource. All such processes are made computable. If the new priority of any of these processes is larger than or the same as the priority of the currently executing process, a rescheduling interrupt is requested. In any event, all processes waiting for the now available resource will compete for that resource based on software priority.

2.5   **VAX/VMS LOCK MANAGEMENT SYSTEM SERVICES**

So far, most of the methods of synchronization described in this chapter have required elevated IPL, execution in kernel access mode, or both. Though these techniques are powerful and effective in synchronizing access to system data structures, there are other system applications in which elevated IPL or kernel mode access are not really necessary, desirable, or allowed (for example, RMS).

The VAX/VMS lock management system services (or the lock manager) provide synchronization tools that can be invoked from all access modes. Furthermore, the lock manager is the fundamental VAXcluster-wide synchronization primitive. Lock management system services are used by RMS, the file system, job controller, device allocation, and Mount Utility to provide clusterwide synchronization. The use of the VAX/VMS lock management system services is described fully in the *VAX/VMS System Services Reference Manual*; Chapter 13 in this book describes the internal workings of the lock manager on a nonclustered VMS system.

Dynamic Memory

3

In this bright little package, now isn't it odd?
You've a dime's worth of something known only to God!
Edgar Albert Guest, *The Package of Seeds*

Some of the data structures described in this book are created when the system is initialized; many others are created when they are needed and destroyed when their useful life is finished. To store the data structures, virtual memory must be allocated and deallocated in an orderly fashion.

The VMS operating system maintains a number of different areas for dynamic allocation of storage with different characteristics. This chapter describes the various areas of dynamic storage, their uses, and the algorithms for allocation and deallocation of these areas.

DYNAMIC DATA STRUCTURES AND THEIR STORAGE AREAS

Almost all the VMS data structures that are created after system initialization are volatile, allocated on demand and deallocated when no longer needed. These data structures have similarities of form (see Section 3.1.4), although their memory requirements vary.

Memory requirements for dynamic data structures differ in a number of ways:

- Pageability
  Data structures accessed by code running at IPL 2 or below can be pageable, whereas data structures accessed at higher IPLs cannot.
- Virtual location
  Some data structures are local to one process, mapped in its per-process address space; others must be mapped in system space, accessible to multiple processes and to system context code.
- Protection
  Many dynamic data structures are created and modified only by kernel mode code, but some data structures are accessed by outer modes.

Storage Areas for Dynamic Data Structures

VMS provides different storage areas to meet the memory requirements of dynamic data structures. There are several "pools" of storage for variable

Table 3-1   Comparison of Different Pool Areas

Pool Area	Protection	Synchronization Technique	Type of List	Allocation Quantum	Minimum Request	Characteristics
			SYSTEM SPACE			
Nonpaged pool	ERKW	Elevated IPL	Variable	16 bytes	16 bytes	Nonpageable, extendable
LRP lookaside list	ERKW	None required	Fixed	@IOC$GL_LRPSIZE	@IOC$GL_LRPMIN	Nonpageable, extendable
IRP lookaside list	ERKW	None required	Fixed	208 bytes	1+@IOC$GL_SRPSIZE	Nonpageable, extendable
SRP lookaside list	ERKW	None required	Fixed	@IOC$GL_SRPSIZE	16 bytes	Nonpageable, extendable
Paged pool	ERKW	Mutex	Variable	16 bytes	16 bytes	Pageable
			PER-PROCESS SPACE			
Process allocation region	UREW	Access mode	Variable	16 bytes	16 bytes	Pageable, extendable into P0 space
KRP lookaside list	URKW	None required	Fixed	CTL$C_KRP_SIZE	Nonapplicable	Pageable

length allocation: a nonpageable system space pool, a pageable system space pool, a pageable per-process space pool, and a nonpageable shared memory pool. In addition, "lookaside" lists of preformed fixed length packets enable faster allocation and deallocation of the most frequently used sizes and types of storage. These storage areas are summarized in Table 3-1 and described in more detail in later sections of this chapter. One additional storage area, the shared memory pool, is described in Chapter 14.

The next sections describe the basic methods for allocating and deallocating variable length storage and fixed length packets.

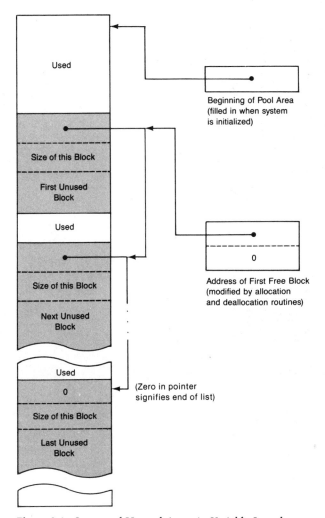

Figure 3-1   Layout of Unused Areas in Variable Length Memory Pools

Table 3-2 Global Listheads for Each Pool Area

Pool Area	Global Address of Pointer	Use of These Fields	Static or Dynamic[1]
Nonpaged pool	EXE$GL_NONPAGED,	Synchronization IPL for nonpaged pool allocation	Dynamic[2]
	EXE$GL_NONPAGED+4,	Address of next (first) free block	Dynamic
	EXE$GL_NONPAGED+8,	Dummy size of zero for listhead to speed allocation	Static
	MMG$GL_NPAGEDYN,	Address of beginning of nonpaged pool area	Static
	MMG$GL_NPAGNEXT	Address of beginning of unexpanded pool area	Dynamic
Large request packet lookaside list	IOC$GL_LRPFL,	Address of first free block	Dynamic
	IOC$GL_LRPBL,	Address of last free block	Dynamic
	IOC$GL_LRPSPLIT,	Address of beginning of LRP area	Static
	MMG$GL_LRPNEXT	Address of beginning of unexpanded LRP area	Dynamic
I/O request packet lookaside list	IOC$GL_IRPFL,	Address of first free block	Dynamic
	IOC$GL_IRPBL,	Address of last free block	Dynamic
	EXE$GL_SPLITADR,	Address of beginning of IRP area	Static
	MMG$GL_IRPNEXT	Address of beginning of unexpanded IRP area	Dynamic

Table 3-2   Global Listheads for Each Pool Area (continued)

Pool Area	Global Address of Pointer	Use of These Fields	Static or Dynamic[1]
Small request packet lookaside list	IOC$GL_SRPFL,	Address of first free block	Dynamic
	IOC$GL_SRPBL,	Address of last free block	Dynamic
	IOC$GL_SRPSPLIT,	Address of beginning of SRP area	Static
	MMG$GL_SRPNEXT	Address of beginning of unexpanded SRP area	Dynamic
Paged pool	EXE$GL_PAGED,	Address of next (first) free block	Dynamic
	EXE$GL_PAGED+4,	Dummy size of zero for listhead to speed allocation	Static
	MMG$GL_PAGEDYN	Address of beginning of paged pool area	Static
Process quota block lookaside list	EXE$GL_PQBFL,	Address of first free block	Dynamic
	EXE$GL_PQBBL	Address of last free block	Dynamic
Process allocation region	CTL$GQ_ALLOCREG,	Address of next (first) free block	Dynamic
	CTL$GQ_ALLOCREG+4,	Dummy size of zero for listhead to speed allocation	Static
	CTL$GQ_P0ALLOC,	Address of next (first) free block	Dynamic
	CTL$GQ_P0ALLOC+4	Dummy size of zero for listhead to speed allocation	Static
Kernel request packet lookaside list	CTL$GL_KRPFL,	Address of first free block	Dynamic
	CTL$GL_KRPBL,	Address of last free block	Dynamic
	CTL$GL_KRP	Address of beginning of area	Static

[1]Static pointers are loaded at initialization time, and their contents do not change during the life of the system. The contents of dynamic pointers change as pool is allocated, deallocated, and expanded.
[2]The synchronization IPL is changed to 31 by INIT and by certain device driver initialization routines but is reset to 11 and generally remains at 11.

3.1.2   **Variable Length List Allocation Strategy**

The variable length pools have a common structure. Each pool has a listhead which contains the virtual address of the first unused block in the pool. The first two longwords of each unused block in one of the pool areas are used to describe the block. As illustrated in Figure 3-1, the first longword in a block contains the virtual address of the next unused block in the list. The second longword contains the size in bytes of the unused block. Each successive unused block is found at a higher virtual address. Thus, each pool area forms a singly linked memory ordered list. Table 3-2 lists the global names of the variable length pool listheads.

Each variable length pool has its own set of allocation and deallocation routines. All the allocation routines for the variable length pools round the requested size up to the next multiple of 16 bytes to impose a granularity on both the allocated and unused areas. Because all the pool areas are initially page aligned, this rounding causes every structure allocated from the pool areas to be at least octaword aligned.

The various allocation and deallocation routines call the lower-level routines EXE$ALLOCATE and EXE$DEALLOCATE, which support the structure common to the variable length lists. Each routine has two arguments: the address of the pool listhead and the size of the data structure to be allocated or deallocated. These general purpose routines are also used for several other pools, including DCL's symbol table space, the NETACP's process space pool, and the global page table. All the allocation and deallocation routines described in this chapter are in module MEMORYALC.

3.1.2.1   **Allocation of Variable Length Pool.** When the allocation routine EXE$ALLOCATE is called, it searches from the beginning of the list until it encounters the first unused block large enough to satisfy the request. If the fit is exact, the allocation routine simply adjusts the previous pointer to point to the next free block. If the fit is not exact, it subtracts the allocated size from the original size of the block, puts the new size into the remainder of the block, and adjusts the previous pointer to point to the remainder of the block. That is, if the fit is not exact, the low address end of the block is allocated, and the high address end is placed back on the list. The two possible allocation situations (exact and inexact fit) are illustrated in Figure 3-2.

3.1.2.2   **Example of Allocation of Variable Length Pool.** The first part of Figure 3-2 (Initial Condition) shows a section of paged pool and the pointer MMG$GL_PAGEDYN, which points to the beginning of paged pool, and EXE$GL_PAGED, which points to the first available block of paged pool. In this example, allocated blocks of memory are indicated only as the total number of bytes being used, with no indication of the number and size of the individual data structures within each block.

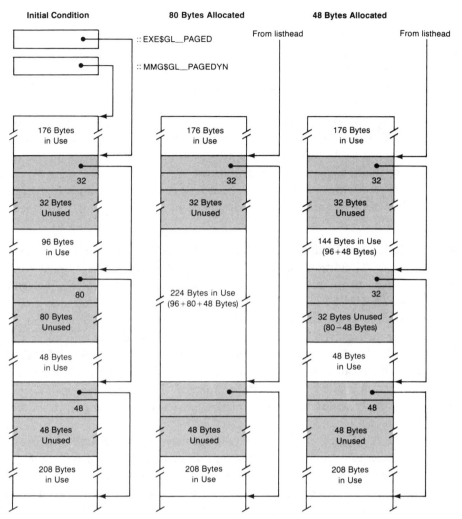

Figure 3-2   Examples of Allocation of Variable Length
Pool

Following the allocation of a block of 80 bytes (an exact fit), the structure of the paged pool looks like the second part of Figure 3-2 (80 Bytes Allocated). Note that the discrete portions of 96 bytes and 48 bytes in use and the 80 bytes that were allocated are now combined to show simply a 224-byte block of paged pool in use.

The third part of Figure 3-2 (48 Bytes Allocated) shows the case where a 48-byte block was allocated from the paged pool structure shown in the first part of the figure. The 48 bytes were taken from the first unused block large enough to contain it. (Note that allocation is done from the low address end of the unused block.) Because this allocation was not an exact fit, an unused block, 32 bytes long, remains.

3.1.2.3 **Deallocation of Variable Length Pool.** When a block is deallocated, it must be placed back into the list in its proper place, according to its address. EXE$DEALLOCATE follows the unused area pointers until it encounters an address larger than the address of the block to be deallocated. If the deallocated block is adjacent to another unused block, the two blocks are merged into a single unused area.

This merging, or agglomeration, can occur at the end of the preceding unused block or at the beginning of the following block (or both). Because merging occurs automatically as a part of deallocation, there is no need for any externally triggered cleanup routines.

Three sample deallocation situations, two of which illustrate merging, are shown in Figure 3-3 and are described in Section 3.1.2.4.

3.1.2.4 **Example of Deallocation of Variable Length Pool.** The first part of Figure 3-3 (Initial Condition) shows the structure of an area of paged pool containing logical name blocks for three logical names: ADAM, GREGORY, and ROSAMUND. These three logical name blocks are bracketed by two unused portions of paged pool, one 64 bytes long, the other 176 bytes long.

If the logical name ADAM is deleted, the structure of the pool is altered to look like the structure shown in the second part of Figure 3-3 (ADAM Deleted). Because the logical name block was adjacent to the high address end of an unused block, the blocks are merged. The size of the deallocated block is simply added to the size of the unused block. (No pointers need to be adjusted.)

If the logical name GREGORY is deleted, the structure of the pool is altered to look like the structure shown in the third part of Figure 3-3 (GREGORY Deleted). The pointer in the unused block of 64 bytes is altered to point to the deallocated block; a new pointer and size longword are created within the deallocated block.

The fourth part of Figure 3-3 (ROSAMUND Deleted) shows the case where the logical name ROSAMUND is deleted. In this case, the deallocated block is adjacent to the low address end of an unused block, so the blocks are merged. The pointer to the next unused block that was previously in the adjacent block is moved to the beginning of the newly deallocated block. The following longword is loaded with the size of the merged block (240 bytes).

3.1.3 **Fixed Length List Allocation Strategy**

The fixed length lists have a common structure. Each is a doubly linked queue with a listhead which points to the first and last unused block in the list. A list of fixed length packets available for allocation is known as a "lookaside" list. Figure 3-4 shows the form of a fixed length list.

Lookaside lists expedite the allocation and deallocation of the most com-

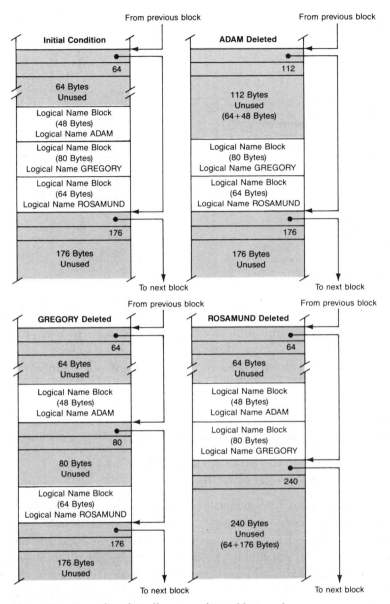

Figure 3-3   Examples of Deallocation of Variable Length
Pool

monly used sizes and types of storage. In contrast to variable length list allocation, fixed length allocation is very simple. There is no overhead of searching for blocks of free memory of sufficient size to accommodate a specific request. Instead the appropriate listhead is selected and a packet is allocated from the front of the list through a simple REMQUE instruction. Deallocation to the back of the list is done by an INSQUE instruction. Examples of allocation and deallocation are shown in Figure 3-4.

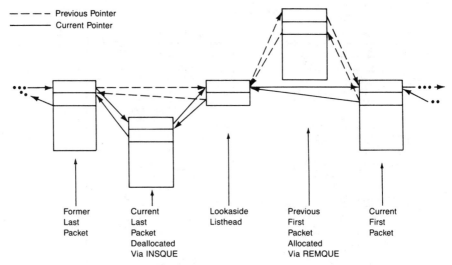

Former Last Packet

Current Last Packet Deallocated Via INSQUE

Lookaside Listhead

Previous First Packet Allocated Via REMQUE

Current First Packet

Figure 3-4 Fixed Length List Allocation and Deallocation

No additional synchronization of access to a lookaside list is required beyond that provided by the queue instructions.

Table 3-2 lists the global names of the fixed length pool listheads.

3.1.4   Dynamic Data Structures

A dynamic data structure, by convention, contains two self-describing fields:

• The size (in bytes) of the data structure in the word at offset 8
• The type code in a byte at offset 10

Data structures with a type code value equal to or larger than 96 also have a one-byte subtype code at offset 11. The macro $DYNDEF in SYS-$LIBRARY:LIB.MLB defines the possible values for the type and subtype fields. The size, type, and subtype fields are defined in the third longword of the data structure, leaving the first two longwords available to link the data structure into a list. Figure 3-5 shows the standard dynamic data structure format.

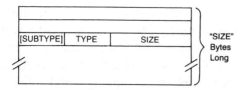

[SUBTYPE]   TYPE   SIZE

"SIZE" Bytes Long

Figure 3-5 Dynamic Data Structure Format

The type field enables VMS to distinguish different data structures and to confirm that a piece of dynamic storage contains the expected data structure type. When a dynamic data structure is deallocated, the size field specifies how much dynamic storage is being returned. At deallocation, a positive value in the type field indicates a structure allocated from local memory, and a negative indicates a structure allocated from shared memory.

The System Dump Analyzer (SDA) Utility uses the type and size fields to produce a formatted display of a dynamic data structure and to determine the portions of variable length pool that are in use.

NONPAGED DYNAMIC MEMORY REGIONS

Nonpaged dynamic memory contains data structures and code used by the portions of the VMS operating system that are not procedure-based, such as interrupt service routines and device drivers. These portions of the operating system can use only system virtual address space and execute at elevated IPL, requiring nonpaged dynamic memory rather than paged dynamic memory.

Nonpaged dynamic memory, more commonly known as nonpaged pool, also contains data structures and code that are shared by several processes and that must not be paged. Nonpageability is dictated by the constraint that page faults are not permitted above IPL 2.

The protection on nonpaged pool is ERKW, allowing it to be read from kernel and executive modes but written only from kernel mode.

Nonpaged pool is the most heavily used of the storage areas. It consists of a variable length list and three lookaside lists. The lookaside lists provide for the most frequently allocated nonpaged pool data structures. Nonpaged pool is sometimes allocated explicitly from a lookaside list and sometimes allocated implicitly from a lookaside list as the result of a call to the general routine that allocates nonpaged pool. Section 3.2.2 discusses allocation in detail.

Initialization of Nonpaged Pool Regions

The sizes of the variable nonpaged pool and the lookaside lists are determined by SYSBOOT parameters. Nonpaged pool is potentially extensible during normal system operation. For each of the four regions of nonpaged pool there are two SYSBOOT parameters, one to specify the initial size of the region and another to specify its maximum size.

The size in bytes of the variable length region of nonpaged pool is controlled by the SYSBOOT parameters NPAGEDYN and NPAGEVIR, both of which are rounded down to an integral number of pages. During system initialization, sufficient contiguous system page table entries (SPTEs) are allocated for the maximum size of the region, NPAGEVIR. Physical pages of memory are allocated for the initial size of the region, NPAGEDYN, and are mapped using the first portion of allocated SPTEs. The remaining SPTEs are left invalid. (PTEs are described in Chapter 14.)

During system operation, the failure of an attempt to allocate from the variable nonpaged pool region results in an attempted expansion of the region, with physical page(s) allocated to fill in the next invalid SPTE(s). See Section 3.2.4 for further details of pool expansion. The deallocation merge strategy described in Section 3.2.3 requires that the newly extended nonpaged dynamic region be virtually contiguous with the existing part and that the four regions be adjacent. It is because of this restriction that the maximum number of SPTEs are allocated contiguously for each region, even if some of them are initially unused.

The lookaside lists are allocated during system initialization in the same manner as the variable length region. A portion of the nonpaged system space following the main portion of pool is partitioned into three pieces. One piece is reserved for the IRP lookaside list, one for the LRP list, and one for the SRP list. Table 3-3 lists the SYSBOOT parameters relevant to each lookaside list. The three pieces are then structured into a series of elements. Figure 3-6 shows the four regions of nonpaged pool. In each of the lists, the elements are inserted into a list with the INSQUE instruction, resulting in a doubly linked list of fixed-size list elements.

The size of an IRP list element is determined by the symbol IRP$C_LENGTH; in VMS Version 4, an IRP is 208 bytes.

The size of the elements in the SRP list is contained in the cell IOC$GL_SRPSIZE, which is defined in module SYSCOMMON. This value is determined from SYSBOOT parameter SRPSIZE. INIT rounds up SRPSIZE to a multiple of 16.

The size of the elements in the LRP list is contained in the cell IOC$GL_LRPSIZE, also defined in module SYSCOMMON. This value is determined from SYSBOOT parameter LRPSIZE. SYSBOOT computes IOC$GL_LRPSIZE by adding 76 to LRPSIZE and rounding up the sum to a multiple of 16. The parameter LRPSIZE is intended to be the DECnet buffer size, exclusive of a 76-byte internal buffer header. (Note that the output of SHOW MEMORY displays the inclusive packet size.)

Table 3-3 SYSBOOT Parameters Controlling Lookaside List Sizes

List Type	Size of Packet	Initial Count	Maximum Count
SRP	SRPSIZE	SRPCOUNT	SRPCOUNTV
IRP	208	IRPCOUNT	IRPCOUNTV
LRP	LRPSIZE + 76[1]	LRPCOUNT	LRPCOUNTV

[1]The actual packet size is the sum of LRPSIZE and 76, rounded up to a multiple of 16.

3.2.2 Allocation of Nonpaged Pool

There are a number of routines in module MEMORYALC that allocate nonpaged pool. Some of these routines, such as EXE$ALLOCPCB or EXE$AL-LOCTQE, allocate pool for a particular data structure, filling in its size and type. Some routines, intended for use only within process context, conditionally place the process into resource wait, waiting for resource RSN$_NPDYNMEM if pool is unavailable. (Chapter 10 discusses process resource waits.) All of these routines invoke EXE$ALONONPAGED, the general nonpaged pool allocation routine.

There are several instances in VMS of explicit allocation from a lookaside list. When a routine such as the Queue I/O Request ($QIO) system service

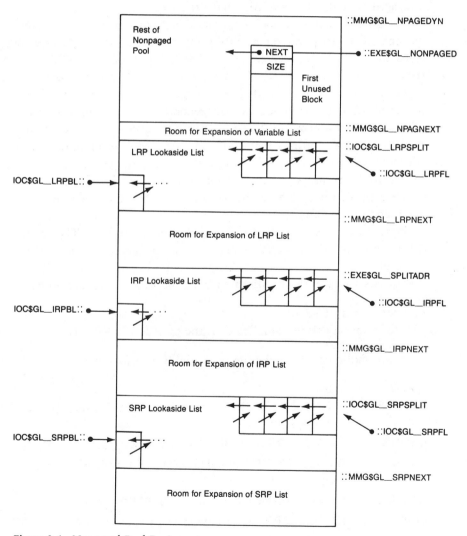

Figure 3-6 Nonpaged Pool Regions

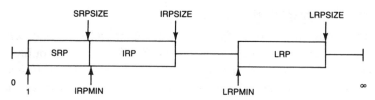

Figure 3-7 Lookaside List Allocation Ranges

needs an I/O request packet (IRP), it simply issues a REMQUE from the beginning of this list (found through global label IOC$GL_IRPFL). Several other system routines allocate IRPs this way. Only if the lookaside list is empty (indicated by the V-bit set in the PSW following a REMQUE) would the general nonpaged pool allocation routine have to be called.

Similarly, the Enqueue Lock Request ($ENQ) system service allocates pool for lock blocks by removing an SRP from the lookaside list, located by the global label IOC$GL_SRPFL. The SYSBOOT parameter SRPSIZE is constrained to be at least the size of a lock block. The $ENQ system service must check, however, whether SRPSIZE is large enough to accommodate a resource block and, if it is not, call the general nonpaged allocation routine.

Because allocation and deallocation from a lookaside list are so much faster than the general routines that allow any size block to be allocated or deallocated, special checks are built into the general nonpaged pool allocation routine to determine whether the requested block can be allocated from one of the lookaside lists. These checks compare the request size to the lists' upper and lower limits.

Figure 3-7 shows the size ranges for the lookaside lists. The ranges are defined so that the majority of requests can be satisfied from one of the lookaside lists.

Requests which must be allocated from the variable list are either

• Larger than an LRP, or
• Larger than an IRP but smaller than the parameter LRPMIN

The symbolic names in the figure are defined as follows:

Symbol	Meaning
SRPSIZE	IOC$GL_SRPSIZE, the parameter SRPSIZE rounded up to a multiple of 16
IRPMIN	IOC$GL_IRPMIN, the sum of IOC$GL_SRPSIZE and 1
IRPSIZE	IRP$C_LENGTH rounded up to a multiple of 16, the constant 208
LRPMIN	IOC$GL_LRPMIN, parameter LRPMIN
LRPSIZE	IOC$GL_LRPSIZE, the sum of parameter LRPSIZE and 76

EXE$ALONONPAGED allocates nonpaged pool by the following steps:

1. It compares the requested size to the ranges just described to determine which, if any, lookaside list it can use.
2. If none of the lookaside lists is appropriate, the pool must be allocated from the variable length list.
3. If one of the lookaside lists is appropriate and the list is not empty, the first packet is removed from the list and returned to the caller.
4. If one of the lookaside lists is appropriate but is empty, an attempt is made to extend the list (see Section 3.2.4). If the list is extended, the allocation is attempted again. If the lookaside list cannot be extended, the pool must be allocated from the variable length list.
5. For variable length list allocation, EXE$ALONONPAGED rounds the allocation size up to a multiple of 16 and calls the lower-level routine EXE$ALLOCATE (described in Section 3.1.2).

EXE$ALONPAGVAR is a separate entry point to EXE$ALONONPAGED, used to allocate pool explicitly from the variable length list. This entry point should be used whenever multiple pieces of pool are allocated as a single larger piece but deallocated in a piecemeal fashion. See Section 3.2.3 for more information.

Deallocation of Nonpaged Pool

A consumer of nonpaged pool invokes EXE$DEANONPAGED to deallocate nonpaged pool to any of the four regions. When EXE$DEANONPAGED is called, it first checks whether the block was allocated from the main portion of the pool or from one of the lookaside lists. The lookaside lists are divided by the contents of the following global locations, beginning with the smaller addresses:

IOC$GL_LRPSPLIT	Boundary between the main part of pool and the LRP list
EXE$GL_SPLITADR	Boundary between the LRP and the IRP list
IOC$GL_SRPSPLIT	Boundary between the IRP and the SRP list

These addresses were determined by INIT when the lookaside lists were initialized. Figure 3-6 shows the relationship of the lookaside lists to the rest of nonpaged pool.

EXE$DEANONPAGED determines the list to which the piece of pool is being returned by the following steps:

1. The address of the block being deallocated is compared to the contents of global location IOC$GL_SRPSPLIT. If the address is greater, the block came from the SRP list.

2. If the address was less than the contents of IOC$GL_SRPSPLIT, the address is compared to the contents of EXE$GL_SPLITADR. If the address is greater, the block came from the IRP list.
3. If the address was less than the contents of EXE$GL_SPLITADR, the address is compared to the contents of IOC$GL_LRPSPLIT. If the address is greater, the block came from the LRP list.
4. If the address was less than the contents of IOC$GL_LRPSPLIT, the block came from the main part of pool.

If the block was originally allocated from one of the lookaside lists, it is returned there by inserting it at the end of the list with an INSQUE instruction. The ends of the lookaside lists are indicated by the global labels IOCGL_SRPBL, IOCGL_IRPBL, and IOC$GL_LRPBL. Note that by allocating packets from one end of the list and putting them back at the other end, a transaction history as long as the list itself is maintained. If the block was originally allocated from the variable length list area, EXE$DEANONPAGED calls EXE$DEALLOCATE, the lower-level routine described in Section 3.1.2.

EXE$DEANONPAGED also calls SCH$RAVAIL to declare the availability of nonpaged pool for any process that might be waiting for resource RSN$_NPDYNMEM. The consequences of this declaration are discussed briefly in Section 3.2.5 and at greater length in Chapter 10.

Deallocating a block back to a list based on the address of the block has an important implication. Lookaside list corruption will result if a nonpaged pool consumer deallocates part of a lookaside list packet. That is, VMS treats all lookaside packets as indivisible. A partial packet deallocated to a lookaside list eventually will be allocated as a whole packet, resulting in double use of the same memory. The entry point EXE$ALONPAGVAR should be used for allocating nonpaged pool that may be deallocated in a piecemeal way. EXE$ALONPAGVAR always allocates from the variable length list.

3.2.4 Expansion of Nonpaged Pool

Dynamic nonpaged pool expansion is the creation of additional nonpaged pool as it is needed. At system initialization, SYSBOOT allocates enough system virtual address space for the maximum size of each nonpaged pool region, but it only allocates enough physical memory for the initial size of each region. When an attempt to allocate nonpaged pool is unsuccessful, the pool can be expanded by allocating more physical memory for it and altering the system page table accordingly.

When routine EXE$ALONONPAGED fails to allocate nonpaged pool from any of the four regions, it attempts to expand nonpaged pool by invoking the routine EXE$EXTENDPOOL (in module MEMORYALC).

EXE$EXTENDPOOL examines each list (lookaside lists and variable list) in turn. If a list is empty and is not at its maximum size, EXE$EXTENDPOOL attempts to allocate a page of physical memory. First a check is made to see if a physical page can be allocated without reducing the number of physical pages available to the system below the minimum required. Expansion of pool must leave sufficient pages to accommodate the sum of the maximum working set size, the modified list low limit, and the free list low limit. If a page can be allocated, EXE$EXTENDPOOL places its page frame number (PFN) in the first invalid SPTE for that list, and sets the valid bit. The new virtual page and any fragment from the previous virtual page are formatted into packets of the appropriate size and placed on the list. EXE$EXTENDPOOL records the size and address of any fragment left from the new page.

If EXE$EXTENDPOOL is able to expand any of the nonpaged lists, it reports that resource RSN$_NPDYNMEM is available for any waiting processes. (See Chapter 10 for more information on scheduling and event reporting.)

For proper synchronization of system databases, the resource availability report and the allocation of physical memory must not be done from a thread of execution running as the result of an interrupt above IPL$_SYNCH. For this reason, EXE$EXTENDPOOL examines the PSL to determine at what IPL the system is running and whether the system is running on the interrupt stack. If EXE$EXTENDPOOL has been entered from an interrupt service routine running above IPL$_SYNCH, EXE$EXTENDPOOL creates an IPL 6 fork process to expand the lists at some later time when IPL drops below 6 and returns an allocation failure status to its invoker.

Nonpaged pool expansion enables automatic system tuning. The penalty for setting an inadequate initial allocation size is the increased overhead in allocating requests that cause expansion. An additional minor physical penalty is that unnecessary PFN database is built for those physical pages that are subsequently added to nonpaged pool as a result of expansion. The cost is about 4 percent of the size of the page per added page.

The penalty for a maximum allocation that is too large is one SPTE for each unused page, or less than 1 percent. If the maximum size of a lookaside list is too small, system performance may be adversely affected when the system is prevented from using the lookaside mechanism for pool requests. If the maximum size of the variable length region is too small, processes may be placed into the MWAIT state, waiting for nonpaged pool to become available.

3.2.5   Nonpaged Pool Synchronization

Elevated IPL is used to serialize access to the nonpaged pool variable length list. The IPL used is that stored in the longword immediately preceding the pointer to the first unused block in the variable length list (see Table 3-2).

The allocation routine for the nonpaged pool variable list raises IPL to the value found here before proceeding. While the system is running, this longword usually contains an 11. The value of 11 was chosen because device drivers running at fork level frequently allocate dynamic storage and IPL 11 represents the highest fork IPL currently used in the operating system. (An implication of this synchronization IPL value is that device drivers must not allocate nonpaged pool while executing at device IPL in response to a device interrupt.)

During initialization, the contents of this longword are set to 31 because the rest of the code in the system initialization routines (module INIT) executes at IPL 31 to block all interrupts. INIT is described in detail in Chapter 25. Changing the contents of this longword avoids lowering IPL as a side effect of allocating space from nonpaged pool. The value is reset to 11 after INIT has finished its allocation but before INIT passes control to the scheduler.

The nonpaged pool allocation routines that run in process context raise IPL to IPL$_SYNCH before invoking EXE$ALONONPAGED. If EXE$ALONONPAGED fails to allocate the pool, these routines test PCB$V_SSRWAIT in PCB$L_STS. If it is set, they place the process into resource wait, waiting for RSN$_NPDYNMEM. They run at IPL$_SYNCH to block deallocation of pool and the accompanying report of resource availability between the time of the allocation failure and the time the process is actually placed into a wait.

IPL is also a consideration for deallocation of nonpaged pool, but for a different reason. Although nonpaged pool can be allocated from fork processes running at IPL levels up to IPL 11, it may not be deallocated as a result of an interrupt above IPL$_SYNCH. The reason for limiting the IPL is that nonpaged pool is a systemwide resource that processes might be waiting for. EXE$DEANONPAGED notifies the scheduler that the resource RSN$_NPDYNMEM is available. The scheduler in turn checks whether any processes are waiting for the nonpaged pool resource. All these modifications to the scheduler database must take place at IPL$_SYNCH, and the interrupt nesting scheme requires that IPL never be lowered below the IPL value at which the current interrupt occurred. This rule dictates that all pool be deallocated from a thread of execution running as the result of an IPL 8 or lower interrupt.

Code executing as the result of an interrupt at IPL 9 or above deallocates nonpaged pool through routine COM$DRVDEALMEM (in module COMDRVSUB). If COM$DRVDEALMEM is called from IPL 8 or below, it merely deallocates the pool, jumping to EXE$DEANONPAGED. If, however, COM$DRVDEALMEM is called from above IPL 8, it transforms the block that is to be deallocated into a fork block (see Figure 6-2), and requests an IPL 6 software interrupt. (Note that the block to be deallocated must be at least

24 bytes, large enough for a fork block. If it is not, COM$DRVDEALMEM issues a nonfatal bugcheck and returns to its invoker.) The code that executes as the IPL 6 fork process (the saved PC in the fork block) simply issues a JMP to EXE$DEANONPAGED to deallocate the block. Because EXE$DEANON-PAGED is entered at IPL 6, the synchronized access to the scheduler's database is preserved. (This technique is similar to the one used by device drivers that need to interact with the scheduler by declaring ASTs. The attention AST mechanism is briefly described in Chapter 2 and discussed in greater detail in Chapter 7.)

By convention, process context code which allocates a nonpaged pool data structure executes at IPL 2 or above as long as the data structure's existence is recorded solely in a temporary process location, such as in a register or on the stack. Running at IPL 2 blocks AST delivery and prevents the possible loss of the pool if the process were to be deleted.

3.2.6 Uses of Nonpaged Pool

Nonpaged pool serves many purposes. This section describes typical uses of the nonpaged pool lists. Note, however, that nondefault choices for SYSBOOT parameters LRPSIZE, LRPMIN, and SRPSIZE may result in different usage.

The variable length list is used for allocating nonpaged pool that does not fit the allocation constraints of the lookaside lists. Typically, device drivers and the larger unit control blocks describing I/O device units are allocated from the variable length list. Also, process control blocks (PCBs), which contain process-related information that must remain resident, are allocated from the variable length list. Nonpaged pool is also allocated during early stages of system initialization. SYSBOOT loads several images into nonpaged variable length pool. These include the system disk driver, terminal driver, and CPU-dependent routines. The detailed use of nonpaged pool by the initialization routines is described in Chapter 25.

The LRP lookaside list is typically used by DECnet for receiving messages from other nodes. On a system connected to a CI bus, CI datagrams, used to provide best-effort message service among the nodes on the CI, may be allocated from the LRP lookaside list. On a system with a relatively large value for LRPSIZE, many loaded images, such as device drivers, may be allocated from the LRP lookaside list rather than from the variable length list.

The IRP lookaside list is typically used for the following data structures:

- I/O and class driver request packets, which describe a particular I/O request
- Job information blocks, which contain the quotas and limits shared by processes in a job
- Resource blocks, used by the lock management system services

- Volume control blocks, which describe the state of a mounted disk or tape volume
- File control blocks, which describe the state of an open file
- Unit control blocks, which describe the state of an I/O device unit
- Larger device driver buffered I/O buffers
- On a system with a CI bus, CI messages, used to provide highly reliable communication among the nodes on the CI

The SRP lookaside list is typically used for the following data structures:

- Lock and resource blocks, used by the lock management system services
- Window control blocks, which contain the location of a file's extents
- Timer queue elements, which describe time-dependent requests such as Schedule Wakeup ($SCHDWK) system service requests
- Smaller device driver buffered I/O buffers
- Interrupt dispatch and channel (controller) request blocks, which describe the state of a device controller

3.3   PAGED POOL

Paged dynamic memory contains data structures that are used by multiple processes but that are not required to be permanently memory resident. Its protection is ERKW, allowing it to be read from kernel and executive modes but written only from kernel mode.

During system initialization, SYSBOOT reserves system virtual address space for paged pool, placing its starting address in MMG$GL_PAGEDYN. The SYSBOOT parameter PAGEDYN specifies the size of this area in bytes. Paged pool is created as a set of demand zero pages. System initialization code running in the context of the swapper process initializes the pool as one data structure encompassing the entire pool and places its address in EXE$GL_PAGEDYN. That initialization incurs a page fault and thus requires process context.

Process context kernel mode code calls the routine EXE$ALOPAGED to allocate paged pool and EXE$DEAPAGED to deallocate paged pool. These routines (all in module MEMORYALC) call the lower-level variable length allocation and deallocation routines described in Section 3.1.2.

If an allocation request cannot be satisfied, EXE$ALOPAGED returns to its caller with a failure status. The caller may return an error, for example, SS$_INSFMEM, to the user program, or the caller may place the process into resource wait, waiting for resource RSN$_PGDYNMEM.

Whenever paged pool is deallocated, EXE$DEAPAGED calls SCH$RAVAIL to declare the availability of paged pool for any waiting process. Chapter 10 describes process resource waits.

Paged pool requires little system overhead, one SPTE per page of pool. Because paged pool is created as demand zero system page table entries (see Chapter 14), it expands on demand through page faults.

Because this storage area is pageable, code which accesses it must run at IPL 2 or below while accessing it. Elevated IPL, therefore, cannot be used for synchronizing access to the paged pool list or to any data structures allocated from it. A mutex called EXE$GL_PGDYNMTX serializes access to the paged pool list. Both EXE$ALOPAGED and EXE$DEAPAGED lock this mutex for write access.

By convention, process context code which allocates a paged pool data structure executes at IPL 2 or above as long as the data structure's existence is recorded solely in a temporary process location, such as in a register or on the stack. Running at IPL 2 blocks AST delivery and prevents the possible loss of the pool if the process were to be deleted.

The following data structures are located in the paged pool area:

- The shareable logical name tables and logical name blocks
- The Files-11 XQP "I/O buffer cache," which is used for data such as file headers, index file bit map blocks, directory data file blocks, and quota file data blocks
- Global section descriptors, which are used when a global section is mapped or unmapped
- Mounted volume list entries, which associate a mounted volume name with its corresponding logical name and unit control block address
- Access control list elements, which specify what access to an object is allowed for different classes of users
- Data structures required by the Install Utility to describe known images
  Any image that is installed has a known file entry created to describe it. Some frequently accessed known images also have their image headers permanently resident in paged pool. These data structures are described in more detail in Chapter 21.
- Process quota blocks (PQBs), which are used during process creation temporarily to store the quotas and limits of the new process

PQBs, initially allocated from paged pool, are not deallocated back to the paged pool list. Instead, they are queued to a lookaside list whose listhead is at global label EXE$GL_PQBFL. Process creation code attempts to allocate a PQB by removing an element from this queue, as a faster alternative to general paged pool allocation.

3.4   PROCESS ALLOCATION REGION

The process allocation region contains variable length data structures that are used only by a single process and are not required to be permanently memory resident. Its protection is set to UREW, allowing executive and kernel modes to write it and any access mode to read it.

The process allocation region consists of a P1 space variable length pool and, with VMS Version 4, may include a P0 space variable length pool as well. The P0 space allocation pool is useful only for image-specific data structures that do not need to survive image exit. The P1 space pool can be used for both image-specific data structures and data structures, such as logical name tables, that must survive the rundown of an image.

During process startup, EXE$PROCSTRT reserves P1 address space for the process allocation region. SYSBOOT parameter CTLPAGES specifies the number of pages in the P1 pool. There is no global pointer that locates the beginning of the process allocation region. The routine EXE$PROCSTRT initializes the pool as one data structure, encompassing the whole pool, and places its address in CTL$GQ_ALLOCREG. As pool is allocated and deallocated, the contents of CTL$GQ_ALLOCREG are modified to point to the first available block.

Executive or kernel mode code running in process context calls EXE$ALOP1PROC or EXE$ALOP1IMAG to allocate from the process allocation region and EXE$DEAP1 to deallocate a data structure to the region. These routines are in module MEMORYALC. When the data structure must be allocated from the P1 pool, EXE$ALOP1PROC is used. When the data structure is image-specific, EXE$ALOP1IMAG is used.

Initially, both these routines call EXE$ALLOCATE with the address of CTL$GQ_ALLOCREG. However, if the process allocation region reaches a threshold of use specified by SYSBOOT parameter CTLIMGLIM, EXE$ALOP1IMAG cannot allocate from P1 space. If the current image has not been linked with the option NOP0BUFS, EXE$ALOP1IMAG creates a P0 process allocation region of at least 16 pages using the Expand Region ($EXPREG) system service; EXE$ALOP1IMAG initializes it as a data structure encompassing the entire region and places its address in CTL$GQ_P0ALLOC. At image rundown, P0 space is deleted and CTL$GQ_P0ALLOC is zeroed. If the current image has been linked with NOP0BUFS, the allocation fails and status SS$_INSFMEM is returned.

Both EXE$ALOP1IMAG and EXE$ALOP1PROC put the address of the appropriate listhead in a register and call EXE$ALLOCATE to perform the variable length allocation described in Section 3.1.2. The EXE$DEAP1 routine determines whether the block being deallocated is from the P0 or P1 space pool and calls EXE$DEALLOCATE with the address of the appropriate listhead.

There is no locking mechanism currently used for either the process allocation region or the process logical names found there. However, the allocation routine executes in kernel mode at IPL 2, effectively blocking any other mainline or AST code from executing and perhaps attempting a simultaneous allocation from the process allocation region.

The following data structures are located in the process allocation region:

- The process-private logical name tables and logical name blocks
- Data structures, called image control blocks, built by the image activator to describe what images have been activated in the process
- Rights database identifier blocks, which contain RMS context (internal file and stream identifiers) for the rights database file
- A context block in which the Breakthrough ($BRKTHRU) system service maintains status information as the service asynchronously broadcasts messages to the terminals specified by the user

There is enough room in the process allocation region for privileged application software to allocate reasonably sized process-specific data structures.

3.5 KRP LOOKASIDE LIST

VMS Version 4 adds a P1 space lookaside list for process-private kernel mode data structures that are not required to be permanently memory resident. The protection on this storage area is URKW, allowing it to be read from any mode but modified only from kernel mode.

Virtual address space for this list is defined at assembly time of the SHELL module, which defines the fixed part of P1 space. Space is defined based on the two globals CTL$C_KRP_COUNT and CTL$C_KRP_SIZE, the number of the KRP packets to create, and the size of a packet. The EXE$PROCSTRT routine, in module PROCSTRT, initializes the list, forming packets and inserting them in the list at CTL$GL_KRPFL and CTL$GL_KRPBL.

A KRP packet is used as pageable storage, local to a kernel mode subroutine. KRPs should be used only for temporary storage that is deallocated before the subroutine returns. The most common use of KRPs is to store an equivalence name returned from a logical name translation. Formerly, space was allocated on the kernel stack for this purpose, but the VMS Version 4 increase in size of equivalence names to 255 bytes made use of the kernel stack impractical.

Allocation and deallocation to this list is through INSQUE and REMQUE instructions. Both allocation and deallocation are always done from the front of the list. There is no need for synchronization other than that provided by the queue instructions. Because KRPs are used only for storage local to the execution of a procedure, a failure to allocate a KRP is very unexpected and indicates a serious error rather than a temporary resource shortage. Kernel mode code which is unsuccessful at allocating from this list thus generates the fatal bugcheck KRPEMPTY.

PART II/Control Mechanisms

Condition Handling

"Would you tell me, please, which way I ought to go from
here?"
"That depends a good deal on where you want to get to," said
the Cat.

Lewis Carroll, *Alice's Adventures in Wonderland*

The VAX architecture defines a generalized uniform condition handling facility for two classes of conditions:

• Conditions detected and generated by hardware/microcode are called exceptions.
• Conditions detected and generated by software are called software conditions.

The VAX/VMS operating system provides this facility for users and also uses the facility for its own purposes.

This chapter describes how VMS dispatches on exceptions and software conditions to user-defined procedures called condition handlers. It also briefly describes how VMS services exceptions which it handles itself.

1 OVERVIEW OF CONDITIONS

1.1 Overview of Exceptions

An exception is the CPU's response to an anomaly or error it encounters while executing an instruction, for example, a divisor of zero in a DIVL instruction. The hardware/microcode responds by changing the flow of instruction execution to an exception service routine pointed to by an anomaly-specific longword vector in the system control block (SCB).

The VAX architecture defines approximately 20 different exceptions, each with its own SCB vector and exception service routine. The exceptions defined by the VAX architecture can be divided into two categories based on whether VMS allows user-defined procedures to handle the exception.

VMS does not allow user-defined procedures to handle

• Inner mode exceptions indicating fatal software or hardware errors (for example, machine checks)
• Exceptions used by VMS in the course of normal system operations (page faults, CHMK, CHME, and subset instruction emulation exceptions)

These exceptions are always handled by exception service routines that are part of VMS.

VMS allows all other exceptions to be handled by a user-supplied procedure, if any is provided. Characteristically these exceptions affect only the current process. A user-defined procedure to handle an exception is called a condition handler.

When an exception occurs for which VMS allows condition handling, VMS performs a search algorithm on a list of possible condition handlers. VMS calls any condition handlers it finds.

The condition handler can examine the parameters of the exception and either take some action (possibly to remove or bypass the exception) or resignal it to another condition handler. If the condition handler resignals, VMS continues its search.

4.1.2   Overview of Software Conditions

A software condition is an error or anomaly detected by an image and treated in a particular way. When the software detects such an error, it transforms it into a software condition by calling one of two Run-Time Library procedures. By calling LIB$SIGNAL (if the image is to continue) or LIB$STOP (if the image is to be aborted), the same VMS condition handler search used for exceptions is invoked.

4.2   OVERVIEW OF THE VAX CONDITION HANDLING FACILITY

The VAX condition handling facility defines the declaration of a condition handler, the search for a condition handler, and the responses available to a condition handler. The condition handling facility provides that software conditions (errors detected by software rather than by CPU microcode) be directed to the same condition handlers as exceptions. Thus, application software can centralize its handling of errors, both hardware and software.

The term "condition" refers to an exception or software condition on which VMS dispatches to user-defined condition handlers. VMS calls a condition handler with an argument, sometimes called a signal or signal name, which identifies what type of condition occurred.

The *VAX/VMS System Services Reference Manual* and the *VAX/VMS Run-Time Library Routines Reference Manual* describe the declaration and coding of condition handlers.

4.2.1   Goals of the VAX Condition Handling Facility

A major goal of the VAX condition handling facility is to provide an easy-to-use, general purpose mechanism with the operating system so that application programs and other layered products, such as compilers, can use this mechanism rather than inventing their own application-specific tools. Other explicit and implicit goals of the VAX condition handling facility are the following:

- The condition handling facility should be included in the base system architecture so that it is available as a part of the base system and not as part of some software component. The space reserved for condition handler addresses in the first longword of the call frame accomplishes this goal.
- By including the handler specification in the procedure call frame, condition handling is made an integral part of a procedure rather than merely a global facility within a process. Including the handler specification as part of the call frame contributes to the general goal of modular procedures and allows condition handlers to be nested. The nested inner handlers can either service a detected exception or pass it along to some outer handler in the calling hierarchy.
- Some languages, such as BASIC and PL/I, have signaling and error handling as part of the language specification. These languages can use the general mechanism rather than inventing their own procedures.
- There should be little or no cost to procedures that do not establish handlers. Further, a procedure that does establish a handler should incur little overhead for establishing it, with the expense in time being incurred when an error actually occurs.
- As far as the user or application programmer is concerned, there should be no difference in the appearance of exceptions and software conditions.

2.2   **Features of the VAX Condition Handling Facility**

Some of the features of the VAX condition handling facility show how these goals were attained. Others show the general desire to produce an easy-to-use but general condition handling mechanism. Features of the VAX condition handling facility include the following:

- A condition handler has three options available to it. The handler can fix the condition (continuing). If the handler cannot fix the condition, it passes the condition on to the next handler in the calling hierarchy (resignaling). The handler can alter the flow of control (unwinding the call stack).
- Because a condition handler is itself a procedure, it has its own call frame with its own slot for a condition handler address. This condition handler address gives a handler the ability to establish its own handler to field errors that it might cause.
- Space and time overhead was minimized by using only a single longword per procedure activation for handler address storage. There is no cost in time for a procedure that does not establish a handler. A procedure that does establish a handler can do so with a single MOVAx instruction. No time is spent looking for a condition handler until a signal is actually generated.

- The mechanism is designed to work even if a condition handler is written in a language that does not produce reentrant code. Thus, if a condition handler written in FORTRAN generated an error, that error would not be reported to the same handler.

  In fact, the special actions that are taken if multiple signals are active has a second benefit, namely that no condition handler has to worry about errors that it generates, because a handler can never be called in response to its own signals.

- Uniform dispatching for exceptions and software conditions is accomplished by providing the same dispatcher for both. Software conditions are generated by calling either LIB$SIGNAL or LIB$STOP, procedures in the Run-Time Library. These procedures jump to SYS$SRCHANDLER, a global location in the system service vectors. SYS$SRCHANDLER transfers control to the executive routine EXE$SRCHANDLER (in module EXCEPTION). Exception service routines also transfer control to EXE$SRCHANDLER. While the initial execution of these two mechanisms differs slightly, reflecting their different initial conditions, they eventually transfer to the same routine so that the information reported to condition handlers is independent of the initial detection mechanism.

- By making condition handling a part of a procedure, high-level languages can establish handlers that can examine a given signal and determine whether the signal was generated as a part of that language's support library. If so, the handler can attempt to fix the error in the manner defined by the language. If not, the handler passes the signal along to procedures further up the call stack.

4.3 EXCEPTIONS

The primary differences between exceptions and software conditions are the mechanism that generates them and the initial state of the stack that contains the condition parameters.

4.3.1 Exception Mechanism

Exceptions are anomalies detected by the hardware/microcode. When an exception is detected, the processor may change access mode and stack. It pushes the exception PC and PSL (and possible exception-specific parameters) onto the stack on which the exception is to be serviced. After the exception information has been pushed onto the stack, control is passed to an exception-specific service routine whose address is stored in a vector in the SCB. Figure 4-1 shows the SCB and Figure 5-1 shows the format of an SCB vector.

The stack on which the exception is serviced depends on the access mode in which the exception occurred, whether the CPU was previously executing on the interrupt stack and what type of exception occurred.

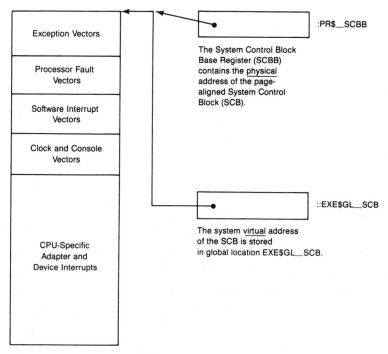

Figure 4-1   System Control Block

In general, a VAX CPU uses the low two bits of the SCB vector to determine on which stack the exception is serviced. Table 4-1 summarizes the stack choices resulting from the architectural mechanisms and VMS SCB vector definitions. Its first column lists the exception name. The second column specifies the access mode in which the exception occurred. The third column specifies whether the interrupt stack is in use at the time of the exception. The fourth column shows the stack on which the exception is serviced.

The exception PC that the processor pushes depends on the nature of the exception, that is, whether the exception is a fault, trap, or abort:

- An exception that is a fault (see Table 4-2) causes the PC of the faulting instruction to be pushed onto the stack. When a fault is dismissed with an REI instruction, the faulting instruction executes again.
- An exception that is a trap (see Table 4-2) pushes the PC of the next instruction onto the destination stack. An instruction that causes a trap does not reexecute when the exception is dismissed with an REI instruction.
- An exception that is an abort causes the PC of the next instruction to be pushed onto the stack. Aborts are not restartable. Exceptions that are aborts include kernel stack not valid, some machine check codes, and some reserved operand exceptions.

Table 4-1   Selection of Exception Stack

Exception Name	PSL<PRVMOD>	PSL<IS>	Stack
Machine check	Any	0 or 1	ISP
Kernel stack not valid	K	0	ISP
Subset exception (MicroVAX)	Any	0 or 1	Same[1]
Change mode to *x*	Any	0	*x*SP[2]
Change mode to *x*	K	1	Halt[3]
All others	U, S, E	0	KSP
All others	K	0	KSP
All others	K	1	ISP[4]

[1]If the exception was a VAX subset instruction emulation exception, then the current stack is used. Section 4.3.5 briefly describes these exceptions.

[2]The stack used is the destination of the CHMx instruction. Note, however, that a CHMx instruction issued from an inner access mode in an attempt to reach a less privileged (outer) access mode will not have the desired effect. The mode indicated by the instruction is minimized with the current access mode to determine the actual access mode that will be used. The exception is generated through the indicated SCB vector, but the final access mode is unchanged. In other words, as illustrated in Figure 1-4, the CHMx instructions can only reach equal or more privileged access modes.

[3]Execution of a CHMx instruction while the CPU is running on the interrupt stack is prohibited by the VAX architecture and results in a CPU halt.

[4]VMS does not expect exceptions to occur when it is operating on the interrupt stack. If an exception other than subset instruction emulation occurs on the interrupt stack, the exception dispatcher generates an INVEXCEPTN fatal bugcheck (see Chapter 8).

The VAX exception vectors are listed in Table 4-2. Most of the exceptions that are listed in this table are handled in a uniform way by the operating system. The actions that the VMS executive takes in response to these exceptions are the subject of most of this chapter. Some of the exceptions, however, result in special action on the part of the operating system. These exceptions, noted in Table 4-2, are discussed in the next section.

4.3.2   Exceptions That the VMS Executive Treats in a Special Way

Although the operating system provides uniform handling of most exceptions generated by users, several possible exceptions are used as entry points into privileged system procedures. Other exceptions can only be acted upon by the executive. It makes no sense for these procedures to pass information about the exceptions along to users' programs.

- The machine check exception is a processor-specific condition that may or may not be recoverable. Machine checks are serviced on the interrupt stack at IPL 31. The machine check exception service routine generates a fatal bugcheck in response to a nonrecoverable kernel or executive mode ma-

Table 4-2   Exception Vectors in the System Control Block

Vector Offset	Exception Name	Extra Parameters	Type
4	Machine check[1]	0	Abort/Fault
8	Kernel stack not valid[1]	0	Abort
16	Reserved/privileged instruction[1]	0	Fault
20	Customer reserved instruction	0	Fault
24	Reserved operand	0	Abort/Fault
28	Reserved addressing mode	0	Fault
32	Access violation	2	Fault
36	Translation not valid[1]	2	Fault
40	Trace pending	0	Fault
44	BPT instruction	0	Fault
48	Compatibility mode	1	Abort/Fault
52	Arithmetic	1	Fault/Trap
64	CHMK[1]	1	Trap
68	CHME[1]	1	Trap
72	CHMS	1	Trap
76	CHMU	1	Trap
200	Subset instruction emulation[1]	10	Trap
204	Suspended instruction emulation[1]	0	Trap

[1]These exceptions result in special action on the part of the operating system.

chine check. Nonrecoverable machine checks in supervisor and user modes are reported through the normal exception dispatch method. Chapter 8 discusses the machine check exception service routine and the bugcheck mechanism.

• A kernel-stack-not-valid exception indicates that the kernel stack was not valid while the processor was pushing information onto the stack during the initiation of an exception or interrupt. This exception is serviced on the interrupt stack at IPL 31. Its exception service routine generates a KRNLSTAKNV fatal bugcheck. (See Chapter 8 for more information on bugchecks.)

• A reserved/privileged instruction exception can indicate an attempt to execute an opcode not supported by the CPU. This can occur, for example, when a floating-point instruction is attempted on a CPU without microcode for that type of floating-point format. Software emulation of floating-point instructions is invoked through a condition handler for this exception.

Two other opcodes not supported by the CPU are reserved for use by VMS as bugchecks. The service routine for this exception must therefore test whether it was entered as the result of executing one of the bugcheck op-codes. If one of the bugcheck opcodes was executed, the service routine transfers control to the bugcheck routine, EXE$BUG_CHECK. The handling of bugchecks is described in Chapter 8.

- The translation-not-valid exception is a signal that a reference was made to a virtual address that is not currently mapped to physical memory. This exception is the entry path into the VMS paging facility. Its service routine, the page fault handler, is discussed in detail in Chapter 15.

- The CHMK and CHME exceptions are the mechanisms used by RMS services and system services to reach a more privileged access mode. The dispatching scheme for these services is described in Chapter 9. These two exceptions are paths into the operating system that allow nonprivileged users to reach an inner access mode in a controlled fashion.

- The VAX subset instruction emulation exceptions assist VMS in emulating string and decimal instructions not present in MicroVAX hardware. When the MicroVAX CPU encounters a string or decimal opcode not present in its instruction set, it evaluates the operands and pushes exception parameters on the stack describing the opcode and its operands. The CPU then dispatches through the SCB to the service routine, VAX$EMULATE (in module [EMULAT]VAXEMUL). The second emulation vector is used to dispatch back into the instruction emulation code at VAX$EMULATE_FPD, following an exception which the emulation code reflects back to the user.

    For more details on these exceptions, see the *MicroVAX I CPU Technical Description*.

4.3.3 Other Exceptions

The rest of the exceptions are handled uniformly by their exception service routines. These exceptions are all reported to condition handlers established by the user or by the system, rather than resulting in special system action such as occurs following a change-mode-to-kernel exception or a translation-not-valid fault (page fault).

For all exceptions that will eventually be reported to condition handlers, the CPU has pushed a PC/PSL pair onto the destination stack. In addition, from zero to two exception-specific parameters are pushed onto the destination stack (see Table 4-2). Finally, the CPU passes control to the exception service routine whose address VMS placed into the SCB when the system was initialized.

4.3.4 Initial Action of Exception Service Routines

These exception service routines all perform approximately the same action. The exception name (of the form SS$_*exception-name*) and the total number of exception parameters (from the exception name to the saved PSL inclusive) are pushed onto the stack. The destination stack now contains a list, called the signal array, which is a VAX argument list (see Figure 4-2). The exceptions that the operating system handles in this uniform way, their names, and the total number of signal array elements, are listed in Table 4-3.

After such a service routine has built this array, it jumps to EXE$EXCEPTION (in module EXCEPTION). EXE$EXCEPTION tests whether the exception occurred in process context (see Section 4.7.3.1). If it did not, EXE$EXCEPTION generates the fatal bugcheck INVEXCPTN. Otherwise, EXE$EXCEPTION builds a second argument list, which is called the mechanism array.

The mechanism array, which is pictured in Figure 4-4, serves the following purposes:

• It records the values of R0 and R1 at the time of the exception (the procedure calling standard prohibits their being saved in a procedure entry mask).
• It records the progress made in the search for a condition handler.

All exceptions (except for CHME, CHMS, CHMU, and the subset instruction emulation exceptions) are initially reported on the kernel stack (assuming the processor is not already on the interrupt stack). The exception reporting mechanism assumes that the kernel stack is valid. The decision to use the kernel stack was made to avoid the case of attempting to report an exception on, for example, the user stack, only to find that the user stack is corrupted in some way (invalid or otherwise inaccessible), resulting in another exception. If a kernel-stack-not-valid exception is generated while reporting an exception, the operating system generates a fatal bugcheck.

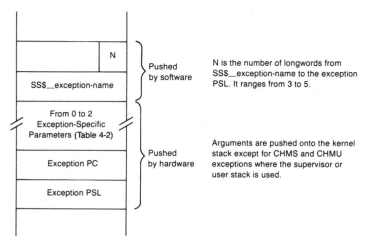

Figure 4-2   Signal Array Built by CPU and Exception Routines

Table 4-3   Exceptions That Use the Dispatcher in Module EXCEPTION

Exception Name	Signal Name	Dispatch Notes[1]	Signal Array Size	Extra Parameters in Signal Array[2]
Access violation	SS$_ACCVIO	① ③d	5	Signal(2) = Reason mask Signal(3) = Inaccessible virtual address
Arithmetic exception	(See Table 4-4)	②	3	None[3]
AST delivery stack fault	SS$_ASTFLT	③c	7	Signal(2) = SP value at fault Signal(3) = AST parameter of failed AST Signal(4) = PC at AST delivery interrupt[4] Signal(5) = PSL at AST delivery interrupt Signal(6) = PC to which AST would have been delivered Signal(7) = PSL at which AST would have been delivered
BPT instruction	SS$_BREAK		3	
Change mode to supervisor	SS$_CMODSUPR	④	4	Signal(2) = Change mode code
Change mode to user	SS$_CMODUSER	④	4	Signal(2) = Change mode code
Compatibility mode	SS$_COMPAT	④	4	Signal(2) = Compatibility exception code
Debug signal	SS$_DEBUG	③e	3	
Machine check	SS$_MCHECK		3	None[5]
Customer reserved instruction	SS$_OPCCUS		3	
Reserved privileged instruction	SS$_OPCDEC	⑤	3	

Table 4-3   Exceptions That Use the Dispatcher in Module EXCEPTION *(continued)*

Exception Name	Signal Name	Dispatch Notes[1]	Signal Array Size	Extra Parameters in Signal Array[2]
Page fault read error	SS$_PAGRDERR	③b	5	Signal(2) = Reason mask Signal(3) = Inaccessible virtual address
Reserved addressing mode	SS$_RADRMOD		3	
Reserved operand	SS$_ROPRAND		3	
System service failure	SS$_SSFAIL	③a	4	Signal(2) = System service final status
Trace pending	SS$_TBIT		3	

[1] These numbers refer to list items in Section 4.3.5.

[2] Additional parameters in the signal array are represented in the following way:

Signal(0) = N	Number of additional longwords in signal array
Signal(1)	Exception name
Signal(2)	First additional parameter
Signal(3)	Second additional parameter
.	.
.	.
.	.
Signal(N − 1)	Exception PC
Signal(N)	Exception PSL

[3] The arithmetic exception has no extra parameters, despite the fact that the hardware pushes an exception code onto the kernel stack. VMS modifies this hardware code into an exception-specific exception name (see Table 4-4) of the form Signal(1) = 8 · code + SS$_ARTRES.

[4] The AST delivery code exchanges the interrupt PC/PSL pair and the PC/PSL to which the AST would have been delivered.

[5] Machine check exceptions that are reported to a process do not have any extra parameters in the signal array. The machine check parameters have been examined, written to the error log, and discarded by the machine check handler (see Chapter 8).

However, the exception must eventually be reported back to the access mode in which the exception occurred. EXE$EXCEPTION creates space on the stack of the mode in which the exception occurred. The exception parameter lists are then copied to that stack, where they will become the argument list that is passed to condition handlers.

EXE$EXCEPTION then passes control to routine EXE$SRCHANDLER, in module EXCEPTION, which locates any condition handlers that have been established for the access mode of the exception. Its search method and the list of information passed to condition handlers is described in Section 4.5.

4.3.5 More Special Cases in Exception Dispatching

Although the procedure previously described is a reasonable approximation to the operation of the exception service routines in the operating system, there are detailed differences that occur in the dispatching of several exceptions that deserve special mention. The following notes refer to Table 4-3:

① User stack overflow is detected by the hardware as an access violation at the low address end of P1 space. The access violation exception service routine tests whether the inaccessible virtual address is at the low end of P1 space. If it is, additional virtual address space is created below the stack and the exception dismissed. Thus, the user stack expands automatically and transparently. User and system condition handlers are notified about such an exception only if the stack expansion is unsuccessful.

② There are ten possible arithmetic exceptions that can occur. They are distinguished in the hardware by different exception parameters. However, the exception service routine does not simply push a generic exception name onto the stack, resulting in a four parameter signal array. Rather, the exception parameter is used by the exception service routine to fashion a unique exception name for each of the possible arithmetic exceptions. The exception parameters and their associated signal names are listed in Table 4-4.

③ There are several conditions listed in Table 4-3 that are detected by software rather than by hardware. However, these software conditions are not generated by LIB$SIGNAL or LIB$STOP. Rather, they are detected by the executive, and control is passed to the same routines that are used for dispatching exceptions. The conditions are dispatched through the executive because they are typically detected in kernel mode but must be reported back to some other access mode. The code to accomplish this access mode switch is contained in EXCEPTION. The conditions that fall into this category are system service failure, page fault read error, insufficient stack space while attempting to deliver an asynchronous system trap (AST), software-detected access violation, and the signal SS$_DEBUG.

Table 4-4   Signal Names for Arithmetic Exceptions

Exception Type	Code Pushed by CPU	Resulting Exception Reported by VMS
	TRAPS	
Integer overflow[1]	1	SS$_INTOVF
Integer divide by zero	2	SS$_INTDIV
Floating overflow[2]	3	SS$_FLTOVF
Floating/Decimal divide by zero[2]	4	SS$_FLTDIV
Floating underflow[2/3]	5	SS$_FLTUND
Decimal overflow[1]	6	SS$_DECOVF
Subscript range	7	SS$_SUBRNG
	FAULTS	
Floating overflow	8	SS$_FLTOVF_F
Floating divide by zero	9	SS$_FLTDIV_F
Floating underflow	10	SS$_FLTUND_F

[1]Integer overflow enable and decimal overflow enable bits in the PSW can be altered either directly or through the procedure entry mask.

[2]The three floating point traps can only occur on VAX-11/780s earlier than microcode revision (rev) level 7.

[3] The floating underflow enable bit in the PSW can only be altered directly. There is no corresponding bit in the procedure entry mask.

(a) The SS$_SSFAIL condition is reported when a process has enabled signaling of system service failures through the Set System Service Failure Mode ($SETSFM) system service and a system or RMS service returns unsuccessfully with a status of either STS$K_ERROR or STS$K_SEVERE. The CHMK and CHME exception service routines, the "change mode dispatchers," push information about the error on the stack of the service execution and transfer control to EXE$SSFAIL (in module EXCEPTION).

(b) The SS$_PAGRDERR condition is reported when a process incurs a page fault for a page on which a read error occurred in response to a previous fault for the same page. Information about the page fault that led to the condition is already on the stack. The translation-not-valid service routine transfers control to EXE$PAGRDERR (in module EXCEPTION).

(c) The SS$_ASTFLT condition is reported when AST delivery code detects an inaccessible stack while attempting to deliver an AST to a process. The AST delivery interrupt service routine pushes information about the error on the AST access mode stack and transfers control to EXE$ASTFLT (in module EXCEPTION).

ⓓ Most access violations are exceptions detected by the microcode. In addition, however, the translation-not-valid exception service routine can generate an access violation. If it detects a process faulting a page in the process header of another process, then it transfers to EXE$ACVIOLAT (in module EXCEPTION), the access violation exception service routine. (Information about the error is already on the current stack.) This is a very unusual situation, typically the result of a software failure in executive or kernel mode code.

ⓔ The signal SS$_DEBUG is generated by either the DCL or MCR command language interpreter (CLI) in response to a DEBUG command while an image exists in an interrupted state. The DEBUG command processor pushes the PC and PSL of the interrupted image, the condition name (SS$_DEBUG), and the size of the signal array (3) onto the supervisor stack and jumps to routine EXE$REFLECT (in module EXCEPTION).

A CLI uses this mechanism for the DEBUG signal rather than simply calling LIB$SIGNAL, because the DEBUG command is issued from supervisor mode but the condition has to be reported back to user mode. EXE$REFLECT can accomplish this access mode switch, whereas LIB$SIGNAL and LIB$STOP have no corresponding function.

④ The exception dispatching for the CHMS and CHMU exceptions and compatibility mode exceptions can be short-circuited by use of the Declare Change Mode or Compatibility Mode Handler ($DCLCMH) system service. The $DCLCMH system service enables a user to establish a per-process change-mode-to-supervisor, change-mode-to-user, or compatibility mode handler. This service fills the locations CTLGL_CMSUPR, CTLGL_CMUSER, or CTL$GL_COMPAT, respectively, in the P1 pointer page with the address of the user-written change mode or compatibility handler.

When the exception service routine for the CHMS or CHMU exception finds nonzero contents in the associated longword in P1 space, it transfers control to the routine whose address is stored in that location with the exception stack (supervisor or user) in exactly the same state it was in following the exception. That is, the operand of the change mode instruction (the change mode code) is on the top of the stack and the exception PC and exception PSL occupy the next two longwords.

The DCL command language interpreter uses the $DCLCMH service to create a special CHMS handler. The use of the CHMS handler is briefly described in Chapter 23. The job controller uses a CHMU handler for its processing of error messages.

The exception service routine for compatibility mode exceptions transfers control to the user-declared compatibility mode handler (if one was declared) with the user stack in the same state it was in before the compatibility mode exception occurred. That is, no parameters are passed to the compatibility mode handler on the user stack. The compatibility mode code, exception PC and PSL, and contents of R0 through R6 are saved in the first ten longwords of the compatibility mode context page in P1 space at global location CTL$AL_CMCNTX.

⑤ The reserved instruction fault is generated whenever an unrecognized opcode is detected by the instruction decoder. The same exception is generated when a privileged instruction is executed from other than kernel mode.

VMS uses this fault as a path into the operating system crash code called the bugcheck mechanism. Opcode FF, followed by FE or FD, tells the reserved instruction exception service routine that the exception is actually a bugcheck. Control is passed to the bugcheck routine that is described in Chapter 8.

.4   SOFTWARE CONDITIONS

One of the goals of the design of the VAX architecture was to have a common condition handling facility for both exceptions and software conditions. The dispatching for exceptions (and for the errors described in Section 4.3.5) is performed by the routines in the executive module EXCEPTION. The Run-Time Library procedures, LIB$SIGNAL and LIB$STOP, provide a similar capability to any user of a VAX/VMS system.

.4.1   Passing Status from a Procedure

There are usually two methods available for a procedure to indicate to its caller whether it completed successfully. One method is to indicate a return status in R0. The other is the signaling mechanism. The signaling mechanism employs a call to the Run-Time Library procedure LIB$SIGNAL or LIB$STOP to initiate a sequence of events exactly like those that occur in response to an exception. One of the choices in the design of a modular procedure is the method for reporting exceptional conditions back to the caller.

There are two reasons why signaling may be preferable to returning completion status. In some procedures, such as the mathematics procedures in the Run-Time Library, R0 is already used for another purpose, namely the return of a function value, and is therefore unavailable for error return status. In this case, the procedure must use the signaling mechanism to indicate exceptional conditions, such as an attempt to take the square root of a negative number.

The second common use of signaling occurs in an application that is using an indeterminate number of procedure calls to perform some action, such as a recursive procedure that parses a command line, where the use of a return status is often cumbersome and difficult to code. In this case, the VAX signaling mechanism provides a graceful way not only to indicate that an error has occurred but also to return control (through $UNWIND) to a known alternate return point in the calling hierarchy.

4.4.2   **Initial Operation of LIB$SIGNAL and LIB$STOP**

A procedure calls LIB$SIGNAL or LIB$STOP with the name of the condition to be signaled and whatever additional parameters are to be passed to the condition handlers that were established by the user and the system. LIB$STOP is an alternate entry point to LIB$SIGNAL. (This chapter refers to the combined procedures as "LIB$SIGNAL/STOP.") LIB$SIGNAL and LIB$STOP differ in whether normal execution may be resumed after the condition handler for the signaled error returns. Use of LIB$SIGNAL enables the program to continue if the condition handler returns SS$_CONTINUE. Use of LIB$STOP does not. The two entry points store different values in a stack flag tested by the code to which a condition handler returns.

The state of the stack following a call to either of these procedures is pictured in Figure 4-3.

Before LIB$SIGNAL/STOP begins its search for condition handlers, it removes the call frame (and possibly the argument list) from the stack. Removing the call frame causes the stack to appear almost exactly the same to LIB$SIGNAL/STOP as it does to the routines in EXCEPTION following an exception (see Figure 4-3). After building the exception argument list, LIB$SIGNAL/STOP jumps to EXE$SRCHANDLER (in module EXCEPTION) to search for condition handlers. (In fact, LIB$SIGNAL/STOP jumps to SYS$SRCHANDLER in the system services vector pages, and then SYS$SRCHANDLER jumps to EXE$SRCHANDLER. The indirection gives the Run-Time Library a constant address to get to the routine in EXCEPTION.) The search for condition handlers takes place on the stack of the caller of LIB$SIGNAL/STOP.

4.5   **UNIFORM CONDITION DISPATCHING**

Once information concerning the condition has been pushed onto the stack, the differences between exceptions and software conditions are no longer important. In the following discussion, the operation of condition dispatching is discussed in general terms and explicit mention of EXCEPTION or LIB$SIGNAL/STOP is only made where they depart from each other in their operation.

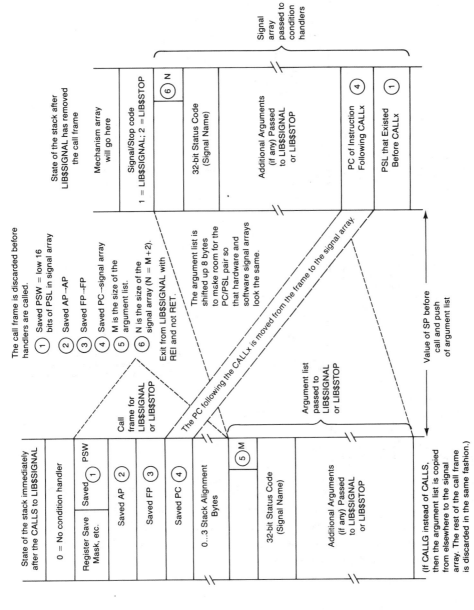

Figure 4-3 Removal of Call Frame by LIB$SIGNAL/STOP

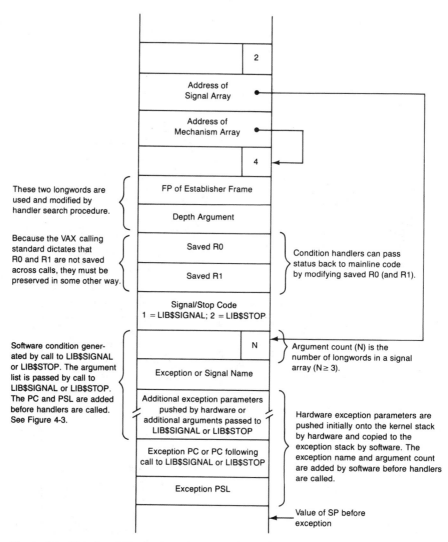

Figure 4-4 Signal and Mechanism Arrays

Before the search for a condition handler begins, EXE$SRCHANDLER builds a second data structure on the stack called the mechanism array. The address of the mechanism array and the address of the signal array are the two arguments that are passed to any condition handlers called by EXE$SRCHANDLER (see Figure 4-4).

4.5.1   **Establishing a Condition Handler**

VMS provides two different methods for establishing condition handlers:

• One method uses the stack associated with each access mode. Each procedure call frame includes a longword to contain the address of a condition handler associated with that frame. Figure 4-3 illustrates a call frame.

• The second method uses software vectors, set aside in the control region (P1 space) for each of the four access modes. Vectored handlers do not possess the modular properties associated with call frame handlers and are intended primarily for debuggers and performance monitors.

Call frame handlers are established by placing the address of the handler in the first longword of the currently active call frame. Thus, in assembly language, call frame handlers can be established with a single instruction:

```
MOVAB   new-handler,(FP)
```

Because direct access to the call frame is generally not available to high-level language programmers, LIB$ESTABLISH, the Run-Time Library procedure, can be called in the following way to accomplish the same result:

```
old-handler = LIB$ESTABLISH (new-handler)
```

Condition handlers are removed by clearing the first longword of the current call frame, as in the following assembly language instruction:

```
CLRL    (FP)
```

The Run-Time Library procedure LIB$REVERT removes the condition handler established by LIB$ESTABLISH.

Software-vectored condition handlers are established and removed with the Set Exception Vector ($SETEXV) system service, which simply loads the address of the specified handler into the specified software vector, located in the P1 pointer page.

4.5.2 The Search for a Condition Handler

At this point in the dispatch sequence, the signal and mechanism arrays have been set up on the stack of the access mode to which the condition will be reported. The establisher frame argument in the mechanism array (see Figure 4-4) will be used by the condition handler search routine EXE$SRCHANDLER to indicate how far along the search has gone. The depth argument in the mechanism array not only serves as useful information to condition handlers that wish to unwind but also allows the search procedure to distinguish call frame handlers (nonnegative depth) from software-vectored condition handlers (negative depth).

4.5.2.1 Primary and Secondary Exception Vectors. EXE$SRCHANDLER begins the search for a condition handler with the primary vector of the access mode in which the exception occurred. If the vector contains the address of a condi-

tion handler (any nonzero contents), the handler is called with a depth argument of −2 (third longword in mechanism array, Figure 4-4). If that handler resignals or if none exists, the same step is performed for the secondary vector, with a depth argument of −1.

4.5.2.2   **Call Frame Condition Handlers.** If the search is to continue (no handler yet passed back a status of SS$_CONTINUE), EXE$SRCHANDLER examines the contents of the current call frame. If the first longword in the current call frame is nonzero, that handler is called next. If no handler is found there or if that handler resignals, the previous call frame is examined by using the saved frame pointer in the current call frame (see Figure 4-5). As each handler is called, the depth longword in the mechanism array is set to the number of frames that have already been examined for a handler.

EXE$SRCHANDLER continues the search until some handler passes back a status code of SS$_CONTINUE or until a saved frame pointer is found whose value is not within the bounds of that access mode's stack. An out-of-range frame pointer might, for example, point to the previous mode stack following a call to a system service. Also, a saved frame pointer value may be out of range as a result of stack corruption. A saved frame pointer value of zero indicates the end of the call frame chain. When EXE$SRCHANDLER receives a return status of SS$_CONTINUE (any code with the low bit of R0 set will do), it cleans off the stack, restores R0 and R1 from the mechanism array, and dismisses the condition by issuing an REI, using the saved PC and PSL that formed the last two elements of the signal array.

Note that EXE$SRCHANDLER passes control back with an REI instruction, even if the condition was caused by a call to LIB$SIGNAL/STOP. LIB$SIGNAL/STOP discards the call frame set up when it was called. That is, LIB$SIGNAL/STOP modifies its stack to look just like the stack used by EXCEPTION (see Figure 4-3).

4.5.2.3   **Last Chance Condition Handler.** If all handlers resignal, the search terminates when a saved frame pointer of zero is located. EXE$SRCHANDLER then calls with a depth argument of −3 the handler whose address is stored in the last chance vector. (This handler is also called in the event that any errors occur while searching the stack for the existence of condition handlers.) The usual handler found in the last chance vector is the "catch-all" condition handler established as part of image initiation. The action of this system-supplied handler is described at the end of this chapter.

If the last chance handler returns (its status is ignored) or the last chance vector is empty, EXE$SRCHANDLER indicates that no handler was found. This notification is performed by a procedure called EXE$EXCMSG (see Chapter 29) in the executive. Its two input parameters are an ASCII string containing message text and the argument list that was passed to any condi-

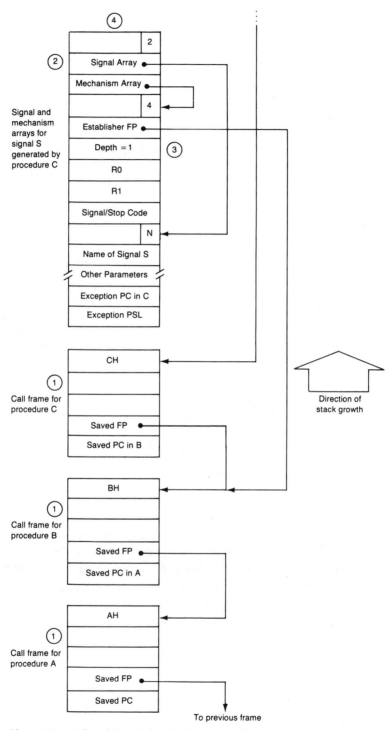

Figure 4-5   Order of Search for Condition Handler

tion handlers. Following the call to EXE$EXCMSG, EXE$SRCHANDLER invokes the $EXIT system service with a status indicating either that no handler was found or that a bad stack was detected while searching for a condition handler.

4.5.3 Multiple Active Signals

If an exception occurs in a condition handler or in some procedure called by a condition handler, a situation called multiple active signals is reached. To avoid an infinite loop of exceptions, EXE$SRCHANDLER modifies its search algorithm so that those frames searched while servicing the first condition are skipped while servicing the second condition.

For this skipping to work correctly, call frames of condition handlers must be uniquely recognizable. The frames are made unique by always calling the condition handlers from a standard call site, located in the system service vector area.

4.5.3.1 Common Call Site for Condition Handlers.

Before the dispatch to the handler occurs, EXE$SRCHANDLER sets up the stack to contain the signal and mechanism arrays and the handler argument list (see Figure 4-4). It loads the handler address into R1 and passes control to the common dispatch site with the following instruction:

```
JSB     @#SYS$CALL_HANDL
```

The code located at SYS$CALL_HANDL simply calls the procedure whose address is stored in R1 and returns to its caller with an RSB.

```
SYS$CALL_HANDL::
        CALLG 4(SP),(R1)
        RSB
```

The call instruction leaves the return address SYS$CALL_HANDL + 4, the address of the RSB instruction, in its call frame. Thus, the unique identifying characteristic of a condition handler is the address SYS$CALL_HANDL + 4 in the saved PC of its call frame. This signature is not only used by the search procedure but also by the Unwind Call Stack ($UNWIND) system service, as described in the following section.

4.5.3.2 Example of Multiple Active Signals.

The modified search procedure can best be illustrated through an example as shown in Figures 4-5 and 4-6. Figure 4-5 shows the stack after Procedure C, called from B, which is called from A, has generated signal S. We are assuming that the primary and secondary condition handlers (if they exist) have already resignaled. Condition handler CH also resignaled.

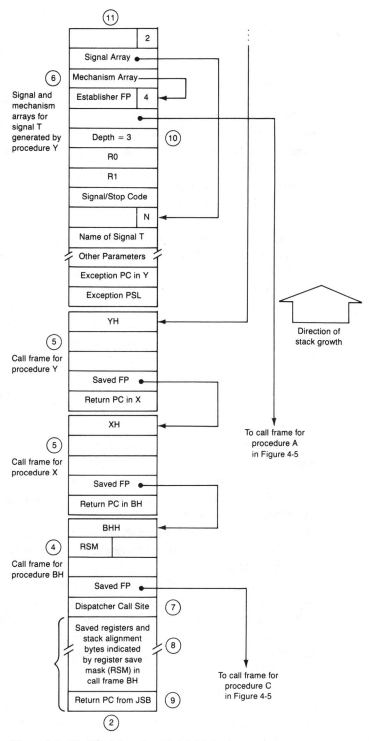

Figure 4-6   Modified Search with Multiple Active
Signals

① Procedure A calls Procedure B, which calls Procedure C.

② Procedure C generates signal S.

③ The search procedure modifies the depth argument and establisher frame argument.

   If handler CH resignals, then the depth argument is 1 when BH is called.

④ The call frame for handler BH is located (at lower virtual addresses) on top of the signal and mechanism arrays for signal S (see Figure 4-6). (The only intervening items are the saved registers and stack alignment bytes indicated by the register save mask in the upper word of the second longword of the call frame for handler BH.) The saved frame pointer in the call frame for BH points to the frame for Procedure C.

⑤ Handler BH now calls Procedure X, which calls Procedure Y (see Figure 4-6).

⑥ Procedure Y generates signal T. The desired sequence of frames to be examined is frame Y, frame X, frame BH, and then frame A. Frames B and C should be skipped because they were examined while servicing condition S.

⑦ EXE$SRCHANDLER proceeds in its normal fashion. The primary and secondary vectors are examined first (no skipping here). Then frames Y, X, and BH are examined, resulting in handlers YH, XH, and BHH being called in turn. Let us assume that all these handlers resignal. After handler BHH returns to EXE$SRCHANDLER with a code of SS$_RESIGNAL, EXE$SRCHANDLER notes that this is the frame of a condition handler, because its saved PC is SYS$CALL_HANDL + 4 (see Figure 4-6).

⑧ The skipping is accomplished by locating the frame that established this handler. The address of that frame is located in the mechanism array for signal S.

   To locate the mechanism array for signal S, the value of SP before the call to BH must be calculated, using the register save mask and stack alignment bits in the call frame.

⑨ One extra longword, the return PC from the JSB to SYS$CALL_HANDL, must be skipped to locate the argument list (and thus the mechanism array) for signal S.

⑩ Because the frame pointed to by the mechanism array element has already been searched, the next frame examined by the search procedure is the frame pointed to by the saved frame pointer in the call frame of Procedure B which, in this case, is the frame for Procedure A. The depths that are passed to handlers as a result of the modified search are 0 for YH, 1 for XH, 2 for BHH, and 3 for AH.

⑪ The frame for the search procedure or for any of the handlers YH, XH, BHH, and AH when they are called is located on top of the signal and mechanism arrays for signal T (at lower virtual addresses). (One example is shown in Figure 4-8, which illustrates the operation of $UNWIND.)

.6   **CONDITION HANDLER ACTION**

A condition handler has several options available to it:

- It can fix the condition and allow execution to continue at the interrupted point in the program.
- It can pass the condition along to another handler by resignaling.
- It can also allow execution to resume at any arbitrary place in the calling hierarchy by unwinding a number of frames from the call stack.

.6.1   **Continue or Resignal**

A handler first determines the nature of the condition by examining the signal name in the signal array (see Figure 4-4). If the handler determines that it is not capable of resolving the current condition for whatever reason, it informs EXE$SRCHANDLER that the search for a handler must go on. This continuation is called resignaling and is performed by passing a return status code of SS$_RESIGNAL back to EXE$SRCHANDLER. (Recall that condition handlers are function procedures that return a status to their caller in R0.)

On the other hand, if the condition handler is able to resolve the condition (in some unspecified way), it indicates to the EXE$SRCHANDLER that the program that was interrupted when the condition occurred can continue. To indicate that the program can now continue, the return status code of SS$_CONTINUE is passed back to the caller.

When EXE$SRCHANDLER detects this return status code, it removes the argument list and mechanism array from the stack (see Figure 4-4), restoring R0 and R1 in the process. It then removes all of the signal array except the condition PC and PSL from the stack. Finally, these are removed with the REI instruction that dismisses the exception and passes control back to the program that was interrupted when the condition occurred.

If the condition that occurred was a hardware fault (such as an access violation), the instruction that caused the exception will be repeated because the PC of that instruction was pushed onto the stack when the exception occurred. If the exception was a hardware trap (such as integer overflow), the next instruction in the instruction stream will be the first to execute. If a condition handler continues from a condition that was initiated through a call to LIB$SIGNAL, the first instruction to execute will be the instruction following the CALLx instruction.

.6.2   **Unwinding the Call Stack**

Another powerful tool available to condition handlers allows them to alter the flow of control when a condition occurs. This tool is called unwinding and allows the condition handler to pass control back to a previous level in the calling hierarchy by throwing away a specified (or default) number of call frames.

The Unwind Call Stack ($UNWIND) system service is called with two optional arguments. The first indicates the number of frames to remove from the call stack, and the second gives an alternate return PC to which control will be returned.

The system service procedure EXE$UNWIND (in module SYSUNWIND) does not actually remove frames from the stack. Rather, it changes the return PC in the specified number of frames to point to a special routine in the executive that will be entered as each procedure exits with a RET instruction. The effect of calling $UNWIND is pictured in Figure 4-7. If the alternate PC argument has also been passed to EXE$UNWIND, the return PC in the next call frame is altered to the specified argument (see Figure 4-7).

As each procedure issues a RET instruction, registers saved in the call frame are restored and control is passed to the executive routine that examines the current frame for the existence of a condition handler. If such a handler exists, it is called with the condition name SS$_UNWIND. When the condition handler returns to EXE$UNWIND, it issues a RET on behalf of the procedure to discard the current call frame. This sequence goes on until the specified number of call frames have been discarded. This technique of calling handlers as a part of the unwind sequence allows handlers that previously resignaled a condition to regain control and perform procedure-specific cleanup and also ensures correct restoration of saved registers.

4.6.3   **Example of Unwinding the Call Stack**

An example of an unwind sequence is illustrated here with the help of Figure 4-7. The situation begins with a sequence exactly like the one pictured in Figure 4-5. Procedure A calls Procedure B, which calls Procedure C. Procedure C generates signal S. The primary and secondary handlers (if they exist) simply resignal. Handlers CH and BH, located next by EXE$SRCHANDLER, also resignal.

Finally, handler AH is called. AH decides to unwind the call stack back to its establisher frame. (This unwinding is not the default case.) To accomplish the unwinding, AH must call $UNWIND with a depth argument equal to the value contained in the mechanism array. In this example, the depth argument is 2. After the call to $UNWIND, which executes in the access mode of its caller, but before the frame modification occurs, the stack has the form pictured on the left-hand side of Figure 4-7. The operation of frame modification by the EXE$UNWIND now proceeds as follows:

① EXE$UNWIND looks down the call stack until it locates a condition handler. Recall that a condition handler is identified by a saved PC of SYS$CALL_HANDL + 4. If handler AH had called another procedure

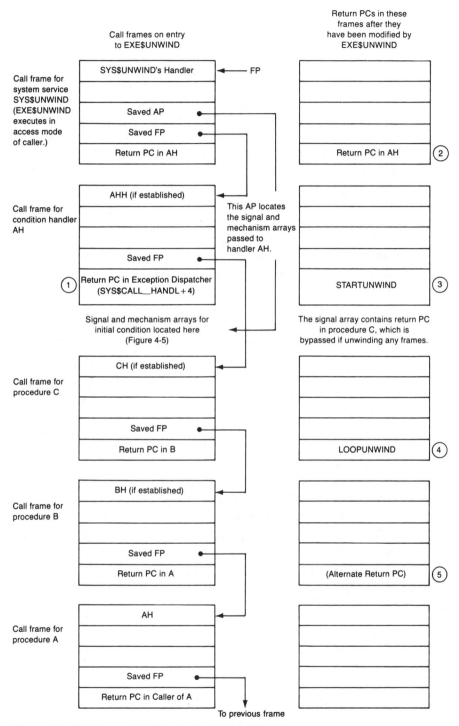

Figure 4-7   Call Frame Modification by EXE$UNWIND

in this example, nothing would have happened to that procedure's call frame. The first call frame modified by EXE$UNWIND is the frame of the first handler that it encounters which, in this example, is the frame for AH.

② EXE$UNWIND does not modify its own frame. When it executes a RET instruction, control returns to handler AH.

③ The first frame that EXE$UNWIND modifies is the frame of the first condition handler that it encounters by tracing back the call stack. It replaces the return address found there with the address of STARTUNWIND, a routine internal to EXE$UNWIND.

When handler AH executes a RET instruction, control will not return to EXE$SRCHANDLER. Instead, the instructions beginning at START-UNWIND execute. Note that not returning to EXE$SRCHANDLER means that control will never get back to Procedure C, because its return PC is stored in the mechanism array and can only be restored by the REI instruction issued by the condition dispatcher.

④ EXE$UNWIND continues to modify the saved PC longwords in successive frames on the call stack until the number of frames specified (or implied) in the $UNWIND argument list have been modified. All frames except the first have their saved PC replaced with address LOOPUNWIND, another label in the internal unwind routine (see Figure 4-7). It is this routine that checks whether the current frame has a handler established and, if so, calls that handler with the signal name SS$_UNWIND to allow the handler to perform procedure-specific cleanup.

If a handler called in this way calls $UNWIND (with the signal array containing SS$_UNWIND as the signal name), then an error status of SS$_UNWINDING is returned, indicating an unwind is already in progress.

⑤ If the alternate PC argument was also supplied to $UNWIND, the call frame into which this argument would be inserted is the next frame beyond the last frame specified (or implied) in the first $UNWIND argument. In this case, if an alternate PC argument were present, it would be placed into the call frame for Procedure B.

Now that all the frames have been modified, the actual unwinding occurs. The sequence of steps is the following:

1. EXE$UNWIND returns control to handler AH.

2. Handler AH does whatever else it needs to do to service the condition. When it has completed its work, it returns to the code beginning at label STARTUNWIND. (Because none of the unwind routines checks return status, it does not matter what status is passed back by AH as it returns.)

3. The routine beginning at STARTUNWIND first restores R0 and R1 from the mechanism array. It then performs the following three steps:

   a. If a handler is established for this frame, the handler is called with the signal name SS$_UNWIND.

b. If either R0 or R1 is specified in the register save mask, the unwind routine replaces the value of that register in the register save area of the call frame with the current contents of the register. Note that this is rather an unusual case. The procedure calling standard (see *Introduction to VAX/VMS System Routines*) specifies that R0 and R1 are to be used to return status codes and function values.

c. Control is returned to whatever address is specified in the saved PC longword of the current call frame by issuing a RET.

4. The RET issued in step 3c discards the call frame for Procedure C, passing control to LOOPUNWIND, where the three steps 3a through 3c are again executed.

5. The RET that discards the call frame for Procedure B passes control back to the point in Procedure A, following the call to Procedure B (if we assume no alternate PC argument), where execution will resume.

In effect, STARTUNWIND and LOOPUNWIND simulate returns from each nested procedure that is being unwound. These procedures never receive control again. However, the outermost procedure receives control as if all of the nested procedures had returned normally.

4.6.4   Potential Infinite Loop

There is one possible problem that can occur with this implementation. The previous section pointed out that EXE$SRCHANDLER takes care (when multiple signals are active) not to search frames for the second condition that were examined on the first pass. If a condition handler generates an exception, it is not called in response to its own signal (unless it establishes itself to handle its own signals!).

However, EXE$UNWIND cannot perform such a check. It must call each condition handler that it encounters as it removes frames from the stack. Thus, a poorly written condition handler (one that generates an exception) could result in an infinite loop of exceptions if a handler higher up in the calling hierarchy unwinds the frame in which this poorly written handler is declared. This loop has no effect on the system but effectively destroys the process in which this handler exists.

4.6.5   Unwinding Multiple Active Signals

There is a slight change in EXE$UNWIND when multiple signals are active. While modifying saved PCs in call frames, EXE$UNWIND counts the number of frames that have been modified until the requested number has been reached. The only change that occurs with multiple active signals is that the loop stops counting while the skipped frames are being modified.

The example of multiple active signals pictured in Figures 4-5 and 4-6 can be used to illustrate the unwinding. Recall that Procedure A called Procedure B, which called Procedure C, which signaled S. Handler CH resignaled. Handler BH called Procedure X, which called Procedure Y, which signaled T. Handlers YH, XH, and BHH all resignaled. Finally, handler AH was called for signal T with a depth of 3.

If AH calls $UNWIND, the top of the stack is as pictured in Figure 4-8, with the continuations of this figure in Figure 4-6. Assume that the depth argument passed to $UNWIND is 3 (taken from the mechanism array and meaning unwind to the establisher of AH), and the alternate PC argument is not present.

The end result of the operation of EXE$UNWIND in this case is as follows:

1. EXE$UNWIND looks down the call stack until it locates a condition

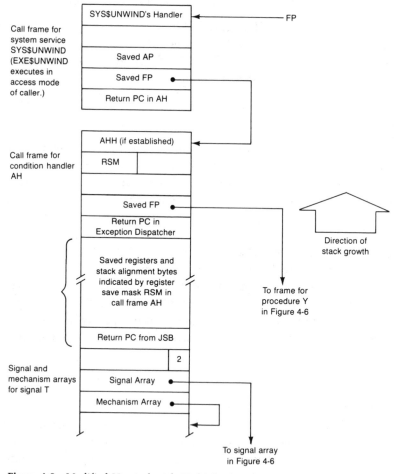

Figure 4-8 Modified Unwind with Multiple Active Signals

handler, which in this case is AH. The saved PC is modified to STARTUNWIND.

2. The saved PC longwords in frames Y and X are altered to contain address LOOPUNWIND. Note that EXE$UNWIND has now altered three frames.

3. Because the next frame on the stack, BH, indicates a condition handler (saved PC of SYS$CALL_HANDL + 4), its associated mechanism array is located (by climbing over saved registers, stack alignment bytes, and a saved PC from the JSB instruction). The saved PCs in all frames up to the frame pointed to by the mechanism array are modified (but not counted toward the number specified in the argument passed to $UNWIND) to contain address LOOPUNWIND. This modification causes frames BH and C to get their saved PCs altered in the example.

4. The saved PC in the frame for Procedure B is not altered so that when the unwind takes place, control will return to the call site of Procedure B in Procedure A.

4.6.6   Correct Use of Default Depth in $UNWIND

A default depth argument of zero to the $UNWIND system service specifies that the stack is to be unwound to the caller of the handler's establisher. In most cases, the caller of the handler's establisher is equivalent to the depth of the handler plus 1. However, because of an inherent ambiguity in counting the stack frames when multiple active signals are present, it is important that the default rather than an explicit depth be used when unwinding to the caller of the establisher.

Consider the two following cases of nested conditions. In Figure 4-9, Procedure A calls Procedure B. A condition causes handler BH to be invoked. An exception within BH causes handler AH to be invoked (because frame B is skipped, as described in Section 4.5.3). The depth of the mechanism vector in AH's argument list is 1. For AH to unwind to its establisher, it must specify an explicit depth of 1 to $UNWIND. EXE$UNWIND removes one frame, as specified by the count. EXE$UNWIND then notices that the next frame is a handler frame and therefore continues to remove stack frames until it finds the establisher of the handler. This discovery completes the unwind to frame A.

Now consider Figure 4-10 in which Procedure A incurs an exception, resulting in the invoking of handler AH. Handler AH then causes an exception, causing its handler AHH to be invoked. The depth of AHH is zero. Now let us suppose that AHH wishes to unwind to the caller of its establisher. Now the establisher of AHH is AH. Since AH is a handler, its caller is the condition dispatcher, *not* Procedure A.

Compare Figure 4-10 with Figure 4-9 carefully and consider what happens if AHH calls the $UNWIND system service with an explicit depth of 1

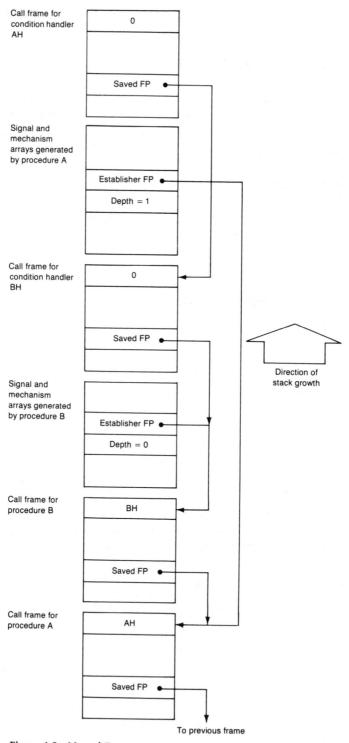

Figure 4-9 Nested Exception, Type 1

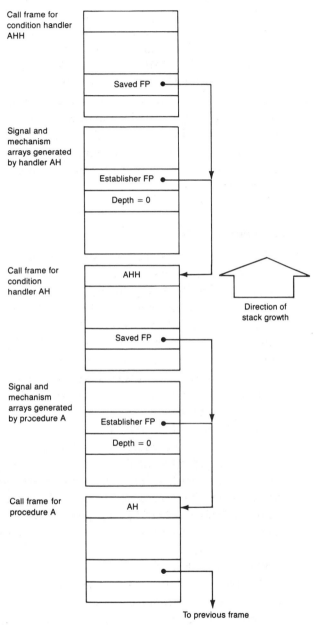

Call frame for
condition handler
AHH

Saved FP

Signal and
mechanism
arrays generated
by handler AH

Establisher FP

Depth = 0

Call frame for
condition
handler AH

AHH

Direction of
stack growth

Saved FP

Signal and
mechanism
arrays generated
by procedure A

Establisher FP

Depth = 0

Call frame for
procedure A

AH

To previous frame

Figure 4-10   Nested Exception, Type 2

(its depth plus 1). The depth of 1 causes AHH's frame to be removed. EXE$UNWIND then notices that the next frame is a handler frame and therefore unwinds it back to its establisher (frame A). Note that once AHH's frame is removed, the stack is indistinguishable from the stack in Figure 4-9 (down to frame B). Thus, invoking $UNWIND with an explicit depth of 1 results in control's returning to Procedure A, which is incorrect.

Therefore, for AHH to unwind to the caller of its establisher (EXE$SRCHANDLER), it must specify a default depth. When this is done, EXE$UNWIND's behavior upon encountering a handler frame after the count has been exhausted is modified so that the stack is not unwound further, and control passes correctly back to the condition dispatcher.

Because of the inherent ambiguity of these two cases, it is important that handlers always use the default depth when unwinding to the caller of their establisher.

4.6.7 Unwinding ASTs

EXE$UNWIND must perform special processing to unwind out of ASTs; simply removing the stack frames would ignore the presence of the AST and fail to dismiss the AST properly.

This situation is depicted in Figure 4-11. If handler XH unwinds to the caller of its establisher (Procedure A), it will also unwind out of the AST. The problem is handled by having EXE$UNWIND recognize the return PC of the AST call frame, which is set to the value EXE$ASTRET, the AST return point in the executive. When this PC is seen in a call frame, EXE$UNWIND knows that the AST parameter list is located immediately beneath the call frame. In this case, the unwind PC (STARTUNWIND or LOOPUNWIND) is stored not in the call frame, but rather in the PC of the AST parameter list.

When the AST procedure returns during the actual unwinding of the stack, it returns to EXE$ASTRET, which dismisses the AST and returns to the interrupted code with an REI. The REI then returns back to STARTUNWIND or LOOPUNWIND because of the modified PC. In addition, immediately before returning to EXE$ASTRET, EXE$UNWIND also stores the current R0 and R1 in the AST parameter list so that they will propagate through the unwind process.

While it is technically possible to unwind out of an AST, this must be done with some caution. If the AST routine has any sort of side effects, it is essential to have a condition handler declared by the AST routine to clean up the side effects when the AST is unwound. (Note that issuing an I/O operation is a side effect of the highest order!) Note that cleaning up any procedures of the main line program from which an unwind was executed may be more difficult, because the asynchronous nature of ASTs means that unwinding could take place at any instant during the execution of a program.

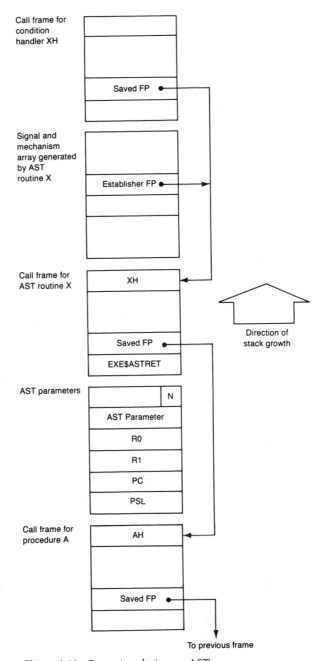

Call frame for
condition
handler XH

Saved FP

Signal and
mechanism
array generated
by AST
routine X

Establisher FP

Call frame for
AST routine X

XH

Direction of
stack growth

Saved FP

EXE$ASTRET

AST parameters

N

AST Parameter

R0

R1

PC

PSL

Call frame for
procedure A

AH

Saved FP

To previous frame

Figure 4-11   Exception during an AST

4.7 DEFAULT (VMS-SUPPLIED) CONDITION HANDLERS

The use of condition handlers is totally general and completely in the hands of the user. However, some actions will always occur as the result of default condition handlers that are established by the executive as a part of process creation or image activation.

The discussions of process creation in Chapter 20 and image initiation in Chapter 21 point out exactly when and how each of the handlers described in this section is established. The action of each of these handlers, once they are invoked, is briefly described in the following sections.

4.7.1 Traceback Handler Established by Image Startup

When an image includes either the debugger or the traceback handler, another frame is put on the user stack before the image itself is called (see Chapter 21). The code that executes before calling the image, EXE$IMGSTA (in module SYSIMGSTA), places the address of a condition handler local to itself into this frame so that subsequent conditions that are not handled by an intervening condition handler will be picked up by this traceback handler.

This handler first checks whether the condition that occurred is SS$_DEBUG. If so, it maps the debugger into P0 space (if not already mapped) and passes control to it. The condition SS$_DEBUG is signaled by a CLI in response to a DEBUG command. This feature allows an image that was not linked or run with debugger support to be interrupted and have a debugger invoked.

For all other conditions, if the severity level is warning, error, or severe error, the handler maps the traceback facility above the end of defined P0 space and passes control to it. The traceback facility passes information about the exception to SYS$OUTPUT and terminates the image.

If the severity level is other than the three listed in the previous paragraph, the traceback condition handler resignals the condition, which usually means that the condition is being passed on to the catch-all condition handler.

4.7.2 Catch-All Condition Handler

The address of this handler, EXE$CATCH_ALL, is placed in an initial call frame on the user stack and in the last chance vector for user mode by either EXE$PROCSTRT when the process is created or by a command language interpreter before an image is called. This handler is always called if no other handlers exist or if all other handlers resignal. Because the address of the handler is duplicated in the last chance vector, it will also be called in the event of some error while looking through the user stack.

The first step that EXE$CATCH_ALL takes is to call SYS$PUTMSG (see

Chapter 29). If the handler was called through the last chance vector (the depth argument in mechanism array is −3) or if the severity level of the condition name in the signal array indicates severe (condition-name <2:0> GEQU 4), then EXE$EXCMSG (see Chapter 29) is called to print a summary message, and the image is terminated; otherwise, the image is continued.

.7.3   Handlers Used by Other Access Modes

In addition to the handlers that the operating system supplies to handle conditions that occur in user mode, it also sets up handlers that will determine system behavior if a condition occurs in one of the other three access modes.

.7.3.1   Exceptions in Kernel or Executive Mode.

In response to an exception in kernel mode, the condition dispatcher makes special checks to determine whether the processor was operating on the interrupt stack when the exception occurred, whether the process was the swapper or null process, or whether IPL was above IPL$_ASTDEL (IPL 2). Any of these could indicate that the exception is not associated with a normal process. In any case, if any of these holds, an Invalid Exception fatal bugcheck (INVEXCPTN) is generated. Routines that may not incur exceptions include interrupt service routines, device drivers (except for their FDT routines), and process-based code that happens to be executing above IPL$_ASTDEL (such as portions of certain system services).

If a kernel mode exception is associated with process-based code for which exceptions are allowed (IPL is less than or equal to 2 and the exception occurred on the kernel stack), then exception dispatching proceeds in its usual manner. The last chance exception vectors for both kernel and executive modes are initialized in module SHELL (see Chapter 20) to contain the addresses of routines that generate a bugcheck code of Unexpected System Service Exception (SSRVEXCEPT). The difference between the bugchecks for the two access modes is that the bugcheck generated by the kernel mode last chance handler is fatal while the corresponding bugcheck generated by the executive mode last chance handler is not. Fatal bugchecks cause the system to crash. Nonfatal bugchecks generally result in error log entries and the deletion of the process that caused the bugcheck. The handling of bugchecks is described in Chapter 8.

Routines that execute in executive mode include RMS, parts of the executive, and any user-written procedure that is entered through either a user-written system service dispatcher or through the Change Mode to Executive ($CMEXEC) system service. Routines that execute in kernel mode (that can cause this bugcheck and not the INVEXCPTN bugcheck because they execute at IPL 0 or IPL 2) include portions of all system services, many exception service routines, device driver FDT routines, including those that are written by users, and procedures that are called by either a user-written system service dispatcher or by the Change Mode to Kernel ($CMKRNL) system service.

4.7.3.2   **Condition Handler Used by DCL or MCR.** The DCL and MCR CLIs establish nearly identical condition handlers at the beginning of their command loops to field conditions that occur in supervisor mode.

The LOGINOUT image activates a CLI (DCL or MCR). The first step that the CLI takes is to establish the supervisor mode condition handler that the CLI uses to handle its own internal errors. The condition handler performs two tasks when it is called:

• It cancels any exit handlers that have been established.
• It resignals the error.

The CLI is then allowed to run to completion, as a result of which the process is deleted.

5   Hardware Interrupts

While I nodded, nearly napping, suddenly there came a tapping,
As of someone gently rapping, rapping at my chamber door.
Edgar Allan Poe, *The Raven*

VAX/VMS is interrupt driven. It contains interrupt service routines that execute in response to hardware interrupts from external and internal devices, such as the interval clock. VAX/VMS does not have a software-based central dispatching module that receives notification of all system events (that is, interrupts) and decides what to do next. Instead, it relies on a hardware-controlled interrupt dispatching scheme that always forces the highest priority interrupt on the system to be serviced first.

5.1   HARDWARE INTERRUPT DISPATCHING

The VAX architecture provides 16 hardware interrupt priority levels (IPLs), from IPL 31 down to IPL 16. The top eight levels are used by CPU-specific errors and power failure and, on certain types of VAX processor, by the interval clock. These interrupts are discussed in Chapters 8, 26, and 11. The lower levels are used by external devices.

An external device requests an interrupt at a particular hardware IPL (fixed for a given device). If the requested IPL value is higher than the level at which the processor is currently running (PSL <20:16>), then the interrupt request is granted. The processor reads the vector in the system control block (SCB) associated with that device and dispatches to the service routine identified by the vector. If the requested value is lower or equal to the current IPL, the interrupt is deferred until IPL drops below that of the interrupt request.

When an interrupt is serviced, the current processor status must be preserved so that the interrupted thread of execution (either process-based code or an interrupt service routine executing at lower IPL) can continue after the interrupt is dismissed. VAX microcode preserves the processor status by saving the PC and PSL on the stack. These are later restored when the interrupt service routine executes an REI instruction to dismiss the interrupt. Other elements of the process context, such as general registers, must be saved and restored by the routines handling the interrupt.

To reduce overhead, no memory mapping information is changed when an interrupt occurs. Therefore, the instructions executed and data referenced by an interrupt service routine must be in system address space. Furthermore, because VAX/VMS does not allow page faulting at IPLs above 2, all instructions and data must be resident.

5.1.1 Interrupt Dispatching

The primary sequence of events in interrupt dispatching is as follows:

1. An interrupt is requested.
2. The current instruction finishes or reaches a well-defined point where the instruction state is completely contained in the general registers, PC, and PSL (which happens in the execution of the string instructions). Some instructions can be interrupted at well-defined points so that, after the interrupt dismissal, they are restarted rather than continued.
3. The interrupt sequence is initiated by VAX microcode. As described in Chapter 4, it examines the SCB vector to determine on which stack the interrupt is to be serviced. Figure 5-1 illustrates the format of an SCB vector and the meaning of the low-order two bits. VMS specifies that all hardware interrupts be serviced on the interrupt stack. The VAX microcode switches stacks, if necessary, and pushes the current PC and PSL onto the new stack.

    Most software interrupts are also serviced on the interrupt stack. However, the per-process interrupt associated with AST delivery and nearly all exceptions are serviced on the per-process kernel stack.
4. A new PC is loaded (from the appropriate SCB vector), and a new PSL is created (with PSL <20:16> containing the IPL associated with the interrupt, and the previous access mode, current access mode, CM, TP, FPD, DV, FU, IV, T, N, Z, and C bits cleared by the hardware). The current access mode bits are cleared to indicate that the service routine runs in

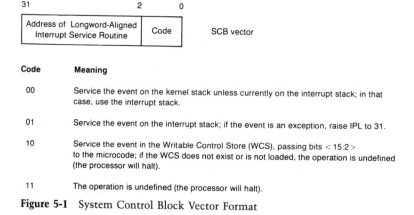

Code	Meaning
00	Service the event on the kernel stack unless currently on the interrupt stack; in that case, use the interrupt stack.
01	Service the event on the interrupt stack; if the event is an exception, raise IPL to 31.
10	Service the event in the Writable Control Store (WCS), passing bits < 15:2> to the microcode; if the WCS does not exist or is not loaded, the operation is undefined (the processor will halt).
11	The operation is undefined (the processor will halt).

Figure 5-1 System Control Block Vector Format

kernel mode. The IS bit is set to indicate that the processor is running on the interrupt stack.

5. The interrupt service routine identified by the SCB vector executes and eventually exits with an REI instruction that dismisses the interrupt.

6. The PC and PSL are restored by the execution of the REI instruction, and the interrupted thread of execution (a process or lower priority interrupt service routine) continues where it left off.

Unlike software interrupt dispatching, there is no one-to-one correspondence between hardware IPL and an interrupt service routine vector in the SCB (see Figure 5-2). The SCB contains the addresses of several interrupt

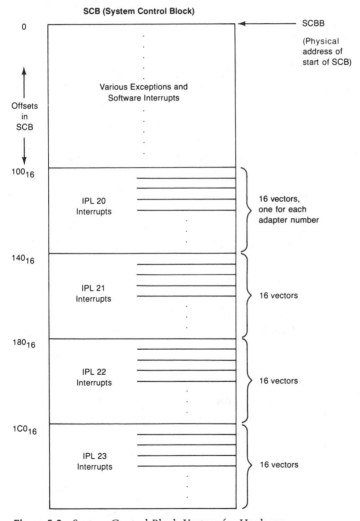

Figure 5-2   System Control Block Vectors for Hardware Interrupts

service routines for a given device IPL. There are no registers corresponding to the Software Interrupt Request Register or Software Interrupt Summary Register (see Chapter 6). Instead, the processor notes that a lower priority interrupt has been requested, but not granted. If the device is still requesting the interrupt when IPL falls below the device interrupt level, the interrupt is granted.

If, however, the device is no longer requesting an interrupt, the system will be unable to determine which interrupt service routine to call. Such an occurrence is called a passive release. If the device is no longer requesting an interrupt, the system is unable to determine which adapter requested the interrupt; in this case, a nexus 0 interrupt service routine is entered. It increments the counter IO$GL_SCB_INT0 and dismisses the interrupt.

5.1.2 System Control Block

The SCB contains the vectors used to dispatch all interrupts and exceptions. Its starting physical address is stored in the System Control Block Base Register (PR$_SCBB). Its starting virtual address is stored at global location EXE$GL_SCB. Its size varies with processor type and configuration.

The first page of the SCB is the only page defined by the VAX architecture. The layout of the first SCB page is pictured in Figure 4-1. Table 6-1 contains more details about the SCB vectors used for software interrupts. Figure 5-2 shows how the second half of the first page is divided among 16 possible external devices, each interrupting at four possible IPL values from 20 to 23.

The nature and type of the external devices vary on different VAX processors. Each device has an identifying number which, along with the IPL of the interrupt, selects a particular SCB vector. The name of the identifying number varies: on some processors, it is called a slot number; on others, a VAXBI node number; on others, a nexus number. For simplicity, this chapter uses the term nexus in a generic way.

The following sections briefly describe the configurations and SCB size of various VAX processors.

5.1.2.1 Adapter Configuration.
Typically, the presence of an adapter at a particular nexus number is checked by testing the first longword in the adapter's I/O register space and checking for nonexistent memory. The presence or absence of an external adapter is determined during system initialization. Specifically, the machine check vector in the SCB is loaded with the address of a special routine. System initialization code then tests the first longword. If a nonexistent memory machine check occurs, there is no connected adapter at the location being tested.

On some CPU types, VMB, the primary bootstrap program, determines the adapter configuration. On other CPU types, the configuration is determined at a later step of initialization. See Chapters 24 and 25 for further information.

The result of this testing is stored in several arrays in nonpaged pool. Chapter 25 describes these arrays. During later stages of system initialization, this information is used when specific adapters are configured into the system.

5.1.2.2   **Direct and Indirect Interrupt Vectors.** An interrupt can be characterized as directly or indirectly vectored. The SCB vector for a directly vectored interrupt contains the address of its interrupt service routine. An indirectly vectored interrupt is dispatched first to a service routine that identifies the device requesting the interrupt and dispatches to its service routine.

The following VAX CPUs implement directly vectored interrupts:

- VAX-11/730
- VAX-11/750
- MicroVAX I
- MicroVAX II
- VAX 8200 family
- VAX 8800 family

UNIBUS interrupts on the following VAX CPUs are indirectly vectored through a UNIBUS adapter (UBA):

- VAX-11/780, VAX-11/782, and VAX-11/785
- VAX 8600 and VAX 8650

Section 5.2.2 describes these two types of interrupt dispatching in more detail.

5.1.2.3   **VAX-11/730 SCB and External Adapters.** On the VAX-11/730, the CPU, UNIBUS adapter, and memory controller are connected by the array bus. In addition to the array bus, communications between the CPU and the integrated disk controller (IDC) are performed over the accelerator bus (so-named because the floating-point accelerator communicates over it). The IDC controls RL02 and R80 disks. The VAX-11/730 is not expandable and does not have expansion slots.

The VAX-11/730 SCB is two pages long. The second page is used for directly vectored UNIBUS interrupts. Each vector in the second page corresponds to a UNIBUS vector in the range from 0 to 774_8.

5.1.2.4   **VAX-11/750 SCB and External Adapters.** The VAX-11/750 SCB is two pages long or, if there is a second UNIBUS on the VAX-11/750, three pages long. The second SCB page on the VAX-11/750 is used for directly vectored UNIBUS device interrupts. Each SCB vector corresponds to a UNIBUS vector in the range from 0 to 774_8. A third SCB page is used for directly vectored UNIBUS device interrupts on the second UNIBUS.

The backplane interconnect on the VAX-11/750, called the CPU to memory interconnect (CMI), connects the CPU, memory controllers, UNIBUS

Table 5-1   Fixed Slots on the VAX-11/750

Adapter Type	Slot Number
Memory controller	0
Up to three MASSBUS adapters	4 through 6
UNIBUS adapter	8
Second UNIBUS adapter	9

adapters, and MASSBUS adapters. Each connection to the CMI is identified by its slot number.

There are a total of 16 slots which can be used to connect adapters. The first ten of these are reserved for a memory controller, UNIBUS adapters, and MASSBUS adapters. These ten slots are called fixed slots because the mapping of controller/adapter to slot number is fixed. That is, a particular slot can have only a particular adapter placed in it. Table 5-1 lists these adapters.

The last six slots are reserved for adapters with configuration registers and are called floating slots. A CI750 port adapter or a DR750 would be connected to a floating slot.

Each slot is assigned four SCB vectors in the first SCB page, one for each IPL value from 20 to 23 (see Figure 5-2).

5.1.2.5   **VAX-11/780, VAX-11/782, and VAX-11/785 SCB and External Adapters.** The SCB for the VAX-11/780, VAX-11/782, and VAX-11/785 is one page. On these processors, the synchronous backplane interconnect (SBI) connects the CPU, memory controllers (including MA780s), DR780s, CI780s, UNIBUS adapters, and MASSBUS adapters. Each connection to the SBI is identified by its transfer request (TR) number.

The TR number determines SBI priority. TR numbers range from 0 (highest priority) to 15 (lowest priority). There is a limit of 15 connections to the SBI (see Table 5-2). TR number 0 is used for a special purpose on the SBI and has no corresponding external adapter. The lowest priority level is reserved for the CPU, and it requires no actual TR signal line. The TR number defines the physical address space through which the device's registers are accessed and through which vectors the device will interrupt. The SCB has four vectors for each possible TR, one vector each for IPLs 20, 21, 22, and 23. UNIBUS interrupts are indirectly vectored (see Section 5.2.2.2).

An adapter is not restricted to having a specific TR number. However, the relative priorities of the various adapters may not change. That is, a system cannot have an MBA with a higher priority (lower TR number) than a UBA. For instance, if a system has two local memory controllers and an MA780 shared memory controller, the first UNIBUS adapter on that system could have TR number 4, with the MA780 having TR number 3, and the memory controllers having TR numbers 1 and 2.

Table 5-2   Standard SBI Adapter Assignments on the VAX-11/78x

External Adapter Type	Nexus Number	Comments
	TR 0	Hold line for next cycle. TR 0 is the highest TR level and is not assigned to a device.
First memory controller	TR 1	
Second memory controller	TR 2	
First MA780 shared memory		If present, follows local memory controllers
Second MA780 shared memory		
First UNIBUS adapter	TR 3	Follows any MA780 controllers present
Second UNIBUS adapter	TR 4	
Third UNIBUS adapter	TR 5	
Fourth UNIBUS adapter	TR 6	
	TR 7	Reserved
First MASSBUS adapter	TR 8	
Second MASSBUS adapter	TR 9	
Third MASSBUS adapter	TR 10	
Fourth MASSBUS adapter	TR 11	
DR780 SBI interface	TR 12	
CI780	TR 14	
	TR 15	Reserved

5.1.2.6   **MicroVAX I SCB and External Adapters.** On the MicroVAX I, the CPU, memory, and external devices are connected to the Q22 bus. Interrupt requests from external devices go directly to the CPU, which arbitrates interrupts. IPLs 20 to 23 correspond to Q22 bus interrupt request lines BIRQ4 to BIRQ7.

MicroVAX I Q22 bus interrupts are somewhat different from those on most other VAX processors. An interrupt is arbitrated in the same way, by comparing its IPL to the processor's IPL. However, when a Q22 bus interrupt is granted, processor IPL is raised to 23. For further details, refer to the manual *MicroVAX I CPU Technical Description*.

The MicroVAX I SCB is two pages long. The second page is used for directly vectored Q22 bus device interrupts. Each vector in the second page corresponds to a Q22 bus vector in the range from 0 to 774_8.

5.1.2.7   **MicroVAX II SCB and External Adapters.** The memory interconnect on the MicroVAX II connects the CPU and optional memory expansion modules. The CPU board contains an interface to the Q22 bus, to which all I/O devices are connected. Interrupt requests from external I/O devices go directly to the CPU, which arbitrates interrupts. IPLs 20 to 23 correspond to Q22 bus interrupt request lines BIRQ4 to BIRQ7.

The MicroVAX II SCB is two pages long. The second page is used for directly vectored Q22 bus device interrupts. Each vector in the second page corresponds to a Q22 bus vector in the range from 0 to 774_8.

MicroVAX II Q22 bus interrupts are like those of the MicroVAX I. An interrupt is arbitrated by comparing its IPL to the processor's IPL. However, when a Q22 bus interrupt is granted, processor IPL is raised to 23.

5.1.2.8   **VAX 8200 Family SCB and External Adapters.** The VAX 8200 family consists of the VAX 8200 and VAX 8300. The SCB for a member of the VAX 8200 family consists of the standard page defined by the VAX architecture, plus an additional page for each UNIBUS adapter present. UNIBUS interrupts are directly vectored.

The bus on a VAX 8200 is called the VAX backplane interconnect (VAXBI). It is a 32-bit, synchronous bus interconnect for up to 16 processors, memory controllers, and adapters. Each node has a unique node number from 0 to 15 determined by an ID plug in the node's VAXBI slot. The node number determines the physical location of the node's registers and its interrupt vectors. (See Chapter 27 for a block diagram of a VAX 8300.)

Each VAXBI node has an 8K-byte block of addresses known as its node space. The first 256 bytes are used to address VAXBI registers implemented by the BIIC (a chip which is the primary interface between the VAXBI bus and the user interface logic on each node). The remaining space is used to address registers on the device. In addition, each node has 256K bytes in I/O space, called window space, for use in mapping addresses to the other bus's memory space (for example, the UNIBUS address space). The physical locations of the node and window spaces are determined by the node number.

Each node has four vectors in the first SCB page, one for each level at which it can request an interrupt. VAXBI interrupt levels 4 through 7 correspond to IPLs 20 through 23.

5.1.2.9   **VAX 8800 Family SCB and External Adapters.** The VAX 8800 family includes the VAX 8500, VAX 8550, VAX 8700, and VAX 8800. A synchronous backplane interconnect bus, called the VAX 8800 memory interconnect (NMI), connects CPUs, memory, and one or two I/O adapters called NMI to BI (NBI) adapters. The VAXBI is the VAX 8800 family I/O bus. Each NBI adapter can interface with up to two VAXBIs. Each VAXBI can have up to 15 interfaces apart from the NBI, which is node 0. (See Chapter 27 for a block diagram of a VAX 8800.)

A VAX 8800 family member processor has a 32-page SCB. Memory and NBI interrupts vector through the architecturally defined page of the SCB. Interrupts from each of four possible VAXBIs vector through pages 28 through 31. Pages 1 through 27 are reserved for "offsettable" VAXBI nodes, nodes that are directly vectored, such as the UNIBUS adapter.

5.1.2.10   **VAX 8600 and VAX 8650 SCB and External Adapters.** The VAX 8600 and VAX 8650 have a four-page SCB to support the theoretical maximum configuration of four synchronous backplane interface (SBI) adapters (SBIAs). On these processors, I/O adapters are connected to an SBI. Each SBI is connected through an SBIA to a bus called an adapter bus (ABUS). The ABUS connects the SBIAs to the memory subsystem. Current configurations support a maximum of two SBIAs. The supported I/O adapters are the UNIBUS, MASSBUS, and CI780 adapters supported on a VAX-11/78*x* system.

Exceptions, software interrupts, and memory errors are dispatched through vectors in the first page of SCB. Hardware interrupts for adapters on the first SBI are vectored through the first page of SCB. Interrupts for adapters on the second SBI use the second page of SCB. A hardware interrupt vector is determined by the combination of interrupt level, TR number, and SBI number.

UNIBUS interrupts are indirectly vectored, as they are on the VAX-11/78*x* (see Section 5.2.2.2).

5.2   **VAX/VMS INTERRUPT SERVICE ROUTINES**

The following sections briefly describe VAX/VMS adapter interrupt service routines and dispatching of device interrupts. Chapter 18 presents an overview of the I/O database, the basis for interrupt dispatching. The manual *Writing a Device Driver for VAX/VMS* describes the I/O database in more detail and contains a more complete discussion of driver interrupt service routines than that presented here.

5.2.1   **Restrictions Imposed on Interrupt Service Routines**

Interrupt service routines operate in the limited system or interrupt context described in Chapter 1. These routines execute at elevated IPL on the interrupt stack outside the context of a process.

There are several restrictions imposed on interrupt service routines by either the VAX architecture or synchronization techniques used by VAX/VMS. Many of these result from the limitations of system context. The following list indicates some of the constraints placed on an interrupt service routine. The description of system context in Chapter 1 contains a more general list of these and other restrictions.

- An interrupt service routine should be very short and do as little processing as possible at elevated IPL.
- Any registers used by an interrupt service routine must first be saved. VMS

saves some registers (usually R0 through R5) prior to calling a device driver interrupt service routine. See the manual *Writing a Device Driver for VAX/VMS* for further details.

- Although an interrupt service routine can raise IPL, it should not lower IPL below the level at which the original interrupt occurred.
- An interrupt service routine should be conservative in its use of stack space. The interrupt stack is not very large on most systems. Its size is determined by the SYSBOOT parameter INTSTKPAGES, which has a default value of two pages.
- Because the low two bits of the interrupt service routine address in an SCB vector are used for stack selection, an interrupt service routine dispatched through an SCB vector must begin on a longword boundary. (An indirectly vectored interrupt service routine need not begin on a longword vector.)
- An interrupt service routine may not access pageable routines or data structures. The page fault exception service routine generates a fatal bugcheck if a page fault occurs while IPL is above 2.
- An interrupt service routine cannot access data structures synchronized by a mutex without destroying their synchronization.
- An interrupt service routine that runs as a result of an interrupt above IPL$_SYNCH (8) may not access data structures synchronized at IPL$_SYNCH without destroying their synchronization. This restriction applies to all hardware interrupts and many software interrupts.
- No references to per-process address space (P0 space or P1 space) are allowed.
- Prior to executing an REI instruction, an interrupt service routine must remove anything it pushed on the stack and restore all saved registers.

5.2.2 Servicing UNIBUS and Q22 Bus Interrupts

Each device on a UNIBUS or Q22 bus has one or more vector numbers and a bus request priority. The bus request priority enables the bus to be arbitrated among devices when multiple interrupts are requested.

On a UNIBUS, there are four bus request (BR) levels, called BR4, BR5, BR6, and BR7. BR7 is the highest priority. If interrupts are requested concurrently for multiple devices with the same BR level, the device electrically closest to the UNIBUS interface has the highest priority. On a Q22 bus, there are also four request levels, called bus interrupt request (BIRQ) levels. BIRQ7 is the highest priority.

In either case, the device IPL of the requested interrupt is the bus request level plus 16. For example, BR4 corresponds to IPL 20.

5.2.2.1 Directly Vectored UNIBUS and Q22 Bus Interrupt Service Routines. VAX

CPUs that implement directly vectored interrupts use additional pages of the SCB for these interrupts.

The System Generation Utility is responsible for building the I/O database for devices and their drivers (see Chapter 18). For a device whose interrupts are directly vectored, SYSGEN initializes the SCB vector with the address of code that dispatches the interrupt to the interrupt service routine. This dispatching code is contained in a data structure called a channel request block (CRB) and resembles the following:

```
PUSHR    #^M<R0,R1,R2,R3,R4,R5>
JSB      @#driver_interrupt_service_routine
```

The second instruction dispatches to the driver interrupt service routine (see Figure 5-3). The longword following the JSB instruction contains the address of another data structure, the interrupt dispatch block (IDB). Its address is pushed onto the stack as the return PC for the JSB instruction. (Control never returns there because that address is removed from the stack by the driver interrupt service routine, as are the saved registers.)

After the JSB instruction in the CRB transfers control, the following events occur:

1. The driver interrupt service routine removes the IDB pointer from the stack and uses it to obtain both the address of the device controller's control/status register (CSR) and the address of the unit control block (UCB) for the device generating the interrupt.
2. Having found the UCB, the interrupt service routine determines whether the interrupt is expected or not. If the interrupt is unsolicited, the interrupt service routine may either take some appropriate action or simply dismiss the interrupt by restoring the saved registers and executing an REI.
3. If the interrupt is expected, the interrupt service routine restores the driver context saved in the UCB by the driver fork process. The driver interrupt service routine then executes a JSB instruction to transfer control to the saved PC.
4. The driver fork process transfers control back to the interrupt service routine. Most often, the driver fork process does this indirectly by forking or waiting for another interrupt. In either case, the fork process invokes a routine that saves the fork process context and returns to its caller by executing an RSB instruction. The driver interrupt service routine then restores the saved registers and dismisses the interrupt with an REI instruction.

.2.2.2   **Indirectly Vectored UNIBUS Interrupt Service Routines.** When an indirectly vectored device on the UNIBUS requests an interrupt, the UBA receives the interrupt request and requests a CPU interrupt on behalf of the interrupting device. It is actually the UBA interrupt that is vectored through the SCB (using the interrupting device's IPL and the adapter's TR number) to an adapter interrupt service routine.

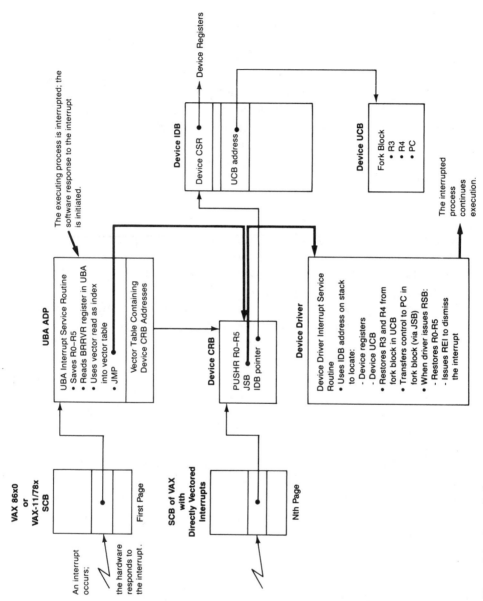

Figure 5-3 Control Flow in Servicing a UNIBUS or Q22 Bus Interrupt

The adapter interrupt service routine saves registers R0 through R5, determines which device actually requested the interrupt, and then passes control to an interrupt service routine in the device driver for the interrupting device. The driver interrupt service routine can then respond to the interrupt in a device-dependent fashion. After servicing the interrupt, the registers saved by the adapter interrupt service routine must be restored and an REI instruction executed to dismiss the interrupt.

There are four interrupt service routines for each UBA, one for each BR level at which UNIBUS devices request interrupts. They differ only in which internal UBA register they read to determine which device requested the interrupt. These interrupt service routines are found in a data structure describing the UBA, the adapter control block (ADP). The UBA ADP is created during system initialization by the CPU-specific routine INI$UBADP. The CPU-specific routine and the actual UBA interrupt service routines are in module [SYSLOA]INIADP*xxx*, where *xxx* is either 780 for the VAX-11/78*x* processors or 790 for the VAX 86*x*0 processors.

Indirectly vectored UNIBUS interrupt servicing begins in one of four UNIBUS adapter interrupt service routines. Each of these routines takes the following steps:

1. The routine (see Figure 5-3) saves registers R0 through R5.
2. A UBA internal register (BRRVR) is read to determine the identity of the interrupting device. Each BRRVR register contains either the vector number corresponding to the device interrupt or an indication that the UBA is interrupting on behalf of itself, not for some device. (There are four BRRVRs in the UBA, one for each BR level.)
3. The UBA interrupts on its own behalf to indicate an adapter error. Certain adapter errors result when a reference is made to a nonexistent address in UNIBUS I/O space. They can indicate a transient hardware error or a bug in a device driver. These errors are logged, up to a maximum of three in any given 15-minute period, and the interrupt is dismissed.

   Another possible error is that power on the UNIBUS or UBA is about to fail. Chapter 26 describes how adapter powerfail is handled.
4. For a device interrupt, the vector number is used as an index into a vector table, which is part of the ADP. The vector table contains a pointer to the JSB instruction in the CRB. The service routine transfers control by executing a JMP to the JSB instruction.

   The vector table entry pointing to the CRB and address fields in the CRB are initialized by SYSGEN in response to the CONNECT command.

The JSB instruction in the CRB transfers control to the driver interrupt service routine. The longword following the instruction contains the address of another data structure, the interrupt dispatch block (IDB). This address is pushed onto the stack as the return PC for the JSB instruction. However, control is never returned there, because that address is removed from the stack by the driver interrupt service routine.

At this point, interrupt dispatching is identical to that on directly vectored processors, as described in the previous section. Device driver interrupt service routines are entered in the same way regardless of processor type.

5.2.3   MASSBUS Adapter Interrupt Service Routine

MASSBUS adapter (MBA) interrupt dispatching is identical across all VAX CPUs that support an MBA. During system initialization, four SCB vectors for each MBA are initialized by the CPU-specific routine INI$MBADP in module [SYSLOA]INIADP*xxx* (where *xxx* designates one of the CPU types listed in Appendix G). The SCB vectors contain an address within the MBA CRB. The CRB contains a PUSHR instruction to save R2 to R5 and a JSB instruction to transfer control to the MBA interrupt service routine, MBA$INT in [SYSLOA]ADPSUB*xxx*.

MBA interrupts are handled differently from UNIBUS interrupts, partly because one MBA interrupt may indicate that multiple devices on the adapter need servicing. The MBA interrupt service routine reads an attention summary register to determine its response to an interrupt.

If the interrupt enable bit in the MBA is set, an MBA interrupt can be caused by any of the following operations:

• Completion of a data transfer
• Assertion of an attention line while the MBA is not busy
• Occurrence of an MBA error while the MBA is not busy
• Power recovery on the MBA

A device on the MASSBUS asserts its attention line under the following circumstances:

• If an error occurs, whether or not a transfer is taking place
• When a mechanical motion such as a disk seek or tape rewind completes
• When a device changes its state

In general, a MASSBUS device driver does not request ownership of the MBA until it is needed to perform a transfer. MBA$INT assumes that if the MBA owner is expecting an interrupt, then the interrupt currently being serviced indicates that a transfer has completed or been aborted. That is, when an MBA interrupt occurs and the current owner of the MBA is expecting an interrupt, MBA$INT dispatches immediately to the owner's driver.

Because data transfer functions block the interrupts from nontransfer functions until the data transfer completes, MBA$INT always checks the MBA attention summary register after a driver interrupt service routine returns control. It tests whether another device on the MASSBUS requested an inter-

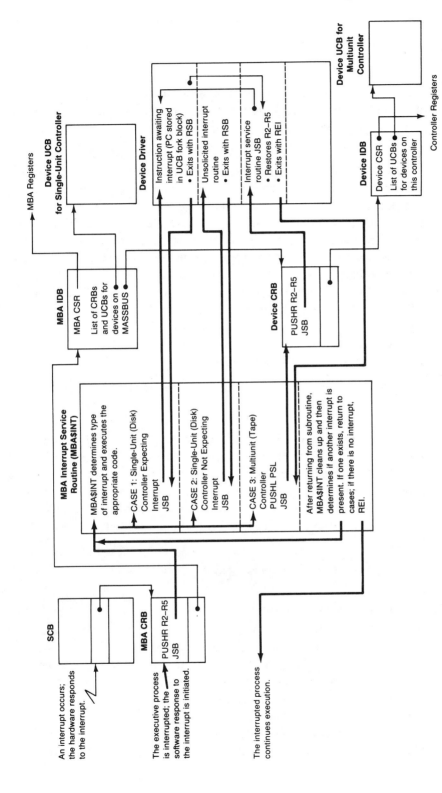

Figure 5-4 Control Flow in Servicing a MASSBUS Interrupt

121

rupt either while the MASSBUS owner was transferring data or while the current interrupt was being processed. The UCB list contained in the IDB allows MBA$INT to associate UCB addresses with devices that are requesting service.

MBA$INT responds to an interrupt in one of three ways (see Figure 5-4). It may perform all three of these actions to service multiple attention requests in response to a single interrupt.

- For an expected interrupt (bit UCB$V_INT set in UCB$W_STS) on a single unit device, MBA$INT restores the driver fork process context and executes a JSB instruction to the fork PC. The driver fork process returns to MBA$INT when it has completed its work.
- For an unsolicited interrupt (bit UCB$V_INT clear in UCB$W_STS) on a single unit device, MBA$INT executes a JSB instruction that transfers control to a driver-supplied unexpected interrupt service routine, which will return to MBA$INT.
- For a multidevice controller (a magnetic tape formatter), MBA$INT transfers control to the CRB for the device controller. The device controller CRB dispatches to a controller interrupt service routine that saves R2 to R5 and transfers control to the driver interrupt service routine. This service routine eventually returns control to MBA$INT.

MBA$INT uses the unit number of a device asserting attention as an index into the list IDB$L_UCBLIST. It identifies the type of the selected longword entry by checking its low-order bit. If the bit is set, then the entry is for a multidevice controller. If the bit is clear, the entry is the UCB address for a single unit device. UCBs, like CRBs, are always longword aligned (the low-order two bits are clear). When a CRB is created for a multidevice controller, and its address stored in the MBA IDB, the address is incremented by 1 so the low-order bit will be set. Control is actually transferred to the PUSHR instruction in the CRB with the following instruction (where R5 contains the MBA IDB entry):

```
JSB   -(R5)   ;autodecrement address to subtract 1
```

5.2.4   VAXBI Interrupt Service Routine

VAXBI interrupts are directly vectored. During system initialization, four SCB vectors are assigned to each node found on the VAXBI. A vector for an I/O adapter transfers control to a location in the CRB for that VAXBI adapter. The instructions in the CRB are a PUSHR for R0 through R5 and a JSB . The IDB address follows the JSB instruction in the CRB (see Figure 5-5).

Initially, the JSB in the CRB transfers control to one of several routines within the ADPSUB8SS module in SYSLOA8SS or ADPSUB8NN in SYSLOA8NN. These routines field interrupts generated by the adapters prior

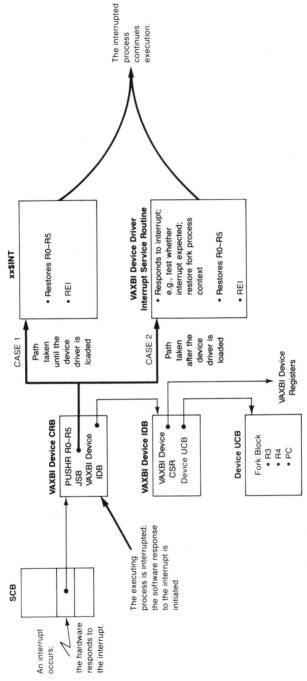

Figure 5-5   Control Flow in Servicing a VAXBI Interrupt

to the loading of the device driver. They each merely clean off the stack and dismiss the interrupt.

When a VAXBI device driver is loaded, the destination of the JSB instruction is modified to the address of the interrupt service routine within the driver. From this point, interrupt dispatching is driver-dependent but generally resembles dispatching for directly vectored interrupts (see Section 5.2.2.1).

5.2.5   **CI Interrupt Service Routine**

CI interrupts are dispatched directly through the SCB. During system initialization, four SCB vectors for each CI port adapter are initialized by the CPU-specific routine INI$CIADP in module [SYSLOA]INIADP*xxx*. The SCB vectors contain an address within the CI CRB. The CRB contains a PUSHR to save R2 to R5 and a JSB instruction to transfer control to the interrupt service routine.

Initially, the JSB in the CI CRB transfers control to routine CI$INT in module ADPSUB*xxx*. This routine simply performs the following operations:

1. It clears the adapter power-up and power-down bits in the CI control register.
2. It sets the maintenance initialization bits in the CI control register.
3. It restores registers R2 to R5.
4. It executes an REI instruction to dismiss the interrupt.

When the CI device driver, PADRIVER, is loaded, the destination of the JSB instruction is modified to the address of the interrupt service routine within the driver. There are several of these, one for each different type of CI port adapter. They are all in module [DRIVER]PAADP and have names such as INTERRUPT_CI780. They are very similar, differing primarily in their methods of testing for error conditions. The following list summarizes their actions, which are pictured in Figure 5-6:

1. The interrupt service routine removes the address of the IDB pointer from the stack, retrieving the address of the UCB.
2. The interrupt service routine examines various adapter registers to determine whether the CI port adapter interrupted because it queued a response packet to a formerly empty response queue or because an error occurred.
3. If there was no error, the interrupt service routine invokes the routine INT$FORK in module [DRIVER]PAINTR.
4. INT$FORK sets and tests a fork block interlock bit in the UCB. If the bit is already set, the UCB is already in use as a fork block and INT$FORK merely returns to the interrupt service routine. If the bit was not already set, INT$FORK forks, using the UCB. That is, a fork PC is stored in the UCB and the UCB is inserted on the IPL 8 fork queue (see Chapters 6 and 19).

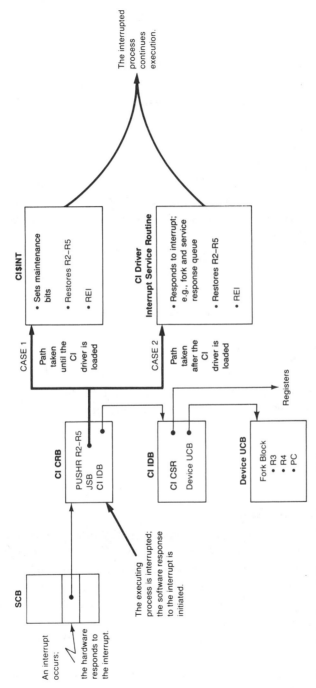

Figure 5-6 Control Flow in Servicing a CI Interrupt

5. INT$FORK returns to the interrupt service routine, which restores the registers saved on the stack and executes an REI instruction to dismiss the interrupt.
6. When the driver fork process is entered, it updates the maintenance timer on the CI port to indicate that the system is still active.
7. It then removes a response packet from the response queue and processes it. It continues dequeuing response packets and processing them until either the queue is empty or it has handled 100 response packets.

5.2.6   DR32 Interrupt Service Routine

DR32 interrupts are dispatched directly through the SCB. During system initialization, entries are made in the SCB to transfer control to locations in the CRB for the DR32. The instructions in the CRB are a PUSHR for R2 through R5 and a JSB instruction. The DR32 IDB address follows these instructions in the DR32 CRB (see Figure 5-7).

Initially, the JSB instruction in the DR32 CRB transfers control to routine DR$INT in module [SYSLOA]ADPSUB*xxx*. This routine simply performs the following operations:

1. Clears the adapter power-up and power-down bits in a DR32 control register
2. Restores registers R2 to R5
3. Executes an REI instruction

When the DR32 driver (module [DRIVER]XFDRIVER) is loaded by SYSGEN, the destination of the JSB instruction is changed to the interrupt service routine in the driver. This routine performs the following operations:

1. Responds to the various types of DR32 interrupts
2. Restores registers R2 to R5
3. Executes an REI instruction

5.2.7   MA780 Interrupt Dispatching

Although the standard MS780 memory controller does not generate interrupts, the shared memory (MA780) controller does. An interrupt can be requested by a driver or the executive to interrupt another processor connected to the shared memory. An interprocessor interrupt is requested whenever a shared memory event flag is set, a shared memory mailbox message is written, or there is interprocessor communication in the VAX-11/782. In addition, when certain types of error occur, the MA780 interrupts through a second SCB vector.

Note that this discussion applies only to MA780 used as shared memory among VAX-11/780s or VAX-11/785s. Interrupt handling in the VAX-11/782 is somewhat different and is briefly discussed in Section 5.2.8. Chapter 27

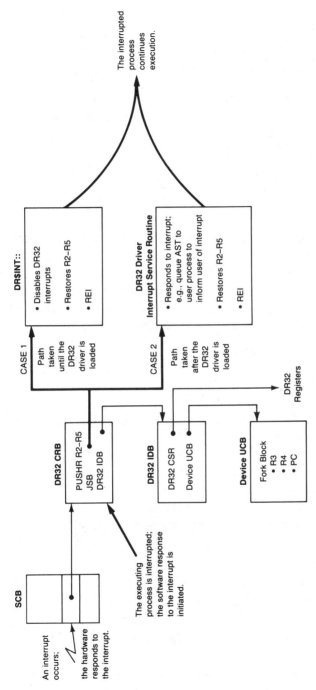

Figure 5-7 Control Flow in Servicing a DR32 Interrupt

127

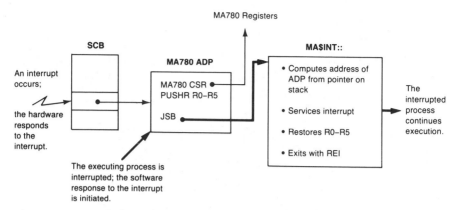

Figure 5-8 Control Flow in Servicing an MA780
Interrupt

gives a more complete description of MA780 interrupts in the VAX-11/782.

During system initialization, module [SYSLOA]INIADP780 initializes SCB vectors to transfer control to locations in the MA780 ADP when MA780 interrupts occur (see Figure 5-8). The locations in the ADP contain a PUSHR instruction saving R0 through R5, and a JSB instruction that transfers control to routine MA$INT in module [SYSLOA]ADPSUB780.

1. When MA$INT obtains control, it removes the value pushed onto the stack by the JSB instruction in the ADP and uses it to determine the address of the MA780's ADP.
2. It uses fields in the ADP to locate adapter registers in the MA780 and to determine which port requested an interrupt and what kind of interrupt was requested.
3. If the interrupt is for a processor being connected to the memory, the interrupt is dismissed by restoring R0 through R5 and executing an REI instruction.
4. Otherwise, MA$INT services the interrupt.
5. Finally, the interrupt is dismissed by restoring R0 through R5 and executing an REI instruction.

5.2.8 MA780 Interrupts on the VAX-11/782

The VAX-11/782 asymmetric multiprocessing system uses the MA780 interprocessor interrupts for different functions than the MA780 support previously described. Thus, the MA780 interrupts must be handled somewhat differently on the VAX-11/782.

When the asymmetric multiprocessing code is loaded, the MA780 interprocessor interrupt vectors in the primary processor's SCB are redirected to point to a multiprocessing MA780 interrupt routine (only for the first

MA780). The interrupt service routine serves interrupts from the attached processor. A new SCB is created in nonpaged pool for the attached processor. The new SCB contains vectors that point to multiprocessing MA780 interrupt service routines for the attached processor. The interprocessor interrupt vector for the remaining MA780s is pointed to an unexpected interrupt handler.

For more information on VAX-11/782 asymmetric multiprocessing, see Chapter 27.

CONNECT-TO-INTERRUPT MECHANISM

The connect-to-interrupt mechanism enables a process to be notified of a UNIBUS device interrupt by the delivery of an asynchronous system trap (AST), setting of an event flag, or both. The process can also specify an interrupt service routine to respond to device interrupts.

A suitably privileged process (with CMKRNL and PFNMAP privileges) can respond to an interrupt by reading or writing device registers and possibly by initiating further device activity. However, to directly manipulate device registers, the process must first map the UNIBUS space containing the registers for the device into its own process space (P0 or P1). The manual *Writing a Device Driver for VAX/VMS* describes mapping UNIBUS I/O space and using the connect-to-interrupt capability. Chapter 16 of this book contains more detailed information on how the mapping is actually performed.

Note that the physical address range of UNIBUS I/O space differs on different types of VAX processors. *Writing a Device Driver for VAX/VMS* contains a list of symbols defined by the processor-specific macros (for example, $IO730DEF) that define the physical addresses symbolically.

The connect-to-interrupt facility is an extension of the interrupt dispatching scheme. To use it, the connect-to-interrupt driver (module [DRIVER]CONINTERR) must be associated with the interrupt vector. The association is made using the SYSGEN command CONNECT, specifying all of the following:

- A name for the device (to be used by the process that connects to the interrupt)
- The CSR address of the device
- The interrupt vector at which the device generates interrupts
- The CONINTERR driver, which initially responds to the device interrupts

When the device generates an interrupt, the normal UNIBUS interrupt dispatching sequence is followed, as discussed in Sections 5.2.1 and 5.2.2. However, the CONINTERR interrupt service routine transfers control to the user-supplied interrupt service routine (if one was supplied), using a JSB or CALL instruction (as requested by the user). This transfer is illustrated in Figure 5-9.

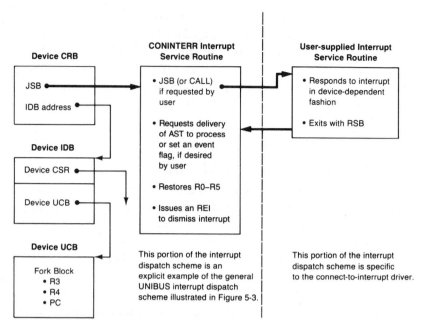

Figure 5-9 Extending Interrupt Dispatch Mechanism
with the Connect-to-Interrupt Facility

When the user-supplied interrupt service routine executes an RSB or RET instruction, the CONINTERR interrupt service routine regains control. Before restoring the registers and dismissing the interrupt, the CONINTERR interrupt service routine queues an AST to the process (if requested) to notify it that an interrupt has occurred. CONINTERR's AST routine sets an event flag, queues the user-requested AST, or both.

For the process-supplied interrupt service routine to be accessible to the CONINTERR interrupt service routine, the CONINTERR driver must double map the user routine into system address space. The double mapping requires enough system page table entries (reserved by the REALTIME_SPTS SYSBOOT parameter) to map the user-supplied routines. When the process disconnects from the interrupt, the SPTEs used to map its routines are made available for later use by other processes.

Note that the connect-to-interrupt driver has no provision for DMA I/O. It does not allocate map registers and data paths. Its fork IPL, IPL$_QUEUEAST, is lower than IPL 8, the IPL at which access to these adapter resources is arbitrated. Furthermore, the driver does not perform the tasks required to deal with VMS direct I/O buffers.

Software Interrupts

And now I see with eye serene
The very pulse of the machine.
William Wordsworth, *She Was a Phantom of Delight*

Software interrupts are fundamental to VAX/VMS. Software interrupt service routines running at interrupt priority levels (IPLs) between 2 and 15 perform many of the most important system functions of VMS. These include dispatching fork processes (IPLs 6 and 8 to 11), servicing processes' time-dependent requests (IPL 7), I/O postprocessing (IPL 4), scheduling (IPL 3), and delivering ASTs (IPL 2). This chapter describes how software interrupts are requested and granted and how VMS uses them.

THE SOFTWARE INTERRUPT

A software interrupt is an interrupt requested by a write to the software interrupt request register rather than through a signal from an external device. The VAX interrupt microcode responds to software interrupt requests as it does to hardware interrupts; it dispatches through the appropriate system control block (SCB) vector, which contains the address of the interrupt service routine.

The VMS operating system requests a software interrupt to cause an interrupt service routine to execute and perform its designated function. That is, VMS uses software interrupts as a way of scheduling operating system functions and as an alternative to periodic checking whether these operating system functions need to be done. IPLs are assigned to the different operating system functions, in part, as an indication of their relative importance.

VMS also uses specific IPLs and interrupt requests at those IPLs to synchronize access to shared data structures. Chapter 2 discusses synchronization through raising IPL.

Hardware Mechanism of Software Interrupts

The VAX architecture provides 15 vectors in the SCB for software interrupts at IPLs 1 through 15. Figure 4-1 shows the SCB, and Figure 5-1 shows the format of an SCB vector. The VAX architecture also provides a means for kernel mode code and CPU console commands to request software interrupts.

A software interrupt at a particular IPL is requested by writing that IPL into the software interrupt request register (PR$_SIRR). VMS code generally uses the SOFTINT macro to write the PR$_SIRR. This macro expands into the following instruction:

```
.MACRO SOFTINT IPL
        MTPR    IPL,S^#PR$_SIRR
.ENDM   SOFTINT
```

The PR$_SIRR can also be written by the following CPU console command:

```
>>>D/I 14 ipl       !for ipl, substitute a hex digit
```

VMS requests the software interrupt service routines for IPLs 3, 4, 6, 7, 8, and 11 from within a hardware interrupt service routine or another software interrupt service routine. Software interrupts at IPLs 5, 12, and 15 are requested only through a CPU console command. The VAX architecture specifies that the IPL 2 software interrupt service routine be requested by REI microcode to deliver ASTs. VMS does not use software interrupts at IPLs 13 and 14. Although VMS provides for fork dispatching at IPLs 9 and 10, VMS itself does not use those IPLs. The software interrupt at IPL 1 is unused.

Writing to PR$_SIRR causes the bit with the same number as the IPL to be set in another processor register, the software interrupt summary register (PR$_SISR). Figure 6-1 shows the layouts of these two registers. At any given time, PR$_SISR contains a bit set for each level at which a software interrupt has been requested but not yet granted. The VAX microcode reads PR$_SISR to test for pending software interrupts. When the microcode grants a software interrupt request, it clears the corresponding bit in PR$_SISR.

The VAX architecture provides both these processor registers to simplify synchronization of access to PR$_SISR. If VMS were to modify the

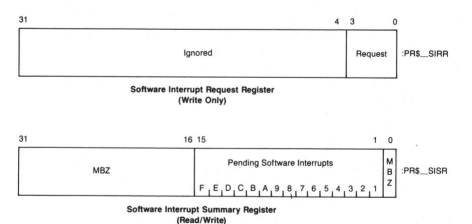

Software Interrupt Request Register
(Write Only)

Software Interrupt Summary Register
(Read/Write)

Figure 6-1 Format of Software Interrupt Request Register and Software Interrupt Summary Register

PR$_SISR directly, several instructions would be required to preserve already set bits in the register. VMS would have to raise IPL to block all interrupts, read PR$_SISR, set the new bit, write PR$_SISR, and restore the previous IPL. (MTPR and MFPR are the only instructions that access these processor registers.) Instead, when kernel mode code (or CPU console command) writes PR$_SIRR, the microcode modifies PR$_SISR with interrupts blocked.

The VAX microcode responds similarly to hardware and software interrupt requests. The microcode tests for pending interrupts between each instruction and at well-defined points during the evaluation and execution of more complicated instructions. The microcode determines the IPL of the highest outstanding interrupt request, whether it is hardware or software. The microcode compares that IPL to the one at which the processor is running and takes one of two actions based on the comparison.

If the processor is running at an IPL equal to or higher than the interrupt request, the interrupt request is deferred until the IPL drops below the requested level. Typically, when VMS requests a software interrupt, the interrupt request is deferred. The lowering of IPL usually occurs as the result of an REI instruction but can also occur if kernel mode code alters IPL by writing to the PR$_IPL register (usually with the SETIPL or ENBINT macros, described in Chapter 2).

If the processor is running at a lower IPL than the interrupt request, the interrupt is granted. There are a few occurrences in the VMS operating system of a software interrupt request at an IPL greater than that at which the processor is currently running. For example, device driver FDT routines may signal completion by calling the routine EXE$FINISHIO or EXE$FINISHIOC. These routines execute at IPL 2 and terminate by requesting the I/O postprocessing software interrupt at IPL 4. In this case, the interrupt is taken immediately.

To grant the interrupt request, the microcode first selects the vector in the SCB that corresponds to the particular interrupt request. That vector contains the address of the interrupt service routine and a flag that specifies whether the interrupt is to be serviced on the interrupt or kernel stack. The microcode records the state of the interrupted thread of execution by pushing the PSL and then the PC onto the appropriate stack. It then sets the IPL to that of the interrupt request and transfers control to the interrupt service routine. When the interrupt service routine is done, it executes an REI instruction, which resumes the previous thread of execution by restoring the PC and PSL from the stack.

6.1.2   Software Mechanisms of Software Interrupts

The VAX architecture constrains software interrupt service routines by providing only one bit to indicate that a software interrupt has been requested at a particular IPL. The service routine is thus unable to determine how many times its bit number was set in PR$_SISR before the IPL dropped and the interrupt request was granted.

As a result, either the software must supply some protocol for determining this number or the number must be irrelevant to the execution of the interrupt service routine. The scheduling interrupt service routine is an example of a routine which has one function to do, regardless of how many times that function has been requested. Other interrupt service routines use queues to keep track of their work. Each element in the queue represents a specific item of work for the interrupt service routine and an instance of the interrupt's having been requested.

An interrupt service routine that uses a queue generally performs all the work in the queue before dismissing the interrupt. It tries to remove an element from the queue with the REMQUE instruction. The REMQUE instruction indicates the presence of a list element by clearing the V-bit in the PSL condition codes. If the V-bit is clear, the interrupt service routine processes that element and does another REMQUE. If the V-bit is set, the queue is empty and no item was removed from it. Thus, the set V-bit indicates that the interrupt service routine's work is complete. The interrupt service routine then exits through an REI instruction. Because such a software interrupt service routine removes work items from its queue until the queue is empty and then dismisses the interrupt, the service routine reacts gracefully to any interrupt granted when there is no work for the interrupt service routine.

6.2 SOFTWARE INTERRUPT SERVICE ROUTINES

There is no central monitor routine in VMS that controls the sequencing of operating system functions. Instead, the need to perform a particular function is indicated by a request for the associated interrupt. Scheduling operating system functions as software interrupts eliminates any requirement for polling whether these functions need to be done. It also enables more important functions to interrupt less important ones.

Table 6-1 shows the software interrupt service routines and their associated IPLs. In some cases, the assigned IPL only indicates the relative importance of the interrupt, and the interrupt service routine runs primarily at a higher IPL for synchronization.

VMS interprets all software interrupts, except the AST delivery and rescheduling interrupts, as systemwide events that are serviced independently of the context of a specific process. The rescheduling interrupt, discussed briefly in this chapter and in greater detail in Chapter 10, is taken on the kernel stack of the current process. The interrupt service routine immediately executes a SVPCTX instruction, saving the process's context and switching onto the interrupt stack. The AST delivery interrupt, discussed briefly at

Table 6-1 Software Interrupt Levels Used by the Executive

IPL	Use	Stack
15	XDELTA on a multiprocessor	Interrupt
14–13	Unused	Interrupt
12	IPC intervention	Interrupt
11	Fork dispatching	Interrupt
10	Fork dispatching	Interrupt
9	Fork dispatching	Interrupt
8	Fork dispatching	Interrupt
7	Software timer service routine	Interrupt
6	Fork dispatching	Interrupt
5	XDELTA, or scheduling on a multiprocessor	Interrupt
4	I/O postprocessing	Interrupt
3	Rescheduling	Kernel
2	AST delivery	Kernel
1	Unused	n/a

the end of this chapter and in greater detail in Chapter 7, is the only interrupt that is serviced in the context of a specific process.

The software interrupt service routines vary. Some perform the same functions every time they are executed. The rescheduling interrupt service routine, for example, takes the current process out of execution, selects another one to run, and places it into execution. The functions of other software interrupt service routines are quite variable. The I/O postprocessing interrupt service routine has a specific function to perform but is data driven by the I/O request packets that are in its work queue. A fork dispatching interrupt exists solely to dispatch to system routines. Which routines a fork dispatching interrupt service routine executes is determined dynamically as a result of system operation.

The software interrupts are described briefly in the following sections. Some are described at more length in subsequent chapters. The use of IPL 5 for scheduling on an asymmetric multiprocessor system is described in Chapter 27. The following sections are in order by interrupt level, except that the service routines for interrupts requested through console command are discussed last.

6.2.1 Fork Processing

Five software interrupts (IPLs 6 and 8 to 11) are used for fork dispatching. Each of the interrupt service routines has its own work queue of fork blocks (FKBs).

When a fork dispatching interrupt is granted, the interrupt service routine

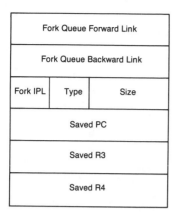

Fork Queue Forward Link		
Fork Queue Backward Link		
Fork IPL	Type	Size
Saved PC		
Saved R3		
Saved R4		

Figure 6-2   Layout of Fork Block

saves the low general registers and removes from its queue the first FKB and dispatches to the fork process it describes.

The following sections describe fork process data structures and service routines in more detail.

6.2.1.1   **Fork Process Data Structures.** A fork block describes a routine to be called by a fork dispatching interrupt service routine. A minimal fork block, shown in Figure 6-2, includes the address, or saved PC, of the fork routine (FKB$L_FPC) and the contents of two registers. The field FKB$B_FIPL specifies in which fork block queue this FKB is inserted and at what IPL its routine will run.

Most often, a fork block is part of a larger data structure, such as a unit control block or class driver request packet, which contains additional data. The combination of standard fork block fields, additional fork block data, and the routine that is to be executed is called a fork process.

Figure 6-3 shows the array of fork queue listheads. The listheads of these queues are ordered in an array that includes a placeholder listhead for IPL 7. Since the IPL 7 interrupt is serviced by the software timer routine, there is no fork process dispatching at IPL 7. However, having the placeholder listhead simplifies the fork process creation code.

6.2.1.2   **Reasons for Creating a Fork Process.** Fork processing exists, in part, so that device drivers do not have to run at high IPLs for long periods of time, blocking other device interrupts. Hardware interrupt service routines within device drivers are entered at device IPLs between 20 and 23. Often these routines must perform lengthy processing that does not require device interrupts to be blocked, the usual reason for maintaining high IPL. The interrupt nesting scheme defined by the VAX architecture does not work correctly if an interrupt service routine lowers IPL below the level at which the interrupt

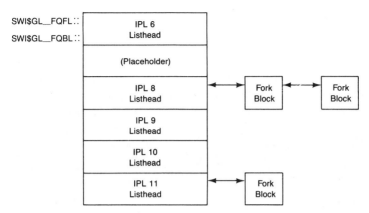

Figure 6-3   Fork Block Queues

occurred. A driver creates a fork process to lower IPL without violating the interrupt nesting scheme. Typically, device interrupt service routines create a fork process as soon as they are able to execute at lower IPL.

A driver might also create a fork process at a lower IPL to access system databases synchronized at that lower IPL, for example, if the driver were to queue an AST to a process.

2.1.3   **Creating a Fork Process.** To fork, a driver calls routine EXE$IOFORK or EXE$FORK (in module FORKCNTRL) specifying the address of the fork block, the fork process context, and a return address. Fork process context consists of the fork block, the contents of R3 and R4, and the address of the routine the fork process is to execute (the fork PC). (EXE$IOFORK clears a bit to disable an I/O timeout on the device and continues in the EXE$FORK routine.) Routine EXE$FORK stores the specified fork process context in the fork block, inserts the fork block at the tail of the appropriate fork queue, and requests a software interrupt at that IPL. EXE$FORK then transfers control to the return address the driver specified, sometimes to the driver but more often to the code that entered the driver. This form of return is known as "returning to caller's caller." The instructions in EXE$FORK that perform these functions are listed in Example 6-1.

2.1.4   **Dispatching a Fork Process.** When a fork interrupt is granted, its interrupt service routine is entered. The fork interrupt service routine saves R6, loads it with the address of the corresponding fork queue listhead, and transfers control to common fork dispatching code. The interrupt service routines for IPLs 6 and 8 and the common fork dispatching code, EXE$FORKDSPTH, are listed in Example 6-2. (These routines are all in module FORKCNTRL.) EXE$FORKDSPTH saves R0 through R5, removes each fork block in turn from the associated queue, and processes it. The removal and processing con-

Example 6-1 EXE$FORK Routine

```
EXE$FORK::                                  ;Create fork process
        MOVQ    R3,FKB$L_FR3(R5)            ;Save registers R3, R4
        POPL    FKB$L_FPC(R5)              ;Get fork process PC
        MOVZBL  FKB$B_FIPL(R5),R4          ;Get fork IPL
        MOVAQ   W^SWI$GL_FQFL-<6*8>[R4],R3 ;Get address of
                                            ; fork queue listhead
        INSQUE  (R5),@4(R3)                ;Insert fork block
                                            ; in fork queue
        BNEQ    10$                        ;If queue populated,
                                            ; avoid extra interrupts
        SOFTINT R4                         ;Request software
10$:    RSB                                ; interrupt and return
```

tinue until the queue is empty, when the dispatcher dismisses the interrupt with an REI instruction.

Because the fork process routine runs on the interrupt stack at IPLs above 2, it must be in nonpageable system space; it must not incur page faults, execute change mode instructions, or incur any exceptions which are dispatched to user-defined condition handlers (see Chapter 4). While the fork process is executing, it may use R0 through R5 and, if saved and restored, the other general registers. The fork process may also use the interrupt stack. However, when the fork process returns control to the fork dispatcher, the stack must be in the same state as when the fork process was entered.

6.2.1.5   **Stalling a Fork Process.** A fork process may be stalled for various reasons and have to wait. When a fork process waits, its context is saved by storing R3, R4, and the PC in the FKB. The FKB is then placed in a queue of FKBs. One example of such a wait is a fork process waiting in the fork dispatcher queue while the system is running at a higher IPL. Another example is a driver fork process which tries to allocate unavailable system resources, such as UNIBUS map registers. The fork process is stalled until another fork process deallocates map registers. The routine called to deallocate map registers restores the context of the waiting fork process so that it can repeat its attempt to allocate map registers. (Note that all fork processes that may stall waiting for a particular resource must use the same fork IPL.)

VMS Version 4 adds a "fork and wait" wakeup mechanism so that fork processes can stall themselves for a short while and be awakened automatically. To fork and wait, a fork process invokes the macro FORK_WAIT, which generates a call to EXE$FORK_WAIT (in module FORKCNTRL). The EXE$FORK_WAIT merely saves the fork process's context (PC, R3, and R4) in the fork block and inserts it at the tail of a queue located through the global pointer EXE$GL_FKWAITFL.

This queue is serviced once a second by the routine EXE$TIMEOUT (in module TIMESCHDL). Thus, on average, the fork process waits for half a second. EXE$TIMEOUT removes each fork block in turn from this queue, restores the fork process context, and reenters the fork process. Part of the restoration of context involves changing IPL from IPL$_TIMER to FKB$B_FIPL. Because lowering IPL would violate the interrupt nesting scheme, use of the fork and wait mechanism is limited to fork processes with fork IPLs at or above IPL$_TIMER.

The disk and tape class drivers use this mechanism after an unsuccessful attempt to allocate nonpaged pool, assuming that nonpaged pool will become available. When the fork process is reentered, it repeats its attempt to allocate nonpaged pool. In this example, the fork and wait mechanism is used in lieu of nonpaged pool availability reporting, the mechanism used by full processes (see Chapters 3 and 10).

The fork and wait mechanism is also used by the IPL 12 interrupt service routine when it recomputes quorum, following an unsuccessful attempt to send a message to the cluster connection manager (see Section 6.2.7).

Chapter 11 contains further information about EXE$TIMEOUT.

.2.1.6   **Use of Fork IPLs.** There are five different fork IPLs; three are used by device drivers supplied as part of VMS:

- IPL 6 is used by the connect to interrupt driver and by drivers that support attention ASTs. Chapter 2 discusses IPL 6 fork processing.
- IPL 11 is used by the mailbox driver and shared memory mailbox driver. The mailbox driver runs at the highest fork IPL so that any driver fork process can write mailbox messages, primarily, to the OPCOM process's mailbox.
- IPL 8 is the most commonly used driver fork IPL. With the exception of the connect to interrupt driver and the mailbox drivers, all drivers shipped with VMS use IPL 8.

The following considerations affect the choice of fork IPL for any particular driver:

- Higher fork IPLs are serviced first.
- All device drivers on a Q-bus or UNIBUS competing for resources such as map registers or datapaths must use the same fork IPL. In particular, if any such VMS drivers exist, all DMA drivers servicing devices on that bus must use fork IPL 8.
- All SCS class and port drivers must use fork IPL 8.
- A driver which accesses a systemwide database synchronized at IPL$_SYNCH can do so without forking if its fork IPL is 8, the value of IPL$_SYNCH.

Software Interrupts

Example 6-2   Fork Dispatching Routine

```
        .ALIGN  LONG                            ;Entry point must be longword
                                                ; aligned
EXE$FRKIPL6DSP::                                ;Fork IPL 6 entry point
        PUSHL   R6                              ;Save R6
        MOVAQ   W^SWI$GL_FQFL,R6                ;Get address of fork queue
                                                ; listhead
        BRB     EXE$FORKDSPTH                   ;Branch to common code
        .
        .
        .

        .ALIGN  LONG                            ;Entry point must be longword
                                                ; aligned
EXE$FRKIPL8DSP::                                ;Fork IPL 8 entry point
        PUSHL   R6                              ;Save R6
        MOVAQ   W^SWI$GL_FQFL+16,R6             ;Get address of fork queue
                                                ; listhead
        NOP                                     ;Pad out to longword boundary
        ;
        ; Drop through to common code
        ;
EXE$FORKDSPTH::                                 ;Software interrupt fork
                                                ; dispatcher

        PUSHL   R5                              ;Save R5 .
        PUSHL   R4                              ;Save R4   .
        PUSHL   R3                              ;Save R3    . PUSHLS are fastest!
        PUSHL   R2                              ;Save R2  .
        PUSHL   R1                              ;Save R1 .
        PUSHL   R0                              ;Save R0.
        BRB     20$                             ;Branch to body of dispatcher
;
; Dispatch fork process when queue is not yet empty
; Dispatch fork process with:
;
;       R0 thru R2 = scratch registers
;       R3 and R4 = restored from fork block
;       R5 = address of fork block
;
10$:    MOVQ    FKB$L_FR3(R5),R3                ;Restore registers R3 and R4
        JSB     @FKB$L_FPC(R5)                  ;Dispatch fork
```

xample 6-2   Fork Dispatching Routine *(continued)*

```
0$:REMQUE@(R6),R5                          ;Remove next entry from fork
                                           ; queue
NEQ10$                                     ;Branch if queue not yet empty
VS30$                                      ;If vs no entry removed
                                           ;Here when last entry dequeued


   Dispatch last entry in the queue
   Dispatch fork process with:

        R0 thru R2 = scratch registers
        R3 and R4 = restored from fork block
        R5 = address of fork block

OVQFKB$L_FR3(R5),R3                        ;Restore registers R3 and R4
SB@FKB$L_FPC(R5)                           ;Dispatch fork
0$:POPR#^M<R0,R1,R2,R3,R4,R5,R6>           ;Restore fork process
                                           ; register set
        REI                                ;Dismiss interrupt
```

.2.2   **Software Timer**

VMS includes both a hardware clock interrupt service routine and a software timer interrupt service routine. Together these routines service time-dependent requests. Chapter 11 describes these interrupt service routines in detail; this section summarizes some of their interaction.

The hardware interrupt service routine, EXE$HWCLKINT, runs every ten milliseconds in response to a hardware interval clock interrupt. Some of its duties are to update the system time, check for quantum expiration of the current process, and check whether the first timer queue element (TQE) has come due. TQEs describe time-dependent requests usually made through the Schedule Wakeup ($SCHDWK) and Set Timer ($SETIMR) system services. The queue of TQEs is kept ordered by expiration time, with most imminent first. Quantum end processing and TQE servicing require lengthier execution than is appropriate at device IPL and require modification to the scheduler database, which is synchronized at IPL$_SYNCH. For these reasons, if either the current process has run out of quantum or if the first TQE has come due, EXE$HWCLKINT requests an IPL$_TIMERFORK interrupt for EXE$SWTIMINT.

Entered as an IPL$_TIMERFORK interrupt, the software timer service routine, EXE$SWTIMINT, raises IPL to IPL$_TIMER (equal to IPL$_SYNCH). At IPL$_TIMER, EXE$SWTIMINT checks for quantum expiration and performs quantum end processing, if necessary. EXE$SWTIMINT then examines the timer queue for expired TQEs. It removes and processes any TQE with an expiration time the same as or earlier than the current system time. EXE$SWTIMINT continues removing and processing TQEs until it reaches one which has not yet expired. EXE$SWTIMINT then executes an REI instruction, dismissing the interrupt and leaving the unexpired TQEs in the queue.

6.2.3 I/O Postprocessing

When a device driver or FDT routine detects that a particular I/O request is complete, it calls a routine that places the I/O request packet (IRP) at the tail of the I/O postprocessing queue, located through global pointer IOC$GL_PSBL, and requests a software interrupt at IPL 4, IPL$_IOPOST. The following instructions, extracted from routine IOC$REQCOM (in module IOSUBNPAG), show this sequence. Other routines that request an IPL$_IOPOST software interrupt execute similar instructions.

```
        .
        .
        .
INSQUE (R3),@IOC$GL_PSBL      ;Insert IRP on IOPOST list
SOFTINT #IPL$_IOPOST          ;Request an IPL 4 interrupt
        .
        .
```

The I/O postprocessing interrupt software routine, IOC$IOPOST (in module IOCIOPOST), removes each IRP in turn from the beginning of the queue, located through global pointer IOC$GL_PSFL, and processes it. The details of the processing vary with the type of IRP. For example, IOC$IOPOST distinguishes between VMS buffered and direct I/O requests. When a direct I/O request completes, IOC$IOPOST unlocks the buffer pages from memory. When a buffered output request completes, IOC$IOPOST deallocates the buffer to nonpaged pool and returns process byte count quota. Chapter 18 contains further information about I/O postprocessing.

When IOC$IOPOST has processed all IRPs in the queue, it dismisses the interrupt with an REI instruction. Example 6-3, an extract from module IOCIOPOST, illustrates the similarity between the fork dispatching and I/O postprocessing sequences.

6.2.4 Rescheduling Interrupt

The executive requests a rescheduling interrupt at IPL 3 whenever a resident process becomes computable whose priority is greater than or equal to that of the current process. The IPL 3 interrupt service routine, SCH$RESCHED (in

Example 6-3 IOC$IOPOST Interrupt Service Routine

```
IOC$IOPOST::                          ;I/O posting interrupt
         MOVQ    R4,-(SP)             ;Save
         MOVQ    R2,-(SP)             ;  normal
         MOVQ    R0,-(SP)             ;  registers (R0-R5)
IOPOST:  REMQUE  @W^IOC$GL_PSFL,R5    ;Get head of post queue
         BVC     10$                  ;Queue not yet empty
         MOVQ    (SP)+,R0             ;Restore
         MOVQ    (SP)+,R2             ;  registers
         MOVQ    (SP)+,R4             ;  and exit
         REI                          ;  if queue empty

10$:     .                            ;Postprocess this
                                      ;  I/O request packet
         .

         .

         BRx     IOPOST               ;Get next I/O request packet
```

module SCHED), removes the current process from execution, selects the
highest priority resident computable process, and places it into execution. It
begins execution at IPL 3 on the kernel stack of the current process. It immediately raises IPL to IPL$_SYNCH and executes a SVPCTX instruction, saving
the context of the current process and switching onto the interrupt stack.

Many of the events that make a process computable occur as part of servicing software interrupts between IPL 4 and IPL$_SYNCH. That the sched-
uler database is modified from these software interrupts has the following
implications:

• SCH$RESCHED must raise IPL to IPL$_SYNCH to block any other accesses to the scheduler database while it takes one process out of execution
  and selects another one to run.
• The IPL 3 interrupt may be requested a number of times before it is granted.
  The number of times the interrupt has been requested is irrelevant, since
  the interrupt service routine always has the same task to do.
• When the IPL 3 interrupt is granted, all events that might affect the choice
  of which process to run have been serviced. That is, the higher priority
  software interrupt service routines that affect the scheduler database have
  completed all their work. Thus, SCH$RESCHED can make the best possi-
  ble choice at the time it raises IPL to block further alterations to the
  database.

Chapter 10 discusses the scheduler database, events that affect the scheduler database, and the rescheduling interrupt.

6.2.5 AST Delivery Interrupt

The asynchronous system trap (AST) delivery interrupt means that there is an AST for the current process to execute. This interrupt is unique: it is the only software interrupt requested by microcode and the only one that runs entirely in process context.

An AST is a mechanism for signaling an asynchronous event to a process. A designated AST routine runs in the context of the process at a specified access mode. Some ASTs are requested by the process, for example, as notification of I/O request completion. Some ASTs are queued to the process by VMS as part of normal system operations, such as automatic working set adjustment.

Chapter 7 describes the details of AST delivery.

An additional use of this interrupt on an asymmetric multiprocessor system is described in Chapter 27.

6.2.6 IPL 15 and IPL 5 XDELTA Interrupts

XDELTA, the executive debugger, can optionally be made memory resident at system initialization. If XDELTA is resident, the SCB vectors for breakpoint and T-bit exceptions contain addresses of service routines within XDELTA. XDELTA remains quiescent, transferring control to the usual exception service routines for breakpoint and T-bit exceptions, until the breakpoint (BPT) instruction at global location INI$BRK is executed.

When that breakpoint instruction is executed, XDELTA accepts command input from the CPU console terminal. These commands can include setting other breakpoints, setting single-step mode, and examining system space. Often programmers debugging kernel mode code, such as a device driver, insert a JSB to INI$BRK in their code to activate XDELTA. The *VAX/VMS Delta/XDelta Utility Reference Manual* provides further information about XDELTA (and DELTA) commands.

VMS provides a software interrupt service routine to enable a person to activate XDELTA at will by writing the PR$_SIRR register at the CPU console terminal. The interrupt service routine to activate XDELTA is INI$MASTERWAKE (in module INIT). The code of this interrupt service routine follows:

```
        .ALIGN LONG
INI$MASTERWAKE:
        JSB     INI$BRK
        REI
```

INI$MASTERWAKE is the IPL 15 interrupt service routine on an asymmetric multiprocessor system or the IPL 5 interrupt service routine on a single processor system. Whether XDELTA is activated through the IPL 5 or IPL 15 interrupt, it runs at IPL 31.

When XDELTA is not resident, the instruction at INI$BRK is a NOP rather than a BPT. Thus, a system without XDELTA reacts gracefully to an XDELTA interrupt or a JSB to INI$BRK.

.2.7   **IPL 12 Interrupt Service Routine**

The IPL 12 interrupt is similar to the XDELTA interrupt; it is only requested by depositing 12 into PR$_SIRR at the CPU console terminal. The IPL 12 interrupt service routine, EXE$IPCONTROL (in module IPCONTROL), facilitates certain types of human intervention when the system might otherwise have to be crashed. When the IPL 12 interrupt request is granted, the interrupt service routine prompts on the console with the following text:

        IPC>

(IPC is a shortened form of IPL C, where C_{16} is 12.) The IPL 12 interrupt service routine accepts the following commands:

Command	Meaning
C	Cancel mount verification in progress
Q	Recalculate quorum for the VAXcluster
X	Activate XDELTA (if it is resident)
CTRL/Z	Return the system to normal operation

The C command is issued with a device specification to cancel mount verification on the specified disk. Mount verification is a mechanism that enables the system to recover gracefully from certain kinds of transient disk failures, by stalling I/O requests to a disk while it is off line or inaccessible. If the disk comes back on line, the system confirms that this is the same disk as was previously mounted and resumes normal I/O processing on the volume. If SYSBOOT parameter MVTIMEOUT seconds elapse before the disk comes on line, mount verification times out and the system aborts I/O requests in progress to that disk.

While the disk is in a state of mount verification in progress, all users' I/O requests to the disk are stalled until the mount verification times out or the disk comes back on line. An impatient user can type CTRL/C or CTRL/Y and STOP to abort the image and cancel its I/O requests. However, the user cannot cancel any I/O request the Files-11 XQP may have made on the user's behalf, and subsequent file system activity in the process will be blocked until mount verification times out or is canceled.

Therefore, if the disk failure is known to be permanent, it may be appropriate to cancel mount verification before the mount verification timeout period has elapsed. In most cases, the DISMOUNT/ABORT command is the preferred way to cancel mount verification. (See the *VAX/VMS DCL Dictionary* for further information on this command.) However, if the state of the system prevents that command from being entered, the C command to the IPL 12 interrupt service routine may be used instead.

For additional information on mount verification, see the *VAX/VMS System Manager's Reference Manual*.

In response to a Q command, EXE$IPCONTROL creates an IPL 8 fork process (see Section 6.2.1 for more information about fork processing) to request the VAXcluster system connection manager to recalculate dynamic quorum based on the current cluster configuration. The Q command can be issued when a VAXcluster system hangs because of quorum loss, after a node crashes and fails to reboot. Creating an IPL 8 fork process is required for synchronization with the connection manager, which runs as an IPL 8 fork process.

The fork process calls a connection manager routine to recompute quorum. If any error occurs, the fork process issues a fork and wait request (see Section 6.2.1.5), retrying its call whenever it is reentered. Once the call to the routine is successful, the fork process exits.

In response to an X command, EXE$IPCONTROL calls INI$BRK to activate XDELTA, as described in Section 6.2.6.

In response to CTRL/Z, EXE$IPCONTROL exits, dismissing the IPL 12 interrupt with an REI instruction.

ASTs

What you want, what you're hanging around in the world
waiting for, is for something to occur to you.
Robert Frost

An asynchronous system trap (AST) is a mechanism for signaling an asynchronous event to a process. Specifically, as soon as possible after the asynchronous event occurs, a procedure or routine designated by either the process or the system executes in the context of the process.

A process may request an AST as notification that an asynchronous system service has completed. ASTs requested by the system result from operations such as I/O postprocessing, process suspension, and process deletion. These operations require that VMS code execute in the context of a specific process. ASTs fulfill this need.

To signal the asynchronous event, the executive queues an AST to the process. Queuing of an AST eventually results in that process's becoming current. AST delivery, the actual dispatch into the AST procedure, occurs in the context of that process. This chapter discusses the queuing and delivery of ASTs and describes some examples of their use by VMS.

.1   AST HARDWARE COMPONENTS

VAX hardware/microcode assists VMS in the queuing and delivery of ASTs. Three mechanisms contribute:

- The REI instruction
- The PR$_ASTLVL processor register
- The IPL 2 software interrupt

The first two features are discussed in this section. Software interrupts are discussed in Chapter 6. The IPL 2 interrupt service routine for AST delivery, SCH$ASTDEL, is discussed in Section 7.5.

.1.1   REI Instruction

The return from exception or interrupt instruction (REI) initiates the delivery of an AST to a process by requesting an IPL 2 interrupt if appropriate. (Note that the requested IPL 2 interrupt will not actually be granted until IPL drops below 2.) The REI microcode performs the following tests to determine whether to request the interrupt:

1. The REI microcode checks whether process context is being restored. If the interrupt stack bit is set in the PSL to be restored, the REI microcode makes no further test and does not request an IPL 2 interrupt. AST delivery has no meaning outside of process context.

2. The REI microcode compares the value in PR$_ASTLVL to the access mode being restored. If the value in PR$_ASTLVL is smaller or equal to the current mode field in the PSL to be restored (that is, if it represents a more or equally privileged access mode) the REI microcode requests a software interrupt at IPL 2. This test prevents a process running in an inner mode from being interrupted to deliver an AST to an outer mode.

7.1.2 ASTLVL Processor Register (PR$_ASTLVL)

The processor register PR$_ASTLVL is used in conjunction with the REI instruction to control IPL 2 software interrupts. This register is part of the hardware context of the process and has a save area in the hardware process control block field PHD$B_ASTLVL (see Chapter 10). The LDPCTX instruction copies PHD$B_ASTLVL to PR$_ASTLVL when a process is placed into execution. Because the SVPCTX instruction does not save PR$_ASTLVL in PHD$B_ASTLVL, any code which changes PR$_ASTLVL must also make the same change to PHD$B_ASTLVL.

PR$_ASTLVL normally contains the access mode of the first AST in the process's AST queue. (Inner mode ASTs are more privileged than outer mode ASTs and are queued and delivered first.) Specifically, PR$_ASTLVL contains the mode of the first AST in the queue:

- After an AST has been queued
- After an AST routine has completed and exited
- After ASTs at a given mode have been enabled or disabled by the Set AST Enable ($SETAST) system service
- After an AST routine has left AST level by invoking the Clear AST ($CLRAST) system service

Occasionally, PR$_ASTLVL contains a value that is 1 greater than the current AST's mode. This is done to prevent IPL 2 interrupt requests until ASTs are again deliverable at that mode. Specifically, PR$_ASTLVL contains the current AST's mode plus 1:

- While an AST routine is in progress
- After an AST has been blocked, because ASTs at that mode are active or disabled

If no AST is queued, PR$_ASTLVL contains a value of 4, chosen so that the REI test previously described will fail, regardless of the access mode being restored by the REI instruction.

.2   **AST DATA STRUCTURES**

The executive queues ASTs to a process as the corresponding events (I/O completion, timer expiration, etc.) occur. The AST queue is maintained as a queue of AST control blocks (ACBs) with the listhead in the process control block (PCB). Section 7.4 describes AST queues in more detail.

.2.1   **Process Control Block**

The PCB contains several fields related to AST queuing and delivery. Figure 7-1 illustrates these fields.

The fields PCB$L_ASTQFL and PCB$L_ASTQBL are the listhead for ACBs queued to the process. The list is doubly linked.

The field PCB$W_ASTCNT specifies how many concurrent ASTs the process can request at the moment. It is initialized to the process's AST quota, typically from the user authorization file. When a process calls an asynchronous system service, requesting AST notification of completion,

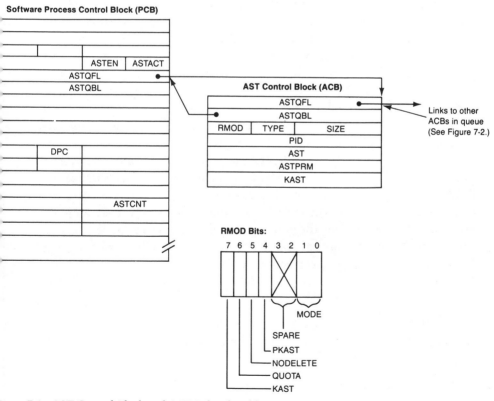

Figure 7-1   AST Control Block and AST-Related Fields
 Software PCB

149

and when a process declares an AST by calling the Declare AST ($DCLAST) system service, the service checks that PCB$W_ASTCNT is greater than zero. If so, the service decrements PCB$W_ASTCNT.

It is the responsibility of the service and of any code decrementing PCB$W_ASTCNT to set the ACB$V_QUOTA bit in the ACB (see Section 7.2.2) as a flag that PCB$W_ASTCNT must be incremented for this AST when it is done. When an AST with ACB$V_QUOTA set is delivered, the AST delivery interrupt service routine, SCH$ASTDEL, increments PCB$W_ASTCNT.

The process delete pending count, PCB$B_DPC, can be incremented for every reason the process should not be deleted or suspended. Currently its value should be zero or 1. A value of 1 indicates that an XQP operation is in progress and that the process should not be suspended or deleted. Section 7.7 discusses the use of this field in more detail.

Both PCB$B_ASTEN and PCB$B_ASTACT contain four bits, one per access mode, with bit 0 corresponding to kernel mode.

Each PCB$B_ASTEN bit, when set, indicates that AST delivery to that access mode is enabled. By default, all four bits are set. A process toggles a PCB$B_ASTEN bit through the $SETAST system service. The $SETAST service allows a process to affect delivery of ASTs to the mode from which the process requested the system service. It enables synchronization between a normal thread of execution and an AST thread. The concept of AST reentrancy and ways of achieving it are described in the *Guide to Creating Modular Procedures on VAX/VMS*.

Each PCB$B_ASTACT bit, when set, indicates that an AST is active at that access mode in the process. The AST delivery interrupt service routine sets the bit, and AST exit code clears it. The executive uses these bits to serialize ASTs for each access mode; that is, the executive will not interrupt an AST thread to deliver another AST to the same access mode. This serialization limits the number of concurrent threads of execution within a process and helps ensure that AST procedures are not entered recursively, thus simplifying synchronization among the different threads in an access mode. It is possible, though not usual, to reset the PCB$B_ASTACT bit using the $CLRAST system service (see Section 7.5.3).

7.2.2 AST Control Block

The AST control block (ACB) includes the following information:

- The PID of the target process
- The AST procedure or routine address
- The access mode
- An optional argument to the AST procedure

The ACB is allocated from nonpaged pool, often as part of a larger structure associated with the requested asynchronous event. The ACB is actually included as the first section of several larger data structures. The I/O request packet (IRP), lock block (LKB), and timer queue element (TQE), for example, all have data structures whose first section is an ACB. (Compare the ACB format pictured in Figure 7-1 with the TQE format shown in Figure 11-1, the LKB format shown in Figure 13-3, or the IRP layout shown in Figure E-11 in Appendix E.)

Both ACB$L_ASTQFL and ACB$L_ASTQBL link the ACB into the AST queue in the PCB. The listhead of this queue is the pair of longwords PCB$L_ASTQFL and PCB$L_ASTQBL.

The field ACB$B_RMOD contains five bit fields:

- Bits <0:1> (ACB$V_MODE) contain the value corresponding to the access mode in which the AST routine is to execute.
- Bit <4> (ACB$V_PKAST), when set, indicates the presence of a piggyback "special" kernel mode AST (see Section 7.6.4).
- Bit <5> (ACB$V_NODELETE), when set, indicates that the ACB should not be deallocated after the AST is delivered.
- Bit <6> (ACB$V_QUOTA), when set, indicates that the process AST quota, PCB$W_ASTCNT, has been charged for this ACB.
- Bit <7> (ACB$V_KAST), when set, indicates the presence of a special kernel mode AST (see Section 7.6). If ACB$V_KAST is clear, this is a "normal" AST.

The field ACB$L_PID identifies which process is to receive the AST.

The fields ACB$L_AST and ACB$L_ASTPRM are the entry point of the designated AST procedure and its optional argument.

The field ACB$L_KAST contains the entry point of a system-requested special kernel mode AST routine if the ACB$V_PKAST or ACB$V_KAST bit of ACB$B_RMOD is set.

7.3 CREATING AN AST

ASTs can be created by three types of actions. The first is a process request for AST notification of the completion of an asynchronous system service, such as Queue I/O Request ($QIO) or Enqueue Lock Request ($ENQ). The arguments for these services include an AST procedure address and an argument to be passed to the AST procedure. The system service charges the AST against the process AST quota (see PCB$W_ASTCNT in Section 7.2.1). The second is the system's queuing an AST to execute code in the context of the selected process. An ACB used in this situation is not deducted from the AST quota of the target process because of its involuntary nature; the ACB$V_QUOTA bit is clear to indicate this.

The system's ability to execute code in a particular process context is crucial to VMS operations. Only the AST mechanism provides this capability. The executive employs this mechanism primarily to access the process's virtual address space.

In a virtual memory operating system such as VMS, resolving a per-process address outside of its process context is difficult at best. The process's pages, as well as page table pages, may not be resident; they may be in a page file, swap file, or in transition. Rather than attempt to locate the relevant page table page(s) and per-process page(s), VMS resolves the address in process context through the AST mechanism so that standard memory management mechanisms can be used.

Examples of the system's queuing an AST include the following:

- I/O postprocessing
- The Force Exit ($FORCEX) system service
- Expiration of CPU time quota
- Working set adjustment as part of the quantum end event (see Chapter 10)
- The Get Job/Process Information ($GETJPI) system service

The third way to create an AST is an explicit declaration of an AST by the process through the $DCLAST system service. This system service simply allocates an ACB, fills in the ACB information from its argument list, and requests the queuing of the ACB. The access mode in which the AST is to execute must be no more privileged than the mode from which the $DCLAST was requested. The system service charges the AST against the process AST quota (see PCB$W_ASTCNT in Section 7.2.1).

7.4   QUEUING AN AST TO A PROCESS

The routine SCH$QAST (in module ASTDEL) is invoked to queue an ACB to a process. It can be invoked from a thread of execution running at any IPL from 0 to IPL$_SYNCH. The routine SCH$QAST uses the ACB$V_KAST bit and ACB$V_MODE bits of the ACB$B_RMOD field to decide where in the process's AST queue to insert the ACB. The AST queue for a process is a doubly linked list with its head and tail at PCB fields PCB$L_ASTQFL and PCB$L_ASTQBL.

SCH$QAST maintains the queue as a first-in/first-out (FIFO) list for each access mode. ASTs of different access modes are placed into the queue in ascending access mode order, that is, kernel mode ASTs first and user mode ASTs last. Special kernel mode ASTs precede normal kernel mode ASTs. Piggyback special kernel mode ASTs are inserted in the AST queue according to the mode of the normal AST on which they ride.

SCH$QAST performs the following steps:

1. SCH$QAST raises IPL to IPL$_SYNCH to synchronize access to the scheduler database and to the process's AST-related data: the AST queue,

PCB$B_ASTACT and PCB$B_ASTEN bits, and possibly PR$_ASTLVL and PHD$B_ASTLVL.

2. If the process is nonexistent, SCH$QAST returns an error status. If bit ACB$V_NODELETE is clear, SCH$QAST deallocates the ACB before returning.

3. If the AST queue is empty (the contents of PCB$L_ASTQFL are equal to its address), then the ACB is inserted as the first element in the AST queue.

4. Otherwise, SCH$QAST scans the queue of ACBs. It inserts a normal ACB before the first ACB whose ACB$V_MODE bits indicate a less privileged access mode or, if it finds none, at the end of the queue. SCH$QAST inserts a special kernel AST before the first normal ACB, or if it finds none, at the end of the queue. Figure 7-2 shows the organization of the AST queue.

5. SCH$QAST calculates ASTLVL as the mode of the first (innermost mode) ACB in the queue and stores it as follows:

   —If the process is currently executing, SCH$QAST stores the new ASTLVL value in both PHD$B_ASTLVL and the processor register, PR$_ASTLVL.

   —If the process is memory resident but not currently executing, SCH$QAST stores the new value for ASTLVL in PHD$B_ASTLVL but not in the processor register.

   —If a process is outswapped, PHD$B_ASTLVL cannot be updated because the process header (including the hardware PCB) is not available. When the process becomes resident and computable at a later time, the swapper calculates and stores a value for PHD$B_ASTLVL by invoking SCH$NEWLVL (in module ASTDEL).

   When setting ASTLVL, SCH$QAST does not check whether an AST is already active for this mode or whether ASTs at this mode are disabled. When either of these conditions is true, the next REI to drop IPL below 2 will cause an IPL 2 interrupt, and SCH$ASTDEL will dismiss it as undeliverable (blocked). This is felt to be an infrequent enough occurrence to be less costly than having SCH$QAST make the checks.

6. It calls SCH$RSE to report to the scheduler that an AST has been queued to the process. SCH$RSE makes the process computable if it is not current, already computable, or suspended.

7. SCH$QAST restores the previous IPL and returns to its invoker.

7.5 DELIVERING AN AST

AST delivery is initiated when an REI instruction determines from the destination access mode and the PR$_ASTLVL register that a pending AST is deliverable (see Sections 7.1 and 7.4) and requests a software interrupt at IPL 2. The amount of time before the AST is actually delivered depends upon the

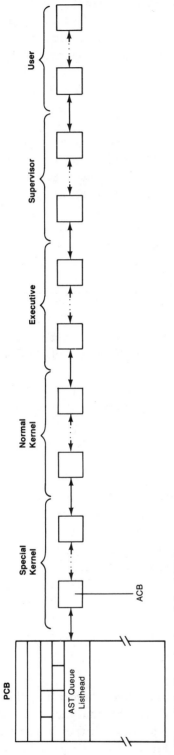

Figure 7-2 Organization of the AST Queue

interrupt activity of the system. When IPL drops below 2, the AST delivery interrupt service routine will execute.

Note that a rescheduling interrupt at IPL 3 may be requested and granted, prior to the granting of the IPL 2 AST delivery interrupt request. In this case the REI will have set the IPL 2 bit in the software interrupt service request (SISR) register PR$_SISR. Conceptually, the IPL 2 bit of the SISR is part of process context; but, for reasons of optimization, both saving and restoring of process context ignore it. Thus, it is possible for a newly scheduled process to inherit a stale SISR; an AST delivery interrupt is then granted in the context of a different process than was originally requested. The AST delivery interrupt service routine detects and ignores such "spurious" AST interrupts. The AST delivery interrupt in question will be requested again, when the process for which it is intended is placed back into execution by the REI from the rescheduling interrupt.

5.1   AST Delivery Interrupt

The IPL 2 software interrupt is unique. It is the only one requested by microcode (REI) rather than by MTPR instructions in the executive, and the only one whose service routine runs entirely in process context. When the IPL 2 interrupt occurs, control is transferred to SCH$ASTDEL (in module ASTDEL), the address in the IPL 2 system control block (SCB) vector. The interrupt service routine's functions are to remove the first pending AST from the queue, determine that the interrupt request is not a spurious one, and dispatch to the specified AST routine at the specified access mode.

Figure 7-3 shows the major steps in SCH$ASTDEL's flow. The circled identifiers in the figure correspond to the following steps. The column headings in the figure describe the environment of that step, for example, its access mode and IPL.

1. SCH$ASTDEL raises IPL to IPL$_SYNCH to synchronize access to the process's AST-related data: the AST queue, PCB$B_ASTACT and PCB$B_ASTEN bits, and ASTLVL as represented in the processor register and PHD field.

2. SCH$ASTDEL tries to remove the first ACB from the process AST queue. If the queue is empty, the IPL 2 interrupt must have been spurious. The routine sets ASTLVL to 4 and exits with an REI instruction.

3. Testing ACB$V_KAST in ACB$B_RMOD, SCH$ASTDEL determines whether the ACB is a special kernel mode AST. It delivers a special kernel mode AST with the following steps:

   a. SCH$ASTDEL drops IPL from IPL$_SYNCH back to IPL 2.

   b. SCH$ASTDEL dispatches to the special kernel AST routine by executing an effective JSB instruction. (It pushes a return address on the stack and executes a JMP instruction.)

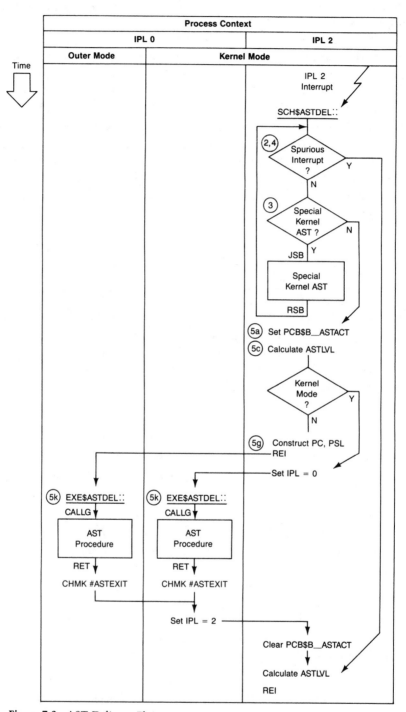

Figure 7-3 AST Delivery Flow

c. On return from the special kernel mode routine, SCH$ASTDEL returns to step 1 to check the AST queue again in case the special kernel AST queued a normal AST to the process.

4. If the AST removed from the queue is a normal AST, then SCH$ASTDEL checks that the mode of the AST is at least as privileged as the destination mode of the REI instruction that initiated AST delivery. This test is accomplished by checking the saved PSL on the kernel stack. If the mode of the AST is less privileged, SCH$ASTDEL reinserts the ACB at the head of the queue and dismisses the interrupt with an REI instruction. This test detects a spurious AST delivery interrupt.

   Two other checks for spurious AST delivery interrupts are required. The first is that the appropriate PCB$B_ASTACT bit must be clear; this test prevents an AST from being interrupted by another AST at the same access mode. The second test is that the appropriate PCB$B_ASTEN bit is set, indicating that AST delivery for that access mode is enabled. If either test fails, SCH$ASTDEL sets ASTLVL to the blocked access mode plus 1, requeues the ACB, and dismisses the interrupt.

5. If the AST is deliverable, then SCH$ASTDEL performs the following operations before dispatching to the AST routine:

   a. SCH$ASTDEL sets the bit corresponding to the current access mode in PCB$B_ASTACT to indicate that there is an active AST at this mode and to block concurrent delivery of another AST.

   b. If ACB$V_QUOTA is set in the ACB, SCH$ASTDEL increments PCB$W_ASTCNT quota to return the quota charged for the AST.

   c. SCH$ASTDEL stores a new value of ASTLVL in PR$_ASTLVL and PHD$B_ASTLVL. The new value of ASTLVL is the access mode of the AST plus 1 (the next outer mode). The access mode is calculated in this manner to prevent another AST interrupt when SCH$ASTDEL switches to the access mode in which the AST procedure is executed.

   d. Modifications to the process's AST-related data are complete and IPL is restored to ASTDEL.

   e. Delivery of a kernel mode AST is simpler than delivery to other modes because the process is already executing in kernel mode and on the appropriate stack. If the AST is for a mode other than kernel, SCH$ASTDEL obtains the stack pointer for that mode.

   f. As described in the next section, SCH$ASTDEL builds an argument list on the stack of the AST's access mode.

   g. If the AST is not a kernel mode AST, SCH$ASTDEL builds a PC/PSL pair of longwords on the kernel stack. The stored PC is the location EXE$ASTDEL, the AST dispatcher. The stored PSL contains the AST access mode in both its current mode and previous mode fields.

   h. If a piggyback special kernel mode AST is associated with the current

AST, the special kernel mode AST routine is dispatched through a JSB instruction. When the piggyback AST routine returns, SCH$ASTDEL continues with the next step.

i. If the AST does not include a piggyback special kernel mode, SCH$ASTDEL tests the ACB$V_NODELETE bit. If the bit is set, processing continues with the next step; if the bit is clear, SCH$ASTDEL deallocates the ACB to nonpaged pool.

j. The code which actually calls an AST procedure, EXE$ASTDEL, must execute in the access mode of the AST.

For AST access modes other than kernel, transfer of control to EXE$ASTDEL and change of access mode is accomplished through an REI instruction, the only way to reach a less privileged access mode (see Figure 1-4). The PC and PSL used by the REI instruction are described in step 5g.

To deliver a kernel mode AST, SCH$ASTDEL merely drops IPL to 0 and falls through to EXE$ASTDEL.

k. EXE$ASTDEL executes a CALLG instruction, transferring control to the AST procedure, with the argument pointer (AP) pointing to the argument list. The use of a CALLx instruction to enter ASTs enables them to be written in any high-level language that supports the VAX Calling Standard. A CALLG instruction is used, rather than a CALLS, so that the argument list will remain on the stack after the AST procedure RETS.

7.5.2 Argument List

AST procedures can be written in any language. By definition, a procedure begins with an entry mask, is passed an argument list, and returns control to its caller (in this case, the AST dispatcher) with a RET instruction.

Figure 7-4 shows the argument list which SCH$ASTDEL passes to an AST procedure. SCH$ASTDEL copies the AST parameter from the ACB where it was initially stored by a system service such as $QIO, $ENQ, or $DCLAST. The AST parameter was originally an argument to the service. The interpretation of the AST parameter is dependent on the application.

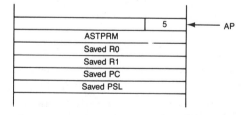

Figure 7-4   Argument List Passed to AST by Dispatcher

SCH$ASTDEL saves the general purpose registers R0 and R1 in the argument list. The AST procedure may not save them through its register save mask, because the procedure calling standard specifies that R0 and R1 be used to return status. The asynchronous nature of ASTs implies that the R0 and R1 contents are unpredictable and therefore must be preserved. The registers are saved and restored by the AST delivery mechanism.

The saved PC and PSL values are the register contents originally saved when the IPL 2 interrupt was granted. The values are normally the pair that was about to be used by the original REI instruction requesting the AST delivery.

AST Exit Path

When an AST procedure is done, it must invoke the Clear AST ($CLRAST) system service, directly or indirectly. The $CLRAST system service, also known as the ASTEXIT system service, clears the appropriate PCB$B_ASTACT bit and recomputes ASTLVL. In most cases, the AST procedure indirectly invokes the ASTEXIT system service by executing a RET instruction. Direct invocation of $CLRAST is discussed later in this section.

When the AST procedure executes the RET instruction, its call frame is removed from the stack and control returns to EXE$ASTRET in the access mode of the AST. The AST argument list, which is still necessary, remains on the stack. The following steps then occur:

1. EXE$ASTRET removes the argument count and the AST parameter from the stack, leaving the R0, R1, PC, and PSL values.
2. EXE$ASTRET executes the instruction

   ```
   CHMK    #ASTEXIT
   ```

   This instruction invokes the change-mode-to-kernel system service dispatcher, EXE$CMODKRNL (in module CMODSSDSP), described in Chapter 9. EXE$CMODKRNL makes a special test for the system service code of zero (ASTEXIT = 0) to shorten the dispatching to that service.
3. The ASTEXIT system service is responsible for resetting ASTLVL and PCB$B_ASTACT, which can only be altered from kernel mode. Thus, it is necessary for the AST dispatcher to reenter kernel mode after the AST returns control to the dispatcher and before the AST delivery interrupt is dismissed. The ASTEXIT system service performs the following steps:

   a. It raises IPL to IPL$_ASTDEL.
   b. It clears the appropriate PCB$B_ASTACT bit to indicate that no AST procedure is active at that mode.
   c. It recomputes the ASTLVL value as the access mode of the first ACB in the queue.

d. It executes an REI instruction, which lowers IPL to 0 and returns to EXE$ASTRET.

4. EXE$ASTRET resumes at the previous access mode:

   a. It restores R0 and R1 from the stack.
   b. EXE$ASTRET executes another REI instruction to dismiss the interrupt. The REI instruction returns control to the access mode and location originally interrupted by AST delivery.

The REI instruction in the ASTEXIT system service may cause another IPL 2 interrupt to occur, depending upon the ASTLVL value and the access mode transitions.

If another IPL 2 interrupt occurs at the REI instruction from the ASTEXIT service, the access mode stack of the first AST still contains the saved R0, R1, PC, and PSL. To prevent a stack from filling with these values as a result of recurring ASTs, SCH$ASTDEL checks whether an AST interrupt occurred at the instruction following the ASTEXIT service. If so, SCH$ASTDEL checks further whether the current AST and the previous AST are for the same access mode. If they are, SCH$ASTDEL pops from the stack the newer copy of the saved values and reuses the original ones in the argument list it builds for the current AST.

If an AST procedure invokes $CLRAST directly without returning through EXE$ASTRET, the appropriate PCB$B_ASTACT bit is cleared and PR$_ASTLVL is set to the mode of the new first ACB in the queue. This has the effect that another AST can be delivered to the same mode; the current procedure is now an ordinary thread interruptible by ASTs. The frame built on the stack from calling the AST procedure remains on the stack. The former AST procedure is responsible for removing it. Furthermore, the former AST procedure is now responsible for any synchronization with another AST thread of execution.

The VAX BASIC Run-Time Library requests the $CLRAST system service from within CTRL/C attention AST procedures. VAX BASIC requires that user programs be notified of CTRL/C through an error signal, rather than through the AST mechanism. The VAX BASIC Run-Time Library, therefore, dismisses the CTRL/C attention AST by invoking $CLRAST and then signals the condition by invoking LIB$SIGNAL (see Chapter 4).

Note that the $CLRAST system service is not supported by Digital, except for use within Digital software, and is not documented in the *VAX/VMS System Services Reference Manual*.

7.6 **SPECIAL KERNEL MODE ASTs**

Special kernel mode ASTs differ from normal ASTs in several ways:

• A special kernel mode AST routine is dispatched at IPL 2 and executes at that level or higher. Synchronization is provided by the interrupt mechanism itself, rather than requiring additional PCB$B_ASTACT and PCB$B_ASTEN bits. Only one special kernel mode AST can be active at any time because the AST delivery interrupt is blocked.

• Special kernel mode ASTs cannot be disabled through $SETAST. Delivery of a special kernel mode AST can only be blocked by raising IPL to 2 or above.

• All special kernel mode ASTs result from the operations of kernel mode code. That is, a user cannot directly request special kernel mode AST notification of an asynchronous event.

• A special kernel mode AST routine is invoked by a JSB instruction, which is a simpler and thus faster means of transferring control than a CALLG instruction.

   The arguments passed to a special kernel AST routine are the PCB address in R4 and the ACB address in R5. When the special kernel mode AST routine executes its RSB instruction, the stack must be in the same state as when the routine was entered. The routine may use R0 through R5 freely but must save R6 through R11 before use and restore them before exiting.

• A special kernel mode AST routine is responsible for the deallocation of the ACB to nonpaged pool, unless it is a piggyback special kernel AST. (For normal ASTs, this deallocation is done by the AST delivery routine.)

The next several sections briefly describe examples of the special kernel mode AST mechanism.

.6.1   **I/O Postprocessing in Process Context**

Completing an I/O request requires the delivery of a special kernel mode AST to the process whose I/O completed. I/O postprocessing is described in more detail in Chapter 18. The I/O postprocessing interrupt service routine queues a former I/O request packet (IRP) as an ACB to the process whose I/O completed. The operations performed by the I/O completion AST routine are those that must execute in process context, particularly those that reference per-process virtual addresses. The special kernel mode AST routines BUFPOST and DIRPOST (in module IOCIOPOST) perform the following operations (DIRPOST is actually a subentry point of BUFPOST):

1. For buffered read I/O operations only, BUFPOST copies the data from the system buffer to the user buffer in per-process address space and deallocates the system buffer to nonpaged pool.

2. DIRPOST increments either PHD$L_DIOCNT or PHD$L_BIOCNT, the process's cumulative totals of completed direct I/O and buffered I/O requests.

3. If a user diagnostic buffer was associated with the I/O request, DIRPOST

copies the diagnostic information from the system diagnostic buffer to the user's buffer and deallocates the system buffer.

4. DIRPOST decrements the channel control block field CCB$W_IOC, the number of I/O requests in progress on this channel. Channel control blocks are in P1 space.

5. If a common event flag is associated with the I/O request, it is set. (Local event flags are set in IOC$IOPOST, as described in Chapter 18.)

6. If the I/O request specified an I/O status block (IOSB), the routine copies information from the I/O request packet to the IOSB.

7. If ACB$V_QUOTA is set in IRP$B_RMOD (the same offset as ACB$B_RMOD), then the user asked for AST notification of I/O completion. The AST procedure address and the optional AST argument were originally stored in the IRP (now an ACB). The former IRP is queued again as an ACB, this time as a normal AST in the access mode at which the I/O request was made.

8. Otherwise, if ACB$V_QUOTA is clear, DIRPOST deallocates the IRP/ACB to nonpaged pool.

7.6.2 $GETJPI System Service

Chapter 29 describes the $GETJPI system service. A process requests the $GETJPI system service to obtain information about itself or about another process. If the request is for information in the virtual address space of another process, $GETJPI queues an AST to the target process. Running in the context of the target process, $GETJPI's special kernel AST routine can easily examine per-process address space.

In general terms, $GETJPI performs the following steps:

1. It allocates and fills in an ACB to describe a special kernel AST and the desired items of information; $GETJPI also allocates a nonpaged pool buffer to return the data and saves its address in the ACB.

2. The special kernel AST routine, executing in the context of the target process, moves the requested information into the system buffer. It modifies the ACB so that it can be used to queue a second special kernel mode AST back to the requesting process.

3. The second special kernel AST routine moves data from the system buffer into a user buffer in the requesting process. Its other actions include the following:

   —Deallocating the system buffer
   --Setting an event flag
   —Delivering an AST in the access mode of the caller, if requested

If the process has requested AST notification, the ACB is used for the third time. Otherwise, it is deallocated to nonpaged pool.

6.3   **Power Recovery ASTs**

The implementation of power recovery ASTs relies on special kernel mode ASTs. A power recovery AST enables a process to receive notification that a power failure and successful restart have occurred. Chapter 26 describes this feature in more detail.

When a power recovery occurs, VMS queues a special kernel mode AST to each process that has requested power recovery AST notification. The special kernel mode AST routine copies the address of the user-requested AST procedure, which is stored in P1 space, to ACB$L_AST and requeues the ACB as a normal AST. The special kernel mode AST routine is required to access the process's P1 space.

6.4   **Piggyback Special Kernel Mode ASTs**

Piggyback special kernel mode ASTs (PKASTs) allow a special kernel mode AST to ride piggyback in the ACB$L_KAST field of a normal mode AST.

The AST delivery interrupt service routine JSBs to the piggyback special kernel AST routine just before calling the normal AST. When the special kernel mode AST returns, the normal mode AST is called.

There are several reasons for using piggyback special kernel mode ASTs:

- It is faster to deliver two ASTs from one interrupt than to deliver two ASTs separately.
- There are times when delivering an AST requires some additional work in kernel mode in the context of the calling process. Piggyback special kernel mode ASTs facilitate this work.

   The lock manager uses piggyback special kernel mode ASTs to load the fields of the caller's lock status block and lock value block. To copy the information from the lock manager's database to the caller's process space, a piggyback special kernel mode AST is required.

   Piggyback special kernel ASTs are also used in terminal out-of-band ASTs (see Section 7.8.5.3).

- A piggyback special kernel AST can be used to queue other normal mode ASTs to a process. The lock manager uses this feature to deliver both blocking and completion ASTs to one process.

.7   **SYSTEM USE OF NORMAL ASTs**

Several other executive features are implemented through normal ASTs. The automatic working set adjustment that takes place at quantum end is implemented with normal kernel mode ASTs. (See Chapter 10 for information on quantum end activities and Chapter 16 for a detailed description of automatic working set adjustment.) CPU time limit expiration is implemented with potentially multiple ASTs. Beginning with user mode, the AST procedure calls the Exit ($EXIT) system service. If the process is not deleted, a supervisor mode time expiration AST is queued. This loop continues with higher access modes until the process is deleted. The Force Exit ($FORCEX) system service (see Chapter 12) causes a user mode AST to be delivered to the target process to request the $EXIT system service.

The executive also uses the AST mechanism for the Suspend Process ($SUSPND) and Delete Process ($DELPRC) system services. In VAX/VMS Version 4, these system services queue normal kernel mode ASTs to their target processes to implement suspension or deletion through code running in the context of the target processes. (In earlier versions of VMS, these system services queued special kernel mode ASTs to their target processes.) These system services must now take care to synchronize their actions with activity of the Files-11 XQP.

The Files-11 XQP runs in process context as a kernel mode AST thread, taking out locks and issuing I/O requests in response to the process's file system requests. The XQP indicates that it is active by incrementing the PCB field PCB$B_DPC. When the XQP must wait for a lock to be granted or an I/O request to complete, it returns from the AST procedure so that the process can wait at the access mode in which the file system request originated. Waiting in the outer mode allows delivery of ASTs to that mode and more privileged modes. While the XQP is executing or waiting, suspension of the process would risk blocking other processes on the system or cluster with interests in the same locks. Deletion of the process would risk relatively minor on-disk corruption, such as dangling directory entries and lost files.

Therefore, $SUSPND and $DELPRC queue normal kernel mode ASTs which cannot be delivered until the XQP AST completes. Furthermore, the SUSPND and DELETE AST procedures check that PCB$B_DPC is zero before proceeding with actual process suspension or deletion.

If PCB$B_DPC is not zero, these AST procedures place the process into a wait. They clear bit 0 of PCB$B_ASTACT so that another kernel mode AST can be delivered, call SCH$NEWLVL to recompute ASTLVL, and place the process into the resource wait RSN$_ASTWAIT. The process waits in kernel mode at IPL 0. Thus, special and normal kernel mode ASTs can be delivered to it. The resource wait PC is an address within the SUSPND or DELETE AST procedure, so that after the XQP AST completes, the SUSPND or DELETE AST will be reentered to finish its job.

Sometime later, queuing of an AST makes the process computable, and delivery of an XQP completion AST causes the XQP to be reentered. When the XQP is done, it decrements PCB$B_DPC and returns from the AST procedure. The SUSPND or DELETE AST is reentered and can proceed now that PCB$B_DPC is zero.

7.1   Process Suspension

The $SUSPND system service causes a target process to be placed into a suspended state. After checking the capability of the initiating process to affect the target process (see Chapter 12), the system service procedure queues a normal kernel AST to the target process so that the suspension and waiting will occur in that process's context. The wait mechanism in VMS requires that a process be placed into a wait from its own context.

When the AST is delivered, the SUSPND AST procedure raises IPL to IPL$_SYNCH and tests whether PCB$V_RESPEN in PCB$L_STS is set. The bit, when set, indicates that a Resume Process ($RESUME) system service has been issued for this process. If the bit is set, the SUSPND procedure clears it and RETS, leaving the process unsuspended.

If a $RESUME has not been issued for this process, SUSPND tests PCB$B_DPC to determine whether an XQP operation is in progress. If PCB$B_DPC is greater than zero, SUSPND places the process into a wait as previously described.

If PCB$B_DPC is zero, SUSPND places the process into a suspended wait state. The process waits in kernel mode at IPL 0. Its saved PC is an address within SUSPND, so that when the process is later placed into execution, it again tests whether a $RESUME has been issued.

7.2   Process Deletion

The $DELPRC system service causes a target process to be deleted. After checking the capability of the initiating process to affect the target process (see Chapter 12), the system service procedure queues a normal kernel AST to the target process so that the deletion will occur in the context of that process. Chapter 22 provides a detailed explanation of process deletion. The use of the AST mechanism provides the following advantages:

- Queuing the AST makes the process computable, regardless of its wait state, unless the process is suspended. The $DELPRC service ensures the deletion of a suspended process by issuing a $RESUME before queuing the AST.
- The process must be resident for the AST to be delivered. Therefore, special cases, such as the deletion of a process that is outswapped, simply do not exist.
- The DELETE AST procedure, running in process context, is able to request standard system services, such as $DASSGN, $DALLOC, and $DELTVA, to implement process deletion. These system services and the AST procedure reference per-process address space, and thus they must run in process context.

7.8   **ATTENTION AND OUT-OF-BAND ASTs**

Several VMS device drivers use ASTs to notify a process that a particular attention condition has occurred on a device. The terminal driver and mailbox driver use ASTs in this way. The terminal driver, for example, queues an attention AST to notify an interested process that CTRL/C or CTRL/Y has been typed on its terminal. The terminal driver can also queue an out-of-band AST as notification that a control character other than CTRL/C and CTRL/Y has been typed. The mailbox driver can queue an attention AST as notification that an unsolicited message has been put in a mailbox or that an attempt to read an empty mailbox is in progress.

The basic sequence for both attention ASTs and out-of-band ASTs follows:

1. A process assigns a channel and issues a Queue I/O ($QIO) system service request for AST notification of an attention condition on that device.
2. The device driver builds a data structure to describe the attention AST request, inserts it on a list connected to the device unit control block, and completes the I/O request.
3. If the attention condition occurs, the device interrupt service routine delivers the attention AST by queuing an AST to the process.

The major distinction between the attention AST and the out-of-band AST mechanisms is that out-of-band ASTs automatically repeat, whereas attention ASTs must be "rearmed." That is, a process must repeat its $QIO request for each attention notification.

Attention ASTs are described in the following sections, and out-of-band ASTs are described in Section 7.8.5.

7.8.1   **Set Attention AST Mechanism**

To establish an attention AST for a particular device (whose driver supports this feature), the user issues a $QIO request with the I/O function IO$_SETMODE (or IO$_SETCHAR for some devices). The kind of attention AST requested is indicated by a function modifier.

The IO$_SETMODE FDT action routine for such a device invokes COM$SETATTNAST (in module COMDRVSUB), which performs the following actions:

1. If the user AST routine address (the $QIO P1 parameter) is zero, the request is interpreted as a flush attention AST list request (see Section 7.8.3).
2. COM$SETATTNAST allocates an expanded ACB from nonpaged pool and charges it against the process AST quota, PCB$W_ASTCNT. The expanded ACB will be used as both a fork block (FKB) and an ACB and is therefore referred to as a FKB/ACB.

3. COM$SETATTNAST copies information into the FKB/ACB, such as the AST procedure address, AST argument, channel number, and PID.

4. It raises IPL to UCB$B_DIPL, the IPL at which the attention AST list is synchronized, and inserts the FKB/ACB into a singly linked, last-in/first-out (LIFO) list of FKB/ACBs connected to the unit control block (UCB) of the associated device.

   The location of the FKB/ACB listhead is device-specific; some UCBs have multiple listheads—one for each attention condition the driver supports. The FDT action routine passes the address of the listhead in a register to COM$SETATTNAST.

8.2   Delivery of Attention ASTs

When the driver (typically the device interrupt service routine) determines that the attention condition has occurred, it calls COM$DELATTNAST with the address of the FKB/ACB listhead.

A driver uses an alternate entry point, COM$DELATTNASTP, to specify that only ASTs requested by a particular process be delivered.

COM$DELATTNAST executes at device IPL, the IPL at which the FKB/ACB list is synchronized. The queuing of ASTs is an operation using IPL$_SYNCH as a synchronization mechanism (see Chapter 2). Specifically, IPL must not be lowered to IPL$_SYNCH. To accomplish correct synchronization and not block activities at IPL 7 and IPL 8, COM$DELATTNAST creates an IPL$_QUEUEAST (6) fork process to queue each AST.

The following steps summarize the delivery of attention ASTs:

1. COM$DELATTNAST scans each FKB/ACB in the list.

   In the case of entry through COM$DELATTNASTP, the routine compares the PID in the FKB/ACB to the requested PID. If they are not equal, the routine leaves the data structure in the queue and goes on to the next entry. If the PIDs match, the routine performs the actions described in the next listed item.

2. The routine removes the FKB/ACB from its list and dispatches to EXE$FORK, specifying the address of a fork process to be stored in FKB$L_FPC of the FKB/ACB. EXE$FORK records the fork process address and queues the fork block to the listhead specified by the FKBB_FIPL, IPL_QUEUEAST, and requests an interrupt at that IPL.

3. When IPL drops below 6, the fork interrupt is granted. The IPL 6 fork dispatcher removes the FKB/ACB from the IPL 6 fork block queue and dispatches to COM$DELATTNAST's fork process.

4. At IPL 6, COM$DELATTNAST's fork process reformats the fork control block into an ACB, describing the AST procedure and the access mode of the original attention AST request.

5. The fork process calls SCH$QAST to queue the ACB to the process.

7.8.3   Flushing an Attention AST List

The list of attention ASTs is flushed as the result of an explicit user request: a Cancel I/O ($CANCEL) request or a Deassign Channel ($DASSGN) request for the associated device.

An explicit user request to flush the attention AST list is a set attention AST request with an AST routine address of zero (see Section 7.8.1). When COM$SETATTNAST is invoked with an AST procedure address of zero, it branches to COM$FLUSHATTNS.

COM$FLUSHATTNS is entered with the PID and channel number of the attention ASTs to be deleted. COM$FLUSHATTNS performs the following operations:

1. It raises IPL to UCB$B_DIPL of the device.
2. It scans the FKB/ACB list looking for any FKB/ACBs with a PID and channel number that match those of the requested flush operation.
3. If the PIDs and channel numbers match, COM$FLUSHATTNS removes the FKB/ACB from the attention AST list.
4. COM$FLUSHATTNS restores the IPL at which it was entered.
5. COM$FLUSHATTNS increments the process AST quota, PCB$-W_ASTCNT, and deallocates the FKB/ACB to nonpaged pool.
6. COM$FLUSHATTNS continues processing until it has scanned the entire attention AST list.

7.8.4   Examples in the VAX/VMS Executive

Users frequently request attention ASTs for terminals and mailboxes. Brief descriptions follow of the terminal driver and mailbox driver's support of attention ASTs.

7.8.4.1   Terminal Driver and CTRL/Y Notification.

A process requests CTRL/C notification and CTRL/Y notification by issuing the $QIO system service request, specifying IO$_SETMODE (or IO$_SETCHAR) with the function modifier IO$M_CTRLCAST or IO$M_CTRLYAST. When an interactive user spawns a new process, that new process may also request CTRL/C and CTRL/Y attention ASTs. If the user types CTRL/C or CTRL/Y, the AST should be delivered only to the process currently associated with the terminal, rather than to every process in the job. As the user spawns new subprocesses and attaches to already created processes, DCL tells the terminal driver the PID of the process currently associated with the terminal. When CTRL/C is typed, the terminal driver invokes COM$DELATTNASTP to deliver only the ASTs requested by the process associated with the terminal.

If no CTRL/C attention AST has been requested, then the CTRL/C is interpreted as a CTRL/Y, and the terminal driver searches the CTRL/Y AST list instead. If a CTRL/Y is typed, only the CTRL/Y attention AST list is searched.

Because the FKB/ACB data structures are not reused, both types of attention ASTs must be reenabled each time they are delivered to a process.

8.4.2   **Mailbox Driver.** A process requests mailbox attention ASTs by issuing a $QIO request with function code IO$_SETMODE (or IO$_SETCHAR). The possible function modifiers are IO$M_READATTN and IO$M_WRTATTN. IO$M_WRTATTN requests notification of an unsolicited message written to that mailbox. IO$M_READATTN requests notification when any process issues a read to that mailbox and there is no message in it.

Attention ASTs of each type may be declared by multiple processes for the same mailbox. When a condition corresponding to an attention AST occurs, all ASTs of the appropriate type are delivered. Only the first process to issue a corresponding I/O request will be able to complete the transfer of data signaled by the attention ASTs.

Read and write attention ASTs must be reenabled after delivery because the entire attention AST list is delivered and removed after each occurrence of the specified condition.

8.5   **Out-of-Band ASTs**

The terminal driver uses a newer form of AST mechanism to notify a process that an "out-of-band" character has been received from its terminal. Out-of-band characters are control characters, the ASCII codes 00 to 20_{16}. (Although CTRL/C and CTRL/Y are in this range, the terminal driver provides the attention AST mechanism described previously to notify a process of their receipt for compatibility with earlier versions of VMS.) Out-of-band ASTs are similar to attention ASTs in that the terminal driver forks down to IPL$_QUEUEAST to queue an ACB to the process.

The most significant difference between the attention AST mechanism and the out-of-band AST mechanism is that out-of-band ASTs are repeating; that is, once declared, out-of-band ASTs are delivered to the process for the life of the process or until the $CANCEL system service is called to flush the AST list. Another difference is that the out-of-band AST mechanism employs a piggyback special kernel AST routine.

8.5.1   **The Terminal AST Block.** The terminal driver builds a data structure called a terminal AST block (TAST) to describe an out-of-band AST request. Figure 7-5 illustrates the TAST.

The TAST can be in two lists at once because of its structure. Through TAST$L_FLINK, the TAST is always queued to the terminal UCB in a singly linked list. Through the first two longwords of the TAST, it can be inserted

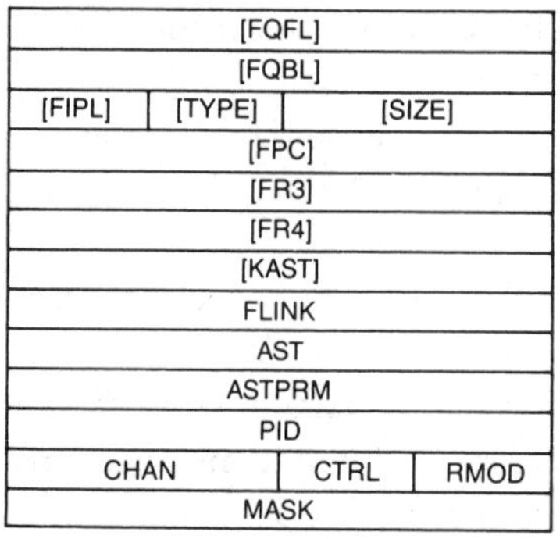

```
           [FQFL]
           [FQBL]
 [FIPL]  [TYPE]         [SIZE]
           [FPC]
           [FR3]
           [FR4]
          [KAST]
          FLINK
           AST
          ASTPRM
           PID
   CHAN          CTRL    RMOD
           MASK
```

Figure 7-5   Terminal AST Block

into a fork queue or a process's ACB queue. The terminal driver sets the bit TAST$V_BUSY in TAST$B_CTRL when the TAST is in use as a fork block or ACB. The TAST includes space for fork process context (that is, a fork PC, fork R3, and fork R4) and the AST information (address of the AST procedure and its argument, PID, and RMOD fields).

7.8.5.2   **Set Out-of-Band AST Mechanism.** A process requests out-of-band notification by issuing the $QIO system service request, specifying IO$_SETMODE (or IO$_SETCHAR) with the function modifier IO$M_OUTBAND.

The terminal driver's FDT action routine for IO$_SETMODE invokes COM$SETCTRLAST (in module COMDRVSUB), which performs the following steps:

1. If the user AST procedure address ($QIO P1 parameter) is zero or the character mask ($QIO P2 parameter) is zero, COM$SETCTRLAST interprets the request as a flush out-of-band AST list request (see Section 7.8.5.4).
2. COM$SETCTRLAST scans the list of out-of-band ASTs, searching for an out-of-band ACB with the same characteristics as the caller. The following items are checked:

   —The PID

   Out-of-band ASTs can be issued to the same terminal device from a process and its subprocesses (which will have different PIDs).
   —The channel number

3. If COM$SETCTRLAST finds a TAST with the same characteristics which is not in use, it modifies the existing TAST by replacing the AST address and the control mask. If the TAST is in use (perhaps queued as an ACB to the process), COM$SETCTRLAST marks it as "lost," removes the TAST from the UCB list, and builds a new TAST to describe the request.
4. If it does not find a similar TAST, it allocates a new TAST from nonpaged pool and charges the process AST quota, PCB$W_ASTCNT. It copies in-

formation from the I/O request packet (the AST procedure address, channel number, and PID) and the $QIO character mask into the TAST. It places the TAST at the tail of the control block list.

5. COM$DELCTRLAST ORs the $QIO character mask into the terminal's out-of-band AST summary mask, the field UCB$L_TL_OUTBAND. This mask represents all the control characters for which the terminal driver must deliver an out-of-band AST.

.8.5.3   **Delivery of Out-of-Band ASTs.** When a control key is typed at a terminal, the terminal driver checks whether that control character is represented in the terminal's out-of-band AST summary mask. If the bit in the summary mask is set, an out-of-band AST has been requested for that control character. The terminal driver interrupt service routine invokes COM$DELCTRLAST (in module COMDRVSUB) to deliver the out-of-band AST. The terminal driver uses an alternate entry point, COM$DELCTRLASTP, to specify that only ASTs requested by a particular process be delivered.

The following steps summarize the delivery of out-of-band ASTs:

1. At device IPL, COM$DELCTRLAST scans the list of TASTs for one whose character mask contains the character typed at the terminal. When COM$DELCTRLAST finds a TAST with a matching character mask, it checks the busy bit to see whether the control block is already in use. In the case of entry through COM$DELCTRLASTP, the routine also compares the PID in the TAST to the requested PID. If they are not equal, the routine goes on to the next TAST in the queue.

   If TAST$V_BUSY is set, COM$DELCTRLAST skips that TAST. If TAST$V_BUSY is clear, COM$DELCTRLAST sets it, marking the TAST in use, and records in TAST$L_ASTPRM the control character that was received.

2. COM$DELCTRLAST executes at device IPL, the IPL at which the TAST list is synchronized. The queuing of ASTs is an operation using IPL$_SYNCH as a synchronization mechanism (see Chapter 2). Specifically, IPL must not be lowered to IPL$_SYNCH. To accomplish correct synchronization and not block activities at IPL 7 and IPL 8, COM$DELCTRLAST creates an IPL$_QUEUEAST (IPL 6) fork process to queue each AST.

   COM$DELCTRLAST dispatches to EXE$FORK, specifying the address of a fork process to be stored in FKB$L_FPC of the TAST. EXE$FORK records the fork process address and queues the TAST to the listhead specified by FKB$B_FIPL (IPL$_QUEUEAST) and requests an interrupt at that IPL. The TAST also remains linked to the terminal UCB list of TASTs. Figure 7-6 shows the TAST in the terminal UCB's TAST list and in the fork block queue.

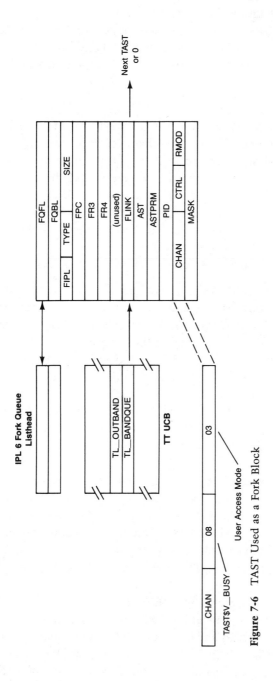

Figure 7-6 TAST Used as a Fork Block

3. When IPL drops below 6, the fork interrupt is granted. The IPL 6 fork dispatcher removes the TAST from the IPL 6 fork block queue and dispatches to COM$DELCTRLAST's fork process.

4. At IPL 6, COM$DELCTRLAST's fork process reformats the fork control block into an ACB describing the AST procedure and the access mode of the original out-of-band AST request. The no delete and piggyback special kernel mode AST flags are set in the ACB, and the special kernel mode AST field is loaded with the address of COM$DELCTRLAST's piggyback special kernel mode AST.

5. The fork process calls SCH$QAST to queue the ACB to the process. Figure 7-7 shows the TAST in use as an ACB.

6. When the process receives the AST, the piggyback special kernel mode AST routine is executed first. The piggyback special kernel mode AST performs two functions:

   a. It clears TAST$V_BUSY.
   b. If the TAST is marked as "lost," the piggyback special kernel AST routine deallocates it. "Lost" control blocks take place when COM$FLUSHCTRLS cannot deallocate a TAST because the busy bit is set (see Section 7.8.5.4). Once the AST has been delivered, the TAST is no longer needed. The piggyback special kernel AST routine deallocates it and returns quota to the process by incrementing PCB$W_ASTCNT.

8.5.4   **Flushing an Out-of-Band AST List.** The list of out-of-band ASTs is flushed as the result of an explicit user request: a cancel I/O request or a deassign channel request for the associated device.

An explicit user request to flush the out-of-band AST list is a set out-of-band AST request with an AST routine address of zero or a character mask of zero (see Section 7.8.5.2). When COM$SETCTRLAST receives such a request, it branches to COM$FLUSHCTRLS.

COM$FLUSHCTRLS is entered with the PID and channel number of the attention ASTs to be deleted. COM$FLUSHCTRLS performs the following operations:

1. It raises IPL to UCB$B_DIPL of the device.
2. It scans the TAST list and compares the PID and channel number in the TAST with those of the requested flush operation. As it scans the list, it builds a new out-of-band AST summary mask. If COM$FLUSHCTRLS finds a TAST that does not match, COM$FLUSHCTRLS ORs its control characters into the summary mask being built and goes on to the next TAST.
3. If the PIDs and channel numbers match, COM$FLUSHCTRLS checks TAST$V_BUSY to see whether the TAST is in use as a FKB or ACB. If TAST$V_BUSY is set, the "lost" bit is set so that the control block will be

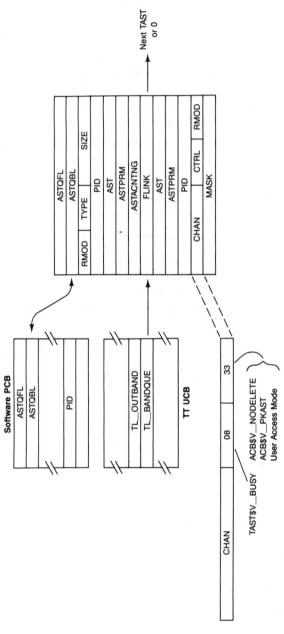

Figure 7-7 TAST Used as an ACB

deallocated once its AST is delivered. Otherwise, the TAST is removed from the out-of-band AST list.

4. If the TAST is not busy, COM$FLUSHCTRLS increments the process AST quota, PCB$W_ASTCNT, and deallocates the TAST to nonpaged pool.

5. COM$FLUSHCTRLS continues processing until it has scanned the entire TAST list. It then replaces the old summary mask with the one just built.

6. COM$FLUSHCTRLS restores the IPL at which it was entered.

8   Error Handling

There is always something to upset the most careful of
human calculations.

Ihara Saikaku, *The Japanese Family Storehouse*

There are several mechanisms for reporting systemwide errors in VAX/VMS.
(Process-specific and image-specific errors are handled by the exception
mechanism described in Chapter 4.)

- The error logging subsystem enables device drivers and other system components to record errors and other events for later inclusion in an error log report.
- The bugcheck mechanism is used by VMS to shut down the system when it detects internal inconsistencies or other unrecoverable errors.
- A machine check is an exception that indicates that the processor has detected some CPU-specific error.

8.1   ERROR LOGGING

The error logging subsystem records device errors, CPU-detected errors, and
other noteworthy events, such as volume mounts, system startups, system
shutdowns, and bugchecks.

8.1.1   Overview of the Error Logging Subsystem

Error logging occurs in three steps:

1. A component, such as a device driver, that wishes to log an error calls a routine in the executive to reserve a portion of one of two error log allocation buffers that are part of the system image. The component writes its error message into the reserved portion and calls another executive routine to indicate that the message has been written.
2. When an allocation buffer is full, the ERRFMT process is awakened to copy the buffer contents to the error log file SYS$ERRORLOG: ERRLOG.SYS.
3. The Error Log Utility selectively reports the contents of the error log file.

If the system is shut down or crashes, the error log allocation buffers are
recorded in the dump file to prevent the loss of error log messages. On the
next system boot, SYSINIT processes the error log allocation buffers saved in

the dump file and writes any valid error log messages to the error log allocation buffers in memory. When ERRFMT runs, it writes those messages and any new ones to the error log file. In this way, no error log information is lost across a system crash or an operator-requested shutdown.

8.1.2   **Device Driver Errors**

There are several routines, all in module ERRORLOG, which device drivers use to log errors. Two commonly used routines are ERL$DEVICERR and ERL$DEVICTMO. These routines log an error associated with a particular I/O request. ERL$DEVICERR is used to report a device-specific error. ERL$DEVICTMO can be called by a driver to report a device timeout. Each routine executes the following sequence:

1. The routine invokes ERL$ALLOCEMB to reserve a portion of the current error log allocation buffer.
2. It records information, which it obtains from the unit control block (UCB) and current I/O request packet (IRP), in the error log message buffer.
3. The routine calls the device driver's register dump routine entry point to store device-specific information into the error log message buffer.
4. It returns control to the device driver. When the device driver finishes processing the I/O request, it invokes IOC$REQCOM (in module IOSUBNPAG).
5. IOC$REQCOM, when it finds that there is an error log message in progress, records the final I/O request status, device status, and error retry counters in the error log buffer. It then invokes ERL$RELEASEMB to indicate that the error message has been completely written.

Some device drivers report conditions that are not associated with a particular I/O request; these conditions are called device attention errors. The CI port driver (PADRIVER), for example, reports an error if the port's microcode is not at the required revision level. To log errors when there is no IRP, drivers call ERL$DEVICEATTN. This routine records in the error log buffer information which is from the device UCB and from the driver's register dump routine.

In addition to ERL$DEVICEATTN, the system communications services (SCS) port and class drivers call four other error log routines:

- ERL$LOGSTATUS—Used by the disk and tape class drivers to log an error status code returned in a mass storage control protocol (MSCP) end packet. The end packet itself is written to the error log buffer with ERL$LOGMESSAGE.
- ERL$LOGMESSAGE—Used by the port and class drivers to log an error condition associated with a command packet, for example, a packet that contains invalid data or is an HSC error log datagram.

- ERL$LOG_DMSCP—Used by the disk class drivers (DUDRIVER and DSDRIVER) to log controller errors and reasons for a controller reset.
- ERL$LOG_TMSCP—Similar to ERL$LOG_DMSCP, this is used by the tape class driver (TUDRIVER) to log controller errors and reasons for a controller reset.

8.1.3   Other Error Log Messages

VMS uses the error log subsystem to record information other than device errors. Other kinds of entries written to the error log include the following:

- Warm start, a successful recovery from a power failure
- Cold start, a successful system bootstrap
- Fatal and nonfatal bugchecks (see Section 8.2)
- Machine check (see Section 8.3)
- Volume mount and dismount
- A message written by the Send Message to Error Logger ($SNDERR) system service (see Chapter 29)

8.1.4   Error Log Data Structures

There are two error log allocation buffers, each 512 bytes, which are built as part of the system image. A two-longword array at the global location ERL$AL_BUFADDR records their starting addresses. The global ERL$GB_BUFIND is a flip-flop switch indicating from which buffer allocations are currently being made. Figure 8-1 shows these data structures and globals.

A header at the beginning of each allocation buffer describes the buffer. The SYS$LIBRARY:LIB.MLB macro $ERLDEF defines symbolic names for fields in the buffer header. The field ERL$B_BUSY contains the number of pending messages in the buffer, messages for which space has been reserved but which have not been completely written. ERL$B_MSGCNT contains the number of completed messages.

The field ERL$B_BUFIND (note, not the global ERL$GB_BUFIND) is a 0 or 1 to identify in which allocation buffer the header is. One flag is defined in the field ERL$B_FLAGS; ERL$V_LOCK is set to inhibit further allocation in the buffer. ERL$L_NEXT points to the next available space in the buffer. ERL$L_END points one byte past the end of the buffer and is used in testing whether the buffer is full.

8.1.5   Operation of the Error Logger Routines

ERL$ALLOCEMB is invoked with the size of the requested error log message buffer. It raises IPL to 31 to synchronize access to the allocation buffer

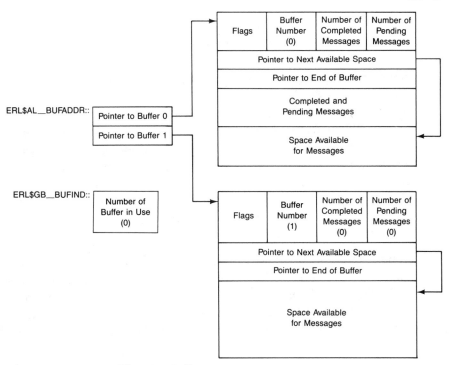

Figure 8-1   Error Log Allocation Buffers

header, since it can be called from an interrupt or exception service routine at any IPL. Using ERL$GB_BUFIND as a subscript into the array ERL$AL_BUFADDR, ERL$ALLOCEMB obtains the address of the current buffer. If its lock flag is clear (its usual state), ERL$ALLOCEMB tests whether the message will fit in the buffer.

If the message does not fit, ERL$ALLOCEMB forces a wakeup of the ERRFMT process (as described in the next section) and switches to the other allocation buffer. If the other buffer is full or its lock flag is set, ERL$ALLOCEMB increments the universal error sequence number (ERL$GL_SEQUENCE), lowers IPL, and returns a failure status. Incrementing the error sequence number for each attempted error log facilitates the detection of lost messages.

If the message does fit in the allocation buffer, ERL$ALLOCEMB allocates an error log message buffer of the requested size, advances the ERL$L_NEXT pointer, and increments the pending message count. ERL$ALLOCEMB copies to the error message buffer the system ID, the size of the buffer, a 0 or 1 to indicate in which allocation buffer this message buffer is, and the universal error sequence number. It increments the error sequence number, lowers IPL, and returns a success status and the address of the allocated buffer.

When the component logging the error has written its information in the error log message buffer, it invokes ERL$RELEASEMB. ERL$RELEASEMB

179

sets a flag in the error log message buffer to indicate that the message is valid, subtracts 1 from the pending message count, and adds 1 to the completed message count. If the ERRFMT process is not currently running and there are ten or more completed messages in the buffer, ERL$RELEASEMB forces a wake of ERRFMT.

Although ERL$RELEASEMB can be called from an interrupt or exception at any IPL, it does not raise IPL to 31. In the allocation buffer header, ERL$RELEASEMB accesses only the completed and pending message counts. ERL$RELEASEMB decrements the one and increments the other with one interlocked instruction and thus requires no further synchronization. It uses the instruction ADAWI to add the number FF_{16} to the adjacent fields, thereby subtracting 1 from the pending message count and adding 1 (the carry) to the completed message count.

8.1.5.1   **Waking the ERRFMT Process.** The routine ERL$WAKE is called once a second from EXE$TIMEOUT (see Chapter 11). The routine does not necessarily wake the ERRFMT process. Rather, it decrements a counter at global location ERL$GB_BUFTIM and only wakes ERRFMT if the counter reaches zero.

When the counter reaches zero, it is reset. The starting value for the error log timer is 30. (This value is an assembly-time parameter, not adjustable with SYSGEN.) Thus, a maximum of 30 seconds can elapse before ERRFMT is awakened. This ensures that error messages are written to the error log file at reasonable intervals, even on systems that have very few errors occurring.

This timing mechanism is exploited by both ERL$ALLOCEMB and ERL$RELEASEMB to force an awakening of ERRFMT. These routines simply set ERL$GB_BUFTIM to 1 so that the next call to ERL$WAKE will wake ERRFMT. ERL$WAKE must be invoked from no higher than IPL$_SYNCH to synchronize access to the scheduler database (see Chapters 2 and 10). ERL$ALLOCEMB and ERL$RELEASEMB run at higher IPLs and thus are unable to invoke ERL$WAKE directly.

ERL$ALLOCEMB forces a wake whenever the current error log allocation buffer fills up and ERL$ALLOCEMB must switch to the other one. ERL$RELEASEMB forces a wake if the current message buffer contains ten or more messages.

If the ERRFMT process is not running, there is no way for error log messages to be written to the error log file. Initially, attempts to log errors by allocating error log message buffers would be successful. However, once the error log allocation buffers fill with messages, any subsequent attempt to allocate an error log message buffer would fail. System operation is otherwise normal.

8.1.6   **Overview of the ERRFMT Process**

When ERRFMT is started, it enters kernel mode and invokes the Set Timer ($SETIMR) system service to request asynchronous system trap (AST) notification at ten-minute intervals. Its AST procedure invokes ERL$ALLOCEMB, writes a time stamp message, and invokes ERL$RELEASEMB. Thus, every ten minutes, ERRFMT's kernel mode AST procedure writes a time stamp to an error log allocation buffer.

Back in user mode, ERRFMT hibernates until it is awakened through ERL$WAKE. When ERRFMT is awakened, it must copy the current error log allocation buffer, process any error messages that were in it, and record them in SYS$ERRORLOG:ERRLOG.SYS. A description of its actions follows:

1. Having changed mode to kernel, ERRFMT determines which error log allocation buffer is to be copied and sets the LOCK flag in it to prevent any further allocations.

2. It tests the pending message counter in the buffer to determine whether there are error messages for which space has been allocated but not yet released.

   If there are pending messages, ERRFMT sets a timer and waits for half a second before testing the counter again. ERRFMT repeats its wait and test sequence until there are no pending messages or until it has waited 255 times.

3. ERRFMT then copies the error log allocation buffer to its own P0 space and compares the copy to the original to detect any changes that might have occurred during the copy. If the two are not equal, ERRFMT repeats the copy, trying to get a consistent copy of the buffer. If necessary, ERRFMT repeats the copy and compare sequence 255 times. ERRFMT performs this sequence as an alternative to copying the buffer at IPL 31.

4. Once ERRFMT has a consistent copy of the message buffer, it clears the pending and completed message counts in the buffer it copied, resets ERL$L_NEXT, and clears the LOCK flag. It then returns to user mode.

5. Running in user mode, ERRFMT processes the messages in the buffer. Whenever ERRFMT finds one of its time stamp messages, it checks whether the previous message written to the error log file is also a time stamp. If so, ERRFMT updates the record containing the older time stamp with the newer one. This avoids filling the error log file with time stamps and ensures that the newest time stamp is recorded.

6. If a process has declared an error log mailbox (see Section 8.1.7), ERRFMT writes each message in the error log buffer to that mailbox.

7. If ERRFMT detects a volume mounted or dismounted message within the error log buffer, it checks the SYSBOOT parameter MOUNTMSG or DISMOUMSG. If the appropriate parameter is set, ERRFMT sends a volume mounted or dismounted message to terminals enabled as disk or tape operators. By default, the SYSBOOT parameters are zero, disabling these messages to operator terminals.

8. After ERRFMT has completed its output operations, it reenters hibernation.

8.1.7   Error Log Mailbox

The error logging subsystem provides the capability for a process to monitor error logging activity as it happens, rather than wait for offline processing with the Error Log Utility. This capability is provided through the undocumented Declare Error Log Mailbox ($DERLMB) system service. This system service is provided only for use by DIGITAL's software, such as the layered software product VAXsim.

A process with DIAGNOSE privilege can call the $DERLMB system service with a single argument, the unit number of the mailbox to receive error log messages. If this mechanism is not in use by another process (the error log mailbox descriptor EXE$GQ_ERLMBX contains a zero), the unit number is stored in the first word of the mailbox descriptor and the process identification (PID) of the requesting process is stored in the second longword.

If this service is called with a unit number of zero, the descriptor is cleared, canceling use of the error log mailbox mechanism. The descriptor is also unconditionally cleared by the image rundown routine (see Chapter 21).

8.2   SYSTEM CRASHES (BUGCHECKS)

When VAX/VMS detects an internal inconsistency, such as a corrupted data structure or an unexpected exception, it generates a bugcheck. If the inconsistency is not severe enough to prevent continued system operation, the bugcheck generated is nonfatal and merely results in an error log entry. If the error is serious enough to jeopardize system operation and data integrity, a fatal bugcheck is generated.

A fatal bugcheck typically results in the following actions:

1. IPL is raised to 31, preventing any further normal system operation.
2. If the SYSBOOT parameter DUMPBUG is 1 (its default value), the contents of physical memory are written to the system dump file. The system dump file is SYS$SYSTEM:SYSDUMP.DMP or, in its absence, the primary page file.
3. The system is halted and automatically rebooted (unless the SYSBOOT parameter BUGREBOOT is zero).

8.2.1   Bugcheck Mechanism

Source code generates a bugcheck by invoking the BUG_CHECK macro. The macro has one required argument, the bugcheck type, and one optional argument, the keyword FATAL. This macro expands into the two-byte opcode FEFF$_{16}$ and one word that identifies the bugcheck type and, in bits <2:0>, its severity. If the keyword FATAL is present, the severity is set to the value STS$K_SEVERE; otherwise it is zero.

The following fatal bugcheck example is extracted from the routine SCH$SCHED in module SCHED:

```
QEMPTY:   BUG_CHECK   QUEUEMPTY,FATAL
```

Its invocation generates the following code:

```
.WORD      ^XFEFF
.WORD      BUG$_QUEUEMPTY ! 4
```

The execution of the bugcheck opcode results in a reserved instruction exception (SS$_OPCDEC, opcode reserved to DIGITAL), causing control to be transferred through the system control block to the service routine for that exception, EXE$OPCDEC in module EXCEPTION.

EXE$OPCDEC checks whether the reserved opcode is either FEFF$_{16}$ or FDFF$_{16}$. (The two-byte opcode FDFF$_{16}$ indicates that the bugcheck code is contained in the next longword. VMS does not currently use longword bugcheck codes.)

If either opcode is present, EXE$OPCDEC interprets this exception as a bugcheck and transfers control to routine EXE$BUG_CHECK (in module BUGCHECK). Otherwise, the illegal opcode exception is treated in the usual manner described in Chapter 4.

The actions of EXE$BUG_CHECK vary, depending on the access mode in which the bugcheck occurred and the severity of the bugcheck. EXE$BUG_CHECK first confirms the read accessibility of the bugcheck operand from the mode that issued the bugcheck and advances the exception PC saved on the stack to point to the instruction following the bugcheck. (As a result, the bugcheck PC shown in a crash dump is an address four bytes higher than the actual bugcheck.) EXE$BUG_CHECK then determines in which access mode the bugcheck occurred.

8.2.2   Bugchecks from User and Supervisor Modes

If a bugcheck is generated from either user or supervisor mode, and the process has BUGCHECK privilege, EXE$BUG_CHECK writes an error log message (of type user-generated bugcheck), invoking ERL$ALLOCEMB and ERL$RELEASEMB.

If the bugcheck is fatal, EXE$BUG_CHECK executes an REI instruction to return to the access mode of the bugcheck and invokes the Exit ($EXIT) system service. The code SS$_BUGCHECK is the final image status. What happens as a result of this call depends on whether the process is executing a single image (no supervisor mode termination handler has been established) or the process is an interactive or batch job.

• If the process is executing a single image, a fatal bugcheck from user or supervisor mode results in process deletion.

- With the current use of supervisor mode termination handlers, a fatal bug-check issued from an interactive or batch job causes the currently executing image to exit and control to be passed to the command language interpreter (CLI) to receive the next command.

In either case, the only difference between user and supervisor mode is that user mode termination handlers are not called if a fatal bugcheck is issued from supervisor mode.

If the bugcheck is not fatal, the exception (the initial path into the bug-check code) is dismissed, and execution continues with the instruction following the BUG_CHECK macro.

The SYSBOOT parameter BUGCHECKFATAL has no effect on bugchecks issued from user or supervisor mode. The severity field in the bugcheck code is used to determine whether a given bugcheck is fatal. User and supervisor mode bugchecks affect only the current process.

8.2.3   Bugchecks from Executive and Kernel Modes

VAX/VMS generates executive and kernel mode bugchecks.

If an executive or kernel mode bugcheck is not fatal and the SYSBOOT parameter BUGCHECKFATAL is zero, EXE$BUG_CHECK proceeds as it does for nonfatal bugchecks for the outer two access modes. A message is sent to the error logger and the exception is dismissed, passing control back to the caller at the instruction following the BUG_CHECK macro.

Typically, execution continues with no further effects. However, the routine that detects the error and generates the bugcheck can take further action. One example of such a routine is the last chance handler for executive mode exceptions. It generates the nonfatal SSRVEXCEPT (unexpected system service exception) bugcheck. On the presumption that process data structures are inconsistent, it then requests the Exit ($EXIT) system service. Exiting from executive mode results in process deletion.

If the bugcheck is fatal or BUGCHECKFATAL is 1, EXE$BUG_CHECK aborts all normal system operation, records information about the fatal bug-check in the dump file, and reboots. If BUGCHECKFATAL is 1, any executive or kernel mode bugcheck is treated as fatal, independent of the severity code in the low-order bits of the bugcheck code. By default, BUGCHECK-FATAL is zero, which means that a nonfatal inner access mode bugcheck does not cause the system to crash.

The fatal bugcheck routine and all the bugcheck codes and associated text are not resident. They are stored in the system image SYS.EXE and must be read into memory, overlaying part of the read-only executive in memory. EXE$BUG_CHECK cannot rely on the normal I/O mechanisms. Instead, it calls the bootstrap system device driver for all its I/O (reading the fatal bug-check code and writing the dump file). The bootstrap system device driver is

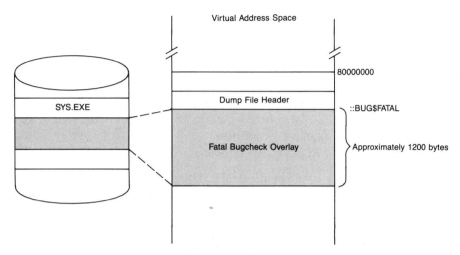

Figure 8-2   Fatal Bugcheck Overlay

the one used by the initialization programs VMB and SYSBOOT (see Chapter 24) and loaded into nonpaged pool by INIT (see Chapter 25). EXE$BUG_CHECK cannot invoke the file system to look up SYS.EXE or the dump file; instead, it uses information about their locations which is recorded and checksummed at system initialization.

Before reading the fatal bugcheck overlay, EXE$BUG_CHECK takes the following steps:

1. It validates the checksum of the boot control block, the data structure containing the locations of the bugcheck overlay and the dump file.
2. EXE$BUG_CHECK invokes SCS$SHUTDOWN (in [SYSLOA]SCSLOA) to shut down any SCS circuits.
3. It invokes EXE$SHUTDWNADP and EXE$INIBOOTADP to shut down all adapters and initialize the one containing the system device. These routines are in the CPU-specific module [SYSLOA]ERRSUBxxx, where xxx identifies the CPU type (see Appendix G).
4. It invokes INI$WRITABLE to change the protection of the pages containing the read-only executive so that they can be overwritten by the bugcheck overlay.
5. It calls a device initialization routine in the bootstrap driver.

The fatal bugcheck code and data are read into system space on top of a read-only portion of the executive. Global label BUG$FATAL defines the beginning of the buffer into which the bugcheck code and data will be read. This label immediately precedes the blank program section (named ". BLANK ."). Its value can be determined by reading the system map. The bugcheck overlay is shown in Figure 8-2.

The code and data read into memory include the following:

- The fatal bugcheck service routine
- A template for the message that is typed on the console terminal
- Some primitive console terminal output routines
- The text of all bugcheck messages

A header block for the dump file is constructed in the 512 bytes immediately preceding the label BUG$FATAL. This area overwrites more read-only portions of the nonpaged executive.

There are two implications of overlaying existing code:

- The routines overlaid by the fatal bugcheck code, data, and dump header are not available for use by the bugcheck code. This requirement is most important in deciding how the nonpaged executive is laid out.
- Portions of the dump may look strange when inspected by the System Dump Analyzer (SDA) Utility. For example, it is impossible to determine if overlaid code is corrupted because SDA can only display the bugcheck code, data, and dump header instead of the original instructions and read-only data.

The contents of the dump file header block are listed in Table 8-1. Note that the error log entry associated with this bugcheck is written into the header to avoid loss of information in case the error log allocation buffers are full when the bugcheck occurs. Table 8-2 shows the layout of the error log message. The error log entry for a nonfatal bugcheck contains the same information as the entry for a fatal bugcheck, except for the 35 longwords set aside

Table 8-1   Contents of the Dump File Header Block

Description	Size
Last error log sequence number (unused)	Longword
Dump file flag (low bit set if dump file analyzed)	Word
Dump file version (contains a 2)	Word
Contents of SBR, SLR, KSP, ESP, SSP, USP, ISP	7 longwords
Quadword memory descriptors for eight memory controllers	8 quadwords
Each quadword is broken down as follows:	
• Page count	3 bytes
• TR number for this controller	Byte
• Base PFN for this controller	Longword
System version number	Longword
One's complement of previous longword	Longword
Error log entry for crash/restart (see Table 8-2)	132 words

Table 8-2   Contents of Error Message Buffer for Crash/Restart Entry

Description	Size
Error message buffer header	Longword
Size in bytes of buffer	Word
Allocation buffer number	Byte
Error message valid indicator	Byte
System ID	Longword
Entry type (contains EMB$K_CR = 37_{10})	Word
System time when crash occurred (from EXE$GQ_SYSTIME)	Quadword
Error log sequence number (low-order word of ERL$GL_SEQUENCE)	Word
Contents of KSP, ESP, SSP, USP, ISP	5 longwords
Contents of R0 to R11, AP, FP, SP, PC, PSL	17 longwords
Contents of P0BR, P0LR, P1BR, P1LR, SBR, SLR, PCBB, SCBB, ASTLVL, SISR, ICCS	11 longwords
Contents of CPU-specific registers	24 longwords
Bugcheck code	Longword
Process ID of current process	Longword
Name of current process	16 bytes

for architectural and CPU-specific processor registers. EXE$BUG_CHECK invokes the CPU-specific routine EXE$DUMPCPUREG to copy CPU-specific processor registers to the error log entry. This routine is in module [SYSLOA]LIOSUB*xxx*, where *xxx* identifies the CPU type (see Appendix G).

The crash dump error log entry will be written into one of the error log allocation buffers by SYSINIT (see Chapter 25) when the rest of the error log messages (blocks 2 and 3 in the dump file) are put back into the error log allocation buffers. (If there is no room in the error log allocation buffers, the bugcheck entry will never be written to the error log file, although the entry is preserved in the dump file.)

EXE$BUG_CHECK writes some information describing the bugcheck to the console terminal. This information includes the contents of general registers, stacks relevant to the crash, contents of processor internal registers, and a summary of the reason for the bugcheck. This output occurs before the dump file is written and should not be interrupted by halting the VAX processor from the console terminal. Such an interruption would prevent the dump file from being written.

Next, EXE$BUG_CHECK writes the dump header and the contents of the two error log allocation buffers to the system dump file. Then, if the SYS-

BOOT parameter DUMPBUG is 1, EXE$BUG_CHECK writes the contents of physical memory to the system dump file. The system dump file is described in the next section.

The last step in EXE$BUG_CHECK either loops or reboots the system. If the SYSBOOT parameter BUGREBOOT is zero, EXE$BUG_CHECK writes a message on the console terminal and loops at IPL 31, waiting for a command to be entered at the console terminal. If BUGREBOOT is 1, its default value, EXE$BUG_CHECK reboots the system by invoking the routine CON$-SENDCONSCMD (in module OPDRIVER) to send a special boot command to the console and halt. When the HALT instruction is executed, the console microcode gains control and processes the boot command.

8.2.4 System Dump File

The most important operation of the bugcheck routine is to write the contents of the error log allocation buffers and physical memory to the dump file. The dump file can be examined using SDA to determine the reason for the crash. SDA is invoked by the DCL command ANALYZE/CRASH_DUMP. The dump file contains three distinct pieces:

1. The dump header (see Table 8-1) is written to the first block in the file.
2. The two error log allocation buffers are written to the next two blocks.
3. The rest of the dump file is filled with the current contents of physical memory. EXE$BUG_CHECK uses the memory descriptors in the restart parameter block (RPB) constructed by VMB (see Chapter 24) to provide an accurate layout of physical address space. If MA780 shared memory is present on the system, its contents are also written to the dump file.

The size of the dump file must be four blocks larger than the number of physical pages in the system. (The first three blocks are used as previously described; there is no current use of the fourth block.) To ensure that a crash dump can be analyzed with SDA, the dump file must be large enough. If a dump file is too small, only the physical pages that fit into the undercon-figured dump file will be written. In a typical VMS configuration, the most crucial contents of physical memory, the system page table, are located at the largest physical addresses (see Chapter 24) and will not be written, making a partial dump useless. That is, SDA cannot analyze a dump file that does not contain the system page table.

8.3 MACHINE CHECK MECHANISM

A machine check is an exception that is reported when the CPU detects an internal error during the attempted execution of an instruction. Machine check errors are CPU-specific; possible types of machine checks include memory cache parity error, translation buffer parity error, and CPU timeout.

Many, but not all, machine checks are caused by some sort of hardware condition. Some hardware conditions are transient; others are persistent.

During a machine check exception, the CPU logs information, called the machine check frame, on the interrupt stack. The machine check frame identifies the type of machine check and includes the contents of relevant CPU registers. Its exact form varies on each type of CPU. Consult CPU-specific literature for information on the form of the machine check frame and the layout of the associated CPU registers.

The exception is dispatched through the SCB to a machine check exception service routine. The exception is serviced on the interrupt stack at IPL 31. The actual machine check exception service routine is contained in the CPU-specific module SYSLOA*xxx* and is loaded during system initialization. The module name has the form MCHECK*xxx*. In both names, *xxx* indicates the CPU type (see Appendix G).

The actual processing of a machine check exception is CPU specific. This section contains an overview of machine check handling. VMS determines from the machine check frame what type of machine check occurred. Although VMS treats each type of machine check somewhat differently, its general response is to log an error and increment the global counter EXE$GL_MCHKERRS. The DCL command SHOW ERROR displays the contents of this counter as CPU errors.

VMS then determines whether the error is recoverable. Recoverability depends on whether the machine check exception was a fault or an abort. The distinction between them is whether register and memory operands have been restored to their state prior to the attempted execution of the instruction. In the case of a fault, they have been restored. In the case of an abort, they cannot be restored, and it is therefore impossible to restart the instruction. Recoverability also depends on whether the instruction is a resumable one. The details of recoverability are CPU-specific.

The basic philosophy of the machine check service routine is to keep as much of the system running as possible. How serious a particular machine check is depends upon whether it is recoverable and the access mode in which the machine check occurred. If the machine check is recoverable, the service routine removes the machine check frame from the interrupt stack and executes an REI to dismiss the exception and return control to the instruction which incurred the exception.

If the machine check is not recoverable, the action taken by the machine check handler depends on the access mode in which the machine check occurred. If the previous mode was supervisor or user, a machine check exception is reported to that access mode. (Unless the process has declared a condition handler for this type of exception, this step results in image exit.) If the previous mode was executive or kernel, the machine check service routine generates the fatal bugcheck MACHINECHK.

8.3.1   **Machine Check Recovery Blocks**

VAX/VMS provides the capability for a block of kernel mode code to protect itself from machine checks while the protected code is executing. For example, this feature is used if an interrupt is generated from a previously unconfigured adapter. If the code that read the configuration register were not protected and the interrupt were spurious, then the configuration register would not exist and the reference to a nonexistent I/O space address would crash the system.

There are several restrictions on the protected code:

- It must be executing in kernel mode.
- The stack cannot be used across the entry into or the exit out of the protected code block. This restriction exists because a coroutine mechanism is used to pass control between the protected block and the VMS routines that establish the protected code.
- VMS elevates IPL to 31, so a limited number of instructions should be included in the block.
- R0 is destroyed by the mechanism.

The basis for the recovery mechanism is several routines in the module EXCEPTION. Most of them are invoked indirectly through macros. Several macros are provided in the macro library SYS$LIBRARY:LIB.MLB. The following macro invokes EXE$MCHK_PRTCT to define the beginning of the block:

```
$PRTCTINI       LABEL,MASK
```

The label argument is identical to the label argument associated with the following macro which defines the end of the block:

```
$PRTCTEND       LABEL
```

If no error occurred while the protected code was executing, R0 contains the success status SS$_NORMAL. Otherwise, R0 contains the error status SS$_MCHECK.

The mask argument allows the block of code to protect itself from different classes of errors. The following list describes the specific types of protection that are defined by the $MCHKDEF macro:

MCHK$M_LOG	Inhibit error logging for the error
MCHK$M_MCK	Protect against machine checks
MCHK$M_NEXM	Protect against nonexistent memory
MCHK$M_UBA	Protect against UNIBUS adapter error interrupts

There are two other features used by the VMS operating system that are a part of this protection mechanism. Invoking the following macro enables kernel mode code to determine whether a recovery block is in effect and take action accordingly:

```
$PRTCTEST       ADDRESS,MASK
```

This macro invokes the routine EXE$MCHK_TEST, which returns status in R0. The low bit set indicates that a recovery block is in effect and that the specified mask is being used. This routine is typically used to determine whether a machine check should be logged in the error log.

There is another related routine in EXCEPTION, one which is invoked directly. EXE$MCHK_BUGCHK is invoked from a machine check exception service routine to determine whether a recovery block is in effect. If no recovery block is in effect, the routine returns, usually to code which generates a bugcheck. If a recovery block is in effect, the routine returns control to the end of the protected block with R0 containing an error code of SS$_MCHECK.

9 System Service Dispatching

Between the idea
And the reality
Between the motion
And the act
Falls the Shadow.

T.S. Eliot, *The Hollow Men*

Many of the operations that VAX/VMS performs on behalf of the user are implemented as procedures called system services. Most of these procedures are linked as part of the executive and reside in system space; others are contained in privileged shareable images.

System services typically execute in kernel or executive access mode so that they can read or write data structures protected from access by less privileged access modes. Some services are invoked directly by application programs. Others are called on behalf of the user by components such as RMS. This chapter describes how control is passed from a user program to the procedures that execute service-specific code.

9.1 SYSTEM SERVICE VECTORS

A system service vector is a system global procedure name called to invoke a particular service. A system service vector contains a small procedure which executes in the mode of the caller and serves as a bridge between the caller and the actual procedure(s) which implement the service request. The actual procedure may be part of SYS.EXE or RMS.EXE and may execute in an inner access mode. The global entry point name of a system service vector is SYS$*service*, as compared to EXE$*service* or RMS$*service*, the usual global name of the procedure in SYS.EXE or RMS.EXE that performs the actual work of the system service.

9.1.1 Location of System Service Vectors

The value of a system service vector, that is, its address, is constant for all versions of VMS, so that existing user programs will not have to be relinked for a new version of VMS. Prior to VAX/VMS Version 3, system service vectors were defined as the lowest pages of system address space, beginning at location 80000000. In VAX/VMS Version 3 and subsequent versions, system service vectors are also defined at P1 space addresses beginning at 7FFEDE00.

The P1 space definitions allow system services to be intercepted on a per-process basis.

The linker, by default, resolves a system service vector global to its P1 space value. The system space and P1 space addresses for the system service vectors access the same physical pages. That is, the physical pages containing the system service vectors are mapped both in system space and in the P1 space of each process.

The VAX/VMS Version 4 system services occupy five pages of memory, with space reserved for expansion up to 16 pages. As new services are added to future releases of VAX/VMS, the vector area will grow to accommodate new entry points.

9.1.2   Contents of System Service Vectors

Each service entry point contains at least eight bytes of code and data called a system service vector. Many vectors consist solely of a global entry point named SYS$*service*, a register save mask, a single instruction that transfers control eventually to a service-specific procedure in the executive, and an instruction (usually a RET) that passes control back to the caller. Other vectors called "composite" vectors transfer control to multiple service-specific procedures.

Most of the system services execute in kernel mode; their system service vectors contain a CHMK instruction. A few system services and all of the RMS services contain a CHME instruction. Some services, such as the text formatting services, execute in the access mode of the caller and dispatch directly to the service-specific code in the VMS operating system with a JMP instruction. The three sets of instructions found in simple system service vectors are illustrated below. Table 9-1 lists the VMS system services that use each of the three methods of initial dispatch illustrated below.

Vectors for system services that change mode to kernel contain the following code:

```
SYS$service::                   ;Entry point for services that
                                ; execute in kernel mode
        .WORD   entry-mask      ;This mask is identical to the
                                ; mask found at location
                                ; EXE$service
        CHMK    I`#service-specific-code
        RET                     ;Return to caller
        .BLKB   1               ;Spare byte to make vector
                                ; eight bytes long
```

Vectors for system services that change mode to executive contain the following code:

```
SYS$service::                     ;Entry point for services that
                                  ; execute in executive mode
       .WORD    entry-mask        ;This mask is identical to the
                                  ; mask found at location
                                  ; EXE$service
       CHME     I^#service-specific-code
       RET                        ;Return to caller
       .BLKB    1                 ;Spare byte to make vector
                                  ; eight bytes long
```

Vectors for system services that do not change mode contain the following code:

```
SYS$service::                     ;Entry point for services that
                                  ; execute in the access mode
                                  ; of the caller
       .WORD    entry-mask        ;This mask is identical to the
                                  ; mask found at location
                                  ; EXE$service
       JMP      @#EXE$service + 2 ;Transfer control to
                                  ; first instruction after the
                                  ; entry mask at EXE$service
```

Some system service vectors are "composite." They include either multiple CHMx instructions or calls to other system service vectors to ensure synchronization of the service request. Many RMS services and all of the "synchronous" system services are composite. A synchronous system service is one which guarantees completion of its normally asynchronous system service counterpart.

Synchronous system service vectors first invoke the asynchronous system service, which returns to its invoker when the request is initiated, and then wait for completion of the asynchronous request. A synchronous system service is named for the asynchronous service it invokes; a trailing "W" in the name of the synchronous services distinguishes the two, $QIO and $QIOW, for example. The asynchronous service procedure clears the event flag and status block (I/O status block or lock status block) associated with the request. The synchronous system service vector code uses a combination of event flag and status block to test for request completion, placing the process into event flag wait if the request has not completed.

This combination of waiting for an event flag and testing a status block is new with VAX/VMS Version 4, replacing the simple wait for event flag used by earlier versions. The newer mechanism prevents a premature return to the synchronous service caller as the result of concurrent uses of the same event flag. (Note, however, that if the caller omits an optional status block, the newer mechanism reverts to being a simple wait for event flag.) The new mechanism is invoked explicitly as the $SYNCH system service and implicitly as part of each synchronous system service.

An example synchronous system service vector, SYS$QIOW, follows. Note that its entry mask is the logical OR of the masks of all service procedures to which this composite vector dispatches. The actual synchronization code is described in Section 9.3.7. Table 9-1 lists the synchronous system service vectors.

```
SYS$QIOW::
        .WORD   <QIO_MASK!WAITFR_MASK!CLREF_MASK!SETEF_MASK>
        CHMK    #QIO
        BLBC    RO,QIOW_RET     ;Don't wait if error queueing
                                ; request
        PUSHL   QIO$_IOSB(AP)   ;Fetch IOSB address if
                                ; specified
        BRW     QIO_ENQ_SYNCH   ;Use common QIOW, ENQW synch
                                ; code

           .

           .

           .
QIOW_RET:
        RET                     ;Return to caller of service
```

An RMS composite vector branches to RMS synchronization code which conditionally stalls the process until all I/O associated with its request is done. An example RMS composite vector, SYS$FIND, is illustrated below. The actual synchronization code is described in Section 9.3.6. Table 9-1 lists the RMS services which branch to synchronization code and those which do not.

```
SYS$FIND::
        .WORD   ^M<R2,R3,R4,R5,R6,R7,R8,R9,R10,R11>
        CHME    #FIND
        BRB     RMS_CHECK_STALL
```

9.2   CHANGE MODE INSTRUCTIONS

Executing a change mode instruction generates an exception. Exception processing VAX microcode alters access mode and pushes the PSL, the PC of the next instruction, and the code that is the single operand of the change mode instruction onto the stack indicated in the instruction. (As pointed out in Chapter 4, the actual access mode is the outermost of the access mode indicated by the instruction and the current access mode contained in the PSL.)

Table 9-1　System Services and RMS Services That Use Each Form of System Service Vector

The following services execute initially in kernel mode.

$ADJSTK	$CREMBX	$DISMOU	$MGBLSC	$SETPRT
$ADJWSL	$CREPRC	$DLCEFC	$MTACCESS	$SETPRV
$ALLOC	$CRETVA	$ENQ	$PURGWS	$SETRWM
$ASCEFC	$CRMPSC	$ERAPAT	$QIO	$SETSFM
$ASSIGN	$DACEFC	$EXIT	$READEF	$SETSSF
$BRKTHRU	$DALLOC	$EXPREG	$RESUME	$SETSTK
$CANCEL	$DASSGN	$FORCEX	$RUNDWN	$SETSWM
$CANEXH	$DCLAST	$GETCHN[1]	$SCHDWK	$SNDERR
$CANTIM	$DCLCMH	$GETDEV[1]	$SETAST	$SUSPND
$CANWAK	$DCLEXH	$GETDVI	$SETEF	$TRNLNM
$CHKPRO	$DELLNM	$GETJPI	$SETEXV	$ULKPAG
$CLRAST	$DELMBX	$GETLKI	$SETIME	$ULWSET
$CLREF	$DELPRC	$GETPTI	$SETIMR	$UPDSEC
$CMKRNL	$DELTVA	$GETSYI	$SETPFM	$WAITFR
$CNTREG	$DEQ	$HIBER	$SETPRA	$WAKE
$CRELNM	$DERLMB	$LCKPAG	$SETPRI	$WFLAND
$CRELNT	$DGBLSC	$LKWSET	$SETPRN	$WFLOR

The following system services execute initially in executive mode.

$ADD_HOLDER	$CREATE_RDB	$GETTIM	$NUMTIM	$SNDJBC
$ADD_IDENT	$FIND_HELD	$GETUAI	$PARSE_ACL	$SNDOPR
$ASCTOID	$FIND_HOLDER	$IDTOASC	$REM_HOLDER	$SNDSMB[1]
$CHANGE_ACL	$FINISH_RDB	$IMGACT	$REM_IDENT	
$CHECK_ACCESS	$FORMAT_ACL	$MOD_HOLDER	$SETUAI	
$CMEXEC	$GETQUI	$MOD_IDENT	$SNDACC[1]	

Table 9-1   System Services and RMS Services That Use Each Form of System Service Vector (continued)

The following system services execute initially in the mode of the caller. Several of them change to a more privileged mode during their execution. Unless otherwise noted, each service can be called from any access mode.

$ASCTIM	$DELLOG[1]	$GETMSG[2]	$IMGSTA[3]	$REVOKID[2]
$BINTIM	$EXCMSG[2]	$GRANTID[2]	$MOUNT[2]	$TRNLOG[1]
$BRDCST[1]	$FAO	$IMGFIX	$PUTMSG[3]	$UNWIND
$CRELOG[1]	$FAOL			

The following RMS services execute in executive mode and branch to a synchronization routine before returning to the caller.

$CLOSE	$ENTER	$GET	$READ	$SPACE
$CONNECT	$ERASE	$MODIFY	$RELEASE	$TRUNCATE
$CREATE	$EXTEND	$NXTVOL	$REMOVE	$UPDATE
$DELETE	$FIND	$OPEN	$RENAME	$WAIT
$DISCONNECT	$FLUSH	$PARSE	$REWIND	$WRITE
$DISPLAY	$FREE	$PUT	$SEARCH	

The following RMS services execute in executive mode. The vectors for these RMS services contain RET instructions rather than a branch to an RMS synchronization routine.

$FILESCAN	$RMSRUNDWN	$SETDDIR	$SETDFPROT	$SSVEXC

The following synchronous system services use composite vectors. Unless otherwise noted, each service executes initially in kernel mode.

$BRKTHRUW	$GETJPIW	$GETQUIW[4]	$QIOW	$SYNCH[5]
$ENQW	$GETLKIW	$GETSYIW	$SNDJBCW[4]	$UPDSECW
$GETDVIW				

[1]This service has been superseded.
[2]This system service can be called only from executive and less privileged access modes.
[3]This system service can be called only from supervisor and user mode.
[4]This service executes initially in executive mode.
[5]This service executes initially in the caller's mode.

For example, the execution of a

```
CHME    #5
```

instruction will push a PSL, the PC of the instruction following the CHME instruction, and a 5 onto the executive stack. Control is then passed to the exception service routine whose address is located in the appropriate entry in the system control block (SCB).

During system initialization, VAX/VMS fills in the SCB entries for CHMK and CHME with the addresses of change mode dispatchers that pass control to the procedures that perform service-specific code. These dispatchers are EXE$CMODKRNL, for CHMK exceptions, and EXE$CMODEXEC, for CHME exceptions. The action of these two dispatchers is discussed in the next section.

The SCB entries for CHMS and CHMU contain the addresses EXE$-CMODSUPR and EXE$CMODUSER. These two exceptions are treated much like any other which VMS passes to a user-declared condition handler. See Chapter 4 for more information.

9.3 CHANGE MODE DISPATCHING IN THE VMS EXECUTIVE

The change mode dispatcher that receives control from the CHMK or CHME instruction in the system service vector must dispatch to the procedure indicated by the code that is found on the top of the stack. In addition, because the service routines are written as procedures, the dispatcher must construct a call frame on the stack. Building the call frame could be accomplished by using a CALLx instruction and a dispatch table of service entry points.

However, the call frame that must be built is identical for each service. In addition, the registers that the service-specific procedure will modify have already been saved because the register save mask in the vector area (at global location SYS$*service*) is the same as the register save mask at location EXE$*service*. So the dispatcher avoids the overhead of the general purpose CALLx instruction and builds its call frame by hand.

Further speed improvement is achieved in this commonly executed code path by overlapping memory write operations (building the call frame) with register-to-register operations and instruction stream references. The actual dispatch to the service-specific procedure is then accomplished with a CASEW instruction that uses the CHMx code as its index into the case table. Figure 9-1 illustrates the control flow from the user program all the way to the service-specific procedure. This flow is shown for both kernel and executive access modes. Figure 9-2 shows the corresponding flow for those services that do not change mode.

3.1   **Operation of the Change Mode Dispatcher**

The operations of the change mode dispatchers are almost identical for kernel and executive modes. This section discusses the common points of the dispatchers for kernel and executive modes. The next sections point out the differences between the dispatchers for the two access modes.

The first instruction of the dispatcher pops the exception code, unique for each service, from the stack into R0. In both the kernel mode dispatcher and the executive mode dispatcher, the call frame is built on the stack by the following four instructions:

```
PUSHAB  B^SRVEXIT
PUSHL   FP
PUSHL   AP
CLRQ    -(SP)
```

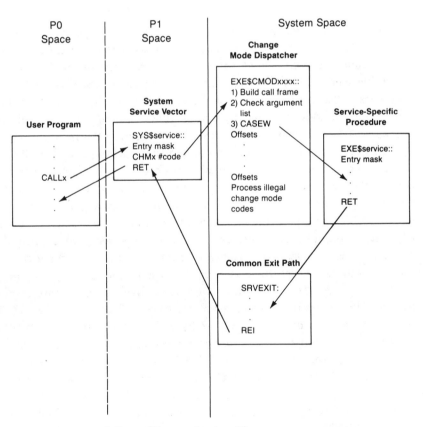

Figure 9-1   Control Flow of System Services That Change Mode

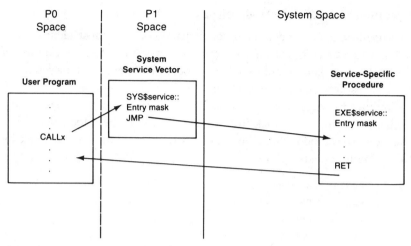

Figure 9-2 Control Flow of System Services That Do
Not Change Mode

While the call frame is being built, two checks are performed on the argument list. The number of arguments actually passed (found in the first byte of the argument list) is compared to a service-specific entry in a prebuilt table to determine whether the required number of arguments for this service have been passed. Read accessibility of the argument list is checked (with the PROBER instruction generated by the IFNORD macro). If either of these checks fails, the error processing described in Section 9.4 is performed.

Finally, a CASEW instruction is executed, using the unique code in R0 as an index into the case table. The case table has been set up at assembly time to contain the addresses of the first instruction of each service-specific routine. Because each service is written as a procedure with a global entry point named EXE$*service* pointing to a register save mask, the case table contains addresses of the form EXE$*service* + 2. If control is passed to the end of the case table, then a CHMx instruction was executed with an improper code and the error processing described in Section 9.4 is performed.

There are several services which are not reachable through case displacements. The maximum displacement of a CASEx instruction is 32,767. The services which are more than 32,767 bytes from the case table (and those which are close to that limit) must be reached more indirectly. A case table entry for such a service points to an EXE$*service* entry point which is local to the CMODSSDSP module. The EXE$*service* entry point contains a JMP to the real procedure, whose global entry point name is EXE$$*service*.

Example 9-1 compares the code for the two dispatchers, copied from the module CMODSSDSP. The entries containing the string "* * * * * *" indicate places where the change mode dispatchers differ.

The instructions are not listed in exactly the same order that they appear in the source module. Rather, the instructions are shown in the order that they are found when all the PSECTs have been sorted out at link time.

Example 9-2 lists the error routines to which the change mode dispatchers branch. These routines are described in Section 9.4.

Example 9-1 Change Mode Dispatchers

```
Change Mode to Kernel Dispatcher       Change Mode to Executive Dispatcher
EXE$CMODKRNL::                          EXE$CMODEXEC::
        POPL    R0                              POPL    R0
        BEQL    ASTEXIT                         ******
        PUSHAB  B^SRVEXIT                       PUSHAB  B^SRVEXIT
        MOVZBL  R0,R1                           MOVZBL  R0,R1
        PUSHL   FP                              PUSHL   FP
        MOVZBL  W^SYS$GB_KRNLARG[R1],R1         MOVZBL  W^B_EXECNARG[R1],R1
        PUSHL   AP                              PUSHL   AP
        MOVAL   @#4[R1],FP                      MOVAL   @#4[R1],FP
        CLRQ    -(SP)                           CLRQ    -(SP)
        IFNORD  FP,(AP),ACCVIO                  IFNORD  FP,(AP),EXACCVIO
                prober  #0,fp,(ap)                      prober  #0,fp,(ap)
                beql    accvio                          beql    exaccvio
        MOVL    SP,FP                           MOVL    SP,FP
        CMPB    (AP),R1                         CMPB    (AP),R1
        BLSSU   KINSARG                         BLSSU   EXINSARG
KERDSP:                                 EXEDSP:
        MOVL    G^SCH$GL_CURPCB,R4              ******
        CASEW   R0,#1,#KCASMAX                  CASEW   R0,#0,S^ECASMAX
          .                                       .
          .                                       .
          .                                       .


        offset to EXE$service + 2               offset to EXE$service + 2
          .                                       .
          .                                       .
                                                  .
        ******                                  JSB     @CTL$GL_RMSBASE
          .                                       .
          .                                       .
                                                  .
        check inhibit bits                      check inhibit bits
```

(continued)

Example 9-1   Change Mode Dispatchers *(continued)*

```
              .                                              .
              .                                              .
              .                                              .
         MOVL    @#CTL$GL_USRCHMK,R1           MOVL    @#CTL$GL_USRCHME,R1
         BEQL    10$                           BEQL    10$
         JSB     (R1)                          JSB     (R1)
10$:     MOVL    L^EXE$GL_USRCHMK,R1   10$:    MOVL    L^EXE$GL_USRCHME,R1
         BEQL    20$                           BEQL    20$
         JSB     (R1)                          JSB     (R1)
20$:     NOP                          20$:    BRW     ILLSER
         NOP
ILLSER:  MOVZWL  #SS$_ILLSER,R0
         RET
```

Example 9-2   Change Mode Dispatcher Error Routines

```
EXACCVIO:                           ;From EXE$CMODEXEC
         MOVL    SP,FP              ;Point FP to call frame
                                    ; so that RET works
         CMPW    R0,#RCASCTR        ;Only report ACCVIO for RMS
                                    ; and built-in functions
         BGEQU   EXEDSP             ;Otherwise, get back in line
         BRW     ACCVIO_RET         ;
EXINSARG:
         CMPW    R0,#RCASCTR        ;Only report INSARG for RMS
                                    ; and built-in functions
         BGEQU   EXEDSP             ;Otherwise, get back in line
         BRW     INSARG             ;Report error to caller
ACCVIO:
         MOVL    SP,FP              ;Set FP so that RET works
         CMPW    R0,#KCASCTR        ;Is this a recognized code?
         BGEQU   KERDSP             ;No. Get back in line
ACCVIO_RET:
         MOVZWL  #SS$_ACCVIO,R0
         RET
KINSARG:
         CMPW    R0,#KCASCTR        ;Is this a recognized code?
         BGEQU   KERDSP             ;No - not necessarily INSARG
INSARG:
         MOVZWL  #SS$_INSFARG,R0 ;Insufficient number of arguments
                                    ; error
         RET
```

The routine in Example 9-3 is the common exit path for all system service and RMS service calls. Its usual action is to execute an REI instruction to return control to the service vector. Alternatively, this routine reports a SS$_SSFAIL exception.

Example 9-3   Change Mode Dispatcher Common Exit Path

```
SRVEXIT:
        BLBC    R0,SSFAIL
SRVREI:
        REI
SSFAIL:
        BITL    #7,R0                   ;Check for mere warning
        BEQL    SRVREI                  ;If so, do not generate
                                        ; exception
        BRW     SSFAILMAIN              ;Go to SSFAIL logic
SSFAILMAIN:
        MOVL    G^CTL$GL_PCB,R1
        TSTW    PCB$W_MTXCNT(R1)        ;Check for ownership
                                        ; of a mutex
        BNEQ    20$                     ;If so, BUGCHECK
        EXTZV   #PSL$V_CURMOD,#PSL$S_CURMOD,4(SP),-(SP)
        ADDL    #PCB$V_SSFEXC,(SP)      ;Are system service
                                        ; failure exceptions enabled
                                        ; for caller's access mode?
        BBC     (SP)+,PCB$L_STS(R1),10$ ;If not, dismiss the
                                        ; exception

        MOVPSL  -(SP)                   ;Get current PSL
        EXTZV   #PSL$V_CURMOD,#PSL$S_CURMOD,(SP),(SP)+
                                        ;If the current mode
                                        ; is kernel
        BNEQ    5$                      ;
        SETIPL  #0                      ;IPL must be lowered to 0
5$:     JMP     EXE$SSFAIL              ;Pass control to the
                                        ; general exception
                                        ; dispatcher
10$:    REI                             ;Return from service with
                                        ; error status
20$:    EXTV    #PSL$V_IPL,#PSL$S_IPL,-4(SP),-(SP)
        CMPL    (SP)+,#IPL$_ASTDEL      ;Test if at elevated IPL
        BGEQ    10$                     ;If yes, do not bugcheck
        BUG_CHECK   MTXCNTNONZ,FATAL
```

9.3.2 **Change-Mode-to-Kernel Dispatcher**

There are two steps performed by the change-mode-to-kernel dispatcher, EXE$CMODKRNL, that are not performed by the change-mode-to-executive dispatcher. Before control is passed to those services that execute in kernel mode, the address of the PCB for the current process (found at global location SCH$GL_CURPCB) is placed into R4. The second difference is that

```
CHMK    #0
```

is a special entry path into kernel mode for the $CLRAST service. If the CHMK code removed from the stack is a zero, control is passed to a routine called ASTEXIT. The action of this routine is described in Chapter 7.

9.3.3 **Change-Mode-to-Executive Dispatcher**

The change-mode-to-executive dispatcher, EXE$CMODEXEC, performs one step unique to executive mode. If the CHME code is not a recognized system service, the CASEW instruction passes control to the end of the case table. At that point, EXE$CMODEXEC transfers control to the RMS dispatcher to determine whether this might be a valid RMS service request before dropping into the error processing described in Section 9.4.

9.3.4 **RMS Dispatching**

The RMS dispatcher, illustrated in Figure 9-3, consists of two instructions. The CASEW instruction dispatches to an RMS service-specific procedure for a legitimate RMS service code. The RMS service-specific procedure exits with a RET back to SRVEXIT. The RSB instruction in the RMS dispatcher following the CASEW instruction passes control back to EXE$CMODEXEC for normal error processing if the CHME code is out of range.

9.3.5 **Return Path for System Services**

When the service-specific procedure has completed its operation, it places a status code in R0 and executes a RET instruction. In the case of a mode of caller system service, dispatched via a JMP, the RET returns control to the caller of the service. In the case of an executive or kernel mode system service, the RET returns control to the code at label SRVEXIT (shown in Example 9-3), because this address was put into the saved PC area of the call frame built by the change mode dispatcher.

The routine SRVEXIT first checks whether an error occurred. If no error occurred or if the error was merely a warning (R0<2:0>=0), the CHMx exception is dismissed with an REI instruction that passes control to the instruction following the CHMx in the system service vector area.

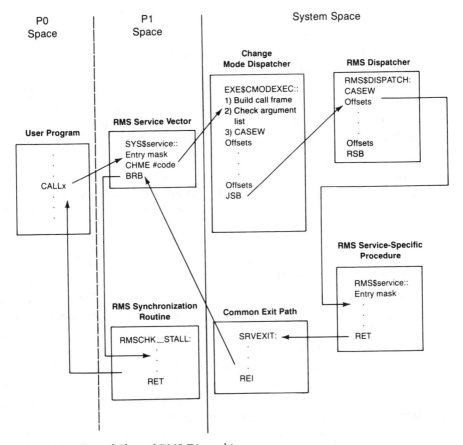

Figure 9-3   Control Flow of RMS Dispatching

If an error or severe error occurred, a check is made to see whether the process owns any mutexes. If the process owns a mutex and is still running at IPL 2 or greater, the CHMx exception is dismissed with an REI instruction, passing control to the instruction following the CHMx in the system service vector. If the process owns a mutex but is running at IPL 0, the system service has not released all of its mutexes on exit but has lowered IPL (an erroneous error path), and a fatal bugcheck is generated. (Chapter 8 describes bugcheck processing and Chapter 2 describes mutexes.)

If the process does not own a mutex and is running in kernel mode, IPL is explicitly lowered to 0. This step is unnecessary unless the process has enabled system service failure exceptions, because the REI instruction that dismisses the CHMK exception will lower IPL. However, if a system service failure exception is to be generated, the exception routines must be entered with IPL set to 0. (A similar check is not needed for executive mode services because elevated IPL requires kernel mode operation.)

If the process has enabled system service exceptions for the calling access mode, control is passed to the exception dispatcher at global label EXE$SSFAIL. The exception that is reported to the caller in the signal array is SS$_SSFAIL. Otherwise, control is passed back to the caller with R0 containing the error status code.

Unless a system service failure is to be signaled, SRVEXIT dismisses the CHMx exception, returning control to the system service vector at the instruction following the CHMx. In most cases, this instruction is a RET, which returns control to the instruction following the CALLx to the system service vector.

However, for most RMS services and the synchronous system services, the system service vector contains code that conditionally stalls the process until its request is complete. The next two sections describe these synchronization methods.

9.3.6 Return Path for RMS Services

The return path for RMS services is slightly more complicated than the return path for system services. The last two bytes of most RMS vectors contain a branch (BRB) to RMS_CHECK_STALL, an RMS synchronization routine (in module CMODSSDSP). RMS_CHECK_STALL checks whether the caller of the RMS service wishes to wait. This is the usual case, but RMS does allow asynchronous I/O operations. The return status code is set to RMS$_STALL by RMS in the usual case, in which the process must wait until the completion of the RMS operation.

If the status code is not RMS$_STALL, then RMS_CHECK_STALL executes a RET, returning control to the caller of the RMS service. If the status code is RMS$_STALL, RMS_CHECK_STALL branches to routine RMSWAIT_IO_DONE.

9.3.6.1 Wait State Associated with RMS Requests. If a stall is indicated, RMSWAIT_IO_DONE places the caller into an event flag wait state, waiting for the event flag associated with the I/O request that RMS has just issued. The crucial point in this implementation is that the caller is waiting at the access mode associated with the original call to RMS and not in executive access mode, thus allowing AST delivery for all access modes at least as privileged as the caller of RMS. (In the usual case where RMS is called from user mode, the access mode of the wait state allows both user and supervisor ASTs as well as executive and kernel ASTs to be delivered while waiting for the RMS operation to complete.)

When the original I/O request completes, RMS gains control first in an executive mode AST that is associated with its $QIO request. If it determines that the original request is complete, it sets final status in the data structure (FAB or RAB) associated with the operation and returns from its AST. The caller now drops through the event flag wait in the RMSWAIT_IO_DONE synchronization routine (because the I/O completion routine set the event flag). The synchronization routine determines that the RMS operation is complete (because the FAB or RAB status field contains nonzero) and executes a RET, passing control back to the point where the initial call to RMS was issued.

If the RMS executive mode AST determines that more I/O is required to complete the original request (such as occurs when reading a large record from a sequential file with small internal buffers or when operating on an indexed file), RMS issues the next $QIO and returns from its AST. Because the previous I/O completion set the associated event flag, the process is now computable. However, the RMS operation is not yet complete. For this reason, RMSWAIT_IO_DONE (executing in the caller's access mode) checks the status field in the RAB or FAB for zero, indicating that RMS has more to do. In this case, the caller is again placed into the LEF state by the RMS synchronization routine. In other words, at a primitive level, the process is placed into a LEF state by RMS one or more times. However, the actual indication that the RMS operation has completed is nonzero contents in the status field of the FAB or RAB.

.3.6.2   **RMS Error Detection.** When the RMS synchronization routine finally decides that RMS has completed its work, it checks the final status. If this status indicates either success or warning, a RET is executed. If either an error or a severe error occurred, a special RMS call ($SSVEXC) is issued. This service simply reports the error status through the normal VMS service exit path (SRVEXIT) that determines whether the process has enabled system service failure exceptions. Because RMS errors are reported through the system service dispatcher, they are treated in exactly the same manner as system service errors.

.3.7   **Return Path for Synchronous Services**

A synchronous system service vector invokes an asynchronous service procedure and tests its return status for successful initiation of the request. If the asynchronous service procedure returns an error, that status is immediately returned to the caller of the synchronous service. If the return status indicates success, the system service vector code branches to one of two synchronization routines (within module CMODSSDSP) which differ only in minor detail and which converge within the SYS$SYNCH composite system service vector.

SYS$SYNCH first tests whether a status block was specified by the caller. For $GETLKIW and $ENQW, the lock status block serves this purpose; in all other cases, the I/O status block is used. If no status block was specified,

SYS$SYNCH executes a

```
CHMK    #WAITFR
```

on the specified event flag, placing the process into event flag wait until the flag is set. When the flag is set, the process is taken out of its wait state, and SYS$SYNCH returns to the caller of the synchronous service. If a status block was specified, SYS$SYNCH executes the following sequence:

1. It tests the status word of the status block. A nonzero status word indicates that the asynchronous service has completed, and SYS$SYNCH returns to the caller of the synchronous service.
2. A zero status word indicates the asynchronous service has not completed, and SYS$SYNCH executes a

```
CHMK    #WAITFR
```

to wait for the specified event flag.
3. When the event flag is set and the process placed into execution, SYS$SYNCH tests the low word of the status block. If it is nonzero, SYS$SYNCH returns to the caller of the synchronous service.
4. If the status word is zero, then the flag has been set spuriously, perhaps by another concurrent use. SYS$SYNCH clears the event flag by executing a

```
CHMK    #CLREF
```

and then proceeds with step 2.

A crucial point in this implementation is that the caller is waiting at the access mode associated with the original synchronous system service call, thus allowing AST delivery for all access modes at least as privileged as the synchronous service call. (In the usual case where a synchronous system service is called from user mode, the access mode of the wait state allows both user and supervisor ASTs, as well as inner access mode ASTs, to be delivered while waiting for the service to complete.)

9.4 DISPATCHING TO PRIVILEGED SHAREABLE IMAGE SYSTEM SERVICES

The VMS operating system does not require that all system services be part of the system or RMS images. A privileged user may write system services as part of a privileged shareable image. Moreover, a number of VMS system services are supplied as privileged shareable images:

- $MOUNT in SYS$SHARE:MOUNTSHR.EXE
- $DISMOU in SYS$SHARE:DISMNTSHR.EXE
- System services relating to system security in SYS$SHARE:SECURE-SHR.EXE and RDBSHR.EXE

Implementing these less frequently used services as privileged shareable images means that they are resident only when explicitly invoked and that they do not contribute to a larger executive image.

The requirements for writing privileged shareable images are described in the *VAX/VMS System Services Reference Manual*. This section describes how control is passed to system services that are part of privileged shareable images.

EXE$CMODKRNL attempts to dispatch to a privileged shareable image whenever a CHMK instruction is executed with a code outside the range of its case table. EXE$CMODEXEC first checks whether RMS recognizes the change mode code before dispatching to a privileged shareable image. VMS system services in privileged shareable images have large positive codes (for example, 16527). The VAX architecture reserves CHMx instructions with negative codes for customer use.

Occasionally, EXE$CMODKRNL and EXE$CMODEXEC spuriously detect an error in the change mode request prior to the CASEW dispatch. They are both optimized for the most common case, dispatching VMS system and RMS services. Each assumes the change mode instruction operand is a positive number less than 255 and uses its low-order byte as an index into the required argument list.

If the argument list does not have the required number of arguments or it is inaccessible, each routine must test its assumption. It compares the entire change mode instruction operand with the maximum valid value for that access mode. Example 9-2 shows these comparisons. If the operand is within the range of valid values, then an appropriate error status is returned to the caller.

If the operand is not within the range, then it may be a request for a system

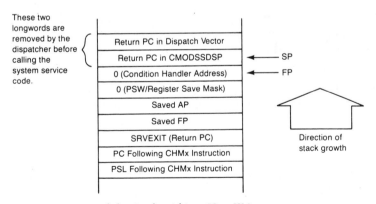

These two longwords are removed by the dispatcher before calling the system service code.

Return PC in Dispatch Vector
Return PC in CMODSSDSP ← SP
0 (Condition Handler Address) ← FP
0 (PSW/Register Save Mask)
Saved AP
Saved FP
SRVEXIT (Return PC)
PC Following CHMx Instruction
PSL Following CHMx Instruction

Direction of stack growth

Figure 9-4 State of the Stack within a User-Written Dispatcher

service in a privileged shareable image. The routine cases, using the entire argument, to reach the out-of-range processing code as shown in Example 9-1.

9.4.1 Per-Process System Service Dispatcher

When a CHMK or CHME instruction is executed with a code that is out of range, the change mode dispatcher attempts to pass control to a privileged shareable image change mode dispatcher. First, a location in P1 space (CTL$GL_USRCHMK or CTL$GL_USRCHME) is checked to see whether a per-process dispatcher exists. Nonzero contents of this location are interpreted as the address of a dispatcher within a privileged shareable image and control is passed to it with the stack as shown in Figure 9-4. The change mode dispatcher assumes that if the per-process dispatcher accepts the change mode code, the service-specific procedure will eventually return to SRVEXIT by executing a RET instruction. If the per-process dispatcher rejects the code, it returns control to the code listed in Section 9.3.1 with an RSB instruction.

9.4.2 Privileged Shareable Images

The usual contents of CTL$GL_USRCHMK and CTL$GL_USRCHME are addresses within the two pages in P1 space set aside by the VMS operating system for user-written system services and image-specific message processing. Kernel mode and executive mode each have one half page (256 bytes) devoted to system service dispatching. The initial content of the first byte of each dispatch area (set up by PROCSTRT) is an RSB instruction. With the dispatch scheme described in the previous section, there is effectively no per-process change mode dispatching.

However, if an image executes that was previously linked with a privileged shareable image (linked with the /PROTECT and /SHAREABLE options and installed with the /PROTECTED and /SHARED options), the image activator replaces the RSB instruction with a JSB to the user-written change mode dispatcher specified as a part of the privileged shareable image (see Figure 9-5). The VMS operating system allows multiple privileged shareable images to be linked into the same executable image. (There is a limit of 42 user-written dispatchers of each type. How these dispatchers are collected into privileged shareable images determines the number of privileged shareable images that can be included in a single executable image.) An RSB instruction follows the last JSB instruction in the dispatch area. The example pictured in Figure 9-5 shows three privileged shareable images.

When the image activator (see Chapter 21) encounters a reference to a privileged shareable image in the executable image it is activating, it maps the

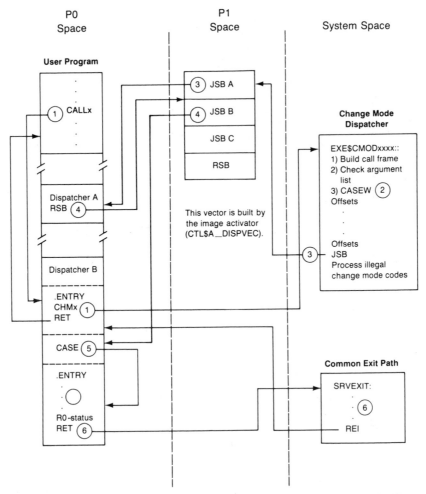

Figure 9-5   Dispatching to System Services in a
Privileged Shareable Image

section(s) containing the user-written system services, using information
stored in a protected image section (a privileged library vector, pictured in
Figure 9-6) to modify the P1 space dispatch area. For example, if a privileged
shareable image contained a change-mode-to-kernel dispatcher, the image
activator would insert a JSB instruction in P1 space that transferred control
to the dispatcher specified by the PLV$L_KERNEL longword in the privi-
leged library vector.

Once the image containing user-written system services is activated, execution proceeds normally until one of the services is invoked. Dispatching
proceeds as follows (see Figure 9-5):

① A CALLx instruction transfers control to a service-specific entry mask in P0

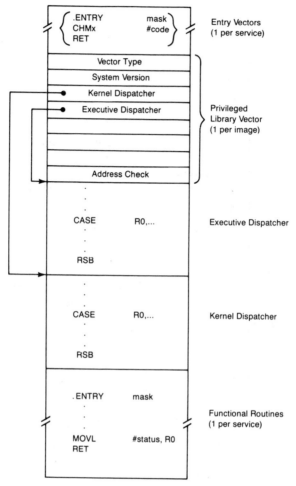

Figure 9-6 Structure of Privileged Shareable Image

space. The CHMK or CHME instruction located there transfers control to the VMS change mode dispatcher.

② Execution proceeds as if a VMS service were invoked except that the change mode code is not recognized by the VMS dispatcher and control passes to the end of the case table (see the examples in Section 9.3.1).

③ The JSB instruction in CMODSSDSP passes control to the P1 space dispatch area where another JSB instruction passes control to the first dispatcher.

④ The first dispatcher rejects the change mode code simply by executing an RSB back to the P1 space vector where a second JSB is executed.

⑤ The second dispatcher recognizes the change mode code as valid and dispatches (probably with a CASEx instruction) to a service-specific procedure that is also a part of the second privileged shareable image.

⑥ When the service completes (successfully or unsuccessfully), it loads a final status into R0 and exits with a RET which passes control to SRVEXIT. At this point, privileged shareable image system service dispatching merges with VMS system service dispatching.

If each dispatcher executed an RSB to reject the change mode code, control eventually would reach the RSB instruction in the P1 space vector. This RSB instruction passes control back to the VMS change mode dispatcher, which checks next for a systemwide dispatcher.

.4.3   Systemwide User-Written Dispatcher

If no per-process dispatcher exists or if the last per-process user-written dispatcher returns to the routine in CMODSSDSP with an RSB, a location in system space (EXE$GL_USRCHMK or EXE$GL_USRCHME) is checked for the existence of a systemwide user-written dispatcher. If none exists (contents are zero, its usual contents in a VMS system), or if this dispatcher passes control back with an RSB, an illegal system service call (SS$_ILLSER) is reported back to the user in R0. This scheme assumes that privileged shareable image system services that complete successfully will exit with a RET back to SRVEXIT, where an REI instruction will dismiss the CHMK or CHME exception. Note that there is no standard documented way to add a systemwide user-written dispatcher to a system.

.5   RELATED SYSTEM SERVICES

There are five system services in the VMS operating system that are closely related to system service dispatching and the change mode instructions. The Declare Change Mode or Compatibility Handler ($DCLCMH) system service is described in Chapter 4. This section describes the Set System Service Failure Exception Mode ($SETSFM) system service, the Set System Service Filter ($SETSSF) system service, and the change mode system services.

.5.1   Set System Service Failure Exceptions System Service

The $SETSFM system service either enables or disables the generation of exceptions when an error is detected by the system service common exit path. The service itself simply sets (to enable) or clears (to disable) the bit in the process status longword (PCB$L_STS in the software PCB) for the access mode from which the system service was called. Section 9.3.5 describes the use of these bits in more detail.

.5.2   Change Mode System Services

The Change Mode to Kernel ($CMKRNL) and Change Mode to Executive ($CMEXEC) system services provide a simple path for privileged processes to execute code in kernel or executive mode. These services check for the appropriate privilege (CMKRNL or CMEXEC) and then dispatch (with a CALLG instruction) to the procedure whose address is supplied as an argument to the service. (Note that if $CMKRNL is called from executive mode, no privilege check is made.)

The procedure that executes in kernel or executive mode must load a return status code into R0. If not, the previous contents of R0 will be used to determine whether an error occurred.

9.5.3   System Service Filtering

Some applications (especially user-written CLIs) require that user mode programs have no direct access to system and RMS services. The Set System Service Filter ($SETSSF) system service was provided for this purpose.

When the module CMODSSDSP is assembled in order to create the system service vectors, two tables of bytes are created, one for kernel mode system services (at the symbol SYS$GB_KMASK), and one for executive mode system services (at the symbol B_EMASK). Each entry in these tables contains a mask that indicates whether or not the system service can be disabled by $SETSSF. If the service can be disabled by $SETSSF, the mask also indicates the system service filter groups for which the service is disabled. Group 0 specifies all services, except $EXIT; group 1 specifies most services, with the exception of $EXIT and those services required for condition handling or image rundown. The *VAX/VMS System Services Reference Manual* lists the services that are not disabled by $SETSSF.

The byte at offset CTL$GB_SSFILTER in the per-process control region contains the system service filter mask for a particular process. Usually this mask contains the value zero. When $SETSSF is called, the mask value specified in the call to $SETSSF is written into this mask.

When the system is bootstrapped, module INIT checks the bit EXE$V_SSINHIBIT at global location EXE$GL_DEFFLAGS. This bit corresponds to the SYSBOOT parameter SSINHIBIT. If the bit is set, the SCB vectors for CHME and CHMK are revectored to the entry points EXE$CMODEXECX and EXE$CMODKRNLX, respectively.

These alternate change mode service routines first test whether the CHMx was executed in user mode. These routines branch to the standard change mode dispatchers for CHMx instructions executed in inner modes. If the CHMx instruction was executed in user mode, then these alternate routines AND the value in CTL$GB_SSFILTER with the value in the system service filter tables (found at locations B_EMASK or SYS$GB_KMASK). The CHMx code is used as an index into these tables. If the result of the AND is zero, the routines branch to the standard change mode dispatchers. If the result of the

AND is nonzero, these routines return the error status SS$_INHCHME or SS$_INCHMK, depending on whether the system service was an executive or kernel mode service.

If CTL$GB_SSFILTER is not zero, access to services in privileged shareable images is also denied. Attempts to invoke those services result in the error SS$_INHCHME or SS$_INCHMK, depending on the mode of the service.

PART III/Scheduling and Time Support

10 Scheduling

It is equally bad when one speeds on the guest unwilling to
go, and when he holds back one who is hastening. Rather one
should befriend the guest who is there, but speed him when
he wishes.

Homer, *The Odyssey*

The scheduler identifies and selects for execution the highest priority computable memory resident process. A process currently executing enters a wait state by making a direct or indirect request for a system operation which cannot complete immediately. A waiting process becomes computable as the result of system events, such as the setting of an event flag and queuing of an AST.

This chapter describes the interactions of priorities, process scheduling states, and system events. It also discusses the operation of the scheduler and the hardware mechanisms that assist process context switching.

10.1 PROCESS CONTROL BLOCK

The data structure fundamental to scheduling is the software process control block (PCB). It specifies the scheduling state and priority of a process. When the term "PCB" is used without a modifier, it refers to the software PCB. The data structure that contains copies of the general registers is always called the "hardware PCB." Figure 10-1 illustrates the fields of the PCB that are particularly important to scheduling.

The field PCB$W_STATE contains a numeric value equivalent to a particular process scheduling state. The state of a process defines its readiness to be scheduled for execution, its computability or lack thereof. In addition, the state may indicate whether the process is memory resident or out-swapped. Table 10-1 lists the process state names and the corresponding PCB$W_STATE values. The various process scheduling states and the transitions among them are discussed throughout this chapter.

The PCBs of processes in most scheduling states are queued together with those of other processes in the same state so that they can be located more easily by scheduling routines. The state queue link fields, PCB$L_SQFL and PCB$L_SQBL, link a PCB into a state queue. The various state queues are described in Section 10.3.

The data structure which contains the hardware context of the process is the hardware PCB. Its physical address is stored in the software PCB field

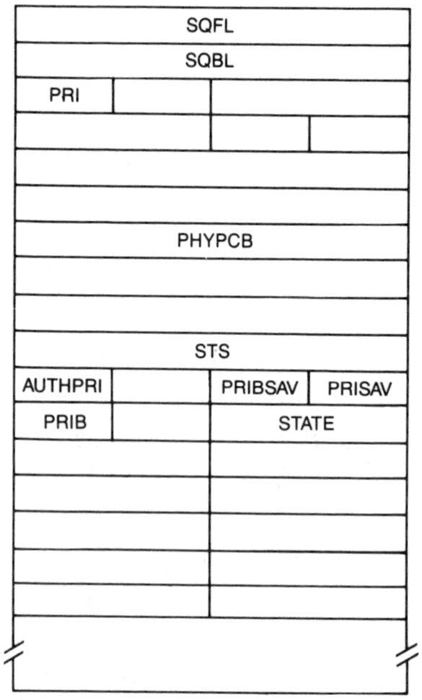

Figure 10-1 Process Control Block Fields Used in Scheduling

PCB$L_PHYPCB. Section 10.5.1 describes the hardware PCB.

Several PCB fields define the priority of the process. Section 10.2 describes the use and contents of these fields.

PCB$L_STS, the process status longword, contains various flags describing the status of the process. The bit PCB$V_RES is of particular significance to scheduling. When set, it indicates that the process is in memory rather than outswapped. Table 12-2 describes all the flags in the process status longword.

10.2   PROCESS PRIORITY

Process scheduling priority (as distinct from interrupt priority level, a hardware mechanism) is used in determining the relative precedence of processes for execution and memory residence. Priority is a value in the range from 0 to 31. The null process executes at priority level 0, and the highest priority real-time process executes at priority level 31. The range of 32 priority levels is divided evenly between the normal process levels of 0 to 15 and the real-time process levels of 16 to 31. The execution behavior of a process is significantly affected by the type of process (normal or real-time) and its assigned priority level.

Several fields of the PCB describe the priority of the process. The values in these fields are stored internally in an inverted order. For example, the priority value of 0 for the null process is stored internally in the PCB fields as 31.

Table 10-1   Process Scheduling States

State Name	Mnemonic	Value
Collided page wait	COLPG	1
Miscellaneous wait	MWAIT	2
Mutex wait		
Resource wait		
Common event flag wait	CEF	3
Page fault wait	PFW	4
Local event flag wait (resident)	LEF	5
Local event flag wait (outswapped)	LEFO	6
Hibernate wait (resident)	HIB	7
Hibernate wait (outswapped)	HIBO	8
Suspend wait (resident)	SUSP	9
Suspend wait (outswapped)	SUSPO	10
Free page wait	FPG	11
Computable (resident)	COM	12
Computable (outswapped)	COMO	13
Currently executing process	CUR	14

The highest priority process possible has internally stored software priority values of 0. The internal priority value is 31 minus the external priority value.

As a result of this inversion, priority promotions or boosts are implemented through subtract or decrement instructions. Inverting the values facilitates selection of the next process to execute and the next process to be inswapped; these functions use the find first set (FFS) instruction, which begins its search for a set bit at bit position 0.

System utilities, such as SDA, MONITOR, and the DCL command SHOW SYSTEM, interpret these inverted values and display external values. An external value is also returned by the $GETJPI system service when a process priority is requested. Conversion in various user interfaces occurs because systems and users generally associate higher priority numbers with higher priority processes.

Note that all discussions in this book treat process priority as an increasing entity from 0 (for the null process) to 31 (for the highest priority real-time process). Please take this convention into account when relating descriptions in this book to the actual routines in the listings, where inverted priorities are used.

The field PCB$B_PRI (see Figure 10-1) defines the current priority of the process, which is used to make scheduling decisions. PCB$B_PRIB defines the base priority of the process, from which the current priority is calculated.

For normal or time-sharing processes, these priority values are sometimes different, while real-time processes always have identical current and base priority values.

When a process is created, its current and base priority are initialized from an argument to the Create Process system service. For an interactive process, this value is taken from the system authorization file. A process with the alter priority privilege can raise and lower its priority through the Set Priority ($SETPRI) system service or the DCL command SET PROCESS/PRIORITY. Chapter 12 describes the operation of the $SETPRI system service.

The field PCB$B_AUTHPRI contains the base priority authorized at the time the process was created. A process without the alter priority privilege may raise and lower its priority between 0 and the contents of PCB$B_AUTHPRI.

The fields PCB$B_PRIBSAV and PCB$B_PRISAV record the base and current priority values at the time a process first locks a mutex, before it receives a temporary elevation into the real-time range. When the process unlocks the mutex, its priority values are restored from these fields. Chapter 2 contains further details.

10.2.1 Real-Time Priority Range

Processes with priority levels 16 through 31 are considered real-time processes. There are two scheduling characteristics that distinguish real-time processes:

- The priority of a real-time process does not change over time, unless there is a direct program or operator request to change it. The fact that the priority does not change implies that the base priority and the current priority of a real-time process are identical, and no dynamic priority adjustment (see Section 10.2.3) is applied by the operating system.
- A real-time process executes until it is either preempted by a higher or equal priority process or it enters one of the wait states (see Section 10.3.3). Thus, a real-time process is not susceptible to quantum end events (see Section 10.4.2) and is not removed from execution (rescheduled) because some interval of execution time has expired.

Taken in isolation, the real-time range of VMS priorities provides a scheduling environment like traditional real-time systems: preemptive, priority driven scheduling without a time slice or quantum.

10.2.2 Normal Priority Range

Normal processes include interactive terminal sessions, batch jobs, and all system processes except the swapper and Files-11 XQP cache server process.

The scheduling behavior of a normal process differs from that of a real-time process in several ways.

The current priority of a normal process varies over time, while its base priority remains constant unless there is a direct program or operator request to change it. This behavior is the result of dynamic priority adjustment applied by the VMS system to favor I/O-bound and interactive processes at the expense of compute-bound (and frequently also batch) processes. The mechanism of priority adjustment is discussed in the following section.

Normal processes run in a time-sharing environment that allocates CPU time slices (or quanta) to processes in turn. An executing normal process controls the CPU until one of the following events occurs:

- It is preempted by a higher or equal priority computable process (see Figure 10-6, event 5, for an example).
- It enters a resource or event wait state (see Figure 10-6, event 7, for an example).
- It has used the current quantum or time slice (see Figure 10-6, event 17, for an example).

Processes with identical current priorities are scheduled on a round-robin basis. That is, each process at a given priority level executes in turn before any other process at that level executes again.

Normal processes experience round-robin scheduling because the default behavior (from Create Process system service arguments or from the user authorization file) is to assign the same base priority to all user processes. The default base priority is the value of SYSBOOT parameter DEFPRI. Its usual value is 4. Thus priority levels 4 through 10 tend to be occupied by several processes simultaneously.

0.2.3   **Priority Adjustment**

Normal processes do not generally execute at a single priority level. Rather, the priority of a normal process changes over time in a range of 0 to 6 priority levels above the base process priority. Two mechanisms provide this priority adjustment.

As a condition for which the process has been waiting is satisfied or a needed resource becomes available, a boost or priority increment may be applied to the base priority to improve the scheduling response for the process (see Section 10.4.3.2). Each time the process executes without further system events (see Section 10.4.3) or quantum expiration (see Section 10.4.2), the current priority is moved toward the base priority (or demoted) by one priority level (see Section 10.5.4). Over time, compute-bound process priorities tend to remain at their base priority levels, while I/O-bound and interactive processes tend to have average current priorities somewhat higher than their base priorities.

An example of priority adjustment that occurs over time for several processes is illustrated in Figure 10-6.

Priority adjustment can also occur as a result of locking a mutex (see Chapter 2) or through action by the routine EXE$TIMEOUT (see Chapter 11).

10.3   PROCESS SCHEDULING STATES

All processes in the system are in either the current state, a wait state, computable resident state, or computable outswapped state. The scheduling state of a process is specified by its PCB$W_STATE field. The symbolic name for a scheduling state has the form SCH$C_*mnemonic,* for example, SCH$C_COM. These symbolic names are defined by the macro $STATEDEF in SYS$LIBRARY:LIB.MLB. Table 10-1 lists the process scheduling state names and the corresponding PCB$W_STATE values.

Certain wait conditions are represented by two different scheduling states: one resident and one outswapped. A process waiting for a local event flag is in the LEF or the LEFO state, depending on its residence. Other scheduling states, common event flag wait (CEF), for example, include both resident and outswapped processes. The PCB$V_RES bit in the PCB status longword for a particular process in such a state specifies whether the process is resident or outswapped.

The listheads for all wait queues, computable resident (COM) queues, and computable outswapped (COMO) queues, are defined in the module SDAT. SCH$GL_CURPCB, the pointer to the PCB of the current (CUR) process, is also defined in SDAT.

The rest of this section describes the various scheduling states and the transitions among them.

10.3.1   Current State

A process in the CUR state is currently being executed. A computable process enters the CUR state after having been selected as the highest priority resident process by SCH$SCHED (see Section 10.5.4). Its PCB address is recorded in the global location SCH$GL_CURPCB.

A CUR process makes a transition to the COM state when it is preempted by a higher or equal priority process. A CUR process of normal priority also makes this transition when it reaches quantum end. A CUR process can also make a transition to any of the resident wait states by making a direct or indirect request for a system operation which cannot complete immediately.

Direct requests, such as $HIBER and $SUSPND, place the process in the voluntary wait states HIB and SUSP. Direct requests, such as $QIOW, $SYNCH, and $WAITFR, place the process in the voluntary wait states LEF or CEF. Subsequent outswapping (from the process viewpoint, an unrequested system operation) can move a process to the LEFO, HIBO, or SUSPO states.

Indirect wait requests occur as a result of paging or contention for system resources. A process does not request PFW, FPG, COLPG, or MWAIT transitions. Rather, the transitions to these wait states occur because direct service requests to the system cannot be completed or satisfied at the moment.

Deletion of processes can only occur from the CUR state. The process's address space and process header are accessible only while it is current. Furthermore, process deletion in the context of the process being deleted enables the use of system services, such as Deassign I/O Channel and Delete Virtual Address Space.

10.3.2 Computable States

Processes in the COM or executable state are not waiting for events or resources, other than acquiring control of the CPU for execution. Processes must be in the computable resident state to be considered for scheduling. There are 32 queues for computable resident processes, one for each software priority. The quadword listheads of these queues are defined as an array whose starting address is global location SCH$AQ_COMH (see Figure 10-2). A process is inserted into the queue corresponding to the internal value of its current software priority.

There is a similar array of 32 quadword listheads for the COMO state, at global location SCH$AQ_COMOH. Processes in the COMO state are waiting for the swapper process to bring them into memory. As COM processes, they can then be scheduled for execution. Processes are created in the COMO state.

The condition (empty or not) of each computable queue is summarized by a bit. If the queue contains one or more PCBs, the bit is set; if the queue is empty, the bit is clear. The 32 bits describing the COM queues are in the longword at global location SCH$GL_COMQS; the COMO queues are summarized in the longword SCH$GL_COMOQS. Bit 0 in each longword corresponds to the external priority 31 queue, bit 1 to priority 30, and so forth. These summary longwords facilitate selection of the next process to execute and selection of the next process to be inswapped.

A process in a wait state makes the transition to COM or COMO through a system event (see Section 10.4.3). The availability of a requested resource or the satisfaction of a wait condition (such as an event flag setting or a $WAKE system service call) makes the process computable. In all process wait states except SUSP and SUSPO, the queuing of an asynchronous system trap (AST) makes a process computable even if the wait condition is not satisfied. Process deletion, implemented with a kernel mode AST, makes any process that is being deleted computable (even if the process is in the SUSP or SUSPO state) because the target process is resumed before the AST is queued.

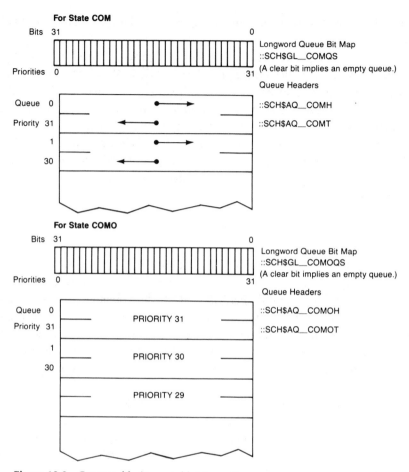

Figure 10-2 Computable (Executable) State Queues

10.3.3   Wait States

A process which is not current or computable is waiting for the availability of a system resource or the occurrence of an event. The process is in one of several distinct wait states. The wait state reflects the particular condition that must be satisfied for the process to become computable again.

Figure 10-3 illustrates a scheduler wait queue header, a listhead for processes in a wait state. The first two longwords in it are the links to the PCBs in this queue. The field WQH$W_STATE contains the numerical value corresponding to the process scheduling state. All PCBs in a state queue have PCB$W_STATE values identical to the state value of the wait queue header. The field WQH$W_COUNT contains the number of PCBs currently in this state and queue.

The wait queue headers for all wait states except CEF are defined within an array ordered by increasing state number, with the collided page wait state first. Each wait queue header (except for CEF) has its own global pointer. A scheduling routine can access a particular wait queue by specifying its global name or using its state number as an index into the wait queue header array. The global location SCH$AQ_WQHDR is the address of the beginning of the array.

Figure 10-4 illustrates the array of wait queue headers. Note that the global location SCH$AQ_WQHDR is defined to be 12 bytes (the length of a wait queue header) before the collided page wait queue header. This definition enables the array to be treated as though it were zero-based, simplifying the address arithmetic. Note also that there is no actual header with an index value of 3, although space is reserved. The wait queue for state 3, or CEF, is allocated elsewhere.

A process waiting for one or more common event flags is queued to a wait queue in the common event block (CEB) defining the common event flag cluster with which the process is associated. A CEB includes three longwords that correspond to a wait state queue header. The entire format of the CEB is shown in Chapter 12. The number of different CEF wait queues depends upon the number of common event flag clusters that exist on a particular system at any given time. Having a wait queue in each CEB makes it easier to determine which CEF processes are computable when a common event flag is set. The wait queue in the CEB contains both resident and outswapped processes and thus there is no CEFO state.

0.3.3.1   **Voluntary Wait States.** There are several scheduling states associated with event flag waits: LEF, LEFO, and CEF. A process enters the LEF or CEF state as a result of issuing $WAITFR, $WFLOR, $WFLAND, and $SYNCH system services directly or indirectly (for example, with a $QIOW or $ENQW system service call, issued either by the user or on his behalf by some system component such as RMS). A process enters the LEF state when it waits for local

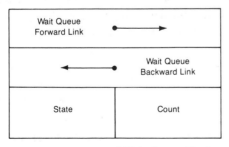

Figure 10-3   Layout of Wait Queue Header

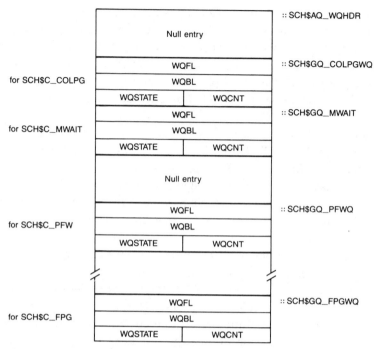

Figure 10-4 Array of Wait Queue Headers

event flags or the CEF state when it waits for flags in a common event flag cluster.

An LEF process enters the LEFO state when it is outswapped. The transition from the LEF, LEFO, or CEF states to the computable (COM or COMO) states can occur as a result of matching the event flag wait mask, queuing an AST, or process deletion (a special case of AST queuing). There are separate resident and outswapped states and queues for hibernating and suspended processes. The $HIBER and $SUSPND system services cause processes to enter the resident wait states. Outswapping a SUSP or HIB process causes it to enter the SUSPO or HIBO state. A process makes the transition from the HIB or HIBO state to COM or COMO as a result of execution of a $WAKE system service, AST queuing, or process deletion. A suspended process is sensitive only to the $RESUME system service and process deletion (because ASTs cannot be delivered to suspended processes).

10.3.3.2 **Memory Management Wait States.** Three process wait states are associated with memory management. Each state is represented by a single queue and listhead of the form shown in Figure 10-3. The PCB$V_RES bit in the PCB status longword for a particular process in one of those states specifies whether that process is resident or outswapped. (Memory management wait states are discussed from another point of view in Chapter 15.)

A process enters the page fault wait state (PFW) when it refers to a page that is not in physical memory. While the page read is in progress, the process is placed into the PFW state. Completion of the page read, AST queuing, or process deletion can cause the process to become COM or COMO, depending upon its PCB$V_RES bit value when the satisfying condition occurs.

A process enters the free page wait state (FPG) when it requests a page to be added to its working set but there are no free pages to be allocated from the free page list. This state is essentially a resource wait until the supply of free pages is replenished through modified page writing, working set trimming, process outswapping, or virtual address space deletion.

A process enters the collided page wait state (COLPG) when several processes cause page faults on the same shared page at the same time. The initial faulting process enters the PFW state, while the second and succeeding processes enter the COLPG state. The COLPG state can also be entered when a process refers to a private page that is already in transition from the disk. All COLPG processes are made COM or COMO when the read operation completes. (A more detailed discussion of collided pages is contained in Chapter 15.)

10.3.3.3   **Miscellaneous Wait State.** The miscellaneous wait state (MWAIT) is used to indicate a process waiting for a resource not managed by any of the other process wait states. There is a single MWAIT queue for memory resident and outswapped processes. A small integer identifying the resource is stored in the PCB$L_EFWM field. The resource values are defined symbolically by the $RSNDEF macro in SYS$LIBRARY:LIB.MLB.

Table 10-2 lists the resources associated with the MWAIT state. System utilities such as SDA, MONITOR, and the DCL command SHOW SYSTEM display the state of a process in a resource wait using one of the mnemonic names in this table.

The MWAIT state is used to wait for the availability of a depleted or locked resource. A process may enter a resource wait if the resource it requests is not available. Common examples are the depletion of nonpaged dynamic memory or no room in a mailbox. The process becomes computable when the resource becomes available again.

Whether queuing an AST to a process makes it executable depends on the interrupt priority level (IPL) at which the process was placed into resource wait. If the IPL in the saved PSL in the hardware PCB is 2 or larger, the AST delivery interrupt is blocked. Thus, the process reexecutes the resource wait code and is placed back into the MWAIT state immediately. If the saved IPL is less than 2, an AST delivery interrupt occurs, causing the execution of the queued AST. When the AST completes, the process reexecutes the resource wait code. Section 10.4.1 describes the mechanism that causes reexecution of the resource wait code.

Table 10-2 Types of MWAIT State

Resource Wait Name	Mnemonic	Symbolic Name	Numeric
AST wait (wait for system or special kernel AST)	RWAST	RSN$_ASTWAIT	1
Mailbox full	RWMBX	RSN$_MAILBOX	2
Nonpaged dynamic memory	RWNPG	RSN$_NPDYNMEM	3
Page file full[1]	RWPFF	RSN$_PGFILE	4
Paged dynamic memory	RWPAG	RSN$_PGDYNMEM	5
Breakthrough[1]	RWBRK	RSN$_BRKTHRU	6
Image activation lock[1]	RWIMG	RSN$_IACLOCK	7
Job pooled quota[1]	RWQUO	RSN$_JQUOTA	8
Lock identifier[1]	RWLCK	RSN$_LOCKID	9
Swap file space	RWSWP	RSN$_SWPFILE	10
Modified page list empty	RWMPE	RSN$_MPLEMPTY	11
Modified page writer busy	RWMPB	RSN$_MPWBUSY	12
Distributed lock manager wait	RWSCS	RSN$_SCS	13
Cluster transition	RWCLU	RSN$_CLUSTRAN	14

[1]This resource wait is not currently used.

Most of the resource names are self-descriptive. RWAST, however, is a general purpose resource used primarily when the wait is expected to be satisfied by the queuing or delivery of an AST to the process. There is no concrete resource named RSN$_ASTWAIT. The $QIO system service can place a process into this resource wait when the process is not allowed to issue another buffered or direct I/O request until one completes. Another use of RSN$_ASTWAIT is to wait for all the I/O requests on a channel to complete after the process has issued a Deassign I/O Channel ($DASSGN) system service. In Version 4, a process about to be suspended or deleted waits for the RSN$_ASTWAIT resource until all its Files-11 XQP activity completes (see Chapter 7).

The Set Resource Wait Mode ($SETRWM) system service can force the immediate return of an error status code, rather than placing the process in the MWAIT state. $SETRWM does this by setting the PCB$V_SSRWAIT bit of the PCB$L_STS field. Disabling resource wait affects many directly requested operations (such as I/O requests or timer requests) but has no effect on allocation requests by the system on behalf of the user. An example of this situation is the pager requiring an I/O request packet to perform a page read operation. If nonpaged dynamic memory is depleted, the process enters the MWAIT state, even if $SETRWM has been used to disable resource waits. The reason for this distinction is that a process can respond to a depleted resource error from a system service call or an RMS request but has no means of reacting to a similar error in the event of an unexpected event such as a page fault.

System routines that access data structures protected by mutexes place a process in the MWAIT state if the requested mutex ownership cannot be granted (see Chapter 2). Thus, the mutex wait state indicates a locked resource and not necessarily a depleted one. When the owner of the requested mutex releases it, the requesting process becomes COM or COMO if it has been outswapped. Eventually, the process is selected as the current process. Once it is placed into execution, it requests ownership of the mutex again. AST queuing cannot make a mutex-waiting process computable for long because the IPL in the stored PSL is IPL$_ASTDEL (IPL 2), blocking the AST delivery interrupt.

The mutex wait state is distinguished from the resource wait state by the contents of the PCB$L_EFWM field. Interpreted as a signed integer, the contents of this field are positive and small when the process is waiting for a resource. When the process is waiting for a mutex, the field contains the system virtual address of the requested mutex. Interpreted as a signed integer, a system virtual address is a negative number. Table 2-2 lists the names of mutexes whose addresses may be stored in PCB$L_EFWM. System utilities such as SDA, MONITOR, and the DCL command SHOW SYSTEM display the state of a process which is waiting for a mutex as MUTEX.

For example, if a process wishes to allocate a block of paged dynamic memory, it must first acquire the paged pool mutex before searching the linked list of available blocks of paged pool (see Chapter 3). If another process is already examining that list, the second process is put into a mutex wait state with the address of the paged pool mutex stored in PCB$L_EFWM. Once the mutex is released by the first process, it can be acquired by the second process, which can then search paged pool for a block of the requested size. If there is no block large enough to satisfy the allocation request, the process is placed into a resource wait state (with 5, the value of RSN$_PGDYNMEM, stored in PCB$L_EFWM). The process remains in this state until a block of paged pool is deallocated and the resource RSN$_PGDYNMEM declared available.

10.4   EVENTS THAT LEAD TO RESCHEDULING

Three kinds of events can result in rescheduling:

- Placement of the current process into a wait state
- Quantum expiration for the current process
- System events, reported for both current and noncurrent processes

The following sections describe these events.

10.4.1   **Placing a Process into a Wait State**

When a process directly or indirectly requests a system operation for which it must wait, the process is placed into the appropriate wait state. The actions to place a process into a wait state are centralized in the routine SCH$WAIT, in module SYSWAIT. This routine is entered in process context at IPL$_SYNCH. Register arguments specify the addresses of the software PCB of the current process and the wait queue into which the process is to be inserted.

Depending on which subentry point of SCH$WAIT is invoked, some or all of the following operations are performed:

1. SCH$WAIT assumes it has been entered from a system service. It removes the call frame from the kernel stack and establishes the PC at which the process will wait as described in the following section.
2. The routine changes the process state to that in WQH$W_STATE, inserts the PCB into the wait queue, and increments the field WQH$W_COUNT to show the addition of a process to the queue.
3. The routine executes a SVPCTX instruction to remove the current process from execution.
4. The routine charges the SYSBOOT parameter IOTA against the process quantum as described in Section 10.4.2. Another process header field, PHD$L_TIMREF, is also adjusted by the value of IOTA. PHD$L_TIMREF and the process quantum must be adjusted together for automatic working set list adjustment to be responsive. (For further details, see Chapter 16.)
5. The contents of the global location EXE$GL_ABSTIM, the system time in seconds, are copied to the field PCB$L_WAITIME, to record the time at which the process began its wait. If the process remains in a wait state for long, it becomes a candidate for working set shrinkage and possibly outswapping. (See Chapter 17.)
6. The routine tests PR$_ASTLVL and the process's wait PSL to determine whether a deliverable AST has been queued to the process but not yet delivered. This test prevents the possibility that an AST event is ignored which otherwise should take the process out of its wait. If a deliverable AST has been queued, SCH$WAIT reports an AST queuing event to SCH$RSE (see Section 10.4.3), which changes the process state to COM.
7. SCH$WAIT then branches to SCH$SCHED (see Section 10.5.4), the second half of the rescheduling interrupt service routine, to select a new process to run.

One of the responsibilities of the routines which invoke SCH$WAIT and its subentry points is to ensure that a process can correctly reenter the appropriate wait state after successful delivery of an AST. There are three different techniques used, depending on the particular wait state being entered.

10.4.1.1   **System Service Wait States.** In the case where a process is entering a wait state as a result of executing a system service (HIB, LEF, or CEF), the wait routine is entered with the PC and PSL of the the system service CHMK exception (see Chapter 9) on the top of the stack. The first implication of this arrangement is that the process waits in the access mode in which the system service was issued. Because ASTs are queued and delivered based on access mode, a supervisor mode AST can be delivered to a process waiting on an event flag as a result of a $QIOW call issued from user or supervisor mode.

In addition, the wait code backs up the saved PC by 4 so that it points to the CHMx instruction in the system service vector (see the code examples in Chapter 9). If a process receives an AST while in such a wait state, the AST is delivered and executes. When the AST delivery routine dismisses its interrupt through an REI instruction, the system service executes again, typically placing the process right back into the wait state it was in before the AST was delivered.

10.4.1.2   **Memory Management Wait States.** Only the page fault handler (see Chapter 15) places processes into the three wait states associated with memory management. This routine places a process into a wait state with the PC and PSL associated with the page fault as the saved process context. Once again, because the PSL reflects the access mode in which the fault occurred, ASTs can be delivered for that and all inner access modes. (Note that this routine does not need to change the PC that it finds on the stack because page fault exceptions are faults and not traps. Faults, discussed in full in Chapter 4, cause the PC of the faulting instruction and not the PC of the next instruction to be pushed onto the exception stack.)

If an AST is delivered to and executes in such a process, the process executes the faulting instruction again. If the reason for the fault has been removed (a free page became available or the page read completed) while the AST was being delivered or was executing, the process simply continues with its execution. If, on the other hand, the situation that caused the process to wait still exists, the process reincurs the page fault and is placed back into one of the memory management wait states. (Note that a process that was initially in a PFW state would be placed into a COLPG state by such a sequence of events.)

10.4.1.3   **Special Cases.** The two remaining wait states (SUSP and MWAIT) are handled in a special way by the wait routine. A process suspension occurs as a result of executing a kernel AST. ASTs cannot be delivered to suspended processes. That is, an AST queued to a suspended process has its AST control block inserted into the AST queue in the software PCB. However, the AST event is ignored by the scheduler. (In fact, while a process is suspended, the saved PC is an address in the kernel AST that caused the process to enter the suspend state. The saved PSL indicates kernel mode and IPL 0.)

When a process is placed into a wait state waiting for a mutex (see Chapter 2), its saved PC is either SCH$LOCKR or SCH$LOCKW, depending on whether it is attempting to lock the mutex for read access or write access. The saved PSL indicates kernel mode and IPL 2, which implies that processes in an MWAIT state waiting for a mutex cannot receive ASTs.

A process can also be placed into an MWAIT state while waiting for an arbitrary system resource. In this case, the caller of routine SCH$RWAIT (in module MUTEX) controls the PC and PSL that are saved when the process is placed into the MWAIT state. In particular, the current access mode and IPL in the saved PSL determine whether any ASTs can be delivered to a process that is waiting for a resource.

10.4.2 Quantum Expiration

The SYSBOOT parameter QUANTUM defines the size of the time slice for the round-robin scheduling of normal processes. The quantum also determines, for most process states, the minimum amount of time a process remains in memory after an inswap operation, but it is not an absolute guarantee of memory residence. (The swapper's use of the initial quantum flag in selecting an outswap candidate is described in Chapter 17.) The value of QUANTUM is the number of 10-millisecond intervals (clock ticks) in the quantum. The default QUANTUM value of 20, therefore, produces a scheduling interval of 200 milliseconds.

A process's quantum is expressed as a negative number of clock ticks. After each 10-millisecond interval, the hardware clock interrupt service routine increments the quantum-remaining field in the process header of the current process. When this value becomes zero or positive, the hardware clock service routine requests a software timer interrupt. The software timer routine signals a quantum end event by invoking the subroutine SCH$QEND in module RSE.

An additional deduction from the QUANTUM is governed by the special SYSBOOT parameter IOTA. This value (in units of 10 milliseconds) is deducted from the remaining quantum value each time a process enters a wait state. The default IOTA value of 2 represents a 20-millisecond charge against the quantum of the process. This mechanism is provided to ensure that all processes experience quantum end events with some regularity. Processes that are compute-bound experience quantum end as a result of using a certain amount of CPU time. Processes that are I/O-bound experience quantum end as a result of performing a reasonable number of I/O requests. This scheme guarantees that processes that spend most of their time in some wait state proceed in an orderly fashion toward quantum end.

The routine SCH$QEND is executed at the end of every quantum. For a real-time process, its only actions are to reset the field PHD$W_QUANT to the full quantum value and to clear the initial quantum flag, PCB$V_INQUAN in the field PCB$L_STS.

For a normal process, however, the occurrence of quantum expiration involves several different operations:

1. Like a real-time process, a normal process has its process header quantum field reset and initial quantum flag cleared. The cleared initial quantum flag makes a process more likely to be outswapped if process swap mode has not been disabled.

2. The CPU limit field of the process header is next checked to determine if a CPU limit has been imposed and if that limit has expired. If the CPU limit has expired, each access mode has an interval of time to clean up or run down before the image exits and the process is deleted. The size of the warning interval given to each access mode is defined by the SYSBOOT parameter EXTRACPU (which has a default value of ten seconds).

3. If no CPU limit expiration has occurred, then the automatic working set adjustment calculations take place if they are enabled. The size of the process working set list may be expanded or contracted by amounts specified by the SYSBOOT parameters WSINC or WSDEC. Chapter 16 describes the details of automatic working set adjustment.

4. If there is an inswap candidate (if SCH$GL_COMOQS is nonzero, indicating at least one nonempty COMO state queue), the current priority of the process is set to its base priority. (If SCH$GL_COMOQS contains a zero, the priority is left alone.)

5. Routine SCH$SWPWAKE is called to determine whether swapper activity is required. The swapper process is awakened from hibernation if any of the following is true:

   —There is at least one computable outswapped process.
   —Modified page writing is required as indicated by the upper and lower limit thresholds for the free and modified page lists.
   —There is at least one process header of a deleted process still in the balance slots.
   —A powerfail recovery has just occurred.

These checks avoid awakening and rescheduling the swapper with the associated context switch overhead when the swapper has no useful work to do.

The swapper process does not execute immediately but must be scheduled for execution. As a computable (after waking), resident, real-time process of software priority 16, the swapper is likely to be the next process scheduled.

6. Finally, a rescheduling interrupt at IPL 3 is requested to remove the current process from execution and select the next process for execution. Note that on a quiet system, the process just removed from execution can be the highest priority computable resident process and thus be placed back into execution immediately.

10.4.3   **System Events**

System events are occurrences of operations that change the states of processes. A system event may make a process computable, memory resident, or outswapped. System events provide some of the transitions among the process states. The movement of a process into and out of the balance set is handled by the swapper process (see Chapter 17).

Figure 10-5 diagrams the transitions among states.

10.4.3.1   **Event Reporting.** Events are reported to the scheduler from many system routines through the RPTEVT macro, which generates the following code:

```
JSB SCH$RSE
.BYTE EVT$_event_name
```

The byte event value identifies the event to be declared by the system routine. The address of the event value is pushed onto the stack by the JSB instruction. Additional parameters (priority increment class and PCB address of the affected process) are passed in registers.

The routine SCH$RSE (in module RSE) performs the following operations:

1. The event number is loaded into a register and the return PC value (on the stack as a result of the JSB instruction) is adjusted to point to the address after the stored byte event value.
2. The state and the event are checked for a significant transition.

   Each event (or state transition) has a bit mask defining which states this event can affect. The state of the process is obtained from the PCB$W_STATE field.

   —For example, a wake event is only significant for processes that are hibernating (HIB or HIBO states).
   —An outswap event is only significant for the four states (COM, HIB, LEF, and SUSP) where a wait queue change is required.
   —The queuing of an AST is significant to all process states, except SUSP, SUSPO, COM, COMO, and CUR states and results in a transition to COM or COMO.

3. If the event is not significant for the current process state, the event is ignored and SCH$RSE simply executes an RSB instruction.

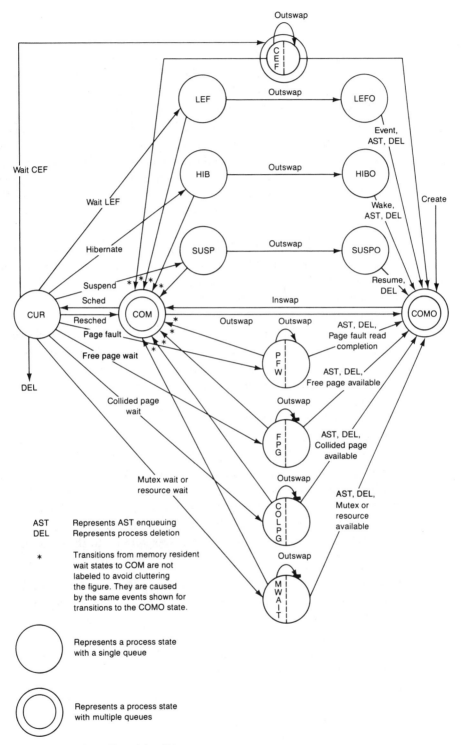

Figure 10-5   State Transition Diagram

4. For significant events, the actions of SCH$RSE vary:

   —For an outswap event producing an LEF to LEFO, HIB to HIBO, or SUSP to SUSPO transition, SCH$RSE simply removes the PCB of the process from the resident wait queue and inserts it in the corresponding outswapped wait queue. The corresponding wait queue header count fields and the process state (PCB$W_STATE) are also adjusted.

   —For an outswap event producing a COM to COMO transition, SCH$RSE removes the PCB from the COM priority queue corresponding to PCB$B_PRI and inserts it into the corresponding COMO priority queue. The value in PCB$W_STATE is changed to the value SCH$C_COMO. The SCH$GL_COMQS status bit vector is also modified if the COM queue is now empty. The appropriate SCH$GL_COMOQS bit is unconditionally set.

   —For transitions from the LEF (implied resident) or CEF resident state to the COM state, SCH$RSE adds 4 to the saved PC in the hardware PCB stored in the process header so that it points past the CHMx instruction. This modification to the PC value allows the process to begin execution immediately following the system service call rather than going through a Wait for Event Flag system service for a flag that is already set. The residence check is necessary because the saved PC of nonresident processes is usually not available. (The saved PC is stored in the hardware PCB in the process header, which may be outswapped if the process is not resident.)

   —For any transition which makes a process computable, SCH$RSE removes the process from the wait queue and decrements the wait queue header count. Priority adjustment is attempted (see Section 10.4.3.2). The process state is changed to COM or COMO, depending upon whether the process is memory resident or outswapped. SCH$RSE inserts the process into the compute queue appropriate for its residence and priority and unconditionally sets the SCH$GL_COMQS or SCH$GL_COMOQS summary bit corresponding to the selected priority queue.

5. Subsequent scheduling or swapping activity is necessary to execute or inswap the now computable process. The swapper is awakened (routine SCH$SWPWAKE is called) if the now computable process is presently outswapped (see Section 10.4.2).

   The scheduler is requested, through an IPL 3 software interrupt, if the now computable process is memory resident and has a priority greater than or equal to that of the currently executing process. This priority check avoids a needless context switch with its associated overhead, when the previously executing process will again execute.

10.4.3.2   **System Events and Associated Priority Boosts.** System routines that report events to SCH$RSE not only describe the event and the process to which it applies, but also specify one of five classes of priority increments or boosts that may be applied to the base priority of the process. Table 10-3 lists the events, priority class, and potential amount of priority increment applied to the process. The table does not show AST queuing, because system routines queuing ASTs to a process can select any of the priority increment classes to be associated with the queuing of an AST.

The actual software priority of the process is determined by the following steps:

1. The priority increment for the event class (see Table 10-3) is added to the base priority of the process (PCB$B_PRIB).
2. If the process has a current priority higher than the result of step 1, the current priority is retained (such as occurs in Figure 10-6, event 13).
3. If the higher priority of steps 1 and 2 is more than 15, then the base priority of the process is used. (Note that this test accomplishes two checks at the same time. First, all real-time processes fit this criterion, with the result that real-time processes do not have their priorities adjusted in response to

Table 10-3   System Events and Associated Priority Boosts

Event	Priority Class[1]	Priority Boost
Page fault read complete	0 (PRI$_NULL)	0
Quantum end	0	0
Other events with no boost	0	0
Direct I/O completion	1 (PRI$_IOCOM)	2
Nonterminal buffered I/O completion	1	2
Update section write completion	1	2
Set priority	1	2
Resource available	2 (PRI$_RESAVL)	3
Wake a process	2	3
Resume a process	2	3
Delete a process	2	3
Timer request expiration	2 (PRI$_TIMER)	3
Terminal output completion	3 (PRI$_TOCOM)	4
Terminal input completion	4 (PRI$_TICOM)	6
Process creation	4	6

[1]Routines that report system events pass an increment class to the scheduler. The scheduler uses this class as a byte index into a table of values (local label B_PINC in module RSE) to compute the actual boost.

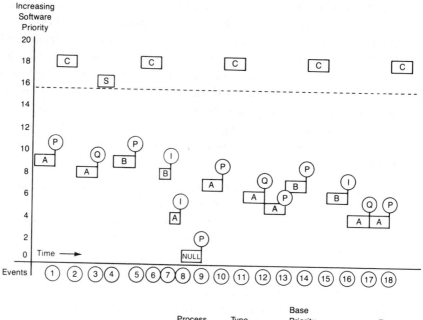

Figure 10-6 Priorities and Priority Adjustments

system events. Second, priority boosts cannot move a normal process into the real-time priority range.)

A side effect of step 3 is that real-time processes always execute at their base priorities. Further, note that normal processes with base priorities from 10 to 15 do not always receive priority increments as events occur. As the base priority of a normal process is moved closer to 15, the process spends a greater amount of time at its base priority. Priority 14 and 15 processes experience no priority boosts. Thus, this strategy benefits those processes that most need it—I/O-bound and interactive processes with base priorities of 4 through 9. Processes with elevated base priorities do not require this assistance as they are always at these levels.

An example of priority adjustment that occurs over time for several processes is illustrated in Figure 10-6. The following notes relate to the numbers at the bottom of Figure 10-6:

① Process C becomes computable. Process A is preempted.
② C hibernates. A executes again, one priority level lower.

③ A experiences quantum end. Because there is a computable outswapped process (which is B), A is rescheduled at its base priority.

④ The swapper process now executes to inswap B, and B is scheduled for execution.

⑤ B is preempted by C.

⑥ B executes again, one priority level lower.

⑦ B requests an I/O operation to a device other than a terminal. A executes at its base priority.

⑧ A requests a terminal output operation. The null process executes.

⑨ A executes following I/O completion at its base priority + 3. (The applied boost was 4, and A's priority was decremented when it was rescheduled.)

⑩ A is preempted by C.

⑪ A executes again, one priority level lower.

⑫ A experiences quantum end and is rescheduled at one priority level lower. A's priority is not lowered to its base because there is no computable outswapped process.

⑬ A is preempted by B. A priority boost of 2 is not applied to B's base priority because the result would be less than B's current priority.

⑭ B is preempted by C.

⑮ B executes again, one priority level lower.

⑯ B requests an I/O operation. A executes again, one priority level lower. (A has reached its base priority.)

⑰ A experiences quantum end and is rescheduled at the same priority (its base priority).

⑱ A is preempted by C.

10.5   **RESCHEDULING INTERRUPT**

The IPL 3 interrupt service routine schedules processes for execution. The function of this interrupt service routine is to remove the currently executing process by storing the contents of the process-private processor (hardware) registers and to replace the register contents with those of the highest priority computable resident process. This operation, known as context switching, is accompanied by modifications to the process state, current priority, and state queue of the affected processes.

The VAX architecture was designed to assist the software in performing critical, commonly performed operations. The mechanism of replacing the hardware context of the current process with the context of a different process is an example of hardware assistance to the operating system. The switching of hardware context is performed by two special purpose instructions, SVPCTX and LDPCTX, which, respectively, save and load the hardware context of a process.

10.5.1   Hardware Context

The definition of a process from the viewpoint of the hardware is contained in the hardware context. This collection of data is the set of hardware processor registers whose contents are unique to the process. These include the following:

- General registers: R0 through R11, AP, FP, and PC
- Per-process stack pointers for kernel, executive, supervisor, and user mode stacks
- PSL
- AST level processor register, PR$_ASTLVL
- Memory mapping registers for the program and control regions (P0BR, P0LR, P1BR, and P1LR)

With the exceptions of the ASTLVL register value and the contents of the memory mapping registers, the current values for the various registers forming the hardware context of the current process are maintained only in the processor registers. When a process is not executing, the complete hardware context is contained in a portion of the process header called the hardware PCB.

The hardware PCB (see Figure 10-7) is a part of the fixed portion of the process header (PHD) for each process. It is resident in memory whenever the corresponding process is in the balance set. Access by the operating system occurs normally through offsets from the starting address of the particular PHD. However, during context switching operations, the hardware must access this data structure directly without address translation. This access uses the value in the PCB base register (PR$_PCBB), which contains the physical address of the hardware PCB for the currently executing process. The swapper stores the physical address of the hardware PCB for each resident process (calculated when the process is swapped into memory) in the PCB$L_PHYPCB field of the corresponding software PCB. Figure 10-8 illustrates access to the hardware PCB.

10.5.2   SVPCTX Instruction

The save process context instruction, svpctx, performs several operations and assumes a special set of initial and final conditions. The following initial conditions are assumed:

- The current access mode is kernel.
- The PC and PSL to be saved for the process are on the kernel stack. If the svpctx instruction that executes is the one in the rescheduling interrupt service routine, the PC and PSL are on the kernel stack as a result of the IPL 3 software interrupt.

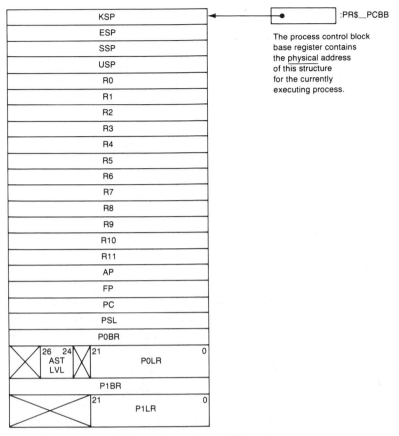

Figure 10-7   Layout of the Hardware Process Control Block

- The register PR$_PCBB contains the physical address of the hardware PCB for the current process.
- The current values of ASTLVL, P0BR, P0LR, P1BR, and P1LR are already stored in the hardware PCB.

When the SVPCTX instruction is executed, the following operations are performed by the VAX hardware:

1. The per-process stack pointers for the four access mode stacks are stored in the hardware PCB.
2. The general registers (R0 through R11, AP, and FP) are moved to the hardware PCB.
3. The PC and the PSL are popped from the current stack and moved to the hardware PCB.

Finally, if the current stack is the kernel stack, the SVPCTX instruction saves the current stack pointer (SP) in the kernel stack field of the hardware

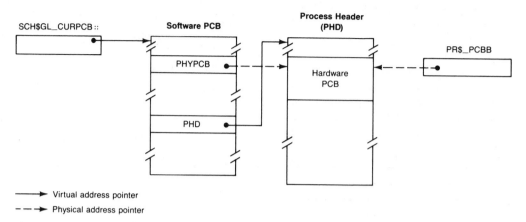

Figure 10-8 Access to the Hardware Process Control
Block

PCB and switches to the interrupt stack (by setting the PSL$V_IS bit and copying the PR$_ISP register contents into the SP register). Switching to the systemwide interrupt stack is essential because there is no current process once the instruction completes.

The ASTLVL, P0BR, P0LR, P1BR, and P1LR fields of the hardware PCB are not changed. It is the responsibility of the various system components that alter these fields always to update both the hardware PCB fields and the per-process processor registers. ASTLVL is unusual in that it is altered as a result of normal system operation when the process is not current. In that case, only the hardware PCB field is altered. The processor register is not altered because the process does not own that register when it is not the current process.

These fields do not change frequently compared to the frequency of context switching. The overhead of storing these fields in the hardware PCB is incurred only when the field values change.

The SVPCTX instruction occurs in several locations in the executive:

- The rescheduling interrupt service routine executes this instruction to remove the current (and still computable) process from execution.
- Module SYSWAIT executes this instruction to place the current process into a scheduling wait state.
- The page fault handler (module PAGEFAULT) executes a SVPCTX instruction to place a process into one of the memory management wait states (PFW, FPG, COLPG).
- At the end of process deletion, the process being deleted is removed from execution with a SVPCTX instruction.

10.5.3   **LDPCTX Instruction**

The load process context instruction, LDPCTX, performs the operations required in establishing the hardware context of the process. The instruction assumes the following initial conditions:

- The processor is in kernel mode on the interrupt stack.
- The register PR$_PCBB contains the physical address of the hardware PCB for the process which is to become current.

When the LDPCTX instruction is executed, the following operations are performed by the VAX hardware:

1. Per-process translation buffer entries are invalidated. All of the previous translation buffer entries belonged to the previous process. They are invalidated to prevent mistranslation of virtual addresses and to protect the data of the previous process.
2. The per-process stack pointers (KSP, ESP, SSP, and USP) are loaded from the hardware PCB.
3. The general registers (R0 through R11, AP, and FP) are loaded into the corresponding processor registers.
4. The memory mapping registers (P0BR, P0LR, P1BR, and P1LR) are checked for legal values, and then they are loaded from the hardware PCB. Until they are loaded, the values in the registers belong to the previous process.
5. The PR$_ASTLVL register is loaded.
6. The contents of the current stack pointer register (SP) are saved in the interrupt stack pointer register (ISP).
7. The PSL$V_IS bit is cleared in order to indicate the switch to the kernel stack.
8. The current stack pointer is updated with the contents of the kernel stack pointer register (KSP).
9. Finally, the saved PC and PSL are pushed onto the kernel stack from the hardware PCB. These values are not stored into the appropriate registers. This particular operation occurs because the next instruction is expected to be an REI instruction. The REI pops the two longwords. It then verifies the PSL format, and inserts the two longwords into the appropriate registers.

The only occurrence of a LDPCTX instruction in the VMS executive is the one shown in Example 10-1, the rescheduling interrupt service routine. (Chapter 27 describes the use of another LDPCTX instruction to place a process into execution on the attached processor of an asymmetric multiprocessing system.)

10.5.4 Rescheduling Interrupt Service Routine

The IPL 3 interrupt service routine contains two parts. SCH$RESCHED preserves the hardware context of the currently executing process and removes it from execution. The SCH$RESCHED logic flows directly into SCH$SCHED, which selects the next process to be scheduled for execution.

SCH$RESCHED is requested as an IPL 3 software interrupt by several different routines:

- SCH$RSE—when a resident process whose priority is greater than or equal to that of the current process becomes computable.
- SCH$QEND—when the current process uses up its quantum if the process is normal and not real-time.
- SCH$UNLOCK—when the current process unlocks a mutex and has a priority restored which is lower than that of another resident computable process.
- EXE$SETPRI—when the current process lowers its priority to a value lower than that of another resident computable process.

Under some circumstances (such as system initialization, placing the previous process into a wait state, or deletion of the previous process), there may not be a current process to be saved by SCH$RESCHED. In these cases, system routines transfer control directly to SCH$SCHED for process selection. (The difference between the two entry points is determined by whether the previous process is still computable. Typically, a process entering a wait state causes entry at SCH$SCHED, while a higher priority process becoming computable causes entry through a software interrupt at SCH$RESCHED.)

SCH$RESCHED performs the following steps. (The numbers in the following list correspond to numbers in the listing of the code, Example 10-1.)

① SCH$RESCHED first raises IPL to IPL$_SYNCH to block concurrent access and modification of the scheduler database by other system components.

② It then executes a SVPCTX instruction to save the hardware context of the current process in its hardware PCB. The register PR$_PCBB contains the physical address of the current process hardware PCB. The detailed operation of the SVPCTX instruction is described in Section 10.5.2.

③ The address of the software PCB for the current process is obtained from the pointer SCH$GL_CURPCB in the module SDAT.

④ The current priority of the process is determined from the PCB$B_PRI field. The current priority is used to determine which of the resident computable state queues is to include this PCB.

⑤ The state of the process is changed to COM from CUR by updating the PCB$W_STATE field.

⑥ The process is inserted at the tail of the corresponding priority queue.

At this point, there is no current process, and the search begins for the next process to execute.

SCH$SCHED raises IPL to IPL$_SYNCH. As with rescheduling, the search for and modification of the next process to be executed must be performed at IPL$_SYNCH to block other potential system operations on the scheduler database.

Note that the search for the highest priority computable resident process and the removal of its PCB from the COM queue are achieved in three instructions (see Example 10-1). The efficiency of this operation is attributable to the instruction set and the design of the scheduler database for the computable states (see Figure 10-2).

SCH$SCHED performs the following operations. (The numbers in the following list correspond to numbers in the listing of the code, shown in Example 10-1.)

⑦ It executes an FFS instruction to locate the least significant set bit in the longword SCH$GL_COMQS. The located bit position indicates the highest priority nonempty computable resident state queue.

⑧ The listhead of the selected computable resident queue is found by using the nonempty queue bit position as an index into the contiguous listheads.

⑨ The first PCB in the selected queue is removed by indirect reference through the forward link of the listhead.

⑩ If the removed PCB was the only one in the queue, the corresponding SCH$GL_COMQS bit must now be cleared because the queue is now empty.

⑪ SCH$SCHED changes the state of the process to current by storing the value SCH$C_CUR into the PCB$W_STATE field.

⑫ SCH$SCHED stores the address of the new current process PCB in SCH$GL_CURPCB.

⑬ It examines the current process priority and potentially modifies it. If the process is a real-time process or a normal process already at its base priority, then the process is scheduled at its current or base priority (they are the same). If the current process is a normal process above its base priority, then a decrease of one software priority level is performed before scheduling. Thus, priority "demotions" always occur before execution, and a process executes at the priority of the queue to which it will be returned (and not the priority of the queue from which it was removed). See Figure 10-6, event 2, for an example.

⑭ The physical address of the hardware PCB for the scheduled process is loaded into the PR$_PCBB register from the PCB$L_PHYPCB field.

⑮ A LDPCTX instruction is executed (see Section 10.5.3).

⑯ SCH$SCHED executes an REI instruction to pass control to the scheduled process. This transfer of control is possible because the LDPCTX instruction

Scheduling

Example 10-1   Scheduler Interrupt Service Routine

```
         .SBTTL   SCH$RESCHED RESCHEDULING INTERRUPT HANDLER
;++
; SCH$RESCHED - RESCHEDULING INTERRUPT HANDLER
;
; This routine is entered via the IPL 3 rescheduling interrupt.
; The vector for this interrupt is coded to cause execution
; on the kernel stack.
;
; ENVIRONMENT:
;        IPL = 3   Mode = kernel   IS = 0
; INPUT:
;        00(SP) = PC at reschedule interrupt
;        04(SP) = PSL at interrupt
;- -
         .ALIGN   LONG
MPH$RESCHED::                                ;Multiprocessing code hooks in here
SCH$RESCHED::                                ;Reschedule interrupt handler
         SETIPL   #IPL$_SYNCH                ;Synchronize scheduler with event  ①
                                             ; reporting
         SVPCTX                              ;Save context of process  ②
         MOVL     L^SCH$GL_CURPCB,R1         ;Get address of current PCB  ③
         MOVZBL   PCB$B_PRI(R1),R2           ;Current priority  ④
         BBSS     R2,L^SCH$GL_COMQS,10$      ;Mark queue nonempty
10$:     MOVW     #SCH$C_COM,PCB$W_STATE(R1) ;Set state to res compute  ⑤
         MOVAQ    SCH$AQ_COMT[R2],R3         ;Compute address of queue
         INSQUE   (R1),@(R3)+                ;Insert at tail of queue  ⑥
;+
; SCH$SCHED - SCHEDULE NEW PROCESS FOR EXECUTION
;
; This routine selects the highest priority executable process
; and places it in execution.
;-
MPH$SCHED::                                  ;Multiprocessing code hooks in here
SCH$SCHED::                                  ;Schedule for execution
         SETIPL   #IPL$_SYNCH                ;Synchronize scheduler with event
                                             ; reporting
         FFS      #0,#32,L^SCH$GL_COMQS,R2   ;Find first full state  ⑦
         BEQL     SCH$IDLE                   ;No executable process?
         MOVAQ    SCH$AQ_COMH[R2],R3         ;Compute queue head address  ⑧
         REMQUE   @(R3)+,R4                  ;Get head of queue  ⑨
         BVS      QEMPTY                     ;Br if queue was empty (BUGCHECK)
```

Example 10-1 Scheduler Interrupt Service Routine *(continued)*

```
          BNEQ     20$                      ;Queue not empty
          BBCC     R2,L`SCH$GL_COMQS,20$    ;Set queue empty ⑩
20$:                                        ;
          CMPB     #DYN$C_PCB,PCB$B_TYPE(R4)  ;Must be a process control block
          BNEQ     QEMPTY                   ;Otherwise fatal error
          MOVW     #SCH$C_CUR,PCB$W_STATE(R4) ;Set state to current ⑪
          MOVL     R4,L`SCH$GL_CURPCB       ;Note current PCB loc ⑫
          CMPB     PCB$B_PRIB(R4),PCB$B_PRI(R4)   ;Check for base ⑬
                                            ;Priority = current
          BEQL     30$                      ;Yes, don't float priority
          BBC      #4,PCB$B_PRI(R4),30$     ;Don't float real-
                                            ; time priority
          INCB     PCB$B_PRI(R4)            ;Move toward base priority
30$:      MOVB     PCB$B_PRI(R4),L`SCH$GB_PRI  ;Set global priority
          MTPR     PCB$L_PHYPCB(R4),#PR$_PCBB  ;Set PCB base phys address ⑭
          LDPCTX                            ;Restore context ⑮
          REI                               ;Normal return ⑯
SCH$IDLE:                                   ;No active, executable process
          SETIPL   #IPL$_SCHED              ;Drop IPL to scheduling level
          MOVB     #32,L`SCH$GB_PRI         ;Set priority to -1(32) to signal idle
          BRB      SCH$SCHED                ; and try again

QEMPTY:   BUG_CHECK QUEUEMPTY,FATAL         ;Scheduling queue empty ⑰
          .END
```

left the PC and PSL of the scheduled process on the kernel stack. Execution of the REI instruction has the following additional effects:

- The interrupt priority level is dropped from IPL$_SYNCH.
- The access mode is typically changed from kernel to a less privileged one.
- If ASTs are queued to the PCB, they are likely to be delivered at this time, depending on their access mode and the access mode at which the process is reentered (see Chapter 7).

⑰ Consistency checks are made to ensure that the queue really had at least one PCB and that the data structure removed was actually a PCB. Failure of either of these tests results in a QUEUEMPTY fatal bugcheck.

11   Time Support

Love, all alike, no season knows, nor clime,
Nor hours, days, months, which are the rags of time.

John Donne, *The Sun Rising*

Support for activities that require either the date and time or the measurement of an interval of time is implemented in both the VAX hardware and the VAX/VMS operating system.

A hardware component called the interval clock interrupts at regular intervals. VAX/VMS uses this clock to keep time and to service time-dependent requests. VAX/VMS keeps two different times, the current date and time (the "system time") and the time elapsed since the system was bootstrapped (the "system uptime"). On most VAX processors, another hardware component called the time-of-year clock maintains the date and time across system reboots and power failures.

VAX/VMS provides two system services to support users' time-dependent requests, Schedule Wakeup ($SCHDWK) and Set Timer ($SETIMR). Another system service, Set Time ($SETIME), enables the system manager to change the system date and time. The Get Time ($GETTIM) system service enables users to read the current date and time. Several other services, described briefly in Chapter 29, convert the date and time between ASCII and binary formats.

Keeping time and servicing time-dependent requests require both a hardware interrupt service routine for the interval clock and a software interrupt service routine. The hardware interrupt service routine keeps the system time and requests the software timer interrupt as necessary. The software interrupt service routine supports time-dependent services such as scheduled wakeups, by examining a time-ordered queue of requests and delivering them as their expiration times occur.

1.1   HARDWARE CLOCKS

The hardware clocks are updated regularly by timing circuitry. Initialization, calibration, and interpretation of the clocks are performed by VMS routines during system initialization and normal operations.

The processor registers that implement the hardware clocks are summarized in Table 11-1, along with the memory locations that implement the various software time values.

The implementations of the interval and time-of-year clocks vary on the different VAX CPUs.

11.1.1   Interval Clock

All VAX CPUs implement an interval clock that can interrupt at ten-millisecond intervals. The minimum implementation is the processor register PR$_ICCS containing a single bit which, when set, enables interrupts every ten milliseconds. The MicroVAX I and MicroVAX II implement the minimum interval timer.

Other VAX processors have two additional processor registers to control the interval clock, PRxxx$_ICR and PRxxx$_NICR. The additional processor registers are defined by the CPU-specific macros $PRxxxDEF, where xxx is the CPU designations. Table G-1 in Appendix G lists the CPU designations and their corresponding CPU types.

A description of the full interval clock implementation follows. It applies to all the VAX processors listed in Table 11-2 except the MicroVAX I and MicroVAX II.

The full implementation of the interval clock is the set of three processor registers. The clock "ticks" at one-microsecond intervals with an accuracy of at least 0.01 percent (an error of less than nine seconds per day). The frequency at which the interval clock causes an interrupt is determined by the value in one of the processor registers, PRxxx$_NICR.

Table 11-1   VAX/VMS Hardware Clocks and Software Timers

Name	Use	Units	Frequency	Updated by
PRxxx$_ICR[1]	Interval count	1 μsec	1 μsec	CPU hardware
PRxxx$_NICR[1]	Next interval count	1 μsec		EXE$INIPROCREG[2]
PR$_ICCS	Interval clock control/status		10 msec	EXE$HWCLKINT, EXE$INIPROCREG
PRxxx$_TODR[1]	Time-of-year clock	10 msec	10 msec	CPU hardware, EXE$INIT_TODR, EXE$SETIME[3]
EXE$GQ_SYSTIME	System date and time	100 nsec	10 msec	EXE$HWCLKINT, EXE$SETIME, EXE$RESTART
EXE$GL_ABSTIM	System uptime	1 sec	1 sec	System initialization, EXE$TIMEOUT
EXE$GL_TODR	Time-of-year base value	10 msec		EXE$SETIME
EXE$GQ_TODCBASE	Time-of-year base value (in system time form)	100 nsec		EXE$SETIME

[1]This is a CPU-specific register that does not exist on all processors.
[2]PRxxx$_NICR is written only at system initialization and after powerfail recovery.
[3]PRxxx$_TODR is actually modified through the CPU-specific routine EXE$WRITE_TODR.

Table 11-2   VAX Interval Clock Interrupt Priority Level

Processor Type	Interval Timer IPL
MicroVAX I	22
MicroVAX II	22
VAX-11/730	24
VAX-11/750	24
VAX-11/780	24
VAX-11/782	24
VAX-11/785	24
VAX 8200	22
VAX 8300	22
VAX 8500	22
VAX 8550	22
VAX 8600	24
VAX 8650	24
VAX 8700	22
VAX 8800	22

The three interval clock registers (see Table 11-1) are used as follows:

- The interval clock control/status register (PR$_ICCS) controls the interrupt status of the interval clock. This register is set by the CPU hardware and then reset by the interval clock interrupt service routine (see Section 11.6).
- The next interval count register (PRxxx$_NICR) defines how often the interval clock will cause a hardware interrupt. At system initialization, this processor register is initialized with a value of −10000. This value specifies an interval clock interrupt period of ten milliseconds (10,000 microseconds).
- Every microsecond the hardware increments the interval count register (PRxxx$_ICR). Thus, it counts from the PRxxx$_NICR value toward zero. When PRxxx$_ICR becomes zero, the register overflows, with the following results:

  a. The hardware copies the contents of PRxxx$_NICR into PRxxx$_ICR to define the next interval.
  b. The hardware sets a bit in PR$_ICCS to indicate the overflow condition. The setting of the bit causes an interval clock interrupt to occur.

The interrupt priority level (IPL) at which the hardware interrupt occurs is either 22 or 24, depending on the processor type. Earlier VAX CPU models use IPL 24. The VAX architecture now defines 22 as the IPL associated with the interval clock. Table 11-2 lists the different CPU types and the IPL associated with their interval clocks.

PR$_ICCS is reset by the interval clock interrupt service routine to indicate servicing of the interrupt and reenabling of the interval clock.

Because the interval clock implementation varies, the interval clock register or registers are initialized by the routine EXE$INIPROCREG, which is in CPU-specific code loaded during system initialization (the SYSLOA*xxx* image).

11.1.2 Time-of-Year Clock

A time-of-year clock is a hardware clock updated by hardware timing circuitry to maintain the date and time across system reboots and power failures. On most VAX CPUs, the time-of-year clock is powered by a battery when there is no power to the system so that the clock keeps correct time. At system initialization, the operating system uses the time-of-year clock and the system global locations EXE$GQ_TODCBASE and EXE$GL_TODR to determine the date and time (see Section 11.2.1). If there is no time-of-year clock or if its battery lacks power, VMS cannot determine the correct date and time without human intervention.

On many VAX CPUs, the time-of-year clock is implemented as a processor register, PR*xxx*$_TODR. The register is an unsigned 32-bit counter, the least significant bit of which represents a resolution of ten milliseconds.

The base time for the time-of-year clock is 00:00:00.00 hours on January 1 of the current year. The number 10000000_{16} represents this base time. That is, the time-of-year clock is initialized to that number rather than 0 to facilitate detection of loss of power to the clock (which causes a reset to 0).

Initialized to 10,000,000, the time-of-year clock can count to a maximum of about 15 months. To prevent overflow, the time-of-year clock must be adjusted during the first three months of the year. This can be accomplished by rebooting the system or invoking the $SETIME system service (see Section 11.3).

The implementation of the time-of-year clock varies on different VAX CPUs. The following summarizes implementations of the time-of-year clock on the various VAX CPUs:

- The MicroVAX I has no time-of-year clock.
- The MicroVAX II has a watch chip with battery backup and no time-of-year processor register.
- The VAX-11/730 has a time-of-year processor register. Certain VAX-11/730 configurations have battery backup for the register.
- The VAX-11/750, VAX-11/780, VAX-11/782, VAX-11/785, VAX 8600, and

VAX 8650 have a time-of-year processor register with battery backup.

- The VAX 8200 and VAX 8300 have a watch chip with battery backup and a time-of-year processor register without battery backup.
- The VAX 8500, VAX 8550, VAX 8700, and VAX 8800 have a time-of-year clock in the console subsystem and no time-of-year processor register. The time-of-year clock has battery backup. VMS must communicate with the console subsystem to read the time-of-year clock.

Access to the time-of-year clock is through routines in CPU-specific code loaded during system initialization (SYSLOAxxx). Thus, the actual implementation of the time-of-year clock is transparent to the rest of VMS.

The SYSLOAxxx routines for accessing the time-of-year clock are the following:

- EXE$INIT_TODR, which uses the clock to initialize the system time
- EXE$READ_TODR and EXE$READP_TODR, which read the clock
- EXE$WRITE_TODR and EXE$WRITEP_TODR, which write the clock

On many VAX CPUs, EXE$READ_TODR and EXE$READP_TODR are identical, as are EXE$WRITE_TODR and EXE$WRITEP_TODR. On a CPU with a watch chip or console time-of-year clock, EXE$READP_TODR and EXE$WRITEP_TODR usually access those. On a CPU with no time-of-year processor register, EXE$READ_TODR simulates one, using EXE$GL_TODR and the amount of time (64-bit format) that has elapsed since the system was booted.

.2 TIMEKEEPING IN VAX/VMS

During system initialization, VMS determines the date and time from the time-of-year clock and the system global locations EXE$GQ_TODCBASE and EXE$GL_TODR. During normal system operation, VMS uses the interval clock interrupts to keep time. Global location EXE$GQ_SYSTIME contains the system date and time. Global location EXE$GL_ABSTIM contains the system uptime. Table 11-1 summarizes these global locations.

.2.1 Initializing the Date and Time

The contents of EXE$GQ_TODCBASE and EXE$GL_TODR are maintained in the system image file, SYS$SYSTEM:SYS.EXE, as a record of the system time on which the contents of the time-of-year clock are based. Both represent the same time in different formats. EXE$GQ_TODCBASE represents the time of last adjustment in standard 64-bit time (the same format as EXE$GQ_SYSTIME). EXE$GL_TODR represents the time of last adjustment in the same 32-bit format as the time-of-year clock.

These base time values represent the more recent of the following times:

- The time when the system was booted
- The last time that the time-of-year was redefined by $SETIME

These values are recorded in the system image whenever the system is booted or the $SETIME system service is requested through either the DCL command or some other program. These values are recorded at system shutdown as well, through the command SET TIME in the shutdown command procedure.

Recording up-to-date values of these variables ensures that

- VMS can determine the current year from EXE$GQ_TODCBASE. A 32-bit time-of-year clock can represent only date and time within year, but not year.
- VMS can use the recorded value of EXE$GL_TODR as a validity test for the time-of-year clock.
- The date and time are as recent as possible for a system which is without battery backup for the time-of-year clock and is to boot unattended.

During system initialization, SYSINIT invokes the routine EXE$INIT_TODR in SYSLOAxxx to validate the time-of-year and to initialize EXE$GQ_SYSTIME from either the time-of-year clock and system global locations or from a date and time entered by the operator. For a node joining a VAXcluster System, SYSINIT obtains the date and time from a node which has already joined and invokes EXE$SETIME_INT to set the date and time. When a new VAXcluster System is being formed, the time from one system is sent to all other nodes, each of which invokes EXE$SETIME_INT. (See Section 11.3 for a description of EXE$SETIME_INT.) After the system disk is mounted, SYSINIT invokes the $SETIME service to record new values for the time-of-year global locations in the system image on disk.

The basic algorithm in EXE$INIT_TODR is similar for all VAX CPUs, although there are some CPU-specific variants:

1. EXE$INIT_TODR examines the SYSBOOT parameter SETTIME.
2. If SETTIME is zero, EXE$INIT_TODR reads the time-of-year clock and compares its contents to those of EXE$GL_TODR. If EXE$GL_TODR is more than one day ahead of the time-of-year clock, the time of year must be reset. This test detects a clock which has lost power. It also prevents losing a year in the date, for example, when a disk with a December date in the system image is booted on a processor whose time-of-year clock has been reset to reflect a new year.

   If the time-of-year clock appears valid, then its contents and those of EXE$GL_TODR and EXE$GQ_TODCBASE are used to reset the system time.

3. If SETTIME is 1 or the time-of-year clock is invalid, EXE$INIT_TODR examines the SYSBOOT parameter TIMEPROMPTWAIT to determine how to reset the time of year:

   a. A negative TIMEPROMPTWAIT value causes the routine to prompt for the date and time on the console terminal and wait until the operator enters valid data.

   b. A positive TIMEPROMPTWAIT value represents an upper limit on the amount of time EXE$INIT_TODR waits for the operator to enter a new date and time. If that time elapses without the input of valid data, EXE$INIT_TODR computes the time of year as in the next item.

   c. A TIMEPROMPTWAIT value of zero means that the routine is to reset the time without human intervention. EXE$INIT_TODR computes a new value for the time of year, based on the contents of EXE$GL_TODR plus ten milliseconds.

4. EXE$INIT_TODR invokes EXE$SETIME_INT, an internal entry point for the system service $SETIME, to initialize the system time and update EXE$GQ_TODCBASE and EXE$GL_TODR. The system image on disk is not modified.

1.2.2   Maintaining the Date and Time

The system time, EXE$GQ_SYSTIME, is the number of 100-nanosecond intervals since 00:00 hours, November 17, 1858 (the base time for the Smithsonian Institution astronomical calendar). EXE$GQ_SYSTIME (see Table 11-1) is updated every ten milliseconds by the interval clock interrupt service routine (see Section 11.6). This quadword is the reference for nearly all user-requested time-dependent software activities in the system. For example, the $GETTIM system service simply writes this quadword value into a user-defined buffer.

EXE$GL_ABSTIM measures the number of one-second intervals that have elapsed since the system was bootstrapped. EXE$GL_ABSTIM is defined as zero at assembly time and incremented by the routine EXE$TIMEOUT (see Section 11.7.2).

EXE$GL_ABSTIM is the reference time for several system-requested time checks. For example, its contents are recorded in the field PCB$L_WAITIME, whenever a process is placed into a voluntary wait, is removed from a voluntary wait, or incurs quantum end. A comparison between PCB$L_WAITIME and EXE$GL_ABSTIM enables outswap scheduling code to determine if the process can be considered to be in a long wait or if the process is dormant. (See Chapter 17.)

In addition, EXE$GL_ABSTIM is used to check periodically for I/O device, I/O controller, mount verify, and lock request timeouts. This variable is also the source for system uptime, interpreted and displayed by the DCL command SHOW SYSTEM.

EXE$GQ_SYSTIME is adjusted at power failure recovery and through the system service $SETIME. EXE$GL_ABSTIM is never adjusted.

11.3 SET TIME SYSTEM SERVICE

The $SETIME system service allows a system manager or operator to change the system time while the operating system is running. This may be necessary because of a power failure longer than the battery backup time of the time-of-year clock or changes between standard and daylight saving time, for example. The new system time (absolute time format, not relative) is passed as the optional single argument of the system service.

The $SETIME system service is also invoked directly at a special entry point, EXE$SETIME_INT. This entry point is used during system initialization to compute the system time from the contents of the time-of-year clock and system variables. The difference between the two entry points is that EXE$SETIME_INT sets a flag to prevent recording the values of EXE$GL_TODR and EXE$GQ_TODCBASE in the system image. (SYSINIT invokes EXE$SETIME_INT before the system disk is mounted.)

The system service procedure EXE$SETIME, in module SYSSETIME, first validates the request. If the requesting process does not have the privileges OPER and LOG_IO, EXE$SETIME returns the error SS$_NOPRIV. If the input quadword cannot be read, the procedure returns the error SS$_ACCVIO.

The procedure diverges into two paths described in the following sections based on the presence or absence of the new time argument.

11.3.1 $SETIME System Time Recalibration Requests

If no argument was passed to the system service or the time argument is a zero value, then the request is considered a request to recalibrate EXE$GQ_SYSTIME from the time-of-year clock, EXE$GL_TODR, and EXE$GQ_TODCBASE. Sometimes recalibration is done during normal operation, because on many VAX CPUs the time-of-year clock is more accurate than the interval clock.

EXE$SETIME performs the following actions:

1. EXE$SETIME invokes EXE$READP_TODR to read the "physical" time-of-year clock. (Its contents are referenced in the items and equations following as TOY_CLOCK.)
2. EXE$SETIME compares the TOY_CLOCK to EXE$GL_TODR. If the latter represents a time more than one day later, the TOY_CLOCK is not valid and EXE$SETIME returns the error status SS$_IVTIME.

3. The new system time, EXE$GQ_SYSTIME, is computed by the following equation:

```
EXE$GQ_SYSTIME

    = EXE$GQ_TODCBASE + ((TOY_CLOCK - EXE$GL_TODR) * 100000)
```

EXE$GQ_SYSTIME and EXE$GQ_TODCBASE are quadword system times in units of 100 nanoseconds. TOY_CLOCK and EXE$GL_TODR are longword time-of-year times in units of ten milliseconds. The multiplier of 100,000 represents the number of 100-nanosecond intervals in ten milliseconds.

4. The values in TOY_CLOCK, EXE$GL_TODR, and EXE$GQ_TODCBASE are corrected if TOY_CLOCK represents a value larger than one year. This prevents the time-of-year clock from overflowing its limit.

5. Each element in the timer queue (see Section 11.4) that specified a relative (or delta) time has its expiration time adjusted by the difference between the previous system time and the new system time. This modification prevents the actual relative time value from being changed by a modification to system time. A timer queue element (TQE) containing an absolute time is not adjusted; this ensures that the TQE will come due at the time specified by the user. Bit TQE$V_ABSOLUTE in TQE$B_RQTYPE distinguishes an absolute request from a relative request: a zero value indicates a relative request; 1, an absolute request. Section 11.4 describes the form and use of TQEs.

6. The pages of the system image in memory that contain EXE$GQ_TODCBASE and EXE$GL_TODR are written back to the system image file if the procedure was entered at EXE$SETIME.

11.3.2 $SETIME Time-of-Year Readjustment Requests

If a nonzero time value is supplied as an argument to $SETIME, then EXE$SETIME performs the following operations:

1. The input argument, specified in system time units of 100 nanoseconds, is converted into time-of-year units (the number of ten-millisecond intervals after 00:00 hours on January 1 of the base year).

2. The specified time, converted to 32-bit time-of-year format, is written into the time-of-year clock and EXE$GL_TODR.

3. The specified time is written into EXE$GQ_TODCBASE and EXE$GQ_SYSTIME.

4. Finally, the timer queue is updated and, if the procedure was entered at EXE$SETIME, the new values for the time-of-year clock base are written to the system image file. (See steps 5 and 6 previously described in Section 11.3.1.)

11.4   TIMER QUEUE AND TIMER QUEUE ELEMENTS

VMS maintains a list of time-dependent requests as a doubly linked list of timer queue elements, ordered by the expiration time of the requests. EXE$GL_TQFL and the following longword (defined in the module SYS-COMMON) form the listhead of the timer queue. TQEs are generally allocated from nonpaged dynamic memory and initialized as a result of $SETIMR and $SCHDWK system service calls (see Section 11.5). The allocation of TQEs is governed by the pooled job quota JIB$W_TQCNT.

The format of a TQE is shown in Figure 11-1. The link fields (TQE$L_TQFL and TQE$L_TQBL), the TQE$W_SIZE field, and the TQE$B_TYPE field are characteristic of system data structures allocated from dynamic memory.

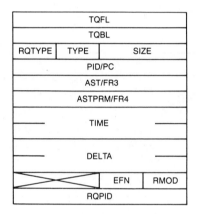

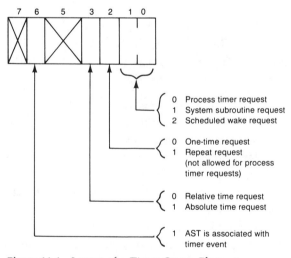

Figure 11-1   Layout of a Timer Queue Element

The TQE$B_RQTYPE field describes the timer request. Its low-order two bits define the type of timer request (process timer request, periodic system routine request, or process wake request). Bit TQE$V_REPEAT in TQE$B_RQTYPE is set if the request is a repeating request, rather than a one-time request. Bit TQE$V_ABSOLUTE in TQE$B_RQTYPE is set if the timer event was requested at a particular absolute time, rather than at a relative interval from the current time. Bit ACB$V_QUOTA of TQE$B_RMOD is set if an AST is to be delivered when the timer event occurs. Figure 11-1 summarizes the bits in TQE$B_RQTYPE.

The interpretation of the next three longword fields depends upon the type of timer request. For system routine requests, these fields contain the PC, R3, and R4 register values to be loaded before control is passed to the routine. For process requests, these fields define the process ID of the process to which to report the event, the address of an AST routine to execute (if requested), and an optional AST parameter.

For both process and system routine requests, the field TQE$Q_TIME is the quadword system time at which a particular timer event is to occur. TQE$Q_DELTA is the repeat interval time for repeating requests.

Several fields are meaningful only for process requests. The access mode of the requesting process is stored in TQE$B_RMOD. The event flag to be set when the timer event occurs is stored in TQE$B_EFN. TQE$L_RQPID contains the process ID of the process that made the initial timer request. (The requesting process is not necessarily the same as the target process whose ID is stored in TQE$L_PID.)

1.5   TIMER SYSTEM SERVICES

Two system services are used to request time-dependent services, Schedule Wakeup ($SCHDWK) and Set Timer ($SETIMR). Both of these services are in the module SYSSCHEVT. Two complementary services cancel time-dependent requests, Cancel Wakeup ($CANWAK) and Cancel Timer Request ($CANTIM). These system service routines are in the module SYSCANEVT.

1.5.1 $SETIMR Requests

The $SETIMR system service creates TQEs of the single process request type. The system service procedure, EXE$SETIMR, performs the following steps:

1. The event flag specified as an argument to the system service is cleared in preparation for a subsequent setting at expiration time.
2. The request is checked to make sure that the following are true:

   —The delta time location is accessible to the requesting process.
   —The PCB$W_ASTCNT of the requesting process is not exceeded (if an

AST is to be associated with this timer request).

—The JIB$W_TQCNT of the requesting job is not exceeded.

3. A TQE is allocated from nonpaged dynamic memory and initialized from the system service arguments (delta time, request type, and process ID).

4. If the expiration time was expressed as a relative time (a negative argument), then the absolute expiration time of the request is calculated by adding the delta time of the request to the current system time, EXE$GQ_SYSTIME. The absolute expiration time is stored in the TQE$Q_TIME field. Bit TQE$V_ABSOLUTE in TQE$B_RQTYPE is cleared if the expiration time was expressed as a relative time; otherwise, it is set.

5. The JIB$W_TQCNT field of the pooled job quotas is decremented to indicate the allocation of the TQE.

6. The access mode of the system service caller is stored in the TQE$B_RMOD field. If an AST routine was specified as an argument to the $SETIMR call, then the process PCB$W_ASTCNT is decremented to indicate the future AST delivery and bit ACB$V_QUOTA of TQE$B_RMOD is set to indicate the AST accounting.

7. The AST parameter (which is used as request identification) and event flag number arguments are copied to the TQE.

8. EXE$SETIMR invokes EXE$INSTIMQ (in module EXSUBROUT) to insert the TQE into the right place in the timer queue and then returns.

The $CANTIM system service removes one or more TQEs before expiration. Two arguments, the request identification parameter and the access mode, control the actions taken by this routine. Each TQE in the timer queue that meets all of the following criteria is removed and deallocated:

- The process ID of the $CANTIM system service caller is the same as the process ID stored in the TQE.
- The access mode of the caller is at least as privileged as the access mode stored in the TQE. (That is, no request can be deleted for an access mode more privileged than that of the caller.)
- The request identification parameter argument is the same as that stored in the TQE. If the argument value is zero, then all TQEs meeting the first two criteria are removed.

11.5.2 Scheduled Wakeup Operations

The logic for managing scheduled wakeup requests is similar to that of $SETIMR requests. Two differences are the ability to specify repeating scheduled wakeup requests and the ability to schedule wakeup requests for another process. The system service procedure EXE$SCHDWK, in module SYSSCHEVT, performs the following actions:

1. The target process ID specified in the system service argument is verified. If the target process is not in the system, the scheduled wakeup request is ignored.
2. EXE$SCHDWK checks whether the target process exists and invokes EXE$NAMPID (see Chapter 12) to determine whether the current process is allowed to affect it. If it is, EXE$SCHDWK tests the repeat time to determine whether the request is a one-time or repeating scheduled wakeup.
3. The requested repeat time is formatted for insertion in the TQE. If the repeat time is less than ten milliseconds, it is increased to that value (the resolution of the interval clock interrupt).
4. A TQE is allocated from nonpaged dynamic memory.
5. The repeat time, request type, and target process ID are initialized in the TQE.
6. If the initial scheduled wakeup time was expressed as a relative time, then bit TQE$V_ABSOLUTE is cleared and the initial expiration time is calculated as in $SETIMR from the initial delta time and the current system time. If the initial scheduled wakeup time was expressed as an absolute time, bit TQE$V_ABSOLUTE is set.
7. The ASTCNT quota of the requesting process is decremented to account for the allocation of the TQE.
8. It invokes EXE$INSTIMQ (in module EXSUBROUT) to insert the TQE into the right place in the timer queue.

When the expiration time is reached, the target process is awakened (see Section 11.7.3). Deallocation of the TQE occurs after delivery of a one-time scheduled wakeup request or as a result of a $CANWAK system service call.

The $CANWAK system service cancels all one-time and repeat scheduled wakeup requests for a target process. EXE$CANWAK, the system service procedure, first invokes EXE$NAMPID to check that the requesting process has the ability to affect the target process (see Chapter 12). Each canceled TQE is deallocated to nonpaged dynamic memory and, if the initial requesting process still exists, its PCB$W_ASTCNT is incremented to indicate the deallocation.

11.6 INTERVAL CLOCK INTERRUPT SERVICE ROUTINE

The interval clock interrupt service routine, EXE$HWCLKINT in module TIMESCHDL, services the hardware interrupt signaled by the interval clock every ten milliseconds.

On some CPUs, this is an IPL 24 interrupt; on others, it is an IPL 22 interrupt. Table 11-2 lists the CPUs and the IPL of their interval clock interrupts. The interval clock interrupt service routine has two major functions:

- Updating the system time (and possibly process accounting)
- Checking the timer queue for timer events that have timed out

Updating the system time and process accounting fields requires the following actions:

1. EXE$HWCLKINT resets the PR$_ICCS register to indicate the servicing of the interrupt and the reenabling of the interval clock.
2. It updates the system time, EXE$GQ_SYSTIME, by adding the equivalent of ten milliseconds to the quadword value.
3. EXE$HWCLKINT analyzes the PSL at the time of the interrupt to determine which of the six timer statistics to increment: kernel mode, executive mode, supervisor mode, user mode, interrupt stack, or compatibility mode. This statistics array is defined at global location PMS$GL_KERNEL and displayed by Monitor Utility MODES display.
4. If the interval clock interrupts while a process is executing (if the interrupt stack bit is clear in the interrupt PSL), then the accumulated CPU utilization (PHD$L_CPUTIM) and quantum value (PHD$W_QUANT) are incremented in the process header. The quantum value is used to determine quantum end (see Section 11.7 and Chapter 10). If the quantum value reaches zero, an IPL$_TIMERFORK, or IPL 7, software interrupt is requested.

   The check for whether the interrupt occurred while the system was already on the interrupt stack prevents a process from being charged for CPU time that the system was using to service interrupts.
5. EXE$HWCLKINT determines whether the software timer interrupt should be requested to service the timer queue. If the first TQE has an expiration time less than or equal to the newly updated system time, then the timer event is due. The software timer is requested through an interrupt at IPL$_TIMERFORK, which is IPL 7.

11.7   SOFTWARE TIMER INTERRUPT SERVICE ROUTINE

The software timer interrupt service routine, EXE$SWTIMINT in module TIMESCHDL, is invoked through the IPL$_TIMERFORK software interrupt. The software timer interrupt can be requested because either the current process has reached quantum end or the first TQE must be serviced. EXE$SWTIMINT immediately raises IPL to IPL$_TIMER (equal to IPL$_SYNCH) to serialize access to systemwide data, such as the scheduler database.

EXE$SWTIMINT tests PHD$W_QUANT to determine whether the current process has reached quantum end. This field is initialized to the negative value of the SYSBOOT parameter QUANTUM and incremented by the interval clock interrupt service routine. A zero or positive quantum value indicates quantum expiration. If the process has reached quantum end, EXE$SWTIMINT invokes routine SCH$QEND to service the quantum end event (see Chapter 10).

If the system time, EXE$GQ_SYSTIME, is greater than or equal to the expiration time of the first element in the timer queue, then the timer event is due. The multiple-instruction comparison with the system time must be performed at IPL$_HWCLK to block a possible interval clock interrupt.

If the timer request is due, then EXE$SWTIMINT removes its TQE from the timer queue, lowers IPL to IPL$_TIMER, and performs one of three sequences of code (depending upon the type of request). The following sections describe these sequences.

1.7.1   Timer Request Servicing

If the TQE is a process timer request (created by a $SETIMR system service call and indicated by a type of 0), then EXE$SWTIMINT performs the following operations:

1. The event flag associated with this timer event is set by using the TQE$L_PID and TQE$B_EFN fields and invoking the SCH$POSTEF routine. A software priority increment of 3 may be applied when the process next executes (see Chapter 10).
2. If the target process is no longer in the system or the event flag number is illegal, the TQE is simply deallocated without further action.
3. The process's JIB$W_TQCNT quota is incremented to indicate the delivery of the timer event and the pending deallocation of the TQE.
4. If ACB$V_QUOTA in TQE$B_RQTYPE is set, the user requested AST notification. EXE$SWTIMINT copies the TQE$B_RMOD field to TQE$B_RQTYPE to reformat the TQE into an AST control block (ACB). EXE$SWTIMINT calls SCH$QAST to queue the ACB to the process in the access mode of the original timer request (see Chapter 7).

When the processing of this TQE has been completed, EXE$SWTIMINT checks whether the next TQE is due.

Note that process timer requests are strictly one-time requests. Any repetition of timer requests must be implemented by the requesting process. A process can request $SETIMR events only on its own behalf.

1.7.2   Periodic System Routines

The second type of TQE is a system routine request, indicated by a type of 1. A request of this type is not the result of any process request, but is a system-requested, time-dependent event. EXE$SWTIMINT handles this type of TQE by performing the following actions:

1. It loads R3 and R4 from the TQE$L_FR3 and TQE$L_FR4 fields (normally defined as the TQE$L_AST and TQE$L_ASTPRM fields). R5 points to the beginning of the TQE.
2. It executes a JSB instruction using the TQE$L_FPC field (normally defined as the TQE$L_PID field).

On return from the system subroutine, R5 is assumed to point to a TQE. Its TQE$V_REPEAT bit is tested. If the bit is set, then the TQE is reinserted in the timer queue using the TQE$Q_DELTA time field. EXE$SWTIMINT next checks the timer queue for further TQEs to service.

Note that even if the TQE is not reinserted in the queue, EXE$SWTIMINT does not deallocate the TQE. This type of TQE can be defined in a static nonpaged portion of system space or within a device driver data structure. For example, the TQE for EXE$TIMEOUT is permanently defined in the module SYSCOMMON, and the timer queue is initialized at bootstrap time with this data structure as the first element in the queue.

One example of this type of request, a repeating system subroutine request, is the once-per-second execution of the subroutine EXE$TIMEOUT in module TIMESCHDL. EXE$TIMEOUT performs the following:

1. The routine SCH$SWPWAKE is called to awaken the swapper process if appropriate (see Chapter 17).
2. EXE$TIMEOUT increments the EXE$GL_ABSTIM field to indicate the passing of one second of system uptime.
3. The routine ERL$WAKE is called to awaken the ERRFMT process if appropriate (see Chapter 8).
4. EXE$TIMEOUT calls ECC$REENABLE, a routine in CPU-specific loaded code. ECC$REENABLE scans the memory controllers to log any unreported corrected read data (CRD) errors and possibly to reenable CRD interrupts.
5. EXE$TIMEOUT scans the I/O database for devices that have exceeded their timeout intervals. Drivers for such devices are called at their timeout entry points at device IPL. This scan also checks for terminal timed reads that have expired. If any is found, EXE$TIMEOUT invokes its driver's timeout routine.
6. EXE$TIMEOUT scans for channel (controller) request blocks (CRBs) that have timed out. The CRB timeout mechanism, new with VMS Version 4, enables a driver to be entered periodically for controller-related functions. The driver stores the address of a timeout routine in the field CRB$L_TOUTROUT and an expiration time in CRB$L_DUETIME. EXE$TIMEOUT compares the expiration time to EXE$GL_ABSTIM and invokes the timeout routine if the CRB due time has arrived.

    The system communications services (SCS) class and port drivers employ this mechanism. The disk class driver, for example, must send its server periodic messages to inform the server that the host system is running. The disk class driver timeout routine also checks that the server has made progress on the oldest outstanding request.

7. If a process is running the Monitor Utility to display disk and disk queue length information, EXE$TIMEOUT scans the I/O database to collect information about disk queue lengths. (Note that this function is implemented through a Version 4.4 patch and is therefore not visible in the Version 4.0 source listing of this module.)

8. Next, EXE$TIMEOUT scans the "fork and wait" queue. Chapter 6 describes this queue and its use by fork processes.

9. The first entry on the lock manager timeout queue is checked to see if it has expired. If it has, a deadlock search is initiated (see Chapter 13).

10. EXE$TIMEOUT examines a number of processes to locate normal priority (priority less than 16) processes in the COM or COMO state, whose priority is less than that of the current process (or the highest normal priority computable process). The current priority of these lower priority processes is boosted to be equal to that of the highest normal priority COM or CUR process.

   This feature was implemented to prevent a high priority, compute-intensive job from causing other processes to be unable to release system or other resources. The number of processes checked depends upon the special SYSBOOT parameter PIXSCAN. EXE$TIMEOUT examines PIXSCAN elements in the PCB pointer list each time it runs. It searches the list in a circular fashion, so that all normal processes eventually receive the priority boost.

11. Invoking SCH$RAVAIL, EXE$TIMEOUT declares available several system resources, RSN$_NPDYNMEM, RSN$_PGDYNMEM, and RSN$_MAILBOX. This is necessary because, in certain rare cases, these resources are not declared available when they should be.

The terminal driver also uses a repeating system timer routine to implement its modem polling. The controller initialization routine in the terminal driver loads the expiration time field in a TQE in the terminal driver with the current system time, sets the repeat bit, and loads the repeat interval with the SYSBOOT parameter TTY_SCANDELTA. When the timer routine expires, it polls each modem looking for state changes.

11.7.3   Scheduled Wakeup

The third type of TQE, indicated by a type of 2, is associated with a request for a scheduled wakeup ($SCHDWK) of a hibernating process. This type of request may be either one-time or repeating and may be requested by a process other than the target process.

EXE$SWTIMINT performs the following operations for a scheduled wakeup TQE:

1. EXE$SWTIMINT invokes SCH$WAKE to awaken the target process (indicated by TQE$L_PID). If the target process is no longer in the system, the control block is deallocated to nonpaged dynamic memory. If the requesting process (TQE$L_RQPID) still exists, its PCB$W_ASTCNT quota is incremented.

2. If the request is a one-time request (indicated by a zero TQE$V_REPEAT bit in the TQE$B_RQTYPE field), then the cleanup described in step 1 is performed.

3. If the request is a repeating type, then the repeat interval (TQE$Q_DELTA) is added to the request time (TQE$Q_TIME), and the TQE is reinserted in the timer queue by its expiration time.

EXE$SWTIMINT then checks to see whether the next TQE is due.

12 Process Control and Communication

The VMS operating system provides many services that allow processes to communicate with one another and allow one process to control the execution of another.

Communication mechanisms include event flags, mailboxes, the lock management system services (lock manager), global shared data sections, and shared files. This chapter explains the event flag mechanism and briefly describes the other mechanisms.

VMS provides system services that enable a process to affect its own scheduling state or that of another process. It also provides services that enable a process to alter some of its parameters (such as name or priority). This chapter describes the implementation of these services. Table 12-1 summarizes the process control services.

12.1 EVENT FLAG SYSTEM SERVICES

Event flags are status posting bits maintained by VAX/VMS for general programming use. Each event flag is a variable which can be either set or clear and whose status can be tested. Event flags are used within a single process for synchronization of I/O requests, lock requests, various information requests (for example, Get Job/Process Information), and timer requests. Event flags can also be used as application-specific synchronization tools. Event flags used for synchronization can be local to one process or shared among processes in the same group.

System services are provided to read, set, or clear collections of event flags. Other services allow a process to wait for one or several event flags.

Each process has available to it 64 local (process-specific) event flags and 64 common event flags shareable among processes in the same group. The event flags are organized into four clusters of 32 flags each. Before a process can refer to a common event flag cluster, it must explicitly "associate" with the cluster (see Section 12.1.2).

Table 12-1 Summary of Process Control System Services

Service Name	Affect Other Processes	Privilege Checks
$ASCEFC	Same group only	PRMCEB (to create permanent cluster)
$DLCEFC	Same group only	PRMCEB
$WAITFR		
$WFLOR		
$WFLAND		
$SYNCH		
$HIBER	No[1]	None
$WAKE	Yes	GROUP or WORLD
$SCHDWK	Yes	GROUP or WORLD
$CANWAK	Yes	GROUP or WORLD
$SUSPND	Yes	GROUP or WORLD
$RESUME	Yes	GROUP or WORLD
$EXIT	No	None
$FORCEX	Yes	GROUP or WORLD
$CREPRC	Yes	DETACH for different UICs
$DELPRC	Yes	GROUP or WORLD
$SETAST	No	Access mode check
$SETPRA	No	Access mode check
$SETPRI	Yes	ALTPRI and either GROUP or WORLD
$SETPRN	No	None
$SETRWM	No[2]	None
$SETSM	No[2]	PSWAPM
$SETSFM	No[2]	Access mode check
$GETJPI	Yes	GROUP or WORLD

[1] As part of the Create Process system service, a process can specify that the process being created hibernate before a specified image executes.

[2] This feature can be specified as a part of the Create Process system service.

12.1.1 Local Event Flags

The 64 local event flags are stored directly in each process's PCB, at offsets PCB$L_EFCS and PCB$L_EFCU (see Figure 12-1). Local event flags 0 to 31 comprise cluster 0 and are located in longword PCB$L_EFCS. Local event flags 32 to 63 comprise cluster 1 and are located in longword PCB$L_EFCU.

12.1.2 Common Event Flags

A common event flag cluster is stored in a nonpaged data structure called a common event block (CEB), whose layout is pictured in Figure 12-2. A partic-

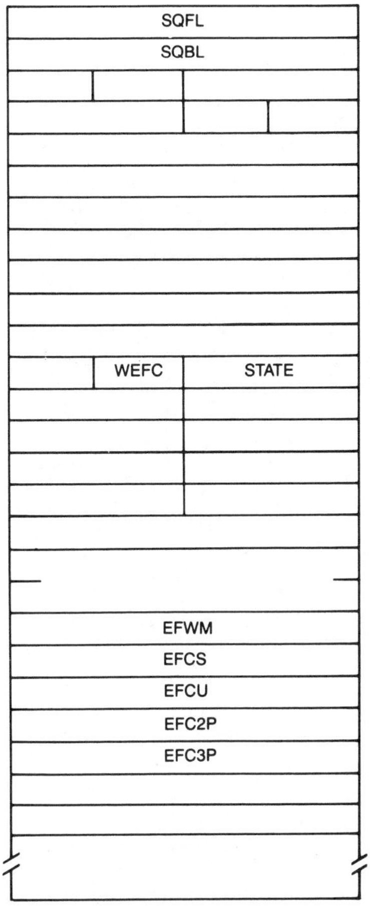

SQFL		
SQBL		
WEFC	STATE	
EFWM		
EFCS		
EFCU		
EFC2P		
EFC3P		

Figure 12-1 Software PCB Fields That Support Event Flags

ular common event flag cluster is identified by its name, CEB$T_EFCNAM, and UIC group, CEB$W_GRP. There cannot be more than one cluster with the same name and group. The CEBs are queued in a systemwide, doubly linked list located by global listhead SCH$GQ_CEBHD (see Figure 12-3). The mutex EXE$GL_CEBMTX synchronizes access to the list of CEBs. (Chapter 2 describes mutexes.)

A process invokes the Associate Common Event Flag Cluster ($ASCEFC) system service to have access to the flags in a common event flag cluster. The process specifies the name of the cluster and implicitly, through its PCB$L_UIC field, the UIC group of the cluster. The process also specifies whether it will access the flags in that cluster using event flag numbers 64 through 95 (cluster 2) or 96 through 127 (cluster 3).

The system service procedure EXE$ASCEFC, in module SYSASCEFC,

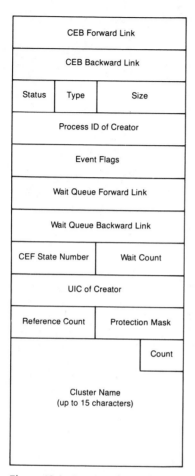

Figure 12-2 Layout of Common Event Block

searches the CEB list for one with the same name and group. If none exists, EXE$ASCEFC creates one and links it into the CEB list. If the process specifies creation of a permanent common event flag cluster and has the privilege PRMCEB, EXE$ASCEFC sets the bit CEB$V_PERM in CEB$B_STS to indicate that the cluster is a permanent one. Whether or not the cluster existed previously, EXE$ASCEFC associates the process and the cluster by incrementing the cluster's reference count, CEB$W_REFC, and by storing the address of the CEB in either PCB$L_EFC2P (for cluster 2) or PCB$L_EFC3P (for cluster 3). (The creation of MA780 shared memory common event clusters is discussed in Section 12.4.6.)

A process dissociates itself from a common event flag cluster by invoking the Disassociate Common Event Flag Cluster ($DACEFC) system service. The system service procedure EXE$DACEFC, in module SYSASCEFC, locates the CEB using the pointer to the cluster in the PCB, decrements the

SCH$GQ_CEBHD::

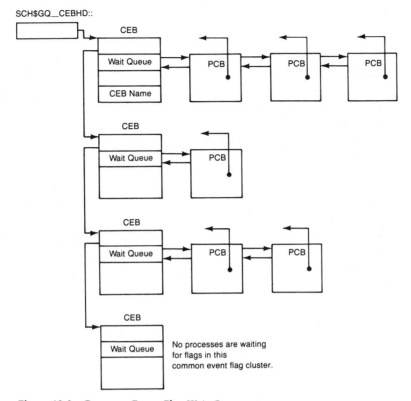

Figure 12-3   Common Event Flag Wait Queues

cluster's reference count, and clears either PCB$L_EFC2P or PCB$L_EFC3P, as appropriate. If the cluster is a temporary one (if CEB$V_PERM is clear) and if its reference count is now zero, EXE$DACEFC removes the CEB from the CEB list and deallocates it to nonpaged pool.

To delete a permanent event flag cluster, a process invokes the Delete Common Event Flag Cluster ($DLCEFC) system service. The system service procedure EXE$DLCEFC, in module SYSASCEFC, clears bit CEB$V_PERM. If the cluster's reference count is zero, EXE$DLCEFC removes it from the list and deallocates it to nonpaged pool. If the cluster's reference count is not zero, its deletion is deferred until all processes have dissociated from it.

12.1.3   Waiting for an Event Flag

A process can be placed into an event flag wait state when it performs any of the following actions:

• Executing one of the three event flag wait services

—Wait for Single Event Flag ($WAITFR)

—Wait for Logical OR of Event Flags ($WFLOR)

—Wait for Logical AND of Event Flags ($WFLAND)

- Executing a Synchronize ($SYNCH) system service (which invokes $WAITFR)
- Executing a Queue I/O Request and Wait ($QIOW), Enqueue Lock Request and Wait ($ENQW) system service, or any of the other synchronous system services which invoke $SYNCH
- Invoking the RMS services as synchronous operations (the usual way they are called)

If the flag or flags in question are already set, the system service immediately returns to its caller. Otherwise, the process is placed into either a local or common event flag wait state. The saved PC in the hardware PCB is altered to contain the address of the CHMK instruction in the system service vector. When the process is placed back into execution, it will reexecute the event flag wait system service. This enables ASTs to be delivered to the process while it is waiting for the flag(s) to be set. (See Chapter 10 for additional information.)

There is an important implication of this implementation—flags for which a process is waiting should not be toggled (set and then cleared) by other threads of execution. The result of toggling an event flag might be that the process becomes computable but reenters the event flag wait when it reexecutes the event flag wait service.

The event flag cluster number (either 0 or 1 for local clusters or 2 or 3 for global clusters) is stored in the PCB (at offset PCB$B_WEFC). The list (mask) of event flags being waited for is stored (in one's complement form) in PCB$L_EFWM.

- If the process is waiting for a single event flag ($WAITFR), the PCB$L_EFWM mask contains a 1 in every bit except the bit number corresponding to the specified flag.
- If the process is waiting for any one of several flags to be set ($WFLOR), the PCB$L_EFWM mask contains the one's complement of the mask passed to the $WFLOR system service. (The $WAITFR mask is thus a special case of a wait for any one of a group of flags to be set.) If any of the flags in the requested mask is set when $WFLOR is called, the process is not placed into a wait state. Instead, the service immediately returns a success code to its caller.
- If a process calls the $WFLAND system service, indicating a wait for all flags in a given mask to be set, the PCB$V_WALL ("wait all" bit in PCB$L_STS) is set. Each of the flags specified in the system service argument must have been set for the wait to be satisfied. However, the flags need not be set simultaneously. The $WFLAND system service complements the argument mask, then clears any bits in it corresponding to cur-

rently set flags, and then stores the mask in PCB$L_EFWM.

Subsequently, each time the process is placed back into execution as a result of AST delivery, the process reexecutes the $WFLAND service. Each time, the event flag wait mask is built anew. One implication of this implementation is that flags for which the process is waiting should not be cleared by other threads of execution.

There are two local event flag wait states (LEF and LEFO) and two corresponding wait queue listheads (SCH$GQ_LEFWQ and SCH$GQ_LEFOWQ) for the entire system. However, there is one common event flag wait queue listhead for each common event flag cluster. Each common event flag wait queue listhead is located in the corresponding CEB (see Figure12-2) and has the same overall structure as any other wait queue listhead (see Figure 12-3). Both resident and outswapped processes waiting for flags in a common event flag cluster are queued to the same CEB wait queue.

12.1.3.1   **Setting an Event Flag.** A process sets an event flag directly by calling the Set Event Flag ($SETEF) system service. A process can use this service at AST level to communicate with its mainline code. It can also use this service to set common event flags to communicate with other processes.

Event flags are also set in response to I/O completion, timer expiration, the granting of a lock request, and completion of any of the following system services:

- Breakthrough [and Wait] ($BRKTHRU[W])
- Get Device/Volume Information [and Wait] ($GETDVI[W])
- Get Job/Process Information [and Wait] ($GETJPI[W])
- Get Lock Information [and Wait] ($GETLKI[W])
- Get Systemwide Information [and Wait] ($GETSYI[W])
- Get Queue Information [and Wait] ($GETQUI[W])
- Send to Job Controller [and Wait] ($SNDJBC[W])
- Update Section File on Disk [and Wait] ($UPDSEC[W])

The routine SCH$POSTEF, in module POSTEF, is called to set an event flag. It is invoked by the $SETEF system service and by any other executive code which must set an event flag. SCH$POSTEF performs the actual event flag setting and checks for possible scheduling implications. SCH$POSTEF first determines what kind of event flag is being set.

If a local event flag is being set, SCH$POSTEF checks whether this flag satisfies the process's wait request. In a $WFLOR wait, this flag merely has to match one of the flags being waited for. In a $WFLAND wait, all of the flags being waited for must be set to satisfy the process's wait request and report an event to the scheduler. If the process's wait is satisfied, SCH$POSTEF reports an event-flag-setting event for the process by invoking routine SCH$RSE (see Chapter 10).

If a common event flag is being set, SCH$POSTEF must scan the list of PCBs in the common event block wait queue to determine which, if any, of the processes waiting for flags in this cluster has its wait request satisfied. SCH$POSTEF reports an event-flag-setting event for each such process.

When an event-flag-setting event is reported for a process in an event flag wait state, SCH$RSE changes its state to COM or COMO and, if appropriate, applies a priority boost. SCH$RSE places the process's PCB into the COM or COMO queue corresponding to its new current priority. SCH$RSE clears and sets, as appropriate, the bits in SCH$GL_COMQS or SCH$GL_COMOQS. SCH$RSE requests a rescheduling interrupt if the target process is resident and has a priority equal to or higher than that of the current process. If the target process is outswapped, SCH$RSE awakens the swapper process (see Chapter 10). If the process is resident, SCH$RSE adds 4 to the saved PC in the hardware PCB so that the process does not reexecute the event flag wait service.

When a common event flag located in MA780 shared memory is being set, the event flag must be set in the master CEB located in shared memory and in the slave CEB on this processor. Other processors connected to this shared memory unit must be notified that a shared memory common event flag was just set. An event-flag-setting event is reported for any process whose wait request is now satisfied. (Shared memory common event flag data structures are discussed at the end of this chapter.)

Any other processor connected to the same global event flag cluster receives initial notification through an MA780 interprocessor interrupt. The interrupt service routine determines that the interrupt was a result of an event flag in shared memory being set, copies the entire set of event flags from the master CEB to the slave CEB, and checks whether any of the processes waiting for flags in this cluster are now computable.

12.1.4   Reading and Clearing Event Flags

The Read Event Flag ($READEF) system service is simply informational. It has no effect on the computability of any process on any processor. The event flag cluster is read from one of the following locations:

- Local event flag clusters are read from the PCB.
- Regular common event flag clusters are read from the CEB.
- Common event flag clusters located in shared memory are read from the master CEB located in shared memory.

The Clear Event Flag ($CLREF) system service simply clears the specified event flag either in the PCB or in a CEB, depending on what type of flag it is.

Note that clearing a flag in a common event flag cluster in MA780 shared memory causes only the event flag in the master CEB to be cleared. It is not necessary to copy the set of flags from the master CEB to the slave CEBs on this or other processors when an event flag is cleared for the following two reasons:

- The event flag wait services only use the master CEB when checking whether to place a process into a wait state or return immediate success.
- The event flag posting routine copies the master set of flags to the local slave CEB before testing whether any process wait requests are satisfied. The master set of flags is copied into all other slave CEBs as a result of notifying other processors that a flag has been set.

The implication of this design is that processes cannot synchronize on the clearing of an event flag in shared memory.

12.2 AFFECTING THE COMPUTABILITY OF ANOTHER PROCESS

In any multiprocessing application, it is necessary for one process to control whether and when other processes in the application can execute. The VMS operating system includes several mechanisms that provide this control.

12.2.1 Common Event Flags

The use of common event flags is one method of synchronization control. One process can reach a critical point in its execution and wait on a common event flag. Another process can allow this process to continue its execution by setting the flag in question.

A common event flag can also be used as a semaphore to gain access to a resource shared among processes. Such an application would require creation of a common event flag cluster with its flags all set to 1. Each flag can be used as an individual lock. Each cooperating process must associate to the common event flag cluster.

Before any process uses the resource represented by a particular event flag, it must execute the following sequence using the appropriate event flag number:

```
5$:     $CLREF_S EFN=#65          ;Clear the event flag
        CMPL     R0,#SS$_WASSET   ;Was its previous state = 1?
        BEQL     10$              ;Branch if yes
        $WAITFR_S EFN=#65         ;Else wait for flag
        BRB      5$
10$:                              ;Proceed to access resource
            .
            .
            .
        $SETEF_S  EFN=#65         ;Set the event flag
```

Clearing an event flag is an interlocked operation implemented by VAX/ VMS (except for MA780 shared memory common event flags). Only one process at a time can clear the flag and cause the transition in its state from set to clear. That process then "owns" the flag and its associated resource. Any other process that clears the flag receives a was-clear status and must wait for the flag to be set.

The process that owns the flag can then access the resource without synchronization problems. When the process's accesses to the resource are complete, the process sets the flag, relinquishing ownership of the flag and resource. The processes which were waiting for the flag are made computable and repeat their attempts to cause the event flag transition from set to clear.

12.2.2 Process Control Services

Several system services allow one process directly to alter the scheduling state of another process. These services have arguments that specify the target process by process name and process identification (PID). The invoker of the service specifies one or the other of these arguments. Process name is always implicitly qualified by UIC group. That is, a process can identify by name only processes with the same UIC group as itself.

It should be noted that with VMS Version 4 there are two forms of PID, an externally visible PID and an internally visible PID. The externally visible PID, new with VMS Version 4, is called an EPID. It is an extension of the internal PID and specifies on what node of a VAXcluster System a process is located. Its value is stored in PCB$L_EPID. System utilities, such as SHOW SYSTEM, display EPIDs. System services use the EPID in a process identification argument passed to or from a service invoker.

The internally visible PID, which is unchanged from earlier versions of VMS, is sometimes called an IPID to distinguish it from the EPID. It is stored in PCB$L_PID. See Chapter 20 for information on its layout and creation. System routines, such as EXE$EPID_TO_IPID (in module SYSPCNTRL), convert an EPID to an IPID for use by VMS executive code. Unless otherwise noted, the term PID in this book refers to the IPID.

12.2.2.1 Privilege Checks.
Regardless of how the target process is specified, VMS must determine whether the process exists and whether the requesting process has the ability to affect the target process. This check is centralized in a routine called EXE$NAMPID (in module SYSPCNTRL) which is called by all such system services.

EXE$NAMPID first determines which process is the target of the system service by translating its argument process name or EPID to an IPID and confirming that the target process exists. If the target process specification is not valid, EXE$NAMPID returns the error SS$_NONEXPR (nonexistent process), which becomes the system service's return status.

If the target process specification is valid, EXE$NAMPID determines whether the requesting process has the ability to affect its target. EXE$NAMPID makes the following tests, proceeding until one is successful or until there are no more:

1. If the requesting and target processes are in the same job tree (have the same JIB), EXE$NAMPID returns successfully. (A process trying to affect itself passes this test.)
2. If the requesting and target processes have the same UIC, EXE$NAMPID returns successfully. (This behavior is new with VMS Version 4.)
3. If the requesting process has WORLD privilege, EXE$NAMPID returns successfully.
4. If the requesting and target processes are members of the same UIC group and the source process has GROUP privilege, EXE$NAMPID returns successfully.

If any test is successful, EXE$NAMPID returns control at IPL$_SYNCH with the address of the target process PCB in R4. Note that this return alters the contents of R4 which, on entry, usually contains the PCB address of the requesting process.

If all these tests fail, EXE$NAMPID returns the error SS$_NOPRIV, which becomes the system service's return status.

2.2.2.2 **Process Creation and Deletion.** A first step in a multiprocess application requires that a controlling process create other processes for designated work. These processes may be deleted when they have completed their work or they may exist in some wait state in anticipation of additional work. The detailed operation of process creation is described in Chapter 20. Process deletion is described in Chapter 22.

2.2.2.3 **Hibernate/Wake.** There are two different ways that a process can be temporarily halted, hibernation and suspension. Hibernation and suspension are implemented through the system services Hibernate ($HIBER) and Suspend Process ($SUSPND).

A process invokes the $HIBER service to place itself into hibernation. (A process cannot put another process into the HIB state.) The $HIBER system service procedure EXE$HIBER, in module SYSPCNTRL, tests whether the wake pending flag (PCB$V_WAKEPEN in PCB$L_STS) is set and clears it. If the flag was clear, indicating that an associated wake has not preceded the hibernate call, EXE$HIBER causes the process to be placed into the hibernate wait state. As described in Chapter 10, the saved PC is altered to contain the address of the CHMK instruction in the system service vector. This enables the process to receive ASTs while it is hibernating. Furthermore, the reexecution of EXE$HIBER with its test of the wake pending flag enables a hibernating process to be awakened by a $WAKE call issued from an AST.

The Wake Process ($WAKE) and Schedule Wakeup ($SCHDWK) system services are the complementary services to $HIBER. Both services can remove a process from hibernation. A process can awaken itself by calling $WAKE from an AST procedure or by having previously scheduled a wake through $SCHDWK. Another process with the ability to affect the hibernating process can request $WAKE or $SCHDWK to awaken it.

The $WAKE system service procedure EXE$WAKE, in module SYSPCNTRL, invokes SCH$WAKE (in module RSE) to set the wake pending flag in the PCB and report the awakening event to the scheduler routine SCH$RSE, with a priority boost class of PRI$_RESAVL. SCH$RSE removes the process from the HIB or HIBO queue and places it in the COM or COMO queue corresponding to its updated priority. (See Chapter 10 for further details on SCH$RSE, priority boosts, and process state queues, and Chapter 11 for more information on $SCHDWK.)

The next time the process executes, EXE$HIBER executes again (because the PC was backed up by 4). Because the wake pending flag is now set, the process returns immediately from the hibernate call (with the wake pending flag now clear). Notice that if the process is in any state other than HIB or HIBO when it is awakened, the net result is to leave the wake pending flag set with no other change in its scheduling state.

12.2.2.4   **Suspend/Resume.** The implementation of process suspension is more complicated than that of hibernation because a process can be placed into the SUSP state by other processes. The scheduling philosophy of the VMS operating system, illustrated in Figure 10-5, assumes that processes enter various wait states from the state of being the current process and in no other way. This assumption requires that the process being suspended (the target) become current, replacing the currently executing process, the requester of the $SUSPND system service.

VMS accommodates this scheduling constraint by using a kernel AST, the same tool that it uses when it needs access to a portion of process address space. In this case, it is not the process address space that is so important. Rather, the process must first be made current before it is placed into the SUSP state.

12.2.2.4.1   *Process Suspension.* Process suspension occurs in two parts, both of which are in module SYSPCNTRL. The first is the $SUSPND system service procedure, EXE$SUSPND, which executes in the context of the requesting process. EXE$SUSPND first checks whether the delete pending bit in the PCB (PCB$V_DELPEN in PCB$L_STS) is set, indicating that the process is being deleted. If the bit is set, EXE$SUSPND returns the error status

SS$_NONEXPR. Otherwise, it tests and sets the suspend pending bit in the PCB of the target process (PCB$V_SUSPEN in PCB$L_STS). If the bit was already set, EXE$SUSPND merely returns with status SS$_NORMAL. Otherwise, it queues the kernel AST (the second part of suspension) to the target process. This implementation provides for the case in which a process suspends itself.

Through the normal scheduling selection process, the target process eventually executes. The kernel AST that performs the suspension executes first unless there are previously queued special and normal kernel ASTs. The SUSPND AST procedure first checks (and clears) the resume pending flag (PCB$V_RESPEN in PCB$L_STS). (This check prevents the deadlock that might otherwise occur if the associated call to the Resume Process ($RESUME) system service preceded the execution of the SUSPND procedure.) If the resume pending flag is set, the AST procedure simply clears the suspend pending bit and returns, enabling the process to continue executing.

If the resume pending flag is clear, the SUSPND AST procedure checks whether there is a Files-11 XQP operation in progress. (Chapter 7 discusses this check and the action taken if there is an operation in progress.) If there is none, the procedure places the process into the SUSP wait state. ASTs cannot be delivered to the process because queuing an AST to a suspended process is ignored by SCH$RSE. The saved PSL indicates kernel mode and IPL 0. The saved PC is an address within the SUSPND AST procedure. When the process is resumed (the only way that a suspended process can continue with its execution), it reexecutes the check of the resume pending flag, which is now set, causing the process to return successfully from the AST.

2.2.2.4.2   *Operation of the $RESUME System Service.* The $RESUME system service is very simple. The resume pending flag in PCB$L_STS of the target process is set and, if the target process of the resume request is in either the SUSP or SUSPO state, a resume event is reported by invoking SCH$RSE. As with all other system events, this report may result in a rescheduling interrupt request, a request to wake the swapper process, or nothing at all.

2.2.2.5   **Exit and Forced Exit.** The Exit ($EXIT) system service terminates the currently executing image. If the process is executing a single image without a command language interpreter, image exit usually results in process deletion. A detailed discussion of the $EXIT system service is given in Chapter 21.

The Force Exit ($FORCEX) system service enables one process to force a target process to request the $EXIT system service. The system service procedure EXE$FORCEX, in module SYSFORCEX, simply sets the force exit pending flag (PCB$V_FORCEPEN in PCB$L_STS) and queues a user mode AST to the target process. This AST procedure, executing in user mode, calls the

$EXIT system service after clearing the AST active flag by executing the following instruction:

```
CHMK    #ASTEXIT
```

(For more information on this instruction, see Chapter 7.) The call to $EXIT is executed in the context of the target process. Execution proceeds in exactly the same manner as it would if the target process had called the system service itself.

12.3 MISCELLANEOUS PROCESS ATTRIBUTE CHANGES

Finally, there are several system services that allow a process to alter its characteristics, such as its response to system service failures, its priority, and its process name. Some of these changes (such as priority elevation or swap disabling) require privilege. The Set Priority ($SETPRI) system service is the only service described in this section that can be issued for a process other than the caller.

12.3.1 Set Priority

The $SETPRI system service allows a process to alter its own priority or the priority of other processes that it is allowed to affect. A process with the ALTPRI privilege can change priority to any value between 0 and 31. A process without this privilege is restricted to the range between 0 and the authorized base priority of its target process (PCB$B_AUTHPRI).

The system service procedure EXE$SETPRI, in module SYSSETPRI, changes the base priority in the PCB at offsets PCB$B_PRIBSAV and PCB$B_PRIB. If the target process is currently executing, its current priority, at offsets PCB$B_PRISAV and PCB$B_PRI, is also changed. If the target process has been running at elevated priority while it has a mutex locked, only PCB$B_PRIBSAV and, if appropriate, PCB$B_PRISAV are altered. (See Chapter 10 for further information on these PCB fields.)

If a process is altering its own priority, EXE$SETPRI compares the priority of the highest priority computable resident process against the current process's new current priority. If there is a computable resident process of higher priority, EXE$SETPRI requests an IPL 3 rescheduling interrupt.

EXE$SETPRI then reports a set-priority system event for the target process by invoking SCH$RSE with a priority boost class of PRI$_IOCOM. If the target process is COM or COMO, SCH$RSE removes it from its current COM or COMO queue and places it into the COM or COMO queue corresponding to its new current priority. SCH$RSE clears and sets, as appropriate, the bits in SCH$GL_COMQS or SCH$GL_COMOQS. SCH$RSE requests a rescheduling interrupt if the target process is resident and has a higher or equal priority to that of the current process. If the target process is outswapped, SCH$RSE attempts to awaken the swapper process. (See Chapter 10 for further details.)

2.3.2   Set Process Name

The Set Process Name ($SETPRN) system service allows a process to change its process name. The new name cannot contain more than 15 characters. If no other process in the same group has the same name, the new name is placed into the PCB (at offset PCB$T_LNAME). (Note that this service allows more flexibility in establishing a process name than is available from the usual channels, such as the authorization file, $JOB card, or DCL command SET PROCESS /NAME because there are no restrictions imposed by the service on characters that can make up the process name.)

2.3.3   Process Mode Services

There are several miscellaneous system services whose only action is to set or clear a bit in some field in the PCB. In particular, the PCB contains a status longword (not to be confused with the hardware entity, the PSL) that records the current software status of the process. Table 12-2 lists each of the flags in this longword and the direct or indirect ways that these flags can be set or cleared. The symbolic name for each of these flags is of the form PSL$V_*name*, where *name* is one of those listed in the table.

The Set Resource Wait Mode, Set System Service Failure Exception Mode, and Set Swap Mode system services all set (or clear) bits in this status longword. The ability to disable swapping is protected by the PSWAPM privilege. The other two services require no privilege. Several other system services (such as $DELPRC, $FORCEX, $RESUME, or $SUSPND) set or clear bits in the status longword as an indication of their primary operation.

The Set AST Enable system service sets or clears (enables or disables) delivery of ASTs to a given access mode. The AST enable flags are stored at offset PCB$B_ASTEN within the PCB. The use of these flags is discussed in Chapter 7.

2.4   INTERPROCESS COMMUNICATION

In any application involving more than one process, it is necessary for data to be shared among the several processes or for information to be sent from one process to another. The VMS operating system provides various mechanisms that accomplish this information exchange. These mechanisms vary in the amount of information that can be transmitted, transparency of the transmission, and amount of synchronization provided by the VMS operating system.

Table 12-2 Meanings of Flags in PCB Status Longword (PCB$L_STS)

Name	Meaning of Flag If Set	Flag Set By	Flag Cleared By
RES	Process is resident	Swapper	Swapper
DELPEN	Process deletion is pending	$DELPRC	
FORCPEN	Forced exit is pending	$FORCEX	Image rundown, Process rundown
INQUAN	Process is in initial quantum after inswap	Swapper	SCH$QEND
PSWAPM	Process swapping is disabled	$SETSWM, $CREPRC	$SETSWM
RESPEN	Resume is pending (skip suspend)	$RESUME	Suspend AST
SSFEXC	Enable system service exceptions for kernel mode	$SETSFM	$SETSFM, Process rundown
SSFEXCE	Enable system service exceptions for exec. mode	$SETSFM	$SETSFM, Process rundown
SSFEXCS	Enable system service exceptions for super. mode	$SETSFM	$SETSFM, Process rundown
SSFEXCU	Enable system service exceptions for user mode	$SETSFM, $CREPRC	$SETSFM, Image rundown
SSRWAIT	Disable resource wait mode	$SETRWM, $CREPRC	$SETRWM
SUSPEN	Suspend is pending	$SUSPND	Suspend AST
WAKEPEN	Wake is pending (skip hibernate)	$WAKE, $SCHDWK	$HIBER
WALL	Wait for all event flags in mask	$WFLAND	Next $WFLOR or $WAITFR

Table 12-2   Meanings of Flags in PCB Status Longword (PCB$L_STS) (continued)

Name	Meaning of Flag If Set	Flag Set By	Flag Cleared By
BATCH	Process is a batch job	$CREPRC	
NOACNT	No accounting records for this process	$CREPRC	
SWPVBN	Modified page write to swap file is in progress	Swapper	Swapper
ASTPEN	AST is pending (not used)		
PHDRES	Process header is resident	Swapper	Swapper
HIBER	Hibernate after initial image activation	$CREPRC	
LOGIN	Login without reading the authorization file	$CREPRC	
NETWRK	Process is a network job	$CREPRC	
PWRAST	Process has declared a power recovery AST	$SETPRA	Queuing of recovery AST, Image rundown, Process rundown
NODELET	Do not delete this process (not used)		
DISAWS	Disable automatic working set adjustment on this process	SET WORK /NOADJUST, $CREPRC	SET WORK /ADJUST
INTER	Process is interactive job	$CREPRC	
RECOVER	(Reserved)		
SECAUDIT	Perform mandatory process auditing	LOGINOUT	

This section discusses event flags, lock management system services, mailboxes, logical names, and global sections. In addition to these, VMS provides file sharing and DECnet task-to-task communication. The *Guide to VAX/VMS File Applications* describes use of the former and the *VAX/VMS Networking Manual* the latter.

12.4.1   Event Flags

Common event flags can be treated as a method for several processes to share single bits of information. In fact, the typical use of common event flags is as a synchronization tool for other more complicated communication techniques.

The internal operations of common event flags are described in the beginning of this chapter.

12.4.2   Lock Management System Services

The lock management system services (also known as the lock manager) enable processes to name a shared resource and request locks on that resource. If access to a resource cannot be immediately granted to a lock, a queuing mechanism is provided for a process to wait until it can be granted access to the resource. The lock manager provides a number of lock modes to control how the resource is to be shared with other processes. Blocking ASTs and a lock value block are also provided to pass information about, or synchronize access to, a resource. The internals of the lock manager are described in Chapter 13.

12.4.3   Mailboxes

Mailboxes are software-implemented I/O devices that can be read and written through RMS requests or the $QIO system service. Although process-specific or systemwide parameters may control the amount of data that can be written to a mailbox in one operation, there is no limit to the total amount of information that can be passed through a mailbox with a series of reads and writes.

There are two forms of synchronization provided for mailbox I/O. A simple but restrictive technique is that the receiving process issue a read from the mailbox and wait until the read completes. The read cannot complete until the process writing to the mailbox completes its I/O request. The limitation of this technique is that the receiving process cannot do anything else while it is waiting for data. Even if the process were to issue an asynchronous I/O request, it must have an I/O request outstanding at all times to receive notification when some other process writes to the mailbox. In some applications, these limitations may be acceptable so that this technique can be used.

Other applications may have a receiving process that performs different tasks, depending on the information available to it. Putting such a process into a wait state for one task prevents it from servicing any of its other tasks. For such applications, the VMS operating system provides a special $QIO request called Set Attention AST that enables a process to receive AST notification when a message is written to its mailbox. This technique allows a process to continue its mainline processing and handle requests from other processes only when such work is needed, without having an I/O request outstanding at all times.

Chapter 18 discusses the implementation of mailboxes and Chapter 7 that of attention ASTs.

2.4.4 Logical Names

Logical names (see Chapter 28) are used extensively by the VMS operating system to provide total device independence in the I/O system. However, logical names can be used for many other purposes as well. Specifically, one process can pass information to another process by creating a logical name in a shared logical name table with information stored in the equivalence string. The receiving process simply translates the name to retrieve the data.

Although some form of synchronization is provided by an error return (SS$_NOTRAN) from the Translate Logical Name ($TRNLNM) system service, processes using such a technique should use event flags (or an equivalent method) to synchronize this communication technique. One use of this technique where synchronization is not required occurs when a process creates a subprocess or detached process and passes the new process data in the equivalence strings for SYS$INPUT, SYS$OUTPUT, or SYS$ERROR. Using this method, there is no possibility for the translation to occur before the creation.

2.4.5 Global Sections

Global sections provide the fastest method for one process to pass information to another process. Because the processes have the data area mapped into their address space, no movement of data takes place. Instead, the method provides for a sharing of the data. The method is not transparent because each process must map the global section that will be used to share data.

In addition, the processes must use event flags, lock management system services, or their own synchronization to prevent the receiver from reading data before it has been made available by the sender and to notify the receiver that new data is available.

If the global section is in shared memory or implemented on a multiprocessor system, simultaneous access by multiple processes is possible. Synchronization in such an application requires use of interlocked instructions or a protocol based on event flags or locks. Chapters 2 and 14 briefly describe synchronization of shared memory.

Chapter 16 describes the implementation of global sections.

12.4.6 Interprocessor Communication with the MA780

VAX-11/780 and VAX-11/785 CPUs can be connected to memory accessible by multiple processors. The controller for this shared memory is an MA780. VMS provides interprocessor communication in shared memory through common event flags, mailboxes, and global sections. This VMS support requires data structures located in shared memory that describe the memory and the shared memory common event flag clusters, mailboxes, and global sections used. Chapter 14 describes the shared memory control structures.

Each processor mapped to the shared memory requires data structures located in local memory that describe processor-specific information. A shared memory common event flag cluster, for example, is represented by a master CEB in shared memory and slave CEBs in local memory. Each processor with one or more processes associated to the master cluster has a slave CEB.

VMS determines that a process is attempting shared memory interprocessor communication by the object name the process specifies in its system service request. The service procedure for each of the relevant services ($ASCEFC, Create Mailbox, Create and Map Section, and Map to Global Section) performs a logical name translation on the name of the object. An equivalence name of the following form indicates that the object is a shared memory object:

> shared-memory-name:object-name

Each service procedure determines whether the specified shared memory object already exists or must be created. If it exists, the service makes the appropriate connection between the process and the data structure describing the object that exists in shared memory. If the shared memory data structure does not exist, the service procedure creates it. (The Map to Global Section service procedure, however, requires that the specified global section already exist.)

12.4.6.1 Shared Memory Common Event Flag Clusters.
When a process associates to a common event flag cluster in shared memory, EXE$ASCEFC must locate or create a master CEB in shared memory and a slave CEB in local memory. Figure 12-4 shows the layouts of shared memory master and slave CEBs. For contrast, see Figure 12-2, the layout of a local memory CEB.

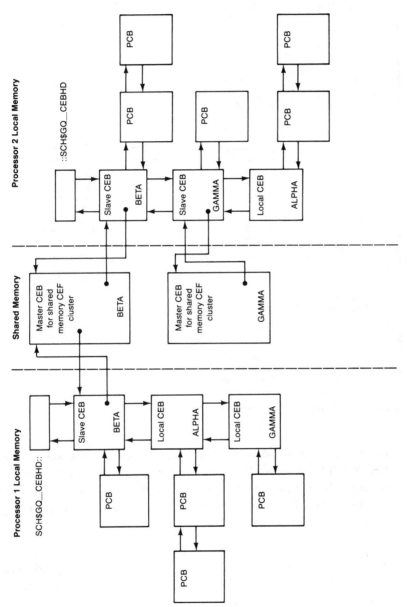

Figure 12-4 Shared Memory Common Event Flag Data
Structures

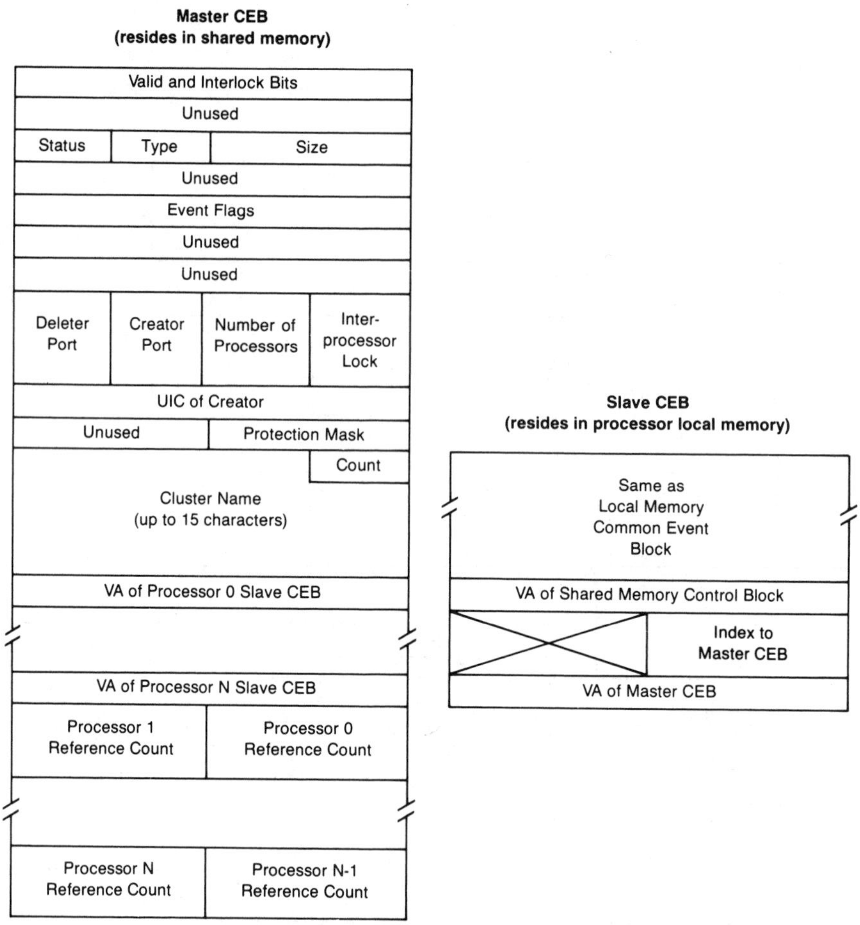

Master CEB
(resides in shared memory)

Valid and Interlock Bits			
Unused			
Status	Type	Size	
Unused			
Event Flags			
Unused			
Unused			
Deleter Port	Creator Port	Number of Processors	Inter-processor Lock
UIC of Creator			
Unused		Protection Mask	
			Count
Cluster Name (up to 15 characters)			
VA of Processor 0 Slave CEB			

Slave CEB
(resides in processor local memory)

Same as Local Memory Common Event Block
VA of Shared Memory Control Block
Index to Master CEB
VA of Master CEB

VA of Processor N Slave CEB	
Processor 1 Reference Count	Processor 0 Reference Count
Processor N Reference Count	Processor N-1 Reference Count

Figure 12-5   Relationship Between Master and Slave CEBs

Figure 12-5 shows the relationship between master and slave CEBs.

EXE$ASCEFC searches the shared memory table of existing master CEBs, comparing the common event flag cluster names and UIC groups to the service arguments to determine whether a cluster with that name already exists. Its actions vary with its findings:

- If the slave CEB already exists, EXE$ASCEFC simply stores the address of the local processor's slave CEB in the appropriate pointer field in the PCB (PCB$L_EFC2P or PCB$L_EFC3P). The slave CEB contains information that identifies the master CEB located in shared memory.
- If the slave CEB does not exist but the master does (there are currently no references to this cluster on this CPU), then a slave CEB is created; the address of the master is stored in the slave; and the address of the slave is stored in the master and in the PCB.

• If the master CEB does not exist either, it is created first in shared memory. Then the slave is created and execution proceeds as described in the previous case.

How common event flags are set and cleared is described at the beginning of this chapter.

12.4.6.2   **Shared Memory Mailboxes.** When a process invokes the Create Mailbox ($CREMBX) system service to create a mailbox in shared memory, EXE$CREMBX (in module SYSMAILBX) must locate or create a shared memory mailbox control block and a unit control block (UCB) in local memory. Figure 18-4 shows the relationship between these control blocks. Figure 18-3 shows the layout of a shared memory mailbox control block.

EXE$CREMBX searches the shared memory mailboxes table, comparing the mailbox names and UIC groups to the service arguments to determine whether a mailbox with that name exists.

• If the shared memory mailbox control block does not exist, it is created.
• If the mailbox already exists on this processor, EXE$CREMBX simply assigns a channel to it. (The UCB pointer in an available channel control block is loaded with the address of the UCB describing the shared memory mailbox.)
• If the mailbox is being created on this node for the first time, a UCB is allocated from nonpaged pool and initialized with parameters that describe the mailbox. A bit is set in a mailbox-dependent field, indicating that this mailbox UCB describes a mailbox in shared memory. Finally, the address of the shared memory mailbox control block is loaded into the UCB.

Mailbox creation is described in more detail in Chapter 18.

12.4.6.3   **Shared Memory Global Sections.** For a global section in shared memory, a special global section descriptor is allocated that describes the global section in shared memory. Unlike global sections that exist in local memory, there are no global page table entries set up for global sections in shared memory.

When a process maps to the shared memory global section, its process page tables are set up to contain the PFNs of the shared memory pages and marked as valid. Such pages are not counted against the process working set. That is, pages in shared memory do not incur page faults. They are always valid. Therefore, they can be described with a simple descriptor that is contained in the global section descriptor, rather than a set of global page table entries required for global pages that exist in local memory. Memory management data structures are described in Chapter 14. The memory management system services are discussed in Chapter 16.

13 Lock Management

'Tis in my memory lock'd,
And you yourself shall keep the key of it.
Hamlet, 1, iii

VAX/VMS lock management system services enable cooperating processes to synchronize their access to shared memory, files, and other entities. Using these services, a process assigns a name to an entity and requests a lock on it. In response to the first request to lock any given name, VMS creates a data structure called a resource block, commonly referred to as a resource. VMS lock management system services do not maintain any linkage between that structure and any actual VMS entity. Processes requiring synchronized access to an entity must explicitly cooperate by locking the resource representing that entity.

A lock is characterized by its lock mode, the extent to which it allows shared access with other locks on the same resource. Locks which permit mutual shared access are termed compatible. Processes holding compatible locks on a resource have concurrent access to it and, if they behave consistently, to the entity it represents. A process requesting an incompatible lock is denied access. Optionally, such a process can be placed into a wait state until blocking locks are released and the resource becomes available.

This chapter discusses first the lock management data structures and then the operations of the lock management system services:

- Enqueue Lock Request [and Wait] ($ENQ[W])
- Dequeue Lock Request ($DEQ)
- Get Lock Information [and Wait] ($GETLKI[W])

The last section in this chapter describes deadlock detection.

The treatment in this chapter assumes that the reader is familiar with the description of the VAX/VMS lock management system services found in the *VAX/VMS System Services Reference Manual*. This chapter briefly discusses VAXcluster distributed lock management, the details of which are beyond the scope of this book.

13.1 LOCK MANAGEMENT DATA STRUCTURES

The lock database consists of the following four kinds of structures:

- Resource blocks (RSBs) that represent the entities for which locks have been requested

- One resource hash table that locates the RSBs
- Lock blocks (LKBs) that describe locks requested by processes
- One lock ID table that locates the LKBs

3.1.1 Resource Blocks

A new RSB is allocated from nonpaged pool whenever a process calls the $ENQ system service, specifying a resource name not already in use. A resource can be created for any desired use but is usually used to represent an actual VMS entity, such as a file or global section. Because the representation is arbitrary, VMS lock management cannot maintain any linkage between the resource and the entity it represents. VMS provides tools which cooperating processes can use to synchronize access to the resource. If the processes honor the relationship of the resource to the entity it represents, access to that entity is synchronized as well.

Resources can be hierarchical. For example, a resource can be defined to represent a particular file, with subresources for particular records in the file. The file resource is a "parent" resource to the resources representing records in the file. A record subresource may be a parent resource to subresources that represent fields in the record. The combination of a resource and all its subresources is called a resource tree. The top-level resource in the tree, the one with no parent, is called the root resource.

The maximum depth of a resource tree is, by default, 32. This value is related to the SYSBOOT parameters INTSTKPAGES and DLCKEXTRASTK (see Section 13.3.2.2).

Some resource names are systemwide; others are qualified by UIC group number. All resource names are qualified by access mode. A resource is uniquely identified by the following combination:

- Resource name string, of 1 to 31 characters
- UIC group number (or zero if the resource is systemwide)
- Access mode
- Address of parent RSB, if any

Figure 13-1 shows the layout of an RSB. The resource name string and length of the name are stored in the fields RSB$T_RESNAM and RSB$B_RSNLEN. The fields RSBW_GROUP, RSBB_RMOD, and RSB$L_PARENT contain the rest of the information uniquely identifying a particular resource. RSB$B_DEPTH indicates the position of the resource in a resource tree; a root resource has a depth of zero. If the resource has a parent resource, its depth is set to 1 more than its parent's RSB$B_DEPTH.

If the resource has a parent resource, its access mode is taken from the parent. Otherwise, the access mode is specified by the $ENQ system service argument ACMODE. The argument is maximized with the mode from which the service was called, which is the default if the argument is omitted. The

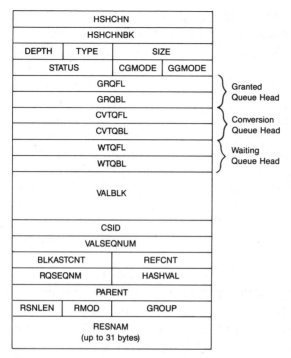

Figure 13-1   Layout of a Resource Block

resource's access mode specifies the least privileged mode from which locks can be queued to the resource and from which information about the locks can be obtained.

An RSB contains listheads for the granted, conversion, and waiting queues of LKBs associated with the resource. The listhead for the granted LKB queue is at offsets RSB$L_GRQFL and RSB$L_GRQBL. The listhead for the conversion queue is at offsets RSB$L_CVTQFL and RSB$L_CVTQBL. The listhead for the waiting queue is at offsets RSB$L_WTQFL and RSB$L_WTQBL. Section 13.1.3 contains information about the significance of these queues.

An RSB also contains 16 bytes which form the value block for the resource at offset RSB$Q_VALBLK. The sequence number associated with the contents of the value block is the field RSB$L_VALSEQNUM. The field RSB$W_REFCNT is a count of how many subresources have this RSB as a parent.

Other RSB fields are described in later sections of this chapter.

13.1.2   Resource Hash Table

The resource hash table locates all the RSBs in use. The combination of the resource name string and its length, resource access mode, UIC group number, and parent RSB hash value is hashed and the result stored in

RSB$W_HASHVAL. The hashing algorithm is similar to the algorithm used for hashing logical names (see Chapter 28). The contents of RSB$W_HASH-VAL index a particular entry in the resource hash table. More than one resource name can hash to the same value. Each longword entry in the hash table is either zero or a pointer to a list of RSBs with that hash value. If a longword entry in the resource hash table contains a zero, there is no RSB with that hash value.

Because the RSBs are maintained in a list that is doubly linked but not circular (the resource hash table itself contains no backward pointers), the list of RSBs is termed a chain. The first two longwords in each RSB contain the forward and backward pointers for the resource hash chain. The last block in each chain has a zero forward pointer.

The resource hash table is allocated from nonpaged pool. The global location LCK$GL_HASHTBL contains its address. The number of longword entries in the resource hash table is determined by the SYSBOOT parameter RESHASHTBL. Note that the parameter does not limit the number of RSBs that can be created. However, a combination of a small hash table and many RSBs can result in longer hash chains than might be desirable.

Figure 13-2 shows the structure of the resource hash table and its relationships to hash chains.

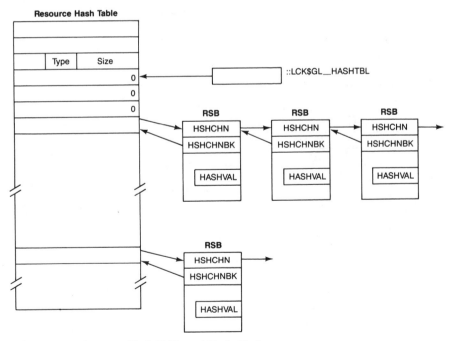

Figure 13-2 Resource Hash Table and Hash Chains

13.1.3   Lock Blocks

An LKB is allocated from nonpaged pool when a process calls the $ENQ system service. The LKB is assigned a unique lock ID used to identify the lock in later lock conversion or dequeue requests. The LKB is owned only by that process. When a process dequeues a lock, the LKB is deallocated. Figure 13-3 shows the layout of a lock block.

The lock is characterized by its lock mode—one of six degrees of shareability. (The *VAX/VMS System Services Reference Manual* lists the lock modes and with which other granted modes each is compatible.) LKB$B_RQMODE specifies the requested lock mode of the lock, and LKB$B_GRMODE, the granted lock mode. A lock granted at one mode can later be converted to another mode.

The lock can be in one of several states, depending on the lock modes of other locks on the resource. If its lock mode is compatible with those of locks granted on the resource and if the conversion queue is empty, the lock is granted and its LKB placed on the RSB granted queue. A subsequent attempt to convert the lock to a more restrictive lock mode can result in the LKB's insertion on the conversion queue. Conversion requests have precedence

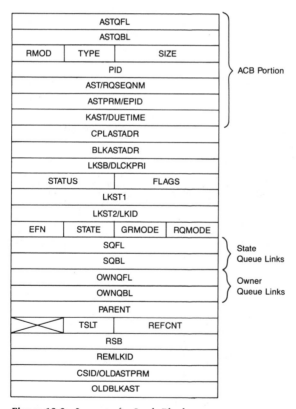

Figure 13-3   Layout of a Lock Block

over new lock requests. A new lock request incompatible with granted lock requests is placed on the waiting queue.

LKB$B_STATE specifies in what state the lock is, for example, granted, waiting, or in a conversion queue. LKB$L_SQFL and LKB$L_SQBL link the LKB into the appropriate queue in its RSB. Typically, a lock in the conversion or waiting queue is also queued to the lock timeout queue through the fields LKB$L_ASTQFL and LKB$L_ASTQBL. If the lock request is not granted within a certain amount of time, a deadlock search will be triggered (see Section 13.3.1).

A lock with a parent lock and resource is termed a sublock. An LKB describing a sublock contains the address of the parent LKB (at offset LKB$L_PARENT); the parent LKB has no corresponding pointer to the sublock. The RSB associated with the sublock points to the parent resource (at offset RSB$L_PARENT); the parent resource has no corresponding pointer to the subresource. This relationship is shown in Figure 13-4. LKB$W_REFCNT specifies how many sublocks have that LKB as their parent.

The first part of an LKB is an asynchronous system trap (AST) control block (ACB). When a lock request is granted, the LKB/ACB can be queued to the process's PCB through the fields LKB$L_ASTQFL and LKB$L_ASTQBL. Queued as an ACB, it describes a special kernel mode AST, a blocking AST, or completion AST (see Section 13.2.4). LKB$L_PID contains the internal process ID of the process which requested the lock.

LKB$B_RMOD specifies the access mode at which completion and blocking ASTs for this lock will be delivered. The access mode from which the $ENQ service is requested determines the value of LKB$B_RMOD. This field also specifies the least privileged access mode from which the lock can be converted or dequeued. If a lock has a parent, the lock's access mode must be the same or less privileged than that of its parent.

LKB$L_EPID contains the extended process ID (see Chapter 20). LKB$L_CPLASTADR and LKB$L_BLKASTADR contain the addresses of the process's AST procedures. LKB$L_LKSB contains the address of the process's lock status block. LKB$L_LKST1 contains the information to be copied to the lock status block. The second longword of lock status, LKB$L_LKID, contains the lock ID itself.

Other LKB fields are described in later sections of this chapter.

13.1.4   Lock ID Table

The lock ID table locates all LKBs. A lock ID consists of an index into the lock ID table and a sequence number identifying this particular use of that index. When a lock index is in use, its entry in the lock ID table contains the address of the associated LKB.

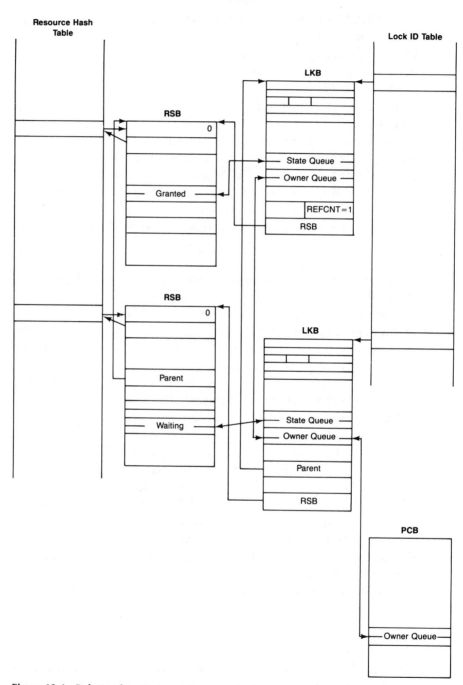

Figure 13-4 Relationships Between Locks and Sublocks

The entry for an unused index has two pieces of information. The high-order word contains the updated sequence number for that index. The low-order word contains the index of the next unused entry in the lock ID table. The unused entries in the lock ID table are linked together, with the listhead at global location LCK$GL_NXTID. When a new lock is requested, its index is taken from LCK$GL_NXTID, which is updated to point to the next unused entry.

A lock to be dequeued is identified by its lock ID. The lock ID locates the corresponding lock ID table entry. The table entry has the address of the LKB to be deallocated. After the LKB is deallocated, the lock ID of the dequeued lock is stored in LCK$GL_NXTID.

Because it is possible that an erroneous value can be passed as a lock ID to a lock management system service, the system services validate the lock ID. They compare the caller's process identification (PID) and access mode with the PID and access mode stored in the LKB. The PIDs must match and the caller's access mode must be equally or more privileged than that of the lock. If the comparison fails, the service exits with the return status code SS$_IVLOCKID.

The global symbol LCK$GL_IDTBL points to the lock ID table. Figure 13-5 shows its structure. Its size is controlled by the SYSBOOT parameters LOCKIDTBL and LOCKIDTBL_MAX. The global location LCK$GL_MAXID contains the index to the last entry in the lock ID table. The lock ID table entry at that location always contains a zero.

During system initialization, a table of LOCKIDTBL longwords is allocated from nonpaged pool. If more locks are requested than can fit in the table, the $ENQ system service builds a new table which is LOCKIDTBL entries longer than the old one. It copies the old table's entries to the new table, initializes the additional entries in the new table, and deallocates the old table. The maximum size of the table, and thus the maximum number of locks, is specified by LOCKIDTBL_MAX.

13.1.5   Relationships in the Lock Database

There are three ways in which the lock database can be accessed:

- As described in Section 13.1.2, the RSB for a given resource name can be located through the resource hash table. All locks associated with the resource can be located through the RSB state queue heads.
- As described in Section 13.1.4, the LKB for a given lock ID can be located through the lock ID table. The resource address field in the LKB points to the resource associated with the lock.
- All locks owned by a specific process can be located through its lock queue header.

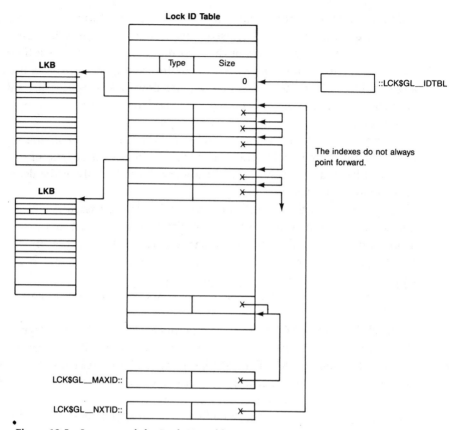

Figure 13-5 Structure of the Lock ID Table

Each process has a doubly linked list of all the locks it has requested. The listhead is in the PCB at offsets PCB$L_LOCKQFL and PCB$L_LOCKQBL. An LKB is linked into this list through fields LKB$L_OWNQFL and LKB$L_OWNQBL. All granted locks are first, followed by converted and waiting locks. The locks are ordered this way to facilitate deadlock detection (see Section 13.3.2.2).

13.1.6   VAXcluster Lock Database

VAX/VMS Version 4 expanded the scope of resources and locks to the VAXcluster System. All resource names are clusterwide, and processes running on any node can cooperate in sharing resources. Lock management is the fundamental VAXcluster synchronization primitive. Lock management system services are used by RMS, the file system, device allocation, the Mount Utility, and user applications to provide clusterwide synchronization.

Lock management data structures, RSBs and LKBs, are distributed among the nodes of a VAXcluster System. This section provides an overview of how the lock management database is organized.

A resource tree is "mastered" on one node. The master node keeps track of all locks taken out on that resource tree and performs the actual locking. A resource is initially mastered on the first node to define that resource. When an $ENQ service is requested for a root resource name which is not currently in use, a master RSB is created on that node.

There is an RSB on the master node and one on each node with a lock on the resource. The RSB on a node not mastering the resource contains the cluster system ID (CSID) of the mastering node in the field RSB$L_CSID. The RSB on the mastering node contains zero in that field to indicate that it is the master RSB. (This field is also zero on a system which is not a member of a VAXcluster System.)

A directory is maintained to keep track of what root resources are defined and on which system each resource is mastered. The directory itself is distributed, consisting of RSBs on various nodes of the VAXcluster System. A directory entry RSB has bit RSB$V_DIRENTRY set in the field RSB$W_STATUS.

To determine which node is the directory node for a particular resource tree, the root resource name is hashed and the hash value is used as an index into a list of CSIDs. All nodes have an identical copy of the list and perform the directory determination with identical results. (The list of CSIDs is called the directory vector. Its address is stored in global location LCK$GL_DIRVEC.) If the same node is the master and directory node for a resource, there is only one RSB.

On a VAXcluster System, there are three types of LKB. Under some circumstances, a process's lock is represented by more than one LKB on more than one node.

A local lock is an LKB on one system for a resource mastered on that system. This LKB is the only one representing the process's lock. (This is similar to the nonclustered case.)

A process copy is an LKB on one system for a resource mastered on another system. The process copy describes the process's interest in the resource. The other system has the master copy of the lock. The field LKB$L_REMLKID in the process copy identifies the lock ID of the master copy. (Lock IDs are specific to a single VAXcluster node.) RSB$L_CSID identifies which node is the master.

A master copy is an LKB which is on the node mastering the resource but which represents the lock of a process on a different node. The field LKB$L_REMLKID in the master copy identifies the lock ID of the process copy. The field LKB$L_CSID in the master copy identifies the node of the process copy. A process copy and master copy are always paired.

The three types of LKB can be distinguished based on the setting of the bit

LKB$V_MSTCPY in LKB$W_FLAGS and the contents of RSB$L_CSID in the associated resource's RSB:

- Local copy—LKB$V_MSTCPY is zero and RSB$L_CSID is zero.
- Process copy—LKB$V_MSTCPY is zero and RSB$L_CSID is nonzero.
- Master copy—LKB$V_MSTCPY is nonzero and RSB$L_CSID is zero.

13.2 LOCK MANAGEMENT SYSTEM SERVICES

The $ENQ service attempts to grant a requested new lock or lock conversion immediately. If the new lock or conversion cannot be granted, the LKB is placed on the waiting or conversion queue. The $DEQ service dequeues the lock from the resource and then searches the resource's state queues for locks to grant that are compatible with the currently granted locks. The $GETLKI service returns information about a specified lock or locks.

The following sections describe the operations of the $ENQ[W], $DEQ, and $GETLKI[W] system services on a single system. VAXcluster System operation is beyond the scope of this book.

13.2.1 The $ENQ[W] System Service

The $ENQ system service procedure, EXE$ENQ in module SYSENQDEQ, runs in kernel mode. EXE$ENQ first validates the event flag and lock mode arguments and tests accessibility of the lock status block. If any of these tests fails, EXE$ENQ returns to its caller with an error status. If the tests succeed, EXE$ENQ tests whether LCK$V_CONVERT is set in the FLAGS argument to determine whether this is a new lock request or conversion of an existing lock. Section 13.2.2 describes lock conversions.

When a new lock is requested, EXE$ENQ allocates an LKB and RSB from nonpaged pool and initializes them. EXE$ENQ allocates the RSB on the assumption that the resource is being defined for the first time. EXE$ENQ then raises IPL to IPL$_SYNCH to synchronize access to the lock database.

If the PARID argument was specified, EXE$ENQ validates the parent lock ID. It checks that the lock ID is valid, that the access mode of the $ENQ caller is less or equally privileged than that of the parent lock, and that the parent's lock PID matches that of the current process. If any of these tests fails, EXE$ENQ returns the error status SS$_IVLOCKID to its caller. If those checks pass, but the parent lock request has not been granted, EXE$ENQ returns the error status SS$_PARNOTGRANT. If the parent lock request has been granted, EXE$ENQ increments the reference count in the parent's lock and stores its address in LKB$L_PARENT.

If the caller specified a systemwide resource name, EXE$ENQ checks that the process either has the SYSLCK privilege or was running in kernel or executive mode when it requested the $ENQ service. If neither condition is true, EXE$ENQ returns the error status SS$_NOSYSLCK to its caller.

EXE$ENQ charges the lock against the job quota JIB$W_ENQCNT, unless the caller specified the FLAGS argument bit LCK$V_NOQUOTA, which requires an executive or kernel mode caller. (Use of this flag is reserved to DIGITAL.) If the job is out of quota, then EXE$ENQ returns the error status SS$_EXENQLM. Otherwise, EXE$ENQ allocates a lock ID, expanding the lock ID table if necessary, and stores the address of the LKB in the table entry for that lock ID.

Next, EXE$ENQ determines whether the resource already exists. It computes the resource hash value to index into the resource hash table and then searches the resource hash chain for the named RSB. EXE$ENQ compares the following fields in an RSB with the same hash value to determine whether it is the named resource:

- Parent RSB address
- UIC group number (or zero for systemwide locks)
- Access mode
- Resource name string

If the RSB for the named resource is not found, the new RSB is added to the end of the hash chain. EXE$ENQ initializes the rest of the RSB fields, including the three lock queue headers, the value block and its sequence number, and the RSB reference count. If the resource has a parent (that is, if the argument PARID was specified), the parent RSB's reference count is incremented. The new lock is granted (see Section 13.2.4). If the FLAGS argument bit LCK$V_SYNCSTS is set, EXE$ENQ returns the success status code SS$_SYNCH to its caller.

If the RSB for the named resource is found, the new RSB is superfluous and is deallocated. EXE$ENQ first tests whether the conversion queue is empty. If it is, EXE$ENQ tests the requested mode in the LKB for compatibility with the currently granted locks. If the new lock is compatible, it is granted (see Section 13.2.4).

If the FLAGS argument bit LCK$V_SYNCSTS is set, EXE$ENQ returns the success status code SS$_SYNCH to its caller. The event flag is not set and no completion AST is queued for such a synchronous return.

If the conversion queue is not empty or if the requested lock mode is incompatible and cannot be granted, EXE$ENQ examines the FLAGS argument bit LKB$V_NOQUEUE. If the flag is set, EXE$ENQ deallocates the LKB and returns the failure status SS$_NOTQUEUED to its caller. If the flag is clear, EXE$ENQ places the LKB at the end of the waiting queue in the RSB. The waiting queue is ordered first-in/first-out (FIFO).

The asynchronous form of the system service ($ENQ) returns to the caller. The caller can either wait for the lock to be granted or continue processing.

The synchronous form of the system service ($ENQW) waits for the event flag associated with the request to be set and status to be returned. (See Chapter 9 for more information concerning synchronous and asynchronous system services.)

To speed checks for compatibility with the currently granted locks, each RSB contains a field indicating the highest granted lock mode of all locks in the granted and conversion queue for that resource. This field is termed the group grant mode. Note that locks on the conversion queue retain their granted mode. It is the granted mode of these locks that is used in calculating the group grant mode, not their requested mode.

The value of the group grant mode is stored in the RSB at offset RSB$B_GGMODE. Because this value is calculated only when a new lock is granted and is maintained in the RSB, compatibility checking involves only one compare operation. (Note that on a VAXcluster System, the group grant mode is maintained only in the master RSB.)

13.2.2   Lock Conversions

A process requests the $ENQ service to do a lock conversion, passing the lock ID of the lock to be converted and the new lock mode. EXE$ENQ compares the new lock mode with the value of the group grant mode. If the new lock mode is compatible with the current granted locks, EXE$ENQ grants the lock (see Section 13.2.4).

If the requested mode of the conversion is not compatible with the group grant mode, EXE$ENQ compares the requested lock mode to the value of the conversion grant mode (stored at offset RSB$B_CGMODE). If the lock is compatible with the conversion grant mode, EXE$ENQ grants the lock. If the lock is incompatible, it is placed at the tail of the conversion queue. The conversion queue is maintained as a FIFO queue. EXE$ENQ also moves the LKB to the end of the PCB queue. The PCB queue has granted locks first, followed by waiting locks and locks in the conversion queue.

Most of the time the conversion grant mode contains the same value as the group grant mode. The only time the conversion grant mode is different from the group grant mode is when both of the following are true:

- The current lock mode of the lock at the head of the conversion queue is the most restrictive lock mode for the resource.
- That lock is the only lock at the current mode.

If both of these conditions are true, the granted lock mode of the lock on the conversion queue is omitted from the calculation of the conversion grant mode. The use of the conversion grant mode ensures that lock conversions between incompatible lock modes will not block themselves.

Suppose that a resource has one lock in its granted queue at null (NL) mode. If a lock request is issued for the resource at protected write (PW) mode, the group grant mode is NL mode, so the PW mode lock is granted. When the new lock is granted, the group grant and conversion grant modes are recalculated; both equal PW mode.

Now the PW mode lock requests a conversion to exclusive (EX) mode. If the group grant mode was used to determine compatibility, the conversion to EX mode could not be granted, because the PW mode lock is actually blocking its own conversion (remember that group grant mode includes both the granted and conversion queues). However, the lock at the head of the conversion queue has the most restrictive lock mode currently granted. In calculating the conversion grant mode, the lock at the head of the conversion queue is omitted. Thus, the conversion grant mode is NL mode and the conversion can be granted.

13.2.3   The $DEQ System Service

A process requests the $DEQ system service to cancel one or more locks. The $DEQ system service procedure, EXE$DEQ in module SYSENQDEQ, runs in kernel mode. EXE$DEQ examines the LOCKID and DEQ_FLAGS arguments to determine if only a specific lock or a number of locks are to be canceled.

If the DEQ_FLAGS argument has the LCK$V_DEQALL bit clear, then the process is requesting that one lock be dequeued. If only one lock is being canceled, EXE$DEQ uses the lock ID to locate the LKB. It then verifies that the access mode of the $DEQ caller is more or equally privileged than that of the lock (LKB$B_RMOD) and that the lock PID matches that of the current process. If either of these tests fails, EXE$DEQ returns the error status SS$_IVLOCKID to its caller. If they pass, EXE$DEQ then checks that the lock has no sublocks. If it does, they must be dequeued first, and EXE$DEQ returns the error status SS$_SUBLOCKS.

EXE$DEQ removes the LKB from whichever resource queue it was on. If the lock was at the head of the wait queue and the conversion queue is empty, EXE$DEQ checks whether the first lock in the wait queue can now be granted. If it can, EXE$DEQ grants it and then goes on to the next lock in the wait queue. It repeats this until it reaches a lock whose lock mode is incompatible with the resource group grant mode.

If the lock being canceled was in the conversion queue, EXE$DEQ checks whether any locks can be granted as the result of a group grant mode that does not include the grant mode of the canceled lock. EXE$DEQ checks whether the first lock in the conversion queue can be granted. If it can, EXE$DEQ grants it and goes on to the next lock in the queue. It repeats this with the conversion and wait queues until it reaches a lock whose mode is incompatible with the resource group grant mode.

If the lock being canceled was in the grant queue, EXE$DEQ checks whether the LKB was the only lock on the resource. If so, EXE$DEQ removes the RSB from its resource hash chain and deallocates it. If there are any other locks, EXE$DEQ recomputes the resource group grant mode and checks whether locks on the conversion and waiting queues can be granted.

If the lock being canceled was a sublock, EXE$DEQ decrements its parent lock's reference count. It releases the lock ID and removes the LKB from the process's PCB lock queue.

If the lock was waiting or in the conversion queue, EXE$DEQ sets the event flag associated with the lock request and queues the LKB as an ACB to the process to return final lock status. The LKB will be deallocated when the AST is delivered.

If the lock was granted, its LKB may still be queued as an ACB. If the ACB was merely to deliver a blocking AST, EXE$DEQ removes the LKB/ACB from the ACB queue and deallocates the LKB. Otherwise, the LKB/ACB will be deallocated when the AST is delivered. Whenever the LKB is deallocated, the lock quota is returned to the process.

If the DEQ_FLAGS argument has the LCK$V_DEQALL bit set, then the process is requesting the dequeuing of multiple locks. Locks are dequeued selectively, in part, based on their access mode. If the PARID is nonzero, EXE$DEQ must examine all sublocks of that lock. If it is zero, then EXE$DEQ must examine all locks the process has taken out. Those locks with an access mode greater or equal to the dequeue access mode are canceled. The dequeue access mode is the argument DEQ_ACMODE, which is maximized with the access mode from which the $DEQ request was made. If the argument is omitted, the dequeue access mode is the mode from which the system service was requested.

13.2.4 Granting a Lock

The routine LCK$GRANT_LOCK, in module SYSENQDEQ, is invoked to grant a lock request. LCK$GRANT_LOCK is invoked under three different sets of circumstances:

- EXE$ENQ receives a request for a lock on a new resource or a resource with locks whose modes are compatible. The lock request can be granted immediately, synchronously with the original system service call.
- EXE$ENQ converts a lock on a resource to a less restrictive lock mode. Another lock that was blocked can now be granted, asynchronously to its original lock request.
- EXE$DEQ cancels a lock on a resource. A lock that was blocked can now be granted, asynchronously to its original lock request.

LCK$GRANT_LOCK takes the following steps in granting a lock:

1. It recomputes the resource's group grant mode.
2. It places the LKB on the granted queue, changing its state to granted.

LCK$GRANT_LOCK writes the requested lock mode in LKB$B_GRMODE.

3. LCK$GRANT_LOCK invokes SCH$POSTEF to set the event flag associated with the lock request (LKB$B_EFN). If the process was waiting for this event flag to be set, the process scheduling priority and state may be altered. (See Chapter 12 for information about event flags and Chapter 10 for information about process scheduling.)

LCK$GRANT_LOCK then makes a series of tests to determine whether it should queue an AST to the process whose lock request it granted. There are three possible requirements for an AST:

- A special kernel AST
- A user-requested blocking AST
- A user-requested completion AST

The three are independent of each other. Thus, it is possible that no AST be requested or as many as three AST routines be required.

LCK$GRANT_LOCK must queue a blocking AST to the process if it requested one and if the newly granted lock is blocking another lock. No blocking AST is necessary if none was requested or if the lock is not blocking another lock.

If the process requested a completion AST, LCK$GRANT_LOCK queues one unless the lock request was granted synchronously and the FLAGS argument bit LCK$V_SYNCSTS was set.

The special kernel AST routine must be queued if the lock request completed asynchronously. It writes the status to the process's lock status block and possibly a value to the lock value block. Even if the lock request completed synchronously, the special kernel AST routine is necessary to perform cleanup if a completion or blocking AST is to be queued.

An ACB can describe one normal AST procedure or one special kernel AST routine. An ACB can also describe a special kernel AST routine "piggybacked" on a normal AST procedure. (See Chapter 7 for a detailed description of ASTs.) If an AST is required, LCK$GRANT_LOCK invokes SCH$QAST to queue an ACB to the process. The LKB is used as the ACB.

LCK$GRANT_LOCK chooses one of the following:

- It does not queue an ACB if the lock request is synchronous and neither a blocking nor completion AST is required.
- It queues an ACB specifying a special kernel AST if the lock request is asynchronous and neither a blocking nor completion AST is required.
- It queues an ACB specifing a piggyback special kernel AST if either or both a blocking and completion AST are required.

Because the ACB can contain the address of only one AST procedure, special treatment is required when both a completion and blocking AST must be delivered. When the lock is granted, LCK$GRANT_LOCK writes the address of the completion AST procedure (stored at offset LKB$L_CPLASTADR) in the field LKB$L_AST. It then queues the LKB as an ACB.

Just before entering the completion AST procedure, the AST delivery service routine dispatches to the piggyback special kernel AST. This routine writes the address of the blocking AST (stored at offset LKB$L_BLKASTADR) in LKB$L_AST. It then requeues the LKB as an ACB. When the routine exits, the completion AST procedure executes. When the completion AST procedure exits, the blocking AST is delivered.

13.2.5 System-Owned Locks

Certain locks, called system-owned locks, are not associated with any process. A system-owned lock and its resource remain in existence when no process has any interest in the resource. A system-owned lock has zero in its LKB$L_PID field and is not queued to any PCB lock queue.

A system-owned lock begins as a process lock requested from kernel or executive mode. A special FLAGS argument passed to the $ENQ service indicates that the lock should be converted to a system-owned lock. The only possible state of a system-owned lock is granted. That is, a process lock which is in the waiting or conversion queue cannot be converted to system-owned. This restriction is partly because delivery of a completion AST or special kernel AST requires a process context. Furthermore, locks in the waiting and conversion queues are examined during deadlock detection with the assumption that each lock is owned by a process.

There is a mechanism defined, however, for delivery of a blocking AST for a system-owned lock. The field LKB$L_BLKASTADR in a system-owned lock contains the address of a blocking AST routine in system space. Instead of queuing a blocking AST to a process, the lock management services dispatch to that routine at IPL$_SYNCH.

Certain components of VAX/VMS, such as the Files-11 XQP, use system-owned locks. The XQP, for example, synchronizes access to its buffer cache through a system-owned lock. The XQP, running in the context of each process in the system, maintains a systemwide cache of blocks read from the on-disk file structure. A process's XQP requests a lock on the buffer cache only while it is reading or writing a block in the cache. The cache exists, however, even when no process is accessing it. The lock management data structures representing the cache must also continue to exist.

The use of system-owned locks is reserved to VAX/VMS. Any other use is strongly discouraged by DIGITAL and completely unsupported.

13.2.6 The $GETLKI[W] System Service

The $GETLKI[W] system service enables a process to get information about one or more locks which it is allowed to interrogate. The process may only get information about locks on resources defined from an access mode greater or equal to that of the $GETLKI caller. For example, a process running in user mode cannot obtain information about locks taken out on inner access mode resources. (The field RSB$B_RMOD defines the resource access mode.)

The process can be further limited to a subset of the resource name space by its lack of privilege. Without any privilege, a process can interrogate only locks on resources with the same UIC group number as its own. With WORLD privilege, a process can interrogate locks on resources of any UIC group. Obtaining information about the locks of systemwide resources requires either that the process have SYSLCK privilege or that it make the $GETLKI request from kernel or executive mode.

The $GETLKI system service procedure, EXE$GETLKI in module SYS-ENQDEQ, runs in kernel mode. The system service is called with a LOCKID argument that either identifies a particular lock or specifies a wildcard operation. First, EXE$GETLKI locates the LKB associated with the specified lock ID and verifies that the process can interrogate it. If the process specified a wildcard operation, EXE$GETLKI locates the first LKB that the process can interrogate. EXE$GETLKI begins with lock index 1 and scans the lock ID table. On each successive call, it returns information about one lock, maintaining the lock index context for the next call.

EXE$GETLKI is called with the address of an item list that includes, for each specified item, which kind of lock information is to be returned, the size and address of the buffer to receive the information, and a location to insert the size of the information returned. EXE$GETLKI checks each item in the item list for correctness: its item code must be valid; its buffer descriptor and buffer must be readable. In general, it then copies the requested information, either from the LKB or its RSB, to the buffer.

Certain types of information are not obtainable through simply copying data structure fields, for example, a list of all locks blocking the specified lock. EXE$GETLKI contains special routines for such information.

When EXE$GETLKI has either processed all items in the item list or found one which is incorrect or has an inaccessible buffer, it is done. It sets the event flag associated with the request. A completion AST is queued if one was requested and if the system service completed without error. It returns to its caller. Under VAX/VMS Version 4, EXE$GETLKI always completes synchronously.

13.3 HANDLING DEADLOCKS

A deadlock occurs when several locks are waiting for each other in a circular fashion. VAX/VMS resolves deadlocks by choosing a participant in the deadlock cycle and refusing that participant's lock request. The participant that is chosen to break the deadlock is termed the victim. The victim's lock or conversion request fails and the error status code SS$_DEADLOCK is returned in the victim's lock status block.

None of the victim's already granted locks are affected, even when they are part of the deadlock. Resolution of the deadlock is the responsibility of the victim.

There are three phases of deadlock handling:

- A deadlock is suspected.
- A deadlock search proves that a deadlock actually exists.
- A victim is chosen.

These three phases are described in subsequent sections. The descriptions are limited to handling of deadlocks within one system which is not a member of a VAXcluster System. VAXcluster deadlock handling is beyond the scope of this book.

13.3.1 Initiating a Deadlock Search

Because deadlock detection is time-consuming, it is not desirable to search for deadlocks every time a lock or conversion request is blocked. Instead, VAX/VMS searches for a deadlock only when a lock request has been waiting for a resource for a specified amount of time. The SYSBOOT parameter DEADLOCK_WAIT specifies how many seconds a blocked lock request must have been waiting before a deadlock search is initiated.

Whenever an LKB is placed in a conversion or waiting queue, it is also placed at the end of the lock timeout queue whose listhead is at global location LCK$GL_TIMOUTQ. The AST queue fields in the LKB link it into the lock timeout queue. Figure 13-6 shows LKBs on the timeout queue. When an LKB is placed on the timeout queue, the time at which the lock request will time out is computed and stored in LKB$L_DUETIME. (LKB$L_DUETIME is actually a double use of the special kernel AST routine address field, LKB$L_KAST.) The due time is the sum of DEADLOCK_WAIT and the current system time in seconds (EXE$GL_ABSTIM).

Once every second, the routine EXE$TIMEOUT (in module TIMESCHDL) executes. EXE$TIMEOUT has various functions (see Chapter 11). One

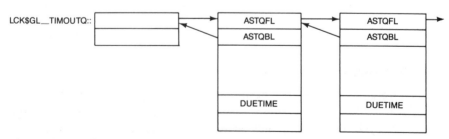

Figure 13-6 Lock Timeout Queue Ordered by
LKB$L_DUETIME

of them is to check whether the first entry in the lock timeout queue has timed out by comparing its LKB$L_DUETIME to the contents of EXE$GL_ABSTIM. Because the queue is time-ordered, checking the due time of the first entry is sufficient to determine whether a deadlock search is necessary. If the first entry has not timed out, no other entry could have. If the first entry has timed out, EXE$TIMEOUT initiates a deadlock search by invoking the routine LCK$SEARCHDLCK (in module DEADLOCK).

3.3.2   **Deadlock Detection**

There are two forms of deadlock, each requiring a different method to detect it. A conversion deadlock is easily detected, because it is restricted to locks for a single resource. A multiple resource deadlock is harder to detect, requiring a more complex search.

3.3.2.1   **Conversion Deadlocks.** A conversion deadlock can occur when there are at least two LKBs in an RSB's conversion queue for a resource. If the requested mode of one lock in the queue is incompatible with the granted mode of another lock in the queue, a deadlock exists.

For example, assume that there are two protected read (PR) mode locks on a resource. The process with one PR mode lock requests a conversion to EX mode. Because PR mode is incompatible with EX mode, the conversion request must wait. While the first conversion request is waiting, the process with the second PR mode lock also requests a conversion to EX mode. The first lock cannot be granted because its requested mode (EX) is incompatible with the second lock's granted mode (PR). The second conversion request cannot be granted because it is waiting behind the first.

The search for a conversion deadlock begins with the first LKB on the lock timeout queue. The LKB's state queue backward link points to the previous LKB in the conversion queue. The granted mode of the previous lock is compared with the requested mode of the lock that timed out. If the modes are compatible, the next previous lock in the conversion queue is examined. The test is repeated until an incompatible lock is found or the beginning of the queue is reached.

If a lock with an incompatible grant mode is found, a deadlock exists. A victim LKB is selected (see Section 13.3.3). If the beginning of the queue is reached, a conversion deadlock does not exist, and a search for a multiple resource deadlock is initiated.

3.3.2.2   **Multiple Resource Deadlocks.** Multiple resource deadlocks occur when a circular list of processes are each waiting for one another on two or more resources.

For example, assume Process A locks Resource 1 and Process B locks Re-

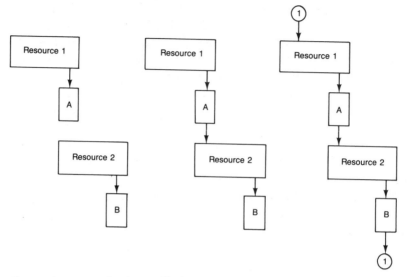

Figure 13-7   Example of a Deadlock Occurring

source 2. Process A then requests a lock on Resource 2 that is incompatible with B's lock on Resource 2, and thus Process A must wait. Note that at this point, a circular list does not exist. When Process B then requests a lock on Resource 1 that is incompatible with A's lock on Resource 1, it must wait. A multiple resource deadlock now exists. Processes A and B are both waiting for each other to release different resources. These steps are shown in Figure 13-7. In the figure, locks that are blocking a resource (incompatible with waiting locks) are shown beneath the RSB; locks that are waiting on a resource are shown above the RSB.

This type of deadlock normally involves two or more resources, unless one process locks the same resource twice. (Usually a process does not lock the same resource twice. However, if the process is multithreaded, double locking can occur. Double locking can result in a multiple resource deadlock.)

To verify that a multiple resource deadlock exists, LCK$SEARCHDLCK uses a recursive algorithm. Its approach is based upon the following:

- A waiting lock is waiting for locks owned by other processes.
- Any of the other processes might themselves have waiting locks.
- Those waiting locks are waiting for locks owned by other blocking processes.

LCK$SEARCHDLCK starts with the lock that timed out on the lock timeout queue. It saves the extended process ID (EPID) of the owner process of the lock that timed out and invokes the multiple resource deadlock routine (LCK$SRCH_RESDLCK). If it finds a lock with the same owner EPID blocking a resource, a deadlock exists.

Each time LCK$SRCH_RESDLCK is invoked, a stack frame is pushed onto the stack. Each stack frame contains information on the current position in the search. Figure 13-8 shows the contents of the stack frame.

The recursive nature of the deadlock search algorithm limits the maximum depth of the resource tree as a function of the SYSBOOT parameters INTSTKPAGES and DLCKEXTRASTK. INTSTKPAGES is the size of the interrupt stack, and DLCKEXTRASTK is the amount of interrupt stack space that should not be used for deadlock searches. The difference between them is the amount of stack available for LCK$SRCH_RESDLCK's stack frames.

Each call to LCK$SRCH_RESDLCK specifies the address of a waiting LKB. The resource associated with the LKB is located and the resource state queues are searched for LKBs whose granted or requested lock mode is incompatible with that of the waiting LKB. If an incompatible LKB is found, that lock is considered to be blocking the waiting LKB.

When a blocking lock is found, its EPID is compared to that of the lock that initiated the deadlock search. If they are the same, the list is proven to be circular and a deadlock exists. A victim lock is chosen (see Section 13.3.3 for details on victim selection), and deadlock detection returns control to EXE$TIMEOUT. If the EPID of the blocking lock is not the same as the saved EPID, another call is made to LCK$SRCH_RESDLCK, specifying the address of the new blocking LKB.

Each time LCK$SRCH_RESDLCK is called, it searches the state queues associated with the specified LKB to see if it is waiting on a resource.

When all the state queues for a given resource have been searched and no blocking lock has been found for that LKB, the routine removes the stack frame and returns control to its caller. If the caller itself was LCK$SRCH_RESDLCK, the previous search for blocked locks on the resource can now be resumed.

A process bitmap is maintained to reduce the number of repeated searches for blocking locks on a particular process. Each time a new blocking PCB is

Saved R2
Saved R3
Saved R4 (PCB + PCB$L_LOCKQFL)
Saved R5
Saved R6 (Address of LKB)
Return Address

Figure 13-8 Stack Frame Built for LCK$SRCH_RESDLCK

located, a bit corresponding to that process is set. If the bit for the PCB is set already, the search for locks blocking that process is terminated, because its locks have been searched already.

13.3.2.3 **Unsuspected Deadlocks.** Note that the use of the process bitmap speeds the location of the suspected deadlock, but prevents the accidental detection of unsuspected deadlocks. An unsuspected deadlock is one that exists within the lock management database, but that has not been detected so far, because none of its locks have timed out on the lock timeout queue. This behavior is accepted for the following reasons:

- Deadlocks should be rare.
- Finding a process a second time in a deadlock search does not necessarily indicate that an unsuspected deadlock exists.
- The occurrence of unsuspected deadlocks should be rarer still.
- Any deadlock search that does not find a deadlock is a waste of processor time.
- The unsuspected deadlock will become a suspected deadlock when one of its own locks times out on the lock timeout queue and a deadlock search is initiated on its behalf.

Figure 13-9 shows two deadlocks. In the figure, locks that are blocking a resource (incompatible with waiting locks) are shown beneath the RSB; locks that are waiting on a resource are shown above the RSB. One deadlock is suspected and a search is in progress for it. The heavy arrows in the figure

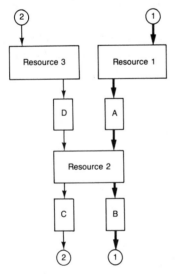

Figure 13-9 Suspected and Unsuspected Deadlocks

show the path of that deadlock cycle. The other is unsuspected. This figure is an extension of the deadlock cycle shown in Figure 13-7.

In this case, the deadlock search was initiated as a search for the locks blocking Process A. Because Process C's lock is the first one found granted for Resource 2, it is the first lock that is investigated for participation in the deadlock cycle. Process C is waiting for Resource 3. The bit corresponding to Process C is set in the process bitmap. The context of the search is saved on the stack and LCK$SRCH_RESDLCK is called to search for processes blocking Process C's lock.

Process D has a blocking lock on Resource 3. Process D is also waiting for Resource 2. The bit corresponding to Process D is set in the process bitmap. The context of the search is saved on the stack and LCK$SRCH_RESDLCK is called to search for processes blocking Process D's lock. Process C has a blocking lock on Resource 2. This situation is a deadlock. However, because the bit corresponding to Process C was set in the process bitmap, the deadlock search for Process C is abandoned. One by one the stack frames are removed and the search whose context was saved continues. Eventually the deadlock search will continue with locks blocking Resource 2, and the deadlock cycle of Processes A and B will be discovered.

Eventually one of the locks requested by Processes C and D will time out, and a deadlock search will be initiated.

3.3.2.4 **Example of a Search for a Multiple Resource Deadlock.** Figure 13-10 shows a series of locks that result in a deadlock. In the figure, locks that are blocking a

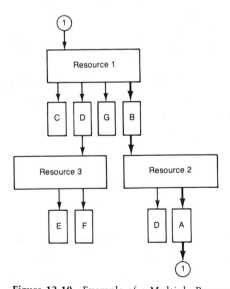

Figure 13-10 Example of a Multiple Resource Deadlock

resource (incompatible with waiting locks) are shown beneath the RSB; locks that are waiting on a resource are shown above the RSB. The heavy arrows in the figure show the path of the deadlock cycle.

Assume that the lock owned by Process A timed out. Process A is waiting for a lock on Resource 1. The deadlock search routine saves Process A's EPID and calls LCK$SRCH_RESDLCK, passing the address of Process A's LKB.

The incompatible lock on Resource 1 is owned by Process C. Process C has no other waiting locks, so LCK$SRCH_RESDLCK moves on to the next incompatible lock. This lock is owned by Process D. When LCK$SRCH_RESDLCK follows the PCB queue for Process D, it finds that this process is waiting for a lock on Resource 3.

LCK$SRCH_RESDLCK calls itself, passing the address of the LKB owned by Process D. The new invocation of LCK$SRCH_RESDLCK pushes a stack frame detailing the position of the search on Resource 1, and LCK$SRCH_RESDLCK starts to search for locks on Resource 3 that are incompatible with Process D's lock. Resource 3 has two incompatible locks, owned by Processes E and F. Neither of these processes is waiting for a lock, so the search on Resource 3 terminates. The contents of the stack frame are restored and LCK$SRCH_RESDLCK returns to its previous invocation. The search for processes blocking Process A resumes.

The next incompatible lock found on Resource 1 is owned by Process G. Process G has no waiting locks, so the search continues with Process B. The PCB queue for Process B shows that it is waiting for a lock on Resource 2.

Again, LCK$SRCH_RESDLCK calls itself, passing the address of the LKB owned by Process B. The new invocation of LCK$SRCH_RESDLCK pushes a new stack frame onto the stack, and LCK$SRCH_RESDLCK finds that Process D owns a lock that is incompatible with the lock owned by Process B. However, because locks owned by Process D have been searched already (the bit for Process D is set in the process bitmap), the search moves on to the next process.

The next incompatible lock is owned by Process A. Because the EPID of Process A matches the EPID that was saved initially, the list is proven to be circular and a deadlock exists. Now a victim must be chosen.

13.3.3   Victim Selection

Because conversion deadlocks involve only two processes, the victim selection routine simply chooses the process with the lower deadlock priority (stored in the PCB at offset PCB$L_DLCKPRI).

For a multiple resource deadlock, the victim selection routine is only slightly more complicated. The frames that were pushed onto the stack in each recursion into the deadlock location routine are searched for the lowest deadlock priority. Each time a lower deadlock priority value is found, the priority and the owner process are noted. If a deadlock priority of zero is found, that process is immediately chosen as the victim. When all frames have been searched or a deadlock priority of zero is found, the stack pointer is restored and the process with the lowest deadlock priority is chosen as the victim.

Note that the current implementation of the VAX/VMS operating system initializes the deadlock priority of all new processes to zero. Thus, it is not possible to determine which process will be chosen as the victim. With the current implementation, victim selection depends primarily on timing.

PART IV/Memory Management

14 Memory Management Data Structures

... but there's one great advantage in it, that one's memory works both ways.

Lewis Carroll, *Through the Looking Glass*

VAX/VMS virtual memory support is implemented partly in VAX hardware/microcode and partly in VMS software. VAX microcode translates a virtual address to a physical address. The *VAX Architecture Reference Manual* documents virtual address translation. In this book, the reader is assumed to be familiar with address translation.

This chapter and the three that follow it describe the data structures and mechanisms that implement software virtual memory support. Chapter 15 describes the translation-not-valid fault handler (pager). The pager is the exception service routine that responds to page faults and brings virtual pages into memory on behalf of a process. Chapter 16 describes system services an image invokes to alter the process's virtual address space and affect its paging. Chapter 17 describes the swapper process. The swapper manages physical memory. It writes modified pages, shrinks process working sets, and outswaps processes to keep the highest priority computable processes in memory.

These components maintain a number of memory management data structures, some process-specific and others systemwide. This chapter describes the following memory management data structures:

- Process-specific memory management data structures in the process header
- Data structures that account for physical memory, the page frame number (PFN) database
- Structures that are used for system and global pages
- Structures that keep track of processes in memory
- Structures that support process swapping
- Structures that describe the page and swap files
- Structures that support MA780 shared memory

14.1 PROCESS DATA STRUCTURES (PROCESS HEADER)

The most important process-specific data structures used by the memory management subsystem are contained in the PHD (Figure 14-1). The address of the process header (PHD) is stored in the software PCB.

Figure 14-1 shows the portions of the PHD that are of special interest to memory management. The smaller figure to the right shows the relative sizes of the portions of the PHD on a typical system. Appendix F describes how the sizes of the pieces of the PHD are related to SYSBOOT parameters.

The following pieces of the PHD are related to memory management:

- The P0 and P1 page tables are the largest contributors to the size of the PHD and contain the complete description of the per-process virtual address space currently being used by the process.
- The working set list (WSL) describes the subset of process page table entries that are currently valid.
- The process section table (PST) is used by the pager to locate a virtual page in a section file. It contains information about the location of the file on a mass storage medium and in virtual address space.
- Because the sizes of the different pieces of the PHD vary from system to system, there must be some method of determining where each piece is

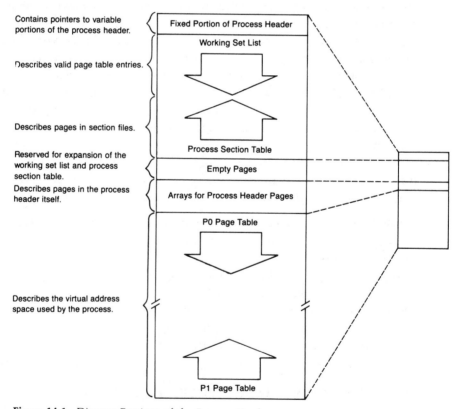

Figure 14-1 Discrete Portions of the Process Header

located. Pointers or indexes in the fixed portion of the PHD serve this purpose. Process accounting information, some of which is used by the pager or the swapper, is also located in this area.

• There are several arrays that contain information about each PHD page. This information is used by the swapper when it is necessary to outswap the PHD.

14.1.1 Process Page Tables

A large part of the PHD is devoted to the P0 and P1 page tables. A page table contains page table entries (PTEs), each of which describes one page of virtual address space. The combined number of PTEs in the two tables is determined by the SYSBOOT parameter VIRTUALPAGECNT. Figure 14-2 shows these page tables in the PHD and the fields in the fixed portion of the PHD that are used to locate the P0 and P1 page tables.

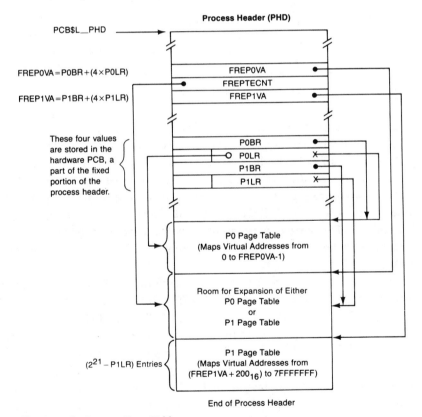

Figure 14-2 Process Page Tables

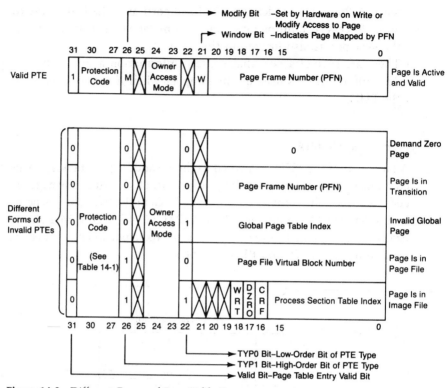

Figure 14-3 Different Forms of Page Table Entry

Figure 14-3 shows the format of a PTE.

The P0 page table contains PTEs for all pages currently defined in P0 space (these are called P0PTEs). The starting virtual address of the P0 page table is stored in offset PHD$L_P0BR and copied to the P0 base register (PR$_P0BR) by LDPCTX when the process is placed in execution. The number of pages in P0 space is stored in offset PHD$L_P0LR and copied to the P0 length register (PR$_P0LR). The virtual page number of the first unmapped page in P0 space (the index of the first nonexistent P0PTE) is stored at offset PHD$L_FREP0VA.

In a similar manner, the P1 page table contains PTEs for the pages currently stored in P1 space (called P1PTEs). The base address and length of the P1 page table are stored in fields PHD$L_P1BR and PHD$L_P1LR. The LDPCTX instruction copies these fields to the processor registers PR$_P1BR and PR$_P1LR. Like P1 space itself, the P1 page table grows toward smaller addresses. To simplify VAX address translation, the base address of the P1 page table is the virtual address of the P1PTE that would map virtual address 40000000. This allows a P1 virtual page number to be used as an index into the P1 page table. PHD$L_P1LR contains the number of P1PTEs that do not exist. The virtual page number of the high address end of the unmapped portion of P1 space (Figure 14-2) is stored at offset PHD$L_FREP1VA.

The processor registers that describe the page tables are not stored by the SVPCTX instruction. These registers change relatively rarely. Thus, having VMS explicitly record changes to them in the hardware PCB saves the memory writes that would otherwise be required every time the process context is saved.

The number of PTEs available for the expansion of either P0 space or P1 space is stored in offset PHD$L_FREPTECNT. This number is the SYSBOOT parameter VIRTUALPAGECNT, minus the current sizes of the P0 and P1 page tables.

A valid PTE is used by the VAX microcode to translate a virtual address to its physical counterpart. Figure 14-3 shows the form of a valid PTE. Bit <31> in the PTE is set to indicate that it is valid and that the microcode can use the page frame information. When a process references a virtual address whose PTE is not valid, a page fault occurs. One of the exception-specific parameters pushed onto the stack by the microcode identifies the invalid virtual page; it is an address within the page, typically the virtual address referenced. This enables the pager to retrieve the PTE for the invalid page to determine where the page is located.

A PTE for an invalid page contains either the location of the page or a pointer to further information about the page. Figure 14-3 shows the different forms of invalid PTE. Notice that bits <31> (valid bit), <30:27> (protection code), and <24:23> (owner access mode) have the same meaning in all possible forms of PTE.

The VAX microcode makes protection checks on both valid and invalid pages. This enables the legality of an intended access to an invalid page to be checked without having to fault the page into memory. Thus, PTE <30:27> must always contain a protection code. Table 14-1 lists the symbolic and numeric forms of possible protection codes.

The pager uses bits <26> and <22> in the invalid PTE to distinguish the different forms of invalid PTE. These are described in the following paragraphs, starting with the PTE at the bottom of Figure 14-3. One form of invalid PTE not pictured in Figure 14-3 is a "null page," a longword of zero. A PTE with a zero protection code disallows any access to the page by any mode. This form of PTE describes an unmapped page of address space.

14.1.1.1 **Process Section Table Index.** When a virtual page is located in a section file (other than a page file), its PTE contains an index into the process section table (PST). This index locates a process section table entry (PSTE). Initially, the PTE of each page in a process section contains the index of its PSTE. The PSTE has information about the location of the file mapped into the process address space and the virtual block in the file containing each section page. The PSTE contains control bits which are copied to the PTE:

- Bit <18> is set to indicate the page is writable.
- Bit <17> is set to indicate the page is demand zero.
- Bit <16> is set to indicate the page is copy-on-reference.

The PST is described in Section 14.1.3 and further in Chapter 15.

14.1.1.2 **Page File Virtual Block Number.** When a virtual page is located in a page file, its PTE contains the virtual block number of the page within the page file. A virtual block number of zero indicates that a block in the page file will exist for the page, but has not yet been allocated. The field PHD$B_PAGFIL indi-

Table 14-1   Memory Access Protection Codes in Page Table Entries

Protection	Symbol	Binary Value	Protection Mask Hexadecimal
No access allowed	PRT$C_NA	0000	00000000
Reserved	PRT$C_RESERVED	0001	00000001
Kernel write (kernel read)	PRT$C_KW	0010	10000000
Kernel read (no write)	PRT$C_KR	0011	18000000
User write (user read)	PRT$C_UW	0100	20000000
Executive write (executive read)	PRT$C_EW	0101	28000000
Executive read, kernel write	PRT$C_ERKW	0110	30000000
Executive read (no write)	PRT$C_ER	0111	38000000
Supervisor write (supervisor read)	PRT$C_SW	1000	40000000
Supervisor read, executive write	PRT$C_SREW	1001	48000000
Supervisor read, kernel write	PRT$C_SRKW	1010	50000000
Supervisor read (no write)	PRT$C_SR	1011	58000000
User read, supervisor write	PRT$C_URSW	1100	60000000
User read, executive write	PRT$C_UREW	1101	68000000
User read, kernel write	PRT$C_URKW	1110	70000000
User read (no write)	PRT$C_UR	1111	78000000

Note that the following rules govern memory access protection:

- If a given access mode has write access to a specific page, then that access mode also has read access to that page.
- If a given access mode can read a specific page, then all more privileged access modes can read the same page.
- If a given access mode can write a specific page, then all more privileged access modes can write the same page.
- Access that is implied (rather than explicitly a part of the symbolic protection name) is included in parentheses.

cates which page file contains the virtual page. This byte is used as an index into the page-and-swap-file vector (see Section 14.5.2). Since a process is assigned to only one page file, PHD$B_PAGFIL applies to all such PTEs.

PHD$B_PAGFIL is part of the longword field PHD$L_PAGFIL, which contains zero in its low-order three bytes. This field is used as a template for a PTE that acquires a page file backing store address.

4.1.1.3   **Global Page Table Index.** The PTE of an invalid process page mapped to a global page contains an index into the global page table, where an associated global PTE contains further information used to locate the page. The global page table is described in Section 14.3. Page faults involving global pages are discussed in Chapter 15.

4.1.1.4   **Page in Transition.** There are several situations in which an invalid virtual page is associated with a physical page. For example, when a page is removed from a process working set, it is not discarded but put on the free or modified page list. Such a page is called a transition page. The PTE contains a PFN, but the valid bit is clear. The two type bits (PTE <26> and <22>) are also clear. Retaining the connection to a transition page minimizes the cost of faulting the page back into the working set.

Transition pages are described by the entries for the physical page found in the PFN database (see Section 14.2). In particular, the PFN STATE array designates the particular transition state the physical page is in.

4.1.1.5   **Demand Zero Pages.** One form of the transition PTE has a zero in the PFN field. This zero indicates a special form of page called a demand-allocate, zero-fill page or demand zero page for short. When a page fault occurs for such a page, the pager allocates a physical page, fills the page with zeros, inserts the PFN into the PTE, sets the valid bit, and dismisses the exception. (For this reason, and a second reason explained in Section 14.2.5, the virtual state of physical page zero cannot change.)

4.1.2   **Working Set List**

The working set list (WSL) describes the subset of a process's pages that are currently valid. Pages described in a process's WSL are either P0, P1, or PHD pages. The WSL is used by the pager and swapper to determine which virtual page to discard (to mark invalid) when it is necessary to take a physical page away from the process. The swapper also uses the WSL to determine which virtual pages need to be written to the swap file when the process is outswapped.

Figure 14-4 shows the WSL in the PHD and the various fields in the fixed

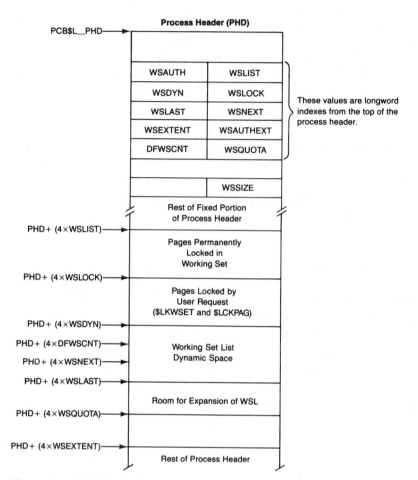

Figure 14-4   Working Set List

portion that locate different pieces of the list. Each of these fields, including the quota fields, contains a longword index (multiply contents by 4 or use longword context index addressing) to the working set list entry (WSLE) in question. The following operations compute the address of the beginning of the WSL:

1. Multiply the contents of PHD$W_WSLIST by 4.
2. Add the result to the address of the PHD.

PHD$W_WSSIZE is the only field shown which is a count rather than a longword index.

Certain types of page are valid for the entire time that they are mapped and do not appear in the WSL. These include PFN-mapped pages, P1 space system service vector pages (see Chapter 9), pages in a resident global section, and pages in MA780 shared memory.

4.1.2.1   **Division of the Working Set List.** The WSL consists of three pieces: entries for pages that are permanently locked, entries for pages locked by user request, and the dynamic portion. The quota fields in the fixed portion of the PHD determine how large the WSL may grow in response to different working set size adjustments. The contents of the three pieces are as follows:

- The permanently locked portion of the WSL (from WSLIST to WSLOCK) describes the pages that are forever a part of the process working set. These include the following:

    —Kernel stack
    —P1 pointer page
    —P1 page table page that maps the kernel stack and the P1 pointer page
    —P1 page table page that maps the P1 window to the PHD
    —PHD pages that are not page table pages. These include the fixed portion, WSL, PST, and PHD page arrays.

- The portion of the WSL between WSLOCK and WSDYN describes all pages that are locked by user request, specifically with the Lock Pages in Working Set ($LKWSET) or Lock Pages in Memory ($LCKPAG) system services. Any per-process page table page that maps a PFN-mapped section or an MA780 shared memory section is placed in this portion of the WSL.

- The dynamic portion of the WSL is a ring buffer used for page replacement. It describes per-process pages and the page table pages that map them. It begins at WSDYN. WSLAST is the offset to the end of the working set list. It marks the end of the ring buffer. The WSL is not necessarily dense; there may be empty entries between WSDYN and WSLAST. The entry most recently inserted into the WSL is pointed to by WSNEXT. The page replacement algorithm, explained in detail in Chapter 15, is a modified first-in/first-out scheme.

The current size of the WSL is PHD$W_WSSIZE, the potential number of valid process or global pages. The actual number of pages that a process currently occupies is the sum of the process private page count (PCB$W_PPGCNT) and the global page count (PCB$W_GPGCNT).

Normally, the maximum size to which the working set can grow is WSQUOTA. However, if there are more than the SYSBOOT parameter BORROWLIM pages on the free page list, the WSL can be extended up to WSEXTENT (at quantum end). If there are more than the SYSBOOT parameter GROWLIM pages on the free page list, pages can be added to a process's working set above WSQUOTA (on resolution of a page fault). WSQUOTA can be altered in interactive and batch jobs by the SET WORKING_SET/QUOTA command. Part of the image reset logic, invoked at image exit, resets the end of the WSL to its default working set count (DFWSCNT). The meanings of the various WSL quotas and limits are summarized in Table 16-1.

Memory Management Data Structures

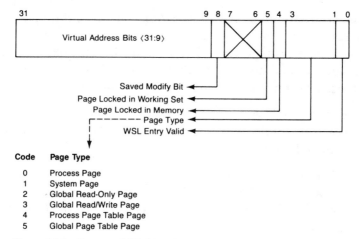

Code	Page Type
0	Process Page
1	System Page
2	Global Read-Only Page
3	Global Read/Write Page
4	Process Page Table Page
5	Global Page Table Page

Figure 14-5 Format of Working Set List Entry

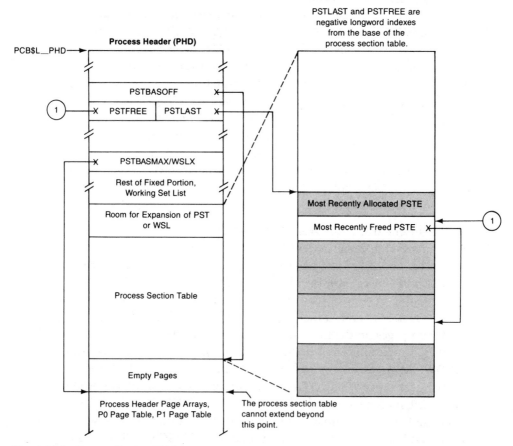

Figure 14-6 Process Section Table

The format of a valid working set list entry (WSLE) is shown in Figure 14-5. Notice that the upper 23 bits are the same as the upper 23 bits of a virtual address. This format allows the WSLE to be passed as a virtual address to several utility routines which ignore the byte offset bits (WSLE control bits).

Table 14-2 shows the meanings of the WSLE control bits.

14.1.3 Process Section Table

The process section table (PST) contains process section table entries (PSTEs). A PSTE is used to locate a section within a file mapped in the process's address space. A process section is a contiguous portion of virtual address space consisting of pages with identical characteristics (for example, protection, owner access mode, writability, file location). When an image is activated (see Chapter 21), the file containing the image is opened and a process section is created for each private image section.

Other process sections can be created when

- An image opens a file and requests the Create and Map Section system service to map that file into its address space

Table 14-2 WSLE Control Bits

Field Name	Bit Number	Meaning
VALID	<0>	This bit is set to indicate that the WSLE is in use.
PAGTYP	<1:3>	This field (a duplicate of the contents of the PFN TYPE array) distinguishes pages that require different action when removed from a working set.
PFNLOCK	<4>	This bit is set to indicate that the page has been locked into physical memory with the $LCKPAG system service. Such a page is also locked into the working set by moving its WSLE into the portion that contains pages locked by user request. However, its WSLOCK bit is not set.
WSLOCK	<5>	This bit is set when one of the following types of page is locked into the process working set: • Permanently locked page • Page locked by user request • Per-process page table page that maps a currently valid page
MODIFY	<8>	This bit is used when the process is outswapped to record the logical OR of the modify bit in the PTE and the saved modify bit in the PFN STATE array.

• A shareable image is activated which is not shared (that is, which has not been installed with the /SHARE qualifier through the Install Utility)

PSTEs enable the memory management subsystem to keep track of process pages in different sections potentially in different files on different mass storage devices.

The location of the PST within the PHD is pictured in Figure 14-6. Figure 14-7 shows the format of a PSTE. Field PHD$L_PSTBASOFF contains the byte offset from the beginning of the PHD to the base of the PST. The base of the PST is at its high address end.

All PSTEs within the table are located through negative longword indexes from the base of the PST. The first PSTE has an index of -8, the second -10_{16}. Successive PSTEs are at lower addresses.

The following operations compute the address of a particular PSTE:

1. Add the contents of PHD$L_PSTBASOFF to the address of the PHD. The result is the address of the PST.
2. Multiply the negative process section table index by 4.
3. Add the negative result to the address of the PST.

Since all references to a PSTE are relative to PHD$L_PSTBASOFF, the PST is position-independent.

A PST is organized into a variable number of linked lists of PSTEs. Figure 14-6 shows a typical PST with free and allocated PSTEs; the allocated PSTEs are shaded. The negative index PHD$W_PSTLAST is the largest index of any entry ever allocated and is a "high-water mark."

All the entries in use for process sections from the same file are linked together. (This is somewhat simplified. Actually, the list consists of all the process sections which page from the section file using the same assigned channel.) The entries are linked together through the backward and forward link index fields of each entry.

When a section is deleted, the PSTE that mapped the section is placed on the list of free entries so that it can be reused. The negative index PHD$W_PSTFREE points to the most recent addition to the free list. If no entry has been deleted, PHD$W_PSTFREE contains zero. The first longword in a PSTE on the free list contains the negative index to the previous element on the free list. When a section is created, the PSTE allocation routine first checks the free list. If there is no free PSTE, a new PSTE is created from the expansion region between the WSL and the PST, and PHD$W_PSTLAST is modified.

VMS attempts to keep the WSL and PST virtually adjacent to simplify and shorten manipulation of the PHD during outswap and inswap. When it is necessary to expand the WSL into the area already occupied by the PST or expand the PST into the area already occupied by the WSL, space is allocated

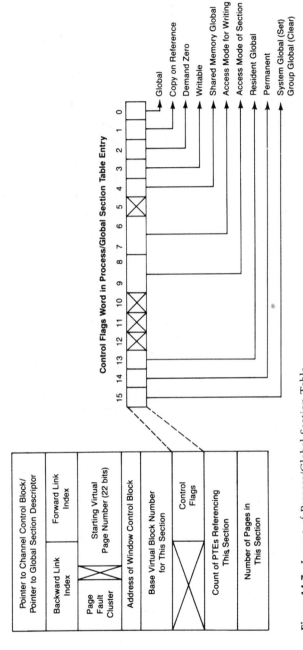

Figure 14-7 Layout of Process/Global Section Table Entry

from existing empty page area (see Figure 14-6). Then, the entire PST is moved into the allocated space at higher addresses, and the new base address is stored in PHD$L_PSTBASOFF. Another reason for their adjacency is to minimize the chances of wasting physical memory for partial pages of PST and WSL.

The longword at PHD$L_PSTBASMAX/PHD$L_WSLX specifies the maximum size of the PST. This longword points to the high address end of the empty page area. Its contents are in WSL index form; that is, PHD$L_WSLX is a longword context index from the beginning of the PST.

The maximum PST and the WSL sizes are limited by the SYSBOOT parameters PROCSECTCNT and WSMAX. Room is reserved in the PHD for the maximum PST and WSL. It is possible for the PST to grow larger than PROCSECTCNT specifies, at the expense of the WSL.

Figure 14-7 shows the format of a process/global section table entry. (Section 14.3.2 describes global section table entries.) Note that the field names within a section table entry are defined by the SYS$LIBRARY: STARLET.MLB macro $SECDEF and begin with SEC$.

The following steps are used to locate a virtual page in a section file using information in the PSTE:

1. The WCB address points to the window control block (WCB) for the file. The WCB contains the mapping information that relates virtual block numbers in a file to logical block numbers on a volume.
2. The starting virtual page number for the section, when subtracted from the virtual page number of the faulting page, gives the page offset into the section.
3. The starting virtual block number of the section is added to the page offset computed in step 2 to give the virtual block number of the virtual page within the file.

14.1.4   Process Header Page Arrays

When a PHD is outswapped, some information about each PHD page must be stored in the outswapped header. The PHD page array portion of the PHD provides an area where this information can be stored (Figure 14-8). Two of the arrays, the BAK and WSLX arrays, save information from the PFN database about each PHD page in the working set.

In the case of a process-private page in P0 or P1 space, the WSLE and PTE record information about the page, such as whether it is valid and where its backing store is. A system page in a released balance slot, however, can be reused for another process header. Any information in its SPTE is overwritten. The BAK array records this information that would otherwise be lost. The WSLX array records the location in the WSL of each PHD page. Without

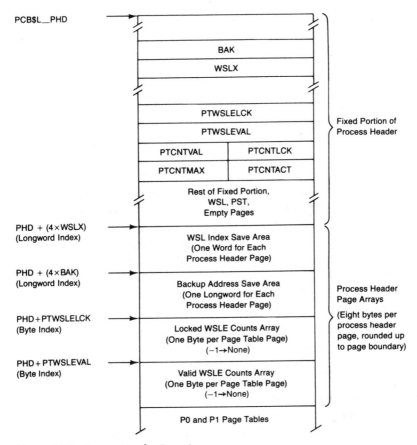

Figure 14-8 Process Header Page Arrays

this information, locating the PHD pages in the WSL at inswap would require searching the WSL.

The other two arrays (locked WSLE count and valid WSLE count) contain a reference count for each page table page. These four arrays are described in greater detail in Chapter 17.

14.1.5   Unusual Characteristics of the Process Header

The PHD has several unusual characteristics that distinguish it from other data structures:

• The PHD is swappable.

When a process is outswapped, its PHD can be outswapped as well. The entire PHD address space is not written to process swap space, only that part of the space in use. In particular, empty pages reserved for expansion of the PST and WSL are not written out and only those page table pages which map pages in the WSL are outswapped.

When later inswapped, the PHD is likely to be placed in a different balance slot at a different system space address (see Section 14.4.1). This means that system space accesses to the PHD must be made while at an IPL high enough to block rescheduling. (Blocking a reschedule means that the swapper process cannot execute and therefore cannot outswap the process while it is accessing its PHD.)

- The PHD is referenced using both system space addresses and P1 space addresses.

The PHD is located in system space partly so that the swapper can access it. Furthermore, VAX address translation requires that per-process page tables be in system space (whose address translation is physically based).

The PHD, excluding the per-process page tables, is also mapped in P1 space and accessed through global pointer CTL$GL_PHD. This "P1 window" to the PHD is at a fixed virtual address range and remains the same across outswaps and inswaps. The exact location and size of the window vary with system version and several SYSBOOT parameters. Most system code that runs in process context accesses the PHD through the P1 window and thus is not constrained to run at IPL 3 or above to block swapping. Chapter 17 contains more information on double mapping of the PHD.

- The PHD is both pageable and nonpageable. The per-process page tables are pageable; the rest of the PHD is not pageable.

The pageable portion of the PHD is paged in the process's WSL; its nonpageable portion is locked into the process's WSL.

In contrast, other pageable system space pages are paged in the system working set (see Section 14.3.2).

An attempt by one process to fault a page in another process's PHD is viewed as an error. The pager simulates an access violation for any such attempted fault.

- The PHD has four variable-length pieces: the two per-process page tables, the WSL, and the PST. The maximum sizes of these pieces are fixed by SYSBOOT parameters, but their actual sizes vary in response to process needs.

The per-process page tables are at a fixed place (fixed for a given set of SYSBOOT parameters) at the high-address portion of the PHD. The P0 page table grows toward increasing addresses and the P1 page table toward decreasing addresses. Enough PHD space must be reserved for their maximum sizes, because the system virtual addresses of the page tables must remain stable while the process is in the balance set. Any outstanding I/O request refers to its buffer using the system virtual address of the PTEs, and every resident page has a back pointer to the address of the PTE that maps it in its associated PFN database.

The dynamic growth area of the PHD must accommodate the growth of both the PST and the WSL. Expansion in either of these can result in moving the PST to higher addresses in the PHD. Section 14.1.3 briefly describes header expansion.

14.2   PFN DATABASE

The memory management data structures include information about the available pages of physical memory. The fact that this information must be available while the page is in use means that it cannot be stored in the page itself. In addition, the caching strategy of the free page list and modified page list requires physical page information to be available, even when pages are not currently active and valid. A portion of the nonpaged executive is set aside for this data, called the page frame number (PFN) database.

The PFN database consists of eight arrays, each of which contains a different kind of information about physical pages of memory. Information about one page of memory is at the same element of each array. The same item of information about all physical pages is stored in successive elements of an array (see Figure 14-9). Table 14-3 lists each kind of information in the PFN database, including the global name of the pointer to the beginning of each array.

PFN is used as an index into each array in the PFN database. The global location MMG$GL_MINPFN contains the lowest valid subscript into the PFN database. It is currently initialized to zero, and thus the PFN arrays are zero-based. Global location MMG$GL_MAXPFN contains the highest valid subscript in the PFN database. Its contents are not the highest PFN on the system but rather the number of the highest physical page for which there are corresponding PFN data array elements, the highest PFN that can be used for paging.

During system initialization, the highest physical pages of memory are allocated for permanent uses, such as the resident executive, nonpaged pool, and system page table. To save physical memory, VMS does not create PFN database to describe such pages because their virtual state does not change (that is, they do not page).

14.2.1   PTE Array

When a physical page is assigned to another use, the pager must be able to find the transition PTE that maps the page. The connection between the physical page and the process which used it must be severed. The PFN PTE longword array contains the system virtual address of the PTE that maps each physical page. A PFN PTE array element for a global page points to the global PTE.

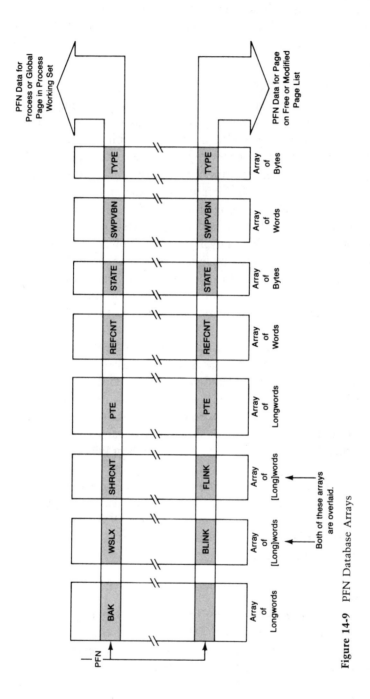

Figure 14-9 PFN Database Arrays

14.2.2   **BAK Array**

A PFN BAK array element stores the backing store information for a PTE. When a physical page is assigned to another use, all links with the PTE that currently maps the page must be broken. The PTE is altered to indicate where the contents of the page can be obtained the next time that they are needed. The BAK array element contains the information that goes back into the PTE.

The PFN PTE array element is used to locate the PTE that must be altered. Figure 14-10 shows the possible contents of a PFN BAK array element. The only forms of PTE (see Figure 14-3) that can go into the BAK array are a process section table index, a global section table index, and a page file virtual block number.

Table 14-3   PFN Database Arrays

Array Element Contents	Global Address of Pointer to Start of Array	Size of Array Element	Comments
System virtual address of PTE	PFN$AL_PTE	Longword	
Backing store address	PFN$AL_BAK	Longword	(Figure 14-10)
Physical page state	PFN$AB_STATE	Byte	(Figure 14-11)
Page type	PFN$AB_TYPE	Byte	(Figure 14-12)
Forward link	PFN$AX_FLINK	[Long]word[1]	(Figure 14-13); Overlays the SHRCNT array
Backward link	PFN$AX_BLINK	[Long]word[1]	(Figure 14-13); Overlays the WSLK array
Reference count	PFN$AW_REFCNT	Word	
Global share count	PFN$AX_SHRCNT	[Long]word[1]	Overlays the FLINK array
Working set list index	PFN$AX_WSLX	[Long]word[1]	Overlays the BLINK array
Swap file virtual block number	PFN$AW_SWPVBN	Word	

[1]The size of this array element is a function of the amount of physical memory on the system (see Section 14.2.5).

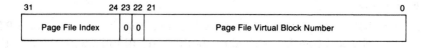

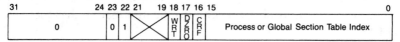

Figure 14-10 Possible Contents of PFN BAK Array Element

14.2.3 STATE Array

The PFN STATE array (see Figure 14-11) indicates the physical state of each physical page. The low three bits contain the page location code. The upper bit in a STATE array element is the modify bit. It determines whether a physical page is put on the free page list or the modified page list when the page is released.

There are a number of paths that can cause the modify bit in the STATE array to be set:

- When a page is removed from a process working set, the modify bit in its PTE is logically ORed into the saved modify bit in the STATE array. The modify bit is recorded in the STATE array element because that bit in an invalid PTE has another use as the TYP1 bit.
- When a page is used as a direct I/O read buffer, the executive routine that locks down pages, MMG$IOLOCK in module IOLOCK, sets the modify bit

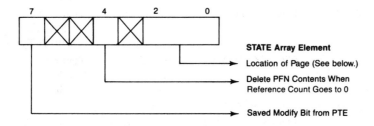

Code	Location
0	Page on Free Page List
1	Page on Modified Page List
2	Page on Bad Page List
3	Release Pending (When Reference Count Goes to 0, Put Page on Free or Modified Page List)
4	Read Error Occurred While Page Read Was in Progress
5	Write in Progress by Modified Page Writer
6	Read in Progress by Page Fault Handler
7	Page Is Active and Valid

Figure 14-11 Contents of PFN STATE Array Element

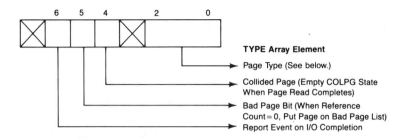

Code	Page Type
0	Process Page
1	System Page
2	Global Read-Only Page
3	Global Read/Write Page
4	Process Page Table Page
5	Global Page Table Page

Figure 14-12   Contents of PFN TYPE Array Element

in the PTE. When the page is removed from the process's working set, the OR operation will cause the bit to be set in the PFN STATE array.

• When a copy-on-reference page is faulted into a process's working set, the modify bit in the STATE array element is set. The set bit forces a write to the page file when the page is removed from the process working set. When a demand zero page is faulted into a process's working set, the modify bit in the STATE array element is set.

The delete bit in the PFN STATE array element affects physical page contents. When the reference count becomes zero of a physical page whose delete bit is set, all ties with its virtual page (PFN PTE array contents) are destroyed. The physical page is then put at the front of the free page list, where it will be reused as quickly as possible.

14.2.4   TYPE Array

The PFN TYPE array (see Figure 14-12) distinguishes the different types of valid pages. This information is required because the pager and swapper must take different action, depending on what type of page is being acted on. The collided page bit in the TYPE array element is set when a page fault occurs while the page is already being read in from its backing store address. Collided pages are described briefly in Chapter 15.

14.2.5   Forward and Backward Link Arrays

A physical page which does not contain a valid virtual page is in one of three lists: free page list, modified page list, or bad page list. The heads of these lists are in an array of longwords which begins at global location PFN$AL_HEAD. The list tails are in the array PFN$AL_TAIL. Each array has three elements: the first for the free list, the second for the modified list, and the third for the bad page list.

The three page lists must all be doubly linked lists because an arbitrary page is often removed from the middle of the list. However, the links cannot exist in the pages themselves because the original contents of each page must be preserved. The FLINK and BLINK arrays implement the links for each page. The FLINK contains the PFN of the successor page, and the BLINK, that of the predecessor page.

A zero in one of the link fields indicates the end of the list (and is not a pointer to physical page zero). For this reason, physical page zero cannot be used in any dynamic function by the VMS operating system but may be mapped by some system virtual page that is always resident. Physical page zero usually contains the restart parameter block (see Chapter 24).

The maximum page frame number depends on how much memory is present on a particular system. On certain VAX CPUs, enough memory can be connected to the system that the maximum page number cannot be expressed in 16 bits. On such a system, the FLINK and BLINK arrays are longword arrays rather than word arrays. During system initialization, VMS determines how much memory is to be described by the PFN database. (Appendix F describes how this number is calculated.) If there are 32 or more megabytes to be described in the PFN database, the FLINK and BLINK arrays must contain longword elements. The global location MMG$GW_BIGPFN contains zero if the element size is a word; otherwise, it contains 1.

Any code which accesses these arrays (and the arrays which overlay them) must use an instruction appropriate to the element size. Two techniques are employed: one, which adds no overhead, for critical code paths and one for less frequently used code paths. References to these arrays made within critical code paths in the nonpaged executive are assembled to be word-context instructions. If the system has 32 or more megabytes, system initialization code alters these references to longword-context instructions. Code in less frequently used code paths which is dependent on the size of a PFN tests the contents of MMG$GW_BIGPFN and executes the appropriate instruction.

Figure 14-13 shows an example of pages on the free list, along with their corresponding FLINK and BLINK array elements. The STATE array element for each of these pages contains zero, indicating that the physical page is on the free page list.

14.2.6   REFCNT Array

The PFN REFCNT array counts the number of reasons why a page should not be put on the free or modified page list. One reason for incrementing the reference count is that a page is in a process working set. Another reason is that a page is part of a direct I/O buffer with I/O in progress.

I/O completion and working set replacement use the same routine to decrement the reference count. If the reference count goes to zero, the physical page is released to the free or modified page list as indicated by the saved modify bit in the PFN STATE array. Manipulations of the reference count are illustrated in the discussion of paging dynamics in Chapter 15.

4.2.7 SHRCNT Array

A second form of reference count is kept for global pages. The PFN share count (SHRCNT) array counts the number of process PTEs that are mapped to a particular global page. When the share count for a particular page goes from zero to 1, the PFN REFCNT array element is incremented. Further additions to the share count do not affect the reference count.

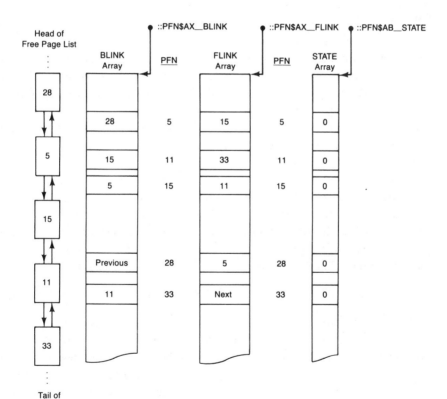

Figure 14-13 Example of Free Page List Showing Linkage Method

As the global page is removed from the working set of each process mapped to the page, the share count is decremented. When the share count finally reaches zero, the REFCNT array element for the page is also decremented.

When a physical page has a nonzero share count, it cannot be on one of the page lists. The forward and backward links are not needed. The SHRCNT array overlays the forward link array. (PFN$AX_FLINK and PFN$AX_SHRCNT are the same global location in system space.) Thus, the size of elements in the SHRCNT array can be a word or longword, depending on the size of a FLINK array element. The SHRCNT array is only used for global pages.

The SHRCNT array is used for a second purpose when the physical page in question is a process page table page or global page table page. In either of these cases, the array element counts the number of active PTEs in the process or global page table page. When this value passes from zero to nonzero, process page table pages are dynamically locked into the process working set and global page table pages are locked into the system working set.

14.2.8 WSLX Array

A working set list index (WSLX) array element for a valid page contains an index into a process or system WSL. The content of an array element is a longword context index from the beginning of the process (or system) header to the WSLE in question. The WSLX element is used, for example, in the deletion of a page of memory. Its PFN is used to locate the PTE that maps it. If the virtual page is valid, the WSLE that describes it must be altered. Without the WSLX array, it would be necessary to search the WSL to locate the WSLE.

Because a physical page in a working set is not on one of the page lists, the forward and backward links are available for other uses. The WSLX array overlays the backward link array. (PFN$AX_BLINK and PFN$AX_WSLX are the same global location in system space.) Thus, the size of elements in the WSLX array can be a word or longword, depending on the size of a BLINK array element. The WSLX array is not used for global pages.

14.2.9 SWPVBN Array

The swap virtual block number (SWPVBN) array is used to support the outswap of a process with I/O in progress. When such an outswap occurs, the virtual block number in the swap file where the locked down page would go is recorded in the SWPVBN array. The modified page writer checks this array for nonzero contents and, if they are nonzero, diverts the page from its normal backing store address to the designated block in the swap file.

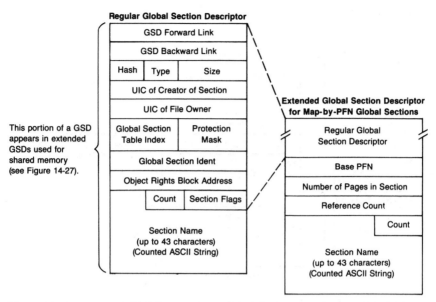

Figure 14-14 Layout of Global Section Descriptor

DATA STRUCTURES FOR GLOBAL PAGES

The treatment of global pages is not much different from process private pages. However, VMS must keep a systemwide database for the various global pages in the system.

Global Section Descriptor

When a global section is created, a structure called a global section descriptor (GSD) is allocated from paged pool to describe the section (see Figure 14-14). A GSD maps the name of a global section to its global section table entry (see Section 14.3.2). The information in the GSD is only used when the section is created or deleted or when some process attempts to map to the section. The pager does not use this data structure.

The GSD is linked into one of two doubly linked GSD lists maintained by the system. All system global sections are put into one list; group global sections (independent of group number) are put into the other list. Global locations EXE$GL_GSDSYSFL and EXE$GL_GSDSYSBL form the listhead for system GSDs; EXE$GL_GSDGRPFL and EXE$GL_GSDGRPBL, the listhead for group GSDs. The mutex EXE$GL_GSDMTX (see Chapter 2) serializes access to both these lists. When a request is made to delete a global section to which processes are still mapped, its GSD is inserted onto a list of delete-pending GSDs.

The global section table index field of the GSD contains an index that allows a second structure (called a global section table entry) to be located.

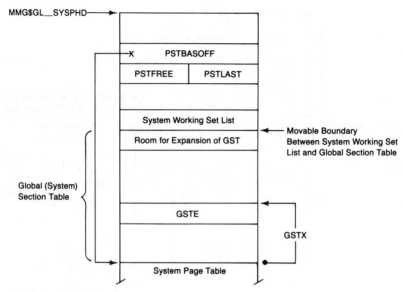

Figure 14-15   System Header Containing the System
Working Set List and the Global Section Table

14.3.2   The System Header and Global Section Table Entries

The system maintains two data structures for itself that parallel structures
maintained for each process in the system. The system PCB and system
header are used by the pager to allow page faults of system pages to be treated
almost identically to page faults for process pages.

The system header (see Figure 14-15) contains a WSL and a section table.
The WSL governs page replacement for pageable system pages (other than
those within the balance set slots). The size of the WSL is determined by
SYSBOOT parameter SYSMWCNT. The section table in the system header
contains section table entries for the files that contain pageable system pages
and global section table entries. The size of the section table is determined by
SYSBOOT parameter GBLSECTIONS.

The files that contain pageable system pages include the executive image
(SYS.EXE), record management services image (RMS.EXE), and system message file (SYSMSG.EXE). These are all paged in the system WSL. In addition
to these, the system WSL is also used for paged pool and the global page table.

The section table in the system header serves a second purpose. When a
global section is created, a section table entry that describes the global section file is created. The new section table entry is allocated from the section
table in the system header. This table is called the global section table (GST).
The format of a global section table entry (GSTE) is nearly identical to the
format of a PSTE. Figure 14-7 illustrates both kinds of section table entry.

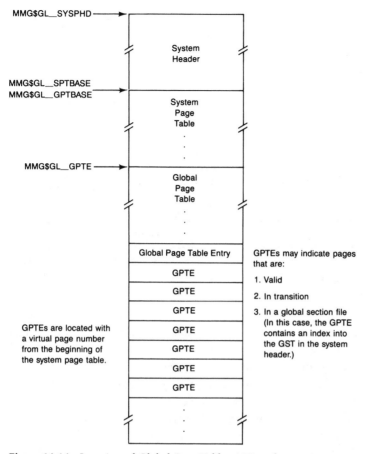

Figure 14-16   Location of Global Page Table at Virtual
End of System Page Table

GSTEs are accessed in exactly the same way as PSTEs, with a negative
longword index from the bottom of the GST (see Section 14.1.3). The global
section table index (GSTX) in the GSD is such an index, associating a GSD
with a GSTE.

.3.3   Global Page Table Entries

A third set of data is also created for each global section. Each page in the
global section is described by a global page table entry (GPTE) in the global
page table (see Figure 14-16). The pager uses GPTEs, just like process PTEs, to
locate global pages.

GPTEs are restricted to the following forms of PTE. The first three are
illustrated in Figure 14-3. The others are illustrated in Figure 14-17.

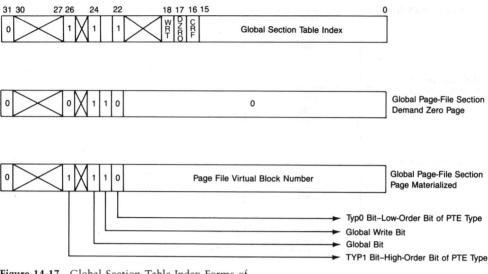

Figure 14-17 Global Section Table Index Forms of GPTE

- The GPTE can be valid, indicating that the global page is in at least one process working set.
- The GPTE can indicate a demand zero page.
- The GPTE can indicate some transition state. The PFN STATE array indicates which transition state is involved.
- The global page can be in a global section file, in which case the GPTE contains a global section table index (GSTX).
- The GPTE can indicate a demand zero page in a global page-file section.
- The GPTE can indicate a global page-file section page which has been created and is in use.

14.3.4 Global Page Table and System Page Table

GPTEs are located in exactly the same manner as process or system PTEs. Location MMG$GL_GPTBASE contains the address of the base of the global page table. All references to GPTEs use what can be thought of as a virtual page number as an index into the global page table.

The interesting thing to note about this approach is that the base of the global page table coincides with the base of the system page table. Further, the virtual page numbers that are used as indexes into the global page table are system virtual page numbers. In fact, when looking at system virtual address space, the global page table simply appears as an extension to the system page table. The global page table index associated with the first global page is 1 greater than the largest system virtual page number for a given configuration.

This logical extension of the system page table exists only when looking at system virtual address space. The global page table does not exist in physical pages adjacent to the system page table. The system length register only records the number of real system page table entries, not the logical extensions. In other words, global pages are not mapped into system virtual address space and are not accessible through system virtual addresses. This pseudo extension to the system page table is only available to the software routines in the memory management subsystem.

Figure 14-18 shows how the global page table relates to the system page table. It also shows the relationship among the GSD, GSTE, and GPTEs for a given section. There are several relationships among these three structures:

- The central structure is the GSTE (see Figure 14-7 for its layout). The first longword in the GSTE points to the GSD.

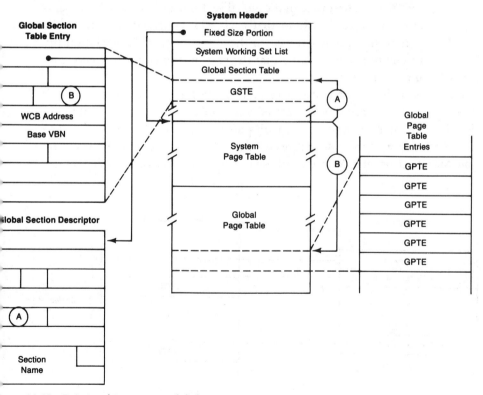

Figure 14-18   Relationships among Global Section Data Structures

349

- The virtual page number field (labeled B in Figure 14-18) contains the pseudo system virtual page number that serves as a longword index to the first GPTE that maps this section. This number is called a global page table index (GPTX).
- The GSD contains a GSTX (labeled A in the figure) that allows the GSTE to be located from the GSD.
- The original form of each GPTE is a section table index (identical to the GSTX found in the GSD), effectively pointing to the GSTE. When any given GPTE is either valid or in transition, the GSTX is stored in the PFN BAK array. Note that GPTEs for global page-file sections contain the page file backing store address.

14.3.5   **Process PTEs for Global Pages**

When a process maps a portion of its virtual address space to a global section, its process PTEs that map the section are in the form used for global page table indexes. The process PTE that maps the first global section page contains the GPTX of the first page in the global section. Each successive process PTE contains the next GPTX, so that each PTE effectively points to the GPTE that maps that particular page in the global section. This relationship is shown in Figure 14-19. Assume that the section shown in the figure contains N number of pages.

Figure 14-3 shows the global page table index form of a process PTE.

All of the data structures associated with global sections are described in detail in Chapter 15, where page faults for global pages are discussed. The initial allocation of these structures is briefly described along with the Create and Map Section and Map Global Section system services in Chapter 16.

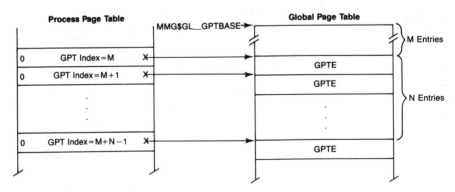

Figure 14-19   Relationship Between Process PTEs and Global PTEs

4.4   **SWAPPING DATA STRUCTURES**

There are three data structures that are used primarily by the swapper but indirectly by the pager:

• Balance slots
• PHD reference count array
• Process index array

The SYSBOOT parameter BALSETCNT is the number of elements in each array.

4.4.1   **Balance Slots**

A balance slot is a piece of system virtual address space reserved for a PHD. The number of balance slots, the SYSBOOT parameter BALSETCNT, is the maximum number of concurrently resident processes.

When the system is initialized, an amount of system virtual address space equal to the size of a PHD times BALSETCNT is allocated (see Figure 14-20). The location of the beginning of the balance slots is stored in global location SWP$GL_BALBASE. The size of a PHD (in pages) is stored in global location SWP$GL_BSLOTSZ. The calculations performed by SYSBOOT to determine the size of the PHD are described in Appendix F.

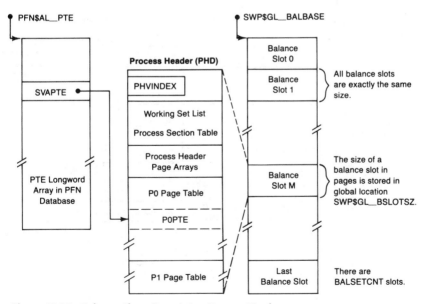

Figure 14-20 Balance Slots Containing Process Headers

14.4.2 Balance Slot Arrays

The system maintains two word arrays describing each process with a PHD stored in a balance slot (see Figure 14-21). Both of the word arrays are indexed by the balance slot number occupied by the resident process. The balance slot number is stored in the fixed portion of the PHD at offset PHD$W_PHVINDEX. Entries in the first array contain the number of references to each PHD. Entries in the second array contain an index into a longword array that points to the PCB for each PHD.

The global location PHV$GL_REFCBAS contains the starting address of the reference count array. Each of its elements counts the number of reasons why the corresponding PHD cannot be removed from memory. Specifically, an array element counts the number of page table pages that contain either valid or transition PTEs. A -1 in a reference count array element means that the corresponding balance slot is not in use.

The global location PHV$GL_PIXBAS contains the starting address of the process index array. Each of its elements contains an index into the longword array, based at the global pointer SCH$GL_PCBVEC. A zero in the process

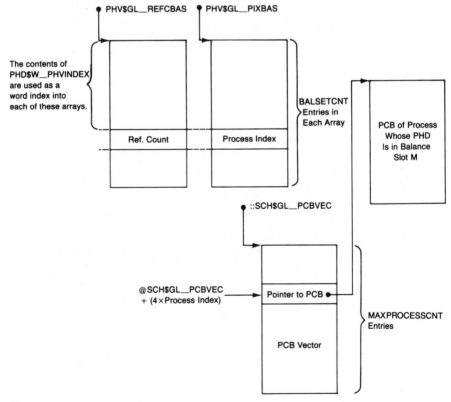

Figure 14-21 Process Header Vector Arrays

index array entry means that the corresponding balance slot is not in use. An element in the longword PCB vector contains the address of the PCB of the process with that process index. Figure 14-21 illustrates how the address of a PHD is transformed into the address of the PCB for that process, using the entry in the process index array.

If the PHD address is known, the balance slot index can be calculated (as described in the next section). By using this as a word index into the process index array, the longword index into the PCB vector is found. The array element in the PCB vector is the address of the PCB (whose PCB$L_PHD entry points back to the balance slot). A more detailed description of the PCB vector can be found in Chapter 20, where its use by the Create Process system service is discussed.

14.4.3   Comment on Equal Size Balance Slots

The choice of equal size balance slots, at first sight seemingly inefficient, has some subtle benefits to portions of the memory management subsystem. There are several instances, most notably within the modified page writer, when it is necessary to obtain a PHD address from a physical page's PFN. With fixed size balance slots, this operation is straightforward.

The contents of the PFN PTE array point to a PTE somewhere in the balance slot area. Subtracting the contents of SWP$GL_BALBASE from the PFN PTE array contents and dividing the result by the size of a balance slot (the size of a PHD) in bytes produces the balance slot index. If this index is multiplied by the size of the PHD in bytes and added to the contents of SWP$GL_BALBASE, the final result is the address of the PHD that contains the PTE that maps the physical page in question.

14.5   DATA STRUCTURES THAT DESCRIBE THE PAGE AND SWAP FILES

Page and swap files are used by the memory management subsystem to save physical page contents or process working sets. Page files are used to save the contents of modified pages that are not in physical memory. Both the swap and page files are used to save the working sets of processes that are not in the balance set.

14.5.1   Page File Control Blocks

Each page and swap file in use is described by a data structure called a page file control block (PFL). A page or swap file can be placed in use either automatically during system initialization or manually through the SYSGEN commands INSTALL/PAGEFILE and INSTALL/SWAPFILE. In either case, code in module [BOOTS]INITPGFIL allocates a PFL from nonpaged pool and initializes it. Figure 14-22 illustrates the fields in a PFL.

Initializing the PFL includes the following operations:

1. The file is opened and a special window control block (WCB) is built to describe all the file's extents. The special WCB, called a "cathedral window," ensures that the memory management subsystem does not have to take a window turn (see Chapter 18), which could lead to system deadlock conditions.
2. The address of the WCB is stored in the PFL.
3. A bitmap is allocated from nonpaged pool and initialized to all bits set. Each bit in the map represents one block of swap or page file. A bit set indicates the availability of the corresponding block.

Note that the locations of the WCB field, the virtual block number field, and the page fault cluster factor field are in the same relative offsets in this structure as they are in a section table entry. Because the offsets are the same, I/O requests can be processed by common code, independent of the data structure that describes the file being read or written.

14.5.2   Page-and-Swap-File Vector

Pointers to the PFLs are stored in a nonpaged pool array called the page-and-swap-file vector. The number of longword pointers in this array is the maximum number of page and swap files that can be in use on the system (the sum of SYSGEN parameters SWPFILCNT and PAGFILCNT) plus 1. A page or swap file is identified by an index number indicating the position of its PFL address in this array.

During system initialization, the routine EXE$INIT (see Chapter 25) allocates and initializes the page-and-swap-file vector, which is a standard dynamic data structure. The first two longwords of its header are unused. The third longword of its header contains the size of the data structure, a type value of DYN$C_PTR, and a subtype value of DYN$C_PFL.

The fourth longword contains the number of pointers in the array. The data begins at the fifth longword. The address of the beginning of the actual data is stored in global location MMG$GL_PAGSWPVC. Figure 14-22 shows the use of the page-and-swap-file vector data area to point to PFLs.

EXE$INIT initializes each pointer with the address of the "null page file control block," MMG$GL_NULLPFL. For the most part, this address serves as a zero value, indicating that no page or swap file with this index is in use. The null PFL, however, is also used to describe the shell process.

The shell process, a module in the system image, is accessed as page file index zero. It is the prototype for creating a new process. The information in the null PFL is optionally used during process creation to read a copy of the shell process into memory.

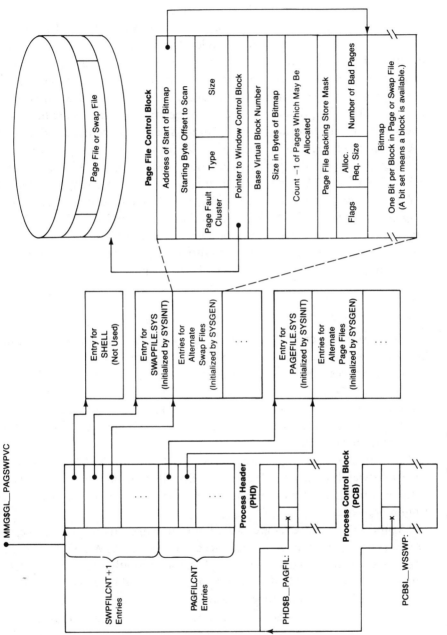

Figure 14-22   Page and Swap File Database

The process SYSINIT (see Chapter 25) places in use the primary page file, SYS$SYSTEM:PAGEFILE.SYS. SYSINIT builds a PFL and places its address in the page-and-swap-file vector. The primary page file has an index value equal to 1 more than the SYSBOOT parameter SWPFILCNT.

SYSINIT also places in use the primary swap file, SYS$SYSTEM:SWAP-FILE.SYS. The primary swap file is index 1. If there is no swap file, index 1 points to the null PFL. If the value of the SYSGEN parameter SWPFILCNT is zero, index 1 points to the primary page file. If there are no swap files, all swap operations are performed to the page files. Although the system can run this way, Digital Equipment Corporation recommends that there be at least one swap file. The allocation algorithm for swap files and dynamics of their use are quite different from those for page files. As a result, page files tend to become internally fragmented into pieces that are smaller than MPW_WRTCLUSTER and thus much smaller than the average swap space.

Any additional page and swap files are placed in use by SYSGEN in response to commands INSTALL/PAGEFILE and INSTALL/SWAPFILE. Installing page files other than the primary one on different disks allows for balancing the paging load. A system with alternate swap files can support a greater number of processes or processes with larger working sets.

14.5.3 Use of Swap Files

When a process is created, it is assigned swap space. Its swap space must contain room for the PHD and the process body (the P0 and P1 pages belonging to the process). The initial amount of swap space is equal to the value of the SYSGEN parameter MPW_WRTCLUSTER. If the value of MPW_WRTCLUSTER is less than the size of the shell process, the initial amount of swap space is set to the size of the shell (20 pages). Figure 14-23 shows how swap space is structured.

When the system assigns swap space, it scans from the beginning of the page-and-swap-file vector and selects the first file with sufficient space. Thus, if there is insufficient swap file space or none, swap space can be allocated from a page file.

If a process's working set grows so that it no longer fits its swap space, the process is reassigned to new swap space, which is MPW_WRTCLUSTER pages bigger than its old swap space. (The code actually uses the SYSBOOT parameter SWPALLOCINC, which is set to the value of MPW_WRTCLUSTER at system initialization. If the two parameters had different values and swapping to page files occurred, fragmentation problems would be more severe.) The process's new swap space can be in a different swap (or page) file than its old swap space. A process's swap space can grow up to WSQUOTA pages. At image exit and process creation, routine MMG$IMGRESET (in module PHDUTL) reduces the process's working set

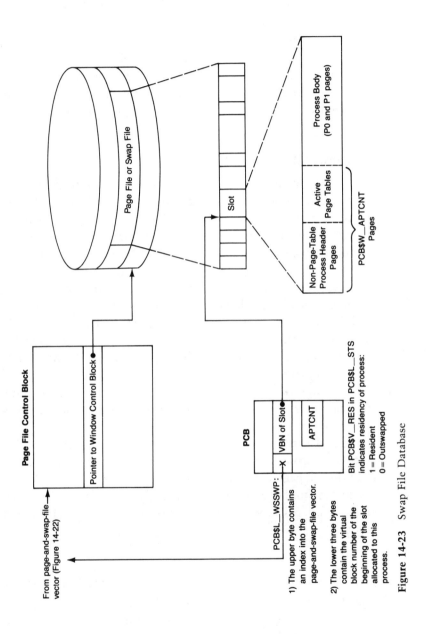

Figure 14-23   Swap File Database

back to PHD$W_DFWSCNT, and the process is reassigned to an initial size swap space.

Dynamically allocated swap space represents a significant change from early versions of VAX/VMS. Prior to VAX/VMS Version 3, swap files were composed of a number of fixed size areas known as swap slots. These swap slots were permanently allocated. The size of the swap slots was tied directly to the SYSGEN parameter WSMAX. This rigidity placed some restrictions on the system. The fixed size of the swap slots limited the possible growth of process working sets. Because each swap slot was the maximum required size (for WSMAX), this limited the number of processes that could be created.

14.5.4   Use of Page Files

When a process is created, it is assigned for its life to the page file with the most available space, the one with the largest value in PFL$L_FREPAGCNT. Installing alternate page files can enhance system performance by reducing paging activity to the existing page files (and sometimes by making more room available for swap spaces). The field PFL$L_FREPAGCNT contains the number of blocks or pages currently available for use in a page file. It is decreased when the modified page writer allocates space in a page file and increased when page file pages are released at address space deletion.

The primary page file, SYS$SYSTEM:PAGEFILE.SYS, is the only one in use until late in system initialization. Thus, the processes created during system initialization (for example, the job controller and OPCOM) are all assigned to the primary page file.

In addition, the primary page file is the backing store for system writable and pageable sections, notably paged pool. It is also the backing store for all global page-file sections.

A global page-file section is used to store temporary global data. It is a section of virtual memory not mapped to a file, whose only backing store is the primary page file. The SYSBOOT parameter GBLPAGFIL specifies the maximum number of pages or blocks of page file that can be used for this type of section. This type of global section is used to implement RMS global buffers.

14.6   SWAPPER AND MODIFIED PAGE WRITER PAGE TABLE ARRAYS

The VAX/VMS I/O subsystem enables an image to make a direct I/O request (DMA transfer) to a virtually contiguous buffer. There is no requirement that pages in a buffer be physically contiguous, only virtually contiguous. This capability is called "scatter-read/gather-write" or, more simply, "scatter/gather."

4.6.1   Direct I/O and Scatter/Gather

A combination of VAX hardware and VMS I/O subsystem software supports I/O to physically noncontiguous pages. The manner in which this is supported varies with processor type and I/O adapter type. For example, on a VAX processor with a UNIBUS or MASSBUS adapter, the device driver maps the memory buffer to I/O bus space. The result of this mapping is a set of contiguous addresses in the I/O bus space. Certain I/O adapters, such as CI adapters, read the relevant PTEs to determine the physical location of the buffer pages. On some processors, such as a MicroVAX I, there is no adapter hardware to support bus mapping. The device driver must transform the request into multiple transfers to or from physically contiguous memory.

Regardless of the manner of the support, a direct I/O request results in the locking of the buffer pages into memory. The I/O locking mechanism invoked at the FDT level brings each page into the working set of the requesting process, makes it valid, and increments that page's reference count (in PFN REFCNT array) to reflect the pending read or write. The buffer is generally described in the I/O request packet (IRP) through three fields:

- IRP$L_SVAPTE contains the system virtual address of the first PTE that maps the buffer.
- IRP$W_BOFF and IRP$L_BCNT together describe the buffer size that is used to calculate how many PTEs are required to map the buffer.

A driver processes this I/O request in a manner suitable to the processor and I/O adapter. For example, it may allocate adapter mapping registers and load them with the PFNs found in the PTEs or it may simply pass the system virtual address of the first PTE to an I/O adapter.

14.6.2   Swapper I/O

The swapper is presented with a more difficult problem. It must write a collection of pages to disk that are not even virtually contiguous. It solves this problem elegantly.

When the system is initialized, an array of WSMAX longwords is allocated from nonpaged pool for use as the swapper's I/O table. The starting address of this array is stored in global pointer SWP$GL_MAP. (The address is also stored in the saved P0 base register in the swapper's PHD so the pages mapped by this array are effectively the swapper's P0 space. This use is discussed in Chapter 20.)

When the swapper scans the WSL of the process being outswapped, it copies the PFNs in every valid PTE to successive entries in its I/O table. The swapper places the address of the base of the table into the field IRP$L_SVAPTE before the IRP is passed to the driver. (The swapper can exercise this control because it builds a portion of its own IRP.) The I/O table looks just like any other page table to the hardware/software combination that implements scatter/gather I/O.

What the swapper has succeeded in doing is making pages that are not virtually contiguous appear to be virtually contiguous to the I/O subsystem. (A different interpretation is that the pages are virtually contiguous in the P0 space of the swapper, the process that is actually performing the I/O.) At the same time that each PTE is being processed, any special actions based on the type of page are also taken care of. The whole operation of outswap and the complementary steps taken when the process is swapped back into memory are discussed in Chapter 17.

14.6.3 Modified Page Writer PTE Array

The modified page writer, in its attempt to write many pages to backing store with a single write request (so-called modified page write clustering), is faced with a problem similar to that of the swapper. The modified page writer builds a table of PTEs in a manner similar to the swapper.

When the modified page writer is building an I/O request, it can encounter three different types of page:

- Pages that are bound for a swap file (SWPVBN nonzero) are written individually.
- Pages that are bound for a section file are not necessarily virtually contiguous; these pages will be written as a group only if they are virtually contiguous.

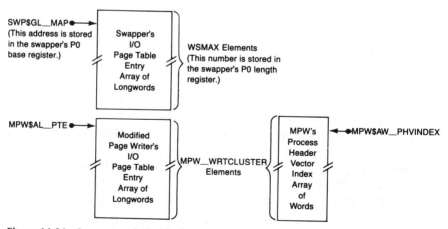

Figure 14-24 Swapper and Modified Page Writer PTE Arrays

• Pages on the modified page list that are to be written to a particular page file may be not only noncontiguous within one process address space, but may also belong to several processes. It is these pages that the modified page writer must cluster so they appear virtually contiguous.

At initialization time (in module INIT), two arrays are allocated from nonpaged pool for the modified page writer (see Figure 14-24). Each array contains MPW_WRTCLUSTER elements. The longword array will be filled with PTEs containing PFNs analogous to the swapper map. The word array contains an index into the PHD vector for each page in the map. In this way, each page that is put into the map and written to its backing store location is related to the PHD containing the PTE that maps this page. The operation of the modified page writer, including its clustered writes to a page file, is discussed in detail in Chapter 15.

14.6.4 Use of the Swapper and Modified Page Writer PTE Array

Each of these arrays supports only one use at a time.

If an inswap or outswap operation is in progress, the swapper map is in use. The swap in progress flag (SCH$V_SIP), in location SCH$GB_SIP, is set to indicate its use.

If the modified page writer is active, the modified page write in progress flag (SCH$V_MPW), in the same global location (SCH$GB_SIP), is set.

14.7 DATA STRUCTURES USED WITH SHARED MEMORY

An MA780 is a multiport memory that can be connected to multiple VAX-11/780 processors or VAX-11/785 processors. The MA780 shared memory unit can be used as an interprocessor communication path with common event flags, mailboxes, or global sections. This VMS support requires data structures located in the shared memory that describe the shared memory itself and its common event flag clusters, mailboxes, and global sections.

In addition, each processor connected to the shared memory requires data structures located in local memory that describe processor-specific information (such as the starting PFN or port number). Information common to both processors (for example, the size of the global section descriptor tables) is maintained in the shared memory data structures.

Note that this use of shared memory differs significantly from the use of MA780 shared memory in the VAX-11/782. In the VAX-11/780 and VAX-11/785, shared memory is used as a common data area or communications path among multiple processors; in the VAX-11/782, the MA780 is used as main memory. (Chapter 27 describes the VAX-11/782.)

14.7.1 Shared Memory Control Structures

The shared memory unit consists of a series of pages of physical memory. The bootstrap sequence records the presence of the shared memory unit but does not configure the physical pages into the system, allowing the user to include shared memory in a site-specific way (for example, whether to reinitialize the MA780 shared memory after each reboot). Once system initialization is complete and memory management is enabled, the physical memory pages must be virtually mapped to be accessible to program code.

The virtual mapping used by one processor to access shared memory pages may be different from the virtual mapping used by another processor. For this reason, some of the data structures that the VMS operating system uses to manipulate its data structures located in shared memory are self-relative queue elements. (Self-relative queue elements are described in the *VAX Architecture Reference Manual*.)

VMS cannot use one of its usual synchronization techniques, elevated IPL, to control access to shared memory data structures. Elevated IPL blocks interrupts on only one processor. Instead, all accesses to shared memory data that must be synchronized are done with one of the interlocked instructions provided for just this purpose in the VAX architecture. User programs that must synchronize their access to shared memory global sections must also use interlocked instructions.

These instructions are as follows:

INSQHI	Insert entry into queue at head, interlocked
INSQTI	Insert entry into queue at tail, interlocked
REMQHI	Remove entry from queue at head, interlocked
REMQTI	Remove entry from queue at tail, interlocked
BBSSI	Branch on bit set and set, interlocked
BBCCI	Branch on bit clear and clear, interlocked
ADAWI	Add aligned word, interlocked

The four instructions that manipulate self-relative queues actually provide two levels of interlocking. Because self-relative queue elements must be quadword aligned, the low three address bits (all zero) are available for other uses. The low-order bit in the forward link is used as a secondary interlock. When this bit is set, interlocked access to the head or tail of the queue is denied. This interlock bit is read in the same interlocked fashion as the other three instructions in the list (BBSSI, BBCCI, and ADAWI).

14.7.1.1 Physical Layout of Shared Memory.

If the shared memory is to be supported by the VMS operating system, it must be configured into the system with the System Generation Utility. This installation step is described in the *VAX/*

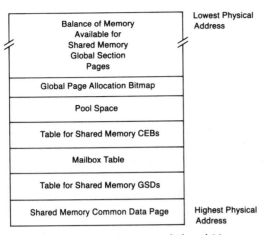

Figure 14-25   Physical Layout of Shared Memory

VMS System Manager's Reference Manual. The resulting physical layout of shared memory is illustrated in Figure 14-25. The VMS data areas located in the shared memory are initialized when the first processor (port) connects the shared memory unit. As other ports make their connection, their local memory data structures are simply initialized to point to the shared structures.

14.7.1.2   **Shared Memory Common Data Page.** The shared memory page with the highest physical address is used by the VMS operating system to contain the information that describes this shared memory unit. This page is called the common data page. Because this page may be virtually mapped to different addresses on each port (and may not even exist at the same physical address), each pointer in the common data page is a relative pointer from the base virtual address of the common data page. The contents of the common data page are listed in Table 14-4.

14.7.1.3   **Processor-Specific Control.** As each processor connects itself to the shared memory unit, a data structure in processor local memory is initialized that allows that processor to locate the common data page. That structure also contains physical page information that allows the shared physical memory to be virtually mapped on that processor. The layout of the shared memory control block is pictured in Figure 14-26.

14.7.2   **Global Sections in Shared Memory**

The creation and mapping of a global section in shared memory are slightly different from the corresponding actions for local memory global sections. The global section is recognized as a shared memory global section because

Table 14-4   Contents of Shared Memory Common Data Page

Field Name	Item	Size
SHD$L_MBXPTR	Relative pointer to mailbox table	Longword
SHD$L_GSDPTR	Relative pointer to GSD table	Longword
SHD$L_CEFPTR	Relative pointer to CEB table	Longword
SHD$L_GSBITMAP	Relative pointer to global page bitmap	Longword
SHD$L_GSPAGCNT	Total count of pages for global sections	Longword
SHD$L_GSPFN	Relative PFN of first global section page	Longword
SHD$W_GSDMAX	Number of entries in GSD table	Word
SHD$W_MBXMAX	Number of entries in MBX table	Word
SHD$W_CEFMAX	Number of entries in CEB table	Word
	(spare word for alignment)	Word
SHD$T_NAME	Name of shared memory	16 bytes
	(counted ASCII string)	
SHD$Q_INITTIME	Initialization time	Quadword

This is the end of the constant area of the shared memory common data page.

SHD$L_CRC	CRC of fields in constant area	Longword
SHD$W_GSDQUOTA	Count of GSDs created (one word per port)	16 words
SHD$W_MBXQUOTA	Count of mailboxes created (one word per port)	16 words
SHD$W_CEFQUOTA	Count of CEBs created (one word per port)	16 words
SHD$B_PORTS	Number of ports	Byte
SHD$B_INITLCK	Owner of initialization lock	Byte
SHD$B_BITMAPLCK	Owner of global page bitmap lock	Byte
SHD$B_FLAGS	Flags for locking data structures	Byte
SHD$B_GSDLOCK	Owner of GSD table lock	Byte
SHD$B_MBXLOCK	Owner of MBX table lock	Byte
SHD$B_CEFLOCK	Owner of CEF table lock	Byte
	(spare byte for alignment)	
SHD$W_PRQWAIT	Ports waiting for interprocessor request blocks (one bit per port)	Word
SHD$W_POLL	Ports actively using the memory (one bit per port)	Word
SHD$W_RESWAIT	Ports waiting for a resource (one bit per port) (one word mask per resource)	16 words
SHD$W_RESAVAIL	Ports needing to report resource available (one bit per port) (one word mask per resource)	16 words
SHD$W_RESSUM	Ports with resources to report (one bit per port)	Word
	(three spare words for alignment)	3 words
SHD$Q_PRQ	Free interprocessor request block listhead	Quadword
SHD$Q_POOL	Free pool block listhead	Quadword
SHD$Q_PRQWRK	Interprocessor request work queue listheads (one listhead per port)	16 quadwords

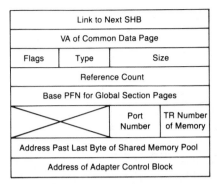

Link to Next SHB		
VA of Common Data Page		
Flags	Type	Size
Reference Count		
Base PFN for Global Section Pages		
	Port Number	TR Number of Memory
Address Past Last Byte of Shared Memory Pool		
Address of Adapter Control Block		

Figure 14-26   Contents of Shared Memory Control
Block

its name translates to an equivalence name of the form

shared-memory-name:section-name

The Create and Map Section system service then creates the data structures necessary to describe this section:

- The GSD for such a section (see Figure 14-27) is located in shared memory and contains information used to map the section.
- Only the port that creates the global section has a GSTE (in the local memory of the creating processor) describing the section. This section table entry is used by the VMS operating system to load the physical pages of the section with the contents of the designated file when the section is created. The GSTE is also used if the Delete Global Section or Update Section system services are called to write the contents of a writable global section located in shared memory back to its original file. (Either system service will not have any effect if it is issued from any port other than the creator port, because only the creator port has a GSTE for the section.)
- Because the pages of a shared memory global section are always valid, there is no need to page those pages. Therefore, no GPTEs are created for the section. Instead, when a process maps to such a section, its process PTEs are loaded with the PFNs of the shared memory section pages and marked valid. These pages are not charged against the process's working set.

Because of the way in which the VMS operating system uses shared memory for global sections, putting global sections into shared memory, even when the memory unit is not connected to another processor, improves system utilization. Each process using the shared sections receives a free extension to its working set. There is no demand placed on the global page table. Local physical memory that would otherwise be required to contain such entities as DCL or the screen management routines in the Run-Time Library is available for other uses, like an expanded physical page cache (free page list).

365

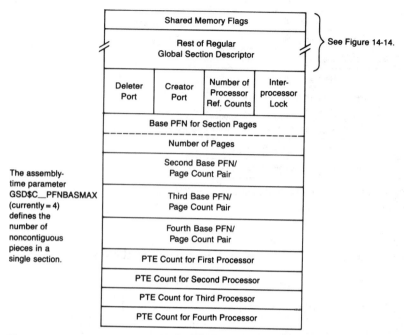

The assembly-
time parameter
GSD$C__PFNBASMAX
(currently = 4)
defines the
number of
noncontiguous
pieces in a
single section.

Figure 14-27 Contents of Shared Memory Global
Section Descriptor

14.7.3 Mailboxes in Shared Memory

A mailbox is recognized as a shared memory mailbox because its name translates to an equivalence name of the form

    shared-memory-name:mailbox-name

When a mailbox is created in shared memory, it is described by a shared memory mailbox descriptor block (MBX) located in the shared memory (see Figure 18-4). In addition, each port connected to the shared memory mailbox has a unit control block (UCB) in its local memory I/O database that makes the connection between the local I/O system and the shared memory mailbox. The relationships among shared memory mailbox data structures are pictured in Figure 18-5.

14.7.4 Common Event Flag Clusters in Shared Memory

A common event flag cluster is recognized as a shared memory event flag cluster because its name translates to an equivalence name of the form

    shared-memory-name:event-flag-cluster-name

As with global sections and mailboxes (and the shared memory itself), there are data structures in shared memory and other structures in local memory required to fully describe a common event flag cluster located in shared memory. The shared memory data structure is called a master common event block (CEB) and contains the only valid set of event flags. Each port connected to this common event flag cluster has a slave CEB in local memory that locates the master. The relationship between the master CEB and the slave CEBs is pictured in Figure 12-5. The layouts of the master and slave CEBs are pictured in Figure 12-4.

15   Paging Dynamics

I consider that a man's brain originally is like a little empty
attic, and you have to stock it with such furniture as you
choose.... Now, the skillful workman is very careful indeed as
to what he takes into his brain-attic. He will have nothing but
the tools which may help him in doing his work, but of these
he has a large assortment, and all in the most perfect order. It
is a mistake to think that that little room has elastic walls
and can distend to any extent. Depend upon it, there comes a
time when for every addition of knowledge you forget something that you knew before. It is of highest importance, therefore, not to have useless facts elbowing out the useful ones.

Sir Arthur Conan Doyle, *A Study in Scarlet*

This chapter shows how the various memory management data structures
are manipulated by the pager in response to different forms of page faults.

Although pager action is described here, it is not presented in a flowchart
or decision fashion. Rather, the actions are described in terms of modifications to data structures and state transitions.

15.1   OVERVIEW OF PAGER OPERATION

Before discussing how the pager reacts to different forms of page faults, this
chapter briefly describes the overall operation of the pager.

15.1.1   Hardware Action

When memory management is enabled, all program references generated by
the CPU are virtual addresses. Each address must be translated to a physical

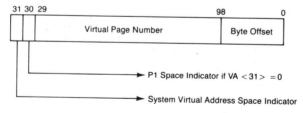

VA < 31:30 > Selects the page table:
    0 = P0 Page Table
    1 = P1 Page Table
    2 = System Page Table
    3 = Reserved
VA < 29:9 > is used as a longword index into the selected table.

Figure 15-1   Format of Virtual Address

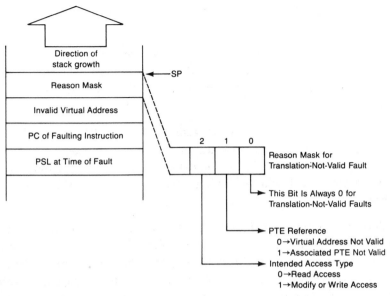

Figure 15-2   State of the Kernel Stack Following
a Translation-Not-Valid Fault

address before a reference to memory or I/O space can be made. The virtual
address (see Figure 15-1) is used by the VAX hardware/microcode address
translation mechanism to find the page table entry (PTE) that is used to translate the address.

   If the PTE is valid, its contents are used to translate the virtual address to a
physical address and execution continues. If the PTE is invalid (PTE<31> =
0), then the VAX microcode generates a translation-not-valid exception, better known as a page fault. The VMS page fault exception service routine,
MMG$PAGEFAULT in module PAGEFAULT, is known as the pager. Figure
15-2 shows the state of the kernel stack following a page fault.

15.1.2   Initial Pager Action

MMG$PAGEFAULT immediately raises IPL to IPL$_SYNCH to serialize
access to the memory management database. Before the pager does any work,
it checks at what IPL the page fault occurred. If the page fault IPL is higher
than 2, the pager generates the fatal bugcheck PGFIPLHI. Page faults above
IPL 2 are not allowed for the following two reasons:

• Code that is executing at a higher IPL needs to perform a series of instructions without being interrupted. If a page fault happens, the faulting process
  might be removed from execution, allowing another process to execute the
  same routine or access the same protected data structure.
• Page faults are exceptions that happen to a process. When the system is
  executing at an IPL higher than 2, it is often on the interrupt stack, running

in system context. There is not necessarily a process in whose context the page can be made valid.

The next step that the pager takes is to retrieve the invalid virtual address from the kernel stack. It uses this address to locate the PTE that maps this page by performing the same operations that the VAX address translation mechanism uses:

1. The upper two bits of the virtual address (VA<31:30>) select which page table (or which base register) to use.
2. The virtual address field (VA<29:9>) is used as a longword index into the page table. The low-order bits specify byte offset in the page and are ignored.

Before examining the PTE, the pager determines whether the SPTE for the page containing the PTE is itself valid. (This check avoids the necessity of making the pager recursive.) If not, the page table page is made valid first. Note that the pager does not perform this check using the page table valid bit in the exception parameter; rather, it checks the valid bit in the system PTE for the page table page. The pager checks the PTE rather than the exception parameter because between the time of the page fault and the time of the check, the PTE could have been altered, invalidating the exception parameter.

Once the PTE is available, the pager takes different actions, depending on the nature of the invalid PTE. (See Figure 14-3 for the different forms of invalid PTE. The next several sections describe some of the major paths through the pager. Extraordinary conditions, such as read and write errors, are only mentioned in passing.

15.2 PAGE FAULTS FOR PROCESS-PRIVATE PAGES

This section describes page faults for process-private pages. The different path through the pager for shared pages is discussed in the next section. There are four cases in the category of private pages:

- Two of the cases involve a page that is originally faulted from a section file. The two cases are distinguished by whether or not the section is copy-on-reference.
- A third case is a fault for a page in a private section of demand zero pages.
- A fourth case that can result from either a copy-on-reference page or a demand zero page is a fault for a page in a page file.

15.2.1 Page Located in a Section File

There are two different types of page that can initially reside in a private section file: a page that is copy-on-reference and one that is not. The PTE for either type of page contains a process section table index (PSTX). The only initial difference between the two types of page is the setting of the copy-on-reference bit in the PTE (see Figure 14-3).

15.2.1.1   **Private Page That Is Not Copy-on-Reference.** The first type of fault is for a page that is not copy-on-reference. The various transitions that such a page can possibly make are illustrated in Figure 15-3. The numbers in circles are keyed to explanations of each of the following transitions. (For simplicity, clustered reads and writes are ignored in the discussion that follows. Section 15.5 discusses all aspects of paging I/O.) The PTE initially contains a PSTX with the copy-on-reference bit (PTE<16>) clear.

①A page fault occurs. The pager uses the virtual address exception parameter to locate the PTE. The PTE contains a PSTX. Information contained in the process section table entry (PSTE) indicates which virtual block in the file contains the virtual page. The pager invokes MMG$FREWSLE (in module PAGEFAULT) to make room in the WSL for a new page. This may require the removal of a page from the working set. The pager then allocates a physical page from the head of the free list and adds the page to the WSL. The field PCB$W_PPGCNT is incremented to indicate one more page in the working set.

The PFN array elements for the physical page allocated are initialized. The STATE array element indicates that a read is in progress. The PTE array element points to the process PTE. The WSLX array element locates the working set list entry (WSLE) just set up. The BAK array element contains the initial contents of the PTE (the PSTX). The REFCNT array element contains the value 2, one reference because the page is in the process working set and one for the read in progress.

The pager builds and queues an I/O request packet (see Section 15.5) that describes the read to be done. The process is placed into a page fault wait state until the page read completes.

②Because most of the work was done in response to the initial fault, there is little left to do when the page read completes. Page read completion occurs as part of I/O postprocessing (see Chapter 18) and runs in system context. Routine PAGIO (in module IOCIOPOST) decrements the REFCNT array element (but, in the usual case, its contents stay above zero so nothing special happens). It changes the PFN STATE array element to active and valid and sets the valid bit in the process PTE. PAGIO reports the scheduling event page fault completion for the process so that it is made computable. (Chapter 10 describes how scheduling events are reported.) The next time that the process is selected for execution, it executes the same instruction that caused the initial page fault.

③One transition that a valid page can undergo (and still remain valid) occurs when the page is modified as a result of instruction execution. The VAX

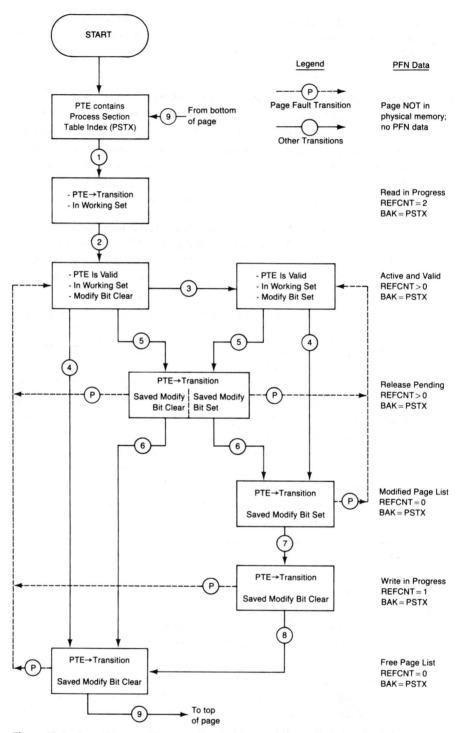

Figure 15-3 State Diagram Showing Page Transitions
for Private Section Page That Is Not Copy-on-Reference

hardware sets the modify bit in the PTE. The change is not noted at this time in the PFN database.

④ When a non-copy-on-reference page is removed from the process working set by the routine MMG$FREWSLE, several things happen:

a. The modify bit in the PTE is logically ORed into the PFN STATE array element, saving its value.

b. The valid, modify, TYP0, and TYP1 bits in the PTE are all cleared. The PFN field is left alone.

c. The CPU translation buffer is invalidated to remove cached but now obsolete contents of the PTE.

d. The REFCNT array element is decremented. If the reference count goes to zero, MMG$RELPFN (in module ALLOCPFN) is invoked to put the page on the free or modified page list, according to the setting of the saved modify bit in the PFN STATE array element. Since the BLINK array overlays the WSLX array, inserting the page into the free or modified list supplants the WSLX array contents. The new location of the page is inserted into the STATE array.

e. The WSLE is made available (that is, zeroed), and PCB$W_PPGCNT is decremented to indicate one less private page.

A page remains in the working set until one of the following occurs:

—Room is required for another page.
—The virtual page is deleted.
—The Purge Working Set ($PURGWS) system service is requested.
—Swapper trimming (see Chapter 17) removes it.
—Working set list adjustment removes it.

⑤ If the reference count (decremented in 4d) does not go to zero, there is outstanding I/O for this page. The state is changed to release pending. The ultimate destination for the page (free or modified list) is recorded in the saved modify bit in the STATE array.

⑥ The I/O completion routine, MMG$UNLOCK in module IOLOCK, decrements reference counts for pages that are locked down. When this routine detects that the count has gone to zero, it invokes MMG$RELPFN to place the page on either the free list or the modified list as appropriate. The STATE array element is changed.

⑦ The modified page writer eventually writes this physical page to its backing store address, which is stored in the BAK array. Writable pages that are not copy-on-reference are written back to the file where they originated.

The STATE of the page is set to write in progress. The saved modify bit is cleared. The REFCNT of 1 reflects this outstanding output operation.

Note that writable private pages that are not copy-on-reference are not produced by the linker. Such a section must be created with the Create and Map Section system service.

⑧ When the modified page write completes, the page's REFCNT is decremented to zero. Because the saved modify bit is clear, the page is placed on the free list.

⑨ While the physical page remains attached to the process, the PTE contains a PFN, and the PFN PTE array contains the address of the process PTE.

When the physical page is reused for another purpose, several steps must be taken to break the ties between the process virtual page and the physical page that is about to be reused.

The process PTE must be altered to reflect the backing store address of the page. (The PFN PTE array is used to locate the PTE.) In this case, the PTE is reset so it contains a PSTX, the same contents it had before the initial page fault.

The PFN array elements for this physical page are all cleared before the page is passed on to the new owner of the physical page. In particular, the PTE array element, the only connection from the PFN database to the process page table, is cleared.

15.2.1.2   **Page Faults Out of Transition States.** Figure 15-3 also shows the transitions that a page makes when a page fault occurs while the physical page is in the transition state. While the changes back to the active state are straightforward, there are details about each fault that should be mentioned. Note that in each case a new WSLE must be acquired, and its acquisition can involve the removal of some other page from the process working set.

1. A page fault from the free page list is resolved by changing the STATE of the page to active, setting the valid bit in the PTE, and incrementing the REFCNT array element.

2. A page fault from the modified list is resolved in exactly the same way. By putting the page back into its modified state, the figure shows that the page was previously modified but never written to its backing store address.

   In fact, the modify bit in the PTE is not set by the pager. Rather, the saved modify bit in the PFN STATE array records the fact that the page has not been backed up.

3. A page fault from the release pending state is similar. The STATE of the page is changed to active, the valid bit in the PTE is set, and the REFCNT is incremented.

   Artistic license is taken in the figure to differentiate physical pages that were modified from pages that were not. Again, the only difference between the two pages is the setting of the saved modify bit in the PFN STATE array, not the setting of the modify bit in the PTE.

4. The transition that deserves special comment is a page fault that occurs while the modified page writer is writing the page to its backing store address. The saved modify bit is cleared before the write begins so that the page will be placed on the free list when the write completes. Although the page has not yet been completely backed up, the assumption is made that the write will complete successfully. Page faults can thus put the page into the active but unmodified state. The only difficulty occurs in the event of a write error. The modified page writer's I/O completion routine, WRITEDONE in module WRTMFYPAG, detects this state of affairs and turns the saved modify bit back on.

5.2.1.3   **Copy-on-Reference Page.** A more common type of writable process-private page is called copy-on-reference. Figure 15-4 illustrates the transitions that such a page makes from its initial page fault until it is written to some backing store address.

Many of the transitions that occur here are the same as the case just described. This section notes each transition but elaborates only those areas that are different.

① The initial setting of the PTE (START 1 in the figure) is the PSTX, but the copy-on-reference bit (PTE<16>) is set. The writable bit, PTE<18>, is also usually set. When a page fault occurs, the pager allocates a physical page, copies its PFN to the PTE, and initiates the read. Two important steps are taken that differ from the previous case.

First, the saved modify bit in the PFN STATE array is turned on. Setting the bit guarantees that the page will be written to its backing store address when removed from the process working set, regardless of what instructions or I/O operations the process chooses to execute.

Second, the BAK array element is set to point to the page file, with an indication that no block has yet been allocated. At this time, all ties to the original section file are broken. Before the modified page writer writes this page to its backing store address (as it certainly will because the saved modify bit was just turned on), it must allocate a block in the page file.

② When the read completes, the page STATE is made active and the PTE set valid (and effectively modified).

④ When the copy-on-reference page is removed from the process working set (and its REFCNT is zero), the page is unconditionally placed on the modified page list.

⑤ If the REFCNT did not go to zero when the page was removed from the process working set, the physical page is placed into the release pending state until the I/O completes.

⑥ At that time, the page is placed on the modified page list.

A page fault from either the release pending state or from the modified page

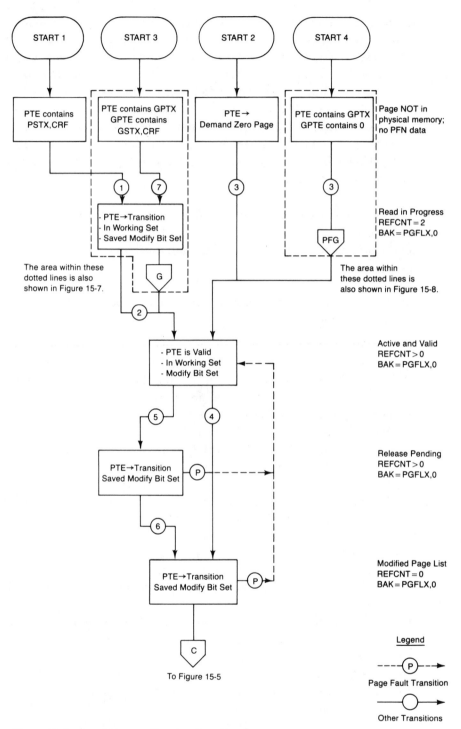

Figure 15-4 State Diagram Showing Page Transitions for Private and Global Copy-on-Reference Pages and for Demand Zero Pages

list puts the page back into the active (but effectively modified) state. That is, the saved modify bit in the PFN STATE array remains set, causing the page to be put back on the modified page list when it is removed from the working set again.

When the modified page writer writes the page to its backing store address (in the page file), the page makes a transition from the modified page list. Figure 15-5, the diagram for faults from the page file, shows this transition. The connection between Figure 15-4 and Figure 15-5 is indicated by path C in the two figures.

5.2.2   Demand Zero Pages

A demand zero PTE can be created by invoking the Create Virtual Address and Expand Region system services. One of these services can be issued explicitly by the process or on its behalf by the system (as part of image activation or in the LIB$GET_VM Run-Time Library procedure).

When the pager detects a page fault for a demand zero page, it takes the following steps:

1. The pager invokes MMG$FREWSLE to make room in the WSL for a new page.
2. It invokes MMG$ININEWPFN to allocate a physical page from the beginning of the free page list.
3. The PFN array elements are initialized. The PTE array element points to the process PTE.
4. The BAK array element denotes a not-yet-allocated block in the page file.
5. The page is filled with zeros. This is done with a MOVC5 instruction that uses a zero-length source string and a null fill character.
6. The page's REFCNT is incremented, the page is added to the process working set, and its STATE is set active. The WSLX array element is filled in, and the process's private page count is incremented.
7. Finally, the pager dismisses the fault by executing an REI instruction, passing control back to the user.

These steps all take place along path 3 in the upper right-hand portion of Figure 15-4.

5.2.3   Global Copy-on-Reference and Page-File Section Pages

There are two forms of pages that merge into the same set of state transitions as private copy-on-reference sections and demand zero pages. These forms are global copy-on-reference pages and global page-file section pages. The details of global page fault resolution are discussed in Section 15.3.

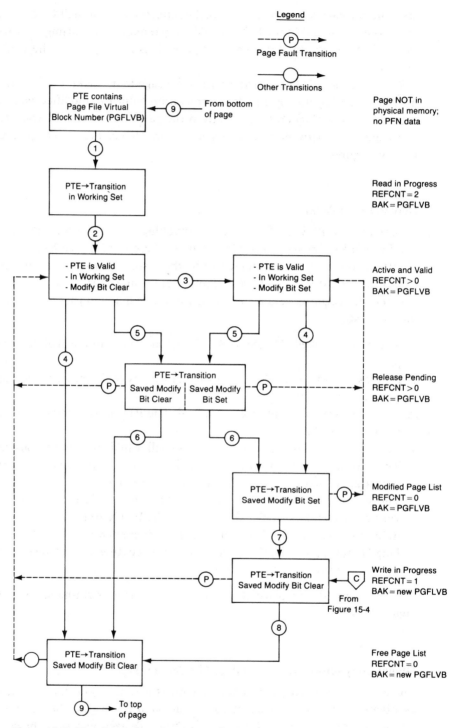

Figure 15-5 Transitions for a Page Located in a Page File

Suffice it to say here that a global copy-on-reference page is initially faulted from a global file but is subsequently indistinguishable from other process-private pages. A global page-file section page is initially faulted as a demand zero page and from then on is indistinguishable from other global writable pages, except that its backing store is in the page file.

5.2.4   Page Located in a Page File

The transitions that a page faulted from the page file goes through (see Figure 15-5) are the same as the transitions described for pages that are not copy-on-reference (see Figure 15-3). The only difference in the PFN data between the two figures is that the BAK array element in Figure 15-5 indicates that the page belongs in the page file. The BAK array element in Figure 15-3 contains a PSTX.

The other difference between the two figures is the entry point into the transition diagram. A page can start out in a section file (PTE contains PSTX) but a page can never start out in a page file. The entry into Figure 15-5 is from Figure 15-4, from one of three initial states that eventually result in the physical page contents being written to the page file.

5.3   PAGE FAULTS FOR GLOBAL PAGES

The page fault resolution for global pages can be described in exactly the same way as process-private pages are described. Following the transition of a global page table entry (GPTE) and its associated PFN database entries adds nothing to the information already presented in Figure 15-3.

A more interesting approach is to look at the interaction of the process PTEs and the GPTEs that they point to. The following discussion uses a specific example, rather than a general case, to allow specific numbers to be used.

5.3.1   Page Fault for Global Read-Only Page

Figure 15-6 illustrates the transitions that occur for a global read-only page that is mapped by two processes. The mapping is shown separately from the operation of section creation to simplify the figure. A second simplification in the figure is that the page is assumed to be read-only. The implications of a read/write global page are described in the next section.

When the global section is initially created, the data structures described in the previous chapter are all set up. The GPTE for the page represented in the figure contains a global section table index (GSTX), which locates the global section table entry (GSTE) containing information about the global file.

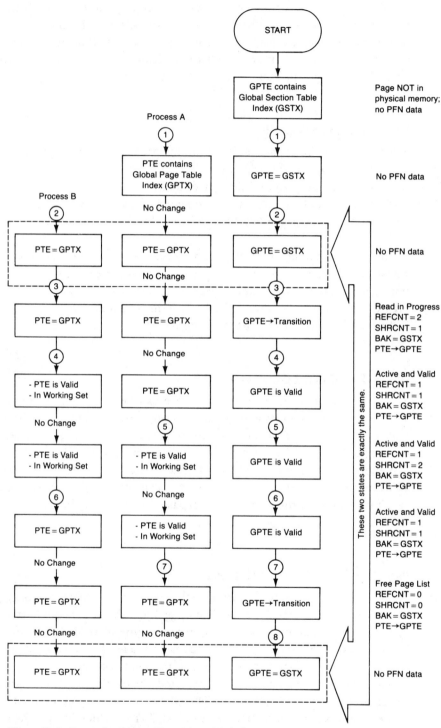

Figure 15-6 Example of Page Transitions Made by a
Global Page Mapped by Two Processes

①When Process A maps to the section, the process PTE contains a global page table index (GPTX), effectively a pointer to the GPTE.

②When Process B maps to the section, its PTE contains exactly the same GPTX as found in Process A's PTE.

③Process B happens to incur a page fault on this global page first. Several things happen:

   a. The pager notes that the process PTE contains a GPTX. This index is used to locate the GPTE.

   b. The GPTE contains a GSTX, indicating that the global page resides on disk somewhere. Exactly the same things are done to initiate the read here as in the case of a process-private page.

   c. A physical page is allocated. A WSLE is created and Process B's global page count, PCB$W_GPGCNT, is incremented.

   d. The STATE of that page is set to read in progress.

   e. Its REFCNT array element is incremented.

   f. Its BAK array element is loaded with the GSTX.

   g. Note that the PFN PTE array element is loaded with the address of the GPTE, not the address of the process PTE. Note also that, while the read is in progress, the GPTE contains a transition PTE but the process PTE still contains the GPTX.

   h. The REFCNT array element indicates two references: one for the read in progress and one because the page is in some process working set (the SHRCNT array element is nonzero). The SHRCNT array element contains a 1 while the read is in progress.

④When the read completes, the I/O postprocessing routine, IOC$IOPOST, queues a special kernel AST to Process B. The special kernel AST routine is the page I/O-done routine, PAGIO. Running in the context of Process B, PAGIO takes the following steps:

   a. The STATE of the page is changed to active.

   b. The GPTE is set to valid to record the fact that this page is in some process working set.

   c. The process PTE, located through its address stored in the I/O request packet, is set up to contain the low-order 21 bits from the GPTE, with the valid bit set and bits 21 and 26 cleared.

   d. The REFCNT and SHRCNT are both 1 at this point.

⑤When Process A faults the same global page, the initial pager action is the same as it was in step 3, because the PTE is a GPTX. Now, however, the pager finds a valid GPTE. Resolution of this page fault is simple.

   A WSLE is created for Process A and its global page count is incremented. The low-order 21 bits of GPTE are simply copied to Process A's

PTE. The valid bit is set and bits 21 and 26 are cleared. The SHRCNT is incremented, and the fault is dismissed.

⑥ When MMG$FREWSLE removes the global page from Process B's working set, it decrements B's global page count and the SHRCNT for the page of memory. Because the SHRCNT is still positive, nothing dramatic happens to the physical page.

Process B's PTE must be restored to its previous state. (The PTE does not assume some transition form.) The PTE array element contains the address of the GPTE so the GPTX must be recalculated.

The calculation is straightforward. The contents of MMG$GL_GPTBASE are subtracted from the PTE array element, the result is divided by 4 (to create a longword index), and the quotient is stored in the process PTE in the GPTX field.

⑦ When MMG$FREWSLE removes the global page from Process A's working set, it restores the process PTE as described in step 6.

The SHRCNT is decremented, this time to zero. Therefore, the REFCNT is also decremented. If the page is unmodified and there is no outstanding I/O, the physical page is placed on the free page list.

The GPTE contains a transition PTE. The STATE array element indicates the free page list. The other PFN array elements are unchanged.

⑧ When the physical page is reused, the ties must be broken between the physical page and, in this case, the GPTE. (None of the processes mapped to this page are affected in any way by this step.)

The contents of the BAK array element (a GSTX) are inserted into the GPTE, located by the contents of the PFN PTE array element. The PFN PTE array element is then cleared, breaking the connection between the physical page and the global page table.

These steps put the process and global page tables back to the state they were in following step 2 (although it is pictured here as a different state to make the figure simpler).

15.3.2   Global Read/Write Pages

The transitions that occur for global writable pages are the same as the transitions for a process-private page that is not copy-on-reference. The only difference between such transitions and the transitions illustrated in Figure 15-3 is that the GPTE, not the process PTE, is affected by the transitions of the physical page.

The process PTE for global pages contains a GPTX up until the time that the page is made valid. Only then is a PFN inserted into the process PTE. As soon as the page is removed from the process working set, the GPTX is placed back into the process PTE. All ties to the PFN database are made through the GPTE, which retains the PFN while the physical page is in the various transition states.

15.3.3   **Global Copy-on-Reference Pages**

The global pages previously described are all shared pages. One type of global page is shared only in its initial state. As soon as the fault occurs, the page is treated exactly like a process-private page. This type of page is a global copy-on-reference page.

Figure 15-7 illustrates the transitions that occur for a global copy-on-reference page:

① The initial conditions are identical to those used in Figure 15-6. The section is created and each of the GPTEs contains a GSTX although, in this case, the copy-on-reference bit is set.

② Process A maps the page and has its PTE set to contain a GPTX.

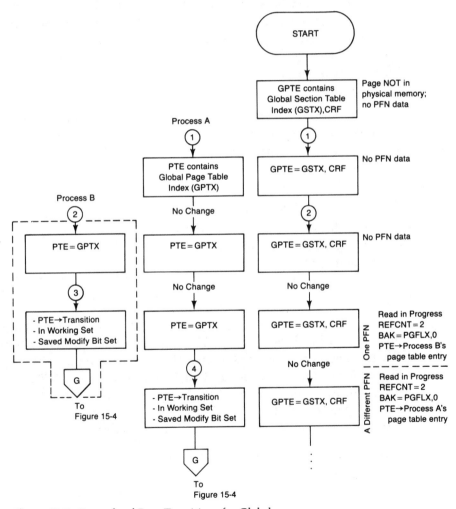

Figure 15-7   Example of Page Transitions for Global Copy-on-Reference Pages

Process B maps the page and gets the same GPTX in its PTE. Up to this point, nothing is different from Figure 15-6.

③ Now when Process B incurs a page fault, the pager follows the GPTX to the GPTE, noting that the page is located in a global section file and is copy-on-reference. A read is initiated and the following modifications are made to the process PTE and the PFN database:

a. The GPTE is not touched. It retains its GSTX contents.
b. The process PTE is set to a transition PTE.
c. The STATE of the physical page is set to read in progress.
d. Its BAK array element contains a page file index (with no block allocated yet).
e. Its PTE array element contains the address of Process B's PTE.

Note that all ties between Process B and the global section are broken. The page is now treated exactly like a private copy-on-reference page. The two boxes for Process B in Figure 15-7 are the boxes within the dashed outline in Figure 15-4.

④ When Process A faults the same page, exactly the same steps are taken, this time with a totally different physical page.

Thus, both Process A and Process B get exactly the same initial copy of the global page from the global file but, from that point on, each process has its own private copy of the page to modify.

15.3.4   Global Page-File Section Pages

A global page-file section provides a means for processes to share global pages without the need of a backing store file. By its nature, such a page has no initial contents and is thus initialized as a demand zero page.

Figure 15-8 illustrates the transitions that occur for a global page-file section page:

① The initial conditions are identical to those used in Figure 15-6. The section is created and each of the GPTEs contains a zero in the PFN field.

② Process A maps the page and has its PTE set to contain a GPTX.
Process B maps the page and has its PTE set to contain a GPTX.

③ When Process B incurs a page fault, the pager follows the GPTX to the GPTE and notes that the GPTE is demand zero. The following modifications are made to the PTEs and to the PFN database:

a. A physical page of memory is allocated.
b. Its PTE array element points to the GPTE.
c. Its BAK array element contains the primary page file index (with no block allocated).
d. The newly allocated PFN is stored in the GPTE.

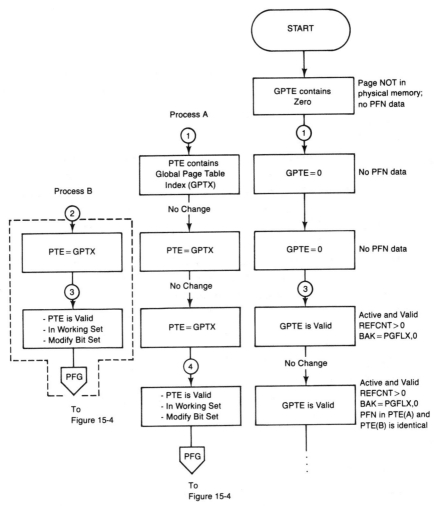

Figure 15-8   Example of Page Transitions for Global
Page-File Section Pages

e. The valid bit is set in the GPTE.

f. The PFN is copied to Process B's PTE and the valid bit is set.

④ When Process A incurs a fault on the page, the pager follows the GPTX to
the GPTE and finds that the GPTE is valid. The valid GPTE is copied to
Process A's PTE.

Transitions for a global page-file section page are the same as the transitions for a page located in a page file (see Figure 15-5). However, for a global
page-file section page, the GPTE, not the process PTE, is affected by the transitions that the physical page makes. Once the global page is removed from
the working set, the process PTE reverts to the GPTX form.

15.4 WORKING SET REPLACEMENT

The WSL (see Figure 14-4) is a circular buffer that describes the process pages that are valid. When a process references an invalid virtual page, the pager must take whatever steps are necessary to make the page valid. It must also add a description of the page to the WSL. In principle, the size (or capacity) of the WSL is used as a brake on memory growth. That is, if there is no room in the WSL for another entry, one must be removed. The pager uses the WSL to decide which virtual page to discard.

The size of a process's WSL is adjusted in response both to process paging and system needs for memory (see Chapter 16). When the WSL is made smaller and pages are removed from the working set, empty entries are not immediately compressed from the circular buffer. Instead, the field PCB$W_WSSIZE is decreased. This field specifies the maximum number of entries in the WSL a process may use.

Leaving empty entries in the WSL reduces CPU overhead. However, it makes adding a page to the working set slightly more complex. That a WSLE is empty does not necessarily mean the process can make use of it; the size of the working set must be less than PCB$W_WSSIZE. If the process is already at its maximum size, a nonempty WSLE must be found whose virtual page can be replaced in the working set by the new page.

The WSL replacement algorithm that the VMS executive uses is a modified first-in/first-out (FIFO) scheme. The entry that has been in the WSL for the longest time (the one pointed to by PHD$W_WSNEXT) is the one first considered for replacement.

15.4.1 Scan of Working Set List

When the pager needs an empty WSLE, it calls routine MMG$FREWSLE (in module PAGEFAULT). This routine selects a WSLE for use. The following steps summarize its flow. Subsequent sections describe more details of particular aspects of its flow.

MMG$FREWSLE scans the WSL, beginning at the WSLE whose index is in PHD$W_WSNEXT:

1. If the WSLE is empty (contents are zero), MMG$FREWSLE checks whether the entry can be used (see Section 15.4.2). If the WSLE can be used, it is selected.
2. If the WSLE is not empty (its contents are nonzero), but is an active page table page (one which maps valid pages), the WSLE cannot be used.
3. If the WSLE is not empty and is an inactive page table page, it may be usable. MMG$FREWSLE takes the steps described in Section 15.4.3 to determine whether the page table page can be released and its WSLE reused.

4. If the WSLE is not empty, but its virtual page has been recently enough accessed that it appears in the translation buffer, the WSLE is skipped (see Section 15.4.4).

5. If the WSLE is selected for reuse and is not empty, MMG$FREWSLE takes the actions described in Section 15.4.5.

6. If the WSLE is not selected, the index is incremented, and the steps in this list are repeated until a WSLE that can be used is found. If the index exceeds the end of the list, it is reset to the beginning of the dynamic WSL.

5.4.2 Using an Empty Entry in the Working Set List

If an empty WSLE is found, checks are made to see if a page can be added to the working set. If there are fewer pages in the working set than are indicated by WSQUOTA, a new physical page can be added to the working set. It may also be possible to add physical pages to the WSL above WSQUOTA (up to WSEXTENT), depending on the size of the free page list.

The following checks are required for an empty WSLE to be usable:

1. If the size of the working set (process page count, PCB$W_PPGCNT, plus global page count, PCB$W_GPGCNT) equals the maximum number of valid WSLEs allowed to the process (PHD$W_WSSIZE), the empty WSLE cannot be used. That is, the working set is full and a page in it must be replaced.

2. If the working set is not full, the size of the working set is compared to WSQUOTA. If the size of the working set is less than WSQUOTA, a new page is allowed in the working set. The empty WSLE pointed to by PHD$W_WSNEXT is used.

3. If there are more than WSQUOTA pages in the working set, the number of pages on the free page list is compared to the SYSBOOT parameter GROWLIM. If there are more than GROWLIM pages on the free page list, a new page is allowed in the working set. The empty WSLE pointed to by PHD$W_WSNEXT is used.

   Note that to extend the working set above WSQUOTA, the WSL itself must have been extended above WSQUOTA. To extend the WSL above WSQUOTA, the free page list must contain more than the SYSBOOT parameter BORROWLIM pages. For more information on working set limits, BORROWLIM, and automatic working set limit adjustment, see Chapter 16.

If an empty but unusable WSLE is found at the end of the WSL, PHD$W_WSLAST is reset to point to the last unavailable (nonzero) WSLE in the WSL. In other words, empty entries at the end of the WSL are compressed if it contains more entries than the size of the working set allowed to the process.

15.4.3 Releasing a Dead Page Table Page

An inactive page table page (also known as a "dead" page table page) is one which maps no valid pages. If an inactive page table page contains transition PTEs for pages on the free page list, the PFN database for those pages must be modified before the page table page can be released from the WSL. If an inactive page table page contains transition PTEs for pages on the modified page list, those pages must be written to their backing store before the page table page can be released from the WSL.

To determine whether an inactive page table page contains any transition PTEs requires examining all its PTEs. MMG$FREWSLE avoids the overhead of this scan whenever possible. That is, it checks how full the WSL is. If the WSL has room for growth, the dead page table scan is postponed. MMG$FREWSLE skips this WSLE and continues its scan of the WSL.

If the WSL does not have room for growth, the inactive page table page is scanned. MMG$FREWSLE severs the connection between the process and any transition page on the free page list. If the page table page contains no modified pages, it is released from the WSL and its WSLE reused.

If, however, the page table page does describe pages on the modified list, they must be written to their backing store before the page table page can be released from the working set. MMG$FREWSLE forces a flush of the modified page list and returns to the pager. The pager places the process into a resource wait until the modified page list is flushed (see Section 15.6.4.2).

15.4.4 Skipping Working Set List Entries

The working set replacement routine is not strictly FIFO. It uses the special SYSBOOT parameter TBSKIPWSL to permit recently referenced pages to remain in the working set. This allows the operating system to modify its strict FIFO page replacement algorithm with some frequency of use information maintained by VAX hardware.

The modified algorithm works in the following manner. Before a valid WSLE is reused, a check is made to see if the virtual page described by that WSLE is in the translation buffer. If the PTE for that page is cached in the TB, the search for an available WSLE starts again with the next WSLE. After TBSKIPWSL WSLEs have been skipped in this manner, the translation buffer checks are abandoned and the next valid WSLE is simply reused. If the value of TBSKIPWSL is set to zero, the mechanism is disabled and no entries are checked in the translation buffer. The default value of TBSKIPWSL is 8.

15.4.5 Reusing Working Set List Entries

The virtual page indicated by the WSLE must be removed before this WSLE can be reused. Typically, the virtual page is valid and must be made invalid.

The modify bit from the associated PTE is saved in the PFN STATE array element. The valid and modify bits in the PTE are cleared. Any cached copy of the PTE is invalidated in the translation buffer.

If the page is a global page, the PFN SHRCNT array element is decremented. If the SHRCNT goes to zero, the REFCNT array element is decremented. The GPTX is copied to the process PTE.

For a process-private page, the REFCNT is decremented. If the page is placed into a transition state, the balance slot reference count for this PHD is incremented to prevent its outswap.

The WSLE is zeroed and its index is stored in PHD$W_WSNEXT.

5.5   **INPUT AND OUTPUT THAT SUPPORT PAGING**

There is very little special purpose code in the I/O subsystem to support pager and swapper I/O. The pager and swapper each build their own I/O request packets (IRPs), but queue these packets to the device driver in the normal fashion. These are the only differences:

- There are special Queue I/O Request entry points for pager and swapper I/O (in module SYSQIOREQ). These entry points bypass many of the usual QIO checks to minimize overhead. An IRP describing a pager or swapper request is distinguished from other IRPs by a flag in the IRP status word.
- These flags are detected by the I/O postprocessing routine. There are special completion paths for page read and other forms of memory management I/O.

To make reading and writing as efficient as possible, the pager supports a feature called clustering. The pager checks to see whether pages adjacent to the virtual page that it is reading are located in the same file in adjacent virtual blocks. If so, the pager requests a multiple-block read, and a cluster of pages is brought into the working set at one time. One N-block request has less CPU and I/O overhead than N one-block requests.

The modified page writer and the Update Section ($UPDSEC) system service also cluster their write operations, both to make their writes as efficient as possible and to allow subsequent clustered reads for the pages that are being written.

Tables 15-1 and 15-2 summarize the I/O requests issued by memory management components. The first table lists the process identification, priority of each I/O request, and information about the priority boost the process receives at I/O completion. (For more information on priority classes and boosts, see Chapter 10.) Table 15-2 summarizes the unusual uses to which the memory management components put several fields in the IRP. These fields are not required for their more typical uses and can thus be used for storage by these components.

Table 15-1 Summary of I/O Requests Issued by Memory Management—Part I

Type of I/O Request	*Priority* *IRP$B_PRI*	*Process ID* *IRP$L_PID*	*Priority Boost at* *I/O Completion*
Process page read	16—Base priority of faulting process	PID of faulting process	0
System page read	Base priority of "system" process	PID of faulting process	0
Modified page write	MPW_PRIO[1]	PID of swapper[2]	None[3]
$UPDSEC page write	Base priority of caller	PID of caller	2
Swapper I/O	SWP_PRIO[1]	PID of swapper	None[3]

[1]This is a SYSBOOT parameter.
[2]The modified page writer is a subroutine of the swapper process.
[3]The swapper is a real-time process and is therefore not subject to priority boosts.

The second table lists more information about each type of I/O request. The columns SVAPTE, AST, and ASTPRM contain the contents for those fields in the IRP for each type. The column "Source of WCB" specifies from which memory management data structure the address of the window control block is obtained. (This address is stored in the field IRP$L_WIND.) The last column contains the limit to the clustering done for each type of I/O request.

15.5.1 Page Reads and Clustering

When the pager determines that a read is required to satisfy a page fault, it allocates an IRP and fills it with parameters that describe the read. Table 15-2 lists those fields that are used for special purposes by the pager.

The pager attempts to create a cluster of pages to read. The manner in which this cluster is formed depends on the initial state of the faulting PTE.

15.5.1.1 Terminating Condition for Clustered Reads.
The pager scans PTEs that map larger virtual addresses, checking for more virtual pages that are located in the same backing store location, until the desired cluster size is reached or until one of the following other terminating conditions is reached:

- A PTE different from the original faulting PTE is encountered (see Section 15.5.1.2)
- The page table page is itself not valid. (Satisfying this fault first, to make a larger cluster, would offset the benefits gained by clustering.)
- No more WSLEs are available. (Each page in the cluster must be added to the working set.)
- No physical page is available.

If, after scanning the adjacent PTEs toward higher virtual addresses, no pages have been clustered, the process is repeated toward lower virtual addresses with the same terminating conditions. The scan is made initially toward higher virtual addresses because programs typically execute sequentially toward higher virtual addresses and these pages are likely to be needed soon. If the forward attempt fails, the pager attempts to read pages adjacent to the faulting page at lower virtual addresses on the assumption that even pages at lower virtual addresses but near the faulting page are likely to be needed soon.

5.5.1.2 **Matching Conditions while Scanning Page Table.** The match that is looked for when scanning the adjacent PTEs depends on the form of the initial PTE:

- If the original PTE contains a PSTX, successive PTEs must contain exactly the same PSTX.
- If the original PTE contains a page file virtual block number, successive PTEs must contain PTEs with successively increasing (or decreasing) virtual block numbers.
- If the original PTE contains a GPTX, successive PTEs must contain successively increasing (or decreasing) indexes. In addition, the GPTEs must all contain exactly the same GSTX.

5.5.1.3 **Maximum Cluster Size for Page Read.** The maximum number of pages that can be in a cluster is determined in several ways, depending on the type of page being read:

- Global page table pages are not clustered.
- The cluster factor for process page table pages is taken from PHD$B_PGTBPFC. The default value of this field is the special SYSBOOT parameter PAGTBLPFC.

   The default value for this parameter is 2. This value is chosen to avoid an artificial end to building a cluster when the page table page also had to be faulted. Decreasing this value may defeat clustered reads. Increasing it above 2 is likely to have a negligible effect in most systems.
- The cluster factor for page file pages is taken from the PFL$B_PFC field of the page file control block (see Figure 14-22). The usual contents of this field are zero. In that case, the cluster factor is taken from the process's PHD$B_DFPFC. The default value of this field is the SYSBOOT parameter PFCDEFAULT.
- The cluster factor for a process or global section is taken from the SEC$B_PFC field of the process or global section table entry (see Figure 14-7). This field usually contains zero, in which case the default page fault cluster is used. (Just as for clustered reads from the page file, this default is taken from PHD$B_DFPFC.)

Table 15-2   Summary of I/O Requests Issued by Memory Management—Part II

Type of I/O Request	SVAPTE	AST	ASTPRM	Source of WCB	Cluster Factor
PROCESS PAGE READ					
Page in mapped file	P0PT/P1PT	0	0/PSTX[1]	PSTE	pfc/PFCDEFAULT[2]
Page in page file	P0PT/P1PT	0	0	PFL	PFCDEFAULT[3]
Page table page	SPT	0	0	PFL[4]	PAGTBLPFC[3]
SYSTEM PAGE READ					
System page[5]	SPT	0	0	SSTE	SYSPFC[3]
Paged pool page	SPT	0	0	PFL	PFCDEFAULT[3]
Global page	GPT	Slave PTE address	0	GSTE	pfc/PFCDEFAULT[2]
Global CRF page	P0PT/P1PT	Master PTE contents	GSTX	GSTE	pfc/PFCDEFAULT[2]
Global page table page	SPT	0	0	PFL[4]	1

Table 15-2 Summary of I/O Requests Issued by Memory Management—Part II (continued)

Type of I/O Request	SVAPTE	AST	ASTPRM	Source of WCB	Cluster Factor
MODIFIED PAGE WRITE					
To page file	MPW map	0	MPW's KAST (WRITEDONE)	PFL	MPW_WRTCLUSTER[3]
To private file	MPW map	0	MPW's KAST (WRITEDONE)	PSTE	MPW_WRTCLUSTER[3]
To global file	MPW map	0	MPW's KAST (WRITEDONE)	GSTE	MPW_WRTCLUSTER[3]
To swap file (SWPVBN = 0)	MPW map	0	MPW's KAST (WRITEDONE)	PFL	1
UPDATE SECTION PAGE WRITE					
Private section	P0PT/P1PT	AST address	AST argument	PSTE	MPW_WRTCLUSTER[3]
Global section	GPT	AST address	AST argument	GSTE	MPW_WRTCLUSTER[3]
SWAPPER I/O					
Swapper I/O	Swapper map	0	Swapper KAST (IODONE)	PFL	n/a

[1] If the page is copy-on-reference, IRP$L_ASTPRM contains the PSTX.

[2] The cluster factor for a private or global section can be specified at link time or when the cluster is mapped by explicitly declaring a cluster factor (pfc). If unspecified, the SYSBOOT parameter PFCDEFAULT is used.

[3] This is a SYSBOOT parameter.

[4] Process page tables and global page tables originate as demand zero pages whose backing store is the page file.

[5] Pageable executive routines originate in one of three files (SYS.EXE, RMS.EXE, and SYSMSG.EXE) described by three system section table entries (SSTEs) located in the system header.

There are two methods available to the user to control the cluster factor of a process or global section. Specifying PFC in the following line from a linker options file enables the page fault cluster factor in the image section descriptor to be set to nonzero contents:

```
CLUSTER = cluster-name,[base-address],pfc,file-spec[,...]
```

A section that is mapped through the Create and Map Section system service can have its page fault cluster factor specified by the optional PFC argument to the system service call.

15.5.1.4   **Page Read Completion.** The I/O postprocessing routine, IOC$IOPOST in module IOCIOPOST, detects page read completion, using the flag IRP$V_PAGIO in the IRP status word.

Page read completion is not reported to the faulting process in the normal fashion with a special kernel mode asynchronous system trap (AST) because none of the postprocessing has to be performed in the context of the faulting process. The routine PAGIO performs the postprocessing needed and makes the process computable.

When a page read completes successfully, PAGIO performs the following steps for each page:

1. The PFN REFCNT array element is decremented, indicating that the read in progress has completed.
2. The page STATE is set to active.
3. The valid bit in the PTE is set.
4. If the page is a global page, the valid bit set in step 3 was in the GPTE. In this case, the process (slave) PTE must be loaded with the PFN and made valid.

After the individual pages have been tended to, PAGIO reports the scheduling event page fault completion for the process so that it is made computable. The priority increment class is 0, so there is no boost to the process's scheduling priority. (If any of the pages just read were collided pages, the collided page wait queue is also emptied. That is, all processes in that state are made computable. Collided pages are discussed in Section 15.6.3.)

15.5.2   **Modified Page Writing**

The modified page writer (a subroutine of the SWAPPER process) also attempts to cluster when writing modified pages to their backing store addresses. The three different cases encountered by the modified page writer depend on the three possible backing store locations that pages on the modified page list can have.

15.5.2.1 **Operation of the Modified Page Writer.** The modified page writer, MMG$WRTMFYPAG in module WRTMFYPAG, proceeds in approximately the following fashion:

1. The first page is removed from the modified page list, and SCH$GL_MFYCNT, the number of pages on the list, is decremented. The PTE address of the page is retrieved from the PFN PTE array.

2. Adjacent PTEs are scanned (first toward lower virtual addresses and then toward higher virtual addresses) looking for transition PTEs that map pages on the modified page list until either the desired cluster size is reached or until one of the other terminating conditions is reached.

   This scan begins first toward smaller virtual addresses for the same reason that the page read cluster routine begins toward larger addresses. If the program is more likely to reference higher addresses, the modified page writer does not want to initiate a write operation, only to have the page immediately faulted (and likely modified again). The modified page writer chooses to first write those pages with a smaller likelihood of being referenced in the near future.

3. If the backing store for the page is a page file, the modified page writer tries to build a larger cluster as described in Section 15.5.2.3. When it can no longer cluster (see Section 15.5.2.2), it initiates a write. The PFN STATE array element for each of the pages is changed to write in progress, and the REFCNT element for each page is incremented.

4. The modified page writer subroutine exits. When the modified page write completes, MMG$WRTMFYPAG's special kernel AST routine, WRITEDONE, is entered.

15.5.2.2 **Modified Page Write Clustering.** The terminating conditions for the scan of the page table include the following:

- The page table page is not valid, implying that there are no transition pages in this page table page. The special check is made to avoid an unnecessary page fault.
- The PTE does not indicate a transition format.
- The PTE indicates a page in transition, but the physical page is not on the modified page list.
- The physical page number is greater than the contents of global location MMG$GL_MAXPFN. This check avoids pages in shared memory, which have no PFN data associated with them.
- The SWPVBN array element must be zero. Pages with nonzero SWPVBN contents are treated in a special way by the modified page writer.
- If the contents of the BAK array indicate that the backing store location for the page is a private or global file, the section index must be the same for all pages in the cluster.

- If the BAK array element indicates that the pages are to be written to the page file, the contents of the virtual block number field are ignored. However, all pages must contain the same page file index in their BAK array elements.

15.5.2.3   **Backing Store Addresses for Modified Pages.** There are three different kinds of backing store address that the modified page writer encounters as it removes pages from the modified page list.

A nonzero SWPVBN array element indicates that the process has been outswapped and this page remained behind, probably as the result of an outstanding read request. The modified page writer issues a write of a single page to the designated block in the swap file. It does not attempt to cluster because virtually contiguous pages in an I/O buffer are unlikely to be adjacent in the outswapped process body. The process body is outswapped with pages ordered as they appear in the WSL, not in virtual address order. A description of how the SWPVBN array element is loaded is found in Chapter 17, where the entire outswap operation is discussed.

If the backing store address is a section, the modified page writer creates a cluster (up to the value of the SYSBOOT parameter MPW_WRTCLUSTER). Any of the terminating conditions listed in the previous section can limit the size of the cluster.

If the backing store address is a page file, adjacent pages bound for the same page file are also written at the same time. The modified page writer attempts to allocate a number of blocks in the page file equal to MPW_WRTCLUSTER. The desired cluster factor is reduced to the number of blocks actually allocated. (Section 15.5.2.4 describes allocation of space within the page file.)

The actual cluster created for a write to the page file consists of several smaller clusters, each one representing a series of virtually contiguous pages (see Figure 15-9):

1. The modified page writer creates a cluster of virtually contiguous pages, all bound for the same page file.
2. If the desired cluster size has not yet been reached, the modified page list is searched until another physical page bound for the same page file is found.
3. Pages virtually contiguous to this page form the second minicluster that is added to the eventual cluster to be written to the page file.
4. The modified page writer continues in this manner until either the cluster size is reached or no more pages on the modified page list have the designated page file as their backing store address. The modified page writer is building a large cluster that consists of a series of smaller clusters. The large cluster terminates only when the desired size is reached or when the modified page list contains no more pages bound to the page file in ques-

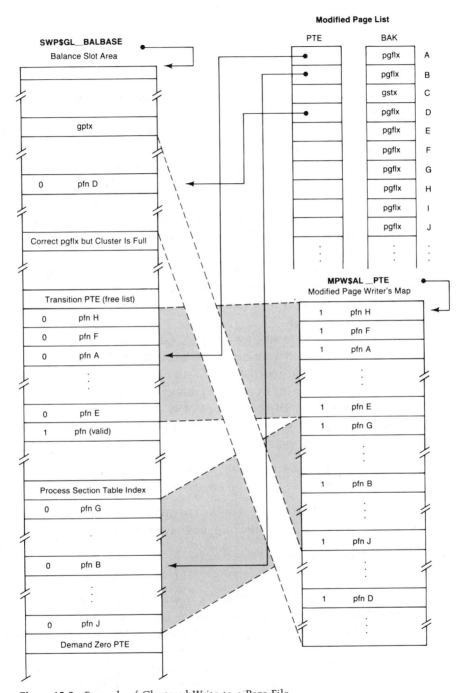

Figure 15-9 Example of Clustered Write to a Page File

tion. Each smaller cluster can terminate on any of the conditions listed in the previous section, or on the two terminating conditions for the large cluster.

15.5.2.4   **Page File Space Allocation.** Before the modified page writer searches for pages to write, it must first determine the size of the write cluster. To do this, it must determine the number of contiguous blocks in the page file that can be allocated.

The modified page writer invokes MMG$ALLOCPAGFIL1 (in module PAGEFILE) to allocate a cluster of blocks in the page file. The number of blocks it tries to allocate is stored in the page file control block at the offset PFL$B_ALLOCSIZ and is usually equal to MPW_WRTCLUSTER. If that many blocks are not available, MMG$WRTMFYPAG reduces the PFL$B_ALLOCSIZ size by 16 blocks, if it can, and invokes MMG$AL-LOCPAGFIL1 again to search for contiguous blocks starting back at the beginning of the page file.

The allocation size is raised sometime later when space frees up in the page file. When the page file deallocation routine determines that it has freed a large enough cluster, it increases the allocation size by 8, to a maximum of MPW_WRTCLUSTER.

When the allocation size for the page file is less than or equal to 16, a special-case allocation routine, MMG$ALLOCPAGFIL2 is invoked. This special-case allocation routine searches for and allocates the first available cluster of blocks, starting from the beginning of the page file. The routine can allocate between 1 and 16 contiguous blocks. If the first available cluster of blocks is not in the first quarter of the page file, MMG$ALLOCPAGFIL2 issues the following message on the console terminal:

```
%SYSTEM-W-PAGEFRAG, Pagefile badly fragmented,
                 system continuing
```

If the first available cluster is in the last quarter of the page file, MMG$AL-LOCPAGFIL2 issues the following message on the console terminal:

```
%SYSTEM-W-PAGECRIT, Pagefile space critical,
                 system trying to continue
```

Each of these messages is issued only once during a boot of the system, even if more than one page file becomes full. The first message is issued when one page file becomes fragmented or full; the second, when the same or a different page file becomes very fragmented or full. These messages on the console terminal may be a good indication that the system requires an(other) alternate page file. However, because of the nature of the checks, it is possible for the system to run out of page file space without any message having been displayed.

If the modified page writer is unable to allocate any blocks in the page file, it exits, returning to the swapper. If the modified page list is still above its high limit, the swapper will be awakened periodically to repeat its call to MMG$WRTMFYPAG.

15.5.2.5   **Example of Modified Page Write to a Page File.** Figure 15-9 illustrates a sample cluster for writing to a page file. The modified page list (pictured in the upper right-hand corner of the figure) is shown as a sequential array to simplify the figure.

1. The first page on the modified page list is pfn A. By scanning backwards through the process's page table, first pfn F and then pfn H are located. The PTE preceding the one that contains pfn H is also a transition PTE, but the page is on the free page list. This page terminates the backward search.
2. The modified page writer map begins with pfn H, pfn F, and pfn A. The search now goes in the forward direction, with each page bound for the page file added to the map up to and including pfn E. The next PTE is valid so the first minicluster is terminated.
3. The next page on the modified page list, pfn B, leads to the addition of a second cluster to the map. This cluster begins with pfn G and ends with pfn J. The backward search was terminated with a PTE containing a section table index. The forward search terminated with a demand zero PTE.

   Note that this second cluster consists of pages belonging to a different process from the first cluster. The difference is reflected in the word array element for each PTE in the map that contains a process header vector index for each page (see Figure 14-24).
4. The next page on the modified page list is pfn C. This page belongs in a global image file and is skipped over during the current write attempt.
5. Pfn D leads to a third cluster that was terminated in the backward direction with a PTE that contains a GPTX. The search in the forward direction terminated when the desired cluster size was reached, even though the next PTE was bound to the same page file. The cluster size is either MPW_WRTCLUSTER or the number of adjacent blocks available in the page file, whichever is smaller. In any case, this cluster will be written with a single write request.
6. Note that reaching the desired cluster size resulted in leaving some pages on the modified page list bound for the same page file, such as pfn I.

15.5.2.6   **Modified Page Write Completion.** When the modified page write is complete, the modified page writer's special kernel AST routine, WRITEDONE, is entered. WRITEDONE decrements various reference counts that indicated the write in progress. If a page's REFCNT is now zero, the page is placed on the free page list. If the number of pages on the modified page list

(SCH$GL_MFYCNT) is still above the low-limit threshold for the modified page list (SCH$GL_MFYLOLIM), then the modified page writer removes the new first page from the modified page list and starts all over.

15.5.3 Update Section System Service

The $UPDSEC[W] system service allows a process to write pages in a section to their backing store addresses in a controlled fashion, without waiting for the modified page writer to do the backup. This system service is especially useful for frequently accessed pages that may never be written by the modified page writer, because they are always being faulted from the modified page list back into the working set before they are backed up.

This system service is a cross between modified page writing and a normal write request. As for any I/O request, the caller can request completion notification with an event flag and I/O status block or an AST. The number of pages written is specified by the address range that is passed as an input parameter to the service. The cluster factor is the minimum of MPW_WRTCLUSTER and the number of pages in the input range. The direction of search for modified pages is determined by the order that the address range is specified to the service.

15.5.3.1 Page Selection.
If the section that is being backed up is a process-private section, only those pages that have the modified bit set in the PTE (or in the PFN state array for transition pages) are written out.

If the section is a global section, then determining which pages have been modified is not feasible. The system service runs in the context of one process and can scan its PTEs for set modify bits. However, to determine whether a particular page has been modified requires looking at the PFN database and the PTEs of all processes mapped to this global page. (The modify bit in the GPTE is inaccessible to hardware and contains no useful information.) Because there are no back pointers for valid global pages, this information is unavailable. Therefore, all pages in a global section are written to their backing store location, regardless of whether the pages have been modified.

If the FLAGS parameter passed to the service has its low bit set, the caller indicates that it is the only process whose modifed pages should be written. In that case, the process's PTEs (and the PFN database) are used to select candidate pages for backing up. Only pages modified by this process are written.

15.5.3.2 Write Completion.
The process that issued the $UPDSEC system service is first notified of write completion with a special kernel mode AST. This AST routine first checks whether all the pages requested by the system service

call have been written or whether another write is required. If more pages have to be written, another cluster is set up and an I/O request queued. If all requested pages have been written, the normal I/O completion path involving event flags, I/O status blocks, and user-requested ASTs is entered, and the process is notified.

5.6   PAGING AND SCHEDULING

Page fault handling can influence the scheduling state of processes in several different ways. If a read is required to satisfy a page fault, the faulting process is placed into a page fault wait state. If a resource such as physical memory or page file space is not available, the process is placed into an appropriate wait state. There are several other wait states that a process may be placed into as a result of a page fault. (Chapter 10 describes process scheduling, wait states, priority increment classes, resource waits, and the reporting of scheduler events.)

5.6.1   Page Fault Wait State

The most obvious wait state is page fault wait, in which a process is placed when a read is required to resolve a page fault. The process that requires the read to resolve its page fault is placed in a page fault wait state. The I/O postprocessing routine, PAGIO, detects that a page read has completed and reports the scheduling event page fault completion for the process. The scheduler removes the process from the page fault wait state and makes it computable. There is no priority boost associated with page fault read completion.

5.6.2   Free Page Wait State

If there is not enough physical memory available to satisfy a page fault, the faulting process is placed in a free page wait state. The physical page manager (routine MMG$DALLOCPFN in module ALLOCPFN) checks for processes in this state whenever a page is deallocated and the free list was formerly empty. It reports the scheduling event free page available so that each process in the free page wait state is made computable.

The physical page manager makes no scheduling decision about which process will get the page. There is no FIFO approach to the free page wait state. Rather, all processes waiting for the page are made computable. The next process to execute will be chosen by the scheduler, using the normal algorithm that the highest priority resident computable process executes next.

15.6.3   **Collided Page Wait State**

It is possible for a page fault to occur for a page which is already being read from disk. Such a page is referred to as a collided page. The collided bit (in the PFN TYPE array) is set and the process placed into the collided page (COLPG) wait state.

One of the details that the page read completion routine checks is the collided bit in the TYPE array element for the page. If the collided bit is set, it reports the scheduling event collided page available for each process in that wait state. It does not check that each process is waiting for the collided page that was faulted in.

This lack of check has two advantages:

- There is no special code to determine which process executes first. All processes are made computable, and the normal scheduling algorithm selects the process that executes next.
- The probability of a collided page is small. The probability of two different collided pages is even smaller. If a process waiting for another collided page is selected for execution, that process will incur a page fault and get put right back into the collided wait state. Nothing unusual occurs and the operating system avoids a lot of special-case code to handle a situation that rarely, if ever, occurs.

15.6.4   **Resource Wait States**

There are several types of resource wait associated with memory management. A process waiting for one of these "resources" is placed in the miscellaneous wait state (see Chapter 10) until the resource is available.

15.6.4.1   **Resource Wait for RWMPB.** When the modified page list contains more pages than the SYSBOOT parameter MPW_WAITLIMIT, any process which faults a modified page out of its working set is placed into this resource wait. The modified page writer declares the availability of the resource RSN$_MPWBUSY when it writes enough modified pages that the list has fewer than MPW_LOLIMIT pages on it.

15.6.4.2   **Resource Wait for RWMPE.** When a process faults a page, the pager invokes MMG$FREWSLE to find a WSLE to describe the page to be added to the process's working set. One possible WSLE is a process page table page that is now inactive; that is, the page table page maps no valid pages. Such a WSLE can be reused. If, however, the page table page contains a transition PTE for a modified page, the modified page must be written to its backing store before the WSLE used by the page table page can be released.

In such a case, the modified list high limit is temporarily set to zero so that the modified page writer will flush it. The process is placed in resource wait for RSN$_MPLEMPTY until its modified page has been written to its backing store. The modified page writer declares the availability of the resource RSN$_MPLEMPTY when it empties the modified page list.

15.6.4.3   **Resource Wait for RWSWP.** When a process is first created, minimal swap space is allocated for it, as described in Chapter 14. As the process faults pages and its working set grows, more swap space must be allocated. If more swap space is not available when the process's working set is increased beyond the size of its current swap space, the process is placed in resource wait for RSN$_SWPFILE. This resource is declared available when a new page or swap file is installed with the SYSGEN Utility and whenever space is deallocated in a page or swap file in which there had previously been an allocation failure.

16 Memory Management System Services

A place for everything and everything in its place.

Isabella Mary Beeton, *The Book of Household Management*

The previous two chapters discussed the data structures used by the memory management subsystem to describe physical and virtual memory and the action of the pager when an invalid page was referenced. This chapter describes the system services available to the user (and also used internally by the executive) to allocate these structures and initialize their contents.

These services enable the user to perform the following memory management services, subject to limitations imposed by process quotas, limits, privileges, and SYSBOOT parameters:

- Create or delete virtual address space
- Create private and global sections that map the blocks of a file to a portion of process address space
- Lock a portion of the process address space into the working set, to avoid the overhead of page faults or to allow portions of code to execute at elevated IPL
- Lock a portion of the process address space into physical memory
- Change the protection on a page of virtual address space
- Disable swapping of a process to prevent it from being removed from memory
- Force the contents of all modified pages in a section to be written to their backing store addresses
- Purge pages from the process's working set list (WSL)

16.1 CHARACTERISTICS OF MEMORY MANAGEMENT SYSTEM SERVICES

Almost all the memory management system services specify a desired virtual address range as an input argument. The page table entry (PTE) associated with each page of virtual address space contains an owner field (see Figure 14-3). The owner field specifies which access mode owns the page. The memory management system service checks the owner field to determine whether the caller of the service is more or equally privileged than the owner of the page and thus can manipulate the page in the desired fashion.

Another characteristic of the memory management system services is that many of the services can partially succeed, that is, affect only a portion of the specified address range. The system service indicates partial success by returning an error status and also the address range for which the operation completed (in the optional RETADR argument).

A common dispatch method is used by most of the memory management system services:

1. Information about the specific service, including the input parameters, is placed on the stack for later retrieval.
2. Page ownership is checked to ensure that a less privileged access mode is not attempting to alter the properties of some pages owned by a more privileged access mode.
3. The address of a single page service-specific routine to accomplish the desired action of the original service is placed into R6.
4. A common routine, MMG$CREDEL in module SYSCREDEL, is called that performs general page processing and calls the single page service-specific routine for each page in the desired range.
5. The address range actually operated on is returned to the caller (in the optional RETADR argument).

16.2   VIRTUAL ADDRESS CREATION AND DELETION

The most basic memory management services available to a process are the creation and deletion of virtual address space. These services are used by the system when an image first begins executing (the image activator calls several services to create process address space) and as part of image exit (the image reset routine deletes all of P0 space and a small part of P1 space). The memory management performed by the system as part of image activation and process deletion is described in Chapter 21.

16.2.1   Address Space Creation

Address space creation is essentially a simple operation in which a series of demand zero pages is created. If necessary, the process page table is expanded. PTEs are initialized to the demand zero form. For the Expand Region ($EXPREG) system service, the demand zero pages are created at the end of the designated per-process address space. For the Create Virtual Address Space ($CRETVA) system service, the pages are created in the specified address range; however, if any pages already exist in the requested range, they must be deleted first.

These two system services can partially succeed. That is, a number of pages smaller than the number originally requested may be created. After several pages have already been successfully created, it is possible to run into one of the limits on the number of pages that can be created. For this reason, it is especially important for the caller of either $CRETVA or $EXPREG to look at the RETADR argument to determine whether the service was partially successful.

16.2.1.1   **Limits on Virtual Address Space Creation.** There are three limitations on the amount of virtual address space that can be created.

The SYSBOOT parameter VIRTUALPAGECNT controls the total number of page table entries (P0PTEs plus P1PTEs) that any process can have in its process header. The division of these pages between P0 space and P1 space is totally arbitrary and process-specific. It is only the sum of P0 and P1 pages that is limited by the SYSBOOT parameter.

The size of a process working set also controls the size of that process's address space. When a process page is valid, the page table page for that page is not only valid but also dynamically locked into the working set. For small address spaces, the set of valid process pages can be represented by a small number of page table pages.

As the address space grows, the probability that a given page table page maps more than one valid process page decreases. The limiting case, one that can usually be reached only with very large process address spaces, requires two working set list entries (WSLEs) for each valid process page. In any case, there is an implicit limit to the process address space imposed by the process working set quotas.

The specific check that is made is whether there is enough room in the dynamic WSL for the fluid working set (PHD$W_WSFLUID), plus the worst case number of page table pages required to map PHD$W_WSFLUID pages, in order to allow the process to perform useful work. The number of page table pages that results is the minimum of PHD$W_WSFLUID and the number of page table pages not already locked down. If this check succeeds, the WSL is expanded. If the working set is full (see Section 16.4), the virtual address creation fails with the status of SS$_INSFWSL.

The third constraint on the total size of the process address space is the page file quota. Each demand zero page and each copy-on-reference section page is charged against the job's page file quota (JIB$L_PGFLCNT).

16.2.1.2   **Create Virtual Address Space System Service.** The $CRETVA system service procedure, EXE$CRETVA in module SYSCREDEL, runs in kernel mode. As an optimization, it first checks whether the entire address space can be created. If so, EXE$CRETVA creates it all at once rather than page by page, invoking the routine MMG$FAST_CREATE (also in module SYSCREDEL).

If EXE$CRETVA encounters any of the limits to virtual address space creation described in the previous section, the address space must be created a page at a time. Page-by-page creation is also necessary if the specified address space overlaps already existing space, since the existing pages must also be deleted. In either of these cases, EXE$CRETVA invokes MMG$CREDEL, specifying MMG$CREPAG as the single page service-specific routine.

16.2.1.3   **Expand Region System Service.** The $EXPREG system service is very similar to the $CRETVA system service. Its system service procedure, EXE$EXPREG in module SYSCREDEL, runs in kernel mode. Depending on the region that is to be expanded, EXE$EXPREG uses either PHD$L_FREP0VA or PHD$L_FREP1VA as one end of the address range.

As an optimization, EXE$EXPREG first checks whether the entire address space can be created. If so, EXE$EXPREG creates it all at once rather than page by page, invoking the routine MMG$FAST_CREATE (also in module SYSCREDEL). Otherwise, it invokes the routine MMG$CREDEL, specifying MMG$CREPAG as the single page service-specific routine.

16.2.1.4   **Automatic User Stack Expansion.** A special form of P1 space expansion occurs when a request for user stack space exceeds the remaining size of the user stack. Such a request can be reported by the hardware as an access violation exception or by software when insufficient user stack space is detected.

Several software routines detect the need to expand the user stack:

- The AST delivery interrupt service routine (see Chapter 7), when it is unable to build the AST argument list on the user stack
- The Adjust Stack ($ADJSTK) system service (only for user mode stack expansion)
- The exception dispatching routine (EXE$EXCEPTION in module EXCEPTION) when it is unable to copy the signal and mechanism arrays onto the user stack (see Chapter 4)

These routines invoke EXE$EXPANDSTK (in module EXCEPTION) to try to expand the user stack. EXE$EXPANDSTK is also invoked by the access violation exception service routine (EXE$ACVIOLAT in module EXCEPTION) for an access violation that occurred in user mode. EXE$EXPANDSTK checks that a length violation (as opposed to a protection violation) occurred and that the inaccessible address is in P1 space. If so, EXE$EXPANDSTK invokes $CRETVA to expand P1 space from its current low address end to the specified inaccessible address. For the usual case, one in which a program requires more user stack space than requested at link time, the expansion typically occurs one page at a time.

Because this automatic expansion cannot be disabled on a process-specific or systemwide basis, a runaway program that uses stack space without returning it is not aborted immediately. Instead, the program runs until it exceeds the virtual address size determined by the SYSBOOT parameter VIRTUALPAGECNT. ($CRETVA indicates this quota violation by returning the error status SS$_VASFULL.)

Another side effect of automatic expansion occurs when a program makes a random (and probably incorrect) reference to an arbitrary P1 address lower than the top of the user stack. Rather than exiting with some error status, the program probably will continue to execute (after the creation of many demand zero pages).

If the stack expansion fails for any reason, the process is notified in a way that depends on the invoker of EXE$EXPANDSTK:

- The $ADJSTK system service can fail with several of the error codes returned by $CRETVA.
- An attempt to deliver an AST to a process with insufficient user stack space results in an AST delivery stack fault condition being reported to the process. (Enough information is removed from the stack by the error routine that the exception dispatcher can at least get started in reporting the exception.)
- If the user stack cannot be expanded in response to a P1 space length violation, then an access violation fault is reported to the process.
- If there is not enough user stack to report an exception, EXE$EXCEPTION first tries to reset the user stack pointer to the high address end of the stack. If that fails, EXE$EXCEPTION invokes $CRETVA in an attempt to recreate the address space. If that fails, EXE$EXCEPTION bypasses the normal condition handler search and reports the exception directly to the last chance handler. Typically, this handler aborts the currently executing image. (See Chapter 4 for more details.)

16.2.2 Address Space Deletion

Page deletion is more complicated than page creation. Creation involves taking the process from one known state (the address space does not yet exist) to another known state (the PTEs contain demand zero PTEs). Page deletion must deal with initial conditions that include all possible states of a virtual page. Page deletion also requires a check that the access mode that owns the page is not more privileged than the mode requesting deletion of the page.

Page creation may first require that the specified pages be deleted to put the process page tables into their known state. Thus, page deletion is often an integral part of page creation.

16.2.2.1 Page Deletion and Process Waits.

A page that has I/O in progress cannot be deleted until the I/O completes. A process trying to delete such a page is placed into a page fault wait state (with a request that a system event be reported when I/O completes) until the page read or write completes. Trying to delete a page in the write-in-progress transition state has the same effect.

A page in the read-in-progress transition state is faulted, with the immediate result that the process is placed into the collided page wait state. Special action must be taken for a global page with I/O in progress because there is no way to determine if the process deleting the page is also responsible for the I/O. In such cases, the process is placed into a miscellaneous wait state (MWAIT) until its direct I/O completes. (If the process has no direct I/O in progress, the problem does not arise in the first place, and the deletion is allowed to proceed.)

16.2.2.2   Delete Virtual Address Space System Service. The $DELTVA system service procedure, EXE$DELTVA in module SYSCREDEL, runs in kernel mode. EXE$DELTVA invokes MMG$CREDEL, specifying MMG$DELPAG as the single page service-specific routine.

When a virtual page is deleted, MMG$DELPAG (and routines it invokes) must return all process and system resources associated with the page. These can include the following:

• A physical page of memory for a valid or transition page
• A page file virtual block for a page whose backing store address indicates an already allocated block
• A WSLE for a page in the process WSL
• Page file quota for a page with a page file backing store address, even if the page has not yet been allocated a block in the page file

Deleting a private section page results in decrementing the reference count in the PSTE (see Figure 14-7). If the reference count goes to zero, the PSTE itself can be released.

In addition, a valid or modified page with a section backing store address (as opposed to a page file backing store address) must have its latest contents written back to the section file. (The contents of a page with a page file backing store address are unimportant after the virtual page is deleted and do not have to be saved before the physical page is reused.)

Deletion of a physical page means that the PFN PTE array element is cleared, destroying all ties between the physical page and any process virtual address. In addition, the page is placed at the head of the free page list, causing it to be used before other pages whose contents might still be useful.

16.2.2.3   Contract Region System Service. The $CNTREG system service procedure, EXE$CNTREG in module SYSCREDEL, runs in kernel mode. The $CNTREG system service is a special case of the $DELTVA system service. EXE$CNTREG simply converts the requested number of pages into a P0 or P1 page range and passes control to a page deletion routine that is common to the two services. That routine invokes MMG$CREDEL, specifying MMG$DELPAG as the single page service-specific routine.

16.2.3   Controlled Allocation of Virtual Memory

There is a second level of memory management available to a process. The Run-Time Library procedures LIB$GET_VM and LIB$FREE_VM provide a mechanism for allocating small blocks of virtual memory in a controlled fashion. Allocation from the free memory pool is performed in much the same way as pool space is allocated by the VMS operating system (see Chapter 3). If there is not a block of memory in the pool large enough to satisfy the request, P0 space is expanded (by calling $EXPREG), and the pool is extended to include the newly created virtual address space.

16.3   PRIVATE AND GLOBAL SECTIONS

In addition to the $CRETVA and $EXPREG system services, another method of creating address space is available. The Create and Map Section ($CRMPSC) system service allows a process to associate a portion of its address space with a specified portion of a file. The section may be specific to a process (private section) or shared among several processes (global section). The Map Global Section ($MGBLSC) system service allows a process to map a portion of its virtual address space to an already existing global section. These two services are used by the image activator (see Chapter 21) to map portions of process address space to either the image file or previously installed global sections.

The $CRMPSC system service also provides special options. Rather than mapping a portion of process address space to a file, a suitably privileged process (with PFNMAP privilege) can map virtual address space to specific physical addresses. In addition, the $CRMPSC service enables the creation of global sections in MA780 shared memory and global page-file sections.

16.3.1   Create and Map Section System Service

The $CRMPSC system service creates a private or global section and maps the process to it. (The $MGBLSC system service is a special case of $CRMPSC in which the global section has already been created.) The $CRMPSC system service procedure, EXE$CRMPSC in module SYSCRMPSC, runs in kernel mode.

The particular actions EXE$CRMPSC takes are determined by the options or flags with which the service is invoked. (The *VAX/VMS System Services Reference Manual* lists the flags that can be used together and those that are incompatible.)

The following sections describe the various actions of EXE$CRMPSC through its effects on memory management data structures.

16.3.1.1   Private Section Creation. When a process-private section is created, a process section table entry (PSTE, pictured in Figure 14-7) is allocated from the PHD.

The information that associates the virtual address range with virtual blocks in the file is loaded into the PSTE. When the private section is being created as a part of image activation as described in Chapter 21, the original source for much of the data stored in the PSTE is an image section descriptor contained in the image file. Each process PTE in the designated address range is loaded with identical contents, namely a process section table index (see Figure 14-3) that locates the PSTE.

The memory management subsystem cannot take a window turn (see Chapter 18) on pages within a section. Therefore, it requires that all the mapping information for the newly mapped file be available in the window control block associated with the mapped file. If EXE$CRMPSC determines that the mapping information is incomplete, it makes a file system request to extend the window control block. Because the window control block occupies nonpaged pool, the extension of the window control block is charged against the process's BYTCNT quota.

Because the quota is charged until the section is deleted, this charge is also made against the process's BYTLM. BYTLM limits the maximum charge against BYTCNT. When a process has insufficient BYTCNT for a request, VMS checks that the request is not larger than BYTLM before placing the process in resource wait. Charging the window control block extension against BYTLM prevents placing the process into what might otherwise be a never-ending resource wait.

16.3.1.2   **Global Section Creation.** The creation of a global section in local memory is similar to the creation of a private section except that the data structures are located in the system header (see Figures 14-15 and 14-18) instead of the PHD:

1. A global section descriptor (GSD, pictured in Figure 14-14) is allocated from paged pool and initialized with the name and protection attributes of the section. This data structure is used by subsequent $MGBLSC system service calls to determine whether the named section exists and to locate the global section table entry (GSTE), which more fully describes the section.
2. A GSTE (see Figure 14-7) is the structure analogous to the process section table entry (PSTE). It is allocated from the system header and initialized.
3. A set of contiguous global page table entries (GPTEs) is allocated from the global page table. There must be one GPTE for each global page plus two additional GPTEs, one at the beginning of the set and one at the end. The two additional GPTEs are cleared and serve as "stoppers," limits to modified page write clustering (see Chapter 15 and Figure 14-16). Except for the stoppers, each GPTE contains information that describes the current state of one global page in the section. GPTEs are not used by the memory management hardware but are used by the pager when a process incurs a page fault for a global page.

4. A global section can be created and mapped by a single system service call. Alternatively, the section can be created in one step and mapped later by either the creating process or by any other process allowed to map the section. In any case, mapping to a global section results in no changes to the PFN database. Rather, a series of PTEs that each contain a global page table index (GPTX) is added to the process page table to describe the designated address range (see Figure 14-19). The process PTEs for global pages can be in one of two states, either valid or containing the appropriate GPTX.

16.3.1.3   **Global Sections in MA780 Shared Memory.** Global sections that are located in MA780 shared memory are treated in a slightly different fashion from local memory global sections. The sections are created after shared memory has been initialized. (See Chapter 14 for a description of the data structures that describe global sections in shared memory.) Global sections in shared memory have the following characteristics:

1. A shared memory GSD (see Figure 14-27) is created that contains, among other things, a list of the physical pages in shared memory that will contain the section. Each page of the section is loaded from the mapped file.
2. A GSTE is created only on the CPU that originally creates the section. This GSTE allows the initial read to be performed and allows subsequent section updates (with the Update Section system service) for writable sections. Pages are also written back to the mapped file on the creating CPU when the section is deleted.
3. No GPTEs are needed for global sections in shared memory because each page is always valid. The PFN information necessary to allow processes to map into this section is contained in the shared memory GSD.
4. When a process maps to the shared memory global section, the process PTEs are loaded with the appropriate PFNs and set valid. These pages are not counted against the process working set.

16.3.1.4   **Global Page-File Sections.** The $CRMPSC system service can create a global page-file section, a temporary demand zero global section. Its backing store is the primary page file, SYS$SYSTEM:PAGEFILE.SYS. The SYSBOOT parameter GBLPAGFIL specifies the maximum number of page file pages that can be put to this use.

When a global page-file section is created, a GSD and GSTE are allocated and initialized. GPTEs are allocated and initialized. Each process PTE is initialized with the appropriate GPTX.

16.3.1.5   **Map by PFN.** The $CRMPSC system service enables a privileged process (one with PFNMAP privilege) to map a portion of its virtual address space to specific physical addresses. Although the primary intention of this service is to allow process address space to be mapped to I/O addresses, it can also be used to map specific physical memory pages.

When a private PFN-mapped section is created, the only effect is to add a series of valid PTEs to the process page table. The PFN fields in these PTEs contain the requested physical page numbers. The PTE$V_WINDOW bit (see Figure 14-3) is set in each PTE to indicate that each of these virtual pages is PFN-mapped. These pages are not counted against the process working set. In addition, no record is maintained in the PFN database that such pages are PFN-mapped.

When a global PFN-mapped section is created, the only data structure created to describe such a mapping request is a special form of GSD (see Figure 14-14). There are no GPTEs nor is there a GSTE. When a process maps to such a section, its process PTEs are set valid, mapped by PFN (PFN$V_WINDOW is set), and the PFN fields are filled in according to the contents of the extended GSD (see Figure 14-14).

16.3.2   Map Global Section System Service

The $MGBLSC service can be considered a special case of the $CRMPSC system service, where the global section already exists. This service usually has no effect on the global database (other than to include the latest mapping in various reference counts). Rather, this service allows a range of process addresses to become mapped to the named global section.

The actual effect of this service is to load each of the designated process PTEs with a GPTX (see Figures 14-3 and 14-19). These GPTXs are effectively pointers to GPTEs in the system header, where the current state of each global page is actually recorded.

When a process maps to a global section in shared memory or to a section that is PFN-mapped, there are no GPTEs to be pointed to. Instead, each process PTE is set valid with the PFN field containing a physical page number either in shared memory (for shared memory global sections) or anywhere in physical address space (as indicated by the extended GSD for PFN-mapped global sections).

16.3.3   Delete Global Section System Service

The Delete Global Section ($DGBLSC) system service is more complicated than global section creation because the section must be reduced from one of many states to nonexistence. In addition, global writable pages must be written to their backing store addresses before a global section can be fully deleted. For these reasons, the actual deletion of a global section is often separated in time from the system service call and return.

The $DGBLSC system service procedure, EXE$DGBLSC in module SYSDGBLSC, runs in kernel mode. It locates the GSD associated with the named section and moves it from the normal GSD list to the delete pending list, at global location EXE$GL_GSDDELFL. The permanent indicator in the GSD is cleared.

The actual section deletion cannot occur until the reference count in the GSTE, the count of process PTEs mapped to the section, goes to zero. Although the reference count can be zero when the $DGBLSC service is invoked, the more typical global section deletion occurs as a side effect of virtual address deletion (which itself might occur as a result of image exit or process deletion).

A reference count of zero indicates that no more process PTEs are mapped to the section. At that time, the following data structures that describe the section can be deallocated:

• The GPTEs in the system header that describe the global section are scanned. If any indicates a transition page on the modify list, that page must be written to its backing store before the section is deleted. To force the modify list to be flushed, the longword at global location SCH$GL_MFYLOLIM and the low word of global SCH$GL_MFYLIM are cleared. When an entire page of GPTEs is freed, the page can be unlocked from the system working set.
• The GSTE in the system header is removed from its active list and placed on the free list of system section table entries for possible later use.

Global sections in shared memory and PFN-mapped global sections exercise some of the same logic when the sections are deleted, but the effects are different because not all of the global data structures exist for these special global sections. A PFN-mapped section is described entirely by an extended GSD (see Figure 14-14). No reference counts are kept for such sections, so the GSD can be placed on the free list of GSDs immediately.

When a shared memory global section is deleted, there are no GPTEs to delete. Furthermore, a GSTE exists only on the CPU from which the section was created.

16.3.4 Update Section System Service

A process invokes the $UPDSEC[W] system service to request that a specified range of process private or global pages be written to their backing store addresses. The system service procedure, EXE$UPDSEC in module SYSUPDSEC, runs in kernel mode. It first clears the event flag associated with the I/O request, charges process direct I/O quota, and allocates nonpaged pool to serve as an "extended" I/O packet. The pool is used to queue one or more modified page write I/O requests and to keep track of how much of the section the service has processed.

EXE$UPDSEC then invokes MMG$CREDEL, specifying MMG$UPDSEC-PAG (in module SYSUPDSEC) as the single page service-specific routine.

This service and its similarities to modified page writing are described in more detail in Chapter 15.

16.4   WORKING SET ADJUSTMENT

The term working set refers to the physical pages which the process currently occupies. The number of pages in a process's working set is the sum of two fields in the PCB: PCB$W_PPGCNT, private pages in use, and PCB$W_GPGCNT, global pages in use. There are two possible limits to the growth of a process's working set.

One limit is the working set limit, PHD$W_WSSIZE. This field contains the maximum number of valid WSLEs the process can have. At any given time, the sum of PCB$W_PPGCNT and PCB$W_GPGCNT cannot exceed PHD$W_WSSIZE.

Sometimes the space available for the WSL limits the growth of the process's working set. A process cannot have more valid pages than its WSL has capacity to describe. As described in Chapter 14, the WSL is variable length and grows toward the process section table (PST). When the working set must expand into the area already occupied by the PST, the PST is moved to higher addresses. However, there is not always room in the PHD to accommodate the expanded WSL. The PST can grow so large that there is not enough WSL area available.

The field PHD$W_WSLAST points to the end of the WSL. That is, there can be no valid WSLEs past the offset described by PHD$W_WSLAST. Because the WSL is not necessarily dense, the capacity of the list may be larger than the process's working set limit.

The size of the process working set limit can be altered with the Adjust Working Set Limit ($ADJWSL) system service either manually by explicit call or automatically as part of the quantum end routine. When the working set limit is increased, new pages can be added to the working set without removing already valid entries. Adding pages to a process's working set decreases the probability that the process will incur a page fault.

It is unlikely that a program will voluntarily reduce its working set limit, unless the program has a good understanding of its paging behavior. The system reduces a process working set as part of the automatic working set adjustment. The swapper process can shrink a process's working set in an attempt to gain more pages, before resorting to swapping a process out of the balance set. In addition, a process working set limit is reset to its default value by MMG$IMGRESET (see Chapter 21) when the image exits.

Table 16-1 lists the process-specific and systemwide WSL parameters.

Table 16-1 Working Set Lists: Limits and Quotas

Description	Location or Name	Comments
Beginning of working set list	PHD$W_WSLIST	Always contains 63_{16}
Working set limit	PHD$W_WSSIZE	Set by LOGINOUT; Altered by $ADJWSL; Altered by automatic working set adjustment
Beginning of list of locked entries	PHD$W_WSLOCK	The same for all processes in a given system
Beginning of dynamic portion of working set list	PHD$W_WSDYN	Altered by $LKWSET and $LCKPAG
Index of most recently inserted working set list entry	PHD$W_WSNEXT	Updated each time an entry is added to working set
End of current working set list	PHD$W_WSLAST	May be altered by $ADJWSL, by pager, by image exit, or by automatic working set adjustment
Default working set size	PHD$W_DFWSCNT	Set by LOGINOUT; Altered by command SET WORK/LIMIT
Normal limit to working set size	PHD$W_WSQUOTA	Set by LOGINOUT; Altered by command SET WORK/QUOTA
Maximum limit to working set size	PHD$W_WSEXTENT	Set by LOGINOUT; Altered by command SET WORK/EXTENT
Upper limit to working set quota	PHD$W_WSAUTH	Set by LOGINOUT; Cannot be altered
Upper limit to working set extent	PHD$W_WSAUTHEXT	Set by LOGINOUT; Cannot be altered

Table 16-1   Working Set Lists: Limits and Quotas *(continued)*

Description	Location or Name	Comments
Lower limit to size of dynamic working set	PHD$W_WSFLUID	Set by SHELL to the value of MINWSCNT
Dynamic working set size not counting PHD$W_WSFLUID process pages and a reasonable number of page table pages	PHD$W_EXTDYNWS	Updated each time size of dynamic working set is changed
Number of pages in use by process	PCB$W_PPGCNT + PCB$W_GPGCNT	Updated each time a page is added to or removed from the working set
Authorized default working set size	UAF$W_DFWSCNT	Copied to PHD$W_DFWSCNT
Authorized default working set limit	UAF$W_WSQUOTA	Copied to PHD$W_WSAUTH and PHD$W_WSQUOTA
Authorized default working set maximum	UAF$W_WSEXTENT	Copied to PHD$W_WSEXTENT and PHD$W_WSAUTHEXT
Systemwide minimum working set size	MINWSCNT	SYSBOOT parameter
Systemwide maximum working set size	WSMAX	SYSBOOT parameter
Working set size for system paging	SYSMWCNT	SYSBOOT parameter
Default value for working set size default (used by $CREPRC)	PQL_DWSDEFAULT	SYSBOOT parameter
Minimum value for working set size default (used by $CREPRC)	PQL_MWSDEFAULT	SYSBOOT parameter
Default value for working set quota (used by $CREPRC)	PQL_DWSQUOTA	SYSBOOT parameter
Minimum value for working set quota (used by $CREPRC)	PQL_MWSQUOTA	SYSBOOT parameter
Minimum value for working set extent (used by $CREPRC)	PQL_MWSEXTENT	SYSBOOT parameter
Default value for working set extent (used by $CREPRC)	PQL_DWSEXTENT	SYSBOOT parameter

417

16.4.1   Adjust Working Set Limit System Service

The $ADJWSL system service procedure, EXE$ADJWSL in module SYSADJWSL, runs in kernel mode. It is invoked to alter the process's working set limit, PHD$W_WSSIZE. There are two different paths in the procedure, one to increase the limit and the other to reduce it.

To increase the working set limit, EXE$ADJWSL first checks and possibly decreases the size of the increase. The new limit must be less than or equal to WSMAX, less than or equal to the process's WSEXTENT, and within the system's physical memory capacity. If the new working set limit is within the capacity of the WSL (PHD$W_WSLAST minus PHD$W_WSLIST), EXE$ADJWSL computes a new value for PHD$W_EXTDYNWS and returns. Otherwise, EXE$ADJWSL must first invoke MMG$ALCPHD (in module PHDUTL) to expand the WSL and then initialize the extra WSLEs.

To reduce the working set limit, EXE$ADJWSL first checks and possibly decreases the size of the reduction. The new limit must allow for at least MINWSCNT WSLEs in the dynamic portion of the WSL. In addition, the extra dynamic working set size (PHD$W_EXTDYNWS) cannot be reduced below zero. If the process's working set (PCB$W_PPGCNT plus PCB$W_GPGCNT) is already less than or equal to the new limit, EXE$ADJWSL simply modifies PHD$W_WSSIZE and returns. Otherwise, EXE$ADJWSL must repeatedly invoke MMG$FREWSLE (in module PAGEFAULT) for each page to be removed from the process's working set. (Chapter 15 describes MMG$FREWSLE.) The reduced list can have holes in it; the PHD$W_WSLAST pointer is only moved back as a side effect of freeing excess WSLEs (above the new limit).

16.4.2   SET WORKING_SET Command

The SET WORKING_SET DCL command enables the default working set size (PHD$W_DFWSCNT), the normal limit to the working set size (PHD$W_WSQUOTA), or the working set maximum (PHD$W_WSEXTENT) to be altered at the command level. Neither the default size nor the maximum can be set to a value larger than the authorized upper limit (PHD$W_WSAUTHEXT).

If the normal limit to the working set size is altered, it affects the maximum size of the working set when physical memory is scarce. If the working set maximum is altered, it changes the upper limit for future calls to the $ADJWSL system service. If the limit (default size) is altered, it affects the WSL reset operation performed by the routine MMG$IMGRESET invoked at image exit. If the limit is set to a value larger than the current quota, both the quota and the limit are altered to the new value.

With the /[NO]ADJUST qualifier to this command, a user can also disable (or reenable) automatic working set adjustment. Use of that qualifier sets (or clears) the process control block (PCB) status longword bit PCB$V_DISAWS.

.4.3   Automatic Working Set Size Adjustment

In addition to adjusting working set through an explicit $ADJWSL request or
as a side effect of image exit, VMS also provides automatic working set adjustment to keep a process's page fault rate within limits set by one of several
SYSBOOT parameters (see Table 16-2). All of the SYSBOOT parameters listed
in this table are dynamic and can be altered without rebooting the system.

The automatic working set adjustment takes place as part of the quantum

able 16-2   Process and System Parameters Used by Automatic Working Set Size Adjustment

escription	*Location or Name*	*Comments*
otal amount of CPU time charged to this process	PHD$L_CPUTIM	Updated by hardware timer interrupt service routine
mount of CPU time since last adjustment check	PHD$L_TIMREF	Updated by quantum end routine when adjustment check is made; Altered when process is placed into a wait
otal number of page faults for this process	PHD$L_PAGEFLTS	Updated each time this process incurs a page fault
umber of page faults at last adjustment check	PHD$L_PFLREF	Updated by quantum end routine when adjustment check is made
lost recent page fault rate for this process	PHD$L_PFLTRATE	Recorded at each adjustment check; Compared to PFRATH and PFRATL
rocess automatic working set adjustment flag	PCB$V_DISAWS	Disables automatic adjustment for process if equal to 1
mount of CPU time process must accumulate before page fault rate check is made	AWSTIME[1]	
ower limit page fault rate	PFRATL[1]	
mount by which to decrease working set list size	WSDEC[1]	
ower bound for decreasing working set list size	AWSMIN[1]	Do not adjust if PCB$W_PPGCNT is less than or equal to this
Jpper limit page fault rate	PFRATH[1]	
mount by which to increase working set list size	WSINC[1]	Disables automatic adjustment for entire system if equal to zero
ree page list size to allow growth of working set	GROWLIM[1]	Do not add working set list entry if @SCH$GL_FREECNT is less than or equal to this value
ree page list size to allow extension of working set list	BORROWLIM[1]	Do not adjust working set list size if @SCH$GL_FREECNT is less than or equal to this value; Disables working set extension for entire system if equal to −1

[1] This value is a SYSBOOT parameter.

end routine (see Chapter 10), because a process that cannot execute for even a single quantum will not benefit from an increased working set size. (Note that no adjustment takes place for real-time processes.)

The quantum end routine, SCH$QEND in module RSE, adjusts the working set in several steps:

1. If the WSINC parameter is set to zero, the adjustment is disabled on a systemwide basis, so nothing is done. If automatic working set adjustment for the process has been turned off by the DCL command SET WORKING_SET/NOADJUST, nothing is done.

2. If the process has not been executing long enough since the last adjustment (if the difference between accumulated CPU time, PHD$L_CPUTIM, and the time of the last adjustment attempt, PHD$L_TIMREF, is less than the SYSBOOT parameter AWSTIME), no adjustment is done at this time. If the process has accumulated enough CPU time, the reference time is updated (PHD$L_CPUTIM is copied to PHD$L_TIMREF), and the rate checks are made.

   Between adjustment checks, PHD$L_TIMREF is also altered when the process is placed in a wait. As described in Chapter 10, when a process goes into a wait, the SYSBOOT parameter IOTA is charged against its quantum. To balance the quantum charge, IOTA is subtracted from PHD$L_TIMREF. Without this balancing effect, a process that undergoes many page fault waits can reach quantum end without having accumulated AWSTIME worth of CPU time and thus not be considered for automatic working set adjustment. This Version 4 change helps ensure the expansion of the working set of a heavily page faulting process.

3. The current page fault rate is calculated. The philosophy for automatic working set adjustment consists of two premises. If the page fault rate is too low, the system can benefit from a smaller working set size (because more physical pages become available) without harming the process (by causing it to incur many page faults). If the page fault rate is too high, the process can benefit from a larger working set size (by incurring fewer faults), without degrading the system.

   —If the current page fault rate is too high (greater than or equal to PFRATH), a determination is made to see if the working set limit should be increased. If the process is not making use of its current WSL (if the sum PCB$W_PPGCNT and PCB$W_GPGCNT is less than 75 percent of PHD$W_WSSIZE), the WSL is not expanded. If the size of the WSL is below WSQUOTA, the WSL is extended by WSINC. If the size of the WSL is greater than or equal to WSQUOTA, the number of pages on the free page list is compared to the SYSBOOT parameter BORROWLIM. If there are more than BORROWLIM pages on the free page list, the WSL is increased by WSINC. However, if there are fewer than BORROWLIM pages on the free page list, the WSL is not extended. The WSL can only be extended up to WSEXTENT. Setting BORROWLIM to −1 disables working set extension for the entire system.

Note that the adjustment taking place here affects only the size of the WSL, not the working set itself. Once the WSL has been extended, newly faulted pages can be added to the working set. The pager adds pages to the working set above WSQUOTA only when there are more than the SYSBOOT parameter GROWLIM pages on the free page list (see Chapter 15).

—If the current page fault rate is too low (strictly, less than PFRATL), the working set is decreased (by WSDEC). However, if the contents of PCB$W_PPGCNT are less than or equal to AWSMIN, no adjustment takes place. This decision is based on the assumption that many of the pages in the working set are global pages and therefore the system will not benefit (and the process may suffer) if the working set is decreased. Note that PFRATL is zero by default. This default value effectively disables this method of working set reduction in favor of swapper working set trimming. The rationale for this change is explained at the end of this list.

4. The actual working set adjustment is accomplished by a kernel mode AST that requests an $ADJWSL system service. The AST parameter passed to this AST is the amount of previously determined increase or decrease. This step is required because the system service must be called from process context (at IPL 0) and the quantum end routine is executing in system context in response to the IPL 7 software timer interrupt.

Two other pieces of the executive control the size of a process's working set: the pager and the swapper. As described previously, the pager can add a page to a process's working set if the size of the free page list is greater than GROWLIM. In an effort to gain pages, the swapper reduces the working sets of processes in the balance set before actually removing processes from the balance set. This working set reduction is known as swapper trimming or working set shrinking. Process selection is performed by a table driven, prioritized scheme (see Chapter 17).

Two problems are inherent in using the quantum end scheme of automatic working set adjustment: processes that are compute-intensive will reach quantum end many times and images that have been written to be efficient with respect to page faults (a low page fault rate) will qualify for working set reduction, because their page fault rate is lower than PFRATL. In both of these cases, working set reduction is not desirable. In contrast, swapper trimming selects its processes starting with those that are least likely to need large working sets.

In what can be seen as an evolutionary change to the operating system, working set reduction at quantum end was disabled in VAX/VMS Version 3.1 by setting the default value of PFRATL to zero. Swapper trimming and the image exit reset are now the primary methods used to reduce working set size.

16.4.4 Purge Working Set System Service

The Purge Working Set ($PURGWS) system service requests that all virtual pages in the specified address range be removed from the working set. A program might invoke this service if a certain set of routines or data were no longer required. By voluntarily removing entries from the working set, a process can exercise some control over the WSL replacement algorithm, increasing the chances for frequently used pages to remain in the working set.

The VMS executive uses this service as part of the image startup sequence (see Chapter 21) to ensure that a program starts its execution without unnecessary pages (such as command language interpreter command processing routines) in its working set.

The $PURGWS system service procedure, EXE$PURGWS in module SYSPURGWS, runs in kernel mode. EXE$PURGWS invokes MMG$-CREDEL, specifying MMG$PURGWSPAG (also in SYSPURGWS) as the single page service-specific routine.

16.5 LOCKING AND UNLOCKING PAGES

Four system services are provided to lock pages into the process working set or into memory:

- Lock Pages in Working Set ($LKWSET)
- Lock Pages in Memory ($LCKPAG)
- Unlock Pages from Working Set ($ULWSET)
- Unlock Pages in Memory ($ULKPAG)

16.5.1 Locking Pages in the Working Set

A set of virtual pages can be locked into the process working set to prevent page faults from occurring on references to these pages. Locking pages in the working set guarantees that when this process is executing (is the current process), the locked pages are always valid. This service has obvious benefit for time-critical applications and other situations in which a program must access code or data without incurring a page fault.

This service is also used by process-based kernel mode routines that execute at IPLs above 2 to ensure the validity of code and data pages. VMS prohibits page faults at IPLs above 2. In response to such a page fault, the pager generates the fatal bugcheck PGFIPLHI.

Pages locked into a process working set do not necessarily remain resident when the process is not current; the entire working set might be outswapped. To guarantee residency of the pages requires either the $LCKPAG system service or the combination of the $LKWSET and the Set Swap Mode ($SETSWM) system services.

The $LKWSET system service procedure, EXE$LKWSET in module SYSLKWSET, executes in kernel mode. EXE$LKWSET invokes MMG$-CREDEL, specifying MMG$LCKULKPAG (also in SYSLKWSET) as the single page service-specific routine.

MMG$LCKULKPAG faults each page in the specified range into the working set if it is not already valid. The WSL (see Figure 14-4) must be reorganized so that the locked page is in the portion of the list following the WSLOCK pointer. MMG$LCKULKPAG accomplishes this reorganization by exchanging the locked WSLE with the entry pointed to by WSDYN, and then incrementing WSDYN to point to the next element in the list. It must also exchange the WSLX PFN array elements for the two valid pages. In addition, the WSL$V_WSLOCK bit is set in the WSLE of the locked page.

MMG$LCKULKPAG checks to ensure that the process will have enough dynamic WSLEs after the page is locked into its working set. The test is that the extra dynamic working set size, the size of the dynamic working set after space has been allocated for page table pages and a minimum working set size, is greater than zero.

When a process is being outswapped, global read/write pages are dropped from the process working set (see Chapter 17) to avoid cumbersome accounting problems about whether the outswapped page contains the most up-to-date information. For this reason, a global read/write page cannot be locked into the process working set. (Such a page can be locked into memory because the $LCKPAG system service prevents outswap of either the PHD or the locked page, avoiding an outswap altogether.) The swapper also performs an optimization with a global read-only page by dropping it from the working set on outswap if the global share count is larger than 1. If such a page is locked into the working set, it is not dropped from the working set, regardless of the contents of the PFN SHRCNT array.

16.5.2   Locking Pages in Memory

The $LCKPAG system service is similar to the $LKWSET system service. The $LCKPAG system service procedure, EXE$LCKPAG in module SYSLKWSET, runs in kernel mode. Like EXE$LKWSET, it invokes MMG$CREDEL, specifying MMG$LCKULKPAG (also in SYSLKWSET) as the single page service-specific routine. MMG$LCKULKPAG is invoked with a flag that identifies its target as a page locked in memory, rather than a page locked in the working set.

The results of invoking the two lock services are similar. One difference is that the WSL$V_PFNLOCK bit in the WSLE is set (rather than the WSL$V_WSLOCK bit). Another difference is that the PHD must be locked in memory because it maps a page locked in memory.

This service performs an implicit working set lock in addition to guaranteeing permanent residency to the specified virtual address range. Because this operation permanently allocates a system resource, physical memory, it requires the privilege PSWAPM.

16.5.3 Unlocking Pages

The unlock pages system services unlock pages from either the working set or physical memory. The two system procedures are EXE$ULWSET and EXE$ULKPAG, both in SYSLKWSET. Both, executing in kernel mode, invoke MMG$CREDEL with MMG$LCKULKPAG as the single page service-specific routine. MMG$LCKULKPAG is invoked with one flag that identifies its target as a page locked in the working set or a page locked in memory and with a second flag that requests an unlock operation.

The WSLE for the page being unlocked may have to be exchanged with another locked entry to place the unlocked entry back into the dynamic portion of the list. As with the exchange associated with locking a page, the WSLX PFN array elements must also be exchanged. Finally, the appropriate bit in the WSLE (WSL$V_WSLOCK or WSL$V_PFNLOCK) is cleared.

16.6 PROCESS SWAP MODE

A process with PSWAPM privilege can prevent itself from being removed from memory by invoking the Set Process Swap Mode ($SETSWM) system service. The $SETSWM system service procedure, EXE$SETSWM in module SYSSETMOD, runs in kernel mode. EXE$SETSWM checks that the process has privilege and simply sets (or clears) the PCB$V_PSWAPM bit in the status longword (PCB$L_STS) in the software PCB. When the swapper is searching for suitable outswap candidates, a process whose PCB$V_PSWAPM bit is set is passed over.

16.7 ALTERING PAGE PROTECTION

A process can alter the protection of a set of pages in its address range with the Set Protection on Pages system service ($SETPRT).

The $SETPRT system service procedure, EXE$SETPRT in module SYS-SETPRT, runs in kernel mode. EXE$SETPRT invokes MMG$CREDEL, specifying MMG$SETPRTPAG as the single page service-specific routine.

In general, the operation of this service is straightforward. However, its actions have one interesting side effect. If a section page for a read-only section has its protection set to writable, the copy-on-reference bit is set. This set bit forces the page to have its backing store address changed to the page file when the page is faulted, preventing a later attempt to write the modified section pages back to a file to which the process may be denied write access.

The VAX/VMS debugger uses this service to implement its watchpoint facility. The page containing the data element in question is set to no-write access for user mode. When the program being debugged attempts to access the page, an access violation occurs, which is fielded by the debugger's condition handler. This handler performs the following actions:

1. Checks whether the inaccessible address is the one being watched and reports the modification if it is
2. Sets the page protection to PRT$C_UW to allow the modification
3. Sets the TBIT in the PSL to give the debugger control after the instruction completes
4. Dismisses the exception

When the instruction completes, the debugger's TBIT handler gains control, sets the page protection back to no-write access for user mode, and allows the program to continue execution.

17 The Swapper

A time to cast away stones and a time to gather stones together . . .
Ecclesiastes 3:5

VAX/VMS does not let the amount of physical memory limit the number of processes in the system. Physical memory is effectively extended by keeping only a subset of active processes resident at once. The number of active processes is kept at a maximum by limiting the number of pages that each process has in memory at any given time. Processes not resident in memory reside on disk in swap file locations; that is, they are outswapped.

The swapper process is the systemwide physical memory manager. Its responsibilities include maintaining an adequate supply of physical memory and ensuring that the highest priority computable processes are resident in memory.

17.1 SWAPPING OVERVIEW

This section reviews some basic swapper concepts.

17.1.1 Comparison of Paging and Swapping

VAX/VMS uses two different techniques to make efficient use of available physical memory. The ability to support programs with virtual address spaces larger than physical memory is the responsibility of the pager. The swapper allows a running system to support more active processes than can fit into physical memory at one time. The swapper's responsibilities are more global or systemwide than those of the pager. Table 17-1 compares the pager and swapper in several details.

17.1.2 Swapper Responsibilities

The swapper has several main responsibilities:

- The subset of processes that are currently resident should represent the highest priority computable processes in the system. When a nonresident process becomes computable, the swapper must bring it back into memory if its priority allows.
- The number of pages on the free page list must be above the low-limit

426

Table 17-1   Comparison of Paging and Swapping

DIFFERENCES

PAGING	SWAPPING
The pager moves pages in and out of process working sets.	The swapper moves entire processes in and out of physical memory.
The pager is an exception service routine that executes in the context of the process that incurs the page fault.	The swapper is a separate process that is awakened from its hibernating state by components that detect a need for swapper activity.
The unit of paging is the page, although the pager attempts to read more than one page with a single disk read.	The unit of swapping is the process or, actually, the pages of the process currently in its working set.
Page read requests for process pages are queued to the driver according to the base priority of the process incurring the page fault.	Swapper I/O requests are queued according to the value of the SYSBOOT parameter SWP_PRIO. Modified page write requests are queued according to the SYSBOOT parameter MPW_PRIO.
Paging supports images with very large address spaces.	Swapping supports a large number of concurrently active processes.

SIMILARITIES

The pager and swapper work from a common database. The most important structures that are used for both paging and swapping are the process page tables, the working set list, and the PFN database.

The pager and swapper do conventional I/O. There are only slight differences in detail between pager and swapper I/O on the one hand and normal Queue I/O requests on the other.

Both components attempt to maximize the number of blocks read or written with a given I/O request. The pager accomplishes this with read clustering. The swapper attempts to inswap or outswap the entire working set in one (or a small number of) I/O request(s). The modified page writer writes clusters of pages.

---

threshold established by the SYSBOOT parameter FREELIM. The free page list is depleted by requests for physical pages for resolving page faults and inswapping computable processes. The swapper must maintain the free list at or above its low limit.

• The number of pages on the modified page list must be below the high-limit threshold established by the SYSBOOT parameter MPW_HILIM. When the modified page list grows above this limit, the modified page writer (which is a subroutine of the swapper) writes pages to their backing store and moves them to the appropriate page list, typically the free list.

There are four operations that the swapper performs to keep the free page list above its low limit. These are described in subsequent sections of this chapter.

1. Process headers (PHDs) of previously outswapped process bodies may be eligible for outswap. If so, they are outswapped. PHDs for already deleted processes are simply deleted.
2. The swapper invokes the modified page writer subroutine to write modified pages.
3. The swapper can shrink the working set of one or more resident processes.
4. If necessary, the swapper selects an eligible process for outswap and removes that process from memory. The table which determines outswap selection also determines the order in which processes are selected for working set reduction.

17.1.3 System Events That Trigger Swapper Activity

The swapper spends its idle time hibernating. Those components that detect a need for swapper activity wake the swapper by calling routine SCH$SWPWAKE (in module RSE). In addition, SCH$SWPWAKE is invoked once a second from system timer code. SCH$SWPWAKE performs a series of checks to determine whether there is a real need for the swapper to run. If so, it awakens the swapper. If not, it simply returns. Performing these checks in SCH$SWPWAKE, rather than in the swapper process itself, avoids the overhead of two needless context switches.

Table 17-2 lists the system events that trigger a possible need for swapper activity, the module that contains the routine that detects each need, and the reason the swapper must be informed about the system event.

17.1.4 Swapper Implementation

The swapper is implemented as a separate process with a priority of 16, the lowest real-time priority. It is selected for execution like any other process in the system. The swapper has its own resources and quotas that are charged when it issues I/O requests.

The swapper executes entirely in kernel mode. All of the swapper code resides in system space. The swapper uses its P0 space when it swaps processes. It has no P1 space.

The swapper serves as a convenient process context for several system functions. In particular, during system initialization, it performs those initialization tasks that require process context and must be performed prior to the creation of any other process, for example, initializing paged pool and creating the SYSINIT process. Chapter 25 describes the system initialization functions of the swapper.

Table 17-2 Events That Cause the Swapper or Modified Page Writer to Be Awakened

Event	Routine Name (Module)	Comments
Process that is outswapped becomes computable	SCH$CHSE (RSE)	The swapper attempts to make this process resident.
Quantum end	SCH$QEND (RSE)	An outswap previously blocked by initial quantum flag setting or process priority may now be possible.
Modified page list exceeds upper limit	MMG$DALLOCPFN, MMG$INSPFNH/T (ALLOCPFN)	Modified page writing is performed by the swapper.
Free page list drops below low limit	MMG$REMPFN (ALLOCPFN)	The swapper must balance free page count by • Reclaiming deleted process headers • Writing modified pages • Swapping headers of previously outswapped process bodies • Swapper trimming • Outswapping
Balance slot of deleted process becomes available	DELETE (SYSDELPRC)	A previously blocked inswap may now be possible.
PHD reference count goes to zero	MMG$DECPHDREF (PAGEFAULT)	A PHD can now be outswapped to join a previously outswapped process body.
System timer subroutine executes	EXE$TIMEOUT (TIMESCHDL)	The swapper may be awakened every second if there is any work to be done.

17.1.5 Swapper Main Loop

The swapper does not determine why it was awakened. Every time it is awakened, it tends to all of its responsibilities. The main loop of the swapper performs the following steps:

1. It compares the size of the free page list to its low limit. If the list is large enough, the swapper performs any necessary cleanup of PHDs belonging to previously deleted processes.

   If the free page list is too small, it must be replenished. The number of additional pages needed is the difference between the SYSBOOT parameter FREEGOAL and its current size.

   The swapper tests whether the modified page list contains that many pages in addition to its low limit. If it does, the swapper triggers modified page writing by changing the modified page list upper limit to the value of its lower limit.

If the modified page list has insufficient pages, the swapper attempts to reclaim memory by releasing the PHD of a previously deleted process or by outswapping the PHD of a previously outswapped process.

If there is no PHD from which memory can be reclaimed, the swapper invokes SCH$OSWPSCHED to shrink working sets and possibly select a process to outswap. Section 17.2.2 describes these operations. Section 17.5 describes the outswap of a process.

Whenever SCH$OSWPSCHED shrinks a process working set, it checks whether the deficit has been made up. If the deficit has not yet been made up, SCH$OSWPSCHED checks whether writing the modified page list would satisfy the deficit. If it would, SCH$OSWPSCHED changes the modified page list upper limit to the value of its lower limit to trigger modified page writing.

2. Next, the swapper calls the modified page writer routine, MMG$WRTMFYPAG in module WRTMFYPAG. If the size of the modified page list exceeds its current upper limit, modified pages are written until the size of the list falls below the current low limit. Section 17.3 describes the initiation of modified page writing.

3. The swapper selects a process in the computable outswap (COMO) state (if one exists) to inswap. Section 17.2.1 describes this selection.

If there is a COMO process and sufficient pages for its working set, the swapper reads the process into memory (see Section 17.6).

If there is a COMO process but insufficient pages for its working set, the swapper attempts to outswap a PHD of a previously outswapped process or to delete a PHD of a previously deleted process.

If there is no PHD from which memory can be reclaimed, the swapper invokes SCH$OSWPSCHED. The deficit to be made up is the difference between how many pages the process needs and how many can be allocated from the free page list without reducing it below its low limit. (The actions of SCH$OSWPSCHED were summarized previously in step 1.)

4. Because the swapper is a separate process that executes fairly frequently, it is a convenient vehicle for testing whether a powerfail recovery has occurred and, if so, notifying all processes that have requested power recovery asynchronous system trap (AST) notification (with the Set Powerfail Recovery AST system service). This delivery mechanism is described in Chapter 26.

5. Finally, the swapper puts itself into the hibernate state, after checking its wake pending flag. If anyone (including the swapper itself in one of its three main subroutines) has requested swapper activity since the swapper began execution, the hibernate is skipped and the swapper goes back to step 1.

17.2   SWAP SELECTION

This section describes the actions that the swapper takes to select a particular process to inswap, shrink, or outswap.

17.2.1   Selection of Inswap Process

The scheduler maintains 32 quadword listheads for COMO processes, one for each software priority (see Figure 10-2). These queues are identical to the 32 queues maintained for the computable resident (COM) processes. The steps that the swapper takes to decide what process to inswap parallel the steps that the rescheduling interrupt service routine takes (see Chapter 10) to select the next process for execution. This parallel is shown in Example 17-1, which contains code extracts from the modules SWAPPER, SCHED, and RSE.

The first half of the parallel listed in the example shows the swapper's selection of the next inswap process and the nearly identical instructions in the scheduler. These routines perform the following operations. (The numbers in the following list correspond to numbers in Example 17-1.)

① IPL is raised to IPL$_SYNCH to synchronize access to the scheduler's database.

② The highest priority nonempty (COMO/COM) queue is selected.

③ The address of its forward pointer is loaded into R3.

④ The address of the selected process control block (PCB) is loaded into R4.

At this point, the swapper has found a process to inswap. The swapper tests whether there are enough pages on the free page list to hold the inswap process and leave at least FREELIM pages on the list. If so, the inswap proceeds. If not, the swapper attempts to make more pages available by shrinking working sets, outswapping one or more processes, writing modified pages, or deleting PHDs of already deleted process bodies. After there are enough pages available, the swapper takes the steps necessary to bring the selected process into memory.

The scheduler, on the other hand, continues execution. The REMQUE instruction shown in the example for the scheduler is duplicated to emphasize that, while a long time elapses between inswap selection and completion of the inswap, there is no time lapse for execution selection.

Some time later, the inswap operation completes. The swapper rebuilds the working set list (WSL) and process page tables. The parallel resumes when the swapper calls routine SCH$CHSEP, in module RSE, to change the state of the newly inswapped process to computable.

⑤ The selected PCB is removed from its former state (COMO/COM).

⑥ If the removal of the PCB emptied the queue, the associated priority bit in the summary longword is cleared. (Note that SCH$CHSEP has biased R1 so that it points to SCH$GL_COMOQS, the summary longword for the COMO state.)

The Swapper

Example 17-1 Parallels Between Inswap Selection and
Execution Selection

```
Swapper's Inswap Selection                          Scheduler's Execution Selection

QEMPTY:
        BUG_CHECK QUEUEMPTY,FATAL                   SCH$IDLE:
                                                            SETIPL  #IPL$_SCHED
                                                            MOVB    #32,W^SCH$GB_PRI
                                                            BRB     SCH$SCHED
SWAPSCHED:                                          SCH$SCHED::
    SETIPL  #IPL$_SYNCH                 ①              SETIPL  #IPL$_SYNCH
    BBSS    S^#SCH$V_SIP,W^SCH$GB_SIP,5$
    FFS     #0,#32,W^SCH$GL_COMOQS,R2   ②              FFS     #0,#32,L^SCH$GL_COMQS,R2
    BNEQ    10$                                         BEQL    SCH$IDLE
    BBCC    S^#SCH$V_SIP,W^SCH$GB_SIP,5$
5$:
    SETIPL  #0
    RSB
10$:
    PUSHR   #^M < R6,R7,R8,R9,R10,R11,AP,FP >
    MOVAQ   W^SCH$AQ_COMOH[R2],R3       ③              MOVAQ   SCH$AQ_COMH[R2],R3
    MOVL    (R3),R4                     ④              REMQUE  @(R3)+,R4
    CMPB    #DYN$C_PCB,PCB$B_TYPE(R4)                   BVS     QEMPTY
    BNEQ    QEMPTY
      .
      .
      .
```

Example 17-1 Parallels Between Inswap Selection and
Execution Selection *(continued)*

State Change from COMO to COM   State Change from COM to CUR

```
SCH$CHSEP::
    REMQUE  (R4),R1              ⑤          REMQUE  @(R3)+,R4
                                            BVS     QEMPTY
    BNEQ    10$                             BNEQ    20$
    MOVZWL  PCB$W_STATE(R4),R1
    BBC     R1,EXESTATE,10$
    MOVZBL  PCB$B_PRI(R4),R1
    BLBC    PCB$W_STATE(R4),5$
    ADDL    #32,R1
5$:
    BBCC    R1,L`SCH$GL_COMQS,10$   ⑥       BBCC    R2,L`SCH$GL_COMQS,20$
10$:
    MOVB    R0,PCB$B_PRI(R4)
    MOVL    #SCH$C_COM,R1
        .                           20$:
        .                               CMPB    #DYN$C_PCB,PCB$B_TYPE(R4)
        .                               BNEQ    QEMPTY
30$:
    BBSS    R0,L`SCH$GL_COMQS,35$
35$:
    MOVW    R1,PCB$W_STATE(R4)      ⑦       MOVW    #SCH$C_CUR,PCB$W_STATE(R4)
    MOVAQ   L`SCH$AQ_COMT[R0],R1
40$:
    INSQUE  (R4),@(R1)+             ⑧       MOVL    R4,L`SCH$GL_CURPCB
    RSB
```

⑦ The STATE field in the PCB is loaded with the new state (COM/CUR) of the process.

⑧ Finally, the address of the PCB is stored appropriately: the PCB for the inswapped process is inserted into a COM queue; the address of the current process's PCB is stored in SCH$GL_CURPCB.

At this point, the parallel ends. If the newly inswapped process is of higher priority than the swapper, that process will be scheduled as soon as the IPL is lowered below 3 and the rescheduling interrupt occurs. Otherwise, the process will not execute until it becomes the highest priority computable process.

There is one optimization that the swapper performs that may prevent an eventual outswap. This optimization is intended to decrease swapping I/O on systems with more compute-bound processes than can fit into available memory. It is controlled by two SYSBOOT parameters, DEFPRI (the default process priority) and SWPRATE (a time interval with a default value of five seconds). The swapper abandons the inswap of a process whose priority is DEFPRI or lower if there is not enough memory for the inswap and if an interval less than SWPRATE has elapsed since the last inswap of a process with priority of DEFPRI or lower.

17.2.2 Selection of Shrink and Outswap Processes

When the swapper must make physical memory available, it invokes the subroutine SCH$OSWPSCHED, in module OSWPSCHED, specifying how many pages of memory it needs. SCH$OSWPSCHED can shrink the working sets of selected processes and/or select a process to be outswapped. To shrink a working set means to remove pages of physical memory from it.

SCH$OSWPSCHED scans the scheduler database looking for processes to be shrunk or swapped. Whenever it gains free pages from shrinking a process working set, it checks whether there are enough pages on the free and modified page lists to satisfy the swapper's need. If enough pages are available, SCH$OSWPSCHED returns.

The search for a candidate process is table driven. The following sections describe first the table and then information about the multiple passes through the table.

17.2.2.1 The Table.
The OSWPSCHED table is divided into sections, each specifying one or more resident process scheduling states and a set of conditions associated with each state. Table 17-3 lists the individual entries and sections in the OSWPSCHED table. States in the same section are considered equivalent.

SCH$OSWPSCHED scans the scheduling queues in the order shown in the column labeled "Process State." It checks whether any process in that state

Table 17-3 Selection of Shrink and Outswap Candidates

	SELECTION DEPENDENT ON:					FLAGS	
Process State	Direct I/O?	Priority?	Initial Quantum?	Long Wait?	Dormant?	SWAP-ASAP	SWPO-GOAL
SUSP	n/a	n/a	No	n/a	n/a	1	0
COM	n/a	Yes	No	n/a	Yes	1	0
HIB	n/a	n/a	No	Yes	n/a	0	1
LEF	No	n/a	No	Yes	n/a	0	1
CEF	No	n/a	No	n/a	n/a	0	1
HIB	n/a	n/a	No	No	n/a	0	1
LEF	No	n/a	No	No	n/a	0	1
FPG	n/a	Yes	No	n/a	n/a	0	0
COLPG	n/a	Yes	No	n/a	n/a	0	0
MWAIT	n/a	n/a	No	n/a	n/a	0	0
CEF	Yes	Yes	Yes	n/a	n/a	0	0
LEF	Yes	Yes	Yes	n/a	n/a	0	0
PFW	n/a	Yes	Yes	n/a	n/a	0	0
COM	n/a	Yes	Yes	n/a	No	0	0

queue satisfies the conditions in the second column through the sixth column. If a process satisfies those conditions, it is a candidate for shrinking and possibly for swapping. When SCH$OSWPSCHED finds such a process, its subsequent action depends on the flags in the last two columns.

The conditions in the table entries discriminate among processes, based on their likelihood of becoming computable in a short while and the effects of shrinking or swapping them. In general, the intent is to prevent the outswap of a process which is about to become computable when the only reason for the swap is to bring a computable process of equal priority into memory. Overall system performance may be improved by shrinking processes, rather than swapping them. However, a process in a certain state may be affected less by being swapped than by having its working set reduced.

Descriptions of the various conditions and flags follow:

• Direct I/O

When a process which is in a local event flag (LEF) or common event flag (CEF) scheduling state has an outstanding direct I/O request, there is a high probability that the process is waiting for the direct I/O to complete. If so, the process will soon become computable and thus be a less desirable shrink or outswap candidate.

• Priority

A process that is computable or likely to be computable soon is not considered a candidate, unless its priority is less than or equal to that of the potential inswap process (stored in global location SWP$GB_ISWPRI).

- Initial Quantum

    A process likely to become computable soon is not considered a candidate if it is within its initial memory residency quantum, unless the inswap process has a real-time priority. The intent is to leave the process in memory long enough to do useful work, after the system has expended the overhead of inswapping it. This reduces the possibility of swap thrashing, a condition in which the system spends a larger percent of time swapping in and out than in process execution.

- Long Wait

    A process waiting in an LEF or hibernate (HIB) state can be characterized by whether it has been in that state longer than the SYSBOOT parameter LONGWAIT. A process that has been waiting a long time is likely to wait longer still; one which has been waiting a short time is more likely to become computable soon. For example, a process waiting for terminal input longer than a LONGWAIT interval is likely to remain in LEF longer still.

- Dormant

    A dormant process is a computable process whose priority is less than or equal to the SYSBOOT parameter DEFPRI and one to which no scheduling event of any kind has happened within the interval specified by the SYSBOOT parameter DORMANTWAIT. Such a process is considered a very good candidate to be shrunk or outswapped. An example of such a process is a compute-bound process with a priority too low to get CPU time. This condition was added to expedite the shrinking and outswap of a process such as a low priority batch job. While the process runs at night on a lightly loaded system, its working set is expanded to WSEXTENT and it acquires lots of physical memory, but once interactive users log in, the process cannot get CPU time.

In addition to conditions imposed by the table entries, there are several implicit constraints on the suitability of a particular process to be shrunk or outswapped. A process cannot be outswapped if it has locked itself into the balance set. The working set of a process which has disabled automatic working set adjustment cannot be shrunk, nor can the working set of a real-time process. A process which is already outswapped cannot be shrunk or outswapped.

Two flags direct SCH$OSWPSCHED to take specific action on a particular pass through the table. The SWAPASAP flag indicates that SCH$OSWPSCHED should swap out a process selected by this entry, after reducing its working set to WSQUOTA. If the system needs memory, one of these processes will be swapped out at its current size. When the outswapped process becomes computable again, it will not have to waste compute time rebuilding its working set. The SWPOGOAL flag indicates that SCH$OSWPSCHED must try to shrink the working set size of a process selected by that table entry to SWPOUTPGCNT. Shrinking the working set of such a process may reclaim enough memory that the process need not be outswapped.

17.2.2.2   **Passes Through the OSWPSCHED Table.** SCH$OSWPSCHED makes two passes through the table. On its first pass, it goes through all the sections of the table, trimming any candidate processes back to WSQUOTA. This is known as "first-level swapper trimming." It continues reclaiming memory from working sets that had been extended until it has reclaimed enough free pages to satisfy the deficit or until it finds a process to be outswapped. A suitable outswap candidate is one that meets the scheduling state and conditions of a table entry that includes the SWAPASAP flag (and which has not locked itself into the balance set).

If the first pass does not satisfy the deficit and does not locate an outswap candidate, SCH$OSWPSCHED scans the table again. This is known as "second-level swapper trimming." In second-level swapper trimming, SCH$OSWPSCHED can scan each section of the table twice. First, if the entry contains the SWPOGOAL flag, SCH$OSWPSCHED shrinks the working set of a process selected by this entry (unless the process has disabled automatic working set adjustment). The working set is reduced, if possible, to the SYSBOOT parameter SWPOUTPGCNT. If the deficit is not satisfied, SCH$OSWPSCHED continues scanning through processes selected by the table section. When it gets to the end of the section, it restarts at the beginning of the section, looking for a process to outswap. When SCH$OSWPSCHED gets to the end of the section for the second time, it goes to the next section. The pass ends when the deficit is satisfied or a process is found to outswap.

The swapper maintains a failure counter that records the number of times that it has attempted to locate a candidate to shrink or swap and failed. This count is maintained across invocations of SCH$OSWPSCHED. It is intended to loosen the constraints in situations where the normal conditions have failed to produce candidates. When this count reaches a value equal to SWPFAIL, the swapper ignores the priority and initial quantum conditions when selecting a process to shrink or outswap. The counter is reset each time that an outswap candidate is successfully located.

When the swapper scans a series of processes in a particular scheduling queue, the scan begins with the least recently queued entry (at the tail of the queue). This starting point ensures that the longer a process has been in a wait queue, the more chance it has of being shrunk or swapped. (A process is inserted into a wait queue at the front of the list, not the tail.)

17.3 WRITING THE MODIFIED PAGE LIST

The modified page writer, MMG$WRTMFYPAG, writes modified pages to their backing store locations. Modified page writing is initiated when the modified page list has exceeded its high limit, defined by the SYSBOOT parameter MPW_HILIMIT. As described in Chapter 15, the modified page writer attempts to write a number of pages at once. After MMG$WRTMFYPAG has written a cluster of pages to their backing store, the pages are removed from the modified page list and placed on the appropriate page list, typically the free page list. Once modified page writing is initiated, the modified page writer continues writing modified pages until the size of the list is at or below its low limit, defined by the SYSBOOT parameter MPW_LOLIMIT.

The actual limits which drive the modified page writer are the system global locations SCH$GL_MFYLIM, the upper limit threshold, and SCH$GL_MFYLOLIM, the low-limit threshold. At system initialization, these globals are initialized from SYSBOOT parameters.

Modified page writing is sometimes triggered when the list is not yet as large as its upper limit by setting SCH$GL_MFYLIM to the same value as SCH$GL_MFYLOLIM. The swapper does this when the free page list can be replenished by writing modified pages. SCH$OSWPSCHED also triggers modified page writing in this way, but only after testing that the modified page list contains at least as many pages as the SYSBOOT parameter MPW_THRESH. MPW_THRESH sets a higher minimum than MPW_LOLIMIT to be met before SCH$OSWPSCHED can trigger writing the modified page list to gain pages.

Only the low-order word of SCH$GL_MFYLIM is used as an upper limit. The high-order word is set to a value of 0100_{16}, as a flag that modified page writing is in progress. By temporarily making the value of the upper limit very large, threshold checks are altered in the various routines which try to wake the swapper when the modified page list reaches its upper limit. This eliminates the overhead of unnecessary wake events for the swapper while processing of the modified page list is already underway.

There are times when all pages in the modified page list must be written to their backing store. This is known as "flushing the modified page list." Flushing the modified page list is triggered by setting both the lower and upper limits for the modified page list to zero. Clearing the upper limit guarantees that a nonempty list has exceeded its threshold, initiating a request for modified page writing. Clearing the lower limit causes modified page writing to continue until the list is empty (below the low limit). Before the modified page writer exits, it restores its two limits to the values contained in the SYSBOOT parameters MPW_HILIMIT and MPW_LOLIMIT.

There are four circumstances in which the modified page list is flushed:

- When a process body has been outswapped but its PHD maps transition pages on the modified page list (as described in Section 17.5.3.1)
- When a writable global section with transition pages still on the modified page list is deleted
- When a process needs to reuse a working set list entry (WSLE) which describes a page table page that is now inactive but still maps transition pages on the modified page list (described in Chapter 15)
- When the OPCCRASH image runs during system shutdown

7.4 SWAPPER'S USE OF MEMORY MANAGEMENT DATA STRUCTURES

In Chapter 16, the memory management data structures that are used by both the pager and the swapper were described. The discussion here reviews those structures and adds descriptions of those structures that are used exclusively by the swapper.

7.4.1 Process Header

Most of the information that the swapper uses in managing the details of either inswapping or outswapping is contained in the PHD. The process page tables contain a complete description of the address space for a given process.

The WSL describes those page table entries (PTEs) that are valid. This list is crucial for the swapper because it is only the process working set that will be written to its swap space when the process is outswapped. In a similar fashion, when a process is inswapped, the WSL in its PHD describes what the rest of the process looks like in the swap file.

7.4.1.1 Working Set List. The WSL describes the portion of a process virtual address space that must be written to the swap file when the process is outswapped. A page in the process working set can be in one of the following three states:

- The page is valid.
- The page is currently being read into memory. The swapper treats page reads like any other I/O in progress when swapping a process. This treatment is described in Section 17.5.
- The process PTE contains a global page table index (GPTX) and the indexed global page table entry (GPTE) indicates a transition state. The swapper handles global pages in a special manner when outswapping a process. This treatment is also described in Section 17.5.

The operation of the swapper's scan of the process WSL at outswap is discussed in Section 17.5.

17.4.1.2 **Process Page Tables.** The WSL does not supply the swapper with all the information necessary to outswap a process. Other information about a virtual page is contained in either the valid (or transition) PTE or in one of the PFN array elements associated with the physical page. Each WSLE effectively points to a different process (or system) PTE that contains a page frame number (PFN). The PTE is copied to the swapper's I/O map and then the contents of the BAK array element for this physical page are put back into the process PTE. These actions eliminate any ties between an outswapped process's page tables and physical memory.

17.4.1.3 **Process Header Page Arrays.** The breaking of ties between process PTEs and physical memory is straightforward for process pages. The contents of the BAK array element are simply merged into the PTE. However, PHD pages are also a part of the process working set. These pages reside in system space and are mapped by system page table entries (SPTEs) that map the balance slot in which the PHD resides.

The relinquishing of the balance slot implies that these SPTEs must also be surrendered. There is no analogous way to store the BAK array contents for PHD pages. For this reason, the PHD page arrays (see Figure 14-8) save the BAK array contents. There is an array element for each page in the PHD. When a process is outswapped, each PHD page currently in the working set has its BAK address put into the corresponding array element in the PHD page BAK array. When the process is swapped back into memory, the PHD header page arrays can be scanned and the BAK contents copied from the array back into the PFN BAK array elements for the physical pages that contain the PHD.

In a similar manner, it is necessary to remember where each PHD page fits into the WSL. This record keeping is done by storing the WSLX PFN array element into the corresponding PHD page WSLX array element. The use of this array while the PHD is being rebuilt following inswap prevents a prohibitively long search of the WSL for each PHD page.

17.4.2 **Swapper I/O Data Structures**

Like the pager, the swapper uses the conventional VMS I/O subsystem. It allocates its own I/O request packet and fills in some of the fields that will be interpreted in a special manner by the I/O postprocessing routine. After these fields have been filled in, it jumps to one of the swapper I/O entry points in module SYSQIOREQ (EXE$BLDPKTSWPR or EXE$BLDPKTSWPW) that fills in an appropriate function code and queues the packet to the appropriate disk driver. Tables 15-1 and 15-2 show how the I/O request packet is used by the swapper for its I/O activities.

The swapper uses a special I/O map that allows it to read or write a process working set, a collection of virtually noncontiguous pages, in one or a small number of I/O requests.

The use of the swapper I/O map to write virtually noncontiguous pages of a process being swapped is described in Chapter 14. This array contains WSMAX longwords and is used for both outswap and inswap operations.

At outswap, the PFN of each page that will be written to the swap file is stored in an array element. The address of this array is passed to the I/O system as the system virtual address of the PTE that maps the first page of the I/O buffer. At inswap, the swapper allocates physical pages of memory for the process working set and records their PFNs in the I/O map. The swap image is read into these pages. As the swapper rebuilds the process's WSL and page tables, it copies the PFN from each entry of its I/O map to the appropriate process PTE.

17.4.3   Swap File Data Structures

The system maintains a page file control block for each page and swap file in the system. Figure 14-23 shows the layout of a page file control block, the structure that allows a page or swap file to be located on disk. Notice that the window control block pointer and virtual block number field are located at the same offsets in page file control blocks and in process or global section table entries. Thus, these data structures can be used by common routines that need not distinguish the type of structure being used to describe a memory management I/O request.

When the system is initialized, the SYSINIT process initializes the primary swap file SYS$SYSTEM:SWAPFILE.SYS. If an alternate swap file is installed (with the SYSGEN command INSTALL), the page file control block for the new swap file is initialized by SYSGEN.

For each process, the indication of which page file control block to use is contained in the software PCB in field PCB$L_WSSWP. The page file control block then indicates the file in which swapping space is assigned to the process. The upper byte is a longword index into the array of pointers to page file control blocks (see Figure 14-22).

When a process is first created, its initial swap space is allocated by the Create Process ($CREPRC) system service. The initial size of the swap space is the size of the shell process, unless SYSBOOT parameter MPW_WRTCLUSTER is larger. The page file index and the virtual block number of the beginning of the space are recorded in the PCB as negative values. A negative value indicates to the swapper that this PCB requires an inswap from the SHELL. After the SHELL has been swapped in, the values are restored to their positive form.

A zero value in PCB$L_WSSWP indicates to the swapping and paging systems that the process is permanently memory resident. Only the processes that are created before the page and swap files are located (null process, swapper process, and SYSINIT process) are permanently memory resident.

When a process's working set is extended, a check is made to see if the new working set fits in the currently allocated swap space. If the new sized working set does not fit in the current swap space, a new swap space (that is MPW_WRTCLUSTER pages larger) is allocated. The old swap space is deallocated.

17.5 OUTSWAP OPERATION

Outswap is described before inswap because it is easier to explain inswap in terms of what the swapper puts into the swap file. The swapper does not remove processes from the balance set indiscriminately. In practice, the swapper tries hard not to swap. A process is removed only if there is a need for physical pages that cannot be satisfied by shrinking working sets and flushing the modified page list or if the system needs a balance set slot (PHD slot).

17.5.1 Selection of Outswap Candidate

As described in Section 17.2, the outswap selection is driven by an ordered table of scheduling states and associated conditions. The swapper selects the process that benefits the least from remaining in memory. Once a candidate is selected, the swapper prepares the working set of that process for outswap.

17.5.2 Outswap of the Process Body

The swapper outswaps the process body (P0 and P1 pages) separately from the PHD. There are two reasons for doing this:

- Fields in the PHD (most notably WSLEs and process PTEs) are modified as the WSL is processed.
- The PHD may not be swappable at the same time as the body because of outstanding I/O, pages on the modified page list, or some other reason.

17.5.2.1 Scanning the Working Set List.

The process body is prepared for outswap by scanning the WSL. Each page in the WSL must be looked at to determine if any special action is required. The swapper looks at a combination of the page type (found in the WSLE, as well as the PFN TYPE array) and the valid bit. Table 17-4 lists all combinations of page type and valid bit setting that the swapper encounters and the action that it takes for each. Several combinations are discussed further in the following sections.

The basic step that the swapper must take as it scans the WSL is to move each swappable page into the swapper's I/O map. This causes the virtually

Table 17-4   Scan of Working Set List of Outswap Process

Type of Page WSL<3:1>	Valid Bit PTE<31>	Action of Swapper for This Page
Process page	Transition	(STATE = Read in Progress) Treat as page with I/O in progress. Special action may be taken at inswap or by modified page writer. (STATE = Active) Outswap. The page will be put back into active transition state at inswap time. (STATE = Read Error) Drop from working set. No other transition states are possible for a page in the working set.
Process page	Valid	Outswap page. If there is outstanding I/O and the page is modified, load SWPVBN array element with block in swap file where the updated page contents should be written when the I/O completes.
System page		It is impossible for a system page to be in a process working set. The swapper generates an error.
Global read only	Transition	If the process PTE still contains a PFN, this page is an active transition page. Outswap the page. If the process PTE contains a GPTX, then the global page table must contain a transition PTE. The page is dropped from the process working set.
Global read only	Valid	If SHRCNT = 1, then outswap. If SHRCNT > 1, drop from working set. It is highly likely that a process can fault such a page later without I/O. This check avoids multiple copies of the same page in the swap file.
Global read/write		Drop from working set. It is extremely difficult to determine whether the page in memory was modified after this copy was written to the swap file.
Page table page		Not part of the process body. However, while the swapper is scanning the process body, the virtual address field in the WSL is modified to reflect the offset from the beginning of the PHD because page table pages will probably be located at different virtual addresses following inswap.

noncontiguous pages in the process's working set to appear virtually contiguous to the I/O system (see Figures 17-2 and 17-5). For each page, the swapper performs the following steps:

1. Locates the PTE from the virtual page number field in the WSLE
2. Determines any special action, based on page validity and page type
3. Copies the PFN from the PTE to the swapper map
4. Records the modify bit (logical OR of PTE modify bit and PFN STATE array saved modify bit) in the WSLE
5. Sets the Delete Contents bit in the PFN STATE array element. This bit causes the page to be placed at the head of the free page list when its reference count goes to zero (which in normal circumstances is when the swap write completes).

Note that the swapper does not have to explicitly put the contents of the PFN BAK array into each PTE. The contents are replaced when the page is released (after the swap write completes and all other references to the page are eliminated).

17.5.2.2   **Pages with Direct I/O in Progress.** If a (modified) page has outstanding I/O while the process is being outswapped, the swapper takes note of this by loading the SWPVBN PFN array element with the virtual block number in the swap file where the page is being written to. The page is nevertheless swapped at this time to reserve a place for it in the swap file.

If the I/O operation is a read (or it is a write and some other action has caused the page to be modified), the physical page is placed on the modified page list when the I/O completes. MMG$RELPFN, the routine that releases the page, puts a page on the modified page list if either the modify bit in the PFN STATE array is set or if the PFN SWPVBN array has nonzero contents.

The modified page writer takes special action for a modified page with nonzero contents in the SWPVBN array. That is, it writes each page to the designated block in the swap file rather than to its normal backing store address.

If the I/O operation is a write (from memory to mass storage) and the page was not otherwise modified, the contents that are currently being written to the swap file are good. The page is placed on the free list when the write completes.

17.5.2.3   **Global Pages.** Global pages are also given special treatment at outswap. If the global page is writable, it is dropped from the process working set before the process is swapped to disk. The task of recording whether the contents that are swapped are up to date when the process is brought back into memory is more complicated than simply refaulting the page (often without I/O) when the process is swapped back into memory.

Global read-only pages are only swapped if the global share count (PFN SHRCNT array) is one. In all other cases, the page is dropped from the working set and must be refaulted (most likely without I/O) when the process is inswapped. (Global pages that are explicitly or implicitly locked into the process working set are not dropped from the working set.) Global transition pages are also dropped from the process working set.

17.5.2.4   Example of Process Body Outswap. Figures 17-1 through 17-3 show some of the special cases encountered by the swapper while it is scanning the process WSL. As mentioned in connection with Table 17-4, the key information about each page is a combination of the PTE valid bit and the physical page type. The order of the scan is determined by the order defined by the WSL. Figure 17-1 shows the process working set, the process page tables, and the associated PFN database entries before the swapper begins its working set scan. Figure 17-2 shows the modified working set and the swapper map after the WSL scan but before the I/O request is initiated. Figure 17-3 shows the

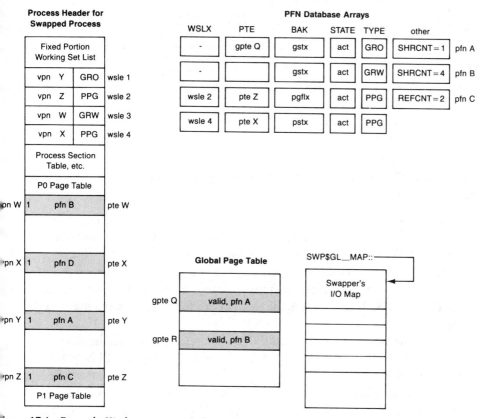

Figure 17-1   Example Working Set List before Outswap Scan

445

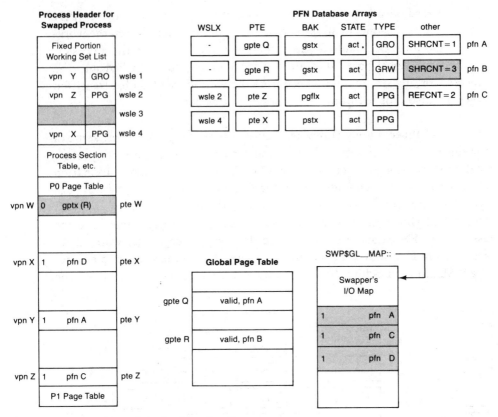

Figure 17-2 Example Working Set List after Outswap Scan

state of the PTEs after the swap write has completed and the physical pages have been released.

1. The first WSLE is a global read-only page. The VPN field of the WSLE locates the PTE. The PFN field of the PTE locates the PFN data associated with this physical page. In particular, the global share count for this page is 1. (This process is the only process that currently has this page in its working set.) The swapper writes this page out as part of the swap image for this process. Thus, pfn A is the first page in the swapper's I/O map (see Figure 17-2).

   When the swapper's write operation completes, the page will be deleted. That is, the PTE array element will be cleared and the page will be placed at the head of the free page list (see Figure 17-3).

2. The second WSLE is a process page that also has I/O in progress (a REFCNT of 2). This page will be swapped. This fact is illustrated by the inclusion of pfn C in the swapper map.

   If the page was previously modified (either the PTE modify bit or saved

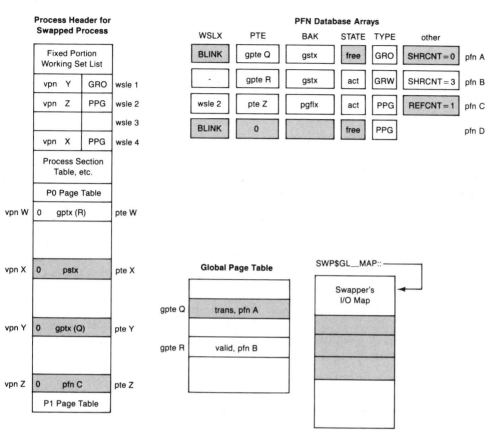

Figure 17-3   Process Page Table Changes after Swapper's
Write Completes

modify bit in the PFN STATE array was set), the virtual block number in
the swap file will be loaded into the SWPVBN array. Loading the SWPVBN
array will force the page to the modified page list when it is released. If the
process is still outswapped by the time the modified page writer gets
around to writing this page, the page will be written to the block reserved
for it when the process is first outswapped.

The page is marked for deletion. That is, when the reference count for
the page reaches zero (because of completion of both the outstanding I/O
and the swapper's write), the page is placed at the head of the free page list
and its PTE array element cleared.

3. The third WSLE is a global read/write page. The page is dropped from the
process working set (see Figure 17-2), meaning that the process PTE is
replaced with a GPTX (that locates gpte R) and the share count for pfn B is
decremented. Notice that pfn B is not a part of the swapper map, which
contains a list of the physical pages that will be written to the swap file.

4. The last WSLE in this example is a process page with nothing special about it. This page is added to the swapper map (pfn D) and its contents are marked for deletion. The deletion will actually occur when the swapper's write operation completes.

17.5.3   Outswap of Process Header

The PHD is not outswapped until after the process body has been successfully written to the swap file. The reason for this illustrates two other cases that can keep the PHD in memory. Before the PHD can be outswapped, all ties to physical memory that exist in the process page tables must be severed, including not only those pages that were in the process working set and written to the swap file but also those pages that are in some transition state, most notably pages on the free and modified page lists.

17.5.3.1   Partial Outswap.
After the process body has been outswapped, the PHD becomes eligible for outswap. In fact, the header of an outswapped process is the first thing that the swapper looks for in an attempt to balance the free page list.

The indication that the PHD cannot be outswapped yet is found in the PHD vector reference count array (see Figure 14-21). This array counts the number of reasons (transition pages, active page table pages, and so on) that prevent the PHD from being outswapped.

Because the outswap of the header does not have to immediately follow the body outswap, it is possible (even probable) that a PHD will not be swapped in the time between when a process body is outswapped and when that process is brought back into memory. Such a situation is referred to as a partial outswap. It has an obvious counterpart, a partial inswap, where the swapper does not have to allocate a balance slot and bring the PHD into memory because the header is already resident.

An important system management point is illustrated here. Process bodies, which consume physical memory, are relatively easy to remove from memory. PHDs consume a smaller amount of physical memory but they also occupy a balance slot. The balance slot is not freed for other use until the entire header is outswapped. If the SYSBOOT parameter BALSETCNT is too small, the system can reach the unfortunate state where there is more than enough physical memory, but computable processes cannot be brought into memory because the balance slots are still tied to already outswapped processes. This situation can be avoided by setting BALSETCNT to an adequate value. See the *Guide to VAX/VMS Performance Management* for details on determining the correct value for SYSBOOT parameters.

When the swapper locates a PHD that can be removed from its balance slot, it takes whatever actions are required to remove the ties that bind the PHD to physical memory. The first such step is to eliminate any transition

PTE whose physical page is on the free page list.

A transition PTE is located by scanning the free page list for a page whose PTE array element contents lie within the P0 or P1 page tables of the PHD being examined. The swapper scans the free page list, starting at the back of the list with the most recently queued entries. The assumption is that, on average, the transition page is in the back half of the list. Whenever such a page is found, the process PTE is reset to the contents of the BAK array. The reference count and PTE array elements are cleared and the page is moved from its current location to the head of the free page list.

Because the free page list is only one of several transition states, the scan of the free page list may not free the PHD for removal. Pages may be in some other transition state. Transition states that represent some form of I/O in progress (release pending, read in progress, write in progress) are left alone because there is nothing that the swapper can do until the I/O completes. After the free page list is scanned, if the process still has transition pages, the swapper forces the modified page list to be flushed. A modified page written to its backing store is released to the free page list. Thus, after the modified page list is flushed (see Section 17.3), the swapper must scan the free list again.

7.5.3.2   **Outswap of the Process Header.** Once the reference count for the PHD reaches zero, the header can be outswapped and the balance slot freed. The outswap of the PHD is entirely analogous to the outswap of a process body. That is, the header pages that are not page table pages and the active page table pages are scanned and put into the swapper's I/O map to form a virtually contiguous block for the I/O subsystem.

There are several differences between the outswap of a PHD and a process body. When a process body is outswapped, the header that maps that body is still resident. When the swapper's write completes and each physical page is deleted, the contents of the BAK array element for each page are put back into the process PTE.

PHD pages are mapped by SPTEs for that balance slot. The SPTEs are not available to hold the BAK array contents because they will be used by the next occupant of this balance slot. One of the PHD page arrays (see Section 17.4.1.3) is set aside for exactly this purpose. As the PHD is processed for outswap, the contents of the BAK array for each active header page are stored in the corresponding PHD page array element.

At the same time, the location of each header page within the WSL is stored in the WSLX array. This array prevents a prohibitively long search to rebuild the PHD when the process is swapped back into memory.

Once the header is successfully outswapped, PCB$V_PHDRES in PCB$L_STS, the header-resident bit, is cleared and the balance slot is available for further use.

17.6 INSWAP OPERATION

The inswap is exactly the opposite of the outswap operation. The swapper brings the PHD, including active page tables, and the process body back into physical memory. It then uses the contents of the WSL to rebuild the process page tables, an operation that primarily involves updating each valid PTE to reflect the new PFN used by that PTE. At the same time that each page is being processed, the swapper can resolve any special cases that existed when the process was outswapped.

17.6.1 Selection of an Inswap Candidate

As described in Section 17.2.1, the swapper selects a process for inswap, exactly as the scheduler selects a candidate for execution. The following processes may be potential candidates for inswap:

• Newly created processes
• Processes in some outswapped wait state that were just made computable
• Processes that were outswapped while in the computable state

The highest priority process in this collection is the one selected for inswap.

17.6.2 Inswap of the Process Header

If the PHD was outswapped, it must be brought back into memory before the process body can be reconstructed. Unlike the special operations that took place when the process was outswapped, an outswapped PHD merely adds two details to the inswap operation:

• If the header is resident, the number of header pages is subtracted from the size of the outswap image in the swap file. That is, whether the header is resident determines the total number of blocks that must be read from the swap file and the virtual block number where the read should begin.
• If the header was swapped, those process parameters that are tied to a specific balance slot (that is, specific system virtual or physical addresses) must be adjusted to reflect the new locations in virtual or physical address space. These include the following:

—Each SPTE must be loaded with the PFN that contains the contents of each PHD page.
—The virtual addresses of the P0 and P1 page tables must be calculated and loaded into their locations in the hardware PCB.
—The physical address of the hardware PCB must be calculated and loaded into software PCB field PCB$L_PHYPCB.

—Finally, the P1 pages that double map the PHD pages that are not page table pages must be loaded with the new PFNs that contain these pages.

7.6.2.1   **Rebuilding the Process Header.** When a PHD is read from the swap image into a new balance slot, the SPTEs that map each balance slot page must be loaded with the PFNs from the swapper map that contain each header page. In addition, the PFN database must be set up for each of these physical pages. The swapper does all this work in a very simple loop that it executes for each header page.

The simplicity (and speed) of the loop results from the use of the two PHD page arrays in the PHD. These arrays enable the PFN BAK and WSLX arrays to be loaded with their previous contents (because their previous contents were copied to the two header arrays when the process was outswapped).

To access these arrays, the swapper needs a virtual mapping to the PHD. It actually reads the PHD into its P0 space, using the swapper I/O map. It then generates the appropriate P0 address.

7.6.2.2   **P1 Window to the Process Header.** All of the PHD pages except process page tables are double mapped with a range of P1 addresses. This double mapping is done because whenever a process is swapped out and then back in, its PHD may shift to a different balance set slot. The system space addresses of the PHD fields are thus not constant. No routine could safely store a PHD address in a register, because the address could change between the storage and its use. To provide constant addresses for the PHD, the swapper sets up a second mapping in P1 space of the pages containing the PHD. The swapper keeps the P1 addresses constant across swaps.

The conventions that the operating system observes about header references are these:

- Any process context reference to the PHD should use the P1 address (CTL$GL_PHD contents point to the P1 map of the PHD).
- Any reference to the system space header must execute at an IPL high enough to block rescheduling and thus swapping.
- Any reference to process page tables must execute at IPL$_SYNCH because the page table pages are not double mapped.

There are two implications for the operating system here:

- These physical pages are not kept track of in any way through reference counts or any other technique. However, all of these header pages are a permanent part of the process working set.
- The P1 page table page that maps these pages must also be a permanent member of the process working set.

17.6.3 Rebuilding the Process Body

The PHD must be put into a known state before the process body can be put back into the approximate shape it was in before the process was outswapped. If the header was never outswapped, there is very little that has to be done. If the header was outswapped, the steps previously described are taken to restore the PHD.

17.6.3.1 Rebuilding the Working Set List and Process Page Tables.

The rebuilding of the process body involves a simple scan of both the swapper map and the process WSL. Recall that at outswap, the key to each special case was the combination of physical page type and the setting of the valid bit in the PTE. On inswap, the key to each special case is the contents of the PTE located by the virtual address field in the WSLE. An approximation of swapper activity for each page is as follows:

1. The PTE is located from the virtual address field of the WSLE.
2. In the usual case, the original contents of the PTE are put into the PFN BAK array, and the PFN from the swapper map is loaded into the now valid PTE.
3. If, for some reason, a copy of the page already exists in memory, then that page is put into the process working set. The duplicate page from the swapper map is released to the front of the free page list.

If the virtual address field represents a system space address, then the WSLE describes a page in the PHD. The swapper must calculate the new system virtual address corresponding to that page and modify the WSLE.

Table 17-5 contains a detailed list of the different cases that the swapper can encounter when rebuilding the process page tables. At inswap time, the swapper uses the contents of the PTE to determine what action to take for each particular page. Several cases deserve special comment.

17.6.3.2 Pages with I/O in Progress when Outswap Occurred.

Pages that had I/O in progress when the process was outswapped were written to the swap file anyway to reserve space. If the page was previously unmodified, then it would be put onto the free page list when both the swap write and the outstanding write operation completed. If the page was previously modified, then it would be put onto the modified page list when both the swap write and the outstanding write operation completed (because the contents of the SWPVBN array were nonzero).

In either case, it is possible for the process to be swapped back in before one of these physical pages was reused. The swapper uses the physical page that is already contained in the process PTE (as a transition page) and releases the duplicate physical page from the swapper map to the front of the free page list.

Table 17-5   Rebuilding the Working Set List and the Process Page Tables at Inswap

Type of Page Table Entry	*Action of Swapper for This Page*
PTE is valid.	Page is locked into memory and was never outswapped.
PTE indicates a transition page (probably because of outstanding I/O when process was outswapped).	Fault transition page into process working set. Release duplicate page that was just swapped in.
PTE contains a GPTX. (Page must be global read-only because global read/write pages were dropped from the working set at outswap time.)	Swapper action is based on the contents of the GPTE: • If the GPTE is valid, copy the PFN in the GPTE to the process PTE and release the duplicate page. • If the GPTE indicates a transition page, make the GPTE valid, add that physical page to the process working set, and release the duplicate page. • If the GPTE indicates a GSTX, then keep the page just swapped in and make that the master page in the GPTE, as well as the slave page in the process PTE.
PTE contains a page file index or a process section table index.	These are the usual contents for a page that did not have outstanding I/O or other page references when the process was outswapped. The PFN in the swapper map is inserted into the process page table. The PFN arrays are initialized for that page.

In the case of a page on the free page list, this decision is simply one of convenience. In the case of a page on the modified page list, the contents of the page in the swap image are out of date, and the swapper has no choice but to use the physical page that is already in memory.

17.6.3.3   Resolution of Global Read-Only Pages. The only possible global page that could be in the swap file is a global read-only page that had a share count of 1 when the process was outswapped (or a page that was explicitly locked). All other global pages were dropped from the process working set before the process was outswapped.

There are two different cases that the swapper will find when rebuilding the process page tables. In either case, the process PTE contains a GPTX so the determining factor is the contents of the GPTE.

• The GPTE contains a GPTX. In this case, the PFN trom the swapper map is stored in the GPTE as well as in the process PTE.

- It is possible that the global page was referenced by some other process while this process was outswapped. In that case, the GPTE might contain a transition or valid PTE. In either case, the PFN that is already in the GPTE is kept. (If the GPTE is in transition, it is made valid.) The duplicate PFN from the swapper map is released to the front of the free page list.

17.6.3.4 **Example of an Inswap Operation.** To illustrate at least some of the special cases that the swapper encounters when a process body is swapped back into memory, Figures 17-4 through 17-6 contain an example of an inswap operation. Note that this example is not related to the outswap example used before (see Figures 17-1 to 17-3). This example is tailored to illustrate the interesting cases the swapper can encounter during an inswap operation.

Figure 17-4 shows the state of the PHD after the process has been selected

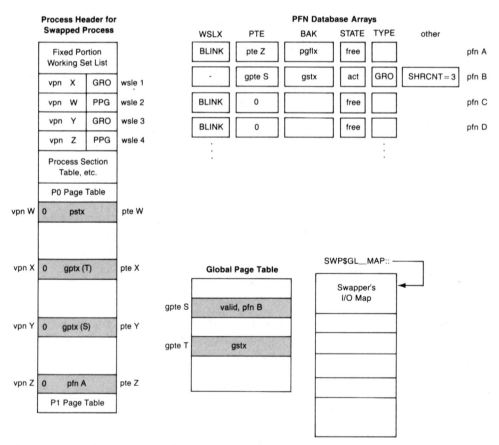

Figure 17-4 Working Set List and Swapper Map before Physical Page Allocation

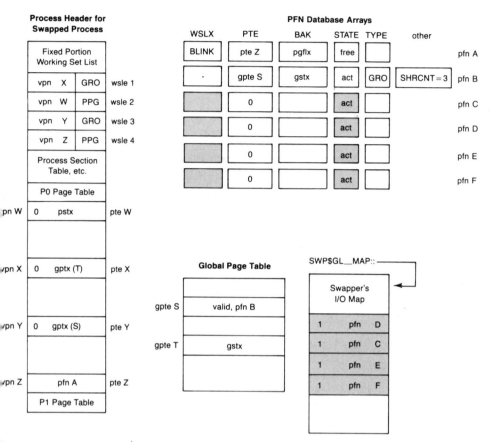

Figure 17-5   Working Set List and Swapper Map after Physical Page Allocation

to be inswapped. Figure 17-5 shows that four physical pages have been allocated to contain the four working set pages that the example is describing. Figure 17-6 shows the rebuilt process page tables and the PFN database changes that result from rebuilding the working set and process page tables.

1. The first WSLE locates virtual page number X. This PTE contains a GPTX. The referenced GPTE (gpte T) contains a GSTX, indicating that the GPTE is not valid.

    Pfn D is put into the process page table. It is also added to the global page database by making the GPTE valid (see Figure 17-6), putting pfn D into the GPTE and updating the PFN data for physical page D to reflect its new state.

2. The next WSLE is a process page mapped by pte W (see Figure 17-5). This PTE contains a process section table index. The PTE is updated to contain pfn C, and the PSTX is stored in the BAK array element for that page (see Figure 17-6). Other PFN arrays are updated accordingly.

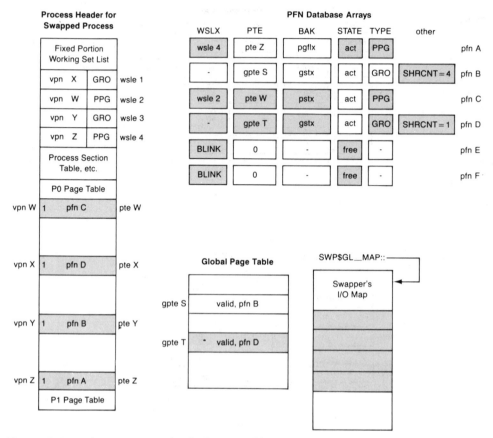

Figure 17-6   Working Set List and Rebuilt Page Tables

3. The next WSLE (that locates pte Y) is exactly like the first, as far as the process data is concerned. However, the GPTE (gpte S) is valid, indicating that another copy of this page already exists. (This second copy could only have happened if another process faulted the page while this process was outswapped.)

   The duplicate page (pfn E) is released to the front of the free page list. The process PTE is updated to contain the physical page that already exists (pfn B) and the share count for that page is incremented (from 3 to 4).

4. The fourth WSLE looks just like the second. However, the process PTE indicates a transition page. (This implies that the header in this example was never outswapped.)

   The action taken here is similar to step 3, where a duplicate global page was discovered. The page just read (pfn F) is released to the head of the free list. The transition page (pfn A) is faulted back into the process working set by removing the page from the free list, setting its state to active, and turning the valid bit in the PTE back on.

7.6.3.5   **Final Processing of the Inswap Operation.** After the WSL has been scanned and the process page tables rebuilt, the process is ready to have its state changed from COMO to COM. Several other scheduling actions must be completed before the scheduler is notified:

1. A new value of ASTLVL is calculated and stored in the hardware PCB in the PHD. (ASTs may have been queued to the process while it was outswapped. The hardware PCB, which contains a copy of the ASTLVL register, was not available while the header was not resident.)
2. The resident bit and the initial quantum bit in the status longword in the software PCB are set.
3. A new quantum interval is loaded into the PHD.
4. Finally, SCH$CHSEP is called to make the process computable.

PART V/Input/Output

18   I/O System Services

Delay not Caesar. Read it instantly.
Julius Caesar, 3, i

Here is a letter, read it at your leisure.
Merchant of Venice, 5, i

All I/O operations performed on a device are requested using the I/O system services. The I/O system services also are called on behalf of a user by system components, such as Record Management Services (RMS). This chapter discusses the following topics:

- The major components of the I/O subsystem
- How an image reserves a particular device for exclusive use and relinquishes the device (device allocation and deallocation)
- How an image creates a logical link to a device and deletes the logical link (channel assignment and deassignment)
- How an image makes an I/O request
- How an image is notified of the completion of an I/O request
- How an image creates and deletes mailbox devices
- How an image performs a breakthrough write to a terminal
- How an image obtains information about a particular device

This chapter assumes a knowledge of device naming conventions. For a detailed discussion of local and VAXcluster System device naming conventions, refer to the *Introduction to VAX/VMS* and *Guide to VAXcluster* manuals.

18.1   LOGICAL NAME TRANSLATION

All of the system service routines discussed in this chapter that have a device-name argument accept a logical name instead of a device name. Each routine uses the same logic to process the device-name argument.

Each system service routine attempts to translate the argument. If the initial attempt at translation is unsuccessful, the routine assumes that the argument specified a physical name, not a logical name, and concludes the logical name translation successfully.

If the initial attempt at translation is successful, the system service routine does one of two things, depending on the nature of the equivalence string returned by the translation. If the equivalence string has the TERMINAL attribute, the routine concludes the logical name translation successfully. The routine uses the equivalence string in place of the original argument.

If the equivalence string does not have the TERMINAL attribute, the system service routine attempts to translate the equivalence string until either an equivalence string that has the TERMINAL attribute is obtained or LNM$C_MAXDEPTH number of translations have been performed without producing an equivalence string with the TERMINAL attribute. (In VAX/VMS Version 4, LNM$C_MAXDEPTH is 10.)

If the system service routine terminates this iteration because an equivalence string with the TERMINAL attribute is obtained, the routine concludes the logical name translation successfully. The routine uses the TERMINAL equivalence string in place of the original argument.

If the system service routine terminates this iteration because LNM$C_MAXDEPTH translations have been done without obtaining an equivalence string with the TERMINAL attribute, the routine terminates with the error status SS$_TOOMANYLNM.

The Create Mailbox and Assign Channel ($CREMBX) system service has an argument that specifies a logical name. This argument is subject to the same logical name translation described in this section.

Logical names and logical name translation are discussed in Chapter 28. The *VAX/VMS System Services Reference Manual* discusses logical names in the context of the I/O system services.

18.2   I/O SUBSYSTEM COMPONENTS

There are four major components of the I/O subsystem: I/O system services, device drivers, the I/O database, and ancillary control processes (ACP). The I/O system services are discussed in subsequent sections. A brief discussion of device drivers, the I/O database, and ACPs follows.

18.2.1   Device Drivers

A device driver controls I/O operations on a peripheral device by performing the following functions:

- Defining the peripheral device for the rest of the operating system
- Preparing a device unit and/or its controller for operation at system startup, during connection of the device via SYSGEN, and during recovery from a power failure
- Performing device-dependent I/O preprocessing
- Translating requests for I/O operations into device-specific commands
- Activating a device unit
- Responding to hardware interrupts generated by a device unit
- Responding to device timeout conditions

- Responding to requests to cancel I/O on a device unit
- Reporting device errors to an error logging program
- Returning status from a device unit to the process that requested the I/O operation

8.2.2   **Driver Components**

Normally, a device driver module can consist of the routines and tables discussed in this section.

8.2.2.1   **Driver Tables.** The three driver tables—driver prolog table, driver dispatch table, and function decision table—are defined in every driver.

The driver prolog table (DPT) defines the identity and size of the driver to the system routine that loads the driver into virtual memory and creates the associated database. With the information provided in the DPT, the driver loading procedure can both load and reload the driver and perform the required I/O database initialization.

The driver dispatch table (DDT) lists the addresses of the entry points of standard routines within the driver and records the size of the diagnostic and error log buffers for drivers that perform error logging.

The function decision table (FDT) lists all valid function codes for the device and associates valid codes with the addresses of I/O preprocessing routines called FDT routines. The FDT consists of a series of entries. Each entry has a quadword mask. Each bit in the mask corresponds to a function code. (For example, bit 33 in a mask corresponds to function code 33.) The first entry consists of just a mask. This mask has bits set to indicate which functions are legal for the associated device. The second entry also consists of just a mask. This mask has bits set to indicate which functions are buffered I/O operations. The subsequent entries consist of a mask and the address of an FDT routine. The mask indicates which functions correspond to the associated FDT routine. FDT routines are discussed in Section 18.5.2. FDT routines are discussed in detail in the manual *Writing a Device Driver for VAX/VMS*.

8.2.2.2   **Driver Routines.** In addition to any FDT routines it may contain, a device driver generally contains both a start I/O routine and an interrupt service routine.

The start I/O routine performs additional device-dependent tasks such as translating the I/O function code into a device-specific command, storing the details of the request in the device's unit control block (UCB) in the I/O database and, if necessary, obtaining the access to controller and adapter resources. Whenever the start I/O routine must wait for these resources to become available, VAX/VMS suspends the routine, reactivating it when the resources become available.

The start I/O routine ultimately activates the device by suitably loading the device's registers. At this stage, the start I/O routine invokes a VAX/VMS macro that causes the routine's execution to be suspended until the device completes the I/O operation and posts an interrupt to the processor. The start I/O routine remains suspended until the driver's interrupt service routine handles the interrupt.

When a device posts an interrupt, its device driver's interrupt service routine determines whether the interrupt is expected or unexpected and takes appropriate action. If the interrupt is expected, the interrupt service routine reactivates the driver's start I/O routine at the point of suspension. The general course of action of the start I/O routine is to perform device-dependent I/O postprocessing and transfer control to VAX/VMS for device-independent I/O postprocessing.

The unit and controller initialization routines prepare a device or controller for operation when the driver loading procedure loads the driver into memory and when VAX/VMS recovers from a power failure.

The timeout handling routine retries the I/O operation and performs other error handling when a device fails to complete an operation within a reasonable period of time. Chapter 11 discusses timeout handling in more detail.

The cancel I/O routine handles requests to cancel I/O on a unit. It is called when an image issues a Cancel I/O on Channel ($CANCEL) system service for the unit, and when the device reference count for the unit goes to zero. Section 18.8 discusses cancel I/O routines in more detail.

18.2.3   I/O Database

Because a device driver and the VAX/VMS executive cooperate to process an I/O request, they must have a common and current source of information about the request. This is the function of the I/O database. Under VAX/VMS, the I/O database consists of three parts:

• Driver tables that allow the system to load drivers, validate device functions, and call drivers at their entry points (see Section 18.2.2)
• Data structures that describe every I/O bus adapter, device type, device unit, controller, and logical path from a process to a device
• I/O request packets (IRP) that define individual requests for I/O activity

Illustrations of I/O database structures and detailed descriptions of their fields appear in the manual *Writing a Device Driver for VAX/VMS*. Figure 18-1 illustrates some of the relationships among VAX/VMS I/O routines, the I/O database, and a device driver.

18.2.3.1   Data Structures. I/O database data structures describe peripheral hardware and are used by VAX/VMS to synchronize access to devices. VAX/VMS

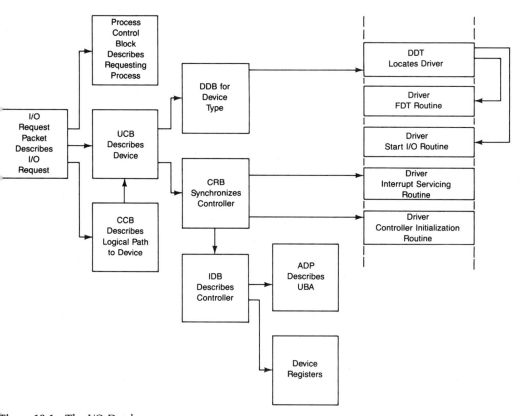

Figure 18-1   The I/O Database

creates these data structures either at system startup or when a driver is loaded into the system.

VAX/VMS creates a UCB for each device unit attached to the system. A UCB defines the characteristics and current state of an individual device unit.

When a driver is suspended or interrupted, the UCB keeps the context of the driver in a set of fields collectively known as a fork block. (See Chapter 6 for more detail about fork blocks and fork routines.) In addition, the UCB contains the listhead for the queue of pending IRPs for the unit.

A device data block (DDB) contains information common to all devices of the same type that are connected to a particular controller. It records the generic device name concatenated with the controller designator (for example, LPA) and the name and location of the associated device driver. In addition, the DDB contains a pointer to the first UCB for the device units attached to the controller.

The channel request block (CRB) defines the current state of a given controller and lists the devices waiting for the controller's data channel. It also contains the code that dispatches a device interrupt to the interrupt service routine for that unit's driver. (See Chapter 5 for more information on device interrupts.)

VAX/VMS also creates an interrupt dispatch block (IDB) for each controller. An IDB lists the device units associated with a controller and points to the UCB of the device unit that the controller is currently serving. In addition, an IDB points to the device registers and the controller's I/O adapter.

An adapter control block (ADP) defines the characteristics and current state of an I/O adapter, such as the VAX UNIBUS and MASSBUS adapters, and the MicroVAX Q22 bus interface. An ADP contains the queues and allocation bit maps necessary to allocate adapter resources. VAX/VMS provides routines that drivers can call to interface with the appropriate adapter.

A channel control block (CCB) describes the logical path between a process and the UCB of the specific device unit. Unlike the data structures mentioned earlier, CCBs are not located in nonpaged system space, but in the P1 space of each process. CCBs are discussed in more detail in Section 18.4.1.

A window control block (WCB) describes the virtual to logical correspondence for the virtual blocks in a file. The WCB is pointed to by the CCB. The WCB contains a base virtual block number and a variable number of map entries (controlled by the /WINDOWS = n qualifier to the DCL command INITIALIZE, by the SYSBOOT parameter ACP_WINDOW for disks mounted with the /SYSTEM qualifier, and by the FAB field RTV at file open time). The map entries form a subset of the file retrieval information for the file. Each map entry consists of an extent size and a starting logical block number (LBN). The map entries represent a virtually contiguous set of blocks that are not necessarily logically contiguous on the disk.

18.2.3.2 **Synchronizing Access to the I/O Database.** There are three methods used to synchronize access to the I/O database: IPL, mutexes, and the lock management system services. Chapter 2 discusses the use of IPL and mutexes for synchronization. Chapter 13 discusses resources, locks, and the lock management system services. The manual *Writing a Device Driver for VAX/VMS* discusses the use of IPL for synchronization from the perspective of device drivers.

The I/O database mutex, IOC$GL_MUTEX, is used to lock the I/O database for either read or write access by process-based code.

If the system is a member of a VAXcluster System, lock management system services are used to synchronize access to the UCBs for devices that are cluster-available (DEV$V_CLU set in UCB$L_DEVCHAR2). The resource name is the string SYS$ concatenated with the allocation class device name. In this chapter, any reference to taking out a lock on a device means using lock management system services.

18.2.3.3   **I/O Request Packets.** The third part of the I/O database is a set of IRPs. When a process requests I/O activity, VAX/VMS constructs an IRP that describes the I/O request in a standard format. The IRP contains fields into which system and driver I/O preprocessing can write information. For instance, the device-dependent arguments specified in the Queue I/O Request ($QIO) system service call are placed in the IRP. The IRP also includes buffer addresses, a pointer to the UCB for the target device, and the I/O function codes.

18.2.4   **Ancillary Control Processes**

An ACP is a process that assists device drivers in processing I/O requests. ACPs perform functions that are device-independent, such as opening files and establishing a network link. VAX/VMS provides the following ACPs:

- F11AACP—Files-11 structure level 1 ACP
- MTAAACP—Magnetic tape ACP
- NETACP—DECnet-VAX ACP
- REMACP—Remote terminal ACP

For VAX/VMS Version 4, the Files-11 structure level 2 ACP, F11BACP, was converted to the Extended QIO Processor (XQP), F11BXQP. Unlike an ACP, the XQP runs in the context of the process making the I/O request. For purposes of this chapter, there is no essential difference between ACPs and the XQP. Any reference to ACPs is equally applicable to the XQP unless stated otherwise.

18.3   **DEVICE ALLOCATION AND DEALLOCATION**

The Allocate Device ($ALLOC) system service allocates a device for exclusive use by a process and its subprocesses. No other processes can allocate the device or assign channels to it until the image that invoked $ALLOC exits or explicitly deallocates the device with the Deallocate Device ($DALLOC) system service. Their system service procedures, EXE$ALLOC and EXE$DALLOC in module SYSDEVALC, run in kernel mode.

There are two exceptions to the restriction just stated. SHARE privilege, which is new in VAX/VMS Version 4, allows a process to assign a channel to a device that is allocated to another process. Processes that are subprocesses of the process that allocated the device can assign channels to the device.

18.3.1   **Explicit and Implicit Device Allocation**

There are two forms of device allocation, explicit and implicit. In both cases, the process ID of the process that allocated the device is stored in the UCB device owner field, UCB$L_PID. In the case of explicit allocation, the device allocated bit (DEV$V_ALL in UCB$L_DEVCHAR) is set. In the case of implicit device allocation, this bit is clear. In the case of explicit allocation, the device reference count (UCB$W_REFC) is incremented. In the case of implicit allocation, the device reference count is not changed.

The system services $ALLOC and $DALLOC explicitly allocate and deallocate a device. A device can be explicitly deallocated only if it has been explicitly allocated.

The Assign I/O Channel ($ASSIGN) system service and the Deassign I/O Channel ($DASSGN) system service perform implicit allocation and deallocation if the device has not been explicitly allocated, it is not shareable (DEV$V_SHR in UCB$L_DEVCHAR is clear), and it is not cluster-available.

18.3.2 Allocate Device System Service

The $ALLOC system service has five arguments:

- The device to allocate, DEVNAM.
- The PHYBUF argument specifies where $ALLOC should return the name of the device.
- The PHYLEN argument specifies where $ALLOC should return the length of the device name.
- The access mode to be associated with the device, ACMODE.
- The FLAGS argument contains only one flag, the low bit. When set, the low bit indicates that any device of a particular type can be allocated, not just a specific device.

Only the DEVNAM argument is required.

EXE$ALLOC takes the following steps to allocate a device:

1. It locks the I/O database mutex for write access.
2. It verifies that the DEVNAM argument's string descriptor and string buffer are read accessible.
3. It invokes IOC$SEARCH (in module IOSUBPAGD) to locate a suitable device. If the FLAGS argument is not specified or is zero, EXE$ALLOC requests IOC$SEARCH to search for the exact device specified by the DEVNAM argument. If the FLAGS argument is 1, EXE$ALLOC requests IOC$SEARCH to search for the first available device having the type specified by the DEVNAM argument.

   IOC$SEARCH translates the DEVNAM argument, as specified in Section 18.1. It then searches the I/O database for either the specific device or one of the particular type. IOC$SEARCH and routines it invokes verify the suitability of the device and its accessibility to this process.

If the appropriate device is found, IOC$SEARCH checks that the process has access to the device. If the system is a member of a VAXcluster System and the device is cluster-available, IOC$SEARCH invokes IOC$LOCK_DEV (in module IOSUBPAGD). IOC$LOCK_DEV invokes the Enqueue Lock Request ($ENQ) system service to queue an exclusive mode lock on the device. (This defines the device as a cluster-available resource.) IOC$LOCK_DEV then stores the lock ID in UCB$L_LOCKID.

4. EXE$ALLOC returns the translated device name if the PHYLEN and PHYBUF arguments are specified, the descriptor is readable, and the buffer is writable.

5. It sets the device-allocated bit.

6. It maximizes the ACMODE argument with the access mode of the caller and stores the result in UCB$B_AMOD.

7. It increments the device reference count.

8. It copies the process ID, PCB$L_PID, to the UCB device owner field.

9. It releases the I/O database mutex.

The device cannot be allocated if any one of the following conditions is true:

- The device is already allocated by another process (UCB$L_PID is nonzero).
- The device reference count is nonzero.
- A volume is mounted on the device.
- The device is spooled (DEV$V_SPL in UCB$L_DEVCHAR is set), and the process does not have ALLSPOOL privilege.
- The requesting process does not have access rights to allocate the device, based on the device owner's UIC (UCB$L_OWNUIC), device protection (UCB$W_PROT), and access control list (ACL).
- The device is not available (DEV$V_AVL in UCB$L_DEVCHAR is clear) or not online (UCB$V_ONLINE in UCB$L_STS is clear).
- The device is a template device (UCB$V_TEMPLATE in UCB$W_STS is set).
- The device is cluster-available and a conflicting lock exists elsewhere in the VAXcluster System.

18.3.3 **Deallocate Device System Service**

An image can deallocate a single device or all devices allocated to the process by invoking the $DALLOC system service. $DALLOC has two optional arguments:

- The DEVNAM argument specifies the device to be deallocated. If the DEVNAM argument is specified, it must translate to a physical device name. If the

DEVNAM argument is not specified, all devices allocated by the process from access modes equal to or less privileged than that specified by the DEVNAM argument are deallocated.

- The ACMODE argument specifies the access mode on behalf of which the deallocation is to be performed. The ACMODE argument is maximized with the access mode of the caller.

EXE$DALLOC performs the following steps:

1. It locks the I/O database mutex for write access.
2. It maximizes the ACMODE argument with the access mode of the caller.
3. It determines if the DEVNAM argument is present. If the argument is present, EXE$DALLOC invokes IOC$SEARCHDEV (in module IOSUBPAGD) to locate the specified device. If the argument is absent, EXE$DALLOC invokes IOC$SCAN_IODB (in module IOSUBNPAG) to find the first UCB in the I/O database.
4. In either case, EXE$DALLOC makes the following checks before deallocating the device.

   —The UCB$L_PID field must match the PCB$L_PID field of the process issuing the $DALLOC request.
   —The access mode in UCB$B_AMOD must be greater than or equal to the access mode computed in step 2.
   —The device must be explicitly allocated.
   —The device must not be mounted (DEV$V_MNT in UCB$L_DEV-CHAR is clear).

5. EXE$DALLOC deallocates the device by invoking IOC$DALLOC_DEV (in module IOSUBPAGD). IOC$DALLOC_DEV takes the following steps:

   a. It clears the device allocated bit.
   b. If the device is shareable, it clears the device owner field.
   c. It decrements the device reference count.
   d. If the reference count is now zero, EXE$DALLOC_DEV invokes IOC$LAST_CHAN, which performs last channel processing. Last channel processing is discussed in Section 18.4.4.
   e. IOC$DALLOC_DEV invokes IOC$UNLOCK_DEV (in module IOSUBPAGD) to deal with the resource lock on the device. IOC$UN-LOCK_DEV tests UCB$L_LOCKID to determine whether there is a lock, and the device reference count to determine whether there are still channels assigned to the device. If there is no lock, the routine returns. Otherwise, if there are still channels assigned to the device, the routine invokes the $ENQ system service to convert the lock to concurrent read mode. If there are no channels assigned to the device, the routine invokes the Dequeue Lock Request ($DEQ) system service to dequeue the lock.

6. If the DEVNAM argument is not present, EXE$DALLOC goes back to step 3 to get the next UCB in the I/O database. When no more UCBs are found, EXE$DALLOC unlocks the I/O database mutex and returns.

   If the DEVNAM argument is present, EXE$DALLOC unlocks the I/O database mutex and returns.

18.4   ASSIGNING AND DEASSIGNING CHANNELS

To request an I/O operation on a device, an image must identify the device to the system. The software mechanism used to link a process to a device is called a channel. A channel to a device is established through the $ASSIGN system service. The image can then issue I/O requests to that device by specifying the channel number assigned to the device. An I/O request is made through the $QIO system service. When the image no longer wants to use the device, it invokes the $DASSGN system service to break the link between the process and the device.

18.4.1   Channel Control Block

A channel is described by a process-specific data structure called a CCB. A process's CCBs are contained in a table located in its P1 space (see Figure 1-7 and Table F-5). The global location CTL$GL_CCBBASE contains the address of the table's high address end. The table is accessed using negative byte displacements. That is, a particular CCB is identified by its displacement from the contents of CTL$GL_CCBBASE. The number of CCBs in the table is determined by the SYSBOOT parameter CHANNELCNT; its value is stored in CTL$GW_NMIOCH.

Figure 18-2 shows the layout of a CCB. The field CCB$B_AMOD contains zero if the channel is unassigned. Otherwise, it identifies the access mode from which the channel was assigned, containing the access mode biased by 1. For example, the value 1 indicates the channel was assigned from kernel mode. CCB$L_UCB contains the address of the UCB of the device to which the channel is assigned. If a file has been opened on the channel, CCB$L_WIND contains the address of its WCB. (If the file is associated with a process section, CCB$L_WIND contains the process section index.)

CCB$L_UCB		
CCB$L_WIND		
CCB$W_IOC	CCB$B_AMOD	CCB$B_STS
CCB$L_DIRP		

Figure 18-2   Layout of Channel Control Block

CCB$B_STS contains several status bits.

Any comparison of the CCB$B_AMOD with an access mode value must be a signed comparison. The XQP reserves a channel for itself by storing −1 in CCB$B_AMOD when the XQP is not actively using the channel. As a result, any access mode value will be greater than the value in CCB$B_AMOD if a signed comparison is made. The XQP takes this step to prevent the channel from being deassigned when the XQP is not actively using the channel. When the XQP wants to actively use the channel, it modifies the CCB to make the channel look like a normal kernel mode channel to the device of the XQP's choice.

The field CCB$W_IOC indicates how many I/O requests are outstanding on the channel. The field CCB$L_DIRP contains an unnamed flag in the low bit that is set to indicate an outstanding access (open) or a deaccess (close) request on this channel. If the deaccess request is pending, waiting for all other outstanding I/O requests to be completed, CCB$L_DIRP contains the address of the IRP that describes the deaccess request ORed with 1.

18.4.2   Assign I/O Channel System Service

The $ASSIGN system service has four arguments; the first two are required, and the last two are optional:

- The name of the device to which to assign the channel, DEVNAM.
- The address of the word in which to store the assigned channel number, CHAN.
- The access mode to be associated with the channel, ACMODE.
- The name of the mailbox to be associated with the channel, MBXNAM. (An image associates a mailbox with a nonshareable device to receive status information, such as the arrival of unsolicited input from a terminal. The device driver for the device either uses or ignores this associated mailbox.)

The $ASSIGN system service procedure, EXE$ASSIGN in module SYSASSIGN, runs in kernel mode. There are two major paths through EXE$ASSIGN. The first path handles assignment to a local device. The second path handles assignment to a remote device. Both paths have the same initial steps.

18.4.2.1   Common Initial Steps.
EXE$ASSIGN performs the following steps for both local and remote device assignment:

1. It verifies that the CHAN argument is write accessible.
2. If the MBXNAM argument is specified, EXE$ASSIGN verifies that it is read accessible and names an existing mailbox.
3. It verifies that the DEVNAM argument is read accessible.
4. It verifies that the ACMODE is read accessible and maximizes the argument

with the access mode of the caller.

5. It invokes IOC$FFCHAN (in module IOSUBPAGD) to find a free CCB.
   IOC$FFCHAN begins its search for a free CCB at the high address end of
   the CCB table. It examines offset CCB$B_AMOD to determine whether
   the CCB is free. If the CCB is in use, IOC$FFCHAN examines the previous
   CCB, repeating its test. This sequence continues until IOC$FFCHAN lo-
   cates a free CCB or comes to the end of the table.

   If no free CCB is located, IOC$FFCHAN returns the error status
   SS$_NOIOCHN. If IOC$FFCHAN locates a CCB, it returns the address of
   the free CCB and a positive index that is the offset into the CCB table.
   This index is the channel number returned from the system service
   request.

6. EXE$ASSIGN locks the I/O database mutex for write access.

7. If the MBXNAM argument was specified, EXE$ASSIGN invokes
   IOC$SEARCHDEV to search the I/O database to locate the device speci-
   fied in the MBXNAM argument. IOC$SEARCHDEV returns the address of
   the mailbox UCB.

8. EXE$ASSIGN invokes IOC$SEARCH to locate the device whose name
   was specified in the DEVNAM argument. If the device name is a logical
   name, IOC$SEARCH performs logical name translation of the DEVNAM
   argument as described in Section 18.1. It then scans the I/O database for a
   device with the name that was the result of the logical name translation. If
   IOC$SEARCH locates the device in the I/O database, it returns the ad-
   dress of the device's UCB.

At this point, the two major paths through EXE$ASSIGN diverge. The cri-
teria used by IOC$SEARCH to distinguish between remote and local devices
is the presence or absence of a node delimiter (::) in the device name. (If the
device is remote, IOC$SEARCH returns the error status SS$_NONLOCAL.)
The local device path is discussed in Section 18.4.2.2. The remote device path
is discussed in Section 18.4.2.3. The two paths do not converge.

8.4.2.2   **Local Device Assignment.** EXE$ASSIGN distinguishes between two types
of local devices, template and nontemplate. Template devices have
UCB$V_TEMPLATE in UCB$L_STS set; nontemplate devices have this bit
clear. The beginning and end of the local device assignment path are common
to both types of local devices.

• If the UCB is a redirected UCB (DEV$V_RED in UCB$L_DEVCHAR2 is
  set), EXE$ASSIGN replaces the original UCB address with the address of
  the logical UCB by using the value in field UCB$L_TT_LOGUCB of the
  original UCB. This mechanism connects a physical terminal to its virtual
  terminal. Only terminal UCBs can be redirected.

• If the device is set spooled, EXE$ASSIGN skips the test for a template
  device.

18.4.2.2.1 *Nontemplate Device Processing.* Nontemplate device processing is the typical case. Most local devices are nontemplate devices. Devices that are cluster-available are considered local, nontemplate devices as far as EXE$ASSIGN is concerned.

- If the device is nonshareable and allocated (UCB$L_PID is nonzero), one of the following two conditions must be true:

  —The requesting process is the owner of the device or is a descendant of the owner process.
  —The requesting process has the SHARE privilege and the volume protection and owner UIC allow access.

- If the device is not allocated, EXE$ASSIGN implicitly allocates it to the process by storing the process ID into UCB$L_PID. This can happen only for devices that are not cluster-available.

  The rest of the steps EXE$ASSIGN takes are common to the template and nontemplate cases.

18.4.2.2.2 *Template Device Processing.* If the device is a template device, EXE$ASSIGN does not assign the channel to that device (the template device). It creates a new UCB (the cloned UCB) using the template UCB as a template (hence the name) and assigns the channel to the cloned UCB. The cloned UCB will have a unique unit number. EXE$ASSIGN accomplishes this as follows:

1. If the template device is a network device, EXE$ASSIGN verifies that the calling process has NETMBX privilege.
2. EXE$ASSIGN invokes IOC$CHKUCBQUOTA (in module UCBCREDEL) to verify that the process has sufficient BYTLM quota (at least the sum of the following):

   —The size of the template UCB
   —The size of an object rights block (ORB)
   —256 bytes left to satisfy process deletion needs

3. It invokes IOC$CLONE_UCB (in module UCBCREDEL) to create the cloned UCB and an ORB.
   IOC$CLONE_UCB makes several modifications to the cloned UCB once it creates the cloned UCB. The following modifications are of interest here:

   —Set the reference count to 1.
   —Mark the unit online.
   —Clear the template bit.
   —Store the sum of the size of the UCB and the size of the ORB in UCB$W_CHARGE.

—Give the UCB a unique unit number between 1 and 9999. (If all of these units already exist, the cloning and thus the $ASSIGN fail.)

—Link the UCB into the UCB chain of the related DDB.

4. EXE$ASSIGN stores the current process's UIC (PCB$L_UIC) in the ORB owner field (ORB$L_OWNER). The object in this case is the UCB. At this point, the owner field of the cloned UCB is still clear.

5. It sets UCB$V_DELETEUCB in UCB$L_STS to mark the cloned UCB for deletion when the reference count goes to zero.

6. If the template UCB is a mailbox UCB (DEV$V_MBX in UCB$L_DEV-CHAR is set), EXE$ASSIGN sets the mailbox delete bit (UCB$V_DELMBX in UCB$W_DEVSTS). This is done because special steps are required to delete a mailbox UCB.

7. EXE$ASSIGN reduces the process's byte count quota and limit by the value stored in UCB$W_CHARGE by IOC$CLONE_UCB. Both are decreased by the charge to prevent infinite asynchronous system trap (AST) waits.

   EXE$BUFFRQUOTA and EXE$BUFFQUOPRC test and charge both values. If a process does not have sufficient byte count but does have sufficient byte limit, these routines will place the process in an AST wait, if the process has system service resource wait mode enabled. The objective is to wait until an I/O completion AST has increased the byte count as a result of I/O completion. Since the amount charged by EXE$ASSIGN will not be restored until the UCB is deleted, the process has effectively had its byte limit reduced by the amount of the charge. EXE$ASSIGN decrements the byte limit as well to reflect this fact.

8. EXE$ASSIGN invokes the driver at entry point DDT$L_CLONEUCB.

   EXE$ASSIGN passes the driver the address of the template UCB as well as the address of the cloned UCB. The driver can perform any additional checks necessary. If the driver returns any error status, the process of cloning the UCB is undone and the $ASSIGN completes with failure.

   The driver's cloned UCB routine runs in the context of the process that invoked the $ASSIGN system service at IPL$_ASTDEL (IPL 2) because the I/O database mutex is owned by the process.

9. If the device is not shareable, EXE$ASSIGN copies the process's PID to UCB$L_PID.

The rest of the steps EXE$ASSIGN takes are common to the template and nontemplate cases.

8.4.2.2.3   *Local Device Final Processing.* At this point, EXE$ASSIGN has found a free channel, verified the existence of the device (creating the UCB in the case of a template device), and verified that the process has access to the device. It completes the assignment of an I/O channel to a local device in the following steps:

1. If an associated mailbox was requested, EXE$ASSIGN stores the address of the associated mailbox UCB in the UCB$L_AMB field of the UCB to which the channel is being assigned. It increments the reference count in the associated mailbox UCB and sets CCB$V_AMB in R6 to indicate that there is an associated mailbox.

    No association can be made if any of the following is true:

    —The device is a file-oriented device (DEV$V_FOD in UCB$L_DEV-CHAR is set).
    —The device is shareable.
    —The device already has an associated mailbox (UCB$L_AMB is nonzero), and the MBXNAM argument specifies a different mailbox.

2. If appropriate, it invokes IOC$LOCK_DEV to define the device as a cluster-available resource and queue a concurrent read mode lock on it. The following conditions must all be met for EXE$ASSIGN to take this action:

    —The device reference count is zero.
    —The system is an active member of a VAXcluster System.
    —The device is cluster-available.

3. It copies the device's UCB address to CCB$L_UCB.
4. It increments the device reference count.
5. It stores the access mode biased by 1 in CCB$B_AMOD. The access mode specified by the ACMODE argument was maximized with the access mode of the caller.
6. It stores R6 in CCB$B_STS. (The only bit that may be set as a result of this step is CCB$V_AMB.)
7. It unlocks the I/O database mutex.
8. It writes the channel number (the index into the CCB table) in the word specified by CHAN argument.
9. It returns to the caller with the success status SS$_NORMAL.

18.4.2.3   **Assigning a Channel to a Remote Device.** If the device is a remote device (the device name contains "::"), EXE$ASSIGN performs the first step in transparent network communication, converting the transparent network communication into the related nontransparent network communication. Transparent and nontransparent network communication are described in the *VAX/VMS Networking Manual*. This section assumes familiarity with transparent and nontransparent network communication.

1. EXE$ASSIGN unlocks the I/O database mutex and lowers IPL to 0. It takes these steps because it will invoke the $ASSIGN system service. This can be done only at IPL 0. When it is invoked as a result of this second $ASSIGN, it will try to lock the I/O database mutex for write access. If it did not unlock the I/O database mutex before requesting the $ASSIGN system service, the system would become deadlocked.

2. It allocates a kernel request packet (KRP). (See Chapter 3 for a description of KRPs.) It uses the KRP as the data area for logical name translation.

3. It verifies that the remote device name descriptor is accessible and the string is the proper length.

4. It translates the DEVNAM argument, as discussed in Section 18.1. This step is a repetition of the logical name translation done at the beginning of EXE$ASSIGN. It is done again because the result of the earlier translation was not saved.

   The result of this step should be a network connect block suitable for use in an outbound connection request operation. EXE$ASSIGN makes no attempt to ensure that the result of this step is in the proper format. If the result is not in the proper format, an error will be returned when the connection is attempted in the next step.

5. It invokes the $ASSIGN system service with the following items in the argument list:

   —The DEVNAM argument is the network device name, _NET.
   —The CHAN argument is a stack location to temporarily hold the assigned channel number.
   —The ACMODE argument is the ACMODE argument of the original $ASSIGN maximized with the access mode of the caller.
   —The MBXNAM argument is the same argument passed in the original $ASSIGN system service request.

6. It invokes the $QIOW system service to establish a connection to the remote device:

   —The function code is IO$_ACCESS ORed with IO$M_ACCESS.
   —The event flag is EXE$C_SYSEFN.
   —The channel number is the one returned by $ASSIGN in the previous step.
   —The network connect block is the result of translating the original DEVNAM argument.

7. It writes the channel number obtained as a result of the original $ASSIGN system service call in the word specified by the CHAN argument of the original $ASSIGN system service call.

8. The system service returns to the caller with the success status SS$_REMOTE.

18.4.3   **Deassign I/O Channel System Service**

The $DASSGN system service deassigns a previously assigned I/O channel and clears the linkage and control information in the corresponding CCB, freeing the CCB for reuse. $DASSGN has only one argument, the CHAN argument, which specifies the channel to be deassigned. The channel can be deassigned only from the same mode from which it was allocated or from a more privileged access mode.

The $DASSGN system service routine, EXE$DASSGN in module SYS-DASSGN, runs in kernel mode. It takes the following steps:

1. It invokes IOC$VERIFYCHAN (in module IOSUBPAGD). IOC$VERIFYCHAN performs the following steps:

    a. It verifies that the channel is a legal channel for the process: there must be at least one channel assigned (CTL$GW_NMIOCH is nonzero), and the channel in question must be assigned.
    b. It verifies that the channel was assigned from an access mode at least as privileged as the access mode from which it is to be deassigned (CCB$B_AMOD must be greater than or equal to the PSL previous mode field).
    c. It returns the address and the index of the CCB for the channel.

2. It invokes EXE$CANCELN with a reason code of CAN$C_DASSGN (channel is being deassigned) to cancel all outstanding I/O on the channel. EXE$CANCELN is an entry point in the $CANCEL system service routine, which is discussed in Section 18.8.

3. It invokes IOC$VERIFYCHAN again. This is because the cancel I/O operation could have activated a kernel mode AST routine that did another $DASSGN.

4. If a file is open on the channel (CCB$L_WIND is nonzero), EXE$DASSGN invokes the $QIOW system service to close the file. (The function code is IO$_DEACCESS; the event flag is number 30. Event flag 30 is used to avoid conflict with the use of event flag 31 by $CANCEL.) A network logical link appears to be a file; the $QIOW dissolves the link.

5. If any I/O is still outstanding (indicated by CCB$W_IOC being nonzero), EXE$DASSGN waits for the I/O completion ASTs to occur. (I/O completion ASTs are discussed in Section 18.7.3. Chapter 7 discusses ASTs in more detail.) This is done in one of two ways:

    —If there is a kernel mode AST pending (the AST level register is zero), EXE$DASSGN lowers IPL to 0 to allow it to be delivered. EXE$DASSGN lowers IPL by pushing the address of step 4 onto the stack and executing an REI instruction, because only the REI instruction causes AST delivery interrupts to be requested. (EXE$DASSGN pushes a PSL onto the stack as part of the check for a pending kernel mode AST.)

—If there is no kernel mode AST pending (the AST level register is non-zero), EXE$DASSGN invokes SCH$RWAIT (in module MUTEX) to place the process in an AST wait state to wait for the I/O completion ASTs to be delivered. Chapter 10 discusses wait states in detail.

6. It locks the I/O database mutex for write access.
7. It clears CCB$B_AMOD.
8. If there is an associated mailbox (CCB$V_AMB in CCB$B_STS is set), EXE$DASSGN disassociates the mailbox by taking the following steps:

   a. It clears UCB$L_AMB in the device UCB.
   b. It decrements the reference count in the mailbox UCB.
   c. If the mailbox reference count is now zero, EXE$DASSGN invokes IOC$LAST_CHAN_AMBX to perform last channel processing for an associated mailbox. Last channel processing is discussed in Section 18.4.4.

9. It decrements the reference count in the device UCB.
10. If the device reference count is now zero, EXE$DASSGN clears the device owner field, which deallocates the device. (Note that the device reference count will be zero only if the allocation was implicit, not explicit. If the allocation was explicit, the device reference count will still be non-zero.)

    Also, if the reference count is now zero and the device is cluster-available, EXE$DASSGN invokes IOC$UNLOCK_DEV to remove the device lock.
11. If the device reference count is 1 and the device has been explicitly allocated, EXE$DASSGN invokes IOC$LAST_CHAN to perform last channel processing. Last channel processing is discussed in Section 18.4.4.
12. It unlocks the I/O database mutex and exits with success status SS$_NORMAL.

18.4.4   Last Channel Processing

EXE$DASSGN performs last channel processing when the last channel to a device is deassigned. There are two circumstances under which this processing will occur:

- If the device reference count goes to zero, the device is not explicitly allocated.
- If the device reference count goes to 1 and the device allocated bit is set, the device is explicitly allocated—the one outstanding reference to the device is the explicit allocation.

Last channel processing is performed by IOC$LAST_CHAN (in module IOSUBNPAG). ICC$LAST_CHAN has two entry points, IOC$LAST_CHAN and IOC$LAST_CHAN_AMBXDGN. The latter routine is called when the device is an associated mailbox; the former routine is called in all other cases. They differ only in their initial steps:

- IOC$LAST_CHAN is called with the UCB address in R5 and the channel index in R2. The UCB address in this case is the UCB of the device assigned to the channel. IOC$LAST_CHAN loads the address of the current IRP (contained in UCB$L_IRP) in R3. It loads the reason code CAN$C_DASSGN in R8.
- IOC$LAST_CHAN_AMBXDGN is called with the UCB address in R5. The UCB in this case is the mailbox UCB, not the UCB of the device assigned to the channel. IOC$LAST_CHAN_AMBXDGN clears R2 and R3. It loads the reason code CAN$C_AMBXDGN in R8. (The channel is not assigned to the mailbox and is not needed by the mailbox driver. The current IRP is also not needed by the mailbox driver.)

At this point, IOC$LAST_CHAN and IOC$LAST_CHAN_AMBXDGN converge. The steps of this path are as follows:

1. It raises IPL to UCB$B_DIPL. This is to synchronize access to the UCB.
2. It invokes the device driver's cancel I/O routine with the registers set as indicated previously.
3. It lowers IPL to IPL$_ASTDEL. This is to prevent process deletion.
4. It tests whether the device is explicitly allocated. If it is, the routine returns to its caller.
5. The routine tests whether the device is a terminal or mailbox. If it is, the routine clears DEV$V_OPR in UCB$L_DEVCHAR, which disables the device as an operator terminal.
6. It tests whether UCB$V_DELETEUCB in UCB$L_STS is set. If this bit is set, the routine takes the following two steps:

   a. It invokes IOC$CREDIT_UCB (in module UCBCREDEL) to return the quota charged against the process's byte count and byte limit.
   b. It invokes IOC$DELETE_UCB (in module UCBCREDEL) to delete the UCB and the associated ORB.

7. The routine returns to its caller.

18.5 $QIO SYSTEM SERVICE

The $QIO[W] system service queues an I/O request to the device driver for the device associated with a channel. The $QIO system service routine, EXE$QIO in module SYSQIOREQ, runs in kernel mode. EXE$QIO performs device-independent preprocessing and, via FDT routines, device-dependent preprocessing. Once the FDT routines have completed, EXE$QIO has completed. Any additional work to be done will be performed by the device driver's start I/O routine.

$QIO has the following arguments:

- The number of the event flag to be associated with the I/O request, EFN. Since this argument is passed by value, omitting the argument is the same as specifying event flag zero.
- The number of the I/O channel, CHAN. This is the same as the CHAN argument returned by the $ASSIGN system service.
- The function code, FUNC. This identifies what operation is to be performed by the device driver. The FUNC argument is divided into two portions, the function code proper and function modifiers. In the following discussion, "function code" means just the function code proper. The term FUNC means the entire argument. EXE$QIO does not perform any processing on the function code modifiers. See the *VAX/VMS System Services Reference Manual* for a detailed description of the FUNC argument.
- The address of the I/O status block (IOSB), IOSB. The IOSB is a quadword to receive final status of the I/O operation. See the *VAX/VMS System Services Reference Manual* for a detailed description of the format of the IOSB.
- The address of an AST routine to be executed when the I/O operation completes, ASTADR.
- The AST parameter to be passed to the routine specified by the ASTADR argument, ASTPRM.
- Six optional device and function-specific parameters, P1 through P6.

The CHAN and FUNC arguments must be specified. All other arguments are optional. Any argument not specified defaults to a value of zero.

8.5.1 Device-Independent Preprocessing

EXE$QIO validates and processes all of the arguments except for arguments P1 through P6. This activity constitutes device-independent preprocessing. EXE$QIO takes the following steps to perform the device-independent preprocessing:

1. It clears the specified event flag. It takes this step so that the process will be placed into a wait state until the I/O operation completes, should the caller invoke either the Wait for Single Event Flag ($WAITFR) or Synchronize ($SYNCH) system services to wait for the I/O operation to complete.
2. It verifies that the channel number is valid and usable. The channel number is considered valid and usable if the following conditions are true:

   —The channel number is greater than zero and less than or equal to the contents of CTL$GW_CHINDX. CTL$GW_CHINDX contains the number of the highest assigned channel. Note that not all of the channels whose number is less than the contents for CTL$GW_CHINDX are necessarily currently assigned. They could have been deassigned since the channel whose number is stored in CTL$GW_CHINDX was last assigned.

—The access mode of the caller (specified by the previous mode field, PSL$V_PRVMOD, of the current PSL) is less than or equal to the access mode specified by the CCB access mode field. This ensures that the channel is used only from access modes at least as privileged as the access mode from which the channel was assigned.

3. If an access or deaccess request is pending on the channel (low bit in CCB$L_WIND is set), the process is placed in an AST wait state, to wait for the access or deaccess to complete. When the AST wait is satisfied, EXE$QIO will be restarted at the beginning. (Resource wait states are discussed in Chapter 10.)

4. It extracts the function code from the FUNC argument.

5. If the device is spooled and the function code specifies a virtual I/O function, EXE$QIO substitutes the intermediate device UCB for the UCB specified in the CCB. (The intermediate device UCB address is stored in UCB$L_AMB of the UCB specified by the CCB.)

6. It verifies the protection on the device when all of the following conditions are true:

   —The device is not file oriented.
   —The device is shareable.
   —The I/O function is a read or a write.

   If all of the previously mentioned conditions are true, EXE$QIO invokes the appropriate routine (EXE$CHKRDACCES or EXE$CHK-WRTACCES in module EXSUBROUT). If the process has the needed access, the appropriate bit (CCB$V_RDCHKDON or CCB$V_WRTCHK-DON) is set in CCB$B_STS.

   Note that EXE$QIO contains two lists of functions, one for reads and one for writes. While the interpretation of function codes is almost entirely up to the device driver, EXE$QIO does know that the "correct" interpretation of certain codes is a read or a write operation and performs access checking based on this interpretation. (In addition, EXE$QIO divides function codes into virtual, logical, and physical, and performs access checking in a later step based on this division.)

7. It verifies that the function code is a legal function by checking the legal function mask in the FDT.

8. If the device is offline, EXE$QIO ensures that the function code is either IO$_DEACCESS or IO$_ACPCONTROL.

9. If the IOSB argument is nonzero, EXE$QIO verifies that the IOSB can be written by the caller. It then clears the IOSB.

10. It uses the buffered I/O function mask in the FDT to determine if the function code specifies a direct or buffered operation.

11. It raises IPL to IPL$_ASTDEL to prevent process deletion. This step is necessary for two reasons:

    —EXE$QIO will allocate an IRP. The fact that this IRP is allocated to this process will not be reflected in any data structure until much later. If the process were to be deleted before this allocation were recorded, the IRP would become lost.

    —In steps 12 and 14, EXE$QIO indicates that this process has outstanding I/O. If the process were to be deleted after these steps, the process would become deadlocked, trying to run down nonexistent I/O.

12. It determines if the process has sufficient quota (direct or buffered, depending upon the previous determination). If the process does have sufficient quota, the quota is reduced.

    If the process does not have sufficient quota, EXE$QIO invokes EXE$SNGLQUOTA (in module EXSUBROUT) to place the process in an AST wait if the process has resource wait mode enabled.

13. It allocates an IRP. (Chapter 3 discusses IRP allocation.)

14. It increments the outstanding I/O count in the CCB.

15. It initializes the IRP. Most of this initialization is straightforward, for example, storing the EFN argument in IRP$B_EFN. There are some steps that deserve special comment:

    —If the ASTADR argument is nonzero, EXE$QIO charges the process AST quota for an AST control block (ACB). It also sets ACB$V_QUOTA in IRP$B_RMOD, to indicate that the process has been charged for the ACB.

    —If the function code specifies a buffered I/O operation, EXE$QIO sets IRP$V_BUFIO in IRP$W_STS. Otherwise, it clears the bit.

    —EXE$QIO clears the fields that describe the buffer, IRPL_SVAPTE, IRPW_BOFF, and IRP$L_BCNT.

    —If CCB$L_WIND is nonzero, the channel is associated with either a file or a process section. If the channel is associated with a file, the value in CCB$L_WIND is the address of a WCB. This address is a system space address, a negative number. EXE$QIO stores this address in IRP$L_WIND.

    If the channel is associated with a process section, the value in CCB$L_WIND is the process section index, a positive number. EXE$QIO uses the process section index as an index into the process section table (PST). This PST entry contains the address of the WCB associated with the process section. (See Chapter 14 for details on the

PST.) EXE$QIO stores the address of this WCB in IRP$L_WIND.

—If the function code is a virtual read or write to a non-file-oriented device, EXE$QIO converts the function code into the corresponding logical function code. It stores the converted function code in IRP$W_FUNC and uses the converted function code for all further checking it performs. (EXE$QIO stores the function modifiers specified in the FUNC argument in IRP$W_FUNC without change.)

16. If the device is not spooled, shareable, or file oriented, EXE$QIO does not perform any additional privilege checks. Otherwise, it verifies that the process has the necessary privilege to access the device.

17. If the request specifies a diagnostic buffer, EXE$QIO allocates the buffer and stores its address in IRP$L_DIAGBUF.

18. If the image requested an I/O completion AST, EXE$QIO verifies that the process has sufficient AST quota.

The device-independent preprocessing is complete. EXE$QIO now performs the device-dependent preprocessing.

18.5.2 FDT Routines

FDT routines are device-specific extensions to EXE$QIO. Their primary purpose is to validate the device-dependent $QIO parameters (P1 to P6). A device driver can include customized FDT routines or use some of the general purpose routines that are a part of the system image. Although FDT routines can be included in a driver image, they are logically device-dependent extensions of the $QIO system service.

FDT routines execute in the context of the process that issued the $QIO request. Therefore, they have access to data in the process's P0 and P1 address space. FDT routines communicate information about the I/O request to the driver by passing information to the driver in the IRP. FDT routines may also modify I/O database structures associated with the device assigned to the channel.

FDT routines for direct I/O (I/O done directly between a user buffer and the device) ensure that each buffer page is valid and locked into memory. (Buffer pages are locked into memory by incrementing the reference count in the PFN database for each physical page involved in the transfer. The PFN database is discussed in Chapter 14.)

FDT routines for buffered I/O operations must allocate a buffer from nonpaged pool that will be used by the driver for the actual transfer. If the operation is a buffered write, the data that is being written is copied into this buffer.

The use of system space buffers permits the device driver to access the data in the buffer from system context.

Transfers that may take a long time to complete (such as a terminal read or write) are usually buffered I/O operations. Transfers that should complete quickly (such as a disk read or write) are usually direct I/O operations.

EXE$QIO searches the FDT entries looking for a mask that specifies the function code. When such a mask is found, EXE$QIO invokes the associated FDT routine. If the FDT routine returns control to EXEQIO, EXEQIO continues its search. Successive FDT routines are called until an FDT routine invokes one of the routines that terminates FDT processing. These routines are described in the next section.

.5.3 $QIO Completion

There are a variety of circumstances under which the $QIO system service completes. This section discusses these circumstances.

.5.3.1 **Error Detected by EXE$QIO.** As discussed previously, EXE$QIO makes certain checks before it allocates an IRP; for example, the CHAN argument must specify a usable channel. If EXE$QIO detects an error before allocating an IRP, it takes the following steps:

1. It invokes SCH$POSTEF (in module POSTEF) to set the event flag specified by the EFN argument.
2. It returns to the caller with an error status in R0.

If the synchronous form of the system service was used, EXE$QIO still returns to the caller because the service has completed with error. (See Chapter 9 for more information concerning synchronous and asynchronous system services.)

EXE$QIO may detect an error after it has allocated an IRP. In this case, it will abort the I/O. EXE$QIO behaves differently in this case than in the previous case because the IRP must be deallocated.

.5.3.2 **$QIO Completion by an FDT Routine.** FDT routines complete the $QIO system service under three different circumstances:

- The request is aborted by the FDT routine.
- The request is completed by the FDT routine.
- The request must be completed by the device driver's start I/O routine.

In all three cases, the final step is to return to the system service dispatcher via a RET instruction. (This step is not listed in any of the following discussions.) The asynchronous form of the system service returns to the caller. The caller can either wait for I/O completion or continue processing. The synchronous form of the system service waits for the event flag associated with the request to be set and status to be returned. (See Chapter 9 for more information concerning synchronous and asynchronous system services.)

18.5.3.2.1   *Aborting the I/O Request.* If EXE$QIO or an FDT routine detects a device-independent error (for example, insufficient privilege), it invokes EXE$ABORTIO (in module SYSQIOREQ) to abort the I/O. Before invoking EXE$ABORTIO, EXE$QIO or the FDT routine loads the final status of the $QIO in R0. EXE$ABORTIO takes the following steps:

1. It clears IRP$L_IOSB, the address of the IOSB.
2. It clears ACB$V_QUOTA in IRP$B_RMOD and increments the process's AST quota if the bit was set.
3. It inserts the IRP in the I/O postprocessing queue and requests an IPL$_IOPOST (IPL 4) interrupt. Note that the interrupt will occur immediately. (Chapter 6 discusses software interrupts in general. Section 18.7 discusses the IPL$_IOPOST interrupt in particular.)

The effect of these steps is to finish the I/O operation without any user AST and without posting I/O status.

18.5.3.2.2   *Completing the I/O Request in the FDT Routine.* Some I/O requests can be completed by an FDT routine. There are two circumstances under which this can occur. In both cases, the driver's start I/O routine does not have to take any action. In one case, the FDT routine detects a device-specific error, for example, a buffer not properly aligned. In the second case, the FDT routine can perform all requested operations, for example, an IO$_SENSEMODE operation that returns only fields in the UCB. The FDT routine takes essentially the same action in both cases; the difference is the status it returns.

The FDT routine invokes either EXE$FINISHIO or EXE$FINISHIOC (both in module SYSQIOREQ). These are alternate entry points to the same routine.

1. EXE$FINISHIOC clears R1. It then continues as if entered at EXE$FINISHIO.
2. EXE$FINISHIO increments the operation count in the UCB (UCB$L_OPCNT).
3. It stores R0 and R1 in IRP$L_MEDIA and IRP$L_MEDIA + 4. R0 on entry to both routines contains the first longword to be stored in the IOSB. R1 on entry to EXE$FINISHIO contains the second longword to be stored in the IOSB.
4. It loads the success status SS$_NORMAL in R0. This will be the final status of the $QIO system service. Note that the final status of the I/O operation (now in the low-order word of IRP$L_MEDIA) may be a failure status.
5. It inserts the IRP in the I/O postprocessing queue and requests an IPL$_IOPOST interrupt. (Chapter 6 discusses software interrupts in general. Section 18.7 discusses the IPL$_IOPOST interrupt in particular.)

18.5.3.2.3   *Queuing the Request to the Driver's Start I/O Routine.* Most I/O requests involve device action. The device action is initiated by the driver's start I/O routine. An FDT routine passes the IRP to the start I/O routine by invoking either EXE$QIODRVPKT or EXE$ALTQUEPKT (both in module SYSQIOREQ).

EXE$QIODRVPKT is the standard method used to queue an I/O request for device activity. This routine initiates driver action only if the device unit is currently idle. If the device unit is busy, EXE$QIODRVPKT queues the request to the unit so that the device driver's start I/O routine will process it when the unit becomes available.

EXE$ALTQUEPKT initiates driver action at the driver's alternate start I/O routine entry point without regard for the device unit's activity status.

18.6   I/O COMPLETION BY A DRIVER START I/O ROUTINE

When a device driver start I/O routine completes an I/O operation, it invokes the REQCOM macro. This macro jumps to the IOC$REQCOM (in module IOSUBNPAG). IOC$REQCOM performs the following steps:

1. If there is an error log buffer (UCB$V_ERLOGIP in UCB$W_STS is set), IOC$REQCOM transfers the necessary information to the error log buffer and invokes ERL$RELEASEMB (in module ERRORLOG) to complete the error log activity for this I/O operation.
2. It increments the I/O operation count in the UCB.
3. It stores the final I/O status in IRP$L_MEDIA and IRP$L_MEDIA + 4. As is the case with IOC$FINISHIO, the status was in R0 and R1 when IOC$REQCOM was invoked.
4. If the I/O request completed with an error and the device is a disk, IOC$REQCOM checks if mount verification is pending or in progress (UCB$V_MNTVERPND or UCB$V_MNTVERIP in UCB$L_STS is set). If either bit is set, IOC$REQCOM invokes EXE$MOUNTVER (in module [SYSLOA]MOUNTVER) to start mount verification.
5. IOC$REQCOM inserts the IRP in the I/O postprocessing queue and requests an IPL$_IOPOST software interrupt.
6. If mount verification is in progress, IOC$REQCOM determines what additional action is necessary and takes it.

18.7   I/O POSTPROCESSING

VAX/VMS performs I/O postprocessing after an I/O operation has been completed by the associated driver. It consists of performing device-independent processing necessary to complete the I/O request.

18.7.1   I/O Postprocessing Routine

The I/O postprocessing routine, IOC$IOPOST (in module IOCIOPOST), is the interrupt service routine for the IPL$_IOPOST (IPL 4) software interrupt. It implements the device-independent facets of I/O completion and handles paging and swapping I/O completion as well (see Chapter 15).

Some I/O postprocessing operations (for example, unlocking buffer pages and deallocating buffers) are performed in the I/O postprocessing interrupt service routine. Other operations (such as writing the IOSB) are performed by a special kernel mode AST routine. The special kernel mode AST routine used by IOC$IOPOST is discussed in Section 18.7.5.

IOC$IOPOST removes the first IRP in the I/O postprocessing queue. It takes one of two paths, depending upon the value in IRP$L_PID. If the value in IRP$L_PID is negative (a system space address), IOC$IOPOST performs system I/O completion. If the value in IRP$L_PID is positive, IOC$IOPOST performs normal I/O completion.

18.7.2   System I/O Completion

If the value in IRP$L_PID is negative, it is the system space address of the system routine (a system completion routine) to be called when the I/O completes. IOC$IOPOST invokes the system completion routine. Upon return from the system completion routine, IOC$IOPOST removes the next IRP in the I/O postprocessing queue and processes it.

18.7.3   Normal I/O Completion

If the value in IRP$L_PID is positive, it is the process ID of the requestor. IOC$IOPOST determines if the I/O operation was buffered or direct by testing IRP$V_BUFIO in IRP$W_STS. If the bit is set, the I/O operation is a buffered one. If the bit is clear, the I/O operation is direct. IOC$IOPOST performs action appropriate to the type of I/O operation and then queues a special kernel mode AST to the requestor. The AST routine will perform the completion that must be done in the context of the requestor.

18.7.3.1   Buffered I/O Completion.
The portions of buffered I/O completion that take place in the IPL$_IOPOST interrupt service routine differ from the direct I/O case because of the differences in the way the two kinds of requests are processed. Buffered I/O involves a transfer to or from a system space buffer, rather than a per-process space buffer.

IOC$IOPOST takes the following initial steps in the case of buffered I/O:

1. It increments the process buffered I/O count (PCB$W_BIOCNT), the number of concurrent allowed buffered I/O requests.

2. If IRP$V_FILACP in IRP$W_STS is set, IOC$IOPOST also increments PCB$W_DIOCNT, the number of concurrent allowed direct I/O requests. This bit is set if the original I/O request involved an ACP that had to perform direct I/O to accomplish the original request.

3. It adds the contents of IRP$W_BOFF to JIB$L_BYTCNT. This restores the byte count quota that was allocated for the system buffer. Note that IRP$W_BOFF does not contain a buffer offset in this case; it contains a byte count.

4. It stores the address of the special kernel mode AST routine in the IRP. The address is stored at offset ACB$L_KAST because the IRP is used as the ACB for the special kernel mode AST. ACB$L_KAST and IRP$L_WIND are the same offset. At this point, the WCB address is no longer needed and that location can be reused safely.

   The special kernel mode AST routine (in module IOCIOPOST) has two entry points: BUFPOST for buffered read completion and DIRPOST for direct read, direct write, and buffered write completion. The first case differs from the other cases in that data must be copied from the system buffer to the process buffer before the process is informed that the I/O is complete. In the case of a buffered write, there is no need to copy data between the process buffer and the system buffer. It was copied from the process buffer to the system buffer by an FDT routine. In the case of direct I/O, there is no system buffer.

   It is possible that there was no need for a system buffer (I/O requests that do not involve the transfer of data are usually buffered I/O requests, not direct I/O requests). If one was needed, its address is in IRP$L_SVAPTE.

   —If IRP$L_SVAPTE is nonzero and IRP$V_FUNC in IRP$W_STS is set, the I/O function is a read requiring a buffer. In this case, IOC$IOPOST stores the address of BUFPOST in ACB$L_KAST.

   —Otherwise, IOC$IOPOST stores the address of DIRPOST in ACB$L_KAST. If IRP$L_SVAPTE is nonzero, IOC$IOPOST deallocates the buffer.

5. It performs the steps described in Section 18.7.3.3.

18.7.3.2   **Direct I/O Completion.** The portions of direct I/O completion that take place in the IPL$_IOPOST interrupt service routine differ from the buffered I/O case because of the differences in the way the two kinds of requests are processed. Direct I/O requests involve the transfer of data directly to or from the process buffer; system buffers are not used. Unlike system buffers, process buffers can be paged. Since paging must not occur during the processing of the I/O request, the pages are locked in memory by one of the FDT routines invoked by EXE$QIO.

Paging and swapping I/O requests are direct I/O requests. IOC$IOPOST takes special steps in the interrupt service routine when the I/O request is a paging or swapping I/O request. Paging and swapping I/O requests are discussed in Chapter 15.

IOC$IOPOST takes the following initial steps for direct I/O other than paging and swapping I/O:

1. It increments PCB$W_DIOCNT, the number of concurrent allowed direct I/O requests.
2. It performs the steps necessary to handle segmented transfers, if needed. Segmented transfers are described in Section 18.7.4.
3. It unlocks the buffer pointed to by IRP$L_SVAPTE, using the IRP$L_BCNT and IRP$W_BOFF fields to determine the size of the locked buffer. It unlocks the pages by invoking MMG$UNLOCK (in module IOLOCK), which decrements the pages' associated reference counts in the PFN database. (The PFN database is discussed in Chapters 14 and 15.) This step may result in the pages being placed on the free or modified page list.
4. If an IRP extension (IRPE) is present (IRP$V_EXTEND in IRP$W_STS is set), IOC$IOPOST unlocks any buffers described by the IRPE. (The address of the IRPE is in IRP$L_EXTEND.) Each IRPE may describe up to two locked buffers (pointed to by IRPE$L_SVAPTE1 and IRPE$L_SVAPTE2, with sizes determined by IRPE$W_BOFF1 and IRPE$L_BCNT1, and IRPE$W_BOFF2 and IRPE$L_BCNT2). IOC$IOPOST then determines if IRPE$V_EXTEND in IRPE$W_STS in the IRPE is set. If so, it repeats this step until the last IRPE in the linked list is found and all buffers described by the IRPEs are unlocked.
5. It stores the address of DIRPOST in ACB$L_KAST.
6. It performs the steps described in Section 18.7.3.3.

18.7.3.3   **Final Steps in IOC$IOPOST.** IOC$IOPOST performs the same final steps for both buffered and direct I/O requests. After completing these steps, it attempts to remove another IRP from the I/O postprocessing queue. If it is successful, it processes that IRP. Otherwise, it executes an REI instruction to exit the interrupt service routine.

If the event flag to be set upon completion of the I/O request is a local event flag, IOC$IOPOST invokes SCH$POSTEF to set the flag. It does not set the event flag if the event flag is common to avoid a race condition. If the event flag is common, some other process could be in a common event flag wait state that would be satisfied by setting the event flag associated with this request. In that case, it is possible that the other process would be scheduled to run before completion status is posted to the process that invoked the $QIO system service. (Event flags are discussed in Chapter 12. Process scheduling is discussed in Chapter 10.)

A similar race condition is possible in a multiprocessor system. In this case, the event flag could be either local or common. The race condition is that it is possible for the requestor to be scheduled before the special kernel mode AST is queued. Since IOC$IOPOST does not set a common event flag at this point, it avoids the race condition in the case of common event flags. It avoids the race condition in the case of local event flags by always raising IPL to IPL$_SYNCH (IPL 8) before setting the local event flag and not lowering IPL until after the special kernel mode AST is queued. Although this raising of IPL is not needed if the system is not a multiprocessor system, IOC$IOPOST always raises IPL to IPL$_SYNCH to block rescheduling before setting the event flag.

IOC$IOPOST sets ACB$V_KAST in IRP$B_RMOD (to indicate that this is a special kernel mode AST) and invokes SCH$QAST (in module ASTDEL) to queue the AST to the process (using the IRP$L_PID field to identify the process to which the AST should be queued). The IRP is used as the ACB for SCH$QAST (as described in Chapter 7). Note that the size of the ACB in this case is the size of the IRP. Except for ACBL_KAST, IOCIOPOST has not changed any fields in the IRP/ACB.

18.7.4   Segmented Virtual and Logical I/O

When an image issues a read or write virtual I/O request for a file on a block-structured device, the image must specify a starting virtual block number (VBN) and the number of virtually contiguous bytes to be transferred. Since the device driver requires LBNs, the I/O subsystem must convert the VBNs into the related LBNs. The conversion is performed in at least one, and possibly two, places: an FDT routine and IOC$IOPOST. In either case, the same basic steps are taken.

When an image issues a read or write logical I/O request for a file on a block-structured device, the image must specify a starting logical block number and the number of logically contiguous bytes to be transferred. If the size of the transfer is greater than 64K bytes, the steps described in Section 18.7.4.3 must be taken.

18.7.4.1   Common Virtual and Logical I/O FDT Processing.
Usually, the device driver specifies the following FDT routines: ACP$READBLK for virtual and logical reads, and ACP$WRITEBLK for virtual and logical writes (both routines are in module SYSACPFDT). These routines store the total byte count of the request in the original byte count field of the IRP (IRP$L_OBCNT) and set the accumulated byte count field of the IRP (IRP$L_ABCNT) to zero. If the transfer is a virtual I/O transfer, these routines then invoke IOC$MAPVBLK (in module IOSUBRAMS) to perform the actual conversion from VBNs to LBNs.

In the case of virtual I/O, the FDT routines take the steps necessary to handle transfers greater than 64K bytes if IOC$MAPVBLK is successful. (If IOC$MAPVBLK is unsuccessful, the FDT routines take the steps discussed in the next section.)

In the case of logical I/O, the FDT routines always take the steps necessary to handle transfers greater than 64K bytes.

The routines then queue the IRP to the driver. The driver performs the transfer without regard for whether the entire range is to be transferred. IOC$IOPOST will check whether the entire range has been transferred when the driver completes the I/O request and take the necessary action.

18.7.4.2   **Virtual I/O FDT Processing.** IOC$MAPVBLK uses the information passed (via registers and the IRP) to convert the VBNs to LBNs. The goal is to convert the starting VBN to the related LBN. The gating factor is the information stored in the WCB (the address of the WCB is passed by the caller) that was created by an ACP when the file was opened.

If the WCB contains enough mapping information to convert the entire virtual range of the transfer into corresponding LBNs on the volume, then the virtual I/O transfer will be handled directly by the driver and IOC$IOPOST, even if the transfer consists of several logically noncontiguous pieces. If the WCB does not contain enough information to completely map the virtual range of the transfer, the intervention of an ACP will be required at some time to complete the transfer. This intervention is known as a window turn. (The number of window turns per unit of time can be displayed by the Monitor Utility with the DCL command MONITOR FCP.)

Because a deadlock situation could occur if a file mapped by the memory management subsystem requires a window turn, the memory management subsystem must avoid window turns. To do this, each file mapped by the memory management subsystem must have all its mapping information in the WCB. This large WCB is called a cathedral window. The format of a WCB is discussed in Section 18.2.3.1.

IOC$MAPVBLK can encounter five possible cases:

• The virtual range is logically contiguous and the needed mapping information is contained in the WCB. In this case, all that IOC$MAPVBLK needs to do is convert the starting VBN into the related LBN. The driver can transfer the data without further conversion of VBNs into LBNs.

• The WCB contains mapping information for the beginning of the virtual range, but more than two map entries are required to map the range. In this case, IOC$MAPVBLK converts the starting VBN into the related LBN. The driver can transfer the start of the virtual range, but will need further conversion of VBNs into LBNs to transfer the rest of the range.

IOC$MAPVBLK uses only the map entry that maps the starting VBN and the next map entry (if that map entry is logically contiguous with its predecessor). Since the field in the map entry that contains the count of blocks covered by the entry is a word in size, it is possible that a logically contiguous range will require more than one map entry to cover the entire logical range.

- The WCB contains mapping information for the beginning of the virtual range, but not for the entire virtual range. In this case, IOC$MAPVBLK converts the starting VBN into the related LBN. The driver can transfer the start of the virtual range, but will need further conversion of VBNs into LBNs to transfer the rest of the range.

  In this case, the virtual range may be logically contiguous, but not enough mapping information is contained in the WCB to verify this. A window turn will be needed later.

- The virtual range is not logically contiguous, but the WCB does contain mapping information for the beginning of the virtual range. IOC$-MAPVBLK handles this case in the same way it handles the previous case.

  The driver can transfer the start of the virtual range, but will need further conversion of VBNs into LBNs to transfer the rest of the range. The WCB may or may not contain the needed information. If it does not, a window turn will be needed. Whether a window turn will be needed later is irrelevant at this point.

- The mapping information that maps the first virtual block in the range to its logical counterpart is not in the WCB. A window turn is needed before any data can be transferred.

In all five cases, IOC$MAPVBLK returns the number of bytes not mapped. In the first four cases, the FDT routines take the following steps:

1. They compute the number of bytes mapped (by subtracting the number of bytes not mapped from IRP$L_OBCNT) and store this number in IRP$L_BCNT.
2. They store the starting LBN in IRP$L_MEDIA.
3. They store the starting VBN in IRP$L_SEGVBN.

The routines then queue the IRP to the driver. The driver performs the transfer without regard for whether the entire virtual range has been mapped. IOC$IOPOST will check whether the entire virtual range has been mapped when the driver completes the I/O request and take the necessary action.

In the fifth case, the FDT routines store the starting VBN in IRP$L_SEGVBN, the number of bytes not mapped (in this case, the total number of bytes requested) in IRP$L_BCNT, and then invoke EXE$QIOACPPKT (in module SYSQIOREQ) to send the IRP to the ACP.

When the ACP processes this IRP, it detects that the WCB does not map the requested virtual range and performs a window turn. It reads the file header to obtain the mapping information necessary for the transfer in question and stores the information in the WCB, replacing other mapping information already contained there. The ACP then performs the equivalent steps that IOC$MAPVBLK performs in the first four cases and queues the IRP to the driver.

18.7.4.3 **Transfers Greater Than 64K Bytes.** VMS supports virtual and logical I/O transfers greater than 64K bytes for disk devices, even though a device and its driver may only support transfers up to 64K bytes. This is done using the UCB$L_MAXBCNT field. This field contains the largest transfer size supported by the driver. If it is zero, it is assumed to be 65024 (64K bytes minus 512).

There are two cases in which a request for a logical I/O transfer greater than 64K bytes can arise:

- A virtual I/O transfer request is made. As described earlier, the FDT routines ACP$READBLK and ACP$WRITEBLK convert the request into a logical I/O transfer request.
- A logical I/O transfer request is made by the image.

The two FDT routines handle the two cases identically once the virtual I/O request has been turned into a logical I/O request. If the IRP$L_BCNT is greater than the maximum transfer size specified by UCB$L_MAXBCNT, the FDT routines set IRP$L_BCNT to the maximum transfer size accepted by the driver. Otherwise, they do not modify IRP$L_BCNT.

18.7.4.4 **IOC$IOPOST Processing.** Whenever IOC$IOPOST encounters an IRP for a direct I/O data transfer request, it determines if the data transfer request requires only one transfer by comparing the original byte count to the number of bytes just transferred (IRP$L_IOST + 2). If the difference is not zero, the request cannot be completed in one transfer. In this case, the accumulated byte count is incremented by the number of bytes just transferred. The accumulated byte count is then compared with the original byte count. If the two numbers agree, the request is completed exactly like other direct I/O requests.

If the two numbers do not agree, IOC$IOPOST prepares the IRP for the transfer of the next segment by taking the following steps:

1. It places the lesser of the remaining byte count and the maximum transfer size accepted by the driver in IRP$L_BCNT.
2. It updates the starting VBN in IRP$L_SEGVBN by the number of blocks transferred in the last transfer.
3. If the transfer is a virtual I/O transfer, IOC$IOPOST invokes IOC$MAPVBLK.

The same five cases exist here as do when IOC$MAPVBLK is invoked by the FDT routines. IOC$IOPOST takes the equivalent steps in each case for the transfer that starts at the VBN in IRP$L_SEGVBN.

4. If the transfer is a logical I/O transfer, IOC$IOPOST queues the IRP to the driver.

Thus, in a fashion transparent to the requestor, the original request is divided into several requests to satisfy the limitations of the WCB and/or maximum transfer size permitted by the device.

8.7.5   I/O Completion Special Kernel Mode AST Routine

The I/O completion special kernel mode AST routine has two entry points: BUFPOST and DIRPOST. BUFPOST performs certain steps unique to buffered read completion and then falls into DIRPOST.

8.7.5.1

Buffered Read Completion. BUFPOST copies data from the system buffer to the user buffer in per-process address space and deallocates the system buffer to nonpaged pool. If the I/O request was a mailbox read (IRP$V_MBXIO set in IRP$W_STS), BUFPOST invokes SCH$RAVAIL (in module MUTEX) to declare the mailbox resource (RSN$_MAILBOX) available in case a process is waiting for this resource. (Resources are discussed in Chapter 10.)

8.7.5.2

Common Completion. DIRPOST performs the completion common to buffered and direct I/O requests:

1. It increments either PHD$L_DIOCNT or PHD$L_BIOCNT, the process's cumulative totals of completed direct I/O and buffered I/O requests.
2. If a user's diagnostic buffer was associated with the I/O request, DIRPOST copies the diagnostic information from the system diagnostic buffer to the user's diagnostic buffer and deallocates the system diagnostic buffer.
3. It decrements the CCB count of I/O requests in progress on this channel.
4. If this was the last I/O for the channel and there is a deaccess request for the channel pending, DIRPOST queues that deaccess request to the ACP by invoking IOC$WAKACP (in module IOC$IOPOST).
5. If a common event flag is associated with the I/O request, DIRPOST invokes SCH$POSTEF to set the flag.
6. If the I/O request specified an IOSB, DIRPOST copies the quadword at IRP$L_MEDIA to the IOSB.
7. If any IRPEs were used, it deallocates them.
8. If ACB$V_QUOTA is set in IRP$B_RMOD, then the user requested AST notification of I/O completion. The AST procedure address and the op-

tional AST argument were originally stored in the IRP (now an ACB). DIRPOST invokes SCH$QAST to queue the IRP as an ACB, this time for a normal AST in the access mode at which the I/O request was made.

9. Otherwise, if ACB$V_QUOTA is clear, DIRPOST deallocates the IRP/ACB to nonpaged pool.

10. It returns to its caller (SCH$ASTDEL in module ASTDEL).

18.8   CANCEL I/O ON CHANNEL SYSTEM SERVICE

The $CANCEL system service cancels all pending I/O requests on a specified channel. In general, this includes all I/O requests that are queued as well as the request currently in progress. The $CANCEL system service may be invoked by an image. It is also invoked by the $DASSGN system service. The $CANCEL system service routine, EXE$CANCEL in module SYSCANCEL, runs in kernel mode. The $CANCEL system service has only the CHAN argument, which specifies the I/O channel on which I/O is to be canceled.

There is a second form of the $CANCEL system service that can be invoked only by calling the system service routine directly at an alternate entry point, EXE$CANCELN. When called at this entry point, the system service has two arguments:

- The CHAN argument
- The optional CODE argument, the reason for the cancellation.

EXE$CANCELN determines if the CODE argument is present. If it is present, the routine saves it for later use. If the CODE argument is not present, the routine saves a reason code of CAN$C_CANCEL. EXE$CANCEL, on the other hand, always saves a reason code of CAN$C_CANCEL. Once the reason code has been saved, EXE$CANCEL and EXE$CANCELN take the same steps:

1. It invokes IOC$VERIFYCHAN to verify the channel. (IOC$VERIFYCHAN is discussed in Section 18.4.3.)

2. It page faults the CCB into memory, raising IPL to UCB$B_FIPL. The CCB is effectively locked into memory.

3. It then searches the IRPs queued to the UCB (starting at UCB$L_IOQFL), looking for IRPs that meet the following criteria:

   —The request is not a virtual request (IRP$V_VIRTUAL in IRP$W_STS is clear). In general, I/O cannot be canceled on disk or tape devices. Drivers for these devices ensure that IRP$V_VIRTUAL is set on all requests that cannot be canceled.

   —The requesting process ID (PCB$L_PID) matches the process ID in IRP$L_PID.

   —The channel number in IRP$W_CHAN matches the channel specified by the CHAN argument. (Note that the CHAN argument specifies the channel number. IOC$VERIFYCHAN converted that value to the associated channel index. It is the latter value that must match the value in IRP$W_CHAN.)

When an IRP that satisfies these criteria is found, EXE$CANCEL takes the following steps and then resumes the search:

a. It clears the buffered read bit (IRP$V_FUNC in IRP$W_STS) for buffered I/O functions.
b. It places the error status SS$_CANCEL in the low-order word of IRP$L_MEDIA and clears the high-order word. This field is used to return the final status of the I/O operation.
c. It inserts the IRP at the tail of the I/O postprocessing queue and requests an IPL$_IOPOST interrupt. The IPL$_IOPOST interrupt service routine is discussed in Section 18.7.

4. When all IRPs meeting these criteria have been found and processed, EXE$CANCEL invokes the driver cancel I/O routine (the address of this routine is stored in DDT$L_CANCEL in the driver's DPT). The driver is passed the cancel reason saved at the start of EXE$CANCEL or EXE$CANCELN. The driver should perform any actions appropriate to canceling I/O.

   Some driver cancel I/O routines will execute a RET instruction if an error occurs. If the driver cancel I/O routine invoked in this step does this and an error occurs, control does not return to EXE$CANCEL but to the routine that called EXE$CANCEL.

5. If the device is a disk, EXE$CANCEL lowers IPL to 0, and returns to the caller with the success status SS$_NORMAL. (As noted in step 11, the ACP control function issued in step 11 is applicable only to the magnetic tape ACP.)

6. If there is no outstanding I/O (CCB$W_IOC is zero) and there is no file activity (CCB$L_WIND is zero), EXE$CANCEL lowers IPL to 0 and returns to the caller with the success status SS$_NORMAL. (If there is file activity, then CCB$L_WIND contains the address of the WCB associated with the channel or a process section index. At this point, the distinction is not significant.)

7. If the device is not mounted or is mounted foreign, EXE$CANCEL lowers IPL to 0 and returns to the caller with the success status SS$_NORMAL.

8. If there is a process section associated with the channel, EXE$CANCEL lowers IPL to 0 and returns to the caller with the success status SS$_NORMAL.

9. At this point, EXE$CANCEL has determined that there is a file open

on this channel. If WCB$V_NOTFCP in WCB$B_ACCESS is set, EXE$CANCEL lowers IPL to 0 and returns to the caller with the success status SS$_NORMAL.

The WCB$V_NOTFCP bit identifies files that were opened during the system startup process before the XQP was available by special routines that exist only during the system startup process. The files associated with these WCBs are not served by any ACP or by the XQP.

10. At this point, EXE$CANCEL has determined that there is a user file open on the channel. It attempts to issue an IO$_ACPCONTROL function. If it cannot allocate an IRP, it does one of two things:

—If the process does not have resource wait mode enabled, it lowers IPL to 0 and returns to the caller. The status indicates the reason that EXE$CANCEL could not allocate an IRP.

—If the process does have resource wait mode enabled, EXE$CANCEL invokes SCH$RWAIT to place the process in an RSN$_NPDYNMEM wait.

11. It initializes the IRP as follows:

   a. The process ID of the requestor is set to the value in PCB$L_PID.
   b. The AST routine address and parameter are cleared (no user AST).
   c. The WCB address is set to the value in CCB$L_WIND.
   d. The UCB address is stored in IRP$L_UCB.
   e. The function code is set to IO$_ACPCONTROL.
   f. The event flag is set to EXE$C_SYSEFN.
   g. The priority is set to the value in PCB$B_PRIB (the process's base priority).
   h. The IOSB address is set to zero.
   i. The channel number is stored in IRP$W_CHAN.
   j. The I/O is marked as buffered I/O with no buffer.
   k. The access rights block address is set to the value in PCB$L_ARB.

This ACP control function is special by virtue of there being no I/O buffer. It is ignored by disk ACPs and the XQP. It is recognized by the magnetic tape ACP as a special I/O abort function (equivalent to calling the driver's cancel I/O routine) which causes the ACP to abort the mounting of a multivolume tape file.

12. It charges the user's buffered I/O quota, PCB$W_BIOCNT, for an I/O request.

13. It invokes EXE$QIOACPPKT to queue the packet to the ACP. (EXE$QIOACPPKT will execute a RET instruction, returning control to the caller of the system service.)

18.9 **MAILBOX CREATION AND DELETION**

Mailboxes are virtual devices used for interprocess communication. They are created by the $CREMBX system service. There are two kinds of mailboxes, temporary and permanent. Temporary mailboxes are deleted automatically when no more processes have channels assigned to them. Permanent mailboxes must be explicitly marked for deletion using the Delete Mailbox ($DELMBX) system service. (After being marked for deletion, permanent mailboxes are deleted when no more processes have channels assigned to them.)

18.9.1 **Create Mailbox and Assign Channel System Service**

The $CREMBX system service routine, EXE$CREMBX in module SYS-MAILBX, runs in kernel mode. It creates a virtual mailbox device named MBA*n* and assigns an I/O channel to it. $CREMBX has seven arguments:

- A flag specifying whether the mailbox is to be permanent or temporary, PRMFLG
- The address of a word into which to write the channel number assigned to the mailbox by EXE$CREMBX, CHAN
- The maximum size of a message that can be sent to the mailbox, MAXMSG
- The number of bytes of nonpaged pool that can be used to buffer messages sent to the mailbox, BUFQUO
- The protection mask to be associated with the created mailbox, PROMSK
- The access mode to be associated with the channel to which the mailbox is assigned, ACMODE
- The logical name to be assigned to the mailbox, LOGNAM

The CHAN argument is required; all others are optional.

EXE$CREMBX takes the following initial steps for local and shared memory mailboxes:

1. It verifies that the CHAN argument is write accessible.
2. It performs logical name translation of the LOGNAM argument if that argument is specified. EXE$CREMBX invokes MMG$MBXTRNLOG (in module SHMGSDRTN) to attempt the translation, as discussed in Section 18.1. MMG$MBXTRNLOG returns two strings:

   —The first string is the name of the shared memory in which the mailbox resides (or will reside if the mailbox does not yet exist). If the LOGNAM argument did not specify a shared memory mailbox, this string is null.
   —The second string is the physical name of the mailbox (MBA*n*).

3. It invokes IOC$FFCHAN to find a free CCB. (IOC$FFCHAN is discussed in Section 18.4.2.1.)

4. It locks the I/O database mutex for write access.

5. It determines if the mailbox is a local mailbox or a shared memory mailbox by examining the LOGNAM argument and the two strings returned by MMG$MBXTRNLOG. If the LOGNAM argument was omitted, or if the LOGNAM argument was not omitted and MMG$MBXTRNLOG returned a null shared memory name, the mailbox is a local mailbox. Otherwise, the mailbox is a shared memory mailbox. (The *VAX/VMS System Services Reference Manual* discusses the format of logical names for shared memory objects, including mailboxes.)

The rest of the steps EXE$CREMBX takes in the case of a local mailbox are similar to those it takes in the case of a shared memory mailbox. Section 18.9.1.1 discusses the steps taken for local mailbox creation. Section 18.9.1.2 discusses the special considerations that apply to shared memory mailboxes.

18.9.1.1   **Mailbox Creation in Local Memory.** Permanent local mailboxes must be named; temporary local mailboxes can be either named or unnamed. EXE$CREMBX determines which type of local mailbox (named or unnamed) is specified by the presence or absence of the LOGNAM argument. (Note that the LOGNAM argument cannot specify a null string.)

EXE$CREMBX tests whether the process has the necessary privilege: TMPMBX for a temporary mailbox, PRMMBX for a permanent mailbox. In the case of a temporary mailbox, the mailbox will have to be created. Thus, EXE$CREMBX is not premature in checking for privilege. In the case of a permanent mailbox, EXE$CREMBX is premature in checking for privilege in that the mailbox may already exist. This means that $CREMBX can be used to assign a channel to an existing permanent mailbox only if the process has PRMMBX privilege. $CREMBX cannot be used to assign a channel to an existing temporary mailbox.

If a logical name has been specified, EXE$CREMBX invokes the Translate Logical Name ($TRNLNM) system service to obtain the address of the mailbox UCB. It passes the following arguments to $TRNLNM:

• The logical name specified by the LOGNAM argument
• An item-list element requesting the back pointer

If the logical name exists, EXE$CREMBX verifies that the back pointer returned by $TRNLNM points to a UCB. The only UCBs that should be pointed to by a logical name back pointer are mailbox UCBs.

If the mailbox exists and the process has the privilege to access the mailbox or owns the mailbox, EXE$CREMBX increments the reference count for that mailbox and assigns a channel to the mailbox by taking the following steps:

1. It stores the mailbox UCB address in CCB$L_UCB.
2. It stores the access mode at which the channel was assigned (plus 1) in

CCB$B_AMOD. As usual, the access mode at which the channel is assigned is the less privileged of the access mode specified by the ACMODE argument and the access mode of the caller.

EXE$CREMBX stores the channel number in the address specified by the CHAN argument and returns to the caller with the success status SS$_ NORMAL.

If the mailbox did not previously exist, EXE$CREMBX must create it. If the mailbox to be created is a temporary mailbox, EXE$CREMBX invokes IOC$CHKMBXQUOTA (in module UCBCREDEL) to determine if the process buffered I/O byte count quota (JIB$L_BYTCNT) is at least the sum of the following:

- The size of a mailbox UCB.
- The overhead to allow for process deletion (256 bytes).
- The space to buffer mailbox messages, the buffer quota. (This value is the BUFQUO argument if the argument was specified or the SYSBOOT parameter DEFMBXBUFQUO if the BUFQUO argument is absent.)

EXE$CREMBX invokes IOC$CLONE_UCB to clone the UCB for MBA0:. EXE$CREMBX initializes the cloned UCB as follows:

1. It stores the buffer quota in the buffer quota and initial buffer quota fields, UCB$W_BUFQUO and UCB$W_INIQUO.
2. It clears the owner field.
3. It modifies the ORB associated with the UCB to specify the system, owner, group, and world format protection mask, and stores the PROMASK argument in ORB$W_PROT.
4. It stores the current process's UIC in the ORB owner UIC field.
5. It stores the maximum message size in the UCB device buffer size field. This value is the MAXMSG argument, if the argument is specified; otherwise, it is the SYSBOOT parameter DEFMBXMXMSG.
6. It clears the current message count, UCB$L_DEVDEPND.
7. It stores the sum of the UCB size, the buffer byte count quota, and the overhead for process deletion in UCB$W_CHARGE.
8. If the mailbox is permanent, EXE$CREMBX sets UCB$V_PRMMBX in UCB$L_DEVSTS.
9. If the mailbox is temporary, EXE$CREMBX takes the following two steps:

   a. It sets UCB$V_DELMBX in UCB$L_DEVSTS. This marks the mailbox for deletion on last channel deassign.
   b. It invokes IOC$DEBIT_UCB (in module UCBCREDEL) to reduce the process's byte count quota (JIB$L_BYTCNT) and byte limit (JIB$L_ BYTLM) by the value stored in UCB$W_CHARGE.

If the LOGNAM argument was omitted, EXE$CREMBX clears the pointer in

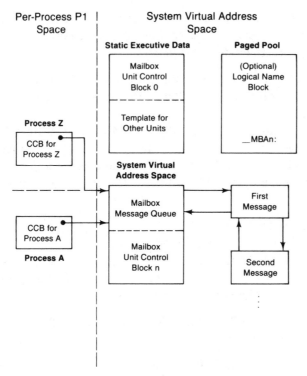

Figure 18-3   Data Structures Associated with Mailbox
Creation

the UCB to the logical name (UCB$L_LOGADR). Otherwise, EXE$CREMBX
invokes the Create Logical Name ($CRELNM) system service to create the
logical name specified by the LOGNAM argument. $CRELNM stores the ad-
dress of the logical name in UCB$L_LOGADR. Finally, EXE$CREMBX assigns a channel in the same way as if the mailbox had already existed. The
relationships among the data structures associated with mailbox creation are
pictured in Figure 18-3.

In VAX/VMS Version 4.4, the behavior just described was changed. If the
logical name is located in a process-private table, $CRELNM clears
UCB$L_LOGADR. As a result, the logical name is not deleted when the
mailbox is deleted. This change only applies when one of the table names,
such as LNM$TEMPORARY_MAILBOX or LNM$JOB, is redirected to a
process-private table, such as LNM$PROCESS_TABLE.

18.9.1.2   **Mailbox Creation in Shared Memory.** Although the format of a shared memory mailbox UCB is somewhat different from a local memory mailbox UCB,
EXE$CREMBX takes the same general steps in the case of a shared memory
mailbox as for a local memory mailbox when the LOGNAM is specified. (The
caller of $CREMBX must specify a logical name if the mailbox is a shared

memory mailbox.) This section discusses the special considerations for shared memory mailboxes.

EXE$CREMBX tests whether the caller has SHMEM privilege. The caller must also have either TMPMBX or PRMMBX privilege. Which privilege depends on whether the caller specified that the mailbox is to be permanent or temporary via the PRMFLG argument. Shared memory mailboxes are always permanent, regardless of the value of the PRMFLG argument.

One extra level of data structure is required to describe a shared memory mailbox. This structure, called a shared memory mailbox control block (Figure 18-4), is located in the shared memory. The UCBs on each port associated with the shared memory mailbox contain the (processor-specific) virtual address of the mailbox. There are three cases that EXE$CREMBX can encounter when creating a mailbox in shared memory:

• If the shared memory mailbox control block does not exist (if the mailbox does not already exist on any processor), EXE$CREMBX creates it before creating the mailbox UCB in local memory. It then creates the logical

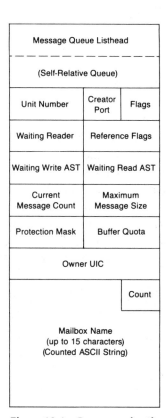

Figure 18-4   Contents of a Shared Memory Mailbox Control Block

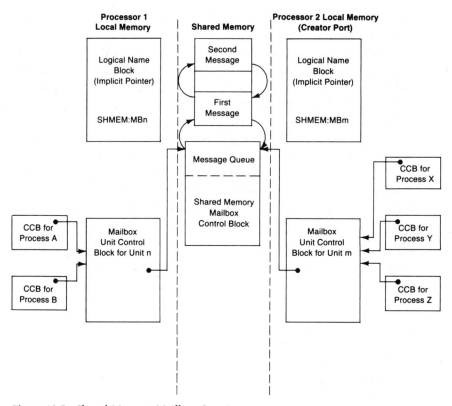

Figure 18-5   Shared Memory Mailbox Creation

name, because shared memory structures always have a logical name associated with them. Finally, it assigns a channel for the creating process.

- If the mailbox is being created on this processor for the first time (but already exists on another processor), EXE$CREMBX invokes IOC$CLONE_UCB to clone the template UCB for the shared memory unit. It sets UCB$V_SHMMBX in UCB$W_DEVSTS, indicating that this mailbox UCB describes a mailbox in shared memory. Finally, it stores the address of the shared memory mailbox control block in UCB$L_MB_MBX.

- If the mailbox already exists on this processor, EXE$CREMBX assigns a channel to it.

The data structures required to describe a shared memory mailbox are pictured in Figure 18-5.

18.9.2   Mailbox Deletion

The $DELMBX system service, EXE$DELMBX in module SYSMAILBX, marks a mailbox for deletion. Invoking $DELMBX to mark a temporary mailbox for deletion is superfluous. The mailbox is actually deleted by IOC$DELETE_UCB when its reference count goes to zero (after the last channel assigned to it has been deassigned). The mailbox driver, MBDRIVER (in module MBDRIVER), will delete the logical name, if any, as part of the last channel processing. See Section 18.4.4 for a discussion of last channel processing.

The $DELMBX system service has only one argument: CHAN, the number of the channel assigned to the mailbox to be deleted.

EXE$DELMBX invokes IOC$VERIFYCHAN to verify the channel number and get the address of the CCB. Once it has located the CCB, EXE$DELMBX gets the UCB address from CCB$L_UCB and then verifies the following:

- That the UCB is a mailbox (DEV$V_MBX in UCB$L_DEVCHAR is set)
- That, if the mailbox is a permanent mailbox, the process has PRMMBX privilege

If these conditions are met, EXE$DELMBX marks the mailbox for deletion by setting bit UCB$V_DELMBX in UCB$W_DEVSTS.

8.10   BREAKTHROUGH SYSTEM SERVICE

The Breakthrough ($BRKTHRU[W]) system service sends a message to one or more terminals, even if an I/O operation is currently in progress on the terminal. There are eleven arguments to $BRKTHRU. All of the arguments except MSGBUF are optional.

- The number of the event flag to be set when the message has been written to the specified terminals, EFN
- The message buffer containing the text to be written, MSGBUF
- The name of the terminal or user name to which to send the text, SENDTO
- The type of terminal to which to send the message, SNDTYP
- The address of an IOSB that will receive the I/O completion status of the $BRKTHRU system service, IOSB
- The carriage control to be used with the message, CARCON
- Options for the $BRKTHRU system service, FLAGS
- The class requestor identification, which identifies the application or image that is requesting the $BRKTHRU system service, REQID
- The number of seconds that must elapse before an attempted write by the $BRKTHRU system service is considered to have failed, TIMOUT
- The address of the AST routine to be executed after the message has been sent to the specified terminals, ASTADR
- The AST parameter to be passed to the AST routine specified by the ASTADR argument, ASTPRM

The $BRKTHRU system service routine, EXE$BRKTHRU in module

SYSBRKTHR, runs in kernel mode. It takes three major steps:

1. It allocates and initializes a breakthrough message descriptor block (BRK) for the request and stores the formatted message in the BRK. This step is discussed in Section 18.10.1. (See Figure 18-6 for the format of a BRK.)
2. It initiates a write to a given terminal. This step is discussed in Section 18.10.2.
3. It responds to the completion of a given write. This step is discussed in Section 18.10.3.

There are two messages sent by EXE$BRKTHRU. One message is the text specified by the MSGBUF argument, the unformatted message. The other message is the message to be sent to video terminals, the screen message. The screen message consists of the following fields:

- An escape sequence to save the cursor position and attributes.
- An escape sequence to position the cursor in column 1 of the correct line.
- An escape sequence to erase to the end of the line.
- One or more escape sequences to erase lines. The number of lines (and thus the number of escape sequences) is specified by the low byte of the FLAGS argument.
- The text specified by the MSGBUF argument.
- An escape sequence to restore the cursor position and attributes.

18.10.1 Initial Processing

EXE$BRKTHRU begins by clearing the event flag specified by the EFN argument. Since the EFN argument is passed by value, it defaults to zero. If an IOSB is specified, EXE$BRKTHRU verifies that the caller has write access to the IOSB and clears the IOSB. It takes these steps so that the caller will wait until the system service completes, should the caller invoke either the $WAITFR or $SYNCH system services to wait for the $BRKTHRU system service to complete.

It invokes EXE$PROBER_DSC (in module EXSUBROUT) to verify the accessibility of the message buffer specified by the MSGBUF argument.

It computes the size of the breakthrough message descriptor block needed for the current request. The size of the BRK is the sum of the following items, rounded up to an integral number of longwords:

- The basic size (BRK$C_LENGTH) of the BRK
- Space for the name of the terminal to which to send the mailbox message (16 bytes)
- The size of the unformatted message
- Space for the screen message (208 bytes plus the size of the unformatted message)

- Space for four QIO context areas

It invokes EXE$ALOP1IMAG (in module MEMORYALC) to allocate space from the process allocation region in P1 space for the BRK, and initializes the BRK as follows:

1. It clears the BRK from BRK$Q_PRIVS up to BRK$T_MSGBUF.
2. It stores the size of the BRK in BRK$W_SIZE.
3. It stores the address of the QIO context area in BRK$L_QIOCTX.
4. It stores the length of the screen message in BRK$L_SCRMSGLEN.
5. It stores the address of the requestor's PCB in BRK$L_PCB.
6. It stores the address of the IOSB specified by the IOSB argument in BRK$L_IOSB.
7. It stores the length of the unformatted message in BRK$W_MSGLEN and copies the unformatted message text to the buffer starting at BRK$T_MSGBUF.
8. It stores the address of the first byte after the message in BRK$L_SCRMSG. It will store the screen message at this address.
9. It validates the SNDTYP argument.
10. It sets up the BRK to reflect the SNDTYP and SENDTO arguments. It handles the four cases as follows (the last two cases are handled identically):

    —If the SNDTYP argument is BRK$C_USERNAME (send message to a single user name), EXE$BRKTHRU invokes EXE$PROBER_DSC to verify the accessibility of the user name specified by the SENDTO argument. It copies the SENDTO argument to BRK$T_SENDNAME and compares it to the current user name (stored in the Job Information Block at offset JIB$T_USERNAME). If the two names are equal, it has completed this step. If they are not equal, it verifies that the process has OPER privilege.

    —If the SNDTYP argument is BRK$C_DEVICE (send message to a specific device), EXE$BRKTHRU invokes EXE$PROBER_DSC to verify the accessibility of the device name specified by the SENDTO argument. It then invokes the Get Device/Volume Information ($GETDVI) system service to get the physical name of the device. EXE$BRKTHRU copies the name returned by $GETDVI to BRK$T_DEVNAM and sets BRK$V_CHKPRV in BRK$B_STS to indicate that it should check the requestor's privilege to send to the specified device at a later step.

    —If the SNDTYP argument is either BRK$C_ALLUSERS (send message to all users) or BRK$C_ALLTERMS (send message to all devices), EXE$BRKTHRU verifies that the requestor has OPER privilege.

11. If the TIMOUT argument is specified, EXE$BRKTHRU ensures that it is at least BRK_C_MINTIME (four seconds). It converts the argument to clock ticks and stores the resulting quadword in BRK$Q_TIMEOUT.

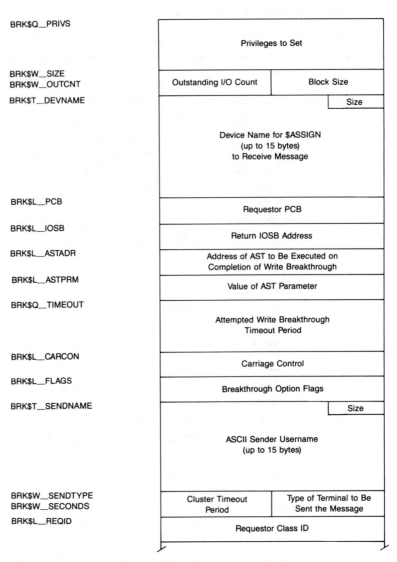

Figure 18-6 Layout of a Breakthrough Message Descriptor Block

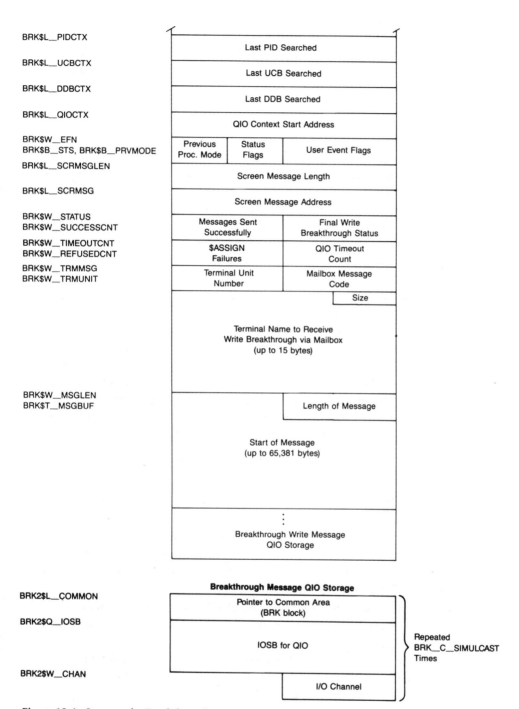

Figure 18-6 Layout of a Breakthrough Message Descriptor Block *(continued)*

(See Chapter 11 for details on timer support.)

12. It stores a privilege mask in BRK$Q_PRIVS. This mask has at most two bits set, the ones for BYPASS and SHARE privileges. These bits are set only if they are not already set in PCB$Q_PRIVMSK. In other words, the mask specifies which of the two privileges the process does not already have.

13. It stores the default cluster timeout value BRK_C_CLUTIMEOUT (four seconds) in BRK$W_SECONDS.

14. It copies the remaining $BRKTHRU arguments to the BRK.

15. It verifies that the REQID argument is legal (a value less than or equal to 63).

16. It stores the success status SS$_NORMAL in BRK$W_STATUS.

17. It stores the mailbox prefix code MSG$_TRMBRDCST in BRK$W_TRMMSG. Note that the BRK contains a mailbox message in fields BRK$W_TRMMSG through the end of the unformatted message stored at BRK$T_MSGBUF.

18. It stores the previous processor access mode in BRK$B_PRVMODE.

19. It stores −1 in BRK$L_PIDCTX.

20. It invokes the Formatted ASCII Output ($FAO) system service to format the message. $FAO stores the length of the screen message in BRK$L_SCRMSGLEN and the screen message at the address in BRK$L_SCRMSG. At this point, the BRK contains the unformatted message (starting at BRK$T_MSGBUG) and the screen message (immediately following the unformatted message). BRK$L_SCRMSGLEN and BRK$L_SCRMSG constitute a descriptor for the screen message.

EXE$BRKTHRU is now ready to commence sending messages. It does so in the following steps:

1. It invokes the Set AST Enable ($SETAST) system service to disable AST delivery for the current process. (Since it executes in kernel mode, invoking $SETAST to disable AST delivery effectively disables AST delivery for all access modes.) This is necessary to prevent image exit before the image temporary bit (CCB$V_IMGTMP) is set in the CCB. This is discussed in further detail in Section 18.10.2.2.

2. It attempts to initiate BRK_C_SIMULCAST (four) message writes. The specific steps it takes to initiate the writing of a message are discussed in Section 18.10.2.

3. If the system is a member of a VAXcluster System, EXE$BRKTHRU invokes EXE$CSP_BRKTHRU (in module [SYSLOA]CSPCLIENT) to send the message to all other nodes in the VAXcluster System.

4. It checks if all writes have been completed. If so, it deallocates the BRK. The specific steps it takes are discussed in Section 18.10.3.3.

5. It invokes $SETAST to enable AST delivery for the current process.

The asynchronous form of the system service returns to the caller. The caller can either wait for I/O completion or continue processing. The synchronous form of the system service waits for the event flag associated with the request to be set and status to be returned. (See Chapter 9 for more information concerning synchronous and asynchronous system services.)

18.10.2 **Writing the Breakthrough Message**

EXE$BRKTHRU takes two major steps when it attempts to initiate writing a message: selecting the next terminal to which to write, and starting the actual I/O operation. If it does not find a terminal to which to write, the second major step is skipped. Each time it finds an acceptable terminal UCB, it initiates a write.

18.10.2.1 **Finding a Terminal.** The steps EXE$BRKTHRU takes to find the next terminal depend upon the SNDTYP argument.

18.10.2.1.1 *Finding a Specific Terminal.* If the SNDTYP argument was BRKC_DEVICE, EXEBRKTHRU has already found the terminal. It did this using the $GETDVI system service when it initialized the BRK. All that it does now is set BRK$V_DONE in BRK$B_STS.

18.10.2.1.2 *Finding All Terminals and All Users.* If the SNDTYP argument was BRK$C_ALLTERMS or BRK$C_ALLUSERS, EXE$BRKTHRU must find all terminals on the system. It does this by invoking IOC$SCAN_IODB to find each UCB in the system.

The caller must pass context to IOC$SCAN_IODB on each call. (The context consists of a DDB address and a UCB address.) IOC$SCAN_IODB uses this context to determine where to start its search of the I/O database. EXE$BRKTHRU uses BRK$L_UCBCTX and BRK$L_DDBCTX to save this context between calls to IOC$SCAN_IODB. EXE$BRKTHRU set these fields to zero when it initialized the BRK, causing IOC$SCAN_IODB to begin its search at the beginning of the I/O database. Each time IOC$SCAN_IODB finds a UCB, it returns a success status. When IOC$SCAN_IODB has reached the end of the I/O database, it returns a failure status.

After each successful call to IOC$SCAN_IODB, EXE$BRKTHRU makes sure that the UCB is acceptable:

- It must be a terminal UCB.
- It must be online.
- If the terminal is not allocated, the terminal must not be set autobaud.

If the UCB is not acceptable, EXE$BRKTHRU invokes IOC$SCAN_IODB again to get another UCB. If IOC$SCAN_IODB finds another UCB,

EXE$BRKTHRU checks that UCB. EXE$BRKTHRU continues this loop until it gets an acceptable UCB or all UCBs have been found. When all UCBs have been found, EXE$BRKTHRU sets BRK$V_DONE in BRK$B_STS.

18.10.2.1.3 *Finding All Terminals for a Specific User.* If the SNDTYP argument was BRK$C_USERNAME, EXE$BRKTHRU must find all terminals on which the given user is logged in. It accomplishes this by finding all processes belonging to that user and the terminal, if any, associated with those processes.

EXE$BRKTHRU invokes the Get Job/Process Information ($GETJPI) system service to perform a wildcard operation. (See the *VAX/VMS System Services Reference Manual* for details on performing wildcard operations with $GETJPI.) EXE$BRKTHRU stores the PID to be passed to $GETJPI in BRK$L_PIDCTX. (The initial value of BRK$L_PIDCTX is −1, the value required to initiate a wildcard operation.) On each invocation of $GETJPI, EXE$BRKTHRU requests the user name and the name of the process's login terminal. Upon completion of each invocation of $GETJPI, EXE$BRKTHRU verifies that the process is an interactive process (the terminal name has a nonzero length) and belongs to the correct user (the name stored in BRK$T_SENDNAME matches the user name returned by $GETJPI). If the process does not meet these criteria, EXE$BRKTHRU invokes $GETJPI to get information about the next process.

Once EXE$BRKTHRU finds an interactive process belonging to the correct user, it invokes IOC$SEARCHDEV to locate the UCB and the DDB for the terminal. EXE$BRKTHRU then verifies that the UCB meets the following criteria:

- It must be a terminal UCB.
- It must be available.
- It must not be for a network device or a spooled device.
- It must not be for a detached terminal.
- It must not have the specific broadcast class disabled (the bit whose number is specified by the REQID argument in UCB$Q_TT_BRKTHRU must be clear).
- It must not have broadcasts disabled or pass-all enabled unless there is a broadcast mailbox associated with the UCB (TT$V_BRDCSTMBX in UCB$L_DEVDEPND2 set).

If the UCB does not meet these criteria, EXE$BRKTHRU invokes $GETJPI to get information about the next process.

If the UCB does meet these criteria, EXE$BRKTHRU verifies that the requestor has the privilege to access the device. If BRK$V_CHKPRIV in BRK$B_STS is set, EXE$BRKTHRU verifies that at least one of the following conditions is met. If this bit is not set, EXE$BRKTHRU proceeds as if one of the following conditions were true:

- The requestor is the owner of the terminal. (PCB$L_PID of the requestor's PCB matches UCB$L_PID; the address of the requestor's PID is obtained from BRK$L_PCB.)
- The requestor is a descendant of the owner of the UCB. EXE$BRKTHRU follows the PCB process owner chain until it finds a process whose process ID matches the device owner or it finds a process with no owner.
- The process has OPER privilege.

If the requestor has the necessary privilege to access the device, EXE$BRKTHRU invokes IOC$CVT_DEVNAM (in module IOSUBNPAG) to convert the device name to the form *ddcn* and store the name starting at BRK$T_DEVNAM + 1. EXE$BRKTHRU stores the length of the name in BRK$T_DEVNAM. EXE$BRKTHRU then stores the UCB$W_UNIT field in BRK$W_TRMUNIT and DDB$T_NAME in BRK$T_TRMNAME.

18.10.2.2   **Performing the Breakthrough I/O.** EXE$BRKTHRU now has in the BRK the information necessary to send the message to a specific terminal. It takes the following steps to send the message:

1. If TT2$V_BRDCSTMBX in UCB$L_DEVDEPND2 is set and UCB$L_AMB is nonzero, EXE$BRKTHRU invokes EXE$WRTMAILBOX (in module MBDRIVER) to write the message to the associated mailbox. Note that the BRK contains the message already formatted for the mailbox write starting at BRK$W_TRMMSG.
2. It verifies that broadcasts to the terminal are not disabled and that the terminal is not in pass-all mode. There are two reasons for checking these bits now. If they were checked earlier, they could have changed since the earlier check was performed. If the terminal has an associated mailbox (actually, if TT2$V_BRDCSTMBX in UCB$L_DEVDEPND2 is set), EXE$BRKTHRU did not check these bits earlier.
3. If BRK$Q_PRIVMSK is nonzero, EXE$BRKTHRU invokes the Set Privilege ($SETPRIV) system service to enable the privileges specified by BRK$Q_PRIVMSK. The result of this step is to give the process BYPASS and SHARE privilege if it does not already have them.
4. It invokes the $ASSIGN system service to assign a channel to the terminal UCB, with the CHAN argument specifying BRK2$W_CHAN. If BRK$Q_PRIVMSK is nonzero after the $ASSIGN system service completes, EXE$BRKTHRU invokes $SETPRIV to disable the privileges specified by BRK$Q_PRIVMSK.
5. It sets CCB$V_IMGTMP in the CCB of the channel just assigned. As a result, SYS$RUNDWN will deassign this channel on image exit if the channel has not been deassigned previously. This ensures that the channel will be deassigned if the image exits before EXE$BRKTHRU completes. (Image termination is discussed in Chapter 21.)

6. It invokes the $QIO system service to write the message to the terminal. (Note that each concurrent write uses a different QIO context area. Since there are four such areas, only four writes can be outstanding at any one time.) The following arguments are specified:

—If BRK$V_SCREEN was specified in the FLAGS argument and TT2$V_DECCRT in UCB$L_DEVDEPND2 is set, the screen message is written. The message and carriage control are specified as follows: the message length is the value in BRK$L_SCRMSGLEN; the message is the one at the address stored in BRK$L_SCRMSG; the carriage control is a zero.

Otherwise, the unformatted message is written. The message and carriage control are specified as follows: the message length is the value in BRK$W_MSGLEN; the message is the one stored at BRK$T_MSGBUF; the carriage control is the value in BRK$L_CARCON.

—The channel is the one specified by BRK2$W_CHAN.

—The IOSB is the one at BRK2$Q_IOSB.

—The AST address is QIO_DONE (in module SYSBRKTHRU). This routine is discussed in Section 18.10.3.2.

—The AST parameter is the address of the QIO context area, BRK2$L_COMMON.

—The function code is write virtual block, with the refresh, cancel CTRL/O, and breakthrough modifiers.

—The event flag is BRK_C_EFN (31).

7. EXE$BRKTHRU increments BRK$W_OUTCNT to reflect another outstanding write request.

8. If the TIMOUT argument was specified (BRK$Q_TIMEOUT is nonzero), EXE$BRKTHRU invokes the Set Timer ($SETIMR) system service, specifying QIO_TIMEOUT (in module SYSBRKTHRU) as the AST routine to be activated when the timer expires and the value in BRK$Q_TIMEOUT as the time. QIO_TIMEOUT is discussed in Section 18.10.3.1.

EXE$BRKTHRU has now completed all the work necessary to initiate the writing of the breakthrough message to a given terminal.

18.10.3 Completion Actions

EXE$BRKTHRU performs three distinct actions related to completion:

• It responds to the expiration of a timer.
• It responds to the completion of a write to a terminal.
• It checks for completion of the $BRKTHRU system service.

It performs the first two actions in AST routines. It performs the latter action in a subroutine.

8.10.3.1   **Timer Expiration.** If the timer expires before the I/O completion AST is executed, the executive invokes QIO_TIMEOUT as an AST routine. The only argument to QIO_TIMEOUT is the address of the QIO context area. QIO_TIMEOUT invokes the $CANCEL system service to cancel the write request. This will result in QIO_DONE being invoked as part of completing the I/O request; any further processing required will be performed by QIO_DONE.

8.10.3.2   **I/O Completion AST.** The I/O completion AST, QIO_DONE, is activated when the I/O operation requested via the $QIO system service completes. The one argument to QIO_DONE is the address of the QIO context area for the completed write. QIO_DONE takes the following steps:

1. If BRK$Q_TIMEOUT is nonzero, QIO_DONE invokes the Cancel Timer ($CANTIM) system service to cancel the timer requested via the $SETIMER system service. Note that the timer may have expired already.
2. It invokes $DASSGN to deassign the channel.
3. It decrements BRK$W_OUTCNT to reflect the completion of the write request.
4. It attempts to initiate another write operation by taking the steps described in Section 18.10.2.
5. It then checks for completion of the $BRKTHRU request by taking the steps described in Section 18.10.3.3.

8.10.3.3   **Completion Checks.** CHECK_COMPLETE is invoked to check for completion of the $BRKTHRU request:

1. It checks BRK$W_OUTCNT. If it is nonzero, there is at least one write request outstanding, and CHECK_COMPLETE exits.
2. It stores the final status in the IOSB if the requestor specified one (BRK$L_IOSB is nonzero). Note that CHECK_COMPLETE always runs in the context of the requestor. Thus, the IOSB, if specified, is accessible.
3. If the requestor specified an AST routine (BRK$L_ASTADR is nonzero), CHECK_COMPLETE invokes the Declare AST system service, giving the AST routine address as that stored in BRK$L_ASTADR and the AST parameter as that stored in BRK$L_ASTPRM.
4. It invokes the Set Event Flag ($SETEF) system service to set the event flag specified by the requestor.
5. It invokes EXE$DEAP1 (in module MEMORYALC) to deallocate the BRK.

18.11   **BROADCAST SYSTEM SERVICE**

The Broadcast ($BRDCST) system service sends messages to one or more terminals, even if an I/O operation is currently in progress on the terminal.

The $BRDCST system service has been superseded by the $BRKTHRUW system service, which should be used for future software development. $BRDCST has four arguments:

- The message buffer containing the text to be written, MSGBUF
- The device to which to send the message, DEVNAM
- The carriage control to be used with the message, CARCON
- Options for the $BRDCST system service, FLAGS

The $BRDCST system service routine, EXE$BRDCST in module SYS-BRKTHR, runs in the access mode of the caller. EXE$BRDCST invokes the $BRKTHRUW system service to perform the breakthrough operation equivalent to the requested broadcast operation. EXE$BRDCST specifies the following arguments to the $BRKTHRUW system service:

- The EFN argument is BRK_C_BRDCSTEFN, event flag 31.
- The $BRKTHRUW MSGBUF argument is the same as the $BRDCST MSGBUF argument.
- The SNDTYP argument is as follows:

  —If the DEVNAM argument is zero, the SNDTYP argument is BRK$C_ALLTERMS (send to all terminals).
  —If the DEVNAM argument is nonzero, it is taken as the address of a descriptor. If the descriptor specifies a length of zero, the SNDTYP argument is BRK$C_ALLUSERS (send to all users). If the descriptor specifies a nonzero length, the SNDTYP argument is BRK$C_DEVICE (send to the specified device).

- If the SNDTYP argument is BRK$C_DEVICE, the SENDTO argument is the same as the DEVNAM argument to the $BRDCST system service. Otherwise, the SENDTO argument is irrelevant.
- The $BRKTHRUW FLAGS argument is the same as the $BRDCST FLAGS, if the latter argument is specified. Otherwise, the $BRKTHRUW FLAGS argument is zero. Note that the $BRDCST FLAGS argument has no bits equivalent to the BRK$V_ERASE_LINES and BRK$V_CLUSTER bits of the $BRKTHRU FLAGS argument.
- The $BRKTHRUW CARCON argument is the same as the $BRDCST CARCON argument, if the latter argument is specified. Otherwise, the $BRKTHRUW CARCON argument is an ASCII blank.
- The TIMOUT argument is 10, which specifies a timeout of ten seconds.
- The IOSB argument specifies an IOSB allocated on the stack by EXE$BRDCST.

Upon completion of the $BRKTHRUW system service, EXE$BRDCST examines the return status. If the status is an error, EXE$BRDCST returns that status to the caller. If the return status of the $BRKTHRUW system service is a success status, EXE$BRDCST returns the status in the IOSB to the caller. Note that if either return status is SS$_NOOPER, EXE$BRDCST replaces it with SS$_NOPRIV. This is done to maintain compatibility with previous implementations of $BRDCST.

18.12 INFORMATIONAL SERVICES

Images frequently require information about particular devices on the system. VAX/VMS provides several system services to obtain specific information about a particular device.

Device-independent information refers to information that is present for each device on the system, such as the device unit number (UCB$W_UNIT), device characteristics (UCB$L_DEVCHAR), and the device type (UCB$B_DEVTYPE). It is obtained by reading fields in the UCB that have the same interpretation for all devices on the system.

Device-dependent information refers to information that is present for each device on the system but whose interpretation is device-dependent (such as the device-dependent information fields UCB$L_DEVDEPEND and UCB$L_DEVDEPND2) or information that is present only for certain devices, such as the logical UCB address in a terminal UCB, UCB$L_TT_LOGUCB.

There are two sets of information, the primary and secondary device characteristics, for each device. These two sets are identical unless one of the following conditions holds:

- If the device has an associated mailbox, the primary characteristics are those of the assigned device and the secondary characteristics are those of the associated mailbox.
- If the device is spooled, the primary characteristics are those of the intermediate device and the secondary characteristics are those of the spooled device.
- If the device represents a logical link on the network, the secondary characteristics contain information about the link.

The $GETDVI system service (in module SYSGETDEV) obtains device-independent information about a device. See the *VAX/VMS System Services Reference Manual* for a listing of the fields that can be returned. $GETDVI uses an item list argument mechanism, which allows it to be extended in an upwardly compatible fashion.

Support still exists for the Get I/O Channel Information ($GETCHN) and Get I/O Device Information ($GETDEV) system services, which are both in module SYSGETDVI. The $GETDVI system service supersedes the $GETCHN and $GETDEV system services and should be used in future software development.

The $QIO system service can be used to obtain device information. Two function codes, IO$_SENSEMODE and IO$_SENSECHAR, can be used to request the device driver to return device-dependent information to the caller. The specific information that can be returned depends on the device. See the *VAX/VMS I/O Reference Volume* manual for details about what information is returned by specific device drivers.

19 VAX/VMS Device Drivers

"Open the pod-bay doors, HAL."
Arthur C. Clarke, *2001: A Space Odyssey*

A VAX/VMS device driver is a collection of tables and routines that control I/O operations on a peripheral device. The manual *Writing a Device Driver for VAX/VMS* describes the general structure of a driver and introduces the system routines commonly called by device drivers.

This chapter highlights various techniques used by selected drivers and documents some of their device-specific processing. The intent is to present techniques which are helpful in understanding the VAX/VMS I/O subsystem but which are not described in the manual *Writing a Device Driver for VAX/VMS*. No attempt is made to discuss each VAX/VMS device driver, nor is every feature of a particular driver described. For detailed descriptions of the features and capabilities provided by each supported device driver, see the *VAX/VMS I/O Reference Volume*.

19.1 DISK DRIVERS

Disks are random access mass storage devices placed either on the MASSBUS, UNIBUS, IDC (VAX-11/730 only), computer interconnect (CI), Q22 bus, or VAXBI.

The drivers written for these devices perform some of the functions in the following list. Newer disks, known as Digital Storage Architecture (DSA) disks, have more intelligent controllers, which perform several of these functions.

- Use hardware error recovery and correction capabilities, such as data checking, offset recovery, and error correction code (ECC)
- Optimize controller operations by overlapping seek and data transfer operations
- Perform dynamic bad block handling (in conjunction with the file system)
- Support online diagnostics and error logging
- Support I/O requests at the logical and physical levels and cooperate with the file system to support virtual I/O requests

The following sections describe some of these functions.

19.1.1 ECC Error Recovery

ECC errors occur only on the following read operations:

- Read data
- Read header and data
- Write check data
- Write check header and data

A disk driver corrects these errors by applying a hardware-specified correction mask to the appropriate memory data. The transfer is then continued as if an error never occurred. Note that a DSA disk has a different ECC scheme, which is implemented within its controller (for example, the UDA or HSC).

The actual error correction information consists of the following:

- An 11-bit mask that must be XORed with the appropriate memory data
- The number of the bit within the sector that specifies the start of the error burst

A disk driver calls routine IOC$APPLYECC (in module IOSUBRAMS) to apply the ECC correction. IOC$APPLYECC requires the use of a system page table entry (SPTE). A device driver that supports ECC recovery specifies the DPT$V_SVP flag in the FLAGS argument to the DPTAB macro. When a device supported by such a driver is connected by SYSGEN, an SPTE is allocated for each unit. Its system virtual page number in stored in field UCB$L_SVPN in the unit control block (UCB). The SPTE is used to double map a data block to be corrected.

The driver must also specify the number of bytes that were transferred into memory (up to, but not including, the block to be corrected). This number can be calculated by adding the remaining byte count to the transfer byte count (UCB$W_BCNT).

IOC$APPLYECC applies the correction by taking the following steps:

1. The transferred byte count is decremented and then ANDed with $1FF_{16}$. The result is the byte offset from the start of the buffer to the block that contains the data in error.
2. The starting bit number of the error burst (a number in the range from 1 to 4096) is decremented to convert it to a relative bit number. The result is separated into a byte offset within the block and a mask shift count.
3. The byte offset within the block is added to the byte offset from the buffer calculated in step 1. The result is the byte offset within the buffer to the start of the error burst.
4. The XOR pattern mask is shifted left by the mask shift count calculated in step 2.

   At this point, the longword XOR pattern and the byte offset within the buffer to the first byte to be corrected have been calculated. All that remains is to double map the data block to be corrected and XOR the pattern mask with memory. However, the following considerations must be accounted for:

—The transfer may have been satisfied part way through the last block, and the error correction is outside the data of interest. For example, suppose the byte count terminated after 20 bytes into the sector and the correctable data starts at byte 35.

—The transfer may have been satisfied part way through the last block, and the error correction is partly inside and partly outside the data of interest. For example, the byte count terminated after 20 bytes into the sector, and the correctable data started at byte 19.

Thus, the correction must be applied one byte at a time. Steps 5 through 7 are repeated four times, if necessary.

5. The offset to the next byte to be corrected is compared with the transfer byte count. If the offset byte count is greater than or equal to the transfer byte count, the remaining corrections are outside the area of interest. Step 8 is executed next.

6. The byte to be corrected is double mapped, using the system virtual page number stored in UCB$L_SVPN. The translation buffer entry for that page is invalidated.

7. The next byte (lowest) of the longword pattern mask is XORed with the memory data, the offset in the buffer is incremented, and the pattern mask is shifted right by eight bits. If all four correction bytes are not applied, steps 5, 6, and 7 are repeated.

8. The transfer is continued by reexecuting the appropriate function after updating the current transfer parameters (byte count, disk address, and system virtual address of the next PTE that maps the transfer).

19.1.2   Offset Recovery

Offset recovery is a technique whereby the drive read heads are moved in small increments (usually 200 to 400 microinches) from the track centerline in an attempt to pick up a stronger signal. A disk driver uses this technique only for read operations. Offset recovery for a DSA disk is implemented by its controller, not the device driver.

When encountering an error that may be correctable using offset recovery, a disk driver takes the following steps:

1. The read heads are returned to the centerline.
2. Up to 16 attempts are made to read the data at the centerline.
3. The heads are offset by an increment, and two retries are performed at that offset. This procedure is repeated up to six times.
4. If after 28 attempts (16 at the centerline and two at each of six offset positions) the data still cannot be retrieved, a failure is returned.

19.1.3   Dynamic Bad Block Handling

A non-DSA disk is typically tested to detect bad blocks before the disk is put into use. The bad blocks are allocated to a special file called

[000000]BADBLK.SYS, so that they cannot be allocated to user files. This is known as static bad block handling. As the disk is used, additional blocks may become bad. Dynamic bad block handling deals with those blocks.

Dynamic bad block handling is a cooperative effort among driver FDT routines, I/O postprocessing, and the Files-11 Extended QIO Processor (XQP). FDT routines for IO$_READVBLK and IO$_WRITEVBLK construct an I/O request packet (IRP) and set the virtual bit in the IRP status word (IRP$V_VIRTUAL in IRP$W_STS). When the I/O postprocessing routine (in module IOCIOPOST) discovers a transfer error on a virtual I/O function, it routes the IRP to the XQP.

The XQP, using information in the IRP, calculates the bad block address and stores that information in [000000]BADLOG.SYS. (This file contains a list identifying suspected bad blocks on the volume that are not currently contained in the volume's bad block file.) In addition, it sets a bit in the file control block to indicate the presence of a bad block. When the file is closed, an equivalent bit is set in the file's header on disk.

When such a file is deleted, the XQP creates a process running the image BADBLOCK.EXE to diagnose the file. It writes worst-case test patterns over the blocks of the file and reads them back, comparing the data to the original pattern. If a bad block is found, the image uses privileged file system functions to allocate the cluster containing the block to the bad block file ([000000]BADBLK.SYS;1), because the smallest unit of file system allocation is the disk cluster.

Note that a dynamic bad block is not discovered until it is already part of a file and is not allocated to the bad block file until that file is deleted. When a bad block is discovered while writing a file, the bad block information is recorded. A bit is set in the FCB for the file and an error indication is returned to the requesting process.

Dynamic bad block handling is restricted to virtual I/O functions (that is, file I/O). Processes performing logical or physical I/O functions must provide their own bad block handling.

Dynamic bad block handling is performed only for non-DSA disks. A DSA disk appears to the system as a perfect medium. When a bad block is detected on a DSA disk, the controller (or the controller and the device driver) remap that block to a new location on the disk.

19.2   **MAGNETIC TAPE DRIVERS**

Magnetic tapes are sequential access mass storage devices.

To perform data transfer operations, the MASSBUS magnetic tape driver (in [DRIVER]TMDRIVER or [DRIVER]TFDRIVER) has to obtain ownership of both the TM03 or TM78 controller (primary channel) and the MASSBUS adapter (secondary channel) by issuing the REQPCHAN and REQSCHAN macros, respectively. At times, the secondary channel may be released (using the RELSCHAN macro) so that other disks may use the MASSBUS. The manual *Writing a Device Driver for VAX/VMS* contains information on how drivers are written for devices on the MASSBUS.

The *VAX/VMS I/O Reference Volume* describes the features and capabilities provided by the magnetic tape drivers and discusses the general error recovery and data check logic employed by them.

The specific algorithm used to correct non-return-to-zero-inverted (NRZI) read errors is the following:

1. If the error occurred while reading in the forward direction, the tape is backspaced and the record is read again.
2. If an error occurred while reading in the reverse direction, the following steps are taken:

   a. The record is read in the forward direction to set up the error correction in the hardware.
   b. The tape is backspaced over the record just read.
   c. The record is reread in the forward direction to apply the error correction.
   d. The tape is backspaced over the record to position the tape properly (because the initial request was for a read in the reverse direction).

A magnetic tape ancillary control process (ACP) is called from various driver FDT routines to perform functions such as writing tape labels.

19.3   CLASS AND PORT DRIVERS

VAX/VMS has a layered strategy for certain device drivers and I/O. A number of drivers are divided into a class driver and a port driver. The class driver handles operations that depend on the actual device (the functional layer). The port driver handles operations that depend on the protocol and hardware used to communicate with a device (the communications layer).

The class and port strategy is applied to the terminal driver (see Section 19.4) and to drivers written for devices that communicate using a DIGITAL protocol known as systems communication architecture (SCA). Figure 19-1 shows a conceptual diagram of SCA.

19.3.1   Implementation of SCA on VAX/VMS

SCA defines a communications layer and the external interface to that layer. The VMS implementation of SCA is known as the system communications services (SCS). An SCA port driver implements SCS on a specific port device. VAX/VMS supplies the following SCA port drivers:

• PADRIVER for the CI780, CI750, BCI750, and CIBCI

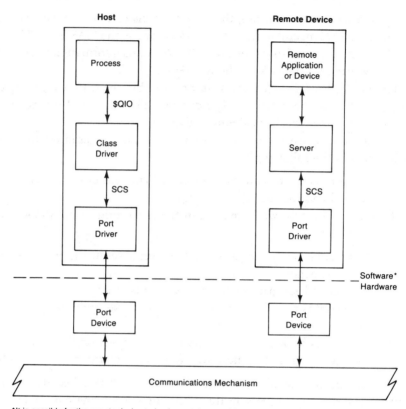

Figure 19-1 Conceptual Diagram of Systems
Communication Architecture (SCA)

* PUDRIVER for UNIBUS port devices, such as UDA50 and TU81; Q22 bus port devices, such as RD52 and TK50; and VAXBI port devices, such as KDB50

An SCA class driver uses SCS as a communications medium for some higher level functions or protocols. A class driver implements the functional layer within the layered strategy and performs operations on a user-visible device without regard for the SCA communications transport used.

Currently there are three protocols in the function layer that call SCS to communicate information:

* DECnet-VAX

    DECnet-VAX uses SCS for communication over the CI. The DECnet CI driver is CNDRIVER.
* Mass storage control protocol (MSCP)

    MSCP is a general protocol designed to describe all types of disk operation. It is implemented by controllers for DSA disks and by the software

MSCP server supplied with VMS. The MSCP disk class driver is DUDRIVER.

• Tape mass storage control protocol (TMSCP)

TMSCP is a general tape protocol designed to describe all types of tape operations. It is implemented by controllers for tape drives, such as the TA78, TU81, and TK50. The TMSCP class driver is TUDRIVER.

The disk class driver can use either the CI, the UNIBUS and Q22 bus, or any other SCA port driver to communicate to an MSCP server. Similarly, the tape class driver can use any SCA port driver to communicate to a TMSCP device. The DECnet class driver uses the CI port driver exclusively.

19.3.2   **I/O Processing**

When a user application performs I/O through a class and port driver, a channel must be assigned to the class driver. $QIOs are issued to that channel.

The following sequence illustrates how SCA class and port drivers communicate information from a process on a host system to a remote device. The disk class driver is used as an example.

1. The process on the host system issues a $QIO to a class driver. The $QIO system service validates the I/O request and describes it in an I/O request packet (IRP). The $QIO system service passes the IRP to the class driver.
2. The class driver translates portions of the IRP to an MSCP request. It then initializes fields in a class driver request packet (CDRP). A CDRP contains information necessary for SCS operations. (Figure 19-2 shows the layout of a CDRP.) As a convenience to the $QIO/class driver interface, a CDRP is designed to be an extension of an IRP.
3. The class driver then calls SCS to transmit the MSCP request to the MSCP server.
4. The SCS operations are interpreted by the port driver, which then communicates the I/O request to a remote port driver.
5. The remote port driver communicates the request to the MSCP server.
6. The server acts on the MSCP request and passes the I/O request to the remote application or device.

19.4   **TERMINAL DRIVER**

The terminal I/O subsystem is a collection of routines that provide a flexible approach to terminal input and output (as described in the *VAX/VMS I/O Reference Volume*). The terminal I/O subsystem is divided into one terminal class driver and a number of device-specific port drivers.

Note that the terminal class and port drivers do not communicate using the SCS protocol, nor do the terminal port devices conform to the SCA stan-

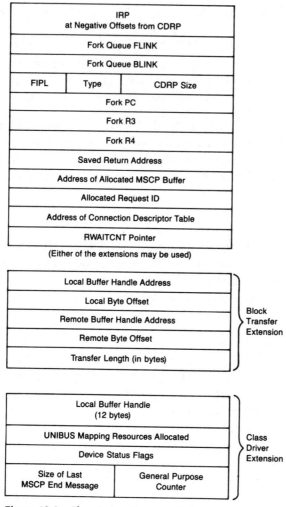

Figure 19-2 Class Driver Request Packet

dards. The terminal class driver, TTDRIVER.EXE, contains FDT and device-independent routines. The port drivers contain interrupt service routines and controller-specific control subroutines.

The following port drivers are supplied with VAX/VMS Version 4.4:

- DZDRIVER for DZ11 and DZ32 controllers
- DZVDRIVER for DZV11 controllers
- YCDRIVER for DMF32 and DMZ32 controllers
- YFDRIVER for DHU11 and DHV11 controllers
- YIDRIVER for DMB32 controllers
- Various CPU-specific console port drivers built into the SYSLOA*xxx* images

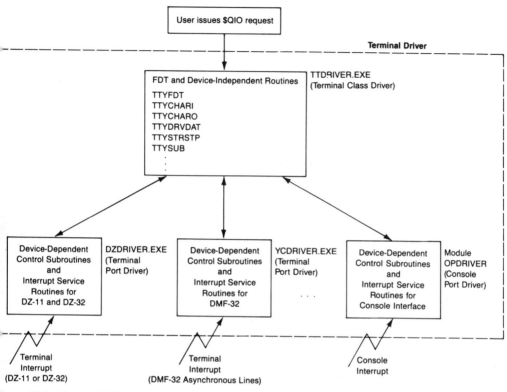

Figure 19-3   Terminal I/O System

The logical components of the terminal I/O subsystem are illustrated in Figure 19-3. (The console interface is discussed in Section 19.6.)

The class and port driver images are separate, loadable images. Therefore, changes can be made to any of them without rebuilding the system image. Support for a new terminal controller can be added in a new port driver.

When the system is bootstrapped, SYSBOOT reads the terminal class driver image into nonpaged pool. INIT creates the necessary linkages between the class and port drivers by linking the console port and terminal class drivers. The device-specific extension of a terminal UCB contains pointers to the class and port vector dispatch tables. INIT locates the address of the dispatch tables for the two drivers and stores them in the console UCB.

Later in system initialization, during autoconfiguration, SYSGEN identifies the terminal controllers present and loads the appropriate port drivers. The controller and unit initialization routines of these port drivers initialize the UCB extensions.

The relationships among the terminal class driver, console port driver, and the console UCB are shown in Figure 19-4.

The fact that the terminal class driver is loaded by SYSBOOT has im-

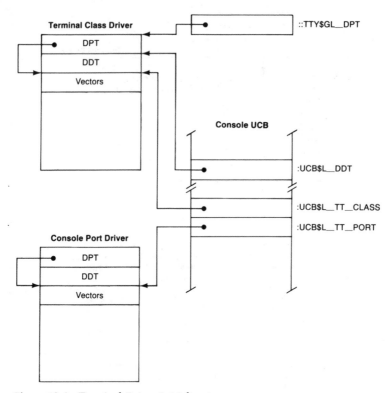

Figure 19-4   Terminal Driver Initialization

plications for anyone who writes a new terminal class driver. Maintain a backup copy of the terminal class driver in SYS$SYSTEM with a different name. If the new terminal driver contains errors that prevent the system from completing its initialization sequence, the SYSBOOT parameter TTY_CLASSNAME can be set during a conversational bootstrap to the name of the backup class driver.

To test a new terminal class driver or a replacement port driver, the system must be rebooted, because the SYSGEN command RELOAD will not reload terminal class or port drivers.

19.4.1   **Full-Duplex Operation**

The terminal driver implements partial full-duplex operation by default. Full-duplex operation is based upon an alternate start I/O entry point to the terminal class driver. Whenever a write request is issued to a full-duplex terminal, the write FDT routine (TTY$FDTWRITE in module [TTDRVR]TTYFDT) allocates and initializes a write buffer packet to describe the write request. It then calls routine EXE$ALTQUEPKT (in module SYSQIOREQ) to enter the alternate start I/O routine of the driver.

Normally, FDT routines invoke EXE$QIODRVPKT (in module SYSQIOREQ) to enter the driver start I/O routine. EXE$QIODRVPKT tests whether the driver is already active for that unit (the bit UCB$V_BSY in UCB$W_STS). If the unit is already busy, EXE$QIODRVPKT queues the IRP to the UCB rather than entering the start I/O routine.

EXE$ALTQUEPKT differs from EXE$QIODRVPKT in the following respects:

- It does not test the UCB busy flag. The flag may be set as the result of a read request in progress. Full-duplex operation means that a read request can be interrupted by a write request.
- It does not clear the cancel and timeout bits in the UCB (UCB$V_CANCEL and UCB$V_TIMOUT in UCB$W_STS) because they may be in use by the current IRP for a read request.
- It does not copy the SVAPTE, BCNT, and BOFF fields from the IRP to the UCB because this would affect the current I/O operation if the UCB is busy.
- It enters the alternate start I/O routine in the driver rather than the regular start I/O routine.

TTY$WRTSTARTIO (in module [TTDRVR]TTYSTRSTP) is the alternate start I/O routine entry point. It raises IPL to device IPL to block device interrupts from the current I/O operation in case the device is busy, and processes the packet as follows:

1. If a write is currently in progress, the write buffer packet is queued.
2. If a read is in progress but the I/O function (IRP$W_FUNC) specifies write breakthrough (IRP$V_BREAKTHRU), the write is started.
3. If a read is occurring but no read data has echoed yet (TTY$W_RB_TXTOFF equals zero), the write is started.
4. Otherwise, the write buffer packet is queued to the UCB.

To complete a write I/O request for full-duplex operation, the driver start I/O routine exits by calling routine COM$POST (in module COMDRVSUB) rather than issuing the REQCOM macro. COM$POST places the IRP on the postprocessing queue, requests an IPL$_IOPOST software interrupt (see Chapter 6), and returns.

Routine IOC$REQCOM is avoided because it would attempt to initiate the next IRP queued to the UCB, and there is still an active IRP. However, all read requests (and half-duplex writes) are terminated through IOC$REQCOM, so that the next request of this type can be processed in the normal fashion.

In full-duplex operation, the device can be expecting more than one interrupt at a time (one for a read request and one for a write request). Therefore, two fork PCs must be stored. (Usually a driver expects only one interrupt at a time and stores the fork PC in UCB$L_FPC.) The terminal driver stores more than one fork PC by altering the value of R5 (which normally points to the UCB) to point to the write buffer packet or the IRP before forking (by invoking the FORK macro).

A fork block is therefore formed in the write buffer packet or in the IRP. The fork block in the UCB is not used for read or write requests, although it is used at other times, for example, when a type-ahead buffer is allocated or when unsolicited input is being handled.

The technique of altering R5 before forking can be copied by any driver to allow more than one outstanding interrupt for a particular device. Any number of outstanding I/O requests could be handled by a driver entered at the alternate start I/O entry point. The driver, however, must be able to distinguish which interrupt is associated with which fork block and synchronize I/O operations. Such a driver might maintain queues for outstanding I/O requests and operate almost exclusively at device IPL (as the terminal port drivers do), blocking out device interrupts to achieve synchronization with multiple I/O request processing.

19.4.2 Channels and Terminal Controllers

The VMS terminal port drivers do not need to synchronize access to a terminal controller using the channel mechanism. Therefore, the terminal driver never requests or releases a controller channel (with the REQCHAN and RELCHAN macros). The locations normally used in the channel request block (CRB) as the controller wait queue are redefined and contain modem control status information.

19.4.3 Type-Ahead Buffer

A type-ahead buffer is allocated from nonpaged pool for each terminal. The size of the type-ahead buffer is usually specified by the SYSBOOT parameter TTY_TYPAHDSZ. If the terminal has the characteristic TT2$V_ALTYPEAHD, then the parameter TTY_ALTYPAHD specifies the type-ahead buffer size. Every character typed is placed into the buffer, even if a read request is active.

If the terminal is in host-synchronous mode when the buffer is within eight characters of being full, the driver sends an XOFF character to the terminal to tell it to stop sending data. (If the terminal has the alternate size type-ahead buffer, the SYSBOOT parameter TTY_ALTALARM is the threshold for determining when to send an XOFF.) The driver sends an XON character to the terminal to tell it to start sending data when the buffer is emptied. This technique prevents loss of characters during block I/O transmission from high-speed terminals.

19.5   PSEUDO DEVICE DRIVERS

VMS supports drivers for virtual devices (pseudo devices). These include the null device (NL:), network device (NET:), remote terminal device (RT:), and mailbox (MB:). Users can assign channels to these devices and issue I/O requests just as though they were real devices. The following sections highlight some of the features of these pseudo device drivers.

19.5.1   Null Device Driver

The null device driver (in NLDRIVER) is assembled and linked with the system image (SYS.EXE). It is a very simple driver, consisting of two FDT routines (one to complete read requests and one to complete write requests). The read FDT routine in the null driver responds to read requests by returning an SS$_ENDOFFILE status code to the user. The write FDT routine in the null driver responds to write requests by returning an SS$_NORMAL status code. No data is transferred, nor are any privilege or quota checks made.

19.5.2   Network Device Driver

The network device (NET:) is best viewed as a mechanism for DECnet-VAX users to access network functions. When a process assigns a channel to NET, a network UCB is created and given a unique number, such as NET100. The channel number returned to the user points to the newly created UCB. This channel can then be used to perform access, control, and I/O operations on the network. When the user deassigns the last channel to the network UCB, the UCB is deleted.

The network device driver and the communication drivers support two I/O request interfaces: $QIOs and "internal" IRPs.

- When a user issues a $QIO, the executive and the driver's FDT routines cooperate to build an IRP. The driver then processes the IRP (normally by passing it to its own STARTIO routine).
- So-called internal IRPs are built by kernel mode modules (device drivers) and passed to another driver's alternate start I/O interface.

    The remote terminal drivers (CTDRIVER and RTTDRIVER) use NETDRIVER's internal IRP interface in communication across the network. NETDRIVER uses the internal IRP interface to pass I/O requests to communication device drivers.

There are actually two images that are used for network communication: the network device driver (NETDRIVER) and the network ACP (NETACP). NETDRIVER creates links to other CPUs, performs routing and switching functions, breaks user messages into manageable pieces on transmission, and reassembles the messages on reception. The actual I/O in network communication is performed by the communication device driver (for example, XMDRIVER performs network communication through DMC-11s).

NETACP performs the following tasks:

- Creates processes to accept inbound connects
- Parses network control blocks and supplies defaults when a user issues an IO$_ACCESS function code to create a logical link
- Transmits and receives routing messages to maintain a picture of the network
- Maintains the volatile network database

Figure 19-5 illustrates some network I/O functions. For more information on DECnet, see the *VAX/VMS Networking Manual* and the *VAX/VMS Network Control Program Reference Manual*.

19.5.3   Remote Terminals

DECnet-VAX allows users to log in on a remote VAX/VMS processor and perform operations on that remote processor just as they would at the local processor. The communication from the remote processor to the controlling terminal is performed through a pseudo device on the remote processor called a remote terminal. The driver for remote terminals is CTDRIVER.EXE.

Note that while DECnet-VAX can communicate with other DIGITAL operating systems running DECnet, the focus of this discussion is on DECnet communication between two VAX processors running VAX/VMS Version 4. A different protocol is used when the remote VAX processor is running a version of VAX/VMS prior to Version 4, in which case the remote terminal driver is RTTDRIVER.EXE.

In addition to DECnet, three images are required to support remote terminals: the local processor uses the image RTPAD.EXE; the remote processor uses the images REMACP.EXE and CTDRIVER.EXE.

When a user on a local system issues the DCL command SET HOST, RTPAD uses DECnet-VAX to request a connection to a network object on the specified node. On remote processors running VAX/VMS, the object is REMACP. The image REMACP creates a UCB for the remote terminal and links the UCB into the driver tables by calling CTDRIVER at its unsolicited input entry point. REMACP then returns information about the remote processor to RTPAD.

RTPAD has routines for communicating with a number of different DIGITAL operating systems (including RSTS/E, RSX-11M, TOPS-20, and VAX/VMS). The information returned from REMACP is used to determine which operating system is communicating with the local processor. In VAX/VMS, REMACP sends unsolicited data to CTDRIVER; sending this data to

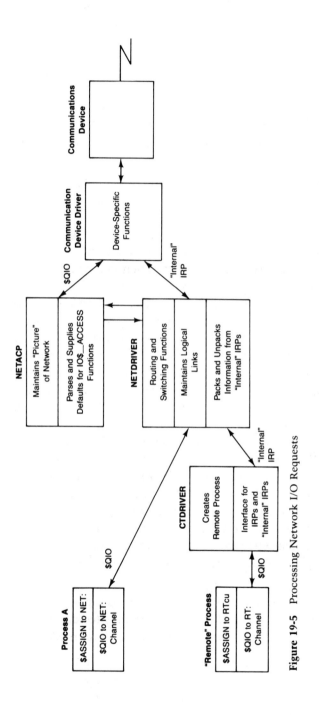

Figure 19-5   Processing Network I/O Requests

CTDRIVER is equivalent to pressing the RETURN key on a terminal that is not logged in. CTDRIVER creates a detached process running LOGINOUT. The user is now logged in to the remote system.

In communicating information across the network, CTDRIVER receives $QIOs from the remote processor, packs the information into a block, and uses the "internal" IRP interface to pass the request to NETDRIVER. RTPAD unpacks the information and reissues the $QIO for the local terminal. If the $QIO is a read, RTPAD packs the input information into a block and passes the packets of information back to CTDRIVER.

When the user logs off from the remote system, REMACP deletes the remote terminal UCB.

19.5.4 Mailbox Driver

Mailboxes are software-implemented devices that can be read and written. Normally, mailboxes are used for communication between processes. Although mailboxes transfer information in much the same way that other I/O devices do, they are not actual devices.

The messages written to a mailbox are stored in nonpaged pool until they are read. The space available for messages is determined when the mailbox is created. The mailbox driver uses two locations in the UCB to keep track of how much space is available. UCB$W_INIQUO contains the space originally allocated for messages. No message written to the mailbox can be greater than this value. UCB$W_BUFQUO contains the space currently available for messages. Originally, UCB$W_BUFQUO contains the value stored in UCB$W_INIQUO.

The following sections describe how the mailbox driver (in module MBDRIVER) buffers messages written to mailboxes and serializes mailbox read requests. Note that mailboxes in shared memory are supported by a separate, loadable driver, MBXDRIVER (in module [DRIVER]MBXDRIVER).

MBDRIVER uses the highest fork IPL (IPL$_MAILBOX, IPL 11) as its fork IPL. It does this to prevent possible synchronization problems with other drivers that reference mailboxes while in their respective fork processes (for example, to send a "device is off line" message to the operator's mailbox).

19.5.4.1 Processing Set Mode Requests. A process can use the IO$_SETMODE function to request MBDRIVER to perform three different operations. The specific operation is determined by the function modifier.

- IO$M_READATTN—Request an attention asynchronous system trap (AST) when a read request is issued for the mailbox
- IO$M_WRTATTN—Request an attention AST when a write request is issued for the mailbox

• IO$M_SETPROT—Set the volume protection on the mailbox

Only one of the modifiers can be specified at a time. If no modifier is specified, MBDRIVER assumes that IO$M_WRTATTN was specified.

9.5.4.1.1 *AST Notification of Mailbox Read or Write Requests.* When an image requests a set mode function to establish either a read or write attention AST, MBDRIVER's set mode FDT routine, FDTSET, takes the following steps:

1. It verifies that the process may access the mailbox.
2. It invokes COM$SETATTNAST (in module COMDRVSUB) to allocate, initialize, and queue an AST control block (ACB) to the appropriate listhead in the mailbox UCB. FDTSET passes the address of the listhead, either UCB$L_MB_W_AST for write attention AST requests or UCB$L_MB_R_AST for read attention AST requests. (See Chapter 7 for further details.)
3. It raises IPL to IPL$_MAILBOX to synchronize access to the UCB.
4. It determines if the notification condition is met. The condition is met in the following cases:

   —If the request is for a write attention AST, there must be at least one message queued to the mailbox (UCB$W_MSGCNT not equal to zero).
   —If the request is for a read attention AST, the UCB must be busy (UCB$V_BSY in UCB$W_STS is set).

   If the appropriate condition is met, FDTSET invokes COM$DELATTN-AST (in module COMDRVSUB) to queue the attention AST to the requesting process (see Chapter 7 for details).

   If the appropriate condition is not met, FDTSET invokes EXE$FINISHIOC (in module SYSQIOREQ) to complete the I/O request. (See Chapter 18 for details.) The attention AST will be queued to the process when a read or write request, as appropriate, is issued for the mailbox.

9.5.4.1.2 *Specifying Access Protection of a Mailbox.* When an image requests a set mode function to set the protection on the mailbox, FDTSET takes the following steps:

1. It examines the mailbox UCB object rights block (ORB) to verify that the requesting process is the owner of the UCB.
2. It raises IPL to IPL$_MAILBOX to synchronize access to the UCB.
3. It sets the flag specifying that the standard system, owner, group, world protection mask is valid (ORB$M_PROT_16 in ORB$B_FLAGS) and moves the P2 argument of the I/O call to the protection mask word (ORB$W_PROT) of the ORB.
4. It invokes EXE$FINISHIOC to complete the I/O request.

19.5.4.2   **Processing a Mailbox Write Request.** When an image invokes the $QIO system service to request a mailbox write, MBDRIVER's write FDT routine, FDTWRITE, takes the following steps:

1. It invokes WRITECHECKIO (in module MBDRIVER) to validate the request. The following criteria must be met:

   —The process must have write access to the mailbox.
   —The message size must be less than or equal to the maximum message size for the mailbox (UCB$W_DEVBUFSIZ).
   —The process must have read access to the buffer specified (from which the mailbox message will be read).

   WRITECHECKIO saves the address of the specified buffer in IRP$L_MEDIA.

2. FDTWRITE invokes EXE$ALONONPAGED (in module MEMORYALC) to allocate a message block from nonpaged pool.
3. It initializes the block, as shown in Figure 19-6.
4. It copies the data to be written to the mailbox from the specified buffer to the message block.
5. It saves the current IPL and raises IPL to IPL$_MAILBOX.
6. It determines if there is enough space for the message.
7. If not, it restores the saved IPL and deallocates the message block.

   If the message size is less than the total space allowed for messages (UCB$W_INIQUO) and the no-resource-wait modifier (IO$M_NORSWAIT) was not specified, FDTWRITE invokes EXE$IORSNWAIT (in module SYSQIOFDT) to place the process in a resource wait state waiting for the mailbox resource. (See Chapter 10 for details on resource waits.)

   If the message size is larger than UCB$W_INIQUO or if the no-resource-wait modifier was specified, FDTWRITE invokes EXE$ABORTIO (in module SYSQIOREQ) to abort the I/O request with a completion status of SS$_MBTOOSMALL.

8. If there is enough room for the message, it invokes INSMBQUEUE (in module MBDRIVER). INSMBQUEUE takes the following steps:

   a. INSMBQUEUE increments the count of outstanding messages (UCB$W_MSGCNT).
   b. If the UCB is busy (in other words, if there is a read in progress), it jumps to FINISHREAD (in module MBDRIVER), performing no further processing.
   c. If the UCB is not busy, it inserts the message block at the tail of the queue of messages at listhead UCB$L_MB_MSGQ.
   d. It invokes COM$DELATTNAST to queue any write attention ASTs to the appropriate processes.

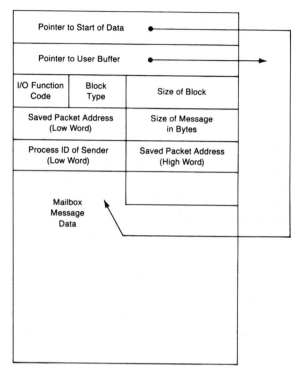

Figure 19-6   Layout of Mailbox Message Block

9. FDTWRITE restores the saved IPL.
10. If the IO$M_NOW modifier was specified, it invokes EXE$FINISHIOC to complete the I/O request with a completion status of SS$_NORMAL.
11. If the IO$M_NOW modifier was not specified, it invokes EXE$QIORETURN (in module SYSQIOREQ) to complete the $QIO system service. The processing of the write I/O request is suspended until a read request is issued.

9.5.4.3   **Processing a Mailbox Read Request.** MBDRIVER takes three major steps to process a read request: FDT processing, start I/O processing, and request completion.

9.5.4.3.1   *FDT Read Processing.* When an image invokes the $QIO system service to request a mailbox read, MBDRIVER's read FDT routine, FDTREAD, takes the following steps:

1. It invokes READCHECKIO (in module MBDRIVER) to validate the request. The following criteria must be met:

   —The process must have read access to the mailbox.
   —The message size must be less than or equal to the maximum message

size for the mailbox (UCB$W_DEVBUFSIZ).

—The process must have write access to the specified buffer (into which the mailbox message will be placed).

READCHECKIO saves the address of the specified buffer in IRP$L_MEDIA.

2. FDTREAD sets the mailbox I/O bit in the IRP (IRP$V_MBXIO in IRP$W_STS). The I/O postprocessing special kernel mode AST routine announces the availability of the mailbox resource when it processes an I/O request with the mailbox I/O bit set (see Chapter 18).

3. If the IO$M_NOW modifier was not specified, FDTREAD invokes EXE$QIODRVPKT to queue the IRP. MBDRIVER's start I/O routine will perform the rest of the processing of this request.

4. If the IO$M_NOW modifier was specified, it takes the following steps:

   a. It raises IPL to IPL$_MAILBOX.
   b. If any messages are available (UCB$W_MSGCNT is nonzero), it invokes EXE$QIODRVPKT to queue the IRP. MBDRIVER's start I/O routine will perform the rest of the processing of this request.
   c. If no messages are available, it invokes EXE$FINISHIOC to complete the I/O operation with a final I/O status of SS$_ENDOFFILE.

19.5.4.3.2 *Start I/O Read Request Processing.* MBDRIVER's start I/O routine, START-IO, performs the following steps:

1. It tries to dequeue a message written to the mailbox (messages are queued to the UCB listhead at UCB$L_MB_MSGQ).

2. If the message queue is empty, STARTIO invokes COM$DELATTNAST to queue any pending read attention ASTs to the appropriate processes. The mailbox UCB busy bit remains set. As a result, subsequent read requests will be queued to the UCB. The current read request will not complete until a write request is issued. When the current read request is completed, STARTIO will process the next read request in the queue.

3. If STARTIO dequeued a message, it invokes FINISHREAD (in module MBDRIVER).

19.5.4.3.3 *Read Request Completion.* FINISHREAD is invoked by STARTIO and INSMBQUEUE to complete the current read request. STARTIO invokes FINISHREAD when it processes a read request and there is at least one message in the queue. INSMBQUEUE invokes FINISHREAD when a write request is to be queued and there is a read request in progress.

FINISHREAD takes the following steps:

1. It stores the address of the message block built by FDTWRITE (see Figure 19-6) in IRP$L_SVAPTE in the read request's IRP. The I/O postprocessing

routine uses this field to determine the address of the message to be copied to the user's buffer. (See Chapter 18 for more information on I/O postprocessing.)

2. It initializes the first two longwords in the message block with the values expected by the I/O postprocessing routine. (The first longword points to the message data, stored in the message block, and the second longword points to the user buffer, where the data will be copied by the I/O completion special kernel mode AST.)

3. It stores the address of the user's buffer (which is in IRP$L_MEDIA) in the message block.

4. It increases the message quota (UCB$W_BUFQUO) by the size of the message to reflect the delivery of this message.

5. It invokes SCH$RAVAIL to declare the availability of the mailbox resource.

6. It stores the final byte count in the read request IRP.

7. It places the process ID of the process that issued the read request in IRP$L_MEDIA + 4 (so that it will become the high-order longword of the I/O status block (IOSB) for the write request $QIO) and the SS$_NORMAL success code in the low-order word of the IOSB (IRP$L_MEDIA) of the write request IRP.

8. It invokes COM$POST (in module COMDRVSUB) to insert the write request's IRP on the I/O postprocessing queue. FINISHREAD calls this routine, rather than issuing the REQCOM macro, so that another IRP is not dequeued (because only read request IRPs are queued to the UCB waiting to enter the start I/O routine).

9. It places the process ID of the process that issued the write request in R1 and invokes the REQCOM macro to complete the read request. The value in R1 will become the high-order longword of the read request's IOSB. IOC$REQCOM will dequeue the next request and the start I/O sequence will be repeated. If no read request is outstanding, the busy bit will be cleared.

CONSOLE SUBSYSTEM

The console subsystem is the portion of the processor that initiates a bootstrap operation and permits microdiagnostics to execute. The details of the console subsystem are not specified by the VAX architecture, but are CPU-specific. The *Guide to VAX/VMS Software Installation* contains more details about the console subsystem of each CPU.

Some console features are common to most VAX processors. On these processors, there are at least four internal processor registers for communication with a console terminal. On some processors, these registers also communicate with a console block storage device; on others there are additional regis-

Table 19-1   VAX Console Processor Registers

Register Name	Use
PR$_RXCS	Console receive control and status register
PR$_RXDB	Console receive data buffer register
PR$_TXCS	Console transmit control and status register
PR$_TXDB	Console transmit data buffer register

ters. Table 19-1 lists the registers common to all VAX processors.

Transfers to console devices are made through internal processor registers and, on certain processors, device registers in I/O space. No direct memory transfer is made between a VAX CPU and any console device.

The VAX architecture specifies that the PR$_TXDB register is also used for communication from code executing VAX instructions to the console subsystem. Some special uses of this register are listed in Table 19-2. Some VAX processors support additional uses.

19.6.1   VAX-11/730 Console Subsystem

The console subsystem on the VAX-11/730 consists of a terminal, two TU58 cartridge devices, an optional remote diagnosis port, and a console microprocessor. The console program executes on the console microprocessor. When the console program has control, the VAX-11/730 cannot execute VAX instructions.

There are eight internal processor registers on the VAX-11/730 for communication with the console devices, four for the console terminal and four for the TU58s.

Table 19-2   Special Uses of the Console PR$_TXDB Register

Register Contents	Meaning	Comments
F01	Software done	This value notifies the console program that a program started by means of a console command file has completed successfully.
F02	Reboot the CPU	This value is written to request a system reboot from the default boot device.
F03	Clear warm-start flag	This flag is maintained to prevent nested restart attempts.
F04	Clear cold-start flag	This flag is maintained to prevent nested bootstrap attempts.

VAX-11/750 Console Subsystem

The console subsystem on the VAX-11/750 consists of a terminal, a TU58 cartridge device, an optional remote diagnosis port, and console microcode in the VAX-11/750 processor. When the console program has control, the VAX-11/750 processor is not executing user or system instructions but, rather, console microcode.

There are eight internal processor registers on the VAX-11/750 for communication with the console devices, four for the terminal and four for the TU58 console block storage device.

VAX-11/780 and VAX-11/785 Console Subsystem

The console subsystem on the VAX-11/780 and VAX-11/785 consists of an LSI-11 microcomputer, a floppy disk, the console terminal, and an optional remote diagnosis port. The console program executes on the LSI-11, and the console devices are on the LSI-11 bus. Because the console program executes on a separate processor, the console subsystem can perform a limited set of functions without halting the VAX CPU.

The VAX-11/780 or VAX-11/785 CPU has four internal processor registers for communication with both console devices. The device ID is encoded into control bits to distinguish between the two devices. In fact, the console program reads the registers and performs the appropriate I/O function to the appropriate device.

MicroVAX I Console Subsystem

The console subsystem on the MicroVAX I system consists of console microcode and a console terminal.

When the console program has control, the MicroVAX I processor is not executing user or system instructions but, rather, the console program microcode. The console program gains control of the processor whenever any halt condition occurs, such as execution of a HALT instruction.

The MicroVAX I has four internal processor registers for communication with the terminal.

MicroVAX II Console Subsystem

The console subsystem on the MicroVAX II system consists of a console program stored in ROM in the processor's local I/O space and a console terminal.

When the console program has control, the MicroVAX II processor is not executing user or system instructions but, rather, the console program's VAX instructions. The console program gains control of the processor whenever any halt condition occurs, such as execution of a HALT instruction.

The MicroVAX II has four internal processor registers for communication with the console terminal.

19.6.6 VAX 8200 Family Console Subsystem

The VAX 8200 family consists of the VAX 8200 and VAX 8300. The console subsystem on a VAX 8200 family member consists of a console terminal, two RX50 floppy disk drives, an optional remote diagnosis port, and console microcode in the VAX CPU. When the console program has control, the VAX processor is not executing user or system instructions but, rather, console microcode. The console program gains control of the processor whenever any halt condition occurs, such as execution of a HALT instruction.

The VAX 8200 CPU has four internal processor registers to communicate with the console terminal. Communication with the disk drives is through device registers in I/O space.

On a VAX 8300, only the primary CPU can communicate with the console terminal (using the same four internal processor registers as a VAX 8200 CPU). The secondary CPU communicates with the console terminal via the primary CPU. The primary and secondary CPUs use the internal processor register PR8SS$_RXCD to pass console data between them. The primary CPU uses the previously mentioned four internal processor registers to communicate with the console terminal on behalf of the secondary CPU.

19.6.7 VAX 8600 and VAX 8650 Console Subsystem

The console subsystem on the VAX 8600 and VAX 8650 consists of a PDP-11 microcomputer, an RL02 disk console block storage device, the console terminal, and an optional remote diagnosis port. The console program executes on the PDP-11. Because the console program executes on a separate processor, the console subsystem can perform a number of functions without halting the VAX CPU.

The VAX 8600 or VAX 8650 CPU has six internal processor registers to communicate with the two console devices, four for the console terminal and two for the disk.

19.6.8 VAX 8800 Family Console Subsystem

The VAX 8800 family consists of the VAX 8500, VAX 8550, VAX 8700, and VAX 8800. The console subsystem on a VAX 8800 family member consists of a microprocessor with a fixed disk, two floppy diskettes, a console terminal, and an optional remote diagnosis port. The console program executes on the console subsystem microcomputer. Because the console program executes on a separate processor, the console subsystem can perform a number of functions without halting the VAX CPUs.

Each VAX 8800 family member has four internal processor registers to communicate with all the console devices. The device ID is encoded into control bits to distinguish among the devices.

19.6.9   Data Transfer Between the VAX CPU and Console Devices

The internal processor registers PR\$_TXCS and PR\$_RXCS are used for control and status information (to enable interrupts and indicate that a device is ready). The other two internal processor registers, PR\$_RXDB and PR\$_TXDB, are used to transfer data. (For information about other CPU-specific internal processor registers that communicate with console devices, see the CPU-specific hardware documentation.) The TX*xx* registers are used for transmit operations (with respect to the VAX CPU), while the RX*xx* registers are used for receive operations.

Most other drivers treat device registers as if they were memory locations, using MOVB or MOVW instructions to read or write data in those registers. In the case of the console, the MTPR and MFPR instructions must be used to transmit and receive data, control, and status information.

For example, the following instructions on the VAX-11/780 transmit and receive data:

```
MTPR    data,#PR$_TXDB   ;  Transmit data
MFPR    #PR$_RXDB,data   ;  Receive data
```

The data is sent or received as a longword, with bits <7:0> containing the ASCII character and bits <11:8> identifying which console device (terminal or block storage device) is sending or receiving the data.

On some VAX CPUs, the distinction between devices is made by choice of register instead of by including a device code in a data buffer register. Note that all data is passed a character at a time, even to the block storage device.

19.6.10   Console Interrupt Dispatching

As the previous discussion of processor registers indicates, the terminal and console block storage device are treated slightly differently. On some CPUs, the block storage device has its own control registers and interrupt vectors. On others, the two devices are handled more as a single entity, with common routines distinguishing terminal operations from console block storage operations.

19.6.10.1   Console Terminal Interrupts.

When the system is bootstrapped, the system control block (SCB) is initialized (from the SCB template in module

[SYS]SCBVECTOR) so that the vectors at offsets $F8_{16}$ and FC_{16} point to console interrupt service routines (CON$INTDISI for console input and CON$INTDISO for console output).

Both routines respond to an interrupt by saving registers R0 through R5 and transferring control to a console driver in the CPU-specific image SYS-LOA*xxx* (CON$INTINP for console input, CON$INTOUT for console output). For many processors, the name of the driver is [SYSLOA]OPDRIVER. Other console drivers have names of the form OPDRV*xxx*. (See Appendix G for a list of VAX processors and their *xxx* designations.)

CON$INTINP reads the data and console device identification from the PR$_RXDB register and determines whether the interrupt was from the console terminal or block storage device. If the interrupt was from the console terminal, then the chapter read operation is handled by the terminal driver's character buffering routine whose address is stored in the console terminal UCB. The character is also echoed back to the console terminal by being placed in the PR$_TXDB register.

Routine CON$INTOUT transmits data to the console terminal through the PR$_TXDB register and determines whether the resulting interrupt is from the terminal or the console block storage device. If the interrupt was caused by the terminal, then the terminal output routine (whose address is stored in the console terminal UCB) is called to get the next character for output.

Note that the handling of console terminal I/O is done by the normal terminal driver routines. Only the initial fielding of interrupts and the device registers that are read or written distinguish console terminal I/O from operations through the regular terminal subsystem. Note also that the console terminal always interrupts at IPL 20 (the lowest device IPL) on all VAX processors.

19.6.10.2 **Console Block Storage Device I/O.** The device driver and associated database for the console block storage device are not loaded until an explicit CONNECT CONSOLE command is issued to SYSGEN. At that time, the device driver and data structures appropriate to the specific processor are loaded into memory and initialized.

A SYSGEN CONNECT CONSOLE command on a VAX-11/730 or VAX-11/750 causes the TU58 driver (called DDDRIVER) to be loaded. Data structures for a device called CSA1 are built. (On the VAX-11/730, a unit control block for CSA2 is also created.) In addition, two dedicated vectors in the SCB (at offsets $F0_{16}$ and $F4_{16}$ are loaded to point to interrupt dispatch code contained in the console device CRB.

DDDRIVER responds to console TU58 interrupts in exactly the same way that it responds to interrupts generated by a TU58 on the UNIBUS. The only difference between the two interrupts may be the device IPL at which each is dispatched. On a VAX-11/750, a console TU58 interrupt occurs at IPL 23, while UNIBUS TU58 interrupts and VAX-11/730 console TU58 interrupts occur at IPL 20.

A SYSGEN CONNECT CONSOLE command on a VAX-11/780 causes the console floppy disk driver (called DXDRIVER) to be loaded and data structures for a device called CSA1 to be built. Because the console floppy interrupts through the same vectors used by the console terminal, no further SCB modification is required.

When a console device interrupt occurs, the interrupt service routine determines whether the interrupt was from the console terminal or from the block storage device. If the interrupt was from the block storage device, the console has been connected (a UCB exists for device CSA1), and the interrupt was expected (the UCB$V_INT bit is set in the status word in the UCB), then the driver context is restored from the UCB and the driver process is resumed at the saved PC (UCB$L_FPC). Otherwise, the interrupt is considered spurious and is simply dismissed.

In response to the CONNECT CONSOLE command on a VAX 8600 or VAX 8650, SYSGEN loads the console RL02 driver, CVDRIVER, and builds data structures for CSA1. The SCB vector at offset $F0_{16}$ is initialized to point to interrupt dispatching code in the console CRB.

The VAX 8800 family is similar to the VAX 8600, except that the console block storage driver name is CWDRIVER and there are three block storage units. On the VAX 8200 and VAX 8300, the console block storage driver is RXDRIVER.

19.6.10.3   **Double Mapping of Buffer Pages.** One interesting feature of the console block storage device drivers is that they double map a page in the user's data buffer into system address space so that data can be transferred directly to and from the user's buffer. User buffer pages are not normally accessible because device drivers execute in system context and do not have process address space available to them. By double mapping a buffer page into a system address range, the driver can access the entire user buffer one page at a time. The SPTE used to map the page is reserved in the driver by setting the DPT$V_SVP bit in the FLAGS argument to the DPTAB macro.

By making the user buffer accessible through system virtual addresses, these drivers can use VMS direct I/O, even though they are not DMA devices. Use of direct I/O enables them to issue virtual I/O requests, call existing file system FDT routines, and use the virtual I/O completion routines in the I/O postprocessing code.

PART VI/Process Creation and Deletion

20 Process Creation

All things in the world come from being.
And being comes from non-being.

Lao-tzu, *Tao Tê Ching*

The creation of a new process requires the cooperation of several pieces of the executive:

- Creation begins in the context of an existing process that requests the Create Process ($CREPRC) system service. The $CREPRC system service performs the following steps:

  a. It makes privilege and quota checks.
  b. It allocates and initializes the process control block (PCB); a job information block (JIB), if it is creating a detached process; and the process quota block (PQB), with explicit $CREPRC arguments and implicit parameters taken from the context of the creator.
  c. It places the new process into the scheduler database.

- The initial scheduling state of the new process is computable outswapped (COMO). Thus, execution of the new process is suppressed until the swapper process moves the new process into the balance set. The following steps are performed in the context of the swapper process:

  a. The swapper moves the template for the new process context into the balance set from SHELL, a module in the system image.
  b. It builds the process header (PHD) according to the values of SYSBOOT parameters for this configuration.

- The final steps of process initialization take place in the context of the new process in the routine EXE$PROCSTRT. EXE$PROCSTRT performs the following steps:

  a. It copies the arguments from the PQB to the PHD and various locations in P1 space.
  b. It calls the image activator to activate the image.
  c. It calls the image at its entry point.

20.1 CREATE PROCESS SYSTEM SERVICE

The $CREPRC system service establishes the parameters of the new process. Some of these parameters are passed to the system service by the caller. The

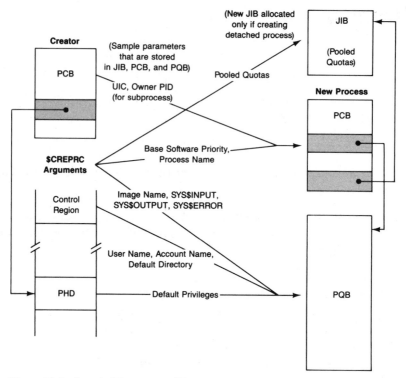

Figure 20-1 Sample Movement of Parameters in Process Creation

system service copies others from the context of the caller: the caller's PCB, PHD, JIB, and control region are all used (see Figure 20-1).

The $CREPRC system service can copy information to the PCB or the JIB of the new process, but cannot access its PHD or control region because neither exists at this stage of process creation. The parameters to be copied to either of these are stored in a temporary data structure until the new process comes into existence and has a virtual address space and PHD. The PQB is this temporary data structure. Its contents are listed in Table 20-1.

20.1.1 Control Flow of the Create Process System Service

The $CREPRC system service procedure, EXE$CREPRC in module SYSCREPRC, runs in kernel mode. It takes the following steps:

1. The caller specifies the UIC argument to request creation of a detached process. EXE$CREPRC tests whether the specified user identification code (UIC) is the same as that of the caller. If it is, no privilege is necessary. (This behavior is new with VAX/VMS Version 4.) Otherwise, the process needs either the DETACH or CMKRNL privilege. If the process is

Table 20-1   Contents of the Process Quota Block

Item	Size (Bytes)
Privilege mask	8
Size of PQB	2
Type code	1
Status	1
AST limit	4
Buffered I/O limit	4
Buffered I/O byte limit[1]	4
CPU time limit	4
Direct I/O limit	4
Open file limit[1]	4
Paging file quota[1]	4
Subprocess limit[1]	4
Timer queue entry limit[1]	4
Working set quota	4
Working set default	4
Lock limit	4
Working set extent	4
Logical name table quota	4
Flags	2
Default message flags	1
Reserved	1
Authorization file flags	4
Process creation flags	4
Minimum authorized security class	20
Maximum authorized security class	20
SYS$INPUT attributes	4
SYS$OUTPUT attributes	4
SYS$ERROR attributes	4
SYS$DISK attributes	4
CLI image name	256
CLI command table name	256
Spawn CLI image name	256
Spawn CLI command table name	256
Equivalence name for SYS$INPUT	256
Equivalence name for SYS$OUTPUT	256
Equivalence name for SYS$ERROR	256
Equivalence name for SYS$DISK	256
Default directory string	256
Image name	256

[1]This quota or limit is now pooled in the JIB; hence, the PQB is no longer used to transfer this value.

requesting creation of a detached process without the necessary privilege, EXE$CREPRC returns the error status SS$_NOPRIV to its caller.

2. EXE$CREPRC allocates a PCB from nonpaged pool and a PQB from either the PQB lookaside list or paged pool. (Chapter 3 describes nonpaged pool, paged pool, and the PQB lookaside list.) EXE$CREPRC zeros all of both data structures except their headers. After allocating the pool, EXE$CREPRC is running at IPL 2.

3. If EXE$CREPRC is creating a detached process, it allocates a JIB from nonpaged pool and initializes it. EXE$CREPRC initializes the jobwide list of mounted volumes as an empty list. It copies account and user name from the creating process's JIB and zeros all other fields.

   If EXE$CREPRC is creating a subprocess, no JIB allocation is necessary; the subprocess shares the JIB of its creator. The relationship between the JIB and the PCBs of several processes in the same job is shown in Figure 20-2. EXE$CREPRC increments JIB$W_PRCCNT, the count of subprocesses in the job. It tests whether the field is less than or equal to JIB$W_PRCLIM, the maximum number of processes in the job tree. If the job tree is at its maximum size, EXE$CREPRC returns the error status SS$_EXQUOTA to its caller.

   Note that the process count fields within each PCB (PCB$W_PRCCNT) count the number of subprocesses created by that process. JIB$W_PRCCNT counts the total number of subprocesses in the job.

   Whether a detached process or subprocess is being created, EXE$CREPRC stores the address of the JIB in PCB$L_JIB.

4. If a subprocess is being created, EXE$CREPRC charges the number of SHELL pages against JIB$L_PGFLCNT, the page file quota. If the job has insufficient page file quota, EXE$CREPRC returns the error status SS$_EXQUOTA to its caller.

5. Several fields in the PCB are initialized to nonzero values:

   a. The AST queue is set up as empty.
   b. AST delivery to all access modes is enabled.
   c. The lock queue in the PCB is set up as empty.
   d. The default file protection is copied from the creating process's PCB.
   e. The entire access rights block (ARB) is copied from the creating process's ARB. If the creator has an extended rights list, EXE$CREPRC allocates a nonpaged pool buffer into which it copies the extended rights list.

      The ARB is currently located within the PCB. However, routines such as ACPs and device drivers that wish to check a process's access rights use the ARB pointer to locate the privilege mask and UIC. If, in the future, the ARB becomes an independent structure, the programs that use the ARB pointer will continue to work without modification.

   f. The unit number of a termination mailbox is copied from the

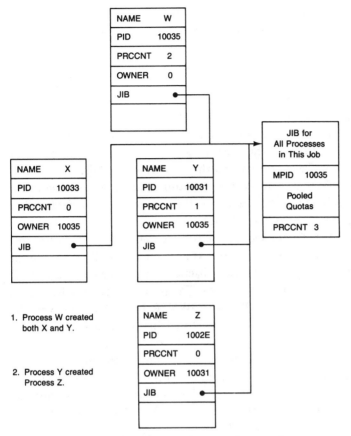

Figure 20-2 Relationship Between the JIB and PCBs of
Several Processes in the Same Job

$CREPRC MBXUNIT argument. A unit number of zero will indicate to
the process deletion routine that no termination message is to be sent
back to the creator.

g. The process page count, PCB$W_PPGCNT, is initialized to the count
of pages in the shell process.

h. EXE$CREPRC copies the process name into the PCB.

6. The process privileges of the new process are determined and stored into
the PQB. If no privilege argument is present, the current privileges of the
creator are used. (Table 21-2 summarizes the various privilege masks associated with a process.)

If a privilege argument is present and the creator has SETPRV privilege,
then the privilege argument is used with no modification.

If a privilege argument is present and the creator does not have
SETPRV privilege, then the privileges passed to the new process are the
logical AND of the privileges of the creator and the privileges specified in

the argument to $CREPRC. In short, a created process cannot receive privileges that its creator does not have.

7. The software priority of the new process is determined and stored in the PCB in the base priority, initial priority, and current priority fields. (Because the BASPRI argument is passed by value, it is always present, with a default value determined by the treatment of missing arguments by the language processor.)

   If the creator has ALTPRI privilege, the priority specified in the argument list is used. If the creator does not have ALTPRI privilege, the smaller of its base priority and the priority in the argument list is used.

8. The UIC of the new process is determined and stored in the PCB. If the caller specified the UIC argument, the new process is a detached process and the argument is the UIC for that detached process.

   If the caller did not specify the UIC argument, the UIC of the creator is used. If the caller specified the STSFLG bit DETACH, then the process being created is detached. The absence of that flag and a zero UIC indicate the creation of a subprocess. The (internal) process ID (PID) of the creator is stored in the PCB$L_OWNER field of the PCB of the new subprocess. Its extended PID is stored in the field PCB$L_EOWNER. (Section 20.1.4 describes internal and extended PIDs.)

9. EXE$CREPRC tests that the process name is unique within the UIC group. It examines the process name fields of all PCBs in the system with the same group number. If the process name is not unique, EXE$CREPRC returns the error status SS$_DUPLNAM to its caller. Process name is always qualified by UIC group number.

10. Several text strings are copied to the PQB. The image name and the equivalence names for SYS$INPUT, SYS$OUTPUT, and SYS$ERROR are taken from the $CREPRC argument list. EXE$CREPRC translates the logical name SYS$DISK in the table LNM$FILE_DEV and stores its equivalence name in the PQB. For compatibility with previous releases, SYS$DISK is translated once. Thus, its equivalence name must be either a shareable logical name or physical device name.

11. The default message flags and flags from the authorization file record are copied from the control region of the creator to the PQB.

12. EXE$CREPRC copies the minimum and maximum authorized security clearance records from the creator's PHD to the new process's PQB.

13. It copies the following information from the P1 space of the creator process:

    —Default directory string
    —Command language interpreter (CLI) name
    —Command table name
    —CLI name for use by spawned subprocesses
    —Command table name for use by spawned subprocesses

Table 20-2   Flags in the Status Longword in the PCB (PCB$L_STS) That Can Be Set at
Process Creation

Flag in PCB$L_STS	Meaning (If Set)	Privilege Required
PCB$V_SSRWAIT	Disable system service resource wait mode	None
PCB$V_SSFEXCU	Enable system service exceptions for user access mode	None
PCB$V_PSWAPM	Inhibit process swapping	PSWAPM
PCB$V_NOACNT	Suppress accounting	NOACNT
PCB$V_BATCH	Batch (noninteractive) process	DETACH
PCB$V_HIBER	Hibernate process before calling image	None
PCB$V_LOGIN	Log in without reading the authorization file	None
PCB$V_NETWRK	Process is a network connect object	DETACH
PCB$V_DISAWS	Disable system initiated working set adjustment	None
PCB$V_INTER	Process is interactive	None

14. The status flags for the new process are extracted from the $CREPRC argument list and set in the PCB$L_STS field in the new PCB. Some of these flags require privileges (see Table 20-2). The privilege mask that is checked is that of the creator process.

15. If the process being created is a detached process (that is, not a subprocess, batch, network, or interactive process), then EXE$CREPRC copies JIB$W_MAXJOBS and JIB$W_MAXDETACH from the JIB of the creator to that of the new process. If either count is nonzero, indicating a limit, EXE$CREPRC must check whether creation of this process would exceed one of those limits. To check, it raises IPL to IPL$_SYNCH (8) and scans all existing processes. It looks for one which is not a network process or a subprocess and which has the same user name as the process being created. If it finds one, it increments the total count of jobs with that user name. If the process is neither interactive nor batch, it also increments the total count of detached processes with that user name. After scanning all the processes, if either limit has been exceeded, EXE$CREPRC returns the error status SS$_EXPRCLM to its caller.

16. The quotas are determined for the new process and stored in the PQB. Section 20.1.2 describes the steps taken to determine the quota list for the new process.

17. The address of the PQB is stored in the field PCB$L_PQB (see Figure 20-1). PCB$L_PQB uses the same longword as the event flag wait mask field, PCB$L_EFWM. This field is available because the process cannot yet be waiting for any event flags.

18. EXE$CREPRC processes the ITMLST argument, if one was supplied. This argument is reserved for use by VAX/VMS. Its use is to pass logical name attributes for SYS$INPUT, SYS$OUTPUT, and SYS$ERROR, which

EXE$CREPRC copies to the PQB.

19. IPL is raised to IPL$_SYNCH to synchronize access to the scheduler database. Swap space is allocated for the process. Its address and size are stored in the PCB. If sufficient swap space cannot be allocated, EXE$CREPRC returns the error status SS$_INSSWAPSPACE to its caller.

20. EXE$CREPRC searches the PCB vector (pictured in Figure 20-3 and described in Section 20.1.3) for an empty slot. If it finds none, it returns the error status SS$_NOSLOT to its caller.

21. If the maximum process count has been exceeded (SCH$GW_PROC-CNT's contents are larger than those of SCH$GW_PROCLIM), EXE$CREPRC returns the error status SS$_NOSLOT to its caller. Otherwise, internal and extended PIDs are fabricated (see Section 20.1.4) and stored in the PCB of the new process.

22. If a detached process is being created, its internal PID (IPID) is stored in the master PID field of the JIB (JIB$L_MPID).

23. EXE$CREPRC invokes the routine SCH$CHSE to make this process COMO. A boost of 6 is given to the base priority. It is this boosted priority that will determine when the new process is copied in from the SHELL.

24. If a subprocess is being created, the count of subprocesses owned by the creator (PCB$W_PRCCNT in the creator's PCB) is incremented. In addi-

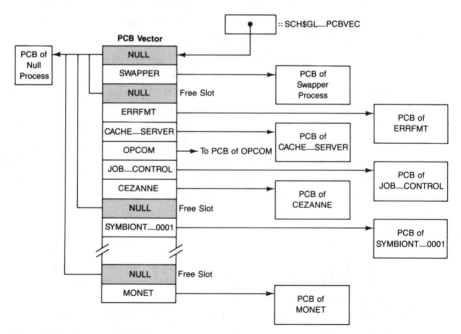

Figure 20-3   Sample PCB Vector

tion, if the creator has a nonzero CPU time limit (there is a CPU time limit in effect), the amount of CPU time passed to the new process is deducted from the creator.

25. Finally, the extended PID (EPID) of the new process is returned to the creator (if requested), IPL is lowered to 0, and control is passed back to the caller of $CREPRC.

20.1.2 Establishing Quotas for the New Process

Two tables in the executive are used by the $CREPRC system service when quotas are set up for the new process: a minimum quota table and a default quota table. Each quota or limit in the system has an entry in both tables. The contents of the minimum table are determined by the SYSBOOT parameters whose names are of the form PQL_M*quota-name*; the contents of the default table are of the form PQL_D*quota-name*. Following is a list of the steps taken to determine the value for each quota or limit that is passed to the new process:

1. The default values for each quota are put into the PQB as initial values.
2. Each quota that is included in the argument list to $CREPRC replaces the default value in the list.
3. Each quota is forced to at least its minimum value.
4. A check is made to ensure that the creator possesses sufficient quota to cover the quotas that it is giving to the new process. This check is performed in the following way:

   a. If the creator has either DETACH or CMKRNL privilege and is creating a detached process, then no check is performed. If the creator has neither privilege and is creating a detached process with the same UIC, then the new process quotas must be less than or equal to those of the creator. This type of process creation is termed "restricted detached." Pooled quotas are placed directly into the newly allocated JIB.

   b. If a subprocess is being created and the quota is neither pooled nor deductible (the only deductible quota currently implemented is CPU time limit), then the subprocess quota must be smaller than or equal to the creator's quota.

   c. Pooled quotas require no special action when a subprocess is being created because they already reside in the JIB, a structure that is shared by all processes in the job (see Figure 20-2).

   d. If a subprocess is being created and the quota in question is the CPU time limit quota, what happens depends on how much quota the creator process possesses. If the creator has infinite CPU time limit, then no check is performed. If the creator has a finite CPU time limit and specifies an infinite CPU time limit for the subprocess, half of the creator's CPU time limit is passed to the subprocess. If the creator has a finite CPU time limit and specifies a finite CPU time limit for the subprocess, the amount passed to the subprocess must be less than the creator's original quota, or the creation is aborted.

5. The quotas and working values that belong in the PCB are moved to the PCB.

Table 20-3 lists the quotas that are passed to a new process when it is created, whether each quota is deductible or pooled, and where the limit is stored in the context of the new process. Further discussion of quotas can be found in the *VAX/VMS System Manager's Reference Manual* and in the *VAX/ VMS System Services Reference Manual*.

With the exception of CPU time limit and subprocess count, all active counts start at their process limit values and decrement to zero. An active count of zero indicates no quota remaining. An active count equal to the corresponding process limit indicates no outstanding requests.

20.1.3   The PCB Vector

When the system is initialized, an array of MAXPROCESSCNT longwords is allocated from nonpaged pool. This array locates the PCB of each process in the system at any given time. The first two entries in the table point to the PCBs of the null process and the swapper process. All other entries in the table initially point to the PCB of the null process.

An entry that points to the PCB of the null process but has nonzero index is considered an empty slot. (The entry that locates the PCB of the null process that has an index of zero is the "real" pointer.) The scan for an empty slot begins with the slot most recently allocated. System processes created during system initialization have low indexes.

An example of the contents of this table is shown in Figure 20-3.

20.1.4   Fabrication of Process IDs

Under VAX/VMS Version 4, a process has two forms of PID, an internal one and an extended one. In this book, the unqualified term "process ID" refers to the internal and traditional form. Internal PID and extended PID are referred to as IPID and EPID. The EPID is a version of the IPID that is compressed so that it can also specify the VAXcluster node of a process.

The following PCB fields contain information related to process identification:

- PCB$L_PID—Internal process ID
- PCB$L_EPID—Extended process ID

Table 20-3   Storage Areas for Process Quotas

Quota/Limit Name	Location of Active Count	Location of Process Limit	Count/Limit Stored by[1]
	NONDEDUCTIBLE QUOTAS		
AST limit	PCB$W_ASTCNT	PHD$W_ASTLM	C/P
Buffered I/O limit	PCB$W_BIOCNT	PCB$W_BIOLM	C/C
Direct I/O limit	PCB$W_DIOCNT	PCB$W_DIOLM	C/C
Working set quota	n/a[2]	PHD$W_WSQUOTA	/P
Working set default	n/a[2]	PHD$W_DFWSCNT	/P
Working set extent	n/a[2]	PHD$W_WSEXTENT	/P
	DEDUCTIBLE QUOTA		
CPU time limit	PHD$L_CPUTIM	PHD$L_CPULIM	P/P[3]
	POOLED QUOTAS (SHARED BY ALL PROCESSES IN THE SAME JOB)		
Buffered I/O byte limit	JIB$L_BYTCNT	JIB$L_BYTLM	[4]
Open file limit	JIB$W_FILCNT	JIB$W_FILLM	[4]
Page file page limit	JIB$L_PGFLCNT	JIB$L_PGFLQUOTA	[4]
Subprocess limit	JIB$W_PRCCNT	JIB$W_PRCLIM	[4]
Timer queue entry limit	JIB$W_TQCNT	JIB$W_TQLM	[4]
Enqueue limit	JIB$W_ENQCNT	JIB$W_ENQLM	[4]

[1]The slash (/) separates the count from the limit:

C/ indicates that the count value is stored by EXE$CREPRC.
/C indicates that the limit value is stored by EXE$CREPRC.
P/ indicates that the count value is stored by EXE$PROCSTRT.
/P indicates that the limit value is stored by EXE$PROCSTRT.

[2]Working set list quotas are handled differently from other quotas (see Chapter 15).
[3]CPUTIM starts at zero and increments for each clock tick that the process is current. If limit checking is in effect (CPULIM nonzero), then CPUTIM may not exceed CPULIM.
[4]The contents of the JIB are loaded by EXE$CREPRC when a detached process is created. Subprocess creation uses an existing JIB.

- PCB$L_OWNER—Internal process ID of process's creator
- PCB$L_EOWNER—External process ID of process's creator

The executive generally identifies a process by its IPID, although code such as the lock management system services may use both forms. System services accept and return EPIDs. System utilities display EPIDs.

The low-order word of the IPID contains the index into the PCB vector that locates the PCB of the identified process. The high-order word is taken from an array of words that is allocated from nonpaged pool and cleared during system initialization. There is one element (called a sequence number) in

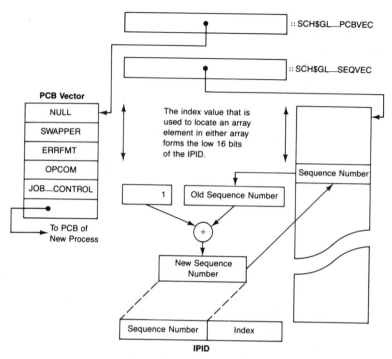

Figure 20-4 Fabrication of Internal Process IDs (IPIDs)

this array for each possible PCB vector index. The element is used as a consistency check to determine that a number alleged to be an IPID corresponds to a real process in the system.

When an empty slot in the PCB vector is located, the corresponding sequence number (see Figure 20-4) is incremented and used as the high-order 16 bits of the IPID. When a process is referenced by its IPID, the validity of the IPID is checked by using the low-order 16 bits as an index into the sequence vector and comparing the value found there with the high-order 16 bits of the IPID. With this scheme, a second check must also be made. The entry in the PCB vector must be compared to the address of the null process. If the addresses are equal, the process has been deleted but no new process has been assigned to the empty slot.

Sequence numbers cycle to 0 after reaching 32767. Thus, IPIDs, when interpreted as signed integers, are always positive. Negative values in the IRP$L_PID field of an I/O request packet are used in a special form of I/O completion. The I/O postprocessing interrupt service routine interprets a negative IRP$L_PID value as the (system virtual) address of an internal I/O completion routine.

The two checks described in the previous paragraphs are actually performed in one step (routine EXE$NAMPID in module SYSPCNTRL) by using

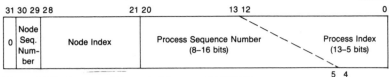

Figure 20-5 Layout of Extended Process ID (EPID)

the low-order word of the IPID as an index into the PCB vector. The PCB indexed by the IPID contains its IPID at offset PCB$L_PID. The IPID in the PCB is compared to the IPID that is being checked. If the process specified has been deleted (the PCB vector now points to the PCB of the null process) but the slot has not yet been reused (the sequence number is not yet incremented), the sequence number array element will match the high-order word in the IPID but the full 32-bit IPIDs will not match.

The EPID is constructed from the IPID. Figure 20-5 shows its format. Its low-order 21 bits contain the IPID in two fields. The widths of these two fields vary, depending on the value of the SYSBOOT parameter MAXPROCESSCNT. The first field, beginning at bit zero, contains the process index. The size of the field is computed at system initialization and stored in global location SCH$GL_PIXWIDTH. The second field contains the sequence number. Its size is 21 minus the size of the first field.

Bit 31 of the EPID is zero. The other ten high-order bits identify the VAXcluster node. The node identification is similar to process identification in that it consists of an index into a node table and a sequence number that counts how many times the index has been reused. On a system that is not a VAXcluster node, these bits are all zero.

After a system joins a VAXcluster System, the EPIDs of any existing processes must be updated with the node information, which comes from the node's cluster system identification (CSID). The low-order ten bits from the global location SCH$GW_LOCALNODE are inserted into the field PCB$L_EPID of each process and, if appropriate, into the field PCB$L_EOWNER.

The format of the EPID, like any other internal interface, is subject to change in future releases of VAX/VMS. Kernel mode software should not attempt to partition the fields in the EPID and, instead, should use one of the following routines when transformation or manipulation of an EPID is necessary:

- EXE$EPID_TO_PCB—Convert an EPID to address of corresponding PCB
- EXE$EPID_TO_IPID—Convert an EPID to IPID
- EXE$IPID_TO_EPID—Convert an IPID to EPID
- EXE$IPID_TO_PCB—Convert an IPID to address of corresponding PCB

These routines are in the module SYSPCNTRL.

20.2 **THE SHELL PROCESS**

A process comes into existence in the COMO scheduling state. However, the swap image of a newly created process does not reside in the swap file. Instead, a special swap image exists in the paged portion of the system image file, SYS$SYSTEM:SYS.EXE (see Figures 20-6 and 14-22). Table F-2 shows the relative location of SHELL within the paged executive. This image contains a minimal PHD and P1 space.

The actual contents of the swap image found in SHELL are listed in Table 20-4. As shown in the table, there are five P1 pages, two P1 page table pages, and a variable number of PHD pages that contribute to SHELL. The swapper process reads seven of these pages when it creates a new process.

20.2.1 **Moving SHELL into Process Context**

The selection of a newly created process for inswap and the actual inswap operation are performed by the swapper. If all SHELL's pages are valid, the swapper copies them to the new process's P1 space by a MOVC instruction. If any is invalid, the swapper reads all the pages from the system image on disk, rather than pagefault several times. This optimization is especially effective at times when many processes are being created.

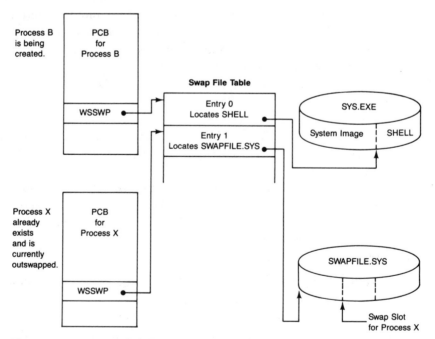

Figure 20-6   Location of Shell Process in the System Image File

Table 20-4   Contents of the Initial Swap Image in the Shell Process

Item	Size	Permanently Locked in Working Set	Page Number in SHELL	Is Page Read from SHELL by Swapper Process?
PHD (fixed + WSL + PST)	n/a[1]	Yes	1	Yes, 1 page only
P1 page table pages	2	Yes	2, 3	Yes, 2 pages
P1 pointer page	1	Yes	4	Yes, 1 page
RMS data area	1	No	5	Yes, 1 page
Kernel stack	3	Yes	6, 7	Yes, first 2 pages
Rest of PHD	n/a[1]	Yes		No
Page table page arrays	n/a[2]	Yes		No

[1]The size of the top of the PHD depends on the values of several SYSBOOT parameters. See Appendix F for details on how the size of the PHD is calculated by SYSBOOT.

[2]There are eight bytes per PHD page in these arrays. See Appendix F for details.

20.2.2   Configuration of the Process Header

When the system image SYS.EXE is linked, the shell process is constructed to look exactly like an outswapped process. However, a PHD cannot be entirely configured without taking into account several SYSBOOT parameters.

To accomplish the final configuration of the PHD, the swapper makes one check (after the process has been read in, but before the working set is rebuilt) to determine whether this is a new process created from SHELL. If it is, a special subroutine is called to configure the PHD before the final operations of inswap are completed.

This subroutine of the swapper, SWP$SHELINIT in module SHELL, executes only as part of the creation of a new process. To avoid using up space in the resident executive, the routine is put into some of the pages that are read in from SHELL. Recall from Chapter 17 that the swapper's pseudo page table (as far as the I/O system is concerned) is also its P0 page table (as far as address translation routines are concerned). This special subroutine executes from P0 addresses in the context of the swapper process. After the new process page tables are set up, the physical pages that contain this code become the kernel stack.

Running in kernel mode, the routine SWP$SHELINIT performs the following actions:

1. It zeros pages that are a part of SHELL (and also permanently locked into the working set), but which are not read from the copy of SHELL in the system image. The pages zeroed are all but the first page of the beginning of the PHD, one page of the kernel stack, and the page table page arrays

(see Table 20-4). None of the information to be put into these pages is assembled into the system image. Their contents are determined dynamically and stored by EXE$PROCSTRT.

2. The system page table entries (SPTEs) that map the fixed portion of the PHD, the working set list (WSL), and the process section table (PST) are temporarily mapped so that SWP$SHELINIT can access them. The initial contents of each SPTE are simply the contents of the swapper's I/O map (see Figure 14-24).

3. The SPTEs that map the empty pages of the PHD (used for WSL expansion, see Chapter 14) are left as no-access pages. The SPTEs that map the page table page arrays in the PHD (see Chapters 14 and 17) are also temporarily mapped so that SWP$SHELINIT can access them.

4. The translation buffer is invalidated.

5. The balance slot index is stored in the PHD. This number is supplied to SHELL by the swapper, which records the number of the slot that has just been filled.

6. The SYSBOOT parameters that determine the default page fault cluster size and the default page table page fault cluster size are stored in the PHD.

7. The page file with the most free space is selected as the page file for the new process. The page file number is recorded in the PHD at offset PHD$B_PAGFIL.

8. The index to the beginning of the WSL (PHD$W_WSLIST) and the pointer to the end of the PST (PHD$L_PSTBASOFF) are calculated and stored.

9. The pointers to the four arrays in the page table page array portion of the PHD (see Figure 14-8) are calculated and stored. The page table page arrays (which count valid and locked pages in each page of PTEs) are initialized to −1, indicating no valid or locked pages. The next to last page table page in P1 space has its entries corrected to reflect four locked pages and five valid pages. The four locked pages are the P1 pointer page and three pages of kernel stack. The page that is valid but not locked is one page of Record Management Services (RMS) data area.

10. The four counters in the fixed portion of the header that count page table pages with locked pages, valid pages, active page table pages, and those PTEs with nonzero entries (see Figure 14-8) are initialized to the number of active P1 page table pages. There are two such pages for VAX/VMS Version 4.

11. Three WSL pointers (WSLOCK, WSDYN, WSNEXT) are adjusted from their initial values assembled into SHELL to reflect the additional pages from the top of the PHD that are a permanent part of the working set. The WSL entry (WSLE) for the one page that is valid but not locked (step 9) is slid down to make room for the WSLEs for the PHD pages.

12. The pages that comprise the top of the PHD (fixed portion, WSL, PST, and page table page arrays) are added to the process WSL. In addition, the page frame number (PFN) database arrays for the physical pages that are mapped are updated to indicate that these pages are page table pages (TYPE array), active and modified (STATE array), and in the process working set (WSLX array).

13. The SPTEs that map the process PTEs are initialized to demand zero pages. The two P1 page table pages that are a permanent part of the working set are added to the WSL. The PFN arrays for the physical pages to which the P1 page table pages are mapped are updated as in step 12. Finally, the SPTEs that map these P1 page table pages are set up so that these pages are accessible.

14. The offsets from the beginning of the PHD to the beginning of the P0 page table and the end of the P1 page table are calculated, reflecting the size of the beginning of the PHD (see Chapter 14 and Appendix F). The address of the first free virtual address in P1 space (stored in the PHD at offset PHD$L_FREP1VA) and the contents of the copy of the P1 length register (stored in the hardware PCB in the PHD) are also adjusted to reflect the size of the PHD which is mapped into P1 space.

15. The swapper I/O map (see Figure 14-24) is adjusted to reflect the current state of the WSL. The address of the P1 window to the top of the PHD is calculated and stored in location CTL$GL_PHD. (Although the swapper is the current process, it is able to access the P1 address of the newly created process because its pages are mapped as swapper P0 addresses in the swapper I/O page table.) When SWP$SHELINIT returns control to the swapper, the completion of the inswap operation will reflect the correct state of the WSL and the location of the P1 window to the PHD.

16. The PHD is marked resident by setting bit PCB$V_PHDRES in PCB$L_STS.

17. The WSQUOTA, WSAUTH, WSEXTENT, and WSAUTHEXTENT pointers are initialized to the value of the SYSBOOT parameter WSMAX. The WSFLUID counter is initialized to the value of the SYSBOOT parameter MINWSCNT. The end of the WSL (WSLAST) and the default count (DFWSCNT) initially reflect the value of the SYSBOOT parameter PQL_DWSDEFAULT. PHD$W_WSSIZE is initialized to the value of PQL_DWSDEFAULT.

18. The calculations in step 14 adjusted the values of the P0 and P1 base registers relative to the beginning of the PHD. The virtual address of the PHD is added to these two registers so that they contain the virtual addresses of the beginning of the P0 and P1 page tables, exactly what is required for address translation.

19. The P1PTEs that map the system service vectors are initialized with the contents of the SPTEs that map the system service vectors in system

space. The P1 mapping of the system service vectors enables them to be replaced on a per-process basis, simply by modifying that process's P1PTEs.

20. Finally, the size of the initial swap space allocation is copied from the PCB to the PHD (PHD$L_SWAPSIZE).

SWP$SHELINIT returns control to the swapper's main inswap routine, where the final steps of the inswap operation are completed. The operation of the swapper process is described in Chapter 17.

20.3 PROCESS CREATION IN THE CONTEXT OF THE NEW PROCESS

The final steps of process creation take place in the context of the newly created process. SHELL contains an initial hardware context for the process. In particular, the saved PC in the hardware PCB is the address of the routine EXE$PROCSTRT in module PROCSTRT. The saved PSL indicates kernel mode at IPL 2. Thus, the first code that executes in the context of a newly created process is the same for every process in the system.

20.3.1 Operation of EXE$PROCSTRT

EXE$PROCSTRT begins execution in kernel mode at IPL 2. It also executes in executive and user modes. When EXE$PROCSTRT is entered, the PCB and the PHD have been properly configured. In addition, all PCB information passed from the creator process has been copied by EXE$CREPRC. EXE$PROCSTRT must copy the information from its temporary location in the PQB to the PHD and P1 space (see Figure 20-7). EXE$PROCSTRT then prepares for execution and calls the image whose name was passed by the creator process.

EXE$PROCSTRT performs the following steps:

1. It stores the addresses of the RMS dispatcher and the base of the control region in the P1 pointer page. The base of the control region is the address of the P1 map to the PHD, which is the part of P1 space currently at the lowest virtual address.

2. The P1 space vectors for user-written system services, user-written run-down handlers, and per-process or image-specific messages are initialized to point to RSB instructions. (The use of these vectors in dispatching to user-written system services is discussed in Chapter 9.)

3. The address of the process's PCB is stored in CTL$GL_PCB.

4. EXE$PROCSTRT initializes the kernel request packet (KRP) lookaside list (see Chapter 3), forming the space into KRPs and inserting them on the list.

5. Those quotas that are stored in the PHD (currently only CPU time limit

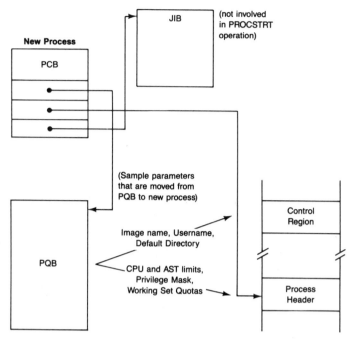

Figure 20-7   Removal of Process Parameters from the
Process Quota Block

and asynchronous system trap (AST) limit) are moved from the PQB to
the PHD (see Table 20-3).

6. The WSL pointers are initialized to reflect the quotas passed from the
   creator (after minimization with the systemwide working set maximum).

7. The process's base priority is copied to PHD$B_AUTHPRI and
   PCB$B_AUTHPRI. Saving the base priority enables a process without
   ALTPRI privilege to lower its base priority and later raise it as high as the
   original base priority.

8. The process privilege mask is copied to the first quadword of the PHD
   (the working privilege mask), the permanent privilege mask
   (CTL$GQ_PROCPRIV in the P1 pointer page), and the authorized privi-
   lege mask (PHD$Q_AUTHPRIV). The use of each of these privilege
   masks is described in Chapter 21.

9. The default message flags are copied into P1 space.

10. The login time is saved in CTL$GQ_LOGIN.

11. EXE$PROCSTRT copies the minimum and maximum authorized secu-
    rity clearance records from the PQB to the PHD.

12. It initializes to empty three image activator lists (see Chapter 21):

    —Image control blocks (ICBs) representing activated images

       —ICBs representing work in progress
       —ICB lookaside list

13. EXE$PROCSTRT creates P1 virtual address space for four uses:

       —Channel control block table
       —Process allocation region
       —Process I/O segment
       —Image I/O segment

    Appendix F describes these areas and the SYSBOOT parameters that affect their size. EXE$PROCSTRT records the address of each portion and writes the new low P1 space address in CTL$GL_CTLBASVA.

14. It allocates space from the P1 allocation region for the process logical name hash table and initializes it. EXE$PROCSTRT also allocates space for the process-private logical names and tables which it will create. (Chapter 28 describes the logical name data structures and their use.)

15. It initializes the process directory logical name table, LNM$PROCESS_DIRECTORY, and the process logical name table and inserts them into the hash table.

16. EXE$PROCSTRT creates the logical name table logical names LNM$PROCESS, LNM$GROUP, and LNM$JOB. It inserts them into the hash table and in LNM$PROCESS_DIRECTORY.

17. Using the PQB equivalence strings and logical name attributes, EXE$PROCSTRT creates the logical names SYS$INPUT, SYS$OUTPUT, SYS$ERROR, TT, and SYS$DISK.

18. If this process is not a subprocess, EXE$PROCSTRT creates the job and group logical name tables. (If the process is a subprocess, then the tables have already been created.) These tables are accessed by multiple processes and must be in system space. EXE$PROCSTRT allocates paged pool for them and locks the logical name table mutex for write access. (See Chapter 2 for a description of mutexes.)

    EXE$PROCSTRT initializes the two tables and inserts the job table into the shareable logical name hash table. It then checks whether the group table already exists (created by some other process with the same UIC group number). If the group table exists, EXE$PROCSTRT deallocates its pool. Otherwise, it inserts the logical name into the shareable logical name hash table.

19. EXE$PROCSTRT then allocates space from the P1 allocation region for the process-private logical name table cache. It formats the space into a lookaside list of logical name cache entries.

20. The image name is moved to the image header buffer for subsequent use by the image activator.

21. EXE$PROCSTRT copies the default directory string from the PQB to the

control region. It also copies the two sets of CLI and command table information.

22. It copies the $CREPRC and user authorization file (UAF) flags from the PQB to P1 space.

23. It stores, redundantly, the user name and account name in the P1 pointer page. (With VAX/VMS Version 4, this information is also in the JIB.)

24. EXE$PROCSTRT deallocates the PQB by inserting it on the PQB lookaside list (see Chapter 3). Once the PQB has been deallocated, IPL can be lowered to 0, allowing the process to be deleted. By keeping IPL at 2 until the PQB has been released, the need for special case code in the Delete Process ($DELPRC) system service is avoided. There is no need to check in $DELPRC whether the process being deleted is only partially created and still owns a PQB.

    Another more philosophical interpretation is that at this point in the creation of a process, there exists something that is capable of being deleted, a full-fledged process.

25. EXE$PROCSTRT merges the Files-11 XQP into P1 space. During system initialization, a global section is created from the XQP image, which is pure code and read-only data to be shared among all processes. EXE$PROCSTRT invokes the Map Global Section ($MGBLSC) system service to map the shareable XQP section.

    EXE$PROCSTRT writes the lowest XQP address into CTL$GL_CTLBASVA to record the new P1 base virtual address. It dispatches to initialization code within the XQP image. The initialization code requests the Expand Region ($EXPREG) system service to create a process-private copy of XQP impure area and space for a kernel stack. It then updates CTL$GL_CTLBASVA. After performing other Files-11 initialization, it returns to EXE$PROCSTRT.

26. The shareable image list for the Address Relocation Fixup ($IMGFIX) system service is initialized to point to a dummy element. (This system service is described in Chapter 21.)

27. EXE$PROCSTRT changes access mode to executive by fabricating a PSL and PC on the stack and executing an REI instruction. Execution of an REI instruction is the only way to get to an outer (less privileged) access mode.

    At this point, EXE$PROCSTRT has moved all the information from the creator to the context of the new process and is now ready to activate the image that will execute in the context of the new process. It must change mode to executive to call the image activator, which is an executive mode system service.

28. The image activator is called to set up the page tables and perform the other steps necessary to activate the image. Image activation is described in Chapter 21.

29. An executive mode termination handler, EXE$RMSEXH in module PROCSTRT, is declared that calls SYS$RMSRUNDWN for each open file. This handler is invoked when the Exit ($EXIT) system service is called from executive access mode, which usually happens when the process is deleted.
30. EXE$PROCSTRT changes access mode to user by fabricating a PSL and PC on the stack and executing an REI instruction.
31. The frame pointer (FP) is cleared, guaranteeing that the search of the user mode stack for a condition handler by the exception dispatcher will terminate (see Chapter 4).
32. EXE$PROCSTRT sets up an initial call frame on the user mode stack by executing a CALLG instruction to an inline procedure:

```
        CALLG   (AP),B^90$
        REI
90$:    .WORD   0               ;Entry mask
        .                       ;Procedure code
        .
        .
```

   EXE$PROCSTRT establishes the catch-all condition handler, EXE$CATCH_ALL, as the condition handler for this call frame and also as the last chance exception vector for user mode. The purpose and action of this handler are discussed in the next section.
33. EXE$PROCSTRT requests the $IMGFIX system service to perform fixups on the image.
34. An argument list that is nearly identical to the one used by one of the CLIs (see Chapter 23) is built on the stack. This argument list allows an image to execute with no concern over whether it was activated from EXE$PROCSTRT or from a CLI. The address of a dummy CLI call back routine is stored in location CTL$AL_CLICALBK. If an image that was activated from EXE$PROCSTRT attempts to communicate with a nonexistent CLI, the dummy CLI call back routine will return the error status CLI$_INVREQTYP.
35. EXE$PROCSTRT tests the PCB$V_HIBER bit in PCB$L_STS to determine whether the process was created with the hibernate STSFLG. If it was, EXE$PROCSTRT requests the Hibernate ($HIBER) system service. When the process is awakened, EXE$PROCSTRT proceeds.
36. EXE$PROCSTRT calls the image at its initial transfer address. If the image terminates with a RET instruction (instead of calling the $EXIT system service directly), control returns to EXE$PROCSTRT. If the process was created with the hibernate STSFLG, EXE$PROCSTRT places the process back into hibernation. If it is awakened, EXE$PROCSTRT calls the image again. An effect of this implementation is that the image is not exited and no exit handlers (user-declared or system-declared, such as

EXE$RMSEXH) are invoked.

If the process was not created with the hibernate flag, EXE$PROCSTRT calls the $EXIT system service itself. In general, there is no difference between an image terminating with a RET instruction or with a call to $EXIT. If the process was initially created with the hibernate flag, there is a difference between RET and $EXIT. If a process is to be put into hibernation for future awakenings, it must use the RET instruction to return to EXE$PROCSTRT rather than terminate with a call to $EXIT.

0.3.2 Catch-All Condition Handler

This condition handler is established in the outermost call frame by EXE$PROCSTRT and the CLIs before calling an image. Any condition that is resignaled (not properly handled) by other handlers (or unfielded because no other handlers have been established) is eventually passed to this handler. The handler issues a message using the Put Message ($PUTMSG) system service. Depending on the severity level of the condition, it may force image exit.

The catch-all condition handler, EXE$CATCH_ALL in module PROC-STRT, performs the following actions:

1. If the condition is SS$_SSFAIL, then it disables system service failure mode to avoid an infinite loop.
2. If the exception was generated by a call to LIB$SIGNAL (that is, the exception did not pass through the module EXCEPTION in the executive), the argument list is adjusted to contain only those arguments passed to LIB$SIGNAL and not the PC and PSL fabricated into the signal array by that procedure (see Chapter 4).
3. Unless system services are inhibited for this process, EXE$CATCH_ALL requests the $PUTMSG system service to write an error message to SYS$OUTPUT (and to SYS$ERROR if different from SYS$OUTPUT). (The $PUTMSG system service is discussed in Chapter 29.)
4. If this handler was called as a last chance handler (indicated by a depth of −3) or if the error level is severe or greater (and if system services are not inhibited for this process), it calls EXE$EXCMSG to write an exception summary to SYS$OUTPUT. (EXE$EXCMSG is described in Chapter 29.) EXE$CATCH_ALL then dispatches to EXE$IMGDUMP_MERGE, described in Section 20.3.3, to write the process address space to a file for later analysis. When it returns, EXE$CATCH_ALL requests the $EXIT system service.
5. If the handler was not called as a last chance handler and if the error level is less than severe, EXE$CATCH_ALL returns the status SS$_CONTINUE to the exception dispatcher, which returns to the image.

20.3.3   **Image Dump Facility**

EXE$IMGDMP_MERGE, in module PROCSTRT, provides the capability to write a dump file of the process's address space in a format which can be mapped later for analysis by the debugger. It is invoked when the image terminates as the result of an exception which it cannot handle. It is normally invoked from the condition handler established by the Image Startup system service (see Chapter 21), but, if not, it can also be invoked from the last chance handler.

If the exception occurred in a mode more privileged than user, then no dump may be taken and EXE$IMGDMP_MERGE returns to its invoker. If the exception occurred in user mode, the routine requests the Get Job or Process Information ($GETJPI) system service to obtain process privileges, installed image privileges, and the PHD flags. EXE$IMGDMP_MERGE tests whether the PHD$V_IMGDMP flag is set. If it is clear, the process has not requested image dump and EXE$IMGDMP_MERGE returns. This flag can be specified as part of the $CREPRC stsflg argument and with the DCL commands SET PROCESS/DUMP and RUN/DUMP.

If the flag is set, EXE$IMGDMP_MERGE checks whether the image was installed with more privileges than the process has. If the image was and the process has neither CMKRNL nor SETPRV privilege, no dump can be taken and EXE$IMGDMP_MERGE returns. Otherwise, EXE$IMGDMP_MERGE requests the $IMGACT and $IMGFIX system services to activate the image SYS$LIBRARY:IMGDMP.EXE and transfers control to the image.

Image Activation and Termination

I would have you imagine, then, that there exists in the mind
of man a block of wax . . . and that we remember and know
what is imprinted as long as the image lasts; but when the
image is effaced, or cannot be taken, then we forget or do not
know.

Plato, *Dialogs, Theaetetus* 191

Before an image can execute, VAX/VMS must take several steps to prepare
the process. Process page tables and other data structures must be set up to
locate the correct image files on disk. Address references among shareable
images must be resolved. The term "image activation" refers to the combination of these steps. In addition, if the debugger, Image Dump Utility, or
traceback handler is expected to run when the image executes, the correct
hooks must be present to allow these images to be invoked.

At image exit, exit handlers declared by the user or VAX/VMS must be
called. If the image is executing in a batch or interactive environment, all
traces of the image must be eliminated so that the next image can begin
execution with no side effects from the execution of the previous image.

This chapter describes the following system services related to image activation and termination:

- Image Activate ($IMGACT)
- Address Relocation Fixup ($IMGFIX)
- Image Startup ($IMGSTA)
- Declare Exit Handler ($DCLEXH)
- Exit ($EXIT)
- Rundown ($RUNDWN)

It also describes the initialization and use of the various privilege masks
maintained for each process.

1.1 IMAGE INITIATION

VAX/VMS contains no special code to load images into memory for initial
execution. Instead, it uses the page fault mechanism that brings in pages on
demand from an image file. For this scheme to work, the process page tables
must reflect the state of all the pages in the main image file and its shareable
images' files. The image activator initializes the process page tables and
makes other necessary preparations, such as creating address space for the
user stack.

In this chapter, the term "main image" refers to a main, controlling image that has been invoked by a user. A main image can be linked with multiple shareable images, which themselves can be linked with other shareable images.

Before control can be transferred to the main image, .ADDRESS and G^ references that point to locations within shareable images must be resolved. This resolution is performed at activation time rather than at link time so that shareable images can change in size without requiring a relink of all images that use them.

The actual transfer of control to the main image also takes place through the executive so that hooks can be inserted to allow later inclusion of a debugger, the Image Dump Utility, or the traceback facility. This path, called the debug bootstrap, always executes unless explicitly excluded at link time with a /NOTRACEBACK qualifier to the LINK command.

21.1.1   Image Activation

Although the concept of image activation is straightforward, there are several special cases of image activation. Some of these cases are discussed explicitly. Others are mentioned only in passing.

The following types of image activation are discussed explicitly:

- Activation of a simple main image, one linked with no shareable images
    This is an artificial separation from the next case, simply to illustrate the difference in the image activator's actions.
- Activation of an image linked with one or more shareable images
    Because almost every high-level language processor generates calls to library routines, this case includes most images.
- Activation of a known image
    The activation of images that have been installed is streamlined by the data structures that were created by the Install Utility.
- Activation of a compatibility mode image
    When the image activator is called to activate a compatibility mode image, it actually activates the RSX-11M Application Migration Executive (AME) and passes the compatibility mode image name to the AME for further processing. (The RSX-11M AME is part of the optional software product VAX-11 RSX.)

There are several other special cases that the image activator must check for. These are mentioned in the specific parts of image activation where they cause special action to be taken. Some specific cases are the following:

- Image activation at system initialization time
    During initialization of the system, image files must be opened without the support of either Record Management Services (RMS) or the file system.

The image activator calls special code in the executive that performs the simpler file system operations in the absence of a file system. These routines are briefly described with system initialization in Chapters 24 and 25.

• Merged image activation

A merged image activation occurs subsequent to the activation and transfer of control to a main image. This can be used for mapping a debugger, the Image Dump Utility, traceback handler, message file, or command language interpreter (CLI) into an unused area of P0 or P1 space. It is also used to activate a shareable image when an already activated image calls the Run-Time Library procedure LIB$FIND_IMAGE_SYMBOL.

Rather than using the virtual address descriptors found in the merged image, the image activator simply uses the next available portion of P0 or P1 space. The user stack and image I/O segment are not mapped for a merged image. The RMS initialization routines are not called either, because an image is already executing and has RMS context that cannot be destroyed.

• Message sections

Message sections add per-process or image-specific entries to the message facility.

• P0-only images

The VAX/VMS Linker can produce images that map all temporary structures, including the user stack and the I/O segment in P0 space. The image activator must recognize this type of an image so that the two structures usually located in the lowest address portion of P1 space are correctly mapped.

P0-only images are used whenever it is necessary to extend the permanent part of the low address end of P1 space. For example, the SET MESSAGE command causes a P0-only image called SETP0.EXE to execute. This image maps the indicated message section into the low address end of P1 space and alters location CTL$GL_CTLBASVA to reflect the new boundary between the temporary and permanent parts of P1 space. This last step is critical if the message section is to remain mapped when later images terminate.

• Privileged shareable images

Privileged shareable sections implement user-written system services and rundown routines. System service procedures that are not part of the system image (for example, $MOUNT and $DISMOU) are implemented as privileged shareable images.

• Images that do not reside on a random access mass storage device

The image activator can activate images from sequential devices (certain magnetic tape devices) and images located on another node of a network. An address space large enough to contain the entire image is first created. The image is then copied into this address space, thus requiring all image pages, including read-only pages, to be set up as writable.

21.1.1.1 **Overview of the Image Activator.** There are essentially two steps that the image activator performs each time that it activates an image. First, it calls RMS to open the image file, which enables the system to perform all of its file protection checks. Then it reads the image header (IHD). The IHD contains information about the virtual address space requirements of each section in the image. The image activator requests memory management system services to map each image section.

21.1.1.2 **Data Structures That Describe Images.** An image file begins with an IHD that describes the image and its sections. The IHD contains image section descriptors (ISDs), one for each section in the image. Each ISD describes a portion of the image's virtual address space, including its size and starting address. Figure 21-1 shows the layout of an IHD and its position in an image. Figure 21-2 shows the layout of an ISD.

There are three types of ISD:

- ISD for a private section—The code or data is in the image file (or this section represents a private mapping of a global section)
- Demand zero ISD—The range of virtual address space begins as zero-filled pages

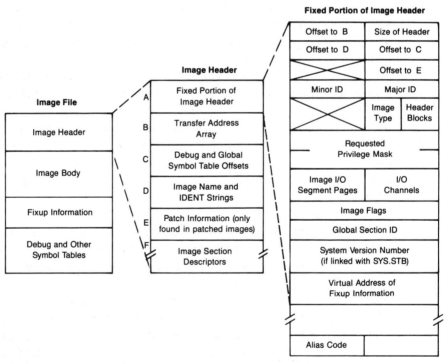

Figure 21-1   Contents of an Image Header

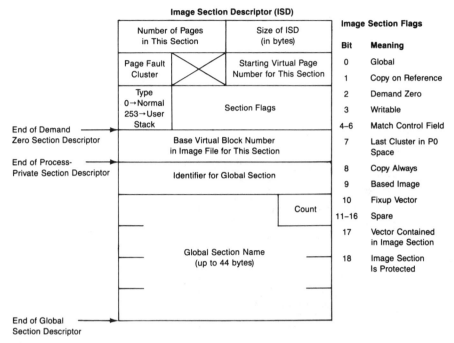

Figure 21-2   General Form of an Image Section
Descriptor

• Global ISD—The code or data is in a shareable image

A main image linked without any shareable images contains the first two types of ISD.

A main image linked with a shareable image contains an ISD that describes the shareable image. This type of ISD, called a global ISD, primarily serves to name the shareable image. The shareable image contains its own IHD and ISDs to describe its own virtual address space. Address space for the shareable image is not usually assigned when the main image is linked. Instead, the address space for the shareable image is assigned and allocated when it is activated. Thus, the size of the shareable image can change without requiring the main image to be relinked.

A shareable image linked with another shareable image contains a global ISD to point to the second shareable image. If the main image refers only to symbols in the first shareable image but not the second, it need not contain a global ISD for the second shareable image. The entire collection of shareable images implied by a main image is not determined until image activation. Thus, a shareable image can be relinked to reference additional shareable images without requiring the relink of the main image linked with it.

Activating a main image can result in the activation of many shareable images. After a main image has begun to execute, the image activator can be

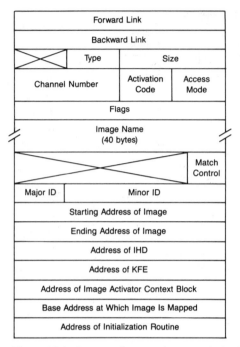

Forward Link

| Backward Link |

| | Type | Size |

| Channel Number | Activation Code | Access Mode |

| Flags |

| Image Name (40 bytes) |

| | Match Control |

| Major ID | Minor ID |

| Starting Address of Image |

| Ending Address of Image |

| Address of IHD |

| Address of KFE |

| Address of Image Activator Context Block |

| Base Address at Which Image Is Mapped |

| Address of Initialization Routine |

Figure 21-3   Layout of an Image Control Block

called again to activate additional shareable images. The image activator must keep track of which images are already activated. It uses a data structure called an image control block (ICB) to describe each image. Figure 21-3 shows the layout of an ICB.

ICBs are initially allocated from the P1 allocation region (see Chapter 3), but are deallocated to an ICB lookaside list for faster subsequent allocation. In addition to the lookaside list, the image activator keeps two other ICB lists—one for images already activated and one for images yet to be activated. These doubly linked lists are located in P1 space at the following global locations:

- IAC$GL_ICBFL—Lookaside list
- IAC$GL_IMAGE_LIST—Activated images (known as the "done list")
- IAC$GL_WORK_LIST—Images to be activated (known as the "work list")

21.1.1.3   **Data Structures That Describe Known Images.** Several data structures describe "known images." A known image has special properties that affect its activation. The Install Utility is used to specify known images and their properties. (The *VAX/VMS Install Utility Reference Manual* describes this utility and its commands.)

The known image mechanism has several functions. Its main purpose is to identify images installed with privileges and images installed to be shared in the virtual address space of multiple processes. A subsidiary function is faster image activation.

An image that requires enhanced privileges but must execute in nonprivileged process context (such as MOUNT, SET, or SHOW) is installed with the /PRIVILEGE qualifier. When such an image is activated, the process gains enhanced privileges temporarily. The enhanced privileges are removed when the image is run down.

Several different types of image are installed with the /SHARE qualifier:

• A shareable or executable image with image sections that are to be shared by multiple processes
• A shareable or executable image whose shareable sections are to reside in MA780 multiport memory and be accessed by processes running on multiple VAX-11/780 or VAX-11/785 CPUs
• A shareable image containing a privileged section, such as a user-written system service or rundown routine

An installed image is opened by its file ID rather than its file name, saving the overhead of a file lookup. Image activation can be further shortened if the image is installed /OPEN so that its file remains open. In this case, the image activator's $OPEN call to RMS is essentially a null operation. If such an image is installed /HEADER_RESIDENT, its IHD is stored in paged pool. Keeping the IHD resident saves the additional read operations otherwise required to read it into memory every time the image is activated.

The Install Utility creates and manages the known image database (also called the known file database) to describe images that have been installed. RMS scans the known image database whenever a file is opened with the known file option. (Use of this option is reserved to VAX/VMS and unsupported for any other use.) All of the known image data structures are in paged pool. The two major ones are the known file entry (KFE) and known file directory (KFD).

A KFE is allocated for each known image. It identifies the file name of the image and its properties. If the image is shareable, the KFE specifies how many global sections are in it, the image version, and match control. The KFE also contains either the full file ID or the addresses of the file's resident IHD and its window control block (WCB). (A WCB describes the disk location of the blocks of an open file.) Figure 21-4 shows the layout of the KFE.

Each KFE has the address of its corresponding KFD. The KFD contains the full device and directory names associated with a known image. If multiple known images are installed from a particular device and directory combination, they share the same KFD. Each KFD has a reference count of how many KFEs point to it and a listhead for its KFEs, which are linked together. Keeping the device and directory information in the KFD rather than in each KFE

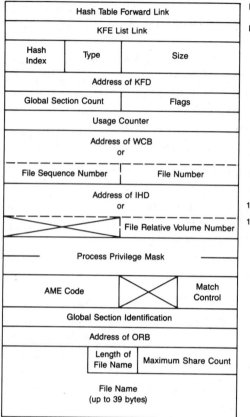

KFE Flags

Bit	Meaning
0	Installed /PROTECT
1	Shareable Image
2	Installed /PRIVILEGE
3	Installed /OPEN
4	Image Header Resident
5	Shared Image
6	Shared Memory Image
7	Compatibility Mode Image
8	Installed /NOPURGE
9	Image Accounting Enabled
10	Has Writable Sections
11	Execute Access Only

Figure 21-4   Layout of a Known File Entry

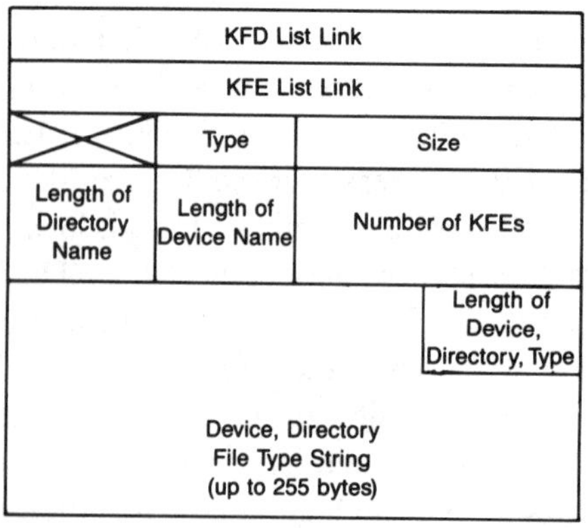

Figure 21-5   Layout of a Known File Directory

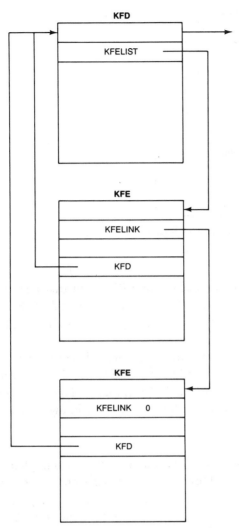

Figure 21-6 Known File Directory and Known File
Entries

saves paged pool. Figure 21-5 shows the layout of the KFD. Figure 21-6 shows
a KFD and its list of KFEs.

A data structure called a known file resident image header (KFRH) exists
for each known image installed /HEADER_RESIDENT. Space for the IHD is
allocated with the KFRH. The KFRH immediately precedes the IHD and
specifies its size and version number. The field KFE$L_IMGHDR contains
the address at which the IHD begins. Figure 21-7 shows the layout of a KFRH.

A KFE hash table locates all the KFEs. A known image name is hashed to a
number between 0 and 127. The number indexes into the hash table, which
has 128 longword entries. An entry value of zero indicates no KFE with that

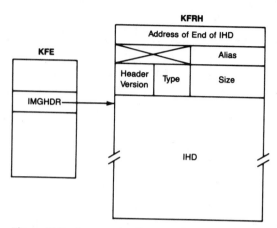

Figure 21-7 Layout of a Known File Resident Image Header

hash index. A nonzero entry is the address of a KFE with that hash index. KFEs with the same hash index are linked together. The end of the list is indicated by a forward link of zero. Figure 21-8 shows the hash table and several KFEs linked to it.

There is one more known image data structure, called the known file pointer block (KFPB). It contains the address of the hash table and also the head of the list of KFDs and the number of KFDs in the list. Figure 21-8 shows the layout of the KFPB and its relationship to the other known image data structures.

21.1.1.4   **Implementation of the Image Activator.** The image activator is implemented as the $IMGACT system service. Direct calls to this system service are reserved for VAX/VMS. Direct calls by users are completely unsupported. Instead, users can call the image activator indirectly through any CLI command that runs an image and through the Run-Time Library procedure LIB$FIND_IMAGE_SYMBOL.

Table 21-1 shows the arguments that can be passed to the $IMGACT system service. The last four arguments are similar to the input arguments for various other memory management system services that are described in Chapter 16.

21.1.1.5   **Activation of a Simple Main Image.** Most of the common operations that are performed by the image activator occur during the activation of a simple main image, that is, one linked with no shareable images. This section describes the general flow through the image activator. Other forms of activation, described in later sections, are mentioned in this section when appropriate.

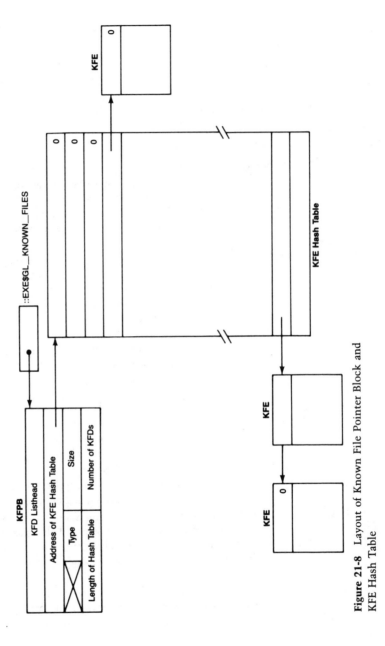

Figure 21-8   Layout of Known File Pointer Block and KFE Hash Table

Table 21-1   Arguments for the Image Activator System Service

Argument Name	*Meaning*
NAME	Descriptor of image name to be activated.
DFLNAM	Descriptor of default file name.
HDRBUF	Address of 512-byte buffer in which the IHD and image file descriptor are returned. The first two longwords in the buffer are the addresses within the buffer of the IHD and the image file descriptor.
IMGCTL	Image activation control flags. These flags control the form that the activation will take. The options are the following:

FLAG	MEANING
IAC$V_MERGE	If set, the image activator is directed to merge one executable image into the address space of another. When this flag is set, the user stack and the image I/O segment are to be ignored. This flag must be set if the image activator is called from user mode.
IAC$V_EXPREG	If set, the INADR argument does not give an actual address range but merely indicates P0 address space, which is expanded as required. This flag is only used during a merged image activation for a P0 image.
IAC$V_P1MERGE	If set, the image activator is directed to merge an executable image into P1 space. This flag is used when mapping a CLI into P1 space. This merge is performed in two parts: first the image is merged into P0 space and then the image is moved into P1 space. The sole purpose of the merge into P0 space is to determine the size of the image. Once the size has been determined, the correct starting address in P1 space can be calculated.
IAC$V_SETVECTOR	If set, the image activator initializes the P1 vectors that dispatch to user-written system services, rundown routines, and message sections.

INADR	Address of a two-longword array containing the virtual address range into which the image is to be mapped. This argument is usually omitted, in which case the address ranges designated by the ISDs in the IHD are used or the image is mapped at the next available location.
RETADR	Address of a two-longword array to receive the starting and ending addresses into which the image was actually mapped.
IDENT	Address of a quadword containing the version number and matching criteria for a shareable image.
ACMODE	Access mode for page ownership and image channel assignment. This defaults to user mode. If specified, it is maximized with the access mode of the $IMGACT caller.

The $IMGACT system service procedure, EXE$$IMGACT, runs primarily in executive mode with some kernel mode subroutines. (The "$$" in the system service procedure name results from its distance from the case table used by the change mode dispatcher. See Chapter 9 for more information.) EXE$$IMGACT is in the module SYSIMGACT; some of the procedures it calls are in modules IMGMAPISD, IMGDECODE, and SYSIMGFIX. EXE$$IMGACT and the procedures it calls are known as the image activator.

To activate a simple main image, the image activator takes the following steps:

1. It initializes its scratch area in P1 space.
2. It resets the P1 space vectors for user-written system services, rundown routines, and message sections.
3. It checks the accessibility of the system service argument list and its arguments and copies them for later use.
4. It calls RM$RESET (in module RMSRESET) to initialize the image I/O segment.
5. It allocates and zeros an ICB.
6. It locks the known file database by invoking the Enqueue Lock Request and Wait ($ENQW) system service. It locks the systemwide resource "INSTALL$KNOWN FILE" for protected read. This blocks any attempt at concurrent changes to the known file database by the Install Utility.
7. The image activator calls RMS to open the image for execute access, specifying the user-open, process-permanent file, and known file database search options. If the image has been installed as a known image, RMS returns the address of its KFE. The image activator stores the image name, channel number, and KFE address in the ICB. If the image is known, the image activator takes note of whether it was installed with the /PRIVILEGE, /ACCOUNT, or /SHARE qualifiers.
8. If the IHD is not resident, the image activator reads the first block of the image file and performs several consistency checks to determine that it is indeed an IHD. At this point, the check for an ordinary native mode image is made. The last word in the first block of the IHD, IHD$W_ALIAS, indicates whether a different image should be activated first. The word can indicate an image produced by the VAX/VMS Linker, an image produced by some other linker, or an image that is a CLI.

   The only other linker supported is the RSX-11M Task Builder. It produces a compatibility mode image with a zero in IHD$W_ALIAS. When the image activator finds such an image, it instead activates SYS$SYSTEM:RSX.EXE. Further details about the activation of a compatibility mode image are found in Section 21.1.1.11.

   If the IHD specifies that the image is a CLI, the image activator instead activates LOGINOUT. Section 21.1.1.12 contains further details about the activation of a CLI.

9. The image activator copies information from the system service argument list into the ICB and inserts the ICB at the tail of its work list.

10. It begins to process its work list. It removes the ICB from its work list and checks whether the image described is already mapped. In the case of a simple main image, the image described by the ICB has not been mapped.

11. It processes the ISDs in the image's header. Its main task is setting up the process page tables to reflect the address space produced by the linker. It performs this task by reading each ISD in the IHD (see Figure 21-2), determining the type of section described, and calling the appropriate memory management system service to perform the actual mapping.

   a. The most common form of ISD in a simple image describes a private section. This type of section can be either read-only or read/write, depending on the attributes of the program sections that made up the image section. Initial page faults for each page in this type of section will be satisfied from the appropriate blocks in the image file.

   The image activator uses the contents of this type of ISD as input arguments to the Create and Map Section ($CRMPSC) system service. The result is a series of page table entries (PTEs) that contain process section table indexes. Figure 21-9 shows the PTEs, section table entry, and ISD. The number of PTEs is equal to the page count in the ISD. Notice that all of the PTEs index the same process section.

   If the image has been installed /SHARE by the Install Utility, then some of its sections are global and can be shared.

   —If the section is read-only and the image was installed /SHARE, it requests the Map Global Section ($MGBLSC) system service. The result is a series of PTEs that are global page table indexes. Figure 21-10 shows the PTEs, global page table, and ISD.
   —If the section is writable and the image was installed /SHARE /WRITE, it requests the $MGBLSC system service.
   —If the section is writable and copy-on-reference, it requests the $CRMPSC system service.
   —If the section is read-only but not shared, it requests the $CRMPSC system service. (An image section containing an .ASCID directive or .ADDRESS reference to a symbol in a shareable image cannot be shared. See Section 21.1.2 for further information.)

   One special kind of private section is a "fixup vector table," which describes addresses in the image that are resolved at image activation, rather than at link time. (Section 21.1.2 describes the processing of fixup vectors.) When the image activator encounters a fixup vector, it adds it to the list of fixup vectors to be processed later.

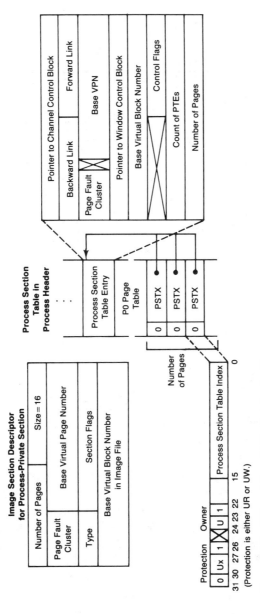

Figure 21-9 ISD and Page Table Entries for Process-Private Section

587

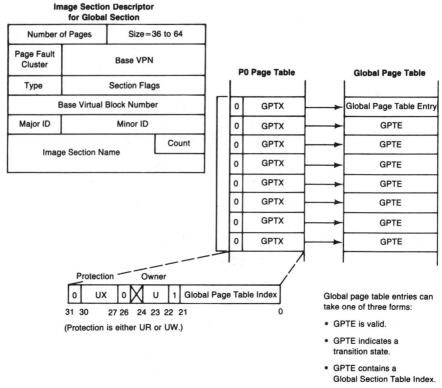

Figure 21-10 ISD and Page Table Entries for Global Section

b. Another form of ISD is a demand zero section. The linker produces such a section whenever there are five (or some user-specified default number of) consecutive pages in the image file that contain all zeros. It also produces a demand zero section for an uninitialized copy-on-reference section of any size. The image file does not contain demand zero section pages but merely an indication (in the ISD) that a certain range of virtual address space contains all zeros.

The image activator uses the contents of this type of ISD as input arguments to the Create Virtual Address Space ($CRETVA) system service. The result is a series of demand zero page PTEs. The number of PTEs is equal to the page count in the ISD. Figure 21-11 shows the PTEs and demand zero section ISD.

Note that one such section is the area in P1 space that contains the user stack. The linker distinguishes this special demand zero section from others by a special code byte in the type designator in the ISD. The image activator records the ISD page count and delays mapping the user stack until later in the activation.

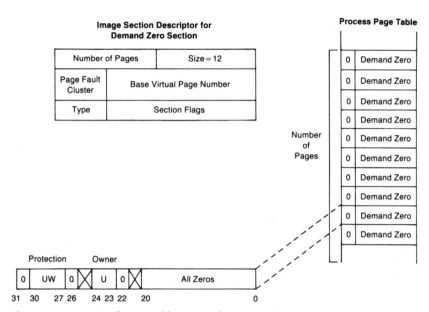

Figure 21-11   ISD and Page Table Entries for Demand
Zero Section

c. The third type of ISD is a global ISD, which indicates that a range of
   virtual address space is to be mapped to a shareable image. When the
   image activator encounters a global ISD, it builds an ICB to describe
   the shareable image and inserts it at the end of its work list. The next
   section describes the activation of a shareable image.

12. If the image is being activated from a sequential device (magnetic tape or
    across a network), then the address range is created and the entire image
    read from the sequential device into virtual address space. All future page
    faults will be resolved from the page file.

13. In the case of a simple image (with no references to shareable images and
    thus no global ISDs), there was only one ICB on the work list. The image
    activator continues with its end processing (see Section 21.1.1.7).

    If ICBs have been added to the work list as a result of processing a main
    image ICB, the image activator processes them as described in the follow-
    ing section.

21.1.1.6   Activation of Shareable Images. Whenever the image activator encounters
a global ISD in the header of an image being activated, it allocates an
ICB, records the image name in it, and inserts it at the tail of the ICB work
list. When the image activator completes the processing associated with, for
example, the main image's ICB, it continues with the following steps. (In
the case of a merged image activation request, perhaps initiated through the

procedure LIB$FIND_IMAGE_SYMBOL, there would be no main image processing.)

1. It removes an ICB from its work list. If there is none, activation is complete and the image activator proceeds with its end processing (see Section 21.1.1.7).

2. It scans the done list to see whether an image with the same name has already been activated in the virtual address space.

   If one has, the image activator deallocates the ICB and goes back to step 1 to process the next ICB on the work list. Commonly referenced shareable images, such as LIBRTL, can appear on the work list multiple times. This could result from the activation of several shareable images, each of which was linked with LIBRTL. No matter how many times a shareable image appears on the work list, the check for an ICB on the done list with the same name results in only one activation of the shareable image.

3. If no image of that name has been activated, the image activator places the ICB on the done list. It is placed on a stack that is maintained in the done list. This stack ensures that ICBs appear on the list in the proper order for image initialization (see Section 21.1.1.8).

4. The image activator calls RMS to open the image named by the ICB. It specifies a default file type of EXE and directory of SYS$SHARE, with file open options of user-open, process-permanent file, and known file database search. If the global ISD specified a writable global section, the image is opened for write access. Otherwise, it is opened for execute access.

   There are two conditions under which the image activator enters a "restricted" mode of operation:

   —If a main image installed with privileges has been activated
   —If a main image has been activated to which the process has only execute access

   If either condition is true, the image activator specifies that RMS use only executive or kernel mode logical names when it tries to translate the image name. Furthermore, the shareable image must be a known image. If not, the activation is aborted and the image activator returns the error status SS$_PRIVINSTALL.

5. If the image is not a known image with its header resident, the image activator reads in its header. See step 8 in Section 21.1.1.5 for further details.

6. It then checks that the match control information in the IHD is consistent with the match requested in the global ISD whose presence caused the activation of this shareable image. If there is a mismatch, the image activator aborts the activation and returns the error status SS$_SHRIDMISMAT.

7. If the IHD indicates that the shareable image has an initialization section, the image activator sets the ICB$V_INITIALIZE flag and records the address of the initialization section (see Section 21.1.1.8).

8. It processes the ISDs for each section in the shareable image.

   If the ISD is a global ISD, representing a different shareable image, the image activator compares its name to the name in the most recently added ICB. If the names are different, it creates an ICB to describe the image and adds it to the front of the work list. The comparison prevents redundant ICBs for one image that might otherwise result from multiple global ISDs in a second image which represent different image sections in the first image.

   If the ISD is not a global ISD, the image activator maps the section into the process address space. If the shareable image has been installed /SHARE, then some of its sections are global and can be shared. Step 11 in Section 21.1.1.5 lists which system service the image activator calls for each type of image section.

   If the section is a protected section, the image activator maps the read-only pages with UR protection and the writable pages with UREW protection. It specifies that the pages are owned by executive mode, preventing user mode code from deleting them or altering them.

9. The image activator is done processing the ICB. It removes the next ICB from its work list and repeats the steps in this section.

   If there is no ICB and if a main image was activated in this call to the image activator, it performs the end processing described in Section 21.1.1.5. Otherwise, the image activator is done and returns to its caller. The caller must request the $IMGFIX system service (see Section 21.1.2) to perform address relocation.

21.1.1.7   **Image Activator End Processing.** The image activator's end processing consists of the following steps:

1. The image activator tests whether the image was linked with an image I/O segment larger than the standard space allocated during process creation. The standard size is determined by the SYSBOOT parameter IMG-IOCNT (default value of 32). However, the size can be overridden with the following entry in the linker options file:

   ```
   IOSEGMENT = n
   ```

   If a larger image I/O segment was requested, the image activator calls the $CRETVA system service to create a replacement image I/O segment.

   If a P0-only image is being activated, the image activator creates the image I/O segment at the high address end of P0 space.

2. The address space for the user stack is created with the Expand Region ($EXPREG) system service. The usual location of the user stack is at the

low address end of P1 space, where the automatic stack expansion facility of the exception dispatcher can add user stack space as needed. The location of the user stack in P0-only images is at the high address end of the P0 image.

The default size of the user stack is 20 pages. This value can be overridden with the following line in the linker options file:

```
STACK = n
```

The image activator creates a user stack with two extra pages for system use during exception processing in case the user stack is corrupted.

3. Running in kernel mode, the image activator stores the address of the high end of the user stack in the P1 pointer page, in the CTL$AL_STACK array. Reserving space for system use during exception processing, the image activator loads an address two pages below the high end of the stack into the processor register PR$_USP. This value is loaded into the SP register when an REI instruction returns the process to user mode, which usually occurs following the return from the image activator.

4. The privileges that will be in effect while this image is executing are calculated. The logical AND of the privilege mask found in the IHD (IHD$Q_PRIVREQS, which currently enables all privileges and so is effectively unused) with the process-permanent privilege mask (found at global location CTL$GQ_PROCPRIV) is then ORed with the privilege enhancements for a privileged known image (KFE$Q_PROCPRIV).

   The result is stored in the process privilege mask in the process control block (PCB) at offset PCB$Q_PRIV and in the process header (PHD) at offset PHD$Q_PRIVMSK (the mask that is actually checked by other routines in the system). The mask at KFE$Q_PROCPRIV is copied to the PHD at offset PHD$Q_IMAGPRIV. The uses of the various privilege masks are described in Section 21.4.

5. A check is made to determine whether any of the images activated were linked with the system symbol table, SYS$SYSTEM:SYS.STB. If so, the image activator checks that the version of the symbol table agrees with the currently running system version. If the version numbers disagree, the image activator turns off CMKRNL and CMEXEC privileges in the current privilege mask and returns the status SS$_SYSVERDIF. Removing these privileges prevents many different spurious errors that could occur if the outdated image were to execute with those privileges intact.

6. The image activator stores the address of the IHD buffer in the global location CTL$GL_IMGHDRBF.

7. It checks whether image accounting was requested for this particular image or enabled for the system as a whole. If so, the image activator records various statistics, such as current CPU time, in their P1 locations.

8. If a known image is being activated, its use count must be incremented. If

the image was installed /OPEN, the share count in its WCB must also be incremented. The image activator then sets the done bit in the ICB to indicate that it has been activated. (The actions in this step are done for each image being activated.)

9. At this point, the image activator has finished its work. It dequeues the known file list lock. It loads a final status into R0 and returns to its caller (either EXE$PROCSTRT or a CLI) to allow the image itself to be called. The caller must request the $IMGFIX system service (see Section 21.1.2) to perform address relocation.

Computing the Proper Order of Image Initialization. As a by-product of its normal work, the image activator computes the order of initialization for multiple shareable images activated by a main image. The basic rule for image initialization is that if shareable image A calls shareable image B, then the initialization routine for image B must be called before the initialization routine for image A. This rule enables image A to call any routine in image B (or in any image that B calls) during A's own initialization.

The initialization routine for each activated image is called as part of image fixup (see Section 21.1.2.4). EXE$IMGFIX first calls the initialization routine specified by the ICB that is at the end of the done list. Then it works its way from the rear to the front of the done list. The image activator must create the correct order of ICBs on the done list by careful placement of ICBs on both the work and done list.

If image A calls image B, then at some point during the activation of image A, the image activator encounters a global ISD that references image B. The image activator builds a global ICB and inserts it at the front of the work list. Inserting these global ICBs at the front of the list ensures that these called, or "son," images will be activated after the calling, or "parent," image and before any brothers of the parent. This list generates a walk of the image call graph known as a preorder traversal.

A stack, implemented at the front of the done list, is used to convert this preorder traversal into the proper initialization order—a postorder traversal. Basically, a parent node is stacked until its last son has been activated. A stack pointer points to the top of this stack in the done list. (Initially, the stack pointer points to the queue header.) Figure 21-12 shows how the ICBs at the front of the done list form this stack.

To pop this stack, the stack pointer is simply moved to the left. The next ICB from the work list is always inserted to the right of the top of the stack and will become the new top of the stack if it has any sons. ICBs to the right of the top of the stack are always in the proper initialization order. ICBs at and to the left of the stack pointer are parent ICBs who still have descendants that have not been activated.

The stack is built so as to ensure that the sons and descendants of an image

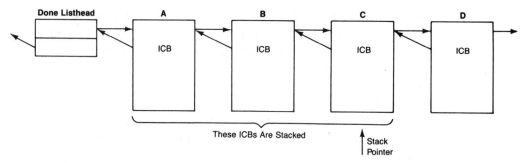

Figure 21-12   ICB Stack in the Done List

are always placed on the done list to the right of the ICB of the parent. Since the done list is processed in reverse order during initialization, this placement ensures that all images called directly or indirectly by some image are initialized before that image itself.

The manipulation of the work and done lists is controlled by the ICB$L_ACTIVE_SONS count in each ICB. This field specifies how many of the image's sons have not yet been activated (their ICBs are still on the work list) and how many have been activated but still have active sons of their own (these ICBs are on the stack in the done list). The ICBs to the right of the stack in the done list have no active sons.

The following steps describe the image activator's manipulation of ICBs on the done and work lists to generate the proper initialization order. The details of image activation are described in Sections 21.1.1.5 and 21.1.1.6 and are not repeated here.

1. The image activator removes an ICB from the front of the work list. If there is none, it goes on to end processing (see Section 21.1.1.7).
2. If this is an image that was already activated (that is, on the done list) and still has active sons, then the image activator has detected a circularity. (The image is one of its own descendants, so no initialization order is possible.) In this rare case, all the images on the done list that are involved in the circularity must be marked. An error will be reported if a subsequent attempt is made to initialize one of those images. The images involved in the circularity are exactly those ICBs on the stack from the top of the stack down to and including the previously activated image.

   Regardless of whether there is a circularity, if the image was previously activated, the image activator deallocates the ICB and continues at step 6.
3. Otherwise, this is a new image needing activation. The image activator inserts its ICB just to the right of the top of the stack in the done list and zeros its ICB$L_ACTIVE_SONS count.

   It then performs the detailed work of activation for this image (steps 4 through 8 in Section 21.1.1.6). During those steps, each time the image activator creates a new global ICB (son), it places the new ICB at the front of the work list and increments ICB$L_ACTIVE_SONS in its parent's ICB. (After the parent image is activated but before its sons have been, this field contains the total number of shareable images referenced by the image.)

4. If the field ICB$L_ACTIVE_SONS in the ICB to the right of the top of the stack is nonzero after the image has been activated, the image activator makes that ICB the top of the stack and continues with step 1. (This new parent remains on the stack until all its sons, which are located at the front of the work list, are activated and no longer have active sons of their own.)

5. Otherwise, the field ICB$L_ACTIVE_SONS in the ICB to the right of the top of the stack is zero, and the image activator continues with step 6.

6. This step is called a "decrement parent" operation. ICB$L_ACTIVE_SONS in the parent ICB waiting at the top of the stack must be decremented to indicate that one of its sons is no longer active. If its count becomes zero, this same step must be repeated for its parent, and so on.

   If the stack is empty, there is no parent to decrement. The image activator continues with end processing (see Section 21.1.1.7). Otherwise, it decrements ICB$L_ACTIVE_SONS in the ICB at the top of the stack.

7. If the count is still positive (the image still has active sons), the ICB remains at the top of the stack. The image activator continues with step 1. Otherwise, if ICB$L_ACTIVE_SONS is now zero, it must decrement the ICB$L_ACTIVE_SONS field in the parent of the ICB.

8. If the ICB at the top of the stack is the one that initiated the activations, it has no parent, so the image activator goes on to its end processing. Otherwise, the image activator pops the stack by moving the stack pointer to the left in the done list and repeats step 6.

21.1.1.9   Example Activation. The details of activating an image linked with several shareable images can be illustrated with an example. The example main image is linked with the shareable images A, B, C, and LIBRTL. A, B, and C are themselves linked with LIBRTL.

At the beginning of the activation, an ICB representing the main image is placed on the work list. As its ISDs are processed, work list items are added for A, B, C, and LIBRTL as the result of references in the main image:

Work List	In Progress	Done List
A (main image)	Main image	
B (main image)		
C (main image)		
LIBRTL (main image)		

After mapping the sections of the main image, the image activator removes the ICB for A from its work list. A's global ISD for LIBRTL makes a contribution to the work list:

Work List	In Progress	Done List
B (main image)	A	Main image
C (main image)		
LIBRTL (main image)		
LIBRTL (A)		

After the sections for B and C are mapped, there are two more entries on the work list, both additional duplicate entries for LIBRTL:

Work List	In Progress	Done List
LIBRTL (main image)		Main image
LIBRTL (A)		A
LIBRTL (B)		B
LIBRTL (C)		C

Mapping the first LIBRTL entry, the image activator adds nothing to the work list, because LIBRTL references no other shareable images:

Work List	In Progress	Done List
LIBRTL (A)		Main image
LIBRTL (B)		A
LIBRTL (C)		B
		C
		LIBRTL

The image activator removes each remaining entry from the work list, discovers the duplication, and discards the entry. It empties its work list and completes the activation without encountering any new images to map.

21.1.1.10   **Activation of a Known Image.** When a known image is activated, the image activator is informed by RMS, which places the address of the KFE in the CTX field of the file access block (FAB). Of course, the open operation may have been shortened as a result of install options (see Section 21.1.1.3).

The activation of a known image proceeds in much the same way as a regular image, although some of the work that the image activator must perform in the regular case can be avoided here. In particular, a known image that has its header resident can be activated more quickly, because the header read operation is avoided.

In any case, the ISDs must still be processed and the PTEs set up so that the image can execute. In addition, the image activator must update the usage statistics for this known image (see Figure 21-4).

21.1.1.11   **Activation of a Compatibility Mode Image.** When the image activator determines from IHD$W_ALIAS that it is attempting to activate a compatibility mode image, it changes its course and instead activates the RSX-11M AME (SYS$SYSTEM:RSX.EXE).

An AME is itself a native mode image that is responsible for mapping the compatibility mode image into the address range between 0 and 10000_{16} (see Figure 1-8), passing control to that image while turning on the compatibility mode bit (with an REI instruction), and fielding all compatibility mode and other exceptions generated by the compatibility mode image. Currently, the RSX-11M AME is the only supported AME.

From the point of view of image activation, once the image activator determines that it is activating a compatibility mode image, it continues with activation, but activation of the AME and not the compatibility mode image. The name of the compatibility mode image is stored in the compatibility mode page (at global location CTL$AG_CMEDATA) in P1 space, whence it is retrieved by the AME.

21.1.1.12   Activation of a Command Language Interpreter. When the image activator determines that it is attempting to activate a CLI and the IAC$V_MERGE flag is clear, it activates instead the image LOGINOUT. First, the image activator closes the CLI image file, because LOGINOUT performs its own file open. Then it activates LOGINOUT and transfers control to it. LOGINOUT maps the CLI into P1 space and passes control to it.

21.1.2   Address Relocation Fixup ($IMGFIX) System Service

The $IMGFIX system service enables the postponement of address assignment from link time to image activation. By delaying address assignment, position independence is maintained in images that are linked with shareable images and within shareable images themselves.

There are several forms of addressing that are modified by $IMGFIX: a G^ reference to an address in a shareable image, an .ADDRESS reference to a location within a nonbased shareable image, and an .ASCID directive within a nonbased shareable image. Resolution of a G^ reference is deferred so that the relative address is not affected by a change in size of any of the intervening shareable images.

The .ADDRESS directive references a fixed address in virtual memory. Resolution of an .ADDRESS reference to a location in a shareable image is deferred so that the fixed address can be determined at run time, not link time. However, if the link options file specified a base address for an image, .ADDRESS references to locations within it do not need to be deferred.

The .ASCID directive builds an ASCII string and a descriptor for it. It incorporates the equivalent of an .ADDRESS directive referencing the string. .ASCID directives within a nonbased shareable image must be fixed up after the base address of the shareable image is determined. In the following sections, text references to .ADDRESS directives include those generated by .ASCID directives.

The *VAX/VMS Linker Reference Manual* explains in more detail the motivation for the $IMGFIX system service and the linker's action in preparing for image fixups.

An image linked under VAX/VMS Version 3 or a later version contains a section called the fixup vector tables. These tables contain data that describe .ADDRESS references, data that describe G^ references, and a list of the shareable images referenced by the image. Figure 21-13 shows the layout of an image and its fixup vector tables.

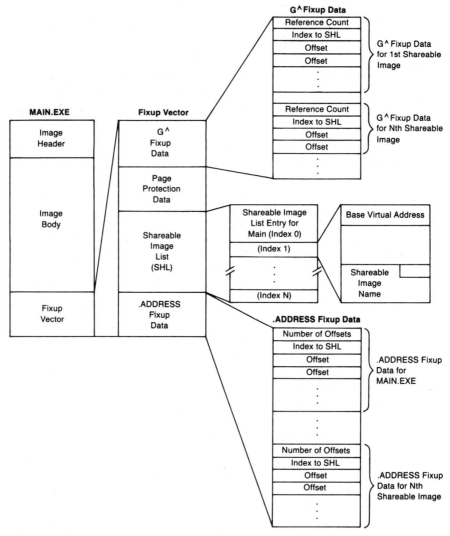

Figure 21-13   Image Layout with Fixup Vectors

21.1.2.1 **Shareable Image List.** There is one shareable image list entry (SHL) for each shareable image referenced by the image, plus one SHL for the image itself. Each SHL contains the base virtual address and name of its shareable image. The base virtual address is copied from the ICB corresponding to the shareable image. The first shareable image list element (index 0) contains information used to resolve .ADDRESS locations.

21.1.2.2 **Resolution of G^ Locations.** When the image is linked, all G^ references to locations in shareable images are changed to @^L references (longword relative deferred). (A G^ reference resolved at link time is changed to @#, absolute addressing mode.) The @^L address points to a location in the fixup vector tables reserved for G^ vectors. The G^ vector table contains one table for each shareable image linked with the main image. All references to a specific global label (within a specific shareable image) use the same G^ vector table entry. The linker loads the entries in the G^ vector tables with the location of the label, expressed as an offset from the base of its shareable image.

When resolving G^ references, the $IMGFIX system service locates each shareable image entry in the G^ vector table and performs the following action:

• The index into the shareable image list is used to locate the appropriate shareable image list entry.
• Using this entry, the base virtual address of the shareable image is located.
• The base address is added to each offset contained in the G^ vector table and the resulting value is stored in the G^ vector table.

When the image is actually executed, the longword relative deferred address points to the cell within the G^ vector table. The cell in the G^ vector table contains the correct virtual address of the reference.

21.1.2.3 **Resolution of .ADDRESS Locations.** When an image is linked, the following actions take place for each .ADDRESS directive:

1. The offset of the specified location from the base of its image is determined. This offset is stored in the longword reserved by the .ADDRESS directive.
2. The offset of the .ADDRESS directive from the base of its image is determined. This offset is stored in the .ADDRESS vector table portion of the fixup vector table.

Like G^ vector table entries, .ADDRESS vector table entries are separated into tables for each specific image. The .ADDRESS vector table also contains a table for entries in the image (if it is not a based image).

Figure 21-14 illustrates the resolution of the .ADDRESS directive by the

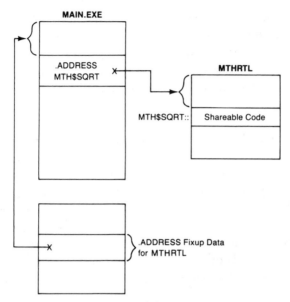

Figure 21-14 Resolution of the .ADDRESS Directive

linker. The address of MTH$SQRT is within the shareable library MTHRTL. The .ADDRESS directive within MAIN.EXE contains the offset of the label MTH$SQRT from the base of MTHRTL.EXE. The entry in the .ADDRESS vector table contains the offset of the .ADDRESS directive from the base of MAIN.

When $IMGFIX resolves the .ADDRESS directives, it performs the following steps to obtain the actual address of the location:

1. The offset to the .ADDRESS cell is added to the base address of the main image (using the previous example, the image MAIN). Separating the offset and base address in this fashion allows the main image to be a position-independent shareable image.
2. The contents of the .ADDRESS cell (the offset to the label MTH$SQRT) are added to the base address of the shareable image (MTHRTL.EXE).
3. The resulting address is loaded into the .ADDRESS cell.

This action is repeated for all .ADDRESS directives in all images in the image file, except in images that have a specified starting base address. Note that an image section containing any .ADDRESS or .ASCID references fixed up in this way cannot be shared among processes, since the resolutions of those directives are specific to the virtual address space in each process.

21.1.2.4 **Additional Functions of EXE$IMGFIX.** After address fixup is complete, EXE$IMGFIX alters the protection on the fixup vector section to UREW. It then tests whether any privileged shareable images have been activated. If any has, it calls the $IMGACT system service, specifying the IAC$V_SET-

VECTOR flag. Running in executive mode, the image activator can initialize the P1 space dispatch vectors for user-written system services, rundown routines, and message sections.

If any shareable image specified an initialization routine, EXE$IMGFIX scans, from back to front, the list of ICBs representing activated images. EXE$IMGFIX, running in user mode, calls the initialization routine of each shareable image that specified one.

1.1.3   Image Startup

After the page tables have been set up by the image activator, the image is called at its transfer address. Depending on how the image was linked, the initial transfer of control may be to a debugger, user-supplied initialization procedure, or the user image itself.

1.1.3.1
Transfer Vector Array. In addition to the ISDs previously discussed, the linker also includes in the image header a data structure called a transfer vector array. This array contains the user-supplied transfer address and also the means for including a debugger or a traceback handler in the user image.

The format of the transfer vector array is pictured in Figure 21-15. If a debugger transfer address is specified or implied, it appears first in the list. An

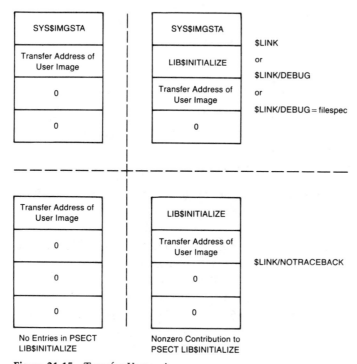

Figure 21-15   Transfer Vector Array

image-specific initialization procedure, if specified, occurs next. The last entry in the list is the transfer address of the user image, either the argument of an .END directive for a VAX MACRO program or the first statement of the main program written in a high-level language. A fourth entry containing a zero is the end of list indication, no matter what options were passed to the linker.

The initialization transfer address is described in the *Guide to Creating Modular Procedures on VAX/VMS* and is not discussed here.

If the DCL command LINK/DEBUG = file-spec is used to link an image, the explicit file specification is the name of a particular debugger object module. The linker places the transfer address found in the specified debugger file into the first element in the transfer vector array. If the /NOTRACEBACK option is included (and not overridden implicitly by including an explicit /DEBUG option), then there is no debug transfer address. In all other cases (including the DCL command LINK/DEBUG, which does not specify an explicit debugger module), the linker places the address of SYS$IMGSTA (found in the system service vector area) in the first element of the transfer vector array.

21.1.3.2 **Image Startup System Service.** Unless explicitly suppressed (with the /NOTRACEBACK qualifier), all images execute the Image Startup system service, sometimes called the debugger bootstrap. The system service procedure, EXE$IMGSTA in module SYSIMGSTA, runs in user mode. This procedure examines link and CLI flags to determine whether to start the user image directly or map the debugger (specified by translating the logical name LIB$DEBUG) into the user's P0 space and transfer control to it.

EXE$IMGSTA first tests whether it should map a debugger into P0 space. The mapping is done if either of the following conditions is true:

- If the program was linked with the DCL command LINK/DEBUG and simply run (that is, not run with a RUN/NODEBUG command)
- If the program was run with the DCL command RUN/DEBUG, independent of whether the debugger was requested at link time

The debugger is not mapped if the image was run with a RUN/NODEBUG command or if the /DEBUG qualifier was omitted from both the LINK command and the RUN command.

If a debugger is to be mapped, EXE$IMGSTA requests the Translate Logical Name ($TRNLOG) system service to translate the logical name LIB$DEBUG. If there is no translation, EXE$IMGSTA uses the string "DEBUG" as the debugger name. EXE$IMGSTA then requests the $IMGACT system service to activate the debugger image. It specifies flags for a merged activation in P0 space, so that the debugger will be mapped at addresses just higher than the main image and its shareable images. EXE$IMGSTA then requests the $IMG-FIX system service and then transfers control to the debugger image through a self-relative offset at the beginning of the image. The debugger, in response to user commands, transfers control to the image.

If no debugger is mapped, EXE$IMGSTA establishes a condition handler in the current call frame that gains control on signals that the image does not handle directly. One option that this handler can exercise is to map the traceback facility to print a symbolic dump of the exception.

Whether or not a debugger is mapped, EXE$IMGSTA alters the argument list to point to the next address in the transfer vector array and passes control to the next transfer address. This is either the Run-Time Library procedure LIB$INITIALIZE or the transfer address of the user image.

21.1.3.3   **Exception Handler for Traceback.** The condition handler that was established before the image was called has two purposes:

- It invokes a debugger if a DEBUG command is typed after an image is inter-rupted with a CTRL/Y.
- If an unfielded condition occurs, it causes an image dump, if one was re-quested, and invokes the traceback handler to produce a symbolic stack dump.

If a user interrupts execution of a nonprivileged image by typing CTRL/Y and DEBUG, the DCL (or MCR) CLI generates the signal SS$_DEBUG. (Priv-ileged images are simply run down in response to this command sequence.) If all handlers established by the image resignal the SS$_DEBUG exception, the debugger boot handler eventually gains control. Its response to a SS$_DEBUG signal is to map the debugger specified by the logical name LIB$DEBUG (if it is not already mapped) and transfer control to it. Notice that an image that was neither linked nor run with the debugger can still be debugged (albeit, without a debug symbol table) if the program reaches some undesirable state, such as an infinite loop.

The second purpose of the exception handler is to field any error conditions (where the severity level is WARNING, ERROR, or SEVERE) and pass them on to the traceback facility. If an image dump was requested, the handler dispatches to EXE$IMGDMP_MERGE (see Chapter 20) to create an image dump. When EXE$IMGDMP_MERGE returns, the handler maps the traceback facility (denoted by the logical name LIB$TRACE) into P0 space. If the condition has a severity level of either SUCCESS or INFO, the handler merely resignals it. The condition is then handled by the catch-all condition handler established by either EXE$PROCSTRT or the CLI that called the image.

21.2   **IMAGE EXIT**

When an image has completed its work, it passes control back to VMS either by calling the Exit ($EXIT) system service or by returning to its caller, which calls the $EXIT system service. $EXIT calls whatever exit handlers have been declared by the image and then requests the Delete Process ($DELPRC) system service.

Exit handlers are described in the next section, which is followed by a description of the operations of the $EXIT system service.

21.2.1   Exit Handlers and Related System Services

An exit handler is an optional, user-declared procedure that performs image cleanup. To use this option, an image running in a process builds a data structure called an exit control block and passes its address to the Declare Exit Handler ($DCLEXH) system service. Exit handlers can be declared for user, supervisor, and executive access modes. The access mode from which the service is called is the mode in which the exit handler is to execute.

An exit control block contains the address of the exit handler and its arguments. The exit handler's first argument is the address of a longword to receive the final image status. The declarer of the exit handler defines any additional arguments and their use. An exit control block also contains a forward link field. This field contains the address of the next exit control block or, if there is none, zero. The $DCLEXH system service links together

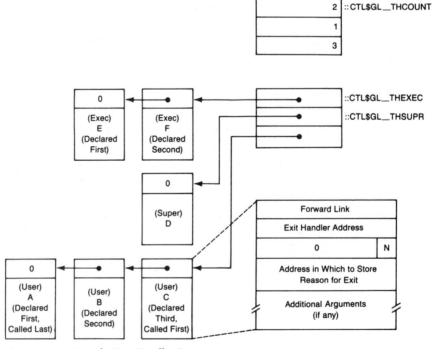

Figure 21-16 Sample Exit Handler Lists

all the exit control blocks for an access mode. Each list is ordered with the most recently declared exit handlers' control blocks first.

The exit handler listheads are in a three-longword array. Another three-longword array contains the number of exit control blocks in each list. Each array is indexed by access mode. Figure 21-16 shows these arrays and exit control blocks.

Both arrays are in P1 space and modifiable only from kernel mode. Exit control blocks, however, are defined by the image in per-process address space it controls. Therefore, the system services that access these lists must exercise particular care. An exit control block corrupted through program error could destroy the integrity of its list.

When inserting or removing an exit control block, for example, each system service must test the accessibility of affected forward links. The count array is used to prevent infinite loops that might otherwise result from multiple declarations of the same exit control block.

Two system services other than $DCLEXH access exit control blocks: Cancel Exit Handler ($CANEXH) and $EXIT (see Section 21.2.2). An image invokes the $CANEXH system service to delete a particular exit control block or all those for one access mode.

The $DCLEXH and $CANEXH system service procedures are EXE$DCLEXH and EXE$CANEXH, both in module SYSDCLEXH. Both execute in kernel mode.

1.2.2   Flow of the Exit System Service

The $EXIT system service procedure, EXE$EXIT in module SYSEXIT, runs initially in kernel mode. It also executes in outer modes, calling exit handlers.

EXE$EXIT is called with a single argument, the final status of the image. It stores the status in the P1 pointer page, at global location CTL$GL_FINALSTS, where it can be copied for image or process accounting. EXE$EXIT clears the force exit pending flag in the process status longword (PCB$L_STS).

If EXE$EXIT was called from kernel mode, it invokes $DELPRC, and the process is deleted. If EXE$EXIT was called from any other access mode, it examines the exit handler listheads (see Figure 21-16). It begins with the one for the mode from which it was called and proceeds to those of inner (more privileged) access modes.

If EXE$EXIT finds a nonzero listhead, it saves the listhead contents and the number of exit control blocks in the list, and clears both the listhead and the count longwords. EXE$EXIT then empties the kernel stack and executes an REI instruction to enter the outer access mode.

Running in the outer mode, EXE$EXIT removes the first exit control block from the list, updates the list pointer, writes the final image status to the address specified in the exit control block, and calls the exit handler. When (if) that handler returns, EXE$EXIT calls the next handler in the list. This continues until the list is exhausted or until EXE$EXIT has exhausted the count of exit handlers.

Once all the exit handlers for a given access mode have been called, EXE$EXIT must return to a more privileged access mode. It changes access mode by requesting the $EXIT system service. If none of the exit handlers in the list just processed has done anything extraordinary (such as declaring another exit handler), then the list for that mode is still empty and EXE$EXIT proceeds to the next inner access mode in its search for more exit handlers.

When EXE$EXIT reaches kernel mode, it invokes $DELPRC to delete the process.

21.2.3 **Example of Exit Handler List Processing**

To illustrate the processing of exit handlers, suppose that a process has its exit handler lists set up as shown in Figure 21-16. When the image requests the $EXIT system service from user mode, EXE$EXIT takes the following steps:

1. EXE$EXIT finds a nonzero listhead for user mode exit control blocks. The listhead points to the exit control block for Procedure C, the most recently declared user mode exit handler.
2. EXE$EXIT stores this address in R0 and clears the listhead. It then executes an REI instruction to change access mode to user and then calls Procedure C. When C returns, EXE$EXIT calls Procedure B and finally Procedure A. When A returns, EXE$EXIT determines that the user mode list is exhausted (because the forward pointer in the last exit handler is zero). EXE$EXIT, running in user mode, requests the $EXIT system service.
3. As in step 1, the search for exit handlers begins with user mode but this list is now empty. EXE$EXIT continues with the supervisor mode list, which has the single exit control block for handler D. The supervisor listhead is cleared, access mode is changed to supervisor, and Procedure D is called. When D returns, EXE$EXIT again requests the $EXIT system service, this time from supervisor mode.
4. Now the search for exit handlers begins with supervisor mode, whose list is empty. The list for executive mode contains two exit handlers, F and E, which are called from executive mode. When they return, the $EXIT system service is again requested, this time from executive access mode. The search that now begins with the executive mode listhead fails and the process is deleted.

The logic illustrated here shows how a process can prevent image termination through the use of exit handlers. Suppose EXE$EXIT invoked a supervisor mode handler which redeclared itself. When EXE$EXIT exhausted the exit handler list and requested the $EXIT system service again, the handler would be back on the supervisor mode exit handler list and would be reentered to redeclare itself again.

In fact, this use of exit handlers is just the mechanism used by the DCL and MCR CLIs to allow multiple images to execute, one after another, in the same process. This mechanism is discussed in more detail in Chapter 23.

Note that an exit handler that is declared later (which implies that it will be called earlier) can prevent previously declared handlers for the same access mode from even being called by simply requesting the $EXIT system service. In the previous example, Procedure C could prevent exit handlers B and A from being called by requesting $EXIT itself.

1.3   IMAGE AND PROCESS RUNDOWN

In an interactive or batch process, multiple images can execute one after another. Several steps must be taken to prevent a later image from inheriting either enhancements (such as elevated privileges) or degradations (such as a reduced working set) from a previous image. In addition, when a process is deleted, all traces of it must be eliminated from the system data structures and all reusable resources returned to the system.

The Rundown ($RUNDWN) system service serves both those needs. (Note that use of the $RUNDWN system service is reserved for VAX/VMS. Any other use is completely unsupported.)

$RUNDWN is called with one argument, access mode. This argument enables $RUNDWN to distinguish between image rundown and process rundown. The service is requested with an argument of user mode by both the DCL and MCR CLIs (see Chapter 23) to clean up between image executions. $RUNDWN is also requested from the $DELPRC system service (see Chapter 22) with an argument of kernel mode to remove traces of a process being deleted.

The $RUNDWN system service performs much of its work by requesting other system services. $RUNDWN passes its access mode argument to these services to allow them to determine how much work to do. For example, the Dequeue Lock Request ($DEQ) system service (see Chapter 13) can be called with an access mode argument to release all locks for that access mode and all outer modes. If $RUNDWN is requested with an argument of user mode, its $DEQ request cancels only user mode locks. If $RUNDWN is called with an argument of kernel mode, then all process locks are dequeued.

1.3.1   Flow of Rundown

The $RUNDWN system service procedure, EXE$RUNDWN in module SYSRUNDWN, runs in kernel mode. It first maximizes the access mode argument with the access mode of its caller. That is, the less privileged access mode is passed to other system services. Used in the following list, the phrase "based on access mode" means "perform this operation for this access mode and all outer (less privileged) access modes."

The following steps describe its actions:

1. EXE$RUNDWN clears any previously requested powerfail asynchronous system trap (AST) and returns AST quota to the process.

2. It requests the Set Resource Wait Mode ($SETRWM) system service, enabling resource wait mode to ensure that image rundown completes successfully.

3. EXE$RUNDWN invokes any per-process user-written rundown routines. Such a routine might perform cleanup for user-written system services.

4. If image accounting is enabled, an image deletion message is written to the accounting log file.

5. EXE$RUNDWN increments the image counter (PHD$L_IMGCNT). This counter prevents the delivery of ASTs to an image that has exited. The use of this synchronization technique in the operation of the Get Job/Process Information ($GETJPI) system service is described in Chapter 29.

6. The four P1 space vectors for user-written system services, user-written rundown routines, and image-specific message sections (see Figure 9-5) are reset to contain RSB instructions.

7. EXE$RUNDWN requests the Set Pagefault Monitoring ($SETPFM) system service to disable any monitoring of process page faults.

8. EXE$RUNDWN searches the channel control block table for channels to deassign. It compares the access mode of each assigned channel to that of the rundown. For each channel assigned in the same or an outer mode, EXE$RUNDWN requests the Deassign Channel ($DASSGN) system service. The deassign completes unless the channel has an open file. The access mode comparison prevents, for example, process-permanent files from being closed when an image is being run down (input access mode is user). Other channels that are not deassigned at this stage of image rundown include the image file and any other file that is mapped to a range of virtual addresses.

   If the channel's assigned mode is more privileged, EXE$RUNDWN makes an additional check of the flag CCB$V_IMGTMP to see whether the channel is associated with the Breakthrough ($BRKTHRU) system service. If it is, EXE$RUNDWN deassigns the channel so that broadcast operations are aborted at image exit.

9. The rights database identifier table is deallocated to the P1 process allocation region.

10. EXE$RUNDWN invokes MMG$IMGRESET (in module PHDUTL) to reset the image pages. MMG$IMGRESET performs the image clean-

up associated with memory management. The steps it performs are as follows:

a. MMG$IMGRESET invokes RM$RESET (in module RMSRESET) to reset the image I/O segment.

b. MMG$IMGRESET releases all ICBs that describe currently mapped images and places them on the ICB lookaside list.

c. All of P0 space is deleted. This frees the main image file and any other mapped file. Physical pages are released and blocks in the page file are deallocated.

d. The nonpermanent parts of P1 space are deleted. These are the user stack and an optional enlarged image I/O segment (see Figure 21-17). Any expansions to P1 space (at smaller virtual addresses than the user stack) are also deleted, as well as VAX DEBUG dynamic memory.

e. The working set list is reset to its default value, undoing any previous expansion or contraction performed by the Adjust Working Set Limit ($ADJWSL) system service. Working set size changes are described in Chapter 16.

f. The process privilege masks in the process header and PCB are reset to their permanent value, found at location CTL$GQ_PROCPRIV. This step eliminates any privilege enhancements to the process resulting from the execution of an image installed with privilege. (Section 21.4 describes the various privilege masks.)

g. The global location CTL$GL_IMGHDRBF is cleared to indicate that no image is active.

h. If any global sections were released as a result of releasing the process address space, the global sections are deleted.

i. The pointer to the end of the active working set list

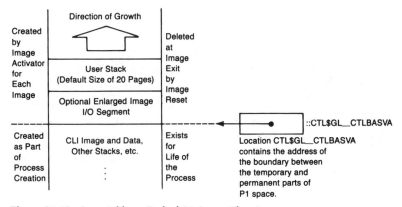

Figure 21-17 Low Address End of P1 Space That Is Deleted at Image Exit

(PHD$W_WSLAST) is reset to the end of the minimum working set list.

j. The process is allocated a new, smaller swap space.

11. The channel deassignment loop performed in step 8 is executed again. However, because the image file and other mapped files have now been disassociated from virtual address space, the channels associated with those files will also be deassigned. As in step 8, this deassignment is based on access mode, so that process-permanent files are unaffected by image rundown.

12. EXE$RUNDWN requests the Deallocate Device ($DALLOC) system service to deallocate devices allocated from this and outer access modes.

13. It requests the Cancel Timer ($CANTIM) and the Cancel Wakeup ($CANWAK) system services to cancel requests made from this and outer access modes.

14. It requests the $DEQ service to release locks for this and outer access modes.

15. It requests the Disassociate Common Event Flag Cluster ($DACEFC) system service to disassociate clusters 2 and 3.

16. It raises IPL to IPL$_SYNCH (8) because the next several steps manipulate systemwide data structures.

17. If this image has declared an error log mailbox, it is eliminated. The method for declaring an error log mailbox is described in Chapter 8.

18. All pending AST control blocks (ACBs) are removed from the list in the PCB, based on access mode. The blocks are then deallocated to nonpaged pool. This operation starts at the tail of the list and proceeds toward the head of the list until an ACB is found with a more privileged (smaller) access mode than the $RUNDWN access mode or until the AST pending queue is empty. (Recall from Chapter 7 that ASTs are enqueued in order of increasing access mode.)

19. Any change mode handlers for this and outer access modes are eliminated. Because change mode handlers only exist for user and supervisor modes, this step results in elimination of a change mode to user handler every time an image exits and the elimination of a change mode to supervisor handler when the process is deleted.

20. Any exit handlers for this and outer access modes are canceled.

21. Exception handlers found in the primary, secondary, and last chance vectors are eliminated for this and outer access modes.

22. The AST active bits for this and outer access modes are cleared. The AST enable bits for this and outer access modes are set.

23. System service failure exceptions are disabled for this and outer access modes.

24. Any compatibility mode handler that has been declared is canceled.

25. A new value of ASTLVL is calculated (by routine SCH$NEWLVL in module ASTDEL) to reflect the change in the AST queue resulting from step 18.

26. The force exit pending and wake pending flags in the PCB are cleared. Clearing these flags is the last step that must be performed at IPL$_SYNCH, and IPL is lowered to 0.

27. EXE$RUNDWN deletes all process logical names based on access mode. At image exit, all user mode logical names are deleted. At process deletion, all process logical names are deleted.

28. EXE$RUNDWN resets any P0 extension made to the process allocation region (see Chapter 3).

29. Resource wait mode is returned to its previous state, normal completion status is set, and control is returned to the caller.

1.4   PROCESS PRIVILEGES

VAX/VMS prevents unauthorized use of the system through process privileges. One or more of these privileges is required to perform particular system services, execute certain commands, or use privileged utilities.

1.4.1   Process Privilege Masks

VAX/VMS maintains several privilege masks for each process (see Table 21-2 and Section 21.1.1.5).

- PHD$Q_PRIVMSK contains the working privilege mask, the one checked by all system services that require privilege. This mask can be altered each time an image executes, can be altered by the Set Privileges ($SETPRV) system service, and is reset to the process-permanent privilege mask as a part of image rundown.

- The process privilege mask (PCB$Q_PRIV) in the access rights block (ARB) is always an exact duplicate of the privilege mask in the PHD. The ARB is currently a part of the software PCB.

- The process-permanent privilege mask is in the P1 pointer page at global location CTL$GQ_PROCPRIV. This mask is copied to the PHD and PCB privilege masks at image exit by MMG$IMGRESET. This mask is initialized when the process is created.

- The authorized privilege mask, PHD$Q_AUTHPRIV, is used by the $SETPRV system service to allow a process without SETPRV privilege to remove one of its permanent privileges and later regain that privilege. This mask is also initialized when the process is created.

- The image privilege mask, PHD$Q_IMAGPRIV, contains the privilege mask from a privileged known image while that image is executing in the process. This mask is used by the $SETPRV system service to allow an

Table 21-2   Process Privilege Masks

Symbolic Name	Use of This Mask	Modified by	Referenced by
PHD$Q_PRIVMSK	Working privilege mask	EXE$PROCSTRT, LOGINOUT, $SETPRV, Image activator, MMG$IMGRESET	System services that require privilege
PCB$Q_PRIV	Duplicate of the PHD mask	Same as PHD$Q_PRIVMSK	Device drivers, Files-11 XQP, ACPs
CTL$GQ_PROCPRIV	Records the permanently enabled privileges	EXE$PROCSTRT, LOGINOUT, $SETPRV	Image activator, MMG$IMGRESET, SET/SHOW commands
PHD$Q_AUTHPRIV	Records the privileges from the authorization file	EXE$PROCSTRT, LOGINOUT	$SETPRV, $GETJPI
PHD$Q_IMAGPRIV	Records the privileges of an installed image	Image activator	$SETPRV, LOGINOUT, $GETJPI
UAF$Q_PRIV	Records the privileges in the authorization file	AUTHORIZE	LOGINOUT
UAF$Q_DEF_PRIV	Records the default privileges in the authorization file	AUTHORIZE	LOGINOUT
KFE$Q_PROCPRIV	Records privileges with which an image is installed	INSTALL	Image activator
IHD$Q_PRIVREQS	Currently unused	Linker	Image activator

image installed with privilege to invoke the $SETPRV service without losing privileges.

- The authorization file record for a user contains two privilege masks: UAF$Q_DEF_PRIV and UAF$Q_PRIV. UAF$Q_DEF_PRIV contains the privileges which LOGINOUT copies to CTL$GQ_PROCPRIV, PHD$Q_PRIVMSK, and PCB$Q_PRIV when a user logs in. LOGINOUT copies the privileges in UAF$Q_PRIV to PHD$Q_AUTHPRIV.
- KFE$Q_PROCPRIV records the privileges with which a known image has been installed. When a process runs such an image, those privileges are temporarily granted to the process.

21.4.2 **Set Privilege System Service**

The $SETPRV system service enables a process to alter its image-specific (PHD$Q_PRIVMSK and PCB$Q_PRIV) or process-permanent (CTL$GQ_PROCPRIV) privilege masks, gaining or losing privileges as a result. In addition, the service can return the previous settings of either the image-specific or process-permanent privileges, if requested.

The $SETPRV system service procedure, EXE$SETPRV in module SYS-SETPRV, runs in kernel mode.

The path through EXE$SETPRV used to disable privileges requires no special privilege and clears the requested privilege bits in the image-specific (and, optionally, the process-permanent) privilege masks.

The path through the code used to enable privileges requires no privilege if the requested privilege is included in the list of privileges authorized for this process (PHD$Q_AUTHPRIV). If a process tries to acquire a privilege that is not in its authorized list, one of two conditions must hold for the requested privilege to be granted:

• The process must have SETPRV privilege. A process with this privilege can acquire any other privilege with either the $SETPRV system service or the DCL command SET PROCESS/PRIVILEGES (which invokes $SETPRV).
• The system service was called from executive or kernel mode. This condition is an escape to allow either VMS or user-written system services to acquire whatever privileges they need without regard for whether the calling process has SETPRV privilege. Such procedures must disable privileges granted in this fashion as part of their return path.

Note that the implementation of the $SETPRV system service does not return an error if a nonprivileged process attempts to add unauthorized privileges. In such a case, the service clears all unauthorized bits in the requested privilege mask, loads the modified privilege mask, and returns the alternate success status SS$_NOTALLPRIV.

22 Process Deletion

> . . . for dust you are and unto dust you shall return.
> *Genesis* 3:19

The Delete Process ($DELPRC) system service enables a process to remove a process from existence. A process can delete itself or any other process in the system which it has the capability to affect.

Process deletion occurs in two steps: the first in the context of the process requesting the deletion, and the second in the context of the process to be deleted. The system service first checks the capability of the current process to affect its target process and then queues a kernel mode asynchronous system trap (AST) to the target process. The AST, executing in the target process context, performs the actual deletion operations.

Process deletion requires the following operations:

- All traces of the process must be removed from the system.
- All system resources it used must be returned.
- Accounting information must be sent to the accounting manager (the job controller).
- If the process being deleted is a subprocess, all quotas and limits taken from its creator must be returned.
- Finally, if the creator requested notification of the subprocess's deletion through a termination mailbox, the deletion message must be sent.

22.1 PROCESS DELETION IN CONTEXT OF CALLER

The initial operation of the $DELPRC system service occurs in the context of the process requesting the system service. This part of the operation performs a simple set of privilege checks and then queues a kernel mode AST that will cause the deletion to continue in the context of the process actually being deleted. (Chapter 7 describes the queuing and delivery of ASTs.)

22.1.1 Delete Process System Service

The $DELPRC system service procedure, EXE$DELPRC in module SYS-DELPRC, runs in kernel mode. It first allocates an AST control block (ACB) to describe the AST to be queued. It then invokes the routine EXE$NAMPID (in module SYSPCNTRL) to convert the specified process name or extended process ID (EPID) to the address of the PCB of the process to be deleted.

EXE$NAMPID checks that the name or EPID corresponds to an actual process and verifies that the process requesting the system service has the capability to delete its target process. (Chapter 12 describes the requirements for one process to affect another.) If EXE$NAMPID returns an error status, EXE$DELPRC deallocates the ACB and returns the error status to its caller.

EXE$DELPRC checks that the target process is neither the swapper nor the null process; neither of these processes can be deleted, regardless of the privileges of the calling process. If the target process is either of these, EXE$DELPRC deallocates the ACB and returns the error status SS$_NONEXPR.

EXE$DELPRC then performs the following steps:

1. It marks the target process for deletion by setting bit PCB$V_DELPEN in the process status longword PCB$L_STS. If the bit was already set, a delete is already in progress for the target process. EXE$DELPRC deallocates the ACB and returns the success status SS$_NORMAL to its caller.
2. If the target process is suspended (scheduling states SUSP or SUSPO), EXE$DELPRC resumes the process. If the process were to remain suspended, no AST (including the delete process kernel mode AST) could be delivered to it.
3. EXE$DELPRC initializes the ACB with the PID of the target process and the address of the DELETE kernel mode AST procedure that performs the actual process deletion.
4. It queues the AST to the target process, with a potential boost of 3 to its software priority.

Queuing the AST to the target process makes it computable. Eventually, the scheduler selects that process for execution.

22.2   PROCESS DELETION IN CONTEXT OF PROCESS BEING DELETED

Most of process deletion occurs in the context of the process being deleted. If the process has no pending special kernel mode or other kernel mode ASTs, the delete process kernel mode AST procedure, which is called DELETE, executes immediately.

Deleting a process in its context means that its address space and process header are readily accessible. The DELETE AST procedure is therefore able to request standard system services, such as $DELTVA and $DASSGN. Special cases, such as the deletion of a process that is outswapped, simply do not exist.

In earlier versions of VAX/VMS, a special kernel mode AST, rather than a normal kernel mode AST, was queued to do process deletion. Chapter 7 discusses this Version 4 change in behavior.

22.2.1 **DELETE Kernel Mode AST**

The following steps are performed by the DELETE AST procedure:

1. DELETE first clears the PCB$B_ASTACT bit to indicate that no kernel mode AST is active and invokes SCH$NEWLVL to determine the mode of the most important pending AST. Taking these steps enables another kernel mode AST to interrupt the DELETE AST. Although interruption of an AST by another at the same mode is usually prohibited, it may be necessary before process deletion can complete.

   In particular, if the process has a Files-11 operation in progress, it must complete before DELETE can proceed. A nonzero field PCB$B_DPC indicates this condition. DELETE places the process into a resource wait. The queuing and delivery of a kernel mode AST ends the resource wait. When the file system operations are complete, control returns to the DELETE procedure. (Chapter 7 documents the field PCB$B_DPC and its use in stalling process deletion.)

2. DELETE then enables resource wait mode.

3. Any user-specified rundown routines are invoked to do image-specific cleanup, if they have not already been invoked once through image rundown. DELETE then resets the P1 cells that control dispatching to privileged shareable images.

4. It calls SYS$RMSRUNDWN to perform an RMS rundown. SYS$RMSRUNDWN is a system service vector that invokes the procedure RMS$RMSRUNDWN, in module [RMS]RMS0RNDWN, to abort RMS I/O for the process. RMS$RMSRUNDWN invokes the routine RM$LAST_CHANCE, which is in module [RMS]RMS0LSTCH.LIS.

   RM$LAST_CHANCE scans the process's open files. It looks for sequential disk files which are not shared and are open for write. For each such file, the routine closes the file to update the RMS record attributes in the file header, particularly the end-of-file pointer. RM$LAST_CHANCE also looks for any file that uses global buffers and detaches the process from the global buffer pool for the file. It makes no attempt to write out modified global buffers, because successful process deletion is considered more important.

5. If the process has any subprocesses (if its PCB$W_PRCCNT field is nonzero), they must be deleted before deletion of the owner can continue. (Section 22.2.2 contains an example of deleting a process with subprocesses.) The following steps are performed to delete the subprocesses:

   a. DELETE scans the PCB vector for all PCBs whose owner field specifies the PID of the process being deleted. DELETE requests the $DELPRC system service to delete each of these subprocesses.

   b. DELETE checks whether PCB$W_PRCCNT is zero. If it is greater than zero, the process is placed into the resource wait state (MWAIT).

The process becomes computable again when a special kernel mode AST is used to return CPU time quota from one of the subprocesses.

  c. After the special kernel mode AST executes, control returns to DE-LETE. It checks the subprocess count. If the count is still nonzero, the process is put back in the MWAIT state until another special kernel AST is queued. If the count is zero, all subprocesses have been deleted and the DELETE procedure can continue.

6. DELETE requests the system service $RUNDWN to run down the process from kernel mode. ($RUNDWN is described in Chapter 21.)

7. DELETE requests the Delete Virtual Address Space ($DELTVA) system service to delete the virtual pages associated with all sections still mapped to the process address space.

8. If the process is not a subprocess, DELETE dismounts each jobwide mounted volume.

9. All allocated devices are deallocated.

10. DELETE ensures that all outstanding process I/O requests have completed. It compares PCB$W_DIOLM to PCB$W_DIOCNT and PCB$W_BIOLM to PCB$W_BIOCNT. The difference between the first two fields is the number of outstanding direct I/O requests; the difference between the latter two is the number of outstanding buffered I/O requests. DELETE loops at IPL 0, waiting for the two sets of counts to be equal.

11. If the current process is not a subprocess, DELETE decrements one of two system process counts. If the process is interactive (if PCB$V_INTER in PCB$L_STS is set), DELETE decrements the number of interactive jobs, SYS$GW_IJOBCNT. If the process is a batch job (if PCB$V_BATCH in PCB$L_STS is set), DELETE decrements the number of batch jobs, SYS$GW_BJOBCNT.

12. If the current process is not a subprocess, DELETE deletes the jobwide logical name table.

13. The process name string in the PCB is cleared by zeroing the count byte.

14. If the process is a subprocess (if the PCB$L_OWNER field is nonzero), any remaining deductible quotas must be returned to the owner process. The following steps are taken to return quotas to the subprocess's owner process:

  a. An I/O request packet (IRP) is allocated for use as an ACB. The extra space at the bottom of the IRP will be used to hold the quotas being returned to the owner.

  b. The address of the return quota special kernel mode AST (RETQUOTA) and the PID of the owner are stored in the ACB.

  c. The unused quotas are put into the bottom of the IRP. The only quota that must be returned to the creator is unused CPU time. All other

> quotas are either pooled or nondeductible (see Chapter 20).
>
> d. Finally, the special kernel mode AST is queued to the creator, giving it a priority boost of 3.

15. If the creator of this process requested a termination mailbox message, a termination message is constructed on the stack. The contents of the message are listed in Table 22-1.

16. Routine EXE$PRCDELMSG (in module ACCOUNT) is invoked to send an accounting message to the job controller. The message is sent to the job controller, unless it was explicitly prevented by the NOACNT flag at process creation time or process termination accounting has been disabled for the entire system. The contents of this message are used to fill in all relevant fields of the accounting identification and resource packets. (The data structures used by the Accounting Utility are described in the *VAX/VMS Accounting Utility Reference Manual*.)

17. Most of the remainder of P1 space is deleted. The P1 pages permanently locked into the working set list, for example, the kernel stack, are not deleted. Some of P1 space, including the user stack, may have already been deleted as a result of a previous image reset call.

Table 22-1   Contents of the Termination Mailbox Message Sent to the Process Creator

Field in Message Block	Source of Information
Message type	MSG$_DELPROC[1]
Message size	
Final exit status	CTL$GL_FINALSTS
Process ID	PCB$L_EPID
Job ID	Not currently used
Logout time	EXE$GQ_SYSTIME
Account name	CTL$GT_ACCOUNT
User name	CTL$GT_USERNAME
CPU time	PHD$L_CPUTIM
Number of page faults	PHD$L_PAGEFLTS
Peak paging file usage	Not currently used
Peak working set size	CTL$GL_WSPEAK
Buffered I/O count	PHD$L_BIOCNT
Direct I/O count	PHD$L_DIOCNT
Count of mounted volumes	CTL$GL_VOLUMES
Login time	CTL$GQ_LOGIN
EPID of owner	PCB$L_EOWNER

---

[1]MSG$_DELPROC is a constant, indicating that this is a process termination message.

18. At this point, the process must be removed from the scheduler's database. To synchronize access to this data, the rest of the code in the DELETE AST executes at IPL$_SYNCH.

    The process is removed from execution with a svpctx instruction. Executing this instruction switches stacks so that the DELETE procedure is running on the interrupt stack.

19. DELETE stores the address of the PCB of the null process in global location SCH$GL_CURPCB, making the null process the current process. DELETE also stores it in the slot in the PCB vector formerly occupied by the process being deleted, freeing this slot for future use.

20. The pages in process space that were permanently locked into the working set (for example, the kernel stack and the P1 pointer page) are deleted and placed at the beginning of the free page list. The process header pages that are a permanent part of the working set will be deleted by the swapper when the process header is deleted.

21. Any remaining ACBs are removed from the PCB queue and deallocated to nonpaged pool.

22. The process swap space is deallocated.

23. If the process had an extended rights list, it is deallocated to nonpaged pool.

24. The process count field in the job information block (JIB) is decremented. If the process being deleted is a detached process (the PID of the process being deleted is equal to the master PID field in the JIB), the JIB is deallocated.

25. The owner process's subprocess count (PCB$W_PRCCNT) is decremented. If the owner process is also being deleted, the owner is currently in a wait state, waiting for the contents of this field to become zero. The parent process is made computable, so that it can check the value of PCB$W_PRCCNT. If the value is now zero, the parent can continue with its own deletion.

26. The PCB is deallocated to nonpaged pool.

27. The number of processes in the balance set is decremented.

28. The routine SCH$SWPWAKE is invoked to awaken the swapper because there is a process header to be removed from the balance slot area (see Chapter 17).

29. Finally, the DELETE AST procedure exits by jumping to the scheduler (at entry SCH$SCHED) to select the next process for execution (see Chapter 10).

22.2.2 Deletion of a Process That Owns Subprocesses

When a process owns subprocesses, the deletion of the owner process must be delayed until all the subprocesses that it owns are deleted. The prior dele-

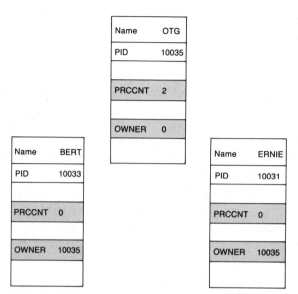

Figure 22-1 Sample Job to Illustrate Process Deletion
with Subprocesses

tion of subprocesses ensures that any quotas taken from the creator are returned. In early versions of VAX/VMS, prior to the existence of the JIB and its jobwide pooled quotas (see Chapter 20), there were several quotas charged against a process when it created a subprocess. At deletion of the subprocess, the subprocess returned those quotas. All of the quotas treated in this way are now pooled except for CPU time limit, which is the only quota returned at subprocess deletion.

During the execution of the DELETE AST procedure, a check is made to see if the process being deleted owns any subprocesses. If it does, these processes must be located and deleted.

As Figure 22-1 shows, there are no forward pointers in the JIB or PCB of an owner process to indicate which subprocesses it has created. The only indication that a process has created subprocesses is a nonzero value in PCB$W_PRCCNT. The process's subprocesses can only be located by scanning all the PCBs in the system until each PCB is located whose owner field contains the PID of interest.

22.2.3 Example of Process Deletion with Subprocesses

The details of this situation can be best illustrated with an example. Figure 22-1 shows a process whose process ID equals 10035 and whose name is OTG. The process OTG owns two subprocesses: the first has a process ID of 10033 and the name BERT; the second has a process ID of 10031 and the name ERNIE.

Neither of these subprocesses owns any further subprocesses. The following steps occur as a result of the process OTG being deleted. Assume that the priorities are such that the processes execute in the order OTG, BERT, and ERNIE.

1. The deletion of process OTG proceeds normally until it is determined that this process has created two subprocesses. The PCB vector is scanned until the two PCBs with 10035 in the owner field are located. These two processes are marked for deletion. This means that the DELETE kernel mode AST is queued to the two subprocesses and they are made computable. Process OTG is placed into a wait state because the count of owned subprocesses is nonzero (actually two, at this point).

2. The previous assumption about priorities implies that process BERT executes next. Its deletion proceeds past the point where process OTG stopped because it owns no subprocesses. However, the next step in the DELETE AST procedure determines that process BERT is a subprocess and must return quotas to its owner. The return of quotas is accomplished by queuing a special kernel mode AST (RETQUOTA) to process OTG, changing its state back to computable. When BERT has finished with all actions that require the presence of the JIB, it decrements the process count in OTG's PCB$W_PRCCNT. However, the count of owned subprocesses is still not zero (down to one now) so process OTG is put right back into the resource wait state.

3. The assumption about priorities indicates that process BERT continues to execute until it disappears entirely from the system. Process ERNIE now begins execution of the DELETE AST procedure. Again, the check for owned subprocesses indicates none, but the check for being a subprocess indicates that it is. A RETQUOTA AST is again queued to process OTG and the count of owned subprocesses decremented (finally to zero).

4. Now process OTG resumes execution as a result of the delivery of the RETQUOTA AST and subsequently finds that the count of owned subprocesses has gone to zero. In fact, process OTG continues to be deleted at this point, even though process ERNIE has not been entirely deleted. This overlapping is simply a result of the timing in this example. The process ERNIE is well on the way to being deleted and is no longer of any concern to process OTG. The important point is that the quotas given to process ERNIE have been returned to OTG. Once OTG's PCB$W_PRCCNT is equal to zero, it is irrelevant which process executes next. Because ERNIE and BERT have finished work that depended on the presence of the JIB, OTG and the JIB can be deleted totally.

In the general case of a series of subprocesses arranged in a tree structure, the deletion of some arbitrary process requires that each subprocess further down in the tree must execute the process deletion step which returns quota to its owner.

23 Interactive and Batch Jobs

In my end is my beginning.
Motto of Mary, Queen of Scots

The previous three chapters describe the creation and deletion of a process that executes a single image. This chapter describes the special actions that must be taken to allow several images to execute consecutively in the context of the same process. Because this mode of operation occurs in all interactive and batch jobs, it merits special discussion. However, the total operation of a VAX/VMS command language interpreter (CLI) is not discussed.

23.1 JOB CONTROLLER AND UNSOLICITED INPUT

The job controller is the process that controls the creation of nearly all interactive and batch jobs. Interactive jobs are usually initiated by unsolicited

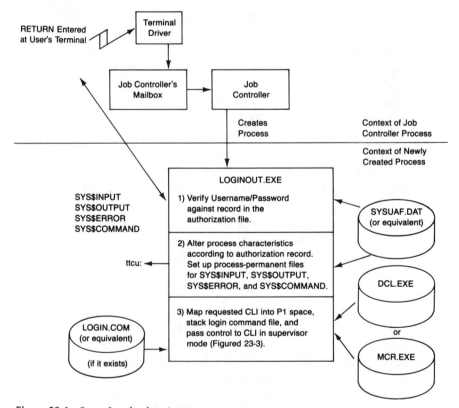

Figure 23-1 Steps Involved in Initiating an Interactive Job

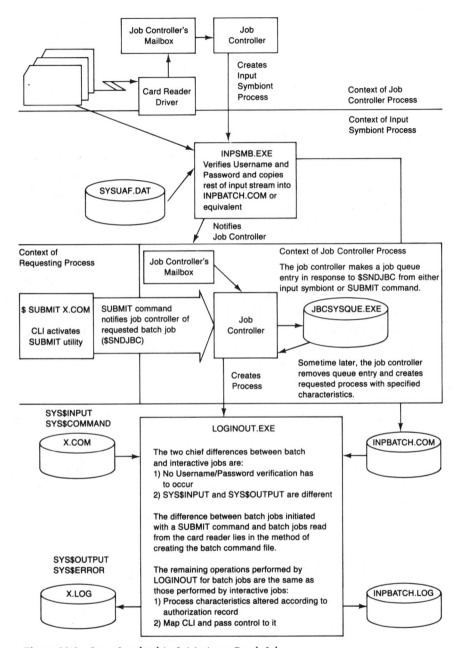

Figure 23-2 Steps Involved in Initiating a Batch Job

terminal input. Batch jobs are usually initiated through the SUBMIT command, although unsolicited card reader input also results in the creation of a batch job.

The crucial step performed by the job controller is the creation of a process that executes the image LOGINOUT. This image is activated and called ex-

623

actly like any other image, as described in Chapters 20 and 21. The actions that LOGINOUT takes, especially mapping a CLI into P1 space, are what differentiate interactive and batch jobs from the single image process described in the previous chapters. The creation of an interactive job is pictured schematically in Figure 23-1. The creation of a batch job is shown in Figure 23-2.

23.1.1   Unsolicited Terminal Input

The terminal interrupt service routine performs special action when an unexpected input interrupt occurs. First, it checks whether the terminal has the characteristic NO_TYPEAHEAD. If the terminal does, unsolicited input is ignored and the interrupt is dismissed. Otherwise, a check is made to determine whether the device is owned. If it is and if the owner process has requested notification of unsolicited interrupts, it is notified. Otherwise, the input characters are placed into a type-ahead buffer.

If the device is unowned, the job controller is notified through its mailbox that an unowned terminal has received an unexpected interrupt. In a sense, the job controller is the default owner of all otherwise unclaimed terminals.

The job controller routine that responds to unsolicited terminal input simply requests the Create Process ($CREPRC) system service. Table 23-1 shows the process parameters it passes to the system service.

The string *ttcu:* indicates the controller and unit of the terminal where the unsolicited input was typed. The terminal device type can be an actual physical device; an LT device, if the terminal is connected through a DECserver; an RT device, if the terminal is remote; a VT device, if virtual terminal support is enabled; or a WT device for a VAXstation window.

Note that each interactive process is initiated with a process name indicating its input device and LOGINOUT as the image to be executed (see Figure 23-1).

Table 23-1 $CREPRC Arguments for an Interactive Process

Argument	Value
Process name	_ttcu:
UIC	[1,4]
Image name	SYS$SYSTEM:LOGINOUT.EXE
SYS$INPUT	ttcu:
SYS$OUTPUT	ttcu:
SYS$ERROR	ttcu:
Base priority	DEFPRI (SYSBOOT parameter)
Privilege mask	TMPMBX, NETMBX, SETPRV
Status flags	Interactive process

23.1.2   **SUBMIT Command**

When the SUBMIT command is executed, a message is sent to the job controller, which places the requested job in one of its job queues. When the number of active jobs in one of the batch queues drops below its maximum value, the job controller selects the highest priority pending job from one of its queues. It creates a process for that job with the specified command procedure as SYS$INPUT and a log file in an appropriate directory as SYS$OUTPUT (see Figure 23-2). The image to be executed is LOGINOUT. Because LOGINOUT maps the appropriate CLI into the process P1 space, the input stream can be a series of command language commands.

23.1.3   **Unsolicited Card Reader Input**

An alternative method for starting batch jobs uses the "hot" card reader feature implemented in the card reader driver interrupt service routine. Like the terminal driver, the card reader driver informs the job controller that an unexpected interrupt has occurred on an unowned device. The job controller creates a process similar to the process created in response to unsolicited terminal input except that the image INPSMB.EXE, the input symbiont, executes in place of LOGINOUT.

Table 23-2 shows the process parameters passed by the job controller to the $CREPRC system service.

The letter c represents the controller number. The fact that this process has a card reader for its output device is irrelevant, because it does no writing to either SYS$OUTPUT or SYS$ERROR.

The input symbiont reads the $JOB and $PASSWORD cards and performs a validation similar to the one performed by LOGINOUT. After determining the user's default directory from the authorization record, the input symbiont opens a file in that directory and reads the rest of the job cards into that file. By default, the file is named INPBATCH.COM. Terminating conditions of

---

Table 23-2 $CREPRC Arguments for Input Symbiont Process

Argument	Value
Process name	_CRc0:
UIC	[1,4]
Image name	SYS$SYSTEM:INPSMB.EXE
SYS$INPUT	CRc0:
SYS$OUTPUT	CRc0:
SYS$ERROR	CRc0:
Base priority	DEFPRI (SYSBOOT parameter)
Privilege mask	TMPMBX, NETMBX, SETPRV

---

this read are an end of file, an $EOJ card, or another $JOB card.

Once the input stream has been read into the user's directory, the input symbiont sends a message to the job controller. The operation proceeds from this point in exactly the same manner as for the SUBMIT command. That is, the job controller eventually creates a process with the card file as SYS$INPUT, a log file as SYS$OUTPUT, and LOGINOUT as the image to be executed (see Figure 23-2).

23.2 THE LOGINOUT IMAGE

The LOGINOUT image is responsible for verifying that the user is authorized to use the system, reading the user's record in the authorization file, and altering the process characteristics to reflect what is found there. The most important step that this image performs in altering the process is to map a CLI into P1 space. (The layout of P1 space is pictured in Figure 1-7 and detailed in Table F-5).

23.2.1 Interactive Jobs

The LOGINOUT image is the first to run in an interactive process. It executes primarily in user mode, with some executive and kernel mode procedures. Its modules are in the facility [LOGIN].

When LOGINOUT executes in response to unsolicited terminal input, it must verify that the user has access to the system before it proceeds with the rest of its operations. It performs the following steps:

1. A user mode call frame condition handler is established to service any hardware exceptions or signaled conditions that occur while LOGINOUT is executing. When this handler is invoked, it first calls the Put Message ($PUTMSG) system service to write an error message. It then checks the type and severity of the condition. If the condition has not already been stored in P1 space, the handler stores it in preparation for writing the code to the termination mailbox.

   If the condition is a severe error, the handler calls the Exit ($EXIT) system service from executive mode, causing the process to be deleted. Otherwise, it returns, and LOGINOUT continues execution.

   When LOGINOUT executes executive mode code, it declares the same condition handler for executive mode.

2. LOGINOUT calls the Get Job/Process Information ($GETJPI) system service to find out the user name, process status flags, job type, and process owner.

3. LOGINOUT calls the Get Device Information ($GETDVI) system service to find out the name and characteristics of SYS$INPUT.

4. The logical names SYS$INPUT, SYS$OUTPUT, and SYS$ERROR are translated in the LNM$PROCESS table. The resultant strings are saved for later use.

5. LOGINOUT initializes the process-permanent data region in P1 space. This region is shared by LOGINOUT and the CLI it maps.

6. LOGINOUT next determines what type of process is being created from the global location CTL$GL_CREPRC_FLAGS, which contains a copy of the flags specified to the $CREPRC system service.

7. For an interactive process, one usually created in response to unsolicited input from a terminal, LOGINOUT performs the following steps:

    a. It initializes the user name and account name fields in the job information block (JIB) and P1 space to the string "<login>".

    b. Process-permanent files are created for the input and output devices by calls to Record Management Services (RMS). In the case of an interactive login, these are typically terminal devices. LOGINOUT redefines the logical names SYS$INPUT and SYS$OUTPUT in the LNM$PROCESS table. LOGINOUT defines the logical names SYS$ERROR and SYS$COMMAND with the same equivalence strings as SYS$OUTPUT and SYS$INPUT. The equivalence names for these logical names are prefixed by four bytes consisting of an escape ($1B_{16}$), a null character (00_{16}), and a two-byte internal file identifier (IFI). When RMS receives such a string as a result of logical name translation, it uses the IFI as an index into one of its internal tables. Using the IFI allows fast access to these commonly used files.

    c. LOGINOUT determines whether the job type is local, dialup, or remote, based on the characteristics of the SYS$INPUT terminal. It stores the terminal name in PCB$T_TERMINAL.

    d. LOGINOUT determines whether there is a system password and whether it applies to this terminal. If there is, it issues a timed, no-echo read to the terminal and checks the password entered by the user.

    e. It then translates the logical name SYS$ANNOUNCE and writes the announcement message defined by the system manager. This message might consist of the system name and a description of its use.

    f. LOGINOUT checks to see if autologins are enabled for the terminal that is logging in. If they are, LOGINOUT looks up the terminal name in SYS$SYSTEM:SYSALF.DAT to determine the user name associated with the terminal. It then reads the user authorization file (UAF) record associated with the user and stores the user name in the JIB.

    g. If autologins are not enabled for the SYS$INPUT terminal, LOGINOUT prompts on it for the user name. It reads and parses the input, noting the presence of qualifiers, such as /CONNECT and /CLI. It opens the system authorization file and reads the record associated with that user. LOGINOUT stores the user's name in the JIB and P1 space.

h. In either case, LOGINOUT then prompts for password, reads it, and verifies it. If there is a secondary password for the account, LOGINOUT prompts for it, reads it, and verifies it.

i. LOGINOUT then performs a scan of the intrusion database in nonpaged pool. The type of scan performed depends on the success of user validation:

—If a user validation error (such as invalid user name or password) has occurred, a suspect scan is performed. If evasion is in effect, the user name is set and a breakin audit is performed. Otherwise, the failed password count is incremented in the user's UAF record, and a corresponding intrusion record is either created or updated.

—If the login was valid, an intruder scan is performed. If the user is found to be an intruder, a breakin audit is performed and the login terminates.

j. If this is a captive or restricted account, LOGINOUT checks that the user did not include login qualifiers to change aspects of the process environment fixed for that account.

k. If SYS$INPUT is not a remote terminal, LOGINOUT then checks whether the user has disconnected from a process that still exists. It performs a wildcard $GETJPI, looking for a process with the same user name and user identification code (UIC) and a disconnected terminal. It displays any matches and asks the user to which, if any, the terminal should be connected. It records the answer for later use.

l. LOGINOUT checks that the interactive job count would not be exceeded by the logging in of this process.

8. Many of the process attributes extracted from the authorization file are put into their proper places, overwriting the attributes placed there when the process was created:

—Default disk and directory string
—User name
—Default privilege mask
—Process quotas and limits
—Information about primary and secondary day restrictions
—Base software priority
—UIC

9. After the process's correct UIC has been set, LOGINOUT recreates the job logical name table and, possibly, the group logical name table.

10. LOGINOUT attempts to change the process name from _ttcu: to the user name. This attempt fails if another process in the same group already has the same name. (A common cause of user name duplication is a user logged in at more than one terminal.) In the case of failure, the process retains its name (_ttcu:), guaranteed to be unique for a given system.

11. LOGINOUT checks a number of other fields in the authorization file record. These fields include the user or account job limit, account and password expiration, the hourly restrictions, the terminal type (dialup or remote terminal), and the DISUSER flag. These checks are waived in the case of the SYSTEM account logging in on the console terminal.

12. LOGINOUT begins initialization for a CLI. It creates logical names PROC0 through PROC9, each equated to the file specification of a command procedure (or indirect command file) to be executed before the CLI enters its input loop. Currently, only PROC0 and PROC1 are used. PROC0 is equated to the system name table translation of the logical name SYS$SYLOGIN.

    PROC1 is equated to the file specified by the LGICMD field of the user's UAF record or the file specified by the login qualifier /COMMAND at login time (by an authorized user). If the contents of the LGICMD field are null and no /COMMAND qualifier was present on the login command, PROC1 is equated to the string LOGIN. The LGICMD field should indicate the null device (using the string NL:) to provide a default of no login command file.

    When the CLI later executes its initialization code, it will translate these logical names and execute the command procedures (or indirect command files).

13. The CLI is mapped into the low address end of P1 space (see Figure 1-7). This mapping is accomplished by a merged image activation of the selected CLI. The procedure LIB$P1_MERGE first merges the CLI into P0 space to determine its size, deletes the P0 space, and maps the correct amount of P1 space. Next, the CLI's command table is mapped into P1 space, using the same procedure.

    The default CLI is specified by the authorization file. However, it can be overridden with the login qualifier /CLI by a user allowed to do so. The default command table is also specified by the authorization file. However, it can be overridden with the login qualifiers /CLI and /TABLE by a user allowed to do so.

14. LOGINOUT calls a kernel mode procedure to change the owner and protection of the CLI and command table pages. The owner access mode for each page is set to supervisor. The protection on all writable pages is changed to prevent writes from user mode.

15. P1 space is expanded by a number of pages equal to the SYSBOOT param-

eter CLISYMTBL to accommodate the CLI symbol table. Global location CTL$GL_CTLBASVA is altered to reflect the new low address end of P1 space.

16. LOGINOUT writes to SYS$OUTPUT, announcing successful login. It translates the logical name SYS$WELCOME and writes the announcement message defined by the system manager. If SYS$WELCOME is not defined, LOGINOUT writes the message below, obtaining the version number from the global location SYS$GQ_VERSION:

```
Welcome to VAX/VMS Version V4.4
```

It also writes the dates of the last logins, the number of login failures for that user since the last succcessful login, and the number of new mail messages for the user. (If the DISNEWMAIL flag is set in the UAF record, the new mail message is omitted.)

17. The logical names SYS$LOGIN, SYS$LOGIN_DEVICE, and SYS$-SCRATCH are also created in the process's job logical name table. If this is a remote login, the name SYS$REM_NODE is also created. The equivalence name for these logical names is the default disk and directory specified by the user's UAF record. The qualifier /DISK = ddcu (used with the user name portion of the login sequence) can be used to override the default disk.

18. LOGINOUT records the time of login in the UAF record.

19. At this point, LOGINOUT has finished its work and must pass control to the CLI. To pass control to the CLI, LOGINOUT calls an executive mode routine that performs the following actions:

    a. Changes the protection on pages in the process-permanent data region so that the pages can only be accessed from supervisor and inner access modes

    b. Modifies the PSL in the call frame so that the current and previous mode fields contain supervisor mode

    c. Writes the transfer address of the CLI into the PC saved in the call frame

    d. Exits from executive mode, by executing an REI instruction, which returns the process to supervisor mode with the PC pointing to the first instruction in the CLI

23.2.2 Batch Jobs

Many of the operations performed by LOGINOUT for an interactive process are also necessary for a batch job. For example, LOGINOUT must open the input and output streams and map the CLI. However, password verification is not performed, either because the input symbiont has already done it or because it is not necessary, in the case of a SUBMIT command.

Rather than describing the steps performed by LOGINOUT again, the following list simply specifies those that are different for a batch process:

1. LOGINOUT determines that it is creating a batch process because the batch flag is set in CTL$GL_CREPRC_FLAGS, a copy of the flags originally specified to the $CREPRC system service.
2. LOGINOUT initializes the account name fields in the JIB and P1 space to the string "<batch>".
3. LOGINOUT requests the Send to Job Controller ($SNDJBC) system service to obtain information about the batch job, for example, its user name, process priority, and working set information.
4. The prompted reads of user name and password and the system announcements that occur in the login of an interactive process are unnecessary for a batch process.
5. It reads the authorization file record for this user. It obtains process attributes to supplement information not specified at batch queue creation or job submission. These values are minimized with the values returned by the job controller.
6. The job parameters, P1 through P8, if present, are defined as user mode logical names which the CLI later translates.

Mapping the CLI and transferring control to it happen in exactly the same way as they do for an interactive job. In both cases, if SYS$SYLOGIN is defined as a system logical name, the first commands that execute are the commands in the site-specific login command file. If the user authorization file does not specify a user login command file, the command file SYS$LOGIN:LOGIN.COM is executed (if the CLI is DCL).

23.2.3   SPAWN and ATTACH

The DCL command SPAWN is used to create interactive subprocesses. The ATTACH command is used to transfer terminal control from one process to another within the same job. An image can also request an ATTACH or SPAWN function by calling the Run-Time Library procedures LIB$ATTACH and LIB$SPAWN. These procedures pass back the request to the DCL CLI. The major difference between the two ways of requesting the function is whether additional information about the request is passed in a command line or an argument list.

The major work involved in spawning a new subprocess is in copying process context information from the creating process to the subprocess. This information includes the process CLI symbols, process logical names, current privileges, out-of-band asynchronous system trap (AST) settings, verify flag settings, prompt string, default disk and directory, keypad definitions and states, and the command line that was passed to SPAWN (if one exists).

In response to a SPAWN request, DCL performs the following operations:

1. It parses the command line to determine what qualifiers are present (or examines an argument list) and validates them.
2. It temporarily disables the current process's out-of-band ASTs, blocking CTRL/Y ASTs during a critical section of code.
3. It creates a mailbox, requesting an attention AST if a message is written to the mailbox. This mailbox will receive termination information from the subprocess (and from up to three other spawned subprocesses) when it is deleted.
4. DCL records the name of the subprocess's CLI and command table files in P1 space locations. The $CREPRC system service will copy them to the process quota block for later use by LOGINOUT running in the context of the subprocess.
5. It creates a second mailbox through which context will be copied to the spawned subprocess. DCL obtains its name from the $GETDVI system service.
6. DCL creates an attach request mailbox. The process receives attach requests from other processes in the job tree in this mailbox. It is created with a logical name of the form DCL$ATTACH_*pid*, where *pid* is the extended process ID.
7. DCL requests the $GETJPI system service to determine the current process's quotas. From them, it builds a quota list used in creation of the spawned subprocess.
8. It requests the $CREPRC system service to create the subprocess. The IMAGE argument specifies LOGINOUT. The ERROR argument specifies the name of the communication mailbox through which context is to be passed. If the creating process does not specify input and output files to the SPAWN command, the INPUT and OUTPUT arguments specify the creating process's SYS$INPUT and SYS$OUTPUT file specifications. The $CREPRC request specifies a termination mailbox to receive a process deletion message from the subprocess. Because the request does not include a privilege mask for the subprocess, the $CREPRC system service creates the subprocess with the current privileges of the current process (see Chapter 20).
9. When the subprocess is created, LOGINOUT maps the specified CLI, typically DCL, and passes control to it. DCL, running in the context of the subprocess, first tests whether it is a subprocess. If it is, it translates the logical name SYS$ERROR. If there is a supervisor mode translation with an equivalence string which is the name of a mailbox, DCL recognizes that a SPAWN operation is in progress and that it must read context information from the creating process.

   The context information is passed in the following manner:

   a. DCL issues read requests to the communication mailbox.

b. The creating process writes context information to the mailbox, one record at a time. Each record has a type code identifying its contents. When the subprocess receives the information, it adds the information to its context.

c. The first record passed contains the permanently enabled privilege mask (CTL$GQ_PROCPRIV), out-of-band AST flag settings, verify flag setting, and prompt string. DCL, running in the context of the spawned subprocess, reads the record and initializes the process accordingly.

It requests the Set Privilege ($SETPRV) system service to reset the process privileges from those passed in the record. Thus, the subprocess has its working and permanently enabled privileges set to the permanently enabled privileges of its creator. Its authorized privilege mask, however, contains the privileges its creator possessed when the spawn occurred. This enables a privileged image to tailor an environment in a spawned subprocess and pass additional privileges onto its first image.

d. Next, the SPAWN command string is passed (if one was specified).

e. The creating process then scans the process logical name directory, which contains a list of process logical name table names. It copies all tables which were defined in user or supervisor mode and which do not have the LNM$V_CONFINE attribute. It then copies all of the logical names defined in those tables. DCL, running in the spawned subprocess context, creates the corresponding logical name tables and then their logical names.

f. The contents of the symbol table are then passed, one symbol at a time, followed by terminal keypad definitions. Note that DCL command tables are not passed to the subprocess.

10. Once it has passed all information to the subprocess, DCL tests whether the creating process is to wait for the subprocess. If it is, DCL requests a write attention AST on the attach request mailbox and hibernates. Otherwise, it restores out-of-band ASTs and resumes normal processing.

11. DCL, running in the context of the spawned subprocess, issues a special I/O request to the terminal driver to specify itself as owner of the terminal and continues normal processing.

The DCL request ATTACH transfers terminal control to a specified process (called the target process in this discussion). The operation of the DCL ATTACH routine is as follows:

1. DCL first disables out-of-band ASTs, to block CTRL/Y ASTs. It gets the name or process identification (PID) of the target process and then checks that the target process is not itself and that it is a process in the same job tree.

2. DCL creates an attach mailbox for the calling process. It will be used if a later attach request names this process as its target. DCL requests a write attention AST for the mailbox.

3. DCL locates the target process's attach mailbox and writes the name of its output stream (usually the equivalence name of SYS$INPUT) to the mailbox, thus triggering the write attention AST that was declared when the target process spawned a subprocess. It then issues a read request on the target process's attach mailbox.

4. The target process wakes in response to the write attention AST. The AST procedure tests whether the current process is detached. If it is, the AST procedure writes an affirmative response (a longword with a value of 1) to its attach mailbox. Otherwise, it writes a zero longword to mean the process is not detached.

5. Once it receives the affirmation, DCL in the calling process deassigns its channel to the target process's attach mailbox and hibernates.

6. The AST procedure in the target process issues a wake request for the process, declares another write attention AST for its attach mailbox, and returns control to the target process.

When one of the subprocesses created by the SPAWN command is deleted, the termination AST is delivered. The termination AST simply performs cleanup work before the subprocess is deleted. The channels to the attach and termination mailboxes are deassigned, and the mailboxes are deleted. If the subprocess was created by a call to LIB$SPAWN and if an event flag or AST routine was specified in the call, the event flag is set or the AST is delivered.

23.3 COMMAND LANGUAGE INTERPRETERS AND IMAGE EXECUTION

There are three VAX/VMS CLIs available from DIGITAL: DCL, MCR, and DEC/Shell. DCL is supplied with VAX/VMS. MCR, once a component of VAX/VMS, is now part of the optional product VAX-11 RSX. This section describes features of DCL and MCR. Discussion of the third CLI, supplied with the optional product VAX DEC/Shell, is beyond the scope of this book.

Once DCL or MCR gains control, it performs some initialization and then reads and processes successive records from SYS$INPUT. This section describes those operations that result in image execution, to contrast interactive and batch jobs with the simple processes described in previous chapters. The operations of both DCL and MCR in activating an image are described in some detail. These steps in the two CLIs are nearly identical. DCL is mentioned explicitly where it differs from MCR.

One of the important steps that either CLI performs is the declaration of a supervisor mode exit handler. It is this handler that prevents process deletion following image exit and allows the successive execution of multiple images within the same process.

A simplified flow of control through either CLI is pictured in Figure 23-3.

3.3.1   CLI Initialization

The first DCL CLI code is the routine DCL$STARTUP in module [DCL]INITIAL. For the MCR CLI, the initialization code is the routine MCR$STARTUP in module [MCR]MCRINIT. The initialization code performs the following steps before it enters the main command processing loop:

1. The CLI clears the FP register and then calls itself, creating an initial call frame on the supervisor stack. Because the saved FP in the call frame is zero, the call frame chain is terminated. It calls itself again and establishes a call frame condition handler.

2. The CLI writes the address of its CLI callback service routine in the global location CTL$AL_CLICALBK. Callback is a mechanism used to obtain services from the CLI, such as symbol creation and lookup.

3. The CLI initializes its work area. It initializes various internal variables based on information from LOGINOUT, passed in the process-permanent data region. It also initializes the CLI symbol table data structures.

4. If this is a batch job, the CLI translates the logical names for parameters P0 through P8 and creates symbols whose values are the equivalence names.

5. The CLI translates PROC0 through PROC9 and saves their equivalence names to identify the command procedures it must execute.

6. The CLI calls the Rundown ($RUNDWN) system service with an argument of user mode to run down the LOGINOUT image.

7. The CLI validates the structure of its command table.

8. DCL enables CTRL/Y and out-of-band ASTs on the terminal. MCR enables CTRL/Y ASTs. (If the UAF record had the DISCTLY flag set, CTRL/Y ASTs are not enabled.)

9. The CLI calls the Declare Change Mode Handler ($DCLCMH) system service to establish a change-mode-to-supervisor handler. This handler allows the CLI to get back to supervisor mode from user mode when it needs to write protected data structures. One instance where this is required is in symbol definition, because CLI symbol tables are protected from write access by user mode.

10. Finally, control is passed to the first instruction of the main command processing loop (routine DCL$RESTART or MCR$RESTART).

3.3.2   Command Processing Loop

The main command processing loop reads a record from SYS$INPUT and takes whatever action is dictated by the command. Some actions can be per-

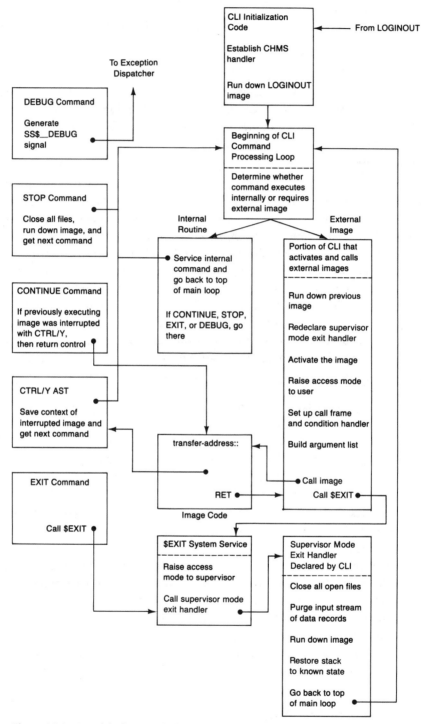

Figure 23-3 Simplified Control Flow Through a
Command Language Interpreter

Table 23-3   General Actions Performed by a Command Language Interpreter

General CLI Operations	Sample Commands
Commands that require external images	COPY, LINK, Some SET commands, Some SHOW commands
Commands that require internal processing and an external image	LOGOUT, MCR, RUN
Foreign commands	string: = =$image-file-spec
Other operations that destroy an image	STOP, EXIT, Invoking a command procedure
Commands that the CLI can execute internally (see Table 23-4)	EXAMINE, SET DEFAULT
Other internal operations	Symbol definition

formed directly by the CLI. Others require the execution of a separate image. Table 23-3 lists the general operations performed by a CLI and indicates those actions that require an external image.

If the record that is read from the input stream is a recognized command, DCL (or MCR) must also determine whether it can perform the requested action itself or activate an external image. Table 23-4 lists the commands that can be executed by DCL or MCR without destroying a currently executing image. (Special commands used by the MCR indirect command file processor are not included in the table.) Any other command either requires an image to execute (such as COPY or LINK) or directly affects the currently executing image (such as STOP).

23.3.3   Image Initiation by a CLI

When an external image is required, the CLI first performs some command-specific steps. It then enters a common routine to formally activate and call the image. The steps that it takes are nearly identical to the steps performed by EXE$PROCSTRT, described in Chapter 20:

1. The previous image (if any) is run down by calling the $RUNDWN system service. This system service removes any traces of a previously executing image. If the previous image terminated normally, this call is unnecessary. However, a CTRL/Y followed by an external command bypasses the normal image termination path, requiring this extra step to

Table 23-4   Commands Handled by CLI Internal Procedures

Command	*Description*
=	Create/modify a symbol
ALLOCATE	Allocate a device
ASSIGN	Create a logical name
ATTACH[1]	Transfer control to another process in job
CALL[1]	Transfer control to a labeled subroutine in a command procedure
CANCEL	Cancel scheduled wakeups for a process
CLOSE[1]	Close a process-permanent file
CONNECT[1]	Connect the physical terminal to a virtual terminal of another process
CONTINUE	Resume interrupted image
CREATE/NAME_TABLE	Create a new logical name table
DEALLOCATE	Deallocate a device
DEASSIGN[1]	Delete a logical name
DEBUG	Invoke the symbolic debugger
DECK[1]	Delimit the beginning of an input stream
DEFINE[1]	Create a logical name
DEFINE/KEY	Associate a character string and attributes with a terminal key
DELETE/KEY	Delete a key definition
DELETE/SYMBOL[1]	Delete a symbol definition
DEPOSIT	Modify a memory location
DISCONNECT[1]	Disconnect a physical terminal from a virtual terminal
EOD[1]	Delimit the end of an input stream
EOJ	Delimit the end of batch job submitted through card reader
EXAMINE	Examine a memory location
EXIT	Exit a command procedure, Run down an image after invoking exit handlers
GOSUB[1]	Transfer control to a labeled subroutine in a command procedure
GOTO	Transfer control within a command procedure
IF[1]	Conditional command execution
INQUIRE[1]	Interactively assign a value to a symbol
ON	Define conditional action
OPEN[1]	Open a process-permanent file
READ[1]	Read a record into a symbol
RECALL[1]	Display previously entered commands for possible reissue
RETURN[1]	Terminate a GOSUB subroutine procedure
SET CONTROL	Determine CTRL actions
SET DEFAULT	Define default directory string
SET KEY	Change current terminal key definition state
SET [NO]ON	Determine error processing
SET OUTPUT_RATE	Set rate at which output is written to a batch job log file

Table 23-4   Commands Handled by CLI Internal Procedures *(continued)*

Command	Description
SET PROMPT[1]	Change the CLI's prompt string
SET PROTECTION	Define default file protection
SET SYMBOL[1]	Alter scope of a symbol
SET UIC	Change process UIC and default directory string
SET [NO]VERIFY	Determine echoing of command procedure commands
SHOW DEFAULT	Display default directory string
SHOW KEY	Display terminal key definitions
SHOW PROTECTION	Display default file protection
SHOW QUOTA	Display current disk file usage
SHOW STATUS	Display status of currently executing image
SHOW SYMBOL	Display value of symbol(s)
SHOW TIME	Display current time
SHOW TRANSLATION	Show translation of single logical name
SPAWN[1]	Create a subprocess and transfer control to it
STOP	Run down an image bypassing termination handlers
WAIT[1]	Wait for specified interval to elapse
WRITE[1]	Write the value of a symbol to a file

[1]These commands are available in the DCL CLI but not in the MCR CLI.

ensure that the previous image is eliminated before another is activated.

2. The supervisor mode exit handler is declared to enable the CLI to regain control at image exit. Recall from Chapter 21 that an exit handler must be redeclared after each use.

3. The image is activated by calling the Image Activate ($IMGACT) system service (see Chapter 21).

4. The CLI pushes a PSL with a current mode of user and an address within itself onto the stack. It then executes an REI instruction to change access mode to user.

5. It clears the FP register and then calls itself, creating an initial call frame on the user stack. Because the saved FP in the call frame is zero, the call frame chain is terminated.

6. It establishes the catch-all condition handler as the handler for this call frame and as last chance exception vector.

7. It calls the Address Relocation Fixup ($IMGFIX) system service to relocate image addresses.

8. The argument list (see Figure 23-4) that is passed to the image (and to any intervening procedures such as SYS$IMGSTA) is built on the user stack. The CLI flags argument specifies, for example, whether the process is

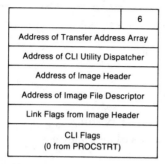

	6
Address of Transfer Address Array	
Address of CLI Utility Dispatcher	
Address of Image Header	
Address of Image File Descriptor	
Link Flags from Image Header	
CLI Flags (0 from PROCSTRT)	

Figure 23-4   Argument List Passed to an Image by
EXE$PROCSTRT or a CLI

batch, whether verify mode is enabled, and whether the image was run
with the /DEBUG qualifier.

9. The image is called at the first address in the transfer address array (described in Chapter 21). As mentioned in the discussion of image startup,
the first transfer address is the address of the debug bootstrap that establishes the traceback exception handler and maps the debugger, if requested.

10. The instruction following the call to the image results in a call to the
$EXIT system service. The code path through either CLI makes it irrele-
vant whether an image terminates with a RET instruction or a call to the
$EXIT system service. For any image that might be called as a procedure
from another image, the RET instruction is the preferred method of image
termination.

23.3.4   Image Termination

When an image in an interactive or batch job terminates, the $EXIT system
service eventually calls the supervisor mode exit handler established by the
CLI before the image was called. This exit handler performs several cleanup
steps before passing control to the beginning of the main command loop to
allow the CLI to process the next command:

1. If the image exited with an error status in R0, DCL writes the corresponding error message.
2. Any files left open by the image are closed by calling SYS$RMSRUNDWN
for each open file.
3. Any data records in the input stream (records that do not begin with a
dollar sign for DCL or a right angle bracket for MCR) are discarded and a
warning message is issued.
4. The image that just terminated is run down by calling $RUNDWN with
an argument of user mode.

5. Finally, control is passed to the beginning of the main command loop so that the CLI can read and process the next command.

3.3.5   Abnormal Image Termination

When an image terminates normally, it is run down as a part of the CLI's exit handler, and control is passed to the CLI at the start of its command loop. An image can also be interrupted by typing CTRL/Y or by using the COBOL or FORTRAN pause capability. Further execution of the image depends on the sequence of commands that execute while the image is interrupted.

3.3.5.1   CTRL/Y Processing.

When CTRL/Y (or possibly CTRL/C) is typed at the terminal, the terminal driver passes control to the AST procedure the CLI established during its initialization. The AST procedure first reestablishes itself, enabling future CTRL/Ys to be passed to the same AST procedure. It then checks whether a SET NOCONTROL = Y command has been executed. If so, the AST procedure returns, dismissing the CTRL/Y. Otherwise, it then checks what access mode was interrupted by the CTRL/Y.

If the previous mode was supervisor, the AST procedure checks whether an ON CONTROL_Y command has been issued previously that specifies a particular command to be executed in response. If this is so, the procedure sets a flag to indicate that the command be executed and returns. If not, DCL is restored to its initial state (with no nesting of indirect levels) and control is passed to the beginning of the main command loop.

If the previous mode was user, then the CTRL/Y must have interrupted an image. If the image was installed with enhanced privileges, the CLI saves the current privileges and resets the process privileges to those it had before the image was activated. A flag is set and the CLI returns to command processing. If, at this point, the user enters the DCL commands ATTACH, CONTINUE, or SPAWN (or the MCR command CONTINUE), the appropriate action is taken and the image is not run down. Any other command causes the privileged image to be run down before the next command is executed. Issuing a STOP command for a nonprivileged image causes the image to be terminated without the invocation of its exit handlers (see Section 23.3.5.7). However, because a privileged image is run down before the STOP command is invoked, its exit handlers are invoked.

3.3.5.2   Pause Capability.

The VAX COBOL and VAX FORTRAN languages provide the capability to interrupt an image under program control. Either of the Run-Time Library procedures that implement this feature could also be called from any other language.

The following COBOL statement generates a call to the Run-Time Library procedure COB$PAUSE, which sends the message "literal" to SYS$OUTPUT and passes control to the CLI at the beginning of its main command loop:

```
STOP literal
```

The following FORTRAN statement generates a call to the Run-Time Library procedure FOR$PAUSE, which sends the message "literal" to SYS$OUTPUT and passes control to the CLI at the beginning of its main command loop:

```
PAUSE [literal]
```

If the "literal" argument is omitted, FOR$PAUSE sends the following message to SYS$OUTPUT:

```
FORTRAN PAUSE
```

23.3.5.3 **State of Interrupted Images.** If a nonprivileged image was interrupted, the image context is saved and control is passed to the beginning of the main command loop to allow the user to execute commands. If the CLI can perform the requested action internally (see Table 23-4), then the image can be continued.

However, execution of any command that requires an external image destroys the context of the interrupted image. In addition, if the user executes an indirect command file while an image is interrupted, that image is destroyed, even though the commands in the indirect command file can be performed internally by the CLI.

Six commands that the user can request when an image has been interrupted by CTRL/Y have special importance. These commands are ATTACH, CONTINUE, DEBUG, EXIT, SPAWN, and STOP. (Note that ATTACH and SPAWN are supported only by DCL.)

23.3.5.4 **CONTINUE Command.** If a CONTINUE command is typed and the previous mode was user, the AST is dismissed and control is passed back to the image at the point where it was interrupted.

23.3.5.5 **DEBUG Command.** As described in Chapter 21, a DEBUG command causes the CLI to generate a SS$_DEBUG signal that will eventually be fielded by the condition handler established in image startup. This handler responds to the SS$_DEBUG signal by mapping the debugger (if it is not already mapped) and transferring control to it. This technique enables the debugger to be used, even if the image was not linked with the /DEBUG qualifier. (For this capability to work, the image cannot be linked with the /NOTRACEBACK qualifier. That qualifier prevents the handler that dynamically maps the debugger from being established.)

23.3.5.6 **EXIT Command.** The EXIT command invokes the $EXIT system service from user mode. Exit handlers are called and the image is run down.

23.3.5.7   **STOP Command.** The STOP command performs essentially the same cleanup operations that occur for a normally terminating image. However, STOP does its own work and does not call the $EXIT system service. Thus, user mode exit handlers are not called when an image terminates with a CTRL/Y STOP sequence.

The STOP command processor first determines whether an image or a process is being stopped. (The various possible STOP commands are described in the *VAX/VMS DCL Dictionary*.) If an image is being stopped, all open files are closed by calling SYS$RMSRUNDWN. The image itself is then run down (by requesting the $RUNDWN system service). Finally, control is passed to the beginning of the main command loop.

Note that STOP performs nearly identical operations to the CLI exit handler invoked as a result of a call to the $EXIT system service or an EXIT command. The only difference between either EXIT sequence and the STOP command is that user mode exit handlers are not called first. Thus, in most cases, the STOP and EXIT commands are interchangeable. One useful aspect of the STOP command is that it can be used to eliminate an image that contains a user mode exit handler which is preventing that image from completely going away, either intentionally or as a result of an error.

23.4   **LOGOUT OPERATION**

LOGINOUT, the image that performs the initialization of an interactive or batch job, also executes to cause the eventual deletion of such a process. When LOGINOUT is entered, it must determine whether to perform login, logout, or batch job step initialization. The indication to LOGINOUT that the process is logged in already is the existence of the process-permanent data (PPD) region, used to communicate between LOGINOUT and the CLI.

If this region exists, LOGINOUT tests whether the process is batch. If it is not, LOGINOUT takes whatever action is required before calling the Delete Process ($DELPRC) system service to perform those parts of process deletion that are independent of the kind of process that is being deleted.

1. If the user specified the /[NO]HANGUP qualifier on the LOGOUT command, LOGINOUT checks whether changing the terminal characteristics is appropriate. If the process is interactive and not a subprocess and the terminal is a local terminal, LOGINOUT reads the current terminal characteristics and resets them, altering the hangup bit.
2. LOGINOUT copies the IFIs for SYS$INPUT and SYS$OUTPUT from PPD locations into RMS data structures. This restores definitions of SYS$INPUT and SYS$OUTPUT made at login.
3. The logout message is written to the restored SYS$OUTPUT. (Thus, it cannot be redirected via a logical name definition.) If the user asked for a

full logout message, LOGINOUT calls $GETJPI to get information, such as CPU time, number of page faults, and number of I/O requests.

4. SYS$INPUT and SYS$OUTPUT are closed.

5. Finally, $EXIT is called from executive mode. As described in Chapter 21, the search for exit handlers is limited to the executive mode list, bypassing the supervisor mode exit handler established by the CLI to prevent process deletion following image exit.

6. After the executive mode exit handler has performed its work, the $EXIT system service calls the $DELPRC system service, which removes the logged out process from the system.

If the process is a batch job, LOGINOUT first closes SYS$INPUT. It calls the $SNDJBC system service again to determine if there is another job step. If the batch job was submitted with multiple command procedures specified, LOGINOUT opens the new SYS$INPUT, reinitializes the batch job environment, and reenters the CLI.

If the message returned from the job controller indicates that the job should be terminated, LOGINOUT terminates it through the following steps:

1. It writes a logout message to the log file.

2. It closes the log file.

3. If the log file is to be printed, then LOGINOUT calls $SNDJBC again, this time to queue the file to a print queue.

4. It then calls the $EXIT system service from executive mode, resulting in the deletion of the process.

PART VII/System Initialization

Bootstrap Procedures

Ante mare et terras et quod tegit omnia caelum unus erat toto
naturae vultus in orbe, quem dixere chaos: rudis indigestaque
moles . . .
[Before the sea was, and the lands, and the sky that hangs
over all, the face of Nature showed all alike, which state has
been called chaos: a rough unordered mass of things . . .]

Ovid, *Metamorphoses* I, 5–7

Before a VAX/VMS system can operate, some initialization or bootstrap programs must execute to configure the system and read the executive into memory. Parts of the bootstrap operation are specific to the type of VAX processor. Others are common across all VAX family members.

This chapter first summarizes all phases of system initialization and then describes those that occur before code contained in the system image (SYS.EXE) executes. Chapter 25 describes the later phases of system initialization.

24.1 OVERVIEW OF SYSTEM INITIALIZATION

There are a number of programs invoked in VAX/VMS system initialization. Some of them run outside an operating system environment; others execute in system context with memory management enabled; others execute in process context. In general, an initialization task is postponed to as late a program as possible. With a larger percentage of the system environment present, a task is easier to implement and debug. These programs are summarized in the following list and described in detail in this and the next chapter.

• The console subsystem is CPU-specific. Regardless of its implementation, it must initialize the CPU, locate 64K bytes of good memory, and load VMB.EXE into it.
• VMB.EXE, the primary bootstrap program, runs stand-alone on the VAX processor. It provides an operating-system-independent bootstrap. Its functions are to size memory, initialize the adapter and device that contain the secondary bootstrap program, and load it.
• SYSBOOT.EXE, the secondary bootstrap program for VAX/VMS, also runs stand-alone. It reads SYSBOOT parameters and, based on their values, lays out system virtual address space. It loads the system image, SYS.EXE, into memory, as well as several other images, such as the system device driver.

It transfers control to EXE$INIT, a module in SYS.EXE.

- After turning on memory management, EXE$INIT runs in system context, on the interrupt stack. It performs those initialization tasks which require memory management enabled and which must be done prior to entering process context. These tasks include initializing the scheduler and memory management databases. EXE$INIT jumps to the scheduling routine SCH$SCHED (see Chapter 10), which places the swapper process into execution.

- EXE$SWAPINIT, a routine in the swapper process, performs the minimum initialization tasks that must be done in process context and before creating a new process. As part of the swapper, it is part of the system image and is thus kept to a minimum size. Because it is pageable code, it eventually disappears from the system working set and thus occupies no physical space. These tasks include initializing paged pool and the pageable logical name database. EXE$SWAPINIT creates the SYSINIT process.

- The SYSINIT process performs initialization tasks which must be done in process context and which do not lend themselves to DCL commands. These include initializing the swap and page files, mapping the Files-11 XQP as a global section, and mapping RMS. The SYSINIT process creates the STARTUP process.

- The STARTUP process executes a series of DCL commands. It creates various system processes such as OPCOM and the job controller. It runs SYSGEN to autoconfigure the I/O database. It runs the Install Utility to alter the default activation of various images. Some images are installed to be activated more quickly; others, so they can be shared among processes; and others, to be activated with privileges not otherwise granted to the process. The STARTUP process executes a series of site-specific commands and enables interactive logins.

24.2   PROCESSOR-SPECIFIC INITIALIZATION

The initial steps that occur in the initialization of a VAX/VMS system depend on the particular VAX processor being booted. The next sections briefly describe the processor-specific steps that occur before VMB gains control and begins execution. (Note that all descriptions assume that the console terminal is in local enable mode, able to receive command input.)

In all processors, the following steps occur:

- 64K bytes of error-free, page-aligned, contiguous memory are located.
- VMB is loaded into the second page of the 64K bytes of memory.
- The bootstrap device code, other bootstrap flags, and additional information are passed to VMB using registers R0 through R5 and R10 through AP.
- VMB executes.

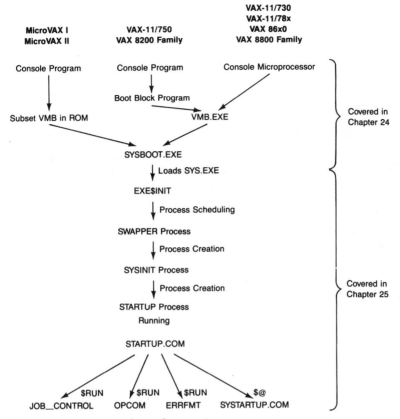

Figure 24-1 Sequence of Initialization Events

The way in which good memory is located and registers are loaded is CPU-dependent. The most obvious processor-specific item that affects the bootstrap operation is the console configuration. Figure 24-1 summarizes the bootstrap sequence.

24.2.1 VAX-11/730 Initial Bootstrap Operation

The console subsystem on the VAX-11/730 consists of a separate microprocessor, two block-addressable storage devices (TU58 cartridge tape drives), and a terminal. The console TU58 is an RT-11 directory structured device. When the CPU is in console mode, only the console program can execute; the CPU cannot execute any VAX instructions.

There are several ways in which a bootstrap sequence may be initiated:

- A power-on occurs (boot switch is pressed, or processor is turned on).
- The console command B(oot) is typed while the processor is in console mode.

- A bootstrap command procedure is invoked while the system is in console mode.
- The following instruction is executed in kernel mode:

```
MTPR    #^XF02,#PR$_TXDB
```

- While the AUTO RESTART switch is in the ON position, a CPU halt condition occurs and auto restart fails.

In the bootstrap sequence, the console subsystem must execute a series of programs to load and execute VMB. Table 24-1 lists these programs.

The initial bootstrap programs are console microprocessor programs. The steps of initial bootstrap are as follows:

1. After performing a self-test, the microprocessor locates the TU58 that contains the boot block (trying DD1 first and, if that fails, then DD0) and loads blocks 0 through 5 from the tape into microprocessor memory. The

Table 24-1   Processor-Dependent Programs Used to Bootstrap the VAX-11/730

Program Executing	Location of Program	Purpose of Program
EXECUTES ON CONSOLE MICROPROCESSOR		
Console microprocessor ROM bootstrap	ROM in console subsystem	Read TU58 boot block into memory and execute code contained there
TU58 boot block program	LBN 0 on console TU58	Locate CONSOL.EXE, read it into memory, and pass control to it
CONSOL.EXE	Console TU58	Initialize VAX-11/730, load general registers, and execute the next two indirect command files
POWER.CMD[1]	Console TU58	Locate 64K-byte block of good memory and check system configuration
CODE0n.CMD[2]	Console TU58	Configuration-dependent
Bootstrap command file	Console TU58	Load VMB into VAX memory and transfer control to it
EXECUTES ON VAX-11/730		
VMB.EXE	Console TU58	Size physical memory, locate secondary bootstrap, load it into memory, and pass control to it

[1]This is actually a command procedure that loads and runs programs written in CPU microcode.

[2]When POWER.CMD determines the configuration of the machine, it returns a value to CONSOL.EXE. This value is then used as n to determine which CODE0n.CMD to execute.

code in the boot block locates the main console microcode program CON-
SOL.EXE on the console TU58.

2. CONSOL.EXE then executes two command procedure files, POWER.
    CMD and CODE0n.CMD. POWER.CMD loads several microcode files
    into the CPU, including one called POWER.CPU. POWER.CPU initializes
    the machine, searches for a page-aligned 64K-byte block of good memory,
    and checks the configuration of the machine. When POWER.CPU exits, it
    returns an address 200_{16} bytes beyond the beginning of the first good page.
    This address is loaded into SP. (In a typical system with no errors in the
    first 64K bytes, the contents of SP are 200_{16}.)

    Each possible configuration of the VAX-11/730 is assigned a value.
    Whichever value POWER.CPU returns is substituted into the file name
    CODE0n.CMD. The CODE0n.CMD routines load the normal run-time
    microcode for the appropriate processor configuration. Table 24-2 lists the
    command files used with specific processor configurations.

3. The AUTO RESTART switch is checked. If it is in the OFF position, the
    processor enters console mode and prints the following console command
    prompt:

    >>>

    If the AUTO RESTART switch is in the ON position, the console
    executes the commands in the default bootstrap command file
    (DEFBOO.CMD).

4. The three console commands that bootstrap a VMS system cause the exe-
    cution of command files located on the console TU58. Table 24-3 shows
    the commands and their associated command files.

    These command files identify the system device and other characteris-
    tics of the bootstrap operation by loading general registers R0 through R5
    with parameters that will be interpreted by the primary bootstrap pro-
    gram, VMB.

5. The following three commands in the bootstrap command files display the
    contents of SP (to identify the starting address in physical memory). They
    then load the primary bootstrap program, VMB, from the TU58 into the

---

Table 24-2   VAX-11/730 Bootstrap Command Files

Command File	*Hardware Configuration*
CODE00.CMD	No FPA, no IDC
CODE01.CMD	No FPA, with IDC
CODE02.CMD	With FPA, no IDC
CODE03.CMD	With FPA, with IDC

Table 24-3   Commands to Boot VAX Processors

Command	Command File[1]
B	DEFBOO.CMD
B *dev*	*dev*BOO.CMD or *dev*BOO.COM
@*filespec*	*filespec*.CMD or *filespec*.COM

[1]The file type of a console command procedure depends on the particular processor and console subsystem. CMD is used by the VAX-11/730, VAX-11/78x, and BOOT58.EXE. COM is used by the VAX 8800 family and the VAX 86x0.

good 64K-byte block of VAX memory, leaving the first page free.

```
E  SP
L/P/S:@  VMB.EXE
S  @
```

The free page will contain a data structure called a restart parameter block (RPB). The RPB is used by VMB and, in the event of powerfail or other system failure, by restart routines in the console subsystem and VMS.

The third command, START, transfers control to the first byte of VMB.

6. VMB.EXE is described in Section 24.3.

24.2.2   VAX-11/750 Initial Bootstrap Operation

The console subsystem on a VAX-11/750 consists of one block-addressable TU58 cartridge tape and a terminal. The VAX-11/750 console program is implemented in CPU microcode stored in read-only memory (ROM) within the CPU. When the CPU is in console mode, the console program (and nothing else, such as a user program or VMS itself) executes.

There are several ways in which a bootstrap sequence may be initiated:

• The system is powered on, or the RESET front panel button is depressed, and the POWER-ON ACTION switch is in the bootstrap position.
• The B(oot) command is entered while the system is in console mode.
• A HALT instruction is executed, or some other halt condition occurs, and the POWER-ON ACTION switch is in the BOOT position.
• The following instruction is executed in kernel mode:

```
MTPR    #^XF02,#PR$_TXDB
```

• An attempt to restart the system after a power failure recovery or some other halt condition does not succeed, and the POWER-ON ACTION switch is in the RESTART/BOOT position.

In the bootstrap sequence, the console subsystem must execute a series of

Table 24-4 Processor-Dependent Programs Used to Bootstrap the VAX-11/750

Program Executing	Location of Program	Purpose of Program
Console program	ROM in VAX-11/750 CPU	Initialize CPU, locate block of good memory, determine boot device, and pass control to device-specific ROM
Device-specific ROM code	I/O address space of VAX-11/750 CPU	Load LBN 0 of boot device into memory and pass control to it
Boot block code	LBN 0 of boot device	Load primary bootstrap program from system device or BOOT58 from console TU58 and pass control to it
VMB.EXE	Specific LBN on system device	Size physical memory, locate secondary bootstrap, load it into memory, and pass control to it
BOOT58.EXE	Specific LBN on console TU58	Process indirect command files or enhanced console commands, boot from an HSC system device

programs to load and execute VMB. Table 24-4 lists these programs.

The steps of initial bootstrap are as follows:

1. The console program initializes the CPU and locates a page-aligned 64K-byte block of good memory. It loads the first 128 map registers in the UNIBUS adapter to address this block of memory (a step not taken when the TU58 is used as a bootstrap device). The console program on the VAX-11/750 does not process command files. Instead, it must construct the contents for R0 through R5 from the device selected by the BOOT DEVICE switch and the bootstrap command itself. It then passes control to the device-specific ROM selected either by the bootstrap device selector switch on the CPU cabinet front panel or by the boot command.

2. The device-specific ROM program is a VAX macro instruction program. It consists of two main pieces, a control routine and a device-specific subroutine. This program simply reads the boot block, LBN 0, of the selected device into the first page of the good memory and passes control to it (at an address 12 bytes past the beginning of the program).

3. The code in the boot block reads VMB or BOOT58 from the console device into memory. The boot block program is described in more detail in Section 24.2.2.1.

4. BOOT58 executes a command procedure that reads VMB from the system device into memory. BOOT58 is described in more detail in Section 24.2.2.2.

5. VMB is described in Section 24.3.

24.2.2.1   **Boot Block Program.** The boot block program loads a single program into memory and passes control to it. The boot block program does not contain any I/O support. It uses the driver subroutine contained in the device ROM program. The boot block program on a system device loads VMB. The boot block program on a console TU58 loads an enhanced command processor program called BOOT58. The boot block program on a stand-alone BACKUP console TU58 loads VMB.

There are three longwords of header information that precede the body of the boot block program. These longwords contain the following:

- The size of the bootstrap program to be loaded
- The starting logical block number (LBN) of the bootstrap program to be loaded
- A relative offset into the block of good memory where this program is to be loaded

The boot block is written during normal system operation by the Writeboot Utility. It uses the file system to look up a user-specified file (VMB.EXE or BOOT58.EXE) on a user-specified device. WRITEBOOT determines values for the three header longwords and writes the boot block program into LBN 0. Notice that the boot block program has the LBN of the bootstrap program hard coded into the block. If the position of the bootstrap program on the volume changes, the Writeboot Utility must be run again to rewrite the boot block with new information.

Note that the location of VMB by the boot block program is one of the few cases in VAX/VMS of a file being located by an LBN coded into another program. Thus, VMB on a VAX-11/750 system device is one of the few files that is not free to move or be superseded by a newer version without some external intervention, in this case, running WRITEBOOT.

24.2.2.2   **BOOT58.** The TU58 on the VAX-11/750 is not necessarily used during a normal bootstrap operation. However, the VAX-11/750 has an alternate bootstrap path that uses the TU58 and provides the following:

- Command procedure capability
- An enhanced console command language
- The ability to bootstrap a system if the boot block on the system device is corrupted
- The ability to bootstrap a system from a hierarchical system controller (HSC) disk

The stand-alone program BOOT58 is an enhanced console command processor loaded from the TU58 that provides the features previously listed. BOOT58 is loaded by selecting the console block storage device (DDA0:) as the bootstrap device, either by the device selector switch or with the following command:

```
>>>B DDA0:
```

Note that the drive DDA0: must contain the TU58 cartridge with console command files and BOOT58.EXE. The TU58 is an RT-11 structured device.

The boot block on the TU58 boots BOOT58. Once BOOT58 prompts, commands or command procedure file specifications can be entered at the console terminal. BOOT58 accepts the commands shown in Table 24-3.

There is no device-specific ROM on the VAX-11/750 that supports loading LBN 0 from an HSC disk through a CI750 adapter and then loading VMB. BOOT58 makes it possible to load VMB from the console. VMB does contain device support for the CI750 and HSC disks. It first loads volatile computer interconnect (CI) microcode from the console TU58 into the CI750 and volatile VAX-11/750 microcode into the VAX-11/750.

BOOT58 is used on the VAX 8200 family processors in an analogous manner (see Section 24.2.6). On those processors, it is booted from the console RX50 and is used to boot VMS from an HSC system disk.

24.2.3   VAX-11/780 and VAX-11/785 Initial Bootstrap Operation

The console subsystem on the VAX-11/780, VAX-11/782, and VAX-11/785 consists of a separate LSI-11 microprocessor, a block-addressable RX01 floppy disk, and a terminal. The console subsystem can perform certain (but not all) operations while the VAX-11/78x CPU is executing instructions.

There are several ways in which a bootstrap sequence may be initiated:

- The B(oot) command is entered while the system is in console mode, or the boot switch is depressed.
- A bootstrap command procedure is invoked while the system is in console mode.
- The following instruction is executed in kernel mode:

```
MTPR    #^XF02,#PR$_TXDB
```

- An attempt to restart the system after a power failure recovery or any other halt condition does not succeed, and the AUTO RESTART switch is in the ON position.

In the bootstrap sequence, the console subsystem must execute a series of programs to load and execute VMB on a VAX-11/78x. The initial bootstrap programs run on the LSI-11 and execute PDP-11 instructions rather than VAX instructions. Table 24-5 lists these programs and those that run on the VAX processor. (Note that this description does not include booting the at-

Table 24-5   Processor-Dependent Programs Used to Bootstrap the VAX-11/780, VAX-11/782, and VAX-11/785

Program Executing	Location of Program	Purpose of Program
	EXECUTES ON LSI-11	
LSI-11 ROM bootstrap	LSI-11 I/O space	Read floppy boot block into memory and execute code contained there
Floppy boot block program	LBN 0 on console floppy	Locate CONSOL.SYS, read it into memory, and pass control to it
CONSOL.SYS	Console floppy	Initialize VAX-11/78x, load general registers, and invoke memory locator program; load VMB into VAX memory and transfer control to it
	EXECUTES ON VAX-11/78x	
Good memory locator[1]	ROM in memory controller	Locate 64K-byte block of error-free memory
VMB.EXE	Console floppy	Size physical memory, locate secondary bootstrap, load it into memory, and pass control to it

[1]This program does not run on a VAX-11/782 system.

tached processor of an asymmetric multiprocessing system; see Chapter 27 for information.)

The steps of initial bootstrap are as follows:

1. The first program that executes in the LSI-11, after self-test, is a bootstrap program located in ROM. It loads the boot block program located on LBN 0 of the console floppy (sectors 1, 3, 5, and 7) into LSI memory.

2. The boot block program at LBN 0 is a copy of the bootstrap program used by the RT-11 operating system. The RT-11 bootstrap, which understands the RT-11 file system, looks for a specific file (the monitor), loads it into memory, and transfers control to it.

   The boot block program found on the console floppy diskette looks for a program called CONSOL.SYS.

3. CONSOL.SYS loads the file WCSxxx.PAT from the floppy diskette into the VAX writable control store and then prompts (>>>) on the console terminal. It verifies that the versions of the microcode are consistent with one another. If there is a version mismatch between the writable control store (WCS) and either the PROM control store (PCS) or the field program-

mable logic array (FPLA), an error message is displayed on the console terminal.

4. The three console commands that bootstrap a VMS system cause the execution of command files located on the console floppy. Table 24-3 shows the commands and their associated command files.

   These command files identify the system device and other characteristics of the bootstrap operation by loading general registers R0 through R5 with parameters that will be interpreted by the primary bootstrap program (VMB).

   Note that the DEFBOO.CMD command files used to bootstrap either processor on a VAX-11/782 multiprocessing system are not the same as the command files described here. The contents and operation of DEFBOO.CMD on a VAX-11/782 are described in Chapter 27.

5. The command files also contain the following commands:

   ```
   START 20003000
   WAIT DONE
   ```

   These two commands cause a program located in ROM in the first memory controller on the synchronous backplane interface (SBI) to execute. The command file waits until the memory ROM program completes before executing its next command. The memory ROM program signals the console program that it is done by writing the "software done" signal with the following instruction:

   ```
   MTPR    #^XF01,#PR$_TXDB
   ```

   The program in the memory controller ROM performs a primitive memory sizing operation in an effort to locate 64K bytes of error-free, page-aligned, contiguous physical memory that can be used by the remaining bootstrap programs. The output of this program is an address 200_{16} bytes beyond the beginning of the first good page. This address is loaded into SP. (In a typical system with no errors in the first 64K bytes, the contents of SP are 200_{16}.)

6. The following three commands cause the primary bootstrap program VMB to be loaded from the floppy disk into the good 64K-byte block of VAX memory, leaving the first page free for the RPB. The START command transfers control to VMB at its first location.

   ```
   EXAMINE SP
   LOAD VMB.EXESTART:@
   START @
   ```

7. VMB.EXE is described in Section 24.3.

24.2.4   **MicroVAX I Initial Bootstrap Operation**

The MicroVAX I console program is implemented in CPU microcode. When the CPU is in console mode, the console microcode, and nothing else, executes. The MicroVAX I has no console block storage device. A subset version of VMB.EXE, specific to the MicroVAX I, is stored in erasable programmable read-only memory (EPROM) in the CPU.

There are several ways in which a bootstrap sequence can be initiated:

- The system is powered on, and the option switches specify that the processor is to boot or warm start and then boot.
- The B(oot) command is entered while the system is in console mode.
- A HALT instruction is executed, or some other error halt condition occurs, and the option switches specify that the processor is to boot.
- An attempt to restart the system after an error halt fails, and the option switches specify that the system should be booted next.
- The following instruction is executed in kernel mode:

```
MTPR     #^XF02,#PR$_TXDB
```

When a MicroVAX I system is initialized, the console microcode locates a page aligned 64K-byte block of good memory, copies VMB.EXE from ROM to the good memory, and transfers control to VMB. Table 24-6 summarizes these two processor-dependent programs.

The steps of initial bootstrap are as follows:

1. On power-up, the MicroVAX I performs a self-test called Microverify to test that the CPU works and can execute VAX instructions. Microverify also checks the integrity of VMB in the EPROM. It adds all the words in the EPROM and checks that the result is zero. (The last word in the EPROM is a two's complement of all the other words.)
2. After the hardware is tested and initialized, the console microcode searches for a 64K-byte block of good memory. The console program on

---

Table 24-6   Processor-Dependent Programs Used to Bootstrap the MicroVAX I

Program Executing	Location of Program	Purpose of Program
Console microcode	MicroVAX I CPU	Locate block of good memory, load VMB from EPROM into memory, and pass control to it
VMB.EXE	EPROM in MicroVAX I CPU	Size physical memory, locate secondary bootstrap, load it into memory, and pass control to it

---

Table 24-7   Register Input to MicroVAX I VMB

Register	Contents
R0	Zero or ASCII name of bootstrap device
R1	Setting of the option switches
R2	Unused
R3	Unused
R4	Unused
R5	Software boot control flags
R10[1]	Halt PC
R11[1]	Halt PSL
AP[1]	Halt code
SP	Address of 64K bytes of good memory plus 200_{16}

[1]The console program sets up these registers after a halt condition. These registers are not used by VMB.

the MicroVAX I does not process command files. It must construct the contents for R0 through R5 from the boot device and/or the bootstrap command. Table 24-7 shows the register arguments.

3. The console program copies VMB from the EPROM into the piece of good memory and passes control to it.
4. MicroVAX I VMB is described in the following section.

24.2.4.1   **MicroVAX I VMB.EXE.** MicroVAX I VMB is based upon the full VMB that runs on other VAX processors. There are, however, a number of significant differences between the two. These differences are summarized in the following list. For a detailed description of MicroVAX I VMB, see the *MicroVAX I CPU Technical Description* manual. For a detailed description of the full VMB, see Section 24.3.

• MicroVAX I VMB is not linked with XDELTA.
• The register arguments are different. Contrast Table 24-14 with Table 24-7.
• Full VMB.EXE tries to boot a system from the system device specified by its register arguments. MicroVAX I VMB is called a "sniffer boot" because it can search for a bootable device. Its search sequence is affected by the setting of option switch 1.

—If option switch 1 is off (its default position), and if a B(oot) command is entered with no device specification, MicroVAX I VMB searches for a bootable disk. It first looks at each floppy diskette in ascending unit order on an RQDX1 controller. If the diskette is Files-11, VMB looks up SYSBOOT. If it is there, VMB boots it. If the diskette is not Files-11, VMB tests whether LBN 0 is a boot block. If it is, VMB boots it. If VMB fails to find anything to boot on any diskette, it checks the fixed head disks next.

If that fails, it scans memory for the signature of a programmable ROM (PROM). Lastly, it looks for a DEQNA to request a down-line bootstrap. If there is no response in 30 seconds, VMB retransmits its request every 30 seconds. If no response is received within two minutes, the bootstrap fails.

—If option switch 1 is on, VMB bypasses searching the disks for a secondary bootstrap and begins looking for a PROM.

—In response to a boot command with a device specification, VMB searches the specified device for the secondary bootstrap.

24.2.5   MicroVAX II Initial Bootstrap Operation

The MicroVAX II console program is implemented in VAX macro instruction code. When the CPU is in console mode, the console program, and nothing else, executes. The MicroVAX II has no console block storage device. A subset version of VMB.EXE, specific to the MicroVAX II, is stored in ROM in the CPU, along with the console program and power-up diagnostics.

There are several ways in which a bootstrap sequence may be initiated:

- The system is powered on, and halts are disabled through the halt enable switch on the CPU patch panel insert, mounted inside the rear of the CPU cabinet. (Chapter 26 describes the significance of this switch in more detail.)
- The B(oot) command is entered while the system is in console mode.
- An $F02_{16}$ is written to the console program mailbox (CPMBX, see Chapter 26).
- An attempt to restart the system after an error halt fails, and the CPMBX has its default contents.

When a MicroVAX II system is initialized, several programs execute before VMB. These are summarized in Table 24-8.

The steps of initial bootstrap are as follows:

1. Following power recovery, the processor performs hardware initialization, writes a power-up code into the AP register, and passes control to the console program in ROM.
2. On power-up, the console program checks its own integrity by computing the checksum of its own code and comparing it to the expected value stored within ROM. The console then looks for a small piece of contiguous good physical memory. It scans from high memory addresses downward. It requires two pages for use as a stack and writable data area and the rest for a bit map of available memory.
3. The console program performs some additional checks, including determination of the console terminal type. It then executes diagnostics, which are also located in ROM, to test the processor and memory. The memory

Table 24-8   Processor-Dependent Programs Used to Bootstrap the MicroVAX II

Program Executing	Location of Program	Purpose of Program
CPU initialization microcode	MicroVAX II CPU	Pass control to the console program
Console program	I/O address space ROM in MicroVAX II CPU	Size physical memory, locate block of good memory, load VMB from ROM into memory, and pass control to it
VMB.EXE	I/O address space ROM in MicroVAX II CPU	Locate secondary bootstrap, load it into memory, and pass control to it

test diagnostic records the memory it finds in the bit map. A bit set indicates a present page of memory. The first bit in the map corresponds to the first page of memory. The bit map does not map itself or the other pages of memory reserved for the console program's use. The address of the bit map and its size will be passed to VMB.

4. To perform a bootstrap, the console program then searches for a 64K-byte block of good memory. It initializes the Q22 bus I/O map registers to map to the first four megabytes of MicroVAX II memory.

5. The console does not process command files. It must construct the contents for R0 through R5 from the boot device and/or the bootstrap command. Table 24-9 shows the register arguments.

Table 24-9   Register Input to MicroVAX II VMB

Register	Contents
R0	Zero or ASCII name of bootstrap device
R1	Contents of MicroVAX II boot and diagnostic register
R2	Memory bit map size in bytes
R3	Address of memory bit map
R4	Unused
R5	Software boot control flags
R10[1]	Halt PC
R11[1]	Halt PSL
AP[1]	Halt code
SP	Address of 64K bytes of good memory plus 200_{16}

[1]The console program sets up these registers after a halt condition. These registers are not used by VMB.

6. The console program copies VMB from the console program ROM into the piece of good memory and passes control to it.

7. MicroVAX II VMB is described in the following section.

24.2.5.1   **MicroVAX II VMB.EXE.** MicroVAX II VMB is based upon the full VMB that runs on other VAX processors. There are, however, a number of significant differences between the two. These differences are summarized in the following list. For a detailed description of MicroVAX II VMB, see the *MicroVAX 630 CPU Module User's Guide*. For a detailed description of the full VMB, see Section 24.3.

• The register arguments are different. Contrast Table 24-14 with Table 24-9.
• Full VMB sizes memory itself. MicroVAX II VMB uses the available memory bit map built by the memory diagnostic.
• Full VMB.EXE tries to boot a system from the system device specified by its register arguments. MicroVAX II VMB has several possibilities:

—In response to a B(oot) command with no device specification, MicroVAX II VMB searches for a bootable disk. In searching for a bootable disk, VMB tries each disk drive of all possible mass storage control protocol (MSCP) controllers. Furthermore, if it does not locate SYSBOOT, it checks whether LBN 0 is a boot block. It then searches for a TK50 magnetic tape to boot. If that fails, it scans memory for the signature of a programmable ROM. Lastly, it looks for a DEQNA to request a down-line bootstrap. If there is no response in 30 seconds, VMB retransmits its request every 30 seconds. If no response is received after 12 retransmits, VMB doubles the timeout interval. It retransmits 12 times with a 60-second timeout. It continues in this manner, up to a maxium delay of 60 minutes.

—In response to a boot command with a device specification, it searches the specified device for the secondary bootstrap.

24.2.6   **VAX 8200 and VAX 8300 Family Initial Bootstrap Operation**

The VAX 8200 family console consists of two block-addressable storage devices (RX50 floppy diskettes) and a console terminal. The console program is implemented in CPU microcode. When the CPU is in console mode, the console program (and nothing else, such as a user program or VMS itself) executes.

There are several ways in which a bootstrap sequence may be initiated:

• The system is powered on, or the RESTART button on the control panel is depressed, and the lower key switch on the CPU control panel is in the Auto Start position.

- The B(oot) command is typed while the system is in console mode.
- The following instruction is executed in kernel mode:

```
MTPR    #^XF02,#PR$_TXDB
```

- An attempt to restart the system after a power failure recovery or some other halt condition does not succeed, and the lower key switch is in the Auto Start position.

When a VAX 8200 family member is initialized, the console program is the first in a series of programs that execute before VMB executes. These programs are summarized in Table 24-10. (Note that this description does not include booting the attached processor of an asymmetric multiprocessing system; see Chapter 27.)

The steps of initial bootstrap are as follows:

1. The console program initializes the CPU. It locates 64K bytes of contiguous, error-free, page aligned memory and loads the bootstrap code from the electrically erasable programmable read-only memory (EEPROM) into a

---

Table 24-10   Processor-Dependent Programs Used to Bootstrap the VAX 8200 Family

Program Executing	Location of Program	Purpose of Program
Console program	ROM in VAX CPU	Initialize CPU, load bootstrap code from EEPROM into boot RAM, locate block of good memory, determine action to take, and pass control to bootstrap code
Bootstrap code	EEPROM	Load LBN 0 of boot device into memory and pass control to it
Boot block code	LBN 0 of boot device	Load primary bootstrap program from system device or BOOT58 from console RX50 and pass control to it
VMB.EXE	Specific LBN on system device	Size physical memory, locate secondary bootstrap, load it into memory, and pass control to it
BOOT58.EXE	Specific LBN on console RX50	Process indirect command files or enhanced console commands, boot from an HSC system device

---

boot random access memory (RAM).

2. The console program does not process command files. Instead, it must construct the contents for R0 through R5 from the default boot device and/or the bootstrap command itself. The system manager identifies the default boot device by running a stand-alone diagnostic to load its name into the EEPROM.

3. The console program passes control to the primary bootstrap code.

4. The bootstrap code consists of two main pieces, a dispatch routine and device-specific routines. The dispatch routine parses the boot device name passed from the console microcode and selects the corresponding device-specific routine. The device-specific routine simply reads LBN 0 of the selected device into the first page of the good memory and passes control to it (at an address 12 bytes past the beginning of the program).

5. The boot block program reads VMB or BOOT58 from the boot device into memory. The boot block program is described in Section 24.2.2.1.

6. VMB is described in Section 24.3.

7. BOOT58 is described in Section 24.2.2.2.

24.2.7   **VAX 8600 and VAX 8650 Initial Bootstrap Operation**

The console subsystem on the VAX 8600 and VAX 8650 consists of a separate T-11 microprocessor, a block-addressable storage device (RL02 disk), and a terminal. The T-11 runs a modified version of the RT-11 operating system; VAX console support is provided by the console program, EDOAA. The console disk is an RT-11 directory structured device. A number of console commands can be executed while the VAX CPU is executing instructions.

There are several ways in which a bootstrap sequence may be initiated:

• The VAX processor is powered on, and the system control panel Restart Control switch is in the BOOT position.

• The console command B(oot) is typed while the console terminal is in console mode and the VAX processor is halted.

• A bootstrap command procedure is invoked while the console terminal is in console mode and the VAX processor is halted.

• The following instruction is executed in kernel mode:

```
MTPR    #`XF02,#PR$_TXDB
```

• While the Restart Control switch is in the RESTART/BOOT position, a CPU halt condition occurs and auto restart fails.

• While the Restart Control switch is in the BOOT position, a powerfail or error halt condition occurs.

In the bootstrap sequence, the console subsystem must execute a series of programs to load and execute VMB. Table 24-11 lists these programs.

Table 24-11   Processor-Dependent Programs Used to Bootstrap the VAX 86x0

Program Executing	Location of Program	Purpose of Program
EXECUTES ON CONSOLE MICROPROCESSOR		
Console micro-processor PROM bootstrap	PROM in console subsystem	Read RL02 boot block into memory and execute code contained there
RL02 boot block program	LBN 0 on console RL02	Locate monitor program, read it into memory, and pass control to it
RT-11 based mon-itor program	Console RL02	Locate EDOAA, read it into memory, and pass control to it
EDOAA	Console RL02	Initialize VAX 86x0, load general registers, and execute the next several indirect command files
LOAD.COM	Console RL02	Initialize VAX CPU, start execution of ULOAD.COM
ULOAD.COM	Console RL02	Load VAX CPU microcode from RL02
Bootstrap com-mand file	Console RL02	Initialize VAX processor and registers, load VMB into VAX memory, and transfer control to it
EXECUTES ON VAX 86x0		
VMB.EXE	Console RL02	Size physical memory, locate secondary bootstrap, load it into memory, and pass control to it

The initial bootstrap programs are console microprocessor programs. The bootstrap steps are as follows:

1. When the console is powered on, code in the console PROM executes. It initializes the console microprocessor and performs self-tests. At successful completion of its self-tests, the PROM code performs some diagnosis of the path to the RL02 and reads the boot block.
2. The boot block program boots the modified RT-11 monitor.
3. The monitor automatically locates and loads the console program.
4. The console program then executes the command procedure LOAD.COM, initializes the CPU, I/O adapters, and physical memory map, and invokes the execution of ULOAD.COM.

5. The console program executes the command procedure ULOAD.COM, which loads microcode from the RL02 into the various CPU microstores.

6. The console program then clears the system cache. The console tests the Restart Control switch. If it is in the RESTART/BOOT position, the console attempts a warm restart. If that fails, the console then executes the command procedure DEFBOO.COM.

7. The three console commands that bootstrap a VMS system cause the execution of command files located on the console TU58. Table 24-3 shows the commands and their associated command files.

8. The following command from a boot command file initiates a search for a 64K-byte block of good VAX memory:

```
FIND/MEMORY
```

9. The following three commands cause the primary bootstrap program VMB to be loaded from the RL02 into the good block of VAX memory, leaving the first page free for the RPB. The START command transfers control to VMB at its first location.

```
EXAMINE SP
LOAD/START:@ VMB
START @
```

10. VMB.EXE is described in Section 24.3.

24.2.8   VAX 8800 Family Initial Bootstrap Operation

The console subsystem on the VAX 8800 family consists of a separate microprocessor, three block-addressable storage devices (two floppy RX50 diskettes and a fixed head disk), and a terminal. The microprocessor runs the P/OS operating system; VAX console support is provided by an application task. The fixed head disk is an ODS-1 directory structured device. The floppies can be ODS-1 or ODS-2, depending on their use. A number of console commands can be executed while the VAX CPU is running.

There are several ways in which a bootstrap sequence may be initiated:

• The console is powered on, and the software keyswitches AUTO_POWERON and AUTO_BOOT are both enabled.

• The console command B(oot) is typed while the console terminal is in console mode and the VAX processor is halted.

• A bootstrap command procedure is invoked while the console terminal is in console mode and the VAX processor is halted.

• The following instruction is executed in kernel mode:

```
MTPR    #^XF02,#PR$_TXDB
```

Table 24-12   Processor-Dependent Programs Used to Bootstrap the VAX 8800 Family

Program Executing	Location of Program	Purpose of Program
EXECUTES ON CONSOLE MICROPROCESSOR		
Console microprocessor microcode	ROM in console subsystem	Perform self-test, read P/OS into memory, and pass control to it
Console P/OS	Console fixed disk	Locate console program, N16PRO.TSK, read it into memory, and transfer control to it
N16PRO.TSK	Console fixed disk	Initialize console database, open log file, and execute next two indirect command files
SYSINIT.COM	Console fixed disk	Turn on VAX CPU power, run diagnostics, load microcode, and start console support microcode
Bootstrap command file	Console fixed disk	Load registers for VMB, load VMB into VAX memory, and transfer control to it
EXECUTES ON VAX 8800 FAMILY MEMBER		
Console support microcode	Console fixed disk	Initialize VAX CPUs, NMI, NBI, and memory; locate 64K-byte block of good memory
VMB.EXE	Console fixed disk	Size physical memory, locate secondary bootstrap, load it into memory, and pass control to it

- While the software keyswitches AUTO_RESTART and AUTO_BOOT are enabled, a CPU halt condition occurs and restart fails.

In the bootstrap sequence, the console subsystem must execute a series of programs to load and execute VMB. Table 24-12 lists these programs. (Note that this description does not include booting the attached processor of an asymmetric multiprocessing system; see Chapter 27.)

The initial bootstrap programs are console microprocessor programs. The steps of initial bootstrap are as follows:

1. When the console microprocessor is turned on, it performs a self-test, loads P/OS from the fixed disk, and starts it.
2. P/OS loads the console program from the fixed disk and transfers control to it.
3. The console program opens a log file to record all console input and output

667

(the terminal is a video monitor) and starts up the real-time interface (RTI) driver which controls communication with the VAX CPU. It executes the command procedure SYSINIT.COM (not to be confused with the SYSINIT process).

4. The SYSINIT.COM command procedure turns on the power on the VAX CPU if AUTO_POWERON is enabled, checks that hardware modules are correctly placed, loads VAX CPU microcode (including console support microcode) from the fixed disk, and checks hardware and microcode revisions. It checks that the revisions are at least the minimum supported and also compatible with one another. The command procedure initializes the NMI, NBIs, and the memory.

5. SYSINIT.COM then tests the software keyswitches AUTO_RESTART and AUTO_BOOT, both of which are most likely on. SYSINIT.COM thus tries auto restart first, but when that fails, it invokes DEFBOO.COM to boot the VAX CPU.

6. The console executes the commands in the default bootstrap command file (DEFBOO.COM). The three console commands that bootstrap a VMS system cause the execution of command files located on the fixed disk. Table 24-3 shows the commands and their associated command files.

7. The following three commands cause the primary bootstrap program VMB to be loaded from the fixed disk into the good 64K-byte block of VAX memory, leaving the first page free for the RPB. The START command transfers control to VMB at its first location.

```
EXAMINE SP
LOAD /MAINMEMORY /START:@ VMB.EXE
START @
```

8. VMB.EXE is described in Section 24.3.

24.3 PRIMARY BOOTSTRAP PROGRAM (VMB)

The first program that is common to VMS systems, generally independent of CPU type, is the primary bootstrap program, VMB. The processor-independent files and programs used in bootstrap operations are listed in Table 24-13. (MicroVAX VMB is somewhat different. See Sections 24.2.4.1 and 24.2.5.1 for more information.)

The main differences in the initiation of VMB on various VAX processors are the following:

• Location of VMB (console block storage device, system device, or ROM)
• Method for determining system device
• Method for determining and loading R0 through R5
• Program that loads and passes control to VMB

VMB performs the following two major steps:

1. It locates and determines the size of physical memory on the system.
2. It locates the secondary bootstrap program, loads it into memory, and transfers control to it.

24.3.1 Motivation for Two Bootstrap Programs

VMB and the secondary bootstrap program, SYSBOOT, are conceptually one program. The VAX-11/780 initialization (initially implemented for VAX/VMS Version 1.0) required that the initial bootstrap program reside on the console floppy diskette, whose capacity of 512 blocks was also used for microcode, the console program, and command procedures. Rather than impose artificial restrictions on the size of the bootstrap program, it was divided into two pieces:

- A primary piece that resides on the floppy disk and one of whose major purposes is to locate the secondary piece
- A secondary piece that resides on the system device (with no real limits on its size) that performs the bulk of the bootstrap operation

Once this division was achieved, VMB became a more flexible tool that could be used to load programs other than VMS. To preserve this flexibility, the division of the bootstrap into primary and secondary pieces was continued in subsequent versions of VAX/VMS.

VMB is a general purpose bootstrap program that is used for several options other than initializing a VMS system. There are three options currently available in addition to initializing a VAX/VMS system by loading SYSBOOT:

- The diagnostic supervisor [SYSMAINT]DIAGBOOT.EXE can be loaded instead of SYSBOOT.
- VMB can prompt for the name of any stand-alone program to be loaded into VAX memory. This program might be a stand-alone diagnostic program, an alternate secondary bootstrap, or another operating system. The file system routines and control transfer mechanism used by VMB place some restrictions on this file.

  —The system device containing the file to be loaded by VMB must be an ODS-2 Files-11 volume.
  —The file must be contiguous.
  —The code in the program must be position-independent.

- VMB can load the contents of a bootstrap block from the system disk and execute the program that it finds there. In general, this boot block is LBN 0 on the volume. The VAX-11/780 and VAX-11/785 bootstrap sequences allow an alternate boot block number to be passed to VMB in R4. Specifying

Table 24-13 Processor-Independent Bootstrap Files

Files Used by This Program	Use of Files
	VMB.EXE[1]
SYSBOOT.EXE[2]	Secondary bootstrap program, loaded into memory
	SYSBOOT.EXE
VAXVMSSYS.PAR and other parameter files	Configure system
SYS.EXE	System image, loaded into memory
TTDRIVER.EXE	Terminal class driver, loaded into nonpaged pool
SYSLOA*xxx*.EXE	CPU-specific routines, loaded into nonpaged pool
SCSLOA.EXE	System communications services, loaded into nonpaged pool
CLUSTRLOA.EXE	Loadable VAXcluster support, loaded into nonpaged pool
*yy*DRIVER.EXE	System device driver, loaded into nonpaged pool
ERAPATLOA.EXE	Optional erase pattern routine, loaded into nonpaged pool
CHKPRTLOA.EXE	Optional protection check routine, loaded into nonpaged pool
FPEMUL.EXE	Floating-point emulation code, loaded into nonpaged pool
VAXEMUL.EXE	String and other emulated instruction code, loaded into nonpaged pool
SYSDUMP.DMP	System dump file, located and sized for later use
	SYSINIT PROCESS
SYSINIT.EXE	Image that runs in this process
RMS.EXE	Record Management Services, mapped as pageable system section
SYSMSG.EXE	System message file, mapped as pageable system section
SWAPFILE.SYS	Opened and initialized
PAGEFILE.SYS	Opened and initialized
F11BXQP.EXE	Activated in P1 space, mapped as global section
QUORUM.DAT	On a VAXcluster System with a quorum disk, opened
	STARTUP PROCESS
STARTUP.COM	SYS$INPUT for STARTUP process

Table 24-13 Processor-Independent Bootstrap Files *(continued)*

Files Used by This Program	*Use of Files*
	STARTUP PROCESS
LOGINOUT.EXE	Image that first runs in STARTUP process
DCL.EXE	Command language interpreter, mapped into P1 space to interpret and execute commands
DCLTABLES.EXE	Command tables, mapped into P1 space and used by DCL.EXE
SYCONFIG.COM	In SYS$MANAGER, site-specific device configuration command procedure
SYSTARTUP.COM	In SYS$MANAGER, site-specific startup command procedure
	INSTALL, STARTUP PROCESS
VMSIMAGES.DAT	List of images to be installed
All installed images	Set up as known images
	SYSGEN, STARTUP PROCESS
VAXVMSSYS.PAR	Written to record SYSBOOT parameters
Various device drivers	Loaded into nonpaged pool, specify I/O database and device initialization

[1]VMB must be contiguous, because it is loaded by either the console subsystem or a boot block program.
[2]This file must be contiguous, because it is located by primitive file system routines in VMB.

an alternate boot block number is only supported on a VAX-11/780 or VAX-11/785.

The ability to pass control to a boot block program makes VMB a flexible tool. One possible use for a bootstrap program is support for a file system other than Files-11, such as that of ULTRIX-32.

If none of these options is selected through the corresponding flags in R5, VMB enters its default path, which loads SYSBOOT into memory and transfers control to it.

In each version of VAX/VMS, enhancements are made to VMB. These enhancements include support for new processor types, support for new devices, and changes to the argument list passed to SYSBOOT. Because a user might attempt to bootstrap a VAX/VMS system with an old version of VMB, it is desirable to maintain forward and backward compatibility between versions of VMB and SYSBOOT. SYSBOOT checks the version of VMB that loaded it and takes appropriate action, depending on the relative versions. Compatibility is maintained by not removing functionality from VMB that is required by older versions of SYSBOOT.

24.3.2   **Operation of VMB**

VMB receives control running in the following environment:

- In kernel mode
- On the boot interrupt stack (SP = RPB base plus 200_{16})
- With memory management disabled
- At IPL 31

Most of the modules that make up full VMB.EXE are from facility [BOOTS].

VMB determines the type of bootstrap that is being performed and the identity of the system device by interpreting the contents of registers R0 through R5.

Tables 24-14 and 24-15 summarize the input parameters passed to VMB. VMB saves these parameters in the RPB (see Table 24-16) for use by later steps in system initialization.

The steps that VMB takes to load SYSBOOT into memory follow. Note that this list does not include error paths. It focuses on booting VMS from a system device and does not discuss booting stand-alone backup.

1. VMB sets up a one-page system control block (SCB) (see Figure 24-2) with all but two interrupt and exception vectors pointing to a single service routine. The vectors for TBIT and BPT exceptions are loaded with the addresses of exception service routines in XDELTA, linked as a part of the VMB image.
2. VMB then reads the processor ID register (PR$_SID) to determine the CPU type. VMB uses the CPU type as the basis of decisions about which piece of CPU-dependent code to execute. A similar step is performed later by SYSBOOT for the use of both SYSBOOT and the executive.
3. VMB switches to a three-page stack in physical pages four pages above the end of the SCB. The four pages immediately above the SCB are reserved for a bit map to describe up to eight megabytes of physical memory.

   Figure 24-2 illustrates the layout of physical memory after VMB begins execution.
4. If the R5 bootstrap breakpoint flag, RPB$V_BOOBPT, is set, VMB executes a BPT instruction, which transfers control to XDELTA, linked as a part of the VMB image. This breakpoint is useful in debugging problems that prevent a system from booting.
5. The input parameters to VMB are stored in the RPB (see Table 24-16).
6. A bit map is set up to describe all physical memory that is to be used as

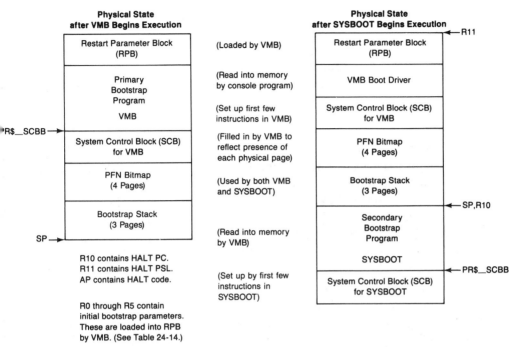

Figure 24-2 Physical Memory Layouts Used by VMB and SYSBOOT

main memory. Each possible page is represented by one bit. If the page is free from error, the bit representing it is set. If the page does not exist or has errors, its bit is clear. The bit map is the basis for the creation of the PFN database, built during a later step in system initialization. The routine that tests for memory errors is CPU-specific.

7. If VMB finds a CI port adapter, it must load the volatile CI microcode. It looks it up and reads it from the console block storage device. The microcode file for a CI780, CI750, or BCI750 adapter is called CI780.BIN; the file for a BCA is called CIBCA.BIN. (If the system is a VAX 8800 family member, the microcode is on CSA3.) VMB sets the flag VMB$V_LOAD_SCS in the SYSBOOT argument list to indicate that the loadable system communications services (SCS) code is to be loaded.

8. If VMB finds a CI750 on a VAX-11/750, VMB must check that the CPU revision level is at or above the minimum level required for CI support. It also tests whether the level is high enough to require the loading of volatile CPU microcode. If it is, VMB locates the file PCS750.BIN on the console TU58, reads it into memory, and loads it into the CPU microstore.

9. VMB relocates the boot driver (see Section 24.3.3).

10. Depending on processor and bus type, the bus and the bus adapter for the system device are initialized. The bootstrap device is initialized, if

673

needed. The CI port adapter initialization routine loads the CI microcode.

11. The secondary bootstrap image is identified (by flags and values in R5 and, optionally, information solicited from the console terminal). The order of precedence in choosing a secondary bootstrap image is the following:

    a. If the R5 flag RPB$V_BBLOCK is set, a boot block program is read from the system device. On a VAX-11/780 or a VAX-11/785, R4 contains the logical number of the disk block that contains the secondary bootstrap image.

    b. If the R5 flag RPB$V_SOLICT is set, VMB prompts for the name of the secondary bootstrap image on the console terminal.

    c. If the R5 flag RPB$V_DIAG is set, the diagnostic supervisor is loaded. This option specifies that the file [SYSMAINT]DIAGBOOT.EXE be used as the secondary bootstrap image.

    d. The absence of any of the three options (a, b, or c) means that [SYSEXE]SYSBOOT.EXE is to be used as the secondary bootstrap image. Before SYSBOOT.EXE can be located, the value in R5 at PRB$V_TOPSYS must be evaluated to determine which of the system root directories on a multiple-system device is being bootstrapped. By default, the high four bits of R5 are zero, so VMB searches [SYS0.SYSEXE] for SYSBOOT. In the case of a VAXcluster common system disk, VMB also searches [SYSn.SYSCOMMON.SYSEXE]. If SYSBOOT is not found in [SYS0.SYSEXE], for backward compatibility VMB looks in [SYSEXE].

    VMB records the file name of the secondary boot image in field RPB$T_FILE.

12. The image is read into memory (see Figure 24-2). Actually, SYSBOOT is read into memory overlaying roughly half of VMB, so that it might fit in the 64K bytes of good memory. Before reading SYSBOOT, VMB disables XDELTA exceptions and moves the SCB, PFN bit map, and stack it is running on.

13. If the R5 flag RPB$V_HALT is set, VMB executes a HALT instruction before passing control to the secondary bootstrap image. This feature enables use of the console subsystem to debug the secondary bootstrap.

14. VMB passes control to the secondary bootstrap image at its transfer address. This address is the first byte in SYSBOOT. However, if an image other than SYSBOOT is being loaded and the flag RPB$V_HEADER in R5 is set, VMB uses the transfer address stored in the image header of the secondary bootstrap program (provided that the secondary bootstrap image was produced by the VAX/VMS Linker).

Table 24-14   Register Input to VMB

Register	Contents
R0	Bootstrap device type code

BIT FIELD	MEANING
<31:16>	
	MASSBUS—MBZ[1]
	UNIBUS—Optional vector address; if zero, use default vector
<15:8>	MBZ
<7:0>	Bootstrap device type code

VALUE	MEANING
0	MASSBUS device (RM03/5, RP04/5/6/7,RM80)
1	RK06/7
2	RL01/2
3	IDC on VAX-11/730
4–16	Reserved for UNIBUS devices
17	UDA-50
18–31	Reserved
32	HSC on CI
33–63	Reserved for UNIBUS devices
64	Console block storage device

Register	Contents
R1	Bootstrap device bus address

CPU	BIT FIELD	MEANING
11/730 and	<31:4>	MBZ
11/78x	<3:0>	TR number of adapter
11/750	<31:24>	MBZ
	<23:0>	Address of I/O page for boot device's UNIBUS
86x0	<31:06>	MBZ
	<5:4>	A-bus adapter number
	<3:0>	TR number of adapter
8200 family	<31:4>	MBZ
	<3:0>	VAXBI node number of adapter
8800 family	<31:6>	MBZ
	<5:4>	VAXBI bus number
	<3:0>	VAXBI node number of adapter

[1]MBZ stands for "must be zero."

(continued)

Table 24-14 Register Input to VMB *(continued)*

Register	Contents		
R2	Bootstrap device controller information		

BUS TYPE	BIT FIELD	MEANING
All types	<31:24>	Optional controller letter
UNIBUS	<31:18>	MBZ
	<17:0>	UNIBUS address of the device's CSR
MASSBUS	<31:4>	MBZ
	<3:0>	Adapter's controller/formatter number
CI	<31:16>	MBZ
	<15:8>	Alternate HSC port number
	<7:0>	HSC port number

Register	Contents
R3	Boot device unit number
R4	LBN of boot block (VAX-11/780 and VAX-11/785 only)
R5	Software boot control flags (see Table 24-15)
R10[2]	Halt PC
R11[2]	Halt PSL
AP[2]	Halt code
SP	Address of 64K bytes of good memory plus 200_{16}

[2]The console subsystem sets up these registers after a halt condition. These registers are not used by VMB.

24.3.3   Bootstrap Driver and I/O Subroutines

VMB contains a skeleton Queue I/O Request ($QIO) routine and device driver to perform its I/O. This driver and routine are loaded into nonpaged pool by SYSBOOT for possible later use by the bugcheck code (see Chapter 8).

The VMB image actually contains simple drivers for all possible system devices. Once it has determined the name of the bootstrap device (from register contents), VMB moves the driver code for the selected device so that it is adjacent to the $QIO routine, thus allowing the entire bootstrap I/O system to be moved with a single MOVC3 instruction. The location and the size of the $QIO routine plus the selected driver are recorded in the RPB for later use by SYSBOOT and EXE$INIT.

This simple operation by VMB prevents nonpaged pool from being loaded with a set of bootstrap device drivers that are never used. That is, the only bootstrap driver that is preserved for the life of a VMS system is the bootstrap device driver for the system device, which is selected through input to VMB. All other bootstrap drivers are linked into the VMB image but disappear along with the rest of VMB when VMS is completely initialized. It also makes more efficient use of the 64K-byte block of memory into which SYSBOOT must fit.

Table 24-15   Bootstrap Control Flags to VMB (Contents of R5)

Bit Position	Symbolic Name	Meaning
0	RPB$V_CONV	Conversational boot. If set, SYSBOOT solicits parameters from the console terminal. On a VAX-11/730, if this and RPB$V_DIAG are set, the diagnostic supervisor enters MENUTEST mode.
1	RPB$V_DEBUG	Debug. If set, VMS makes the XDELTA debugger resident in the running system.
2	RPB$V_INIBPT	Initial breakpoint. If set, VMS executes a BPT instruction after turning on memory management.
3	RPB$V_BBLOCK	Secondary boot from boot block. If set, secondary bootstrap is a single 512-byte block. On a VAX-11/78*x*, its LBN can be specified in R4. On other processors, the boot block is LBN 0. On MicroVAX I and II, this bit causes VMB to bypass its search for a Files-11 secondary bootstrap file.
4	RPB$V_DIAG	Diagnostic boot. If set, secondary bootstrap is image [SYS*n*.SYSMAINT]DIAGBOOT.EXE.
5	RPB$V_BOOBPT	Bootstrap breakpoint. If set, VMB and SYSBOOT execute BPT instructions to transfer control to XDELTA.
6	RPB$V_HEADER	Image header. If set, VMB takes the transfer address of the secondary bootstrap image from that file's image header. If clear, VMB transfers control to the first byte of the secondary boot file.
7	RPB$V_NOTEST	Memory test inhibit. If set, VMB does not test memory pages.
8	RPB$V_SOLICT	Solicit file name. If set, VMB prompts for the name of a secondary bootstrap file.
9	RPB$V_HALT	Halt before transfer. If set, VMB executes a HALT instruction before transferring control to the secondary bootstrap.
10	RPB$V_NOPFND	No PFN deletion (not currently used)
11	RPB$V_MPM	Multiport memory. If set, specifies that the memory bit map is to include only multiport memory for later use by VMS. No local memory is to be used. This bit applies to the VAX-11/782 only.

(continued)

Table 24-15   Bootstrap Control Flags to VMB (Contents of R5) *(continued)*

Bit Position	Symbolic Name	Meaning
12	RPB$V_USEMPM	If set, specifies that the memory bit map is to include both multiport memory and local memory for later use by VMS, as though both were one single pool of pages (not used by VMS).
13	RPB$V_MEMTEST	If set, specifies that a more extensive algorithm is to be used when testing main memory for uncorrectable hardware errors.
14	RPB$V_FINDMEM	If set, requests use of MA780 memory if MS780 memory is insufficient for bootstrap. This flag is only used when performing software installations on a VAX-11/782.
15	RPB$V_AUTOTEST	On a VAX-11/730, if this and RPB$V_DIAG are set, the diagnostic supervisor enters AUTOTEST mode.
16	RPB$V_CRDTEST	If set, specifies that memory pages with correctable errors are not to be used by VMS.
17	RPB$V_DIFSYSDEV	If set, indicates that the system device is different from the boot device, which is magnetic tape. Used for booting stand-alone BACKUP from magnetic tape on MicroVAX systems.
<31:28>	RPB$V_TOPSYS	Specifies the top-level directory number for a system disk with multiple system roots.

24.3.4   File Operations

One of the problems that must be solved in any bootstrap operation is the location of files before the file system itself is in full operation. Many files must be looked up before the Files-11 XQP is initialized.

VMS solves this problem by including two special object modules (FILEREAD and FILERWIO) in the system image. The modules contain subroutines that can perform some primitive file operations on an ODS-2 Files-11 volume. One of these modules (FILEREAD) is also linked into both the VMB and the SYSBOOT images.

VMB and SYSBOOT call a file open routine, FIL$OPENFILE in FILEREAD, to look up files, such as SYS.EXE. To improve its performance, FIL$OPEN-

FILE uses a cache to record information about directories used in file lookup. For example, to locate SYS.EXE might require looking up and reading the master file directory, SYS*n*.DIR, and SYSEXE.DIR.

To avoid repeated lookups and directory and subdirectory reads, FIL$OPENFILE records directory file IDs, size in blocks, starting LBN, and also caches blocks from directory files. While VMB and SYSBOOT run, the cache is physically based. SYSBOOT copies the cache to nonpaged pool for use by EXE$INIT and the SYSINIT process until the XQP is operational.

SECONDARY BOOTSTRAP PROGRAM (SYSBOOT)

The secondary bootstrap program, SYSBOOT, executes when VMB is directed to load a VMS system. VMB has already tested main memory, read SYSBOOT into memory, and transferred control to it.

SYSBOOT performs three major functions:

- The system is configured. That is, SYSBOOT loads a set of adjustable SYS-BOOT parameters. By default, it uses the parameters from the last system initialization, those in the file [SYS*n*.SYSEXE]VAXVMSSYS.PAR. If this is a conversational bootstrap, SYSBOOT prompts on the console terminal. The person booting the system can specify values for selected parameters or a whole different set of parameters loaded from a specified file. SYSBOOT calculates other system parameters whose values depend on the values of the adjustable parameters.
- SYSBOOT maps system virtual address space. The sizes of many of the pieces of system address space depend on the values of one or more SYS-BOOT parameters. The calculations that SYSBOOT performs and the results of these calculations are detailed in Appendix F.

  In addition to sizing the pieces of system space, SYSBOOT also sets up the system page table (SPT) to map many of the pieces of the nonpaged and paged executive. In a related step, SYSBOOT prepares a P0 page table that allows memory management to be turned on. (This last step is described in Chapter 25.)
- The last major step that SYSBOOT performs is reading the various portions of SYS.EXE into the physical pages it allocated when it set up the SPT. It also locates a number of other files (see Table 24-13) and reads them into space it allocates in nonpaged pool. Their locations in pool are passed on to EXE$INIT in a bootstrap parameter block, defined by module BOOPARAM (see Table 24-17).

There is little CPU-dependent code in SYSBOOT. Most of the CPU dependencies have already been taken care of by VMB. However, SYSBOOT does load the CPU-dependent code that is used during normal VMS system execution.

Table 24-16   Contents of the Restart Parameter Block

Field Name	Contents	Size in Bytes	Loaded by	Special Uses
RPB$L_BASE	Physical base address of 64K-byte block	4	VMB	Used to identify RPB
RPB$L_RESTART	Physical address of EXE$RESTART	4	EXE$INIT	Locates restart routine
RPB$L_CHKSUM	Checksum of first 31 longwords of EXE$RESTART	4	EXE$INIT	Consistency check on RPB and EXE$RESTART
RPB$L_RSTSTFLG	Restart in progress flag	4	Console, EXE$INIT, EXE$RESTART	Prevents nested restarts
RPB$L_HALTPC	PC at HALT/restart	4	VMB	
RPB$L_HALTPSL	PSL at HALT/restart	4	VMB	
RPB$L_HALTCODE	Reason for restart	4	VMB	Determines EXE$RESTART's actions
RPB$L_BOOTRx	Saved bootstrap parameters (R0 through R5)	24	VMB	
RPB$L_IOVEC	Address of bootstrap driver	4	VMB, EXE$INIT	Loads system images, writes crash dump
RPB$L_IOVECSZ	Size (in bytes) of bootstrap driver	4	VMB	
RPB$L_FILLBN	LBN of secondary bootstrap file	4	VMB	
RPB$L_FILSIZ	Size in blocks of secondary bootstrap file	4	VMB	
RPB$Q_PFNMAP	Descriptor of PFN bit map	8	VMB	Used by SYSBOOT to locate bit map
RPB$L_PFNCNT	Count of physical pages	4	VMB, SYSBOOT	

Field Name	Contents	Size in Bytes	Loaded by	Special Uses
RPB$L_SVASPT	System virtual address of system page table	4	EXE$INIT	Used by EXE$RESTART
RPB$L_CSRPHY	Physical address of UBA device CSR	4	VMB	Locates boot device
RPB$L_CSRVIR	Virtual address of UBA device CSR	4	INIADPxxx	Locates boot device
RPB$L_ADPPHY	Physical address of adapter configuration register	4	VMB	Locates boot device
RPB$L_ADPVIR	Virtual address of adapter configuration register	4	INIADPxxx	Locates boot device
RPB$W_UNIT	Bootstrap device unit number	2	VMB	
RPB$B_DEVTYP	Bootstrap device type code	1	VMB	
RPB$B_SLAVE	Bootstrap device slave unit number	1	VMB	
RPB$T_FILE	Secondary bootstrap file name (counted ASCII string)	40	VMB	
RPB$B_CONFREG	Byte array of adapter types	16	VMB[1]	
RPB$B_HDRPGCNT	Count of header pages in secondary bootstrap image	1	VMB	
RPB$W_BOOTNDT	Type of boot adapter	2	VMB	Used by boot driver
RPB$B_FLAGS	Miscellaneous flag bits	1		
RPB$L_ISP	Powerfail interrupt stack pointer	4	EXE$POWERFAIL	Restored by EXE$RESTART
RPB$L_PCBB	Saved process control block base register	4	EXE$POWERFAIL	Restored by EXE$RESTART
RPB$L_SBR	Saved system base register	4	EXE$INIT, EXE$POWERFAIL	Restored by EXE$RESTART
RPB$L_SCBB	Saved system control block base register	4	EXE$INIT, EXE$POWERFAIL	Restored by EXE$RESTART

(continued)

Table 24-16 Contents of the Restart Parameter Block (continued)

Field Name	Contents	Size in Bytes	Loaded by	Special Uses
RPB$L_SCBB '	Saved system control block base register	4	EXE$INIT, EXE$POWERFAIL	Restored by EXE$RESTART
RPB$L_SISR	Saved software interrupt summary register	4	EXE$POWERFAIL	Restored by EXE$RESTART
RPB$L_SLR	Saved system length register	4	EXE$INIT, EXE$POWERFAIL	Restored by EXE$RESTART
RPB$L_MEMDSC	Longword array of memory descriptors	64	VMB	Used by BUGCHECK to dump physical memory
RPB$L_BUGCHK	Address of bugcheck loop for attached processor	4	VMB, MP_xxx.EXE	Address of attached processor initialization code or RPB$B_WAIT
RPB$B_WAIT	Bugcheck loop code for attached processor	4	VMB, MP_xxx.EXE	Before MP_xxx.EXE is run, contains a jump to self
RPB$L_BADPGS	Number of bad pages found in memory scan	4	VMB	
RPB$B_CTRLLTR	Controller letter designation	4	VMB	

[1]The byte array of adapter types is loaded by VMB only on the VAX-11/750 and VAX-11/78x. The system configuration is determined at a later stage of system initialization on other processors.

Table 24-17   Information Passed from SYSBOOT to INIT

Global Location	Size	Description
OO$GL_DSKDRV	Longword	Address of bootstrap device driver in nonpaged pool
OO$GL_SYSLOA	Longword	Address of CPU-dependent image in nonpaged pool
OO$GL_TRMDRV	Longword	Address of terminal class driver in nonpaged pool
OO$GQ_INILOA	Quadword	Currently unused
OO$GL_NPAGEDYN	Longword	Size of nonpaged pool remaining (in bytes)
OO$GL_SPLITADR	Longword	Base address of IRP lookaside list
OO$GL_IRPCNT	Longword	Number of IRPs to be initialized
OO$GL_LRPSIZE	Longword	Size of large request packets (in bytes)
OO$GL_LRPMIN	Longword	Minimum size of request that can be allocated an LRP
OO$GL_LRPSPLIT	Longword	Base address of LRP lookaside list
OO$GL_LRPCNT	Longword	Number of LRPs to be initialized
OO$GL_SRPSPLIT	Longword	Base address of SRP lookaside list
OO$GL_SRPCNT	Longword	Number of SRPs to be initialized
OO$GQ_FILCACHE	Quadword	Pool descriptor for FIL$OPENFILE cache
OO$GL_BOOTCB	Longword	Address of boot control block in pool
OO$GT_TOPSYS	10 bytes	Top-level system directory (ASCIC string)
OO$GB_SYSTEMID	6 bytes	48-bit SCS system ID of boot device port
OO$GL_PRTDRV	Longword	Address of port driver in pool
OO$GL_UCODE	Longword	Address of port microcode in pool
OO$GL_SCSLOA	Longword	Address of SCS loadable code in pool
OO$GL_CLSLOA	Longword	Address of cluster loadable code in pool
OO$GL_ERAPATLOA	Longword	Address of $ERAPAT loadable code in pool
OO$GL_CHKPRTLOA	Longword	Address of $CHKPRT loadable code in pool
OO$GL_MTACCESSLOA	Longword	Address of $MTACCESS loadable code in pool
OO$GB_NODENAME	8 bytes	ASCII name of the node containing boot device
OO$GL_VAXEMUL	Longword	Address of instruction emulation loadable code in pool
OO$GL_FPEMUL	Longword	Address of floating-point emulation loadable code in pool
OO$GL_DEVNAME	Longword	ASCII boot device name

24.4.1   Detailed Operation of SYSBOOT

SYSBOOT runs in the environment established by the console subsystem and VMB:

- In kernel mode
- On the interrupt stack
- With memory management disabled
- At IPL 31

Most of the modules that make up SYSBOOT are from facility [BOOTS].
  SYSBOOT begins operation with the physical memory layout pictured in Figure 24-2. R11 points to the beginning of the RPB. The following steps describe the operation of SYSBOOT:

1. SYSBOOT rewrites the SCB so that most vectors contain the address of a service routine in SYSBOOT. The vectors for TBIT and BPT exceptions dispatch to exception service routines in XDELTA, which is linked with the SYSBOOT image. The machine check vector is modified to point to a customized exception service routine. SYSBOOT initializes the vectors for subset instruction emulation to dispatch to service routines for the emulation of certain instructions not supported in CPU microcode. These exceptions are implemented on the MicroVAX I and MicroVAX II to facilitate software emulation of instructions such as MOVTC. Emulation of some of these unsupported instructions is linked into VMB and SYSBOOT.

2. The system identification processor register, PR$_SID, is read to determine the CPU type. On the MicroVAX II, an additional register, called the system type register, is read to determine the CPU subtype. The CPU type and subtype are stored for later use by code whose execution depends on the specific CPU type. This value is used in several ways:

   —It determines which pieces of CPU-dependent code within SYSBOOT execute. For example, SYSBOOT must check whether the hardware revision level is at least the minimum required to support VAX/VMS. Its test is processor-specific.

   —The CPU type and subtype determine the name of the file that contains CPU-specific support, SYSLOAxxx.EXE, where xxx designates the CPU type. See Appendix G for a list of CPU types and their corresponding SYSLOAxxx image names.

   —Those portions of CPU-specific code that are selected at execution time (with suitable test and branch instructions) use the CPU type and subtype as the object of the tests.

   —The size of the SCB, a part of the overall sizing of system address space described in step 18 and Appendix F, depends on the CPU type.

The different strategies used to handle CPU dependencies are described in the next chapter.

3. If the bootstrap breakpoint flag, RPB$V_BOOBPT in R5, is set, SYS-BOOT executes a BPT instruction. The exception transfers control to XDELTA.

   Note that the same flag controls breakpoint execution in both VMB and SYSBOOT. This flag can be used in locating a hardware problem or other problem that is preventing system initialization.

4. SYSBOOT checks which version of VMB loaded it. If an older version of VMB was used, SYSBOOT performs operations not performed by VMB. This step allows backward compatibility for earlier versions of VMB. The following items are checked:

   —Presence and contents of the SYSBOOT argument list
   —Support for more than eight megabytes of memory
   —Bootstrap adapter device type
   —Presence of the FIL$OPENFILE cache
   —Presence of memory descriptors in the RPB
   —Presence of CI microcode read into memory
   —Presence of a system root directory name

5. SYSBOOT looks up SYS.EXE and records the locations of its disk extents.

6. It then looks up and reads VAXVMSSYS.PAR, the file containing the current SYSBOOT parameters. Chapter 25 describes in more detail the movement of parameter information during the initialization sequence.

7. At this point, SYSBOOT tests whether the operator requested a conversational bootstrap by setting the R5 flag RPB$V_CONV. If so, SYSBOOT prompts to allow interactive alteration of the parameter values. In any case, SYSBOOT enters the next step with some set of adjustable parameters.

8. The file SYSDUMP.DMP is opened and its file extents are mapped for later use. If the dump file is not found, SYSBOOT opens and maps the primary page file, PAGEFILE.SYS, instead. Its first blocks will be used as a dump file when the system bugchecks or is shut down. When the SYSINIT process runs (see Chapter 25), it will look in the page file instead of the dump file to see whether there are saved error log messages to be restored.

9. Using the system device information saved in the RPB, SYSBOOT determines the name of the full driver for the system device. It looks in the boot driver data structure to determine the name of any auxiliary driver needed, for example, a CI port driver.

10. It determines the name of the SYSLOA*xxx* image containing CPU-specific code to be loaded. Appendix G lists the name used for each different processor.

11. It tests several SYSBOOT parameters to determine whether optional site-specific images such as CHKPRTLOA.EXE should be loaded.

12. It determines whether SCSLOA.EXE and CLUSTRLOA.EXE must be loaded as a function of system device type and the SYSBOOT parameters VAXCLUSTER and PE6.

13. SYSBOOT then tests which types of instructions, if any, must be emulated in software. Not all VAX processors implement all types of instructions. In particular, certain types of floating-point instruction may not be present. The MicroVAX I and MicroVAX II do not implement many string and decimal instructions. SYSBOOT must decide whether the images VAXEMUL.EXE and/or FPEMUL.EXE must be loaded for string and decimal instruction emulation and floating-point instruction emulation.

14. SYSBOOT then constructs the name of the terminal class driver, prefixing the value of the parameter TTY_CLASSNAME to the string DRIVER.

15. Having constructed a list of all the images to be loaded, SYSBOOT looks up each image in the list to determine its existence and location on the disk. SYSBOOT uses the boot driver built into VMB and primitive file system routines. It then truncates the FIL$OPENFILE cache, because no more file lookups are necessary.

16. SYSBOOT saves the contents of the PR$_SID register and any CPU-specific extended system information. This information will be copied into the system image in memory later at the 16 bytes beginning at EXE$GB_CPUDATA.

17. SYSBOOT determines the page frame number (PFN) of the highest usable page of memory, taking into account the value of the PHYSICALPAGES parameter, and stores it in MMG$GL_MAXMEM. If the parameter is set low to specify only partial use of the memory, it is the lower pages of memory that will be used.

18. The size of each process header and the sizes of the other pieces of system address space, including the SCB, are calculated. In particular, the size of the SPT is calculated. The details of these calculations are described in Appendix F. Pages of contiguous physical memory are allocated at the highest portion of physical memory for the SCB, SPT, and system header. The pages are filled with zeros, and the system page table entries (SPTEs) used to map the pages are filled in.

19. The first page of the SCB is loaded with the contents of module SCBVECTOR, which contains the entry points for the interrupt and exception service routines located in SYS.EXE. Vectors in additional pages of the SCB, if present, are loaded with the address of ERL$UNEXP, an unexpected interrupt handler. For some processors, interrupt vectors used for passive releases are initialized with the address of ERL$VEC_RETURN.

20. The system header is configured. All entries in the system header whose contents depend on configuration parameters are filled in at this time. This step is analogous to the process header configuration that is performed by code in SHELL as a part of process creation (see Chapter 20).

21. Space for the interrupt stack is allocated and mapped. The SPTEs for the global page table are filled in to indicate that they are demand zero pages. Physical memory is allocated for the initial sizes of the three nonpaged pool lookaside lists, and the corresponding SPTEs are filled in. The size and address of each list is recorded.

22. The high end of nonpaged pool is preallocated for the boot driver, any microcode file needed by the boot device, boot control block data structure, images which SYSBOOT looked up earlier, and, below those, the FIL$OPENFILE cache. The pool used for the FIL$OPENFILE cache is deallocated later in the bootstrap operation. Allocating it below the other images eliminates pool fragmentation when it is deallocated.

23. Pieces of the executive that are never paged (see Table F-4) are allocated from the highest pages of physical memory. These include device drivers (for the null device and mailbox), other permanently resident parts of the system image, the interrupt stack, nonpaged pool, the SPT, the SCB, and the system header.

    SYSBOOT estimates the size of the PFN database based on the number of pages left and allocates it. It initializes the pages of the PFN database, and the SPTEs that map them. The physical pages allocated for the nonpaged portions of the executive are not accounted for in the PFN database, because their state will never change. The pages occupied by the PFN database are also not accounted for in the PFN database.

24. The pageable portions of SYS.EXE (the pageable executive routines) are also mapped so that the system image can be read into memory.

25. SYSBOOT calls the boot driver to read the list of loadable images built earlier into nonpaged pool. These files include the following:

    —The system device driver and, if applicable, its port driver
    —Terminal class driver
    —SCSLOA.EXE, if needed
    —SYSLOA*xxx*.EXE
    —CLUSTRLOA.EXE, if needed
    —Optionally, ERAPATLOA.EXE
    —Optionally, CHKPRTLOA.EXE
    —FPEMUL.EXE, if needed
    —VAXEMUL.EXE, if needed
    —Optionally, MTACCESS.EXE

    The addresses of these files are recorded in the argument list passed to EXE$INIT (see Table 24-17) so that they can be stored in appropriate

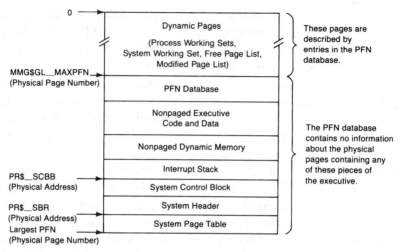

Figure 24-3 Physical Memory Layout Used by the Executive

places in system address space after memory management is turned on.

26. The system image is read into memory.

27. The contents of SYSBOOT's internal parameter table are copied to the portion of the memory image of SYS.EXE that contains all the adjustable parameters. This step preserves the current parameter settings (because SYSBOOT is exiting) until they can be written back to the disk by SYSINIT (see Chapter 25).

28. SYSBOOT copies the FIL$OPENFILE cache into the nonpaged pool allocated for it, where it will facilitate file lookups until the file system is initialized.

29. It also copies to nonpaged pool the boot control block, boot driver, and any microcode associated with the boot device. It modifies RPB$L_IOVEC to reflect the virtual address of the boot driver.

30. SYSBOOT copies the argument list it built for EXE$INIT into the bootstrap parameter block within the memory image of SYS.EXE (see Table 24-17).

31. SYSBOOT loads the base and length registers for the P0 and system page tables so that EXE$INIT can turn memory management on. Enabling memory management is described in more detail in Chapter 25.

32. Finally, SYSBOOT transfers control to module EXE$INIT. This transfer must be done to a physical location, because memory management has not been enabled yet. The state of physical memory is pictured in Figure 24-3.

25 Operating System Initialization

Had I been present at the creation, I would have given some
useful hints for the better ordering of the universe.

Alfonso the Wise

The second phase of system initialization occurs in several components. The most significant ones are as follows:

- Code that is a part of the executive (routine EXE$INIT in module INIT)
- A special process (SYSINIT) created to complete those pieces of initialization that require process context to execute

EXE$INIT turns on memory management and establishes many data structures whose size or contents depend on SYSBOOT parameters. SYSINIT opens system files, creates system processes, maps Record Management Services (RMS) and the message file, and creates the process that invokes the startup command file.

25.1 INITIAL EXECUTION OF THE EXECUTIVE

The final instruction in SYSBOOT transfers control to the (physical) address of EXE$INIT (in module INIT). EXE$INIT turns on memory management, configures the I/O adapters, and initializes scheduling and memory management data structures. Finally, it releases the pages that it occupies so that code that executes only once during the life of the system does not consume system resources.

EXE$INIT begins execution in the environment set up by prior phases of system initialization. It immediately modifies its environment by turning on memory management. Subsequently, it executes under the following conditions:

- At IPL 31
- With memory management enabled
- On the systemwide interrupt stack

25.1.1 Turning on Memory Management

The first (and perhaps most important) step that EXE$INIT takes turns on memory management. Before SYSBOOT transfers control to EXE$INIT, it sets up the system page table (SPT) to map the executive and dynamic data structures. In addition, SYSBOOT builds a small P0 page table that maps the first physical page of EXE$INIT to a virtual page whose virtual page number is identical to its physical page number. Thus, EXE$INIT can be referenced by a P0 virtual address that is identical to its physical address.

P0 space is used for this double mapping because the P0 space address range from 0 to 40000000 is the maximum physical address range permitted by the VAX architecture. That is, even with the maximum possible physical memory on a VAX processor, there is a P0 address range with identical addresses.

25.1.1.1 **Double Mapping of EXE$INIT by SYSBOOT.** This P0 page table is constructed by loading the P0 base and length registers with values that access a portion of the SPT (see Figure 25-1). If EXE$INIT is located in PFN *n*, then

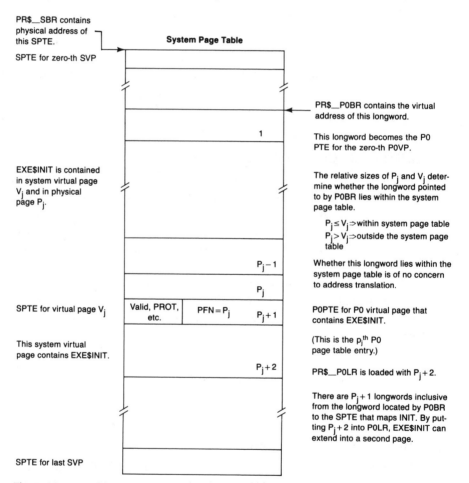

Figure 25-1 Double Use of System Page Table Entries by EXE$INIT

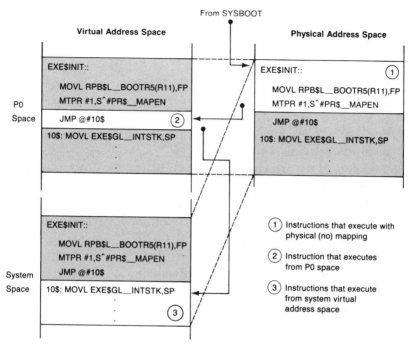

Figure 25-2   Address Space Changes as Memory
Management Is Enabled by EXE$INIT

P0LR is loaded with $n + 2$. P0BR is loaded with a system virtual address that
is n longwords smaller than the system virtual address of the system page
table entry (SPTE) that maps EXE$INIT.

The net result of all this mapping is that the physical page containing
EXE$INIT can and will be accessed in three different ways (see Figure 25-2).
These different mappings are listed here in order of mapping complication,
and not in the order in which they are used. EXE$INIT can be accessed in the
following ways:

- As a physical address
- As a system virtual address (80024EA0 in Version 4) mapped by the SPT
- As a P0 virtual address located by the subset of the SPT that is also used as
  a P0 page table

25.1.1.2   **Instructions That Turn On Memory Management.** When EXE$INIT begins
execution, memory management is disabled. The PC contains the physical
address of EXE$INIT. The following numbered descriptions correspond to
numbers in Figure 25-2.

① The first instruction executes in physical space:

```
MOVL    RPB$L_BOOTR5(R11),FP
```

691

Its effect is not related to turning memory management on.

The next instruction actually turns memory management on:

```
MTPR    #1,S^#PR$_MAPEN
```

That is, all address references from that point on must be translated. Note that the instruction does not cause a transfer of control. The PC is simply incremented by 3, the number of bytes in the instruction. However, the next PC reference will be translated, because memory management has been enabled.

Because of the mapping set up by SYSBOOT, the incremented (physical) PC (the address of the JMP instruction) translated as a P0 address is the physical address of the JMP instruction.

② The next instruction is the only instruction that executes with a P0 PC:

```
JMP     @#10$
```

This instruction immediately transfers control to a system virtual address that was calculated when the system image was linked. When this system virtual address is translated, it results in the physical address of the next instruction in the physical page containing EXE$INIT.

③ The next instruction is the first one to execute in system address space:

```
10$:    MOVL    EXE$GL_INTSTK,SP    ;SET TO USE INTERRUPT STACK
```

Its effect is not directly related to turning on memory management.

The four instructions shown in Figure 25-2 execute in three different mapping contexts. The mapping that was set up by SYSBOOT results in the selection of successive instructions from the same physical page.

25.1.2   Initialization of the Executive

Once EXE$INIT has turned on memory management, it can make references to system addresses. In particular, it can now initialize dynamic data structures whose listheads are in global locations in system space. Some of these steps involve allocation from nonpaged pool. (The nonpaged pool space allocated by EXE$INIT and the SYSBOOT parameters that control its size are listed in Table 25-1.)

EXE$INIT takes the following steps once memory management has been turned on:

1. The address of the systemwide interrupt stack is stored in the SP register.
2. EXE$INIT tests flags in EXE$GL_ARCHFLAG, initialized by SYSBOOT, to determine whether any instruction emulation is required. If subset instruction or floating-point emulation is required, SYSBOOT has already loaded VAXEMUL.EXE or FPEMUL.EXE (or both) into nonpaged

Table 25-1   Use of Nonpaged Pool by EXE$INIT

Item	Global Name of Pointer	Factors That Affect Size
Real-time bit map	EXE$GL_RTBITMAP	RBM$K_LENGTH + (4 · REALTIME_SPTS)
Lock ID table	LCK$GL_IDTBL	12 + (4 · LOCKIDTBL)
Resource hash table	LCK$GL_HASHTBL	12 + (4 · RESHASHTBL)
Deadlock detection process bit map	LCK$GL_PRCMAP	13 + (MAXPROCESSCNT/8)
Adapter control blocks	IOC$GL_ADPLIST	Number and type of external adapters (see Table 25-2)
PCB and sequence number vectors	SCHGL_PCBVEC, SCHGL_SEQVEC	12 + (6 · (MAXPROCESSCNT + 1)) [1]
Process header vectors	PHVGL_PIXBAS, PHVGL_REFCBAS	12 + (4 · (BALSETCNT + 1)) [2]
Swapper map	SWP$GL_MAP	12 + (4 · WSMAX) + 4 [3]
Modified page writer arrays	MPWAL_PTE, MPWAW_PHVINDEX	12 + (6 · MPW_WRTCLUSTER)
Page-and-swap-file vector	MMG$GL_PAGSWPVC	4 · (SWPFILCT + PAGFILCT) + 16
DDB, UCB, and ORB for system device port driver		UCB size for that driver
CRB and IDB for system device class driver		

---

[1]There is one extra slot in each array for system PCB. The system process has a process index of MAXPROCESSCNT.

[2]There is one extra slot in each array for the system header. The system header has a balance slot index of BALSETCNT.

[3]The extra longword contains a zero, an end of list indicator.

pool. EXE$INIT invokes the initialization routine of either or both emulators.

3. EXE$INIT initializes several exception vectors in the system control block (SCB) built by SYSBOOT. If the SYSBOOT parameter SSINHIBIT is set, the CHMK and CHME vectors are redirected to enable system service filtering. System service filtering is briefly described in Chapter 9.

4. The SCB base register is loaded with the physical address of the SCB.

5. Executive debugger support is either initialized or eliminated, according to the setting of the R5 debug flag, RPB$V_DEBUG, on input to VMB.

—If debug support is selected, the BPT and TBIT exception vectors are loaded with the addresses of exception service routines within XDELTA.

—If debug support is not selected, the BPT instruction in EXE$INIT (at address INI$BRK) is converted to a NOP. In addition, the pages containing XDELTA (see Appendix F) are included in the list of pages that EXE$INIT will release to the free page list as part of its exit routine.

6. SYSBOOT has loaded the SYSLOA*xxx*.EXE image into nonpaged pool appropriate for the processor type. EXE$INIT invokes EXE$LINK_VEC (in module LINKVEC) to connect the routines in the SYSLOA image to "vectors" in the system image. Section 25.1.3 describes this in detail. CPU-specific support for the console terminal, part of SYSLOA, is needed to print the announcement message and any others.

7. EXE$INIT initializes the console terminal and prints the announcement message on it. Note that this important milestone, while not very far into EXE$INIT, indicates that the system image has been read into memory and memory management turned on, both significant steps in initializing the executive.

8. The virtual page number of the boundary between the paged and nonpaged executive is loaded into the paged code arrays.

9. The nonpaged pool variable list is initialized (see Chapter 3).

10. If the R5 initial breakpoint flag, RPB$V_INIBPT, was set on input to VMB, then EXE$INIT executes a JSB to INI$BRK. If debug support has been selected, the instruction at INI$BRK contains a BPT instruction, which dispatches to XDELTA.

11. A tentative value for the maximum number of processes is established.

12. The values for the high and low thresholds of the modified page list are set.

13. If the system has more than 32 MB of memory, page frame number (PFN) database references in the nonpaged system image are modified to use longword context opcodes.

14. If the SYSPAGING SYSBOOT parameter is set, indicating that the pageable executive routines will page, then the SPTEs for these pages are initialized with system section table indexes. In addition, the first section table entry in the system section table is initialized to point to the executive image SYS.EXE. (Chapter 14 describes the system section table.) If SYSPAGING is clear, SYSBOOT has allocated physical pages for this portion of the executive and initialized the SPTEs appropriately.

15. The fields in the restart parameter block (RPB) used by the restart routine (see Chapter 26) are initialized.

16. The physical pages represented by the PFN bit map set up by VMB are placed on the free page list. (Note that the pages that contain the PFN bit map must be virtually mapped before they can be accessed.)

17. The SPTEs for paged pool are initialized. If paged pool will page (if the POOLPAGING SYSBOOT parameter flag is set), the SPTEs are initialized to demand zero format PTEs. If pool paging is turned off, physical pages are allocated; a PFN is stored in each SPTE, with a protection code

of ERKW and the valid bit set.

18. The nonpaged pool lookaside list packets are formatted and linked together. (The lookaside lists are described in Chapter 3.)

19. IOC$GL_IRPMIN, the minimum size allocation that can be filled with an I/O request packet (IRP) is initialized to be 1 larger than the size of a small request packet (SRP).

20. The FIL$OPENFILE cache pointers and the top-level system directory name string are set up for FILEREAD. These global parameters were initialized by SYSBOOT.

21. EXE$INIT initializes the permanent local system block (SB). The system ID and VAXcluster node name are taken from the SYSBOOT parameters SCSSYSTEMID, SCSSYSTEMIDH, and SCSNODE.

22. SYSBOOT loads a number of images into nonpaged pool. EXE$INIT must initialize them. In particular, "vectors" in the system image that dispatch to routines within an image must be modified to point to the routines in pool. EXE$INIT invokes a local routine to connect the vectors and call any initialization routine within the image (see Section 25.1.3). The images treated in this way are as follows:

—SYSLOA*xxx*.EXE (where *xxx* is one of the CPU designations listed in Appendix G)

—Optionally, ERAPATLOA.EXE

—Optionally, MTACCESS.EXE

—SCSLOA.EXE, if the system has a computer interconnect (CI) adapter or system communications services (SCS) type system device

—CLUSTRLOA.EXE, if the system is to participate in a VAXcluster System

The initialization routine in the SYSLOA image determines which adapters are present on the system and initializes them and their data structures. Adapter initialization is discussed further in Section 25.1.4.

23. If the SYSBOOT parameter REALTIME_SPTS is nonzero, that number of SPTEs is taken from the list of available SPTEs (see Appendix F) and described in a real-time bit map control block, allocated from nonpaged pool. These SPTEs are used by the connect-to-interrupt driver.

24. Lock management data structures, the lock ID table and the resource hash table, are initialized. A process bit map is set up for deadlock detection; the map has one bit for each possible process.

25. The process control block (PCB) and sequence number vectors (see Chapter 20) are allocated from nonpaged pool and initialized. All sequence numbers are initialized to zero. All PCB vector slots except one are initialized to the address of the PCB of the null process. Process index 1 is the swapper process. An extended process ID is calculated for both the swapper and null processes.

Note that one extra entry is allocated at the end of each array. The extra entry in the PCB vector points to the system PCB. The system PCB is defined in module PDAT; its dynamic contents are loaded by EXE$INIT. It is used by the pager to read faulted pages into the system working set list.

26. The scheduler is called to make computable the two processes that are assembled as part of the executive image, the swapper and the null process.

27. The process header (PHD) vectors (see Chapter 14) are initialized for each balance slot. The reference count array is initialized to contain −1 in each array element. The process index array is zeroed to indicate free balance slots. The null process is the process with a process index of zero. Because the null process does not swap, it does not require a balance slot. An index of zero can thus be used for another purpose, namely to indicate a free balance slot.

As Appendix F illustrates, the system header and system page table (SPT) immediately follow the balance slot area in system address space. In fact, portions of the memory management subsystem treat the system header as the occupant of an additional balance slot, one with a slot number equal to the SYSBOOT parameter BALSETCNT. The two PHD vector arrays have one extra entry at the end to reflect this feature.

28. The swapper map is allocated from nonpaged pool (see Chapters 14 and 17). Its address is stored in global location SWP$GL_MAP and also in the swapper's P0 base register. Pages mapped in the swapper map are accessible as P0 virtual pages when the swapper is the current process.

29. The modified page writer arrays (see Chapters 14 and 15) are allocated from nonpaged pool.

30. PFN database array fields for the page occupied by the RPB are initialized to reflect its use.

31. The page-and-swap-file vector is initialized. Each array element is the address of a page file control block for a page or swap file recognized by the system. The first element is initialized so it can be used to read the shell process into the system working set. (See Chapter 14 for more information.)

32. A number of miscellaneous initialization operations are performed here. The maximum depth of the lock manager resource name tree is calculated. The size of the tree is associated with the size of the interrupt stack. Space is reserved in the system working set for the shell. The address of the system header is stored in the system PCB and the process index for the system process is determined. The map of the file SYS.EXE, contained in the boot control block, is placed in a window control block (WCB).

33. EXE$INIT invokes EXE$INI_TIMWAIT to initialize global variables

used in timed wait loops generated by the macros TIMEWAIT and TIMEDWAIT. EXE$INI_TIMWAIT is in module [SYSLOA]INIADP*xxx*. These macros are invoked, typically from code running at IPL 31, to ensure the passage of a specified relatively small amount of time. For example, the PADRIVER uses the TIMEWAIT macro to wait, after initializing the port adapter, for 100 milliseconds or for it to become ready.

EXE$INI_TIMWAIT calibrates EXE$GL_TENUSEC and EXE$GL_UBDELAY. EXE$GL_UBDELAY is the number of times a particular 1-instruction loop must execute to take three microseconds. EXE$GL_TENUSEC is the number of times a prototype loop executes in ten microseconds. The prototype loop includes an inner loop executed EXE$GL_UBDELAY times. In actual use, the prototype loop is likely to be replaced by code that polls a device register. The delay is incorporated so as to introduce a three-microsecond gap between UNIBUS or other I/O bus references.

34. The driver prolog tables (DPTs) for the three devices (mailbox, null device, and console terminal) that are linked with SYS.EXE are connected to the driver database (located through listhead IOC$GL_DPTLIST).

35. Argument lists to create logical names for SYS$DISK and SYS$-SYSDEVICE are allocated from nonpaged pool. Nonpaged pool is used to pass information to the swapper process, which will create the logical names after it initializes paged pool and the logical name database.

36. SYSBOOT has already loaded the terminal class driver into nonpaged pool. EXE$INIT invokes IOC$INITDRV (in module RELOCDRV) to initialize its data structures as directed by the DPT. Then EXE$INIT inserts the DPT into the list at IOC$GL_DPTLIST. It relocates the terminal class vector table and connects it to the console port driver data structures. (See Chapter 19 for further information.) The data structures for additional terminals will be established later by the System Generation Utility.

37. SYSBOOT has already loaded into nonpaged pool the driver for the system device and, if any, its port driver. EXE$INIT allocates and initializes the associated database. It takes the following actions:

a. It scans the list of adapter control blocks (ADPs) looking for the one with a node number that matches boot R1 (see Chapter 24). As it scans, it fills in each ADP$B_NUMBER to indicate how many adapters of this type have already been found. That is, it determines whether a particular adapter is the first of its kind, or the second, and so on.

b. If there is a port driver, EXE$INIT links it into the list at IOC$GL_DPTLIST. It allocates from nonpaged pool and initializes a DDB, UCB, and ORB, and links them into the I/O database.

    c. EXE$INIT constructs a name for the system device unit using information passed from VMB and the driver name.

    d. It stores the device and driver names in the device data block (DDB) for the system device and unit number in its unit control block (UCB).

    e. It links the system device driver into the list at IOC$GL_DPTLIST.

    f. It stores the system device UCB address in EXE$GL_SYSUCB and in the SYS.EXE WCB.

    g. EXE$INIT then invokes EXE$BOOTCB_CHK to compute a checksum for the boot control block, which contains the SYS.EXE WCB. Bugcheck processing code recomputes the checksum to test the integrity of the boot control block before using it as a source of disk addresses for the fatal bugcheck code overlay and the dump file.

    h. It allocates an SPTE, if requested, for the system device and stores its number in UCB$L_SVPN.

    i. Once the system device name is determined, the equivalence names for SYS$DISK and SYS$SYSDEVICE can be stored in Create Logical Name ($CRELNM) argument lists for later use by the swapper process.

    j. If there is a system device port driver, EXE$INIT connects its channel request block (CRB), interrupt dispatch block (IDB), and UCB and calls IOC$INITDRV to initialize its data structures. It allocates a CRB and an IDB for the system device class driver and calls IOC$INITDRV.

38. All loaded drivers are then called at their controller and unit initialization points.

39. EXE$INIT invokes EXE$INIPROCREG, a CPU-specific routine within the SYSLOA image, to initialize processor registers, for example, to enable interval clock interrupts.

40. A page of physical memory (the "black hole" page) is reserved for adapter powerfail. Its PFN is stored in global location EXE$GL_BLAKHOLE. When power failure occurs, for example, on a UNIBUS, all virtual pages mapped to UBA registers or UNIBUS I/O space (24 pages in all) are remapped to this physical page. This remapping prevents drivers for UNIBUS devices from generating multiple machine checks while the power is off for the UBA. Powerfail operations are discussed in more detail in Chapter 26.

41. A page of physical memory and an SPTE to map it are allocated for use in mount verification. The virtual address of the SPTE is stored in EXE$GL_SVAPTE.

42. A page of physical memory and an SPTE to map it are allocated for both a system erase pattern buffer and a pseudo page table to map the buffer. Their virtual addresses are stored in EXE$GL_ERASEPB and EXE$GL_ERASEPPT. These are used to optimize erasure of disk blocks when an erase-on-delete file is deleted.

43. The maximum allowable working set is readjusted (if necessary) to reflect the amount of available physical memory.

    Specifically, the number of physical pages used by the executive (see Appendix F) is subtracted from available physical memory. System usage includes not only nonpaged code and data but also the system working set, MPW_LOLIMIT pages on the modified page list, and FREELIM pages on the free page list (but not the pages used by EXE$INIT). The value of WSMAX is then minimized with this difference.

44. Two flags used by the restart mechanism (see Chapter 26) are cleared.

45. Finally, EXE$INIT frees up the pages that it occupied and jumps to the scheduler. The protection fields for these system virtual pages are set to no access in the SPT and the physical pages are placed on the free page list. EXE$INIT accomplishes these steps by copying a small routine into nonpaged pool and transferring control to that routine. The routine itself vanishes as a result of the first allocation from pool, because the use of this block of pool was not recorded anywhere.

25.1.3   CPU-Dependent and Other Loadable Routines

There are two different types of CPU-dependent code that appear in the VAX/VMS operating system and two corresponding methods that the VMS operating system uses for incorporating the code:

- When there are one or two instructions or data references that depend on the specific type of CPU being used, the system usually includes the code or data sequence for all CPUs in line and uses the contents of location EXE$GB_CPUTYPE to determine which piece of the code or data to use. (This location was previously loaded by SYSBOOT from the contents of the PR$_SID register.) On some processor types, there is an additional level of dispatch based on CPU subtype.
- In the case of CPU-dependent routines (such as the purge datapath routine, IOC$PURGDATAP) or CPU-dependent modules (such as the machine check handler), a technique of vectored entry points to routines in a separate image is used.

The vectored entry point method works in the following way. Each reference within the executive image to a CPU-dependent routine is dispatched to a JMP instruction in module SYSLOAVEC, which is linked with SYS.EXE. The CPU-dependent routines are linked together into a set of CPU-dependent images with names of the form SYSLOAxxx.EXE. (See Appendix G for a list of SYSLOA images.) SYSBOOT uses the CPU type and subtype to determine which SYSLOA image to load into nonpaged pool.

Another vector module called LOAVEC (actually, SYSLOAVEC with a different setting of a conditional assembly flag), linked into each CPU-dependent image SYSLOA*xxx*.EXE, contains an offset into the loadable image for each of the CPU-dependent subroutines. EXE$LINK_VEC uses the information in this table to adjust the arguments of the JMP instructions (in module SYSLOAVEC) so that they point to the correct routines in the copy of the SYSLOA image in nonpaged pool. The initial destination of all the JMP instructions is EXE$LOAD_ERROR, a global address of a HALT instruction within module SYSLOAVEC. If any of these CPU-dependent routines is referenced before EXE$INIT has invoked EXE$LINK_VEC, the system will halt.

The cost of separating out CPU-dependent routines from the system image, one extra level of indirection, is far outweighed by the benefits, which include fewer execution time decisions and no need for either separate system images for each CPU or one larger system image supporting all CPUs. The linkage established by EXE$INIT for CPU-dependent routines is illustrated in Figure 25-3.

This same mechanism is used for SCSLOA and CLUSTRLOA. SCSLOA routines are required on a system which has any disk or magnetic tape controllers that use the mass storage control protocol (MSCP). SCSLOA and CLUSTRLOA routines are both required for a system that is a member of a VAXcluster System.

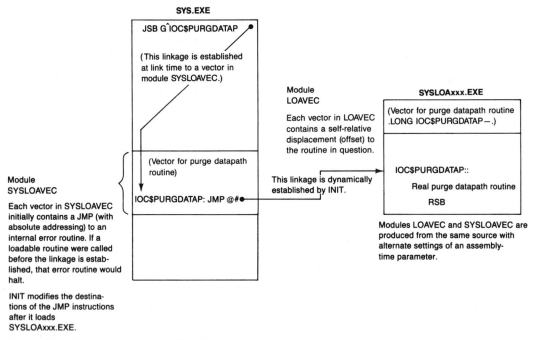

Figure 25-3 Linkage and Control Flow Example for CPU-Dependent Routines

i.1.4   **I/O Adapter Initialization**

The CPU-specific routine [SYSLOA]INIADPxxx is used to determine the location of external adapters and initialize the adapters for later use by the SYSGEN configuration operations. INIADPxxx also records the processor type in the hardware type field of the local system block.

Although some of the initialization that INIADPxxx performs depends on the nature of the external I/O adapter, there are several general steps that are taken for each adapter:

1. An adapter control block (ADP) that identifies the adapter and contains information about how the adapter's internal registers are mapped is allocated from nonpaged pool and initialized.
2. System virtual space is set up to map to the I/O space addresses for internal adapter registers and other I/O space assignments.
3. The adapter hardware is initialized.

Information about the hardware configuration is recorded in several nonpaged pool arrays. The number of elements in each array is specified by the contents of the global EXE$GL_NUMNEXUS. Each array is indexed by nexus number. There are three arrays:

- MMG$GL_SBICONF contains the address of a longword array. Each element contains the starting virtual address to which its adapter registers are mapped.
- EXE$GL_CONFREG contains the address of a byte array that specifies the type of each adapter. On some processors, such as the VAX-11/78x or the VAX 86x0, adapter type codes are one byte long. Type codes are defined by the SYS$LIBRARY:LIB.MLB macro $NDTDEF.
- EXE$GL_CONFREGL contains the address of a longword array which also specifies the type of each adapter.

Table 25-2 lists the differences in ADP size and mapping requirements for each of the possible external adapters.

INIADPxxx also checks for the presence of UNIBUS memory. If UNIBUS memory is found, the associated UBA map registers are disabled.

i.2   **INITIALIZATION IN PROCESS CONTEXT**

Further steps in system initialization must be performed by a process. System services can only be called from process context. A command language interpreter (CLI) can only be mapped into P1 space by code executing in process context.

The process phase of system initialization is divided into several parts:

- Initialization within the swapper process

Table 25-2 External Adapter Initialization

Adapter Type	Size of ADP (in bytes)	Number of System Virtual Pages Mapped for Adapter
Local memory	None exists	1 (or 0 on some CPUs)
MA780 shared memory	132	1
UNIBUS adapter	600 or 1240 [1]	24 [2]
MASSBUS adapter	48	8
DR32 interface	48	4
CI interface	66	16
KDB50	600	8
KLESI-B	600	8
DMB32 interface	48	2
DRB32	48	16
DEBNT	66	16
Unknown VAXBI device	48	16
Unoccupied slot	None exists	1 to allow access

[1] An ADP for a UBA with indirect vectors also contains the interrupt service routines for the UBA and 128 longword vectors, corresponding to UNIBUS vectors from 0 to 774_8.

[2] Eight pages map the UBA internal registers, such as mapping registers, data path registers, and the like. There are 16 pages that map the UNIBUS I/O page to allow virtual access to device CSRs, data registers, and so on.

- SYSINIT process
- Startup process

25.2.1   Swapper Process

When the scheduler executes, it selects the highest priority computable process for execution. There are only two processes in existence at this time, the swapper and null processes. The swapper process is always selected, because it has an external priority of 16 and the null process has an external priority of 0.

The swapper process is entirely resident within system space. Other than that, it is scheduled and placed into execution like any other process. Its PCB and PHD are defined within the module PDAT. Its hardware PCB defines its PC as the address of EXE$SWAPINIT and its PSL as kernel mode and IPL 0. Thus, when the swapper executes for the first time, it enters EXE$SWAPINIT, system initialization code executed only once during the life of the system.

The swapper performs the minimum initialization that requires process context. In particular, it initializes paged pool and the logical name database. The swapper initializes the paged pool listhead, which must be done from process context to handle the resulting page faults.

The swapper then performs the following steps to initialize the logical name database. (See Chapter 28 for a description of logical name data structures.)

1. It allocates paged pool for the shareable logical name hash table.
2. The swapper zeros it, initializes its header, and stores its address in the longword pointed to by LNM$AL_HASHTBL.
3. The swapper initializes the logical name table header (LNMTH) of the system directory. It records the hash table address in the LNMTH. It then hashes the system directory name and inserts it into the appropriate hash chain of the shareable hash table.
4. It initializes the system logical name table, recording the hash table address in its LNMTH. It invokes LNM$INSLOGTAB (in module LNMSUB) to insert the system table into the database.
5. The swapper calls the Create Logical Name ($CRELNM) system service to create the following logical names:

   —LNM$DIRECTORIES, whose equivalence names are the shareable and per-process shareable directories
   —The executive mode table name LNM$FILE_DEV
   —The supervisor mode table name LNM$FILE_DEV
   —The table names that provide upward compatibility from VMS Version 3: LOG$PROCESS, LOG$GROUP, LOG$SYSTEM, TRNLOG$_GROUP_SYSTEM, TRNLOG$_PROCESS_GROUP, TRNLOG$_PROCESS_SYSTEM, and TRNLOG$_PROCESS_GROUP_SYSTEM
   —The table names LNM$PERMANENT_MAILBOX and LNM$TEMPORARY_MAILBOX
   —The table name LNM$SYSTEM
   —The executive mode names SYS$DISK and SYS$SYSDEVICE in LNM$SYSTEM table

6. It deallocates the nonpaged pool used by EXE$INIT to pass information needed for the creation of SYS$DISK and SYS$SYSDEVICE

The swapper then creates a process called SYSINIT that performs much of the system initialization requiring process context.

25.2.2 SYSINIT Process

In one sense, SYSINIT is an extension of the swapper process. However, the initialization code is isolated to prevent encumbering the swapper with more code that only executes once during the life of a system. (This isolation is one of several techniques used during system initialization and process creation to cause seldom-used code to disappear after it is used. A list of such techniques appears in Appendix B.)

The major functions that SYSINIT performs can be grouped into several categories:

- Initiation of VAXcluster initialization for this node
- Opening the swap and page files and recording their extents
- Mapping RMS.EXE and the system message file as system sections
- Creation of the STARTUP process

25.2.2.1   **Pool Usage by SYSINIT.** SYSINIT, like EXE$INIT, allocates nonpaged pool. It also allocates some paged pool. However, the sizes of various blocks are not directly related to SYSBOOT parameters. Structures that are allocated from nonpaged pool as a result of the execution of SYSINIT include the following:

- Software PCBs and JIBs for system processes
- File control blocks and window control blocks for all opened files
- A volume control block for the system disk

25.2.2.2   **Detailed Operation of SYSINIT.** SYSINIT is a normal process, scheduled and placed into execution in the ordinary way. Its image, SYSINIT.EXE, is part of the [SYSINI] facility. SYSINIT begins execution in user mode, but performs much of its work in kernel and executive mode procedures.

SYSINIT takes the following steps:

1. SYSINIT changes mode to kernel to create a system-specific root resource. It calls the Enqueue Lock Request ($ENQ) system service to create an executive mode system resource. Its name is the string SYS$-SYS_ID concatenated with the system's SCS system ID (SYSBOOT parameters SCSSYSTEMID and SCSSYSTEMIDH) and is therefore unique within the VAXcluster System.

    SYSINIT locks the root resource with a system-owned lock that will survive the deletion of SYSINIT. SYSINIT stores its lock ID in EXE$GL_SYSID_LOCK. VMS components use it as a parent resource for resources local to this system. (See Chapter 13 for information on lock management.)

2. SYSINIT changes mode to kernel to set the system time. It invokes the routine EXE$INIT_TODR in the SYSLOA image. (See Chapter 11 for more information on EXE$INIT_TODR and setting system time.)

3. SYSINIT changes mode to kernel to initialize cluster connection management. If this system expects to participate in a VAXcluster System, SYSINIT creates the stand-alone configure process, STACONFIG. This process autoconfigures disks and SCS communication ports. If the SYSBOOT parameter DISK_QUORUM indicates there is to be a quorum disk, STACONFIG starts SCS polling to discover remote MSCP disk

servers in case connection to a quorum disk is necessary for the node to join the VAXcluster System.

SYSINIT sets a flag to tell the cluster connection manager to proceed with cluster formation and prints the following message on the console terminal:

```
Waiting to form or join VAXcluster
```

It waits for 100 milliseconds, during which time the STACONFIG process and the cluster connection manager run, and then tests whether the quorum disk has been found.

If it has, SYSINIT assigns a channel to it, opens the quorum file, and starts the quorum disk polling routine to run every QDISKINTERVAL seconds. It then checks whether the system is a member of a VAXcluster System yet. If not, SYSINIT waits again.

When the system is a member, SYSINIT takes out a concurrent read lock on the system device and resets the time to correspond to the clusterwide time.

4. If the system disk is to be a member of a disk shadow set, SYSINIT changes mode to kernel and establishes the shadow set.

5. Back in user mode, SYSINIT recreates executive mode logical names for SYS$SYSDEVICE and SYS$DISK in the system logical name table. (In the case of an MSCP system disk, their equivalence names are not quite right. At the time EXE$INIT created them, the allocation class of the system disk was not yet known. When SYSINIT runs, the MSCP server for the system disk has communicated its allocation class and SYSINIT can form an equivalence name that contains the allocation class.) It also creates the following logical names:

> SYS$SYSTEM
> SYS$SYSROOT
> SYS$COMMON
> SYS$SHARE
> SYS$MESSAGE

The creation of these names cannot be delayed until the creation of the STARTUP process, because these names are needed as a part of the creation of that process:

—The name of the image that is passed to the STARTUP process is SYS$SYSTEM:LOGINOUT.

—SYS$SYSTEM is defined in terms of SYS$SYSROOT and SYS$-COMMON.

—The LOGINOUT image performs a merged image activation (see Chapter 21) to map the DCL CLI into P1 space. The image activator

uses logical name SYS$SHARE to locate the shareable image DCL-TABLES.EXE, which contains the command database for the DCL CLI.
—The logical name SYS$MESSAGE is required for RMS to open the system message file.

6. If the SYSBOOT parameter UAFALTERNATE is set, SYSINIT creates the executive mode logical name SYSUAF in the system table. Its equivalence name is SYS$SYSTEM:SYSUAFALT.DAT. This feature allows an alternate authorization file to be used. If the alternate authorization file does not exist, all users are denied access to the system.

7. The following files are opened by the file I/O routines located in the executive:

    SYS$SYSTEM:PAGEFILE.SYS
    SYS$SYSTEM:SWAPFILE.SYS
    SYS$SYSTEM:RMS.EXE

If the first part of the page file is being used as the dump file, SYSBOOT has already opened PAGEFILE.SYS; it is not opened again.

8. SYSINIT calls a kernel mode procedure whose first step is to initialize the global page table entry list.

9. Next, the page file is initialized. This requires that the information obtained in SYSBOOT or in step 7 be loaded into a WCB that describes the page file. The address of that WCB is stored in the page file control block (see Figure 14-22) for the initial page file.

    In addition, a bit map that describes the availability of each block in the page file is allocated from nonpaged pool and initialized to all 1's to indicate that all blocks are available. If the page file is being used as a dump file, then the first four blocks of the page file are not reflected in the bit map and will always be reserved for a minimum dump containing pending error log messages and the dump header block. If the page file contains a valid dump and the SYSBOOT parameter SAVEDUMP is set to 1, the blocks in the page file that contain the dump are marked unavailable. When the dump is successfully copied to another file using the SDA command COPY, the blocks are marked available. If the page file contains a valid dump, the second and third blocks of the dump file (error log buffers) are preserved before the page file is initialized.

10. If present, the swap file is initialized. SYSINIT allocates a WCB from nonpaged pool and stores its address in the first swap file entry in the page-and-swap-file vector (see Chapter 14). A bit map identical to a page file bit map is allocated from nonpaged pool and initialized to all 1's to indicate all blocks are available.

11. SYSINIT tests the SYSPAGING parameter. If it is set, SYSINIT allocates and fills in a WCB that describes all of the file extents of RMS.EXE and

creates a pageable system section for RMS. The section table entries that describe it are initialized, starting with the second section table entry in the system header. (The first system section table entry, the one that describes the system image itself, was set up by EXE$INIT.) RMS pages in the system working set. If SYSPAGING is zero, SYSINIT creates writable address space for RMS and reads it into memory. SYSINIT records the starting address of RMS in MMG$GL_RMSBASE.

12. The second and third blocks of the dump file contain the contents of the error log buffers if the system just crashed. These buffers were written to the dump file by the bugcheck code (see Chapter 8) so their contents would not be lost. If the system is rebooting after a crash, SYSINIT copies the valid and complete messages that were in the second and third blocks of the dump file to the error log buffers. Eventually, they will be written to SYS$ERRORLOG:ERRLOG.SYS.

   SYSINIT also reads the first block of the dump file and logs the entry describing the crash. The bugcheck routine wrote this entry in the first block of the dump file when the system crashed. This alternative to typical error logging avoids the loss of the entry that might otherwise result if the two error log buffers had insufficient space at the time of the crash.

   If they were very full at the time of the crash, after SYSINIT processes the second and third blocks of the dump file, they may be very full again. When SYSINIT tries to log the crash entry, there may be insufficient space for it in the error log buffers. In that case, the error log entry that actually describes the crash will never appear in an error log report. However, the crash entry is contained in the dump file and its information can be retrieved until the time the dump file is reused.

13. A cold start is logged in the error log.

14. SYSINIT exits the kernel mode procedure, returning to user mode, and then changes mode to executive. It calls the Image Activate ($IMGACT) and Image Fixup ($IMGFIX) system services to activate the Files-11 extended QIO Processor (XQP) in SYSINIT's P1 space. It then calls an initialization routine in the XQP. From this point on, the file system is available for SYSINIT's file operations.

15. SYSINIT exits the kernel mode procedure, returning to user mode, and then changes mode to executive. It calls a procedure to mount the system disk.

16. SYSINIT requests the Set Time ($SETIME) system service to record the system time in the system image.

17. The FIL$OPENFILE cache can now be deallocated from nonpaged pool.

18. The logical name SYS$TOPSYS is created.

19. SYSINIT changes mode to kernel and calls a procedure to create global sections for the XQP's image sections. If the SYSBOOT parameter ACP_XQP_RES is set, SYSINIT creates resident global sections so that

the pages of the XQP will always be in physical memory. The primitive file system routines that are a part of SYS.EXE are no longer required and will disappear in time as a result of system working set replacement.

20. The system message file (SYS$MESSAGE:SYSMSG.EXE) is opened and mapped. The section table entries that map the message file's sections are initialized following the section table entries for RMS in the system header.

21. Finally, the STARTUP process is created. The important point about this process is that it executes the image LOGINOUT, which maps a CLI (see Chapter 23).

25.2.3 STARTUP Process

The STARTUP process created by SYSINIT completes system initialization. This process is the first in the system to include a CLI. The inclusion of DCL allows the operation of this process to be directed by a DCL command procedure.

25.2.3.1 STARTUP.COM. The steps performed by commands in this file follow:

1. System logical names are created, including the following:

—If the system root is not part of a VAXcluster common disk, redefinitions of

    SYS$COMMON
    SYS$SYSROOT

—VMS-specific names:

    SYS$SPECIFIC
    SYS$SYSDISK
    SYS$ERRORLOG
    SYS$EXAMPLES
    SYS$HELP
    SYS$INSTRUCTION
    SYS$LIBRARY
    SYS$MAINTENANCE
    SYS$MANAGER

—Logical names used for system management, installation, and testing
—Logical names used by the symbolic debugger
—The logical name table LNM$DCL_LOGICAL

2. If the SYSBOOT parameter WRITESYSPARAMS is set, STARTUP runs SYSGEN to issue the command WRITE CURRENT. This preserves the

parameter settings in the file SYS$SYSTEM:VAXVMSSYS.PAR.

3. Detached system processes are started:

—Error logger (ERRFMT)
—Job controller (JOB_CONTROL)
—Operator communication process (OPCOM)

On a system that is a member of a VAXcluster System, several other detached processes are started:

—Files-11 XQP cache server (CACHE_SERVER)
—Cluster server (CLUSTER_SERVER)
—Configure process (CONFIGURE)

4. The Install Utility is invoked to make privileged and shareable images known to the system. Its input is taken from the file SYS$-MANAGER:VMSIMAGES.DAT.
5. If there is a site-specific command procedure SYS$MANAGER:SYCON-FIG.COM, STARTUP invokes it. This command procedure can configure user-written device drivers prior to VMS autoconfiguration or disable autoconfiguration.
6. If the SYSBOOT parameter NOAUTOCONFIG is zero and if SYCON-FIG.COM has not zeroed the DCL symbol STARTUP$AUTOCON-FIGURE, STARTUP runs SYSGEN to configure external I/O devices. If NOAUTOCONFIG is zero and STARTUP$CONFIGURE has not been zeroed, STARTUP.COM creates the CONFIGURE process.
7. If a secondary swap file is to be used, it is installed.
8. If the system is a VAX 8600 or a VAX 8650, STARTUP runs the program ERRSNAP to copy hardware-recorded error information from the console disk to SYS$ERRORLOG.
9. STARTUP enables interactive logins.
10. The site-specific command file SYS$MANAGER:SYSTARTUP.COM is invoked.
11. If the rights database is in use and if the node-specific identifier (the string SYS$NODE_ concatenated with the node name) does not exist, STARTUP creates it.
12. STARTUP then logs out.

25.2.3.2   **Site-Specific Startup Command File.** The site-specific command file, SYS$MANAGER:SYSTARTUP.COM, that is distributed with VAX/VMS contains no commands. It can be edited to do the following:

• Start batch and print queues
• Set terminal speeds and other device characteristics
• Create site-specific system logical names

- Install additional privileged and shareable images
- Load user-written device drivers
- Mount volumes other than the system disk
- Load the console block storage driver (if desired) with a CONNECT CONSOLE command to SYSGEN and mount the console medium
- Issue the DCL command START/CPU to initialize the attached processor on an asymmetric multiprocessing system
- Start DECnet (if present on the system)
- Run the System Dump Analyzer (SDA) to preserve the previous dump file in case the system crashed
- Produce an error log report
- Announce system availability

25.3 SYSTEM GENERATION UTILITY

SYSGEN fits into the initialization sequence in two unrelated ways:

- It is invoked directly by STARTUP.COM to autoconfigure the external I/O devices.
- It interacts indirectly with system initialization by producing parameter files that may be used by SYSBOOT for future bootstrap operations.

The role of SYSGEN in autoconfiguring the I/O system is described in the manual *Writing a Device Driver for VAX/VMS*. This section briefly compares the operations that SYSGEN and SYSBOOT perform on parameter files. Table 25-3 summarizes this comparison.

25.3.1 Contents of Parameter Block

A common module called PARAMETER is linked into both the SYSGEN and SYSBOOT images. This module contains information about each adjustable parameter. Each parameter is defined by a data structure. The SYS$-LIBRARY:LIB.MLB macro $PRMDEF defines the fields in the data structure. Table 25-4 lists the fields. This data never changes. In addition, each parameter occupies a cell in a table of working values. This table is manipulated with the following SYSGEN and SYSBOOT commands:

- Displayed by SHOW parameter-name commands
- Altered by SET parameter-name value commands
- Overwritten by a USE command

There is also a copy of the working table linked into the system image, SYS.EXE. (This table is produced from the same source module as PARAMETER with a different setting of a conditional assembly parameter. The resultant module is called SYSPARAM.)

Table 25-3   Comparison of SYSGEN and SYSBOOT

SYSGEN	*SYSBOOT*
PURPOSE	
SYSGEN has four unrelated purposes: • It creates parameter files for use in future bootstrap operations. • It modifies dynamic parameters in the running system with the WRITE ACTIVE command. • It loads device drivers and builds their associated data structures. • It creates and installs additional page and swap files.	SYSBOOT configures the system using parameters from VAXVMSSYS.PAR or another parameter file.
USE IN SYSTEM INITIALIZATION	
During initialization, SYSGEN can be invoked to autoconfigure all I/O devices and record the current SYSBOOT parameters.	SYSBOOT is the secondary bootstrap program that executes after VMB and before control is passed to the executive.
ENVIRONMENT	
SYSGEN executes in the normal environment of a utility program. The driver and swap/page functions require privilege (CMKRNL). A WRITE ACTIVE command also requires CMKRNL privilege. The parameter file operations are protected through the file system.	SYSBOOT runs in a stand-alone environment with no file system, memory management, process context, or any other environment provided by VMS.
VALID COMMANDS	
USE • USE FILE-SPEC • USE CURRENT • USE DEFAULT • USE ACTIVE	USE • USE FILE-SPEC • USE CURRENT • USE DEFAULT • No equivalent command
SET	SET
SHOW	SHOW
EXIT (CONTINUE)	EXIT (CONTINUE)
WRITE	No equivalent command
Commands associated with device drivers	No equivalent commands
Commands associated with additional page and swap files	No equivalent commands
INITIAL CONDITIONS	
Implied USE ACTIVE	Implied USE CURRENT

Table 25-4   Information Stored for Each Adjustable Parameter by SYSGEN and SYSBOOT

Item	*Size of Item*
Address of parameter in SYS.EXE[1]	Longword
Default value of parameter	Longword
Minimum value that parameter can assume	Longword
Maximum value that parameter can assume	Longword
Parameter flags	Word

- DYNAMIC parameter   SHOW /DYN
- STATIC parameter
- SYSGEN parameter   SHOW /GEN
- ACP parameter   SHOW /ACP
- JBC parameter   SHOW /JOB
- RMS parameter   SHOW /RMS
- SCS parameter   SHOW /SCS
- SYS parameter   SHOW /SYS
- TTY parameter   SHOW /TTY
- SPECIAL parameter   SHOW /SPECIAL
- DISPLAY parameter
- CONTROL parameter
- MAJOR parameter   SHOW /MAJOR
- PQL parameter   SHOW /PQL
- NEG parameter
- CLUSTER parameter   SHOW /CLUSTER
- LGI parameter   SHOW /LGI
- ASCII parameter

Size of this parameter	Byte
Bit position if parameter is flag	Byte
Name string for parameter	16 bytes
Name string for units	12 bytes
Working value of parameter	Longword

[1]The working value of each parameter is found not only in internal tables in SYSBOOT and SYSGEN but also in the executive itself. In fact, the parameter address (first item) stored for each parameter locates the working value of each parameter in the memory image of the executive.

25.3.2   Use of Parameter Files by SYSBOOT

Figure 25-4 shows the flow of parameter value data during a bootstrap operation. The numbers in the figure describe the significant steps in setting values or moving data:

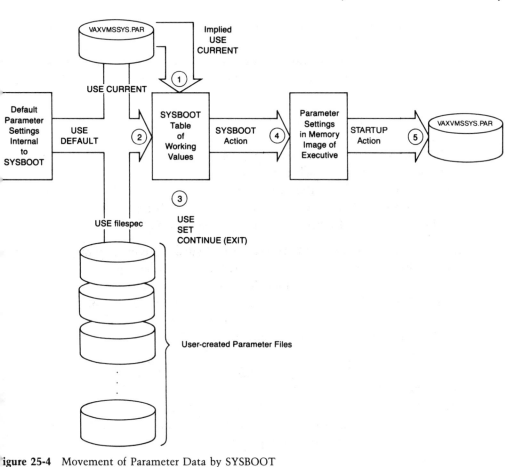

Figure 25-4   Movement of Parameter Data by SYSBOOT and SYSINIT

① The first step that SYSBOOT performs is to locate the file VAXVMS-SYS.PAR in SYS$SYSROOT:[SYSEXE] and read its parameter settings into SYSBOOT's working table. In the language of SYSBOOT and SYSGEN commands, this step is an implied command:

```
USE CURRENT
```

This operation causes the system to be initialized with the parameter settings used during the previous configuration of the system (because of step 5).

In versions of VMS prior to Version 4, the current parameters were stored in SYS.EXE. However, to support sharing of SYS.EXE by multiple members of a VAXcluster System, it was necessary to move the parameters into a separate file, called VAXVMSSYS.PAR. Each member has its own version of this file.

②If a conversational bootstrap was selected (R5<0> was set as input to VMB), then SYSBOOT will prompt for commands to alter current parameter settings. A USE command to SYSBOOT's prompt results in the working table being overwritten with an entire set of parameter values. There are three possible sources of these values:

—USE FILE-SPEC directs SYSBOOT to the indicated parameter file for a new set of values.
—USE DEFAULT causes the working table in SYSBOOT to be filled with the default values for each parameter.
—USE CURRENT causes the parameter values in VAXVMSSYS.PAR to be loaded into SYSBOOT's working table. (A USE CURRENT command is redundant if it is the first command passed to SYSBOOT.)

③Once the initial conditions have been established, individual parameters can be altered with SET commands. The conversational phase of SYSBOOT is terminated with a CONTINUE (or EXIT) command.

④After SYSBOOT has calculated the sizes of the various pieces of system space but before it transfers control to EXE$INIT, it copies the contents of its working table to the corresponding table in the memory image of the executive.

⑤One of the steps performed by the STARTUP process copies the parameter table from the memory image of the executive to SYS$SYSTEM: VAXVMSSYS.PAR. Because SYSBOOT always does an implied USE CURRENT as its first step, this implied command guarantees that all subsequent bootstraps will use the latest parameter settings even if no conversational bootstrap is selected.

25.3.3 Use of Parameter Files by SYSGEN

SYSGEN's interaction with parameter files is not an integral part of the bootstrap operation. However, its action, pictured in Figure 25-5, closely parallels that of SYSBOOT.

①The initial contents of SYSGEN's working table are the values taken from the memory image of the executive. The data movement pictured in Figure 25-5 is a movement from one memory area to another, rather than the result of an I/O operation. In any event, SYSGEN begins its execution with an implied command:

```
USE ACTIVE
```

This set of initial conditions would differ from SYSBOOT's initial state only if someone had already run SYSGEN and written parameters to either CURRENT (VAXVMSSYS.PAR) or ACTIVE (the memory image of the executive) or if SYSBOOT had modified any parameters.

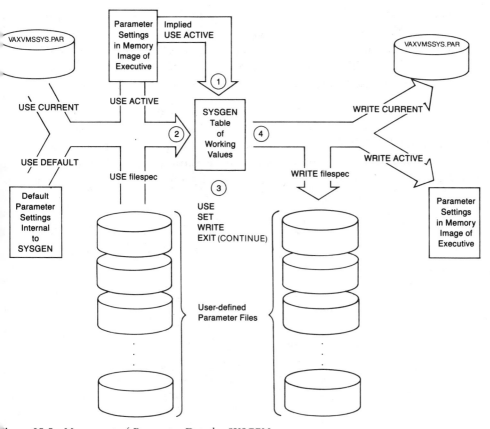

Figure 25-5 Movement of Parameter Data by SYSGEN

②SYSGEN can choose initial settings for its working table in exactly the same fashion as SYSBOOT.

There is an additional reserved file specification available to SYSGEN. A USE ACTIVE command causes the parameter table from the memory image of the executive to be copied into SYSGEN's working table.

③SET commands can be used to alter individual parameter values. Typically, an EXIT (or CONTINUE) command would not be used until the final settings were preserved with a WRITE command.

④This step preserves the contents of SYSGEN's working table in the following way:

—WRITE FILESPEC creates a new parameter file that contains the contents of SYSGEN's working table.

—WRITE CURRENT alters the copy of SYS$SYSTEM:VAXVMSSYS.PAR. The next bootstrap operation will use these values automatically (even without a conversational bootstrap option).

—Several parameters determine the size of portions of system address space. Other parameters determine the size of blocks of pool space allocated by EXE$INIT. These parameters cannot be changed in a running system. However, many parameters are not used in configuring the system. These parameters are designated as DYNAMIC (see Table 25-4).

A WRITE ACTIVE command to SYSGEN alters the settings of dynamic parameters only in the memory image of the executive.

A word of caution is in order here. Before one experiments with a new configuration, the parameters from a working system should be saved in a parameter file. If the new configuration creates a system that is unusable, the system can be restored to its previous state by directing SYSBOOT to use the saved parameters.

Power Failure and Recovery

For there are moments when one can neither think nor feel.
And if one can neither think nor feel, she thought, where is
one?

Virginia Woolf, *To the Lighthouse*

Powerfail recovery support enables a suitably equipped VAX/VMS system to survive power fluctuations and power outages of short duration with no loss of operation. The support is provided by hardware features (battery backup) and VAX/VMS software routines.

VAX/VMS support includes a power failure service routine that saves the volatile state of the machine when the power fails, a restart routine that restores that state when the power is restored, CPU-specific initialization code, and device-specific code within many VAX/VMS device drivers. VAX/VMS also provides process notification by means of power recovery asynchronous system traps (ASTs).

26.1 POWERFAIL SEQUENCE

When a drop in operating voltage occurs, the CPU hardware requests a powerfail interrupt at IPL 30. This interrupt is dispatched through the vector at offset 12 in the system control block (SCB). The VMS powerfail interrupt service routine is EXE$POWERFAIL, in module POWERFAIL. That powerfail is an interrupt means its grant can be blocked by code executing at IPL 30 or 31. A number of routines in VMS do this deliberately for a short sequence of instructions to avoid potential synchronization problems.

EXE$POWERFAIL saves the volatile machine state (those registers whose contents are not preserved by some sort of battery backup) in main memory (which is preserved by battery backup). EXE$POWERFAIL itself saves registers common to all types of VAX processor. To save CPU-specific registers, it invokes the routine EXE$REGSAVE, in module [SYSLOA]ERRSUBxxx, part of the CPU-specific image SYSLOAxxx (see Appendix G). The registers are saved either on the interrupt stack or in the restart parameter block (RPB). The interrupt stack pointer (ISP) is the last value saved. Checking the value of the saved ISP, the restart routine can determine whether the interrupt service routine preserved all the required registers.

Once the registers have been saved, EXE$POWERFAIL waits in the following tight loop until the CPU ceases all operations:

```
10$: BRB     10$
```

Table 26-1   Data Saved by EXE$POWERFAIL and Restored during Power Recovery

The elements in Group A are restored before memory management is reenabled. The RPB is accessed through its physical address.

GROUP A

Element	Where Stored
System base register	RPB
System length register	RPB
System control block base register	RPB

The elements in Group B are restored after memory management has been reenabled, which allows the RPB and interrupt stack to be accessed through system virtual addresses.

GROUP B

Element	Where Stored
Interrupt stack pointer	RPB
Process control block base register	RPB
Software interrupt summary register	RPB
P1 length register	Interrupt stack
P1 base register	Interrupt stack
P0 length register	Interrupt stack
P0 base register	Interrupt stack
AST level register	Interrupt stack
Four per-process stack pointers	Interrupt stack
CPU-specific processor registers (see Table 26.2)	Interrupt stack

The elements in Group C are not restored until the other power recovery steps described in the text are performed and the powerfail interrupt is dismissed. The PC/PSL pair are restored by the REI instruction that dismisses the interrupt.

GROUP C

Element	Where Stored
General registers (R0 through FP)	Interrupt stack
Interrupt PC and PSL	Interrupt stack

The BRB instruction was chosen over an explicit HALT to avoid triggering a restart before the CPU stops.

Tables 26-1 and 26-2 list the registers preserved by EXE$POWERFAIL and restored at powerfail recovery.

26.2   POWER RECOVERY

The console subsystem power recovery logic performs various validity checks in a CPU-dependent fashion and then passes control to the VMS re-

Table 26-2   CPU-Specific Registers Saved at Powerfail

Register[1]	CPU
Performance monitor enable register	VAX-11/730
Performance monitor enable register	VAX-11/750
Translation buffer disable register	VAX-11/750
Memory cache disable register	VAX-11/750
None	MicroVAX I
None	MicroVAX II
Performance monitor enable register	VAX-11/78x
SBI maintenance register	VAX-11/78x
Performance monitor enable register	VAX 8200 family
Translation buffer disable register	VAX 8200 family
Memory cache disable register	VAX 8200 family
Performance monitor enable register	VAX 86x0
Cache state register	VAX 86x0
Fbox state register	VAX 86x0
Performance monitor enable register	VAX 8800 family
Cache on register	VAX 8800 family

[1]These CPU-specific processor registers are saved on and restored from the interrupt stack.

start routine. This routine restores the saved state of the machine and then notifies each device driver in the system that power has failed, so that the drivers can take device-specific action to restore interrupted I/O requests.

26.2.1   Initial Step in Power Recovery

The initial step in recovery from a power failure is performed by the CPU-specific console subsystem. It performs the following tasks:

1. Initializes the CPU
2. Verifies that the contents of memory survived the power outage
3. Locates the restart routine through the RPB
4. Passes control to that routine

The RPB is a page aligned page of physical memory whose first four longwords contain the physical address of the RPB, physical address of the restart routine, checksum of the first 31 longwords in the restart routine, and a warm restart inhibit flag. On most systems, the RPB is located at physical address 0. If the first 64K-byte block of physical memory contains any bad pages, the RPB is at a higher address. (The RPB in the VAX-11/782 must be at address 0.)

When searching for the RPB, the console subsystem looks for a longword on a page boundary that contains its own address. The console subsystem examines the second longword to determine that it contains a valid physical address (and not zero, in case a page of zeros passes the first test). If the address is acceptable, the checksum of the first 31 words of the restart routine is calculated. The checksum is then compared to the checksum in the RPB. If the two checksums are equal, the page contains an RPB and the restart routine is intact.

The subsections that follow contain further information about power recovery on each VAX processor. Many VAX processors have two control panel switches whose settings affect powerfail recovery: a console enable switch and a restart action switch. The console enable switch can allow or inhibit command entry on the local console terminal. The descriptions that follow assume that the local console terminal is enabled and that console commands can be entered at it.

26.2.1.1   **Power Recovery on the VAX-11/730.** When power is restored on a VAX-11/730, the console subsystem tests whether the AUTO RESTART/BOOT switch on the front of the processor cabinet is in the OFF position. If it is, the console subsystem simply prompts on the console terminal and waits for input. (Note that the AUTO RESTART/BOOT switch on the front panel should be switched off when first turning on a VAX-11/730 system to avoid an unnecessary restart attempt.)

If the AUTO RESTART/BOOT switch is in the ON position, the console subsystem searches through physical memory for a valid RPB. In searching for the RPB, it tests whether the contents of memory survived the power outage. Memory contents can fail to be backed up for two different reasons:

- Because the system does not have battery backup, the contents of memory are lost when the power fails.
- Because the power is off for longer than the battery backup could preserve memory contents, the contents of memory are lost when the battery backup fails. (This time depends on the amount of memory present but is generally not shorter than ten minutes.)

If the RPB is not located, the restart fails and the console subsystem attempts to bootstrap the system by executing the command file DEFBOO.CMD.

If the RPB is located, the warm restart inhibit flag (bit <0> in the fourth longword of the RPB) is checked. The bit set indicates that a warm restart has already been attempted and has failed. In that case, the console subsystem then executes the command file DEFBOO.CMD to bootstrap the system.

If the warm restart inhibit flag is clear, the console subsystem performs the following steps:

1. Sets the warm restart inhibit flag to prevent a second restart attempt before the first has succeeded
2. Loads SP with the address of the RPB plus 200_{16}
3. Loads AP with a value indicating the cause of the halt
4. Loads R10 and R11 with the PC and PSL at the time of the halt for use in servicing error halt conditions other than powerfail
5. Transfers control to the restart routine whose address is in the second longword of the RPB

26.2.1.2 **Power Recovery on the VAX-11/750.** When power is restored on a VAX-11/750, the console subsystem tests the setting of the POWER-ON ACTION switch on the front of the processor cabinet. If the switch is in either the HALT or BOOT position, the console subsystem performs the designated action. If the switch is in either the RESTART/BOOT or RESTART/HALT position, the console subsystem attempts a restart. The second option (BOOT or HALT) is used only if the restart fails.

For a restart, the console subsystem first tries to locate the RPB. In searching for the RPB, it tests whether the contents of memory survived the power outage.

If a valid RPB cannot be located or if the warm restart inhibit flag is set, the restart attempt has failed and the console subsystem takes its alternative option. For the BOOT alternative, the console subsystem executes bootstrap read-only memory (ROM) code for unit 0 of the device identified by the device switch on the cabinet. The ROM code reads the boot block, block 0, from that device and then transfers control to it. (See Chapter 24 for more information.)

If a valid RPB is located, the console subsystem transfers control to the restart routine as described in Section 26.2.1.1.

26.2.1.3 **Power Recovery on the VAX-11/780 and VAX-11/785.** When power is restored on the VAX-11/780 or VAX-11/785, the console subsystem (LSI-11) performs the same sequence that it does when a system is being initialized (see Chapter 24). If power is also being restored on the LSI-11, CONSOL.SYS is loaded from the console floppy. No state for the LSI-11 is preserved across a power failure.

The console subsystem then tests the AUTO RESTART switch on the front of the processor cabinet. If it is in the OFF position or if the warm start inhibit flag maintained by the console subsystem is set, the console subsystem simply prompts on the console terminal and waits for input.

If the AUTO RESTART switch is in the ON position and the warm start inhibit flag is clear, the console subsystem executes the command file RESTAR.CMD. Before it executes RESTAR.CMD, it reloads the CPU microcode writable control store (WCS) contents from the console floppy (from file WCS*xxx*.PAT). WCS is not preserved by memory battery backup.

The standard RESTAR.CMD command file contains commands designed to restart a running VMS system. RESTAR.CMD generally contains the following lines:

```
HALT                          ! Halt processor
INIT                          ! Initialize processor
DEPOSIT/I 11 20003800         ! Set address of SCB base
DEPOSIT R0 0                  ! Clear unused register
DEPOSIT R1 3                  ! TR number for UNIBUS adapter
DEPOSIT R2 0                  ! Clear unused register
DEPOSIT R3 0                  ! Clear unused register
DEPOSIT R4 0                  ! Clear unused register
DEPOSIT R5 0                  ! Clear unused register
DEPOSIT FP 0                  ! No machine check expected
START 20003004                ! Start restart referee
```

On systems with more than two memory controllers, the UNIBUS adapter (UBA) is not located at TR 3. For such a system, RESTAR.CMD must be altered so that R1 is loaded with the TR number of the UBA. This step is necessary because the UBA map registers are used by ROM restart code as temporary storage. Note that RESTAR.CMD is different on the VAX-11/782 multiprocessing system; RESTAR.CMD for the VAX-11/782 is described in Chapter 27.

The START command passes control to the same ROM program that is used during system initialization, except that the program is entered at its restart entry point. The ROM program determines whether the contents of main memory are valid. If they are, the ROM program attempts to locate the RPB.

If a valid RPB cannot be found or if the warm restart flag inhibit in the RPB is set, the ROM program sends a reboot (cold start) command to the console subsystem by executing the following instruction:

```
MTPR    #^XF02,#PR$_TXDB
```

(The special uses of the PR$_TXDB register for communication from the VAX CPU to the console program are described in Chapter 19.)

If a valid RPB is found, the ROM program passes control to the restart routine as described in Section 26.2.1.1.

26.2.1.4   **Power Recovery on the MicroVAX I.** The MicroVAX I has no battery backup for its memory. Therefore, when the power recovers, it is not possible to resume normal system operation. When power is restored on a MicroVAX I, the console microcode tests the setting of two option switches (dual-in-line package, or DIP, switches 3 and 4 on the datapath module of the CPU). These two recovery action switches specify the actions that the processor attempts following power recovery or a halt condition.

The four possibilities are as follows:

- Both off—Warm start, boot, halt
- Switch 4 off, 3 on—Boot, halt
- Switch 4 on, 3 off—Warm start, halt
- Both on—Halt

The default setting is the first one, with both switches off. This means that after a power recovery or halt condition, the console microcode first tries to restart. The next activity, boot, is attempted only if the restart fails. If the boot attempt fails, the console microcode halts the processor and prompts on the console terminal.

For a restart, the console microcode first tries to locate the RPB. If a valid RPB is located, the console subsystem transfers control to the restart routine as described in Section 26.2.1.1. Because there is no battery backup, the console is not likely to find a valid RPB except after an error halt.

26.2.1.5   **Power Recovery on the MicroVAX II.** The MicroVAX II has no battery backup for its memory. Therefore, when the power recovers, it is not possible to resume normal system operation. When power is restored on a MicroVAX II, the console program tests the setting of the halt enable switch. The halt enable switch is on the CPU patch panel insert, mounted inside the rear of the CPU cabinet.

It has two positions to specify the actions the processor attempts following power recovery or a halt condition. If the switch is down, as it is by default, halts are "disabled." Otherwise, they are enabled. Following power recovery, the console tests the halt enable switch. If halts are enabled, the console performs a diagnostic self-test and halts the processor. Otherwise, after the self-test, it reboots the processor. If the boot attempt fails, the console halts the processor.

Following an error halt, the console tests the halt enable switch and halt action bits in a register called the console program mailbox (CPMBX). VMS does not set the bits (except when it initiates a reboot directly), so the bits remain at their initialized value of zero. If halts are enabled, the console halts the processor. Otherwise, it tests and sets the CPMBX restart-in-progress flag. If the flag was already set, the restart fails. If the flag was clear, the console tries a warm restart, followed by a boot; if both fail, it halts the processor.

For a restart, the console first tries to locate the RPB. If a valid RPB is located, the console subsystem transfers control to the restart routine as described in Section 26.2.1.1.

26.2.1.6   **Power Recovery on the VAX 8200 Family.** When power is restored on a VAX 8200 family member, the console subsystem tests the settings of the upper and lower key switches on the front of the processor cabinet. If the upper switch is in either the Enable or Secure position and the lower switch is in the Auto Start position, the console subsystem attempts a restart.

The console microcode tests and sets its restart-in-progress switch. It also tests its bootstrap-in-progress switch. If either flag is already set, the restart attempt is aborted. If the bootstrap-in-progress switch is clear, the console subsystem initiates a boot; otherwise, it halts. (See Chapter 24 for more information.) The console subsystem next tries to locate the RPB. In searching for the RPB, it tests whether the contents of memory survived the power outage.

If a valid RPB cannot be located or if the RPB warm restart inhibit flag is set, the restart attempt has failed and the console subsystem initiates a boot. If a valid RPB is located, the console subsystem transfers control to the restart routine as described in Section 26.2.1.1.

26.2.1.7 **Power Recovery on the VAX 8600 and VAX 8650.** When power is restored to the console microprocessor of a VAX 86x0, the console microprocessor initializes itself and the VAX CPU as described in Chapter 24.

In the case of a warm restart, the console program tests the Restart Control switch, which has four positions:

> BOOT
> HALT
> RESTART/BOOT
> RESTART/HALT

If the switch is in the BOOT position, the console program invokes the DEF-BOO.COM command procedure. If it is in the HALT position, the console program halts.

If it is in one of the two RESTART positions, the console program confirms that the battery backup unit was still operational when the power was restored. It tests its warm-start-in-progress flag. A set flag indicates a previously unsuccessful attempt at warm start. If the flag is clear, the console commands the VAX 86x0 console support microcode to locate the RPB.

If the RPB is located, the console program sets the warm-start-in-progress flag and transfers control to the restart routine as described in Section 26.2.1.1.

If restart cannot be attempted and the Restart Control switch is in the RESTART/BOOT position, the console program invokes the DEFBOO.COM command procedure. If the switch is in the RESTART/HALT position, the console program halts the processor.

26.2.1.8 **Power Recovery on the VAX 8800 Family.** When power is restored to the console microprocessor of a VAX 8800 family member, P/OS boots and runs the console program. The console program restores its own state, which had been saved in a log file. It determines whether the power failure included the VAX CPU. If it did, the console program begins the execution of SYSINIT.COM, described in Chapter 24. SYSINIT.COM tests the software keyswitch AUTO_RESTART. If it is set, SYSINIT.COM invokes the command procedure RESTAR.COM. If it is not set but AUTO_BOOT is, SYSINIT.COM invokes DEFBOO.COM.

After an error halt, the console program executes the command procedure RESTAR.COM.

RESTAR.COM tests the state of the AUTO_RESTART switch. If it is set, the command procedure deposits the halt code, PC, and PSL into AP, R10, and R11, initializes the CPU, clears R0 through R5, and searches for an RPB. If a valid RPB is located, RESTAR.COM transfers control to the restart routine as described in Section 26.2.1.1.

If AUTO_RESTART is disabled or if a valid RPB is not found, then RESTAR.COM tests the setting of AUTO_BOOT. If it is enabled, the procedure DEFBOO.COM is executed.

26.2.2   Operations of the Restart Routine

The VMS restart routine, EXE$RESTART in module POWERFAIL, receives control with the following environment:

- In kernel mode
- On the boot-time interrupt stack (SP = RPB base plus 200_{16})
- With memory management disabled
- At IPL 31

These initial conditions are similar to the entry to VMB, except that the RPB has already been initialized. One more similarity between the entry to EXE$RESTART and VMB is the contents of the SP register. This value serves two purposes. First, the SP specifies the location of the RPB. Second, the last several longwords in the page containing the RPB are used as stack space by EXE$RESTART until the saved interrupt stack pointer is restored.

EXE$RESTART first restores information saved in the RPB by EXE$POWERFAIL (see Table 26-1, Group A). Most of this information is necessary to turn memory management back on. A dummy P0 page table is set up (just like the one set up by SYSBOOT) so that the page containing the restart routine is mapped as a P0 virtual address that, when translated, yields the identical physical address. Chapter 25 shows how the contents of P0BR are determined to produce this identity mapping.

After the P0 page table is set up, memory management is enabled using the same two instructions used by EXE$INIT:

```
        MTPR    #1,#PR$_MAPEN
        JMP     @#10$
10$:
```

(This technique is described at the beginning of Chapter 25.)

Once memory management has been enabled, EXE$RESTART checks whether the restart was initiated as a part of powerfail recovery or in response to some other error halt condition detected by the console subsystem.

If the restart did not result from powerfail recovery, EXE$RESTART signals a reason-specific fatal bugcheck. This will result in a cold start, a bootstrap, if the SYSBOOT flag BUGREBOOT is set. By causing a crash, EXE$RESTART preserves information about the error condition in the crash dump file. One example of such an error halt is invalid interrupt stack. The CPU microcode causes this halt if the interrupt stack pointer points to a page which is not valid or to which kernel mode does not have write access when an interrupt or exception must be serviced.

If this is a power recovery, EXE$RESTART clears two warm start inhibit flags, the use of which is discussed in Section 26.3.2.

Before copying the saved value of the interrupt stack pointer to the SP register, EXE$RESTART tests it. If the value is zero, the ISP was not saved by EXE$POWERFAIL, and EXE$RESTART signals the fatal bugcheck STATENTSVD, software state not saved during powerfail.

EXE$RESTART restores the registers listed in Table 26-1, Group B. EXE$RESTART does not use the SP register to restore this data from the stack. Instead, it uses a scratch register (R6) to traverse the stack. Because the SP register is left pointing to the end of the saved information, the data on the stack will not be overwritten if another power failure occurs while the data is being restored. Using a scratch register allows the restart routine to be repeated as many times as necessary without special action.

EXE$POWERFAIL invokes the routine EXE$REGRESTOR, in module [SYSLOA]ERRSUBxxx, part of the CPU-specific image SYSLOAxxx (see Appendix G). After everything except the general registers has been restored, EXE$RESTART takes the following steps:

1. It initializes processor registers by invoking the CPU-specific routine EXE$INIPROCREG, in module [SYSLOA]ERRSUBxxx.
2. It reads the battery backed up time-of-year clock by invoking the CPU-specific routine EXE$READ_TODR, also in [SYSLOA]ERRSUBxxx.
3. The restart time plus three minutes is computed and stored at the global location EXE$GL_PWRDONE. This value represents the time it may take all hardware components to become fully operational again. Device drivers can use the routine EXE$PWRTIMCHK (in module POWERFAIL) to make sure that these three minutes have passed before restarting I/O operations. It may take as long as three minutes for devices such as disks to become operational.
4. It computes the duration of the powerfail and stores the result in global location EXE$GL_PFATIM.

5. It corrects the system time, at global location EXE$GQ_SYSTIME, by adding to it the duration of the powerfail.

6. It scans the timer queue for timer queue elements that have expired. It changes absolute due time in each TQE it finds to the corrected system time. This substitution is done to allow periodic timer requests to reestablish internal synchronization.

   For example, suppose that a periodic timer request is declared with a period of one minute and the power is off for three minutes. With no adjustment of the absolute due time, the request would expire immediately three times following power recovery. The readjustment causes one request to come due immediately, with the next request not occurring until one minute later.

   Note that relative synchronization between several requests may be lost as a result of a power failure. For example, if one request is due to expire in two minutes, a second is due to expire in five minutes (or three minutes after the first), and the power is off for more than five minutes, then both requests will be delivered at the same time. A power recovery AST might be used to allow multiple requests to reestablish their relative synchronization.

7. A power recovery entry is made in the error log.

8. EXE$RESTART invokes CNX$POWER_FAIL. If the system is a member of a VAXcluster System, this notifies the connection manager of power recovery.

9. EXE$RESTART initializes external adapters by invoking the CPU-specific routine EXE$STARTUPADP in [SYSLOA]ERRSUBxxx.

10. All external devices are notified that a power failure and recovery sequence have occurred. This step is detailed in Section 26.2.3.

11. EXE$RESTART lowers IPL to 29 to allow any pending powerfail interrupt to occur (see Section 26.3.1) and then raises it back to IPL 31.

12. It modifies the SP to point to the saved general registers on the interrupt stack and restores them.

13. The last sanity check flag, EXE$GL_PFAILTIM, is cleared (see Section 26.3.1).

14. RPB$L_ISP is cleared (so that EXE$RESTART will find it zero if the state is incompletely saved in a subsequent power failure).

15. EXE$RESTART dismisses the powerfail interrupt by executing an REI instruction.

26.2.3   Device Notification

EXE$RESTART invokes the routine EXE$INIT_DEVICE, also in module POWERFAIL, to initialize devices and device drivers after a powerfail recovery.

While IPL is still at 31 to block all interrupts, EXE$INIT_DEVICE scans the I/O database. It sets the powerfail bit, UCB$V_POWER, in the status word of each unit control block (UCB) it finds (except mailbox UCBs).

For each controller it finds, EXE$INIT_DEVICE invokes the controller initialization routine. If that routine returns successfully, EXE$INIT_DEVICE invokes the unit initialization routine for each unit of that controller. The powerfail bit enables these initialization routines to differentiate between power recovery and ordinary initialization.

EXE$INIT_DEVICE checks each unit to see whether its driver fork process is expecting an interrupt or has I/O being timed. If either is true, EXE$INIT_DEVICE clears its interrupt-expected bit, sets its timeout-expected bit, and sets its due time to zero. These actions cause each such device to time out. Later, when the driver's timeout routine runs, it can differentiate between ordinary timeout and power failure by checking the powerfail bit.

The check for device timeout occurs within EXE$TIMEOUT, the system subroutine that executes once a second (see Chapter 11). EXE$TIMEOUT cannot execute until later, after both of the following occur:

1. The interval clock interrupts (which means that IPL has dropped below 22 or 24, depending on CPU type).
2. The software timer interrupt service routine executes. (This will not happen until IPL is lowered below 7.)

In VMS, most of the work done to recover from a power failure occurs in drivers. VMS disk drivers and magnetic tape drivers are capable of restarting whatever request they were processing when the power failed in such a way that the power failure is totally transparent to them. (If a magnetic tape unit lost vacuum, operator intervention is required to reestablish the vacuum and rewind the tape. Once that is done, the driver automatically restarts the I/O request that was in progress when the power failed.)

26.2.4 Process Notification

VMS can notify a process of powerfail recovery by queuing an AST to it. A process requests this notification by calling the Set Power Recovery AST ($SETPRA) system service.

26.2.4.1 Set Power Recovery AST System Service.

The $SETPRA system service procedure, EXE$SETPRA in module SYSSETPRA, runs in kernel mode. It performs two steps:

1. Stores the address of the AST in global location CTL$GL_POWERAST

and the access mode in which the AST is to be delivered in location CTL$GB_PWRMODE

2. Sets the power AST flag (PCB$V_PWRAST) in the process control block (PCB) status longword

The effect of this system service is disabled at image rundown (see Chapter 21).

26.2.4.2   **Delivery of Power Recovery ASTs.** The delivery of a power recovery AST occurs in several distinct steps:

1. EXE$RESTART stores the duration of the power failure in location EXE$GL_PFATIM. (This value is simply the current contents of the time-of-year clock minus EXE$GL_PFAILTIM, the time at which the power failed.) Nonzero contents in this location act as a trigger to the swapper the next time that it runs.

   Note that no special action is taken at this point to wake up the swapper. In fact, because this routine is running at IPL 31, the swapper scheduling state could not be changed without potential synchronization problems.

2. The swapper's main loop (see Chapter 17) calls routine EXE$POWERAST (in module SYSSETRPA) if location EXE$GL_PFATIM contains a nonzero value.

3. EXE$POWERAST scans the PCB vector and queues a special kernel mode AST to each process that has the PCB$V_PWRAST flag set. That flag is cleared to prevent multiple ASTs in case another powerfail occurs before the process executes. A special kernel mode AST is required because the address and access mode of the recovery AST are stored in the P1 space of the requesting process.

4. The special kernel mode AST copies the address and access mode from their P1 space locations into the AST control block and queues the recovery AST to the requesting process.

5. Finally, the recovery AST itself is delivered to the requesting process. The AST parameter is the duration of the power failure in ten-millisecond units.

To receive notification of a subsequent powerfail recovery, a process must "rearm" the AST by calling the $SETPRA system service again.

26.3   **MULTIPLE POWER FAILURES**

Hardware and software flags exist in combination to prevent infinite looping or related problems in response to a power failure that occurs while either the powerfail service routine or the restart routine is executing.

26.3.1   **Nested Powerfail Interrupts**

Caution is necessary where power failure is concerned. Fluctuating voltages can cause the power repeatedly to fail and be restored. VMS must provide for the possibility of a second powerfail interrupt before an earlier one is dismissed.

The powerfail interrupt code is guaranteed only a brief interval between the powerfail interrupt request and the total loss of power. If the powerfail interrupt is blocked while the CPU is running at IPL 30 or 31, EXE$POWERFAIL will have that much less time to save the volatile machine state.

A second powerfail interrupt can be blocked for a considerable time while EXE$RESTART restores state from a previous interrupt. If the second interrupt were not granted until EXE$RESTART completed restoration and dismissed the first powerfail interrupt, there could be insufficient time to save the machine state.

VMS uses a combination of three things to defend against nested powerfail interrupts:

• EXE$GL_PFAILTIM
• Preserving the machine state saved on the stack
• Temporarily lowering IPL in EXE$RESTART

One of the first steps EXE$POWERFAIL takes is to save the contents of the time-of-year clock in location EXE$GL_PFAILTIM. This location retains nonzero contents until just before EXE$RESTART executes its REI instruction, dismissing the powerfail interrupt. If a powerfail interrupt occurs while this location contains a nonzero value (indicating that another failure/recovery is already in progress), EXE$POWERFAIL does not save the machine state.

Volatile machine state has already been saved as a result of the first powerfail interrupt. That state will be restored eventually by EXE$RESTART. Any state saved at the time of the second interrrupt would merely reflect the interruption of EXE$RESTART's attempts to restore state after the first interrupt. This check prevents nested powerfail interrupts on a system experiencing some obscure behavior that would otherwise be extremely difficult to diagnose.

One more bit of caution is evident in the manner in which EXE$RESTART restores data from the interrupt stack. A scratch register is used to traverse the stack, rather than the SP register. If another powerfail interrupt were to occur while data was being restored, its saved PC and PSL would not overlay the previously saved data.

When EXE$RESTART is nearly done but EXE$GL_PFAILTIM is still nonzero and SP is still intact, it deliberately lowers IPL to 29 to allow any pending powerfail interrupt to be granted. If one is pending and granted,

EXE$POWERFAIL sees that EXE$GL_PFAILTIM is nonzero and saves no state. It branches to self, awaiting the power failure. When the power recovers and EXE$RESTART is reentered, it again restores machine state from the RPB and the state saved on the stack.

If there is no pending powerfail interrupt, EXE$RESTART raises IPL back to 31, clears EXE$GL_PFAILTIM and RPB$L_ISP, and resets the SP register to reflect the removal of all saved machine state. It then executes an REI instruction to dismiss the interrupt.

26.3.2 Prevention of Infinite Restart Loop

There are two flags whose purpose is to prevent an infinite restart loop like the following loop:

1. An error halt condition occurs.
2. The console subsystem locates the RPB and transfers control to EXE$RESTART.
3. Prior to restoring or crashing the system, EXE$RESTART incurs an error halt condition.
4. The console subsystem locates the RPB and transfers control to EXE$RESTART.
5. EXE$RESTART incurs the same error halt condition . . .

The first flag is located in the RPB. During system initialization, EXE$INIT clears it after there is enough of VMS to restart.

The flag is tested and set by the console subsystem during restart after it has found a valid RPB. If it locates an otherwise valid RPB with this flag set, it aborts the restart attempt. Either the RPB is in error or an earlier restart attempt has incurred an error halt.

A second flag, maintained by the console subsystem on some types of VAX CPU, functions in a similar manner. It is set by the console at the beginning of the restart. EXE$RESTART initiates the clearing of it by sending a command to the console subsystem. On some CPUs, the following instruction sends the command:

```
MTPR    #^XF03,#PR$_TXDB
```

If the console subsystem detects that this flag is set while attempting a restart, it aborts the restart and takes the same processor-specific action it would if the RPB flag were set.

26.3.3 Device Driver Action

Drivers do not have to concern themselves directly with the multiple restart problem. Even though the bulk of driver recovery is done in response to an

IPL 7 software interrupt when a second power failure is possible, drivers are protected by one of the following situations:

- The driver controller and unit initialization routines are called at IPL 31 before EXE$GL_PFAILTIM is cleared. Drivers are protected here by the same sanity checks that VMS uses for itself.
- If the driver does not get called at its timeout entry point before the power fails again, the preserved driver state indicates a unit that has already timed out. When power is finally restored permanently, the driver will be called at its timeout entry point.
- If the driver is in the middle of its timeout routine, it still appears to the system as a unit that has timed out. It will be called at its timeout entry point again when the machine finally stabilizes.
- The driver may succeed in returning control to the operating system with, for example, one of the following calls:

```
WFIxxCH
IOFORK
REQCOM
```

If the operating system has received control, the request has either been completed or the driver is back into a state (such as expecting an interrupt) where the power recovery logic will cause the driver to be called at its timeout entry point when the power is finally restored.

26.4 FAILURE OF EXTERNAL ADAPTER POWER

Certain adapters can experience a power failure independently of the processor. These adapters are as follows:

- UNIBUS adapter on a VAX-11/78x, VAX 86x0
- Second UNIBUS interface on a VAX-11/750
- MASSBUS adapter on a VAX-11/78x, VAX 86x0
- CI780, CI750, and CIBCI port adapters

For these adapters, VMS provides service routines for the powerfail and subsequent recovery interrupts.

A key problem is that a reference to the registers or I/O space of a power-failed adapter causes a machine check. If the reference is made in kernel mode, for example, by a device driver trying to access device registers, the machine check would result in a fatal bugcheck. To prevent such machine checks, VMS remaps the system virtual address space reserved for the adapter to point to the "black hole" page. This page is a physical page of memory allocated at system initialization for this purpose. This mapping technique prevents subsequent machine checks or related errors from device drivers that reference a powerfailed adapter.

6.4.1   UNIBUS Power Failure

A UNIBUS failure on a VAX-11/780, VAX-11/782, VAX-11/785, VAX 8600, or VAX 8650 does not necessarily indicate that the entire system is in error. VMS allows UNIBUS errors, including UNIBUS power failure caused by turning off the power to the UBA or the BA-11K, to occur without crashing the entire system.

When such an error occurs, the UBA interrupts on behalf of itself. The interrupt service routine for the affected UBA detects that a UBA interrupt (as opposed to a UNIBUS device interrupt) has occurred and transfers control to an error routine that does the following:

- Checks that the interrupt is a result of the power failure of the UBA or UNIBUS
- Writes an error log entry
- Remaps the system virtual addresses that previously mapped the UBA itself and the UNIBUS I/O page (24 pages in all) so that these pages now point to the so-called black hole page reserved at initialization time
- Modifies the interrupt vector to point to a power-up routine

If the UNIBUS has gone away either because the power was turned off or for some other reason, devices that were waiting for I/O completion will time out. The program that issued the initial I/O request will receive an appropriate error notification, assuming that no driver is sitting in a tight loop at device IPL waiting for a status bit to change state.

When the power is restored, the system virtual pages are remapped to point to the UBA registers and UNIBUS I/O space. EXE$INIT_DEVICE is invoked to reinitialize all devices on the recovered UBA. Its actions in reinitializing devices are described in Section 26.2.3. If any devices were removed while the power was turned off, they will be marked offline as part of the power recovery operation. The interrupt vector is restored to its usual contents.

It is also possible for power to fail on the second UNIBUS interface (UBI) of a VAX-11/750 without failing on the entire system. VMS responds as it does on the systems previously described. The UBI interrupts to indicate powerfail through the vector at SCB offset $1E4_{16}$.

6.4.2   Support for Power Failure of Other Adapters

A MASSBUS adapter (MBA) power failure on a VAX-11/78*x* or VAX 86*x*0 does not necessarily indicate that power is being lost for the entire system. VMS services MBA powerfail on those processors as it does UBA powerfail. It maps the system virtual address space corresponding to the MBA registers to the black hole page. When the power is restored, the address space is mapped back to the MBA registers, the MBA is initialized, and EXE$INIT_DEVICE is invoked to reinitialize the devices on the adapter.

Certain computer interconnect (CI) adapters (CI780, CI750, and CIBCI) can also lose power independently of the rest of the system. The CI device driver, PADRIVER, maps the system virtual address space corresponding to the CI registers to the black hole page. When the power is restored, the driver remaps the address space, reloads the volatile CI microcode, and initializes the CI.

27 Asymmetric Multiprocessing

> The one is independent, and its essential nature is to be for
> itself; the other is dependent, and its essence is life or exis-
> tence for another. The former is the Master, or Lord, the latter
> the Bondsman.
>
> Hegel, *Phenomenology of Mind*

An asymmetric multiprocessing (ASMP) system contains two processors in a
tightly coupled configuration. The primary processor of an ASMP system
does computational work, performs memory management and I/O for the
system, and schedules work for itself and the attached processor. The attached processor does computational work and can perform any user, supervisor, or executive mode service.

The primary processor, however, must execute most kernel mode code
(system services and exception service routines) for user processes. An exception or interrupt that causes a change to kernel mode on the attached processor usually results in an interrupt to the primary processor. The primary
processor selects another process for the attached processor and schedules for
itself the process executing in kernel mode.

This chapter describes the internals of VAX/VMS asymmetric multiprocessing. It is assumed that readers are familiar with the concepts of multiprocessing and the multiprocessing configurations described in the *Guide to
Multiprocessing on VAX/VMS*.

27.1 ASMP DESIGN GOALS

VAX/VMS ASMP was originally designed to join two VAX-11/780 processors
into a tightly coupled, asymmetric multiprocessing system (the VAX-11/782)
to expand the processing power of the VAX-11/780. The system was targeted
for users with multistreamed, compute-intensive jobs.

There were several requirements for the multiprocessing system:

- It must use existing DIGITAL hardware with no changes.
- The same version of VAX/VMS must run on the VAX-11/782 and any other
  VAX processor. In addition, applications must run on all processors.
- Single processor systems must not be penalized by an increase in size of the
  executive.
- There must be no complex changes to existing kernel mode routines.

The last requirement is met by preventing the attached processor from executing most VMS kernel mode code. VMS runs in kernel mode when it modifies system data structures. Its chief means of synchronizing access to these data structures is raising IPL to block interrupts. Raising IPL on one processor does not synchronize two processors' accesses. Implementing multiprocessor synchronization requires complex changes to existing kernel mode routines. ASMP therefore ensures that nothing runs in kernel mode on the attached processor except ASMP code. (Chapter 2 describes the importance of synchronization in maintaining system databases and several methods of achieving it.)

To meet the rest of these requirements, the asymmetric multiprocessing code was designed as a separate component loaded into nonpaged pool when multiprocessing is turned on.

With VAX/VMS Version 4.4, asymmetric multiprocessing support has been extended to the VAX 8300 and VAX 8800 systems, in addition to the VAX-11/782. Each of the systems has its own version of the multiprocessing code with support for its hardware.

27.2 ASMP HARDWARE CONFIGURATIONS

VAX/VMS ASMP requires a hardware configuration of two CPUs of the same model type. Each processor can execute an instruction stream independently of the other. There must be an interprocessor interrupt mechanism that enables software running on one processor to interrupt the other.

The CPUs access common physical memory through the same physical addresses. The CPUs' memory caches are invalidated as needed by the hardware, without software involvement. The memory must be capable of interlocked access. That is, if one CPU accesses the memory with an interlocked instruction (for example, BBSSI), the memory must block any attempted interlocked access by the other CPU.

In addition, the CPUs must be at the same hardware and microcode revision level. If one has a floating-point accelerator or optional microcode, such as G and H floating-point support, both must have it. These requirements exist because a process running on one CPU can be context switched in the middle of an instruction and resumed on the other processor.

The following sections describe the systems on which ASMP is supported.

27.2.1 VAX-11/782

The VAX-11/782 system consists of two VAX-11/780 processors that use from two to four MA780 shared memory units as common memory. Both processors address a common pool of memory in the MA780 shared memory. The local memory on either processor is not used by VAX/VMS but is required for stand-alone diagnostics.

The MA780 shared memory was designed to support multiprocessing. It provides interprocessor interrupts and, optionally, multiprocessor selective cache invalidation. For performance reasons, MA780 selective cache invalidation is required on MA780s used in a VAX-11/782 system.

Although the two processors share a common physical memory, each CPU has its own memory cache of recently referenced physical addresses and their contents. If one processor writes to a location in the shared memory whose contents the other processor has cached, the second processor's cache must be invalidated. The MA780 provides for this by having the second processor's MA780 port adapter send its processor a cache invalidation message. However, use of this technique for every memory write on a VAX-11/782 system would result in more synchronous backplane interconnect (SBI) traffic than is desirable.

Instead, MA780 selective cache invalidation reduces overall SBI traffic. The hardware associates longwords in shared memory with the processor (or processors) using those locations. When one processor performs a write to a longword of shared memory, the other processor is sent a cache invalidation message only if its cache contains the location that was written. Execution of an interlocked instruction forces any pending cache invalidations to be completed before the instruction completes.

Figure 27-1 shows the hardware configuration of a VAX-11/782. The configuration shown in the figure uses two MA780 shared memory units. The configuration is asymmetric, unlike that of the VAX 8300 and VAX 8800. Except for one UNIBUS adapter, all I/O adapters are attached to the SBI of the primary processor. Although I/O devices can be physically connected to the

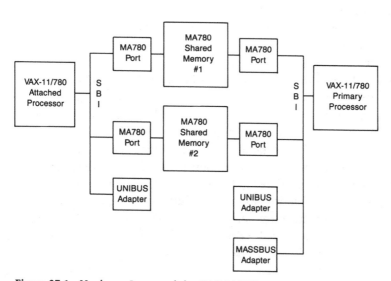

Figure 27-1 Hardware Layout of the VAX-11/782

attached processor, they are not recognized by VMS. One UNIBUS adapter is required on the attached processor for stand-alone diagnostic purposes.

27.2.2   VAX 8300

The VAX 8300 consists of two VAX 8200 processors on a common backplane interconnect, the VAXBI. The processor which is in the first physical VAXBI backplane slot is connected to the console. It is booted as the primary processor; the other one is the attached processor. The processors access common memory on the VAXBI. The VAXBI provides an interprocessor interrupt capability. Although both processors are physically capable of accessing any I/O adapters connected to the VAXBI, ASMP support requires that only the primary processor access I/O adapters and devices.

Any VAXBI node which implements a cache, such as a CPU, must monitor the VAXBI for writes to locations in its cache and invalidate them as required. Because both processors and the memory are on the same VAXBI, that mechanism is sufficient to maintain the validity of both processors' caches.

Figure 27-2 shows the hardware configuration of a VAX 8300. The configuration in the figure shows a VAX 8300 with two I/O adapters on the VAXBI, a VAXBI-to-UNIBUS adapter (DWBUA), and a VAXBI-to-CI adapter (BCI750).

27.2.3   VAX 8800

The VAX 8800 consists of two processors on a common backplane, the VAX 8800 memory interconnect (NMI). The processors access common memory on the NMI. The NMI provides an interprocessor interrupt capability. A processor is either the LEFT or the RIGHT processor, depending on its physical position in the CPU cabinet. A console command allows either processor to be selected as the primary processor. By default, the LEFT processor boots as the primary processor.

Both CPUs and the memory are on the NMI. Each CPU has its own cache of recently referenced locations and their contents. Logic in the cache monitors the bus for modifications to memory whose contents are cached. The cache invalidates itself whenever appropriate. This, however, is not sufficient to ensure the validity of the data in cache, since each processor's writes to memory locations are buffered temporarily in its cache. Execution of an interlocked instruction, however, forces the "write buffer" to be emptied, completing writes to memory. (Other instructions such as REI and SVPCTX also force emptying of the write buffer.) As the other processor's cache monitors the NMI, it sees the forced writes and invalidates itself as appropriate.

A VAX 8800 NMI-to-VAXBI adapter (NBIA) connects one or two VAXBI buses to the NMI. Although both processors are physically capable of accessing any I/O adapters connected to the NMI or VAXBIs, ASMP support requires that only the primary processor access I/O adapters and devices.

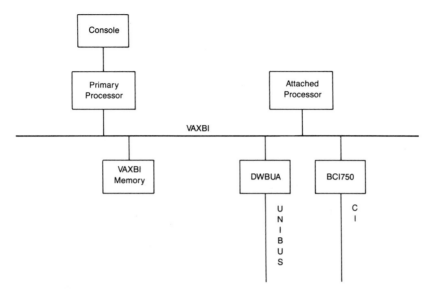

Figure 27-2   Hardware Layout of the VAX 8300

Figure 27-3 shows a possible VAX 8800 hardware configuration. The configuration in the figure shows a VAX 8800 with one NBIA/NBIB connecting one VAXBI bus.

ASMP SOFTWARE COMPONENTS

7.3

The following executable images, each with a corresponding symbol table, contain the ASMP code:

- MP.EXE and MP.STB for the VAX-11/782
- MP_8SS.EXE and MP_8SS.STB for the VAX 8300
- MP_8NN.EXE and MP_8NN.STB for the VAX 8800

Note that ASMP support for either the VAX 8300 or the VAX 8800 is an option licensed separately from VAX/VMS. The executable image for either of these systems is shipped as an encrypted file with VAX/VMS; obtaining the key requires purchase of the license. ASMP support for the VAX-11/782, however, is included in the VAX/VMS license.

To run ASMP on a VAX 8300 or a VAX 8800, the system manager defines the logical name MP to be equivalent to the appropriate image name. For example, the following command specifies support for a VAX 8800:

```
DEFINE/EXEC/SYSTEM MP MP_8NN
```

In response to the DCL multiprocessing commands SHOW CPU, START /CPU, and STOP/CPU, DCL activates the image MP in SYS$SYSTEM. If the

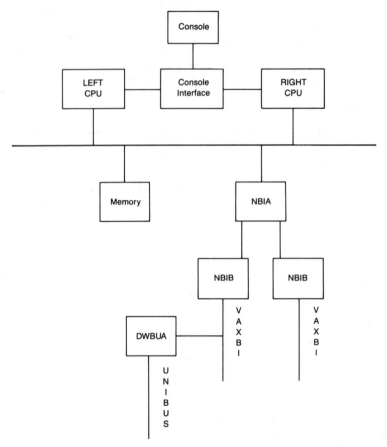

Figure 27-3 Hardware Layout of the VAX 8800

system manager has defined the logical name MP, then DCL activates the image whose name is equivalenced to MP.

Each ASMP image contains support for the DCL multiprocessing commands and the ASMP code that is loaded into nonpaged pool. The symbol tables define symbolic offsets in the ASMP code loaded into nonpaged pool.

The source modules for these images are part of the [MP] facility. Each image contains source modules in common with the others and source modules which are unique to it. The source modules which are hardware-specific have file names that end in _782, _8SS, or _8NN, depending on the system type. For example, the module MPLOAD_782 contains the load code for a VAX-11/782. This chapter refers to the generic hardware-specific source module by using a file name that ends in _xxx, for example, MPLOAD_xxx.

27.3.1 Hooks in the Executive

For the nonpaged pool ASMP code to be included as part of the VMS executive, a number of symbols were added to the executive. These symbols indicate locations which must be patched dynamically to jump into ASMP code when multiprocessing is turned on. These symbols are termed ASMP hooks. The symbols used as multiprocessing hooks are contained in every copy of the VAX/VMS operating system; however, they are used only by the ASMP code.

Three types of hooks are used to link the multiprocessing code into the VMS executive. The following table shows the hooks and the changes they perform:

Symbol Format	Change to Code
MPH$*name*	The instruction indicated by the hook is replaced by a jump to multiprocessing code. This hook is used when the multiprocessing routine MPS$*name* performs the entire set of actions normally performed by the routine *xxx*$*name*.
MPH$*name*HK	The instruction indicated by the hook is replaced by a jump to multiprocessing code. This hook is used when only a few lines need to be changed by multiprocessing, or when supplemental action is necessary.
MPH$*name*CONT	Multiprocessing code returns to the normal flow of code at this point. No change is made to the instruction indicated by this hook.

All the instructions at MPH$*name*HK and MPH$*name* hooks are modified when multiprocessing is turned on. First, however, six bytes at each location are saved in a storage area in nonpaged pool so that they can be restored if multiprocessing is turned off. At each location an instruction is placed that transfers control to corresponding ASMP code. In most cases, the instruction is a JMP:

```
JMP     @#MPS$name
```

All entry points in the loaded multiprocessing code have names of the form MPS$*name*.

The following code fragments illustrate the use of the MPH$*name* hook in the routine SCH$QAST, in module ASTDEL. Because queuing ASTs is significantly different on an ASMP system, the entire routine is superseded by one within the ASMP code.

The following fragment shows the instruction at hook MPH$QAST before multiprocessing is turned on:

```
MPH$QAST::
SCH$QAST::
            MOVZWL   ACB$L_PID(R5),R0
```

After multiprocessing is turned on and the hook altered, the instruction is as follows:

```
MPH$QAST::
SCH$QAST::
        JMP     @#MPS$QAST
```

In such a case, the replacement multiprocessing routine exits by returning control to the modified routine's caller (with an RSB or RET instruction, as appropriate).

The following code fragment illustrates the use of the MPH$*name*HK and MPH$*name*CONT, in the routine SCH$ASTDEL. This hook is used to insert multiprocessing code into the routine, rather than to replace code.

```
            SETIPL  #IPL$_SYNCH
MPH$ASTDELHK::
            REMQUE  @PCB$L_ASTQFL(R4),R5
            BVS     QEMPTY
MPH$ASTDELCONT::
```

When multiprocessing is turned on, the instruction at MPH$ASTDELHK is replaced with a

```
JMP     @#MPS$ASTDELHK
```

The code at MPS$ASTDELHK returns by jumping to MPH$ASTDELCONT.

27.3.2   Hooks in the Primary Processor's SCB

Another form of hook is used to modify the software control block (SCB) of the primary processor. In this case, the contents of specific vectors in the SCB are replaced by the addresses of multiprocessing interrupt service routines. These routines are invoked by interrupts and return through the normal REI mechanism.

When the ASMP code is loaded, the primary processor's SCB is modified. The original contents of the modified vectors are saved so that they can be restored if ASMP is turned off. The IPL 5 software interrupt vector is modified to point to the multiprocessing rescheduling routine (see Section 27.6.1 for a description of its operation). Because this vector is used to awaken XDELTA on a single processor system, the XDELTA interrupt must be moved. The IPL 15 software interrupt vector, which is otherwise unused, is modified to dispatch to the XDELTA interrupt service routine.

These two changes to the software interrupt vectors occur on all ASMP systems. The other SCB changes, however, are specific to each hardware system.

When multiprocessing is enabled on a VAX-11/782, the interprocessor interrupt vector for the first MA780 is modified to point to a multiprocessing routine; the MA780 error interrupt vector remains unchanged. The interprocessor interrupt vectors for any additional MA780s point to unexpected interrupt error handlers. The vectors at IPLs 20 and 21 and IPLs 22 and 23 are loaded redundantly, because the IPL levels interrupted by the MA780 are jumper-selectable. The even-numbered IPLs are the interprocessor interrupts and the odd-numbered IPLs are the error interrupts. The MA780 vectors are located among the nexus interrupt vectors in the second half of the SCB. Their exact location depends on the nexus number(s) of the MA780(s).

For a VAX 8300 or VAX 8800 system, the SCB vector at offset 80_{16} is initialized to contain the address of the primary processor's interprocessor interrupt service routine.

27.4   ATTACHED PROCESSOR STATES

Within the loaded multiprocessing code, the location MPS$GL_STATE contains the state of the attached processor. There are six possible states: INITIALIZE, IDLE, BUSY, EXECUTE, DROP, and STOP.

Figure 27-4 shows the states for the attached processor and the possible transitions among the states. As shown in the figure, certain transitions can be caused only by the primary processor; others can be caused only by the attached processor. This protocol was designed to prevent possible synchronization problems.

When the ASMP code is loaded in response to the DCL command START /CPU, the attached processor is set to the INITIALIZE state. Once the attached processor has executed its initialization code, it changes its execution state to IDLE. The primary processor schedules work for the attached processor only when the attached processor is in the IDLE state.

If no suitable computable process exists, the state of the attached processor remains IDLE and the processor loops, waiting for its state to be set to BUSY by the primary processor.

The primary processor sets the state to BUSY when it schedules a process for the attached processor. The primary processor places the address of the process's PCB in MPS$GL_CURPCB. The attached processor detects the change to BUSY, loads its PR$_PCBB register with the physical address of the

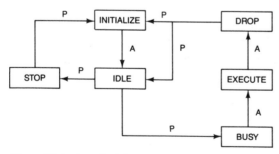

Figure 27-4   Attached Processor States

743

process hardware PCB, and executes a LDPCTX instruction to load the process. The attached processor then sets its state to EXECUTE and executes an REI instruction to place the process into execution. (See Chapter 10 for further information on the hardware PCB and the LDPCTX instruction.)

The BUSY and EXECUTE states must be unique so that special conditions, such as powerfail recovery, can be handled correctly. If a powerfail occurs on the attached processor when its state is BUSY, the processor simply halts. However, if its state is EXECUTE, the attached processor must save the context of its current process before halting.

When the attached processor can no longer execute its process, it saves the process's context, changes its state to DROP, and interrupts the primary processor. The primary processor places the process's PCB into the appropriate resident computable queue, sets the attached processor's state to IDLE, and tries to schedule another process for the attached processor.

Thus, the attached processor usually cycles through IDLE, BUSY, EXECUTE, and DROP. Section 27.6 describes ASMP scheduling in more detail.

The attached processor enters the STOP state at the primary's request when the DCL command STOP/CPU is issued or when the primary processor issues a bugcheck.

27.5   ASMP INITIALIZATION

The primary processor does most of the work of system initialization. It loads the executive into memory and performs all the tasks that are involved in bootstrapping a single processor system.

The sequence to boot VMS varies from system to system. In particular, CPU initialization and loading of the primary bootstrap program, VMB.EXE, differ on each CPU type. However, the steps from VMB through execution of startup command files are basically the same on all systems. After VMS is running as a single processor system, the DCL command START/CPU turns on multiprocessing.

Booting the attached processor differs on each of the three systems. However, once the attached processor is booted, its execution is very similar on all systems.

The following sections describe briefly the parts of each system boot relevant to ASMP and then the operations of the START/CPU and STOP/CPU commands. For additional details on system initialization, see Chapter 24.

27.5.1   System Initialization on the VAX-11/782

As part of the installation procedures used to install the VAX/VMS operating system on the VAX-11/782, two special console floppy diskettes are created: one for the primary processor and one for the attached processor. These floppy diskettes contain special command files used to bootstrap the processors of the multiprocessing system.

In response to a BOOT console command on the primary processor, its console selects one of the bootstrap command files on the console floppy and executes it on the primary processor. The command file clears error bits in the MA780 registers and defines the starting address for each MA780 memory. It initializes the CPU, initializes R0 to R5 as arguments to VMB, loads VMB at location 200_{16}, and starts execution of VMB. Because there is no bootstrap ROM in the MA780, the first 64K bytes in the first MA780 are assumed "good," free of uncorrectable errors. The command file sets the flag RPB$V_MPM in R5, causing VMB to ignore local memory and use only shared memory as main memory.

VMB builds the restart parameter block (RPB) at physical address 0. VMB configures only the shared memory in the bit map it builds to describe main memory. From this point on, initialization continues as it would on a single processor VAX-11/780 system (see Chapter 24). When the initialization is complete on the primary processor, VMS runs normally on the primary processor without multiprocessing, using MA780 memory rather than local memory.

In response to a BOOT console command on the attached processor, its console locates the command file DEFBOO.CMD on the console floppy and executes it on the attached processor. This command file clears error bits in the MA780 registers and defines the starting address for each MA780 memory. These addresses must be identical to those established by the primary processor; hence, the need for the new VAX-11/782-specific console floppies.

The command file initializes the CPU and starts execution at offset RPB$B_WAIT ($100_{16}$) in the RPB. Both processors share the same RPB. Until multiprocessing is turned on, offset RPB$B_WAIT contains a HALT instruction. For this reason, a START/CPU command must be issued on the primary processor before the attached processor can be booted. In response to a START/CPU command, ASMP is loaded and moves a JMP instruction to offset RPB$B_WAIT so that the attached processor jumps to its initialization code.

The instruction at RPB$B_WAIT resembles the following example:

```
RPB$L_BUGCHK:    .ADDRESS EXE$MPSTART
RPB$B_WAIT:      JMP      @RPB$L_BUGCHK
```

RPB$L_BUGCHK, another RPB offset, contains the physical address of EXE$MPSTART. See Section 27.5.4 for information on CPU-independent ASMP initialization.

When multiprocessing is turned off, the location RPB$L_BUGCHK is loaded with the address corresponding to RPB$B_WAIT. This turns the instruction into a jump to itself. If the attached processor is rebooted before multiprocessing is turned on again, the attached processor simply waits in this loop until the DCL command START/CPU is reissued.

27.5.2 System Initialization on the VAX 8300

A VAX 8300 has only one physical console terminal. By default, console commands are intended for the primary processor. CPU console microcode can pass commands and messages between the physical console and the "logical" console of the attached processor. Commands and messages can also be passed to and from the logical console of the attached processor through processor registers accessed with MTPR and MFPR instructions.

In response to a B[oot] console command, CPU console microcode performs the following actions:

1. It locates the first 64K bytes of physically contiguous good memory.
2. It does a node reset for all VAXBI nodes, initializing the primary processor and the attached processor.
3. It initializes R0 to R5 on the primary processor as register arguments for VMB to use.
4. It begins execution on the primary of bootstrap code loaded from an EEPROM in the CPU.

The bootstrap code reads the boot block from the system disk and transfers control to it. The boot block code, in turn, loads VMB at offset 200_{16} in the 64K bytes of memory and transfers control to it. Finally, VMB builds the RPB at offset 0 in the 64K bytes of memory. Initialization continues as it would on a single processor system, bringing up VMS on the primary processor.

After VMS is running, the DCL command START/CPU turns on multiprocessing and boots the attached processor. After ASMP is initialized and offsets RPB$B_WAIT and RPB$L_BUGCHK modified, the ASMP code writes commands to the logical console of the attached processor so that the attached processor begins execution at offset RPB$B_WAIT in the RPB. The initialization of the RPB by the primary processor is identical to that described in Section 27.5.1. See Section 27.5.4 for information on CPU-independent ASMP initialization.

27.5.3 System Initialization on the VAX 8800

A VAX 8800 console is called a VAXCONSOLE. The console subsystem has its own processor with a fixed disk and floppy diskettes. VMB.EXE and the console command procedures are on the fixed disk. Through the console subsystem, a user can issue commands to one or both CPUs.

In response to a BOOT console command, the console locates the command procedure DEFBOO.COM. DEFBOO.COM contains a BOOT command with a device specification. The console locates and executes the command procedure corresponding to the device specification, for example, BCIBOO.COM, to boot from a hierarchical storage controller (HSC) disk. Executing the command procedure, the console performs the following actions:

1. It initializes both CPUs and the NMI.
2. It locates the first 64K bytes of physically contiguous good memory.
3. On the CPU designated to be primary, the console initializes R0 to R5 as register arguments for VMB to use.
4. It loads VMB.EXE from the fixed disk into offset 200_{16} of the 64K bytes of memory.
5. It starts the primary processor executing at the beginning of VMB. VMB builds the RPB at offset 0 in the 64K bytes of memory.

After VMS is running, the DCL command START/CPU turns on multiprocessing and boots the attached processor. After ASMP is initialized and offsets RPB$B_WAIT and RPB$L_BUGCHK are modified, the ASMP code sends a command to the console to boot the attached processor. The console executes the command procedure SECBOO.COM, performing the following actions:

1. It halts the attached processor if it is not already halted.
2. It disables memory management on the attached processor.
3. It initializes the attached processor's PSL to indicate interrupt stack execution at IPL 31.
4. It locates the RPB initialized by the primary processor.
5. It starts the attached processor, executing at offset RPB$B_WAIT, which contains a jump to EXE$MPSTART.

The initialization of the RPB by the primary processor is identical to that described in Section 27.5.1. See the following section for information on CPU-independent ASMP initialization.

27.5.4 Turning On Multiprocessing

Multiprocessing is turned on in response to the DCL command START/CPU, which executes the MP image specified by the system manager. The command invokes routine MPS$LOAD in the hardware-specific module MP-LOAD_*xxx*.

MPS$LOAD performs the following actions:

1. It loads a portion of the MP image into approximately 24 pages of nonpaged pool. These pages contain the following:

   —Data areas used for communication between the two processors

—Replacement code for several VMS kernel mode routines

—All special code executed by the attached processor

—Space for the interrupt stack, SCB, and error log buffers of the attached processor

The global pointer EXE$GL_MP contains the address of the loaded code. The loaded code must begin on a page boundary because it contains data structures and code that must be page aligned. MPS$LOAD allocates enough pool that it can place the loaded code on a page boundary and deallocate any unused portion.

The loaded code is a dynamic nonpaged pool data structure with a standard header. Its first longword, which is usually a FLINK, instead contains the address of the pool allocated for ASMP. The contents of the first longword are used as the address of pool to deallocate when ASMP is unloaded. (This address differs from the contents of EXE$GL_MP only when the unused portion of pool is too small to deallocate at load time.) The second longword is the size of the pool in bytes. The third longword contains the size and type fields.

Symbolic offsets within the loaded code (for example, MPS$GL_STATE) are defined in the symbol table corresponding to the MP image.

2. The communication data areas are initialized, and the attached processor's state is set to INITIALIZE.

3. The current system time is recorded in MPS$GQ_MPSTRTIM as the start time for ASMP.

4. IPL is raised to 31 to block all interrupts, and the pages containing the VMS executive are made writable.

5. Locations within the executive that are multiprocessing hooks are modified so that control is transferred to ASMP code (see Section 27.3.1).

6. The primary processor's SCB is modified to handle multiprocessor scheduling and interprocessor interrupts (see Section 27.3.2).

7. The attached processor's SCB is initialized. Most of its vectors dispatch to interrupt and exception service routines within the loaded code. There are, however, three exceptions which are handled by the usual VMS service routines—CHMU, CHMS, and CHME. These change mode exceptions are serviced by the usual VMS service routines running on the attached processor. CHMU and CHMS exceptions are described in Chapter 4. Chapter 9 describes the CHME exception, which is the path to executive mode system services and RMS services.

8. MPS$LOAD stores the physical address of EXE$MPSTART into offset RPB$L_BUGCHK in the RPB. EXE$MPSTART is the attached processor's initialization and restart routine which is loaded as part of the multiprocessing code.

9. The pages containing the VMS executive that had been made writable are

now made read-only.

10. CPU-specific initialization is performed:

   —On a VAX-11/782, the MA780 port is initialized and its interprocessor and error interrupts are enabled.

   —On a VAX 8300, boot commands are sent to the logical console of the attached processor. Invoked by MPS$LOAD, MPS$MPINIT writes a processor register on the primary processor to send console commands, one character at a time. These commands make the attached processor halt, initialize itself, initialize its SP, and start execution at offset RPB$B_WAIT in the RPB.

   —On a VAX 8800, a miscellaneous console command called "boot other CPU" is sent to the console subsystem. In response, it executes a command procedure to boot the attached processor.

11. IPL is lowered to 0.

When the attached processor is started at offset RPB$B_WAIT, the JMP instruction transfers control to the initialization routine EXE$MPSTART, in MPINIT_*xxx*. EXE$MPSTART begins execution at IPL 31 with memory management turned off. Because memory management is disabled, EXE$MPSTART and all its data references must be contained in a single page of memory. This page of memory is referred to as the attached processor's "boot page." EXE$MPSTART is aligned on a page boundary within the pool allocated by MPS$LOAD.

1. EXE$MPSTART stores the contents of the system ID register and any additional CPU-specific hardware revision level information beginning at offset MPS$GB_CPUDATA, which is within the boot page.

2. It turns on memory management, using information in the RPB. A pointer to the RPB is stored in the boot page. Once memory management is turned on, EXE$MPSTART is no longer confined to the boot page.

3. It compares the hardware revision level information for the attached processor to that of the primary processor to ensure that they are at the same level. If any incompatibility is found, EXE$MPSTART outputs an error message to the attached processor's console.

4. It turns on the interval clock. The attached processor uses its own interval clock to do CPU-time accounting and quantum-end detection for its processes.

5. A cold start message is logged in the error log.

6. IPL is lowered to IPL$_SYNCH.

7. The attached processor's state is set to IDLE.

8. The primary processor is interrupted with a rescheduling request.

9. The attached processor loops, waiting for its state to be altered.

27.5.5 **Turning Off Multiprocessing**

The DCL command STOP/CPU turns off ASMP. This command invokes the routine MPS$UNLOAD, in module MPLOAD_*xxx*. MPS$UNLOAD, running on the primary processor, performs the following functions:

1. IPL is raised to IPL$_SYNCH.
2. MPS$UNLOAD interrupts the attached processor with a stop request and waits for the attached processor to acknowledge the stop request.

   If the attached processor is running a process, it saves the context of the current process and the primary processor adds the process to its scheduling queues.

   In response to the stop request, the attached processor loads a jump to self instruction into RPB$B_WAIT, acknowledges the stop request, and executes a HALT instruction.
3. After the attached processor acknowledges the stop request, MPS$UNLOAD sets the state of the attached processor to STOP.
4. MPS$UNLOAD changes the protection on the pages that contain the VMS executive to make them writable and raises IPL to 31 to block all interrupts.
5. Each location identified by multiprocessing hooks is replaced with its original contents.
6. MPS$UNLOAD restores the primary processor's SCB to its original condition, a single processor SCB.
7. The executive is made read-only.
8. MPS$UNLOAD clears the global pointer EXE$GL_MP.
9. It lowers IPL to 2 and deallocates the pages containing the multiprocessing code to nonpaged pool.
10. It lowers IPL to 0.

When MPS$UNLOAD completes execution, the primary processor runs as a single CPU, and the attached processor either remains halted or restarts, executing the jump to self instruction at RPB$B_WAIT until the DCL command START/CPU is issued.

27.5.5.1 **Timeout of the Attached Processor.** If, for some reason, the attached processor does not respond to an interrupt request for a translation buffer invalidation after a reasonable amount of time (in Version 4.4, three minutes), the primary assumes that the attached processor is no longer functioning. In this case, all the steps in turning off ASMP are executed, with the exception of deallocating the pages in nonpaged pool. The multiprocessing code in nonpaged pool is not deallocated in case the attached processor resumes execution.

If the attached processor times out while it is executing a process, that process is lost. There is no way to recover its context from the attached processor. The process remains visible in the system with a state of CURrent, but it cannot be examined or deleted. Any devices or system resources allocated by the lost process cannot be recovered for use without rebooting the system.

27.6   ASMP SCHEDULING

To simplify synchronization of the scheduler database, the primary processor schedules processes for execution on itself and on the attached processor. Scheduling a process for the attached processor takes precedence over scheduling one for the primary processor.

- The need to reschedule the attached processor is indicated by an IPL 5 interrupt.
- The need to reschedule the primary processor is indicated by an IPL 3 interrupt, as it is on a single processor system. If the attached processor is IDLE, the IPL 3 interrupt service routine schedules a process for the attached processor before scheduling one for the primary processor.

27.6.1   The IPL 5 Interrupt Service Routine

When the attached processor needs to be rescheduled, it interrupts the primary processor by requesting an interprocessor interrupt. The primary processor's interprocessor interrupt service routine requests an IPL 5 interrupt to reschedule the attached processor. The IPL 5 interrupt service routine, MPS$RESCHEDIPL5, running on the primary, selects a process to run on the attached processor.

MPS$RESCHEDIPL5 saves the low general registers and invokes the routine MPS$SCHSCND, which actually schedules the attached processor. (The attached processor is also known as the secondary processor; the routine name is an abbreviated form of the phrase "schedule the secondary.") Both routines are in module MPSCHED. MPS$SCHSCND is also invoked from the IPL 3 interrupt service routine when it detects that the attached processor is IDLE.

MPS$SCHSCND, running on the primary processor, performs the following actions:

1. It raises IPL to IPL$_SYNCH to synchronize access to the scheduler database.
2. If the attached processor's state is DROP, MPS$SCHSCND first tests the flag MPS$V_SECWAITCK in MPS$GL_SECREQFLG. The attached processor sets this flag if its process has invoked an event flag wait system service and the specified flags are clear. If MPS$V_SECWAITCK is set, the primary processor completes the event flag wait system service. (See Section 27.7.2 for further details.)

To remove a process from the attached processor, MPS$SCHSCND reads its PCB address from MPS$GL_CURPCB and places the process into the appropriate resident computable queue. It requests an IPL 3 interrupt and sets the attached processor's state to IDLE.

3. MPS$SCHSCND then searches the resident computable queues for a process suitable for execution on the attached processor. Section 27.6.3 lists the constraints placed on a process which runs on the attached processor.

4. If MPS$SCHSCND finds a suitable process, it sets the process state to CUR, stores its PCB address in MPS$GL_CURPCB, and sets the attached processor's state to BUSY. If no suitable process is available, the attached processor's state remains IDLE.

The attached processor loops until its state is set to BUSY. Then the attached processor executes LDPCTX and REI instructions to place the selected process into execution.

When MPS$SCHSCND returns, the IPL 5 interrupt service routine restores the saved registers and executes an REI instruction to dismiss the interrupt.

27.6.2 The IPL 3 Interrupt Service Routine

The IPL 3 interrupt service routine consists of two routines, MPS$RESCHED and MPS$SCHED, both in module MPSCHED. These routines replace SCH$RESCHED and SCH$SCHED, their counterparts on a single processor system. (Chapter 10 contains a detailed description of SCH$RESCHED and SCH$SCHED.)

The IPL 3 interrupt service routine, running on the primary processor, performs the following actions:

1. MPS$RESCHED raises IPL to IPL$_SYNCH to synchronize access to the scheduler database and removes the current process from execution on the primary.

2. Entry point MPS$SCHED (which can be entered directly, for example, when the primary processor's current process is placed into a wait) invokes MPS$SCHSCND to select a process for the attached processor if it is IDLE. (Sections 27.6.1 and 27.6.3 describe MPS$SCHSCND.)

3. MPS$SCHED selects a process for the primary processor and loads it with a LDPCTX instruction.

4. MPS$SCHED then checks whether the attached processor is IDLE. If the attached processor is still IDLE, there is no suitable process for it to run. MPS$SCHED determines whether it should simulate a pending executive mode AST for the primary processor's current process. An executive mode AST would enable the primary processor to detect when its process leaves kernel mode and thus becomes a candidate to run on an IDLE attached processor. (See the next section for more information.)

5. MPS$SCHED executes an REI instruction, dismissing the interrupt and placing the primary's new current process into execution.

27.6.2.1   **Transitions from Kernel Mode.** The IPL 3 scheduling routine simulates a pending executive mode AST for the process it has just scheduled on the primary processor when all the following are true:

- There is no process suitable to execute on the attached processor.
- There is at least one other resident computable process (excluding the null job).
- The process scheduled on the primary processor has no pending ASTs.
- The process scheduled on the primary processor would be suitable to run on the attached if it were not in kernel mode. (See Section 27.6.3 for the criteria which make a process unsuitable.)

The process then executes on the primary processor. Eventually, when the process issues the REI instruction to leave kernel mode, an AST delivery interrupt is triggered. The AST delivery interrupt service routine determines that this is a simulated AST and that the attached processor is IDLE. The routine then requests an IPL 3 rescheduling interrupt and dismisses the AST delivery interrupt.

The IPL 3 rescheduling interrupt service routine saves the context of the current process and places it on the appropriate compute queue. Then the interrupt service routine looks for a suitable process to schedule on the attached processor. If the process whose context was just saved is the most suitable process, it is scheduled to run on the attached processor. Note that this AST is simulated only when the attached processor is IDLE and there are at least two computable processes (other than the null job).

This mechanism helps to minimize idle time on the attached processor.

27.6.3   **Selecting a Process for the Attached Processor**

The primary processor's routine MPS$SCHSCND is invoked from the IPL 5 and IPL 3 interrupt service routines to select a suitable process to run on the attached processor. MPS$SCHSCND uses a modified form of the scheduling algorithm used on a single processor system. The algorithm for scheduling processes on a single processor or on the primary processor of an ASMP is round-robin within priority level, highest priority processes scheduled first (see Chapter 10). However, not all processes are eligible for execution on the attached processor.

A process in one of the following conditions is unsuitable for execution on the attached processor:

- A process in kernel mode

- A process about to go into kernel mode to service a pending AST delivery interrupt
- A process which has issued the Create and Map Section ($CRMPSC) system service to map particular pages of physical address space
- A process which has issued the DCL command SET PROCESS /CPU = NOATTACHED
- A process with a current priority higher than the SYSBOOT parameter VMSD2

A process executing in kernel mode or about to execute in kernel mode must run on the primary processor and is unsuitable for execution on the attached processor (see Section 27.1).

A process that has created and mapped a section to I/O space physical pages (using the PFNMAP option with the $CRMPSC system service) is not scheduled to execute on the attached processor. For each page the process maps that is in I/O space, a location in the process header (PHD$L_MPINHIBIT) is incremented.

This form of PFN mapping is usually done to access VAX-11/780 UNIBUS I/O space. The process's P0 page table is loaded with PFNs that correspond to particular locations in I/O address space. If such a process were to execute on the attached processor, its translated references to the PFN-mapped section would access the attached processor's I/O address space (instead of the primary's I/O address space where the devices are).

Note that while the processors share common addresses in the MA780 shared memory, each processor has its own I/O address space. Because the attached processor has no devices a process can access, processes with PFN-mapped pages are not allowed to run on the attached processor. Figure 27-5 shows the relative layout of physical address space in the VAX-11/782. Although this restriction arises from the nature of the VAX-11/782 hardware configuration, for reasons of simplicity and consistency, it applies equally to the other ASMP systems.

The DCL command SET PROCESS/CPU = NOATTACHED provides a way to specify that a particular process not run on the attached processor. This DCL command sets bit 29 in PHD$L_MPINHIBIT. Thus, a single test of PHD$L_MPINHIBIT can detect both this condition and a PFN-mapped section.

The system manager sets the SYSBOOT parameter VMSD2 to the value of the highest priority at which a process is eligible to run on the attached processor. The default value for the parameter is 0, indicating no priority constraint. Setting this parameter to a value 1 or 2 larger than the value of the parameter DEFPRI tends to restrict the attached processor to the execution of compute-intensive processes. A process which is not compute-intensive and which issues I/O requests receives priority boosts as those requests complete

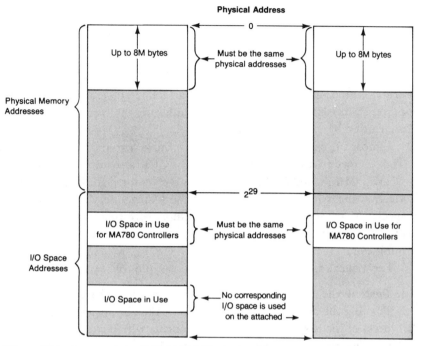

Figure 27-5 Layout of the VAX-11/782 Physical Address Space

and thus runs at higher than default priority. For more details on priority adjustment, see Chapter 10.

System rescheduling overhead is minimized when the attached processor executes compute-intensive processes that do not require frequent kernel mode services. However, if there are no compute-intensive processes, it may be wise to allow a boosted process to run on the attached processor rather than no process.

27.7 EXECUTING A PROCESS ON THE ATTACHED PROCESSOR

A process running on the attached processor is not preempted if a higher priority process becomes available. Instead, a process executes on the attached processor either until it incurs an exception or interrupt that requires a transition to kernel mode or until the process runs out of quantum. This means that VMS does not necessarily execute the two highest priority resident-computable processes.

It also means that when the process is executing kernel mode system services, it runs on the primary processor. The only kernel mode system services which can execute on the attached processor are the event flag wait and Clear AST ($CLRAST) system services.

27.7.1 Transitions to Kernel Mode on the Attached Processor

Because most process context, kernel mode code can be executed only on the primary processor, it is critical for the attached processor to detect when its current process changes access mode to kernel. Transitions to kernel mode are caused by exceptions or interrupts.

Almost all exceptions and interrupts cause a transition to kernel mode. The vectors in the attached processor's SCB are set up so that only the CHME, CHMS, and CHMU exceptions are vectored to the normal VMS service routine. All other exceptions and the AST delivery interrupt dispatch to special ASMP service routines. For the most part, these service routines save the current process context and interrupt the primary processor for a rescheduling event.

The typical actions of such a service routine follow:

1. Pushing the current PSL onto the process's kernel mode stack.
2. Pushing the appropriate PC onto the stack. The appropriate PC is the address of the first instruction in the routine which would service this kind of exception on the primary processor. For example, MPS$PAGEFAULT, the attached processor's page fault exception service routine, pushes onto the stack the address of MMG$PAGEFAULT. Typically, a service routine computes the offset of its SCB vector and pushes the address of the service routine in the corresponding vector in the primary processor's SCB.
3. Branching to MPS$MPSCHED, which removes the process from execution (see Section 27.7.4). When the process is placed back into execution on the primary processor, it resumes execution at the first instruction of the primary's service routine.

The exception service routine for the CHMK exception, MPS$CMODKRNL, in module MPCMOD, differs somewhat from the preceding description because certain kernel mode system services can execute on the attached processor.

27.7.2 Kernel Mode System Services on the Attached Processor

Several kernel mode system services can execute at least partly on the attached processor:

- Clear AST ($CLRAST)
- Wait for Event Flag ($WAITFR)

- Wait for Logical Or of Event Flags ($WFLOR)
- Wait for Logical And of Event Flags ($WFLAND)

MPS$CMODKRNL tests the CHMK operand to see if it represents a request for one of the services just listed. (For a detailed description of the CHMK exception and change mode dispatching on a single processor system, see Chapter 9.)

If the request is not for one of those services, MPS$CMODKRNL pushes a suitable PSL on the stack and the address of its primary processor counterpart, EXE$CMODKRNL, and branches to MPS$MPSCHED, which saves the process context (see Section 27.7.4).

If the request is for the $CLRAST service, MPS$CMODKRNL branches to MPS$ASTEXIT, described in the next section.

If the request is for an event flag wait system service, MPS$CMODKRNL builds a change mode dispatcher call frame and transfers control to the system service procedure. The event flag wait services are described in Section 27.7.2.2.

It should be noted that although MPS$CMODKRNL and these several system services execute on the attached processor, they run primarily at IPL 0 and are interruptible. It is possible for the process to be context switched and for execution in these code sequences to resume on the primary processor. This possibility requires additional tests in MPS$CMODKRNL and in these services to determine on which processor they are running.

27.7.2.1   **The $CLRAST System Service on the Attached Processor.** The $CLRAST system service request is requested automatically at the end of every AST procedure. (Chapter 7 describes this system service in detail and its results on a single processor system.) This service clears the PCB$B_ASTACT bit corresponding to the mode of the AST procedure and computes a new value for PR$_ASTLVL, the mode of the most important AST pending for the process.

The $CLRAST service routine MPS$ASTEXIT, in module MPCMOD, executing on the attached processor, performs the following actions:

1. It determines the access mode of the AST procedure just executed.
2. It reads the address of the process's PCB and clears the appropriate PCB$B_ASTACT bit to indicate that there is no longer an AST active in that mode in this process.
3. MPS$ASTEXIT examines the first AST control block (ACB) queued to the process at PCB$L_ASTQFL. As a result of concurrent activity on the primary processor, the process's AST queue may be changing while the attached processor tries to examine the first ACB in the queue. To ensure valid data, MPS$ASTEXIT first executes an interlocked instruction to flush any pending cache invalidates and then examines PCB$L_ASTQFL.

4. MPS$ASTEXIT computes and stores a new value for ASTLVL in PR$_ASTLVL and in the process header, based on the ACB it found.

5. MPS$ASTEXIT executes another interlocked instruction and reexamines PCB$L_ASTQFL. If its value has changed, MPS$ASTEXIT repeats the preceding step.

6. MPS$ASTEXIT dismisses the CHMK exception, returning to the process.

27.7.2.2   **Event Flag Wait System Services.** The event flag wait system services are among the most frequently executed kernel mode system services. These services begin execution on the attached processor and can complete on the attached processor whenever the event flag wait is unnecessary, that is, if the flags necessary to end the wait are set when the system service first reads them.

Each event flag wait system service procedure (all of which are in module MPWAIT) executes code equivalent to that of its counterpart on a single processor system. (Chapter 12 describes those services in detail.)

Running at IPL$_SYNCH, the service procedure tests whether the wait is satisfied. If the wait is satisfied, the service procedure removes its call frame from the kernel stack and executes an REI instruction to dismiss the exception and return to the system service caller.

If the wait is not satisfied, the service procedure pushes the PSL and the address of MPS$WAITCONT onto the stack. It then sets the flag MPS$V_SECWAITCK in MPS$GL_SECREQFLG and branches to MPS$-MPSCHED, which saves the process context (see Section 27.7.4).

Before the primary processor removes this process from the attached processor, it tests and clears the flag MPS$V_SECWAITCK. If the flag was set, the primary processor must repeat the test for whether the event flag wait is satisfied.

The routine MPS$WAITCK (in module MPWAIT), running at IPL$_SYNCH on the primary processor, repeats the wait test. It checks whether the specified event flags are set. If the wait condition is satisfied, MPS$WAITCK changes the attached processor's state to BUSY so that it will resume execution of this process.

If the wait condition is not satisfied, MPS$WAITCK places the process into a wait state. The process must wait with a saved PC and PSL that will cause reexecution of the system service. Because the process hardware context has already been saved, MPS$WAITCK modifies the hardware PCB, saved PC, and PSL fields directly and changes the attached processor's state to IDLE. The remainder of MPS$WAITCK's actions are similar to those of its counterpart, SCH$WAIT. (See Chapter 10 for detailed information on placing a process into a wait.)

27.7.3   Quantum End on the Attached Processor

The quantum of a process is charged whenever that process is current and executing when the interval timer interrupts. Other events, such as voluntary waits, are also charged against the process quantum. (See Chapter 10 for more details.)

27.7.3.1   **Interval Clock Interrupt Service Routine.** The interval timer interrupt service routine which runs on the attached processor, MPS$HWCLKINT in module MPTIMER, is similar to its counterpart for the primary processor. (See Chapter 11 for a description of EXE$HWCLKINT.)

1. MPS$HWCLKINT increments the appropriate CPU mode field to maintain the statistics displayed by the Monitor Utility MODES screen.
2. If the system was not running in process context at the time of the interrupt, MPS$HWCLKINT increments the null job's CPU time and dismisses the interrupt. (Although the null job does not really execute on the attached processor, idle time is charged against it.)
3. If the system was running in process context at the time of the interrupt, MPS$HWCLKINT increments the CPU time field in the current process header and charges the process quantum.
4. If the process has quantum remaining, MPS$HWCLKINT dismisses the interrupt.
5. If, however, this charge results in quantum runout, MPS$HWCLKINT determines whether the process is real-time or normal, as a function of its base priority.
6. If the process is real-time, it is not subject to quantum end events. MPS$HWCLKINT gives the process another quantum and dismisses the interrupt.
7. If, however, the process is normal, MPS$HWCLKINT requests an IPL$_TIMERFORK (IPL 7) interrupt before dismissing the interval timer interrupt.

27.7.3.2   **Software Timer Interrupt Service Routine.** The IPL 7 interrupt service routine, MPS$SWTIMINT, also in module MPTIMER, runs in process context. As a sanity check, MPS$SWTIMINT checks whether the process has run out of quantum. (There should be no other source of IPL 7 software interrupt requests.) If the process has not, MPS$SWTIMINT dismisses the interrupt.

If the process has reached quantum end, it must be scheduled to run on the primary processor. Quantum end processing must run only on the primary processor because its actions (such as automatic working set adjustment) can result in modifications to systemwide databases synchronized by raising IPL.

If the process has run out of quantum, MPS$SWTIMINT pushes a PC and

PSL on the stack and branches to MPS$MPSCHED, which saves the process context (see Section 27.7.4). The PC saved in the process hardware PCB is the address of a quantum end routine, MPS$QEND. The PSL saved in the hardware PCB indicates IPL 0 and kernel mode. Thus, when the process is placed back into execution on the primary processor, it will resume execution at the quantum end routine, MPS$QEND.

MPS$QEND, also in module MPTIMER, merely establishes an environment suitable for the execution of SCH$QEND, the usual quantum end routine, and dispatches to it. (See Chapter 11 for a description of SCH$QEND.)

27.7.4 Removing a Process from the Attached Processor

A process is removed from the attached processor in two phases. The first, executed on the attached processor, is routine MPS$MPSCHED (and its subentry points in module MPSCHED). The second phase, chiefly the routine MPS$SCHSCND, must execute on the primary processor because the scheduler database is modified.

MPS$MPSCHED, running on the attached processor, performs the following actions:

1. MPS$MPSCHED executes a SVPCTX instruction, saving the context of the process.
2. It sets the state of the attached processor to DROP.
3. It interrupts the primary processor to request rescheduling.
4. MPS$MPSCHED loops at IPL$_SYNCH, waiting for its state to change to BUSY. This loop is known as the attached processor's busy wait.

The primary processor's interprocessor interrupt service routine requests an IPL 5 interrupt. When the interrupt is granted, MPS$SCHSCND executes as the second phase of removing a process from the attached processor. Section 27.6.1 describes how this routine completes rescheduling of the attached processor.

27.8 INTERPROCESSOR INTERRUPT COMMUNICATION

On all systems, the same interprocessor interrupt service routines are used, regardless of which SCB vectors dispatch the interprocessor interrupts. MPS$PINTSR is the primary processor's interprocessor interrupt handler; MPS$SINTSR is the attached processor's interprocessor interrupt handler. Both are in module MPINT_*xxx*.

The primary processor interrupts the attached processor for one of several reasons:

• When an AST is queued to the process running on the attached processor, the primary processor interrupts the attached processor to update its PR$_ASTLVL register. PR$_ASTLVL on the attached processor can be modified only by code executing on the attached processor.

- When a fatal bugcheck occurs on the primary processor, it interrupts the attached processor. The attached processor executes a SVPCTX instruction to save the context of the current process and sets its state to STOP.
- In response to the DCL command STOP/CPU, the primary processor interrupts the attached processor. The attached processor then executes a SVPCTX instruction to save the context of the current process and halts.
- When a system page table entry is altered, the primary processor interrupts the attached processor, requesting it to invalidate the corresponding entry in its translation buffer. The primary processor loops until the attached processor writes a global flag to indicate that the address has been invalidated. After a certain amount of time has gone by with no acknowledgment, the attached processor is presumed no longer running. See Section 27.5.5.1 for further information.

The attached processor interrupts the primary processor for one of several reasons:

- When the attached processor must be rescheduled, it interrupts the primary processor to request a process to execute. A rescheduling request can occur when the attached processor is first initialized or when the current process on the attached processor makes a transition to kernel mode.
- When the attached processor has an error log message, it interrupts the primary processor to copy the error log message to the system error log block buffers.
- When a fatal bugcheck occurs on the attached processor, it interrupts the primary processor and requests the primary processor to crash the system.

PART VIII/Miscellaneous Topics

Logical Names

Call things by their right names. . . . Glass of brandy and
water! That is the current but not the appropriate name: ask
for a glass of liquid fire and distilled damnation.

Robert Hall, *Olinthus Gregory, Brief Memoir of the Life of Hall*

A logical name definition is a mapping of a string to one or more replacement
strings. A replacement string is called an equivalence name. A logical name
can represent a file specification, device name, application-specific information, or another logical name. Replacing an occurrence of the logical name
with an equivalence string is called logical name translation.

VAX/VMS provides automatic logical name translation for a name used in
a file specification or device name. A logical name used to refer to a device or
file enables transparent device independence and I/O redirection. For example, a program or command procedure can refer to a disk volume by logical
name, rather than by the name of the specific drive on which the disk volume
is mounted.

A user can define a logical name as a shorthand way to refer to a file or
directory that is referenced frequently.

This chapter first summarizes the characteristics of logical names. It then
describes the data structures that implement logical names and internal operation of the system services related to logical names:

- Create Logical Name ($CRELNM)
- Create Logical Name Table ($CRELNT)
- Delete Logical Name ($DELLNM)
- Translate Logical Name ($TRNLNM)

Logical name concepts are described in the *VAX/VMS DCL Concepts
Manual*. The *VAX/VMS System Services Reference Manual* documents the
use of the logical name system services.

28.1 GOALS OF EXTENDED LOGICAL NAME SUPPORT

VAX/VMS Version 4 provides extended support for logical name processing.
The goals of this new support are as follows:

- Upward compatibility for Version 3 logical names
  VAX/VMS Version 4 provides the earlier system services as jacket routines for calls to the newer services (see Section 28.9). It automatically de-

fines system, group, and process logical name tables whose properties are similar to those of Version 3 tables.

• Provision of a basis for RMS search lists

A Record Management Services (RMS) search list is an ordered list of file specifications that RMS processes in a special way. Multivalued logical names provide multiple equivalence names for a logical name. Thus, a search list can be built as a set of equivalence names for a logical name used in a file specification.

• More independent name spaces for logical names

Version 3 provided only one shared system table, one table shared among all the processes in the same user identification code (UIC) group, and one process-private name table for each process. A logical name must be unique in a given table. Version 4 allows for creation of an arbitrarily large number of logical name tables, reducing the likelihood of logical name collisions.

• More user control over the order in which logical name tables are searched

In Version 3, the order in which tables were searched was defined as process, group, and system. The only control over the sequence was to disable searching of a particular table. For example, a particular logical name translation might bypass the process table. In Version 4, each request to translate a logical name can determine which tables are to be searched by specifying a logical name whose multiple translations are the tables to be searched.

• More control over sharing of logical names

In Version 3, process-private tables were shared among users in the same group or among all users in the system. In addition to those sorts of sharing, Version 4 supports sharing among processes in the same job tree and sharing based on access control lists (ACLs).

Protection is assigned to a shareable table through a mask specified when the table is created. Section 28.3 describes this mechanism further. The number of different name tables possible also enables a process to control its sharing.

28.2   CHARACTERISTICS OF LOGICAL NAMES

A logical name is uniquely identified by the combination of the logical name string, logical name table that contains its definition, and its access mode. That is, two otherwise identical name strings which have different access modes or which are defined in different logical name tables are two different logical names.

A logical name string is from 1 to 255 bytes long. Each byte can have any value.

The scope of a logical name varies. A logical name definition can be any of the following:

• Private to one process

- Handed down from a process to its spawned subprocesses
- Shared among a detached process and all its subprocesses (job tree)
- Shared among all the processes with the same UIC group code
- Shared among all the processes on the system
- Shared among a subset of processes on the system as specified by an ACL

A logical name definition cannot be shared among processes on different nodes of a VAXcluster System.

The scope of a logical name is determined primarily by the logical name table in which it is defined. If the table is a shareable one, then, by default, the name is shareable.

If the table is a process-private table, then, by default, the logical name can be used by the process and handed down to any subprocess it spawns. When a subprocess is spawned, certain environmental characteristics of the creating process are copied. In particular, all logical names created without the CONFINE attribute are copied to the spawned subprocess. That is, the definitions current at the time of the spawn are copied; any subsequent changes to the definitions are not shared.

The access mode of a logical name can be specified when it is defined. If not specified, access mode defaults to that of the caller of the $CRELNM system service. If the ACMODE argument is specified and if the process has the privilege SYSNAM, the logical name is created with the specified access mode. Otherwise, the argument is maximized with (made no more privileged than) the mode of the system service caller.

A logical name table can contain multiple definitions of the same logical name with different access modes. When a request to translate such a logical name specifies the ACMODE argument, then all names defined at a less privileged mode are ignored.

The access mode of a logical name is really an integrity level. Because kernel and executive access mode logical names can only be created by the system manager or someone of equivalent privilege, they are used where the security of the system is at stake. For example, during certain system operations, such as the activation of an image installed with privilege, only executive and kernel mode logical names are used.

A process-private user mode logical name is deleted at rundown of the image that defined it (or at rundown of the next image if the name was defined by DCL command). Shareable user mode names, however, survive image exit and process deletion.

A logical name can be created with several attributes. The CONFINE attribute indicates that DCL should not propagate the logical name to a spawned subprocess. Logical names of process-permanent files created with the OPEN command have the CONFINE attribute. The NO_ALIAS attribute indicates that the logical name cannot coexist in a logical name table with another definition for that name that has an outer access mode. The CRELOG attribute indicates that the logical name was defined through the VAX/VMS Version 3 $CRELOG system service. RMS uses this attribute to ensure translation compatible with VAX/VMS Version 3. (Section 28.9 briefly describes support for the superseded logical name system services.)

28.3 CHARACTERISTICS OF LOGICAL NAME TABLES

A logical name table is a container for logical names. Each table defines an independent name space. A logical name table has the following characteristics:

• Scope—whether it is shareable or process-private
• Access mode
• Name
• Parent logical name table
• Access control in the case of a shareable logical name table
• Quota to limit the amount of pool occupied by its logical names

During system initialization, several shareable logical name tables are created. During the creation of each process, several other tables, shareable and process-private, are created. (Section 28.3.1 documents these default tables.) The $CRELNT system service enables a process to create additional tables at will. Process-private name tables are created in P1 space. Shareable tables are created in system space.

The access mode of a logical name table can be specified when it is defined. If not specified, the mode defaults to that of the caller of the $CRELNT system service. If the ACMODE argument is specified and if the process has the privilege SYSNAM, the logical name table is created with the specified access mode. Otherwise, the argument is maximized with the mode of the system service caller.

A logical name table can contain logical names of its access mode and less privileged access modes. A logical name table can be a parent table to another table of the same or a less privileged access mode.

A logical name table is identified by its name, which is itself a logical name. In fact, the name table data structure is a special form of equivalence name. As a logical name, each logical name table name must be contained within a logical name table. Two special logical name tables called directories exist as containers for logical name table names. A logical name that is to translate (directly or iteratively) to the name of a logical name table must be contained within a directory table.

The "system" directory, named LNM$SYSTEM_DIRECTORY, contains the names of shareable tables. The process directory, LNM$-PROCESS_DIRECTORY, contains the names of process-private tables. Each directory contains its own table name.

The address of either directory table can be determined, indirectly, through the two-longword array at LNM$AL_DIRTBL. Its first longword points to a longword containing the address of the system directory. Its second longword points to CTL$GL_LNMDIRECT, which contains the address of the process directory. Each process has its own process directory.

A logical name in a directory table is restricted to a length no longer than 31 characters. It can only consist of the characters "$", "_", and the DIGITAL alphanumeric character set (the digits, upper and lowercase alphabet).

Logical name tables have a hierarchy. That is, each logical name table, except for the directory tables, has a parent logical name table. Directories have no parent table and serve as ancestors of all logical name tables. A directory anchors the quota and access hierarchy for its name space. The hierarchical structure enables finer control over quota allocation and access to logical name tables.

The parent of a logical name table is not necessarily a directory table. That is, this hierarchical structure is distinct from the location of logical name table names. Consider the logical name table A, created by the following DCL command:

```
$ CREATE/NAME_TABLE/PARENT = LNM$PROCESS A
```

The parent table of logical name table A is the process-private logical name table LNM$PROCESS. A's table name, however, is contained in LNM$-PROCESS_DIRECTORY, the same directory as its parent table.

A logical name table is restricted in the amount of memory its logical names can occupy. There are two types of table quota: pooled and limited. Quota of either type is derived from the directory table at the top of the hierarchy.

Pooled quota is held by a logical name table called a quota holder and can be used by any other table that specifies this table as its quota holder. When a table is created, its quota is specified. A quota value of zero indicates that the table will use the quota of its parent table's quota holder.

A nonzero quota value indicates a limited amount of quota to be withdrawn from the parent table's quota holder and given to the newly created table. The newly created table is its own quota holder.

A shareable logical name table is protected through UIC-based protection. Each class of user (system, owner, group, and world) can be granted four types of access:

- Read (R) access allows the user to read the contents of the logical name table, that is, to translate logical names.
- Write (W) access allows the user to modify the contents of the table, for example, delete or alter logical name translations.
- Enable (E) access allows the user to withdraw quota from the table to create

a descendant logical name table.

- Delete (D) access allows the user to delete the table itself, including all its logical names and descendant tables and their names. A logical name table is deleted when its name or parent table is deleted.

The default protection mask for a table created through $CRELNT allows RWED access to system and owner users and no access to group or world users.

In addition, an ACL for a logical name table enables fine-tuning of UIC-based protection. (ACLs for logical name tables were introduced in VAX/VMS Version 4.2.) The DCL command SET ACL /OBJECT = LOGICAL_NAME_TABLE creates or modifies access control entries. See the *VAX/VMS DCL Concepts Manual* for further information.

To provide compatibility with Version 3 behavior, a suitably privileged process can read and write certain logical name tables if UIC- and ACL-based mechanisms prohibit access. That is, a process with GRPNAM privilege can access its group table, LNM$GROUP_*gggggg*, to translate, create, or delete logical names. A process with SYSNAM can similarly access the system table, LNM$SYSTEM_TABLE.

28.3.1   Default Logical Name Tables

Table 28-1 lists the default tables created by VMS. The names of the share-able tables are contained in the system directory. The names of the process-private tables are contained in the process directory.

There are a number of predefined logical names for logical name tables that are used in particular VMS contexts for translating and creating logical names. By convention, these names have the prefix LNM$. For example, RMS and other VMS components specify the table LNM$FILE_DEV when-ever file specifications or device names are translated. Table 28-2 lists some of the default logical names that translate to table names.

Some table names are not usually referenced directly. Typically, for exam-ple, LNM$PROCESS and LNM$JOB are specified as table names, rather than LNM$PROCESS_TABLE and LNM$JOB_*xxxxxxxx*. The indirection makes it possible for users to redefine some of the predefined names to modify the search order or the tables to be used. In addition, it enables a "generic" and transparent reference to a process's job table, for example, rather than to the very specific and transient name LNM$JOB_*xxxxxxxx*.

Some table names exist to allow for user redefinition. For example, the table name LNM$DCL_LOGICAL is used for the SHOW LOGICAL and SHOW TRANSLATION commands and for the logical name lexical func-tions. By default, LNM$DCL_LOGICAL translates to LNM$FILE_DEV. However, a user interested in displaying names and translations in the direc-

Table 28-1   Default Logical Name Tables

Table Name	Shareable	Use
LNM$PROCESS_DIRECTORY	No	Contains definitions of process-private logical name table names and names that translate to these table names
LNM$PROCESS_TABLE	No	Contains process-private logical names, such as SYS$DISK and SYS$INPUT
LNM$SYSTEM_DIRECTORY	Yes	Contains definitions of shareable logical name table names and names that translate to these table names
LNM$JOB_*xxxxxxxx*[1]	Yes	Contains names shared by all processes in the job tree, for example, SYS$LOGIN and SYS$SCRATCH
LNM$GROUP_*gggggg*[2]	Yes	Contains names shared by all processes with that UIC group
LNM$SYSTEM_TABLE	Yes	Contains names shared by all processes in the system, for example, SYS$LIBRARY and SYS$SYSTEM

[1]The string *xxxxxxxx* represents an eight-digit hexadecimal number that is the address of the job information block.
[2]The string *gggggg* represents a six-digit octal number containing the process's UIC group number.

tory tables themselves might redefine LNM$DCL_LOGICAL as shown in the following example:

```
$ SHOW LOGICAL TRNLOG$_PROCESS_GROUP
% SHOW-S-NOTRAN, no translation for logical name
        TRNLOG$_PROCESS_GROUP
$ DEFINE/SUPERVISOR/TABLE = LNM$PROCESS_DIRECTORY LNM$DCL_LOGICAL -
_$ LNM$FILE_DEV,LNM$PROCESS_DIRECTORY,LNM$SYSTEM_DIRECTORY
$ SHOW  LOGICAL TRNLOG$_PROCESS_GROUP
   "TRNLOG$_PROCESS_GROUP" = "LOG$PROCESS" (LNM$SYSTEM_DIRECTORY)
       = "LOG$GROUP"
1  "LOG$PROCESS" = "LNM$PROCESS" (LNM$SYSTEM_DIRECTORY)
       = "LNM$JOB"
2  "LNM$PROCESS" = "LNM$PROCESS_TABLE" (LNM$PROCESS_DIRECTORY)
2  "LNM$JOB" = "LNM$JOB_80471670" (LNM$PROCESS_DIRECTORY)
1  "LOG$GROUP" = "LNM$GROUP" (LNM$SYSTEM_DIRECTORY)
2  "LNM$GROUP" = "LNM$GROUP_000100" (LNM$PROCESS_DIRECTORY)
```

Because TRNLOG$_PROCESS_GROUP is defined in LNM$SYSTEM_DIRECTORY, the first SHOW LOGICAL command fails to find it. After redefining LNM$DCL_LOGICAL to include both directory tables, SHOW

Table 28-2   Default Logical Names That Translate to Logical Name Table Names

Logical Name	Equivalence Name
LNM$PROCESS	LNM$PROCESS_TABLE
LNM$JOB	LNM$JOB_*xxxxxxxx*[1]
LNM$GROUP	LNM$GROUP_*gggggg*[2]
LNM$SYSTEM	LNM$SYSTEM_TABLE
LNM$DCL_LOGICAL	LNM$FILE_DEV
LNM$FILE_DEV (supervisor mode)	LNM$PROCESS, LNM$JOB, LNM$GROUP, LNM$SYSTEM
LNM$FILE_DEV (executive mode)	LNM$SYSTEM
LNM$PERMANENT_MAILBOX	LNM$SYSTEM
LNM$TEMPORARY_MAILBOX	LNM$JOB
LOG$PROCESS	LNM$PROCESS, LNM$JOB
LOG$GROUP	LNM$GROUP
LOG$SYSTEM	LNM$SYSTEM
TRNLOG$_GROUP_SYSTEM	LOG$GROUP, LOG$SYSTEM
TRNLOG$_PROCESS_GROUP	LOG$PROCESS, LOG$GROUP
TRNLOG$_PROCESS_SYSTEM	LOG$PROCESS, LOG$SYSTEM
TRNLOG$_PROCESS_GROUP_SYSTEM	LOG$PROCESS, LOG$GROUP, LOG$SYSTEM

[1]The string *xxxxxxxx* represents an eight-digit hexadecimal number that is the address of the job information block.

[2]The string *gggggg* represents a six-digit octal number containing the process's UIC group number.

LOGICAL displays TRNLOG$_PROCESS_GROUP. It can translate iteratively all its equivalence names as well, because they are defined in one of the two directory tables. Note that since LNM$DCL_LOGICAL is a name that translates to a logical name table, its redefinition must be in one of the two directories. (For a description of the SHOW LOGICAL and DEFINE commands, see the *VAX/VMS DCL Dictionary*.)

28.4   CHARACTERISTICS OF LOGICAL NAME TRANSLATION

A logical name with only one equivalence name has only one translation. A multivalued logical name has multiple equivalence names, up to a maximum of 128. Each of its equivalence names can be identified by an index number. An equivalence name is from 1 to 255 bytes. Each byte can have any value.

An equivalence name can be defined with several attributes. Each equivalence name of a multivalued logical name can have different attributes. The CONCEALED attribute means that the equivalence name should not be displayed in system output. Typically, this is used to foster device independence by displaying logical names rather than the names of specific devices. It is also used in the creation of logical names for rooted directories. The TERMINAL attribute means that the equivalence name should not be translated further.

When a logical name is translated, the translation attribute CASE_BLIND can be specified. This attribute means that the search for that logical name is independent of the case (upper or lowercase) in which the logical name was originally defined and that in which the logical name was specified to the $TRNLNM system service.

When access mode is specified for a logical name translation, it applies to both the translation of the name and of the name tables involved. For example, if executive access mode translation is requested, then all outer mode logical names and table names are ignored.

Logical name translation has two dimensions:

• Breadth—A logical name can have multiple equivalence strings.
• Depth—One logical name can translate to another logical name, which, in turn, translates to another logical name, and so on.

These dimensions apply to the name of a logical name table, as well as to a logical name. To translate a logical name, VMS must also translate the name of the tables in which to look for the logical name. The translation for a logical name table name, done implicitly as part of translating a logical name, is different from that for a logical name.

8.4.1 Dimensions of Logical Name Translation

Default logical name translation deals with the breadth of a name, but not its depth. That is, the $TRNLNM system service can return multiple equivalence strings when it translates a logical name. One of the $TRNLNM arguments is an item list through which multiple equivalence names can be returned. The item list must explicitly request multiple equivalence names and supply buffer addresses for them.

However, when $TRNLNM translates a logical name, it does not translate iteratively. That is, it does not check whether an equivalence name is itself a logical name. Further translation must be requested explicitly; the equivalence name returned must be supplied as the logical name argument in another $TRNLNM request. Certain system services, such as Assign Channel

($ASSIGN), make iterative $TRNLNM requests to translate a logical name as deeply as possible. These system services have a maximum iteration count, typically of nine translations.

RMS has a more complex form of iteration. It parses a file specification and calls $TRNLNM iteratively to translate certain components of it. For more details, see the *Guide to VAX/VMS File Applications.*

28.4.2 Dimensions of Logical Name Table Translation

Each of the logical name system services must translate a logical name table name to perform its main function. A table name can be one of the following:

- A logical name whose single equivalence name is the table data structure itself (see Section 28.5.2)
- A name whose equivalence name is itself a logical name that translates iteratively to the table data structure
- A multivalued logical name, each of whose equivalence names is a logical name that translates iteratively to a table data structure

Unlike logical name translation, table name translation must deal with both the depth and the breadth of the name. To locate a particular logical name, for example, a table name and all its equivalence names might have to be translated iteratively. In the $TRNLNM system service, and sometimes $DELLNM, translation of a table name stops as soon as one is found that contains the target logical name. In the system services $CRELNT, $CRELNM, and under some circumstances (see Section 28.8.5) $DELLNM, translation of a table name only goes as far as finding the first table.

The table name translation sequence is depth-first. That is, the first equivalence name is translated until it translates to a table data structure or can be translated no further. If the table name found does not contain the logical name of interest, the second equivalence name is translated, and so on. This algorithm is described in more detail in Section 28.7.

28.5 LOGICAL NAME DATA STRUCTURES

The logical name database consists of the following kinds of structures:

- Logical name blocks (LNMBs) that describe the logical names that are defined
- Logical name translation blocks (LNMXs) that contain equivalence names
- Logical name table headers (LNMTHs) that describe logical name tables
- Hash tables that locate the LNMBs (LNMHSHs)
- Table name cache blocks (LNMCs)

The SYS$LIBRARY:LIB.MLB macro $LNMSTRDEF defines symbolic offsets for all these data structures.

Logical Name Blocks and Logical Name Translation Blocks

Each defined logical name is described by a logical name block (LNMB). An LNMB contains the logical name string, its access mode, and its attributes.

Each LNMB is immediately followed by at least one data structure called a logical name translation block (LNMX). An LNMX contains flags for the equivalence name attributes, an index identifying the equivalence name, and a counted string equivalence name. There is one LNMX for each equivalence name defined for the logical name. The series of LNMXs associated with a given LNMB concludes with a single LNMX that contains no equivalence name and has the bit LNMX$V_XEND set in its flags byte.

Translation to a particular equivalence name can be requested by specifying its index value. A translation index is a byte-sized signed number. The positive values 0 to 127 are available for users. By default, the first equivalence name is assigned an index value of 0, the second a value of 1, and so forth.

The negative values -1 to -128 are reserved for system use. Currently, VMS uses two special index values. The value 82_{16} (or -126) indicates that the equivalence string is a table data structure (see Section 28.5.2). The value 81_{16} (or -127) indicates that the equivalence string is a back pointer. A back pointer can be used to link a mailbox unit control block (UCB) with the LNMB that contains its logical name. It can also be used to connect a mounted volume list entry and its LNMB.

It is possible for the creator of a logical name explicitly to assign an index value to each equivalence name. Translation indexes can be sparse. For example, a particular logical name might have translations 1, 3, 5, and 10. VMS uses this feature itself to create back pointer logical names. Any general use of this feature is discouraged, because RMS and other VMS components assume that equivalence names have dense ascending indexes.

Figure 28-1 shows the layout of the LNMB and LNMX data structures. The field LNMB$W_SIZE contains the size of the LNMB, including the sizes of the LNMXs that follow the LNMB. Before the memory for the LNMB and the LNMXs is allocated, the size required for the sum of all the strings plus the fixed size is rounded up to the next quadword. As a result, although logical name blocks are of variable length, they are always an integral number of quadwords.

A process-private LNMB is allocated from the process allocation region. The LNMB for a shareable logical name must be accessible by multiple processes and is allocated from paged pool.

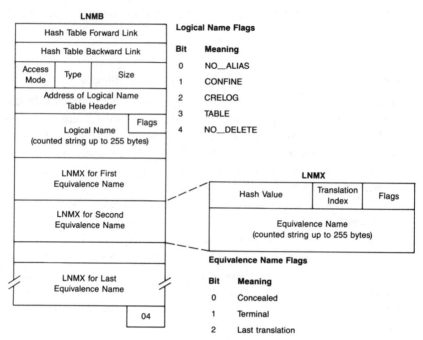

Figure 28-1 Layouts of Logical Name and Logical
Name Translation Blocks

The LNMB specifies the address of the logical name table in which the logical name is defined; the field LNM$L_TABLE contains the address of the logical name table's header (see Section 28.5.2). The LNMB also has two longwords, LNMB$L_FLINK and LNMB$L_BLINK, which link the LNMB into a hash chain of LNMBs whose logical names have the same hash value (see Section 28.5.3).

28.5.2 Logical Name Table Headers

A logical name table is a logical name with one special translation. Its first LNMX has the special index value 82_{16} to indicate that it contains an LNMTH as an equivalence name. The second LNMX merely flags the end of the data structure.

An LNMTH describes a logical name table. Figure 28-2 shows its layout. The field LNMTH$L_HASH contains the address of either the shareable hash table or the process-private hash table (see Section 28.5.3). LNMTH$L_NAME contains the address of the LNMB. The fields LNMTH$L_PARENT, LNMTH$L_CHILD, and LNMTH$L_SIBLING contain addresses of other LNMTHs and link logical name tables into a quota and access hierarchy. LNMTH$L_QTABLE contains the LNMTH address of the table that is the quota holder for the table.

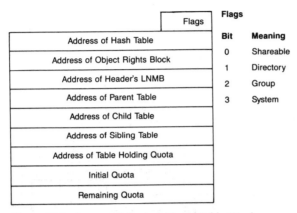

Figure 28-2   Layout of Logical Name Table Header

   Note that an LNMTH contains no listhead for LNMBs. The intuitive view of the relationship between a logical name and its containing table is different from the implementation. A logical name table is a container for logical names in an abstract sense. The only connection between a logical name and its containing table is from the LNMB to the table header; the field LNMB$L_TABLE contains the address of the LNMTH. In other words, it is not possible to examine a table header to locate logical names in that table. Instead, every LNMB of the appropriate hash table must be examined to determine which ones are in the table of interest.

   Figure 28-3 shows the relationship between the process directory, a particular logical name table, LNM$PROCESS_TABLE, and a particular logical name, SYS$LOGIN. (For simplicity, Figure 28-3 omits hash table links, which are pictured in Figure 28-4.)

8.5.3   Logical Name Hash Tables

   Locating a particular logical name and its translation requires hashing the logical name in the appropriate hash table and then determining whether the name and its containing logical name table match the name of interest. Each process has its own hash table to locate all process-private logical names. All shareable logical names are hashed in the shareable hash table.

   A hash table consists of a 12-byte header and a number of longword entries. Each entry in the hash table is either zero or a pointer to a hash chain of LNMBs with the same hash value. The chain is doubly linked through the fields LNMB$L_FLINK and LNMB$L_BLINK. The last LNMB in a chain has a forward pointer of zero.

   The order of LNMBs in a hash chain is determined by the following criteria:

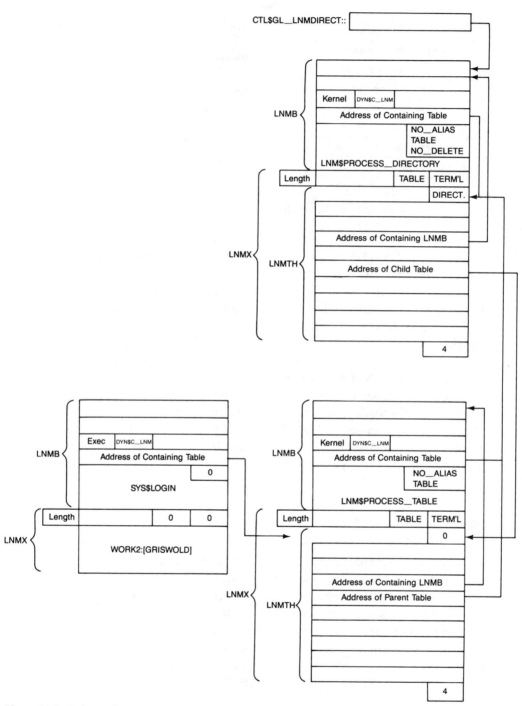

Figure 28-3 Relationship Between Logical Name Table
and Directory Table

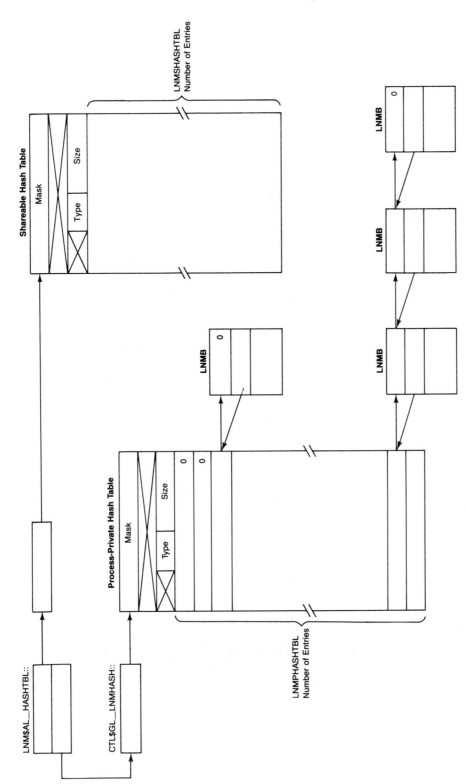

Figure 28-4 Logical Name Hash Tables and Logical Name Blocks

1. Length of the logical name, with shorter strings first
2. Alphabetical order of the logical name string for LNMBs with names of the same length
3. Address of the containing table address, with lowest address first, for LNMBs with the same logical name
4. Access mode of the logical name, with outermost access mode first, for LNMBs with the same logical name string in the same table

The SYSBOOT parameter LNMPHASHTBL specifies the number of longword entries in the process-private hash table. During process creation, EXE$PROCSTRT allocates it from the process allocation region and initializes its header. Because the process allocation region consists of demand zero pages, the table's longword entries are zeroed as a side effect of allocating space from the region for the first time.

The SYSBOOT parameter LNMSHASHTBL specifies the number of longword entries in the shareable hash table. The shareable hash table is allocated from paged pool, its header built, and longword entries cleared during system initialization.

The address of either hash table can be determined indirectly through the two-longword array at global location LNM$AL_HASHTBL. Its first longword points to a longword containing the address of the shareable hash table. Its second longword points to CTL$GL_LNMHASH, which contains the address of the process hash table. The field LNMTH$L_HASH in each logical name table contains the address of the hash table for its logical names.

Figure 28-4 shows this array, the two hash tables, and two hash chains.

The algorithm used to hash the logical names was chosen to be relatively fast and provide a good distribution within the hash table. It is implemented by the routine LNM$HASH (in module LNMSUB).

The hashing algorithm is as follows:

1. The size of the logical name string is moved to a longword. This is the base hash value.
2. Starting at the beginning of the string, four bytes are converted to uppercase and XORed into the hash longword. The hash is then rotated by nine bits to the left.
3. Step 2 is repeated with the next four bytes until there are fewer than four bytes remaining in the string.
4. The remaining bytes are XORed into the hash longword, one byte at a time. After each XOR, the hash is rotated by 13 bits.
5. The hash longword is then multiplied by an eight-digit hexadecimal number (71279461_{16}).
6. A number of high-order bytes in the hash longword are cleared. (LNMHSH$L_MASK contains the mask against which these bytes are cleared.) The result can be stored within a word and is a number no larger

than the number of entries in the hash table. It is used as a longword index into the hash table.

8.5.4   Logical Name Table Name Cache Blocks

To speed up logical name translation, information about logical name tables is cached. The name of a logical name table is itself a logical name that must be translated to translate a logical name. If the name of a logical name table translates to another logical name or, indeed, to a multivalued logical name, iterative translation may be required.

A cache block records the result of a particular table name translation for subsequent use. Figure 28-5 shows the layout of the logical name table cache block.

A cache block contains the address of the LNMB of the table name (LNMC$L_TBLADDR) and addresses of up to 25 LNMTHs obtained from translating that table name. (A table name that resolves to more than 25 table headers cannot be cached.) In the course of resolving a table name, table header addresses are stored in its cache block.

If the target table is found before the table name is exhaustively translated, the cache block contains valid but incomplete data. In this case, a zero longword indicates the end of the series of valid entries. If the table name has been exhaustively translated, a longword containing a −1 indicates that the cache block contains the complete list of table headers for that table name. An incomplete list of table headers can be extended during later resolutions of the logical table name that require more translations.

Each time the contents of a directory change, the sequence number associated with it is incremented. For example, when a process-private logical name table is created or deleted, global location CTL$GL_LNMDIRSEQ is incremented. It is also incremented if a logical name in the process directory, for example, LNM$PROCESS, is redefined. The sequence number for the shareable directory, LNM$GL_SYSDIRSEQ, is similarly incremented whenever the system directory is altered.

The cache block fields LNMC$L_PROCDIRSEQ and LNMC$L_SYS-DIRSEQ record the sequence numbers of the process and system directories current when a table name translation is cached. The fields are used as a validity check on the cached LNMTH addresses. During translation of that table name, the cached sequence numbers are checked against the current ones. The cache is valid only if they both match.

Each process has its own cache, with blocks for the most recently referenced logical name table names. During process startup, EXE$PROCSTRT (in module PROCSTRT) allocates cache blocks from the process allocation region. It initializes and inserts them in a doubly linked list whose head is at CTL$GQ_LNMTBLCACHE. The amount of space used for cache blocks is

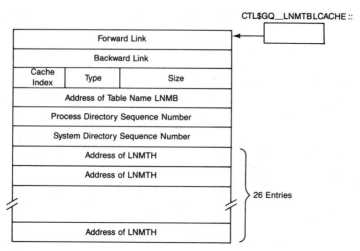

CTL$GQ_LNMTBLCACHE ::

| Forward Link |
| Backward Link |

| Cache Index | Type | Size |

| Address of Table Name LNMB |
| Process Directory Sequence Number |
| System Directory Sequence Number |
| Address of LNMTH |
| Address of LNMTH |

} 26 Entries

| Address of LNMTH |

Figure 28-5   Layout of Logical Name Table Cache Block

approximately twice that used for the process hash table. The size of each cache block is 128 bytes. The number of cache blocks is related to the SYS-BOOT parameter LNMPHASHTBL in the following way:

$$\text{Number\_of\_cache\_blocks} = (\text{LNMPHASHTBL} * 8)/128$$

28.5.5   Synchronization of Access to the Logical Name Database

A single mutex provides synchronization to the logical name database. (Chapter 2 describes the use of mutexes.) Its global name is LNM$AL_MUTEX.

The $TRNLNM system service locks the mutex for read access. Other processes can also lock the mutex for read access and translate logical names. The other logical name system services all modify the database and therefore lock the mutex for write access, blocking any access by another process.

28.6   SEARCHING FOR A LOGICAL NAME

To search for a logical name, the logical name system services invoke the routine LNM$SEARCHLOG (in module LNMSUB).

LNM$SEARCHLOG must first hash the name in the two logical name hash tables to find out whether it exists at all. (If the current process is the swapper, with a system space stack and no P1 space, the search is limited to the shareable logical name hash table.) LNM$SEARCHLOG initializes a stack local data structure called a name translation block (NT) to describe the state of the name translation. It then invokes LNM$PRESEARCH with the address of the process-private hash table. (The DCL SHOW LOGICAL command also builds an NT structure and invokes the routines LNM$PRESEARCH and LNM$CONTSEARCH directly.)

LNM$PRESEARCH invokes LNM$HASH to hash the logical name. The resulting value is used as an index into the hash table. The hash table entry located by the index is a listhead of LNMBs with that hash value. LNM$PRESEARCH invokes routine LNM$CONTSEARCH to search the LNMB list for one with a matching logical name.

LNM$CONTSEARCH compares the length of the logical name in the LNMB with the length of the name being searched for. If the logical name in the LNMB is shorter, the LNMB is passed over. The search continues without the overhead of a string comparison instruction that is bound to fail. If the name in the LNMB is longer, the search has passed the possible LNMBs and fails.

If an LNMB is found whose name is the same length, the logical name strings are compared. If the comparison fails, LNM$CONTSEARCH tests whether the search is a case-blind search, one in which the uppercase version of both strings' characters must be compared. If a caseless search is required, LNM$CONTSEARCH converts the strings one character at a time and compares them. The routine continues converting and comparing until a character comparison fails or the end of string is reached.

If the comparison fails, LNM$CONTSEARCH tests whether the string in the LNMB is alphabetically lower than the logical name of interest. If it is higher, the search has passed the last possible LNMB and fails. If it is lower, the search continues until it reaches the end of the hash chain, an LNMB containing a string higher in the sort sequence, or an LNMB with matching name.

Regardless of the outcome, LNM$SEARCHLOG initializes a second data structure and invokes LNM$PRESEARCH with the address of the shareable hash table.

These searches are independent of the containing table. They are performed to find out whether the logical name has been defined at all. Because many file specifications are translated to check whether they are logical names, attempted logical name translation is most frequent. That is, most translations fail. The data structures and search algorithm were designed to optimize the determination that a particular string is not a logical name.

If LNM$PRESEARCH finds no match in either hash table, LNM$SEARCHLOG cleans off the stack and returns the failure status SS$_NOLOGNAM to its invoker. It also returns the address of the LNMB on which it failed. If the target logical name is subsequently created (as it might be if LNM$PRESEARCH were invoked from $CRELNM to determine whether a logical name already existed), its LNMB will be inserted into the hash chain at this position.

If there is an LNMB containing the logical name of interest, LNM$-

SEARCHLOG must check it to determine whether its containing table and access mode also match. The LNMB may be followed by others with the same logical name but different containing tables or access modes. (Section 28.7 describes table name resolution in detail.) Note that if there are both process-private and shareable LNMBs containing the logical name, the search begins with the process-private ones.

LNM$SEARCHLOG first invokes LNM$SETUP to confirm that the table name passed to it does have a translation in one of the two directories and initialize logical name table processing. If the table name does not exist, LNM$SEARCHLOG cleans up the stack and returns the failure status SS$_NOLOGNAM to its invoker.

If the table name does exist, LNM$SETUP returns in R1 the address of the first LNMTH to which the table name resolves. (Recall that a table name can be a multivalued logical name with equivalence names that are themselves logical names.) LNM$SEARCHLOG invokes LNM$CONTSEARCH again, but this time with the address of the containing table header.

If the table is shareable, LNM$CONTSEARCH looks in the shareable hash table; otherwise, it checks the process-private one. Beginning at a starting point determined by the previous search, it scans the hash chain for a matching logical name. This time, however, when it finds a match, it compares containing table name addresses.

If it comes to a higher address, the search has failed, since LNMBs with the same logical name are ordered by LNMTH address. If the LNMTH address in the LNMB in the hash chain is smaller, LNM$CONTSEARCH goes on to the next LNMB.

If it finds one with the same LNMTH address, LNM$CONTSEARCH must also check the access mode. If the LNMB access mode is greater (less privileged) than the requested mode, it goes on to the next LNMB. If the LNMB mode is equal to or less than the requested mode, the LNMB matches. The first match that satisfies all criteria terminates the search.

If LNM$CONTSEARCH returns, having found a matching logical name, LNM$SEARCHLOG cleans up the stack and returns the success status SS$_NORMAL to its invoker, along with the address of the target LNMB.

If LNM$CONTSEARCH does not find a matching name, the next table to which the table name resolves must be checked. LNM$SEARCHLOG invokes LNM$TABLE to continue the table processing begun with the invocation of LNM$SETUP. LNM$TABLE returns the address of the next LNMTH. LNM$SEARCHLOG invokes LNM$CONTSEARCH again.

This sequence continues until either a matching logical name is found or there are no more tables to check.

There is another path into this search sequence; system services other than logical name services, such as $ASSIGN, invoke the routine LNM$SEARCH_ONE. LNM$SEARCH_ONE locks the logical name database mutex for read access. It invokes LNM$SEARCHLOG to find the LNMB and extracts the translation with index zero. It unlocks the mutex and returns to its invoker.

LOGICAL NAME TABLE NAME RESOLUTION

To resolve a logical name table name, the logical name system services and routines and the DCL SHOW LOGICAL command invoke either the routine LNM$FIRSTTAB or the combination of LNM$SETUP and LNM$TABLE. These three routines are all in module LNMSUB.

LNM$FIRSTTAB is called to return only the first table in the translation of a table name. A typical use of it is to identify the table in which to create a new logical name. LNM$FIRSTTAB itself invokes LNM$SETUP.

LNM$SETUP and LNM$TABLE are used to perform iterative and potentially exhaustive translations of a table name. LNM$SETUP is invoked first to initialize the search context and return the address of the first table header. Each subsequent invocation of LNM$TABLE returns another table header address, until the table name has been exhaustively translated.

When LNM$SETUP is entered, its invoker has allocated and partially initialized a stack local data structure called a recursive table translation block (RT). Its fields include recursion depth, access mode of the request, address of the associated table name cache block, and ten longwords in which to maintain search context. The recursion depth is an index into these longwords.

LNM$SETUP initializes the recursion depth to zero. It checks first the process directory and, if that fails, the system directory for the starting table name. (Recall that all logical names involved in the translation of table names must be contained in one of the two directories.) If the table name does not exist, LNM$SETUP returns the error status SS$_NOLOGNAM to its invoker.

If the name exists, LNM$SETUP saves the address of its LNMB in the RT's top search context longword as the starting point of the translation. It then scans for a valid table name cache block (see Section 28.5.4) describing this table name.

If one is found, its cache entries contain the addresses of some (possibly all) of the table headers to which the table name resolves.

If LNM$TABLE exhausts the valid cache data, it invokes LNM$-TABLE_SRCH to expand the resolution of the table name and add entries to the end of the cache block.

The fundamental recursion loop in resolving a table name is within LNM$TABLE_SRCH. LNM$TABLE_SRCH uses the RT data structure to keep track of the breadth and depth of its position in resolving the table name.

At the beginning of the loop, it examines the next equivalence name at the current recursion depth to determine what to do. There are several possibilities:

a. If the equivalence name is an ordinary string, LNM$TABLE_SRCH updates the contents in the stack longword to point to the next equivalence name.

ⓑ It tests that the maximum recursion depth (10) has not been exceeded. If the depth has been exceeded, LNM$TABLE_SRCH returns the error SS$_TOOMANYLNAM.

   Otherwise, it increments the recursion depth and invokes LNM$-LOOKUP to find the LNMB associated with the string. It positions to the name string in the LNMB and examines its equivalence name, beginning the loop again.

ⓒ If there are no more equivalence names, LNM$TABLE_SRCH decrements the recursion depth and selects the corresponding RT search longword. It begins the loop again.

ⓓ If the equivalence name is a table header (the desired result), LNM$TABLE_SRCH decrements the recursion depth and returns the address of the table header to its invoker.

Figure 28-6 shows an example complete resolution of the logical name LNM$FILE_DEV. The first step is translating LNM$FILE_DEV. It is a shareable name found in the system directory with four equivalence names. The second step is translating the "leftmost" equivalence name, LNM$PROCESS. It is a process-private name with the equivalence name LNM$-PROCESS_TABLE. The third step translates LNM$PROCESS_TABLE to its equivalence name, the first table header for LNM$FILE_DEV.

In the figure, the numbers indicate the sequence of translations. The letters

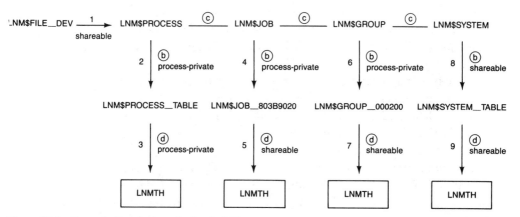

Figure 28-6   Example Resolution of a Logical Name
Table Name

on each step correspond to the possible actions in the recursion loop previously listed.

In this example, each equivalence name of LNM$FILE_DEV is translated as deeply as required to reach a table header. In practice, during logical name translation or deletion, table name resolution stops as soon as the containing table for the logical name is found. During logical name creation, table resolution stops with the first table, in this example, LNM$PROCESS_TABLE.

28.8   LOGICAL NAME SYSTEM SERVICES

The logical name system service procedures all run in kernel mode. The procedures themselves are in the module SYSLNM. Logical name subroutines that they use are in module LNMSUB.

Before describing the specific system service procedures, this section describes some checks common to the services.

28.8.1   Privilege and Protection Checks

Each of the system services has an access mode argument. If the caller explicitly specifies it and has the privilege SYSNAM, the desired access mode is used with no further check. If the caller specifies it but does not have the privilege, the access mode is maximized with the mode from which the system service was called. That is, the less privileged of the two is used.

Any string argument passed to the services must be probed to test accessibility from the mode of the system service caller. An input string is tested for read accessibility and an output string for write accessibility. An item list must be probed for read accessibility and each buffer in it must also be probed.

The logical name system services must check a process's access to a shareable table. (A process always has access to a process-private table, although it may be constrained by access mode considerations.) The system services use standard VMS protection checks. That is, they invoke the routine LNM$CHECK_PROT, which calls an internal entry point of the Check Access Protection ($CHKPRO) system service.

The $CHKPRO system service determines whether the process, given its rights and privileges, can access the table. The system service's checks encompass the process UIC, the protection mask of the table, any ACLs defined for the table, and whether the process has any of the following privileges:

SYSPRV
GRPPRV
BYPASS
READALL

If the $CHKPRO system service returns a failure status, LNM$CHECK_
PROT makes two checks of its own to provide compatibility with earlier
versions of VMS. If the intended access is read or write, LNM$CHECK_
PROT tests whether the table of interest is either a group table or the system
table. If this is the group table and the process has the privilege GRPNAM, its
access is allowed. If this is the system table and the process has the privilege
SYSNAM, its access is allowed.

28.8.2 Logical Name Translation

The $TRNLNM system service procedure, EXE$TRNLNM, confirms the
presence of its required arguments: descriptors for the logical name string
and name of its containing table. EXE$TRNLNM locks the logical name
database mutex for read access and then invokes LNM$SEARCHLOG to lo-
cate the logical name (see Section 28.6).

If LNM$SEARCHLOG returns the error status SS$_NOLOGNAM, indicating that the logical name does not exist, EXE$TRNLNM passes that error
status back to its caller. On a successful search, LNM$SEARCHLOG returns
the address of the logical name's LNMB.

EXE$TRNLNM examines the address of the LNMB to determine whether
it is a process-private or a shareable name. If the name is shareable (a system
space LNMB), EXE$TRNLNM calls LNM$CHECK_PROT to determine
whether the process has read access to the containing table (see Section 28.3).
If the process does not have access, EXE$TRNLNM returns the failure status
SS$_NOPRIV to its caller.

If the process does have access, EXE$TRNLNM processes the item list,
which contains the list of specific information to be returned. EXE$-
TRNLNM probes any specified output buffers for write access and copies
information from the LNMB, its LNMXs, and the LNMTH of its containing
table, as requested. It then unlocks the logical name database mutex and
returns to its caller.

28.8.3 Logical Name Creation

The $CRELNM system service procedure, EXE$CRELNM, confirms the presence of its required arguments, descriptors for the logical name string, and
name of its containing table. If the caller specified the address of an item list
containing equivalence strings and their attributes, EXE$CRELNM scans the
list to determine their cumulative size. The item list is not a required argument, but there is probably little purpose served in creating a logical name
with no translations, other than perhaps the creation of a logical name to
serve as an on-off flag.

EXE$CRELNM raises IPL to IPL$_ASTDEL and allocates enough paged pool for the LNMB and all its LNMXs. The assumption is that the logical name is shareable and will thus require paged pool, rather than P1 pool. Until the containing table is located, EXE$CRELNM cannot determine whether the name is private or shareable. If there is insufficient paged pool, EXE$CRELNM returns the error status SS$_INSFMEM to its caller.

EXE$CRELNM then locks the logical name database mutex for write access and invokes LNM$FIRSTTAB (see Section 28.7) to translate the name of the containing logical name table. A new logical name is always created in the first table of a table name search list.

If LNM$FIRSTTAB returns the error status SS$_NOLOGTAB to indicate that the containing table name did not translate to any existing table, EXE$CRELNM unlocks the logical name database mutex and deallocates the paged pool. It returns the error status to its caller.

On a successful search, LNM$FIRSTTAB returns the address of the containing table's LNMTH. EXE$CRELNM examines a flag in the LNMTH to determine whether it is a shareable table. If the table is process-private, EXE$CRELNM deallocates the paged pool and allocates the same amount from the P1 allocation region. If there is insufficient P1 allocation region, EXE$CRELNM unlocks the mutex and returns the error status SS$_INSFMEM to its caller.

If the table is shareable, EXE$CRELNM calls LNM$CHECK_PROT to determine whether the process has write access to the containing table (see Section 28.3). If the process does not have access, EXE$CRELNM unlocks the mutex, deallocates the pool, and returns the failure status SS$_NOPRIV to its caller.

In either case, EXE$CRELNM then checks that there is sufficient quota for the LNMB in the table that holds the quota for the containing table (LNMTH$L_QTABLE). If there is not, EXE$CRELNM deallocates the pool, unlocks the mutex, and returns the error status SS$_EXLNMQUOTA to its caller.

EXE$CRELNM then begins to fill in the LNMB. If the containing table is one of the directories, EXE$CRELNM tests that the length of the logical name string is less than 32 characters and that it contains no characters other than those allowed for logical names contained in a directory. (Note that if a logical name is being created which is not a table name but whose containing table is one of the directories, it must meet those same requirements.) If the logical name string does not meet those requirements, EXE$CRELNM deallocates the pool, unlocks the mutex, and returns the error status SS$_IVLOGNAM to its caller.

EXE$CRELNM copies the logical name string to the LNMB. It then begins processing the item list, building LNMXs as specified by the caller. After the LNMB is built, EXE$CRELNM invokes LNM$INSLOGTAB to insert the LNMB into the logical name database.

LNM$INSLOGTAB scans any LNMBs with the same name and containing table until there are no more or it encounters one with a more privileged access mode. It compares their access modes to that of the logical name being created and examines the NO_ALIAS attribute of the new name to determine what to do:

- If there is an LNMB with the same access mode, the old LNMB is deleted and superseded by the new one.
- If there is one with a more privileged mode and the NO_ALIAS attribute, the new logical name cannot be inserted. LNM$INSLOGTAB returns the error status SS$_DUPLNAM to EXE$CRELNM. EXE$CRELNM deletes the LNMB, unlocks the mutex, and returns the error status to its caller.
- If there is one with a more privileged mode and without the NO_ALIAS attribute, the new logical name can be created.
- If one is found with a less privileged mode and the new name has the NO_ALIAS attribute, the old LNMB is deleted and the new one is inserted.

LNM$INSLOGTAB charges the size of the LNMB against the containing table's quota holder. If the containing table is a directory, LNM$INSLOGTAB increments the directory sequence number as part of the cache invalidation mechanism (see Section 28.5.4). If the containing table is a directory, EXE$CRELNM computes and stores a hash value for each of its equivalence names. The assumption behind this is that the logical name translates to one or more name table names, whose hash values will be needed whenever a table search involving this name is performed.

28.8.4 Logical Name Table Creation

The $CRELNT system service procedure, EXE$CRELNT, confirms the presence of the descriptor for the name of the parent table, its one required argument. If the caller omits the name of the table to be created, EXE$CRELNT supplies a default name. The form of the default name is LNM$-*xxxxxxxxeeeeeeee*, where *xxxxxxxx* is the address of the LNMB of the table and *eeeeeeee* is the process's extended process ID (EPID). A default table name can be used to ensure that the name of a table does not conflict with any other defined table.

EXE$CRELNT raises IPL to IPL$_ASTDEL and allocates enough paged pool for the LNMB, its single LNMX and LNMTH, the trailer byte flagging the end of translations, and an object rights block (ORB). The assumption is that the logical name table is shareable and thus requires paged pool, rather than P1 allocation region pool. Until the parent table is located, EXE$CRELNT cannot determine whether the new table is private or shareable.

EXE$CRELNT then locks the logical name database mutex for write access and invokes LNM$FIRSTTAB (see Section 28.7) to translate the name of the parent logical name table. If the parent table is a table name search list, its first table name becomes the parent of the new table.

If LNM$FIRSTTAB returns the error status SS$_NOLOGTAB to indicate that the parent table name did not translate to any existing table, EXE$CRELNT unlocks the logical name database mutex and deallocates the paged pool. It returns the error status to its caller.

On a successful search, LNM$FIRSTTAB returns the address of the parent table's LNMTH. If the parent table is process-private, EXE$CRELNT deallocates the paged pool and allocates space from the P1 allocation region. The P1 allocation does not include space for the ORB, because a process-private table does not need an ORB.

If the parent table is shareable, EXE$CRELNT calls LNM$CHECK_PROT to determine whether the process has enable access to the parent table (see Section 28.3). If the process does not have access, EXE$CRELNT deallocates the pool, unlocks the mutex, and returns the failure status SS$_NOPRIV to its caller.

If the parent table is shareable and the process specified the name of the table to be created, EXE$CRELNT checks whether the process has write access to the system directory. If a default table name was constructed, the process does not need write access to the system directory. On error, EXE$CRELNT deallocates the pool, unlocks the mutex, and returns the error status SS$_NOPRIV to its caller.

EXE$CRELNT then checks that there is sufficient quota for the LNMB in the directory table. If a quota for the new table was specified, then EXE$CRELNT also checks that the parent table's quota holder has sufficient quota for the new table. If there is not, EXE$CRELNT deallocates the pool, unlocks the mutex, and returns the error status SS$_EXLNMQUOTA to its caller.

EXE$CRELNT then fills in the LNMB and translation blocks. If the caller specified the name of the table to be created, EXE$CRELNT tests that it is a legal table name. If the table is shareable, EXE$CRELNT initializes its ORB. EXE$CRELNT then invokes LNM$INSLOGTAB to insert the LNMB into the logical name database.

LNM$INSLOGTAB scans any LNMBs with the same name and containing table until there are no more or it encounters one with a more privileged access mode. Its actions depend on the NO_ALIAS attribute of the new name and any old ones, the access modes of the new and old names, and the presence or absence of the CREATE_IF ATTR argument. The CREATE_IF attribute means that the table should be created only if there is not already one with the same name and access mode.

- If there is an LNMB with the same access mode and CREATE_IF was not specified, the old LNMB is deleted and superseded by the new one. Deleting an LNMB whose equivalence name is an LNMTH means that all the logical names contained in that table must be deleted. Any descendant tables and their logical names must also be deleted.

- If there is an LNMB with the same access mode and CREATE_IF was specified, LNM$INSLOGTAB returns the status SS$_NORMAL and the address of the old LNMB. EXE$CRELNT deletes the new LNMB.
- If there is an LNMB with a more privileged mode and the NO_ALIAS attribute, the new LNMB cannot be inserted. LNM$INSLOGTAB returns the error status SS$_DUPLNAM to EXE$CRELNT.
- If there is an LNMB with a more privileged mode and without the NO_ALIAS attribute, LNM$INSLOGTAB can insert the new LNMB. It will return the status SS$_LNMCREATED.
- If an LNMB is found with a less privileged mode and the new name has the NO_ALIAS attribute, the old LNMB is deleted (along with all its logical names and descendants' logical names). The new LNMB is inserted. LNM$INSLOGTAB returns the status SS$_SUPERSEDE.

To insert the new LNMB (and its table), LNM$INSLOGTAB inserts the LNMB into the hash chain and the LNMTH into the name table hierarchy as the first child of its parent table. If there already was one, the address of its LNMTH is stored in the new table's LNMTH$L_SIBLING. If this table is to be its own quota holder, quota is withdrawn from the parent's quota holder and allocated to the new table. The table's LNMB is withdrawn from the appropriate directory table. LNM$INSLOGTAB increments the appropriate directory sequence number.

EXE$CRELNT returns to its caller, if requested, the name of the newly created table. It unlocks the logical name database mutex and returns, passing back the status from LNM$INSLOGTAB.

28.8.5 Logical Name Deletion

The $DELLNM system service procedure, EXE$DELLNM, confirms the presence of the descriptor for the name of the table containing the names to be deleted, its one required argument. The LOGNAM argument is the logical name to be deleted; it can be a logical name table name. The absence of the logical name argument is a request to delete all logical names in the table. Only logical names with an access mode equally or less privileged than that of the request can be deleted.

EXE$DELLNM raises IPL to IPL$_ASTDEL and locks the logical name database mutex for write access.

If the caller requested deletion of a particular logical name, EXE$DELLNM invokes LNM$SEARCHLOG (see Section 28.6) to determine whether the name exists. If the name is not found or if its access mode is more privileged than that of the service request, EXE$DELLNM unlocks the mutex and returns the error status SS$_NOLOGNAM to its caller.

If the name found is shareable, EXE$DELLNM invokes LNM$CHECK_PROT to ensure that the caller has write access to the containing logical name table. If the caller does not, but the name being deleted is a table name, delete access to the table being deleted is sufficient. If the caller does not have access, EXE$DELLNM unlocks the mutex and returns the error status SS$_NOPRIV to its caller.

EXE$DELLNM invokes LNM$DELETE_LNMB to remove the logical name and any outer access mode aliases from the database. As long as the name is not the name of a table, deleting it is straightforward and consists of the following steps for each alias:

• Removing the LNMB from its hash chain
• Returning the quota charged for it
• Deallocating it to the P1 allocation region or paged pool

EXE$DELLNM unlocks the mutex and returns to its invoker.

If, however, the LNMB is a table name, deleting it also requires deleting each LNMB contained within the table. In addition, any descendant tables and their logical names are deleted. LNM$DELETE_LNMB removes the LNMB from its hash chain and inserts it into a holding list. It then invokes a routine called DELETE_TABLE to delete the table.

DELETE_TABLE examines the table header to determine whether this table has any descendants. If it does, DELETE_TABLE finds the first one, removes it from its hash chain, inserts it into the holding list, and branches back to itself. DELETE_TABLE is now one level lower in the logical name table hierarchy. It continues recursively, until it reaches a childless level.

It then deletes all the logical names in that table. This requires scanning the appropriate hash table and examining each LNMB to see whether it is contained within the table. Each such LNMB is removed from its hash chain and deallocated to its pool, with quota returned to the containing table. (If the table is shareable, the LNMB is deallocated to paged pool. Otherwise, it is deallocated to P1 pool.)

After all its names are deleted, the table is then removed from the table hierarchy, its table quota is returned to its quota holder, and the LNMB quota is returned to the appropriate directory. The appropriate directory sequence number is incremented and the LNMB deallocated to its pool.

Control returns to DELETE_TABLE, which processes the first LNMB in the holding list, the parent of the one just deleted. DELETE_TABLE examines the table header of that LNMB to see whether it still has descendants. If it does not, then all the user names in that table and the table itself are deleted. If it does still have descendants, DELETE_TABLE places the LNMB for the first child into the holding list and branches back to itself. Eventually, DELETE_TABLE empties the holding list and returns. EXE$DELLNM unlocks the mutex and returns to its caller.

If EXE$DELLNM is called without the logical name argument, it invokes LNM$FIRSTTAB to find the first table header to which the table name resolves. If the table is shareable, it confirms that the process has write access to the table. DELETE_NAMES is invoked to delete all the names in that table.

As described previously, it scans the appropriate hash table, looking for LNMBs with a matching table header address and an access mode equally or less privileged than that of the delete request. Each such LNMB is removed from the hash chain, its quota is returned, and it is deallocated to pool.

When all the names of suitable access mode in that table are deleted, EXE$DELLNM unlocks the mutex and returns to its caller.

When an image exits, the Rundown Image ($RUNDWN) system service must delete all process-private logical names with an access mode less or equally privileged to the exit mode (see Chapter 21). It invokes the routine LNM$DELETE_HASH, specifying the exit access mode and the address of the process-private hash table. LNM$DELETE_HASH locks the logical name table mutex and invokes DELETE_NAMES with the address of the hash table. Many of its logical names, of course, are names of tables. Deleting each of them requires the steps previously described to delete a table, its descendant tables, and its logical names. When all the the names are deleted, LNM$DELETE_HASH unlocks the mutex and returns to the $RUNDWN system service.

28.9 SUPERSEDED LOGICAL NAME SYSTEM SERVICES

The VAX/VMS Version 4 logical name system services supersede several system services from earlier versions of VAX/VMS:

- Create logical name ($CRELOG)
- Delete logical name ($DELLOG)
- Translate logical name ($TRNLOG)

These services are supported under Version 4 for backward compatibility. Moreover, VAX/VMS creates a process with logical name tables and table name definitions that support these services and the tables they use. Table 28-3 shows the correspondence between Version 3 table numbers and Version 4 table names. Table 28-2 shows the translation of those table names.

It is possible for users of the V3 logical name system services to make some use of Version 4 features without reprogramming. By redefining the table names used by these Version 3 system services, a process can access tables other than the standard process, group, and system logical name tables. In fact, VMS defines the name LOG$PROCESS to equate to both the process and jobwide logical name tables. This enables translation of logical names within the jobwide logical name table by default.

Table 28-3   Correspondence Between Table Numbers and Logical Name Table Names

Table Number	Table Name	Access Mode
0	LOG$SYSTEM	Executive
1	LOG$GROUP	User
2	LOG$PROCESS	Mode of caller[1]

[1]An access mode specified by the caller is used.

The Version 3 system service procedures are in module SYSLOGNAM and are mode-of-caller services. Each service transforms its argument list and invokes the equivalent Version 4 system service. Each service confirms that the minimum number of arguments expected is present and that the argument list is accessible.

The arguments to each service include access mode and table number. Each service checks that its table number argument is valid and converts it to the corresponding Version 4 logical name table name. Table 28-3 shows this correspondence and also the access mode associated with each table.

For the process table, any access mode specified by the caller is used. If the argument is omitted, the caller's access mode is used. This access mode is passed as an argument to the Version 4 logical name system service. The Version 4 service will test that the process has suitable privileges.

The following paragraphs supply a few specific additional details about the implementation of the $CRELOG and $TRNLOG services.

A name created with the $CRELOG service has only one translation, the equivalence name supplied to $CRELOG. The logical name has the CRELOG attribute. The equivalence name is assigned translation index 0. If the equivalence name begins with a leading underscore, the underscore is removed and the equivalence name has the TERMINAL attribute.

$TRNLOG returns translation number 0 of the specified logical name. If the translation has the TERMINAL attribute, $TRNLOG prefixes an underscore to the equivalence name. This manipulation enables most logical names, including file names, to be created and used through either the old or new system services.

Two arguments to the $TRNLOG system service control its actions: the TABLE and DSBMSK arguments. The TABLE argument is the address to receive the translation table number. The DSBMSK argument specifies which subset of the process, group, and system tables is to be searched. (The mask is a "disable" mask; by specifying which tables to omit, it indirectly identifies those to be searched.)

If the TABLE argument is zero, EXE$TRNLOG transforms the DSBMSK argument into a table name search list with the names of the tables to be searched. It selects one of the logical name table names whose name begins with the string TRNLOG$. It calls the $TRNLNM system service and transforms its return arguments into forms compatible with the V3 interface.

A nonzero TABLE argument means that EXE$TRNLOG must return the number of the containing table. To determine the containing table, EXE$TRNLOG calls the $TRNLNM system service once for each table to be searched, until the logical name is found or the end of the table subset is reached.

29 Miscellaneous System Services

> . . . Of shoes—and ships—and sealing wax—
> Of cabbages—and kings—
> And why the sea is boiling hot—
> And whether pigs have wings.
>
> Lewis Carroll, *Through the Looking Glass*

This chapter includes brief discussions of the system services not mentioned in the previous chapters. Although these services do not generally make extensive use of the internal structures and mechanisms of the VMS executive, these descriptions are provided as an informational aid to users of the services and for completeness. Detailed discussions of the arguments, return status codes, required process privileges, and system service options can be found in the *VAX/VMS System Services Reference Manual.*

29.1 COMMUNICATION WITH SYSTEM PROCESSES

Some of the operations often associated with an operating system are performed in the VAX/VMS system by independent processes rather than by code in the linked system image. Examples of this type of system activity include the following:

- Managing print and batch jobs and queues
- Gathering accounting information about utilization of system resources
- Communicating with one or more system operators
- Reporting device errors

29.1.1 Services Supported by the Job Controller

The job controller is a system process, named JOB_CONTROL, which runs the image JOBCTL.EXE. The job controller performs many different functions and supports several system services. It uses several independent threads of execution to perform the following roles:

- As the queue manager of the batch/print subsystem, the job controller is responsible for all transactions to and from the queue file, whose name is SYS$SYSTEM:JBCSYSQUE.DAT. (On a VAXcluster System, the job controllers running on each node all access a single, common queue file.) These transactions include the creation and deletion of job queues and the creation, modification, and dispatching of batch and print jobs. For processing print jobs, the job controller directs the activity of one or more print symbiont processes. A print symbiont process can run the standard image supplied with VAX/VMS, PRTSMB.EXE, or one which has been modified or rewritten by a user.

- As the system accounting manager, the job controller records the use of system resources in the file SYS$SYSTEM:ACCOUNTNG.DAT. (On a VAXcluster System, each job controller accesses a node-specific accounting file.)
- As the job manager, the job controller is responsible for the creation of interactive and batch processes. In response to unsolicited terminal input, the job controller creates a detached process running the image LOGINOUT.EXE. In response to unsolicited card reader input, the job controller creates an input symbiont process, running the image INPSMB. The input symbiont reads the card deck and submits a batch job. When the job controller schedules a batch job to run from an execution queue, it creates a process running the image LOGINOUT.EXE and passes any job parameters to it through the DCL symbols P1 through P8.

The job controller communicates with other processes on the system through mailbox messages. It receives messages from the executive (as the result of system service calls and notification of process deletion), print symbionts, terminal driver, and card reader driver. The job controller sends messages to print symbionts and detached processes during login.

VAX/VMS provides several system services to communicate with the job controller in its roles as queue manager and accounting manager. These system services are described in the following sections and include the following:

- Send Message to Job Controller ($SNDJBC[W])
- Get Queue Information ($GETQUI[W])
- Send Message to Account Manager ($SNDACC, which is obsolete under VAX/VMS Version 4)
- Send Message to Symbiont Manager ($SNDSMB, which is obsolete under VAX/VMS Version 4)

29.1.1.1   **Operation of the $SNDJBC System Service.** The $SNDJBC[W] system service creates, stops, and manages queues and the batch and print jobs in those queues. In addition, it turns accounting on and off. The service requests the job controller to perform those actions by writing messages into its mailbox. A user invokes the $SNDJBC system service to request any of the job controller actions available through DCL commands, for example, PRINT, SUBMIT, INITIALIZE/QUEUE, STOP/QUEUE, and DELETE/QUEUE. The arguments to the $SNDJBC system service include the following:

- The event flag number to be set when the request completes
- The function code specifying which function $SNDJBC is to perform
- A place-holding null argument
- The address of an item list that includes (for each requested item) which item of information is specified or returned, the size and address of the buffer to receive or specify the information, and a location to insert the size of the information returned
- An I/O status block (IOSB) to receive final status information
- The entry point and parameter for an asynchronous system trap (AST) procedure to be called when the request completes

The $SNDJBC system service procedure EXE$SNDJBC, in module SYS-SNDJBC, executes in executive mode. It performs the following operations:

1. The message type is defined as MSG$_SNDJBC and the target mailbox is defined as the job controller's mailbox, SYS$GL_JOBCTLMB.
2. The IOSB, if specified, is checked for write access and is cleared.
3. The FUNC code specified in the $SNDJBC argument list is validated.
4. The message buffer is allocated on the current stack (the executive mode stack). Each item in the item list is checked for correctness: its item code must be valid; its buffer descriptor and buffer must be readable. The following information is placed in the buffer (using code common to the $GETQUI service):

   —Items in the item list
   —The function code
   —Address of the AST procedure and parameter
   —IOSB address
   —Event flag number
   —Image counter (PHD$L_IMGCNT)
   —System time (EXE$GQ_SYSTIME)
   —Terminal name of the requesting process (PCB$T_TERMINAL)
   —Extended owner process ID (PCB$L_EOWNER)
   —Process status longword (PCB$L_STS)
   —Extended process ID (PCB$L_EPID)
   —Access mode of system service caller
   —Process base priority PCB$B_PRIB)
   —Process user name and account name (CTL$T_USERNAME and CTL$T_ACCOUNT)
   —Process UIC (PCB$L_UIC)
   —Process privileges (PHD$Q_PRIVMSK)
   —Message type

5. The common code then invokes the Change Mode to Kernel ($CMKRNL)

system service. The kernel mode procedure called performs the following operations:

a. It clears the specified event flag.
b. If AST notification was requested, the routine checks the process's AST quota. If the AST quota is insufficient, the message is not queued to the job controller, and EXE$SNDJBC returns with status SS$_EXASTLM. If the process has AST quota, its quota is charged.
c. It calls EXE$SENDMSG (in module SYSSNDMSG) to write the buffer to the job controller mailbox. EXE$SENDMSG is invoked by many system services that communicate with system processes. EXE$SENDMSG verifies that the target mailbox has a process reading messages written to the mailbox.

   EXE$SENDMSG raises IPL to 2 and faults the message (which is still on the executive stack) into the process's working set. It then invokes EXE$WRTMAILBOX, part of the mailbox device driver (module MBDRIVER), to do the I/O operation. (Because EXE$WRTMAILBOX runs at IPL$_MAILBOX, IPL 11, the pages containing the message must be valid; page faults are not allowed at IPLs above 2.)

6. The asynchronous form of the system service ($SNDJBC) returns to the caller. The caller can either wait for the information to be returned or continue processing. The synchronous form of the system service ($SNDJBCW) waits for the event flag associated with the request to be set and status to be returned. (See Chapter 9 for more information concerning synchronous and asynchronous system services.)

Section 29.1.1.3 describes how information is returned to the user.

29.1.1.2 **Operation of the $GETQUI System Service.** The $GETQUI[W] system service obtains information about the queues and jobs initiated and managed by the job controller. The $GETQUI system service performs the same operations (using common code) as the $SNDJBC system service (described in the previous section). The message type for $GETQUI messages is MSG$_GETQUI. This service is requested to obtain any of the information available through the DCL command SHOW QUEUE.

Section 29.1.1.3 describes how information is returned to the user.

29.1.1.3 **$SNDJBC and $GETQUI Special Kernel AST.** The job controller queues a special kernel AST (see Chapter 7) to the process when its request has completed. The AST is described by an extended AST control block (ACB). The ACB includes any data requested by the process and information about where and how much data is to be stored. EXE$JBCRSP (in module SYSSNDJBC), the special kernel AST routine, returns status and any requested data from the $SNDJBC and $GETQUI services to the process.

EXE$JBCRSP first tests that the image which requested the system service is still executing. This test is a comparison of the process's current PHD$L_IMGCNT against its value at the time of the service request. PHD$L_IMGCNT is incremented each time that an image is run down (see Chapter 21). If the two values are different, a different image is running now, and addresses in the previous image, such as that of the AST procedure or IOSB, are no longer valid. If the same image is no longer running, EXE$JBCRSP deallocates the extended ACB, returning AST quota to the process, if appropriate, and returns.

If the same image is running, EXE$JBCRSP completes the request through the following actions:

1. It sets the specified event flag by calling routine SCH$POSTEF with a null priority class increment (see Chapters 10 and 12).
2. It stores a status value in the IOSB, if one was specified.
3. It stores data in any output buffer items from the original request.
4. If the user requested AST notification, EXE$JBCRSP calls SCH$QAST to queue the ACB as a completion AST and returns.
5. If the user did not request AST notification, EXE$JBCRSP deallocates the ACB and returns.

29.1.2 Superseded System Services

The $SNDJBC system service supersedes two system services from versions of VAX/VMS prior to Version 4:

• Send Message to Accounting Manager ($SNDACC)
• Send Message to Symbiont Manager ($SNDSMB)

These services are supported under VMS Version 4 for compatibility with earlier versions.

29.1.2.1 Send Message to Accounting Manager System Service. Requests to the accounting manager can be sent through the job controller's mailbox by the $SNDACC system service. A user invokes the $SNDACC service to request actions normally available through the DCL command SET ACCOUNTING and to send messages directly to the accounting manager.

The $SNDACC system service procedure, EXE$SNDACC in module SYSSNDMSG, runs in executive and kernel modes. It performs the following operations:

1. The mailbox message type is defined as MSG$_SNDACC and the target mailbox is defined as the job controller's mailbox, SYS$GL_JOBCTLMB.
2. The request is checked for possible errors, such as too large a message,

insufficient privilege, or inaccessible data references. (The user privilege OPER is required to create a new log file or enable or disable accounting.)

3. The message buffer is allocated on the current stack (the executive mode stack), and the following information is placed in the buffer:

—Mailbox message type
—Reply mailbox channel (if specified as an optional argument)
—Privilege mask, UIC, user name, and account name
—Process base priority
—User-supplied accounting message type that specifies which function is to be performed
—User-defined message text

4. EXE$SNDACC invokes the $CMKRNL system service to call the local procedure SENDMSG.

5. SENDMSG performs the following operations:

   a. It validates the process's reply channel (if one was specified as an optional argument).
   b. It verifies that the target mailbox has read/write access.
   c. It invokes routine EXE$SENDMSG. Section 29.1.1.1 describes the actions of EXE$SENDMSG.

29.1.2.2   **Send Message to Symbiont Manager System Service.** Requests to the symbiont manager are sent to the job controller's mailbox by the $SNDSMB system service. A user invokes the $SNDSMB service to request actions normally available through DCL commands, such as PRINT, SUBMIT, and DELETE /ENTRY.

The $SNDSMB system service performs exactly the same operations (using common code) as the $SNDACC system service (described in the previous section), except that the message type is defined to be MSG$_SNDSMB.

The user privilege OPER is required to use any function of $SNDSMB that affects a queue itself (for example, initializing or deleting a queue). $SNDSMB requires GROUP privilege to affect queue entries owned by processes in the caller's group; WORLD privilege is required to affect entries from outside the group.

29.1.3   **Operator Communications**

Operator communications are handled by a system process named OPCOM, which runs the image OPCOM.EXE). OPCOM has the following responsibilities:

- Defining which terminals are operator terminals and for what class of activity (such as disk or tape operations) these terminals will receive messages

- Replying to or canceling a user request to an operator
- Managing the operator log file

Requests to OPCOM are sent through OPCOM's mailbox by the Send Message to Operator ($SNDOPR) system service. A user invokes the $SNDOPR service to request actions normally available through the DCL user command REQUEST and the operator command REPLY.

The user privilege OPER is required to call $SNDOPR to enable a terminal as an operator's terminal, reply to or cancel a user's request, or initialize the operator log file.

With exceptions of a different mailbox (SYS$GL_OPRMBX) and a different message type (MSG$_OPRQST), $SNDOPR shares common code with $SNDACC and $SNDSMB (described in Section 29.1.2).

29.1.4   Error Logger

As described in Chapter 8, the error logging subsystem contains three pieces:

- The executive itself contains routines that maintain a set of error message buffers. These routines are called by device drivers and other components that log errors so that error messages can be written to some available space in one of these buffers.
- The error formatting process (process ERRFMT running image ERRFMT.EXE) is awakened to copy the contents of these error message buffers to the error log file for subsequent analysis.
- The Error Log Utility reads the error messages in the error log file and produces an error log report, based on the contents of the error log file and the options selected when the utility is run.

A user can invoke the Send Message to Error Logger ($SNDERR) system service to send messages to the error logger (put messages into one of the error message buffers for later transmission to the error log file). Using this system service requires the BUGCHK privilege.

Unlike the $SNDJBC and $SNDOPR system services, the $SNDERR system service has the following characteristics:

- It executes entirely in kernel mode (rather than executive and kernel mode).
- It writes a message to an error message buffer (rather than sending a mailbox message).

The $SNDERR system service procedure, EXE$SNDERR in module SYSSNDMSG, performs the following actions:

1. The request is checked for access and privilege violations.
2. It invokes ERL$ALLOCEMB (in module ERRORLOG) to allocate an error

log message buffer.

3. The message buffer is filled with the message type (EMB$C_SS), the message size, and the message text. An error log sequence number and the current time are also a part of every error message.

4. It invokes ERL$RELEASEMB (also in ERRORLOG) to release the buffer to the error logging routines for subsequent output to the error log file.

Chapter 8 contains a discussion of the error log routines and a brief description of the ERRFMT process.

29.2 SYSTEM MESSAGE FILE SERVICES

VAX/VMS provides three levels of message file capability. The creation and declaration of image-specific and process-permanent message files are discussed in the description of the Message Utility in the *VAX/VMS Message Utility Reference Manual* and the *VAX/VMS DCL Dictionary*. The system message file (SYSMSG.EXE) is mapped into system address space as a pageable section. This initialization is performed by SYSINIT during system initialization (see Chapter 25).

Two system services provide the capability for a user to do the following:

• Search for a message text corresponding to a given status code—the Get Message ($GETMSG) system service
• Write one or more message texts to SYS$OUTPUT—the Put Message ($PUTMSG) system service

A third procedure (EXE$EXCMSG) does not use the various message files but is also one of the message output procedures that can be invoked as part of condition handling.

29.2.1 Get Message System Service

The $GETMSG system service executes in the mode of the caller. It searches each of the three levels of message files for a match to the status code provided as an argument.

29.2.1.1 Finding the Message Files. The first step of the retrieval of a message involves determining which types of message files have been defined.

1. If an image message section has been defined, then it has been incorporated as a program region image section. The control region location CTL$GL_GETMSG points to the per-image message section vector in the control region (see Appendix F). The vector is initialized with a value corresponding to an RSB instruction. If an image has defined any message sections, then this vector is changed by the image activator to the following code sequence:

```
JSB      @#<P0-location_1>
JSB      @#<P0-location_2>
         .
         .
         .
JSB      @#<P0-location_n>
RSB
```

These instructions are not executed; rather, the address serves as a pointer to the message sections. (That there is a JSB instruction is a side effect of the use of a particular code path in the image activator also used in the support of privileged shareable images.) Each P0 location is in a different message section (up to a maximum of 41 distinct message sections in a given image). The message section search routine searches one message section at a time.

2. If no match is found in the current section, the message dispatcher searches the next message section given in the P0 space vector, and so on.

3. If no image message section has been defined or the input status value could not be found in any image message section, then a test is made for a process-permanent message section (established by the SET MESSAGE command). The absence of a process-permanent message section is indicated by a zero in the control region location, CTL$GL_PPMSG. If a process-permanent message section has been defined, CTL$GL_PPMSG points to a control region address in a process-permanent section vector (see Appendix F). The process-permanent message section is searched in a fashion similar to that used for the previous image section case.

4. If a process-permanent message section has not been defined or the input status value could not be found in the process-permanent message section, then the system message file is searched. The location EXE$GL_SYSMSG points to a system location in a system section vector. The message section search routine is called to search for the system message file.

If no message file is found or none of the defined message files contains the specified status code, then the status code is inserted into a message indicating that the message is not in the message file, and the service returns with the status code SS$_MSGNOTFND.

29.2.1.2   **Searching a Located Message Section.** When a message section is located, the starting address and length of the message section index are calculated. A binary search of the message section index is then performed to determine if the specified status code is included.

If no message is defined within the section for the specified status code, a check is made in other message sections of the same type. If no further message sections of the same type exist, the search routine returns to the $GETMSG main search procedure. $GETMSG then checks the next type of message section until the system message file has been searched.

If a message corresponding to the specified status code is located within a message section, then the information selected by the $GETMSG FLAGS argument is copied into the user-defined buffer. If the combine bit is set in the FLAGS argument (bit 4), then the argument is reduced to the information selected by the process's default message flags (CTL$GB_MSGMSK). If the FLAGS argument is not specified, the process default message flags (CTL$GB_MSGMSK) is used to select the information. The search routine returns control to the caller of the $GETMSG system service.

29.2.1.3   **Indirect Message Sections.** Indirect message sections allow users to create more than one message file associated with an executable image. Message files can then be changed without recompiling and relinking the image. Briefly, the executable image contains pointers to a message file rather than the messages themselves. The DCL commands used to create indirect message sections are described in the *VAX/VMS Message Utility Reference Manual*.

As a result of creating an indirect message section, two image files are created. One is an executable image, in which the actual message text areas contain the file specification of the second image. The second image is nonexecutable and contains the message data.

When the $GETMSG system service searches for a message code and finds a file specification (rather than message text) related to the code, it maps the nonexecutable image specified by the file specification to the end of the virtual address space. The newly mapped section contains the actual message text. The search for the message code continues. When the message is found, the information specified by the $GETMSG FLAGS argument is copied into the user-defined buffer. If the combine bit is set in the argument (bit 4), then the argument is reduced to the information specified in the process's default message flags (CTL$GB_MSGMSK). If the FLAGS argument is not specified, the process's default message flags (CTL$GB_MSGMSK) is used to select the information.

If the nonexecutable image has already been mapped, the text for the code is in the newly mapped section. $GETMSG then searches for the second occurrence of the message code and processes the code as usual.

29.2.2   **Put Message System Service**

The $PUTMSG system service provides the ability to write one or more error messages to SYS$ERROR (and SYS$OUTPUT if it is different from SYS$ERROR). It executes in the access mode of its caller and uses $GETMSG to retrieve the associated text for a particular status code.

The following four arguments are passed to $PUTMSG:

- A message argument vector describing the messages in terms of status codes, message field selection flag bits, and $FAO arguments (see Section 29.5.2).
- An optional action routine to be called before writing the message texts.
- An optional facility name to be associated with the first message written. If it is not specified, the default facility name associated with the message is used.
- An optional parameter to be passed to the caller's action routine. If it is not specified, it defaults to zero.

The construction of the message argument vector is discussed in the *VAX/VMS System Services Reference Manual*. Other uses of the $PUTMSG system service are described in the *VAX/VMS Run-Time Library Routines Reference Manual*.

Each argument of the message argument vector is processed as follows:

1. The facility code of the request is determined to be a system, RMS, or standard facility code. Standard facility codes can require $FAO arguments. System messages (facility code 0) and RMS messages (facility code 1) do not use associated $FAO arguments in the message argument vector. System exception messages require $FAO arguments to follow immediately after the message identification in the message vector.
2. $GETMSG is called with the status code and field selections (based upon the selection bits and $FAO arguments).
3. If there are $FAO arguments present and the message is flagged as having at least one $FAO argument, $FAOL is called to assemble all the portions of the message to be written (supplied facility code, optionally specified delimiters, output from $GETMSG).
4. The user's action routine is called, if one was specified.
5. If the action routine returns an error status, the message is not written. Otherwise, the formatted message is written to SYS$ERROR by an RMS $PUT request. If SYS$OUTPUT is different from SYS$ERROR, then the formatted message is also written to SYS$OUTPUT.

When all of the arguments in the message argument vector have been processed, the $PUTMSG system service returns to its caller.

29.2.3   Procedure EXE$EXCMSG

This procedure is used internally by the catch-all condition handler to report a condition that has not been properly handled by any condition handlers further up the call stack. EXE$EXCMSG is also called by EXE$EXCEPTION to write the contents of the general registers to SYS$OUTPUT if a condition is not handled in any other way. (See Chapter 4 for information on condition handling.)

The two input arguments to this procedure are the address of an ASCII string and the address of the exception argument list passed to the condition handlers (see Chapter 4).

The procedure writes a formatted dump of the general registers, signal array, and stack, as well as the caller's message text to SYS$OUTPUT (and to SYS$ERROR if different from SYS$OUTPUT). This message appears for all fatal errors that occur in images that were linked without the traceback handler. (Note that most images shipped with the VAX/VMS operating system are linked without the traceback handler.)

Although this procedure has an associated entry point in the system service vector area, it cannot be conveniently called from any languages, except VAX MACRO and VAX BLISS-32. This restriction is imposed by the specification of the second argument, which requires access to the general register AP, a capability denied to most high-level languages.

29.3 PROCESS INFORMATION SYSTEM SERVICES

The Get Job/Process Information ($GETJPI[W]) system service provides selected information about a specified process (which may not necessarily be the process requesting the $GETJPI service). The information that can be obtained from this service includes selected data from the process control block (PCB), job information block (JIB), process header (PHD), and control region.

The arguments to $GETJPI include the following:

- The event flag number to be set when the request completes
- The process ID of the process from which information is to be collected
- The process name of the target process
- The address of an item list that includes (for each requested item) which item of information is to be returned, the size and address of the buffer to hold the information, and a location to insert the size of the returned information
- An IOSB to receive final status information
- The entry point and parameter for an AST procedure to be called when the request completes

29.3.1 Operation of the $GETJPI System Service

The $GETJPI system service procedure, EXE$GETJPI in module SYSGETJPI, executes in kernel mode. It performs the following operations:

1. It invokes EXE$NAMPID to check that the current process has the ability to obtain information about the target process (see Chapter 12).
2. The IOSB, if specified, is checked for write access and cleared.

3. The event flag is cleared.
4. If AST notification was requested, EXE$GETJPI checks that the process has sufficient AST quota and charges it.
5. Each item in the list is checked for the following conditions:

   —The buffer descriptor must be readable and the buffer writable.
   —The requested item must be a recognized one.

6. If these conditions are met, then the requested item can be retrieved. All data about the current process and PCB and JIB data about another process can be obtained directly without entering the context of the target process. (The PCB and JIB are nonpaged pool data structures allocated for the life of the process and job.) In addition, data from the PHD of another process can be obtained directly if the PHD is resident (if the PCB$V_PHDRES bit in PCB$L_STATUS is set). All such information is moved to the user-defined buffers for each corresponding item.
7. If no information remains to be gathered, then EXE$GETJPI returns to the caller after performing the following actions:

   —Setting the specified event flag
   —Queuing AST notification, if it was requested
   —Writing status to an IOSB, if one was supplied

8. If there is remaining information that could not be retrieved by step 6, the information concerns a process other than the caller and is stored either in the target process's control region or process header. This information must be retrieved by executing in the context of the target process. EXE$GETJPI must queue a special kernel mode AST (see Chapter 7) to the target process so that EXE$GETJPI code can execute in the context of the target process.

   EXE$GETJPI allocates nonpaged dynamic memory for an extended ACB and an information buffer. (The pool is charged to the process's JIB$L_BYTCNT quota.) The normal ACB fields are initialized. The extension is initialized with descriptors of all the information that must be retrieved by executing in the context of the other process. The buffer is created to receive the retrieved information for transmission to the requesting process.
9. EXE$GETJPI checks the status and state of the target process. If the target process is in any of the following states, information from it cannot be obtained:

   —It no longer exists.
   —Deletion or suspension is pending.
   —The process state is suspended (SUSP), suspended outswapped (SUSPO), or miscellaneous wait (MWAIT) states (see Chapter 10).

If the process is any of these states, EXE$GETJPI deallocates the nonpaged pool, restoring the quota charged, and returns an error to its caller. The status of SS$_SUSPENDED is returned for the three wait states of SUSP, SUSPO, and MWAIT. If the process has been deleted or is in the process of being deleted (has the delete pending bit set in the PCB status longword), a status of SS$_NONEXPR is passed back to the caller. Note that the completion mechanisms are all triggered if one of these errors occurs. That is, the event flag is set, a user-requested AST is queued, and an IOSB is written with the failure status.

10. EXE$GETJPI queues the ACB to the target process with a priority increment class of PRI$_TICOM (6). However, if the target process is computable (COM) or computable outswapped (COMO), queuing the AST does not result in a priority boost. (See Chapter 10 for information on event reporting.) In that case, EXE$GETJPI boosts the target process's priority enough to make it equal to the priority of the current process (unless the current process is a real-time process or its priority is lower than that of the target process).

11. The asynchronous form of the system service returns to the caller. The caller can either wait for the information to be returned or continue processing. The synchronous form of the system service waits for the event flag associated with the request to be set and status to be returned. (See Chapter 9 for more information concerning synchronous and asynchronous system services.)

29.3.2   **$GETJPI Special Kernel Mode ASTs**

When the target process is not the caller and the information needed resides in the process header or P1 space of the target process, the special kernel mode AST code must execute in the context of the target process (to access the information). Once the AST has obtained the information, it must be passed back to the caller's context, so that it can be written to the caller's address space. The VMS system uses special kernel mode ASTs for both pieces of this operation.

A summary of the operations performed by these special kernel mode ASTs follows:

1. When the target process is placed in execution, the first special kernel AST routine runs. It examines the extended ACB to determine what information was requested and stores it in the associated system buffer. It reformats the extended ACB to deliver a second special kernel mode AST, this time to the requesting process. It queues the extended ACB to the requesting process and returns.

2. The second kernel mode AST routine executes in the context of the requesting process. If the PHD image counter is not the same as it was when

the service was requested, then the requesting image has been run down. In this case, the block of nonpaged pool is deallocated, the JIB$L_BYTCNT quota is restored, and the special kernel mode AST simply returns.

3. If the image counter in the process header agrees with the image counter in the extended ACB, the special kernel AST routine copies the retrieved data from the system buffer into the user-defined buffers.

   Note that the asynchronous nature of this aspect of the system service requires that the IOSB and all data buffers be probed again for write accessibility. This check ensures that the original caller of $GETJPI has not altered the IOSB and data buffer protection in the interval between the call to $GETJPI and the delivery of the return special kernel AST.

4. The event flag is set and the IOSB is written if it was specified.

5. If a completion AST was requested, the extended ACB is used for the third time to queue an AST to the requesting process in the access mode of the caller. Otherwise, the ACB is deallocated to nonpaged pool.

29.3.3   Wildcard Support in $GETJPI

The $GETJPI system service also provides the ability to obtain information about all processes in the system (in other words, a wildcard search). A wildcard request is indicated by passing a negative process ID to the $GETJPI system service. The internal routine in $GETJPI that determines the identity of the target process recognizes a wildcard request and passes information back to the caller about the first process in the PCB vector after the swapper and the null process (see Chapter 20).

In addition, the process index field of the caller's PID argument is altered to contain the process index of the target process. When the caller of $GETJPI issues a second call, the negative sequence number (in the high-order word of the process ID) indicates that a wildcard operation is in progress, but a positive process index indicates where in the PCB vector the search should continue. Note that the user program will not work correctly if the caller alters the value of the process ID argument between calls to $GETJPI.

The user issues calls to $GETJPI until a status code of SS$_NOMOREPROC is returned, indicating that the PCB vector search routine has reached the end of the PCB vector. An example of the wildcard use of the $GETJPI system service is contained in the *VAX/VMS System Services Reference Manual*.

29.4   SYSTEM INFORMATION SYSTEM SERVICES

The Get System Information ($GETSYI[W]) system service provides selected information about the running system or another node within the VAXcluster System. Although synchronous and asynchronous forms of the service are provided, both forms of the service complete synchronously under VAX/VMS Version 4. Currently, the only information that can be obtained about a target system which is not the running system is contained in nonpaged pool data structures on the local system.

The arguments to $GETSYI include the following:

- Event flag to be set when the request completes
- Node name of the system for which the information is requested
- Address of the Cluster System Identification (CSID) of the system
- Address of the item list that includes (for each requested item) which item of information is to be returned, the size and address of the buffer to hold the information, and a location to insert the size of the returned information
- Address of an IOSB to receive the final status of the information requested
- Entry point and parameter for an AST procedure to be called when the request completes

29.4.1 Operation of the $GETSYI System Service

The $GETSYI system service procedure, EXE$GETSYI in module SYS-GETJPI, executes in kernel mode. It performs the following actions:

1. It invokes local routine NAMCSID to validate the node name/CSID pair. NAMCSID tests CLU$GL_CLUB to determine whether the running system is a member of a VAXcluster System.

   —If the system is a member of a VAXcluster System, NAMCSID (after resolving a wildcard reference) invokes another local routine, EXE$NAMCSID, to obtain the address of the cluster system block (CSB) specified by CSID or node name. If a CSB is located, its address is returned to EXE$GETSYI. Otherwise, the error status SS$_NOSUCH-NODE is returned, which EXE$GETSYI returns as system service status.

   —If the system is not a member of a VAXcluster System and the user specified a CSID, NAMCSID returns the error SS$_NOMORENODE, which EXE$GETSYI returns as system service status.

   —If the system is not a member of a VAXcluster System and the user specified a node name, NAMCSID checks that the node name is that of the running system. If it is, NAMCSID returns successfully with the address of the system block (SB). If the node name is not that of the running system, NAMCSID returns the error status SS$_NOSUCH-NODE, which EXE$GETSYI returns as system service status.

2. The IOSB, if specified, is checked for write access and cleared.
3. The event flag is cleared.
4. If AST notification was requested, EXE$GETSYI checks that the process

has sufficient AST quota and charges it.

5. Each item in the list is checked for the following conditions:

   —The buffer descriptor must be readable and the buffer writable.
   —The requested item must be a recognized one.

6. If these conditions are met, then the requested information is retrieved and copied to the user-defined buffer. Under VMS Version 4, all available information can be obtained immediately and while in the context of the requesting process. The only information available about a nonlocal system is contained in its CSB or SB. Other information about the current system can be obtained from various system global locations.

7. When no information remains to be gathered, then the system service returns to the caller after performing the following actions:

   —Setting the specified event flag
   —Queuing requested AST notification to the process
   —Writing status information to an IOSB, if one was specified

29.4.2   Wildcard Support in $GETSYI

The $GETSYI system service provides the ability to obtain information about all systems in a VAXcluster System, that is, to perform a wildcard search of the cluster vector table. The cluster vector table is a table of CSB addresses, indexed by the low word of the CSID. Its address is stored in global location CLU$GL_CLUSVEC. A wildcard request is indicated through a negative CSID argument to the $GETSYI system service. The internal routine in $GETSYI that determines the identity of the target system recognizes a wildcard request and passes information back to the caller about the first system described in the cluster vector table.

In addition, the cluster system identification field of the caller's CSID argument is altered to contain a node index of the target system. When the caller of the $GETSYI service issues a second call, the negative sequence number (in the high-order word of the CSID) indicates that a wildcard operation is in progress. The positive node index (in the low-order word of the cluster system ID) indicates where in the cluster vector table the search should resume. Note that the user program will not work correctly if the caller alters the value of the CSID argument between calls to $GETSYI.

The user continues to request the $GETSYI system service until a status of SS$_NOMORENODE is returned, indicating that the cluster vector table has been exhausted.

29.5   FORMATTING SUPPORT

The final group of system services provides conversion support for time-related requests and formatted I/O of ASCII character strings.

29.5.1   **Time Conversion Services**

The time conversion system services are defined in the module SYSCVRTIM. The $NUMTIM system service executes in executive mode and converts a binary quadword time value in system time format (described in Chapter 11) into the following seven numerical word length fields:

- Year (AD)
- Month of year
- Day of month
- Hour of day
- Minute of hour
- Second of minute
- Hundredths of seconds

A positive time argument is converted into the corresponding absolute system time. A zero-valued time argument requests the conversion of the current system time. A negative time argument is interpreted as a time interval from the current system time.

The $ASCTIM system service executes in the access mode of the caller and converts a system time format quadword into an ASCII character string. The input binary time argument is passed to $NUMTIM. The seven fields returned from $NUMTIM are then converted into ASCII character fields with the selection determined by whether the input time was an absolute or delta time and whether the conversion flag was set, indicating conversion of day and time or only the time portion. The $FAO system service (described in Section 29.5.2) is used to concatenate and format the string components before returning the string to the caller.

The $BINTIM system service executes in the access mode of the caller and converts an ASCII time string into a quadword absolute or delta time. If the input string expresses an absolute time, then the current system time is converted by $NUMTIM to supply any fields omitted in the ASCII string. Each ASCII field is then converted to numerical values and stored in the seven word fields used by $NUMTIM. The seven word fields are then combined into a binary quadword value. The resulting value is negated if a delta time was specified in the ASCII string.

29.5.2   **Formatted ASCII Output**

The $FAO and $FAOL system services provide formatting and conversion facilities from binary and ASCII input parameters to a single ASCII output string. The two system services execute in the access mode of the caller and use common code. The only difference between them is whether the parameters are passed as a list of arguments ($FAO) or as the address of the first parameter ($FAOL).

The control string is parsed character by character. Information that is not preceded by the control character (!) is copied into the output string without further action. When a control character and operation code are encountered in the control string, the appropriate conversion routine is executed to process zero, one, or two of the input parameters to the system service. When the control string has been completely parsed, the service returns to the caller with a normal status code. If the output string length is exceeded, a buffer overflow error status is returned.

The description of the $FAO system service in the *VAX/VMS System Services Reference Manual* contains details about how to specify $FAO requests.

APPENDIXES

Appendix A

System Processes and Privileged Images

Table A-1 System Processes

Image Name	Linked with SYS.STB	Description
F11AACP.EXE	Yes	Files-11 ODS-1 ACP
MTAAACP.EXE	Yes	Magnetic tape ACP
REMACP.EXE	Yes	Remote terminal ACP
NETACP.EXE	Yes	Network ACP
ERRFMT.EXE	Yes	Error log buffer format process
INPSMB.EXE	Yes	Card reader input symbiont
JOBCTL.EXE	Yes	Job controller/Symbiont manager
OPCOM.EXE	Yes	Operator communication facility
PRTSMB.EXE	Yes	Print symbiont
FILESERV.EXE	Yes	Cluster cache server process
CSP.EXE	Yes	Cluster server process
CONFIGURE.EXE	Yes	Configure cluster devices

Table A-2   Images Installed with Privilege (in a Typical VMS System)

Image Name	Linked with SYS.STB	Description
ANALIMDMP.EXE	Yes	Image Dump Analyze Utility
CDU.EXE	Yes	Command Definition Utility
LOGINOUT.EXE	Yes	Login/logout image
MAIL.EXE	No	Mail Utility
MONITOR.EXE	Yes	System Statistics Utility
PHONE.EXE	No	Phone Utility
REQUEST.EXE	Yes	Operator request facility
RTPAD.EXE	No	Remote Terminal Utility
SET.EXE	Yes	SET command processor
SETP0.EXE	Yes	SET command processor
SHOW.EXE	Yes	SHOW command processor
SHWCLSTR.EXE	Yes	SHOW CLUSTER command processor
SUBMIT.EXE	No	Batch and print job submission facility

Table A-3   Images Requiring Privilege That Are Typically Not Installed

Image Name	Linked with SYS.STB	Description
CIA.EXE	Yes	Show Intrusion Utility
INSTALL.EXE	Yes	Known Image Installation Utility
MP.EXE	Yes	Multiprocessing loadable code
MSCP.EXE	Yes	VAXcluster disk server
NCP.EXE	No	Network control program
OPCCRASH.EXE	Yes	System shutdown facility
QUEMAN.EXE	No	Queue manipulation command processor
REPLY.EXE	No	Message broadcasting facility
RUNDET.EXE	No	RUN process command processor
SDA.EXE	Yes	System dump analyzer
STOPREM.EXE	Yes	Stop REMACP Process Utility
SYSGEN.EXE	Yes	System Generation and Configuration Utility
XFLOADER.EXE	Yes	DR32 microcode loader

Table A-4   Images Whose Operations Are Protected by System UIC or Volume Ownership

Image Name	Linked with SYS.STB	Description
AUTHORIZE.EXE	Yes	Authorize Utility
BADBLOCK.EXE	Yes	Bad block locator
BACKUP.EXE	No	Backup Utility
DISKQUOTA.EXE	Yes	Disk Quota Utility
DISMOUNT.EXE	No	Volume Dismount Utility
ERRFMT.EXE	Yes	Error Log Utility
INIT.EXE	Yes	Volume Initialization Utility
VERIFY.EXE	No	File Structure Verification Utility
VMOUNT.EXE	No	Volume Mount Utility

Table A-5   Miscellaneous Images Linked with SYS$SYSTEM:SYS.STB

Image Name	Linked with SYS.STB	Description
ANALYZOBJ.EXE	Yes	Analyze Object Module Utility
CHECKSUM.EXE	Yes	Checksum File or Image Utility
CLUSTRLOA.EXE	Yes	VAXcluster support
DCL.EXE	Yes	DCL command interpreter
DELTA.EXE	Yes	Executive debugger
DISMNTSHR.EXE	Yes	Dismount service shareable image
F11BXQP.EXE	Yes	ODS-2 file system
FPEMUL.EXE	Yes	Floating-point instruction emulation
IMGDMP.EXE	Yes	Write Image Dump Utility
MOUNTSHR.EXE	Yes	Mount service shareable image
PATCH.EXE	Yes	Patch Utility
PFMFILWRT.EXE	Yes	Page Fault Monitor Utility
RMS.EXE	Yes	Record Management Services image
S0DELTA.EXE	Yes	Executive debugger
SCSLOA.EXE	Yes	System communications services
SECURESHR.EXE	Yes	Security services shareable image
SETSHOACL.EXE	Yes	Set/Show ACL Utility
SMBSRVSHR.EXE	Yes	Print symbiont shareable image
SYSLOA*xxx*.EXE	Yes	CPU-specific support
VAXEMUL.EXE	Yes	Subset instruction emulation

Appendix B

Use of Listing and Map Files

This book has presented a detailed overview of the VAX/VMS executive. However, the ultimate authority on how the executive or any other component of the system works is the source code for that component. This appendix shows how the listing and map files produced by the language processors and the VAX/VMS Linker can be used with other tools to understand how a given component works or why the system is malfunctioning.

B.1 HINTS IN READING THE EXECUTIVE LISTINGS

The sources for the VAX/VMS operating system are available in two forms for customers who purchase a source license. The source listings option includes microfiche listings for most components. The source distribution option provides source files and command procedures on magnetic tape.

The suggestions made in this appendix emphasize reading the modules that make up the executive and the initialization routines, most of which are written in VAX MACRO.

B.1.1 Structure of a MACRO Listing File

The modules that make up the system image are all written from a common template that includes a module header describing each routine in the module. The general format of a VAX MACRO listing file is described in the *VAX MACRO and Instruction Set Reference Volume*. Features that are specific to listings included in the source listing kit are described here.

B.1.1.1 $xyzDEF Macros.

One of the first parts of each module that requires explanation is the invocation of a series of macros that define symbolic offsets into data structures referenced in the module. The general form of these macros is shown in the following example, where *xyz* represents the data structure whose offsets are required:

```
$xyzDEF
```

For example, a module that deals with the I/O subsystem probably invokes the $IRPDEF and $UCBDEF macros to define offsets into I/O request packets (IRPs) and unit control blocks (UCBs). Some of the $xyzDEF macros, such as

$SSDEF, $IODEF, and $PRDEF, define constants (system service status returns, I/O function codes and modifiers, and processor register definitions) rather than offsets into data structures.

Structures and constants that are used in system services and other public interfaces have their $*xyz*DEF macros defined in SYS$LIBRARY: STARLET.MLB, the default macro library that is automatically searched by the assembler. Most of the data structures used by the executive have their macro definitions contained in a special macro library called SYS$LIBRARY:LIB.MLB. The distinction between these two macro libraries is discussed in Appendix E, where many of the data structures described in this book are listed.

One way to obtain the symbol definitions resulting from these macros is to look at the symbol table that appears at the end of the assembly listing. However, the information presented there is often incomplete or not in a suitable form. An alternative representation of the data can be obtained from the following sequence of DCL commands:

```
$ CREATE xyzDEF.MAR
        .TITLE   xyzDEF
        $xyzDEF GLOBAL
        .END
 ^Z
$ MACRO xyzDEF+SYS$LIBRARY:LIB.MLB/LIBRARY
$ LINK/NOEXE/MAP/FULL xyzDEF
$ PRINT xyzDEF.MAP
```

This command sequence produces a single object module that contains all the symbols produced by the $*xyz*DEF macro. The argument GLOBAL makes all the symbols produced by the macro global. (This argument must appear in uppercase to be properly interpreted by the assembler's macro processor.) That is, the symbol names and values are passed from the assembler to the linker so that they appear on whatever map the linker produces. The full map contains two lists of symbol definitions, one in alphabetical order and one in numeric order.

.1.1.2   **Routine Body.** In general, the routines that make up the executive were coded according to strict standards that result in code that is easily maintained. One side effect of these standards is that the code is easy to read for someone attempting to learn how the VMS operating system works.

Several items about the instructions that appear in the module body are worth describing:

• Data structure references are usually made using displacement mode addressing. For example, the following instruction loads the contents of R3 (presumably the address of an IRP) into the IRP pointer field (a longword) in a UCB pointed to by R5:

```
MOVL    R3,UCB$L_IRP(R5)
```

Such instructions are practically self-documenting. The overall arrangement of data in a particular structure does not need to be known to understand such instruction references.

- Whenever a sequence of instructions makes an assumption about the relative locations of fields within a data structure, there is a possibility of failure if the structure were to change. In the following two instances, such assumptions might be used:

—Two adjacent longword fields could be loaded with a single MOVQ instruction.

—A structure could be traversed using autoincrement or autodecrement addressing.

The ASSUME macro (defined in SYS$LIBRARY:STARLET.MLB) is often used to detect these failures immediately by issuing an assembly-time error. For example, if a device driver wanted to clear adjacent fields in a UCB, the following instruction and macro sequence would prevent subtle errors if the layout of the UCB changed in the future:

```
CLRQ    UCB$L_SVAPTE(R5)
ASSUME  UCB$L_BOFF EQ <UCB$L_SVAPTE + 4>
ASSUME  UCB$L_BCNT EQ <UCB$L_SVAPTE + 6>
```

The options available with this macro can be determined by examining its definition in the microfiche listing in the SYS component.

- There are some commonly used instruction sequences that occur so frequently that the author of a module used an assembly-time macro to represent the instruction sequence. Other instruction sequences, particularly those that read or write the internal processor registers, are more readable if hidden in a macro definition. However, because macros are rarely expanded as a part of the assembler listing, the reader of listing files must be able to locate the macro definitions.

There are three levels at which macros are defined in the VAX/VMS operating system:

—A macro may be local to a module. In this case, the macro definition appears as part of module header. Such macros are often used to generate data tables used by a single module.

—A macro may be a part of a specific facility, such as DCL. The macros that are a part of a specific facility are included as part of the microfiche listing for that facility. For example, the DCL microfiche includes not only all modules that make up the DCL images but also the macros that are used to assemble those modules.

—A macro may be used by many components of the operating system. In this case, the macro definition is found on either the SYS microfiche (for example, in SYSDEF*xx*.SDL or SYSMAR.MAR) or the VMSLIB microfiche (for example, in STARDEF*xx*.SDL or SSMSG.SDL). Most of the macro definitions in this category are data structure definitions, but there are many common instruction sequences appearing in several components that are defined in the file called SYSMAR.MAR. Note that SYSDEF and STARDEF were divided into four submodules each. The strings AE, FL, MP, or QZ are used to identify the first letters of the structures defined in each module. These strings should be substituted for the string *xx*.

The definitions of all system macros that are used in building the operating system are included in the macro library SYS$LIBRARY:LIB.MLB, which is supplied as a part of the VAX/VMS binary distribution kit. Applications such as user-written device drivers or user-written system services can also use this macro library. Such applications must be reassembled or recompiled with each new release of LIB.MLB, which usually occurs with each major release of the VAX/VMS operating system.

The definitions of all macros that are intended for use in nonprivileged applications, such as system service calls, can be found in the macro library SYS$LIBRARY:STARLET.MLB, which is also supplied as a part of the VAX/VMS binary distribution kit. This macro library is automatically searched by the assembler to resolve undefined macros. Appendix E contains a description of some of the data structures defined in STARDEF.SDL and SYSDEF.SDL.

• Another search that the reader of listings has to embark on involves looking for destinations of instructions that transfer control or reference static data locations. If the destination or data label is outside the module currently being looked at, the symbol appears in the symbol table at the end of the assembler listing as an undefined global. The module that defines that symbol can be determined with the map file for that component (see Section B.2).

Symbols that are local to a module are usually easy to find, because most of the modules that make up the executive or any other component are not very large. However, the listing files for some modules are longer than 50 pages. There are a couple of steps that can be taken before the reader scans every page of the listing, looking for the place where the symbol is defined:

—The symbol in question or some textual reference to it may appear in the table of contents for this module.

—The value of the symbol appears in the symbol table. Because the assembler includes the value of the current location counter in every line of the listing, the reader can determine approximately where in the listing the symbol is defined. (This technique is not foolproof. The value of the symbol that appears in the symbol table is relative to the beginning of the PSECT in which the symbol is defined. Modules with more than one relocatable PSECT may have to be searched more carefully.)

B.1.2   **VAX Instruction Set and Addressing Modes**

One of the design goals of the VAX instruction set was that it contain useful instructions with a natural number of operands. Thus, there are two- and three-operand forms of the arithmetic instructions ADD, SUB, MUL, and DIV. There are also bit manipulation instructions, a calling standard, character string instructions, and so on. All of these allow the assembly language programmer to produce code that is not only efficient but also highly readable.

However, there are certain places in the executive where the most obvious choice of instruction or addressing mode was not used, because a shorter or faster alternative was available. Interrupt service routines, routines that execute at elevated IPL, and commonly executed code paths, such as the system service dispatcher and the main paths in the pager, are all examples where clarity of the source code was sacrificed for execution speed.

One question that must be answered at this point is why there is a concern over instruction length on a machine with practically unlimited virtual address space. There are at least two answers to that question.

Most of the areas where instruction size is an issue are within the permanently resident executive. This portion of the system consumes a fixed percentage of the physical memory that is present in the configuration. Keeping instruction size small is one way to keep this real memory cost to a minimum.

A second answer is that VAX processors make use of an instruction lookahead buffer that contains the next bytes in the instruction stream. Its size varies on different processors but is at least eight bytes on all current types of VAX. If the buffer empties, the next instruction or operand cannot be evaluated until the buffer is replenished. By keeping instructions small in key areas, this wait can be avoided and the instruction buffer can be filled in parallel with other CPU operations.

B.1.2.1   **Techniques for Increasing Instruction Speed.** This section lists some of the techniques employed to reduce instruction size or increase execution speed. The list is hardly exhaustive but a pattern emerges here that can be applied to other modules in the executive that are not explicitly mentioned here.

Each list element consists of a general technique and may also contain a specific example, including the name of the module where this technique is employed.

- The MOVAx and PUSHAx instructions combined with displacement mode addressing are equivalent to an ADDLx instruction with the addition being performed to calculate the effective address of the operand. For example, the following two instructions are equivalent:

```
PUSHAB   12(R3)
;
ADDL3    #12,R3,-(SP)
```

However, the PUSHAB instruction is one byte shorter than the ADDL3 instruction and also faster.

- The use of MOVAx and PUSHAx described in the previous item can be combined with indexed mode addressing to accomplish a multiply by 2, 4, or 8. For example, the following instruction multiplies the contents of R1 by 4, adds 4 to the product, and places the result back into R1:

```
MOVAL    @#4[R1],R1
```

This instruction is used by the change mode dispatchers (in module CMODSSDSP) to calculate the length of an argument list from the number of arguments.

- The following instruction found in routine EXE$ALLOCATE, in module MEMORYALC, performs two steps at once:

```
MOVAB    (R0)+,R2
```

Its ostensible purpose is to place the address of the allocated block of memory into R2, where it will be picked up by the caller. However, because the allocated block is always at least quadword aligned, the byte context of the instruction forces an increment of R0 by 1, setting the low bit of R0. This set bit will be interpreted as a success indicator by the caller.

- When two successive writes to memory occur, on many types of VAX processors, the second write must wait for the first to complete. If successive write operations can be overlapped with register-to-register operations, instruction stream references, or other operations that do not generate writes to memory, then some other instruction can begin execution while the memory write is completing.

  There are several places in the executive where this technique is used. The three examples that follow are among the most commonly executed code paths in the system:

  —The page fault handler saves R0 through R5 with PUSHL instructions interspersed among instructions that do not write to memory.

—The Queue I/O Request ($QIO) system service procedure intersperses writes to memory, initializing an IRP, with reads from its argument list and register operations.

—The change mode dispatchers for executive and kernel modes build customized call frames on their stacks. As the code examples in Chapter 9 illustrate, the writes to memory (the stack operations) are overlapped with register and instruction stream references.

- There are three ways to push registers onto the stack: with a PUSHR mask instruction, with a series of MOVQ instructions to −(SP), or with a series of PUSHL instructions. Instruction implementation is sufficiently different on various VAX processors that generalization about performance of these instructions is difficult. However, the PUSHR instruction is seldom used in time-critical places because it is slower than either MOVQ or PUSHL. PUSHR must interpret its bit mask operand and then push the registers accordingly. PUSHR, however, does not alter condition codes and is used when their settings must be retained across saving registers.

- When it is necessary to include a test and branch operation, a decision as to which sense of the test to branch on and which sense to allow to continue in line is required. One basis for this decision is to allow the common (usually error-free) case to continue in line, only requiring the (slower) branch operation in unusual cases.

B.1.2.2 **Unusual Instruction and Addressing Mode Usage.** There are several instances in the executive where the purpose of an instruction is not at all obvious. This list includes the most common occurrences of unusual use of the instruction set and addressing modes.

- There are many instances of the following instruction sequence where the initial setting of the bit has no effect on the flow of control:

```
        BBSS    bit arguments , 10$
10$:
```

This sequence is used whenever the bit to be set (or cleared) with an equivalent sequence using BBCC is identified by bit number or bit position.

To set (or clear) the bit with a BISx or BICx instruction, a mask must first be created with a 1 in the designated position, requiring either two instructions or an immediate mask that might occupy a longword. (The only exception to this involves a bit in the first six positions, where the mask can be contained in a short literal constant.)

Note that a BBCS instruction is equivalent to a BBSS instruction when the branch destination is the next instruction. There are some occurrences of BBCS where a BBSS seems to accomplish the same purpose. Probably the choice was made by looking at the usual sense of the bit in question before the instruction and choosing the instruction to avoid the branch in the usual case.

- There are several instances of autoincrement deferred addressing where the need for the increment of the register is not apparent. For example, both of the following instructions occur in the rescheduling interrupt service routine in module SCHED:

```
INSQUE  (R1),@(R3)+
;
REMQUE  @(R3)+,R4
```

In both cases, R3 contains the address of the listhead of some doubly linked list before instruction execution. Its contents after the instruction is executed are irrelevant.

In fact, the increment is totally unnecessary. All that is needed is double deferral from a register. In other words, the addressing mode @0(R3) would be equally appropriate if the contents of R3 were not important. However, deferred byte displacement addressing costs an extra byte to hold the displacement. In this commonly executed code path, the savings of one byte was extremely important.

It is worth noting that there is no similar problem when a single level of deferral from a register is required. The assembler is smart enough to generate simple register deferred mode (code 6) when it encounters byte displacement mode with a displacement of zero (0(Rn)) in the source code.

- The permanent symbol table of the VAX MACRO assembler recognizes the mnemonic POPL, even though there is no POPL instruction in the VAX instruction set. The generated code for the following instructions are identical:

```
POPL    dst
;
MOVL    (SP)+,dst
```

That is, the mnemonic generates two bytes (for instruction opcode and source operand specifier) plus whatever is required to specify the destination operand.

For example, the following pseudo instruction (the first instruction in the change-mode-to-kernel dispatcher in module CMODSSDSP) removes the change mode code from the stack (so that REI will work correctly) and loads it into R0:

```
POPL    R0
```

A combination of the POPL instruction with an unusual addressing mode occurs in the exception dispatcher for change-mode-to-supervisor and change-mode-to-user exceptions where it is necessary to remove the second

POPL dest ≡ MOVL (SP)+,dest

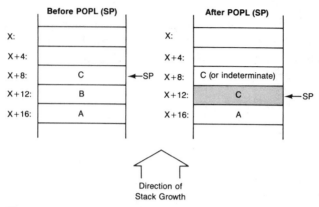

Figure B-1 Stack Modification Due to POPL (SP)
Pseudo Instruction

longword from the stack. The following instruction has the effect of removing the next-to-last item from the stack and discarding it, leaving the stack
in the state pictured in Figure B-1:

```
POPL    (SP)
```

• The following instruction, followed by some conditional branch instruction, performs exactly the same function as a TSTQ instruction, which does
not exist:

```
MOVQ    R0,R0
```

This curious instruction is found in module SYSSCHEVT, where the Set
Timer Request ($SETIMR) and Schedule Wakeup ($SCHDWK) system services are implemented.

B.1.3 Use of the REI Instruction

The only means of reaching a less privileged access mode from a more privileged mode is through the REI instruction. There are two slightly different
techniques that accomplish this mode change.

The most general technique of going to a less privileged access mode alters
the flow of execution at the same time. This technique is used by the RSX-
11M AME to get into compatibility mode. The following instruction sequence accomplishes the desired result:

```
PUSHL   new-PSL
PUSHL   new-PC
REI
```

Note that the many protection checks built into the REI instruction prevent this technique from being used by a nonprivileged user to get into a more privileged access mode or to elevate IPL, two operations that would allow such a user to damage the system. A second technique can be used when it is only necessary to change access mode. No accompanying change in control flow is required. The instruction sequence listed here (patterned after code contained in module PROCSTRT) shows this second technique:

```
        PUSHL   executive-mode-PSL
        BSBB    DOREI
          .                       ;Do processing in
          .                       ; executive access mode
          .

        PUSHL   user-mode-PSL
        BSBB    DOREI
          .                       ;Do processing in
          .                       ; user access mode
          .

DOREI:  REI                       ;REI uses pushed PSL and PC
                                  ; that BSBB put on stack
          .
          .
          .
```

B.1.4   Register Conventions

Each of the major subsystems of the executive uses a set of register conventions in its main routines. That is, the same registers are used to hold the same contents from routine to routine. Some of the more common conventions are listed here:

- R4 usually contains the address of the process control block (PCB) of the current process. Nearly all system service procedures and scheduling routines use this convention. In fact, as illustrated in the examples in Chapter 9, the change-mode-to-kernel system service dispatcher loads the address of the PCB of the caller into R4 before passing control to the service-specific procedure. When it is necessary to store a process header (PHD) address, R5 is usually chosen. (Except during the execution of the swapper and certain memory management code that executes at IPL$_SYNCH, R5 contains the address of the P1 window to the PHD rather than the system space address of the PHD.)
- The memory management subsystem uses R2 to contain an invalid address and R3 to contain the system virtual address of the page table entry (SVAPTE) that maps the page. When a physical page is eventually associ-

ated with the page, the PFN is stored in R0.

- The I/O subsystem uses two nearly identical conventions, depending on whether it is executing in process context (in the $QIO system service or in device driver FDT routines) or in response to an interrupt. The most common register contents are the current IRP address stored in R3 and the UCB address in R5. In process context, R4 contains the address of the PCB of the requesting process. Within interrupt service routines, R4 contains the virtual address that maps one of the CSRs of the interrupting device. A more complete list of register usage by device drivers and the I/O subsystem can be found in the manual *Writing a Device Driver for VAX/VMS*.

B.1.5   Elimination of Seldom-Used Code

There are several different techniques that are used to eliminate code and data that are not used very often. For example, none of the programs used during the initialization of a VMS system remains after its work is accomplished. Process creation is an example of a complex system service that executes relatively infrequently during the lifetime of a typical system. The VMS executive uses several techniques that allow these routines to do their work as efficiently as possible and yet eliminate them after they have done their work.

B.1.5.1   Eliminating the Bootstrap Programs.

The following list illustrates some of the techniques used to remove the bootstrap programs from memory after they have done their work:

- Both VMB and SYSBOOT execute in physical pages whose use is not recorded anywhere. When module INIT places all physical pages except those occupied by the permanently resident executive on the free page list, the pages used by VMB and SYSBOOT are included. Their contents are overwritten the first time that each physical page is used.
- The module INIT is a part of the system image and cannot be eliminated quite so easily. Chapter 24 describes how INIT puts the physical pages that it occupied on the free page list after its work is done.

  The routine that puts the physical pages on the free page list performs a straightforward function. However, the unusual part of this step is that this routine was first copied to an unused portion of nonpaged pool, but the pool space was not formally allocated. When the routine has accomplished its work and returned, the code remains until the portion of pool that it occupied is used later on, eliminating the last traces of INIT from memory. Note that this technique assumes that no pool allocation takes place until it is done. The fact that IPL remains at 31 while INIT executes ensures that no such allocation occurs.

- The system initialization that takes place in process context can be thought of as a part of the swapper process because the swapper creates SYSINIT, which in turn creates the STARTUP process. Because both SYSINIT and STARTUP are separate processes, they disappear after they are deleted (when they have completed their work).

B.1.5.2 **Infrequently Used System Routines.** The simplest technique used by the system to prevent infrequently used code from permanently occupying memory is to put it into the paged portion of the system image. The normal operation of system working set replacement eventually forces those pages that are referenced only occasionally out of the system working set.

This technique is used by several system services that are not called very often, such as the Set Time ($SETIME) system service, which changes the system time. Process creation and deletion are also not used as often as other system services.

Because process creation is spread throughout the system, the following techniques are employed to eliminate the code from the system after the process is created:

- The routines in the Create Process ($CREPRC) system service, Delete Process ($DELPRC) system service, and the kernel mode asynchronous system trap (AST) associated with $DELPRC are located in the paged executive. System working set list replacement will result in the reuse of the pages they occupied.
- The swapper has a special subroutine that it calls when it inswaps a newly created process from SHELL. This subroutine is located in several of the pages that the swapper just read into memory. Because of the way that the swapper does its I/O, these pages are mapped as P0 pages in the swapper's address space. These pages become the kernel stack of the new process (which cannot execute until the swapper changes the process state to computable resident, after it is finished with the special subroutine). The swapper has succeeded in executing several pages worth of code (that are only used the first time a process is inswapped) without requiring the allocation of any additional physical memory.
- The final steps of process creation take place in the context of the new process in routine EXE$PROCSTRT, located in the paged executive. System working set list replacement will result in the reuse of the pages it occupied.

B.1.6 **Dynamically Locking Code or Data into Memory**

The frequency of use is not the only criterion that is used to decide whether to put a routine into the paged or nonpaged executive. The page fault handler assumes that it will never incur a page fault above IPL 2. (This assumption is enforced by issuing a fatal bugcheck if it is violated.)

Several system services that are not used very often (including $CREPRC and $DELPRC) must elevate IPL to IPL$_SYNCH to synchronize access to the scheduler's database. There are several different techniques used to minimize the contribution that these routines make to the nonpaged executive.

B.1.6.1   **Locking Pages in External Images.** The simplest technique for locking down pages while executing at IPL$_SYNCH is used by privileged utilities that use the Change Mode to Kernel ($CMKRNL) system service. These programs can use the Lock Pages in Working Set ($LKWSET) system service to lock down the code and data pages that are referenced while IPL is elevated above 2.

B.1.6.2   **Placing Code in the Nonpaged Executive.** This technique puts the smallest possible block of code into the nonpaged executive and places the rest of the routine into the paged executive. A control transfer allows the nonpaged code to execute. The following variation on a routine within the Get Job/Process Information ($GETJPI) system service illustrates the technique. The reason that the entire routine cannot exist in pageable pages is because routine EXE$NAMPID returns at IPL$_SYNCH and thus may not incur a page fault.

```
        .PSECT YEXEPAGED
        .ENABLE LOCAL_BLOCK

          .
          .                       ;Processing begins
          .                       ;  in paged code
        JSB     25$
          .
          .

          .
        .SAVE_PSECT
        .PSECT AEXENONPAGED
25$:    BSBW    EXE$NAMPID        ;This is only
                                  ;  nonpaged piece
        SETIPL  #0
        RSB

        .RESTORE_PSECT
          .
          .                       ;Processing continues
          .                       ;  in paged code
```

B.1.6.3   **Dynamic Locking of Pages.** The preceding piece of code only contributes seven bytes to the nonpaged executive. The $CREPRC and $DELPRC system services must execute many more instructions at IPL$_SYNCH. They employ a technique that dynamically locks one or two pages into memory. (The executive cannot use the $LKWSET system service to lock pages into the system working set.)

This technique relies on the assumption that once IPL is elevated to IPL$_SYNCH, no events related to page faulting occur, particularly removing a page from the process or system working set.

```
                 .
                 .                      ;Processing begins
                 .                      ; in paged code

        BEGIN_LOCK:
                 DSBINT    LOCK_IPL
                 .
                 .                      ;No page faults
                 .                      ; will occur here
        ENBINT
                 .
                 .                      ;Page faults
                 .                      ; can occur again
                 BRB       END_LOCK

        LOCK_IPL:
                 .LONG     IPL$_SYNCH
        END_LOCK:


        ASSUME <END_LOCK-BEGIN_LOCK> LE 513
```

The key to this technique is that the DSBINT pseudo instruction cannot successfully complete until both the page containing the instruction and the page containing the source operand are valid. Once the instruction completes (implying that both pages are valid), IPL is set at IPL$_SYNCH, preventing further paging activity until the IPL is lowered (with the ENBINT macro). The DSBINT macro expands to the following instructions:

```
        MFPR    #PR$_IPL,-(SP)
        MTPR    src,#PR$_IPL
```

The ASSUME macro is necessary to ensure that the DSBINT macro and source operand are not more than one page apart, preventing the possibility of an invalid page between the two valid pages, an occurrence that would subvert this technique. It is also necessary to transfer control around the long-word containing IPL$_SYNCH.

A natural question at this point is why the first technique, the one used by $GETJPI, is necessary at all. It seems that the call site to EXE$NAMPID could be locked down using this technique. The answer is that EXE$NAM-PID cannot be invoked above IPL 2. It accesses the caller's argument list, a data reference that could potentially cause a page fault, and page faults are not allowed above IPL 2.

B.2 USE OF MAP FILES

One indispensable tool for reading the executive listings is the map file SYS.MAP, found in directory SYS$SYSTEM. This file was produced when the system image was linked and contains the system virtual addresses of all global symbols in the system image. More importantly from the point of view of reading the listings, it contains a cross-reference listing of modules that define and reference each global symbol.

The techniques that are described for using this file are also applicable to other map files. Map files for device drivers are necessary for debugging a new device driver. Use of the map files for Record Management Services (RMS), DCL, and other loadable images is also described, because these images are not activated in the usual way but, rather, are mapped into system or process virtual address space.

B.2.1 System Image Map, SYS.MAP

There are two main uses for the system map file. One of these occurs when the system crashes. The addresses that are reported on either the console terminal or in the system dump file must be related to actual routines in system address space. The portion of the map that lists in ascending order all program sections that contribute to the executive is useful here. The address in question is compared with each PSECT contribution until the module that defines the symbol is found. The base address of this module is subtracted from the address that is being examined to produce an offset into the correct module. This offset can be used with the assembler listing to locate the instruction or data reference that caused the error.

Such an error situation could arise as a result of a bug in the operating system but is more likely a result of some user-written code, such as a device driver, customized system service, or simply a procedure that is called through the $CMKRNL or the Change Mode to Executive ($CMEXEC) system service.

The only limitation to this use of the map is the resolution of a system virtual address larger than the highest address in the executive image. This type of address is most likely found in a routine that is dynamically loaded, such as RMS, a device driver, or CPU-dependent routines. Table F-2 lists the global pointers that locate each dynamically mapped portion of system address space. By examining the contents of these locations, the component that contains the offending address can often be determined.

SYS.MAP is a useful tool for reading most routines in the executive. Because of the modular construction of VMS, many routines referenced by one routine are in some other module. The simplest way to locate these external symbols is to look in the alphabetical cross-reference map for the external symbol name. The first item of information is the name of the module that defines this symbol. All modules that reference this symbol are listed in succeeding columns.

B.2.2   RMS.MAP, DCL.MAP, and MPxxx.MAP

The cross-reference capability mentioned in the description of SYS.MAP is useful for any component of the operating system that contains many modules. A module in DCL, for example, may contain a reference to an external subroutine. The module containing that subroutine can be determined with the cross-reference listing in the map file [DCL]DCL.MAP.

The RMS image, loadable asymmetric multiprocessing (MPxxx.EXE) images, and command language interpreters (CLIs) present a second problem to anyone attempting to relate code or data in virtual memory to references in an assembler listing or a map file. These images are mapped into a virtual address range that is not known until the mapping occurs. The maps, meanwhile, contain addresses beginning at zero.

Despite the fact that RMS and the loadable asymmetric multiprocessing code are mapped into system virtual address space and DCL is mapped into P1 space, the technique employed in these cases is the same. The technique to relate map addresses to virtual memory locations for these images is as follows.

When RMS is mapped by SYSINIT, the base address of the RMS image is stored in global location MMG$GL_RMSBASE. (The contents of this location are copied to location CTL$GL_RMSBASE in the P1 pointer page by EXE$PROCSTRT when a process is created.) The base address of any CLI is stored in the first longword at global location CTL$AG_CLIMAGE. Because both RMS and DCL are linked with a base address of zero, the contents of these two locations can be used as simple offsets to relate an address extracted from the map to a virtual address in a running system.

For example, if an error occurred at location X in system space and X was larger than the contents of MMG$GL_RMSBASE, denoted by Y, then the relative offset into the RMS image is simply Y − X. Obviously, if this difference is larger than the size of the RMS image, then address Y is not in RMS. The RMS map is file [RMS]RMS.MAP.

To present an example that goes in the other direction (from a relative address on an assembler listing to a virtual memory location), suppose that you want to locate a specific instruction in module DCLxyz, part of the DCL image. The relative offset in the assembly listing is added to the base address of module DCLxyz (taken from [DCL]DCL.MAP) to form the offset into the DCL image. This sum is added to the contents of global location CTL$AG_CLIMAGE to form the P1 virtual address of the instruction.

The asymmetric multiprocessing code is described by one of the map files [MP]MPxxx.MAP (see Chapter 27). When multiprocessing is turned on, the multiprocessing code is loaded into locations starting at the address specified in global location EXE$GL_MP. Thus, this address can be used as the base address for the multiprocessing image. Note that only part of the multiprocessing code is loaded (up to the PSECT named _END, defined in module MPLOAD). The remainder of the multiprocessing code is used to interpret the DCL commands START/CPU, STOP/CPU, and SHOW CPU and to load the multiprocessing code into nonpaged pool.

B.2.3 Device Driver Map Files

Device drivers are loaded into nonpaged pool by SYSGEN. The SHOW /DEVICE command to this utility displays among other pieces of information the address range into which the driver image is loaded. The address of the DDT from the driver map (program section $$$115_DRIVER) gives the base address that is used to convert addresses on the assembly listing to system virtual addresses. Debugging device drivers is discussed in more detail in the manual *Writing a Device Driver for VAX/VMS*.

B.2.4 CPU-Dependent Routines

The base address of the CPU-dependent code (see Chapter 25) is stored in the global location MMG$GL_SYSLOA_BASE. The map files for these routines have names of the form [SYSLOA]SYSLOAxxx.EXE. Appendix G contains a list of the SYSLOA images.

B.2.5 Other Map Files

Other map files can also be used for the cross-reference capabilities already mentioned. In addition, many other components of the operating system execute as regular images, so no base addresses have to be used to locate addresses in virtual address space. The addresses on the map correspond to the virtual addresses that are used for an executable image. However, the map file does not include the base address of nonbased, PIC shareable images; their base addresses are determined at image activation time.

SYSTEM DUMP ANALYZER

Because some of the routines and most of the data structures used by the VAX/VMS operating system are loaded or constructed dynamically, the map file is limited in its ability to relate addresses to data structures or routines. In addition, the map file can only supply addresses of static data storage areas in the system, and not their contents. The System Dump Analyzer (SDA) Utility is a tool that overcomes these limitations of the map files. The use of SDA is described in the *VAX/VMS System Dump Analyzer Reference Manual*. This section mentions several of the many SDA commands that are especially useful when studying how the operating system works.

Global Locations

Many of the dynamic data structures, located in parts of system address space that are beyond the last address in the executive image, are located through global pointers in the static part of the executive (the part found in the image SYS.EXE). These static locations are loaded when the structures in question are created or modified, either as a part of system initialization or some other loading mechanism.

One way to display these global pointers is the SDA command SHOW SYMBOLS /ALL. It shows not only the addresses but also the contents of all global locations. This list, together with the map file SYS.MAP, enables any data structure to be located in system address space if the global name of the listhead that locates the structure is known. Alternatively, the EXAMINE command can be used to determine the contents of particular global pointers. Appendix C contains a complete list of the static data locations used by the system.

SDA defines symbols for the base addresses of some of the loadable images described in Section B.2 and a number of other loadable images. These symbols include the following:

- CLUSTRLOA—Base address of VAXcluster support
- *xx*DRIVER (*xx* is a device name)—Base address of device driver
- FPEMUL—Base address of floating-point emulation code
- MP—Base address of asymmetric multiprocessing code
- MSCP—Base address of the mass storage control protocol (MSCP) server
- RMS—Base address of RMS
- SCSLOA—Base address of system communications services (SCS) image

- SYSLOA—Base address of CPU-specific code
- VAXEMUL—Base address of string emulation code

With these symbols it is possible to form simple address expressions to specify a particular location in any of these modules. For example, the following SDA command examines offset 100_{16} in RMS:

```
EXAMINE RMS + 100
```

B.3.2 Layout of System Virtual Address Space

A second useful application of SDA involves creating a picture of system address space. As Figure F-2 shows, many of the pieces of system address space are constructed at initialization time. The sizes of the various pieces are determined by SYSBOOT parameters (see Appendix F). In response to the command SHOW PAGE_TABLE /SYSTEM, SDA lists the contents of the entire system page table. This listing, the symbol table described in the previous section, and the system image map SYS$SYSTEM:SYS.MAP allow an accurate picture of system virtual address space to be drawn.

B.3.3 Layout of P1 Space

SDA can also be used to obtain the layout of P1 space. Most of the pieces of P1 space (see Figure 1-7 and Table F-5) are fixed in size. The P1 page tables defined in module SHELL determine the sizes of these pieces of P1 space. Other pieces may not even exist for some processes. In any case, the SDA command SHOW PROCESS/PAGE_TABLES/P1 produces a complete layout of P1 space.

B.4 INTERPRETING SDL FILES

Most data structures and other systemwide constants used by the executive and other system components are defined with a structure definition language (SDL). SDL enables data structures to be defined in a language-independent way. SDL can generate one or more language-specific versions of a structure.

When a VAX/VMS system is built from source, the SDL preprocessor reads and processes system data structure definitions written in SDL. It produces a set of macro definitions for use by VAX MACRO and another set for the BLISS-32 compiler.

In particular, there are SDL files that generate the macros defining data structures and constants in the VAX MACRO libraries SYS$LIBRARY: LIB.MLB and STARLET.MLB and the BLISS-32 files SYS$LIBRARY:LIB.REQ and STARLET.REQ. These SDL files are supplied with both the VAX/VMS source kit and microfiche listing kit. The SDL definition of a data structure typically includes comments describing the fields of the structure. The SDL definition can thus be a source of information about the meaning of system data structure fields. These comments are not propagated to LIB.MLB and STARLET.MLB, although they do appear in LIB.REQ and STARLET.REQ.

This section shows how the SDL description of a data structure is related to both the resulting VAX MACRO definition and a picture of the structure. Its sole purpose is to assist in the interpretation of SDL files supplied with VAX/VMS. Note that SDL is an internal DIGITAL tool. Any other use is completely unsupported.

B.4.1   A Sample Structure Definition

One way to see how a structure is defined is to look at the resultant symbol definitions. The SDL definition of a given structure can be compared with the resultant VAX MACRO or BLISS-32 symbols. These symbols can be found in any listing that uses the structure in question. Alternatively, the command procedure listed in Section B.1.1.1 can be used.

Example B-1 shows the SDL definition of the AST control block (ACB) and the comments that accompany each field definition. Figure 7-1 shows the layout of an ACB. Table B-1 lists each SDL directive in the ACB definition, its meaning, the symbol it creates, and the value of that symbol. Individual SDL directives are briefly described in the following subsections.

B.4.2   Commonly Used SDL Statements

An SDL statement consists of SDL keywords, user-specified names, and expressions. An SDL statement is terminated by a semicolon. It can be followed by a comment to be included in the output macro. The comment must begin with the character pair "/*".

Valid SDL expressions can contain any of the following:

- Numeric constants
- Local symbols
- The special offset location symbols: period (.), colon (:), and circumflex (ˆ)
- Arithmetic, shift, and logical operators
- Parentheses to define the order of evaluation

The next subsections describe the SDL statements commonly used in defining structures used by VAX/VMS. Emphasis is on reading the SDL files used to build the system. A complete syntax of each statement is not given.

B.4.2.1   MODULE Statement.
A MODULE statement groups related symbols and data structures. It defines a collection of SDL statements to be processed.

Example B-1   SDL Definition of AST Control Block

```
module $ACBDEF;
/*+
/* AST CONTROL BLOCK DEFINITIONS
/*
/* AST control blocks exist as separate structures and as substructures
/* within larger control blocks such as I/O request packets and timer
/* queue entries.
/*
/*-


aggregate ACBDEF structure prefix ACB$;
  ASTQFL longword unsigned;                              /*AST queue forward link
  ASTQBL longword unsigned;                              /*AST queue backward link
  SIZE word unsigned;                                    /*Structure size in bytes
  TYPE byte unsigned;                                    /*Structure type code
  RMOD_OVERLAY union fill;
    RMOD byte unsigned;                                  /*Request access mode
    RMOD_BITS structure fill;
      MODE bitfield length 2;                            /*Mode for final delivery
      FILL_1 bitfield length 2 fill prefix ACBDEF tag $$; /*Spare
      PKAST bitfield mask;                               /*Piggyback
                                                         /* special kernel AST
      NODELETE bitfield mask;                            /*Don't delete ACB
                                                         /* on delivery
      QUOTA bitfield mask;                               /*Account for quota
      KAST bitfield mask;                                /*Special kernel AST
    end RMOD_BITS;
  end RMOD_OVERLAY;
  PID longword unsigned;                                 /*Process ID of request
  AST longword unsigned;                                 /*AST routine address
  ASTPRM longword unsigned;                              /*AST parameter
  KAST longword unsigned;                                /*Internal kernel mode
                                                         /* transfer address
  constant "LENGTH" equals . prefix ACB$ tag K;          /*Length of block
  constant "LENGTH" equals . prefix ACB$ tag C;          /*Length of block

end ACBDEF;


end_module $ACBDEF;
```

Table B-1 SDL Description and Resultant Macro Symbol Definitions for AST Control Block

SDL Directive	Meaning of Directive	Resultant Symbol Name	Symbol Value
module $ACBDEF	Begin $ACBDEF macro		
aggregate ACBDEF structure prefix ACB$	Begin ACB structure		
ASTQFL longword unsigned	Longword field	ACB$L_ASTQFL	0
ASTQBL longword unsigned	Longword field	ACB$L_ASTQBL	4
SIZE word unsigned	Word field	ACB$W_SIZE	8
TYPE byte unsigned	Byte field	ACB$B_TYPE	10
RMOD_OVERLAY union fill	Define beginning of overlay structure		
RMOD byte unsigned	Byte field	ACB$B_RMOD	11
RMOD_BITS structure fill	Begin RMOD_BITS structure		
MODE bitfield length 2	Bit field of length 2	ACB$V_MODE	0
		ACB$S_MODE	2
FILL_1 bitfield length 2 fill prefix ACBDEF tag $$	Skip 2 spare bits		
PKAST bitfield mask	Single bit field	ACB$V_PKAST	4
		ACB$M_PKAST	10_{16}
NODELETE bitfield mask	Single bit field	ACB$V_NODELETE	5
		ACB$M_NODELETE	20_{16}
QUOTA bitfield mask	Single bit field	ACB$V_QUOTA	6
		ACB$M_QUOTA	40_{16}
KAST bitfield mask	Single bit field	ACB$V_KAST	7
		ACB$M_KAST	80_{16}
end RMOD_BITS	End RMOD_BITS structure		
end RMOD_OVERLAY	End the overlay structure		
PID longword unsigned	Longword field	ACB$L_PID	12
AST longword unsigned	Longword field	ACB$L_AST	16
ASTPRM longword unsigned	Longword field	ACB$L_ASTPRM	20
KAST longword unsigned	Longword field	ACB$L_KAST	24
constant "LENGTH" equals . prefix ACB$ tag K	Define a constant	ACB$K_LENGTH	28
constant "LENGTH" equals . prefix ACB$ tag C	Define a constant	ACB$C_LENGTH	28
end ACBDEF	End ACB structure		
end_module $ACBDEF	End $ACBDEF macro		

Typically, each VAX/VMS data structure is defined within its own module. The name of the module is the name of the generated macro. For example, the following statement from Example B-1 defines the beginning of the module that defines the ACB data structure:

```
module $ACBDEF;
```

B.4.2.2   **AGGREGATE Statement.** An AGGREGATE declaration defines a single data structure within a module. There are two types of AGGREGATE declaration:

- STRUCTURE
- UNION

The fields in a STRUCTURE occupy consecutive storage locations; the fields in a UNION reuse the same storage location.

The period character symbolizes the current byte offset within an AGGREGATE declaration.

Each VMS data structure definition begins with an AGGREGRATE STRUCTURE statement. This statement includes a PREFIX keyword that specifies the prefix characters in each symbol definition. For example, the following statement from Example B-1 defines the beginning of the ACB structure, each of whose symbol definitions begin with the characters ACB$:

```
aggregate ACBDEF structure prefix ACB$;
```

B.4.2.3   **Data Structure Fields.** Each field in a data structure is defined in a statement consisting of a name and one or more keywords. A keyword can identify the type of data and/or its size. For example, the keywords BYTE, WORD, LONGWORD, QUADWORD, and OCTAWORD specify integer fields of those sizes. A keyword can specify some attribute of a field. For example, the keyword SIGNED specifies that an integer field is signed. The default is unsigned. Many other keywords are used to define VMS data structures. Examples are F_FLOATING, BITFIELD, and CHARACTER.

The value of the symbol name is set equal to the current value of an internal offset counter. In general, as each field definition is processed, the internal counter value is increased by the size of the field (1, 2, 4, or 8).

B.4.2.4   **Symbol Names.** The naming conventions that apply to VMS symbols defined through SDL are listed in Appendix D. In general, a data structure symbol has the form *structure$type_field-name*. *Structure* identifies its data structure. *Type* identifies the type of data. *Field-name* names the field.

A data structure symbol name is formed from a combination of the following:

- PREFIX keyword value
- Letter indicating type. Data type keywords of BYTE, WORD, LONG-

WORD, QUADWORD, or OCTAWORD generate characters B, W, L, Q, or O. A CONSTANT statement usually specifies a TAG value of C or K.
- Underscore (_)
- Field name on a data type statement

B.4.2.5   **Symbol Values.** It is possible for the user to assign values directly to a symbol defined as part of an SDL structure (for example, with the DEFAULT keyword). Normally, however, SDL assumes that a symbol will be used as an offset from the beginning of its data structure. SDL keeps track of the current offset from the start of the structure, and SDL assigns that value to the symbol.

B.4.2.6   **Unions.** It is often desirable to give a field multiple names. In addition, subfields within a field often exist. The UNION statement defines the beginning of a substructure whose members reuse the same storage locations. The following extract from Example B-1 shows a UNION substructure:

```
RMOD_OVERLAY union fill;
  RMOD byte unsigned;
  RMOD_BITS structure fill;
        .
        .
        .
  end RMOD_BITS;
end RMOD_OVERLAY;
```

This extract defines the symbol ACB$B_RMOD and the structure ACB$R_RMOD_BITS to be the value of the current byte offset.

The FILL qualifier indicates that no symbol is to be generated in the MACRO and BLISS expansion of the structure definition.

B.4.2.7   **CONSTANT Statement.** The CONSTANT statement defines a constant. Depending on what TAG argument is supplied, the C directive produces symbols of the form *xyz$C_name*, *xyz$K_name*, or *xyz$_name*.

Table B-1 illustrates one use of the CONSTANT statement.

```
constant "LENGTH" equals . prefix ACB$ tag K;
```

This statement defines the symbol ACB$K_LENGTH equal to the value of the period character, the current byte offset in the ACB structure.

There are several other examples of constant definitions in both the SYSDEF and STARDEF SDL files. The definitions of the DYN$ symbols describe dynamically allocated structures. The JPI$ symbols describe an information list to the $GETJPI system service.

B.4.2.8   **BITFIELD Statement.** Bit fields require two numbers to completely describe them, a bit position and size. SDL always defines a bit position (indicated by a V_ in the symbol name). The bit position is specified by the current bit offset. The circumflex character symbolizes the current bit offset within the current subaggregate.

The size of a field (indicated by S in the symbol name) is always defined when the field size is specified explicitly with the LENGTH keyword. It is often useful to define a mask symbol (indicated by *type* of M in the symbol name) that has 1's in each bit position defined by the bit field and zeros elsewhere. SDL defines such a symbol if the MASK keyword is present in the BITFIELD statement.

Because this section merely tries to show what symbols result from a given SDL definition, the simplest way to describe the bit field syntax is with some examples. Table B-1 includes SDL BITFIELD statements extracted from the definition of the ACB.

B.4.2.9   **END and END_MODULE Statements.** The structure definition is terminated with an END statement. The module is terminated with an END_MODULE statement.

Appendix C

Executive Data Areas

The writable executive consists of several dynamically allocated tables as well as statically allocated data structures that are a part of the system image SYS.EXE. This appendix summarizes all of these data areas, with an emphasis on the static executive database that is related to other material in this book.

The information presented in this appendix was accumulated by incorporating data from the system map (SYS.MAP) with the contents of specific source modules. Information outside the scope of this book is simply summarized. There is no attempt to include every global symbol in SYS.EXE in this appendix. Data blocks (such as unit control blocks or timer queue elements) are referenced as single entities. Global labels within such structures are ignored. Global labels associated with backward link pointers of doubly linked lists are also omitted. Names that appear in the "Global Symbol" column in lowercase represent local symbols, names that are only used within the module in which they are defined.

C.1 STATICALLY ALLOCATED EXECUTIVE DATA

The cells that contain the data described in this section can be identified with specific source modules in the executive. Those cells that can be addressed directly with a global name are so indicated. Program section names (.PSECT names) are included in each section title to allow easy location of a given data area. Program sections of zero length declared in module MDAT for the purpose of defining global labels that separate major sections of SYS.EXE are not included here. They can be found by examining SYS.MAP.

C.1.1 System Service Vector Area ($$$000)

The first five pages of system virtual address space contain the system service vectors. These pages are read-only. The global label MMG$A_ENDVEC, defined in module MDAT, represents the high address end of the system service vector pages.

C.1.2 File System Performance Monitor Data ($$$000PMS)

Module PMSDAT defines this area. It consists of a block of 95 longwords used to describe the cumulative behavior of the file system. The file system consists of the On-Disk Structure Level 1 (ODS-1) ancillary control process

(ACP) and the On-Disk Structure Level 2 (ODS-2) Extended QIO Processor (XQP). Additional longwords in this area contain information on XQP file operations.

Global Symbol	Size	Description of Data
PMS$GL_FCP \ PMS$GL_FCP2 /	70 longwords	File system statistics
PMS$GL_TURN	Longword	Number of window turns
PMS$GL_SPLIT	Longword	Number of split I/O transfers
PMS$GL_HIT	Longword	Number of transfers not requiring window turns
PMS$GL_DIRHIT	Longword	Number of directory LRU hits
PMS$GL_DIRMISS	Longword	Number of directory LRU misses
PMS$GL_QUOHIT	Longword	Number of quota cache hits
PMS$GL_QUOMISS	Longword	Number of quota cache misses
PMS$GL_FIDHIT	Longword	Number of file ID cache hits
PMS$GL_FIDMISS	Longword	Number of file ID cache misses
PMS$GL_EXTHIT	Longword	Number of extent cache hits
PMS$GL_EXTMISS	Longword	Number of extent cache misses
PMS$GL_FILHDR_HIT	Longword	Number of file header cache hits
PMS$GL_FILHDR_MISS	Longword	Number of file header cache misses
PMS$GL_DIRDATA_HIT	Longword	Number of directory data block hits
PMS$GL_DIRDATA_MISS	Longword	Number of directory data block misses
PMS$GL_STORAGMAP_HIT	Longword	Number of storage bit map cache hits
PMS$GL_STORAGMAP_MISS	Longword	Number of storage bit map cache misses
PMS$GL_OPEN	Longword	Number of currently opened files
PMS$GL_OPENS	Longword	Total number of file opens
PMS$GL_ERASEIO	Longword	Total count of erase $QIOs issued
PMS$GL_VOLLCK	Longword	Number of XQP volume synchronization locks
PMS$GL_VOLWAIT	Longword	Number of times XQP waited for volume synchronization lock
PMS$GL_SYNCHLCK	Longword	Number of XQP directory and file synchronization locks
PMS$GL_SYNCHWAIT	Longword	Number of XQP waits for a directory or file synchronization lock
PMS$GL_ACCLCK	Longword	Number of XQP access locks
PMS$GL_XQPCACHEWAIT	Longword	Number of XQP waits for cache free space

C.1.3 RMS Writable Area ($$$000RMS)

This area, defined in module SYSCOMMON, provides RMS with a system-wide area writable from executive mode.

Global Symbol	Size	Description of Data
RMS$GW_GBLBUFQUO	Word	Current global buffer quota remaining
	31 words	Reserved for future use

C.1.4   Process Database ($$$000_STACKS)

Module PDAT defines kernel mode stacks for two system processes: the null process and the swapper process. Note that the global symbol for the swapper's kernel stack points to the base (high address) of the stack.

Global Symbol	Size	Description of Data
	32 longwords	Kernel mode stack for the null process
SWP$A_KSTK	160 longwords	Kernel mode stack for swapper

C.1.5   Miscellaneous Bugcheck Information ($$$025)

Module BUGCHECK maintains several longwords about a fatal bugcheck in progress.

Global Symbol	Size	Description of Data
bugchk_flags	Longword	Flags used by bugcheck code
fatal_spsav	Longword	Fatal bugcheck in progress stack pointer
EXE$GL_BUGCHECK	Longword	Saved fatal bugcheck code

C.1.6   Data Structures for Drivers Linked with the Operating System ($$$100)

Module DEVICEDAT contains data structures for the devices that are linked as a part of the system image SYS.EXE. These devices include the null device, several mailboxes, and the console terminal.

There are unit control blocks (UCBs) for three mailboxes defined in DEVICEDAT. The UCB for unit 0 is a skeleton UCB that is copied to create a new mailbox. The job controller and OPCOM mailboxes use predefined UCBs.

Global Symbol	Size	Description of Data
IOC$GL_ADPLIST	Longword	Listhead of adapter control blocks
IOC$GL_DPTLIST	Quadword	Listhead of driver prolog tables (DPTs)
TTY$GL_DPT	Longword	Address of terminal class driver DPT
NO$GL_DPT	Longword	Address of asynchronous class driver DPT
TTY$GL_JOBCTLMB	Longword	Address of job controller mailbox
SYS$GL_UIS	Longword	Address of loaded UIS code
UIS$GL_USB	Longword	UIS context block
SYS$GL_FALLBACK	Longword	Systemwide terminal/printer fallback table
SCS$GA_LOCALSB	104 bytes	Permanent local SCS system block
• IOC$GL_DEVLIST		Listhead of DDBs of all devices (part of system block)

Global Symbol	Size	Description of Data
SYS$GL_BOOTDDB	68 bytes	Device data block (DDB) for system disk
SYS$GL_BOOTORB	88 bytes	Object rights block (ORB) for system disk
SYS$GL_BOOTUCB	252 bytes	UCB for nonshadowed system disk
OPA$GL_DDB	68 bytes	DDB for console terminal
OPA$ORB0	88 bytes	ORB for console terminal
OPA$UCB0	372 bytes	UCB for console terminal
OPA$CRB	84 bytes	Channel request block (CRB) for console terminal
OPA$IDB	32 bytes	Interrupt dispatch block (IDB) for console device
MB$GL_DDB	68 bytes	DDB for mailbox
MB$ORB0	88 bytes	ORB for mailbox
MB$UCB0	144 bytes	UCB template used in mailbox creation (not linked into mailbox DDB's UCB list)
SYS$GL_JOBCTLMB	144 bytes	UCB for job controller's mailbox (MBA1)
MB$GL_ORB1	88 bytes	ORB for MBA1
SYS$GL_OPRMBX	144 bytes	UCB for operator's mailbox (MBA2)
MB$GL_ORB2	88 bytes	ORB for MBA2
NL$GL_DDB	68 bytes	DDB for null device
NL$GL_ORB0	88 bytes	ORB for null device
NL$GL_UCB0	144 bytes	UCB for null device
NET$WCB	48 bytes	Window control block for network pseudo device
sys_crb	72 bytes	CRB for mailboxes

C.1.7 Driver Prolog Tables ($$$105_PROLOGUE)

The driver prolog tables for these drivers are assembled and linked into the system image. The contributions to this part of the writable executive come from three modules (MBDRIVER, NLDRIVER, and DEVICEDAT) that are linked with SYS.EXE.

Global Symbol	Size	Description of Data
		MODULE MBDRIVER
MB$DPT	57 bytes	DPT for mailbox driver
		MODULE NLDRIVER
NL$DPT	57 bytes	DPT for null device driver
		MODULE DEVICEDAT
OP$DPT	160 bytes	DPT for console terminal device driver
OPA$VECTOR	60 bytes	Console port dispatch vector

C.1.8   Linked Driver Code ($$$115_DRIVER)

There is a section that contains the driver code for these drivers. This section is bounded by the two global labels MMG$AL_BEGDRIVE and MMG$AL_ENDDRIVE, defined in module MDAT.

C.1.9   Memory Management Data ($$$210)

The memory management data consists mainly of listheads for dynamically allocated structures.

Global Symbol	Size	Description of Data
	MODULE ALLOCPFN	
FN$AL_HEAD	3 longwords	Pointers to the heads of the free, modified, and bad page lists
fn$al_tail	3 longwords	Pointers to the tails of the free, modified, and bad page lists
CH$GL_FREECNT	Longword	Free page count
CH$GL_MFYCNT	Longword	Modified page count
fn$al_count + 8	Longword	Bad page count
FN$GL_PHYPGCNT	Longword	Number of available physical pages
CH$GL_FREEREQ	Longword	Free pages required by the swapper
CH$GL_MFYLIM	Longword	Modified page list high limit
FN$AL_HILIMIT + 8	Longword	Bad page list high limit
CH$GL_FREELIM	Longword	Free page list low limit
CH$GL_MYFLOLIM	Longword	Modified page list low limit
FN$AL_LOLIMIT + 8	Longword	Bad page list low limit
CH$GL_MFYLIMSV	Longword	Saved high-limit threshold of modified page list
CH$GL_MFYLOSV	Longword	Saved low-limit threshold of modified page list
	MODULE PAGEFAULT	
MS$GL_FAULTS	16 longwords	Page fault statistics for Monitor Utility
	MODULE WRTMFYPAG	
MPW$AL_PTE	Longword	Pointer to modified page writer PTE array
MPW$AW_PHVINDEX	Longword	Pointer to PHD vector index array used by the modified page writer
MPW$GL_BADPAGTOTAL	Longword	Number of pages placed on the bad page list
	MODULE SYSLKWSET	
MMG$GL_PFNLOCK	Longword	Count-down counter of pages remaining that may be locked in memory

C.1.10   **Scheduler Data ($$$220)**

The scheduler's database is defined primarily in module SDAT. This module contains the queue headers for each of the scheduling states and related counters. Several other modules (particularly SWAPPER) also contribute to this program section.

Global Symbol	Size	Description of Data
	MODULE SDAT	
	Quadword	Terminates outswap scheduling scan
SCH$AQ_COMH	32 quadwords	Listheads for computable processes at all software priority levels
SCH$AQ_COMOH	32 quadwords	Listheads for computable outswapped processes for all software priority levels
SCH$AQ_WQHDR	132 bytes (132 = 11 * 12)	Wait queue headers for 11 wait states
SCH$GL_CURPCB	Longword	Address of PCB of current process
SCH$GL_COMQS	Longword	Queue summary longword for COM state
SCH$GL_COMOQS	Longword	Queue summary longword for COMO state
SCH$GB_SIP	Byte	Swap flags
• SCH$V_MPW	Bit	Modified page writer active
• SCH$V_SIP	Bit	Swap in progress
SCH$GB_RESCAN	Byte	Queue reordering notification
• SCH$V_REORD	Bit	flags
		RELPFN has reordered the queue
MMG$GB_FREWFLGS	Byte	SWAPPER/FREWSLE communication flags
• MMG$V_NOWAIT	Bit	FREWSLE may not enter resource wait for pages from the modified list
• MMG$V_NOLASTUPD	Bit	FREWSLE may not update WSLAST
SCH$GW_PROCCNT	Word	Current number of processes requiring swap file (does not count NULL or SWAPPER)
SCH$GW_PROCLIM	Word	Maximum number of processes on the system
SWP$GL_SLOTCNT	Longword	Number of available swap slots

Global Symbol	*Size*	*Description of Data*
	MODULE SDAT	
SCH$GQ_CEBHD	Quadword	Listhead for common event blocks
SCH$GW_CEBCNT	Word	Number of common event blocks
SCH$GW_DELPHDCT	Word	Number of PHDs of already deleted processes
SWP$GL_SHELL	Longword	Shell process swap address
SWP$GL_INPCB	Longword	PCB address of process being swapped into memory
SWP$GL_ISPAGCNT	Longword	Inswap page count
SWP$GW_IBALSETX	Word	Balance set slot index for inswap process
SWP$GB_ISWPRI	Byte	Priority of inswap process
	Byte	Spare for alignment
SWP$GL_ISWPPAGES	Longword	Number of inswapped pages
SWP$GL_ISWPCNT	Longword	Number of inswaps performed
SWP$GL_OSWPCNT	Longword	Number of outswaps performed
SWP$GL_HOSWPCNT	Longword	Number of header outswaps
SWP$GL_HISWPCNT	Longword	Number of header inswaps
SCH$GL_RESMASK	Longword	Resource wait mask vector
SCH$GB_PRI	Byte	Priority of current process
	3 bytes	Spare for alignment
	MODULE OSWPSCHED	
SWP$GL_SWTIME	Longword	Earliest time for next exchange swap
saved_r3	Longword	Outswap state table
	MODULE PAGEFILE	
MMG$GL_NULLPFL	36 bytes	Null page file control block
MMG$GL_PAGSWPVC	Longword	Pointer to vector of page/swap file control blocks
MMG$GL_MAXPFIDX	Longword	Maximum page file index currently in use
MMG$GW_MINPFIDX	Word	Minimum page file index currently in use
SGN$GW_SWPFILCT		Number of swap file slots
	MODULE POWERFAIL	
EXE$GL_PWRDONE	Longword	End time for power recovery interval

Global Symbol	Size	Description of Data
	MODULE POWERFAIL	
EXE$GL_PWRINTVL	Longword	Allowable recovery interval in ten-millisecond units
	MODULE SWAPPER	
ioroutine	Longword	Address of read or write build packet routine
ioea	Longword	I/O end action routine
rwsswp	Longword	Remaining working set swap address
rsvapte	Longword	Remaining system virtual address of page table entries
rpgcnt	Word	Remaining page count
oswppgs	Word	Outswap page count
oswppcb	Longword	Address of PCB of outswap process
SWP$GW_BALCNT	Word	Number of processes in balance set excluding swapper and null processes
SCH$GW_SWPFCNT	Word	Number of successive outswap schedule failures

C.1.11   Memory Management Data ($$$222)

This program section contains the data cell contribution of module MDAT to the executive. MDAT also defines global labels that separate data areas from read-only sections and that separate pageable code from nonpaged routines. In addition, MDAT allocates patch areas for the executive.

Global Symbol	Size	Description of Data
PHV$GL_PIXBAS	Longword	Address of process index array
PHV$GL_REFCBAS	Longword	Address of PHD reference count array
EXE$GQ_GBLHOOK1	10 quadwords	Variables for adding loadable routines between major releases
EXE$GL_CPUNODSP	Longword	Virtual address that maps CPU node private space
EXE$GL_CONFREGL	Longword	Address of nexus device type longword array
EXE$GL_CONFREG	Longword	Address of nexus device type byte array
MMG$GL_SBICONF	Longword	Address of a longword array containing nexus slot virtual addresses
EXE$GL_NUMNEXUS	Longword	Maximum nexus number possible
MMG$GL_RMSBASE	Longword	Address of RMS image

Global Symbol	Size	Description of Data
MG$GL_FPEMUL_BASE	Longword	Base address of floating-point instruction emulator
MG$GL_SYSLOA_BASE	Longword	Base address of SYSLOAxxx.EXE
MG$GL_VAXEMUL_BASE	Longword	Base address of decimal/string instruction emulator
MG$GL_GBLSECFND	Longword	Last global section table entry found when deleting page file backing store addresses
MG$GL_GBLPAGFIL	Longword	Remaining page file available for global sections

C.1.12 Process Data for System Processes ($$$230)

Two processes exist as a part of the system image. They are the swapper and the null process. The module PDAT defines their software PCBs and PHDs. In addition, it defines a system header containing the system page table (SPT, see Chapter 14 and Appendix F), a system PCB to support system paging, and some other data.

Global Symbol	Size	Description of Data
nulphd	380 bytes	Minimal PHD (fixed portion only) for null process
SCH$GL_NULLPCB	228 bytes	PCB for null process
swpphd	380 bytes	Minimal PHD (fixed portion only) for swapper process
SCH$GL_SWPPCB	228 bytes	PCB for swapper process
MMG$AL_SYSPCB	228 bytes	System PCB
SCH$GL_PCBVEC	Longword	Address of PCB vector of longwords
SCH$GL_SEQVEC	Longword	Address of sequence vector of words
SCH$GL_MAXPIX	Longword	Maximum process index for this system
SCH$GL_PIXLAST	Longword	Last process index created
SCH$GL_PIXWIDTH	Longword	Width of process index field determined by MAXPROCESSCNT parameter
SCH$GW_LOCALNODE	Word	ID for local VAXcluster node
	Word	Spare for alignment

C.1.13 SYSCOMMON—Miscellaneous Executive Data ($$$260)

Module SYSCOMMON contains most of the miscellaneous listheads, counters, semaphores, and other data that is not directly tied to one of the major subsystems. Module ERRORLOG also makes a significant contribution to this program section.

Executive Data Areas

Global Symbol	Size	Description of Data
EXE$GL_FLAGS	Longword	System flags longword (see Section C.1.16)
EXE$GL_STATE_FLAGS	Longword	State of system control flags
EXE$GQ_ERLMBX	Quadword	Descriptor of error log mailbox
	• Word	Unit number
	• Word	Spare for alignment
	• Longword	Process ID of assigner
EXE$GL_VAXEXCVEC	Longword	Address for intercept VAX CPU exception dispatching
EXE$GL_FPEXCVEC	Longword	Address for intercept of floating exception dispatching
EXE$GL_USRCHMK	Longword	Address of systemwide user-written change mode to kernel dispatcher
EXE$GL_USRCHME	Longword	Address of systemwide user-written change mode to executive dispatcher
SWI$GL_FQFL	6 quadwords	Fork queue listheads for IPLs 6 through 11 (IPL 7 used only as a place holder)
EXE$GL_FKWAITFL	Quadword	Fork and wait work queue listhead
LNM$AL_HASHTBL	3 longwords	Addresses of logical name hash tables
LNM$AL_DIRTBL	3 longwords	Addresses of logical name directory table
LNM$AL_MUTEX	Longwords	Mutex for shareable logical database
LNM$GL_SYSDIRSEQ	Longword	Sequence number for cache of logical name table translations
EXE$GL_SYSUCB	Longword	Address of system disk UCB
FIL$GT_DDDEV	14 bytes	Counted ASCII string of default device (SYS$SYSDEVICE)
FIL$GT_TOPSYS	10 bytes	Counted ASCII string of top-level system directory on default device
FIL$GQ_CACHE	Quadword	File read cache descriptor
EXE$GQ_BOOTCB_D	Quadword	Descriptor for boot control block
EXE$GL_SAVEDUMP	Longword	Number of page file blocks to release when dump is copied from page file
EXE$GL_ERASEPB	Longword	Address of an erase pattern buffer (EPB) containing zeros
EXE$GL_ERASEPPT	Longword	Address of a pseudo page table that maps the EPB filled in by INIT
IOC$GL_PSFL IOC$GL_PSBL	Quadword	Listhead for I/O postprocessing queue
IOC$GL_IRPFL IOC$GL_IRPBL	Quadword	Listhead for IRP lookaside list
IOC$GL_IRPREM	Longword	Address of partial IRP
IOC$GL_IRPCNT	Longword	Current count of allocated IRPs
IOC$GL_IRPMIN	Longword	Minimum request that can be allocated an IRP
IOC$GL_SRPFL IOC$GL_SRPBL	Quadword	Listhead for SRP lookaside list

Global Symbol	*Size*	*Description of Data*
IOC$GL_SRPSIZE	Longword	Size of an SRP
IOC$GL_SRPMIN	Longword	Minimum request that can be allocated an SRP (unused)
IOC$GL_SRPSPLIT	Longword	Boundary between SRP and IRP lookaside lists
IOC$GL_SRPREM	Longword	Address of partial SRP
IOC$GL_SRPCNT	Longword	Current count of allocated SRPs
IOC$GL_LRPFL IOC$GL_LRPBL	Quadword	Listhead for LRP lookaside list
IOC$GL_LRPSIZE	Longword	Size of an LRP
IOC$GL_LRPMIN	Longword	Minimum request that can be allocated an LRP
IOC$GL_LRPSPLIT	Longword	Boundary between LRP lookaside list and the main portion of nonpaged pool
IOC$GL_LRPREM	Longword	Address of partial LRP
IOC$GL_LRPCNT	Longword	Number of LRPs currently allocated
IOC$GL_POOLFKB	6 longwords	Fork block for pool expansion
IOC$GL_PFKBINT	Longword	Fork block interlock (0 = free)
EXE$GL_PQBFL EXE$GL_PQBBL	Quadword	Listhead for PQB lookaside list
IOC$GL_AQBLIST	Longword	ACP queue block listhead
IOC$GQ_MOUNTLST	Quadword	Systemwide mounted volume list
IOC$GQ_BRDCST	Quadword	Unused
IOC$GL_CRBTMOUT	Longword	List of CRBs to scan for timeouts
IOC$GL_DU_CDDB	Longword	Listhead of CDDBs for disk class driver connections
IOC$GL_TU_CDDB	Longword	Listhead of CDDBs for tape class driver connections
IOC$GL_HIRT	Longword	Pointer to host initiated replacement table (used by MSCP disks)
IOC$GL_SHDW_WRK	Longword	Address of area used for processing shadow set generation number comparisons (unused)
EXE$GL_GSDGRPFL EXE$GL_GSDGRPBL	Quadword	Listhead for group GSD list
EXE$GL_GSDSYSFL EXE$GL_GSDSYSBL	Quadword	Listhead for system GSD list
EXE$GL_GSDDELFL EXE$GL_GSDDELBL	Quadword	Listhead for GSD block delete pending list
EXE$GL_WCBDELFL EXE$GL_WCBDELBL	Quadword	Listhead for WCB delete queue for GSD windows
EXE$GL_SYSWCBFL EXE$GL_SYSWCBBL	Quadword	Listhead for system WCBs
EXE$GQ_RIGHTSLIST	Quadword	Systemwide rights list descriptor

Executive Data Areas

Global Symbol	Size	Description of Data
PMS$GL_KERNEL	6 longwords	Timer statistics for time spent in each access mode, on the interrupt stack, and in compatibility mode
EXE$GL_ABSTIM	Longword	System absolute time in seconds
	Longword	Spare for alignment
EXE$GQ_SYSTIME	Quadword	System time in units of 100 nanoseconds
EXE$GQ_BOOTTIME	Quadword	Base time of last boot
EXE$GL_PFAILTIM	Longword	Contents of time-of-year clock at last power failure
EXE$GL_PFATIM	Longword	Duration of most recent power failure in ten-millisecond units
EXE$GL_TQFL	Quadword	Timer queue listhead
EXE$GL_TQBL		
devicetim	32 bytes	Timer queue element for system routine EXE$TIMEOUT
EXE$AL_TQENOREPT	32 bytes	Permanent last entry in timer queue
IOC$GL_MUTEX	2 words	I/O database mutex
EXE$GL_CEBMTX	2 words	Common event block list mutex
EXE$GL_PGDYNMTX	2 words	Paged dynamic memory mutex
EXE$GL_GSDMTX	2 words	Global section descriptor list mutex
EXE$GL_SHMGSMTX	2 words	Shared memory global section descriptor list mutex
EXE$GL_SHMMBMTX	2 words	Shared memory mailbox list mutex
EXE$GL_ENQMTX	2 words	Enqueue/dequeue tables mutex (unused)
EXE$GL_ACLMTX	2 words	ACL modification mutex
EXE$GL_SYSID_LOCK	Longword	System parent lock ID
EXE$GL_KNOWN_FILES	Longword	Address of hash table for known file entries
kfe_lock_name	ASCII	ASCII string of facility name for Install Utility
EXE$GQ_KFE_LCKNAM	Quadword	String descriptor of KFE lock name
EXE$GL_GPT	Longword	Address of first free global page table entry (GPTE)
	Longword	Dummy count of number of GPTEs in listhead
SYS$GQ_VERSION	Quadword	ASCII string containing system version number
SYS$GW_IJOBCNT	3 words	Current counts of interactive, network, and batch logins
EXE$GW_SCANPIX	Word	Process index of next process to check for priority boost
EXE$GL_SYSMSG	Longword	Address of systemwide message section
EXE$GL_USRUNDWN	Longword	Address of systemwide user rundown service vector
EXE$GL_NONPAGED	Longword	IPL at which nonpaged pool allocation occurs
	Longword	Address of first free block of nonpaged pool
	Longword	Dummy size of zero for listhead

Global Symbol	Size	Description of Data
XE$GL_SPLITADR	Longword	Address of boundary between LRP and IRP lookaside lists
XE$GL_PAGED	Longword	Address of first free block of paged pool
	Longword	Dummy size of zero for listhead
MS$GL_SFDBASE	Longword	Unused
XE$GL_SHBLIST	Longword	Address of shared memory control block list
XE$GL_RTBITMAP	Longword	Address of real-time SPTE bitmap
MCHK$GL_MASK	Longword	Function mask for current machine check recovery block
MCHK$GL_SP	Longword	Saved stack pointer for return at end of recovery
XE$GL_MCHKERRS	Longword	Number of machine checks since bootstrap
XE$GL_MEMERRS	Longword	Number of memory errors since bootstrap
IO$GL_UBA_INT0	Longword	Number of UBA interrupts through vector 0
XE$GL_BLAKHOLE	Longword	Physical page used to remap addresses of adapters that have experienced power failure
IO$GL_SCB_INT0	Longword	Number of unexpected SCB interrupts
XE$GL_TENUSEC	Longword	Number of times loop executed in ten microseconds in TIMEDWAIT macro
XE$GL_UBDELAY	Longword	Number of times to execute a three-micro-second loop delay in TIMEDWAIT macro
XE$GL_MP	Longword	Address of loaded multiprocessor code
XE$GL_SITESPEC	Longword	Longword available to privileged users for site-specific purposes
XE$GL_INTSTKLM	Longword	Top of interrupt stack
LCK$GL_IDTBL	Longword	Address of lock ID table
LCK$GL_NXTID	Longword	Address of next lock ID to use
LCK$GL_MAXID	Longword	Maximum lock ID
LCK$GL_HASHTBL	Longword	Address of resource hash table
LCK$GL_HTBLCNT	Longword	Number of entries in resource hash table (expressed as a power of 2)
LCK$GL_TIMOUTQ	Quadword	Listhead for lock timeout queue (for deadlock detection)
LCK$GL_DIRVEC	Longword	Address of directory vector
LCK$GL_PRCMAP	Longword	Address of process bitmap
LCK$GQ_BITMAP_EXP	Quadword	Process bitmap expiration timestamp (exact time)
LCK$GQ_BITMAP_EXPLCL	Quadword	Process bitmap expiration timestamp (approximate local time)
LCK$GB_HTBLSHFT	Byte	Number of entries in hash table (expressed as a shift count)
LCK$GB_MAXDEPTH	Byte	Maximum number of sublocks allowed
LCK$GB_STALLREQS	Byte	Stall lock request flag

Executive Data Areas

Global Symbol	Size	Description of Data
LCK$GB_REBLD_STATE	Byte	Lock rebuild state flag
EXE$GL_ACMFLAGS	Longword	Accounting manager control flags
NSA$GR_JOURNVEC	40 bytes	Security journaling bit vector (unused)
NSA$GR_ALARMVEC	40 bytes	Security alarms bit vector
EXE$GL_SVAPTE	Longword	System virtual address of PTE that maps the black hole page
XQP$GL_SECTIONS	Longword	Number of Files-11 XQP global sections
XQP$GL_DZRO	Longword	Size of XQP demand zero section
XQP$GL_FILESERVER	Longword	PID of CACHE_SERVER process
XQP$GL_FILESERV_ENTRY	Longword	AST entry point of CACHE_SERVER process
SYS$GQ_PWD	Quadword	Encrypted system password
CIA$GL_MUTEX	2 words	Mutex for CIA queues
CIA$GQ_INTRUDER	2 longwords	Listhead of known and suspected intruders
IOC$GT_NOPOOL_TWP	48 bytes	Terminal write packet for pool expansion failure message
IOC$GL_POOLEXP_STS	2 words	Status of pool expansions
	• Word	Status bits
	• Word	Message length
EXE$GL_BADACV_T	Longword	Time of the last bad access violation
EXE$GL_BADACV_C	Longword	Number of incorrect access violations

Module ERRORLOG makes a significant contribution to program section $$$260. Most of the space is occupied by two 512-byte error message buffers.

Global Symbol	Size	Description of Data
buf1	512 bytes	First error log buffer
buf2	512 bytes	Second error log buffer
ERL$AL_BUFADDR	2 longwords	Addresses of two error log buffers
ERL$GB_BUFIND	Byte	Current buffer allocation indicator
ERL$GB_BUFFLAG	Byte	Buffer status flags
ERL$GB_BUFPTR	Byte	Format process (ERRFMT) buffer indicator
ERL$GB_BUFTIM	Byte	Format process wakeup timer
ERL$GL_ERLPID	Longword	Process ID of error format process
ERL$GL_SEQUENCE	Longword	Systemwide error sequence number

Module SWAPPER makes a contribution to program section $$$260. The space is occupied by system logical name tables and translation item lists.

Global Symbol	Size	Description of Data
LNM$SYSTEM_DIRECTORY	43 bytes	System directory logical name table body

Global Symbol	Size	Description of Data
LNM_SYSTEM_DIR_LNMTH	45 bytes	System directory logical name table header
LNM_SYSTEM_DIR_ORB	104 bytes	System directory logical name table ORB
system_table	39 bytes	System logical name table body
system_table_lnmth	41 bytes	System logical name table header
system_table_orb	41 bytes	System logical name table ORB
sys_disk_arg	24 bytes	$CRELNM macro argument list for SYS$DISK
sys_sysdevice_arg	24 bytes	$CRELNM macro argument list for SYS$DEVICE

.1.14   Statistics Used by Performance Tools ($$$270NP)

Module PMSDAT contains data that is used by the Monitor Utility and other performance tools.

Global Symbol	Size	Description of Data
MS$GL_DIRIO	Longword	Number of direct I/O operations
MS$GL_BUFIO	Longword	Number of buffered I/O operations
MS$GL_LOGNAM	Longword	Number of logical name translations
MS$GL_MBREADS	Longword	Number of mailbox read operations
MS$GL_MBWRITES	Longword	Number of mailbox write operations
MS$GL_TREADS	Longword	Number of terminal read operations
MS$GL_TWRITES	Longword	Number of terminal write operations
MS$GL_IOPFMPDB	Longword	Address of performance data block
MS$GL_IOPFMSEQ	Longword	Master I/O packet sequence number
MS$GL_ARRLOCPK	Longword	Number of local packets arriving
MS$GL_DEPLOCPK	Longword	Number of local packets departing
MS$GL_ARRTRAPK	Longword	Number of arriving packets
MS$GL_TRCNGLOS	Longword	Cumulative transit congestion loss
MS$GL_RCVBUFFL	Longword	Number of receiver buffer failures
MS$GL_ENQNEW_LOC	Longword	Number of local new lock requests
MS$GL_ENQNEW_IN	Longword	Number of incoming new lock requests
MS$GL_ENQNEW_OUT	Longword	Number of outgoing new lock requests
MS$GL_ENQCVT_LOC	Longword	Number of local conversion requests
MS$GL_ENQCVT_IN	Longword	Number of incoming conversion requests
MS$GL_ENQCVT_OUT	Longword	Number of outgoing conversion requests
MS$GL_DEQ_LOC	Longword	Number of local dequeues
MS$GL_DEQ_IN	Longword	Number of incoming dequeues
MS$GL_DEQ_OUT	Longword	Number of outgoing dequeues
MS$GL_ENQWAIT	Longword	Number of $ENQ requests waiting
MS$GL_ENQNOTQD	Longword	Number of $ENQ requests not queued

Executive Data Areas

Global Symbol	Size	Description of Data
PMS$GL_BLK_LOC	Longword	Number of local blocking ASTs queued
PMS$GL_BLK_IN	Longword	Number of incoming blocking ASTs queued
PMS$GL_BLK_OUT	Longword	Number of outgoing blocking ASTs queued
PMS$GL_DIR_IN	Longword	Number of incoming directory operations
PMS$GL_DIR_OUT	Longword	Number of outgoing directory operations
PMS$GL_DLCKMSGS_IN	Longword	Number of incoming deadlock detection messages
PMS$GL_DLCKMSGS_OUT	Longword	Number of outgoing deadlock detection messages
PMS$GL_DLCKSRCH	Longword	Number of deadlock searches performed
PMS$GL_DLCKFND	Longword	Number of deadlocks found
	22 longwords	Spare for expansion of monitoring during Version 4
PMS$GL_CHMK	Longword	Number of CHMK exceptions
PMS$GL_CHME	Longword	Number of CHME exceptions
PMS$GL_PAGES	Longword	Number of physical pages of memory in configuration
PMS$GW_BATCH	Word	Number of current batch jobs
PMS$GW_INTJOBS	Word	Number of interactive users
PMS$AL_READTBL	11 longwords	Histogram to count number of characters per terminal read operation
PMS$AL_WRITETBL	11 longwords	Histogram to count number of characters per terminal write operation
PMS$GL_READCNT	Longword	Total number of terminal characters read since bootstrap
PMS$GL_WRTCNT	Longword	Total number of terminal characters written since bootstrap
PMS$GL_PASSALL	Longword	Number of reads in PASSALL mode
PMS$GL_RWP	Longword	Number of read-with-prompt reads
PMS$GL_LRGRWP	Longword	Number of read-with-prompt reads of more than 12 characters
PMS$GL_RWPSUM	Longword	Total number of characters read in prompt mode
PMS$GL_NOSTDTRM	Longword	Number of reads not using standard terminals
PMS$GL_RWPNOSTD	Longword	Number of read-with-prompt reads not using standard terminals
PMS$GL_TTY_CODE1	Longword	Performance code vector 1
PMS$GL_TTY_CODE2	Longword	Performance code vector 2
PMS$GL_LDPCTX	Longword	Number of LDPCTX instructions
PMS$GL_SWITCH	Longword	Number of switches from the current process

Global Symbol	Size	Description of Data
•MS$GB_PROMPT	4 bytes	RTE input prompt
•MS$GL_DOSTATS	Byte	Flag to turn statistics code on and off
	3 bytes	Spare for alignment

C.1.15   Entry Points for CPU-Dependent Routines ($$$500)

Module SYSLOAVEC contains entry points for each CPU-dependent routine. Module SCSVEC contains entry points for the loadable SCS code. (SCS is described in Chapter 19.) Each entry point is a JMP instruction (with absolute addressing). The destination of each JMP is changed to a routine in the CPU-dependent image SYSLOAxxx.EXE loaded into nonpaged pool during system initialization. See Chapter 25 for further information.

There are two types of routine here. Those routines that are entered through the SCB must have their entry point longwords aligned. Each of these routines has two spare bytes to preserve longword alignment. Other routines can have the six-byte JMP instructions packed together.

This program section also has contributions from other modules, including CLUSTRVEC, which describes the entry points for the connection manager and distributed lock manager.

Global Symbol	Size	Description of Data
	MODULE SYSLOAVEC	
EXE$AL_LOAVEC ⎫		Address of start of vectors
EXE$MCHK ⎬	8 bytes	Machine check exception service routine
EXE$INT54	8 bytes	Interrupt service routine for SCB vector 54
EXE$INT58	8 bytes	Interrupt service routine for SCB vector 58
EXE$INT5C	8 bytes	Interrupt service routine for SCB vector 5C
EXE$INT60	8 bytes	Interrupt service routine for SCB vector 60
UBA$INT0	8 bytes	Interrupt service routine for UNIBUS vector 0
UBA$UNEXINT	6 bytes	Interrupt service routine for unexpected UNIBUS interrupts
ECC$REENABLE	6 bytes	Reenable memory error timers
EXE$INIBOOTADP	6 bytes	Initialize boot device adapter
EXE$DUMPCPUREG	6 bytes	Write CPU-specific registers in error log buffer
EXE$REGRESTOR	6 bytes	Restore CPU-specific registers on power recovery
EXE$REGSAVE	6 bytes	Save CPU-specific registers at power failure
EXE$INIPROCREG	6 bytes	Initialize processor registers
EXE$TEST_CSR	6 bytes	Test UNIBUS CSR for existence
IOC$PURGDATAP	6 bytes	Purge UNIBUS buffered data path
INI$MPMADP	6 bytes	Initialize multiport MA780 memory
EXE$STARTUPADP	6 bytes	Start up any adapters

Executive Data Areas

Global Symbol	Size	Description of Data
		MODULE SYSLOAVEC
EXE$SHUTDWNADP	6 bytes	Shut down any (all) adapters
MA$RAVAIL	6 bytes	Multiport MA780 memory resource available
MA$REQUEST	6 bytes	Multiport MA780 memory request
MA$INITIAL	6 bytes	Multiport memory MA780 initialization
CON$STARTIO	6 bytes	Console start I/O
CON$SET_LINE	6 bytes	Set console line
CON$DS_SET	6 bytes	Console data set
CON$XON	6 bytes	XON to console
CON$XOFF	6 bytes	XOFF to console
CON$STOP	6 bytes	Stop console output
CON$STOP2	6 bytes	Stop console output for two seconds
CON$ABORT	6 bytes	Abort console I/O
CON$RESUME	6 bytes	Resume console output
CON$SET_MODEM	6 bytes	Set console modem
CON$NULL	6 bytes	Null routine
CON$DISCONNECT	6 bytes	Console disconnect routine
CON$INITIAL	6 bytes	Initialize console controller
CON$INITLINE	6 bytes	Initialize console line
CON$INTINP	6 bytes	Console input interrupt
CON$INTOUT	6 bytes	Console output interrupt
CON$SENDCONSCMD	6 bytes	Send CPU-dependent command to console
SYS$CLRSBIA	6 bytes	Clear SBIA error bits
CON$OWNCTY	6 bytes	Set up to talk directly to console
CON$RELEASECTY	6 bytes	Restore normal console interface
CON$GETCHAR	6 bytes	Get a character from the console
CON$PUTCHAR	6 bytes	Put a character out to the console
CON$INIT_CTY	6 bytes	Initialization routine for the console
EXE$READ_TODR	6 bytes	Read time-of-year clock
EXE$WRITE_TODR	6 bytes	Write time-of-year clock
EXE$INIT_TODR	6 bytes	Initialize system time-of-year clock
INI$CONSOLE	6 bytes	Initialize console device data structures
EXE$INI_TIMWAIT	6 bytes	Initialize TIMEDWAIT macro loop data cells
EXE$READP_TODR	6 bytes	Read physical time-of-year register
EXE$WRITEP_TODR	6 bytes	Write physical time-of-year register
EXE$MOUNTVER	6 bytes	Mount verification main entry point
EXE$MNTVERSIO	6 bytes	Mount verification start I/O request
EXE$MNTVERSHDOL	6 bytes	Mount verification online shadow unit
EXE$CLUTRANIO	6 bytes	Mount verification VAXcluster state transition block I/O

lobal Symbol	Size	Description of Data
		MODULE SYSLOAVEC
XE$UPDGNERNUM	6 bytes	Mount verification update shadow set generation number
XE$MNTVER_DVI_ASSIST	6 bytes	Mount verification $GETDVI escape
XE$MNTVERSP1	6 bytes	Mount verification spare transfer vector
XE$MNTVERSP2	6 bytes	Mount verification spare transfer vector
XE$GL_MVMSLBAS	6 bytes	Mount verification message list base address
XE$EXTRA6	6 bytes	Extra jump vector; currently targeted to halt in ERRSUB
XE$EXTRA7	6 bytes	Extra jump vector; currently targeted to halt in ERRSUB
XE$EXTRA8	6 bytes	Extra jump vector; currently targeted to halt in ERRSUB
XE$EXTRA9	6 bytes	Extra jump vector; currently targeted to halt in ERRSUB
XE$EXTRA10	6 bytes	Extra jump vector; currently targeted to halt in ERRSUB
XE$MCHK_ERRCNT	Longword	Pointer to error counters in machine check routine
XE$LOAD_ERROR	Byte	HALT instruction (initial destination of JMP instructions in vectors)
		MODULE SCSVEC
CS$GQ_CONFIG	Quadword	Listhead for system descriptor blocks
CS$GQ_DIRECT	Quadword	Listhead for directory of processes in VAXcluster System
CS$GQ_POLL	Quadword	Listhead of SCA poller process blocks (SPPBs) giving process names
CS$GL_BDT	Longword	Buffer descriptor table for SCS block transmissions
CS$GL_CDL	Longword	Connection descriptor table pointing to list of SCS connections
CS$GL_RDT	Longword	Response descriptor table
CS$GL_MCLEN	Longword	Unused
CS$GL_MCADR	Longword	Pointer to CI port microcode in nonpaged pool
CS$GL_MSCP	Longword	Start of MSCP server process
CS$GL_PDT	Longword	Listhead of PDTs
CS$GA_DFLTMSK	Longword	Mask of processes to enable when new systems appear
CS$GW_NEXTBIT	Longword	Next bit available for assignment
CS$GA_EXISTS	Longword	Flag to indicate presence of SCS
CS$AL_LOAVEC		Address of start of vectors
CS$ACCEPT	6 bytes	Perform SCS accept

Global Symbol	Size	Description of Data
		MODULE SCSVEC
SCS$ALLOC_CDT	6 bytes	Allocate connection descriptor table
SCS$ALLOC_RSPID	6 bytes	Allocate response ID
SCS$CONFIG_PTH	6 bytes	Configure with path to remote system
SCS$CONFIG_SYS	6 bytes	Configure with system ID
SCS$CONNECT	6 bytes	Perform SCS connect
SCS$DEALL_CDT	6 bytes	Deallocate connection descriptor table
SCS$DEALL_RSPID	6 bytes	Deallocate response ID
SCS$DISCONNECT	6 bytes	Perform SCS disconnect
SCS$ENTER	6 bytes	Insert an entry in SCS directory
SCS$LISTEN	6 bytes	Perform an SCS listen operation
SCS$LOCLOOKUP	6 bytes	Look up a path block
SCS$REMOVE	6 bytes	Remove an entry in SCS directory
SCS$RESUMEWAITR	6 bytes	Resume when CRB is dequeued
SCS$UNSTALLUCB	6 bytes	Resume when UCB is dequeued
SCS$LKP_RDTCDRP	6 bytes	Search a response descriptor table for a CDRP
SCS$LKP_RDTWAIT	6 bytes	Search a response ID wait queue for a CDRP
SCS$RECYL_RSPID	6 bytes	Recycle a response ID
SCS$FIND_RDTE	6 bytes	Locate and validate the RDTE for a given response ID
SCS$LKP_MSGWAIT	6 bytes	Send credit wait queues for CDRP with given CDT
SCS$DIR_LOOKUP	6 bytes	Search for processes on remote node
SCS$NEW_SB	6 bytes	Called when a system block is created or reused
SCS$POLL_PROC	6 bytes	Declare a process name to the poller
SCS$POLL_MODE	6 bytes	Enable/disable polling of a process
SCS$POLL_MBX	6 bytes	Declare a mailbox to receive poll notifications
SCS$CANCEL_MBX	6 bytes	Cancel notifications to a mailbox
SCS$SHUTDOWN	6 bytes	Shut down all SCS virtual circuits

C.1.16   Table of Adjustable SYSBOOT Parameters ($$$917)

As described in Chapter 25, the system image contains a copy of the working value of each SYSBOOT parameter. This table of values is written into the memory image of the executive by SYSBOOT. Global label MMG$A_SYSPARAM, defined in module MDAT, locates the beginning of the parameter area. Global label EXE$A_SYSPARAM, defined in module SYSPARAM, has the same value. In the following list, the name of each parameter is included as a part of its description.

Global Symbol	Size	Description of Data
XE$GQ_TODCBASE	Quadword	Base value in time-of-day clock in system time format (not a parameter)
XE$GL_TODR	Longword	Base value in time-of-year clock (not a parameter)
GN$GW_DFPFC	Word	Default page fault cluster size (PFCDEFAULT)
GN$GB_PGTBPFC	Byte	Default page table page fault cluster size (PAGTBLPFC)
GN$GB_SYSPFC	Byte	Page fault cluster factor for system paging (SYSPFC)
GN$GB_KFILSTCT	Byte	Number of known file lists (KFILSTCNT)
	Byte	Spare for alignment
GN$GW_GBLSECNT	Word	Global section count (GBLSECTIONS)
GN$GL_MAXGPGCT	Longword	Global page count (GBLPAGES)
GN$GL_GBLPAGFIL	Longword	Global page file page limit (GBLPAGFIL)
GN$GW_MAXPRCCT	Word	Maximum process count (MAXPROCESSCNT)
GN$GW_PIXSCAN	Word	Maximum number of processes to scan for priority boosting (PIXSCAN)
GN$GW_MAXPSTCT	Word	Process section count (PROCSECTCNT)
GN$GW_MINWSCNT	Word	Minimum working set size (MINWSCNT)
GN$GW_PAGFILCT	Word	Number of page files (PAGFILCNT)
GN$GW_SWPFILES	Word	Number of swap files (SWPFILCNT)
GN$GW_SYSDWSCT	Word	Size of system working set count (SYSMWCNT)
GN$GW_ISPPGCT	Word	Size in pages of interrupt stack (INTSTKPAGES)
LCK$GL_EXTRASTK	Longword	Amount of interrupt stack that must remain free when performing deadlock searches (DLCKEXTRASTK)
SGN$GL_BALSETCT	Longword	Balance set count (BALSETCNT)
SGN$GL_IRPCNT	Longword	Number of preallocated I/O request packets (IRPCOUNT)
SGN$GL_IRPCNTV	Longword	Maximum number of IRPs (IRPCOUNTV)
SGN$GL_MAXWSCNT	Longword	Maximum process working set size (WSMAX)
SGN$GL_NPAGEDYN	Longword	Number of bytes of nonpaged pool (NPAGEDYN) (truncated to page boundary by SYSBOOT)
SGN$GL_NPAGEVIR	Longword	Maximum size of nonpaged pool (NPAGEVIR)
SGN$GL_PAGEDYN	Longword	Number of bytes of paged pool (PAGEDYN) (truncated to page boundary by SYSBOOT)

Executive Data Areas

Global Symbol	Size	Description of Data
SGN$GL_MAXVPGCT	Longword	Maximum virtual page count (VIRTUALPAGECNT)
SGN$GL_SPTREQ	Longword	Number of additional SPTEs to allocate (SPTREQ)
SGN$GL_EXUSRSTK	Longword	Extra user stack space (in bytes) allocated by image activator (EXUSRSTK)
SGN$GL_LRPCNT	Longword	Initial number of packets in the LRP lookaside list (LRPCOUNT)
SGN$GL_LRPCNTV	Longword	Maximum number of LRPs allowed on the LRP lookaside list (LRPCOUNTV)
SGN$GL_LRPSIZE	Longword	Size of an LRP (LRPSIZE)
SGN$GL_LRPMIN	Longword	Minimum request that can be allocated an LRP (LRPMIN)
SGN$GL_SRPCNT	Longword	Initial number of packets in the SRP lookaside list (SRPCOUNT)
SGN$GL_SRPCNTV	Longword	Maximum number of SRPs (SRPCOUNTV)
SGN$GL_SRPSIZE	Longword	Size of an SRP (SRPSIZE)
SGN$GL_SRPMIN	Longword	Minimum request that can be allocated an SRP (SRPMIN)
SGN$GW_PCHANCNT	Word	Permanent I/O channel count (CHANNELCNT)
SGN$GW_PIOPAGES	Word	Number of pages of process I/O address space for EXE$PROCSTRT to create (PIOPAGES)
SGN$GW_CTLPAGES	Word	Number of pages of process allocation region space for EXE$PROCSTRT to create (CTLPAGES)
SGN$GW_CTLIMGLIM	Word	Limit on use of the process allocation region by image requests (CTLIMGLIM)
SGN$GW_IMGIOCNT	Word	Default number of pages mapped for image I/O segment (IMGIOCNT)
SCH$GW_QUAN	Word	Length in ten-millisecond units of quantum (QUANTUM)
MPW$GW_MPWPFC	Word	Modified page writer cluster factor (MPW_WRTCLUSTER)
MPW$GW_HILIM	Word	High-limit threshold of modified page list (MPW_HILIM)
MPW$GW_LOLIM	Word	Low-limit threshold of modified page list (MPW_LOLIM)
MPW$GB_PRIO	Byte	Priority at which modified page writes are queued (MPW_PRIO)
SWP$GB_PRIO	Byte	Priority at which swapper I/O requests are queued (SWP_PRIO)
MPW$GL_THRESH	Longword	Limit below which modified page writer does not reclaim pages (MPW_THRESH)

lobal Symbol	Size	Description of Data
IPW$GL_WAITLIM	Longword	Limit above which processes creating modified pages must wait until pages have been released from modified page list (MPW_WAITLIMIT)
GN$GW_WSLMXSKP	Word	Number of working set list entries to skip in modified scan of WSL (TBSKIPWSL)
IMG$GL_PHYPGCNT	Longword	Maximum number of physical pages to use (PHYSICALPAGES)
CH$GL_PFRATL	Longword	Low-limit page fault rate threshold (PFRATL)
CH$GL_PFRATH	Longword	High-limit page fault rate threshold (PFRATH)
CH$GL_PFRATS	Longword	Page fault rate threshold for system paging (PFRATS)
CH$GL_WSINC	Longword	Working set increment (WSINC)
CH$GL_WSDEC	Longword	Working set decrement (WSDEC)
CH$GW_AWSMIN	Word	Minimum value of automatic working set adjustment (AWSMIN)
SCH$GL_AWSTIME	Longword	Working set measurement interval (in ten-millisecond units) (AWSTIME)
SCH$GL_SWPRATE	Longword	Swap rate for compute-bound jobs (SWPRATE)
WP$GL_SWPPGCNT	Longword	Target number of pages for a working set about to be outswapped (SWPOUTPGCNT)
SWP$GL_SWPINC	Longword	Swap file allocation increment value (SWPALLOCINC)
SCH$GW_IOTA	Word	Amount of time in ten-millisecond units charged against quantum when process goes into wait state (IOTA)
SCH$GW_LONGWAIT	Word	Amount of elapsed time for a LEF or HIB process to be scheduled as a longwait process (LONGWAIT)
SCH$GW_DORMANTWAIT	Word	Number of seconds to wait before marking COM process dormant (DORMANTWAIT)
SCH$GW_SWPFAIL	Word	Number of outswap failures to happen before modifying selection algorithm (SWPFAIL)
SGN$GL_VMSD1	Longword	DIGITAL-reserved parameter (VMSD1)
SGN$GL_VMSD2	Longword	DIGITAL-reserved parameter (VMSD2)
SGN$GL_VMSD3	Longword	DIGITAL-reserved parameter (VMSD3)
SGN$GL_VMSD4	Longword	DIGITAL-reserved parameter (VMSD4)
SGN$GL_VMS5	Longword	DIGITAL-reserved parameter (VMS5)
SGN$GL_VMS6	Longword	DIGITAL-reserved parameter (VMS6)

Executive Data Areas

Global Symbol	Size	Description of Data
SGN$GL_VMS7	Longword	DIGITAL-reserved parameter (VMS7)
SGN$GL_VMS8	Longword	DIGITAL-reserved parameter (VMS8)
SGN$GL_USERD1	Longword	Parameter reserved for users (USERD1)
SGN$GL_USERD2	Longword	Parameter reserved for users (USERD2)
SGN$GL_USER3	Longword	Parameter reserved for users (USER3)
SGN$GL_USER4	Longword	Parameter reserved for users (USER4)
SGN$GL_EXTRACPU	Longword	Extra CPU time after CPU time expiration (EXTRACPU)
EXE$GL_SYSUIC	Longword	Maximum group code for system UIC (MAXSYSGROUP)
IOC$GW_MVTIMEOUT	Word	Time before abandoning mount verification attempt (MVTIMEOUT)
IOC$GW_MAXBUF	Word	Maximum buffered I/O request size (MAXBUF)
IOC$GW_MBXBFQUO	Word	Default buffer quota for mailbox creation (DEFMBXBUFQUO)
IOC$GW_MBXMXMSG	Word	Default maximum message size for mailbox creation (DEFMBXMXMSG)
IOC$GW_MBXNMMSG	Word	Default number of messages for mailbox creation (DEFMBXNUMMSG)
SGN$GL_FREELIM	Longword	Low-limit threshold of free page list (FREELIM)
SGN$GL_FREEGOAL	Longword	Target number of pages to free when the size of the free list is less than FREELIM (FREEGOAL)
SCH$GL_GROWLIM	Longword	Minimum number of pages on the free list for a process to expand its working set above WSQUOTA (GROWLIM)
SCH$GL_BORROWLIM	Longword	Minimum number of pages on the free list for a process to extend its working set list above WSQUOTA (BORROWLIM)
EXE$GL_LOCKRTRY	Longword	Number of retries allowed to lock a multiprocessor data structure (LOCKRETRY)
IOC$GW_XFMXRATE	Word	Maximum DR780 data rate (XFMAXRATE)
IOC$GW_LAMAPREG	Word	Number of UNIBUS map registers to preallocate for LPA11 (LAMAPREGS)
EXE$GL_RTIMESPT	Longword	Number of preallocated SPTEs for connect to interrupt driver (REALTIME_SPTS)
EXE$GL_CLITABL	Longword	Number of pages for CLI symbol table (CLISYMTBL)
LCK$GL_IDTBLSIZ	Longword	Size of the lock ID table (LOCKIDTBL)
LCK$GL_IDTBLMAX	Longword	Maximum size of lock ID table (LOCKIDTBL_MAX)

Global Symbol	Size	Description of Data
CK$GL_HTBLSIZ	Longword	Size of the resource hash table (RESHASHTBL)
CK$GL_WAITTIME	Longword	Deadlock detection timeout period (DEADLOCK_WAIT)
CS$GW_BDTCNT	Word	Number of buffer descriptor table entries allocated for SCS (SCSBUFFCNT)
CS$GW_CDTCNT	Word	Number of connection descriptor table entries allocated for SCS (SCSCONNCNT)
CS$GW_RDTCNT	Word	Number of response descriptor table entries allocated for SCS (SCSRESPCNT)
CS$GW_MAXDG	Word	Maximum SCS datagram size (SCSMAXDG)
CS$GW_MAXMSG	Word	Maximum SCS sequenced message size (SCSMAXMSG)
CS$GW_FLOWCUSH	Word	SCS flow control cushion (SCSFLOWCUSH)
CS$GB_SYSTEMID CS$GB_SYSTEMIDH	Quadword	SCS system ID (SCSSYSTEMID and SCSSYSTEMIDH)
CS$GB_NODENAME	Quadword	SCS system node name (SCSNODE)
CS$GW_PRCPOLINT	Word	SCA process poller—polling interval (PRCPOLINTERVAL)
CS$GW_PASTMOUT	Word	Wakeup interval for CI port driver (PASTIMOUT)
CS$GW_PAPPDDG	Word	Number of datagram buffers to queue for START (PASTDGBUF)
CS$GB_PANPOLL	Byte	Number of CI ports to poll each interval (PANUMPOLL)
CS$GB_PAMXPORT	Byte	Maximum port number to poll each interval (PAMAXPORT)
CS$GW_PAPOLINT	Word	Time between polls (PAPOLLINTERVAL)
CS$GW_PAPOOLIN	Word	Time between checks for SCS applications waiting for pool (PAPOOLINTERVAL)
CS$GB_PASANITY	Byte	CI port flags including sanity timer enable/disable (PASANITY)
CS$GB_PANOPOLL	Byte	CI remote port polling enable/disable flags (PANOPOLL)
SGN$GL_PE1	Longword	Enable/disable discarding of datagrams by PEDRIVER (PE1)
SGN$GL_PE2	Longword	Reserved for PEDRIVER (PE2)
SGN$GL_PE3	Longword	Reserved for PEDRIVER (PE3)
SGN$GL_PE4	Longword	Enable/disable PEDRIVER breakpoints (PE4)
SGN$GL_PE5	Longword	PEDRIVER port services parameter (PE5)

Executive Data Areas

Global Symbol	Size	Description of Data
SGN$GL_PE6	Longword	PEDRIVER—CI port group code (PE6)
SGN$GW_TPWAIT	Word	Amount of time to wait for the time of day to be entered when booting (TIMEPROMPTWAIT)
SCS$GB_UDABURST	Byte	Maximum number of longwords that the host is willing to accept per transfer (UDABURSTRATE)
LNM$GL_HTBLSIZS	Longword	Size of shareable logical name hash table (LNMSHASHTBL)
LNM$GL_HTBLSIZP	Longword	Size of process logical name hash table (LNMPHASHTBL)
EXE$GL_DEFFLAGS	Longword	System flags longword (not a parameter itself)
• EXE$V_BUGREBOOT	Bit	Automatic reboot on bugcheck (BUGREBOOT)
• EXE$V_CRDENABL	Bit	CRD error enable (CRDENABLE)
• EXE$V_BUGDUMP	Bit	Write system dump on bugcheck (DUMPBUG)
• EXE$V_FATAL_BUG	Bit	Make all bugchecks fatal (BUGCHECKFATAL)
• EXE$V_MULTACP	Bit	Create separate ACP for each volume (ACP_MULTIPLE)
• EXE$V_NOAUTOCNF	Bit	Inhibit autoconfiguration of I/O devices (NOAUTOCONFIG)
• EXE$V_NOCLOCK	Bit	Do not start interval timer (NOCLOCK)
• EXE$V_NOCLUSTER	Bit	Inhibit page read clustering (NOCLUSTER)
• EXE$V_POOLPGING	Bit	Enable paging of paged pool (POOLPAGING)
• EXE$V_REINITQUE	Bit	Create a new JBCSYSQUEUE.EXE (REINITQUE)
• EXE$V_SBIERR	Bit	Enable detection of SBI errors (SBIERRENABLE)
• EXE$V_SETTIME	Bit	Prompt for system time in SYSBOOT (SETTIME)
• EXE$V_SHRF11ACP	Bit	Enable sharing of file ACP (ACP_SHARE)
• EXE$V_SAVEDUMP	Bit	Save dump from page file (SAVEDUMP)
• EXE$V_SSINHIBIT	Bit	Inhibit system services on a per-process basis (SSINHIBIT)
• EXE$V_SYSPAGING	Bit	Enable paging of pageable system code (SYSPAGING)
• EXE$V_SYSUAFALT	Bit	Select alternate authorization file (UAFALTERNATE)
• EXE$V_SYSWRTABL	Bit	Leave system image in memory writable (WRITABLESYS)

Global Symbol	Size	Description of Data
EXE$V_RESALLOC	Bit	Enable resource allocation checking (RESALLOC)
EXE$V_JOBQUEUES	Bit	Enable job controller queues (JOBQUEUES)
EXE$V_CONCEALED	Bit	Enable use of concealed devices (CONCEAL_DEVICES)
EXE$V_CJFLOAD	Bit	Unused
EXE$V_CJFSYSRUJ	Bit	Unused
EXE$GL_DYNAMIC_FLAGS	Longword	Dynamic system flags (not a parameter itself)
EXE$V_CLASS_PROT	Bit	Perform nondiscretionary classification checks (CLASS_PROT)
EXE$V_WRITESYSPARAMS	Bit	Set by SYSBOOT if a USE DEFAULT, USE "file," or a SET command is executed (WRITESYSPARAMS)
EXE$V_BRK_TERM	Bit	Use the terminal name in the association string used in LOGIN's break-in detection (LGI_BRK_TERM)
EXE$V_BRK_DISUSER	Bit	If enabled, set the DISUSER flag in the user's UAF record if a break-in attempt is detected (LGI_BRK_DISUSER)
EXE$GL_MSGFLAGS	Longword	Mount message flags (not a parameter itself)
EXE$V_DISMOUMSG	Bit	Inform operator console of dismounts (DISMOUMSG)
EXE$V_MOUNTMSG	Bit	Inform operator console of mounts (MOUNTMSG)
SGN$GL_LOADFLAGS	Longword	SYSGEN load flags (not a parameter itself)
SGN$V_LOADERAPAT	Bit	If set, load alternate erase pattern generator (LOADERAPT)
SGN$V_LOADCHKPRT	Bit	If set, load alternate protection check routine (LOADCHKPRT)
SGN$V_LOADMTACCESS	Bit	Control loading of installation-specific accessibility routine (LOADMTACCESS)
TTY$GL_DELTA	Longword	Delta time for dialup line timer scan (TTY_SCANDELTA)
TTY$GB_DIALTYP	Byte	Dialup flag bits (TTY_DIALTYPE)
	• Bit	0 = Bell standard protocol 1 = CCITT standard protocol
	• Bit	0 = disable use of RING signal 1 = require RING signal before setting DTR
	• Bit	0 = enable 30-second timeout for DTR 1 = disable timeout
TTY$GB_DEFSPEED	Byte	Default speed for terminals (TTY_SPEED)

Executive Data Areas

Global Symbol	Size	Description of Data
TTY$GB_RSPEED	Byte	Default receive speed (TTY_RSPEED)
TTY$GB_PARITY	Byte	Default parity (TTY_PARITY)
TTY$GW_DEFBUF	Word	Default terminal line width (TTY_BUF)
TTY$GL_DEFCHAR	Longword	Default terminal characteristics (TTY_DEFCHAR)
TTY$GL_DEFCHAR2	Longword	Default terminal characteristics (second longword) (TTY_DEFCHAR2)
TTY$GW_TYPAHDSZ	Word	Size of type-ahead buffer (TTY_TYPAHDSZ)
TTY$GW_ALTYPAHD	Word	Alternate type-ahead buffer size (TTY_ALTYPAHD)
TTY$GW_ALTALARM	Word	Alternate type-ahead buffer alarm size (TTY_ALTALARM)
TTY$GW_DMASIZE	Word	DMA size (TTY_DMASIZE)
TTY$GW_PROT	Word	Default terminal allocation protection (TTY_PROT)
TTY$GL_OWNUIC	Longword	Default terminal owner UIC (TTY_OWNER)
TTY$GW_CLASSNAM	Word	Default terminal class driver name prefix (TTY_CLASSNAME)
TTY$GB_SILOTIME	Byte	Default silo timeout value for DMF-32 (TTY_SILOTIME)
TTY$GL_TIMEOUT	Longword	Default disconnected terminal timeout value (TTY_TIMEOUT)
TTY$GB_AUTOCHAR	Byte	Autobaud rate recognition character (TTY_AUTOCHAR)
TTY$GL_DEFPORT	Longword	Default port characteristics (TTY_DEFPORT)
SYS$GB_DFMBC	Byte	Default multiblock count (RMS_DFMBC)
SYS$GB_DFMBFSDK	Byte	Default multibuffer count for sequential disk I/O (RMS_DFMBFSDK)
SYS$GB_DFMBFSMT	Byte	Unused (RMS_DFMBFSMT)
SYS$GB_DFMBFSUR	Byte	Unused (RMS_DFMBFSUR)
SYS$GB_DFMBFREL	Byte	Unused (RMS_DFMBFREL)
SYS$GB_DFMBFIDX	Byte	Unused (RMS_DFMBFIDX)
SYS$GB_DFMBFHSH	Byte	Unused (RMS_DFMBFHSH)
SYS$GB_RMSPROLOG	Byte	Default RMS prolog value (RMS_PROLOGUE)
SYS$GW_RMSEXTEND	Word	Default file extend size (RMS_EXTEND_SIZE)
SYS$GW_FILEPROT	Word	Unused (RMS_FILEPROT)
SYS$GW_GBLBUFQUO	Word	Maximum number of global buffers that may be in concurrent use (RMS_GBLBUFQUO)

lobal Symbol	Size	Description of Data
YS$GB_DFNBC	Byte	Number of blocks for RMS DAP network record-mode transfers; defines maximum network record size (RMS_DFNBC)
QL$AL_DEFAULT + 4	12 longwords	Table of process quota list default values (see Table 20-3)
QL$AL_MIN + 4	12 longwords	Table of process quota list minimum values (see Table 20-3)
QL$AB_FLAG + 1	12 bytes	Table of process quota flags
CP$GW_MAPCACHE	Word	Number of blocks in bitmap cache (ACP_MAPCACHE)
CP$GW_HDRCACHE	Word	Number of blocks in file header cache (ACP_HDRCACHE)
CP$GW_DIRCACHE	Word	Number of blocks in file directory cache (ACP_DIRCACHE)
CP$GW_DINDXCACHE	Word	Number of pages in file system directory index cache (ACP_DINDXCACHE)
CP$GW_WORKSET	Word	ACP working set size (ACP_WORKSET)
CP$GW_FIDCACHE	Word	Number of cached index file slots (ACP_FIDCACHE)
ACP$GW_EXTCACHE	Word	Number of cached disk extents (ACP_EXTCACHE)
ACP$GW_EXTLIMIT	Word	Fraction of disk to cache (ACP_EXTLIMIT)
ACP$GW_QUOCACHE	Word	Number of quota file entries to cache (ACP_QUOCACHE)
ACP$GW_SYSACC	Word	Default access for system volumes (ACP_SYSACC)
ACP$GB_MAXREAD	Byte	Maximum number of blocks to read at once for directories (ACP_MAXREAD)
ACP$GB_WINDOW	Byte	Default window size for system volumes (ACP_WINDOW)
ACP$GB_WRITBACK	Byte	Enable deferred cache write back (ACP_WRITEBACK)
ACP$GB_DATACHK	Byte	ACP data check enable flags (ACP_DATACHECK)
• ACP$V_READCHK	Bit	Do data check on reads
• ACP$V_WRITECHK	Bit	Do data check on writes
ACP$GB_BASEPRIO	Byte	ACP base software priority (ACP_BASEPRIO)
ACP$GB_SWAPFLGS	Byte	ACP swap flags (ACP_SWAPFLGS)
• ACP$V_SWAPSYS	Bit	Swap ACPs for /SYSTEM volumes
• ACP$V_SWAPGRP	Bit	Swap ACPs for /GROUP volumes
• ACP$V_SWAPPRV	Bit	Swap ACPs for private volumes
• ACP$V_SWAPMAG	Bit	Swap magnetic tape ACPs

Executive Data Areas

Global Symbol	Size	Description of Data
EXE$GL_STATIC_FLAGS	Longword	XQP control flags (not a parameter itself)
• EXE$V_XQP_RESIDENT	Bit	XQP memory resident (ACP_XQP_RES)
• EXE$V_REBLDSYSD	Bit	System disk rebuild flag (ACP_REBLDSYSD)
SYS$GB_DEFPRI	Byte	Default priority for job initiations; upper limit on "cruncher" process priority (DEFPRI)
SYS$GW_IJOBLIM	Word	Limit for interactive jobs (IJOBLIM)
SYS$GW_BJOBLIM	Word	Limit for batch jobs (BJOBLIM)
SYS$GW_NJOBLIM	Word	Limit for network jobs (NJOBLIM)
SYS$GW_RJOBLIM	Word	Limit for remote terminal jobs (RJOBLIM)
SYS$GB_DEFQUEPRI	Byte	Default queue priority (DEFQUEPRI)
SYS$GB_MAXQUEPRI	Byte	Maximum queue priority (MAXQUEPRI)
SYS$GB_PWD_TMO	Byte	Number of seconds that a dialup user has to enter system password before LOGINOUT exits (LGI_PWD_TMO)
SYS$GB_RETRY_LIM	Byte	Number of retries an interactive user has before the process goes away (LGI_RETRY_LIM)
SYS$GB_RETRY_TMO	Byte	Number of seconds user has to attempt another login before process is deleted (LGI_RETRY_TMO)
SYS$GB_BRK_LIM	Byte	Number of consecutive login failures before LOGINOUT begins evasive action (LGI_BRK_LIM)
SYS$GL_BRK_TMO	Byte	Number of seconds that a suspect must be free of login failures before it is taken off the suspect list (LGI_BRK_TMO)
SYS$GL_HID_TIM	Byte	Number of seconds that LOGINOUT should practice evasive action on an intruder (LGI_HID_TIM)
CLU$GB_VAXCLUSTER	Byte	Controls loading of VAXcluster code • 0 = never load • 1 = load if SCSLOA is being loaded • 2 = always load and also load SCSLOA
CLU$GW_QUORUM	Word	Quorum for an operable VAXcluster System (QUORUM)
CLU$GW_VOTES	Word	Number of votes this system contributes to quorum (VOTES)
CLU$GW_RECNXINT	Word	Interval during which to attempt reconnection to a VAXcluster member (RECNXINTERVAL)
CLU$GB_QDISK	Byte	VAXcluster quorum disk name (DISK_QUORUM)

Global Symbol	Size	Description of Data
CLU$GW_QDSKVOTES	Word	Number of votes contributed by quorum disk (QDSKVOTES)
CLU$GW_QDSKINTERVAL	Word	Disk quorum interval (QDSKINTERVAL)
CLU$GL_ALLOCLS	Longword	Device allocation class for system. Used to derive common lock resource name for multiple access paths to same device (ALLOCLASS)
CLU$GW_LCKDIRWT	Word	Determines portion of lock manager directory entries that will be handled by this system (LOCKDIRWT)
SGN$GB_TAILORED	Byte	Indicates if system is tailored (TAILORED)
EXE$GL_WSFLAGS	Longword	Workstation SYSGEN flags (not a parameter itself)
EXE$V_OPA0	Bit	If set, reserve the first 23 scan lines for an OPA0 window (WS_OPA0)
SGN$GB_STARTUP_P1	Longword	Used to pass information to the system startup procedure (STARTUP_P1)
SGN$GB_STARTUP_P2	Longword	Used to pass information to the system startup procedure (STARTUP_P2)
SGN$GB_STARTUP_P3	Longword	Used to pass information to the system startup procedure (STARTUP_P3)
SGN$GB_STARTUP_P4	Longword	Used to pass information to the system startup procedure (STARTUP_P4)
SGN$GB_STARTUP_P5	Longword	Used to pass information to the system startup procedure (STARTUP_P5)
SGN$GB_STARTUP_P6	Longword	Used to pass information to the system startup procedure (STARTUP_P6)
SGN$GB_STARTUP_P7	Longword	Used to pass information to the system startup procedure (STARTUP_P7)
SGN$GB_STARTUP_P8	Longword	Used to pass information to the system startup procedure (STARTUP_P8)

The rest of module SYSPARAM consists of other systemwide parameters, the values of which are not directly adjustable with SYSBOOT or SYSGEN. Rather, their values depend directly on the values of one or more adjustable parameters.

Global Symbol	Size	Description of Data
SWP$GL_SHELLSIZ	Longword	Pages required for shell process
SWP$GW_BAKPTE	Word	Number of PHD pages for process header page arrays
SWP$GW_EMPTPTE	Word	Number of empty PHD pages for working set list expansion

Global Symbol	Size	Description of Data
SWP$GW_WSLPTE	Word	Number of PHD pages for fixed area, working set list, and process section table
SWP$GB_SHLP1PT	Byte	Number of P1 page table pages required for SHELL
	Byte	Spare for alignment
SWP$GL_BSLOTSZ	Longword	Size (in pages) of balance slot
SWP$GL_MAP	Longword	Address of swapper's I/O page table
SWP$GL_PHDBASVA	Longword	Base address of PHD window
SGN$GL_PHDAPCNT	Longword	Number of SHELL header pages
SGN$GL_PHDLWCNT	Longword	Number of longwords in PHD
SGN$GL_P1LWCNT	Longword	Number of longwords to end of P1 page table
SGN$GL_PHDPAGCT	Longword	Number of all PHD pages excluding page table pages
SGN$GL_PTPAGCNT	Longword	Number of page table pages
MMG$GL_CTLBASVA	Longword	Initial low address end of P1 space
EXE$AL_STACKS	2 longwords	Array of kernel mode system space stacks
	• Longword	Address of swapper's kernel stack
• EXE$GL_INTSTK	• Longword	Address of interrupt stack
MMG$GL_GPTBASE	Longword	Base address of global page table
MMG$GL_GPTE	Longword	Address of first GPTE at end of SPT
MMG$GL_MAXGPTE	Longword	Highest GPTE address
MMG$GL_MAXSYSVA ⎫ MMG$GL_FRESVA ⎬	Longword	Highest system virtual address (plus 1)
MMG$GL_SPTBASE	Longword	Base virtual address of SPT
MMG$GL_SPTLEN	Longword	Length of SPT
MMG$GL_SYSPHD	Longword	Virtual address of system header
MMG$GL_SYSPHDLN	Longword	Size (in bytes) of system header
SWP$GL_BALBASE	Longword	Base virtual address of balance set slots
SWP$GL_BALSPT	Longword	Base virtual address in SPT for mapping balance slots
MMG$GL_SBR	Longword	Physical address of SPT (duplicates contents of PR$_SBR)

Global Symbol	Size	Description of Data
MMG$GL_NPAGEDYN	Longword	Virtual address of beginning of nonpaged pool
MMG$GL_NPAGNEXT	Longword	Next virtual address for nonpaged pool extension
MMG$GL_IRPNEXT	Longword	Next virtual address for IRP list extension
MMG$GL_LRPNEXT	Longword	Next virtual address for LRP list extension
MMG$GL_SRPNEXT	Longword	Next virtual address for SRP list extension
MMG$GL_PAGEDYN	Longword	Virtual address of beginning of paged pool
MMG$GL_MAXPFN	Longword	Maximum PFN accounted for in PFN database
MMG$GL_MINPFN	Longword	Minimum PFN in PFN database
MMG$GL_MAXMEM	Longword	Highest PFN mapped by SYS-BOOT (includes pages not in PFN database)
EXE$GL_RPB	Longword	Virtual address of restart parameter block
BOO$GL_SPTFREL	Longword	Virtual page number of lower end of pool of unused SPTEs
BOO$GL_SPTFREH	Longword	Virtual page number of upper end of pool of unused SPTEs
EXE$GL_SCB	Longword	Virtual address of system control block
EXE$GL_ARCHFLAG	Longword	Architectural flags (bits defined by $ARCDEF)
EXE$GB_CPUDATA	16 bytes	System-specific information
EXE$GB_CPUTYPE	Byte	CPU type read from PR$_SID
PFN$GB_LENGTH	Byte	Number of bytes per page in PFN database
MMG$GW_BIGPFN	Word	Flag to indicate size of PFN FLINK, BLINK
EXE$GW_PGFL_FID	3 words	File ID of PAGEFILE.SYS
PFN$A_BASE	8 longwords	Addresses of eight PFN database arrays
• PFN$AL_PTE	Longword	Address of PTE array
• PFN$AL_BAK	Longword	Address of backing store address array
• PFN$AW_REFCNT	Longword	Address of reference count array of words
• PFN$AX_FLINK • PFN$AX_SHRCNT	Longword	Address of combined forward link/global share count array of words

Global Symbol	Size	Description of Data
• PFN\$AX_BLINK } • PFN\$AX_WSLX }	Longword	Address of combined backward link/working set list index array of words
• PFN\$AW_SWPVBN	Longword	Address of swap image virtual block number array of words
• PFN\$AB_STATE	Longword	Address of STATE array of bytes
• PFN\$AB_TYPE	Longword	Address of TYPE array of bytes
EXE\$GT_STARTUP	33 bytes	Counted ASCII string of name of startup command procedure file

The following table lists the SYSBOOT parameters alphabetically and indicates the names of the cells where each parameter is stored.

SYSBOOT Parameter	Cell Name
ACP_BASEPRIO	ACP\$GB_BASEPRIO
ACP_DATACHECK	ACP\$GB_DATACHK
ACP_DINDXCACHE	ACP\$GW_DINDXCACHE
ACP_DIRCACHE	ACP\$GW_DIRCACHE
ACP_EXTCACHE	ACP\$GW_EXTCACHE
ACP_EXTLIMIT	ACP\$GW_EXTLIMIT
ACP_FIDCACHE	ACP\$GW_FIDCACHE
ACP_HDRCACHE	ACP\$GW_HDRCACHE
ACP_MAPCACHE	ACP\$GW_MAPCACHE
ACP_MAXREAD	ACP\$GB_MAXREAD
ACP_MULTIPLE	EXE\$V_MULTACP (EXE\$GL_DEFFLAGS)
ACP_QUOCACHE	ACP\$GW_QUOCACHE
ACP_REBLDSYSD	EXE\$V_REBLDSYSD (EXE\$GL_STATIC_FLAGS)
ACP_SHARE	EXE\$V_SHRF11ACP (EXE\$GL_DEFFLAGS)
ACP_SWAPFLGS	ACP\$GB_SWAPFLGS
ACP_SYSACC	ACP\$GW_SYSACC
ACP_WINDOW	ACP\$GB_WINDOW
ACP_WORKSET	ACP\$GW_WORKSET
ACP_WRITEBACK	ACP\$GB_WRITBACK
ACP_XQP_RES	EXE\$V_XQP_RESIDENT (EXE\$GL_STATIC_FLAGS)
ALLOCLASS	CLU\$GL_ALLOCLS
AWSMIN	SCH\$GW_AWSMIN
AWSTIME	SCH\$GL_AWSTIME
BALSETCNT	SGN\$GL_BALSETCT
BJOBLIM	SYS\$GW_BJOBLIM
BORROWLIM	SCH\$GL_BORROWLIM
BUGCHECKFATAL	EXE\$V_FATAL_BUG (EXE\$GL_DEFFLAGS)

SYSBOOT Parameter	Cell Name
BUGREBOOT	EXE$V_BUGREBOOT (EXE$GL_DEFFLAGS)
CHANNELCNT	SGN$GW_PCHANCNT
CJFLOAD	EXE$V_CJFLOAD (EXE$GL_DEFFLAGS)
CJFSYSRUJ	EXE$V_CJFSYSRUJ (EXE$GL_DEFFLAGS)
CLASS_PROT	EXE$V_CLASS_PROT (EXE$GL_DYNAMIC_FLAGS)
CLISYMTBL	EXE$GL_CLITABL
CONCEAL_DEVICES	EXE$V_CONCEALED (EXE$GL_DEFFLAGS)
CRDENABLE	EXE$V_CRDENABL (EXE$GL_DEFFLAGS)
CTLIMGLIM	SGN$GW_CTLIMGLIM
CTLPAGES	SGN$GW_CTLPAGES
DEADLOCK_WAIT	LCK$GL_WAITTIME
DEFMBXBUFQUO	IOC$GW_MBXBFQUO
DEFMBXMXMSG	IOC$GW_MBXMXMSG
DEFMBXNUMMSG	IOC$GW_MBXNMMSG
DEFPRI	SYS$GB_DEFPRI
DEFQUEPRI	EXE$GB_DEFQUEPRI
DISK_QUORUM	CLU$GB_QDISK
DISMOUMSG	EXE$V_DISMOUMSG (EXE$GL_MSGFLAGS)
DLCKEXTRASTK	LCK$GL_EXTRASTK
DORMANTWAIT	SCH$GW_DORMANTWAIT
DUMPBUG	EXE$V_BUGDUMP (EXE$GL_DEFFLAGS)
EXTRACPU	SGN$GL_EXTRACPU
EXUSRSTK	SGN$GL_EXUSRSTK
FREEGOAL	SGN$GL_FREEGOAL
FREELIM	SGN$GL_FREELIM
GBLPAGES	SGN$GL_MAXGPGCT
GBLPAGFIL	SGN$GL_GBLPAGFIL
GBLSECTIONS	SGN$GW_GBLSECNT
GROWLIM	SCH$GL_GROWLIM
IJOBLIM	SYS$GW_IJOBLIM
IMGIOCNT	SGN$GW_IMGIOCNT
INTSTKPAGES	SGN$GW_ISPPGCT
IOTA	SCH$GW_IOTA
IRPCOUNT	SGN$GL_IRPCNT
IRPCOUNTV	SGN$GL_IRPCNTV
KFILSTCNT	SGN$GB_KFILSTCT
LAMAPREGS	IOC$GW_LAMAPREG
LGI_BRK_DISUSER	EXE$V_BRK_DISUSER (EXE$GL_DYNAMIC_FLAGS)
LGI_BRK_LIM	SYS$GB_BRK_LIM
LGI_BRK_TERM	EXE$V_BRK_TERM (EXE$GL_DYNAMIC_FLAGS)
LGI_BRK_TMO	SYS$GL_BRK_TMO

SYSBOOT Parameter	*Cell Name*
LGI_HID_TIM	SYS$GL_HID_TIM
LGI_PWD_TMO	SYS$GB_PWD_TMO
LGI_RETRY_LIM	SYS$GB_RETRY_LIM
LGI_RETRY_TMO	SYS$GB_RETRY_TMO
LNMPHASHTBL	LNM$GL_HTBLSIZP
LNMSHASHTBL	LNM$GL_HTBLSIZS
LOADCHKPRT	SGN$V_LOADCHKPRT (SGN$GL_LOADFLAGS)
LOADERAPT	SGN$V_LOADERAPAT (SGN$GL_LOADFLAGS)
LOADMTACCESS	SGN$V_LOADMTACCESS (SGN$GL_LOADFLAGS)
LOCKDIRWT	CLU$GW_LCKDIRWT
LOCKIDTBL	LCK$GL_IDTBLSIZ
LOCKIDTBL_MAX	LCK$GL_IDTBLMAX
LOCKRETRY	EXE$GL_LOCKRTRY
LONGWAIT	SCH$GW_LONGWAIT
LRPCOUNT	SGN$GL_LRPCNT
LRPCOUNTV	SGN$GL_LRPCNTV
LRPMIN	SGN$GL_LRPMIN
LRPSIZE	SGN$GL_LRPSIZE
MAXBUF	IOC$GW_MAXBUF
MAXPROCESSCNT	SGN$GW_MAXPRCCT
MAXQUEPRI	SYS$GB_MAXQUEPRI
MAXSYSGROUP	EXE$GL_SYSUIC
MINWSCNT	SGN$GW_MINWSCNT
MOUNTMSG	EXE$V_MOUNTMSG (EXE$GL_MSGFLAGS)
MPW_HILIMIT	MPW$GW_HILIM
MPW_LOLIMIT	MPW$GW_LOLIM
MPW_PRIO	MPW$GB_PRIO
MPW_THRESH	MPW$GL_THRESH
MPW_WAITLIMIT	MPW$GL_WAITLIM
MPW_WRTCLUSTER	MPW$GW_MPWPFC
MVTIMEOUT	IOC$GW_MVTIMEOUT
NJOBLIM	SYS$GW_NJOBLIM
NOAUTOCONFIG	EXE$V_NOAUTOCNF (EXE$GL_DEFFLAGS)
NOCLOCK	EXE$V_NOCLOCK (EXE$GL_DEFFLAGS)
NOCLUSTER	EXE$V_NOCLUSTER (EXE$GL_DEFFLAGS)
NPAGEDYN	SGN$GL_NPAGEDYN
NPAGEVIR	SGN$GL_NPAGEVIR
PAGEDYN	SGN$GL_PAGEDYN
PAGFILCNT	SGN$GW_PAGFILCT
PAGTBLPFC	SGN$GB_PGTBPFC

SYSBOOT Parameter	*Cell Name*
PAMAXPORT	SCS$GB_PAMXPORT
PANOPOLL	SCS$GB_PANOPOLL
PANUMPOLL	SCS$GB_PANPOLL
PAPOLLINTERVAL	SCS$GW_PAPOLINT
PAPOOLINTERVAL	SCS$GW_PAPOOLIN
PASANITY	SCS$GB_PASANITY
PASTDGBUF	SCS$GW_PAPPDDG
PASTIMOUT	SCS$GW_PASTMOUT
PE1	SGN$GL_PE1
PE2	SGN$GL_PE2
PE3	SGN$GL_PE3
PE4	SGN$GL_PE4
PE5	SGN$GL_PE5
PE6	SGN$GL_PE6
PFCDEFAULT	SGN$GW_DFPFC
PFRATH	SCH$GL_PFRATH
PFRATL	SCH$GL_PFRATL
PFRATS	SCH$GL_PFRATS
PHYSICALPAGES	MMG$GL_PHYPGCNT
PIOPAGES	SGN$GW_PIOPAGES
PIXSCAN	SGN$GW_PIXSCAN
POOLPAGING	EXE$V_POOLPGING (EXE$GL_DEFFLAGS)
PQL_DASTLM	PQL$GDASTLM
PQL_DBIOLM	PQL$GDBIOLM
PQL_DBYTLM	PQL$GDBYTLM
PQL_DCPULM	PQL$GDCPULM
PQL_DDIOLM	PQL$GDDIOLM
PQL_DENQLM	PQL$GDENQLM
PQL_DFILLM	PQL$GDFILLM
PQL_DJTQUOTA	PQL$GDJTQUOTA
PQL_DPGFLQUOTA	PQL$GDPGFLQUOTA
PQL_DPRCLM	PQL$GDPRCLM
PQL_DTQELM	PQL$GDTQELM
PQL_DWSDEFAULT	PQL$GDWSDEFAULT
PQL_DWSEXTENT	PQL$GDWSEXTENT
PQL_DWSQUOTA	PQL$GDWSQUOTA
PQL_MASTLM	PQL$GMASTLM
PQL_MBIOLM	PQL$GMBIOLM
PQL_MBYTLM	PQL$GMBYTLM
PQL_MCPULM	PQL$GMCPULM
PQL_MDIOLM	PQL$GMDIOLM

SYSBOOT Parameter	*Cell Name*
PQL_MENQLM	PQL$GMENQLM
PQL_MFILLM	PQL$GMFILLM
PQL_MJTQUOTA	PQL$GMJTQUOTA
PQL_MPGFLQUOTA	PQL$GMPGFLQUOTA
PQL_MPRCLM	PQL$GMPRCLM
PQL_MTQELM	PQL$GMTQELM
PQL_MWSDEFAULT	PQL$GMWSDEFAULT
PQL_MWSEXTENT	PQL$GMWSEXTENT
PQL_MWSQUOTA	PQL$GMWSQUOTA
PRCPOLINTERVAL	SCS$GW_PRCPOLINT
PROCSECTCNT	SGN$GW_MAXPSTCT
QDSKINTERVAL	CLU$GW_QDSKINTERVAL
QDSKVOTES	CLU$GW_QDSKVOTES
QUANTUM	SCH$GW_QUAN
QUORUM	CLU$GW_QUORUM
REALTIME_SPTS	EXE$GL_RTIMESPT
RECNXINTERVAL	CLU$GW_RECNXINT
REINITQUE	EXE$V_REINITQUE (EXE$GL_DEFFLAGS)
RESALLOC	EXE$V_RESALLOC (EXE$GL_DEFFLAGS)
RESHASHTBL	LCK$GL_HTBLSIZ
RJOBLIM	SYS$GW_RJOBLIM
RMS_DFMBC	SYS$GB_DFMBC
RMS_DFMBFHSH	SYS$GB_DFMBFHSH
RMS_DFMBFIDX	SYS$GB_DFMBFIDX
RMS_DFMBFREL	SYS$GB_DFMBFREL
RMS_DFMBFSDK	SYS$GB_DFMBFSDK
RMS_DFMBFSMT	SYS$GB_DFMBFSMT
RMS_DFMBFSUR	SYS$GB_DFMBFSUR
RMS_DFNBC	SYS$GB_DFNBC
RMS_EXTEND_SIZE	SYS$GW_RMSEXTEND
RMS_FILEPROT	SYS$GW_FILEPROT
RMS_GBLBUFQUO	SYS$GW_GBLBUFQUO
RMS_PROLOGUE	SYS$GB_RMSPROLOG
SAVEDUMP	EXE$V_SAVEDUMP (EXE$GL_DEFFLAGS)
SBIERRENABLE	EXE$V_SBIERR (EXE$GL_DEFFLAGS)
SCSBUFFCNT	SCS$GW_BDTCNT
SCSCONNCNT	SCS$GW_CDTCNT
SCSFLOWCUSH	SCS$GW_FLOWCUSH
SCSMAXDG	SCS$GW_MAXDG
SCSMAXMSG	SCS$GW_MAXMSG
SCSNODE	SCS$GB_NODENAME

SYSBOOT Parameter	*Cell Name*
SCSRESPCNT	SCS$GW_RDTCNT
SCSSYSTEMID	SCS$GB_SYSTEMID
SCSSYSTEMIDH	SCS$GB_SYSTEMIDH
SETTIME	EXE$V_SETTIME (EXE$GL_DEFFLAGS)
SPTREQ	SGN$GL_SPTREQ
SRPCOUNT	SGN$GL_SRPCNT
SRPCOUNTV	SGN$GL_SRPCNTV
SRPMIN	SGN$GL_SRPMIN
SRPSIZE	SGN$GL_SRPSIZE
SSINHIBIT	EXE$V_SSINHIBIT (EXE$GL_DEFFLAGS)
STARTUP_P1	SGN$GB_STARTUP_P1
STARTUP_P2	SGN$GB_STARTUP_P2
STARTUP_P3	SGN$GB_STARTUP_P3
STARTUP_P4	SGN$GB_STARTUP_P4
STARTUP_P5	SGN$GB_STARTUP_P5
STARTUP_P6	SGN$GB_STARTUP_P6
STARTUP_P7	SGN$GB_STARTUP_P7
STARTUP_P8	SGN$GB_STARTUP_P8
SWPALLOCINC	SWP$GW_SWPINC
SWPFAIL	SCH$GW_SWPFAIL
SWPFILCNT	SGN$GW_SWPFILES
SWPOUTPGCNT	SWP$GL_SWPPGCNT
SWPRATE	SCH$GL_SWPRATE
SWP_PRIO	SWP$GB_PRIO
SYSMWCNT	SGN$GW_SYSDWSCT
SYSPAGING	EXE$V_SYSPAGING (EXE$GL_DEFFLAGS)
SYSPFC	SGN$GB_SYSPFC
TAILORED	SGN$GB_TAILORED
TBSKIPWSL	SGN$GW_WSLMXSKP
TIMEPROMPTWAIT	SGN$GW_TPWAIT
TTY_ALTALARM	TTY$GW_ALTALARM
TTY_ALTYPAHD	TTY$GW_ALTYPAHD
TTY_AUTOCHAR	TTY$GB_AUTOCHAR
TTY_BUF	TTY$GW_DEFBUF
TTY_CLASSNAME	TTY$GW_CLASSNAM
TTY_DEFCHAR	TTY$GL_DEFCHAR
TTY_DEFCHAR2	TTY$GL_DEFCHAR2
TTY_DEFPORT	TTY$GL_DEFPORT
TTY_DIALTYPE	TTY$GB_DIALTYP
TTY_DMASIZE	TTY$GW_DMASIZE
TTY_OWNER	TTY$GL_OWNUIC

SYSBOOT Parameter	Cell Name
TTY_PARITY	TTY$GB_PARITY
TTY_PROT	TTY$GW_PROT
TTY_RSPEED	TTY$GB_RSPEED
TTY_SCANDELTA	TTY$GL_DELTA
TTY_SILOTIME	TTY$GB_SILOTIME
TTY_SPEED	TTY$GB_DEFSPEED
TTY_TIMEOUT	TTY$GL_TIMEOUT
TTY_TYPAHDSZ	TTY$GW_TYPAHDSZ
UAFALTERNATE	EXE$V_SYSUAFALT (EXE$GL_DEFFLAGS)
UDABURSTRATE	SCS$GB_UDABURST
USER3	SGN$GL_USER3
USER4	SGN$GL_USER4
USERD1	SGN$GL_USERD1
USERD2	SGN$GL_USERD2
VAXCLUSTER	CLU$GB_VAXCLUSTER
VIRTUALPAGECNT	SGN$GL_MAXVPGCT
VMS5	SGN$GL_VMS5
VMS6	SGN$GL_VMS6
VMS7	SGN$GL_VMS7
VMS8	SGN$GL_VMS8
VMSD1	SGN$GL_VMSD1
VMSD2	SGN$GL_VMSD2
VMSD3	SGN$GL_VMSD3
VMSD4	SGN$GL_VMSD4
VOTES	CLU$GW_VOTES
WRITABLESYS	EXE$V_SYSWRTABL (EXE$GL_DEFFLAGS)
WRITESYSPARAMS	EXE$V_WRITESYSPARAMS (EXE$GL_DYNAMIC_FLAGS)
WSDEC	SCH$GL_WSDEC
WSINC	SCH$GL_WSINC
WSMAX	SGN$GL_MAXWSCNT
WS_OPA0	EXE$V_OPA0 (EXE$GL_WSFLAGS)
XFMAXRATE	IOC$GW_XFMXRATE

C.1.17 Remainder of System Image

The rest of the system image consists of read-only code areas, read-only tables, and patch space. All other data areas are dynamically created as a part of system initialization.

Global label MMG$FRSTRONLY, defined in module MDAT, locates the beginning of the nonpaged executive routines. The paged executive is delimited by the labels MMG$AL_PGDCOD and MMG$AL_PGDCODEN, also defined in MDAT.

DYNAMICALLY ALLOCATED EXECUTIVE DATA

Many of the data structures and areas of system address space are not a part of the executive image but instead are constructed when the system is initialized. The sizes of some of these areas depend on the values of SYSBOOT parameters. Other areas depend on the particular physical configuration.

Restart Parameter Block

The restart parameter block (RPB) is filled in at initialization time with bootstrap parameters. The power failure interrupt service routine loads the volatile machine state into the RPB before the system halts. During power recovery, the RPB allows the console logic to determine whether memory contents survived the power outage. The use of the RPB is discussed in Chapters 24 and 26.

PFN Database

The PFN database consists of several arrays, the contents of which describe the state of each page in physical memory. (To save memory, pages that contain the permanently resident executive are not accounted for in the PFN database.) The PFN arrays are described in Chapter 14. Their use during page fault resolution is discussed in Chapter 15. PFN array manipulation during swapper operations is discussed in Chapter 17.

Paged Dynamic Memory

Paged dynamic memory contains all systemwide dynamically allocated structures that do not have to be permanently resident. Typical structures allocated from paged dynamic memory are listed in Chapter 3.

Nonpaged Dynamic Memory

Nonpaged pool contains all dynamically allocated structures that must be resident at all times. These structures may contain either code or data. There are actually two pool areas here. The normal nonpaged pool uses the same allocation routine as is used for paged pool. This pool area can have blocks of any size allocated from it. A second pool area of nonpaged pool contains three lists of fixed-size blocks linked together so that a block can be inserted or removed with the INSQUE and REMQUE instructions. The contents of this second area are often called the lookaside lists. The use of nonpaged pool is described in Chapter 3.

| C.2.5 | **Interrupt Stack** |

The interrupt stack is used to service all hardware interrupts and all software interrupts except AST delivery.

| C.2.6 | **System Control Block** |

The SCB is, strictly speaking, not a writable data structure, although entries are sometimes modified by the executive debugger XDELTA, the DCL commands START/CPU and STOP/CPU, and SYSGEN code used to connect multiport MA780 memory.

| C.2.7 | **Balance Set Slot Area** |

The balance set slot area is devoted exclusively to PHDs. Any resident process has its PHD in one of the balance set slots. Balance set slots are described in Chapter 14. Their use by the swapper is discussed in Chapter 17.

| C.2.8 | **System Header** |

The system header is a system analog to PHDs. It allows system code to be pageable. The structures within the system header that are often altered are the system WSL and the system section table that contains GSTEs.

| C.2.9 | **System Page Table** |

The portion of the SPT that undergoes the most change is the part that maps the balance slot area. Other operations can cause other areas of the SPT to change.

| C.2.10 | **Global Page Table** |

The global page table is a pseudo extension of the SPT that allows GPTEs to be accessed with system virtual page numbers (SVPNs). The global page table is altered when global sections are created and deleted. In addition, GPTEs can change as a result of page faults.

C.3   PROCESS-SPECIFIC EXECUTIVE DATA

Some process-specific data is stored in the PHD. That data is accessible (subject to synchronization considerations) whenever the process is resident. Most of the process-specific data is found in P1 space. P1 space is only addressable when the process is the current process. The executive uses ASTs that execute in process context when it is necessary to acquire or modify such data from some other process.

C.3.1   P1 Pointer Page

The P1 pointer page is a permanent member of the process working set and is defined in executive module SHELL.

Global Symbol	Size	Description of Data
CTL$GW_NMIOCH	Word	Number of I/O channels
CTL$GW_CHINDX	Word	Maximum channel index
CTL$GL_LNMHASH	Longword	Process logical name hash table pointer
CTL$GL_LNMDIRECT	Longword	Process logical name directory pointer
	Longword	Maximum extent (low address limit) of kernel stack
CTL$AL_STACK	4 longwords	Array of stack pointer values
	• Longword	Initial value of kernel stack pointer
	• Longword	Initial value of executive stack pointer
	• Longword	Initial value of supervisor stack pointer
	• Longword	Initial value of user stack pointer
CTL$GQ_LNMTBLCACHE	2 longwords	Listhead for logical name translation cache
CTL$GL_CMSUPR	Longword	Address of change mode to supervisor handler
CTL$GL_CMUSER	Longword	Address of change mode to user handler
CTL$GL_CMHANDLR	Longword	Address of compatibility mode handler
CTL$AQ_EXCVEC	8 longwords	Addresses of primary and secondary exception handlers for each of the four access modes
CTL$GL_THEXEC	Longword	Executive mode termination handler
CTL$GL_THSUPR	Longword	Supervisor mode termination handler
CTL$GL_THUSER	Longword	User mode termination handler
CTL$GQ_COMMON	Quadword	Descriptor (size and address) of per-process common area
CTL$GL_GETMSG	Longword	Address of per-process message dispatcher
CTL$AL_STACKLIM	4 longwords	Lowest stack value for each access mode
CTL$GL_CTLBASVA	Longword	Low-address end of permanent part of P1 space
CTL$GL_IMGHDRBF	Longword	Address of image activator's image header buffer
CTL$GL_IMGLSTPTR	Longword	Address of ICB list (for debugger)

Executive Data Areas

Global Symbol	Size	Description of Data
CTL$GL_PHD	Longword	Address of P1 window that double maps the PHD pages that are not page table pages
CTL$GQ_ALLOCREG	Quadword	Listhead for the process allocation region
CTL$GQ_MOUNTLST	Quadword	Listhead for the process-private mounted volume list
CTL$T_USERNAME	12 bytes	User name for process (blank-filled ASCII string)
CTL$T_ACCOUNT	8 bytes	Account name for process (blank-filled ASCII string)
CTL$GQ_LOGIN	Quadword	System time at process creation
CTL$GL_FINALSTS	Longword	Exit status of latest image to execute
CTL$GL_WSPEAK	Longword	Peak working set size for process
CTL$GL_VIRTPEAK	Longword	Peak page file used
CTL$GL_VOLUMES	Longword	Number of mounted volumes
CTL$GQ_ISTART	Quadword	Image activation time
CTL$GL_ICPUTIM	Longword	Initial image CPU time
CTL$GL_IFAULTS	Longword	Initial image fault count
CTL$GL_IFAULTIO	Longword	Initial image fault I/O count
CTL$GL_IWSPEAK	Longword	Image working set peak
CTL$GL_IPAGEFL	Longword	Image page file peak usage
CTL$GL_IDIOCNT	Longword	Initial image direct I/O count
CTL$GL_IBIOCNT	Longword	Initial image buffered I/O count
CTL$GL_IVOLUMES	Longword	Initial image volume mount count
CTL$T_NODEADDR	7 bytes	Remote node address
CTL$T_NODENAME	7 bytes	Remote node name (counted ASCII)
CTL$T_REMOTEID	17 bytes	Remote node ID
	Byte	Spare for alignment
CTL$GQ_PROCPRIV	Quadword	Permanent process privilege mask
CTL$GL_USRCHMK	Longword	Address of per-process change mode to kernel dispatcher
CTL$GL_USRCHME	Longword	Address of per-process change mode to executive dispatcher
CTL$GL_POWERAST	Longword	Address of power recovery AST for process
CTL$GB_PWRMODE	Byte	Access mode for power recovery AST
CTL$GB_SSFILTER	Byte	System services inhibit filter mask
	2 bytes	Spare for alignment
CTL$AL_FINALEXC	4 longwords	Address of last chance exception handlers for each of the four access modes
CTL$GL_CCBBASE	Longword	Address of base of I/O channel area
CTL$GQ_DBGAREA	Quadword	Descriptor (size and address) of debug symbol table
CTL$GL_RMSBASE	Longword	Pointer to base of RMS image

Global Symbol	Size	Description of Data
CTL$GL_PPMSG	2 longwords	Address of process-permanent message section
CTL$GB_MSGMASK	Byte	Default message display flags
CTL$GB_DEFLANG	Byte	Default message language
CTL$GW_PPMSGCHN	Word	Channel to process-permanent message section
CTL$GL_USRUNDWN	Longword	Per-process vector to user rundown service
CTL$GL_PCB	Longword	Address of process control block
CTL$GL_RUF	Longword	Pointer to recovery unit process block
CTL$GL_SITESPEC	Longword	Site-specific per-process cell
CTL$GL_KNOWNFIL	Longword	Process known file list pointer
CTL$AL_IPASTVEC	8 longwords	Vector for IPAST addresses
CTL$GL_CMCNTX	Longword	Address of the AME context page
CTL$GL_IAFLNKPTR	Longword	Address of IAF list (used by the debugger)
CTL$GL_F11BXQP	Longword	Address of XQP queue and dispatch vectors
CTL$GQ_P0ALLOC	Quadword	Header of P0 extension to process allocation region
CTL$GL_PRCALLCNT	Longword	Number of bytes of process allocation region usable by image requests
CTL$GL_RDIPTR	Longword	Pointer to rights database identifier
CTL$GL_LNMDIRSEQ	Longword	Sequence number for cache of logical name table translations
CTL$GQ_HELPFLAGS	Quadword	Help flags
CTL$GQ_TERMCHAR	Quadword	Terminal characteristics (unused)
CTL$GL_KRPFL	Quadword	Listhead for KRP lookaside list
CTL$GL_KRPBL		
CTL$GL_CREPRC_FLAGS	Longword	$CREPRC flags used to create this process
CTL$GL_THCOUNT	3 longwords	Number of termination handlers for executive, supervisor, and user modes

C.3.2   Other P1 Space Data Areas

The layout of P1 space is pictured in Chapter 1 and detailed in Appendix F. Table F-5 lists the global labels that delimit each area in P1 space. The remainder of Appendix C summarizes data locations in specific P1 areas that are defined in module SHELL. The areas are presented in order of decreasing P1 virtual addresses. That is, the CLI data pages, presented first, occupy the highest P1 address range. The RMS data area, listed last, occupies the lowest P1 address range of the areas presented here.

C.3.2.1

Data Pages for Command Language Interpreter. Module SHELL sets aside an area for the generic CLI data pages.

Global Symbol	Size	Description of Data
CTL$AL_CLICALBK	2 longwords	Call back vector for CLI
CTL$AG_CLIMAGE	2 longwords	Virtual address range of CLI
CTL$GL_CLITABLE	2 longwords	Virtual address range of CLI command table
CTL$GL_UAF_FLAGS	Longword	Flags from authorization record
CTL$GT_CLINAME	Counted string	CLI name (file name only)
CTL$GT_TABLENAME	Counted string	CLI table name (full file specification)
CTL$GT_SPAWNCLI	Counted string	Spawn CLI name (file name only)
CTL$GT_SPAWNTABLE	Counted string	Spawn CLI table name (full file specification)
CTL$AG_CLIDATA		Rest of CLI data area

C.3.2.2 **Process Allocation Region.** The process allocation area is a per-process pool area constructed exactly like paged and nonpaged dynamic memory. See Chapter 3 for further information.

Global Symbol	Size	Description of Data
CTL$GQ_ALLOCREG	• Longword	Initial forward link (contains zero)
	• Longword	Initial size of region

C.3.2.3 **Compatibility Mode Context Page.** Another P1 data area for which module SHELL defines symbols is the page used by the compatibility mode exception service routine.

Global Symbol	Size	Description of Data
CTL$AL_CMCNTX	10 longwords	General register contents stored by exception service routine
	• 7 longwords	Saved R0 through R6
	• 1 longword	Saved compatibility mode exception code
	• 2 longwords	Saved exception PC and PSL
	Rest of page	Used by compatibility mode emulator

C.3.2.4 **RMS Data Area.** This area contains the RMS context that exists for the life of the process. This includes impure areas to describe process-permanent and image I/O files.

Global Symbol	Size	Description of Data
PIO$GL_FMLH	2 longwords	Free memory listhead for process I/O segment
PIO$GL_IIOFSPLH	2 longwords	Free memory listhead for image I/O segment
PIO$GW_STATUS	Word	RMS overall status
PIO$GT_ENDSTR	16 bytes	End of data string
PIO$GW_DFPROT	Word	Default file protection
PIO$GB_DFMBC	Byte	Default multiblock count (RMS_DFMBC)
PIO$GB_DFMBFSDK	Byte	Default multibuffer count for sequential disk I/O (RMS_DFMBFSDK)
PIO$GB_DFMBFSMT	Byte	Default multibuffer count for magnetic tape I/O
PIO$GB_DFMBFSUR	Byte	Default multibuffer count for unit record devices
PIO$GB_DFMBFREL	Byte	Default multibuffer count for relative files
PIO$GB_DFMBFIDX	Byte	Default multibuffer count for indexed files
PIO$GB_DFMBFHSH	Byte	Default multibuffer count hashed
PIO$GB_DFNBC	Byte	Network block transfer size
PIO$GB_RMSPROLOG	Byte	Structure level for RMS files
PIO$GW_RMSEXTEND	Word	Extend quantity for RMS files
	Byte	Spare for alignment
PIO$GL_DIRCACHE	2 longwords	Directory cache listhead
PIO$GL_DIRCFRLH	Longword	Free list for directory cache nodes (singly linked)
PIO$GL_RULOCK	Longword	List of locks held for recovery units
PIO$GL_NXTIRBSEQ	Longword	Next sequence number for IRB$L_IDENT
	4 bytes	Spare for alignment
PIO$GW_PIOIMPA	9 longwords	Impure area descriptor for process I/O segment
	4 bytes	Spare for alignment
PIO$GW_IIOIMPA	41 longwords	Impure area descriptor for image I/O segment
PIO$AL_RMSEXH	4 longwords	RMS termination handler control block
PIO$GQ_IIODEFAULT	Quadword	Default image I/O area
PIO$GT_DDSTRING	256 bytes	Default directory string

Appendix D

Naming Conventions

The conventions described in this appendix were adopted to aid implementors in producing meaningful public names. Public names are all names that are global (known to the linker) or that appear in parameter or macro definition files.

Public names follow these conventions for the following reasons:

- Using reserved names ensures that customer-written software will not be invalidated by subsequent releases of DIGITAL products that add new symbols.
- Using definite patterns for different uses tells someone reading the source code what type of object is being referenced. For example, the form of a macro name is different from that of an offset, which is different from that of a status code.
- Using length codes within a pattern associates the size of an object with its name, increasing the likelihood that reference to this object will use the correct instructions.
- Using a facility code in symbol definitions gives the reader an indication of where the symbol is defined. Separate groups of implementors choose facility code names that will not conflict with one another.

To fully conform with these standards, local synonyms should never be defined for public symbols. The full public symbol should be used in every reference to give maximum clarity to the reader.

D.1 PUBLIC SYMBOL PATTERNS

All DIGITAL symbols contain a dollar sign. Thus, customers and applications developers are strongly advised to use underscores instead of dollar signs to avoid future conflicts.

Public symbols should be constructed to convey as much information as possible about the entities they name. Frequently, private names follow a similar convention. The private name convention is then the same as the public one, with the underscore replacing the dollar sign in symbol names. Private names are used both within a module and globally between modules of a facility that is never in a library. All names that might ever be bound into a user's program must follow the rules for public names. In the case of internal names, a double dollar sign convention can be used, as shown in item 4 in the following list of formats:

1. System service and RMS service macro names are of the form

   ```
   $service-name
   ```

   In a system service macro name, a trailing _S or _G distinguishes the stack form from the separate argument list form. Details about the names of system service macros can be found in the *VAX/VMS System Routines Reference Volume*.

   These names appear in the system macro library SYS$LIBRARY: STARLET.MLB and represent a call to one of the VAX/VMS system services or RMS services. The following examples show this form of symbol name:

$ASCEFC_S	Associate common event flag cluster
$CLOSE	Close a file
$TRNLNM_G	Translate logical name

2. Facility-specific public macro names are of the form

   ```
   $facility_macro-name
   ```

   The executive does not use any symbol names of this form.

3. System macros using local symbols or macros always use names of the form

   ```
   $facility$macro-name
   ```

   This is the form to be used both for symbols generated by a macro and included in calls to it, and for internal macros that are not documented. The executive does not use any symbol names of this form.

4. Global entry point names are of the form

   ```
   facility$entry-name
   ```

   The following examples show this form of symbol name:

EXE$ALOPAGED	Allocate paged dynamic memory
IOC$WFIKPCH	Wait for interrupt and keep channel
MMG$PAGEFAULT	Page fault exception handler

   Global entry point names that are intended for use only within a set of related procedures but not by any calling programs outside the set are of the form

   ```
   facility$$entry-name
   ```

   The executive contains few symbol names of this form. However, the

Run-Time Library contains several examples of symbol names that follow this convention, for example:

BAS$$NUM_INIT   Initialize the BASIC NUM function
FOR$$SIGNAL_STO   Signal a FORTRAN error and call LIB$STOP
OTS$$GET_LUN   Get logical unit number

5. Global entry point names that have nonstandard calls (JSB entry point names) are of the following form, where _Rn indicates that R0 through Rn are not preserved by the routine:

```
facility$entry-name_Rn
```

Note that the caller of such an entry point must include at least registers R2 through Rn in its own entry mask so that a stack unwind will restore all registers properly.

The executive does not use this convention for its JSB entry points, but the Run-Time Library contains several examples of its use, for example:

COB$CVTFP_R9   Convert floating to packed
MTH$SIN_R4   Single precision sine function
STR$COPY_DX_R8   JSB entry to general string copying routine

6. Status codes and condition values are of the form

```
facility$_status
```

The following examples show this form of symbol name:

RMS$_FNF   File not found
SS$_ILLEFC   Illegal event flag cluster
SS$_WASCLR   Flag was previously clear

7. Global variable names are of the form

```
facility$Gt_variable-name
```

The letter G indicates a global variable. The letter t represents the type of variable as defined in Section D.2. The following examples show this form of symbol name:

CTL$GQ_PROCPRIV   Process privilege mask
EXE$GL_NONPAGED   First free block in nonpaged pool
SCH$GL_CURPCB   Address of PCB of current process

8. Addressable global arrays use the letter A (instead of the letter G) and are of the form

```
facility$At_array-name
```

The letter A indicates a global array. The letter t indicates the type of array element as defined in Section D.2. The following examples show this form of symbol name:

CTL$AQ_EXCVEC	Array of primary and secondary exception vectors
PFN$AX_FLINK	Array of forward links for PFN lists

9. Public structure definition macro names are of the form

```
$facility_structureDEF
```

Invoking this macro defines all symbols of the form *structure$xxxxxx*.

Most of the public structure definitions used by VAX/VMS do not include the string "facility_" in the macros that define structure offsets. Rather, macros of the following form are used to define *structure$xxxxxx* symbols:

```
$structureDEF
```

The following examples show the $*structure*DEF form of the macro:

$ACBDEF	Offsets into AST control block
$PCBDEF	Offsets into software process control block
$PHDDEF	Offsets into process header

Many of the macros of this form are contained in the macro libraries SYS$LIBRARY:LIB.MLB or STARLET.MLB. These macros are initially defined in a language-independent structure definition language, as described in Appendix B.

10. VAX MACRO public structure offset names are of the form

```
structure$t_field-name
```

The letter t indicates the data type of the field as defined in Section D.2. The value of the public symbol is the byte offset to the start of the data element in the structure. The following examples show this form of symbol name:

CEB$L_EFC	Event flag cluster (in common event block)
GSD$W_GSTX	Global section table index (in global section descriptor)
PCB$B_PRI	Current process priority (in software PCB)

11. VAX MACRO public structure bit field offsets and single bit names are of the form

```
structure$V_field-name
```

The value of the public symbol is the bit offset from the start of the field that contains the datum (and not from the start of the control block). The following examples show this form of symbol name:

ACB$V_QUOTA	Charge AST to process AST quota

PSL$V_CURMOD	Current access mode
UCB$V_CANCEL	Cancel I/O on this unit

12. VAX MACRO public structure bit field size names are of the form

    ```
    structure$S_field-name
    ```

    The value of the public symbol is the number of bits in the field. The following examples show this form of symbol name:

ACB$S_MODE	Access mode of requestor (2 bits)
PSL$S_CURMOD	Current access mode (2 bits)
PTE$S_PROT	Memory protection on page (4 bits)

13. For BLISS, the functions of the symbols in the previous three items are combined into a single name used to reference an arbitrary datum. Names are of the following form, where x is the same as t for standard-sized data (B, W, L, and Q) and x stands for V for arbitrary and bit fields:

    ```
    structure$x_field-name
    ```

    The macro includes the offset, position, size, and sign extension suitable for use in a BLISS field selector. Most typically, this name is defined by the following BLISS statement:

    ```
    MACRO
        structure$V_field-name=
        structure$t_field-name,
        structure$V_field-name,   ! VAX MACRO V
                                  ! bit field definition
        structure$S_field-name,
        <sign extension> %;
    ```

14. Public structure mask names are of the form

    ```
    structure$M_field-name
    ```

    The value of the public symbol is a mask with bits set for each bit in the field. This mask is not right-justified. Rather, it has *structure$V_field-name* zero bits on the right. The following examples show this form of symbol name:

CEB$M_VALID	Shared memory master CEB is valid
PSL$M_CURMOD	Current access mode
PTE$M_PROT	Memory protection on page

15. Public structure constant names are of the form

    ```
    structure$K_constant-name
    ```

    The following examples show this form of symbol name:

PCB$K_LENGTH	Length (in bytes) of software PCB
SRM$K_FLT_OVF_F	Code for floating overflow fault
STS$K_SEVERE	Fatal error code

For historical reasons, many of the constants used by the executive have the letter C instead of K to indicate that the object data type is a constant. Examples of this form of symbol name are

DYN$C_PCB	Structure type is software PCB
EXE$C_CMSTKSZ	Size of stack space added by change mode handler
PTE$C_URKW	Protection code of user read, kernel write

16. .PSECT names are of the form

```
facility$mnemonic
```

When these names are put into a library, they have the form

```
_facility$mnemonic
```

The following examples show symbols of the form *facility$mnemonic*:

COPY$COPY_FILE	File copying main routine program section
DCL$ZCODE	Program section that contains most code for the DCL command language interpreter
JBC$MSGOUT	Program section containing the job controller's message output routine

This convention is not adhered to as strictly as the other naming conventions because .PSECT names control the way that the linker allocates virtual address space. Names will often be chosen to affect the relative locations of routines and the data that they reference.

Some sample .PSECT names from the Run-Time Library show examples of the form *_facility$mnemonic*:

_LIB$CODE	General library (read-only) code section
_MTH$DATA	Data section in mathematics library
_OTS$CODE	Code portion of language-independent support library

The executive does not use this convention when forming its .PSECT names. Rather, it uses names that cause the desired sections to be placed in the correct parts of system space. For example, .PSECT names control those pieces of the executive that are pageable. In addition, .PSECT names allow data areas and code that references that data to be placed within 64K bytes so that word displacement addressing (rather than longword displacement) can be used to reference the data. The following examples show .PSECT names that are used in the executive:

$$$220	One of the first data program sections in the executive
$AEXENONPAGED	Nonpaged executive code
YEXEPAGED	Pageable executive routines

OBJECT DATA TYPES

Table D-1 shows some of the letters that are used for the various data types or are reserved for various purposes. N, P, and T strings are typically variable length. In structures or I/O records, they frequently contain a byte-sized digit or character count preceding the string. If so, the location or offset is to the count. Counted strings cannot be passed in procedure calls. Instead, a string descriptor must be generated.

Table D-1   Letters and the Data Types They Indicate

Letter	Data Type or Usage
A	Address
B	Byte integer
C	Character[1]
D	Double precision floating
E	Reserved to DIGITAL
F	Single precision floating
G	G_floating-point values
H	H_floating-point values
I	Reserved for integer extensions
J	Reserved to customers for escape to other codes
K	Constant
L	Longword integer
M	Field mask
N	Numeric string (all byte forms)
O	Reserved to DIGITAL as an escape to other codes
P	Packed string
Q	Quadword integer
R	Reserved for records (structure)
S	Field size
T	Text (character) string
U	Smallest unit of addressable storage
V	Field position (VAX MACRO) Field reference (BLISS)
W	Word integer
X	Context-dependent (generic)
Y	Context-dependent (generic)
Z	Unspecified or nonstandard

[1]In many of the symbols used by VAX/VMS, C is used as a synonym for K. Although K is the preferred indicator for constants, many constants used by VMS are indicated by a C in their name. Some constants, such as lengths of data structures, have both a C form and a K form.

D.3   **FACILITY PREFIX TABLE**

Table D-2 lists some of the facility prefixes used by DIGITAL-supplied software. This list is not inclusive and is intended to show examples of several facility prefixes. Each facility name has a unique facility code.

Note that bit <27>, the customer facility bit, is clear in all of the facility codes listed here. Customers are free to use any of the facility codes listed here, provided that they set bit <27>. The default action of the message compiler is to set this bit.

The location of the facility code within a status code and the meaning of the other fields in the status code are described in the *VAX/VMS Utility Routines Reference Manual*.

Individual products such as compilers also have unique facility codes formed from the product name.

Table D-2   Facility Names and Their Prefixes

Prefix	Facility Description	Condition <27:16>
	EXECUTIVE AND SYSTEM PROCESSES	
SS	System service status codes	0
CLI	Command language interpreters	3
JBC	Job controller	4
OPC	Operator communication	5
ERF	Error logger format process	8
	RUN-TIME LIBRARY COMPONENTS	
SMG	Screen management routines	18
LIB	General Purpose Library	21
MTH	Mathematics Library	22
OTS	Language-independent object time system	23
FOR	VAX FORTRAN Run-Time Library	24
SORT	VAX SORT	28
STR	String manipulation procedures	36
	UTILITIES AND COMPILERS	
DBG	Symbolic debugger	2
LIN	VAX linker	100
DIF	File Differences Utility	108
PAT	VAX Image File Patch Utility	109
LAT	Local area terminal	374

Structure name prefixes are typically local to a facility. Refer to the individual facility documentation for its structure name prefixes. Individual facility structure names do not cause problems, because these names are not global and are therefore not known to the linker. They become known at assembly or compile time only by explicitly invoking the macro defining the facility structure.

For example, the macro $FORDEF defines all of the status codes that can be returned from the VAX FORTRAN support library. The facility code of 24 is included in the upper 16 bits of each of the status codes defined with this macro.

Please note that DIGITAL does not provide a registration service for the customer facility codes.

Appendix E

Data Structure Definitions

This book has described VAX/VMS in terms of the data structures used by various components of the executive. This appendix summarizes those data structures.

LOCATION OF DATA STRUCTURE DEFINITIONS

The data structures used by VMS are defined in a language called SDL (see Appendix B). Two sets of four files contain most SDL definitions.

Four files contain most structure and constant definitions used internally by the VMS executive. These files have names of the form [SYS]SYSDEFxx.SDL, where xx represents the letters AE, FL, MP, or QZ. The two letters indicate the range of initial letters of all the data structures contained in that file. The VAX MACRO definitions based on these files are stored in the file SYS$LIBRARY:LIB.MLB. The BLISS-32 definitions based on these files are stored in the file SYS$LIBRARY:LIB.REQ. Many components of VMS are built with these files. They are also available to users for special applications such as user-written device drivers and system services.

Four files named [VMSLIB]STARDEFxx.SDL contain all structure and constant definitions available for general applications (such as system service calls). Again, xx represents the letters AE, FL, MP, or QZ. The definitions based on these files are stored in the files SYS$LIBRARY:STARLET.MLB and STARLET.REQ.

The distinction between the files in SYSDEFxx.SDL and STARDEFxx.SDL is that a structure or constant defined in STARDEF is considered an external interface and usually does not change from release to release. A structure or constant defined in SYSDEF is considered an internal interface and is subject to change. Consequently, VAX MACRO programs that use LIB.MLB or BLISS-32 programs that use LIB.REQ (or LIB.L32) must be reassembled and relinked with each major release of VAX/VMS.

OVERVIEW

Table E-1 lists the data structures and constants summarized in this appendix. The majority of them are defined in the SYSDEFxx modules. The follow-

Table E-1   Summary of Data Structures in Appendix E

SYSTEMWIDE DATA STRUCTURES

ACB	ACL[1]	ARB	CEB
FKB	GSD	ISD	JIB
KFD	KFE	KFPB	KFRH
LKB	LNMB	LNMC	LNMHSH
LNMTH	LNMX	MBX	MTX
ORB	PCB	PHD	PQB
RPB	RSB	SHB	SHD
TQE			

STRUCTURES USED BY THE I/O AND FILE SUBSYSTEMS

ADP	BRK	CCB	CDDB
CDRP	CRB	DDB	DDT
DPT	FCB	IDB	IRP
TAST	UCB	WCB	

SYMBOLIC CONSTANTS

BTD	CA	DYN	IO*xxx*
IPL	NDT	PR	

[1]This structure or constant is defined in module STARDEF*xx*.

ing classes of structures are in the table:

- Data structures used by memory management, the scheduler, and other components of the system image. There is at least one figure or table in this book that describes each of these structures.
- Data structures used by the I/O and file subsystems. This includes device drivers and utilities such as MOUNT and INIT.
- Constants such as data structure types, IPLs, and processor register definitions.

E.3   EXECUTIVE DATA STRUCTURES

This section contains a brief summary of most of the data structures described in this book. Three data structures, the software process control block (PCB), the process header (PHD), and the job information block (JIB) are partly described in several places throughout the book. They are illustrated here in their entirety, with references to other partial descriptions.

E.3.1   ACB—Asynchronous System Trap Control Block

Purpose:	Describes a pending AST for a process.
Usual Location:	AST queue with listhead in software PCB.
Allocated from:	Nonpaged pool.
Reference:	Figure 7-1.
Special Notes:	ACBs are usually a part of a larger structure, such as an I/O request packet (IRP) or timer queue element (TQE).

E.3.2   ACL—Access Control List

Purpose:	List of entries that grant or deny access to a particular system resource.
Usual Location:	ACL queue with listhead in resource's object rights block (ORB$L_ACLFL).
Allocated from:	Paged pool.
Reference:	Figure E-1.
Special Notes:	An ACL contains access control entries (ACEs) beginning at offset ACL$L_LIST.

E.3.3   ADP—Adapter Control Block

Purpose:	Defines characteristics and current state of an I/O adapter.
Location:	Pointed to by CRB (CRB$L_INTD + VEC$L_ADP).
Allocated from:	Nonpaged pool.
Reference:	Figure E-2.

E.3.4   ARB—Access Rights Block

The ARB is currently a part of the software PCB. The ARB pointer (PCB$L_ARB) points to this overlaid data structure. Figure E-14 shows an ARB within a software PCB. Program references that use the ARB pointer in the software PCB to locate the ARB or any fields within the ARB (such as the privilege mask) will continue to work without modification should the ARB become an independent data structure in a future release of VAX/VMS.

Purpose:	Defines process access rights and privileges.
Location:	Currently a part of the software PCB.
References:	Table 21-2, Figures E-3, E-14.

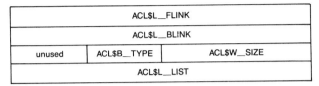

Figure E-1   Layout of an Access Control List

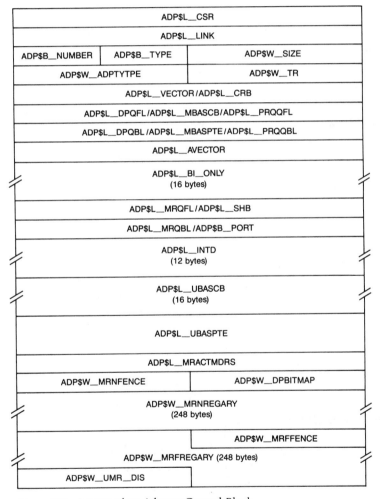

Figure E-2   Layout of an Adapter Control Block

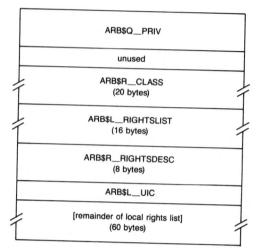

Figure E-3 Layout of an Access Rights Block

E.3.5 BRK—Breakthrough Message Descriptor Block

Purpose: Used to send asynchronous messages to one or more
                    terminals.

Allocated from: Nonpaged pool.

Reference: Figure 18-6.

E.3.6 CCB—Channel Control Block

Purpose: Describes the logical path between the process and the
                    UCB of the specific device.

Location: Within per-process space table, pointed to by
                    CTL$GL_CCBBASE.

Reference: Figure 18-2.

E.3.7 CDDB—Class Driver Data Block

Purpose: Auxiliary data structure for each SCS connection
                    between a disk or tape class driver and a remote
                    MSCP server.

Usual Location: Pointed to by CRB$L_AUXSTRUC.

Allocated from: Nonpaged pool.

Reference: Figure E-4.

Special Notes: There is one CDDB per MSCP controller.

CDDB$L__CDRPQFL			
CDDB$L__CDRPQBL			
CDDB$B__SUBTYPE	CDDB$B__TYPE	CDDB$W__SIZE	
CDDB$B__SYSTEMID (6 bytes)			
CDDB$W__STATUS			
CDDB$L__PDT			
CDDB$L__CRB			
CDDB$L__DDB			
CDDB$Q__CNTRLID			
CDDB$W__CNTRLTMO		CDDB$W__CNTRLFLGS	
CDDB$L__OLDRSPID			
CDDB$L__OLDCMDSTS			
CDDB$L__RSTRTCDRP			
CDDB$W__RSTRTCNT		CDDB$B__DAPCOUNT	CDDB$B__RETRYCNT
CDDB$L__RSTRTQFL			
CDDB$L__RSTRTQBL			
CDDB$L__SAVED__PC			
CDDB$L__UCBCHAIN			
CDDB$L__ORIGUCB			
CDDB$L__ALLOCLS			
CDDB$L__DAPCDRP			
CDDB$L__CDDBLINK			
CDDB$W__WTUCBCTR		CDDB$B__RSVDB	CDDB$B__FOVER__CTR
CDDB$W__CPYSEQNUM		CDDB$B__CHVRSN	CDDB$B__CSVRSN
CDDB$L__MAXBCNT			
CDDB$L__RSVD3			
CDDB$L__RSVD4			
CDDB$L__PERMCDRP			

Figure E-4   Layout of a Class Driver Data Block

E.3.8   **CDRP—Class Driver Request Packet**

Purpose:	Data structure used to communicate between SCS and a class driver.
Usual Location:	Linked into CDDB listhead (CDDB$L_CDRPQFL).
Allocated from:	Nonpaged pool.
Reference:	Figure 19-2.
Special Notes:	Contains within it, at negative offsets, a full IRP.

E.3.9   CEB—Common Event Block

Purpose:	Contains description and wait queue for common event flag cluster.
Location:	In list whose head is at SCH$GQ_CEBHD. (Master CEBs are located in shared memory and pointed to by a field in the slave CEB located in the CEB list on each processor.)
Allocated from:	Nonpaged pool. (Master CEBs are allocated from a CEB table located in shared memory.)
References:	Figures 12-2, 12-3, 12-4, 12-5.

E.3.10   CRB—Channel Request Block

Purpose:	There is one CRB for each set of devices whose access to a controller must be synchronized.
Location:	Pointed to by UCB (UCB$L_CRB).
Allocated from:	Nonpaged pool.
Reference:	Figure E-5.

E.3.11   DDB—Device Data Block

Purpose:	There is one DDB for each controller in a system.
Location:	Linked into device listhead (IOC$GL_DEVLIST).
Allocated from:	Nonpaged pool.
Reference:	Figure E-6.

E.3.12   DDT—Driver Dispatch Table

Purpose:	Specifies the driver entry points for various I/O functions.
Location:	Pointed to by DDB$L_DDT and UCB$L_DDT.
Allocated from:	Nonpaged pool.
Reference:	Figure E-7.

E.3.13   DPT—Driver Prolog Table

Purpose:	Defines the identity and the size of the driver to the system routine that loads the driver into virtual memory.

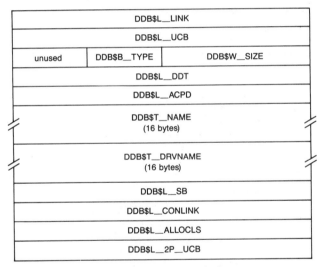

CRB$L__WQFL		
CRB$L__WQBL		
CRB$B__TT__TYPE	CRB$B__TYPE	CRB$W__SIZE
CRB$B__UNIT__BRK	CRB$B__MASK	CRB$W__REFC
CRB$L__AUXSTRUC		
CRB$L__TIMELINK		
CRB$L__DUETIME		
CRB$L__TOUTROUT		
CRB$L__LINK		
CRB$L__INTD (36 bytes)		
CRB$L__INTD2 (36 bytes)		

Figure E-5   Layout of a Channel Request Block

DDB$L__LINK		
DDB$L__UCB		
unused	DDB$B__TYPE	DDB$W__SIZE
DDB$L__DDT		
DDB$L__ACPD		
DDB$T__NAME (16 bytes)		
DDB$T__DRVNAME (16 bytes)		
DDB$L__SB		
DDB$L__CONLINK		
DDB$L__ALLOCLS		
DDB$L__2P__UCB		

Figure E-6   Layout of a Device Data Block

Location:	Beginning of the driver image.
Allocated from:	Nonpaged pool.
Reference:	Figure E-8.
Special Notes:	The size of the DPT is the size of the entire driver, including the DPT itself.

DDT$L__START	
DDT$L__UNSOLINT	
DDT$L__FDT	
DDT$L__CANCEL	
DDT$L__REGDUMP	
DDT$W__ERRORBUF	DDT$W__DIAGBUF
DDT$L__UNITINIT	
DDT$L__ALTSTART	
DDT$L__MNTVER	
DDT$L__CLONEDUCB	
unused	DDT$W__FDTSIZE
DDT$L__MNTV__SSSC	
DDT$L__MNTV__FOR	
DDT$L__MNTV__SQD	

Figure E-7 Layout of a Driver Dispatch Table

DPT$L__FLINK			
DPT$L__BLINK			
DPT$B__REFC	DPT$B__TYPE	DPT$W__SIZE	
DPT$W__UCBSIZE		DPT$B__FLAGS	DPT$B__ADPTYPE
DPT$W__REINITTAB		DPT$W__INITTAB	
DPT$W__MAXUNITS		DPT$W__UNLOAD	
DPT$W__DEFUNITS		DPT$W__VERSION	
DPT$W__VECTOR		DPT$W__DELIVER	
DPT$T__NAME (12 bytes)			
DPT$Q__LINKTIME			
DPT$L__ECOLEVEL			

Figure E-8 Layout of a Driver Prolog Table

..3.14   **FCB—File Control Block**

Purpose: Describes a uniquely accessed file on a volume;
                     provides a means for controlling shared access to a
                     file.

Usual Location: Linked into the volume control block listhead
                     (VCB$L_FCBFL).

Allocated from: Nonpaged pool.

Reference: Figure E-9.

..3.15   **FKB—Fork Block**

Purpose: Stores minimum context for a fork process.

Usual Location: First six longwords of UCB.

Allocated from: Nonpaged pool.

Reference: Figure 6-2.

..3.16   **GSD—Global Section Descriptor**

Purpose: Contains identifying information about a global
                     section.

Location: Group or system GSD list. (Shared memory GSDs are
                     located in shared memory.)

Allocated from: Paged pool. (Shared memory GSDs are allocated from
                     pages in shared memory set aside for shared memory
                     GSDs.)

References: Figures 14-14, 14-27.

Special Notes: There are three different forms of GSD:

                     • Normal GSD
                     • Descriptor for PFN-mapped section
                     • Descriptor for section that resides in
                       shared memory

E.3.17   **IDB—Interrupt Dispatch Block**

Purpose: Provides the information for a controller-specific
                     interrupt dispatcher to dispatch an interrupt to the
                     appropriate driver for that device unit.

Location: Pointed to by CRB$L_INTD + VEC$L_IDB.

Allocated from: Nonpaged pool.

Reference: Figure E-10.

FCB$L__FCBFL		
FCB$L__FCBBL		
FCB$B__ACCLKMODE	FCB$B__TYPE	FCB$W__SIZE
FCB$L__EXFCB		
FCB$L__WLFL		
FCB$L__WLBL		
FCB$W__ACNT		FCB$W__REFCNT
FCB$W__LCNT		FCB$W__WCNT
FCB$W__STATUS		FCB$W__TCNT
FCB$W__FID__SEQ		FCB$W__FID / FCB$W__FID__NUM
FCB$W__SEGN		FCB$W__RVN
FCB$L__STVBN		
FCB$L__STLBN		
FCB$L__HDLBN		
FCB$L__FILESIZE		
FCB$L__EFBLK		
FCB$W__DIRSEQ		FCB$W__VERSIONS
FCB$L__HIGHWATER		
FCB$L__ACCLKID		
FCB$L__LOCKBASIS		
FCB$L__TRUNCVBN		
FCB$L__CACHELKID		
FCB$L__FILEOWNER		
FCB$Q__ACMODE		
FCB$L__SYS__PROT		
FCB$L__OWN__PROT		
FCB$L__GRP__PROT		
FCB$L__WOR__PROT		
FCB$L__ACLFL		
FCB$L__ACLBL		
unused (20 bytes)		
unused (20 bytes)		
FCB$L__DIRINDX		

This part of the FCB is structured like an ORB (see Figure E-13).

Figure E-9 Layout of a File Control Block

IDB$L__CSR			
IDB$L__OWNER			
IDB$B__VECTOR	IDB$B__TYPE	IDB$W__SIZE	
IDB$B__COMBO__CSR__OFFSET	IDB$B__TT__ENABLE	IDB$W__UNITS	
IDB$W__SPARE1		IDB$B__FLAGS	IDB$B__COMBO__VECTOR__OFFSET
IDB$L__ADP			
IDB$L__UCBLST (32 bytes)			

Figure E-10   Layout of an Interrupt Dispatch Block

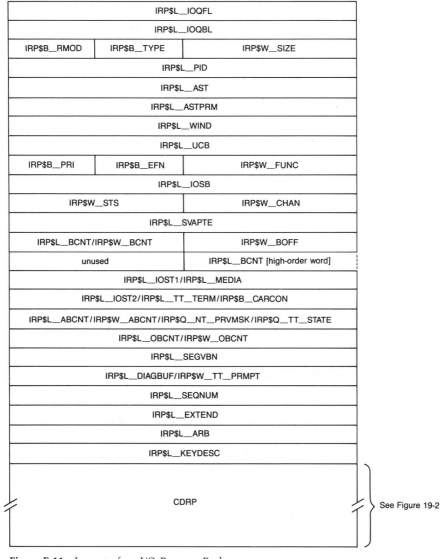

IRP$L__IOQFL	
IRP$L__IOQBL	
IRP$B__RMOD	IRP$B__TYPE	IRP$W__SIZE
IRP$L__PID	
IRP$L__AST	
IRP$L__ASTPRM	
IRP$L__WIND	
IRP$L__UCB	
IRP$B__PRI	IRP$B__EFN	IRP$W__FUNC
IRP$L__IOSB	
IRP$W__STS	IRP$W__CHAN
IRP$L__SVAPTE	
IRP$L__BCNT/IRP$W__BCNT	IRP$W__BOFF
unused	IRP$L__BCNT [high-order word]
IRP$L__IOST1/IRP$L__MEDIA	
IRP$L__IOST2/IRP$L__TT__TERM/IRP$B__CARCON	
IRP$L__ABCNT/IRP$W__ABCNT/IRP$Q__NT__PRVMSK/IRP$Q__TT__STATE	
IRP$L__OBCNT/IRP$W__OBCNT	
IRP$L__SEGVBN	
IRP$L__DIAGBUF/IRP$W__TT__PRMPT	
IRP$L__SEQNUM	
IRP$L__EXTEND	
IRP$L__ARB	
IRP$L__KEYDESC	
CDRP	See Figure 19-2

Figure E-11   Layout of an I/O Request Packet

E.3.18   **IRP—I/O Request Packet**

Purpose: Constructed by the Queue I/O Request ($QIO) system
                        service to describe an I/O function to be performed
                        on a device unit.

Usual Location: All IRPs pending for a particular device unit are linked
                        together, typically at UCB$L_IOQFL.

Allocated from: Nonpaged pool.

References: Figures E-11, 19-2.

E.3.19   **ISD—Image Section Descriptor**

Purpose: Describes virtual address range and corresponding
                        information (virtual block range, global section
                        name) to the image activator.

Location: Image header.

Reference: Figure 21-2.

E.3.20   **JIB—Job Information Block**

The JIB appears in several figures in this book. Figure E-12 shows all of the
fields currently defined in this structure.

Purpose: Contains quotas pooled by all processes in the same
                        job.

Location: Pointed to by PCB$L_JIB field of all PCBs in the same
                        job.

Allocated from: Nonpaged pool.

Reference: Figure E-12.

E.3.21   **KFD—Known File Device and Directory Block**

Purpose: Contains the file device and directory names associated
                        with an image. Multiple known images share the
                        same KFD.

Location: Pointed to by the known file pointer block
                        (KFPB$L_KFDLST).

Allocated from: Paged pool.

Reference: Figure 21-5.

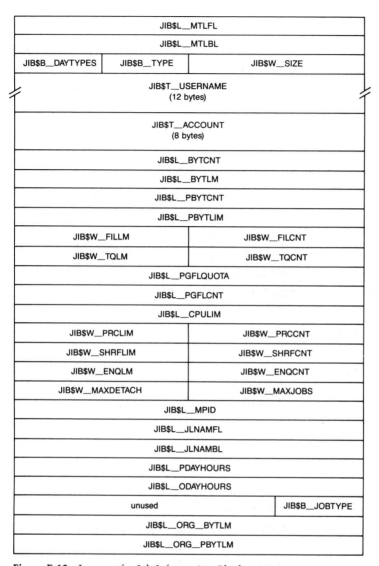

JIB$L__MTLFL		
JIB$L__MTLBL		
JIB$B__DAYTYPES	JIB$B__TYPE	JIB$W__SIZE
JIB$T__USERNAME (12 bytes)		
JIB$T__ACCOUNT (8 bytes)		
JIB$L__BYTCNT		
JIB$L__BYTLM		
JIB$L__PBYTCNT		
JIB$L__PBYTLIM		
JIB$W__FILLM		JIB$W__FILCNT
JIB$W__TQLM		JIB$W__TQCNT
JIB$L__PGFLQUOTA		
JIB$L__PGFLCNT		
JIB$L__CPULIM		
JIB$W__PRCLIM		JIB$W__PRCCNT
JIB$W__SHRFLIM		JIB$W__SHRFCNT
JIB$W__ENQLM		JIB$W__ENQCNT
JIB$W__MAXDETACH		JIB$W__MAXJOBS
JIB$L__MPID		
JIB$L__JLNAMFL		
JIB$L__JLNAMBL		
JIB$L__PDAYHOURS		
JIB$L__ODAYHOURS		
unused		JIB$B__JOBTYPE
JIB$L__ORG__BYTLM		
JIB$L__ORG__PBYTLM		

Figure E-12   Layout of a Job Information Block

3.22   KFE—Known File Entry Block

Purpose:	Identifies the file name of the image and its properties.
Location:	Pointed to by the KFPE hash table, whose address is contained in the known file pointer block (KFPB$L_KFEHSHTAB).
Allocated from:	Paged pool.
References:	Figures 21-4, 21-6.

E.3.23 **KFPB—Known File Pointer Block**

Purpose: Contains address of KFE hash table and the listhead for the KFDs.

Location: Pointed to by EXE$GL_KNOWN_FILES.

Allocated from: Paged pool.

Reference: Figure 21-8.

E.3.24 **KFRH—Known File Resident Image Header**

Purpose: Exists for each known image installed /HEADER_RESIDENT.

Location: Immediately precedes the IHD and specifies its size and version number.

Allocated from: Paged pool.

Reference: Figure 21-7.

E.3.25 **LKB—Lock Block**

Purpose: Contains information about a request to the Enqueue Lock ($ENQ) system service.

Allocated from: Nonpaged pool.

Reference: Figure 13-3.

E.3.26 **LNMB—Logical Name Block**

Purpose: Contains the logical name string, its access mode, and attributes.

Location: Chained from the shared logical name hash table or a process-private hash table.

Allocated from: Paged pool for shared logical names or process allocation region for process logical names.

References: Figures 28-1, 28-4.

E.3.27 **LNMC—Logical Name Table Name Cache Block**

Purpose: Facilitates logical name translation.

Location: Doubly linked from a P1 space listhead (CTL$GQ_LNMTBLCACHE).

Allocated from: Process allocation region.

Reference: Figure 28-5.

3.28   LNMHSH—Logical Name Hash Table

Purpose:	Locates all logical names.
Location:	Indirectly pointed to by the array of addresses at LNM$AL_HASHTBL.
Allocated from:	Paged pool and process allocation region.
Reference:	Figure 28-4.

3.29   LNMTH—Logical Name Table Header

Purpose:	Describes a logical name table.
Allocated from:	Paged pool for the shared table or process allocation region for process tables.
Reference:	Figure 28-2.

3.30   LNMX—Logical Name Translation Block

Purpose:	Describes an equivalence name for a logical name.
Location:	Follows an LNMB.
Allocated from:	Paged pool for shared names or process allocation region for process names.
Reference:	Figure 28-1.

3.31   MBX—Shared Memory Mailbox Control Block

Purpose:	Describes each mailbox that exists in shared memory.
Location:	Pages in shared memory dedicated to mailbox control blocks.
References:	Figures 18-4, 18-5.

3.32   MTX—Mutex (Mutual Exclusion Semaphore)

Purpose:	Controls process access to protected data structures.
Usual Location:	Statically allocated longwords in system space.
Reference:	Figure 2-1.

3.33   ORB—Object Rights Block

Purpose:	Defines the protection information for various objects within the system.

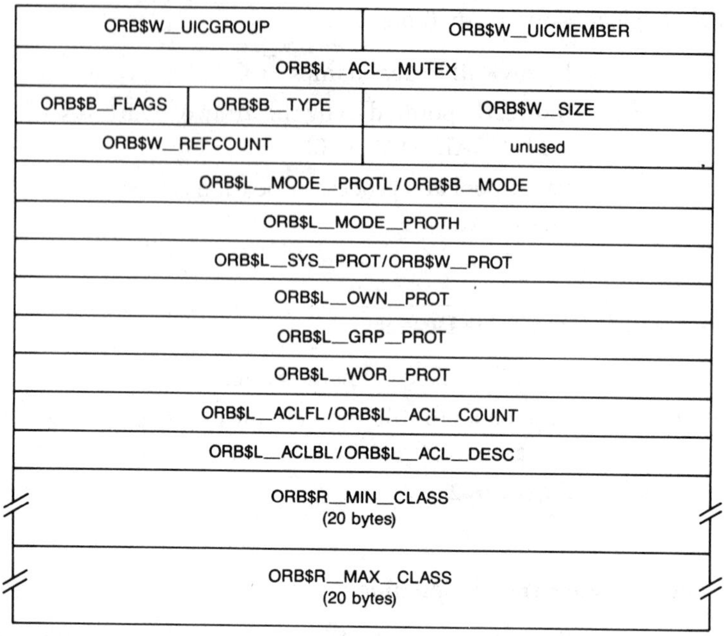

ORB$W__UICGROUP		ORB$W__UICMEMBER	
ORB$L__ACL__MUTEX			
ORB$B__FLAGS	ORB$B__TYPE	ORB$W__SIZE	
ORB$W__REFCOUNT		unused	
ORB$L__MODE__PROTL / ORB$B__MODE			
ORB$L__MODE__PROTH			
ORB$L__SYS_PROT / ORB$W__PROT			
ORB$L__OWN__PROT			
ORB$L__GRP__PROT			
ORB$L__WOR__PROT			
ORB$L__ACLFL / ORB$L__ACL__COUNT			
ORB$L__ACLBL / ORB$L__ACL__DESC			
ORB$R__MIN__CLASS (20 bytes)			
ORB$R__MAX__CLASS (20 bytes)			

Figure E-13 Layout of an Object Rights Block

Usual Location:	Linked to a data structure, such as a UCB, via offset *xxx*$L_ORB.
Allocated from:	Paged pool.
Reference:	Figure E-13.

E.3.34   PCB—Process Control Block

The term "process control block" can refer to two different structures in the VAX literature. All software documentation, including this book, refers to the software process control block as simply PCB and always prefixes the hardware process control block with "hardware."

E.3.34.1   Software Process Control Block

Purpose:	Contains the permanently resident information about a process.
Location:	Linked into a scheduling state queue; also pointed to by one of the PCB vector elements.
Allocated from:	Nonpaged pool.
Reference:	Figure E-14.

E.3.34.2   Hardware Process Control Block

Purpose:	Contains hardware context of a process while it is not executing.
Location:	Part of the fixed portion of the process header.
Reference:	Figure 10-7.

E.3.35   PHD—Process Header

Purpose:	Contains process context data that must reside in system space but can be outswapped.
Location:	Balance slot area in system space. (PHD pages that are not page table pages are double mapped by a range of P1 space addresses.)
References:	Figures E-15, 14-1, 14-2, 14-4, 14-6, 14-8.

E.3.36   PQB—Process Quota Block

Purpose:	Used during process creation to store new process parameters that are copied to the PHD and P1 space after those areas are accessible.
Location:	Pointed to by PCB$L_EFWM.
Allocated from:	Paged pool.
Reference:	Figure E-16.

E.3.37   RPB—Restart Parameter Block

Purpose:	Contains volatile processor state during power failure; locates the bootstrap I/O driver and associated subroutines.
Usual Location:	Physical page zero on system with no bad memory in the first 64K bytes.
Reference:	Table 24-16.

E.3.38   RSB—Resource Block

Purpose:	Contains information about a resource defined to the lock management system services.
Usual Location:	Resource hash table pointed to by LCK$GL_HASHTBL.
Allocated from:	Nonpaged pool.
References:	Figures 13-1, 13-2.

PCB$L__SQFL				
PCB$L__SQBL				
PCB$B__PRI	PCB$B__TYPE	PCB$W__SIZE		
PCB$W__MTXCNT		PCB$B__ASTEN	ACB$B__ASTACT	
PCB$L__ASTQFL				
PCB$L__ASTQBL				
PCB$L__PHYPCB				
PCB$L__OWNER				
PCB$L__WSSWP				
PCB$L__STS				
PCB$L__WTIME				
PCB$B__PRIB	PCB$B__WEFC	PCB$W__STATE		
PCB$W__TMBU		PCB$W__APTCNT		
PCB$W__PPGCNT		PCB$W__GPGCNT		
PCB$W__BIOCNT		PCB$W__ASTCNT		
PCB$W__DIOCNT		PCB$W__BIOLM		
PCB$W__PRCCNT		PCB$W__DIOLM		
PCB$T__TERMINAL (8 bytes)				
PCB$L__PQB				
PCB$L__EFCS				
PCB$L__EFCU				
unused	PCB$B__PGFLINDEX	PCB$W__PGFLCHAR		
PCB$L__SWAPSIZE				
PCB$L__EFC2P				

Figure E-14 Layout of a Software Process Control Block

E.3.39   SHB—Shared Memory Control Block

Purpose:	Describes shared memory connected to specific processor.
Location:	In list at EXE$GL_SHBLIST in processor local memory.
Allocated from:	Nonpaged pool.
Reference:	Figure 14-26.

E.3.40   SHD—Shared Memory Data Page

Purpose:	Initial description of VMS usage of a specific shared memory controller.

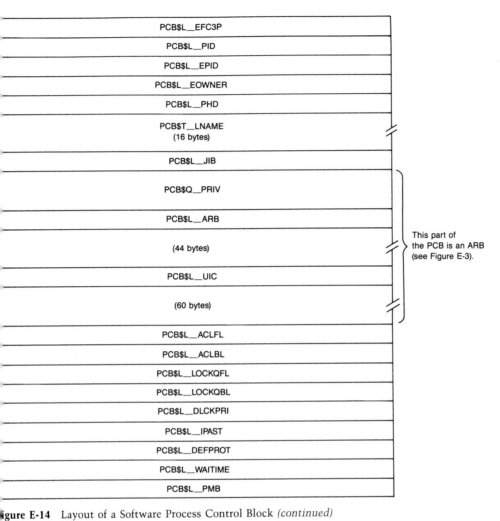

| PCB$L__EFC3P |
| PCB$L__PID |
| PCB$L__EPID |
| PCB$L__EOWNER |
| PCB$L__PHD |
| PCB$T__LNAME
(16 bytes) |
| PCB$L__JIB |
| PCB$Q__PRIV |
| PCB$L__ARB |
| (44 bytes) |
| PCB$L__UIC |
| (60 bytes) |
| PCB$L__ACLFL |
| PCB$L__ACLBL |
| PCB$L__LOCKQFL |
| PCB$L__LOCKQBL |
| PCB$L__DLCKPRI |
| PCB$L__IPAST |
| PCB$L__DEFPROT |
| PCB$L__WAITIME |
| PCB$L__PMB |

This part of the PCB is an ARB (see Figure E-3).

Figure E-14   Layout of a Software Process Control Block *(continued)*

Location:	Last physical pages of shared memory.
Reference:	Table 14-4.

.3.41   TAST—Terminal AST Block

Purpose:	Contains information for delivery of out-of-band character ASTs.
Usual Location:	Queued to the terminal UCB via TAST$L_LINK.
Allocated from:	Nonpaged pool.
Reference:	Figure 7-5.

PHD$Q__PRIVMSK		
PHD$W__WSAUTH	PHD$W__WSLIST	
PHD$W__WSDYN	PHD$W__WSLOCK	
PHD$W__WSLAST	PHD$W__WSNEXT	
PHD$W__WSEXTENT	PHD$W__WSAUTHEXT	
PHD$W__DFWSCNT	PHD$W__WSQUOTA	
PHD$L__PAGFIL		
PHD$L__PSTBASOFF		
PHD$W__PSTFREE	PHD$W__PSTLAST	
PHD$L__FREP0VA		
PHD$L__FREPTECNT		
PHD$L__FREP1VA		
PHD$W__FLAGS	PHD$B__PGTBPFC	PHD$B__DFPFC
PHD$L__CPUTIM		
PHD$W__PRCLM	PHD$W__QUANT	
PHD$W__PHVINDEX	PHD$W__ASTLM	
PHD$L__BAK		
PHD$L__WSLX		
PHD$L__PAGEFLTS		
PHD$W__SWAPSIZE	PHD$W__WSSIZE	
PHD$L__DIOCNT		
PHD$L__BIOCNT		
PHD$L__CPULIM		
unused	PHD$B__AWSMODE	PHD$B__CPUMODE
PHD$L__PTWSLELCK		
PHD$L__PTWSLEVAL		
PHD$W__PTCNTVAL	PHD$W__PTCNTLCK	
PHD$W__PTCNTMAX	PHD$W__PTCNTACT	
PHD$W__EXTDYNWS	PHD$W__WSFLUID	
PHD$L__PCB		
PHD$L__ESP		
PHD$L__SSP		
PHD$L__USP		
PHD$L__R0		
PHD$L__R1		
PHD$L__R2		
PHD$L__R3		

Figure E-15 Layout of a Process Header

PHD$L__R4		
PHD$L__R5		
PHD$L__R6		
PHD$L__R7		
PHD$L__R8		
PHD$L__R9		
PHD$L__R10		
PHD$L__R11		
PHD$L__R12		
PHD$L__R13		
PHD$L__PC		
PHD$L__PSL		
PHD$L__P0BR		
PHD$L__P0LRASTL		
PHD$L__P1BR		
PHD$L__P1LR		
PHD$W__RESPGCNT		PHD$W__EMPTPG
PHD$W__CWSLX		PHD$W__REQPGCNT
PHD$Q__AUTHPRIV		
PHD$Q__IMAGPRIV		
PHD$L__RESLSTH		
PHD$L__IMGCNT		
PHD$L__PFLTRATE		
PHD$L__PFLREF		
PHD$L__TIMREF		
PHD$L__MPINHIBIT		
PHD$L__PGFLTIO		
unused	unused	PHD$B__AUTHPRI
PHD$L__EXTRACPU		
PHD$R__MIN__CLASS (20 bytes)		
PHD$R__MAX__CLASS (20 bytes)		
PHD$L__SPARE		
unused (60 bytes)		
PHD$L__WSL		

Figure E-15   Layout of a Process Header *(continued)*

PQB$Q__PRVMSK			
PQB$B__STS	PQB$B__TYPE	PQB$W__SIZE	
PQB$L__ASTLM			
PQB$L__BIOLM			
PQB$L__BYTLM			
PQB$L__CPULM			
PQB$L__DIOLM			
PQB$L__FILLM			
PQB$L__PGFLQUOTA			
PQB$L__PRCLM			
PQB$L__TQELM			
PQB$L__WSQUOTA			
PQB$L__WSDEFAULT			
PQB$L__ENQLM			
PQB$L__WSEXTENT			
PQB$L__JTQUOTA			
unused	PQB$B_MSGMASK	PQB$W__FLAGS	
PQB$L__UAF__FLAGS			
PQB$L__CREPRC__FLAGS			
PQB$R__MIN__CLASS (20 bytes)			
PQB$R__MAX__CLASS (20 bytes)			

Figure E-16 Layout of a Process Quota Block

E.3.42 TQE—Timer Queue Element

Purpose:	Describes pending timer or scheduled wakeup request.
Location:	Linked to the timer queue at EXE$GL_TQFL.
Allocated from:	Nonpaged pool.
Reference:	Figure 11-1.

E.3.43 UCB—Unit Control Block

Purpose:	Describes the status, characteristics, and current state of a device unit.
Location:	Linked from DDB$L_UCB.
Allocated from:	Nonpaged pool.

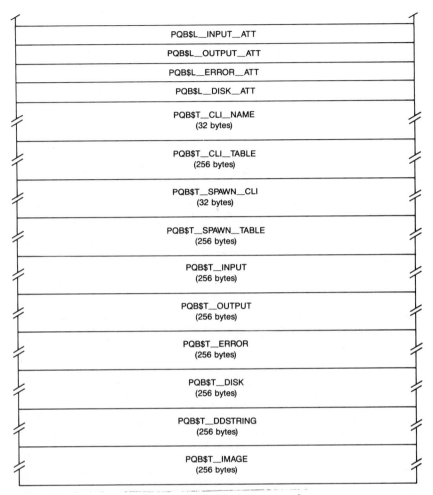

Figure E-16   Layout of a Process Quota Block *(continued)*

Reference:	Figure E-17.
Special Notes:	Figure E-17 shows the part of the UCB common to all device units. See the manual *Writing a Device Driver for VAX/VMS* for information on extensions to the common part of the UCB.

.3.44   WCB—Window Control Block

Purpose:	Describes the virtual to logical correspondence for the blocks of a file.
Location:	Contained in FCB list at FCB$L_WLFL.
Allocated from:	Nonpaged pool.
Reference:	Figure E-18.

UCB$L__FQFL			
UCB$L__FQBL			
UCB$B__FIPL	UCB$B__TYPE	UCB$W__SIZE	
UCB$L__FPC			
UCB$L__FR3			
UCB$L__FR4			
UCB$W__INIQUO		UCB$W__BUFQUO	
UCB$L__ORB			
UCB$L__LOCKID			
UCB$L__CRB			
UCB$L__DDB			
UCB$L__PID			
UCB$L__LINK			
UCB$L__VCB			
UCB$Q__DEVCHAR			
UCB$W__DEVBUFSIZ		UCB$B__DEVTYPE	UCB$B__DEVCLASS
UCB$Q__DEVDEPEND			
UCB$L__IOQFL			
UCB$L__IOQBL			
UCB$W__CHARGE		UCB$W__UNIT	
UCB$L__IRP			
UCB$B__AMOD	UCB$B__DIPL	UCB$W__REFC	
UCB$L__AMB			
UCB$L__STS			
UCB$W__QLEN		UCB$W__DEVSTS	
UCB$L__DUETIM			
UCB$L__OPCNT			
UCB$L__SVPN			
UCB$L__SVAPTE			
UCB$W__BCNT		UCB$W__BOFF	
UCB$W__ERRCNT		UCB$B__ERTMAX	UCB$B__ERTCNT
UCB$L__PDT			
UCB$L__DDT			
UCB$L__MEDIA__ID			

Figure E-17   Layout of a Unit Control Block

SYMBOLIC CONSTANTS

The files [SYS]SYSDEF*xx*.SDL and [VMSLIB]STARDEF*xx*.SDL define many systemwide symbolic codes that identify structures, resources, quotas, priorities, and so on. Many of these constants are listed in the *VAX/VMS System Services Reference Manual* and the *VAX/VMS I/O Reference Volume*. Those that are most closely tied to the material in this book but that are not listed in those manuals are listed here.

BTD—Bootstrap Device Codes

The bootstrap device codes (see Table E-2) are used to interpret the contents of R0 to VMB, the primary bootstrap program. (Note that these do not apply to VMB on a MicroVAX I or MicroVAX II.)

CA—Conditional Assembly Parameters

The conditional assembly parameters (see Table E-3) control whether certain code is included when components of VMS are assembled. The first parameter was important during the initial development of VMS but is no longer used. All measurement code (used by the Monitor Utility) is always included.

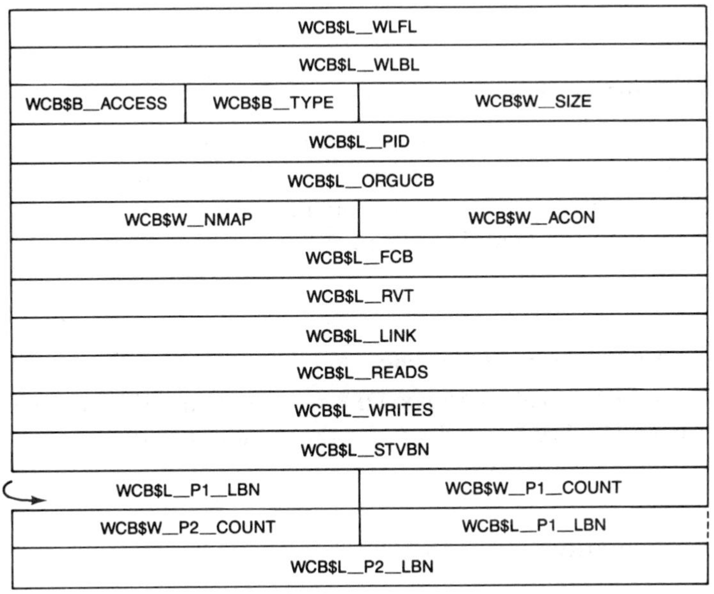

WCB$L__WLFL		
WCB$L__WLBL		
WCB$B__ACCESS	WCB$B__TYPE	WCB$W__SIZE
WCB$L__PID		
WCB$L__ORGUCB		
WCB$W__NMAP		WCB$W__ACON
WCB$L__FCB		
WCB$L__RVT		
WCB$L__LINK		
WCB$L__READS		
WCB$L__WRITES		
WCB$L__STVBN		
WCB$L__P1__LBN		WCB$W__P1__COUNT
WCB$W__P2__COUNT		WCB$L__P1__LBN
WCB$L__P2__LBN		

Figure E-18   Layout of a Window Control Block

Table E-2   Bootstrap Device Codes

Symbolic Name	Code	Device
BTD$K_MB	0	MASSBUS device
BTD$K_DM	1	RK06/7
BTD$K_DL	2	RL02
BTD$K_DQ	3	RB02/RB80
BTD$K_UDA	17	UDA
BTD$K_TK50	18	TK50
BTD$K_HSCCI	32	HSC on a CI
BTD$K_CONSOLE	64	Console block storage device
BTD$K_QNA	96	DEQNA
BTD$K_UNA	97	DEUNA

Table E-3   Conditional Assembly Parameters

Symbolic Name	Code	Feature
CA$_SIMULATOR	1	VMS running on simulator
CA$_MEASURE	2	Accumulate statistics for Monitor Utility
CA$_MEASURE_IOT	4	Accumulate I/O statistics for Monitor Utility

E.4.3   **DYN—Data Structure Type Definitions**

All structures allocated from nonpaged and paged pool have a unique code in the type field, at offset *xxx*$B_TYPE (see Table E-4). SDA uses the contents of this field when formatting dumps of pool and in automatic formatting of a data structure with the FORMAT command.

E.4.4   **IOxxx—I/O Address Space Definitions**

The SYS$LIBRARY:LIB.MLB $IO*xxx*DEF macros define the layout of I/O space for each CPU. See Appendix G for the values of *xxx*.

E.4.5   **IPL—Interrupt Priority Level Definitions**

IPLs that are used by VMS for synchronization and other purposes are given the symbolic names listed in Table E-5.

Table E-4   Data Structure Type Definitions

Symbolic Name	Code	Structure Type
DYN$C_ADP	1	Adapter control block
DYN$C_ACB	2	AST control block
DYN$C_AQB	3	ACP queue block
DYN$C_CEB	4	Common event block
DYN$C_CRB	5	Channel request block
DYN$C_DDB	6	Device data block
DYN$C_FCB	7	File control block
DYN$C_FRK	8	Fork block
DYN$C_IDB	9	Interrupt dispatch block
DYN$C_IRP	10	I/O request packet
DYN$C_LOG	11	Logical name block
DYN$C_PCB	12	Software process control block
DYN$C_PQB	13	Process quota block
DYN$C_RVT	14	Relative volume table
DYN$C_TQE	15	Timer queue element
DYN$C_UCB	16	Unit control block
DYN$C_VCB	17	Volume control block
DYN$C_WCB	18	Window control block
DYN$C_BUFIO	19	Buffered I/O buffer
DYN$C_TYPAHD	20	Terminal type-ahead buffer
DYN$C_GSD	21	Global section descriptor
DYN$C_MVL	22	Magnetic tape volume list
DYN$C_NET	23	Network message block
DYN$C_KFE	24	Known file entry
DYN$C_MTL	25	Mounted volume list entry
DYN$C_BRDCST	26	Broadcast message block
DYN$C_CXB	27	Complex chained buffer
DYN$C_NDB	28	Network node descriptor block
DYN$C_SSB	29	Logical link subchannel status block
DYN$C_DPT	30	Driver prolog table
DYN$C_JPB	31	Job parameter block
DYN$C_PBH	32	Performance buffer header
DYN$C_PDB	33	Performance data block
DYN$C_PIB	34	Performance information block
DYN$C_PFL	35	Page file control block
DYN$C_PTR	37	Pointer control block
DYN$C_KFRH	38	Known file image header

(continued)

Table E-4   Data Structure Type Definitions *(continued)*

Symbolic Name	Code	Structure Type
DYN$C_DCCB	39	Data cache control block
DYN$C_EXTGSD	40	Extended global section descriptor
DYN$C_SHMGSD	41	Shared memory global section descriptor
DYN$C_SHB	42	Shared memory control block
DYN$C_MBX	43	Mailbox control block
DYN$C_IRPE	44	Extended I/O request packet
DYN$C_SLAVCEB	45	Slave common event block
DYN$C_SHMCEB	46	Shared memory master common event block
DYN$C_JIB	47	Job information block
DYN$C_TWP	48	Terminal driver write packet ($TTYDEF)
DYN$C_RBM	49	Real-time SPTE bitmap
DYN$C_VCA	50	Disk volume cache block
DYN$C_CDB	51	X25 LES channel data block
DYN$C_LPD	52	X25 LES process descriptor
DYN$C_LKB	53	Lock block
DYN$C_RSB	54	Resource block
DYN$C_LKID	55	Lock ID table
DYN$C_RSHT	56	Resource hash table
DYN$C_CDRP	57	Class driver request packet
DYN$C_ERP	58	Error log packet
DYN$C_CIDG	59	CI datagram buffer
DYN$C_CIMSG	60	CI message buffer
DYN$C_XWB	61	DECnet logical link context block
DYN$C_WQE	62	DECnet work queue block
DYN$C_ACL	63	Access control list queue entry
DYN$C_LNM	64	Logical name block
DYN$C_FLK	65	Fork lock request block
DYN$C_RIGHTSLIST	66	Rights list
DYN$C_KFD	67	Known file device directory block
DYN$C_KFPB	68	Known file list pointer block
DYN$C_CIA	69	Compound intrusion analysis block
DYN$C_PMB	70	Page fault monitor control block
DYN$C_PFB	71	Page fault monitor buffer
DYN$C_CHIP	72	Internal check protection block
DYN$C_ORB	73	Object rights block
DYN$C_QVAST	74	QVSS AST block
DYN$C_SCS	96	SCS control block
DYN$C_CI	97	CI port structure

Table E-4   Data Structure Type Definitions *(continued)*

Symbolic Name	Code	Structure Type
DYN$C_LOADCODE	98	Loadable code
DYN$C_INIT	99	Structure set up by INIT
DYN$C_CLASSDRV	100	Class driver structure
DYN$C_CLU	101	Cluster structure
DYN$C_PGD	102	Paged pool structure
DYN$C_UIS	103	UIS structure
DYN$C_DSRV	105	Disk server structure
DYN$C_MP	106	ASMP structure
DYN$C_SPECIAL	128	Code that defines beginning of special codes
DYN$C_SHRBUFIO	128	Shared memory buffered I/O buffer

Table E-5   IPL Symbols

Symbolic Name	Code	Function
IPL$_ASTDEL	2	AST delivery interrupt
IPL$_SCHED	3	Rescheduling interrupt
IPL$_IOPOST	4	I/O postprocessing interrupt
IPL$_QUEUEAST	6	Fork level used for AST queuing
IPL$_TIMERFORK	7	IPL for software timer fork routine
IPL$_TIMER	8	IPL for software timer routine
IPL$_SCS	8	SCS synchronization IPL
IPL$_SYNCH	8	Systemwide synchronization level
IPL$_MAILBOX	11	Fork IPL for mailbox driver
IPL$_PERFMON	15	Performance monitor synchronization
IPL$_HWCLK	24	Hardware clock interrupt
IPL$_POWER	31	Block powerfail interrupt

E.4.6 **NDT—Nexus (Adapter) Device Type**

Each external adapter has an associated code that is used by VMB, INIT, and the power recovery routine to determine which adapter-specific action should be taken to (re)initialize each adapter (see Table E-6).

E.4.7   **PR—Processor Register Definitions**

The macro $PRDEF, in SYS$LIBRARY:LIB.MLB, defines symbolic names for the processor registers that are common to all types of VAX. For each CPU type a second LIB.MLB macro, $PR*xxx*DEF, defines symbolic names for the CPU's additional processor registers. See Appendix G for the values of *xxx*.

Table E-6   Nexus (Adapter) Device Types

Symbolic Name	Code	Adapter
NDT$_MEM4NI	8	Memory, 4K, not interleaved
NDT$_MEM4I	9	Memory, 4K, interleaved
NDT$_MEM16NI	16	Memory, 16K, not interleaved
NDT$_MEM16	17	Memory, 16K, interleaved
NDT$_MEM1664NI	18	Memory, 16K and 64K mixed
NDT$_MB	32	MBA 0, 1, 2, or 3
NDT$_UB0	40	UNIBUS adapter or interconnect 0
NDT$_UB1	41	UNIBUS adapter 1
NDT$_UB2	42	UNIBUS adapter 2
NDT$_UB3	43	UNIBUS adapter 3
NDT$_DR32	48	DR32
NDT$_CI	56	CI750, CI780
NDT$_MPM0	64	Multiport memory 0
NDT$_MPM1	65	Multiport memory 1
NDT$_MPM2	66	Multiport memory 2
NDT$_MPM3	67	Multiport memory 3
NDT$_MEM64NIL	104	64K memory, not interleaved, lower controller
NDT$_MEM64EIL	105	64K memory, externally interleaved, lower controller
NDT$_MEM64NIU	106	64K memory, not interleaved, upper controller
NDT$_MEM64EIU	107	64K memory, externally interleaved, upper controller
NDT$_MEM64I	108	64K memory, internally interleaved
NDT$_MEM256NIL	112	256K memory, not interleaved, lower controller
NDT$_MEM256EIL	113	256K memory, externally interleaved, lower controller
NDT$_MEM256NIU	114	256K memory, not interleaved, upper controller

Table E-6   Nexus (Adapter) Device Types *(continued)*

Symbolic Name	Code	Adapter
NDT$_MEM256EIU	115	256K memory, externally interleaved, upper controller
NDT$_MEM256I	116	256K memory, internally interleaved
NDT$_SCORMEM	80000001_{16}	VAX 8200 memory
NDT$_BIMFA	80000101_{16}	DRB32
NDT$_BUA	80000102_{16}	VAXBI UNIBUS adapter
NDT$_BLA	80000103_{16}	KLESI-B
NDT$_NBI	80000106_{16}	VAX 8800 VAXBI adapter
NDT$_BCA	80000108_{16}	CIBCA
NDT$_BICOMBO	80000109_{16}	DMB32
NDT$_BCI750	$8000010B_{16}$	CIBCI
NDT$_BDA	$8000010E_{16}$	VAXBI disk adapter
NDT$_AIE	$8000410F_{16}$	DEBNT

Appendix F

Size of System and
P1 Virtual Address Spaces

The system image SYS$SYSTEM:SYS.EXE contains the operating system code for the VMS system but very little of the data. Many of the data structures that VMS uses are not created until the system is bootstrapped, so that the structure sizes can be determined from the appropriate SYSBOOT parameters. This appendix describes the relationships between these SYSBOOT parameters and the portions of the address spaces whose sizes they determine.

In the equations that appear in this appendix, two common features dominate. One feature is division by 512, the number of bytes in a page. This division is done whenever the input parameter is a number of bytes, such as the NPAGEDYN SYSBOOT parameter or an expression for the number of bytes in a process header. If 511 is added to an expression for a number of bytes before the integer division takes place, this represents a rounding up to the next highest page boundary.

The second feature is the number 128 that appears in expressions that count the number of pages for which system page table entries (SPTEs) are needed. The significance of the number 128 is that a page table entry (PTE) is four bytes long, so that a page of PTEs maps 128 pages. In this case, the rounding factor that is added is 127.

F.1   SIZE OF PROCESS HEADER

Before the various portions of address space are calculated, the size of the process header (PHD) is related to the SYSBOOT parameters that affect its size. Table F-1 lists each portion of the PHD, the SYSBOOT parameters that affect its size, and the global location where the size of that portion is stored. The table also introduces the notation used in the first set of equations to describe each piece of the PHD. Figure F-1 shows the actual layout of the PHD and the relationship of the parts described in Table F-1.

The following global locations contain sums of the sizes of several of the pieces listed in Table F-1:

$$\text{SGN\$GL\_PHDAPCNT} = \text{PHD(wsl\_pst)} + \text{PHD(bak)}$$

Table F-1   Discrete Portions of the Process Header

Symbolic Name or Equations	Items Stored in This Portion	Factors Affecting Size of This Portion	Global Location Where Size of This Portion Is Stored
PHD(wsl_pst)	Fixed portion, PST, WSL	PHD$K_LENGTH, PROCSECTCNT, WSMAX, PQL_DWSDEFAULT	SWP$GW_WSLPTE
PHD(empty)	No access pages for WSL expansion	WSMAX, PQL_DWSDEFAULT	SWP$GW_EMPTPTE
PHD(bak)	PHD page arrays, Page table page arrays	Size of the PHD	SWP$GW_BAKPTE
PHD(page_tables)	P0 and P1 page tables	VIRTUALPAGECNT	SGN$GL_PTPAGCNT

$$SGN\$GL\_PHDPAGCT = PHD(wsl\_pst) + PHD(empty) + PHD(bak)$$

$$SWP\$GL\_BSLOTSZ = PHD(wsl\_pst) + PHD(empty) + PHD(bak) + PHD(page\_tables)$$

F.1.1   Process Page Tables

Most of the PHD is taken up by the P0 and P1 page tables. The total number of pages allocated for the process page tables depends on the parameter VIRTUALPAGECNT:

$$PHD(page\_tables) = \frac{VIRTUALPAGECNT + 127}{128} \tag{F.1}$$

F.1.2   Working Set List and Process Section Table

The working set list (WSL) and process section table (PST) are located at the low address end of the PHD immediately after the fixed size area and grow toward each other. The size of the PST depends on the parameter PROCSECTCNT. On first approach, one would assume that the WSL size depends on the parameter WSMAX. In most systems, many processes have working sets that are much smaller than the allowed maximum. The initial WSL size is calculated to take this into account. It is assumed that most processes have working sets that are approximately equal to the parameter PQL_DWSDEFAULT.

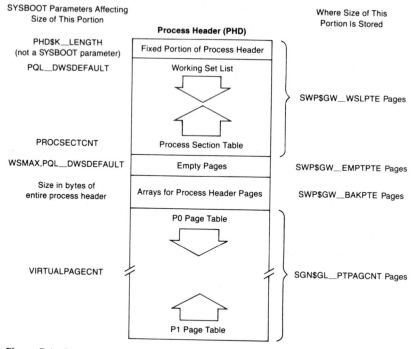

Figure F-1 Process Header and SYSBOOT Parameters

Equation F.2 calculates the maximum number of pages required for the fixed portion of the PHD, WSL, and PST. The extra space reserved for WSL expansion is calculated in Equation F.3. The difference between these two numbers (Equation F.4) is the number of pages initially available for the fixed portion, WSL, and PST. The significance of the numbers 4 and 32 in Equation F.2 is that a working set list entry (WSLE) is four bytes and a process section table entry (PSTE) is 32 bytes.

$$\text{PHD(temp)} = \frac{\left(\begin{array}{c} \text{PHD\$K\_LENGTH} + (4 \times \text{WSMAX}) \\ + (32 \times \text{PROCSECTCNT}) + 511) \end{array}\right)}{512} \tag{F.2}$$

$$\text{PHD(empty)} = \frac{\text{WSMAX} - \text{PQL\_DWSDEFAULT}}{128} \tag{F.3}$$

$$\text{PHD(wsl\_pst)} = \text{PHD(temp)} - \text{PHD(empty)} \tag{F.4}$$

F.1.3   Process Header Page Arrays

The PHD page arrays include two arrays that describe each page in the PHD. These arrays are used by the swapper to store information about PHD pages while the header is outswapped. There are also two arrays of bytes in this portion of the PHD that describe each page table page. To simplify the calculation of the size of this portion of the PHD, space is allocated as if the last two arrays contained an element for each PHD page. Because the page tables constitute approximately 90 percent of the PHD in a typical system, this algorithm results in a very good approximation. Because the result is rounded up to the next page boundary, there is no difference in size for almost all combinations of SYSBOOT parameters.

The PHD page arrays are located in the PHD, so the space allocated for this area depends on its own size. The calculation of this portion of the PHD proceeds iteratively. An approximate size of the area is determined, based on the sizes of the other three areas. The estimates are then refined until two successive calculations reach the same result.

Define the following:

$$\text{PHD(the\_rest)} = \text{PHD(wsl\_pst)} \\ + \text{PHD(empty)} \\ + \text{PHD(page\_tables)} \tag{F.5}$$

$$\text{PHD(bak,0)} = 0$$

Perform the calculation shown in Equation F.7 until the following equality exists:

$$\text{PHD(bak,N)} = \text{PHD(bak,N} - 1) \tag{F.6}$$

$$\text{PHD(bak,N)} = \frac{\left(8 \times [\text{PHD(the\_rest)} + \text{PHD(bak,N} - 1)]\right) + 511}{512} \tag{F.7}$$

Call the result of this calculation PHD(bak):

$$\text{PHD(bak)} = \text{PHD(bak,N)} \tag{F.8}$$

The sum of the four pieces of the PHD yields its size in pages. The result of this calculation is stored in global location SWP\$GL_BSLOTSZ.

$$\text{PHD(total)} = \text{PHD(wsl\_pst)} \\ + \text{PHD(empty)} \\ + \text{PHD(bak)} \\ + \text{PHD(page\_tables)} \tag{F.9}$$

F.2   SYSTEM VIRTUAL ADDRESS SPACE

Once the size of the PHD has been calculated, the size of system address space can be computed. System space is made up of a fixed part and pieces of variable size.

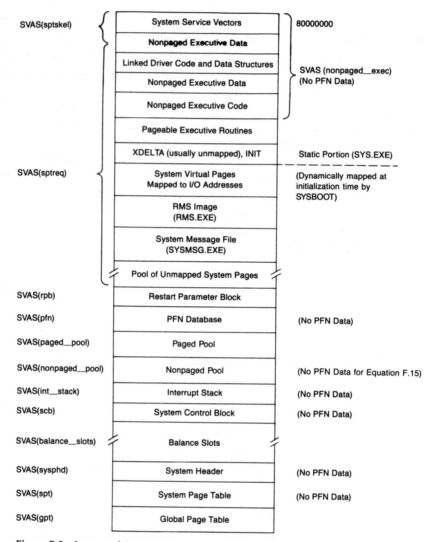

Figure F-2 Layout of System Virtual Address Space

Figure F-2 pictures the fixed part of system address space and the nomenclature used to designate each piece. Table F-2 lists each piece, the global location of the pointer to each piece, and its size. It also shows the protection and pageability of each piece. It does not show page owner mode, because all system space pages are owned by kernel access mode.

F.2.1 System Virtual Address Space and SYSBOOT Parameters

Many of the pieces of system address space vary, depending on one or more SYSBOOT parameters. Table F-3 lists each piece of variable system space, the

Table F-2   Detailed Layout of Fixed System Virtual Address Space

Item[1]	Global Location[2]	Size in Pages[3]	Protection	Pageable
System service vectors	80000000	5	UR	No
Nonpaged executive data	MMG$A_ENDVEC			
File system performance data	PMS$GL_FCP	0.9	UREW[4]	No
Null and swapper process stacks		1.5	URKW	No
Linked driver data	EXE$GL_BUGCHECK	5.5	URKW	No
Linked driver code	MMG$AL_BEGDRIVE	2.6	URKW	No
Nonpaged executive data	MMG$AL_ENDDRIVE	16.6	URKW	No
Nonpaged executive code	MMG$FRSTRONLY	88	UR	No
Extendable patch space	@MMG$GL_PGDCOD[5]	5	UR	Yes
Pageable executive data	EXE$UPCASE_DAT	1	UR	Yes
Pageable executive code	EXE$EXCPTNE − 0D	142	UR	Yes
Shell process	SWP$GL_SHELLBAS	7	UR	Yes
Usually unmapped pages	MMG$AL_PGDCODEN			
XDELTA[6]		18	URKW	No
INIT		12	No access	
BUGCHECK		24	No access	
End of fixed sized portion of system virtual address space	MMG$A_SYS_END			

[1]The pieces of the executive listed in this table originate in the system image file SYS$SYSTEM:SYS.EXE and are mapped by SYSBOOT. The addresses of each of these pieces remain unchanged until a new major release of the operating system.

[2]Numbers in address expressions are hexadecimal. If a global location is not preceded by the symbol @, its value is the address of the area in question. If a global location is preceded by the symbol @, its value is an address that contains the address of the area in question.

[3]Sizes are expressed in decimal numbers. A size that is not an integral number of pages is approximate. Consult the system map for precise numbers.

[4]The protection granularity defined by the VAX architecture is a page. For this reason, the first page in this area is set to UREW protection. The remaining pages are set to URKW.

[5]The cell MMG$GL_PGDCOD points to the second page of the patch area that lies between the nonpaged and paged executive. The end of the executive is established dynamically. If another patch page is required, the symbol is changed to point to the next page.

[6]The pages containing XDELTA only remain mapped if the R5 flag requesting the executive debugger is set at system initialization.

global location of the pointer to each piece, and the SYSBOOT parameter that affects its size. It also shows the protection and pageability of each piece. It does not show page owner access mode, because all system space pages are owned by kernel access mode.

The sizes of most of the pieces of system address space listed in Table F-3 are simply related to one or two SYSBOOT parameters. Their sizes are computed in a straightforward manner by SYSBOOT. The sizes of the system page table (SPT) and the PFN database are a little more complicated. A discussion of their sizes appears in the next section.

When SYSBOOT calculates the size of the SPT, it forms a sum of the sizes of the pieces of system virtual address space and allocates an SPTE for each page. The calculation presented here considers each piece of system space in the order of increasing virtual address rather than in the order that SYSBOOT performs the calculation.

1. The first pages of system address space, containing the system service vectors and file system performance statistics blocks, have their size accounted for in the assembly-time parameter MMG$C_SPTSKEL, defined in module SPTSKEL:

$$SVAS(sptskel) = 6 \tag{F.10}$$

The file system performance statistics data area is less than one page long. However, access protection is on a per-page basis. Part of the first page of the area reserved for the null process and swapper kernel mode stacks falls into the remaining part of this area and thus has a protection of UREW (the protection applied to the statistics area). The remainder of the stacks area is URKW.

2. The area that contains the SYS.EXE image, the RMS image, and the system message file has its size determined by the SYSBOOT parameter SPTREQ. There must be enough extra pages in this area to map the I/O adapters, to reserve a system virtual page for each device unit whose driver requests one, and to map the mass storage control protocol (MSCP) server on a VAXcluster System with local disks served to VAXcluster members. Other uses of this area include a buffer for mount verification and a buffer for the pattern to be written to a disk file, which must be erased when it is deleted.

   If there are any SPTEs required for mapping by PFN for real-time devices, the requested number (SYSBOOT parameter REALTIME_SPTS) is added to system virtual address requirements:

$$SVAS(sptreq) = SPTREQ + REALTIME\_SPTS \tag{F.11}$$

After the size of the SPT is calculated and rounded up to the next page boundary, any extra pages acquired are added to the pool of available SPTEs.

Table F-3   Detailed Layout of Variable System Virtual Address Space

Item[1]	Global Location[2]	Factors That Affect Size[3]	Protection	Pageable
MAPPED TOWARD INCREASING VIRTUAL ADDRESSES BY EXE$INIT				
Mapping for I/O adapters	@(@MMG$GL_SBICONF)[4]	External adapters	KW	No
Connect to interrupt pages	RBM$L_SPTFREL in real-time SPT bitmap[5]	REALTIME_SPTS	No access[6]	No
System disk driver page	UCB$L_SVPN in system disk UCB[5]	1 page	KW	No
Mount verification buffer		1 page	KW	No
Erase pattern buffer	@EXE$GL_ERASEPB	1 page	KW	No
Erase pattern page table	@EXE$GL_ERASEPPT	1 page	KW	No
MAPPED TOWARD INCREASING VIRTUAL ADDRESSES BY THE STACONFIG PROCESS[7]				
Other driver pages	UCB$L_SVPN in UCBs[5]	Number of units	KW	No
MAPPED TOWARD INCREASING VIRTUAL ADDRESSES BY THE SYSINIT PROCESS				
RMS image	@MMG$GL_RMSBASE	Size of RMS image	UR	Yes
System message file	@EXE$GL_SYSMSG	Size of file	UR	Yes
MAPPED TOWARD INCREASING VIRTUAL ADDRESSES BY STARTUP AND SYSTARTUP COMMAND PROCEDURES				
Other driver pages	UCB$L_SVPN in UCBs[5]	Number of units	KW	No
MSCP server data	@SCS$GL_MSCP − 200	1 page	KW	No
MSCP server	@SCS$GL_MSCP	Size of image	EW	No
UNMAPPED SYSTEM VIRTUAL ADDRESS SPACE				
Pool of available system pages	@BOO$GL_SPTFREL[5] @BOO$GL_SPTFREH[5]	SPTREQ	No access	

(continued)

Table F-3   Detailed Layout of Variable System Virtual Address Space (*continued*)

Item[1]	Global Location[2]	Factors That Affect Size[3]	Protection	Pageable
		MAPPED TOWARD DECREASING VIRTUAL ADDRESSES BY SYSBOOT		
Restart parameter block	@EXE$GL_RPB	1 page	URKW	No
PFN database	@PFN$A_BASE	Everything	ERKW	No
Paged pool	@MMG$GL_PAGEDYN	PAGEDYN	ERKW	Yes
Nonpaged pool	@MMG$GL_NPAGEDYN	NPAGEVIR	ERKW	No
LRP lookaside list	@IOC$GL_LRPSPLIT	LRPCOUNTV, LRPSIZE	ERKW	No
IRP lookaside list	@EXE$GL_SPLITADR	IRPCOUNTV	ERKW	No
SRP lookaside list	@IOC$GL_SRPSPLIT	SRPCOUNTV, SRPSIZE	ERKW	No
No access guard page		1 page	No access	
Interrupt stack	@EXE$GL_INTSTKLM	INTSTKPAGES	ERKW	No
No access guard page	@EXE$GL_INTSTK	1 page	No access	
System control block	@EXE$GL_SCB	CPU configuration	ERKW	No
Balance slot area	@SWP$GL_BALBASE	BALSETCNT, Size of PHD	ERKW	Yes, no[8]
System header	@MMG$GL_SYSPHD	SYSMWCNT, GBLSECTIONS	ERKW	No

Table F-3   Detailed Layout of Variable System Virtual Address Space (continued)

Item[1]	Global Location[2]	Factors That Affect Size[3]	Protection	Pageable
MAPPED TOWARD DECREASING VIRTUAL ADDRESSES BY SYSBOOT				
System page table	@MMG$GL_SPTBASE	Everything	ERKW	No
Global page table	@MMG$GL_GPTE	GBLPAGES	URKW	Yes[9]
End of system space	@MMG$GL_MAXSYSVA			

[1]The sizes of the pieces of system space listed in this table depend on the values of specific SYSBOOT parameters or on the particular device and memory configuration. Their starting addresses are stored in global locations.

[2]Numbers in address expressions are hexadecimal. If a global location is not preceded by the symbol @, its value is the address of the area in question. If a global location is preceded by the symbol @, its value is an address that contains the address of the area in question.

[3]Sizes are expressed in decimal numbers.

[4]MMG$GL_SBICONF is the address of an array of longwords. Each array element contains the system virtual address of the first page that maps I/O addresses for that adapter. The number of elements in the array is contained in the global EXE$GL_NUM-NEXUS.

[5]This location does not contain a system virtual address. Rather, it contains a system virtual page number.

[6]The pages set aside for connect to interrupt drivers are mapped "no access" as part of initialization. When one of these SPTEs is allocated in response to specific requests, its protection is altered.

[7]On a member of a VAXcluster System, SYSINIT creates the STACONFIG process. The STACONFIG process autoconfigures local disks and SCS port devices.

[8]The PHDs that reside in the balance slot area are a part of the process working set to which they are associated. Although portions of the PHD do not page, the physical pages locked down in this manner are accounted for in process working sets and do not count toward the executive's use of memory.

[9]Global page tables are pageable. However, if a global page table page contains at least one valid global PTE, then that page is locked into the system working set.

3. The restart parameter block (RPB) is always one page long. In the notation of Figure F-2, this is expressed by the following equation:

$$SVAS(rpb) = 1 \qquad (F.12)$$

The single page required for the RPB is not counted when determining the initial size of the SPT. It is assumed that page rounding or one of the approximations will add the single SPTE required to map the RPB.

4. The number of pages in the PFN database is discussed in Section F.2.2.

5. The space reserved for paged pool depends on the SYSBOOT parameter PAGEDYN. The parameter expresses the pool size in bytes and is truncated to the next smallest page boundary to give the pool size in pages. SYSBOOT modifies the parameter so that the next bootstrap operation will reflect the truncated pool size.

$$SVAS(paged\_pool) = \frac{PAGEDYN}{512} \qquad (F.13)$$

6. The space reserved for nonpaged pool is the sum of the size of the nonpaged variable length list and the sizes of the lookaside lists. The SYSBOOT parameter NPAGEVIR determines the maximum size of the variable length list. The size of each lookaside list is determined by the size of its request packets and the maximum number of packets in each list. The size of each request packet is rounded up to a 16-byte boundary, the granularity of pool allocation. For simplicity, this rounding is not shown in the two equations that follow. The constant IRP$C_LENGTH, rounded, is 208.

$$
\begin{aligned}
SVAS(nonpaged\_pool) = {} & \frac{NPAGEVIR}{512} \\
& + \frac{(SRPSIZE \times SRPCOUNTV) + 511}{512} \\
& + \frac{(IRP\$C\_LENGTH \times IRPCOUNTV) + 511}{512} \\
& + \frac{[(LRPSIZE + 76) \times LRPCOUNTV] + 511}{512}
\end{aligned}
\qquad (F.14)
$$

Note that the size of the nonpaged variable length list is truncated to the next smallest page boundary; the size of each lookaside list is rounded up to the next page boundary.

Enough virtual address space must be reserved for the maximum sizes of each list. The following equation represents the sum of the initial sizes of the lists. During system operations, each list can be expanded up to its maximum size.

$$PHYS(nonpaged\_pool) = \frac{NPAGEDYN}{512}$$

$$+ \frac{(SRPSIZE \times SRPCOUNT) + 511}{512}$$

$$+ \frac{(IRP\$C\_LENGTH \times IRPCOUNT) + 511}{512} \qquad (F.15)$$

$$+ \frac{[(LRPSIZE + 76) \times LRPCOUNT] + 511}{512}$$

7. The SYSBOOT parameter INTSTKPAGES is the size of the interrupt stack in pages:

$$SVAS(int\_stack) = INTSTKPAGES \qquad (F.16)$$

In calculating the total size of the SPT, the guard pages (protection set to no access) at either end of the interrupt stack are not counted. These pages cause access violation exceptions (actually an interrupt stack not valid processor halt) on either stack overflow or stack underflow.

8. The size of the system control block (SCB) is CPU-dependent. All processors have, at a minimum, the one-page architecturally defined SCB (see Figures 4-1 and 5-2):

   —The VAX-11/780, VAX-11/782, and VAX-11/785 have only the one page of architecturally defined SCB.
   —The VAX-11/730, MicroVAX I, and MicroVAX II have a second page for dispatching UNIBUS or Q-bus interrupts.
   —The VAX-11/750 has one additional page for each UNIBUS interface on the system. This results in either a two-page or three-page SCB.
   —The VAX 8200 and VAX 8300 have an additional page for each VAXBI UNIBUS adapter.
   —The VAX 8500, VAX 8550, VAX 8700, and VAX 8800 have a 32-page SCB to support the theoretical maximum number of directly vectored adapters.
   —The VAX 8600 and VAX 8650 have a four-page SCB to support the maximum configuration of four synchronous backplane interface (SBI) adapters.

$$SVAS(scb) = a\ number\ between\ 1\ and\ 32 \qquad (F.17)$$

9. The area devoted to balance slots constitutes more than half of system virtual address space in typical configurations. Its size depends on the SYSBOOT parameter BALSETCNT and the size of a PHD in pages, calculated in Section F.1. The constant size of balance slots makes this a trivial calculation:

$$SVAS(balance\_slots) = BALSETCNT \times PHD(pages) \qquad (F.18)$$

The motivation behind constant size balance slots is explained in Chapter 14.

10. The system header involves a calculation similar to the size of the PHD, described in the previous section. However, there is no optimization technique for empty pages, because there is no large variation in working set sizes. There is also no need for the analog to PHD page arrays because the system header does not describe an object that swaps. The size of the SPT, the system analog to process page tables, is calculated separately from the rest of the system header, which has a simple dependence on two SYSBOOT parameters.

The only system header components are the system equivalent to the WSL and the PST in the PHD. The system equivalents are the system WSL and the global section table. The SYSBOOT parameters that control their sizes are SYSMWCNT and GBLSECTIONS.

$$SVAS(sysphd) = \frac{\left(\begin{array}{c} PHD\$K\_LENGTH + (4 \times SYSMWCNT) \\ + (32 \times GBLSECTIONS) + 511 \end{array}\right)}{512} \qquad (F.19)$$

The system section table contains section table entries not only for all global sections but also for three system sections: the system image itself, the RMS image, and the system message file.

11. The size of the SPT depends on the sizes of the other pieces of system address space. The calculation of its size is discussed in Section F.2.2.

12. The last simple calculation of a portion of system virtual address space involves the size of the global page table, governed by the SYSBOOT parameter GBLPAGES:

$$SVAS(gpt) = \frac{GBLPAGES + 127}{128} \qquad (F.20)$$

F.2.2   System Page Table and the PFN Database

The PFN database contains a description of each page of physical memory. However, it does not contain information about the nonpaged portions of system space. Because the PFN database is a nonpaged part of system space, its size depends on itself. However, the situation is more complicated. The SPT, also nonpaged, maps the PFN database. Thus, the size of the PFN database depends on its own size in two different ways.

Chapter 14 describes the PFN database. Depending on the amount of physical memory present on the system, the PFN database contains either 18 or 22 bytes of information for each page of physical memory it describes. If the global variable MMG\$GW_BIGPFN contains the value zero, there are 18 bytes of information; if it contains the value 1, there are 22 bytes of information. (Chapter 14 describes how this number is determined.) The value

PFN_SIZE in the following equation represents either 18 or 22:

$$\text{SVAS(pfn)} = \frac{\text{PFN\_SIZE} \times (\text{PHYSICAL} - \text{NO\_PFN\_DATA}) + 511}{512} \quad \text{(F.21)}$$

The value PHYSICAL represents the size of physical memory:

$$\text{PHYSICAL} = \text{minimum (size of physical memory, PHYSICALPAGES)}$$

$$\text{(F.22)}$$

NO_PFN_DATA represents the nonpaged portions of system space that are not accounted for in the PFN database:

$$\begin{aligned}
\text{NO\_PFN\_DATA} = \ & \text{SVAS(nonpaged\_exec)} \\
& + \text{SVAS(pfn)} \\
& + \text{PHYS(nonpaged\_pool)} \\
& + \text{SVAS(int\_stack)} \\
& + \text{SVAS(scb)} \\
& + \text{SVAS(sysphd)} \\
& + \text{SVAS(spt)}
\end{aligned} \quad \text{(F.23)}$$

The nonpaged portion of the SYS.EXE image, SVAS(nonpaged_exec), is a subset of SVAS(sptreq). Its size is variable, depending on the size of the paged portion of SYS.EXE:

$$\begin{aligned}
\text{SVAS(nonpaged\_exec)} = \ & @\text{MMG\$GL\_PGDCOD} \\
& - \text{MMG\$A\_ENDVEC}
\end{aligned} \quad \text{(F.24)}$$

Notice that the PFN database depends on its own size explicitly (through the NO_PFN_DATA term) and also implicitly through the size of the SPT (Equation F.25).

In a similar fashion, the size of the SPT depends on its own size explicitly and implicitly through the size of the PFN database:

$$\text{SVAS(spt)} = \frac{\text{THE\_REST} + \text{SVAS(spt)} + \text{SVAS(pfn)} + 127}{128} \quad \text{(F.25)}$$

THE_REST represents all contributions to system address space except for the SPT and the PFN database.

$$\begin{aligned}
\text{THE\_REST} = \ & \text{SVAS(sptskel)} \\
& + \text{SVAS(sptreq)} \\
& + \text{SVAS(rpb)} \\
& + \text{SVAS(paged\_pool)} \\
& + \text{SVAS(nonpaged\_pool)} \\
& + \text{SVAS(int\_stack)} \\
& + \text{SVAS(scb)} \\
& + \text{SVAS(balance\_slots)} \\
& + \text{SVAS(sysphd)} \\
& + \text{SVAS(gpt)}
\end{aligned}$$

F.2.3   **Approximation Used by SYSBOOT**

For some large values of either VIRTUALPAGECNT or physical memory size, an iterative calculation for the sizes of these two quantities does not converge but rather oscillates about a stable solution.

To avoid this problem, a simplification in the calculation is made. The number of SPTEs set aside for the PFN database does not take into account the fact that the pages occupied by the nonpaged executive are not accounted for in the PFN database:

$$SVAS(pfn) = \frac{(PFN\_SIZE \times PHYSICAL) + 511}{512} \qquad (F.26)$$

This relation replaces Equation F.21 in the calculation of the size of the SPT. It also greatly simplifies Equation F.25, because the SVAS(pfn) term no longer depends on SVAS(spt). Instead, SVAS(pfn) is a constant.

Because Equation F.26 errs on the high side in allocating SPTEs for the PFN database, the number of SPTEs set aside for the SPT does not use Equation F.27 iteratively. Instead, there is a single pass on calculating the size of the SPT:

$$SVAS(spt,0) = \frac{THE\_REST + SVAS(pfn)}{128} \qquad (F.27)$$

$$SVAS(spt) = \frac{THE\_REST + SVAS(pfn) + SVAS(spt,0) + 127}{128} \qquad (F.28)$$

Because physical pages are not allocated for the PFN database until the SPT size has been calculated, there is no large waste of physical memory. The only effect of these two approximations might be one more physical page allocated for the SPT than is absolutely necessary. The allocation of an extra page only occurs on systems with very large amounts of memory in the first place, so the loss is practically unnoticed.

F.2.4   **Renormalization of SPTREQ**

The rounding of the size of the SPT to the next highest page boundary can add extra SPTEs to those required to map the entire system. After SYSBOOT has calculated the result of Equation F.28, it maps SYS.EXE beginning at the low address end of system address space (80000000). It maps the dynamic portion of system space beginning at the high address end.

Any pages left over after this mapping are put into the pool of SPTEs located by BOO$GL_SPTFREL and BOO$GL_SPTFREH. As SPTEs are needed for further mapping (for example, by SYSINIT to map RMS and the system message file or by SYSGEN when loading drivers that require a system virtual page number), these pages are taken from the pool. Once the entire system is mapped, any extra pages (as a result of rounding or an overestimate of the SPTREQ parameter) remain in the pool of SPTEs.

3   **PHYSICAL MEMORY REQUIREMENTS OF VAX/VMS**

Once the sizes of the various pieces of system address space have been calculated, it is possible to list the total physical memory requirements of the executive, that is, the number of pages that are not available for user processes.

3.1   **Physical Memory Used by the Executive**

Table F-4 lists each piece of the nonpaged executive and either its size in pages or the number of the equation that describes how its size is computed. This initial sum is the total memory requirement of the nonpaged executive code and data tables. Note that Equation F.15 only accounts for the initial sizes of the nonpaged pool lists. As pools expand, this number increases, with Equation F.14 as its upper limit. The paged executive (see Table F-4) also requires physical memory. However, it is reasonable to assume that the system working set is full at all times, so that the physical memory requirements of the paged executive are simply SYSMWCNT pages.

$$
\begin{aligned}
\text{NONPAGED} = \ &\text{SVAS(nonpaged\_exec)} \\
&+ \text{SVAS(rpb)} \\
&+ \text{SVAS(pfn)} \\
&+ \text{PHYS(nonpaged\_pool)} \\
&+ \text{SVAS(int\_stack)} \\
&+ \text{SVAS(scb)} \\
&+ \text{SVAS(sysphd)} \\
&+ \text{SVAS(spt)}
\end{aligned}
\tag{F.29}
$$

Two other items must be taken into account when calculating the number of physical pages used by the executive. The SYSBOOT parameters FREELIM and MPW_LOLIM set low-limit thresholds on the number of pages on the free and modified page lists. These parameters should be included when calculating the number of available physical pages:

$$
\begin{aligned}
\text{MEMORY} = \ &\text{NONPAGED} \\
&+ \text{SYSMWCNT} \\
&+ \text{FREELIM} \\
&+ \text{MPW\_LOLIM}
\end{aligned}
\tag{F.30}
$$

$$
\text{AVAILABLE} = \text{PHYSICAL} - \text{MEMORY}
\tag{F.31}
$$

An additional item to be considered is the Files-11 XQP. This image is shared in the P1 space of each process. If the SYSBOOT parameter ACP_XQP_RES is 1 (its default value), the XQP is mapped as a resident global section, which means that all its shareable pages are permanently resident. For VAX/VMS Version 4.4, a resident XQP contributes approximately 120 pages to the total memory requirements.

Table F-4   Division of System Virtual Address Space into Nonpaged and Paged Pieces

Item	*Size[1]*

The following portions of system address space are permanently mapped by SYSBOOT. The physical pages that they occupy are not accounted for in the PFN database.

Nonpaged portion of executive image	@MMG$GL_PGDCOD − MMG$A_ENDVEC
PFN database	Equation F.26
Nonpaged pool	Equation F.15
Interrupt stack	Equation F.16
System control block	Equation F.17
System header	Equation F.19
System page table	Equation F.28

The following portions of system address space are permanently mapped.

Mount verification buffer	1 page
Erase pattern buffer	1 page
Erase pattern page table	1 page
MSCP server	Size of MSCP image, @(@SCS$GL_MSCP)

The following are the pageable portions of the executive. Their total memory cost can never exceed SYSMWCNT.

Paged executive data	1 page
Paged executive routines	MMG$AL_PGDCODEN − @MMG$GL_PGDCOD
RMS image	Size of RMS image (205 pages)
System message file	Size of system message file (284 pages)
Paged pool	Equation F.13
Global page table pages	Equation F.20

The following portions of system address space do not require physical memory accounted for in Equation F.28.

XDELTA, INIT, and BUGCHECK	Usually not mapped
I/O space mapping	I/O addresses
SVPNs for disk drivers	I/O addresses or double mapping
Balance slot area	PHD pages and page table pages are charged to process working sets

---

[1]If a global location is not preceded by the symbol @, its value is the address of the area in question. If a global location is preceded by the symbol @, its value is an address that contains the address of the area in question.

By working back from Equation F.31, it is possible to obtain the number of available physical pages in terms of the contents of a SYSGEN parameter file and one more input parameter, the size of physical memory.

3.2   System Processes

When attempting to assess the total memory required by the system, one more factor must be taken into account. All memory resident system processes require a number of pages equal to their respective working set sizes. The following processes are considered to be system processes:

- Job controller
- Print symbionts, if any
- Error logger format process (ERRFMT)
- Operator communication process (OPCOM)
- Magnetic tape ACPs, if any
- Network ACP (NETACP), if present
- Remote terminal ACP (REMACP), if present

In addition, on a node that is a member of a VAXcluster System, there are several other system processes:

- Cluster cache server process
- Cluster server process
- Cluster device configuration process

The amount of memory required by these processes cannot be calculated in closed form, as the executive's memory requirements are, for several reasons:

- The memory consumed by a process is its working set size. Automatic working set size adjustment causes this process attribute to vary over time (assuming, of course, that the process in question reaches its working set limit, a reasonable assumption for system processes). The working set of any process in the system is readily available from the Monitor Utility.
- Sharing confuses the issue. However, the DCL command SHOW SYSTEM lists the physical memory used by each process in the system.
- System processes can be outswapped, temporarily reducing the physical memory requirements of those processes to zero.

Because physical memory requirements of system processes vary over time and can be easily obtained from a utility such as MONITOR or with the SHOW SYSTEM command, they are not included in any equations in this appendix. However, their requirements should be taken into account when any type of configuration calculation is made. This appendix is provided as a tool for calculating the memory requirements of the executive, a number that is not readily available.

F.4   **SIZE OF P1 SPACE**

Many of the pieces of P1 space have predetermined sizes, based on the contents of module SHELL in the executive. This module includes a skeleton P1 page table that is used to set up an initial P1 page table when a process is created.

Some pieces of P1 space are dynamically configured, with sizes that are determined by a variety of techniques. Table F-5 lists the pieces of P1 space and how the size of each is determined. The following list includes details about each dynamic portion of P1 space. Like P1 space itself, the list moves toward lower virtual addresses.

1. All of the pieces of P1 space from the VAX DEBUG dynamic memory to the RMS data pages have their sizes determined by assembly-time parameters in module SHELL. These pieces are implicitly mapped by the swapper when the skeleton P1 page tables are copied from the shell process at the time that the process is created.
2. The P1 window to the PHD includes all of the PHD, except for page table pages (see Table F-1). The empty pages are included in the P1 window. Section F.1 relates the size of the PHD to the relevant SYSBOOT parameters.
3. There are SYSBOOT parameter CHANNELCNT elements in the channel control block (CCB) table. Each CCB is 16 bytes. The global location CTL$GL_CCBBASE points to the high address end of the table. A particular CCB is identified by its negative byte displacement from the contents of CTL$GL_CCBBASE.
4. The process allocation region is a P1 space dynamic memory pool (see Chapter 3). Its size in pages is determined by the SYSBOOT parameter CTLPAGES.
5. The process I/O segment contains RMS data structures describing "process permanent" files, those which can and usually do remain open across image activations. Its size is determined by the SYSBOOT parameter PIOPAGES.
6. The SYSBOOT parameter IMGIOCNT determines the default number of pages that are created by EXE$PROCSTRT for the image I/O segment, the RMS impure area for files opened during the execution of a specific image.

   The default number of image I/O segment pages can be overridden for a specific image by including the following line as a part of the link time option file:

   ```
   IOSEGMENT = n
   ```

   If the IOSEGMENT option specifies more pages than the IMGIOCNT parameter, the image activator allocates an alternate image I/O segment the size specified by the IOSEGMENT.

Table F-5   Detailed Layout of P1 Space

Item	Global Location[1]	Factors That Affect Size[2]	Protection	Owner	Pageable
		MAPPED BY THE IMAGE ACTIVATOR			
Low address end of P1 space	@(@CTL$GL_PHD + PHD$L_FREP1VA)				
User stack		STACK link option	UW	U	Yes
Extra user stack pages		2 pages	UW	U	Yes
Extra image I/O segment		IOSEGMENT link option	UREW	E	Yes
Boundary between process-permanent and image-specific P1 space	@CTL$GL_CTLBASVA[3]				
		MAPPED BY THE DCL COMMAND SET MESSAGE			
Per-process message section	@CTL$GL_PPMSG	Size of section	UR	E	Yes
		MAPPED BY LOGINOUT			
CLI symbol table	@(CTL$AG_CLIDATA + 10)	CLISYMTBL	SW	S	Yes
CLI command tables	@CTL$AG_CLITABLE	Image size	UR	S	Yes
CLI image	@CTL$AG_CLIMAGE	Image size	UR	S	Yes

(continued)

955

Table F-5   Detailed Layout of P1 Space (continued)

Item	Global Location[1]	Factors That Affect Size[2]	Protection	Owner	Pageable
		MAPPED BY EXE$PROCSTRT			
Files-11 XQP data and stack	@(@CTL$GL_F11BXQP + 18)		KW	K	Yes, no[4]
Files-11 XQP image	@(@CTL$GL_F11BXQP + 10)	Image size	ER	E	Yes, no[4]
Image I/O segment	@(PIO$GQ_IIODEFAULT + 4)	IMGIOCNT	UREW	K	Yes
Process I/O segment		PIOPAGES	UREW	K	Yes
Process allocation region		CTLPAGES	UREW	K	Yes
Channel control block table	@CTL$GL_CCBBASE[5]	CHANNELCNT	UREW	K	Yes
Initial end of P1 space for each process in this system	@MMG$GL_CTLBASVA[6]				
		FIXED SIZE PORTION—DEFINED IN SHELL			
P1 window to PHD	@CTL$GL_PHD	Size of the PHD	URKW, ERKW	K	No
RMS data areas	PIO$GL_FMLH	6 pages	UREW	E	Yes
Per-process common for users	CTL$A_COMMON − 800	4 pages	UW	K	Yes
Per-process common for DIGITAL	CTL$A_COMMON	4 pages	UW	K	Yes

Table F-5   Detailed Layout of P1 Space (continued)

Item	Global Location[1]	Factors That Affect Size[2]	Protection	Owner	Pageable
		FIXED SIZE PORTION—DEFINED IN SHELL			
Compatibility mode data pages	CTL$AG_CMEDATA	2 pages	UW	K	Yes
VMS user-mode data page	CTL$GL_DCLPRSOWN	1 page	UW	K	Yes
Not currently used		2 pages	No access	K	
Security audit data pages	NSA$T_IDT	3 pages	KW	K	Yes
Image activator context page	CTL$GL_IAFLINK	1 page	UREW	E	Yes
Generic CLI data pages	CTL$AL_CLICALBK	12 pages	URSW	S	Yes
Image activator scratch pages	IAC$AL_IMGACTBUF	8 pages	UREW	E	Yes
Debugger context pages		4 pages	UW	U	Yes
Vectors for user-written system services and messages	CTL$A_DISPVEC	2 pages	UREW	K	Yes
Image header buffer	MMG$IMGHDRBUF	1 page	URSW	E	Yes
KRP lookaside list	CTL$GL_KRP	8 pages	URKW	K	Yes
No access guard page		1 page	No access	K	
Kernel stack expansion pages		4 pages	No access	K	

(continued)

957

Table F-5   Detailed Layout of P1 Space *(continued)*

Item	Global Location[1]	Factors That Affect Size[2]	Protection	Owner	Pageable
		FIXED SIZE PORTION—DEFINED IN SHELL			
Kernel stack	CTL$GL_KSTKBAS	3 pages	SRKW	K	No
Executive stack	CTL$GL_KSPINI	16 pages	SREW	E	Yes
Supervisor stack	@(CTL$AL_STACK + 4)[7]	32 pages	URSW	S	Yes
System service vectors	P1SYSVECTORS	5 pages	UR	K	No
Reserved for system service vector expansion		11 pages	No access	K	No
P1 pointer page	CTL$GL_VECTORS	1 page	URKW	K	No
VAX DEBUG dynamic memory	@(CTL$GQ_DBGAREA + 4)	128 pages	UW	U	Yes

[1]Numbers in address expressions are hexadecimal. If a global location is not preceded by the symbol @, its value is the address of the area in question. If a global location is preceded by the symbol @, its value is an address that contains the address of the area in question.

[2]Sizes are expressed in decimal numbers.

[3]Global location CTL$GL_CTLBASVA contains the address of the boundary between the image-specific portion of P1 space (deleted at image exit by routine MGM$IMGRESET) and the process-permanent portion of P1 space.

[4]The Files-11 XQP stack and some of its data are not pageable. Those pages are locked into the process's working set list. If the Files-11 XQP is mapped as a resident global section, none of it pages. Otherwise, most of it pages, but those pages that are accessed at elevated IPLs are locked into the working set list.

[5]CTL$GL_CCBBASE points to the high address end of the channel control block table.

[6]Global location MMG$GL_CTLBASVA contains the lowest address in P1 space at system initialization, when EXE$PROCSTRT runs. As a CLI and other dynamic portions of P1 space, such as a process-permanent message section, are added, location CTL$GL_CTLBASVA is updated to reflect the changes.

[7]Global location CTL$AL_STACK is the address of a four-longword array whose elements contain the initial values of the four per-process stack pointers. An array element is indexed by access mode.

7. In VAX/VMS Version 4, the file system is implemented as procedure-based code that runs in process context. The size of the space required is determined partly by F11BXQP.EXE, the size of the image. EXE$PROCSTRT maps the Files-11 Extended QIO Processor (XQP) into the P1 space of each process. It then calls initialization code within the XQP. The initialization code creates additional P1 space for use as an impure area and a private kernel stack.

8. The LOGINOUT image maps the selected command language interpreter (CLI) into P1 space for interactive and batch jobs. (A merged image activation accomplishes this mapping.) The size of the CLI image determines how much space is taken up by the CLI.

9. The SYSBOOT parameter CLISYMTBL determines the number of demand zero pages that are created by LOGINOUT for the CLI symbol table.

10. Two extra pages are allocated for the user stack by the image activator. These pages are not used for the user stack. Instead, they are at a higher virtual address than the initial value of the user stack pointer.

   These pages allow the operating system to recover if the user stack is corrupted.

11. The size of the user stack is determined by the following option in an options file at link time:

```
STACK = n
```

The default user stack size is 20 pages.

   Because the stack is automatically expanded by the system's access violation handler when the user stack overflows, there is little need for using this option. One possible use might be for an image that requires a large amount of stack space but cannot afford the overhead required for automatic stack expansion at run time.

Appendix G

VAX CPU Designations

Most parts of VAX/VMS are independent of CPU type. There are, however, certain CPU-specific components. These components have names that contain CPU designations in the positions shown as *xxx* or *yyy*. They include the following:

- The set of macros $PR*yyy*DEF
- The set of macros $IO*yyy*DEF
- The loadable images SYSLOA*xxx*.EXE

The macro $PRDEF, in SYS$LIBRARY:LIB.MLB, defines symbolic names for the processor registers that are common to all types of VAX processors. For each CPU type, a second LIB.MLB macro, $PR*yyy*DEF, defines symbolic names for the CPU's additional processor registers.

The SYS$LIBRARY:LIB.MLB $IO*yyy*DEF macros define the layout of I/O space for each CPU. Table G-1 shows the CPU designation for each CPU type.

Table G-1 VAX CPU Designations

yyy	*SYSLOAxxx*	*System Types*
UV1	SYSLOAUV1.EXE	MicroVAX I
UV1	SYSLOAWS1.EXE	VAXstation I
UV2	SYSLOAUV2.EXE	MicroVAX II
UV2	SYSLOAWS2.EXE	VAXstation II
UV2	SYSLOAWSD.EXE	VAXstation II/GPX
410	SYSLOA410.EXE	MicroVAX 2000
410	SYSLOA41W.EXE	VAXstation 2000
730	SYSLOA730.EXE	VAX-11/730, VAX-11/725
750	SYSLOA750.EXE	VAX-11/750
780	SYSLOA780.EXE	VAX-11/780, VAX-11/782, VAX-11/785
790	SYSLOA790.EXE	VAX 8600, VAX 8650
8SS	SYSLOA8SS.EXE	VAX 8200, VAX 8300
8NN	SYSLOA8NN.EXE	VAX 8500, VAX 8550, VAX 8700, VAX 8800

The loadable SYSLOA images contain support for CPU-specific implementation details, such as machine check exceptions, memory and bus error interrupts, I/O adapter initialization, and console terminal support. The SYSLOA image names and the names of their CPU-specific source modules contain a CPU designation. Certain VAX processors (such as the MicroVAX II) support sufficiently different console terminals that a different SYSLOA image is required for each type of console terminal. Table G-1 lists the names of the SYSLOA images.

Index